Applied Econometrics

The HarperCollins Series in Economics

Applied Econometrics

Leonard Lardaro

University of Rhode Island

HarperCollins*CollegePublishers*

*To
Mom and Dad,
Georgann,
Beth, Thomas, and Alicia*

Senior Acquisitions Editor: John Greenman
Project Editors: Randee Wire & Ellen MacElree
Design Supervisor: Julie Anderson
Text and Cover Design: Lesiak/Crampton Design Inc: Cynthia Crampton
Cover Illustration: Paul M. Koziarz/Precision Graphics
Production Administrators: Linda Murray/Valerie A. Sawyer
Compositor: Syntax International
Printer and Binder: R. R. Donnelley & Sons Company
Cover Printer: New England Book Components, Inc.

Applied Econometrics

Library of Congress Cataloging-in-Publication Data

Lardaro, Leonard.
    Applied econometrics/Leonard Lardaro.—1st ed.
        p.   cm.
    Includes index.
    ISBN 0-06-043847-9
    1. Econometrics.   2. Econometrics—Problems, exercises, etc.
    I. Title.
HB139.L37   1992
330′.01′5195—dc20   92-12006
                                         CIP

92 93 94 95 9 8 7 6 5 4 3 2 1

Contents

3 A PRIMER ON THE SOURCES, MANIPULATION, AND COMPUTER PROCESSING OF ECONOMIC DATA   96

4 ECONOMETRIC THEORY: THE BIVARIATE REGRESSION MODEL   151

5   EXTENSIONS OF THE BIVARIATE REGRESSION MODEL: STATISTICAL INFERENCE AND FORECASTING   219

6   ECONOMETRIC THEORY: THE MULTIPLE REGRESSION MODEL   269

14   AN INTRODUCTION TO SIMULTANEOUS EQUATIONS MODELS   593

15   THE IDENTIFICATION AND ESTIMATION OF SIMULTANEOUS EQUATION MODELS   621

STATISTICAL TABLES   T-1

INDEX   I-1

Preface

During the last five years, a striking transformation has occurred in the way that undergraduate econometrics texts are written. In the past, virtually all such texts presented a myriad of formulas but excluded most of the major skills that "hands on" courses in this field need. Notably absent were a sufficiently complete review of statistics and a detailed explanation of the economic theory underlying econometric applications. Today, econometrics texts can be divided into two categories: those patterned on the earlier formulaic style, and a lower tier of books that omits most derivations of important results. These lower-tier texts do not include economic theory at a level that enables students to apply concepts from previous courses.

AIMS AND APPROACH OF THIS TEXT

The purpose of this book is to reach a middle ground by presenting important derivations within an understandable frame of reference, while at the same time explaining the underlying theoretical bases for estimated equations. There are three primary advantages to this approach. First, it benefits students who are ill-prepared to take econometrics courses. Second, students are given an opportunity to apply economic theory in a manner that reinforces their understanding of basic concepts. (Economic theory is *not* merely included as an afterthought, as in most other texts; indeed, detailed explanations of the theoretical bases of estimated equations are presented in a manner that presupposes little economics background.) Finally, by understanding both the theoretical and econometric underpinnings of equations, students gain proficiency in formulating, estimating, and interpreting testable relationships on their own.

The purely "cookbook" approach of most lower-tier econometrics texts fails to prepare students to improvise in situations that differ from those in their text. The combination of this approach and the simplicity that current software allows students to estimate regressions poses the danger that students will not understand the *results* of their regressions. I feel that the most frustrating aspect of current available econometric software is that as software becomes more "user friendly," students feel less responsibility to manage the entire process of formulating and estimating equations derived from economic theory. This text underscores the need for students to control both the input into and output from standard computer programs, since today the saying, "garbage in, garbage out" is more relevant than ever before. Throughout this text, both strengths and limitations of the usual measures for evaluating equations are detailed, and ex-post forecast performance is included among the criteria for judging equations.

DISTINGUISHING FEATURES

This text differs in several significant ways from those already on the market. The econometrics chapters (Chapters 4–15) are more applied than those in other books, and the theoretical bases of equations are given throughout. The statistical prerequisites necessary to understand the econometrics chapters are provided early in the book and readers are shown computer printouts from badly constructed equations in order to develop a sense of problem-causing factors that they will likely encounter during this course. Also included are some of the more recent tests and measures in econometrics, such as the Breusch-Pagan test of heteroskedasticity, and a fairly complete but nonmathematical discussion of collinearity diagnostics based on the work of Belsley, Kuh, and Welsch. Finally, this text stresses that econometrics does not end with a computer printout. It presents the types of manipulations that are possible with estimated equations.

There are several content features that set this econometrics text apart from others currently available:

1. Chapters 2 and 3 provide a self-contained review of statistical and computer prerequisites, as well as a detailed explanation of the economic theory that underlies the estimated equations presented. The statistical review integrates directly into the presentation of econometric theory and practice. Derivations (such as the unbiasedness of the least-squares estimators) are thus extensions of previously discussed material. Criteria for judging estimated equations are presented and extended throughtout Chapters 4–15, the econometric chapters. Various criteria are recommended, with both the strengths and weaknesses of each detailed. Ex-post forecasting performance is one such criterion that other texts ignore.

2. An entire chapter (Chapter 7) examines the process of specifying, estimating and evaluating an econometric equation. Using a detailed example, readers learn how to formulate a population regression function from a relationship specified by economic theory. Important factors to consider when selecting the specific variables for the sample regression function are delineated, as well as how to estimate and then critique the resulting sample regression function. This example demonstrates for students the entire process that can be used to empirically investigate relationships from their current or past theory courses. The chapter concludes with a descriptive presentation of influence statistics, as presented by Belsley, Kuh and Welsch,[1] and a suggested format for major papers in this course.

---

[1] D. Belsley, E. Kuh, and R. Welsch, *Regression Diagnostics: Identifying Influential Data and Sources of Collinearity* (New York: John Wiley & Sons), 1980.

3. Chapter 8 on functional form provides realistic economic examples for various equation specifications considered. As is true throughout this text, the economic basis for these equations is provided in the discussion of coefficients of interest.

4. The material on multicollinearity in Chapter 10 follows the presentation of specification error. Since both specification error and multicollinearity often display a number of similar symptoms, it is appropriate to include both of these topics in the same chapter. However, the desirable properties of the least squares estimators are attained only when an equation is properly specified. Thus, any valid discussion of multicollinearity can only proceed when the researcher has confidence in the specification of the equation being critiqued, which presupposes background in the consequences of specification error.

The discussion of multicollinearity in Chapter 10 presents diagnostic material far beyond that in current texts. Besides the condition number of a matrix and variance inflation factors, this text presents in a nonmathematical way an entire section (that is optional) on the methodology of Belsley, Kuh and Welsch,[2] using an automobile demand equation, and the collinearity diagnostics of SAS (the COLLIN option in PROC REG).

5. The discussion of autocorrelation in Chapter 11 presents the methodology and terminology of time-series analysis in a way that parallels the treatment of this topic in business school courses in time series forecasting. The basis for which generalized least squares transformation is appropriate is presented in a way that frees students from memorizing various transformations without an understanding of their basis.

6. The material on simultaneous equations in Chapters 14 and 15 is a balanced presentation of both theory and examples. This text uses the chapters on simultaneous equations as an opportunity to further elaborate on several of the equations discussed earlier in the text, while providing readers with numerous examples of why simultaneous equation relationships arise and practice in determining whether a variable is endogenous or exogenous.

I have used portions of this text for several years in my undergraduate econometrics class. The primary prerequisite for students reading this text is familiarity with principles-level economic theory and facility with basic algebra. Statistical background is not presupposed. The self-contained presentation of statistics in Chapter 2 has enabled students lacking prior statistics exposure to successfully complete my course. Seeing relationships from previous courses, having to focus on key relationships in terms of expected signs and estimated magnitudes only serves to reinforce the knowledge gained from previous classes.

I am indebted to a number of people who have helped bring this project to fruition. First and foremost, I am grateful to HarperCollins economics editor, John

---

[2] *Ibid.*

Greenman, who has given me encouragement and a great deal of moral support throughout our entire association, as has his very capable assistant, Ilana Scheiner. I would also like to thank my project editor, Randee Wire, for her efforts to shepherd the final version of this manuscript into published form. I am indebted to the following reviewers of the manuscript of this text, who made many valuable suggestions for improvements: John Fizel, Pennsylvania State University; Mark P. Karsig, Central Missouri State University; Stuart Low, Arizona State University; Rajan K. Sampath, Colorado State University; and Terry G. Seaks, University of North Carolina, Greensboro. Two reviewers who were particularly helpful deserve recognition, Mary Deily of Lehigh University and Tom S. Witt of West Virginia University, provided extremely thorough and helpful reviews of a number of chapters in this text. Several of my undergraduate and graduate students have also provided helpful comments; I am particularly grateful to Phil Bond, Lisa Matlin Pratt, Lisa Bianchi, Trish Beard and Jeff Hannah for their suggestions. Of course, any errors or ambiguities that remain are entirely attributable to me. I would also like to thank Clarice Coleman for typing several chapters of this manuscript and the Rhode Island Seafood Council, particularly Ralph Boragine and Terry Corr, for assisting me in shipping chapters to HarperCollins. Finally, I must extend my undying gratitude to the members of my family who put up with a great deal as I wrote this book. Thank you Georgann, Beth, Thomas, and Alicia. Without your patience and support, I could never have completed this text.

Leonard Lardaro

1 The Scope and Methods of Econometrics

Much of what economists disagree about centers on questions of magnitude rather than theory. During the 1980s, for example, there was a lively debate about the extent to which the supply-side tax cuts undertaken by the Reagan administration would increase both savings and investment. Another area of controversy concerned the devaluation of the dollar: would the depreciation of the dollar relative to the currencies of America's major trading partners produce a large enough improvement in its balance of trade to effectively eliminate the persistent deficits experienced since the early 1980s? As we begin the 1990s, potential areas of difference continue to persist. Will the mandated increases in the minimum wage have a large effect on the rate of unemployment? If the U.S. government imposes higher gasoline taxes, will the resulting fall in the overall consumption and importation of oil be substantial enough to reduce the rising trend in domestic oil consumption? Will a reduction in the capital gains tax increase or decrease total tax revenue?

The answer to all of these questions involves more than merely determining a direction of change. What matters most is *by how much* the variable of interest changes in response to some type of change. For example, economic theory predicts that dollar depreciation will both raise the prices of imports and lower export prices. Based on theory, we therefore expect the dollar volume of imports to fall and exports to rise, improving our balance of trade. Theory, however, does not indicate the amount by which both imports and exports change. This is an empirical question that theory alone is incapable of answering.

Economic theory provides only the starting point for resolving these debates; it establishes the causal factors that must be considered, along with their direction of influence. Ultimate resolution must be accomplished empirically, using actual data and methods that allow such a determination to be made.

How do economists determine these magnitudes? This is accomplished by the branch of economics called **econometrics**. Perhaps the best way to define econometrics is to provide several quotes relating to what econometrics does:

> Econometrics is concerned with the empirical determination of economic laws. The word 'empirical' indicates that the data used for this determination have been obtained from observation, which may be either controlled experiments designed by the econometrician . . . , or 'passive' observation.[1]

> Its basic task is to put *empirical* flesh and blood on theoretical structures.[2]

This chapter provides a brief overview of what econometrics is, what the study of this subject entails, and how econometrics evaluates questions left unanswered in theory courses. This material is intended to supply the initial conceptual understanding needed to begin the study of econometrics, as well as outlining the topics whose substance is contained in subsequent chapters.

A BRIEF OVERVIEW OF WHAT ECONOMETRICS ENTAILS

Econometrics is a quantitative tool that allows statistical evaluation of economic data to be performed. Econometrics has become an essential tool for both practicing economists and students majoring in economics. Persons with facility in econometrics are able to perform tests of economic theory. The jargon of econometrics is a necessary prerequisite for understanding much of literature in professional journals as well.

The process of deriving econometric estimates begins with a relationship specified by economic theory, which is then translated into a specific functional form. Data on critical variables are then gathered, and, through the methodology of econometrics, actual estimates are obtained and evaluated.

As you can see, the practice of econometrics requires facility with more than just economic theory: translating a theoretical relationship into a specific functional form involves mathematics; the derivation and manipulation of estimates is performed using statistical methods. Putting this all together, the econometrician can be defined in the following way:

> The econometrician is simply an economist who, in trying to understand the workings of economic systems, makes use of techniques which are based primarily on the methodology of statistics and which are often communicated in the language of mathematics.[3]

We will now discuss what econometrics entails by presenting two examples that illustrate how economic theory can be used to specify the theoretical relationships that form the basis for empirically investigating the behavior of variables of interest. The first of these is a macroeconomic relationship: the Quantity Theory of Money.

---

[1] H. Theil, *Principles of Econometrics* (New York: John Wiley & Sons), 1971, p. 1.

[2] J. Johnston, *Econometric Methods*, 3d ed. (New York: McGraw-Hill), 1984, p. 5.

[3] J. Stewart, *Understanding Econometrics.* 2nd ed. (London: Hutchinson Publishing Co.), 1984, p. 11.

The second example, which is continued throughout the remainder of this chapter, is microeconomic: the demand function for a good.

THE THEORETICAL RELATIONSHIP

The steps involved in transforming a theoretical relationship into an empirically estimable function will be illustrated using the Quantity Theory of Money.[4] The quantity theory, as this is called, defines a relationship between the supply of money and the overall level of economic activity, or Gross National Product (GNP). GNP, which is the dollar value of all final goods and services produced by an economy in a year, can be calculated by summing total expenditure during a given year with adjustments to avoid double counting. Since total expenditure is the product of the price level, P, and the aggregate amount produced, Q, GNP is:

$$GNP = P \cdot Q.$$

The quantity theory of money postulates a specific relationship between the supply of money (M) and the level of GNP. Assume, for example, that M equals $10 billion when GNP is $100 billion. How can this money supply support such a large overall level of economic activity? The answer to this question is based on the (income) *velocity of circulation*, V, which denotes the average number of times a dollar changes hands during the course of a year. If the average dollar of M is used 10 times per year, the velocity of circulation equals 10, and a $10 billion money supply can support a $100 billion GNP. Adding the velocity of circulation to this analysis gives the equation of exchange:

$$M \cdot V = P \cdot Q.$$

Total expenditure (and GNP) can therefore be represented either by the product of price and quantity, or of the supply of money and the velocity of circulation. Assuming that the velocity of circulation does not counteract the effect of variations in M on GNP, then changes in the supply of money will cause GNP to change.[5] This relationship, which is the Quantity Theory of Money, thus provides us with a simple **model** for the determination of GNP[6]:

$$GNP = f(M). \tag{1.1}$$

The variable on the left side of this equation, whose behavior the model explains, is called the **dependent variable**. The causal factor associated with this variable, M, is the **explanatory (independent) variable**. Because there is a single explanatory variable in this model, Equation (1.1) is referred to as a **bivariate relationship**.

---

[4] A more complete description than that presented here can be found in virtually any principles of macroeconomics textbook.

[5] This assumption amounts to stating that the demand for money is not interest sensitive.

[6] This relationship is obviously oversimplified, because it excludes all other factors that influence GNP. This example is intended only to provide a starting point for the discussion in the text.

The Quantity Theory of Money postulates a **positive (or direct) relationship** between the supply of money and the level of GNP, indicating that M and GNP move in the same direction, other things being equal. The **expected sign** of the money supply in this model, which indicates the direction of causation between it and the dependent variable, is positive. A graph expressing this relationship is upward sloping.

Microeconomic theory can be utilized to model the demand for a single good. The demand function for a good X, which provides a model of the quantity of a good X demanded (q_x) for an individual, identifies the set of explanatory variables for q_x and their direction of influence. This function, which is a **multivariate relationship**, can be expressed as:

$$q_x = f(p_x, p_y, I, p^e), \tag{1.2}$$

where p_x is the price of good X, p_y is the price of a related good Y, I is the level of income, and p^e is the expected (future) price of X.

To determine the expected sign of a variable in a multivariate relationship, we must consider the theoretical relationship between it and the dependent variable, assuming fixed values for the remaining explanatory variables. This procedure is the basis for the "other things being equal" statement employed so frequently in economics. Consider the expected sign of p_x. According to the Law of Demand, there is an **inverse (negative) relationship** between the price of X and q_x, indicating that these variables change in opposite directions. An increase in p_x, given p_y, I, and p^e causes q_x to fall, since:

  (i) this raises the relative price of good X, causing consumption of X to decrease (substitution effect); and
  (ii) this price increase reduces real income, so that if X is a normal good, less of it will be demanded (income effect).

By similar reasoning, a fall in p_x will tend to raise q_x. The expected sign of p_x is therefore negative, and the graph of this relationship, which produces the demand curve for good X, is downward sloping.

The discussion of these two models should clarify the linkage between economic theory and econometrics: *economic theory postulates the variable(s) whose values determine the behavior of a variable of interest as well as setting forth the causation involved.* Unfortunately, economic theory does not always provide expected signs for explanatory variables. The sign of I in Equation (1.2), for example, depends on whether X is a normal or inferior good. If this classification is not known, the expected sign of I is **indeterminate**, and the latter sign cannot be ascertained without further information.

ADDING A FORM (SPECIFICATION) TO THE THEORETICAL FUNCTION

The next step in estimating either a GNP or demand equation consists of selecting a form for the function, called the **equation specification**. This defines the specific way in which the explanatory variable(s) relate to the dependent variable.

Economic theory does not always provide this information.[7] The right-hand sides of Equations (1.1) and (1.2) are consistent with numerous equation specifications. Should these be linear or nonlinear in the explanatory variables? If a nonlinear functional form is appropriate, what particular form should be used? Answers to these questions are often not apparent. Final determination of the "best" equation specification is frequently judgmental. As an introduction to this topic, we will explore the linear functional form and outline the assumptions it embodies.

A linear specification of Equation (1.2) is:

$$q_x = \alpha_0 + \alpha_1 p_x + \alpha_2 p_y + \alpha_3 I + \alpha_4 p^e. \tag{1.3}$$

The coefficients (α's) in Equation (1.3) are **parameters**, unknown values we can estimate using econometric methods. The first of these, α_0, is the intercept of the demand function. The remaining α's are **partial slopes**. These are partial in the sense that each relates a particular explanatory variable to q_x while keeping the "other things" (i.e., remaining explanatory variables) constant. For example, α_1 is the slope of the demand curve for X, which is the graph of q_x and p_x holding p_y, I, and p^e constant.[8] To see this more clearly, rewrite Equation (1.3) as:

$$q_x = \alpha_0^* + \alpha_1 p_x, \tag{1.4}$$

where $\alpha_0^* = (\alpha_0 + \alpha_2 p_y + \alpha_3 I + \alpha_4 p^e)$. This intercept designates the value of q_x when p_x equals 0. The coefficient of p_x is the slope of the demand curve:

$$\text{slope of demand curve} = \Delta q_x / \Delta p_x,$$

or the rate of change in q_x for a change in the price of this good, other things being equal. If we use the following hypothetical values as the parameters in Equation (1.3):

$$q_x = 10 - 1.5 p_x + 2 p_y + 0.1 I + 1.0 p^e, \tag{1.5}$$

the equation for the demand curve for X is:

$$q_x = (10 + 2 p_y + 0.1 I + 1.0 p^e) - 1.5 p_x, \tag{1.6}$$

which becomes:

$$q_x = 50 - 1.5 p_x \tag{1.6'}$$

when $p_y = 5$, $I = 200$, and $p^e = 10$. Note that these "other things" serve to locate the demand curve by determining its vertical intercept, but do not affect its slope. If one or more of these change, the curve will shift either right or left, depending on the expected sign of the coefficient whose variable changes.

The coefficient of p_x in Equation (1.6′) displays the correct sign, indicating a downwardly sloped demand curve for X. The linear specification of this equation is

---

[7] Unless calculus and advanced microeconomic theory are employed, such uncertainty in functional form will exist, which is the likely situation for readers of this text.

[8] Note that this demand curve reverses the variables on the axes from the traditional graph of such a curve.

consistent with a constant slope, which, when graphed, produces a straight line demand curve. If p_x is measured in dollars, and q_x is expressed in thousands of units per month, the coefficient of p_x in Equation (1.6') indicates that a $1 increase in p_x (i.e., one of its units) lowers q_x by 1,500 units per month (i.e., 1.5 of its units, which are thousands), other things being equal.

The constant slope of the demand equation in this example specifies that the $1 increase in p_x lowers q_x by the same 1,500 units per month, irrespective of whether p_x is $2 or $20. When the data used to estimate an equation consist of observations that span a very long time period, changes in the purchasing power of money can render the linear specification inappropriate, requiring a nonlinear function instead. Thus, the constant slope assumption embodied in the linear specification does not always provide an adequate depiction of reality.

THE TYPE OF FUNCTION USED IN ECONOMETRICS

Each of the functions in the previous examples expresses an exact relationship between the explanatory variable(s) and the dependent variable. The demand function

$$q_x = \alpha_0 + \alpha_1 p_x + \alpha_2 p_x + \alpha_3 I + \alpha_4 p^e,$$

for example, produces a specific q_x for any associated set of values for p_x, p_y, I, and p^e. This demand function implies that:

(i) the only determinants of q_x are the included explanatory variables; and
(ii) the appropriate functional form is linear in these explanatory variables.

This is an example of a **deterministic function**: any set of values for the explanatory variables produces a *single* value of the dependent variable. The distinguishing characteristic of a deterministic function is thus a one-to-one relationship between the explanatory variable(s) and the dependent variable. This can be seen by referring to the demand curve derived from the above demand function:

$$q_x = \alpha_0^* + \alpha_1 p_x.$$

The graph of this relationship is given in Figure 1.1. If the price of X equals p_1, the quantity of X demanded takes the value q_1, which is obtained from point A on this curve. If p_x rises to p_2, q_x falls to q_2, as the consumption point moves to B. The amount by which q_x changes is obtained directly from the numerical value of α_1, the coefficient of the variable whose value has changed.

How accurate a depiction of reality is such a demand function, or its implied demand curve, likely to be? To answer this question, let us focus our attention on the demand function. If this were an econometric equation, the numerical values of its coefficients would be derived from actual data on the demand for X by a sample of individuals or families. While this function includes the major subset of factors that account for the consumption behavior of the persons purchasing good X, it does not incorporate all the determinants. For a given combination of p_x, p_y, I, and p^e values, the same q_x will therefore *not* pertain to all persons in the sample: some will have purchased more, while others less.

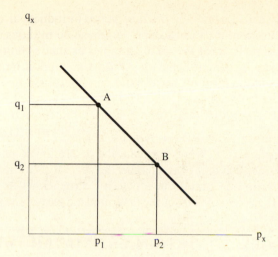

Figure 1.1 Demand curve for good *x*

If the actual values of p_x and q_x are plotted for a sample of individuals, a very different looking graph, called a **scatter diagram**, results. Figure 1.2 illustrates a hypothetical scatter diagram for the demand curve example. The type of function that is the basis of the points in this scatter diagram, one that associates a *range* of values of the dependent variable for each value of the explanatory variable, is called a **stochastic function**. Connecting all the points associated with this type of function does not produce a relationship that is meaningful from the perspective of either economics or econometrics. Stochastic functions are therefore related to deterministic functions

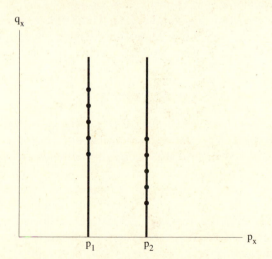

Figure 1.2 Scatter diagram of price-quantity combinations for demand curve

through a modification that accounts for the divergence of individual observations from the deterministic function: the inclusion of a **stochastic error** term.

The stochastic error accounts for the set of variables omitted from the equation, as well as the randomness in human behavior. When this term is included in the original function the stochastic form of the demand curve results:

$$q_x = \alpha_0 + \alpha_1 p_x + \varepsilon,$$

where ε is the stochastic error. Note that this function consists of a *deterministic part*, $\alpha_0 + \alpha_1 p_x$, and a *stochastic part*, ε. When graphed, the deterministic portion of this equation produces a straight line that characterizes the general relationship between p_x and q_x. As the next section illustrates, the stochastic error allows us to associate actual values of q_x with those obtained from the deterministic part of the relationship.

THE METHOD USED TO OBTAIN ESTIMATES

The starting point for econometric estimation is the **population regression function** (PRF), which depicts the actual relationship we are interested in estimating. Returning to the demand function example, the population regression function can be expressed as:

$$q_x = f(p_x, p_y, I, p^e) + \varepsilon$$

where $f(p_x, p_y, I, p^e)$ is the specification of the PRF and ε is a stochastic error. If we utilize a linear specification for this function, the population regression function becomes:

$$q_x = \alpha_0 + \alpha_1 p_x + \alpha_2 p_y + \alpha_3 I + \alpha_4 p^e + \varepsilon \tag{1.7}$$

The coefficients in this equation are unknown values, or population parameters that we can estimate econometrically using sample data. These values are then utilized to construct an estimate of the population regression function called the **sample regression function** (SRF). If we denote these estimated coefficients with a " $\hat{\ }$ ", the sample regression function can be written:

$$\hat{q}_x = \hat{\alpha}_0 + \hat{\alpha}_1 p_x + \hat{\alpha}_2 p_y + \hat{\alpha}_3 I + \hat{\alpha}_4 p^e. \tag{1.8}$$

Equation (1.8) expresses *predicted* q_x in terms of actual values of the explanatory variables. In order to express the sample regression function in terms of actual q_x, we utilize an estimated stochastic error term called the **equation residual**, which is defined as:

$$\hat{\varepsilon} = q_x - \hat{q}_x.$$

The residual is merely the difference between actual and estimated q_x. This term serves as a "balancing term" which allows us to link q_x and $\hat{q}_x$. If we rearrange this equation, we can express q_x as:

$$q_x = \hat{q}_x + \hat{\varepsilon} \tag{1.9}$$

By substituting the right side of Equation (1.8) into (1.9), an equation that expresses q_x in terms of the estimated coefficients and the residual results:

$$q_x = \hat{\alpha}_0 + \hat{\alpha}_1 p_x + \hat{\alpha}_2 p_y + \hat{\alpha}_3 I + \hat{\alpha}_4 p^e + \hat{\varepsilon} \tag{1.9'}$$

Equation (1.9') is the stochastic form of the sample regression function.

The technique utilized to obtain estimates of the coefficients in the sample regression function is called **least squares** or **linear regression analysis**. It estimates these values by minimizing the sum of the squared residuals.[9]

The salient features of this technique can be outlined by returning to the demand curve example discussed previously. The population regression function corresponding to the demand curve for X is:

$$q_x = \alpha_0 + \alpha_1 p_x + \varepsilon \tag{1.10}$$

where the stochastic error includes the omitted variables from the demand function: p_y, I, and p^e, as well as other factors. For each p_x, least squares utilizes an estimate of the population mean of q_x as the basis for the predicted value of q_x. There is a one-to-one relationship between each p_x and the corresponding estimate of the population mean of q_x. Because a single q_x is associated with each p_x, a straight line can be passed through these points. This line is the sample regression function. The least squares technique can thus be viewed as a means of "collapsing" a stochastic function into a deterministic one.

The sample regression function associated with (1.10) can be expressed as either:

$$q_x = \hat{\alpha}_0 + \hat{\alpha}_1 p_x + \hat{\varepsilon},$$

or   (1.11)

$$\hat{q}_x = \hat{\alpha}_0 + \hat{\alpha}_1 p_x.$$

An example of these using hypothetical coefficients is:

$$q_i = 90 - 1.5 p_i + \hat{\varepsilon}_i,$$

or   (1.12)

$$\hat{q}_i = 90 - 1.5 p_i,$$

where the subscript x has been dropped, and i denotes a person in the sample. A graph of Equation (1.12) is given in Figure 1.3. If the price of X is \$2, the predicted quantity of X demanded is:

$$\hat{q}_i = 90 - 1.5(2) = 87.$$

This value is designated by the point on the sample regression function corresponding to $p_x = \$2$. When actual q_i differs from this value, a residual exists. If, for example,

---

[9] This criterion is used because minimizing the sum of the residuals can produce unsatisfactory results. When large negative and positive residuals exist, these will tend to cancel, giving the impression of a good equation when the opposite may be true.

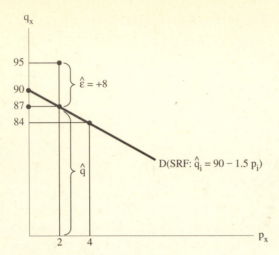

Figure 1.3 Sample regression function for the demand curve for good *x*

actual q_i is 95, the residual is:

$$\hat{\varepsilon}_i = q_i - \hat{q}_i = 95 - 87 = +8.$$

This residual is indicated by the vertical distance between the sample regression function and actual q_i at the $2 price of X. Note that a positive residual indicates an *under*estimate, while the opposite is true for a negative residual. We now turn to other manipulations that are possible with a sample regression function.

MANIPULATING AN ESTIMATED EQUATION

The sample regression function provides an estimate of the relationship between one or more explanatory variables and a dependent variable. One important use of this equation, called forecasting, involves predicting possible values the dependent variable might take.[10] Forecasts can provide us with estimates of values that may occur in the future, or that would have prevailed had the factors underlying the relationship differed from those that actually occurred. This information is useful for considering the merits of different policy options, or for persons interested in planning for the future. A second application of the sample regression function is the estimation of elasticities, which indicate the sensitivity of the dependent variable to changes in its explanatory variables. These too play a prominent role in the application of econometric results to economic policy. The basics of each of these will now be discussed.

---

[10] The connotation associated with forecast is that of creating a prediction for values that will occur at a later date, so that forecasting uses time series data. This is not necessarily the case. Cross-sectional data can also be used to create forecasts.

Predicted Value of the Dependent Variable in an Equation

A **cross-sectional data base** consists of observations on a number of different entities such as individuals, households, or firms, that occur during a single time period. A cross-sectional demand function can provide us with estimates of the quantity of a good demanded for a group of individuals during a specific year, or whenever the sample data were obtained. We obtain predicted quantity demanded by plugging a value for each explanatory variable into our sample regression function. If we utilize the hypothetical bivariate function from the previous section, our sample regression function is:

$$\hat{q}_i = 90 - 1.5p_i,$$

where the subscript i denotes the sample observation number. For example, $i = 1$ might correspond to Robert Smith, while $i = 2$ signifies David Jones, etc. By substituting values for p_i into this equation, we obtain predictions for q. If Robert Smith ($i = 1$) paid \$5 for this good, and David Jones ($i = 2$) paid \$6, our predicted quantities demanded are 82.5 ($= 90 - 1.5(5)$) units for Mr. Smith and 81 ($= 90 - 1.5(6)$) units for Mr. Jones. The value we select for p_i need *not* be one that actually occurred in the sample. Hypothetical values that pertain to contemplated policy changes might be used, for example.

Another type of data that can be used to estimate this demand curve is **time series data**. A time series data base consists of observations on the same (or similar) entities that span a number of different time periods. The frequency of this type of data can be monthly, quarterly, or annually, depending on the data source. The time series version of our bivariate demand function is:

$$\hat{q}_t = 90 - 1.5p_t,$$

where the subscript t denotes a time period. This sample regression function indicates that the relationship between q and p is contemporaneous: the value of q is determined by price during the same time period, so that the time subscript for each of these variables is the same.

Time series equations allow us to produce two different types of predicted values for our dependent variable. The first of these is our prediction for the current time period, t. This is obtained by substituting values for each of our explanatory variables into the estimated equation. If, for example, our bivariate demand function was estimated with quarterly data, and $t = 1$ corresponds to the first quarter of 1980, then if price that quarter was \$10, our prediction of quantity demanded for 1980: 1 is 75 ($= 90 - 1.5(10)$) units.

The second type of prediction pertains to the value of our dependent variable in a future time period. To forecast quantity demanded next period, q_{t+1}, we add 1 to each of the subscripts in our bivariate demand equation:

$$\hat{q}_{t+1} = 90 - 1.5p_{t+1}.$$

Because of the **contemporaneous** nature of this relationship, the prediction for q can only be made using a future value for the price of X. If the value used for p_{t+1} differs substantially from its actual value, the prediction will likely be unsatisfactory, even if the estimated coefficients are correct.[11] Forecasting with time series equations presupposes that the past (in-sample) relationship remains valid into the future as well. When the relationship between the variables in our equation is not contemporaneous, such as:

$$\hat{q}_t = 90 - 1.5p_{t-1},$$

our forecast for q is then based on a known value of the explanatory variable. In the above equation, quantity demanded this period is determined by the price that prevailed last period. Expressing the above relationship for period $t + 1$:

$$\hat{q}_{t+1} = 90 - 1.5p_t$$

gives the forecast at time t for quantity demanded in period $t + 1$. Problems arise in this situation when the estimated coefficients are faulty.

Elasticity Estimates

The law of demand specifies that consumers can be expected to buy less of a product whose price has risen, and more of a good when its price falls (other things being equal). This sensitivity of quantity demanded to price changes can, however, vary significantly among different goods.

Econometric estimates of the coefficient of p_x provide us with further information: *how much* quantity demanded responds to changes in price. However, such estimates are not comparable when the goods being evaluated possess widely different units of measurement for q_x. If, for example, the quantity of good 1 is expressed in hundreds of units per month, while for good 2 the units are millions per month, the sensitivity of good 2's consumption to price changes will typically be much greater than that for good 1. This occurs because these price coefficients fail to take into account the amount of a good that is being consumed. To make these estimates comparable, economists have developed the concept of the elasticity. The elasticity of demand measures the responsiveness of q_x to changes in p_x, where these changes are expressed as *percentages*. Because a percent change is a relative magnitude (it is defined as the change in a variable relative to the size of that variable), large absolute changes do not necessarily constitute large percent changes. We can therefore compare price sensitivities for different goods, if we use this device.

Many other elasticities exist. For the general variables x and y, where $y = f(x)$, the elasticity of y with respect to x is defined as:

(percent change in y/percent change in x)   **(1.13)**

The numerator in this formula, the percent change in y, is given by the expression:

Percent change in $y = (\Delta y/y) \cdot 100$

---

[11] This, of course, rules out pure luck.

The percent change in x is expressed in a similar manner. Using this information we may write elasticity formula (1.13) as:

$$(\Delta y/y)/(\Delta x/x) = (x/y)(\Delta y/\Delta x) \qquad \textbf{(1.14)}$$

When y in Equation (1.14) is q_x and x is p_x, we obtain the price elasticity of demand (η_d), which is defined as:

$$\eta_d = (\text{percent change in } q_x/\text{percent change in } p_x).$$

The elasticity of demand indicates the percent change in q_x that results from a 1 percent change in p_x, other things being equal. If we drop the subscript x and replace it with i to designate a person or family in our sample data, then, using Equation (1.14), the expression for η_d simplifies to:

$$\eta_d = (p_i/q_i)(\Delta q_i/\Delta p_i)$$

The slope coefficient from the sample regression function provides us with an estimate of $(\Delta q_i/\Delta p_i)$. Substituting this into the equation for η_d gives the estimated elasticity of demand ($\hat{\eta}_d$):

$$\hat{\eta}_d = (p_i/q_i)(\hat{\alpha}_1).$$

Final calculation of this measure requires that we select values for p_i and q_i. Typically, a value is chosen for p_i and the associated $\hat{q}_i$ is calculated. This pair of values is then substituted into the first term above. If we return to the hypothetical prices and predicted quantities referred to earlier:

i	Person	p_i	$\hat{q}_i$
1	Smith	$5	82.5
2	Jones	$6	81.0

the estimated elasticity for each person is:

$$(5/82.5)(-1.5) = -0.091 \text{ for Smith}$$

$$(6/81)(-1.5) = -0.111 \text{ for Jones}$$

Note that the use of actual values for p_x (and x in general) is not required when producing elasticity estimates. For cross-sectional data, values for p can be actual or hypothetical, depending on the intended use for this estimate. Sample averages are often utilized with this type of data. Several possible choices for p also exist for time series data: value p for the most recent period, the sample average, and a likely future value of p.

WHERE THEORY COURSES LEAVE OFF

The dividing line between economic theory and econometrics is based on the nature of econometrics: econometrics starts where economic theory leaves off. While theory often fails to furnish information regarding magnitudes, econometrics permits us to arrive at estimates of individual parameters and other measures of interest. An example of this demarcation is provided by an application of the elasticity of demand: when does a price increase raise total spending on a particular good? Recall that total spending for a good is the product of its price and the quantity purchased. If quantity purchased were to remain constant, higher prices would always raise total spending. However, according to the law of demand, price increases also serve to lower quantity demanded, other things being equal. This quantity effect therefore moves total spending in the opposite direction of the change in price.

Economic theory resolves this indeterminacy with the aid of the elasticity of demand. Demand is elastic if the absolute value of η_d exceeds 1, which indicates that the percent change in q exceeds that of p; inelastic when the absolute value of η_d is less than 1, so that the percent change in q is less than that of p; and unit elastic when the absolute value of η_d equals 1, so the percent changes in p and q are equal. Based on economic theory, we expect total spending to fall in response to a price increase if demand is elastic; to increase if demand is inelastic; and to remain unchanged when demand is unit elastic.

The crucial word in each of these statements is "if." As the above statements indicate, theory can be used to arrive at an answer to this question only after an estimate of the elasticity of demand has been obtained. This estimate can be provided using econometric methods: start with a demand function specified by economic theory; gather actual data on the prices paid for this good and the corresponding quantities demanded; and employ least squares to obtain estimates of the slope of the demand curve for this good ($\hat{\alpha}_1$) and predicted quantity demanded ($\hat{q}_i$) that we can use in the elasticity formula given in the previous section:

$$\hat{\eta}_d = (p_i/\hat{q}_i)(\hat{\alpha}_1).$$

Equipped with this estimate, we can determine the outcome of a price increase on total spending as well as the level of total spending that will accompany this new price (p_n), $p_n \cdot \hat{q}_i$.

WHAT ECONOMETRICS CANNOT DO

The coefficients in a population regression function are population parameters whose actual values are unknown. Estimating these requires a methodology such as least squares. Each of the resulting coefficients is in actuality a single outcome associated with a more general entity called an **estimator**. An estimator is a rule (formula) that outlines the way in which sample data are combined to approximate a population parameter of interest. Individual estimates derived from these formulas tend to differ depending on the type of sample used, chance, and so forth. Because of this fact, estimators are random variables, for which a *range* of possible estimates exist.

The properties possessed by various estimators, which are general statements about their behavior under specified conditions, have become a critical consideration in econometric research. This knowledge provides researchers with information about the likely possibilities that can accompany the use of a particular estimator.

An extensive literature exists that explores the properties of the least squares estimators under different circumstances. A major implication of this work can be summarized by the following statement: *there is no guarantee that an estimate obtained from the single use of an estimator will coincide with its population value*. This result pertains even under the "best" set of circumstances any econometric researcher is ever likely to see. The favorable outcomes associated with an estimator therefore pertain to likely values we can expect to observe *on average*, and how the range of possible estimates varies as the size of our sample changes.

Estimated coefficients sometimes differ substantially from their population values. This occurs either when the magnitude itself differs significantly from a population coefficient, or when the sign of a coefficient is the opposite of that expected. Both are potentially serious problems. Knowledge of economic theory, previous econometric results, or intuition can often be helpful in signaling the researcher that a potential difficulty exists with the estimated equation.

An objective determination of the value of the population coefficient can be made utilizing the techniques of **hypothesis testing** and **statistical inference**. The researcher specifies a **testable hypothesis** indicating a value of the unknown population parameter. Because an estimated coefficient is a random variable, associated with it is a probability distribution that indicates the range of "likely" values we can expect to observe if this estimator is used. Final judgment on whether or not to reject this hypothesis is then based on the coefficient estimate and characteristics of this distribution. Estimated values that are "very unlikely" to exist if this variable belongs in the equation (given the hypothesized population parameter value and its distribution) are used as supporting evidence for including this variable.[12]

Unfortunately, this process is not foolproof. A researcher who follows this methodology can conclude that a variable belongs in an equation when, in fact, the opposite is true. The existence of this possibility limits what can be said about equation estimates.

An example of this is provided by the GNP equation based on the Quantity Theory of Money. The Quantity Theory postulates a positive relationship between nominal GNP and the nominal supply of money. Nevertheless, taken by itself, this theory does not provide all the information required to detail the specification of this relationship. Before we can estimate an equation based on this model, we must address an important question: what is the *temporal* relationship between these vari-

---

[12] For those familiar with hypothesis testing, this procedure involves a t-test of a coefficient, where "very unlikely" is defined as a difference of two or more standard deviations between a parameter estimate and the value postulated in the null hypothesis.

ables? In other words, is the linkage between GNP and M contemporaneous? If the data are monthly or quarterly, the answer is no. Lags exist in the process by which money influences economic activity. Past or lagged values of M are therefore relevant. However, if we estimate a GNP equation using quarterly data with M_t as the explanatory variable, the coefficient of this variable indicates that it exerts a significant influence on GNP_t. What causes this result? Lagged M (the cause) is correlated with both the current money supply, M_t, and current GNP, GNP_t. While it appears that it is this quarter's money supply that determines the behavior of GNP_t, this is merely the result of the correlation between current and lagged values of M. The significant coefficient for M_t is therefore the result of **spurious (false) correlation**.

Not only can variables that do not belong in an equation appear to influence the dependent variable; variables that do belong can appear not to be part of a specified relationship. This often results from the omission of a relevant explanatory variable from the sample regression function, which is called **specification error**, or using a data base whose variables are highly correlated with each other, which is known as **multicollinearity**.

The second of these, multicollinearity, is a frequent and potentially serious problem for which remedies do not always exist. Often, this complication arises as the result of the type of data used when estimating econometric relationships. In economics, data are seldom produced as the result of controlled experimentation, where the "other things" that affect a dependent variable are kept at predetermined levels. Economic data, which is typically nonexperimental, include the joint effects of a number of factors changing simultaneously. This greatly complicates the task of estimating the individual effects of explanatory variables on a dependent variable.

An example of this can be seen with reference to the demand function for X given by Equation (1.2). Included among the explanatory variables in this equation are the price of X and the price of a related good, Y. While it might appear that including both of these variables will not cause any problems when we estimate this demand function, according to supply and demand analysis the prices of X and Y will tend to move in a predictable manner. If, for example, Y is a substitute for X, then, as the price of Y rises, consumption of X will tend to increase. This change will manifest itself as an increase in both the demand for X and the price of X (other things being equal). Based on supply and demand analysis, we therefore expect the prices of goods X and Y to be correlated.

For nonexperimental data, q_x, p_x, and p_y will generally all change simultaneously. Estimating the separate effect of p_y on q_x is thus more complicated than were we to utilize experimental data that holds the price of X constant. Because of this correlation between p_x and p_y, either (or both) of the coefficients of these variables may appear not to be significant determinants of q_x in our sample regression function.

In light of these possibilities, it is necessary to state one final limitation of econometric analysis. *A researcher can never prove anything with econometric analysis. Because of problems such as spurious correlation, where "irrelevant" variables appear significant, and both specification error and multicollinearity, which make relevant variables appear nonsignificant, one can never be totally certain about the validity of a set of empirical estimates. Furthermore, the nature of statistical inference as a means of evaluating estimates implies that at best we can only fail to disprove hypotheses about the results we obtain.* Thus, when we "fail to disprove" a hypothesis, we have not proved it. Extreme care must therefore be exercised when conducting econometric research.

A LOOK AHEAD.   The discussion in this chapter has provided a skeletal outline of what econometrics is, what the study of this subject entails, and the things econometrics cannot do. Understanding both the strengths and limitations of econometrics is critical to persons studying the material in this text, since an approach based on this knowledge will foster increased awareness in all aspects of econometric research. The burden is on the *researcher* to provide quality results. The adage "garbage in, garbage out" always looms as a possibility if sufficient care is not exercised when setting up, estimating, and analyzing econometric equations.

The next chapter provides the statistical background necessary to study econometrics within an established frame of reference. This is essential to retaining and using this material both during this course and after its completion. Chapter 3 outlines the different types of economic data, presents data manipulation methods used frequently in econometrics, and illustrates the implementation of this knowledge with "canned" computer programs. The computer discussion emphasizes understanding the way "canned" programs work, and how such programs can be used to perform the types of data manipulation discussed earlier in the chapter. The formal presentation of econometrics, which constitutes the remainder of the text, draws heavily on the background accumulated from these initial chapters.

KEY TERMS

Bivariate relationship

Multicollinearity

Contemporaneous

Cross-sectional data base

Dependent variable

Deterministic function

Econometrics

Equation residual

Equation specification

Estimator

Expected sign

Explanatory (independent) variable

Hypothesis testing

Indeterminate

Inverse (negative) relationship

Least squares (linear regression analysis) model

Multivariate relationship

Parameters

Partial slopes

Population regression function (PRF)

Positive (or direct) relationship

Sample regression function (SRF)

Scatter diagram

Specification error

Spurious (false) correlation

Stochastic error

Stochastic function

Testable hypothesis

Time series data

EXERCISES

1. The text explores a GNP equation based on the quantity theory of money. What other variables should be included in this equation? What are their expected signs? Be sure to explain the basis of these signs.

2. This chapter provides an example of an economic relationship (GNP and M) that is not contemporaneous. In other words, it is *lagged* values of the explanatory variable that affect the dependent variable. Give a microeconomic example of a relationship that is not contemporaneous, discuss the expected signs of the variables in this function, and explain the basis for the lagged relationship.

3. Outline a set of variables that should be included in a sample regression function for the supply of wheat. What are the expected signs of these variables? How might you alter the variables included in this equation based on the type of data used (i.e., cross-section or time series data)?

4. A cross-sectional data base of 10,000 persons who purchased Macintosh apples in 1989 was used to estimate the sample regression function:

$$\hat{q}_i = 150 - 2.5p_i,$$

where q is the quantity of Macintosh apples demanded in 1989, and p is the price per dozen of these apples. If the average price per dozen paid by these persons was $8:

(a) What is the predicted quantity demanded for 1989?

(b) Using the answer from (a), what is the estimated price elasticity of demand for Macintosh apples?

(c) What is estimated total spending on Macintosh apples when price is $5 (calculate the new $\hat{q}$ for this answer).

(d) Graph the demand curve for Macintosh apples implied by this function. Show that the elasticity of demand varies along this curve even though it is a straight line.

5. Assume that the same data as question (4) is used to estimate the following demand function for Macintosh apples:

$$\hat{q}_x = 10 - 1.5p_x + 0.8p_y + 0.05I + 0.2p^e,$$

where the q_x and p_x are defined in question 4, p_y is the price per dozen of oranges, I is income, and p^e is the expected future price per dozen of Macintosh apples.

(a) Does the sign of p_y indicate that Macintosh apples and navel oranges are complements or substitutes? Explain why.

(b) Derive the demand curve for Macintosh apples assuming that $p_y = \$4$, $I = \$200$, and $p^e = \$4$.

(c) Calculate an estimate of the elasticity of demand when $p_x = \$4$.

(d) The following data pertain to the first two persons in the sample:

	q	p_x	p_y	I	p^e
Robert Smith	35	5	7	400	5
David Jones	30	6	6	450	5

(1) What is the predicted quantity demanded for each person?

(2) Calculate the equation residual for each of these persons.

(3) If both Smith and Jones expect the price of apples to rise to $8 per dozen, how much will annual consumption of apples change for each of these persons?

(4) If the price expectation in (2) turns out to be correct, how much will the total spending on apples by each person change?

6. **(Advanced)** How can the information provided by the estimated demand function and part (b) of the previous question be used to calculate the income elasticity of demand? The cross (price) elasticity? (Hint: think of what the coefficients of I and p_y indicate, "other things being equal.")

2

Statistical Prerequisites: Descriptive Statistics; Probability; Mathematical Expectation; and Estimator Theory

At this point, you should have a fairly good idea of what the basic ingredients of econometrics are. It is now necessary for us to create a framework within which it is possible to understand the myriad of topics outlined in Chapter 1 that are discussed in depth throughout the remainder of this text. Such a framework is essential to the practice of applied econometrics, as nowadays almost anyone can gather data and estimate a regression equation with a computer. As the last chapter showed, the practice of applied econometrics entails a great deal more than mechanically cranking out estimated coefficients on a computer. We can only comprehend the validity of such estimates, their strengths and weaknesses, and the specific types of inferences these can be used for when an infrastructure exists that specifies how all the relevant pieces fit together.

This chapter provides the initial set of building blocks that is essential to gaining this kind of understanding: the statistical prerequisites for econometrics. Readers familiar with this material may either skim this subject matter, or skip the chapter entirely. However, this material is presupposed in the chapters that follow. The introduction to summations given in the first section can be ignored by persons comfortable with this tool.

SUMMATION NOTATION

When it is necessary for us to represent the sum of a large number of terms, we can utilize an abbreviation, called **summation notation**, which enables us to greatly simplify this task. Assume we have n observations (called the sample size) on some variable of interest, x.[1] We denote the values taken by x as: $x_1, x_2, \ldots, x_n$, where the

---

[1] In the conventional notation, variables are designated with capital letters, and observations with lowercase letters. In this text, both variables and observations will be denoted using lowercase letters. This should avoid some of the confusion with notation students sometimes encounter.

subscript represents the observation number. The dots in this expression denote the terms between x_3 and x_n that have been omitted. We must frequently obtain sums of values of this variable. If our sample size is 100, the sum of the x terms is:

$$\text{Sum of the } x\text{'s} = x_1 + x_2 + x_3 + \cdots + x_{100}.$$

The summation notation representation of this sum is given simply by:

$$\sum_{i=1}^{100} x_i = x_1 + x_2 + x_3 + \cdots + x_{100},$$

where Σ signifies "the sum of" the x values labeled with the index (subscript) i. The bottom number is the initial value of this index. The number on top denotes the final value. This notation enables us to represent the sum of a large number of terms with a single expression, the left side of the above equation. Furthermore, the summation expression remains the same regardless of whether sample size is 3 or 30,000; all that changes are the values of the indexes.

We can also use summation notation to express the sum of a number of terms, each of which involves the product of two or more variables. For example, total expenditure on good i is given by the product of its price (p) and quantity purchased (q): $p_i \cdot q_i$. Total expenditure on n goods is then:

$$\sum_{i=1}^{n} p_i q_i = p_1 q_1 + p_2 q_2 + \cdots + p_n q_n.$$

We now state several rules of summation notation and provide a proof for each of these rules.

Rules of Summations

$$\sum_{i=1}^{n} k x_i = k \sum_{i=1}^{n} x_i, \tag{I}$$

where k is a constant. To see this, expand the left side of this expression then factor out the constant k:

$$\sum_{i=1}^{n} k x_i = k x_1 + k x_2 + \cdots + k x_n$$

$$= k(x_1 + x_2 + \cdots + x_n) = k \sum x_i$$

$$\sum_{i=1}^{n} (x_i \pm y_i) = \sum_{i=1}^{n} x_i \pm \sum_{i=1}^{n} y_i \tag{II}$$

As with (I), expand the left side then collect individual x and y terms:

$$\sum_{i=1}^{n} (x_i \pm y_i) = (x_1 \pm y_1) + (x_2 \pm y_2) + \cdots + (x_n \pm y_n)$$

$$= (x_1 + \cdots + x_n) \pm (y_1 + \cdots + y_n)$$

$$= \sum x_i \pm \sum y_i.$$

Result (II) illustrates that the sum of a bracketed expression is the summation of each of its individual terms.

$$\sum_{i=1}^{n} k = n \cdot k, \qquad \textbf{(III)}$$

where k is a constant that does not vary with the index i.

$$\sum_{i=1}^{n} k = k + k + \cdots + k$$
$$= k \text{ added } n \text{ times}$$
$$= nk$$

$$\sum_{i=1}^{n} (x_i \pm k) = \sum_{i=1}^{n} x_i \pm nk \qquad \textbf{(III')}$$

This result is a slight modification of (III) that follows from the previous rules.

$$\sum_{i=1}^{n} (x_i \pm k) = (x_1 \pm k) + (x_2 \pm k) + \cdots + (x_n \pm k)$$
$$= (x_1 + x_2 + \cdots + x_n) \pm (k + k + \cdots + k)$$
$$= \sum_{i=1}^{n} x_i \pm nk$$

UNIVARIATE DESCRIPTIVE STATISTICS

When we analyze actual data for a variable of interest, the way we describe its behavior is different from what is said at the level of economic theory. Because we are confronted with a number of different values taken by this variable, it is necessary for us to characterize the behavior of all these values. The measures used for this purpose are called **descriptive statistics**. We will focus on two types of descriptive statistics. The first of these, **measures of central tendency**, characterize the behavior of this variable on average. Such measures produce a representative or average value that pertains to the entire set of observations on a variable. The second type of descriptive statistic, **measures of dispersion**, provides information about the variability of values around central tendency. In the discussion that follows, we assume that the population contains N values and that our sample consists of n values from this population. Formulas for both population and sample descriptive statistics will be stated, but manipulations will be performed only on the sample statistics.

MEASURES OF CENTRAL TENDENCY

The Mean

The **mean** (or **arithmetic mean**) of x is simply the average of individual x values. The formula for the mean is:

$$\mu_x = \frac{1}{N} \sum x_i \quad \text{(population)} \qquad \hat{\mu}_x = \frac{1}{n} \sum x_i \quad \text{(sample)} \qquad \textbf{(2.1)}$$

The symbol "μ" in (2.1) is the Greek letter *mu* that is often used to denote the population mean. The "$\hat{}$" above mu for the sample mean designates that this is an estimate of the actual value. Throughout this text, estimated parameters will be denoted in this way. If we expand the formula for the sample mean, this expression becomes:

$$\hat{\mu}_x = (1/n)(x_1 + x_2 + \cdots + x_n),$$

or

$$\hat{\mu}_x = (1/n)x_1 + (1/n)x_2 + \cdots + (1/n)x_n. \tag{2.2}$$

The recurring term $(1/n)$ in (2.2) is the **weight**, or measure of the importance attached to each observation. If each x value is distinct, $(1/n)$ denotes the probability that a particular x occurs. The **probability** of an x value indicates the number of times this specific value occurs as a proportion of the total number of possible values. This is simply its relative frequency of occurrence. The mean is therefore a weighted average of individual x values, where probabilities serve as weights.

To calculate the sample mean of x, it is necessary that we sum the values of x, then divide by the total number of observations. If the sample values of x are 1, 7, 3, and 9, the sample mean of x is $(1/4)(1 + 7 + 3 + 9)$, or 5. Although none of the sample values equals 5, the central tendency of x, as portrayed by the sample mean, indicates that this value characterizes the value taken by x on average.

An important result that we will frequently refer to characterizes the relationship between sample values of x and the mean: the sum of the deviations of individual x values from the mean, $(x_i - \hat{\mu}_x)$, equals zero. We can derive this result using the summation rules outlined in the previous section and the fact that $\hat{\mu}_x$ is a constant:

$$\sum(x_i - \hat{\mu}_x) = \sum x_i - \sum \hat{\mu}_x \quad \text{(using II)}$$
$$= \sum x_i - n\hat{\mu}_x \quad \text{(using III', where } \hat{\mu}_x \text{ is a constant).} \tag{2.3}$$

By solving (2.1) for Σx_i, we obtain an expression for the first term on the right in the above equation.

$$\hat{\mu}_x = (1/n)\sum x_i$$

so that

$$\sum x_i = n\hat{\mu}_x. \tag{2.3'}$$

Substituting (2.3') into (2.3) completes the derivation of this result:

$$\sum(x_i - \hat{\mu}_x) = \sum x_i - n\hat{\mu}_x$$
$$= n\hat{\mu}_x - n\hat{\mu}_x$$
$$= 0.$$

Above-average sample values are therefore exactly offset by below-average values. This is illustrated in Table 2.1. The amount by which 1 is below the sample average is offset by the deviation of 9 from the average. The same is true for the sample values of 3 and 7. *Because positive and negative deviations from the mean exactly cancel, we cannot construct a meaningful measure of dispersion from either the sum of the deviations from the mean, or the average of these deviations,* $(1/n)\Sigma(x_i - \hat{\mu}_x)$. Any statistic based on these would always indicate zero dispersion.

Table 2.1   *X* Values and
                  Deviations
                  from $\hat{\mu}_x = 5$

x	$(x_i - \hat{\mu}_x)$
1	-4
7	$+2$
3	-2
9	$+4$
Total	0

Geometric Mean

If the unit of measurement for the variable x is a percentage, such as an interest rate or the inflation rate, the correct measure of central tendency is the **geometric mean** of x, denoted $\hat{\mu}_G$:

$$\hat{\mu}_G = \sqrt[n]{x_1 \cdot x_2 \cdots x_n}$$

The reason this measure uses the product of x values and not their sum can be seen from the following example based on inflation rates. If we let x_t denote the ratio of the price level (p) in two successive time periods, p_t/p_{t-1}, then its value is 1 plus the rate of inflation. For example, if $p_t = 105$ and $p_{t-1} = 100$, then $x_t = 1.05$. Prices in period t are 5 percent higher than those in the preceding period. Using three periods for simplicity, then:

$$p_3 = p_0(x_1 \cdot x_2 \cdot x_3),$$

where p_0 is the base period price level and p_3 is the level of prices in the third period. The price level for any period is obtained by multiplying its value in the preceding period by 1 plus the inflation rate. These can be expressed as:

$$p_1 = p_0 \cdot x_1 = p_0(p_1/p_0)$$
$$p_2 = p_1 \cdot x_2 = (p_0(p_1/p_0))(p_2/p_1)$$
$$p_3 = p_2 \cdot x_3 = (p_0(p_1/p_0)(p_2/p_1))(p_3/p_2)$$

We are interested in measuring the average inflation rate. The arithmetic mean of these inflation rates is:

$$\hat{\mu}_x = (x_1 + x_2 + x_3)/3 = (1/3)[(p_1/p_0) + (p_2/p_1) + (p_3/p_2)]$$

The geometric mean is:

$$\hat{\mu}_{Gx} = \sqrt[3]{x_1 \cdot x_2 \cdot x_3} = \sqrt[3]{(p_1/p_0)(p_2/p_1)(p_3/p_2)}$$

Once an estimated mean is calculated, it is used in place of the actual growth rate for each period to convert base period prices into those for period 3. Thus, estimated $p_3 = p_0(\hat{\mu})^3$, where $\hat{\mu}$ is either the arithmetic or geometric mean. The result, using the arithmetic mean, is:

$$\text{estimated } p_3 = p_0(\hat{\mu}_x)^3 = p_0(1/3)^3[(p_1/p_0) + (p_2/p_1) + (p_3/p_2)]^3 \neq p_3$$

For the geometric mean:

$$\text{estimated } p_3 = p_0(\hat{\mu}_{Gx})^3 = p_0\{\sqrt[3]{(p_1/p_0)(p_2/p_1)(p_3/p_2)}\}^3$$
$$= p_0\{(p_1/p_0)(p_2/p_1)(p_3/p_2)\}$$
$$= p_3$$

The arithmetic mean gives an incorrect estimate for p_3, while the geometric mean produces the correct value.

The proper measure to approximate the central tendency for a set of observations that are percentages is thus the geometric mean. If the sample values of x are 0.01, 0.02, and 0.03, the geometric mean is 0.0182, while the arithmetic mean is 0.02.

MEASURES OF DISPERSION

The Variance

The **variance** of x, denoted σ_x^2, is the average of the squared **deviations** of the x's from their mean. The formula for the variance is:

$$\sigma_x^2 = \frac{1}{N} \sum(x_i - \mu_x)^2 \quad \text{(population)}$$

$$\hat{\sigma}_x^2 = \frac{1}{n-1} \sum(x_i - \hat{\mu}_x)^2 \quad \text{(sample)} \qquad \textbf{(2.4)}$$

The denominator of the first term in the sample variance is not n, which would make $\hat{\sigma}_x^2$ the mean of the squared x deviations, but $(n-1)$. Defining the sample variance this way allows it to attain a desirable estimator property that is discussed later in this chapter.[2]

Calculating the sample variance is fairly straightforward. Once we compute the sample mean, we obtain the deviation of each x_i from the mean, square then sum these deviations, then divide by $(n-1)$. An illustration of this is given in Table 2.2 using the data from Table 2.1.

---

[2] For those with a statistical background: the desirable property of this statistic is unbiasedness, and the term $(n-1)$ represents the number of degrees of freedom.

Table 2.2   Calculation of the Variance

x	$(x_i - \hat{\mu}_x)$	$(x_i - \hat{\mu}_x)^2$	
1	$(1 - 5) = -4$	$(-4)^2 = 16$	
7	$(7 - 5) = +2$	$(+2)^2 = 4$	$\hat{\sigma}_x^2 = 1/3(40)$
3	$(3 - 5) = -2$	$(-2)^2 = 4$	$= 13.33$
9	$(9 - 5) = +4$	$(+4)^2 = 16$	
		$\sum(x_i - \hat{\mu}_x)^2 = 40$	

The formulas given in (2.4) require four steps to calculate the sample variance. An alternative method, or "shortcut" formula, exists. To derive this, we first square the bracketed term in (2.4):

$$\hat{\sigma}_x^2 = \frac{1}{n-1} \sum(x_i - \hat{\mu}_x)^2$$

$$= \frac{1}{n-1} \sum(x_i^2 + \hat{\mu}_x^2 - 2\hat{\mu}_x x_i)$$

Using rule (II) for summations, we then sum each term in the bracket:

$$= \frac{1}{n-1} \left(\sum x_i^2 + \sum \hat{\mu}_x^2 - \sum 2\hat{\mu}_x x_i\right).$$

By applying summation rules (I) and (III) along with (2.3'), $\Sigma x_i = n\hat{\mu}_x$, we arrive at the final form of this "shortcut" equation:

$$= \frac{1}{n-1} \left(\sum x_i^2 + n\hat{\mu}_x^2 - 2\hat{\mu}_x \sum x_i\right)$$

$$= \frac{1}{n-1} \left(\sum x_i^2 + n\hat{\mu}_x^2 - 2n\hat{\mu}_x^2\right)$$

$$\hat{\sigma}_x^2 = \frac{1}{n-1} \sum x_i^2 - \frac{n}{n-1} \hat{\mu}_x^2 \tag{2.5}$$

The advantage of using this "shortcut" is that its calculation of $\hat{\sigma}_x^2$ requires that we perform only one step beyond computing $\hat{\mu}_x$: sum the squared x values.

One drawback associated with the variance is its unit of measurement. Since $\hat{\sigma}_x^2$ is defined in terms of squared deviations, its unit of measurement is the square of the unit with which x is measured. If, for example, x is age in years, the variance of x is denominated in years squared, which is a somewhat awkward standard. Fortunately, we can remedy this deficiency by deriving a variant of $\hat{\sigma}_x^2$, called the standard deviation, whose unit of measurement is the same as that for x.

Standard Deviation

The **standard deviation** of x, denoted σ_x, is the (positive) square root of the variance of x. The regular and "shortcut" formulas for the standard deviation of x are:

$$\sigma_x = \sqrt{\frac{1}{N}\sum(x_i - \mu_x)^2} \quad \text{(population)} \qquad \hat{\sigma}_x = \sqrt{\frac{1}{n-1}\sum(x_i - \hat{\mu}_x)^2} \quad \text{(sample)}$$

$$\text{(2.6)}$$

$$\sigma_x = \sqrt{\frac{1}{N}\sum x_i^2 - \mu_x^2} \quad \text{(population)} \qquad \hat{\sigma}_x = \sqrt{\frac{1}{n-1}\sum x_i^2 - \frac{n}{n-1}\hat{\mu}_x^2} \quad \text{(sample)}$$

Calculating the standard deviation involves only one step beyond computing the variance. $\hat{\sigma}_x$ measures the average deviation of x around its mean in a way that eliminates the problem caused by the canceling of positive with negative deviations. Finally, $\hat{\sigma}_x$ has the same unit of measurement as x itself. In the example above, where x denotes the age of an individual in years, both the mean and standard deviation are denominated in years, while the variance is expressed in years squared. Because such differences exist in the units of measurement for descriptive statistics, the mean and standard deviation are typically used together when characterizing the behavior of a variable.

MEASURES OF ASSOCIATION BETWEEN PAIRS OF VARIABLES

The univariate statistics discussed above summarize the behavior of a single variable, or of several variables taken one at a time. These statistics allow us to examine the central tendency of a variable, as measured by its mean, the divergence of each observation from its mean, and dispersion, with either the variance or standard deviation, based on squared deviations from the mean. We now expand this information and present several statistical measures that are used to depict the interrelationship between a pair of variables. We illustrate the basis for these measures by focusing on two macroeconomic variables, the capacity utilization rate (c) in manufacturing and the civilian unemployment rate (u).

The theoretical relationship between these variables is inverse. An increase in the capacity utilization rate, which indicates more intensive use of the existing capital stock, necessitates that firms increase their use of variable inputs, especially labor. As total labor input (manhours) rises, employment also increases, which, other things being equal, lowers the unemployment rate.[3] Thus, according to economic theory, $u = f(c)$, and the expected sign of the capacity utilization rate is negative. Figure 2.1 depicts such an inverse relationship. If the capacity utilization rate rises from c_1 to

---

[3] A more detailed analysis of both the theoretical and empirical relationship between these variables is provided in Chapter 4. It is assumed here that causation runs from the capacity utilization rate to the unemployment rate. A more realistic analysis would consider the fact that these variables may in fact be jointly determined.

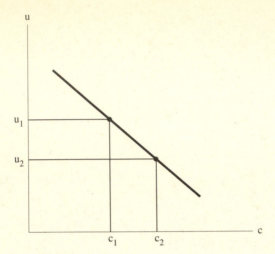

Figure 2.1

c_2, then, other things being equal, the unemployment rate falls from u_1 to u_2. However, other things are *not* equal with actual data. The capacity utilization rate in manufacturing captures only the cyclical behavior of the unemployment rate. It does not account for the secular (long-term) trend in the unemployment rate that is determined by both the size and composition of the labor force. Because changes in the unemployment rate reflect both cyclical and secular factors, a number of different unemployment rates can arise for a single capacity utilization rate. We must therefore distinguish the theoretical relationship between these variables from their statistical association.

Table 2.3 gives the actual values for these variables from 1979 to 1988. The capacity utilization rate ranged from 70.3 percent to 84.6 percent, with an average of 79.1 percent. The unemployment rate varied from 5.8 percent to 9.7 percent, with a mean of 7.3 percent. The graph of these unemployment rate–capacity utilization rate values, which is called a **scatter diagram**, is given in Figure 2.2(a). Each point in this diagram represents the combination of values for a specific year. The solid lines in this figure indicate the mean of each variable, and their intersection denotes the point of means. All but one of the points in Figure 2.2(a) lie in quadrants (II) and (IV). Consider the points in quadrant (II). There, the unemployment rate is above average, while the capacity utilization rate is below average. The opposite is true for quadrant (IV), which indicates the combination of a below-average unemployment rate and an above-average capacity utilization rate. If we were to fit a line to these data, it would clearly have a negative slope. That not all points will lie on such a line results from the fact that we are dealing with a stochastic function, as discussed in Chapter 1.

The statistical relationship between these variables is based on the existence of a pattern in the deviations of individual observations from their means. Consider 1979, for example. As Table 2.3 shows, the capacity utilization rate that year was 84.6 percent, which exceeds its average over this period of 79.1 percent. Where was the

Table 2.3 Capacity Utilization Rate in Manufacturing and
the Civilian Unemployment Rate

YEAR	CAPACITY UTILIZATION RATE	UNEMPLOYMENT RATE
1979	84.6	5.8
1980	79.3	7.1
1981	78.2	7.6
1982	70.3	9.7
1983	73.9	9.6
1984	80.5	7.5
1985	80.1	7.2
1986	79.7	7.0
1987	81.1	6.2
1988	83.5	5.5
Mean	79.1	7.3
Standard Deviation	4.3	1.4

Source: Economic Report of the President, 1989.

unemployment rate in 1979 relative to its mean? The 5.8 percent unemployment rate
in 1979 was below its average of 7.3 percent. Thus, the point corresponding to 1979
lies in quadrant (IV). The data in this diagram thus portray a definite pattern: whenever one of these variables is above average, the other virtually always falls below its
average. The scatter diagram therefore depicts an inverse relationship between the
capacity utilization rate and the unemployment rate for these years. We now discuss
two measures of the *linear* association between a pair of variables: the covariance
and the correlation coefficient. These allow us to quantify the information contained
in this scatter diagram.

The Covariance

The quantifiable information that forms the basis for measuring the linear association
between a pair of variables is contained in the pattern of the deviations of each variable from its mean. If we refer to these variables as x and y, then for each sample
observation, numerical values exist for the deviations of x and y from their means,
$(x_i - \hat{\mu}_x)$ and $(y_i - \hat{\mu}_y)$, respectively. The product of these terms for observation i is:

$$(x_i - \hat{\mu}_x) \cdot (y_i - \hat{\mu}_y)$$

In the previous example, when x was above average, which makes $(x_i - \hat{\mu}_x)$ positive,
y was almost always below its mean, so that $(y_i - \hat{\mu}_y)$ was negative. To obtain the
covariance between x and y, we sum these products, then divide by a term. The result
can be viewed as the mean of these products. It depicts the pattern that pertains *on
average*. If we denote the covariance between x and y as σ_{xy}, the population and

Unemployment Rate and Capacity Utilization Rate: 1979–1988

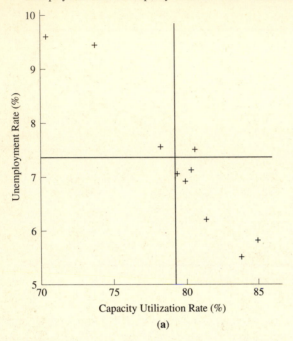

(a)

Unemployment Rate and Capacity Utilization Rate: 1970–1988

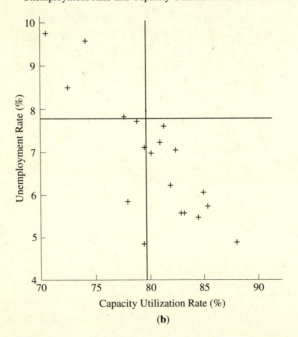

(b)

Figure 2.2

sample formulas are:

$$\sigma_{xy} = \frac{1}{N} \sum (x_i - \mu_x)(y_i - \mu_y) \quad \text{(population)}$$

(2.7)

$$\hat{\sigma}_{xy} = \frac{1}{n-1} \sum (x_i - \hat{\mu}_x)(y_i - \hat{\mu}_y) \quad \text{(sample)}$$

where μ_x and μ_y are the population means of x and y, respectively.

The covariance between the unemployment rate and the capacity utilization rate in the example above is negative. The dominant pattern is thus deviations from means that differ in sign. Patterns as clear as that given in Table 2.3 do not always occur. Typically, a scatter diagram's points lie in all four quadrants. Figure 2.2(b), which is based on the capacity utilization rate–unemployment rate data for 1970 to 1988, displays this more typical pattern, where one or more points are in each of quadrants (I) and (III). Both variables attain above-average values in quadrant (I) and below-average values in quadrant (III). Since an above-average observation implies a positive deviation from the mean, the product of two such values gives a positive value. A below-average value implies a negative deviation. The product of two negative deviations, as in quadrant (III), also gives a positive product. So, the calculation of $\hat{\sigma}_{xy}$ for 1970 to 1988 involves both positive and negative products. The sign of the covariance between two variables is therefore determined by both the signs and magnitudes of the product terms. In this example, the covariance is negative for both the 1979–1988 and the 1970–1988 periods. The positive products in the 1970–1988 data are therefore more than offset by the negative products. Table 2.4 illustrates the calculation of the covariance for the data in Table 2.3.

The covariance between two variables can thus be visualized with the aid of a scatter diagram, as in the previous example. Using this device to depict the statistical relationship between two variables, most points will lie in quadrants (II) and (IV) when these variables are inversely related, and in quadrants (I) and (III) when a positive relationship exists.

Using the products of deviations from means, the covariance is easier to interpret than if it were calculated using products of the actual values of the variables themselves, as x and y might have very different units of measurement. When the dispersion in either or both of these variables is large, however, the covariance will also tend to be large. This limits our ability to compare covariances. An example of this can be seen by referring to the cross-sectional labor demand data given in Table 2.5(a), which consists of the average monthly employment of production and nonsupervisory personnel (employment) and real hourly earnings (real wages) for 1983 by two-digit Standard Industrial Code (SIC) category.[4] There is an inverse relationship

---

[4] Although these data reflect the influences of both labor supply and labor demand, they primarily reflect labor demand. 1983 is the first year of an economic recovery. During that year, unemployment remained close to double-digit levels. Thus the supply of labor was likely fairly elastic during that year and employment primarily demand determined. Second, by using two-digit SIC categories, we are less likely to encounter areas of labor shortage that might exist at either three- or four-digit SIC levels.

Table 2.4 Calculation of the Covariance Between the Capacity Utilization Rate (x) and Unemployment Rate (y)

YEAR	x	y	$(x_i - \hat{\mu}_x)$	$(y_i - \hat{\mu}_y)$	$(x_i - \hat{\mu}_x)(y_i - \hat{\mu}_y)$
1979	84.6	5.8	5.48	−1.52	−8.33
1980	79.3	7.1	0.18	−0.22	−0.04
1981	78.2	7.6	−0.92	0.28	−0.26
1982	70.3	9.7	−8.82	2.38	−20.99
1983	73.9	9.6	−5.22	2.28	−11.90
1984	80.5	7.5	1.38	0.18	0.25
1985	80.1	7.2	0.98	−0.12	−0.12
1986	79.7	7.0	0.58	−0.32	−0.19
1987	81.1	6.2	1.98	−1.12	−2.22
1988	83.5	5.5	4.38	−1.82	−7.97
Mean	79.1	7.3		Total	−51.76

$$\hat{\sigma}_{xy} = (1/(n-1))\sum(x_i - \hat{\mu}_x)(y_i - \hat{\mu}_y)$$
$$= (1/9)(-51.76)$$
$$\hat{\sigma}_{xy} = -5.75$$

between these variables. Other things being equal, an increase in real wages (w) raises the marginal costs of production. This lowers both profit-maximizing production and employment (N). Thus, $N = f(w)$, and the expected sign of w is negative.

The empirical relationship between these variables differs from this since a number of factors in addition to real wages determine the levels of employment for these SIC categories. Again, we are dealing with a stochastic function. Table 2.5(b) illustrates the calculation of the covariance between employment and real wages for these SIC categories. Compared to the real wage data, the magnitudes of the employment figures, along with the variance of this data series, are rather large: mean employment is 7,503 thousand persons per month, and the variance of employment is 38,121,218! The covariance between employment and real wages is −5,763. This is approximately 1,000 times the covariance between the unemployment rate and the capacity utilization rate discussed earlier. Does this indicate that the linear association between N and w is much stronger than that between the unemployment rate and the capacity utilization rate? Not necessarily. The units of measurement for these variables affect the magnitudes of their covariances. If we instead express employment in millions of persons per month, mean employment falls to 7.503, with a variance of 38.12. The covariance between N and w then falls to −5.76. By altering the unit of measurement for only one of our variables, we have obtained a covariance that is almost identical to that between the unemployment rate and the capacity utilization rate! This illustrates a potentially serious limitation of the covariance.

Table 2.5 Nonsupervisory Employment and Real Hourly Earnings by SIC Category for 1983

(a)

	EMPLOYMENT OF PRODUCTION AND NONSUPERVISORY WORKERS (thousands/month)	REAL HOURLY EARNINGS ($/hr) (1977 = 100)
Manufacturing	12,581	$5.39
Mining	678	$6.88
Construction	3,026	$7.28
Transportation and Public Utilities	4,073	$6.59
Wholesale Trade	4,220	$5.21
Retail Trade	13,951	$3.50
Finance, Insurance, and Real Estate	4,066	$4.45
Services	17,428	$4.46

Source: Statistical Abstracts of the United States, 1982.

(b)

	N	w	$(N_i - \hat{\mu}_N)$	$(w_i - \hat{\mu}_w)$	$(N_i - \hat{\mu}_N)(w_i - \hat{\mu}_w)$
Manufacturing	12,581	5.39	5,078.13	−0.08	−406.3
Mining	678	6.88	−6,824.88	1.41	−9,623.1
Construction	3,026	7.28	−4,476.88	1.81	−8,103.1
Transportation and Public Utilities	4,073	6.59	−3,429.88	1.12	−3,841.5
Wholesale Trade	4,220	5.21	−3,282.88	−0.26	853.5
Retail Trade	13,951	3.50	6,448.13	−1.97	−12,702.8
Finance, Insurance, and Real Estate	4,066	4.45	−3,436.88	−1.02	3,505.6
Services	17,428	4.46	9,925.13	−1.01	−10,024.4
Mean	7,503	5.47		Total	−40,342.0
Stand. Dev.	6,174	1.34			

$$\hat{\sigma}_{Nw} = (1/(n-1))\sum (N_i - \hat{\mu}_N)(w_i - \hat{\mu}_w)$$
$$= (1/7)(-40,342.0)$$
$$\hat{\sigma}_{Nw} = -5,763.14$$

The Correlation Coefficient

The **correlation coefficient** between x and y is related to the covariance and is thus a second measure of the linear association between this pair of variables. Unlike the covariance, however, the correlation coefficient is a pure number. As such, it does not suffer from the potential problem with units of measurement the covariance possesses. This feature allows us to compare the correlation coefficients for different pairs of variables.

Recall that the covariance is affected by the dispersion in the values of x and y. The correlation coefficient "loses" the original units of measurement for these variables by standardizing for such dispersion. This is accomplished by dividing the covariance by the product of the standard deviations for x and y. The result is a number that lies between two absolute limits, which we can use as benchmarks for the strength of the relationship between the variables under study. The formula for the correlation coefficient of x and y, ρ_{xy}, is:

$$\rho_{xy} = \frac{\sigma_{xy}}{\sigma_x \cdot \sigma_y} \quad \text{(population)}$$

(2.8)

$$\hat{\rho}_{xy} = \frac{\hat{\sigma}_{xy}}{\hat{\sigma}_x \cdot \hat{\sigma}_y} \quad \text{(sample)}$$

It can be shown that ρ_{xy} always lies between -1 and $+1$. Since the standard deviation is always positive, the sign of ρ_{xy} is determined by the numerator of (2.8), the covariance. A negative covariance therefore implies a negative correlation coefficient, while a positive covariance is associated with a positive correlation coefficient.

A correlation coefficient of -1 indicates a **perfect negative correlation**. All of the points in the scatter diagram fall on a downward sloping line that passes through the point of means. This line, which is called the **population reference line**, passes through the point (μ_x, μ_y) and has slope $-(\sigma_y/\sigma_x)$. In general, the stronger an inverse relationship is, the closer ρ_{xy} will be to -1, and the more tightly points will lie around the reference line, as in Figure 2.3(a). Conversely, a weaker negative relationship implies that ρ_{xy} is closer to 0, and that points are more widely scattered around the reference line, as in Figure 2.3(b). The corresponding graphs for positive correlation are given in Figure 2.3(c) for the weaker relationship and in Figure 2.3(d) for the stronger relationship. The slope of the sample reference line for these points is $+(\hat{\sigma}_y/\hat{\sigma}_x)$. When the correlation coefficient is $+1$, a **perfect positive correlation** exists.

If we refer again to the capacity utilization rate – unemployment rate data in Table 2.3, the covariance between these variables is -5.75 (derived in Table 2.4). The standard deviations are 4.25 for the capacity utilization rate and 1.42 for the unemployment rate. The sample correlation coefficient based on these data is:

$$\hat{\rho}_{xy} = \frac{-5.75}{(4.25)(1.42)}$$

$$= -0.953.$$

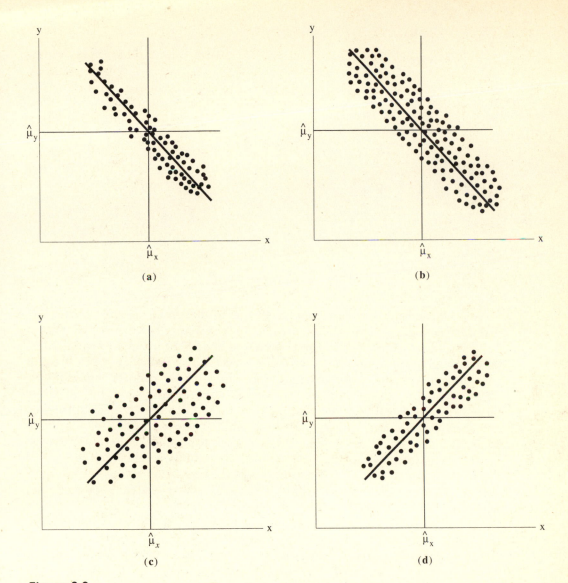

Figure 2.3

These data are fairly tightly spread around the reference line. Using the longer time period of 1970–1988 for these variables, the value of $\hat{\rho}_{xy}$ falls to -0.823. While still indicative of a strong correlation, it is not as large as that for the smaller sample. *Note that a sample correlation coefficient of -0.953 does not imply that when x is above average, y is below average 95.3 percent of the time. Furthermore, a correlation coefficient of -0.953 indicates a stronger negative association than does -0.476, but not by twice as much.*

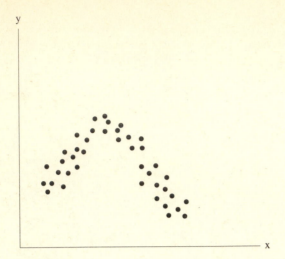

Figure 2.4

Let us compare this correlation coefficient to that from the employment and real wage data discussed in the last section. The covariance between N and w (from Table 2.5(b)) is $-5,763$. The standard deviations are 6,174 for employment and 1.34 for real wages, which gives a correlation coefficient of -0.698. Although it is not valid for us to draw a conclusion about which of these is the stronger empirical relationship based on their covariances, we can make this determination by comparing their correlation coefficients. Because the time series correlation coefficient between the unemployment rate and capacity utilization rate exceeds that of the cross-sectional data on employment and real wages, we conclude that the linear association between the unemployment rate and the capacity utilization rate is the stronger of the two considered here. Of course, one must exercise caution because, as we show later, correlation does not necessarily indicate causation, and it is possible that one of the relationships entails some nonlinearity.

If no systematic *linear* relationship exists between x and y, the correlation coefficient is zero. In this case, either the band of values around the reference line is extremely wide, or the relationship between x and y is nonlinear, as in Figure 2.4.

The Coefficient of Determination

The correlation coefficient is an improvement over the covariance since it permits us to compare the strengths of the relationships between different pairs of variables. Nevertheless, we cannot use this measure to make statements about the frequency with which the deviation terms conform to a specific sign pattern (such as with $\rho_{xy} = -0.953$). There is a measure, called the **coefficient of determination**, that allows us to make statements about percentages. The coefficient of determination, which is the square of the correlation coefficient, indicates the proportion of the total variation in one variable that is associated with changes in the other. If ρ_{xy} is -0.953, as in the first example above, the coefficient of determination, ρ_{xy}^2, equals 0.91 $(= [-0.953]^2)$, and 91 percent of the observed variability in the unemployment rate is associated with the changes in the capacity utilization rate. Note that ρ_{xy} equals ρ_{yx}, so that neither the correlation coefficient nor the coefficient of determination specifies which of these is the dependent variable. It is therefore equally valid to interpret the 0.91 coefficient of determination as indicating that 91 percent of the variability in the capacity utilization rate can be associated with changes in the un- employment rate for this period. The same is true for the employment-real wage data. Its coefficient of determination is 0.49 $(= [-0.698]^2)$. Thus approximately half of the observed variation in employment is associated with differences in real wages, or half of the variation in real wages can be linked to differences in employment levels. As these examples show, correlation does not necessarily indicate causation.

Correlation and Causation

To pursue the last point further, consider again the Quantity Theory of Money. As discussed in Chapter 1, this theory postulates that changes in the nominal supply of money (M) cause nominal Gross National Product (GNP) to change in the same direction. Thus, GNP = $f(M)$, and the expected sign of M is positive. The causality for this equation is derived from the *monetary transmission mechanism*. The Keynesian transmission mechanism for an increase in the money supply consists of the following sequence of events, which are depicted in Figure 2.5(a):

> an increase in money supply (M^s) causes
>
> a decrease in the rate of interest (r), which causes
>
> interest-sensitive spending such as planned investment (I_p) to rise,
>   which, through a multiplier, causes
>
> an increase in nominal GNP (Y)

Unfortunately, this theory has nothing to say about the relevant time period for the explanatory variable. In other words, is the relationship between M and GNP contemporaneous?

This process is not instantaneous. A lag exists between the time at which M changes and the response by GNP. If we were to obtain quarterly data for GNP and M, then, based on theoretical considerations, we would expect the scatter diagram of current period values for these variables to exhibit a weak relationship. In fact, just the opposite occurs, as the scatter diagram of quarterly GNP and M1 for the 1984:3 to 1988:4 period in Figure 2.5(b) illustrates. Note the extremely strong posi- tive relationship displayed by these data. The correlation coefficient for these vari- ables is 0.963, which indicates an almost perfect positive correlation! How can this be possible?

The model implied by this diagram is:

$$\text{GNP}_t = f(M_t),$$

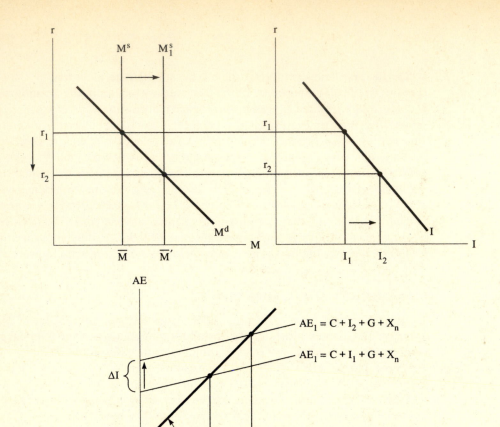

$$AE_1 = C + I_2 + G + X_n$$

$$AE_1 = C + I_1 + G + X_n$$

(a)

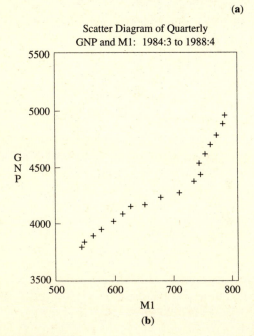

Scatter Diagram of Quarterly
GNP and M1: 1984:3 to 1988:4

(b)

Figure 2.5

where the subscript t denotes the time period. This large correlation coefficient is not the result of M_t affecting GNP_t (remember that with a correlation coefficient, the direction could be the reverse as well). Instead, it reflects the influence of the common time trend shared by both of these variables. Both GNP_t and M_t are rising throughout this entire time period. However, neither the scatter diagram nor the correlation coefficient takes this factor into account when depicting the relationship between these variables. It is therefore the upward time trend in M_t that is responsible for the large correlation with GNP_t, although it appears that M_t is responsible.

The name for this situation, recall, is spurious correlation. Because of the potential for this complication, we must always be mindful of the caveat that *correlation does not necessarily indicate causation*. Causation *does* run from the money supply to GNP, but not from the current quarter's M to current quarter GNP. A more appropriate explanatory variable is a lagged value of M.[5] As lagged M is highly correlated with current M, the appearance that M_t is the correct causal factor emerges.

PROBABILITY AND MATHEMATICAL EXPECTATION

Econometric equations utilize estimators of population parameters as the coefficients in sample regression functions. These estimators are random variables, variables whose values differ depending on factors such as the sample of values utilized to estimate these coefficients. Because of this fact, estimated coefficients can sometimes diverge substantially from their population parameters. For us to judge the potential desirability of different estimators, we must therefore possess a set of *objective* criteria that allow us to:

(i) establish systematic links between estimators and population parameters; and

(ii) judge particular estimates to determine whether these are "acceptable" in some sense (based on hypotheses about the corresponding population coefficients).

The criteria employed for this purpose have as their basis the probability distributions (or density functions) associated with these estimators. These indicate the likelihood, or probabilities, of obtaining different possible values from these estimators. The notion of probability is thus a fundamental ingredient in the evaluation of estimators. The next part of this chapter provides an overview of probability theory that is presupposed throughout the remainder of this text. Mathematical expectation is also presented. This is a tool that allows us to derive expressions for the central tendency and dispersion in probability distributions of interest.

---

[5] Actually, a distributed lag of past money supply values would be more appropriate. Obviously, at this point in the text, we are interested in establishing the difference between current period and lagged values. The topic of distributed lags is considered later.

PROBABILITY AND PROBABILITY FUNCTIONS

Univariate Probability

The concept of probability was introduced earlier in the discussion of the sample mean. Recall that the formula for the sample mean is:

$$\hat{\mu}_x = (1/n)\sum x_i$$
$$= (1/n)x_1 + (1/n)x_2 + \cdots + (1/n)x_n.$$

The expression on the right shows that $\hat{\mu}_x$ is a weighted average of individual x values, where the weight is $(1/n)$ for each sample value.[6] The value $(1/n)$ is the **probability** of each x value occurring. This expresses the number of times a particular sample value occurs relative to the total number of sample values. The probability of observing a particular value is thus related to the relative frequency with which that value occurs; that is, the number of occurrences divided by the total number of possible values. If the value of the sample mean is obtained from a sample where x_1 occurs n_1 times, and x_2 occurs n_2 times, and these account for all n observations, the sample mean is:

$$\hat{\mu}_x = (n_1/n)x_1 + (n_2/n)x_2.$$

The probability of x_1 is thus (n_1/n), while the probability of x_2 is (n_2/n). Since probabilities are relative frequencies (proportions), their sum must equal one.

Probabilities are associated with uncertain events. Variables whose values are based on uncertainty are called **random variables**. Associated with every possible value of a random variable is a probability of that value occurring. Random variables whose possible values do not include intervals are called **discrete random variables**. An example is a variable x that takes only the values 1, 2, 3, 4, and 5. Random variables also exist whose values include those between discrete values. These are called **continuous random variables**. Values taken by a continuous random variable would include all the values in the interval from 1 to 5 in the above example.

A **probability function** is a function that associates a probability with each possible value of a discrete random variable. Initially, we will consider a discrete random variable x that takes the values x_1, x_2, and x_3. If we denote the probability (p) that x takes the value x_1, or $p(x = x_1)$ as $p(x_1)$, with similar notation for x_2 and x_3, then the probabilities associated with our x values are $p(x_1)$, $p(x_2)$, and $p(x_3)$. The relevant probability function for these values is depicted in Table 2.6. Each probability denotes the relative frequency with which the particular x value occurs; p_i equals (n_i/n) if there are n_i occurrences of the ith value of x out of a total of n sample values.

---

[6] The general formula for a weighted average is:

$$\sum w_i x_i / \sum w_i,$$

where w_i is the ith weight. In this more general formulation, the weights need not add to 1.

Table 2.6 Probability Function
of x

VALUE	PROBABILITY
x_1	$p(x_1)$
x_2	$p(x_2)$
x_3	$p(x_3)$
Total	1.0

A probability function can also be depicted graphically. Figure 2.6 shows the probability function for the discrete random variable x based on Table 2.6. Note that $p(x_i)$ is on the vertical axis while x_i is on the horizontal axis. Since x is a discrete random variable, it is not defined between either x_1 and x_2 or x_2 and x_3. In this graph, it is assumed that both x_1 and x_2 are more likely to occur than x_3, since each of their probabilities exceed $p(x_3)$. When the values of x are equally likely, $p(x_i)$ equals 1/3 for each value of x, which gives the **uniform probability function** shown in Figure 2.7.

When x is a continuous random variable, it can assume an infinite number of possible x values, since it is defined over an entire interval. The function that associates probabilities with values of a continuous random variable is called a **probability density function**. Probability for this type of variable is denoted by the area under a continuous curve. To show why this is true, it is necessary for us to consider the way values taken by a continuous random variable are summarized.

Because a continuous random variable can take a large number of possible values, it is necessary to divide the values of this variable into a series of mutually

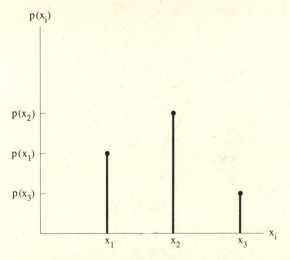

Figure 2.6 Probability function of x

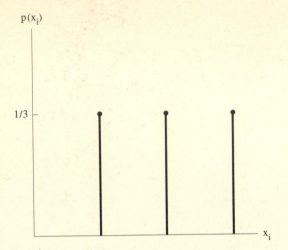

Figure 2.7 Uniform probability function

exclusive ranges called **class intervals**. Each interval should span an equal range of possible values. If, for example, x takes on values from 0 to 100, the class intervals chosen might be[7]:

> 0 to 24.9
>
> 25 to 49.9
>
> 50 to 74.9
>
> 75 to 99.9

Adding the number of observations (n) for each range to these class intervals gives the **frequency distribution of x**. An example of a frequency distribution using these class intervals is:

CLASS INTERVAL	FREQUENCY
0 to 24.9	n_1
25 to 49.9	n_2
50 to 74.9	n_3
75 to 99.9	n_4

The frequency distribution of a random variable can also be represented by a bar graph called a **histogram**. The horizontal axis of a histogram lists the class intervals,

---

[7] There are general rules for selecting this which are not discussed here. The reader is referred to the statistical references at the end of the chapter.

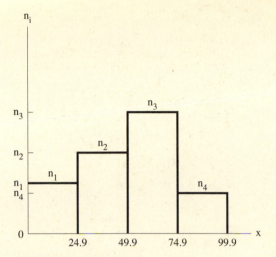

Figure 2.8 Histogram of x

while the vertical axis displays the number of observations. The histogram corresponding to the previous example is given in Figure 2.8. A slight variant of the histogram lists the proportion of the total values occurring in each class interval on the vertical axis, while the horizontal axis displays the class intervals. Such a graph, called the **relative frequency histogram**, is shown in Figure 2.9. The area of any of the bars in a relative frequency histogram is the product of the proportion of values in that class interval and the width of that interval. While the proportions sum to 1, the

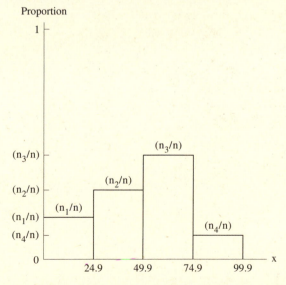

Figure 2.9 Relative frequency histogram of x

total area of all the bars in this type of histogram do not. To make the total area sum to 1, so that area can be related to probability, the vertical axis is converted to what is called the **density scale**. When the density scale is used, the area of each bar gives the proportion of observations falling into that class interval.

Converting to the density scale entails changing the height of each bar to its **relative frequency density**. The height of any bar is then the ratio of the proportion of total observations falling into that class interval to the width of that class (assumed to be identical for each class). The area of each bar is then:

$$\text{area} = \text{height} \cdot \text{width}$$

$$\text{area} = \frac{\text{proportion of } x \text{ values}}{\text{width}} \cdot \text{width}$$

$$= \text{proportion of } x \text{ values.}$$

The probability function associated with continuous random variables is called a density function because of its use of this scale.

The final steps involved in obtaining the probability density function of a random variable consist of increasing both the sample size and the number of class intervals. As sample size increases, the shape of the function tends to stabilize and become more filled in, more closely approximating a continuous function. A histogram with a density scale for a fairly large sample is given by Figure 2.10(a), while the smooth curve based on increasing sample size to a very large value is shown in Figure 2.10(b). The curve in 2.10(b) is the **probability density function** for x. The area between points a and b measures the probability that x takes a value in this interval. Notice that since probability is related to areas under this curve, *the probability that a continuous random variable takes on a specific value is zero, since then the interval width is zero.*[8]

Bivariate Probability

When it is necessary for us to analyze two random variables, the focus of probability shifts to the likelihood of observing a particular *pair* of values, one for each random variable (assuming each is discrete). To make this notion clearer, consider two discrete random variables x and y. If our sample consists of n values of x and m for y, the sample of x and y is then:

$$x: x_1, x_2, \ldots, x_n,$$

$$y: y_1, y_2, \ldots, y_m \quad \text{(where } n \text{ does not necessarily equal } m\text{).}$$

---

[8] For a continuous random variable, probability is found using integral calculus. The probability that x is between a and b is:

$$P(a < x < b) = \int_a^b p(x)\, dx,$$

where $p(x)$ is the probability density function of X.

Relative Frequency
Density

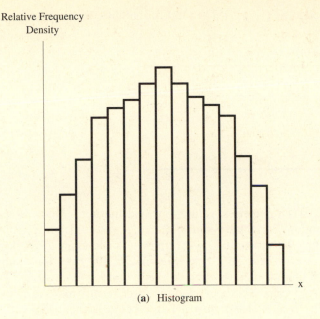

(a) Histogram

Probability
Density

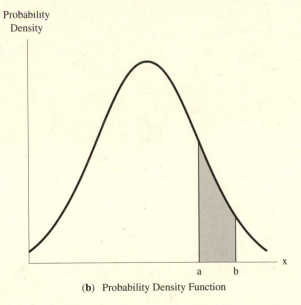

a   b

(b) Probability Density Function

Figure 2.10 Histogram for x and probability density
function

The **joint probability distribution** of x and y, denoted $p(x, y)$, is the function that
assigns a probability to every possible combination of x and y. Using the subscript i
to denote different x values, and j for y values, we will represent the joint probability
that x equals x_i and y takes the value y_j, or $p(x = x_i$ and $y = y_j)$, by $p(x_i, y_j)$. For
example, if i and j are both 1, then we are dealing with the combination x_1, y_1, whose

probability is denoted $p(x_1, y_1)$. The joint probability distribution for these variables is then:

x-y COMBINATION	JOINT PROBABILITY
x_1, y_1	$p(x_1, y_1)$
x_1, y_2	$p(x_1, y_2)$
. . .	. . .
x_n, y_m	$p(x_n, y_m)$

Note that $p(x_i, y_j)$ is a numerical value whose calculation is based on the relationship between the random variables x and y.

When dealing with two random variables, it is necessary to employ double summation. We will now provide a brief overview of the rules for double sums. This information will then be used throughout the remaining discussion of bivariate probability and in Appendix 2A for the derivation of results for bivariate mathematical expectation. The results that follow are numbered sequentially with the rules for single sums presented earlier.

Double sums are relevant when working with two variables, as above, or when two subscripts are associated with a single variable. We will consider the latter case here, where a variable x has two subscripts: x_{ij}. Using this notation, x_{ij} represents the jth member of group i. The total of the x's is then:

$$\sum_{i=1}^{n} \sum_{j=1}^{m} x_{ij} = \sum_{i=1}^{n} x_{i1} + \sum_{i=1}^{n} x_{i2} + \cdots + \sum_{i=1}^{n} x_{im} \qquad \text{(IV)}$$

We can thus break a double sum into a series of terms involving single sums by ranging through the values of the inner index (j). Completing the terms on the right side of (IV) allows us to obtain the sum of the x values:

$$\sum_{i=1}^{n} \sum_{j=1}^{m} x_{ij} = (x_{11} + \cdots + x_{n1}) + (x_{12} + \cdots + x_{n2}) + \cdots + (x_{1m} + \cdots + x_{nm})$$

The starting values for the indexes in these sums need not be 1. Also, the order in which the i and j summations appear does not affect the sum.

Patterns exist for double summation that parallel those for single sums. Constants may be moved outside the summation operators:

$$\sum_{i=1}^{n} \sum_{j=1}^{m} k \cdot x_{ij} = k \cdot \sum_{i=1}^{n} \sum_{j=1}^{m} x_{ij}, \qquad \text{(V)}$$

and summations may be moved inside of a bracketed expression:

$$\sum_{i=1}^{n} \sum_{j=1}^{m} (x_{ij} \pm y_{ij}) = \sum_{i=1}^{n} \sum_{j=1}^{m} x_{ij} \pm \sum_{i=1}^{n} \sum_{j=1}^{m} y_{ij}. \qquad \text{(VI)}$$

One last formula, which is used in the discussion of joint probability that follows, will now be presented and derived:

$$\sum_{i=1}^{n} \sum_{j=1}^{m} x_i y_j = \sum_{i=1}^{n} x_i \sum_{j=1}^{m} y_j$$

$$= \sum_{j} x_1 y_j + \sum_{j} x_2 y_j + \cdots + \sum_{j} x_n y_j \qquad \text{(VII)}$$

Since none of the x values are identified with the subscript j, we can treat these as constants with respect to j and move them outside the summation (via (I)).

$$= x_1 \cdot \sum_{j} y_j + x_2 \cdot \sum_{j} y_j + \cdots + x_n \cdot \sum_{j} y_j.$$

Factoring out the summation of the y terms this becomes:

$$= (x_1 + x_2 + \cdots + x_n) \cdot \sum_{j} y_j$$

$$= \sum_{i} x_i \cdot \sum_{j} y_j.$$

Note that the order of these sums is immaterial. We now return to the discussion of bivariate probability presupposing the results presented above.

The joint probability distribution of x and y, $p(x, y)$, can be related to the univariate probability functions for x and y: $p(x)$ and $p(y)$. We can establish this link using the information given in Table 2.7. Assuming x takes three values and y has two values (i.e., $n = 3$, $m = 2$), each entry in this table represents the joint probability of an x-y combination. We can represent the total of these probabilities using summations:

$$\sum_{i=1}^{3} \sum_{j=1}^{2} p(x_i, y_j) = \sum_{j=1}^{2} p(x_1, y_j) + \sum_{j=1}^{2} p(x_2, y_j) + \sum_{j=1}^{2} p(x_3, y_j) \quad \text{(using VII)}$$

$$= \{p(x_1, y_1) + p(x_1, y_2)\} + \{p(x_2, y_1) + p(x_2, y_2)\}$$
$$+ \{p(x_3, y_1) + p(x_3, y_2)\}$$

Each of these bracketed terms corresponds to a row total in Table 2.7. Since the sum of individual probabilities must equal 1:

$$\sum_{i} \sum_{j} p(x_i, y_j) = 1 \qquad (2.9)$$

Table 2.7 Joint Probability Distribution of x and y

	y_1	y_2	ROW TOTAL
x_1	$p(x_1, y_1)$	$p(x_1, y_2)$	$p(x_1)$
x_2	$p(x_2, y_1)$	$p(x_2, y_2)$	$p(x_2)$
x_3	$p(x_3, y_1)$	$p(x_3, y_2)$	$p(x_3)$
Column Total:	$p(y_1)$	$p(y_2)$	

Next, let us consider the meaning of these bracketed terms. The first of these represents the sum of the terms in the first row of Table 2.7, where x takes the single value x_1. y can assume only two values, y_1 and y_2. Since x can take the value x_1 with y equal to either y_1 or y_2, the sum of the probabilities in the first row denotes the overall probability of observing $x = x_1$. This can be viewed as the probability that $x = x_1$ regardless of the value of y. In other words:

$$p(x_1, y_1) + p(x_1, y_2) = p(x_1). \qquad (2.10)$$

This same result holds for the sum of the terms in either the second or third rows (brackets):

$$p(x_2, y_1) + p(x_2, y_2) = p(x_2)$$
$$p(x_3, y_1) + p(x_3, y_2) = p(x_3) \qquad (2.10\ )$$

It should be evident from both (2.10) and (2.10') that summing over different y values for a *given* x allows us to obtain the probability of that specific x occurring. This is shown in the far right column of the table. Each value in this column is called a **marginal probability**, since it is contained in the margin of the table. We can represent the marginal probabilities for x using summations as:

$$\sum_j p(x_1, y_j) = p(x_1);$$

$$\sum_j p(x_2, y_j) = p(x_2);$$

and

$$\sum_j p(x_3, y_j) = p(x_3)$$

or, for the general case of $x = x_i$:

$$\sum_j p(x_i, y_j) = p(x_i) \qquad (2.11)$$

The columns of Table 2.7 contain marginal probabilities as well. The sum of the entries in the first column gives the marginal probability of y_1, $p(y_1)$. This is obtained by evaluating the likelihood that y equals y_1 as x varies over all three of its possible values. In a similar manner, the sum of the entries in the second column gives the marginal probability of y_2. These marginal probabilities can be represented as:

$$p(x_1, y_1) + p(x_2, y_1) + p(x_3, y_1) = p(y_1)$$
$$p(x_1, y_2) + p(x_2, y_2) + p(x_3, y_2) = p(y_2) \qquad (2.12)$$

or, using summations:

$$\sum_i p(x_i, y_j) = p(y_j). \qquad (2.13)$$

The marginal probability distribution of a random variable, which is a univariate probability distribution, can thus be derived from a bivariate function as shown here. Table 2.8 gives the marginal probability distributions for x and y showing their link with the joint probability distribution.

Table 2.8 Marginal Probability Distributions
for x and y

(a)
MARGINAL PROBABILITY DISTRIBUTION OF x

x	PROBABILITY
x_1	$p(x_1, y_1) + p(x_1, y_2) = p(x_1)$
x_2	$p(x_2, y_1) + p(x_2, y_2) = p(x_2)$
x_3	$p(x_3, y_1) + p(x_3, y_2) = p(x_3)$

(b)
MARGINAL PROBABILITY DISTRIBUTION OF y

y	PROBABILITY
y_1	$p(x_1, y_1) + p(x_2, y_1) + p(x_3, y_1) = p(y_1)$
y_2	$p(x_1, y_2) + p(x_2, y_2) + p(x_3, y_2) = p(y_2)$

The final type of bivariate probability function that will be discussed, which is derived from both joint and marginal probabilities, is called a **conditional probability function (distribution)**. Like joint probability, conditional probability involves a combination of x and y values. Instead of evaluating the likelihood of different pairs of values, conditional probability involves the likelihood of observing values of one of these variables for a *given* value of the other.

This type of probability function is particularly important in econometrics. We can illustrate its importance by referring to the bivariate demand function discussed in Chapter 1:

$$q_x = f(p_x, \varepsilon),$$

where q_x and p_x are the quantity demanded and price of x, respectively, and ε is a stochastic error. The error term reflects the fact that this is a stochastic function, or that a number of different quantities exist for each price of x. All the values of q_x, along with their probabilities, constitute the univariate probability distribution for q. If we focus on a specific price of x, say p_1, the values of q_x that correspond to this price, along with their probabilities, constitute a probability distribution as well. Since these values of q are linked to (conditional upon) the specific value p_1 of price, this set of values is referred to as the conditional distribution of q_x given $p_x = p_1$. A different conditional distribution exists for every value of p_x. Each of these distributions has a mean, which is called a **conditional mean**.

If we now return to the general variables y and x, and assume that $y = f(x, \varepsilon)$, or that the relationship between x and y is stochastic, the formula used to calculate the conditional probability that $y = y_j$ given that $x = x_i$ is:

$$p(y_j | x_i) = p(y_j, x_i)/p(x_i). \tag{2.14}$$

The term on the left should be read "the probability that y equals y_j given that x takes the value x_i." As the right side of this equation shows, this conditional probability is the ratio of the joint probability of observing the pair y_j, x_i to the probability that $x = x_i$ individually, or the marginal probability of x_i. If we assume as before that there are three x values and two y values, then the joint and marginal probabilities needed to construct the conditional distributions for y are contained in Table 2.7. The conditional distribution of y given that $x = x_1$ is:

y	CONDITIONAL PROBABILITY
y_1	$p(y_1 \vert x_1) = p(y_1, x_1)/p(x_1)$
y_2	$p(y_2 \vert x_1) = p(y_2, x_1)/p(x_1)$

Finally, we can derive an expression for the joint probability of y_j and x_i by manipulating (2.14):

$$p(y_j, x_i) = p(y_j \vert x_i)p(x_i) \qquad \textbf{(2.15)}$$

Equation (2.15) is referred to as the **multiplication rule** for probability. If the random variables x and y are independent, the occurrence of y is not affected by whether x takes place. For example, y_j might represent whether or not it rains today, while x_i indicates whether the economy is in a recession. The probability of rain is not a cyclical business phenomenon (as far as we know). The probability of rain is therefore determined without reference to the state of the economy. Generalizing this result:

$$p(y_j \vert x_i) = p(y_j) \quad \text{if } y \text{ and } x \text{ are independent.} \qquad \textbf{(2.16)}$$

We can obtain an expression for the joint probability of two independent random variables by substituting (2.16) into (2.15):

$$p(y_j, x_i) = p(y_j) \cdot p(x_i) \quad \text{if } x \text{ and } y \text{ are independent.} \qquad \textbf{(2.17)}$$

When dealing with independent random variables, joint probabilities coincide with the product of marginal probabilities.

MATHEMATICAL EXPECTATION[9]

Mathematical expectation is an essential tool for the practice of econometrics. It allows us to ascertain expressions for the means and variances of density functions associated with econometric estimators, and to establish systematic links between estimators and population parameters.

---

[9] Only discrete random variables are considered here as knowledge of integral calculus is not presupposed.

Univariate Case

If a random variable x has a probability function such as that in Table 2.6, the mathematical expectation, or expected value, of this random variable is defined as:

$$E(x) = \sum x_i p(x_i) = \mu_x, \tag{2.18}$$

where "E" is the expectation operator. The right side of (2.18) shows that the expected value of x is a weighted average of the values taken by the random variable x, where individual probabilities serve as weights. Mathematical expectation is thus a technique that allows us to determine the mean, or central tendency, of a random variable; or, to phrase this differently, the central tendency of the probability distribution of a random variable. As an illustration, assume that x takes the values: $x_1 = 0$, $x_2 = 1$, and $x_3 = 2$, each with a probability of 1/3. The expected value of x is then:

$$E(x) = 0 \cdot (1/3) + 1 \cdot (1/3) + 2 \cdot (1/3)$$
$$= 1.$$

A number of situations arise where we are not interested in dealing directly with x, but instead with some linear function of this variable. Mathematical expectation allows us to ascertain the mean of this new function. For example, x might be measured in quantity demanded per month, but we wish to view quantity demanded in terms of thousands of units per month. Also, when comparing variables with different units of measurement, we can attain comparability by "standardizing" these variables.

If our original variable is x, we can define a new random variable z, which is a linear function of x, as:

$$z = \alpha_0 + \alpha_1 x, \tag{2.19}$$

where α_0 and α_1 are constants. When (2.19) is graphed, α_0 is the vertical intercept and α_1 is the slope of this line. Note that $z = x$ if $\alpha_0 = 0$ and $\alpha_1 = 1$. The graph of z versus x then passes through the origin with a slope of 1. This gives a 45° line through the origin such as that in the simple Keynesian-cross diagram. If $\alpha_0 = 0$ and $\alpha_1 \neq 0$, the expression for z reduces to:

$$z = \alpha_1 x.$$

This entails changing the slope, while retaining the origin as the vertical intercept. When α_1 does not equal 1, z involves a **change of scale** for x. An example of this, as discussed above, occurs when we desire to change the unit of measurement for x from units per month to thousands of units per month. We then define a new variable, z, whose units are one one-thousandth of those for x. Here, $\alpha_1 = 0.001$, and (2.19) becomes: $z = 0.001x$. When $\alpha_1 < 1$, a scale change makes the values of z more compressed than the corresponding x values. When $\alpha_1 > 1$, the opposite occurs, and values of z are more dispersed than the values of x.

If α_1 equals 1, the scale of z coincides with that of x. Assuming α_0 is not zero, the linear function becomes:

$$z = \alpha_0 + x,$$

which is called a **change of origin** for x. Unlike scale changes, origin changes do not alter dispersion. Instead, the values of x are shifted either right or left, depending on the sign of α_0. When we change only the origin of x, the graph of z versus x has a vertical intercept of α_0 and a slope of 1. This line is parallel to the 45° line through the origin that pertains when $z = x$. An application of origin change occurs when we wish to create a new random variable z with a zero mean from a variable x whose mean is nonzero.

We can determine the mean of this new random variable z using mathematical expectation. In this case, consider that:

$$\alpha_0 + \alpha_1 x = f(x).$$

The mathematical expectation of such a function of x is given by (2.20):

$$E\{f(x)\} = \sum f(x_i) \cdot p(x_i), \tag{2.20}$$

where $f(x_i)$ denotes the value of $f(x)$ when $x = x_i$. We can see what is involved in calculating (2.20) by referring to the information given in Table 2.9. When x equals x_1, $z = f(x_1) = \alpha_0 + \alpha_1 x_1$. What is the probability of z's taking this value? For z to equal $\alpha_0 + \alpha_1 x_1$, x must take the value x_1. The relevant probability is therefore $p(x_1)$. The probabilities for the remaining z values are determined accordingly.

We can obtain the expression for the mathematical expectation of z, $E[z]$, by substituting the information from Table 2.9 into (2.20):

$$E[z] = E[\alpha_0 + \alpha_1 x]$$
$$= \sum (\alpha_0 + \alpha_1 x_i) \cdot p(x_i)$$

According to the rules of summation, we can multiply each of the bracketed terms on the right by $p(x_i)$, which gives:

$$\sum (\alpha_0 + \alpha_1 x_i) \cdot p(x_i) = \sum \alpha_0 p(x_i) + \sum \alpha_1 x_i p(x_i).$$

Since α_0 and α_1 are constants, we can move these outside of the summation sign:

$$\sum \alpha_0 p(x_i) + \sum \alpha_1 x_i p(x_i) = \alpha_0 \sum p(x_i) + \alpha_1 \sum x_i p(x_i).$$

Since probabilities add to 1, the first summation on the right equals 1. The second summation is the definition of $E(x)$, which we denote μ_x:

$$\alpha_0 \sum p(x_i) + \alpha_1 \sum x_i p(x_i) = \alpha_0(1) + \alpha_1 E(x),$$

Table 2.9 Values of x, z, and Probabilities

x	z	PROBABILITY
x_1	$\alpha_0 + \alpha_1 x_1$	$p(x_1)$
x_2	$\alpha_0 + \alpha_1 x_2$	$p(x_2)$
$\vdots$	$\vdots$	$\vdots$
x_n	$\alpha_0 + \alpha_1 x_n$	$p(x_n)$

so:

$$E[\alpha_0 + \alpha_1 x] = \alpha_0 + \alpha_1 \mu_x. \qquad \textbf{(2.21)}$$

Equation (2.21) embodies several important results:

$$E[\alpha_0] = \alpha_0$$

$$E[\alpha_1 x] = \alpha_1 E(x)$$

$$= \alpha_1 \mu_x. \qquad \textbf{(2.22)}$$

The first of these should be fairly obvious: the mean of a constant equals the value of that constant. The second result states that when a scale change is applied to x, the mean is the product of the scale factor (α_1) and the mean of the variable whose scale is changed.

One additional result pertains to a change in the origin of x. If we let α_1 in (2.21) equal 1, then $z = \alpha_0 + x$ and:

$$E[\alpha_0 + x] = \sum(\alpha_0 + x_i)p(x_i)$$

$$= \alpha_0 \sum p(x_i) + \sum x_i p(x_i)$$

$$= \alpha_0(1) + E(x)$$

so that:

$$E[\alpha_0 + x] = \alpha_0 + \mu_x. \qquad \textbf{(2.23)}$$

The mean of a variable whose origin has been changed equals the sum of the original variable's mean plus the amount by which the origin has changed. If, for example, $\alpha_0 = -5$, the values of z are those for x shifted left by 5 units. The mean of z is then five less than μ_x.

A special use of origin change arises when we wish to transform the mean of any variable x from its original value to 0. If we let α_0 equal $-\mu_x$, so that z becomes $x - \mu_x$, or the deviation of x from its mean, then the mean of z is zero. We can establish this result by taking the expected value of z:

$$E(z) = E[x - \mu_x]$$

$$= E(x) - E\{\mu_x\}$$

$$= \mu_x - \mu_x$$

$$= 0$$

since μ_x is a constant, equal to its expectation. This result is analogous to one presented earlier, that $\Sigma(x_i - \hat{\mu}_x) = 0$. However, $E(x)$ is not the same as $\hat{\mu}_x$; $\hat{\mu}_x$ is an estimator of μ_x, which is an unknown population parameter.

Note the patterns implied by (2.21)–(2.23):

  (i) both the expectation and summation operators work the same way with the product of a constant and a variable: the constant may be brought outside the operator; and
 (ii) the expectation of a sum (or difference) equals the sum (or difference) of the separate expected values, which is also similar to the summation rule.

The expected value of x measures the mean, or central tendency of the probability distribution of x. We can also employ mathematical expectation to determine the variance, or dispersion, in the probability distribution of x. Dispersion is defined in terms of deviations from the mean. Since the expected value of the deviation of x from its mean is zero, variance is defined in terms of squared deviations from $E(x)$. Using mathematical expectation, the variance of x is defined as:

$$E[x - E(x)]^2 = E[x - \mu_x]^2$$
$$= \sigma_x^2, \tag{2.24}$$

where σ_x^2 denotes the population variance of x. Note that

$$(x - \mu_x)^2 = f(x),$$

and μ_x is a constant that denotes a change in the origin of x. Using equation (2.20) for the summation definition of $E[f(x)]$, this becomes:

$$E[x - \mu_x]^2 = \sum(x_i - \mu_x)^2 p(x_i) = \sigma_x^2. \tag{2.25}$$

Simple manipulation of the brackets in expressions (2.24) and (2.25) allows us to derive a useful alternative expression for the variance of x. Using (2.24), calculate the square of the bracketed term, then take the expected value of each term separately, noting that μ_x is a constant:

$$E[x - \mu_x]^2 = E[x^2 + \mu_x^2 - 2\mu_x x]$$
$$= E(x^2) + E(\mu_x^2) - E(2\mu_x x)$$
$$= E(x^2) + \mu_x^2 - 2\mu_x E(x)$$
$$= E(x^2) + \mu_x^2 - 2\mu_x^2$$
$$E[x - \mu_x]^2 = E(x^2) - \mu_x^2 \tag{2.26}$$

The corresponding expression with summations is:

$$E[x - \mu_x]^2 = \sum x_i^2 p(x_i) - \mu_x^2.$$

Mathematical expectation can also be used to determine the variance of a linear function of x such as the variable z given by (2.19). The variance of z using the basic formula (2.24) is:

$$\sigma_z^2 = E[z - E(z)]^2.$$

Substituting (2.19) (on page 51) for z, this becomes:

$$\sigma_z^2 = E[(\alpha_0 + \alpha_1 x) - E(\alpha_0 + \alpha_1 x)]^2.$$

Throughout the remainder of this text, we will determine the expected values of random variables before calculating their variances. This procedure provides us with an expression for the expected value term in the variance formula. We saw from (2.21) (on page 53) that:

$$E(z) = \alpha_0 + \alpha_1 \mu_x.$$

Substituting this into the variance equation allows us to obtain the final variance expression:

$$\sigma_z^2 = E[(\alpha_0 + \alpha_1 x) - (\alpha_0 + \alpha_1 \mu_x)]^2$$
$$= E[\alpha_0 - \alpha_0 + \alpha_1(x - \mu_x)]^2$$
$$= E[\alpha_1(x - \mu_x)]^2$$
$$= E[\alpha_1^2(x - \mu_x)^2]$$
$$= \alpha_1^2 E[x - \mu_x]^2$$
$$\sigma_z^2 = \alpha_1^2 \sigma_x^2. \tag{2.27}$$

This result uses the fact that α_1^2 is a constant, which allows us to move it outside the expectation operator, and that the other bracketed term is the definition of the variance of x.

Equation (2.27) embodies a result that is not always obvious; changing the origin of a variable has no affect on its variance. Since this type of change merely displaces the values of x without altering their spread, it is reasonable to find that origin changes do not influence the variance. A direct result of this fact is the following:

$$\text{Var}(x - \alpha_0) = \text{Var}(x + \alpha_0)$$
$$= \sigma_x^2. \tag{2.28}$$

Change of scale does affect the variance of a random variable. When applied to x, the scale factor α_1 (when $\alpha_1 \neq 1$) does not produce a proportional change in the variance of z. Equation (2.27) indicates that the variance of z differs from that of x by the *square* of the scale factor. Since variance involves the square of an expected value, observing the term α_1^2 in the variance of z should not be surprising. If the scale factor is greater than 1, the variance of z exceeds that of x, while for α_1 less than 1, z possesses a smaller variance. If, for example, α_1 equals 3, then σ_z^2 is 9 times the variance of x, while for $\alpha_1 = (1/3)$, the variance of z is one-ninth of σ_x^2.

We will conclude this discussion of univariate mathematical expectation with an application that provides us with a formula that is used frequently in the chapters that follow. A **standardized random variable** is a random variable whose mean is 0 and variance is 1. This type of variable is used to obtain values from several of the probability tables at the end of the text. We generally have to convert random variables into a form that satisfies both of these requirements, which is a process called **standardization**. Given some random variable x, standardization entails defining a new variable z, which is a linear function of x, whose mean is changed from μ_x to 0, and whose variance is transformed from σ_x^2 to 1.

The previous discussion indicated how we can transform a random variable with mean μ_x into a new variable with a zero mean: convert it to a deviation from its mean. If we define a new random variable $z = (x - \mu_x)$, then z has a zero expected value, since $E(x - \mu_x) = \mu_x - \mu_x = 0$. Because this involves only an origin change, then, according to (2.28), the variance of this random variable is:

$$\sigma_z^2 = \text{Var}(x - \mu_x) = \sigma_x^2.$$

Table 2.10   Standardized x Values:
Mean = 7, Variance = 81

x	z
2	$(2 - 7)/9 = -5/9$
7	$(7 - 7)/9 = 0$
10	$(10 - 7)/9 = 1/3$
16	$(16 - 7)/9 = 1$

The variance of z is thus identical to that of x. To make the variance of this random variable 1, it is necessary that we also change the scale of x. When we apply the scale factor α_1 to x, the variance of this product is:

$$\text{Var}(\alpha_1 x) = \alpha_1^2 \sigma_x^2 \quad \text{(using 2.27).}$$

Setting this expression equal to 1 and solving for α_1 gives us the appropriate scale factor to use in standardization, $(1/\sigma_x)$, or the inverse of the standard deviation of x. *To transform any random variable to one with unit variance, divide that variable by its standard deviation.*

To standardize a random variable x, we thus subtract its mean and divide the resulting expression by the standard deviation of x. The equation for a standardized random variable z is[10]:

$$z = (x - \mu_x)/\sigma_x. \tag{2.29}$$

An illustration of the calculations involved in using (2.29) is given in Table 2.10, where it is assumed that x has a mean of 7 and a variance of 81. Note that the new random variable z does not have the same unit of measurement as x. We can ascertain its unit of measurement by referring to the last entry in Table 2.10. The value of z for that entry is 1, which, using the definition of z in (2.29), shows:

$$(16 - \mu_x)/\sigma_x = 1, \quad \text{or} \quad (16 - \mu_x) = 1\sigma_x,$$

The deviation of 16 from the mean of x ($= 7$) is one standard deviation. *The value of a standardized random variable thus measures how many standard deviations an*

---

[10] Perhaps an easier way to arrive at this is to define z as:

$$z = \alpha_0 + \alpha_1 x$$

with the requirements $E(z) = 0$ and $\text{Var}(z) = 1$. This gives two equations:

$$\alpha_0 + \alpha_1 \mu_x = 0 \quad \text{and} \quad \alpha_1^2 \sigma_x^2 = 1$$

that are solved simultaneously for α_0 and α_1. The solution gives $\alpha_1 = (1/\sigma_x)$ and $\alpha_0 = -\mu_x/\sigma_x$. When these are substituted into the equation for z, the desired result is obtained.

observation is from its mean. Standardized random variables are therefore expressed in terms of standard deviations.

Bivariate Case

Extending mathematical expectation to the case of two random variables involves several new results that are easier to remember than to derive. Because of this, the current section only outlines these results, while the derivations are provided in Appendix 2A.

Bivariate mathematical expectation is a tool that allows us to calculate the expected values of expressions involving pairs of random variables. The notation used earlier in this chapter will be continued here: the random variable x takes the values x_i $(i = 1, 2, \ldots, n)$, while the values of y are represented by y_j $(y = 1, 2, \ldots, m)$. In this section we are concerned with evaluating the expectation of a linear function of these variables, $f(x, y)$. The general form of the function considered is:

$$f(x, y) = \alpha_0 + \alpha_1 x + \alpha_2 y. \tag{2.30}$$

For a specific pair of x-y values, this can be expressed as:

$$f(x_i, y_j) = \alpha_0 + \alpha_1 x_i + \alpha_2 y_j,$$

where i can equal j. The probability of observing this function is based on the joint occurrence that $x = x_i$ and $y = y_j$, which is given by the joint probability discussed earlier, $p(x_i, y_j)$. The expected value of (2.30) is a weighted average of the values of x and y with *joint* probabilities as weights. Therefore:

$$E[\alpha_0 + \alpha_1 x + \alpha_2 y] = \sum_i \sum_j (\alpha_0 + \alpha_1 x_i + \alpha_2 y_j) p(x_i, y_j),$$

The use of a double sum is necessitated by the existence of a separate index for each variable. The final expression for this expected value, which is derived in Appendix 2A, is:

$$E[\alpha_0 + \alpha_1 x + \alpha_2 y] = \alpha_0 + \alpha_1 \mu_x + \alpha_2 \mu_y \tag{2.31}$$

where μ_y is the population mean of y. As equation (2.31) shows, the expectation operator can be applied separately to each of the terms in this function. The results established earlier for univariate expectation therefore extend to the bivariate case as well. In fact, this result holds for any number of variables. If we have k different variables, x_1 to x_k, then:

$$E[\alpha_0 + \alpha_1 x_1 + \alpha_2 x_2 + \cdots + \alpha_k x_k] = \alpha_0 + \alpha_1 \mu_1 + \alpha_2 \mu_2 + \cdots + \alpha_k \mu_k$$

where μ_1 is the population mean of x_1, and so forth.

The covariance between x and y can also be defined in terms of mathematical expectation. The basis for this measure is the product of the deviations of these variables from their means. Covariance is therefore:

$$\text{Cov}(x, y) = E[x - E(x)][y - E(y)] = \sigma_{xy}, \tag{2.32}$$

where σ_{xy} denotes the population covariance. We can simplify this formula by multiplying the brackets then taking the expected values of individual terms. The steps involved are:

$$E[x - E(x)][y - E(y)] = E[xy - xE(y) - E(x)y + E(x)E(y)]$$
$$= E(xy) - \mu_x\mu_y - \mu_x\mu_y + \mu_x\mu_y$$
$$\sigma_{xy} = E(xy) - \mu_x\mu_y \qquad (2.33)$$

This derivation uses the fact that both $E(x)$ and $E(y)$ are constants, equal to their expected values. A special case of (2.33) occurs when x and y are independent random variables. If x and y are statistically independent, $E(xy) = E(x)E(y)$, and σ_{xy} equals zero.

When standardized variables are substituted into (2.32), the covariance coincides with the correlation coefficient. If we denote these standardized variables as z_x and z_y, respectively, then, using the fact that each has a zero mean, the following result is obtained:

$$\text{Cov}(z_x, z_y) = E(z_x \cdot z_y) = \frac{\sigma_{xy}}{\sigma_x \cdot \sigma_y} = \rho_{xy}$$

where ρ_{xy} is the population correlation coefficient of x and y.

We can also obtain expressions for the variances of linear functions of x and y using mathematical expectation. For example, we can calculate the variance of the bivariate function given by (2.30) (on page 57) based on mathematical expectation. If we denote this function v, then:

$$\text{Var}(v) = E[v - E(v)]^2$$
$$= E[(\alpha_0 + \alpha_1 x + \alpha_2 y) - E(\alpha_0 + \alpha_1 x + \alpha_2 y)]^2$$
$$= E[(\alpha_0 + \alpha_1 x + \alpha_2 y) - (\alpha_0 + \alpha_1\mu_x + \alpha_2\mu_y)]^2$$
$$= E[\alpha_0 - \alpha_0 + \alpha_1(x - \mu_x) + \alpha_2(y - \mu_y)]^2$$
$$= E[\alpha_1^2(x - \mu_x)^2 + \alpha_2^2(y - \mu_y)^2 + 2\alpha_1\alpha_2(x - \mu_x)(y - \mu_y)]$$
$$= \alpha_1^2 E(x - \mu_x)^2 + \alpha_2^2 E(y - \mu_y)^2 + 2\alpha_1\alpha_2 E(x - \mu_x)(y - \mu_y)$$
$$\text{Var}(\alpha_0 + \alpha_1 x + \alpha_2 y) = \alpha_1^2\sigma_x^2 + \alpha_2^2\sigma_y^2 + 2\alpha_1\alpha_2\sigma_{xy}. \qquad (2.34)$$

The variance of a bivariate function such as (2.30) is therefore a function of the scale factors applied to each variable, the variances of these variables, and the covariance between the pair of variables. In the case where x and y are independent, σ_{xy} is zero, which eliminates the last term in (2.34). The variance of this bivariate function then becomes:

$$\text{Var}(\alpha_0 + \alpha_1 x + \alpha_2 y) = \alpha_1^2\sigma_x^2 + \alpha_2^2\sigma_y^2. \qquad (2.35)$$

When x and y are statistically independent, the variance of a sum thus equals the sum of the individual variances. Two examples of this are given by (2.36):

$$\text{Var}(x + y) = \sigma_x^2 + \sigma_y^2$$
$$\text{Var}(x - y) = \sigma_x^2 + \sigma_y^2. \qquad (2.36)$$

Verification of these equations is left as an exercise.

Finally, mathematical expectation can be used to determine the mean of conditional probability distributions (and density functions). If we again return to the bivariate demand relationship discussed earlier: $q_x = f(p_x, \varepsilon)$, where q_x and p_x are the quantity demanded and price of x, respectively, and ε is a stochastic error term, a range of values for q_x exist for each price of x. These, recall, are the conditional distributions of quantity demanded (given the price of x). If we focus on the single price, p_1, a conditional distribution exists for this price. We can use mathematical expectation to ascertain the mean of this conditional distribution, or the conditional mean of q_x for p_1, denoted $E(q_x|p_1)$.

Like any expected value, this is a weighted average of the individual values taken by the random variable of interest, q_x. The weights, as you might expect, are probabilities. Since we are dealing with a conditional distribution, the probabilities that serve as weights are conditional probabilities. The formula for the conditional mean of quantity demanded given $p_x = p_1$ is:

$$E(q_x|p_1) = \sum q_{xi} \cdot p(q_{xi}|p_1)$$

and for the general case where $y = f(x, \varepsilon)$:

$$E(y|x_j) = \sum y_i \cdot p(y_i|x_j)$$

is the conditional mean of y given that x takes the value x_j. The set of conditional means from the distributions corresponding to the different values of x constitutes the **regression function** of y on x. This is the function we are interested in estimating with econometric methods.

PROBABILITY DENSITY FUNCTIONS USED FREQUENTLY IN ECONOMETRICS

The Normal Distribution

The normal distribution is central to the types of statistical inference performed in econometrics. While it is not utilized directly in a number of the hypothesis tests discussed in Chapters 5 and 6, the probability distributions used are related to this distribution.[11]

The normal distribution is a symmetric, bell-shaped distribution. The behavior of a normally distributed random variable can be characterized by two parameters: a mean and a variance. If we assume that y is a normally distributed random variable, with a mean $E(y) = \mu_y$ and variance $\sigma_y^2 = E[y - E(y)]^2$, the notation used to summarize this distributional information is:

$$y \sim N(\mu_y, \sigma_y^2)$$

---

[11] The normal distribution is not used since knowledge of the population variance is required. The most frequently used distributions in this text are the t-distribution and the F-distribution, which are outlined shortly. Each of these is related to the normal distribution.

which states that y is distributed as (this is the $\sim$) a normal random variable (indicated by the "N"), with mean μ_y and variance σ_y^2.

The values taken by this distribution extend from $-\infty$ to ∞. Since the normal distribution is symmetric, the mean occurs at the maximum height of this distribution, as shown in Figure 2.11(a). Recall that the area between two points of a probability density function designates the probability that a random variable takes a value within that range. For the normal distribution, 68.26 percent of all values occur within one standard deviation of the mean (Figure 2.11(b)), while 95.44 percent of the possible values occur within two standard deviations. As these percentages indicate, practically all the values taken by normally distributed random variables occur within two standard deviations of the mean.

A major result used in statistical inference links the normal distribution to the sample mean. The **central limit theorem** states:

If $y_1, y_2, \ldots, y_n$ are a set of n independent observations from a parent population whose probability function is $p(y)$, then the probability distribution of $\hat{\mu}_y$, the sample mean of y, can be approximated by the normal distribution as

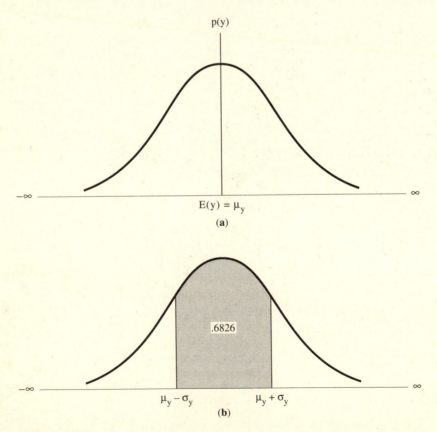

Figure 2.11

sample size (n) approaches infinity. Furthermore, as n approaches infinity, $\hat{\mu}_y \sim N(\mu_y, \sigma_y^2/n)$.

It should be stressed that this is only an approximation; for small n the normal distribution may not provide an adequate characterization.

Exceptions to this theorem exist, but they do not arise in the context of the material presented in this text. For our purposes, this theorem requires only that y values are independent, and that they possess the same parent distribution. *The significance of the central limit theorem to econometrics derives from the fact that it allows us to associate the mean (or sum) of a large number of independent random variables (from a given distribution) with the normal distribution.* Since the stochastic error term in an econometric equation is the sum of a large number of omitted influences (variables), then, based on the central limit theorem, we can associate this error term with the normal distribution.

One final result, which we utilize a great deal throughout the remainder of this text, is the following:

> Any linear function of a normally distributed random variable is itself normally distributed.

Thus, if we have two normally distributed random variables, y_1 and y_2, with $y_1 \sim N(\mu_1, \sigma_1^2)$ and $y_2 \sim N(\mu_2, \sigma_2^2)$, whose covariance is σ_{12}, then the new random variable $y_3 = \alpha_1 y_1 + \alpha_2 y_2$ is also normally distributed. The mean of y_3 is $E(\alpha_1 y_1 + \alpha_2 y_2) = \alpha_1 \mu_1 + \alpha_2 \mu_2$, since α_1 and α_2 are constants. The variance of this variable is: $\alpha_1^2 \sigma_1^2 + \alpha_2^2 \sigma_2^2 + 2\alpha_1 \alpha_2 \sigma_{12}$ (show this).

Actual probabilities for normally distributed random variables are obtained from tables. Because each normal random variable is associated with two parameters, a mean and variance, then, without any standardization, an infinite number of normal distribution tables would be required: one for every possible mean-variance combination. To remedy this, a single table is used that pertains to a **unit normal (standardized) random variable**, z. Using the previous result, if $y \sim N(\mu_y, \sigma_y^2)$, then we can construct a new variable z:

$$z_i = \alpha_0 + \alpha_1 y_i$$

which is a linear function of the normally distributed random variable y. z is then normally distributed. This unit normal random variable is constructed so that $z \sim N(0, 1)$. This involves changing the origin of y, so that $\mu_z = 0$, as well as changing the scale of y in such a way that σ_z^2 equals 1. The steps involved in this transformation were outlined earlier: shifting the mean of y from μ_y to 0 requires that we subtract μ_y from each y_i; creating a variable with unit variance necessitates dividing each y_i by the standard deviation of y. The formula for the unit normal random variable, z, is thus:

$$z_i = (y_i - \mu_y)/\sigma_y. \qquad \textbf{(2.37)}$$

After transforming a normally distributed random variable into a unit normal variable using (2.37), we can use the table at the end of the text to obtain probabilities.

The following examples illustrate the steps involved in this transformation and the use of the normal table.

■ **EXAMPLE 1**   Assume $y \sim N(3, 4)$. Find the probability that y takes a value between -2 and 5; in other words, find $p(-2 < y < 5)$. Think of this expression as: $p(y_1 < y < y_2)$. The solution requires converting y values to z values so that: $p(-2 < y < 5) = p(z_1 < z < z_2)$, where z_1 is the z value corresponding to $y_1 = -2$, and z_2 refers to $y_2 = 5$. Using (2.37): $z_1 = (y_1 - \mu_y)/\sigma_y = (-2 - 3)/2 = -2.5$; $z_2 = (y_2 - \mu_y)/\sigma_y = (5 - 3)/2 = 1$. Therefore $p(-2 < y < 5) = p(-2.5 < z < 1)$. Recall that *the unit of measurement for a z value is standard deviations*. In this example, $z_1 = -2.5$ indicates that the value of -2 taken by y_1 is 2.5 standard deviations below the mean of y. Similarly, the value of 5 for y_2 is 1 standard deviation above μ_y. Figure 2.12(a) shows that $p(-2 < y < 5)$ corresponds to the shaded area between -2.5 and 1 for z.

The Unit Normal Table at the end of the text gives the probability from z_i to infinity, or $p(z \geq z_i)$.[12] Two facts must be used in calculating the probability for this example: (i) $p(z \geq 0) = p(0 \leq z < \infty) = 0.5$, and $p(z \leq 0) = p(-\infty < z \leq 0) = 0.5$; and (ii) since the normal distribution is symmetric, $p(z \leq -z_i) = p(z \geq z_i)$. Using this information, we can obtain the overall probability in two steps as illustrated in Figure 2.12(b). First, $p(0 < z < 1)$ equals 0.5 minus $p(z \geq 1)$. The value of $p(z \geq 1.0)$ in the Normal Table is 0.1587, so $p(0 < z < 1)$ is $0.5 - 0.1587 = 0.3413$. Second, $p(-2.5 < z < 0) = 0.5 - p(z \geq 2.5)$, which equals 0.5 minus $p(z \geq 2.5)$. From the Table, $p(z \geq 2.5)$ equals 0.0062. Thus, $p(-2.5 < z < 0) = 0.5 - 0.0062 = 0.4938$. Adding these two values, $p(-2.5 < z < 1) = 0.3413 + 0.4938 = 0.8351$.   ■

■ **EXAMPLE 2**   If $y \sim N(2, 25)$ find the value y_i for which $p(y \geq y_i) = 0.025$. The solution to this problem reverses the process in the previous example: use the Normal Table to find the z value for which $p(z > z_i) = 0.025$, then solve the z formula for y_i. Using the Normal Table, $p(z > z_i) = 0.025$ occurs with $z = 1.96$. Therefore:

$$(y_i - \mu_y)/\sigma_y = (y_i - 2)/5 = 1.96.$$

Solving for y: $y_i = 2 + 5(1.96) = 11.8$. Check this result by reversing the process: start with $y_i = 11.8$, find the implied z, then use the normal table.   ■

■ **EXAMPLE 3**   From the Normal Table find the z values that leave 0.025 in each tail. Example 2 showed the z value corresponding to 0.025 in the upper tail is 1.96. Because the normal distribution is symmetric, the appropriate value for the lower tail is -1.96. So: $p(-1.96 < z < 1.96) = 1 - 2(0.025) = 0.95$. For a normal distribution, 95 percent of possible values occur within 1.96 standard deviations of the mean.   ■

---

[12] Since we are dealing with continuous distributions, probability is not defined at a specific point. Therefore, the probability that z equals or exceeds z_i is the same as the probability that z is greater than z_i.

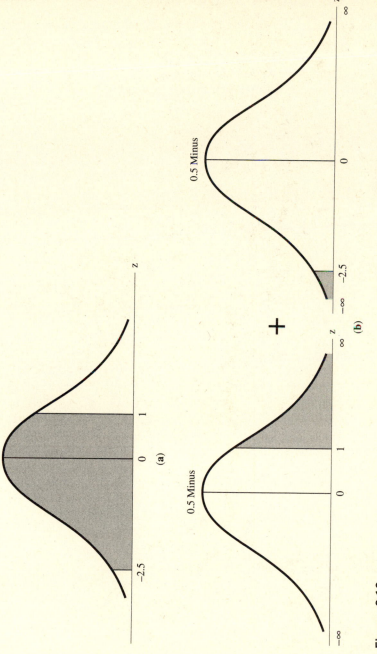

Figure 2.12

The Chi-Square Distribution

The chi-square distribution is used for statistical tests involving the variances of random variables. This distribution starts at the origin and is defined only for positive values of y, as Figure 2.13(a) shows. The shape of the chi-square distribution changes with sample size. As sample size rises, this distribution becomes more symmetric, approaching the normal distribution as n approaches infinity. This is illustrated in Figure 2.13(b).

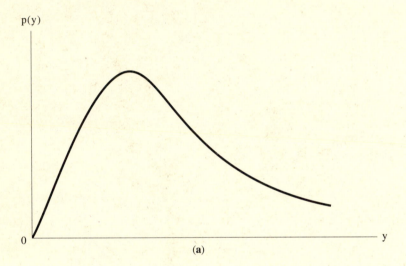

(a)

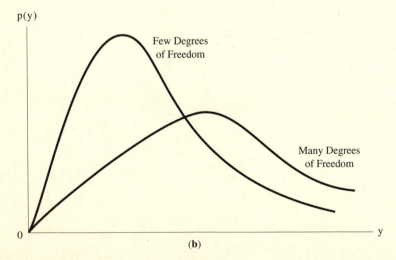

(b)

Figure 2.13 Chi-square distributions

An important parameter associated with the chi-square distribution is the number of **degrees of freedom**, which is the number of independent observations utilized to estimate a parameter. This concept can be explained by referring to the formula for the sample variance of x:

$$\hat{\sigma}_x^2 = \frac{1}{n-1} \sum (x_i - \hat{\mu}_x)^2. \tag{2.38}$$

Although the summation in (2.38) can assume any value, this equation must satisfy the restriction that $\Sigma(x_i - \hat{\mu}_x) = 0$. Because of this, not all sample observations are free to vary. Assume, for example, that $n = 3$ and $\hat{\mu}_x = 5$. If $x_1 = 10$ and $x_2 = 6$, then $\Sigma(x_i - \hat{\mu}_x) = 0$ only if $x_3 = -1$. Therefore, only two of the three observations can assume any value, and there are $2 \ (= n - 1)$ degrees of freedom associated with the sample variance. Viewed in a slightly different manner, if we know x_1, x_2, and $\hat{\mu}_x$, we can always determine x_3.

The chi-square distribution is the probability distribution for the sum of squared independent unit normal random variables:

If $z_1, z_2, \ldots, z_n$ are n independent unit normal random variables, then Σz_i^2 has a chi-square distribution with n degrees of freedom.

This is also the probability distribution for a function of the sample variance:

$(n-1)\hat{\sigma}_x^2/\sigma_x^2$ follows a chi-square distribution with $(n-1)$ degrees of freedom.

Note that the numerator of the above expression equals $\Sigma(x_i - \hat{\mu}_x)^2$, assuming the random variable of interest is x.

This last definition of a chi-square random variable will be used on a number of occasions when we discuss multiple regression. In these applications, the numerator in the above expression is the sum of the squared residuals. We will compare this sum for multiple regression equations that differ in the number of included explanatory variables. This is accomplished by evaluating the difference in the sum of the squared residuals from these equations. The following results will be used in these situations:

If x_1 and x_2 are two independent chi-square random variables, with degrees of freedom n_1 and n_2, respectively, then: (i) the sum $x_1 + x_2$ also has the chi-square distribution with $n_1 + n_2$ degrees of freedom; and (ii) the difference between these magnitudes, $x_1 - x_2$ follows the chi-square distribution with degrees of freedom $n_1 - n_2$, assuming $n_1 > n_2$.

The above is sometimes referred to as the **additivity property of the chi-square distribution**.

The shape of the chi-square distribution approximates the normal distribution as degrees of freedom increase. We will refer to the chi-square table at the end of the text to determine values of a chi-square random variable that delineate specific areas in the right tail of this distribution. Probabilities for chi-square random variables pertain to a specific number of degrees of freedom. The left column in the chi-square table indicates degrees of freedom, while the top row states the probability in the right tail. To find the value of a chi-square random variable that delineates 5 percent (0.05) in the right tail when there are 15 degrees of freedom (df = 15), locate the table entry that corresponds to this row and column. The value from the table is 24.9958. Therefore, the probability that a chi-square random variable with 15 degrees of freedom takes a value greater than or equal to 24.9958 is 5 percent.

The t-Distribution

The normal distribution can be used only when the population variance of a random variable is known. As this is seldom the case, we must employ an alternate distribution which involves estimated variances. This role is filled by the t-distribution. The t-distribution is actually a family of distributions, each corresponding to a different number of degrees of freedom. The following result defines a t-distributed random variable:

If z is a unit normal random variable, and x has a chi-square distribution with n degrees of freedom, then when z and x are independent, the ratio $z/\sqrt{(x/n)}$ follows the t-distribution with n degrees of freedom, denoted t_n.

The basic form of a t-distributed random variable y is:

$$(\hat{\mu}_y - \mu_y)/\hat{\sigma}_y,$$

which has a t-distribution with $n - 1$ degrees of freedom. Except for its denominator, which is an estimated standard deviation, this expression is identical to that for the unit normal random variable. The t-distribution is symmetric around 0.[13]

The variance of this distribution falls as both sample size and the number of degrees of freedom rise. The variance of the t-distribution exceeds that of the normal distribution, since its use of an estimated variance entails greater uncertainty than is true for the normal distribution, which is based on a known variance.[14] The difference between the normal and t-distribution is substantial for "small" samples, which are defined as having fewer than 30 degrees of freedom. As n (and the degrees of freedom) approaches infinity, the t-distribution more closely resembles the normal distribution. The normal distribution table is often used in place of the t-distribution table when the degrees of freedom are 30 or more (a "large" sample). This practice, which allows us to employ "rules of thumb" for important statistical values, has the advantage of freeing us from explicitly considering the number of degrees of freedom when consulting statistical tables.

The t-table at the end of the text gives t-statistic values for areas under the right tail of the t-distribution that equal the probability specified in the top row of the

---

[13] For sufficient degrees of freedom.

[14] The variance of the t-distribution falls as n rises, for $\hat{\sigma}^2$ becomes a better estimator of σ^2 with increased sample size.

table. The left column in this table gives the degrees of freedom. You must select the entry corresponding to the appropriate number of degrees of freedom and probability in the right tail. Like the normal distribution, the t-distribution is symmetric. Values that designate areas in the left tail are thus the negative of the table entry for the right tail. From this table, the t-value that bounds 2.5 percent (0.025) probability in the right tail for a "small" sample with 15 degrees of freedom is 2.131.

Since the t-distribution tends toward the normal distribution as n approaches infinity, t-values move continually closer to normal distribution values for a given area in the right tail. The unit normal value for 2.5 percent probability in the right tail is 1.96. Using the t-table, the corresponding t-value falls from 2.131 with 15 degrees of freedom, to 2.042 with 30 degrees of freedom, then declines to 2.0 when there are 60 degrees of freedom. For 120 degrees of freedom this equals 1.98. The difference between the normal and t-distribution values thus becomes negligible for sufficiently large samples.

The *F*-Distribution

The chi-square distribution is utilized for statistical inference with a single variance. The F-distribution, which is derived from the ratio of two chi-square random variables, is used to make inferences about the variances of a pair of random variables. The F-distribution is skewed, starts from the origin, and ranges to infinity, as shown in Figure 2.14. Since this distribution is related to a pair of chi-square random variables, there are two associated degrees of freedom, as the following shows:

If x_1 and x_2 are two independent chi-square random variables, with n and m degrees of freedom, respectively, then the ratio of these random variables, each divided by

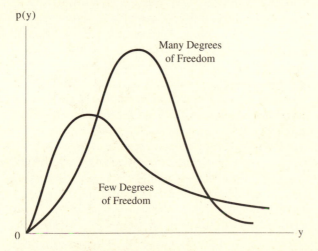

Figure 2.14 *F*-distributions

their degrees of freedom, follows the F-distribution. Specifically,

$$(x_1/n)/(x_2/m) \sim F_{n,m},$$

which denotes an F-distributed random variable with n degrees of freedom in the numerator, and m degrees of freedom in the denominator.

A frequent application of this statistic to the material in this text involves making inferences concerning equation error variances, σ_ε^2. For example, a test of whether the structure underlying a population regression function has remained the same after a major event (such as World War II, the initial OPEC price shock in 1973, or the tenure of Paul Volker at the Federal Reserve Bank) involves estimating the function for each of several subperiods, then comparing estimated error variances. For cross-sectional data, the F-distribution is used to determine whether the error variance is constant for all observations.

The F-distribution table contains F-values beyond which lie either 1 percent (0.01) or 5 percent (0.05) of possible values for this distribution. To find a desired F-value, it is necessary to first select the table with the desired probability in the right tail, then locate the entry that matches the appropriate degrees of freedom for the numerator and denominator. For example, the value of an F-distributed random variable with 15 degrees of freedom in the numerator and 20 degrees of freedom in the denominator is 2.20 with 0.05 in the right tail of this distribution. The probability that an F-distributed random variable with the above degrees of freedom takes a value greater than or equal to 2.20 is therefore 5 percent.

ESTIMATORS AND THEIR PROPERTIES

Estimation theory is a methodology for developing and evaluating different possible formulas that can be used to approximate population parameters. These formulas, which instruct us how to combine sample data to approximate population parameters of interest, are called **estimators**. A **point estimate** is a single value obtained by using an estimator. For example, we can approximate the average age of all persons in the United States (the population parameter μ_x) by taking a sample of persons, then using the sample mean, $\hat{\mu}_x$, as our estimator. We obtain a point estimate of average age by adding the ages for all persons in this sample, then dividing this sum by the number of persons.

How accurate can we expect an estimate such as this to be? Without knowing the value of the relevant population parameter, we cannot assess the accuracy of any point estimate. If we already know the value of the population parameter, it hardly makes sense to generate an estimate of this value. Is there any basis, then, we can use to *systematically* associate the results from using estimators such as $\hat{\mu}_x$ with the population parameters whose values we are interested in? The answer to this question is yes.

Random variables are capable of producing many different point estimates, depending on the particular sample used. Because of this fact, estimators, such as the sample mean, are random variables. We can therefore attach probabilities to different possible point estimates and summarize this information with a probability distribution (or density function). It is this probability distribution that defines the context within which we can make systematic statements about the relationship between an estimator and its population parameter.

The probability distributions associated with different estimators generally possess both central tendency and dispersion. The central tendency of such a distribution, which is the expected value of this estimator, indicates the value we can expect to obtain on average when using this estimator. Its dispersion, or variance, is also an important consideration. The greater is this variation, the more dispersed is the range of possible point estimates we can expect to obtain. This makes it more likely for us to obtain point estimates that differ substantially from our population parameter.

The systematic properties of estimators are defined with reference to the mean and variance of an estimator's probability distribution. Statements about the systematic association between estimators and population parameters are therefore valid only *on average*. Furthermore, since these properties refer directly to the probability distributions of estimators, the implied context is a hypothetical one, where a large number of point estimates are calculated. We now elaborate on these probability distributions in greater detail and define the criteria used to evaluate different estimators.

THE SAMPLING DISTRIBUTION OF AN ESTIMATOR

The previous discussion noted that an estimator is a formula that indicates how sample data should be combined to approximate a population parameter of interest. Furthermore, while we typically use an estimator to produce a single value, the criteria employed to judge its accuracy are based on hypothetical outcomes that would result if a large number of such point estimates were produced. This last fact is crucial to evaluation of estimators.

To make this idea more concrete, let us continue to use the sample mean as our estimator of interest. Assume the data given in Table 2.11 represent the population for some important characteristic. Using a sample size of 5 observations, assume that a researcher carries out the following set of steps:

(a) obtain a randomly selected sample of 5 observations from this population;
(b) record these values and calculate the sample mean, $\hat{\mu}_x$;
(c) return these values to the population, and
(d) repeat the process.

Every time these steps are followed, a sample mean is calculated. If we represent each of these values by an "x" on graph paper (rounding for simplicity), then, after calculating and plotting a series of these, a definite pattern such as that in Figure 2.15 will emerge.

Table 2.11 Table of Random Numbers Used as a Hypothetical Population

5	14	2	1	8
17	2	7	3	1
15	17	9	11	7
1	14	2	18	17
8	3	11	9	16
14	6	3	10	7
1	7	0	6	4
3	13	0	9	1
9	3	2	15	8
0	3	1	0	8
4	1	14	5	13
7	5	5	3	1
8	7	9	7	23
15	3	0	2	14
1	8	0	5	3
12	4	5	8	0
1	6	7	7	18
14	17	10	2	8
9	2	11	8	24
22	3	8	4	5

Figure 2.15(a) is based on 12 samples ($S = 12$). Even with this relatively small number of samples, definite central tendency and dispersion exists. In the lower graph, with 30 samples, the form is more precisely defined, resembling a probability distribution. If we were to continue this process further, the graph would more closely approximate a continuous distribution, or probability density function. This probability density function of possible point estimates is called a **sampling distribution**.

The sampling distribution of the mean associates different values of $\hat{\mu}_x$ with the likelihood of observing these values. In Figure 2.15(b), for example, which is not a continuous sampling distribution, a sample mean of 7 is more likely to occur than a value of either 2 or 12. This indicates that the probability of obtaining a $\hat{\mu}_x$ of 7 is greater than the "very low" or "very high" values of 2 or 12, respectively.

The mean of the hypothetical population used in this example (μ_x) is 7.29, which, with rounding, is 7. This value coincides with the mean of the sampling distribution in Figure 2.15. If we use the estimator $\hat{\mu}_x$ with random samples of 5 observations, then the sampling distribution in this example indicates that we can expect to obtain a value of 7 *on average*.

This is a descriptive derivation of the systematic relationship that exists between this estimator ($\hat{\mu}_x$) and its population parameter (μ_x): $E(\hat{\mu}_x)$, the mean of the sampling distribution, equals μ_x. It should be apparent from Figure 2.15 that using $\hat{\mu}_x$, which gives the correct value on average, can lead to an unsatisfactory point estimate for a single use of this estimator, such as 2 or 12. This points to a sobering fact about estimation: *there are no guarantees. An estimator that produces the correct value on*

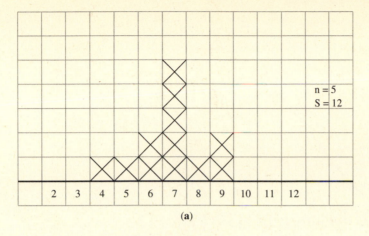

(a)

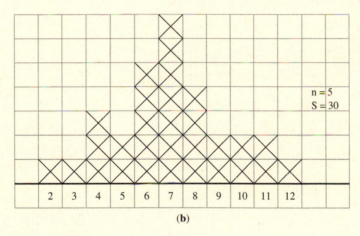

(b)

Figure 2.15 Sampling distributions with sample size (n) of five and different number of samples (S) taken

average can generate a point estimate that is "far" from the population parameter for a single application of this estimator.

This last statement attests to the importance of the dispersion of the sampling distribution, which is related to the likelihood of obtaining values "far" from the mean of the sampling distribution. A look at the diagrams in Figure 2.16 should suggest how the mean and variance affect the likelihood of "good" and "bad" estimates. These diagrams are stated in terms of an estimator $\hat{\alpha}$ of the population parameter α, along with two possible point estimates: $\hat{\alpha}_1$ and $\hat{\alpha}_2$. The area between the points $\hat{\alpha}_1$ and $\hat{\alpha}_2$ in either diagram indicates the probability of obtaining point estimates within that range. Both curves are drawn so that each sampling distribution is centered at the population parameter α. Thus $E(\hat{\alpha})$ equals α for both distributions. The variance of the sampling distribution in Figure 2.16(a) is greater than that for Figure 2.16(b).

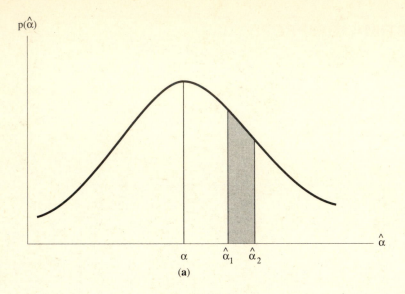

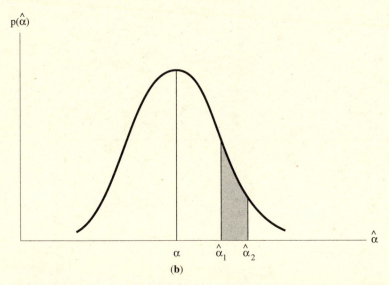

Figure 2.16 Sampling distributions with same mean and different variance

Note that the probability of obtaining point estimates in the interval from $\hat{\alpha}_1$ to $\hat{\alpha}_2$ is greater for the higher variance sampling distribution. This difference is even greater for values farther away from the mean of these distributions. Because an estimator that provides correct point estimates on average can still generate unsatisfactory estimates, we must therefore consider both the mean and variance of the sampling distribution of an estimator when judging its potential performance.

ESTIMATOR PROPERTIES

The properties of estimators define a series of desirable relationships between estimators and various parameters of their sampling distributions. These can be used to contrast various possible estimators of the same population parameter. These properties are defined either in the context of a given sample size, called **small sample properties**, or evaluating performance as sample size increases, which are **large sample (asymptotic) properties**. The small sample properties will be discussed first.

Small Sample Properties

The small sample properties of an estimator are defined with reference to the mean and variance of the sampling distribution of this estimator *for a given sample size*. Because these pertain to the hypothetical context where a large number of point estimates are produced, they are sometimes referred to as **repeated sampling properties**. We will use the general name $\hat{\alpha}$ for an estimator of population parameter α. Examples of $\hat{\alpha}$ are $\hat{\mu}_x$, an estimator of the population mean (μ_x), and $\hat{\sigma}_x^2$ as an estimator of the population variance, σ_x^2. The estimator $\hat{\alpha}$ is a random variable. The mean of its sampling distribution is $E(\hat{\alpha})$, and its variance is $E[\hat{\alpha} - E(\hat{\alpha})]^2$. The first estimator property is related to the mean, or expected value, of $\hat{\alpha}$.

UNBIASEDNESS.   An estimator $\hat{\alpha}$ is an **unbiased estimator** of α if:

$$E(\hat{\alpha}) = \alpha$$

Unbiasedness exists when the mean of the sampling distribution of an estimator coincides with the population parameter it is intended to estimate. On average, point estimates produced by an unbiased estimator are identical to its population parameter. As stated previously, nothing systematic can be stated about the relationship between a single estimate and the population parameter α. Unbiasedness is therefore not the "end all" of estimator properties. Furthermore, unbiasedness says nothing about the variance of the sampling distribution of an estimator. As Figure 2.16 showed, a large variance can imply a substantial likelihood of an unsatisfactory estimate—even if the estimator is unbiased.

The sampling distribution mean is not always centered at α. When this is the case, the estimator is said to be **biased**. On average (but not always) point estimates obtained from a biased estimator will tend to be either above or below the population parameter α. The difference between the expected value of an estimator and the population parameter is the **bias** of the estimator. This magnitude is given by:

$$\text{Bias}(\hat{\alpha}) = E(\hat{\alpha}) - \alpha. \qquad \textbf{(2.39)}$$

If, on average, $\hat{\alpha}$ overestimates α, so that $E(\hat{\alpha})$ exceeds α, $\hat{\alpha}$ is called an **upwardly (positively) biased estimator** of α. When $E(\hat{\alpha})$ falls below α on average, $\hat{\alpha}$ is a **downwardly (negatively) biased estimator** of α.

Just as unbiasedness is not the end-all of estimator properties, bias in an estimator does not necessarily spell doom. The magnitude of any bias that exists (determined from (2.39)) can be used to make judgments concerning how problematic an estimator is likely to be. Figure 2.17 shows two possible sampling distributions for a biased estimator. In each of these diagrams, the horizontal distance between $E(\hat{\alpha})$ and α indicates Bias$(\hat{\alpha})$. When the bias of an estimator is small, $E(\hat{\alpha})$ is close to α. Obtaining a point estimate equal to α is still fairly likely. The greater the bias, the farther $E(\hat{\alpha})$ is from α, implying a reduced likelihood of obtaining point estimates equal to α.

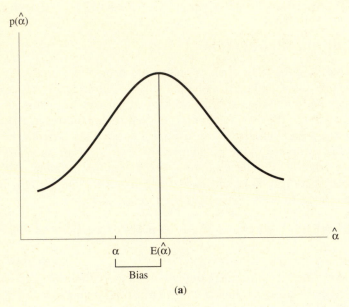

(a)

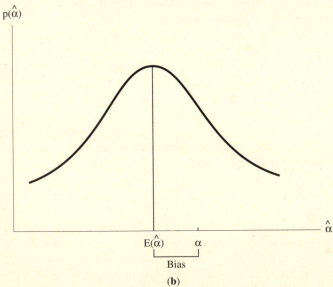

(b)

Figure 2.17 Sampling distributions of biased estimators

Since we have been dealing with $\hat{\mu}_x$, let us determine whether this estimator is unbiased by taking its expected value:

$$E(\hat{\mu}_x) = E[(1/n)\sum x_i]$$
$$= E[(1/n)(x_1 + \cdots + x_n)]$$
$$= (1/n)E(x_1 + \cdots + x_n).$$

Since $(1/n)$ is a constant, it can be moved outside of the expectation operator. Each x_i is a separate random variable from the population x. We can therefore utilize the rule from the last section to evaluate the expected value of the sum on the right:

$$E(x + y) = E(x) + E(y),$$

or the expectation of a sum equals the sum of the expected values. In the present context this becomes:

$$E(x_1 + \cdots + x_n) = E(x_1) + \cdots + E(x_n)$$

At this point it is important to point out two facts that will be used whenever we evaluate estimator properties. First, the term $E(x_i)$ does not represent the mean of a single x value as this notation seems to imply. Each x_i is a random variable since its value is determined by the sample taken. The correct interpretation of $E(x_i)$ is therefore the mean of the population from which the value of x_i originates. Second, completing the determination of whether $\hat{\mu}_x$ is unbiased can only occur if we make assumptions about the population and the sample we are dealing with. In establishing small sample properties, it is therefore necessary for us to assume both a repeated sampling context and something about critical population parameters (namely the mean and variance). For our present purposes, we assume that each x_i comes from the same population whose mean is μ_x, or:

$$E(x_i) = \mu_x \text{ for each value of } i. \tag{2.40}$$

Substituting (2.40) into the derivation gives:

$$E(\hat{\mu}_x) = (1/n)E(x_1 + \cdots + x_n)$$
$$= (1/n)[E(x_1) + \cdots + E(x_n)]$$
$$= (1/n)[\mu_x + \cdots + \mu_x]$$
$$E(\hat{\mu}_x) = (1/n)n\mu_x = \mu_x.$$

Since the mean of the sampling distribution of $\hat{\mu}_x$ equals its population parameter, $\hat{\mu}_x$ is an unbiased estimator of μ_x.

Situations exist where an estimator is biased, but the magnitude of bias diminishes as sample size increases. In this case, it is possible to lower the magnitude of Bias($\hat{\alpha}$) by employing a larger sample. As an example, let us look at a slight variation of $\hat{\mu}_x$ as alternative estimator of the mean:

$$\hat{\mu}'_x = (1/n')\sum x_i$$

where $n' \equiv (n - 1)$. This is a biased estimator of μ_x:

$$E(\hat{\mu}'_x) = (1/n')[E(x_1) + \cdots + E(x_n)]$$

$$= (1/n')[\mu_x + \cdots + \mu_x] \quad \text{using (2.40)}$$

$$= (1/n')(n\mu_x)$$

$$E(\hat{\mu}'_x) = (n/n')\mu_x \neq \mu_x.$$

Consider a sample size of 10 (i.e., $n = 10$). In this case $E(\hat{\mu}'_x)$ equals $(10/9)\mu_x$, or $(1.11\mu_x)$. $\hat{\mu}'_x$ is therefore an upwardly biased estimator of μ_x. If we increase sample size to 100, the expectation of this estimator becomes $1.01\mu_x$ ($= [100/99]\mu_x$). Note that as sample size increases, the bias of this estimator decreases. Next, let us determine the magnitude of the bias of $\hat{\mu}'_x$:

$$\text{Bias}(\hat{\mu}'_x) = E(\hat{\mu}'_x) - \mu_x$$

$$= (n/n')\mu_x - \mu_x$$

$$\text{Bias}(\hat{\mu}'_x) = \mu_x/n'$$

$$= f(n, \mu_x). \tag{2.41}$$

As (2.41) indicates, the bias of $\hat{\mu}'_x$ depends on both sample size (n) and the population parameter (μ_x). For a given μ_x, the bias of this estimator falls as n rises.

Why is $\hat{\mu}_x$ unbiased while $\hat{\mu}'_x$, which is almost identical to $\hat{\mu}_x$, is biased? The answer lies with the weights used for each estimator. Both are weighted averages of individual x values. The weights for $\hat{\mu}_x$ are all $(1/n)$, while for $\hat{\mu}'_x$, each weight is $1/(n - 1)$. The *sum* of the weights is the factor that determines whether these are unbiased estimators. There are n terms in each formula, so the sum of the weights is:

n times $(1/n)$ for $\hat{\mu}_x$

n times $1/(n - 1)$ for $\hat{\mu}'_x$.

Since the sum of the weights is 1 for $\hat{\mu}_x$, this is an unbiased estimator. The sum of the weights is $n/(n - 1)$ for $\hat{\mu}'_x$. Since this sum does not equal one, this estimator is biased. However, the sum of the weights for $\hat{\mu}'_x$ approaches 1 as n rises, which is the basis for the inverse relationship between $\text{Bias}(\hat{\mu}'_x)$ and sample size.

MINIMUM VARIANCE. The property of unbiasedness says nothing about the dispersion in the sampling distribution of an estimator. This is characterized by its variance. The variance of an estimator is related to the precision with which it is estimated. Figure 2.16 (on page 72) showed that the smaller is the variance of an estimator, the more tightly compressed are the range of point estimates around the mean of that estimator. This is consistent with a relatively small probability of obtaining point estimates "very far" from the population parameter. Similarly, a large variance indicates a greater likelihood of obtaining point estimates far from the population parameter, along with a wider spread in possible estimates. Thus, the smaller the variance of an estimator, the more precisely it is estimated. Other things being equal, an estimator with a smaller variance should be preferred to one with a greater variance.

We can calculate the variance of an estimator using mathematical expectation. The variance of $\hat{\mu}_x$ can be determined using the results for variances of sums given earlier in this chapter. To start this calculation:

$$\text{Var}(\hat{\mu}_x) = \text{Var}[(1/n)\textstyle\sum x_i]$$
$$= \text{Var}[(1/n)(x_1 + \cdots + x_n)].$$

For the moment, we will focus on just two x's for convenience. We can employ the following formula as the basis for evaluating the variance of the bracketed expression, where each α equals $(1/n)$:

$$\text{Var}(\alpha_1 x + \alpha_2 y) = \alpha_1^2 \sigma_x^2 + \alpha_2^2 \sigma_y^2 + 2\alpha_1 \alpha_2 \sigma_{xy}$$

Once again it is necessary for us to invoke assumptions about both the population and our sample before we can continue with this determination. If we assume, as before, that each x comes from the same population with mean μ_x, that the x's are pairwise independent (which makes all the covariances 0), and in addition, the variance of this population is σ_x^2, then substituting this information into the original formulation gives:

$$\text{Var}(\hat{\mu}_x) = (1/n)^2[\text{Var}(x_1) + \cdots + \text{Var}(x_n)]$$
$$= (1/n)^2[\sigma_x^2 + \cdots + \sigma_x^2]$$
$$= (1/n)^2(n\sigma_x^2)$$
$$\text{Var}(\hat{\mu}_x) = \sigma_x^2/n.$$

As sample size rises, the variance of $\hat{\mu}_x$ falls (given σ_x^2). We can summarize the information about the mean and variance of the sampling distribution of $\hat{\mu}_x$ presented up to this point in the following way: if we calculate a large number of point estimates of the population mean of some variable using $\hat{\mu}_x$, the average of these estimates will be $\hat{\mu}_x$, no matter whether we use large or small samples. However, if we increase the size of our samples, estimation precision will improve, as the variance of the sampling distribution of this estimator falls.

Let us compare the variance of $\hat{\mu}_x$ to that of the other estimator $\hat{\mu}'_x$ using these same assumptions:

$$\text{Var}(\hat{\mu}'_x) = (1/n')^2[\text{Var}(x_1) + \cdots + \text{Var}(x_n)]$$
$$= (1/n')^2[\sigma_x^2 + \cdots + \sigma_x^2]$$
$$= (1/n')^2(n\sigma_x^2)$$
$$\text{Var}(\hat{\mu}'_x) = \{n/(n')^2\}\sigma_x^2.$$

Note that $\text{Var}(\hat{\mu}'_x)$ also falls as n rises. If sample size is 10, the coefficient of σ_x^2 equals 10/81, or 0.123. When n increases to 50, this coefficient falls to 50/2401, or 0.021, while for $n = 100$, the coefficient equals 0.01. The estimator $\hat{\mu}_x$ thus has the lower variance (given σ_x^2). If $n = 10$, for example:

$$\text{Var}(\hat{\mu}_x) = \sigma_x^2/10$$
$$= 0.1\sigma_x^2$$
$$\text{Var}(\hat{\mu}'_x) = (10/81)\sigma_x^2$$
$$= 0.12\sigma_x^2.$$

In this example, $\hat{\mu}_x$ is the preferable estimator, for it is both unbiased and has the lower variance. When we must choose between unbiased estimators, the one with the smaller variance is the preferred estimator, as the next property shows.

EFFICIENCY.   An estimator $\hat{\alpha}$ of α is **efficient** if:

(a) $\hat{\alpha}$ is an unbiased estimator of α; and
(b) the variance of $\hat{\alpha}$ is no greater than the variance of any other unbiased estimator of α.

The property of efficiency therefore defines the minimum variance unbiased estimator of α.

Efficiency is a very strong property. For a given sample size (remember this is a small sample property), the estimator whose sampling distribution is centered at α with the smallest variance of *all* unbiased estimators is the efficient estimator of α.

In the situations we will encounter throughout this text, it is generally not feasible to compare all possible estimators of α. Instead only two such estimators will likely be considered. In this case, a modification of the efficiency property is used.

RELATIVE EFFICIENCY.   An estimator $\hat{\alpha}_1$ of α is **relatively more efficient** than some other estimator $\hat{\alpha}_2$ if:

(a) both estimators are unbiased; and
(b) $\text{Var}(\hat{\alpha}_1)$ is less than $\text{Var}(\hat{\alpha}_2)$.

A graph of a relatively more efficient estimator is given in Figure 2.18. You might think the two estimators of μ_x discussed previously can be compared to determine which is relatively more efficient. This cannot be done, since $\hat{\mu}'_x$ is a biased estimator

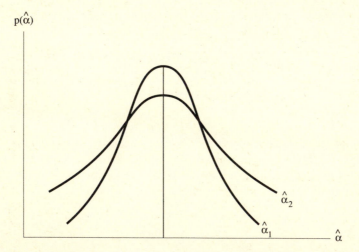

Figure 2.18 Two biased estimators with $\hat{\alpha}_1$ relatively more efficient than $\hat{\alpha}_2$

of μ_x. It therefore does not qualify for consideration in terms of either efficiency or relative efficiency.

MEAN SQUARE ERROR (MSE).   It is possible for an unbiased estimator to possess a greater variance than a biased estimator. This possibility requires an alternative basis for defining estimator preference, one that explicitly deals with possible tradeoffs between bias and variance. The estimator property that does this is the mean square error criterion.

The basis for the mean square error of an estimator is the quantity $(\hat{\alpha} - \alpha)$, which is the **sampling error** of $\hat{\alpha}$. The mean square error is the mean of the squared sampling error:

$$\text{MSE}(\hat{\alpha}) = E[\hat{\alpha} - \alpha]^2 \tag{2.42}$$

Because some of the estimators we will be working with are biased, $E(\hat{\alpha})$ does not necessarily equal α. By adding then subtracting the term $E(\hat{\alpha})$ from the bracket in (2.42) this becomes:

$$\text{MSE}(\hat{\alpha}) = E[(\hat{\alpha} - E(\hat{\alpha})) + (E(\hat{\alpha}) - \alpha)]^2$$

After some algebraic manipulation, we can express the mean square error as[15]:

$$\text{MSE}(\hat{\alpha}) = E[\hat{\alpha} - E(\hat{\alpha})]^2 + [E(\hat{\alpha}) - \alpha]^2$$

The first term on the right is the variance of $\hat{\alpha}$. The second term is the square of Bias($\hat{\alpha}$). The equation for mean square error therefore reduces to:

$$\text{MSE}(\hat{\alpha}) = \text{Var}(\hat{\alpha}) + \{\text{Bias}(\hat{\alpha})\}^2$$

MSE thus provides a basis for evaluating tradeoffs between the bias (if any exists) and the variances of different estimators. Preference is given to the estimator with the smallest mean square error.

Minimizing mean square error leads to the choice of the estimator with the smallest variance when both estimators are unbiased. When considering two unbiased estimators, minimizing MSE therefore implies relative efficiency.

To see how MSE can be used to define preference when evaluating both biased and unbiased estimators, consider the following estimators, assuming (for simplicity) a sample size of 2:

$$\hat{\alpha}_1 = (1/2)x_1 + (1/2)x_2$$

$$\hat{\alpha}_2 = (1/3)x_1 + (1/3)x_2,$$

---

[15] The cross product term is:

$$2[\hat{\alpha} - E(\hat{\alpha})][E(\hat{\alpha}) - \alpha] = 2[\hat{\alpha}E(\hat{\alpha})] - \{E(\hat{\alpha})\}^2 - \alpha\hat{\alpha} + \alpha E(\hat{\alpha})].$$

The expectation of this term is:

$$2[E(\hat{\alpha})E(\hat{\alpha}) - \{E(\hat{\alpha})\}^2 - \alpha E(\hat{\alpha}) + \alpha E(\hat{\alpha})] = 0,$$

since the last two terms cancel and the first product equals the second term.

We will utilize the following assumptions to ascertain the means and variances of these estimators:

$$E(x_i) = \alpha;$$

$$\text{Var}(x_i) = \sigma_x^2;$$

and

$$\text{Cov}(x_i, x_j) = 0 \quad \text{for all } i \neq j.$$

The first estimator (which is really $\hat{\mu}_x$) is unbiased, while the second is biased:

$$E(\hat{\alpha}_1) = (1/2)E(x_1) + (1/2)E(x_2)$$
$$= (1/2)2\alpha$$
$$= \alpha$$

$$E(\hat{\alpha}_2) = (1/3)E(x_1) + (1/3)E(x_2)$$
$$= (2/3)\alpha$$
$$\neq \alpha$$

The bias of the second estimator is:

$$\text{Bias}(\hat{\alpha}_2) = E(\hat{\alpha}_2) - \alpha$$
$$\text{Bias}(\hat{\alpha}_2) = (2/3)\alpha - \alpha$$
$$= -(\alpha/3), \tag{2.43}$$

which indicates that $\hat{\alpha}_2$ is a downwardly biased estimator of α. On average, point estimates produced from $\hat{\alpha}_2$ are one-third below the value of α. If, for example, α equals 12, the magnitude of bias for $\hat{\alpha}_2$ is -4.

We next calculate the variances of these estimators:

$$\text{Var}(\hat{\alpha}_1) = (1/2)^2\text{Var}(x_1) + (1/2)^2\text{Var}(x_2)$$
$$= (1/4)(2\sigma_x^2)$$
$$= \sigma_x^2/2$$

$$\text{Var}(\hat{\alpha}_2) = (1/3)^2\text{Var}(x_1) + (1/3)^2\text{Var}(x_2)$$
$$= (1/9)(2\sigma_x^2)$$
$$= 2\sigma_x^2/9.$$

Note that the variance of the biased estimator $\hat{\alpha}_2$ is smaller than that of the unbiased estimator, $\hat{\alpha}_1$. We can now use the results given by (2.43) and (2.44) to calculate the mean square error of each estimator:

$$\text{MSE}(\hat{\alpha}_1) = \{\text{Bias}(\hat{\alpha}_1)\}^2 + \text{Var}(\hat{\alpha}_1)$$
$$= 0 + \sigma_x^2/2$$
$$= \sigma_x^2/2$$

$$\text{MSE}(\hat{\alpha}_2) = \{\text{Bias}(\hat{\alpha}_2)\}^2 + \text{Var}(\hat{\alpha}_2)$$
$$= (-\alpha/3)^2 + 2\sigma_x^2/9$$

If the mean square error of the biased estimator is the smaller of the two, preference should be given to the biased estimator. In the present example, the biased estimator is preferred if:

$$\alpha^2/9 + 2\sigma_x^2/9 < \sigma_x^2/2,$$

or if $\text{MSE}(\hat{\alpha}_2) < \text{MSE}(\hat{\alpha}_1)$. If the values of α and σ_x^2 are known, this determination can be made. For example, if α equals 0, $\hat{\alpha}_2$ is the preferred estimator, since the bias of this estimator is then zero, and $\hat{\alpha}_2$ has the smaller variance. Note, however, that $\hat{\alpha}_2$ has zero bias only when α equals 0. It is not, however, an unbiased estimator.

BEST LINEAR UNBIASED ESTIMATOR (BLUE).   Most of what this estimator property entails can be inferred from its name. The first requirement is that the estimator in question be a linear estimator, which means that it is possible to express it as a linear function of the sample observations. Unbiased indicates that the sampling distribution of this estimator is centered at its population parameter. "Best" implies that this is a minimum variance (linear) estimator. Combining these properties, $\hat{\alpha}$ is the BLUE of α if it is the minimum variance linear unbiased estimator of α.

The sample mean, $\hat{\mu}_x$, is the best linear unbiased estimator of μ_x. This estimator is linear since it can be expressed as:

$$\hat{\mu}_x = (1/n)x_1 + \cdots + (1/n)x_n,$$

which is a linear function of the sample values of x. $\hat{\mu}_x$ is also unbiased, since, as we saw earlier, $E(\hat{\mu}_x) = \mu_x$. Finally it can be shown that no other linear unbiased estimator of μ_x possesses a smaller variance than $\hat{\mu}_x$. The sample mean is therefore the BLUE of μ_x.[16]

This completes the small sample properties of estimators. We will now discuss the large sample estimator properties.

Large Sample Properties

The small sample properties establish the systematic link between various estimators and their population parameters in the context of a *given* sample size. When judging the performance of an estimator, another important consideration is its behavior as sample size increases. This allows us to evaluate the way a sampling distribution changes when additional information about the population is incorporated into estimation. This perspective, of viewing the behavior of an estimator as sample size is increased, is the basis for the **large sample (asymptotic) properties** of estimators. Knowledge of the large sample properties of an estimator is important, even if we do not intend to alter the size of the sample used to obtain our estimate.

Asymptotic estimation theory is concerned with the behavior of sampling distributions in the limit, or as n approaches infinity. The asymptotic properties of an estimator deal with the behavior of the mean and variance of its sampling distribution

---

[16] This determination is based on the Cramer-Rao lower bound.

as sample size approaches infinity. In this setting, the unbiasedness of an estimator is related to whether its expected value equals the population parameter as sample size is increased. If we denote the value of this estimator based on a sample size of n as $\hat{\alpha}_{(n)}$, the **asymptotic expectation** of $\hat{\alpha}$ is:

$$E[\hat{\alpha}_{(n)}] \text{ as } n \text{ approaches infinity.} \qquad (2.45)$$

Like expected values in general, (2.45) gives the mean of a distribution: the sampling distribution of this estimator that would theoretically exist if sample size were increased toward infinity. This is called the **limiting or asymptotic distribution** of this estimator. In this context, an estimator $\hat{\alpha}$ is an **asymptotically unbiased** estimator of α if the following condition holds:

$$E[\hat{\alpha}_{(n)}] = \alpha \text{ as } n \text{ approaches infinity.} \qquad (2.46)$$

Equation (2.46) states that if sample size is continually increased, point estimates produced with $\hat{\alpha}$ equal the value of the population parameter on average. An estimator that is unbiased will also be asymptotically unbiased. However, an estimator that is biased can still be asymptotically unbiased. We saw in the previous section that it is possible for the bias of an estimator such as μ'_x to be inversely related to sample size. Estimators such as this, while biased for small samples, are asymptotically unbiased.

The final asymptotic property considered here is related to the variance of a sampling distribution as sample size increases.

CONSISTENCY.   An estimator $\hat{\alpha}$ is a **consistent** estimator of α if:

(a) $\hat{\alpha}$ is asymptotically unbiased; and
(b) $\text{Var}(\hat{\alpha})$ decreases as sample size increases.

For a consistent estimator, the range of likely point estimates narrows with increases in sample size, implying more precise estimation.

Consistency can also be defined with reference to the mean squared error of an estimator, if we consider the behavior of MSE as sample size increases. This is called **asymptotic mean square error**. The mean square error of an estimator consists of its variance plus squared bias. Consistency is attained when both bias and variance approach zero as sample size rises. If the asymptotic mean square error of an estimator is 0, it satisfies both of the requirements for consistency, and it is therefore a consistent estimator. Use of the asymptotic mean squared error thus provides an alternative way of ascertaining the consistency of estimator.

We will conclude the discussion of estimator properties by determining whether the two estimators of μ_x discussed earlier are consistent. The sample mean, $\hat{\mu}_x$, was found to possess the following properties:

$$E(\hat{\mu}_x) = \mu_x \quad \text{and} \quad \text{Var}(\hat{\mu}_x) = \sigma_x^2/n.$$

This estimator is both unbiased and asymptotically unbiased. If this is a consistent estimator, its variance must be inversely related to sample size, n. As the variance equation shows, this condition is met. For example, if σ_x^2 equals 10, then with a sample size of 5, the variance of $\hat{\mu}_x$ equals 2. When sample size is 10, this variance falls to

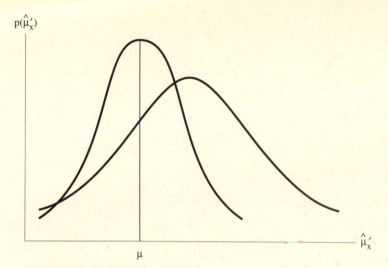

$p(\hat{\mu}'_x)$

μ

$\hat{\mu}'_x$

Figure 2.19 Biased but consistent estimator of the mean

1, while for n greater than 10, $\text{Var}(\hat{\mu}_x)$ is a decreasing fraction. Since $\hat{\mu}_x$ meets both of the conditions required for consistency, it is a consistent estimator of μ_x.

The other estimator of the mean, $\hat{\mu}'_x$, is given by $(1/n')\Sigma x_i$, where $n' \equiv n - 1$. This is a biased estimator, since its expected value is $(n/n')\mu_x$. The magnitude of bias is:

$$\text{Bias}(\hat{\mu}'_x) = \mu_x/n'.$$

For a given value of μ_x, the bias of this estimator approaches 0 as sample size rises. This estimator is thus asymptotically unbiased. The variance of $\hat{\mu}'_x$ is:

$$\text{Var}(\hat{\mu}'_x) = \{n/(n')^2\}\sigma_x^2.$$

For a given σ_x^2, the variance of $\hat{\mu}'_x$ approaches zero as sample size increases, which satisfies the second requirement for consistency. The estimator $\hat{\mu}'_x$ is thus biased but consistent. An illustration of this type of estimator is given by Figure 2.19. The flatter sampling distribution not centered at μ_x represents the smaller sample size. On average, estimates produced with $\hat{\mu}'_x$ differ from μ_x for a given sample size. The difference, which is given by the bias expression above, depends on both sample size and the population parameter μ_x. As n rises, both the dispersion in this sampling distribution and the magnitude of bias fall. As sample size approaches infinity, the sampling distribution more closely resembles the tighter sampling distribution centered at μ_x in Figure 2.19.

A FINAL THOUGHT ABOUT ESTIMATORS

This chapter has provided a thorough analysis of estimator properties. One particular estimator, the sample mean, was evaluated rather extensively. The sample mean is a best linear unbiased estimator of μ_x that also possesses the large sample property of consistency. Since this estimator satisfies the major requirements for a "good" estimator, it might seem reasonable to assume that $\hat{\mu}_x$ will produce excellent results whenever used. Several of the sampling distributions illustrated in the diagrams for this chapter showed instances where this assumption will not be fulfilled.

This fact can be made more forcefully by re-examining the data given in Table 2.11. The use of this hypothetical population allows us to operate with a known population mean, $\mu_x = 7.29$. Consider the values of point estimates of this parameter when we use each row in the table as a sample ($n = 5$). Several of the sample means produced from these row samples are substantially above and below 7.29. Consider the following values:

	VALUES					MEAN
Row 7	1	7	0	6	4	3.6
Row 10	0	3	1	0	8	2.4
Row 15	1	8	0	5	3	3.4
Row 14	15	3	0	2	14	6.8
Row 17	1	6	7	7	18	7.8
Row 3	15	17	9	11	7	11.8
Row 4	1	14	2	18	17	10.4

The first three rows (samples) cited above result in estimates of μ_x that are less than one-half its value. Estimates for the last two rows above are approximately fifty percent higher than μ_x. Yet each of these values was calculated using the same estimator, $\hat{\mu}_x$, which possesses all the desirable estimator properties. The sampling distribution of $\hat{\mu}_x$ for this sample size would have values such as the first three in the lower tail, the second two near the center, and the last two estimates in the right tail. A "good" estimator can therefore produce "bad" point estimates. See if you can determine why the "bad" estimates occurred.

Since the sample mean is a consistent estimator, the variance of estimates (and the sampling distribution of $\hat{\mu}_x$) for $n = 5$ can be expected to exceed those when sample size is increased to (say) 10 or 20. It is therefore possible to improve estimation precision by taking larger samples. Since the variance of the sample mean equals σ_x^2/n, the variance of its sampling distribution for a sample size of 5 will be twice that for samples of size 10 (given σ_x^2). To see this, choose several random samples of size 10 from Table 2.11, calculate the sample means, and note the dispersion in these values.

A LOOK AHEAD.   The statistical prerequisites for the formal presentation of econometric theory that begins in Chapter 4 are now complete. Before proceeding to that material, it is necessary to explore one final topic: data sources and data manipulations. The next chapter does this, and presents background material on methods to carry out such manipulations with canned computer programs. Once that material has been completed, the essential prerequisites will have been laid out. Students entering this course with diverse backgrounds will then have a common point of reference with which they can commence the regularly presented econometrics topics.

KEY TERMS

Additivity property (chi-square)

Asymptotic expectation

Asymptotic mean square error

Asymptotically unbiased

Bias

Central limit theorem

Change of origin

Change of scale

Class interval

Coefficient of determination

Conditional mean

Conditional probability function

Consistency

Continuous random variable

Correlation coefficient

Cross-products

Degrees of freedom

Density scale

Descriptive statistic

Deviation

Discrete random variable

Downwardly (negatively) biased estimator

Efficiency

Estimator

Frequency distribution

Geometric mean

Histogram

Joint probability distribution

Large sample (asymptotic) properties

Limiting or asymptotic distribution

Marginal probability

Mean (arithmetic mean)

Measures of central tendency

Measure of dispersion

Multiplication rule (positive or negative)

Perfect correlation

Point estimate

Population reference line

Probability

Probability density function

Probability function

Random variables

Regression function

Relative frequency density

Relative frequency histogram

Relative efficiency

Repeated sampling properties

Sampling distribution

Sampling error

Scatter diagram

Small sample properties

Standard deviation

Standardization

Standardized random variable

Summation notation

Unbiased estimator

Uniform probability function

Unit normal (standardized) random variable

Upwardly (positively) biased estimator

Variance

Weight

EXERCISES

1. Find the expected value of each of the following expressions using (i) the expectation operator and (ii) the summation definition of expectation.

   (a) $z = x - 5$ (b) $z = 3x + 1$ (c) $z = (1/3)x + 12$.

2. Show that $\Sigma(x_i - \mu_x)^2 p(x_i) = E(x^2) - \mu_x^2$.

3. Using the mathematical expectation definition of variance, show that:

   $$\text{Var}(x - \alpha) = \text{Var}(x + \alpha).$$

4. Show that $\text{Var}(x + y) = \text{Var}(x - y)$ if and only if x and y are independent random variables.

5. Find an expression for $\text{Cov}(\alpha_0 + x, \beta_0 + y)$ using the mathematical expectation definition of covariance.

6. Show that the summation definition of covariance is:

   $$\sum\sum x_i y_j p(x_i, y_j) - \left[\sum_i x_i p(x_i) \sum_j y_j p(y_j) \right].$$

7. (a) Using the expression: $\text{Var}(z) = E(z^2) - \mu_z^2$, find $\text{Var}(\alpha_0 + \alpha_1 x)$.

   (b) Using the expression: $\text{Var}(z) = \Sigma z_i^2 p(z_i) - \mu_z^2$, find $\text{Var}(\alpha_0 + \alpha_1 x)$.

8. Using mathematical expectation find $\text{Var}(x + y + z)$ assuming these variables are *not* independent.

9. The following questions are based on the data in Table 2.11 (on page 70):

   (a) Take seven samples of size 5 (choose any rows you desire) and calculate the mean, $\hat\mu_x$ for each, and the average of these values.

   (b) Compare each of these individual means to the known population mean $\mu_x = 7.29$. Why was each sample above or below μ_x? What does this say about how good the sample is? How would you define an *unbiased* sample?

   (c) Since $\hat\mu_x$ is an unbiased, efficient, and consistent estimator, how do you explain the observations upon which (b) is based?

   (d) Now take three samples of size 20 by choosing any three columns you desire. Take the mean of each column and the mean of these three means. How do these individual means compare to those of (a) in terms of both level and dispersion? How do you account for the difference?

10. Given the following estimators of α:

    $$\hat\alpha_1 = (1/2)x_1 + (1/2)x_2$$
    $$\hat\alpha_2 = (2/3)x_1 + (1/3)x_2$$

    where the x's are independent random variables from a population with mean α and variance σ_x^2:

(a) Are these unbiased estimators (show all work)? If biased, give an expression for the bias.

(b) Calculate the variances of $\hat{\alpha}_1$ and $\hat{\alpha}_2$.

(c) Which of these estimators is preferable? Define your criteria and discuss the factors involved in such a labeling.

11. Show that $\hat{\mu}_x$ is an unbiased estimator of μ_x and derive the formula for the variance of $\hat{\mu}_x$ assuming the x's are independent and come from the same population with mean μ_x and variance σ_x^2.

12. What two conditions must be met for $\hat{\alpha}$ to be an efficient estimator?

13. Explain the need for an estimator property such as Mean Square Error (define), and give an example of two estimators where this criterion allows estimator preference to be defined more clearly than if it did not exist.

14. Consider an estimator $\hat{\alpha} = (1/n')\Sigma x_i$, where $n' = (n - k)$, and the x's are members of a population with mean α and variance σ_x^2.

(a) Show that $\hat{\alpha}$ is a weighted average of the sample values of x.

(b) Show that $\hat{\alpha}$ is a biased estimator of α. Give an expression for the bias, and discuss its behavior in terms of whether bias is constant or varies with some factor.

(c) How do the weights used by an estimator affect whether it is unbiased?

(d) Draw a hypothetical sampling distribution for $\hat{\alpha}$ labeling the locations of both its mean and α.

(e) What "correction factor" (or multiple) would make $\hat{\alpha}$ an unbiased estimator?

(f) What is the variance of $\hat{\alpha}$?

(g) How does the answer to (f) relate to the sampling distribution for $\hat{\alpha}$?

15. Given the following estimators of α:

$$\hat{\alpha}_1 = (1/2)x_1 + (1/2)x_2$$

$$\hat{\alpha}_2 = (1/3)x_1 + (1/3)x_2$$

where the x's are independent and come from a population with mean $\alpha = 10$ and variance $\sigma_x^2 = 36$, define which estimator is "preferable." Explain this result, and show all work.

16. Given the following estimators of α:

$$\hat{\alpha}_1 = (1/3)x_1 + (1/3)x_2$$

$$\hat{\alpha}_2 = (3/4)x_1 + (1/2)x_2$$

where the x's are independent and come from the same population with mean α and variance σ_x^2, indicate which of these estimators is preferable and the basis of your answer.

17.   Define what an upwardly biased estimator is and give an example. Is upward bias always serious?

18.   Define what a downwardly biased estimator is and give an example. When is downward bias serious?

19.   Define the consistency property of estimators. Give an example of a consistent estimator and show that it possesses this property.

20.   We defined a standardized random variable as: $z = (x - \mu_x)/\sigma_x$. Using mathematical expectation show that:

    (a) $E(z) = 0.$ **(b)** $\text{Var}(z) = 1.$

21.   Can an estimator be consistent but not efficient? Explain your answer.

SUGGESTED REFERENCES

For Probability Theory:

Mansfield, E. *Statistics for Business and Economics*, 2d. Ed. New York: W. W. Norton, 1983.

Wonnacott, T. H., and R. J. Wonnacott. *Introductory Statistics for Business and Economics*, 3d. Ed. New York: Wiley and Sons, Inc., 1984.

Smith, G. *Statistical Reasoning*. Boston: Allyn and Bacon, 1984.

For Mathematical Expectation:

Kmenta, J. *Elements of Econometrics*, 2d. Ed. New York: Macmillan, 1986.

APPENDIX 2A   DERIVATION OF THE BIVARIATE RESULTS

This appendix provides complete derivations for several of the bivariate results discussed in Chapter 2. The following equations are used in these derivations:

(2.11) $$\sum_j p(x_i, y_j) = p(x_i)$$

(2.13) $$\sum_i p(x_i, y_j) = p(y_j)$$

(2.17) $p(x_i, y_j) = p(x_i) \cdot p(y_j),$ if x and y are statistically independent

We first illustrate the steps involved in arriving at Equation (2.31): $E[\alpha_0 + \alpha_1 x + \alpha_2 y]$. Using the sigma notation definition of this expression, and multiplying through the bracketed term, we have:

$$E[\alpha_0 + \alpha_1 x + \alpha_2 y] = \sum_i \sum_j (\alpha_0 + \alpha_1 x_i + \alpha_2 y_j)p(x_i, y_j)$$

$$= \sum_i \sum_j \alpha_0 p(x_i, y_j) + \sum_i \sum_j \alpha_1 x_i p(x_i, y_j) + \sum_i \sum_j \alpha_2 y_j p(x_i, y_j)$$

We next move the α's (which are constants) outside the summations:

$$= \alpha_0 \sum_i \sum_j p(x_i, y_j) + \alpha_1 \sum_i \sum_j x_i p(x_i, y_j) + \alpha_2 \sum_i \sum_j y_j p(x_i, y_j).$$

The sum of the joint probabilities, $p(x_i, y_j)$, taken over all values of i and j equals 1. The first term therefore reduces to α_0. In the second term, we can treat x_i as a constant with respect to summation over j. This allows us to move x_i outside the summation involving j. Thus:

$$\alpha_1 \sum_i \sum_j x_i p(x_i, y_j) = \alpha_1 \sum_i x_i \sum_j p(x_i, y_j).$$

From Equation (2.11), we know that summing the joint probabilities over j gives the marginal probability of x_i, $p(x_i)$. Substituting this, we obtain:

$$\alpha_1 \sum_i x_i \sum_j p(x_i, y_j) = \alpha_1 \sum_i x_i p(x_i)$$

$$= \alpha_1 E(x)$$

$$= \alpha_1 \mu_x$$

using the definition of $E(x)$. In a similar manner:

$$\alpha_2 \sum_i \sum_j y_j p(x_i, y_j) = \alpha_2 \sum_j y_j \sum_i p(x_i, y_j)$$

$$= \alpha_2 \sum_j y_j p(y_j) \quad \text{(using (2.13))}$$

$$= \alpha_2 E(y)$$

$$= \alpha_2 \mu_y.$$

The final result is:

$$E[\alpha_0 + \alpha_1 x + \alpha_2 y] = \alpha_0 + \alpha_1 \mu_x + \alpha_2 \mu_y. \tag{2.31}$$

The covariance between x and y is given by either Equation (2.32) (on page 57), or the simplified version, (2.33) (on page 58). The sigma notation definition of (2.32) is:

$$\text{Cov}(x, y) = \sum_i \sum_j (x_i - \mu_x)(y_j - \mu_y) p(x_i, y_j),$$

which is based on the product of the deviations of each pair (x_i, y_j) from their respective means, weighted by the joint probability of (x_i, y_j). We can simplify this expression by multiplying the bracketed terms, then using the manipulations illustrated in the previous derivation:

$$\sum_i \sum_j (x_i - \mu_x)(y_j - \mu_y) p(x_i, y_j) = \sum_i \sum_j x_i y_j p(x_i, y_j) - \mu_y \sum_i x_i \sum_j p(x_i, y_j)$$

$$- \mu_x \sum_j y_j \sum_i p(x_i, y_j) + \mu_x \mu_y \sum_i \sum_j p(x_i, y_j)$$

The first term on the right is the summation definition of $E(xy)$. The expressions involving summations in second and third terms simplify to the expected value of x and y, respectively, which makes each of these $-\mu_x \mu_y$. Since the double sum of the joint probabilities equals 1, the last term is $\mu_x \mu_y$. The right side of the above equation is therefore:

$$E(xy) - 2\mu_x \mu_y + \mu_x \mu_y.$$

The sum of the last two terms in this expression is $-\mu_x \mu_y$, which reduces this equation to: $E(xy) - \mu_x \mu_y$, which is identical to Equation (2.33).

We can use this equation to show that $\text{Cov}(x, y) = 0$ when x and y are independent random variables. To see this, recall that when x and y are statistically independent, their joint probability function is given by the product of the marginal probabilities. In this case, the first term on the right becomes:

$$\sum_i \sum_j x_i y_j p(x_i, y_j) = \sum_i \sum_j x_i y_j p(x_i) p(y_j)$$

$$= \sum_i x_i p(x_i) \cdot \sum_j y_j p(y_j)$$

$$\sum_i \sum_j x_i y_j p(x_i, y_j) = E(x)E(y)$$

$$= \mu_x \cdot \mu_y \quad (x \text{ and } y \text{ independent})$$

When x and y are statistically independent, the expectation of the product xy thus equals the product of the individual expectations. From Equation (2.33):

$$\text{Cov}(x, y) = E(xy) - E(x)E(y).$$

If we substitute the result given above:

$$\text{Cov}(x, y) = E(x)E(y) - E(x)E(y) = 0 \quad \text{when } x \text{ and } y \text{ are independent.}$$

This completes the selected derivations of the bivariate results.

APPENDIX 2B   MATRIX ALGEBRA CALCULATION OF SELECTED STATISTICS IN THIS CHAPTER

This appendix presents a brief introduction to matrix algebra and illustrates how the important statistics discussed in this chapter can be derived using this tool. The reader is referred to *Fundamental Methods of Mathematical Economics* (3d. Ed.) by A. Chiang (McGraw-Hill Publishing Co.) for more in-depth coverage of the topics discussed here. *Subsequent matrix algebra appendixes presuppose the material contained in this appendix.*

Vectors and Matrices

When the observations for two or more variables are listed as columns, these data can be thought of as constituting a **matrix**. A matrix is simply a rectangular array of numbers. The individual numbers in a matrix are called **scalars**. Let us refer to the matrix we are dealing with as X. It is customary to represent such a matrix by referring to a representative element x_{ij}, where the subscript i denotes the row and j the column for this value. This is denoted: $X = [x_{ij}]$.

The observations for our variables constitute a **data matrix**. Each of the rows for such a matrix is a separate observation for the variables in question, while its columns represent the different variables. If our data consist of three observations for each of two variables, then $i = 3, j = 2$, and our data matrix will look like (2B.1):

$$X = \begin{bmatrix} x_{11} & x_{12} \\ x_{21} & x_{22} \\ x_{31} & x_{32} \end{bmatrix} \tag{2B.1}$$

If the number of rows and columns in a matrix are equal, X is a **square matrix**. The matrix (2B.1) is not square, which reflects a necessary condition for econometric estimation, that the number of observations (rows) exceed the number of variables (columns). The **dimension of a**

matrix, which tells its size, is expressed in the form: (number of rows) by (number of columns). For example, X in (2B.1) is a 3×2 matrix.

A **vector** is a matrix with either one row, called a **row vector**, or a single column, called a **column vector**. Examples of each are given by (2B.2).

$$Z = \begin{bmatrix} z_1 & z_2 & z_3 \end{bmatrix} \quad \text{(row vector)}$$

$$Z = \begin{bmatrix} x_1 \\ x_2 \\ x_3 \end{bmatrix} \quad \text{(column vector)} \tag{2B.2}$$

An important manipulation that allows us to obtain sums from vectors or matrices is the transpose. The **transpose of** X, denoted X', is the matrix or vector that results when the row(s) and column(s) of X are interchanged. If $X = [x_{ij}]$, then the transpose of this matrix is: $X' = [x_{ji}]$. If X is a row vector, X' is a column vector, and vice versa. Some examples of transposes are given by (2B.3).

$$X = \begin{bmatrix} x_{11} & x_{12} \\ x_{21} & x_{22} \\ x_{31} & x_{32} \end{bmatrix} \qquad X' = \begin{bmatrix} x_{11} & x_{21} & x_{31} \\ x_{12} & x_{22} & x_{32} \end{bmatrix}$$

$$\tag{2B.3}$$

$$Z = \begin{bmatrix} z_1 & z_2 & z_3 \end{bmatrix} \qquad Z' = \begin{bmatrix} z_1 \\ z_2 \\ z_3 \end{bmatrix}$$

The final building block considered here is the multiplication of vectors or matrices. If we consider the following two matrices:

$$A = \begin{bmatrix} a_{11} & a_{12} \\ a_{21} & a_{22} \\ a_{31} & a_{32} \end{bmatrix} \qquad B = \begin{bmatrix} b_{11} & b_{12} & b_{13} \\ b_{21} & b_{22} & b_{23} \end{bmatrix},$$

then A and B are **conformable for multiplication** if the number of columns in A equals the number of rows in B. The dimension of the resulting matrix is (number of rows in A) $\times$ (number of columns in B). In the present example, A and B are conformable for multiplication (check to see this), and the dimension of the new matrix, say, C is (3×3). The conformability of matrices (or vectors) can also be determined by writing their dimensions in the form:

(the dimension of A) $\times$ (the dimension of B),

then checking that the inner numbers coincide:

new matrix dimension

(3×2) $\times$ (2×3).

conformability

These matrices are conformable since the inside numbers match. The dimension of the resulting matrix is then given by the outermost two numbers.

Let us now see how the product matrix C is calculated. Here, $AB = C$, which is the (3×3) matrix, $C = [c_{ij}]$:

$$\begin{bmatrix} a_{11} & a_{12} \\ a_{21} & a_{22} \\ a_{31} & a_{32} \end{bmatrix} \begin{bmatrix} b_{11} & b_{12} & b_{13} \\ b_{21} & b_{22} & b_{23} \end{bmatrix} = \begin{bmatrix} c_{11} & c_{12} & c_{13} \\ c_{21} & c_{22} & c_{23} \\ c_{31} & c_{32} & c_{33} \end{bmatrix} \tag{2B.4}$$

c_{11} is obtained by multiplying row 1 of A by column 1 of B, which requires taking the following sum:

$$c_{11} = (a_{11} \cdot b_{11} + a_{12} \cdot b_{21}),$$

or adding the product of the first element in row 1 of A and the first element in column 1 of B to the product of the second element in row 1 of A and the second number in column 1 of B. Note that the row (i) value for c_{11} denotes which row of the first matrix (A) to use in this multiplication, while its column (j) value designates the column of the second matrix (B) to use. In other words, think of the subscripts for a given element c_{ij} as denoting:

$$c_{(\text{row of } A, \text{ column of } B)}.$$

When we multiply the terms in the above subscripts, the desired element of C results. Using this information, we obtain c_{12} by multiplying row 1 of A with column 2 of B:

$$c_{12} = (a_{11} \cdot b_{12} + a_{12} \cdot b_{22}).$$

Try calculating the remaining c_{ij} values to practice matrix multiplication.

If A and B are vectors, conformability for multiplication implies that one of these must be a row vector and the other a column vector. Assume, for example, A and B are both column vectors with dimension (3×1). The product AB does not exist, since in their original form these vectors are not conformable for multiplication. The product of A and B does exist when we transpose one of these matrices. For example, A and B' are conformable for multiplication since the inside numbers below match:

$$(3 \times 1) \times (1 \times 3).$$

Their product is a square matrix with 3 rows and 3 columns. Likewise, A' and B can be multiplied, since:

$$(1 \times 3) \times (3 \times 1).$$

The result is a scalar. With this brief introduction, we now show how to derive the univariate statistics presented in this chapter using vectors and matrices.

Univariate Statistics with Matrix Algebra

Assume that our data for a single variable x consists of n observations. We can represent x by the following column vector:

$$X = \begin{bmatrix} x_1 \\ \vdots \\ x_n \end{bmatrix}$$

To calculate the sum of the x's, we require a vector of 1's, which we will denote J. We will assume that J is the following ($n \times 1$) column vector:

$$J = \begin{bmatrix} 1 \\ 1 \\ \vdots \\ 1 \end{bmatrix}$$

Obtaining the sum of the x's, which is a scalar (i.e., 1×1), requires that we multiply a row vector and a column vector. We can obtain the required row vector by transposing either X or J. We will use the transpose of X:

$$X'J = [x_1 \quad x_2 \quad \cdots \quad x_n] \begin{bmatrix} 1 \\ 1 \\ \vdots \\ 1 \end{bmatrix} = x_1(1) + x_2(1) + \cdots + x_n(1) = \sum x_i$$

To obtain $\hat{\mu}_x$, we multiply this product by the scalar $(1/n)$:

$$\hat{\mu}_x = (1/n)X'J. \tag{B.5}$$

Note that if we multiply X' by X a sum also results:

$$X'X = [x_1 \quad x_2 \quad \cdots \quad x_n] \begin{bmatrix} x_1 \\ x_2 \\ \vdots \\ x_n \end{bmatrix} = x_1^2 + \cdots + x_n^2$$

This is the sum of the squares of x:

$$\sum x_i^2 = X'X. \tag{B.6}$$

To calculate the variance of x, we need an expression for the sum of squared deviations from the mean of x. If we define the vector of x deviations, X, as:

$$X = \begin{bmatrix} (x_1 - \hat{\mu}_x) \\ (x_2 - \hat{\mu}_x) \\ \vdots \\ (x_n - \hat{\mu}_x) \end{bmatrix}$$

and use (B.6) to calculate sums of squares, then:

$$\sum(x_i - \hat{\mu}_x)^2 = X'X$$

and:

$$\hat{\sigma}_x^2 = \frac{1}{n-1} \sum(x_i - \hat{\mu}_x)^2$$

$$= \frac{1}{n-1} X'X. \tag{B.7}$$

COVARIANCE AND CORRELATION WITH MATRIX ALGEBRA   Since both covariance and correlation deal with pairs of variables, our data matrix X will now contain n rows and 2 columns, which makes X an $(n \times 2)$ matrix. If we call these variables x and z, the matrix X can be represented:

$$X = \begin{bmatrix} x_1 & z_1 \\ x_2 & z_2 \\ \vdots & \vdots \\ x_n & z_n \end{bmatrix}.$$

The vector J (consisting of 1's) can still be used with this data matrix. The result of multiplying $X'J$ is no longer a sum, but a column vector containing individual sums:

$$X'J = \begin{bmatrix} x_1 & x_2 & \cdots & x_n \\ z_1 & z_2 & \cdots & z_n \end{bmatrix} \begin{bmatrix} 1 \\ 1 \\ \vdots \\ 1 \end{bmatrix}$$

$$= \begin{bmatrix} x_1(1) + x_2(1) + \cdots + x_n(1) \\ z_1(1) + z_2(1) + \cdots + z_n(1) \end{bmatrix} = \begin{bmatrix} \sum x_i \\ \sum z_i \end{bmatrix}.$$

Multiplying this product by the scalar $(1/n)$ creates a column vector consisting of the means of x and z:

$$(1/n)X'J = \begin{bmatrix} (1/n)\sum x_i \\ (1/n)\sum z_i \end{bmatrix}$$

$$= \begin{bmatrix} \hat{\mu}_x \\ \hat{\mu}_z \end{bmatrix} \tag{2B.8}$$

The product $X'X$ also exists when we are dealing with more than one variable. Since X is a matrix, the product $X'X$ is also matrix. If we denote the number of variables (columns) in X as k, $X'X$ is a square matrix with k rows and columns. To see this, consider what $X'X$ looks like for $k = 2$:

$$X'X = \begin{bmatrix} x_1 & x_2 & \cdots & x_n \\ z_1 & z_2 & \cdots & z_n \end{bmatrix} \begin{bmatrix} x_1 & z_1 \\ x_2 & z_2 \\ \vdots & \vdots \\ x_n & z_n \end{bmatrix}$$

$$= \begin{bmatrix} (x_1 \cdot x_1 + \cdots + x_n \cdot x_n) & (x_1 \cdot z_1 + \cdots + x_n \cdot z_n) \\ (z_1 \cdot x_1 + \cdots + z_n \cdot x_n) & (z_1 \cdot z_1 + \cdots + z_n \cdot z_n) \end{bmatrix}$$

$$X'X = \begin{bmatrix} \sum x_i^2 & \sum x_i z_i \\ \sum z_i x_i & \sum z_i^2 \end{bmatrix}. \tag{2B.9}$$

The terms in the first row, first column and second row, second column, called the **principal diagonal** of this matrix, are sums of squares. The off-diagonal elements are the sums of the products of the x's and z's, called the **cross-products**. This type of matrix, which is used extensively in econometrics, is called a **sum of the squares and cross-products matrix** (SSCP). An important property of this kind of matrix is that each of its off-diagonal elements is equal. This implies that the transpose of this matrix is identical to the matrix itself, or that $X'X$ is a **symmetric matrix**. For a matrix larger than 2×2 to be symmetric, it is necessary that every off-diagonal element x_{ij} equals element x_{ji}. In (2B.9) element $x_{12} = x_{21}$. For a 3×3 matrix to be symmetric, it is necessary that $x_{12} = x_{21}$, $x_{13} = x_{31}$, and $x_{23} = x_{32}$. To make this idea clearer, let X consist of three variables (i.e., $k = 3$), derive $X'X$, and explore what is necessary for this to be a symmetric matrix.

In the present context of two variables, a single covariance exists along with two variances. Summarizing all of this information therefore requires a matrix. The first step in deriving this matrix is the calculation of deviations from the mean for each of our variables. If we create a matrix V whose columns are the deviations of x and z from their respective means:

$$V = \begin{bmatrix} (x_1 - \hat{\mu}_x) & (z_1 - \hat{\mu}_z) \\ \vdots & \vdots \\ (x_n - \hat{\mu}_x) & (z_n - \hat{\mu}_z) \end{bmatrix},$$

we can think of this as the deviation form of X. The sum of the squares and cross-products matrix for V, $V'V$ is:

$$V'V = \begin{bmatrix} (x_1 - \hat{\mu}_x) & \cdots & (x_n - \hat{\mu}_x) \\ (z_1 - \hat{\mu}_z) & \cdots & (z_n - \hat{\mu}_z) \end{bmatrix} \begin{bmatrix} (x_1 - \hat{\mu}_x) & (z_1 - \hat{\mu}_z) \\ \vdots & \vdots \\ (x_n - \hat{\mu}_x) & (z_n - \hat{\mu}_z) \end{bmatrix}$$

$$V'V = \begin{bmatrix} \sum(x_i - \hat{\mu}_x)^2 & \sum(x_i - \hat{\mu}_x)(z_i - \hat{\mu}_z) \\ \sum(z_i - \hat{\mu}_z)(x_i - \hat{\mu}_x) & \sum(z_i - \hat{\mu}_z)^2 \end{bmatrix} \tag{2B.10}$$

Like all SSCP matrices, the principal diagonal of $V'V$ consists of sums of squares, and its off-diagonal elements are cross-products (that are equal). If we multiply each of the elements of (2B.10) by the scalar $1/(n-1)$, the diagonal elements are then the variances of x and z, while each off-diagonal element is the covariance between x and z. Thus:

$$\Sigma = \left[\frac{1}{n-1}\right] V'V = \begin{bmatrix} \hat{\sigma}_x^2 & \hat{\sigma}_{xz} \\ \hat{\sigma}_{zx} & \hat{\sigma}_z^2 \end{bmatrix} \tag{2B.11}$$

The matrix given by (2B.11) is the **variance-covariance matrix** (or simply the covariance matrix) of X.

The final topic discussed in this appendix is the derivation of the correlation matrix. Recall that the correlation between x and z is the ratio of their covariance, $\hat{\sigma}_{xz}$, and the product of their standard deviations, $(\hat{\sigma}_x \cdot \hat{\sigma}_z)$. The correlation matrix is derived from the variance-covariance matrix given by (2B.11). However, it is necessary to find a way to obtain the product term $(\hat{\sigma}_x \cdot \hat{\sigma}_z)$ in denominator of each of the terms in this matrix. This is accomplished using the following matrix,

$$D = \begin{bmatrix} 1/\sqrt{\hat{\sigma}_x} & 0 \\ 0 & 1/\sqrt{\hat{\sigma}_z} \end{bmatrix}$$

which is called a **diagonal matrix** (it contains scalars on the principal diagonal and zeros for all off-diagonal elements). The correlation matrix, R, is obtained from the following matrix multiplication:

$$R = D\Sigma D \tag{2B.12}$$

$$R = \begin{bmatrix} 1/\sqrt{\hat{\sigma}_x} & 0 \\ 0 & 1/\sqrt{\hat{\sigma}_z} \end{bmatrix} \begin{bmatrix} \hat{\sigma}_x^2 & \hat{\sigma}_{xz} \\ \hat{\sigma}_{zx} & \hat{\sigma}_z^2 \end{bmatrix} \begin{bmatrix} 1/\sqrt{\hat{\sigma}_x} & 0 \\ 0 & 1/\sqrt{\hat{\sigma}_z} \end{bmatrix}$$

which equals:

$$R = \begin{bmatrix} 1 & \hat{\rho}_{xz} \\ \hat{\rho}_{zx} & 1 \end{bmatrix} \tag{2B.13}$$

Note that R, like Σ, is a symmetric matrix. The 1's in the diagonal represent $\hat{\rho}_{xx}$ and $\hat{\rho}_{zz}$. Since any variable is perfectly correlated with itself, these correlation coefficients must equal 1.

3

A Primer on the Sources, Manipulation, and Computer Processing of Economic Data

The first two chapters provided an overview of econometrics and supplied the statistical prerequisites needed to begin the study of its subject matter. Before proceeding to the formal presentation of econometric theory, we must explore the sources, manipulation, and computer processing of economic data.

Expertise in gathering and manipulating data is an important skill in its own right for several reasons. Available data are not always in the exact form in which we wish to utilize them. For example, the base year for published data may differ from the desired year. Also, the routine practice of data manipulation allows a researcher to observe variables from several different perspectives, some of which may reveal behavior that was not originally anticipated. Finally, when presenting econometric results, it is necessary that we communicate the underlying basis of a model: the included variables, methods used to calculate them, and any interactions that exist. Knowledge of data manipulation thus assists in the formulation and analysis of econometric equations.

Manually performing all the required calculations places severe constraints on available time. The likelihood of calculation error is also high. This is where computers enter the picture. Computers allow the rapid and accurate processing of data, *once you are proficient in using them for this purpose*. Acquiring this capability is no simple task, however. Before embarking on data manipulation with a computer, you must either write your own program in a computer language such as Fortran, or use an existing ("canned") program that is designed to carry out the specific processing you desire without requiring knowledge of a formal programming language.

The first part of this chapter introduces the types and sources of economic data. The mechanics of data manipulation are then discussed. This chapter concludes by illustrating how the previous types of calculations can be performed using a "canned" computer program. Economic examples are provided and discussed along the way.

TYPES OF ECONOMIC DATA

The physical sciences utilize **experimental data**, which is generated through **controlled experimentation**. For this type of data, all factors other than those of primary interest are either absent or kept at predetermined levels. Researchers who utilize experimental data have the luxury of directly observing the relationship of interest, since the "other things" are directly under their control. Problems arise with experimental data when one or more major factors are overlooked, which leads to inaccurate or misleading results.

In contrast, social scientists rely substantially on **nonexperimental data**, for which the researcher is unable to impose controls. The notable feature of nonexperimental data is that a number of factors are often changing simultaneously. This places the burden of isolating the primary elements of interest entirely on the researcher. We control these "other things" by including variables that represent these factors. Fortunately, it is only necessary for us to account for the factors of primary importance that determine the behavior of our dependent variable. While experimental economic data, such as that created from the negative-income tax experiments of the 1970s, does exist, nonexperimental data are by far the primary type of data used in econometric research at the present time. The discussion that follows therefore concentrates on the types of nonexperimental data.

There are three types of nonexperimental data. The first classification, **cross-sectional data**, consists of information on economic units during a single time period. An example of a cross-sectional data base is given by a series of observations on purchases of a specific good by a number of persons in a particular month. The data recorded for each person might consist of the amount purchased, its price, the income of that person, and the price of a substitute good that was considered. This information can be utilized to estimate the demand function for this good. A second example of a cross-sectional data base is observations on a particular date for workers differing in experience and educational attainment. If earnings, age, and other labor supply information are recorded for each employee, a human capital earnings function can be estimated. While each of these examples illustrates the application of cross-sectional data to microeconomic relationships, this type of data can also be utilized to explore macroeconomic models. See if you can visualize other cross-sectional microeconomic and macroeconomic models and the variables needed for each equation.

The second data classification, **time series data**, consists of equally spaced observations covering a number of different time periods. A major source of this type of data is the U.S. government. The frequency of time series data typically ranges from weekly to annually. An example of time series data is quarterly observations over a ten-year period on personal consumption expenditures and disposable personal income (both in real terms). These data can be used to estimate a Keynesian Consumption Function equation. Another example is twenty years of annual data on aggregate automobile purchases (presumably for a given size of automobile), the average selling price of this size auto, income, and related good prices. These data can be used to estimate a time series auto demand function. As this last example illustrates, time series data are not applied exclusively to macroeconomic relationships. Microeconomic models such as demand functions can also be estimated with this type of data.

The final data category is a combination, or "pooling," of cross-sectional and time series data. **Longitudinal data** consist of observations on economic entities over several time periods. If the same economic entities are followed for several time periods, **panel data**, a special variety of longitudinal data, results. If the demand data discussed earlier are extended to track these same individuals for a twenty-four-month period, the cross-sectional data become panel data.

SOURCES OF ECONOMIC DATA

The gathering of economic data—or "data grubbing," as this task is often called—is critical to the practice of applied econometrics. Care must be exercised in obtaining data and understanding the specifics of how each variable is measured. Failure in either of these tasks can produce major errors in the estimation and analysis of empirical relationships. The following references are recommended for learning about the intricacies of various published data:

Heal A., K. Clarkson, and R. Miller. 1985. *Economic Sourcebook of Government Statistics*. Boston: D.C. Heath Publishing Co.

Morton J. 1972. A Student's Guide to American Federal Government Statistics. *Journal of Economic Literature* Vol. 10, 371–397.

Sommers A. 1985. *The U.S. Economy Demystified*. Lexington Books.

Angle E. *Keys for Business Forecasting*, 5th Ed. Federal Reserve Bank of Richmond, 1980.

An excellent and highly readable source that details the ways in which major macroeconomic variables interact, using stories from the *Wall Street Journal* is:

Lehmann M. 1990. *The Dow Jones-Irwin Guide to Using the Wall Street Journal*, 3d Ed. Homewood, IL: Dow Jones-Irwin, Inc.

The following is a listing of what will likely constitute the major sources of time series data for most users of this text:

Economic Report of the President
U.S. Council of Economic Advisers

Survey of Current Business
U.S. Bureau of Economic Analysis

Federal Reserve Bulletin
Board of Governors of the Federal Reserve System

Statistical Abstracts of the United States
U.S. Department of Commerce, Bureau of Census

Historical Statistics of the United States, Colonial Times to 1970
U.S. Department of Commerce, Bureau of Census, 1976

International Financial Statistics
International Monetary Fund

Monthly Labor Review
U.S. Bureau of Labor Statistics

If you are unable to find the data you desire in the above references, the U.S. government provides a complete listing of its statistical information in the *American Statistics Index*. Readers are encouraged to consult several of these sources, noting the particular information each contains. Try to formulate the basis of specific equations that can be estimated using data from the sources you select.

DATA MANIPULATION METHODS

Economists are fortunate enough to have access to continuous data covering many spheres of economic life. Unfortunately, these data are not always available in the exact form desired. The next section discusses the basis of and methods for calculating real values. Included in this material is an overview of the two major price indexes used in this type of calculation. Following this, methods for determining the growth rates of both nominal and real variables are outlined. Economic examples are included to facilitate mastery of this material.

Nominal versus Real Values

The **nominal value** of a variable is simply its dollar amount. Nominal values, which are referred to as current dollar values, do not take inflation into account. Because of this, rising prices can sometimes "inflate" nominal values, causing them to convey a misleading picture of the extent to which change has occurred. Consider nominal income, for example. If a person receives $300 per week from employment, the value of nominal income is $300. In periods of prolonged price increases, the purchasing power of this $300 weekly income will depend on when it is earned. An empirical implication (or complication) is associated with using nominal income in a demand study: if we utilize nominal income as our measure of ability to pay, then, if nominal income rises to $400, we implicitly assume that ability to pay has increased. As should be obvious, this is not always the case, for additional dollars of income do not always enhance ability to pay. Ability to pay rises only when nominal income grows fast enough to offset the loss of purchasing power caused by inflation. Thus it is not the number of dollars but their purchasing power, or *real income*, that is the more appropriate measure of ability to pay.

Economists define the **real value** of a variable as its inflation-adjusted value. These adjust for purchasing power differences that occur through time. Real values are referred to as constant dollar values (i.e., dollars of constant purchasing power). The "common denominator" in real values is the purchasing power (and thus prices) that prevailed in the period that serves as the basis of comparison. Since purchasing power is related to prices, measures representing prevailing prices, or **price indexes**, are required to produce real values.

Price indexes attempt to measure the average level of prices in an economy. Their derivation requires a methodology for assigning the importance, or weight, attached to each of the prices included in the index. The two indexes discussed here, the Consumer Price Index (CPI) and the Implicit (or GDP) Price Deflator (IPD), utilize quantities as weights.

All price indexes are expressed in terms of a temporal basis of comparison, or **base year**. The federal government recently changed the base year for the IPD. The Consumer Price Index is based on a 1982–1984 base year, while the Implicit Price Deflator uses a 1987 base year.[1]

Occasions arise when we must convert the base year from that of the original data source to some other year. Fortunately, all that is required to accomplish this is a simple algebraic manipulation of the initial price index data. The specific choice of base year can sometimes depict time series data in a very different light.

Deciding which price index to utilize for data manipulation requires information on the specific assumptions incorporated in the calculation of the indexes under consideration. The choice of price index weights, for example, must address two questions. First, should the weights be those from the base period or current period? Second, whose expenditure patterns should these quantities reflect? The primary difference between the Consumer Price Index and Implicit Price Deflator arises from the weights utilized. We now examine both of these indexes in detail.

Major Price Indexes[2]

THE CONSUMER PRICE INDEX (CPI).   The CPI attempts to measure the average level of prices paid by consumers for a wide range of goods and services. Separate CPIs are calculated for urban wage earners and clerical workers (CPI-W), and for all urban consumers (CPI-U). The Consumer Price Index is reported monthly. This index is subdivided into seven major expenditure categories: food and beverages; housing; apparel and upkeep; transportation; medical care; entertainment; and other goods and services. Cost-of-living clauses in entitlement programs such as Social Security and many labor contracts are tied to the CPI.

This price index is derived by comparing base year with current period expenditures for the goods and services purchased by the groups indicated above. Expenditure for a single good is the product of its price (p_i) and quantity consumed (q_i). If we assume there are n goods included in the CPI, then the total expenditure on these

---

[1] The previous base year for the IPD was 1982.

[2] For a more complete discussion of these price indexes than that provided here, the reader is referred to either the chapter on Laspeyres and Paasche indexes included in most intermediate microeconomics texts, or the references provided earlier in this chapter.

goods, which is the sum of the expenditure for each good consumed, is:

$$p_1 \cdot q_1 + p_2 \cdot q_2 + \cdots + p_n \cdot q_n = \Sigma p_i q_i.$$

Total expenditure is thus a weighted average of prices, where individual quantities serve as weights. The weights currently used by the CPI are derived from the Consumer Expenditure Surveys of 1982–1984. These replace the weights derived from the 1972–1973 Consumer Expenditure Surveys that were used until the end of 1986.

The CPI utilizes these same quantities continually and is therefore called a **fixed-weight index**. If we denote the base year by the superscript "0" and the current period with t, then base year expenditure is $\Sigma p_i^0 \cdot q_i^0$. This indicates the cost of the base year quantities when valued at the prices prevailing in the base year. Current period expenditure is obtained by valuing base year quantities at current prices: $\Sigma p_i^t \cdot q_i^0$. The CPI is the ratio of current period to base year expenditure:

$$\text{CPI} = \frac{\Sigma p_i^t q_i^0}{\Sigma p_i^0 q_i^0} \cdot 100. \tag{3.1}$$

To visualize what the CPI measures, picture going to a store during the base period and purchasing a specific list of goods (q^0). At this time the price level is p^0, so base period spending is given by the denominator of the CPI expression. Sometime later you return to this store and purchase the *same* goods in the *same* quantities (i.e., q^0). Prices are now p^t, so the amount spent is given by the numerator of (3.1). If this list of goods originally cost \$100 and later costs \$105, the CPI equals 105 for the more recent period. Using this information, it is tempting to conclude that all prices have risen by 5 percent, and that the actual rate of inflation is 5 percent. *Both of these inferences are erroneous, however. The correct interpretation is that the specific list of goods and services included in the CPI is now 5 percent more expensive than it was during the base period (since only q^0 is used).*

The exclusive use of base year weights does not allow for commodity substitution as prices change. The CPI thus implicitly assumes that demand curves are vertical. Because of this, the CPI tends to *overstate* expenditure, and hence price level changes, when prices are rising.[3] Furthermore, the quantities used in this index, which date back to the very beginning of the recovery, which began in 1983, are already somewhat outdated.

THE IMPLICIT PRICE DEFLATOR.   Like the CPI, the Implicit Price Deflator is derived from the ratio of two expenditure levels. The expenditure levels utilized represent nominal and real Gross Domestic Product. Recall that the expenditure calculation of nominal GDP consists of adding expenditures for all domestically produced goods and services for a given year. Using the notation from the previous section, nominal GDP equals $\Sigma p_i^t q_i^t$. Real Gross Domestic Product is derived by

---

[3] The conclusion that the CPI tends to overstate price increases assumes that the cause of higher prices is falling supply and not rising demand. In the latter case, the CPI will tend to understate expenditure.

valuing current output (q^t) at base year prices (p^0): $\Sigma p_i^0 q_i^t$. The Implicit Price Deflator is the ratio of nominal to real GDP:

$$\text{IPD} = \frac{\sum p_i^t \cdot q_i^t}{\sum p_i^0 \cdot q_i^t} \cdot 100. \tag{3.2}$$

Unlike the CPI, the IPD uses current period weights. It does not presuppose constancy in the pattern of consumption. The IPD is not a perfect price measure, however. If prices for a subset of goods rise dramatically during a particular time period, current period weights will tend to understate the trend in consumption for these goods, causing the IPD to understate the actual change in the price level. If the value of the Implicit Price Deflator is 105, nominal GDP is 5 percent higher than real GDP for that time period. Currently produced goods and services are then 5 percent more expensive in the present quarter than in the base year.

Because it is derived from GDP, the Implicit Price Deflator is published quarterly. The IPD is a more appropriate price index than the CPI for converting GDP or its components into real magnitudes, since the available breakdowns for the IPD correspond exactly (or more closely) to the expenditure categories of GDP than do those of the CPI. The IPD component that corresponds most closely to the CPI is the IPD for Personal Consumption Expenditures. This index is preferable to the CPI in two ways: it utilizes current period quantities; and these quantities span all goods consumed in the economy, not merely those of urban wage earners and clerical workers or all urban consumers urban wage earners.

Besides the dissimilar weights utilized by these indexes, two other differences should be mentioned before proceeding. First, the CPI increases when international price shocks occur, since imported goods are included among those consumed by the urban individuals from whom its quantities are derived. The IPD is not affected by foreign price shocks, since it is based on GDP values that are restricted exclusively to domestic factors. Second, until 1983, the treatment of housing expenditure by these indexes differed dramatically. The CPI's previous method for counting housing expenses indicated a more substantial rise in housing costs actually occurred during periods of rising interest rates.[4] In 1983 the CPI adopted the same treatment of housing utilized by the IPD. The inflated CPI values that resulted from this treatment of housing expenditure have never been revised. As a result, the CPI and the IPD for personal consumption expenditure differ substantially from the late 1970s to the early 1980s. Values of the CPI and IPD (using its previous base year) for selected years from 1967 to 1988 are given in Table 3.1. The parenthesis below each variable denotes the base year for that index.

---

[4] The CPI's previous treatment of housing expenditures gave an unrealistically large weight to this component, which, when subjected to the rising interest rates of the late 1970s, produced a substantial overstatement of inflation. While its treatment of housing costs has changed, the CPI has never been revised for this time period.

Table 3.1 CPI and IPDPCE Values for Selected Years

YEAR	CPI (1982–84 = 100)	IPDPCE (1982 = 100)
1967	33.4	36.0
1970	38.8	42.0
1972	41.8	46.5
1975	53.8	59.3
1980	82.4	86.6
1981	90.9	94.6
1982	96.5	100.0
1983	99.6	104.1
1984	103.9	108.1
1985	107.6	111.6
1986	109.6	114.3
1987	113.6	119.5
1988	118.4	124.5

Source: Economic Report of the President, 1989.

Calculations with Price Indexes

CHANGE OF BASE YEAR. The two price indexes in Table 3.1 have different base years. Let us convert the CPI to a 1982 base year, so both indexes use this year as their basis. For annual data, the procedure is simple: first, divide the CPI for each year by the single value of the CPI for the desired new base year; then multiply the resulting proportion by 100. For the first year in this table, 1967, the CPI is 33.4, while the CPI for the new base year, 1982, is 96.5. The 1967 CPI with a 1982 base year is 34.6 (= (33.4/96.5) · 100). Similarly, the CPI for 1970 (1982 = 100) is 40.2 (= (38.8/96.5) · 100). Since prices in both of these years are lower than those in the new base year, the purchasing power of money for these years exceeds that in 1982. As a result, base year quantities (q^0) that cost $100 in 1982 are less expensive in both 1967 and 1970, with the specific amounts given above. The price indexes for years with higher prices than those in the new base year exceed 100. A value such as 110 indicates that base year quantities that cost $100 in 1982 cost $110 in the later year.

It is also possible to convert the base year of monthly and quarterly data. The need for this frequently arises when gathering data that span a long time period. The base year of a variable sometimes reverts from that for the more recent observations to the one previously used. As long as one or more overlapping observations can be found, it is possible to manipulate the data so that we can continue back in time with the desired base year. As an example of this, let us consider gathering quarterly observations on the IPD from 1975 to the present. Until recently, the IPD used a 1982 base year. Prior to 1983, the base year for this variable was 1972. Let us assume that we come across the following data for the 1982–1983 period where only one overlapping observation exists:

	IPD(1972 = 100)	IPD(1982 = 100)
1982:1	203.4	
1982:2	206.2	
1982:3	208.0	
1982:4	210.0	
1983:1	**212.8**	**102.5**
1983:2		103.3
1983:3		104.2
1983:4		105.4

We can convert the earlier values of the IPD to a 1982 base year, if we use the information provided by the overlapping observation. The IPD for 1983:1 with a 1982 base year, 102.5, is 0.4817 the value of the IPD with the 1972 base year, 212.8. If we assume that this ratio pertains to all of the earlier observations we are interested in, then for these earlier periods:

$$IPD(1982 = 100) = 0.4817 \cdot IPD(1972 = 100),$$

and we need only perform this simple manipulation to obtain a time series with a consistent base year. The final values for the IPD with a 1982 base year (along with the original data with a 1972 base) are:

	IPD(1972 = 100)	IPD(1982 = 100)
1982:1	203.4	**98.0**
1982:2	206.2	**99.3**
1982:3	208.0	**100.2**
1982:4	210.0	**101.2**
1983:1	212.8	102.5
1983:2		103.3
1983:3		104.2
1983:4		105.4

REAL VALUES. Calculating real values is fairly straightforward once we have data for the nominal values of a variable or set of variables and an appropriate price index. The phrase "appropriate price index" implies, among other things, an index expressed in terms of a desired base year. Besides this, we will sometimes decide to forego using the overall CPI or IPD, and instead select a finer breakdown of one of these indexes.

Real values can be calculated from both cross-sectional and time series variables. In a cross-sectional data set, for example, persons with nominal income levels may be located in different regions. To calculate real incomes, it is necessary to obtain price index data for each region for the single time period of this data set (the CPI is best suited for this), then use (3.3) below to make the actual calculation.

The formula for the real value of any dollar denominated variable x is:

$$\text{Real } x_i = (x_i/p_i) \cdot 100 \quad \text{(cross-section)}$$

$$\text{Real } x_t = (x_t/p_t) \cdot 100 \quad \text{(time series)}$$

(3.3)

The subscript i designates the cross-sectional unit involved in this calculation, while t denotes time period. In the cross-section example given above, x_i represents the nominal income for person i in a particular region, and p_i is the CPI for the most appropriate geographic breakdown available for this person. As an example in a time series context, real consumption is calculated using x_t, personal consumption expenditure, and p_t, the IPD for the GDP component most closely matched to consumption, the IPD for Personal Consumption Expenditures (IPDPCE), in this time period.

The calculation of real values is illustrated in Table 3.2, which contains time series data on personal consumption expenditures (PCE) and the IPD for Personal Consumption Expenditure for the years 1980–1988. As this table shows, nominal consumption expenditures rose from $1,748.1 billion to $3,296.1 billion, or 88.6 percent, over this time period. However, during periods of rising prices, the growth in nominal values tends to overstate the increase that occurs when differences in purchasing power are accounted for. It is therefore necessary to consider the behavior of real consumption expenditures as well as to obtain a more accurate picture of the extent to which consumption spending has changed over this period. *As a rule, real*

Table 3.2 Calculation of Real Personal Consumption
Expenditures (PCE) Using the Implicit Price
Deflator for Personal Consumption Expenditures

YEAR	PCE (Bil $)	IPDPCE (1987 = 100)	REAL PCE (1987 = 100)
1980	1748.1	71.4	$(1748.1/\ 71.4) \cdot 100 = 2448.3$
1981	1926.2	77.8	$(1926.2/\ 77.8) \cdot 100 = 2475.8$
1982	2059.2	82.2	$(2059.2/\ 82.2) \cdot 100 = 2505.1$
1983	2257.5	86.2	$(2257.5/\ 86.2) \cdot 100 = 2618.9$
1984	2460.3	89.6	$(2460.3/\ 89.6) \cdot 100 = 2745.9$
1985	2667.4	93.1	$(2667.4/\ 93.1) \cdot 100 = 2865.1$
1986	2850.6	96.0	$(2850.6/\ 96.0) \cdot 100 = 2969.4$
1987	3052.2	100.0	$(3052.2/100.0) \cdot 100 = 3052.2$
1988	3296.1	104.2	$(3296.1/104.2) \cdot 100 = 3163.2$
Percent Change 1980–1988	88.6	45.9	29.2

Source: Economic Report of the President, 1992.

values should be considered along with nominal values when the behavior of a time series spans a relatively long period, or when the price level has changed substantially.

The last column of Table 3.2 illustrates the calculation of real personal consumption expenditure based on (3.3). Note that real consumption expenditure varies by a smaller amount than does nominal consumption (29.2 percent versus 88.6 percent). A substantial portion of the growth in nominal consumption is therefore the result of rising prices. For the years prior to 1987, real consumption is greater than nominal consumption. This occurs because the values of the IPDPCE prior to 1987 are below the 1987 value, which causes PCE for these years to be *inflated* to reflect the greater purchasing power of these years relative to 1987. The opposite is true after 1987. Prices for 1988 exceed those in the base year, requiring that nominal PCE be *deflated* to keep these expenditures consistent with the prevailing purchasing power of the 1987 base year.

The choice of which base year to use when computing real values is arbitrary. This decision should be based on the most effective communication of these results to the intended audience. However, the more distant the base year, the greater will be the divergence between nominal and real values for recent periods. The choice of a remote base year can fail to convey a sense of the behavior of the variables being analyzed to persons unfamiliar with real values. When this is a problem, it is advisable to choose a more recent base year, such as the latest year for which data are available, or a year in which some substantial change occurred. The final decision of which base year to use is judgmental. No "right" answer exists.

MEASURING GROWTH

The amount by which a variable is changing often contains important information about its behavior. We can measure such change in several different ways. The first of these evaluates growth in an absolute sense: the difference between the current and previous value of a variable. If we denote the current period value of x as x_t and its value for the previous period x_{t-1}, then the **absolute change in x**, denoted Δx, equals $(x_t - x_{t-1})$.

The unit of measurement for absolute change is the same as that for x. This limits its usefulness as a vehicle for making comparisons between variables with very different units of measurement. For example, if x is measured in hundreds per month, and z, which we wish to contrast with x, is expressed in millions per month, small relative changes in z will translate into large absolute changes. It will thus appear that z is continually growing more rapidly than x, while in reality such change reflects the larger size of z. As this example suggests, valid comparisons can only be made if we can allow for the differences in size, or units of measurement that exist.

Growth rates eliminate this problem by evaluating x_t relative to x_{t-1}. Unlike absolute change, which is given by the difference between these values, growth rates are based on the ratio x_t/x_{t-1}. Dealing with growth rates therefore frees us from the original unit of measurement for a variable. Our measures are now either proportions or percentages.

The **proportionate growth rate** in x, denoted g_x, is the ratio of the absolute change in x to an earlier value (such as x_{t-1}):

$$g_x = (\Delta x_t / x_{t-1}) \tag{3.4}$$

We can express g_x in terms of the ratio x_t/x_{t-1} by substituting for the numerator of (3.4):

$$g_x = (\Delta x_t / x_{t-1}) = (x_t - x_{t-1})/x_{t-1}, \tag{3.5}$$

or

$$g_x = (x_t / x_{t-1}) - 1 \tag{3.6}$$

Since (3.4)–(3.6) evaluate x_t relative to its value one period earlier, each of these is a one-period proportionate growth rate. Either formula allows us to determine the annual growth in x with annual data. If we are interested in measuring annual growth, but our data are either monthly or quarterly, we must evaluate x_t relative to either x_{t-12} (monthly data) or x_{t-4} (quarterly data). We can therefore restate the proportionate growth rate (3.6) as:

$$g_x = (x_t / x_{t-12}) - 1 \quad \text{(twelve-period proportionate growth rate)}$$
$$g_x = (x_t / x_{t-4}) - 1 \quad \text{(four-period proportionate growth rate)} \tag{3.7}$$

Both of the above equations measure annual growth by considering x this period relative to its value one year ago. For this reason, these are sometimes referred to as **year-to-year proportionate growth rates**. For monthly data, this compares the value of x in (say) January of this year with its value the preceding January, while with quarterly data, x in the first quarter of this year is contrasted with x in the first quarter of the previous year.

A slight variant of the proportionate growth rate is the **percent growth rate**, which simply entails multiplying the proportionate growth rate by 100. The equations for the one-period percent growth rate in x that parallel those above are:

$$g_x = \{(x_t - x_{t-1})/x_{t-1}\} \cdot 100, \tag{3.8}$$

or

$$g_x = \{(x_t / x_{t-1}) - 1\} \cdot 100. \tag{3.9}$$

Table 3.3 illustrates the calculation of percent growth rates for the time series of nominal personal consumption expenditure given in Table 3.2. Note that the rate for the first year cannot be obtained, so this becomes a missing value. Calculations for the other years use Equation (3.8). This is likely to be the preferable formula for persons who have never performed this type of calculation, since no short-cuts are involved.

Equations (3.8) and (3.9) can be modified to evaluate either four-period or twelve-period percent growth rates. Using the form of (3.9), these are:

$$g_x = \{(x_t / x_{t-12}) - 1\} \cdot 100;$$

and

$$g_x = \{(x_t / x_{t-4}) - 1\} \cdot 100. \tag{3.10}$$

Table 3.3 Annual Growth in Nominal Personal Consumption Expenditures

YEAR	PCE	GROWTH RATE
1980	1748.1	—
1981	1926.2	$((1926.2 - 1748.1)/1748.1) \cdot 100 = 10.19$
1982	2059.2	$((2059.2 - 1926.2)/1926.2) \cdot 100 = 6.90$
1983	2257.5	$((2257.5 - 2059.2)/2059.2) \cdot 100 = 9.63$
1984	2460.3	$((2460.3 - 2257.5)/2257.5) \cdot 100 = 8.98$
1985	2667.4	$((2667.4 - 2460.3)/2460.3) \cdot 100 = 8.42$
1986	2850.6	$((2850.6 - 2667.4)/2667.4) \cdot 100 = 6.87$
1987	3052.2	$((3052.2 - 2850.6)/2850.6) \cdot 100 = 7.07$
1988	3296.1	$((3296.1 - 3052.2)/3052.2) \cdot 100 = 7.99$

When we use either (3.7) or (3.10) to measure the annual growth in x, we are basing our measure on either the value of x in a given month compared to its value that same month one year ago, or this quarter's x versus x in the same quarter last year. An alternative calculation method exists that is based on the one-period growth rate. This method starts with the one-period growth rate, then compounds (annualizes) this rate for the number of time periods that occur in a year. The **compounded annual (percent) growth rate** in x (cg_x) is given by the formulas:

$$cg_x = \{(x_t/x_{t-1})^{12} - 1\} \cdot 100 \quad \text{(monthly data)} \tag{3.11}$$

$$cg_x = \{(x_t/x_{t-1})^{4} - 1\} \cdot 100 \quad \text{(quarterly data)} \tag{3.12}$$

This method for measuring annual growth implicitly assumes that the one-period growth rate will continue throughout the remainder of a one-year period.

Compound annual growth rates can sometimes differ substantially from the year-to-year measures discussed previously. For example, seasonal factors that affect x may produce a large one-period change that is not representative of its long-term behavior. Compounding this "exceptional" value to produce an annualized growth rate can severely exaggerate the actual growth in this variable. Likewise, supply shocks can cause improbable growth estimates for prices or quantities when compounding is used.

ECONOMIC APPLICATIONS OF GROWTH RATES

The Rate of Inflation

An important application of the growth rate of a variable is the calculation of inflation rates. The *inflation rate* is calculated by taking the percent change in a price index.

A number of price indexes exist that can be used as the basis for such a measure. We have already discussed two of these, the CPI and the IPD, that deal with inflation

Table 3.4 Quarterly Producer Price Index for Finished Goods and Inflation Rates

| | PPI | INFLATION RATE | |
YEAR:QUARTER	(1982 = 100)	YEAR-TO-YEAR	COMPOUND ANNUAL
1987:1	104.1	—	—
1987:2	105.3	—	$((105.3/104.1)^4 - 1) \cdot 100 = 4.69$
1987:3	105.9	—	$((105.9/105.3)^4 - 1) \cdot 100 = 2.30$
1987:4	106.0	—	$((106.0/105.9)^4 - 1) \cdot 100 = 0.38$
1988:1	106.5	$((106.5/104.1) - 1) \cdot 100 = 2.31$	$((106.5/106.0)^4 - 1) \cdot 100 = 1.90$
1988:2	107.4	$((107.4/105.3) - 1) \cdot 100 = 1.99$	$((107.4/106.5)^4 - 1) \cdot 100 = 3.42$
1988:3	108.6	$((108.6/105.9) - 1) \cdot 100 = 2.55$	$((108.6/107.4)^4 - 1) \cdot 100 = 4.54$
1988:4	109.5	$((109.5/106.0) - 1) \cdot 100 = 3.30$	$((109.5/108.6)^4 - 1) \cdot 100 = 3.36$

Source: Federal Reserve Bulletin—various issues.

at the retail level. It is possible to calculate inflation rates for the aggregates of these indexes (overall inflation) or for any of their individual components (e.g.: medical cost inflation using the CPI's medical cost component). Price indexes also exist for the level of the producer, most notably the Producer Price Index.

Annual rates of inflation can be calculated from monthly or quarterly data using either year-to-year percent changes or the compounded annual change (expressed as a percentage). The annual inflation rates reported by the media are usually compound annual growth rates.

Table 3.4 contains quarterly data for the Producer Price Index for Finished Goods (PPI), along with year-to-year and compound annual rates of inflation based on this price index for 1987 and 1988. Only one missing value occurs in the calculation of the compound annual rate of inflation. The loss of only a single value is one of the advantages associated with this method of computing annual inflation. Four missing values occur with the year-to-year annual inflation rate. Annual inflation estimates produced by compounding generally exceed the year-to-year values. During 1988:2 and 1988:3 the disparities are substantial. While it did not occur here, it is possible for annual inflation estimates produced by these two methods to differ in sign. This occurs when the one-period change in x is negative (causing a negative compounded rate) but higher than the value of x one year ago (so the year-to-year change is positive).

Definition of a Recession

A recession is defined as two or more consecutive quarters during which real Gross National Product declines. Since real economic growth occurs when real GDP is rising, a recession is a period of six or more consecutive months with negative real growth.

The data in Table 3.5, which cover the period during which the initial OPEC price increases occurred, can be used to establish when a recession took place. These

Table 3.5   GNP, IPD, Real GNP and Percent Changes

YEAR:QUARTER	GNP	IPD (1982 = 100)	REAL GNP (1982 = 100)	PERCENT CHANGE
1973:1	1311.6	48.0	2732.5	—
1973:2	1342.9	49.0	2740.6	0.30
1973:3	1369.2	50.0	2738.8	−0.07
1973:4	1413.3	51.2	2760.4	0.79
1974:1	1426.2	51.9	2748.0	−0.45
1974:2	1459.1	53.0	2753.0	0.18
1974:3	1489.1	54.8	2717.3	−1.30
1974:4	1516.8	56.3	2694.1	−0.85
1975:1	1524.6	57.7	2642.3	−1.92
1975:2	1563.5	58.6	2668.1	0.98
1975:3	1627.4	59.9	2716.9	1.83
1975:4	1678.2	61.0	2751.1	1.26
Percent Change	28.0	27.1	1.0	

Source: *Survey of Current Business*—various issues.

use Gross National Product (GNP) which was the major measure of aggregate output at that time. The steps involved in this determination are:

(i) converting nominal to real GNP, and;
(ii) calculating the one-quarter percent changes in real GNP.

The results of these calculations are given in the two columns on the right of this table. Nominal GNP consistently increased from $1311.6 billion to $1678.2 billion, or approximately 28 percent over this time period. Real GNP actually declined several times during this interval. Negative real GNP growth occurred during the three quarters from 1974:3 until 1975:1, which indicates that a recession occurred during those quarters. Real GNP fell by 2.8 percent over that period and did not return to its pre-recession value until two quarters into the recovery that followed.

Growth in Real Values

The data in Table 3.5 indicate rather vividly that growth in the nominal value of a variable does not necessarily ensure real growth. The nominal and real growth rates of a dollar denominated variable x can be linked by using the following formula which provides an *approximation* to this relationship:

$$\text{Percent change in Real } x \approx \text{Percent change in Nominal } x - \text{Rate of Inflation} \qquad \textbf{(3.13)}$$

The approximation given by (3.13) is valid when the percent changes in nominal and real x are not large. We can apply (3.13) to the data in Table 3.5. During the time period covered by these data, nominal GNP rose by 28 percent, while inflation, as measured by the percent change in the IPD, was 27.1 percent. The 1 percent growth in Real GNP coincides almost exactly with the difference between these values.

Three very important facts follow directly from this formula:

(i) growth in nominal x does not guarantee that x is growing in real terms;

(ii) during periods of rising prices, real growth occurs only when nominal x grows faster than the rate of inflation; and

(iii) when inflation accelerates, nominal x must grow at ever-increasing rates to preserve real x.

This last point allows us to make an analogy between maintaining a given level of real income and running on a treadmill. Just as it is necessary to run faster and faster to preserve one's position when the speed of a treadmill is increasing, during periods of accelerating inflation, nominal income must rise by greater amounts to keep real income constant. Perhaps this constitutes the economic version of the saying, "The harder I work, the behinder I get."

Real Rate of Interest

Real values are also critical in the evaluation of non-dollar denominated magnitudes, such as interest rates. The distinction between nominal and real interest rates is an important one. The *nominal interest rate* is the stated interest rate on an asset such as a loan or a savings account. It indicates the percent increase in the number of dollars that are paid or received at the end of a year (assuming no compounding) as the result of lending or borrowing money. During periods of rising prices, the purchasing power of dollars paid or received as interest tends to decrease. A more appropriate measure of the cost of lending or borrowing money should therefore account for differences in the purchasing power of money that occur over the life of an asset. This takes us again to the real-nominal distinction discussed earlier for dollar denominated assets. The *real rate of interest* indicates the percent change in *purchasing power* that occurs over the life of an asset. For a given time period:

$$R_r = R_n - \pi^e, \tag{3.14}$$

where R_r denotes the real rate of interest, R_n is the stated or nominal interest rate, and π^e is the expected rate of inflation.

Unlike the nominal interest rate, which can only be positive, the real rate of interest can be either positive, negative, or zero. If, for example, the nominal rate of interest on a savings account is 7 percent while expected inflation is 10 percent, the real interest rate is *−3 percent*. Even though 7 percent more dollars are received at the end of the year, each dollar is expected to buy 10 percent less. The real interest rate in this example is negative because the expected loss in purchasing power more than offsets the growth in the number of dollars gained by saving. *The real interest rate is positive only when the nominal interest rate exceeds expected inflation. The real interest rate is 0 when the nominal interest rate equals the anticipated rate of inflation.*

We do not observe the real rate of interest. Transactions involving interest rates are stated in terms of nominal interest rates. If we are interested in working with real interest rates, it is therefore necessary to approximate these values. The inflation rate that appears in Equation (3.14) is not the actual but the expected inflation rate. Calculating real interest rates requires a measure of expected inflation. The government does not publish a time series called "the expected rate of inflation." Several surveys exist that attempt to measure the inflationary expectations of respondents. We could use the values from such surveys as our inflation measure. Beyond this, the only available course of action is the use of existing data to provide an approximation called a **proxy variable**. The simplest method for constructing a proxy of inflationary expectations is to assume that individuals use past inflation rates as the basis for their projections of future inflation. This framework, which is used in Keynesian economics, is called adaptive expectations. Table 3.6 contains data on interest rates and inflation that we can use to approximate real interest rates based on the adaptive expectations framework. The methodology detailed below reproduces that in the 1987 *Economic Report of the President*.

Starting with the CPI inflation rates in this table, we postulate that individuals formulate inflationary expectations that pertain to long-term interest rates based on the average of *past* rates of inflation. If we use the average of inflation over the past two years as the basis for our expected inflation proxy variable, then:

$$\pi_t^e = (\pi_{t-1} + \pi_{t-2})/2 \tag{3.15}$$

Table 3.6   Real Interest Rates 1977 to 1988

YEAR	10 YEAR GOV'T BOND INTEREST RATE	CPI INFLATION RATE	EXPECTATIONS PROXY*	REAL RATE OF INTEREST
1975	7.99	9.13	—	—
1976	7.61	5.76	—	—
1977	7.42	6.50	7.44	−0.02
1978	8.41	7.59	6.13	2.28
1979	9.44	11.35	7.05	2.39
1980	11.46	13.50	9.47	1.99
1981	13.91	10.32	12.42	1.49
1982	13.00	6.16	11.91	1.09
1983	11.10	3.21	8.24	2.86
1984	12.44	4.32	4.69	7.75
1985	10.62	3.56	3.76	6.86
1986	7.68	1.95	3.94	3.74
1987	8.39	3.65	2.76	5.63
1988	8.85	4.13	2.80	6.05

* Two-year moving average of past CPI inflation rates.

Source: Economic Report of the President, 1989.

where π_t^e represents expected inflation in year t, and π_{t-1} and π_{t-2} represent the measured CPI inflation rates in the previous year and two years earlier, respectively. Note from Table 3.6 that when we construct our proxy variable using Equation (3.15), two missing values occur. This formulation is called a **two-period moving average**. The term "moving average" is derived from the fact that when we calculate a new value for π_t^e, we must move the observations used, as the data below indicate.

π	π_t^e
π_1	missing value
π_2	missing value
π_3	$\pi_3^e = (\pi_2 + \pi_1)/2$
π_4	$\pi_4^e = (\pi_3 + \pi_2)/2$
π_5	$\pi_5^e = (\pi_4 + \pi_3)/2$

For example, π_3^e uses the inflation rates from the first two periods. When we construct π_4^e, we now use the two inflation rates that occur prior to period 4, which requires moving to π_3 and π_2.

The values of expected inflation derived from Equation (3.15) are given in the column labeled "Expectations Proxy" in Table 3.6. Estimated real interest rates are given in the far right column. The real interest rate for 1977 is negative, since the expectations proxy, 7.44 percent, exceeds the nominal interest rate for that year, 7.42 percent. Note also how substantially real interest rates derived from this methodology have risen since 1982. Although nominal interest rates are lower than they were in 1985, real interest rates have risen. This has occurred since the effect on real interest rates of the drop in expected inflation (to just below 3 percent) is more than offset by the rise in the nominal interest rates from 1986 to 1988.

This procedure for calculating real interest rates can be criticized on several grounds. First, its use of adaptive expectations implies that people do not use current information when forming expectations of future inflation. Second, use of the CPI inflation rate for the period spanning the late 1970s and early 1980s overstates actual inflation during that period due to its (then) unsatisfactory treatment of housing expenditure. Third, averaging values of a variable that is expressed as a percentage is more properly accomplished using the geometric mean rather than the arithmetic mean, as discussed in Chapter 2. While use of the geometric mean does not produce large differences in the expected inflation measure, it results in a positive real interest rate for 1977, since π_t^e based on a moving geometric mean equals 7.25 percent in that year.

One final aspect of this topic should be mentioned. By manipulating the real interest rate (3.14), we can express the nominal interest rate in terms of the real rate of interest:

$$R_n = R_r + \pi^e \tag{3.16}$$

The expected inflation term in Equation (3.16) is referred to as the inflationary premium in the (nominal) rate of interest. This equation provides us with a connection between the expected rate of inflation and nominal interest rates. When expected inflation rises, a higher rate of interest is needed to preserve the purchasing power of funds that are loaned (such as savings). We therefore expect the inflationary premium in interest rates to rise, which, other things being equal, will bring about an increase in nominal interest rates. Based on this reasoning, we anticipate a positive relationship be tween these variables, so that an upward trend in nominal interest rates should occur during periods when expected inflation is rising, while falling interest rates should accompany moderating inflationary anticipations.

MEASURING THE SIZE OF A VARIABLE

When analyzing economic data we are frequently confronted with the question of whether or not the value of a dollar denominated variable is large. For example, is a $200 billion deficit excessive? If personal debt rises by $10 billion, does this signal the coming of a recession, since consumers might not be able to sustain this much spending?

There are a number of ways to respond to these questions. In general, though, economists evaluate such magnitudes in *relative* rather than absolute terms. We have already detailed an example of this type of measure. When we convert nominal to real values, these become relative magnitudes since they are defined relative to the purchasing power of the base year. Referring to the questions posed earlier, we would consider the behavior of real deficits and increases in real debt as the basis for determining whether either of their nominal values are excessive.

Another method exists that can be applied to both nominal and real values. When considering whether or not a value is "large," we can evaluate it relative to some measure of size associated with that variable. For example, we can compare nominal budget deficits to the size of the economy, as approximated by GDP. In this example, GDP becomes a measure of our ability to afford deficits. Does a larger deficit pose a problem for the economy? We now answer this question by referring to the deficit (D) as a percentage of GDP, $(D/\text{GDP}) \cdot 100$. If this value is rising, or is well above historical values for the deficit-GDP ratio, we then consider the deficit to be large, indicating that it may well pose a potential problem.

The question of whether an increase in personal debt (D) presages the coming of a recession can be restated in terms of the ratio of debt to income (Y), $(D/Y) \cdot 100$. If debt rises, the debt-income ratio does not necessarily increase. It is possible for an increase in income to exactly offset the effect of higher debt, leaving this ratio constant. This ratio rises only when the growth in debt exceeds that of income.

The importance of such ratios to econometrics can be seen by considering how we should define ability to pay in a demand equation for durable goods. Certainly, income is an important determinant of ability to pay. However, since durable goods are often purchased with credit, we must also consider indebtedness when making this determination. If personal debt rises, are persons less able to pay for durable goods? As discussed above, this depends on the levels of both income and debt. If we include the level of debt in our demand equation, we are building in the assumption that when debt rises, the demand for durable goods falls (other things being equal). However, the ability to afford durable goods can increase at the same time debt is rising. This occurs when income growth outpaces the growth in debt. It is therefore more appropriate to include the debt-income ratio rather than the level of debt in a demand equation for durable goods.

As this discussion illustrates, in a number of situations we must analyze a variable in relative terms, as a percentage of some related variable. The general formula for expressing a variable x as a percentage (P) of some other variable z is:

$$P = (x/z) \cdot 100 \tag{3.17}$$

Equation (3.17) can be thought of as determining the "size relative" value of x, that is, the size of x relative to that of z. A "large" value of x does not necessarily indicate that its size relative value is also large. Similarly, when x is "small," its size relative value might not be small. Whether x is "large" or "small" therefore depends on both its own level and that of z.

An Application of Size Measurement: The Size of Recent Budget Deficits

Since 1980 nominal budget deficits have grown to unprecedented levels, causing concern on the part of both citizens and government alike to deal with this problem. The beneficial and adverse effects of budget deficits will not be debated here. It is appropriate, based on the material in the last section, to examine these deficits in *relative* terms, considering them in both real terms and as a percent of GNP. Table 3.7 shows

Table 3.7   Contrast of Real Deficits and Deficit-GNP Ratios

YEAR	BUDGET DEFICIT	IPD* (1982 = 100)	IPD* (1986 = 100)	GNP	REAL DEFICIT (1986 = 100)	DEFICIT-GNP RATIO
1945	47.6	11.8	10.7	213.4	442.9	22.3
..						
1980	73.8	84.3	76.8	2,731.9	96.1	2.7
1981	78.9	93.3	85.0	3,052.6	92.9	2.6
1982	127.9	100.0	91.1	3,166.0	140.4	4.0
1983	207.8	103.1	93.9	3,405.7	221.3	6.1
1984	185.3	106.8	97.3	3,772.2	190.5	4.9
1985	212.3	109.0	99.3	4,014.9	213.9	5.3
1986	221.2	109.8	100.0	4,240.2	221.2	5.2
1987	149.7	112.7	102.6	4,526.7	145.8	3.3
1988	155.1	115.1	104.8	4,864.2	148.0	3.2

* Implicit Price Deflator for Federal Government Purchases of Goods and Services

Source: Economic Report of the President, 1989.

nominal and real deficits for selected years. Since the largest nominal deficit occurred in 1986, we convert the price deflator to a 1986 base year, then contrast real deficits using that year as a basis. The price index used for this calculation is the IPD for Federal Government Purchases of Goods and Services.

A very striking result is obtained when comparing real deficits: current nominal deficits that seem excessive in terms of a historical perspective are in fact smaller in both real terms and as a percentage of real GNP than past values such as that for 1945. The real deficit for 1945 is twice as large as that for 1986, while the 1945 deficit is approximately four times the multiple of GNP as is that for 1986. Of course, 1945 was a war year, which must be kept in mind if a comparison is made for policy considerations. The fact remains that in relative terms, current deficits are not necessarily astronomical.

THE BASICS OF USING A COMPUTER PROGRAM TO ENTER AND PROCESS DATA

> "Computers do what you tell them to do, not what you want them to."
> (Murphy's Fifth Law of Computing)

The practice of applied econometrics requires the use of computers to perform the numerous and varied calculations that are fundamental to data analysis. Even after the data have been gathered, further steps are necessary before we can empirically investigate relationships within a data set. The most likely first step involves converting the data into a desired form, such as transforming nominal to real values, or calculating growth rates. Once this is completed, information on the central tendency and dispersion of these variables, along with their joint behavior, in terms of covariance or correlation, is useful. Putting all of this information together, we can then estimate a regression equation using the precise form of the dependent variable we are interested in modeling, along with the relevant explanatory variables.

The material in the remainder of this chapter outlines the *general* principles that underlie the ways in which "canned" computer programs perform these types of calculations. Specific examples of data manipulation are provided by detailing two actual "canned" computer programs: Statistical Analysis System (SAS) and TSP (Time Series Processor). Versions of each of these programs exist for both mainframe and personal computers. The discussion that follows will employ the mainframe version of SAS, along with the personal computer version of TSP, MicroTSP. While it is understood that some readers will not have access to either or both of these programs, it is still recommended that you read this material to broaden your understanding of computer usage in applied econometrics.

What Is a "Canned" Computer Program?

No matter what you may think about computers, one fundamental fact must be understood from the outset: computers are basically ignorant. The actions of a computer are based entirely on a series of electrical pulses. To enable communication (interfacing) with computers, it has been necessary for computer scientists to develop languages that enable the instructions of computer users to be conveyed to these machines so that desired tasks might be accomplished. A **computer language** can be thought of as a very detailed set of instructions for the computer to act upon. When presented with a specific command (instruction) from such a language, the computer performs a given action (although not always the one we intend). Examples of computer languages are BASIC, Fortran, and Pascal. A set of commands used to perform a desired set of tasks is called a **computer program.**

As time passed, and computers became more entrenched as a part of empirical research, the inefficiency in having researchers write their own programs with these different languages became apparent. The potential economies that resulted from computer programmers utilizing their comparative advantage to write large, complicated programs were sufficient to lead to the appearance of such programs. These have come to be known as "canned" computer programs. Today, canned programs are readily available for mainframe, mini, and personal computers. Many more persons are able to conduct computer-assisted empirical research than would be the case were all computer users required to be programmers.

Using a canned statistical program to produce the statistical and other information we desire requires only that we know the specific instructions needed to accomplish our desired tasks. These instructions are then translated by the program into code that can be understood and acted upon by the computer. This situation is certainly easier than the alternative of writing our own programs. Don't be fooled, however, into thinking that virtually no time and effort are expended. Existing computer programs require that a command be given in only a certain way—*the program's way.* If we deviate from this form, even in a manner that appears inconsequential, part or all of the entire program execution may need to be redone. For example, if a space or semicolon is inadvertently omitted, the result may be that some or all of the intended output cannot be obtained.

When you first use a canned program, such mistakes will inevitably occur. Experience does matter. For computer users, patience is likely the most important ingredient of all, since you will likely experience a number of Murphy's Laws firsthand. One aim of the material in this chapter is to make your exposure to computers and canned programs a great deal more positive than if you were merely left to your own devices (sorry!). A word of advice: always view the lines you enter into a canned program *from the perspective of the computer.* Following this guideline will allow you to avoid many pitfalls, for you will be more aware of precisely what you are instructing the computer to do.

The general discussion of canned programs that follows focuses on the three essential tasks that all of these programs must perform:

(i) data must be read in and a data set created, so that the computer knows what each variable is and the name you intend for it;

(ii) the entries in this data set are then manipulated prior to statistical analysis, such as creating real from nominal values, or growth rates; and

(iii) part or all of the data set are used to produce desired outputs, such as the printing of data, calculation of summary statistics, or estimating a regression equation. We now examine each of these in detail.

Creating a Data Set

The first step in using a canned program is the creation of a data set. The canned program initially knows nothing about the data you have collected. It is therefore imperative that the computer read the data correctly. Not much can be stated at a very general level about creating a data set and assigning names to variables. Definite naming conventions exist. For example, a data set name might be limited to six or eight characters, with certain symbols (such as %) prohibited. This same naming convention ordinarily applies to both the data set and individual variables. Usually, a single line (command) designates that a data set is being created. It might also indicate a name for this data set. An additional line, often following the first, provides the list of names that will be associated with the variables in the data set. As an example, SAS uses the statements:

```
DATA FIRST;
INPUT X Y;
```

to create a data set called FIRST, then uses the INPUT statement to assign the names X and Y to the variables whose values are entered. The semicolon at the end of each command indicates to SAS where the command ends. Some programs require that we enter the data frequency (e.g.: annual), along with starting and ending dates for time series data or the maximum number of observations for cross-sectional data. In MicroTSP, for example, the commands:

```
CREATE A 55 88
DATA X Y
```

instruct this program to create a data set with annual (A) values for the years 1955 to 1988. If, instead, the data on X and Y consist of 200 cross-sectional observations, the CREATE statement changes to:

```
CREATE U 200
```

where the "U" denotes undated observations.

The computer must next read these data in the exact way we intend it to. Data are often entered in *column form*, which is the convention followed here. When the data are entered in this form, each row consists of a single observation, while columns represent different variables. Assume we have data on two variables we wish to name X and Y, and that our program has been correctly instructed that these are the intended variable names. If the first observation consists of the values of 75 for X and 12 for Y, and we enter these as:

```
7512
```

then, without further information, the program will assume that the initial observation for X is 7512, and that the first value for Y is missing.

As this example shows, the *format* of the data is very important. The computer searches for data to match the names you have given it. When it encounters values, the program has no way of knowing that the first two digits represent X and the last two are Y. We can communicate the precise format of our data to the program in one of several ways. The simplest of these is called *free format*, in which we leave one or more blank spaces between the variables (columns) for each observation. If we write the first observation for X and Y in free format, it becomes:

75   12

The computer will now read the number 75, associate this value with the first variable in the list, note the logical stopping place provided by the space(s), then assign the next set of numbers to the second variable. Free format is probably the easiest way to enter data, since you can check individual values as you go along.

It is possible to enter the data in this example without using the free format. To do this, we must inform the computer that the first two columns designate an observation for X while the last two represent Y. Many programs use a variant of the Fortran input format statement to accomplish this. First, one designates a variable as being either integer (I), where no decimal places are present; a real value (F), which can contain decimal places; or alphanumeric (A), where letters and numbers are combined. If spaces exist between values, the letter x is used to indicate this. The format statement is usually enclosed in brackets. The general form for the data in the original example, 7512 is: (I2, I2), which designates the first two columns as an integer value for the first variable in the list (X), and the next two columns as a second integer value. This can also be represented as (2I2).

To consider a more complicated case, assume the value of Z is 195.22, which, in the terminology of Fortran, represents a *real variable*. We can enter this type of variable either with or without the decimal:

19522 requires using F5.2, or five columns with two decimal places;

195.22 requires using F6.2, but the computer can read the entry as it is.

Both representations are correct. As is often the case, a number of ways exist to accomplish a particular task. If we now enter the values of 75 for X, 12 for Y, and 195.22 for Z as in the following line:

75   1219522

the correct format statement is: (I2,2X,I2,F5.2). Note that this changes only slightly when we enter the data as:

data: 75   12195.22   format: (I2, 2X, I2, F6.2).

As a final example of reading data, let us see how the following information on variables A through G that is entered on two separate lines (lines 2 and 3 in the box below) can be coded with a format statement.

A = 12, B = 261, C = 88.5, D = 1.99, E = 1.7, F = 1, G = 1.00.

12345678901234567890   (these are column numbers)
12   26188.5199   (these two lines represent the entered data)
17 1100

The correct format statement is: (I2 , 3X , I3 , F4 . 1 , F3 . 2/F2 . 1 , 1X , I1 , F3 . 2). The slash informs the computer to move to the next line to find data for the remaining variables. The format statements after the slash give the data format for the second line of each observation. Note that a value such as 12 for A can be expressed as either I2 or F2.0, depending on the way we choose to classify A. In Fortran programs this matters a great deal. In many canned programs, the designation is largely symbolic.

Throughout the previous discussion we have given individual variables simple names, such as X or Y. In actual practice, it is advisable to assign a name that indicates what a variable represents. If, for example, your data set contains variables representing ten components of GDP and you assign the names X1 to X10, you will very likely become confused when trying to remember the correct variable name for a particular GDP component, and possibly use the wrong variable in a data manipulation expression. Instead of the latter naming convention, use abbreviations, such as CONS and INVEST as variable names.

Data Manipulation

Once the data set has been created, variables have been assigned their desired names, and the set of observations has been correctly entered, we must perform manipulations on our variables. The type of data manipulation considered here consists of creating additional variables from those already in the data base. This can be accomplished either by using one or a combination of the existing variables.

Variable Creation Using a Single Variable

Creating a new variable from a single existing variable frequently involves using one of the library functions contained in a canned program. The most commonly used of these functions are the natural logarithm; the lag; the absolute change; and raising a value to the power e (where e is the inverse of the natural log, denoted e^x). When creating a new variable, the correct form is essentially:

new variable = **expression** using an *existing* variable

In SAS, this command must end with a semicolon, while for MicroTSP, variable creation must begin with GENR.

Only existing variables can be used to create new variables. When a canned program creates a new variable, it must be familiar with the variable(s) used in the variable definition statement. If, for example, a variable referred to in a creation expression has not yet been read in, but exists in a SAS INPUT statement, this program will act as though it already possesses information about this variable. Creation of the new variable can thus proceed. In MicroTSP, a variable must already be entered into the data set before we are allowed to use it in any manipulation statement. When this procedure is violated, canned programs either disallow the new variable or create a variable consisting entirely of missing values. Remedial action then consists of rearranging the order in which the variables are formulated, so that their creation is sequential.

Two of the abbreviations for library functions appear to be universal: the natural logarithm of X is denoted LOG(X), and e raised to the power of x is EXP(X). Examples of variable creation statements that utilize these functions are:

SAS	MicroTSP
Y = LOG(X);	GENR Y = LOG(X)
Z = EXP(X);	GENR Z = EXP(X)

The method for creating the lag of a variable differs among canned programs. Some programs include the lag function in their program library. Others use an expression after the variable to denote the desired lag. An example of the latter with the variable **GDP** is:

```
GENR GDPLAG=GDP(-1)    (MicroTSP)
```

In some versions of MicroTSP, the sample time period must be moved forward before this new variable can be created. The corresponding statement for SAS, which has the library function LAG is:

```
GDPLAG=LAG(GDP);
```

Lags that extend beyond a single time period can also be generated with commands such as LAG2(GDP) or GDP(-2).

This lack of uniformity for creating lags results in differences in the statements used to produce absolute changes. Recall that the one-period absolute change in x, Δx, equals $x_t - x_{t-1}$. There are several possible ways to calculate this variable. Some programs contain an absolute change library function, such as DIF(X). We can obtain the absolute change with these programs by using either the DIF function or the LAG function (note: if subtraction is needed, the minus sign is used). Examples of each are:

```
CHGGDP=DIF(GDP);  or  CHGGDP=GDP-LAG(GDP);    (SAS)
```

MicroTSP includes this capability among its "@" functions. The one period absolute change in GDP using this function is:

```
GENR CHGGDP=@DIF(GDP)
```

Without this function, and using lags, the statement that creates CHGGDP is

```
GENR CHGGDP=GDP-GDP(-1)
```

We can also calculate the four period absolute change, which is used to derive year-to-year growth rates from quarterly data. The variable creation statement is similar to those above, with the exception that x_{t-4} replaces x_{t-1}. The expressions are:

```
CH4GDP=DIF4(GDP);  or  CH4GDP=GDP-LAG4(GDP);    (SAS)

GENR  CH4GDP=GDP-GDP(-4)                         (MicroTSP)
```

(note: MicroTSP's @DIF( ) function only defines first differences and cannot be used for either four or twelve-period changes)

Both the one-period and four-period percent growth rates are created with only slight modifications of these expressions. Recall that the percent change in a variable is 100 times its proportionate change, which, in turn, is the ratio of the absolute change to the lag of that variable. The symbol for multiplication in canned programs is the asterisk, "*", while division uses the symbol "/". The following statements, which are based on Equation (3.8), can be used to create the one-period growth rate with SAS that contains both the LAG and DIF library functions:

```
GRGDP=(DIF(GDP)/LAG(GDP))*100;
```

or

```
GRGDP=((GDP-LAG(GDP))/LAG(GDP))*100;
```

Note the use of brackets in the above expressions. There must be a left bracket for each right bracket, so that the expression is "closed off." The corresponding one-period growth rate statements for MicroTSP are:

```
GENR GRGDP=(@DIF(GDP)/GDP(-1))*100
GENR GRGDP=((GNP-GDP(-1))/GDP(-1))*100
```

If we use (3.9) as the basis for this calculation, the expressions become:

```
GRGDP=((GDP/LAG(GDP))-1)*100;        (SAS)
GENR GRGDP=((GDP/GDP(-1))-1)*100    (MicroTSP)
```

As the above illustrates, a number of different methods exist for generating percent changes within a single program. The method you choose should be based on personal preference. The four-period growth rate is calculated by replacing the one-period lag in each of the above expressions with a four-period lag. Try writing the expressions for this variable using the above formats.

Other single-variable expressions involve the absolute value of X, and raising X to various powers. The absolute value of X is often included among the library functions of programs as ABS(X). Raising X to different powers can involve either division, for the reciprocal, multiplication (for square), or the program's exponentiation symbol. The reciprocal of X, using division, is:

```
RECIPX=1/X
```

The square of X, using multiplication, is:

```
SQX=X*X
```

Finally, exponentiation is performed using either the double asterisk, "**", on mainframe and mini computers, or the symbol "^" with most personal computer canned programs. The exponentiation symbol is followed by an integer indicating the desired power. The reciprocal and square of X are given by:

```
RECIPX=X**-1
```

for mainframe and mini computers;

```
RECIPX=X^-1
```

for personal computers;

```
SQX=X**2
```

for mainframe and mini computers;

```
SQX=X^2
```

for personal computers.

Calculating the compound annual growth rate of a variable requires the use of exponentiation. If, for example, we have either monthly or quarterly data on the CPI, we can compute the annualized CPI inflation rate, ANNINF, using the following expressions:

```
ANNINF=(((CPI/LAG(CPI))**12)-1)*100
```

(monthly data — SAS);

```
ANNINF=(((CPI/LAG(CPI))**4)-1)*100
```

(quarterly data — SAS);

```
GENR ANNINF=(((CPI/CPI(-1))^12)-1)*100
```

(monthly data — MicroTSP);

```
GENR ANNINF=(((CPI/CPI(-1))^4)-1)*100
```

(quarterly data — MicroTSP)

Variable Creation Using Several Variables

To construct measures such as real values, it is necessary to use the information from the previous section pertaining to addition, subtraction, multiplication, division, exponentiation, the lag, and absolute differences. If our data set contains the Implicit Price Deflator (IPD) and Gross Domestic Product (GDP), we can create a new variable, real GDP (RGDP) with the base year of our IPD, if we use the statement:

SAS	MicroTSP
`RGDP=(GDP/IPD)*100;`	`GENR RGDP=(GDP/IPD)*100`

If we wish to change the base year of IPD, we must follow the procedure outlined earlier in this chapter: divide each value of the IPD by that of the desired new base year, then multiply by 100. The IPD has a 1987 base year. Let us assume that the desired base year changes to 1980. The IPD for 1980 is 71.7. Using this value, we can create the new IPD (IPD80) and real GDP (RGDP80) using the statements:

SAS	MicroTSP
`IPD80=(IPD/71.7)*100;`	`GENR IPD80=(IPD/71.7)*100`
`RGDP80=(GDP/IPD80)*100;`	`GENR RGDP80=(GDP/IPD80)*100`

Another variable that can be created from several others is the relative price of a good, which is the ratio of the price of that good to the price of some related good. If we have data for the prices of both good X (PRICEX) and some related good Y (PRICEY), the relative price of X is calculated by using the following statement:

SAS	MicroTSP
`RELPX=PRICEX/PRICEY;`	`GENR RELPX=PRICEX/PRICEY`

Finally, the one-period growth rates outlined earlier can be created using several variables. As the following commands illustrate, we can create the variables which serve as "building blocks" for the variable GRGDP sequentially:

SAS	MicroTSP
`CHGGDP=DIF(GDP);`	`GENR CHGGDP=@DIF(GDP)`
`GDPLAG=LAG(GDP);`	`GENR GDPLAG=GDP(-1)`
`GRGDP=(CHGGDP/GDPLAG)*100;`	`GENR GRGDP=(CHGGDP/GDPLAG)*100`

The advantage of using this approach is that it allows us to avoid making mistakes involving brackets. Note, however, that the third line for each program is valid only if both CHGGDP and GDPLAG have been created *prior* to this line. If the line defining GRGDP is placed before either of the first two lines, an error will result.

Obtaining Processed Output from a Canned Program

The range of procedures that exist for obtaining processed information from canned programs precludes discussing them in general terms. The most that can be said here is that canned programs use either a specific command to obtain a given measure, such as MEAN, a more general command that contains this and related measures, such as COVA (abbreviation for covariance), or procedures (called PROC's in SAS) that are similar to the general command like COVA but allow you to tailor the output to the form you desire.

EXAMPLES USING SPECIFIC CANNED PROGRAMS

Statistical Analysis System (SAS)

SAS is one of the most widely used of the mainframe statistical programs. This program enables persons interested in econometric research to enter, summarize, and manipulate data, while performing many of the most frequently demanded econometric procedures with fairly simple commands.

In SAS, the processing of data generally occurs separately from data set creation. Data sets can be created either in a DATA step, or as a joint output generated when data is processed in what are called PROC's. Data manipulation only takes place in a DATA step, however. SAS contains the library functions alluded to in the previous discussion. To see how this program works, let us first enter and manipulate data, then obtain some simple processed data as output. The basis for this example are the data on Personal Consumption Expenditure and the corresponding Implicit Price Deflator from Table 3.2.

The first step in this example is the creation of a data set. The naming convention for both variables and data sets is the same: names are limited to no more than eight characters, where the first must be a letter, and certain characters are prohibited. *All commands (but not the entered data itself) must end in a semicolon. Also, a single command can be entered on more than one line.* Let us call this data set CONSEXPD, so that its name corresponds to its contents, consumer expenditure information. The first line is therefore:

```
DATA CONSEXPD;
```

The next step entails entering information on the names that will be given to the variables in this data set along with any format information (beyond free format). The data here will be entered in free format with columns as variables. The names of the variables and the order in which they will be entered are: YEAR, PCE for Personal Consumption Expenditure, and IPDPCE for the Implicit Price Deflator for Personal Consumption Expenditure (1982 = 100). The second line reflecting this is:

```
INPUT YEAR PCE IPDPCE;
```

Data manipulation statements are only allowed *after* these lines. In this example, we will first calculate real personal consumption expenditures (RPCE) along with the growth rate of consumption expenditures (GRPCE) using the original 1987 base year. We will then change the base year of IPDPCE to 1980 (IPDPCE80) and calculate the corresponding real personal consumption expenditure (RPCE80) as well as the growth rate in real personal expenditures (GRPCE80).

The remaining DATA step lines including all these manipulations are given below. Note that the line CARDS; is used to separate the set of SAS commands from the data that follows, and the value 71.4 in the statement creating IPDPCE80 is the value of IPDPCE (1987 = 100) for the new base year, 1980.

```
RPCE=(PCE/IPDPCE)*100;
GRPCE=(DIF(RPCE)/LAG(RPCE))*100;
IPDPCE80=(IPDPCE/71.4)*100;
RPCE80=(PCE/IPDPCE80)*100;
GRPCE80=(DIF(RPCE80)/LAG(RPCE80))*100;
CARDS;
1980   1748.1    71.4
1981   1926.2    77.8
          . . .
1988   3296.1   104.2
```

Now that we have successfully created a data set, let us obtain summary statistics for each of the variables in this data set. To check for possible data entry errors, it is often informative to view the minimum and maximum for each of these variables, along with the mean and standard deviation. In SAS this constitutes processing of the data, which requires that we include a PROC statement. The name of the PROC that provides this information is **PROC MEANS.**

The different PROCs, what each does, the form for each, and the particular options available are contained in various SAS manuals. The general form for a PROC statement is:

```
PROC name DATA=data set name options;
```

In this statement, *name* is the name of the PROC being used, such as MEANS, *data set name* is the name of the particular data set whose data is input into this PROC, and *options* details the options available to this PROC that we desire to use. If we wish to use the most recently created data set (in this case CONSEXPD) for this PROC, we can omit the DATA = *data set name* statement. This is called a **default condition**, or the situation SAS will assume to exist unless the PROC statement instructs it otherwise. The values we wish to obtain, along with their SAS abbreviations for PROC MEANS (these are given in the manual) are: the mean (MEAN), standard deviation (STD), minimum (MIN) and maximum (MAX) values for each variable. These constitute the options we will select with **PROC MEANS.** The statement that produces these summary statistics is:

```
PROC MEANS MEAN STD MIN MAX;
```

Since we will be using the most recently created data set, CONSEXPD, the DATA = *data set name* portion is omitted from this statement. This statement does not furnish SAS with instructions about which variables to process. By default, **PROC MEANS** will generate the requested statistics for every variable in data set CONSEXPD.

The final step in this example consists of printing this data. In SAS, this is accomplished with **PROC PRINT.** Instead of having SAS print observations for all the variables in CONSEXPD, we can include a second statement that restricts the output of this PROC to a subset of these variables. This is accomplished by placing a VAR statement after the **PROC PRINT** command. The form of the VAR statement is:

```
VAR list;
```

where *list* is the list of variable names that make up our desired subset. If the variables of interest are personal consumption expenditures (PCE), real personal consumption expenditures (1987 = 100), RPCE, and the growth in real personal consumption expenditures, GRPCE, the VAR statement is:

```
VAR PCE RPCE GRPCE;
```

Combining this with the PROC PRINT statement, the commands that print the observations for the above list of variables are:

```
PROC PRINT;
 VAR PCE RPCE GRPCE;
```

The spelling of each variable name in the list must exactly match that in the INPUT line or the variable creation statement that defines it. If one or more names are misspelled, an error results, since SAS only knows the specific variable names contained in the data set CONSEXPD. "Almost" does not count with computers! Note that both of the above statements can be included on the same line in SAS. As long as a semicolon is included at the end of the PROC PRINT statement, SAS will recognize these as two separate commands. Entering these as separate lines has the advantage of simplifying error detection and correction.

The SAS output obtained when these lines are executed (using the VAR statement for PROC MEANS), along with the accompanying SAS notes are shown below.

```
1          DATA CONSEXPD;
2          INPUT YEAR PCE IPDPCE;
3          RPCE=(PCE/IPDPCE)*100;
4          GRPCE=(DIF(RPCE)/LAG(RPCE))*100;
5          IPDPCE80=(IPDPCE/71.4)*100;
6          RPCE80=(PCE/IPDPCE80)*100;
7          GRPCE80=(DIF(RPCE80)/LAG(RPCE80))*100;
8          CARDS;


NOTE: MISSING VALUES WERE GENERATED AS A RESULT OF
      PERFORMING AN OPERATION ON MISSING VALUES.
      EACH PLACE IS GIVEN BY: (NUMBER OF TIMES) AT
      (LINE):(COLUMN). 1 AT 4:7  1 AT 7:9
NOTE: DATA SET WORK.CONSEXPD HAS 9 OBSERVATIONS AND 8
      VARIABLES. 690 OBS/TRK
NOTE: THE DATA STATEMENT USED 0.29 SECONDS AND 764K.
```

The first note indicates that missing values exist in this data set, since lags and absolute changes were used. The first command that produces missing values occurs in line 4, column 7 from the start of the command, the DIF(RPCE) and LAG(RPCE) entries for the variable GRPCE. The second occurrence of missing values is at line 7 column 9. The next note indicates that data set CONSEXPD contains 9 observations (although for some variables there are less, since they have missing values) on a total of 8 variables. This line is helpful in determining whether any errors have occurred up to this point. If the note indicated 0 observations, you would see very quickly that a problem exists with the set of lines you entered.

The SAS output lines for the PROC statements are included next:

```
            PROC MEANS MEAN STD MIN MAX;
                VAR PCE RPCE GRPCE;
  NOTE: THE PROCEDURE MEANS USED 0.21 SECONDS AND 848K
        AND PRINTED PAGE 1.
            PROC PRINT;
                VAR PCE RPCE GRPCE;

  NOTE: THE PROCEDURE PRINT USED 0.20 SECONDS AND 832K
        AND PRINTED PAGE 2.
```

The NOTE following each PROC indicates successful completion of the procedure. If SAS encounters an error, the contents of the NOTE statement can assist us in pinpointing the specific problem(s) that exist. Two problems are likely to arise with the above statements: the misspelling of either a PROC name or a desired summary statistic; or the attempt to process an empty data set. This last problem results from errors committed when creating the data set that should be reflected in the NOTE accompanying the DATA step.

Now that we have viewed the statements used to create data set CONSEXPD and to perform the desired data processing, and have found that no problems exist with either, we can view the resulting SAS output:

VARIABLE	MEAN	STANDARD DEVIATION	MINIMUM VALUE	MAXIMUM VALUE
PCE	2479.73333	498.35660	1748.10000	3296.10000
RPCE	2760.43900	250.74030	2448.30000	3163.20000
GRPCE	3.26324	1.35671	1.12388	4.84786

OBS	YEAR	PCE	RPCE	GRPCE
1	1980	1748.1	2448.3	.
2	1981	1926.2	2475.8	1.12388
3	1982	2059.2	2505.1	1.18240
4	1983	2257.5	2618.9	4.54272
5	1984	2460.3	2745.9	4.84786
6	1985	2667.4	2865.1	4.34182
7	1986	2850.6	2969.4	3.63980
8	1987	3052.2	3052.2	2.78931
9	1988	3296.1	3163.2	3.63816

ERRORS IN SAS LINES AND THEIR CONSEQUENCES.   The most common errors you are likely to commit with SAS involve omitting semicolons, placing variable creation statements in the wrong order, including an incorrect number of brackets in a variable creation expression, and misspelling variable names. We now present the consequences of committing each of these errors, and compare the resulting output to that obtained when the lines are entered correctly.

Omitting a Semicolon.   The most frequent error you are likely to commit with SAS is omitting a semicolon. As a matter of habit, always check the lines to make sure semicolons are present where needed. If you exclude a semicolon in SAS (for other than data lines), SAS will continue to read the information assuming that the two lines constitute a *single* command. In the example that follows, the semicolon is omitted after the INPUT statement.

```
1          DATA CONSEXPD;
2          INPUT YEAR PCE IPDPCE
3          RPCE=(PCE/IPDPCE)*100;
                    503  504
4          GRPCE=(DIF(RPCE)/LAG(RPCE))*100;
5          IPDPCE80=(IPDPCE/71.4)*100;
6          RPCE80=(PCE/IPDPCE80)*100;
7          GRPCE80=(DIF(RPCE80)/LAG(RPCE80))*100;
8          CARDS;

ERROR 503: VARIABLE NAME ONLY.
ERROR 504: FORMAT LIST MISSING, FOR EXAMPLE, (5,2)
NOTE: SAS STOPPED PROCESSING THIS STEP BECAUSE OF ERRORS.
NOTE: SAS SET OPTION OBS=0 AND WILL CONTINUE TO CHECK STATEMENTS.
      THIS MAY CAUSE NOTE: NO OBSERVATIONS IN DATA SET.
NOTE: DATA SET WORK.CONSEXPD HAS 0 OBSERVATIONS AND 8 VARIABLES.
      280 OBS/TRK
NOTE: THE DATA STATEMENT USED 0.23 SECONDS AND 548K.
14         PROC MEANS MEAN STD  MIN MAX;
NOTE: THE PROCEDURE MEANS USED 0.29 SECONDS AND 768K.
ERROR: ERRORS ON PAGES 1.
```

SAS indicates immediately that errors of type 503 or 504 were committed. The two lines from this job:

```
2          INPUT YEAR PCE IPDPCE
3          RPCE=(PCE/IPDPCE)*100;
                    503  504
```

indicate that SAS views RPCE on the second line as a variable name in the INPUT statement. When SAS encounters the equal sign, it does not recognize this as a valid entry in an INPUT statement, and it issues these error messages. The subsequent NOTES indicate that this data set contains 0 observations, so when PROC MEANS looks for data, it is unable to find any.

The NOTE about the number of observations in a data set is an important one. You should use this as an indicator of whether or not problems exist with the data set being created. Here, data set CONSEXPD is created, but with 0 observations, rendering it useless for subsequent processing.

Variable Creation Statements in the Wrong Order. Another common mistake occurs when we attempt to derive a new variable from a variable that has not yet been created. In this case the variable(s) referred to on the right side of variable creation expressions do not yet exist as far as SAS is concerned. A new variable is generated, but it consists entirely of missing values. In this example, the order in which RPCE and GRPCE are created is reversed.

```
1           DATA CONSEXPD;
2           INPUT YEAR PCE IPDPCE;
3           GRPCE=(DIF(RPCE)/LAG(RPCE))*100;
4           RPCE=(PCE/IPDPCE)*100;
5           IPDPCE80=(IPDPCE/71.4)*100;
6           RPCE80=(PCE/IPDPCE80)*100;
7           GRPCE80=(DIF(RPCE80)/LAG(RPCE80))*100;
8           CARDS;

NOTE: MISSING VALUES WERE GENERATED AS A RESULT OF PERFORMING
      AN OPERATION ON MISSING VALUES.
      EACH PLACE IS GIVEN BY: (NUMBER OF TIMES) AT (LINE):(COLUMN).
      9 AT 3:7   1 AT 7:9
NOTE: DATA SET WORK.CONSEXPD HAS 9 OBSERVATIONS AND 8 VARIABLES.
      690 OBS/TRK
NOTE: THE DATA STATEMENT USED 0.29 SECONDS AND 764K.
```

Correct execution of these lines requires that statements 3 and 4 be reversed, since knowledge of RPCE is presupposed when GRPCE is created. No error message appears for this error. Here, the error detection information is contained in the NOTE stating that 9 missing values were produced when executing the statement in line 3 (the GRPCE statement). Everything else appears to be correct. Further evidence of a problem is apparent from the output of PROC MEANS and PROC PRINT, where no values appear for GRPCE.

```
18          PROC MEANS MEAN STD MIN MAX;
               VAR GRPCE RPCE;

NOTE: THE PROCEDURE MEANS USED 0.20 SECONDS AND 848K AND PRINTED PAGE 1.

19          PROC PRINT;
20    .         VAR YEAR RPCE GRPCE;

NOTE: THE PROCEDURE PRINT USED 0.22 SECONDS AND 832K
       AND PRINTED PAGE 2.
```

VARIABLE	MEAN	STANDARD DEVIATION	MINIMUM VALUE	MAXIMUM VALUE
GRPCE	.	.	.	.
RPCE	2760.439	250.74030	2448.30	3163.20

OBS	YEAR	RPCE	GRPCE
1	1980	2448.3	.
2	1981	2475.8	.
3	1982	2505.1	.
4	1983	2618.9	.
5	1984	2745.9	.
6	1985	2865.1	.
7	1986	2969.4	.
8	1987	3052.2	.
9	1988	3163.2	.

Incorrect Brackets in an Expression. A simple rule must be followed when writing expressions with brackets: every left bracket must be matched with a right bracket. In the following example, the right bracket is omitted from the line creating the variable GRPCE (line 4):

```
1          DATA CONSEXPD;
2          INPUT YEAR PCE IPDPCE;
3          RPCE=(PCE/IPDPCE)*100;
4          GRPCE=(DIF(RPCE)/LAG(RPCE)*100;
                                          -
                                   302
5          IPDPCE80=(IPDPCE/71.4)*100;
6          RPCE80=(PCE/IPDPCE80)*100;
7          GRPCE80=(DIF(RPCE80)/LAG(RPCE80))*100;
8          CARDS;
```

SAS issues an error message immediately following the line with the omitted bracket. Since SAS has no way of knowing that the intended location for the bracket is before the asterisk, it acts on the requirement that a right bracket must precede the semicolon that ends this statement. Since this bracket does not appear, SAS issues the error message below:

```
ERROR 302: RIGHT PARENTHESIS NOT FOUND.
NOTE: SAS STOPPED PROCESSING THIS STEP BECAUSE OF ERRORS.
NOTE: SAS SET OPTION OBS=0 AND WILL CONTINUE TO CHECK STATEMENTS.
      THIS MAY CAUSE NOTE: NO OBSERVATIONS IN DATA SET.
NOTE: DATA SET WORK.CONSEXPD HAS 0 OBSERVATIONS AND 8 VARIABLES.
      690 OBS/TRK
NOTE: THE DATA STATEMENT USED 0.25 SECONDS AND 764K.
```

A data set CONSEXPD is therefore created with 0 observations, and the PROC statements using this data set will not execute.

Spelling Error in Entering a Variable Name. The final type of error discussed here occurs when we correctly sequence the SAS lines but misspell the name of an existing variable when creating a new variable. In this example, the name RPCE in the fourth line is incorrectly entered as RPPE.

```
1          DATA CONSEXPD;
2          INPUT YEAR PCE IPDPCE;
3          RPCE=(PCE/IPDPCE)*100;
4          GRPCE=(DIF(RPPE)/LAG(RPPE))*100;
5          IPDPCE80=(IPDPCE/71.4)*100;
6          RPCE80=(PCE/IPDPCE80)*100;
7          GRPCE80=(DIF(RPCE80)/LAG(RPCE80))*100;
8          CARDS;

NOTE: THE VARIABLE RPPE IS UNINITIALIZED.
NOTE: MISSING VALUES WERE GENERATED AS A RESULT OF PERFORMING
      AN OPERATION ON MISSING VALUES.
      EACH PLACE IS GIVEN BY: (NUMBER OF TIMES) AT (LINE):(COLUMN).
      9 AT 4:7   1 AT 7:9
NOTE: DATA SET WORK.CONSEXPD HAS 9 OBSERVATIONS AND 9 VARIABLES.
      616 OBS/TRK
NOTE: THE DATA STATEMENT USED 0.29 SECONDS AND 764K.
```

The first NOTE from SAS indicates that the variable RPPE is uninitialized (does not currently exist). As a result, SAS cannot create GRPCE. Further evidence of a problem is contained in the second NOTE, which states that 9 missing values occurred while executing line 4, and by the third NOTE, which indicates that data set CONSEXPD contains 9 and not the 8 expected variables. Since this data set does contain observations, both PROC MEANS and PROC PRINT will execute. Their output will, however, include missing values that result from the misspelling error. GRPCE consists entirely of missing observations, as does the misspelled variable name RPPE. The output from PROC MEANS shows this:

```
VARIABLE     MEAN      STANDARD    MINIMUM    MAXIMUM
                       DEVIATION    VALUE      VALUE
RPCE       2760.439   250.74000   2448.319   3163.244
GRPCE         .           .           .          .
RPPE          .           .           .          .
```

FURTHER INFORMATION ABOUT SAS.   At this point you should have a fairly good idea of how to use SAS. The following is a list of the SAS PROC's that can perform virtually all the tasks you will need for the material covered in this text: MEANS; PRINT; UNIVARIATE; SORT; REG; AUTOREG; SYSLIN; PLOT; CORR; and IML (for appendix material). Recommended references for SAS are:

SAS Introductory Guide

SAS User's Guide: Basics

SAS User's Guide: Statistics.

Time Series Processor (TSP)—Personal Computer Version

MicroTSP is one of a growing number of mainframe computer programs that have been adapted for use on a personal computer (PC). This powerful and well-documented program allows PC users to perform many of the tasks formerly reserved exclusively for persons working on mainframe computers. The personal consumption expenditure example from the previous section is duplicated with MicroTSP so that readers interested in using both programs can compare the similarities and differences that exist between SAS and MicroTSP.

MicroTSP USING THE PERSONAL CONSUMPTION EXPENDITURE DATA.   MicroTSP commands and procedures differ in several respects from those of SAS. While both programs require that data entry precede manipulation, MicroTSP allows us to create the lag of a variable in a data processing step, since it excludes the LAG library function. Recall that this is forbidden with SAS. In SAS, a data set name must be given before data processing commences, while MicroTSP requires that we assign a data set name only when saving data to a diskette. Finally, MicroTSP does not require an end of command character (such as the semicolon in SAS). Since MicroTSP is an interactive program, the end of a command is indicated by pressing the [**Enter◄┘**] key.

MicroTSP is a "menu driven program," which means that it provides a list (menu) of the commands available, along with the corresponding key to press for each of these, on-screen. When you first enter MicroTSP, the following screen appears:

```
 ┌──────────────────────────────────────────────────────────────┐
 │  range              │  series: current=   maximum=  │ output LPT1:  │
 │─────────────────────┴───────────────────────────────┴──────────────│
 │        No work file in memory -  Use CREATE or LOAD command        │
 │─────────────────────┬───────────────────────────────┬──────────────│
 │  current SMPL       │       path A:                 │   print POFF  │
 │                                                                    │
 │                                                                    │
 │                                                                    │
 │──────────────────────────────────────────────────────────────────│
 │ 1—BREAK 2—LAST │ 3—FILES 4—DATA 5—GRAPH 6—STATS 7—EQUATIONS 8—ESTIMATE 9—CONTROL │
 └──────────────────────────────────────────────────────────────┘
```

The numbers 1 to 9 on the bottom line are abbreviations for the **function keys** [**F1**] through [**F9**] that reside either on the left (for persons with PC or AT keyboards), or at the top of the keyboard (for enhanced keyboards). A separate set of commands (a menu) is associated with each of the function keys F3 through F9. These allow users to move to an appropriate menu, select a command to execute, then press [**Enter◄┘**]. Commands can also be entered directly. This allows users to minimize the extent to which they must rely on the numerous lists associated with the selection areas of DATA, FILES, and STATISTICS. Either way, MicroTSP always prompts its user for whatever additional information is required to execute a command. In the discussion that follows, the function keys are used primarily to facilitate the creation of our data set. The symbol [◄┘] is used to designate pressing the [**Enter◄┘**] key. Although it does not matter whether we enter commands with capital letters on IBM-compatible PCs, we will do so anyway.

The first step in this example consists of creating a data set that contains the annual observations for prices and consumption expenditure. We can accomplish this either by pressing the [**F3**] key (do not follow this with the [**Enter◄┘**] key), or by entering the command CREATE directly following the prompt ">". Assuming we press the [**F3**] key, the following menu appears:

```
              Work Files
(1)  Create a new WF in RAM      CREATE
(2)  Load a WF from disk         LOAD
(3)  Save a WF to disk           SAVE
(4)  Expand the WF range         EXPAND
(5)  Import-Export data file     {F10}
              Disk Operations
(6)  Display file directory      DIR
(7)  Change subdirectory         CD
(8)  Edit a text file            EDIT
(9)  Rename a file               REN
(A)  Delete a file               DEL
(B)  Display a text file         TYPE
 F1  Break (F3-F10 menus)
```

The first item on this list, "(1) Create a new WF in RAM" will be highlighted. Since this is the choice we wish to pursue, we can either press [**Enter◄┘**], or type 1. This begins the process of data set creation. In future MicroTSP sessions, where we will be working with a data set that has been saved to disk, item (2) is the appropriate selection: "Load a WF from disk." To execute this command we can type 2, or move to this choice using the down arrow, then press [**Enter◄┘**]. Having selected (1), the following menu appears:

```
>CREATE
            Frequency
  (U)  Undated
  (A)  Annual
  (Q)  Quarterly
  (M)  Monthly
 F1  Break - cancel procedure
```

The choices are self-explanatory. In the present example, we type A for annual data. MicroTSP then prompts us to supply it with the starting and ending years for this data set. Type 80 for the 1980 start then press [**Enter←**]. MicroTSP next requests the final year. Type 88 for 1988 followed by [**Enter←**].

```
>CREATE[←]
  Frequency // Annual            note: this can be entered with
  Starting date // 80[←]            the single command:
  Ending date ?  88[←]              >CREATE A 80 88[←]
```

When this is completed, the top of the screen then becomes:

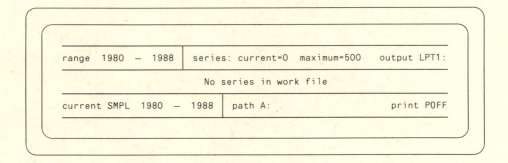

```
range  1980  —  1988  | series: current=0  maximum=500    output LPT1:
                      No series in work file
current SMPL  1980  —  1988  | path A:                        print POFF
```

Starting and ending values are entered differently for monthly, quarterly, and annual data. If we assume that the data start at the beginning of 1980 and extend through to the end of 1988, the starting and ending values are entered:

```
Starting date // 80.01[←]   (monthly)
Ending date ? 88.12[←]      (monthly)
Starting date // 80.1[←]    (quarterly)
Ending date ? 88.4[←]       (quarterly)
```

or, using a single command, this becomes:

```
>CREATE M 80.01 88.12[←]  (monthly data)
>CREATE Q 80.1 88.4[←]    (quarterly data)
```

We must now supply MicroTSP with a list of the names we wish to give the variables in our data set. Press [**F4**], which brings us to the MicroTSP DATA

MANAGEMENT menu:

```
            Data Management
(1) Set sample range        SMPL
(2) Generate by equation    GENR
(3) Data editor             DATA
(4) Seasonal adjustment     SEAS
(5) Groups of series        GROUP
(6) Rename series in WF     R
(7) Delete series from WF   D
(8) Sort WF by series       SORT
(9) Show data table         SHOW
(A) Print data table        PRINT
 F1 Break (F3-F10 menus)
```

then select (3), "Data editor." MicroTSP will now prompt us for a list of variable names. These variable names must be separated by one or more spaces. Enter PCE and IPDPCE:

```
>DATA[◄┘]                          (this can be entered as:
 Series list ? PCE IPDPCE[◄┘]      >DATA PCE IPDPCE[◄┘])
```

At this point, data entry begins. The top of the screen displays the following list of edit commands that pertain to data entry mode:

```
B back up | I# insert at # | N# go to # | D# delete # | X exit
```

The bottom of the screen shows the year and variable name for the particular observation we are entering. Type in the first observation for PCE, then press [**Enter◄┘**].

```
1980           1748.1[◄┘]
_____
OBS            PCE            IPDPCE
_____
```

MicroTSP now moves the cursor to the first observation for IPDPCE. Type in this value, press [**Enter↵**], and continue until the last value is recorded. If a value is entered incorrectly and the [**Enter↵**] key has not yet been pressed, simply use the backspace key [↵], type over the erroneous values, then press the [**Enter↵**] key when finished. If the observation has already been entered (the [**Enter↵**] key has already been pressed), you can either type B (for "backup one observation"), or N followed by the year of the observation you wish to return to (eg: N81). When the cursor arrives at the mistyped value, simply retype the observation, then press [**Enter↵**].

The time period for the last observation will repeat. To conclude data entry, type the letter X (for EXIT), then press [**Enter↵**]. This takes us out of data entry mode, and a usable data set now exists.

1980	1748.1	71.4
1981	1926.2	77.8
1982	2059.2	82.2
1983	2257.5	86.2
1984	2460.3	89.6
1985	2667.4	93.1
1986	2850.6	96.0
1987	3052.2	100.0
1988	3296.1	104.2
1988	X[↵]	

OBS	PCE	IPDPCE

The top of the screen now reflects this data set:

range 1980 — 1988	series: current=2 maximum=500	output LPT1:
IPDPCE PCE		
current SMPL 1980 — 1988	path A:	print POFF

DATA MANIPULATION.   Data manipulation commands must be entered one at a time with MicroTSP.[5] To signal that a new variable is being created, or generated, a GENR statement is required. The form of this command is:

    GENR *expression*

where, in this example, *expression* is either a simple ratio multiplied by 100 or a percent change. We will first change IPDPCE to a 1980 base year, then create real PCE values for each base year. The MicroTSP commands that perform these tasks, along with the accompanying notes below each, are:

    >GENR IPDPCE80=(IPDPCE/71.4)*100[↵]
     IPDPCE80 computed.

    >GENR RPCE=(PCE/IPDPCE)*100[↵]
     RPCE computed.

    >GENR RPCE80=(PCE/IPDPCE80)*100[↵]
     RPCE80 computed.

These variables could have been created using the MicroTSP menus in the following way: press [**F4**], which brings the Data Management menu, then select choice (2), "Generate by equation." MicroTSP then responds with:

    >GENR[↵]
     Equation ? _

We then enter the variable creation statement omitting the GENR. This same procedure must be repeated for every variable we create.

   We next calculate the growth rates for RPCE and RPCE80. *Since growth rate calculations involve lags, if we do not change the original sample period, it will contain missing values for all variables with lags.* MicroTSP will respond with the line "NOTE: Missing values generated as a result of an operation on missing data" after our variable definition statement. At this point, we will illustrate how to change the sample time period so the active period does not contain any missing values.

   The original sample period is set when the data set is created. In the present example, the sample period extends from 1980 to 1988. We can change this time horizon either with a SMPL statement, which takes the form:

    SMPL *first time period final time period*

or by pressing [**F4**], then selecting (1), "Set sample range" from the Data Management menu. Since we will be using a one-year lag in our growth equations, we will move the starting period forward by one year. The SMPL statement that accomplishes this is:

    >SMPL 81 88[↵]

---

[5] MicroTSP also has a facility for creating batch programs with its EDIT command. This is not pursued here.

Now that we have set the sample period, we can create the desired growth rates. The following commands, which are based on percent change Equation (3.8), along with the MicroTSP responses for each, produce these:

```
>GENR GRPCE=((RPCE-RPCE(-1))/RPCE(-1))*100[◄┘]
 GRPCE computed.
```

```
>GENR GRPC80=((RPCE80-RPCE80(-1))/RPCE80(-1))*100[◄┘]
 GRPC80 computed.
```

Note that values for each of these growth rates will exist only for the sample period during which they were created: 1981 to 1988. Each is assigned the value NA, or not available, for the year 1980. Should we attempt to use either of these variables in a calculation when our sample period includes 1980, the 1980 value for this new variable will also be missing. In MicroTSP versions prior to 6.0, this would result in an error, causing MicroTSP to respond with the message "Range Error" (see below).

The variables of interest are now present in our data set. We next illustrate how to generate summary statistics for these variables. This can be accomplished either with the STATS selection [**F6**] on the bottom of the screen, or with the COVA (covariance) command. Using the MicroTSP menus, press [**F6**], which produces the menu:

```
            Descriptive & Test Statistic
  (1) Descriptive (mean.sd.max-min.covar)     COVA
  (2) Descriptive (no covariance matrix)      COVA(M)
  (3) Histogram-Normality test                HIST
  (4) Auto & Partial correlograms/Q-stat      IDENT
  (5) Cross correlogram                       CROSS
  (6) ADF unit root-EG cointegration tests    UROOT
  (7) Pairwise Granger Causality tests        CAUSE
  (8) Equation evaluation tests               TEST
   F1 Break (F3-F10 menus)
```

We choose 1, "Descriptive (mean.sd.max-min.covar)," since we are interested in summary statistics that include variances and covariances. MicroTSP responds to this choice with:

```
>COVA[◄┘]
 Series list ?
```

We then enter the names of the variables for which we desire this summary information. We can instead use the COVA command to perform this task. This approach is quicker than the method outlined above, considering the number of menus and choices involved in the menu driven approach. The form of the COVA command is:

    COVA *list of variables*

The variances and covariances produced by MicroTSP are population values of these measures. MicroTSP thus uses n and not (n − 1) as the denominators in these statistics. To obtain the sample variance or covariance, it is necessary to multiply the population value given with MicroTSP by the ratio n/(n − 1).

    While the variable list allows us to specify the exact set of variables for which summary statistics are calculated, *MicroTSP provides its entire set of summary statistics whenever the COVA command is used unless we include the M option (i.e., COVA(M)).* In the present example, we first change our sample period back to 1980 to 1988, then obtain summary statistics for the variables PCE, IPDPCE, RPCE, and RPCE80. The commands that accomplish this are:

    >SMPL 80 88[◄┘]
    >COVA PCE IPDPCE RPCE [◄┘]

The output that results from these commands is:

```
SMPL range: 1980 - 1988
Number of observations: 9

Series      Mean        S.D.       Maximum      Minimum
  PCE     2479.7333    528.5870   3296.1000    1748.1000
IPDPCE      88.9444     10.6505    104.2000      71.4000
 RPCE     2760.4394    265.9503   3163.2440    2448.3190


                        Covariance           Correlation

  PCE,PCE              248359.31000          1.0000000
  PCE,IPDPCE            4957.54950           0.9906810
  PCE,RPCE            124221.35000           0.9941039
  IPDPCE,IPDPCE          100.82912           1.0000000
  IPDPCE,RPCE           2447.58660           0.9721222
  RPCE,RPCE           62870.72000            1.0000000
```

As you can see, this listing tends to get rather large, since MicroTSP presents the covariance between each pair of variables as a separate line. Note that when the same variable is listed twice in the Covariance-Correlation portion of this output, the covariance entry gives the variance for that variable.

If, instead, you wish to create a variable based on only one of these summary statistics for a single variable, MicroTSP includes a number of "@" functions that allow this to be accomplished. The group of these you are most likely to use include: **@SUM(X)**; **@MEAN(X)**; **@VAR(X)**; **@COV(X)**; **@COR(Y, X)**, and **@OBS(X)**, where X and Y refer to variable names. Their codes for each of these make what each does fairly obvious. To employ one of these, include it in a GENR statement. For example, to create a variable whose (single) value is the mean of X, use the statement:

```
GENR MEANX=@MEAN(X) [↵]
```

MicroTSP can also print the observations for a list of variables. The SHOW command is used to print these to the screen, while the PRINT command sends this output to a connected printer. The format for each is:

```
>SHOW variable list
>PRINT variable list
```

Both of these commands can be executed by pressing [**F4**], then selecting either 9, "Show data table" or A, "Print data table" from the Data Management menu. Either command can also include format strings that instruct MicroTSP how each variable should be printed. In the present case, we use the SHOW command to print the variables PCE, RPCE, and GRPCE to the screen. The command that lists these observations and the resulting output is given below:

```
>SHOW PCE RPCE GRPCE [↵]
```

obs	PCE	RPCE	GRPCE
1980	1748.100	2448.319	NA
1981	1926.200	2475.835	1.123868
1982	2059.200	2505.110	1.182406
1983	2257.500	2618.910	4.542720
1984	2460.300	2745.871	4.847860
1985	2667.400	2865.091	4.341818
1986	2850.600	2969.375	3.639800
1987	3052.200	3052.200	2.789306
1988	3296.100	3163.244	3.638161

We conclude this section by illustrating how MicroTSP can be used to produce line graphs and scatter diagrams. Graphs of one or more series are produced by selecting choice (5), "Graph" from the main menu by pressing [**F5**]. This produces the menu on the left below, after typing 1 for "Line graph." MicroTSP then responds with the command and menu on the right:

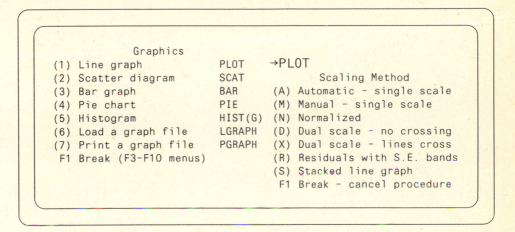

```
              Graphics
  (1) Line graph          PLOT      →PLOT
  (2) Scatter diagram     SCAT            Scaling Method
  (3) Bar graph           BAR       (A) Automatic - single scale
  (4) Pie chart           PIE       (M) Manual - single scale
  (5) Histogram           HIST(G)   (N) Normalized
  (6) Load a graph file   LGRAPH    (D) Dual scale - no crossing
  (7) Print a graph file  PGRAPH    (X) Dual scale - lines cross
  F1 Break (F3-F10 menus)           (R) Residuals with S.E. bands
                                    (S) Stacked line graph
                                    F1 Break - cancel procedure
```

The Scaling Method, along with a brief explanation for each, is:

A for automatic scaling, which maintains variables in their original units of measurement. This is useful for contrasting nominal and real values of the same variable. MicroTSP will, however, alter the range of vertical axis values, so that they do not begin with 0.

M designates manually setting the range of values for the vertical axis. Using this option it is possible to have the vertical axis range from 0 to whatever the highest value of the included variables is.

D which is used when the two variables in the plot have different scales, causes MicroTSP to give each variable a separate scale, but prevents the lines from crossing. This is useful in comparing the turning points in two time series.

X is similar to option D above, with the exception that it permits the two variables with different scales to cross.

N plots the normalized values of the variables in our list. This is useful in comparing turning points and the general movements in two or more variables, since their units of measurement are the same, and they can be entered on a single scale.

After the desired scaling method is entered, MicroTSP prompts you for the variables to include in this line graph. Type in the names, each separated by one or more spaces, then press [**Enter↵**]. The screen now shows the resulting line graph.

It is also possible to produce this same graph with the statement:

```
>PLOT variable list
```

MicroTSP requests the desired scaling method after the variable list has been entered. The letter corresponding to the desired option can also be included in parentheses after the word PLOT. For example, the following command produces a time series plot of PCE and RPCE80 with automatic scaling:

```
>PLOT(A) PCE RPCE80[◄┘]
```

The lines in this time series plot will cross in 1980, which is the base year for RPCE80.

No matter which method is used, MicroTSP produces the graph of these variables along with a number of options at the bottom of this graph:

```
(T)-Type (P)-Print (S)-Save (O)-Options (F)-Plotter & HPGL
(R)-pReview (X)-eXit
```

We can either return to the main program by selecting the X (exit) option, type headings and other information directly into the graph with the T (type) option, print the graph in its present form with the P (print) option, or select O for options which allows customizing of the line graph. The options menu is:

```
                    Graphics Option
     (1) Graph Type (line, scatter, bar, pie)
     (2) Plot Lines & Symbols
     (3) Borders, Grids & Vertical Lines
     (4) Scaling (logarithmic and force zero)
     (5) Axis Labels and Headings
     (6) Legend
     (7) Font (lables and legend)
     (8) Screen Colors
     (9) Bar & Pie Options
     (A) Multiple Graphs
     (B) Get options & titles from another graph
     (C) Save current settings as startup default
     (X) Exit graphics options
```

The most likely choices for customization are (5), "Axis Labels and Headings," and (6), "Legend."

The SCAT command produces a scatter diagram of the relationship between two variables. The form of this command is:

```
>SCAT var1 var2[◄┘]
```

where *var1* denotes the variable that is to be placed on the vertical axis, and *var2* the variable that will be positioned on the horizontal axis. Scatter diagrams are useful for investigating causal relationships that exist between two variables. The dependent variable should be placed on the vertical axis, and therefore appear as the first variable in the list. The same options that pertain to PLOT apply to SCAT as well.

It is possible to produce scatter diagrams using the MicroTSP menus. Select choice (2) in the Graph menu [**F5**], "Scatter diagram." MicroTSP prompts you with:

```
>SCAT [◄┘]
 Series list ?
```

Type the names of the desired variables (separated by spaces) then press [**Enter◄┘**]. Assuming we use the variables RPCE and GRPCE, and that the sample time period does not include missing values, MicroTSP responds with:

```
>SCAT
 Series list // RPCE GRPCE
             Scatter Option
   (S) Simple
   (C) Connect adjacent points
   (R) Regression line
   (B) Both connect & regression
   F1 Break - cancel procedure
```

At this point, select either S or C, depending on whether you desire individual points to be connected. Later in the course, we will select the R option, to depict the scatter diagram of data along with our estimated regression line. The scatter diagram appears on our screen, and the options available with PLOT pertain.

When all the desired tasks have been performed, we can save the data set that has been created. This allows us to avoid the numerous steps involved in data set creation when we use these data in future MicroTSP sessions. To do this, enter the command:

```
>SAVE data set name
```

where *data set name* is a name consisting of 8 or fewer characters which we will assign to these data. If writing the file to other than the default drive, it is necessary to include the drive letter as part of this name. Examples are:

```
>SAVE CONSEXPD [◄┘]        (writes to the default drive)
>SAVE B:CONSEXPD [◄┘]      (writes to drive B:)
```

The alternative method for saving a data set is to use the FILES option, [**F3**], select 3, "Save a WF to disk," then enter the name of the data set when prompted by MicroTSP. To end the session, either type EXIT or press [**F9**], TSP CONTROL, which produces the menu:

```
                    TSP Control
    (1)  End session/Exit to DOS    EXIT
    (2)  Run a MicroTSP program     RUN
    (3)  Run DOS commands           SYSTEM
    (4)  Configure for hardware     CONFIG
    (5)  Session options            OPTION
    (6)  Report on memory use       FREMEN
    (7)  Update & Clear screen      C
                 Printing
    (8)  User specified printing    POFF
    (9)  Print all stat. results    PON
    (A)  Print commands & stats     TRACE
    (B)  Advance page/form feed     FEED
    (C) Redirect print output       OUTPUT
     F1  Break (F3-F10 menus)
```

then type 1. In either case, MicroTSP will prompt you with:

```
Abandon the current work file ? (y/n) _
```

Enter y or yes to end the session.

ERRORS IN MicroTSP LINES AND THE CONSEQUENCES.   The most frequent errors you are likely to commit with MicroTSP are: incorrect spelling of a variable name in the expression to create a new variable; creating variables out of sequence; incorrect brackets; and attempting to create a new variable from an existing variable for which the current sample period includes NA values (versions before 6.0). The feedback from these mistakes is immediate, so the set of lines necessary to follow the consequences is far less involved than was the case with SAS.

Incorrect Variable Spelling.   Even though you know what the variables are and what your command intends to say, you cannot assume that the computer possesses this same knowledge. Almost correctly spelled is the same to a computer as very differently spelled: this indicates the use of a non-existent variable. MicroTSP will not allow a new variable to be created when it is constructed from one or more incorrectly spelled variables. This is illustrated for the creation of IPDPCE with a 1980 base year, where IPD is entered instead of IPDPCE:

```
>GENR IPDPCE80=(IPD/71.4)*100[◄┘]
Undefined series IDP
```

Instead of retyping this entire expression, MicroTSP contains a shortcut method for recalling previous commands: press [**F2**], which repeats the last command. MicroTSP allows us to recall the 20 most recent commands using this procedure. To correct this, we enter [**F2**] to recall this command, move the cursor to the position where letters need to be added (on the /), press the [**Ins**] key, which puts MicroTSP into insert mode, type in the needed letters (PCE in this case), then press the enter key, [   ]. If, instead, it is necessary to delete letters, then after recalling the previous command and moving the cursor to the position of the extra letter(s), press the [**Del**] key as many times as needed, then press the enter key [⏎].

Variables Created Out of Sequence.   The result of creating variables out of order is identical to that from misspelling a variable: as far as the computer is concerned, the variable which is referred to prior to its creation does not exist. It therefore cannot be used to construct a new variable. In the example below, we attempt to create real personal consumption expenditure with a 1980 base year (RPCE80) before creating the relevant price index, IPDPCE80. Since IPDPCE80 has not yet been created, the "Undefined series" message results.

```
>GENR RPCE80=(PCE/IPDPCE80)*100[⏎]
 Undefined series IPDPCE80
```

Incorrect Brackets.   Whenever you create a variable that involves bracketed expressions, it is advisable to write the expression correctly on paper before entering it on the computer. If you attempt to construct it from memory, you may well include an incorrect number of brackets. In the example below, the expression that creates GRPCE omits the far left bracket.

```
>GENR GRPCE=(RPCE-RPCE(-1))/RPCE(-1))*100[⏎]
 Syntax error
```

Note that MicroTSP's message, "Syntax error," does not indicate where the error occurs. We must therefore check the expression to make sure that a right bracket corresponds to each left bracket.

Once we have determined where we have omitted (or over-included) brackets, we can correct this fairly simply by using the shortcut for command recall discussed above. In this case, use the [**F2**] recall option, which will cause the GENR statement above to reappear. Move the cursor with the arrow keys on the right side of the keyboard to the bracket after the equal sign. Press the [**Ins**] key (for insert), then enter the needed bracket, which adds the bracket and moves the rest of the expression one space to the right. We now have the correct statement. When this is completed, press the [**Enter⏎**] key and GRPCE is created.

Incorrect Sample Period (For Versions Prior to 6.0).   If the current sample period coincides with the entire period for which this data set is defined, GENR statements utilizing lagged values of existing variables result in an error. In this case, MicroTSP does not have any observations before the first in the data set that it can use to create a lagged variable. As a result, any calculation involving lags will not be allowed. If we use the creation of GRPCE as the example of this, then, with a current sample period of 1980–1988, the command and response by MicroTSP are:

```
>GENR GRPCE=((RPCE-RPCE(-1))/RPCE(-1))*100[◄┘]
Range Error
```

To rectify this situation, we modify the initial period, adding to it the number of time periods in the highest lag of our expression. Here, we must add an additional year to 1980, but we keep 1988 as final time period. The needed statement is:

```
>SMPL 81 88[◄┘]
```

Once this statement has been entered, we can then create the variable GRPCE by reentering the command that defines this variable. In this instance, we therefore press [**F2**] twice to recall the formula that creates GRPCE.

We can avoid this type of error and directly verify where the SMPL statement should begin by using the SHOW command for the variable(s) on the right side of our variable creation expression. This procedure is especially useful when a range of NA values exists, and the choice of where to begin the SMPL statement is not obvious without such visual inspection.

FURTHER INFORMATION ABOUT MicroTSP. The primary source of information on how to use MicroTSP is its reference manual which is among the most well-written and thorough as any in existence. The sections on regression analysis take the reader through several in-depth examples and provide illustrations of MicroTSP output. This allows readers to gain a sense of both the method being used as well as the calculations MicroTSP performs.

The set of commands you are likely to use for data manipulation and analysis in MicroTSP are: COVA, PLOT, SCAT, LS, TSLS, and FORCST. COVA, as we saw earlier provides summary statistics for variables of interest. PLOT produces a time series plot of one or more variables, while SCAT creates a scatter diagram of two variables. LS (least squares) performs regression analysis. TSLS is a refinement of this, called two-stage least squares, which is the appropriate estimation method when estimating one equation from a set of simultaneous equations. FORCST generates predicted values from regression equations. In addition to these, MicroTSP contains a number of other useful features, such as seasonal adjustment, and the plotting of residuals from regressions (this is the R option with PLOT).

A LOOK AHEAD. These first three chapters span a substantial amout of subject matter, detailing the nature and scope of econometrics, the statistical prerequisites needed to begin the study of this subject, and methods used in manipulating economic data. Now that this framework has been provided, we move to the formal presentation of econometric theory which encompasses the remainder of this text. Subsequent chapters periodically make direct references to the material that has been discussed up to this point. All of what follows presupposes mastery of this subject matter. Do not hesitate to refer back to these chapters when you encounter problems understanding the material that follows.

If you have absorbed the essential elements of these chapters, you should now find yourself thinking more critically about the economic relationships you are studying in your current courses, along with those from previous classes.

KEY TERMS

Absolute change in x
Base year
Compounded annual (percent) growth rate
Computer language
Computer program
Controlled experimentation
Cross-sectional data
Default condition
Experimental data
Fixed-weight index
Function keys

Longitudinal data
Nominal value
Non-experimental data
Panel data
Percent growth rate
Price index
Proportionate growth rate
Proxy variable
Real value
Time series data
Two-period moving average
Year-to-year proportionate growth rate

EXERCISES

1. Compare and contrast the CPI and the Implicit Price Deflator for Personal Consumption Expenditures.

2. Show that choice of base year does not affect the rate of inflation.

3. Explain why nominal values are *less* than real values when prices are below those of the base year.

   The remaining questions pertain to the following data (from the 1992 *Economic Report of the President*):

YEAR	GDP (BIL)	CPI (82–84 = 100)	IPD (1987 = 100)	FEDERAL DEFICIT (BIL)	Aaa INTEREST RATE	AV WAGE MANUF ($/HR)	OUTPUT/HR nonfarm (82 = 100)	MANUF EMPLOYMENT (MIL)
1980	2708.0	82.4	71.7	73.8	11.94	7.27	99.0	20.29
1981	3030.6	90.9	78.9	78.9	14.17	7.99	99.9	20.17
1982	3149.6	96.5	83.8	127.9	13.79	8.49	100.0	18.78
1983	3405.0	99.6	87.2	207.8	12.04	8.83	102.4	18.43
1984	3777.2	103.9	91.0	185.3	12.71	9.19	104.5	19.38
1985	4038.7	107.6	94.4	212.3	11.37	9.54	105.4	19.26
1986	4268.6	109.6	96.9	221.2	9.02	9.73	107.5	19.00
1987	4539.9	113.6	100.0	149.7	9.38	9.91	108.3	19.02
1988	4900.4	118.3	103.9	155.1	9.71	10.18	109.2	19.40
1989	5244.0	124.0	108.4	152.0	9.26	10.47	108.2	19.61

4. **(a)** Have real hourly wages in manufacturing risen or fallen in the 1980s?

    (b) Calculate the real federal deficit and the deficit as a percentage of GDP for each of these years.

    (c) Has the growth rate of productivity (i.e., nonfarm output per hour) risen or fallen in the 1980s? Is this related to inflation rates?

    (d) Overall, has productivity growth kept pace with wage increases? During which periods do these rates diverge the most? Why? How does this affect inflation rates?

5. **(a)** What is the theoretical relationship between wages and employment?

    (b) Explain why real wages are preferable to nominal wages in this relationship.

    (c) Using the data above on average hourly wages in manufacturing and manufacturing employment, obtain a scatter diagram of employment (on the vertical axis) and nominal wages (horizontal axis).

    (d) Obtain the scatter diagram from (c) above using real hourly wages (calculated using the CPI) in place of nominal wages. Does this scatter diagram indicate a higher correlation between real wages and employment than did the diagram in (c) using nominal wages?

    (e) Calculate the correlation coefficient for manufacturing employment and each wage variable. Which is higher?

6. This chapter presented the theoretical basis for an association between inflation and interest rates. Other things being equal, periods of rising inflation should be accompanied by rising interest rates. Using the data above: (i) calculate the inflation rate using the IPD; and (ii) create a scatter diagram of Moody's Aaa Interest Rate (vertical axis) and the IPD inflation rate (horizontal axis). Does the expected relationship hold? If not, why?

7. Calculate the growth rate in productivity (output/hr) in the nonfarm business sector). Using the time series of real wages from (5):

    (a) Obtain the scatter diagram of real wages (vertical axis) and productivity growth (horizontal axis). Is the direction of this relationship consistent with theoretical expectations?

    (b) Now produce the scatter diagram of real wages (horizontal axis) and productivity growth *lagged one year* (horizontal axis). Is the direction of this relationship consistent with theoretical expectations?

    (c) On theoretical grounds, should current or lagged productivity growth be the preferred explanatory variable for the level of real wages (as explored in (a) and (b))? Is this also true on empirical grounds?

8. Does any empirical association exist between the growth rate in the nominal budget deficit and nominal GDP? (Use a scatter diagram and calculate the correlation coefficient between this pair of variables.)

4

Econometric Theory: The Bivariate Regression Model

The first chapter provided a brief sketch of what econometrics entails. This and the remaining chapters supply the substance of econometric theory and practice.

The statistical prerequisites in the proceeding chapters dealt with methods for deriving and judging estimators of unknown population parameters. A great deal of time was spent discussing the sample mean. This estimator is simple to calculate, and it possesses all of the desirable estimator properties. This chapter presents an alternative methodology for estimating the mean of a variable of interest: regression analysis. Unlike the sample mean, which provides a single estimate of the population average of the variable of interest, regression analysis permits us to calculate distinct estimates of this parameter that depend on values taken by an explanatory variable. The building block for this empirical analysis is the theoretical relationship between these variables, which is called the population regression function.

This chapter discusses the population regression function when there is a single explanatory variable and sets forth an estimator of this function, called the sample regression function. The formulas used to calculate this function are presented, along with an analysis of their properties. In addition, several useful criteria for evaluating actual estimates of a population regression function are discussed. The chapter concludes with several examples of sample regression functions.

THE POPULATION REGRESSION FUNCTION

Econometrics is a methodology for estimating economic relationships. Economic theory provides the starting point for econometrics by identifying the factors that determine the behavior of a variable of interest, and indicating their direction of influence. In the terminology outlined in Chapter 1, the variable whose behavior is investigated is the dependent variable. The variables that are causally related to the dependent variable are explanatory variables. The expected sign of an explanatory variable denotes the direction of causation between it and the dependent variable.

A simple example of this is given by demand theory. Economic theory postulates an inverse relationship between the price of a good (p) and its quantity demanded (q), other things being equal. This relationship can be stated as[1]:

$$q = f(p) \tag{4.1}$$

According to the Law of Demand, the expected sign of p is negative. If we represent this theoretical relationship by a linear equation, the demand curve is given by:

$$q = \alpha_0 + \alpha_1 p. \tag{4.1'}$$

Equation (4.1') is a deterministic function, since it generates a single value of quantity demanded for each price. If we were to obtain actual data for use in estimating this function, we would observe a *range* of quantity values for each price. An example of this is given in Figure 4.1(a). Each of these consumption values is not equally likely. *A probability density function* of quantity values therefore exists for each price. Recall (from Chapter 2) that these are called conditional distributions, since each pertains to (is conditional upon) a specific price. The type of function we are actually dealing with is therefore a stochastic function. Figure 4.1(b) illustrates the conditional distributions of q for the prices p_1 and p_2.

The *empirical* association between these variables therefore entails a number of complications that are absent from their theoretical relationship. Most notable of these is the correct interpretation of the inverse relationship between price and quantity demanded. Since our empirical demand function is stochastic, higher prices are not necessarily associated with lower quantities demanded. This will no doubt be true for many of the persons in the data, but not for all persons. In Figure 4.1(b), for example, quantity demanded for persons in the upper half of the distribution for p_2 exceeds that for some of the individuals in the lower half of the conditional distribution for p_1. Our statements about price and quantity demanded must therefore be prefaced in terms of the association between the range of prices and the *average q* value for each price.

The average quantity demanded for price p_i, which is denoted $E(q|p_i)$, is a conditional mean. It is the mean of the conditional distribution of q for price p_i. *For a stochastic function, it is the conditional mean of quantity demanded that is a function of the price of a good.* Stating this relationship symbolically:

$$E(q|p_i) = f(p_i). \tag{4.2}$$

Equation (4.2) is the **population regression function** (PRF), which consists of the population mean of q for each price. The inverse stochastic relationship between price and quantity demanded is based on the fact that in Figure 4.1(b), $E(q|p_2) < E(q|p_1)$. We are thus restricted to making statements about behavior that occurs *on average*.

---

[1] This function is specified in the opposite way the graph of a demand curve is drawn. All explanatory variables other than p are omitted to present this as a bivariate relationship.

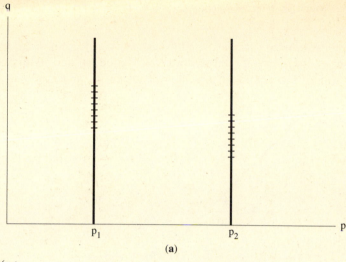

(a)

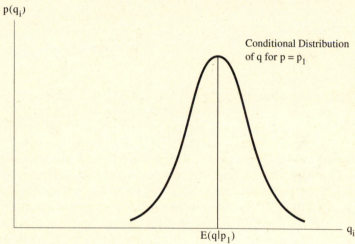

Conditional Distribution
of q for p = p₁

$E(q|p_1)$

(b)

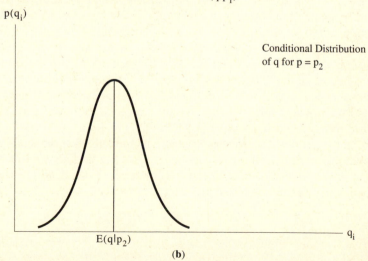

Conditional Distribution
of q for p = p₂

$E(q|p_2)$

Figure 4.1

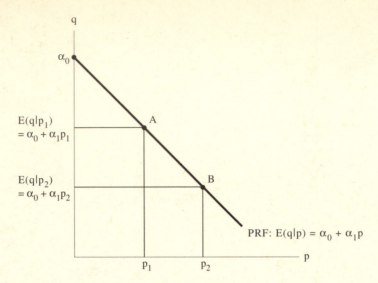

Figure 4.2

If we utilize a linear specification, the population regression function given by Equation (4.2) is:

$$E(q|p_i) = \alpha_0 + \alpha_1 p_i. \tag{4.3}$$

The right side of Equation (4.3) is the **specification** of the population regression function. The graph of Equation (4.3) is given in Figure 4.2. For any price, the value of the population regression function is $E(q|p)$, which equals $\alpha_0 + \alpha_1 p$. This corresponds to the height of the population regression function in Figure 4.2 for that price. For example, when price is p_1, the value of the population regression function is $E(q|p_1)$, which is given by point A on this demand curve. If price rises to p_2, mean quantity demanded falls to $E(q|p_2)$ at point B. The inverse relationship pictured in this graph exists between price and the population *means* of quantity demanded.

It is possible to modify the population regression function into a form that allows us to relate *actual q* to price. This is accomplished by converting Equation (4.2) into a stochastic form. The basis of this conversion can be seen with reference to Figure 4.3, which contains both a scatter diagram of points and the linear version of the population regression function. The actual quantity at point A, q_*, exceeds the mean quantity for p_*. Thus, $q_* > E(q|p_*)$. The difference between actual q and the mean q for a given price is the **stochastic error**, or **random disturbance** of the equation. "Random disturbance" reflects the fact that this term is a random variable and that it "disturbs" an otherwise deterministic relationship. If we denote this term by ε, the stochastic error for the ith observation is:

$$\varepsilon_i = q_i - E(q|p_i). \tag{4.4}$$

In Figure 4.3, the stochastic error, ε_i, is measured by the vertical distance between the actual q, q_*, and the population regression function at that price, $E(q|p_*)$. At point A, q_* exceeds $E(q|p_*)$, and the stochastic error is positive.

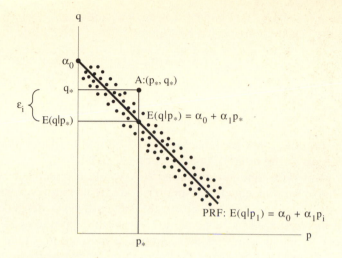

Figure 4.3

If we rearrange Equation (4.4), we can express actual q in terms of its conditional mean:

$$q_i = E(q|p_i) + \varepsilon_i. \tag{4.5}$$

The actual value of q consists of two parts: the population mean of q and a stochastic error. The error term can be viewed as a "balancing item" that enables us to link actual with mean q. Actual q_i can thus be decomposed into an explained portion, $E(q|p_i)$, which is the average quantity demanded for all persons at price p_i, plus a random element, ε_i, which is the unexplained component of q_i. If the linear specification of $E(q|p_i)$ is substituted into Equation (4.5), we obtain the linear form of the stochastic population regression function:

$$q_i = \alpha_0 + \alpha_1 p_i + \varepsilon_i. \tag{4.6}$$

An important question arises when examining either Equation (4.5) or (4.6). Why is part of quantity demanded unexplained? In other words, what factors give rise to the stochastic error? There are a number of reasons why this error term exists. First, the dependent variable might be measured incorrectly. Measured and actual values of q_i can diverge if, for example, coding errors were committed while recording data, or if data on individuals are improperly aggregated. Either type of measurement error will be reflected in ε_i. Second, the population regression function may omit critical variables. In the example used here, price is the only explanatory variable included in the demand equation. This specification is only valid if "other things" such as income, preferences, and the prices of related goods are of secondary importance in determining quantity demanded. If, for example, the correctly specified population regression function is:

$$q_{xi} = \alpha_0 + \alpha_1 p_{xi} + \alpha_2 p_{yi} + \alpha_3 I_i + v_i,$$

where p_y is the price of a related good Y, I is income, and v is a stochastic error, the error term in the demand curve given by Equation (4.6):

$$q_{xi} = \alpha_0 + \alpha_1 p_{xi} + \varepsilon_i$$

is given by the following equation:

$$\varepsilon_i = \alpha_2 p_{yi} + \alpha_3 I_i + v_i.$$

Since ε_i is that part of q_{xi} not accounted for by p_{xi}, points will lie off the population regression function as the result of omitting both p_y and I.

This last point raises another question. Why would a researcher ever omit an influential variable from an equation's specification? By its nature, economic theory is incomplete. Factors that exert a significant influence on a dependent variable might not yet be recognized by economic theory. At the opposite extreme, some of the explanatory variables identified by economic theory are not quantifiable. The specification of the population regression function might not be linear as is the one discussed here. If a different functional form is appropriate, any additional variables used to characterize this form (such as squared terms) are omitted by a linear specification.

Note that every population regression function excludes some variables. *A population regression function should include only the major subset of variables whose behavior determines the values taken by the dependent variable.* Less important variables can thus be omitted. In the demand equation, for example, rainfall might be excluded, even though it influences demand and is in part responsible for the divergence between q_i and $E(q|p_i)$. All excluded variables are reflected in the stochastic error. As we shall see later, proper estimation requires that the net influence of all omitted variables is zero.

Finally, the stochastic error is related to the randomness of human behavior. Modeling human behavior is difficult due to the diversity of responses by persons to economic stimuli. Even if a population regression function possesses the correct functional form, does not omit relevant variables, and contains no measurement error, the element of human behavior results in a stochastic population regression function.

Now that the concept of the population regression function has been presented, we turn our attention to estimating this function. Our estimator of this function, the sample regression function, is calculated based on estimates of the parameters in the population regression function.

THE SAMPLE REGRESSION FUNCTION

The population regression function characterizes the empirical relationship that exists between an explanatory variable and a dependent variable. Economic theory provides the basis of this function by specifying the explanatory variable to include in this equation, as well as its expected sign. The population regression function is, however, based on the entire population of values, and is itself unknown. Econometric estimation of this function uses a sample of the population to calculate the **sample regression function** (SRF). Recall that the population regression function can be expressed as either:

$$E(y|x_i) = f(x_i)$$

or

$$y_i = f(x_i) + \varepsilon_i, \tag{4.7}$$

where the general symbols y for the dependent variable and x for the explanatory variable replace q and p in the previous example from demand theory. If we employ a linear specification to represent $f(x_i)$, the first equation in Equation (4.7) becomes:

$$E(y|x_i) = \alpha_0 + \alpha_1 x_i \tag{4.7'}$$

which indicates that the population mean of y depends on the value selected for x. The estimator for Equation (4.7') provided by the sample regression function involves two estimators: an estimated intercept, $\hat{\alpha}_0$, and an estimate of the slope, $\hat{\alpha}_1$. Our estimator of Equation (4.7'), the sample regression function, is:

$$\hat{y}_i = \hat{\alpha}_0 + \hat{\alpha}_1 x_i. \tag{4.8}$$

In Equation (4.8), $\hat{y}_i$ denotes the predicted value of y for observation i. This is an estimator of the population mean of y, $E(y|x_i)$.

Equation (4.8) is the nonstochastic form of the sample regression function. We can also express this function in stochastic form. This is accomplished by including the estimated error, or **residual**, for a given observation, which is the difference between actual y and the estimate provided by the sample regression function. In equation form, the residual is:

$$\hat{\varepsilon}_i = y_i - \hat{y}_i \tag{4.9}$$

If the sample regression function is plotted along with a scatter diagram of sample values, $\hat{\varepsilon}_i$ represents the vertical distance at any x value between the sample regression function and actual y. The residual in the sample regression function represents the portion of y not explained by the included explanatory variable.

Rearranging Equation (4.9) allows us to derive the stochastic form of the sample regression function. Solving Equation (4.9) for y_i gives:

$$y_i = \hat{y}_i + \hat{\varepsilon}_i. \tag{4.10}$$

Substituting the right side of the sample regression function given by Equation (4.8) into this equation, we obtain:

$$y_i = \hat{\alpha}_0 + \hat{\alpha}_1 x_i + \hat{\varepsilon}_i. \tag{4.11}$$

As this equation shows, the sample regression function includes three estimators: $\hat{\alpha}_0$, $\hat{\alpha}_1$, and $\hat{\varepsilon}_i$. Since α_0 and α_1 are population parameters, ε_i is also unknown. As a result, an estimated error is present in the sample regression function.

A numerical example of a sample regression function is:

$$\hat{y}_i = 15 + 1.5x_i.$$

In this equation, the estimated intercept, $\hat{\alpha}_0$, equals 15. This coefficient is the estimated mean of y when x equals 0. The slope estimator, $\hat{\alpha}_1$, equals 1.5. A one-unit increase in x raises the mean of y by 1.5 of its units, where "units" refer to the units of measurement for x and y. These need not be the same. If x_i is denominated in dollars and y is expressed in units of thousands per month, a \$1 increase in x raises the mean of y by 1,500 units per month.

We can use a sample regression function to predict the population mean of y for hypothetical values of x. If a policy change by government will potentially influence y, then estimating the mean of y under the proposed change requires only that we substitute likely values of x into the sample regression function, then calculate $\hat{y}$. Returning to the demand example, if our sample regression function is:

$$\hat{y}_i = 15 - 1.5x_i$$

where x_i is the average price (in dollars) of a good, and y_i is quantity demanded (in thousands of units per month), we can evaluate the effect of a proposed tariff on foreign producers using this function. If this tariff increases the price of this good by \$2, our sample regression function predicts a fall in mean quantity demanded of three thousand units per month. One caveat should be mentioned. If the selected value of x differs substantially from the sample values for this variable, the estimate of y may be unreliable.

Before outlining the methodology for calculating the coefficients in the sample regression function, it is necessary to define the exact meaning of linearity as it pertains to the population regression function. *A linear specification is one that is linear in the coefficients but not necessarily in the explanatory variable(s).* In other words, an equation is linear (for purposes here), if it can be expressed in the following form:

$$y_i = \alpha_0 + \alpha_1 x_i + \varepsilon_i$$

This requirement is satisfied as long as the α's in the population regression function are not raised to powers other than one or multiplied with each other. Examples of equations that violate the linearity assumption are:

$$y_i = \alpha_0 + \alpha_1^2 x_i + \varepsilon_i$$

$$y_i = \alpha_0 \alpha_1 + \alpha_2 x_i + \varepsilon_i.$$

Equations whose explanatory variables are raised to powers other than one, such as:

$$y_i = \alpha_0 + \alpha_1 x_i^2 + \varepsilon_i$$

$$y_i = \alpha_0 + \alpha_1 (1/x)_i + \varepsilon_i$$

satisfy this definition of linearity. Finally, equations whose variables are transformations or manipulations of y and x, such as absolute changes and natural logarithms, are also considered to be linear. If, for example, the population regression function takes the form of the following *constant elasticity demand function*:

$$q_i = A p_i^\beta$$

then, by applying a logarithmic transformation and adding an error term, this function becomes:

$$\ln(q_i) = \alpha + \beta \ln(p_i) + \varepsilon_i,$$

where "ln" denotes the natural logarithm and $\alpha = \ln(A)$. Since this equation can be expressed as:

$$q_i^* = \alpha_0 + \alpha_1 p_i^* + \varepsilon_i,$$

where $q_i^* = \ln(q_i)$, $\alpha_0 = \alpha$, $\alpha_1 = \beta$, and $p_i^* = \ln(p_i)$, it satisfies the requirements for linearity. This functional form is called the **double-log** specification. Because this specification is linear in its coefficients, it does not violate the requirements for linearity. In fact, the double-log equation is sometimes referred to as a **log-linear specification**. The "linearity" of a linear specification is therefore not as restrictive as it sounds.

DERIVATION OF THE ESTIMATORS: THE LEAST SQUARES TECHNIQUE

A number of different criteria could be employed as the basis for deriving the estimators in the sample regression function. The population function is itself related to the mean of y; it would thus be desirable to have the mean of y as our prediction when x equals its sample mean. Many criteria embody this restriction, however.

Because a sample regression function is stochastic, no estimation method can provide a function capable of predicting every x-y combination. In fact, it is even possible to obtain a sample regression function that fits the scatter of data points well yet fails to predict any x-y pair correctly.[2] Since estimation error is a fact of life, estimators obtained by minimizing the residuals in the sample regression function should ensure accurate prediction. A procedure based on this criterion would select estimators that minimize the sum of the residuals. If this criterion were utilized, however, we could easily conclude that our equation is very precisely estimated, when in fact the opposite is true. This would occur since positive residuals would offset negative residuals, making the sum of the residuals small. Figure 4.4 illustrates this problem. The large positive residuals associated with points A and B are offset by the negative residuals from points C and D, giving this sample regression function a low residual sum.

The criterion actually utilized solves this problem by first squaring the residuals then taking their sum. Since each residual is squared, positive and negative values cannot cancel. In this way, a large residual, *no matter what its sign*, is treated as unsatisfactory. In Figure 4.4, an estimated error of $+5$ associated with A and -5 for B gives 0 as the sum of the residuals, but 50 as the sum of squared residuals. This

---

[2] This situation is analogous to a sample mean that differs from every observation upon which it is based. For example, if x takes values 1, 2, and 6, the mean is 3, which overstates the first two observations and understates the last value.

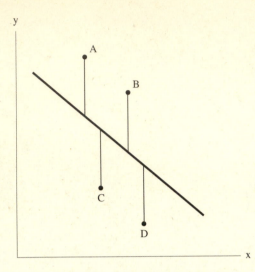

Figure 4.4 Problems with a sample regression function based on minimizing the sum of the square residuals

criterion, which minimizes the sum of the squared residuals, is referred to as the **least squares** technique, or **ordinary least squares** (OLS). The exact procedure involves optimization theory and calculus. At this point only the essential elements and results will be discussed. Actual derivations are presented in the appendix to this chapter.

Deriving the least squares sample regression function involves a procedure where it is necessary to:

$$\text{Minimize } \sum \hat{\varepsilon}_i^2,$$

then solve for $\hat{\alpha}_0$ and $\hat{\alpha}_1$. To explicitly introduce these estimators into this expression for $\hat{\varepsilon}_i$, the residual is written in the form:

$$\hat{\varepsilon}_i = (y_i - \hat{\alpha}_0 - \hat{\alpha}_1 x_i),$$

which is based on Equation (4.11). The sum of the squared residuals equals:

$$\sum \hat{\varepsilon}_i^2 = \sum (y_i - \hat{\alpha}_0 - \hat{\alpha}_1 x_i)^2. \tag{4.12}$$

Determining the values of $\hat{\alpha}_0$ and $\hat{\alpha}_1$ that minimize Equation (4.12) involves partially differentiating this function with respect to each of these coefficients. This produces a set of simultaneous equations called the **normal equations**:

$$\sum (y_i - \hat{\alpha}_0 - \hat{\alpha}_1 x_i) = 0 \tag{4.13}$$

$$\sum x_i (y_i - \hat{\alpha}_0 - \hat{\alpha}_1 x_i) = 0. \tag{4.14}$$

Solving these for $\hat{\alpha}_0$ and $\hat{\alpha}_1$ provides the formulas for these estimators.

The first normal equation, (4.13), can be solved for the estimated intercept. Rearranging terms with the summation brought inside the bracket gives:

$$\sum \hat{\alpha}_0 = \sum y_i - \hat{\alpha}_1 \sum x_i.$$

The left side of this equation equals $n\hat{\alpha}_0$, since $\hat{\alpha}_0$ is a constant. Substituting this and dividing both sides by n:

$$n\hat{\alpha}_0 = \sum y_i - \hat{\alpha}_1 \sum x_i$$

$$\hat{\alpha}_0 = (1/n)\sum y_i - \hat{\alpha}_1(1/n)\sum x_i,$$

or

$$\hat{\alpha}_0 = \hat{\mu}_y - \hat{\alpha}_1\hat{\mu}_x. \tag{4.15}$$

Equation (4.15) is the formula for the least squares intercept estimator. Since the point $(\hat{\mu}_x, \hat{\mu}_y)$ satisfies this equation, the sample regression function passes through the point of means, thus fulfilling one of the desirable prerequisites for an estimation technique.

The calculation of $\hat{\alpha}_0$ presupposes knowledge of $\hat{\alpha}_1$. The formula for the estimated slope is obtained from the second normal equation. First, perform the multiplication that is indicated in Equation (4.14), then apply the summation operation to each of the resulting terms. This produces the equation:

$$\sum x_i y_i = \hat{\alpha}_0 \sum x_i + \hat{\alpha}_1 \sum x_i^2$$

We then substitute Equation (4.15) into this equation, which gives:

$$\sum x_i y_i = (\hat{\mu}_y - \hat{\alpha}_1\hat{\mu}_x)\sum x_i + \hat{\alpha}_1\sum x_i^2$$
$$= \hat{\mu}_y\sum x_i - \hat{\alpha}_1\hat{\mu}_x\sum x_i + \hat{\alpha}_1\sum x_i^2$$

Since $\sum x_i = n\hat{\mu}_x$, this equation simplifies to:

$$\sum x_i y_i = n\hat{\mu}_y\hat{\mu}_x - \hat{\alpha}_1 n\hat{\mu}_x^2 + \hat{\alpha}_1\sum x_i^2$$

Factoring out $\hat{\alpha}_1$, and moving the remaining terms to the left of this equation:

$$\sum x_i y_i - n\hat{\mu}_x\hat{\mu}_y = \hat{\alpha}_1(\sum x_i^2 - n\hat{\mu}_x^2)$$

We then solve for $\hat{\alpha}_1$:

$$\hat{\alpha}_1 = (\sum x_i y_i - n\hat{\mu}_x\hat{\mu}_y)/(\sum x_i^2 - n\hat{\mu}_x^2)$$

Using the results outlined in Chapter 2, the numerator in this expression can be written: $\sum(x_i - \hat{\mu}_x)(y_i - \hat{\mu}_y)$. The denominator equals: $\sum(x_i - \hat{\mu}_x)^2$. The least squares slope estimator is therefore:

$$\hat{\alpha}_1 = \sum(x_i - \hat{\mu}_x)(y_i - \hat{\mu}_y)/\sum(x_i - \hat{\mu}_x)^2 \tag{4.16}$$

If we utilize the notation: $x_i' \equiv (x_i - \hat{\mu}_x)$ and $y_i' \equiv (y_i - \hat{\mu}_y)$, the least squares slope estimator can be written:

$$\hat{\alpha}_1 = \sum x_i' y_i'/\sum x_i'^2 \tag{4.16'}$$

When the slope estimator is expressed in this form, we can establish its link to the building blocks of statistical association presented in Chapter 2. We first associate this estimator with the covariance between x and y, $\hat{\sigma}_{xy}$, and the estimated variance of x, $\hat{\sigma}_x^2$. Recall from Chapter 2 that:

$$\hat{\sigma}_{xy} = \frac{1}{n-1} \sum (x_i - \hat{\mu}_x)(y_i - \hat{\mu}_y)$$

and

$$\hat{\sigma}_x^2 = \frac{1}{n-1} \sum (x_i - \hat{\mu}_x)^2.$$

By manipulating the equation for $\hat{\sigma}_{xy}$, we see that the numerator of Equation (4.16) is related to the covariance between x and y: $\sum (x_i - \hat{\mu}_x)(y_i - \hat{\mu}_y) = (n-1)\hat{\sigma}_{xy}$. Similarly, the denominator of Equation (4.16) can be expressed as $(n-1)\hat{\sigma}_x^2$. Substituting this information into (4.16) gives:

$$\begin{aligned} \hat{\alpha}_1 &= (n-1)\,\hat{\sigma}_{xy}/(n-1)\hat{\sigma}_x^2 \\ &= \hat{\sigma}_{xy}/\hat{\sigma}_x^2. \end{aligned} \tag{4.17}$$

This relationship between the least squares slope estimator and the covariance between x and y should come as no surprise. The mean, variance, and covariance are the primary building blocks for virtually everything discussed in this text. Perhaps less obvious is the fact that regression analysis is directly related to correlation analysis. As we now show, the least squares slope estimator can also be expressed in terms of the correlation coefficient between x and y.

The slope estimator given in Equation (4.17):

$$\hat{\alpha}_1 = \hat{\sigma}_{xy}/\hat{\sigma}_x^2,$$

is a function of the covariance between x and y. Recall from Chapter 2 that the formula for the sample correlation coefficient between x and y ($\hat{\rho}_{xy}$) is:

$$\hat{\rho}_{xy} = \frac{\hat{\sigma}_{xy}}{\hat{\sigma}_x \cdot \hat{\sigma}_y}$$

where $\hat{\sigma}_x$ and $\hat{\sigma}_y$ are the sample standard deviations of x and y, respectively. If we solve this equation for $\hat{\sigma}_{xy}$, the resulting expression can be substituted for the numerator of Equation (4.17), allowing $\hat{\alpha}_1$ to be expressed in terms of the correlation coefficient. Performing this manipulation:

$$\hat{\sigma}_{xy} = \hat{\rho}_{xy} \cdot \hat{\sigma}_x \cdot \hat{\sigma}_y. \tag{4.18}$$

Substituting (4.18) into the numerator of Equation (4.17):

$$\begin{aligned} \hat{\alpha}_1 &= (\hat{\rho}_{xy} \cdot \hat{\sigma}_x \cdot \hat{\sigma}_y)/\hat{\sigma}_x^2 \\ &= \hat{\rho}_{xy}(\hat{\sigma}_y/\hat{\sigma}_x). \end{aligned} \tag{4.19}$$

The least squares slope estimator is therefore the product of the correlation coefficient and the ratio $(\hat{\sigma}_y/\hat{\sigma}_x)$. This last term is the slope of the reference line (discussed in Chapter 2) that passes through the point of means and provides a direction for the points given by the scatter diagram of x and y. The reference line and sample regression function for a downward sloping function are shown in Figure 4.5. The slope of the

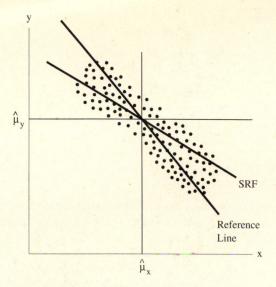

Figure 4.5 Relationship between the reference line and the sample regression function

reference line is $-(\hat{\sigma}_y/\hat{\sigma}_x)$. This curve is not constructed in the same manner as the sample regression function, whose points correspond to mean values of y for different x values. Equation (4.19) indicates that the slope of the sample regression function is only a fraction, $\hat{\rho}_{xy}$, of the slope of the reference line.[3] This result can be interpreted in the following way: a one standard deviation rise in x produces a change in y of $\hat{\rho}_{xy}$ standard deviations, on average. If, for example, $\hat{\rho}_{xy}$ equals -0.8, the slope estimate predicts that a one standard deviation increase in x lowers y by 0.8 standard deviations.[4]

The least squares normal equations embody two conditions that are met with this estimation technique. The bracketed term in each normal equation is the residual, $\hat{\varepsilon}_i$. The normal equations can thus be rewritten:

$$\sum \hat{\varepsilon}_i = 0 \qquad\qquad (4.13')$$

$$\sum x_i \hat{\varepsilon}_i = 0. \qquad\qquad (4.14')$$

The first of these is based on Equation (4.13); both the sum and the average of the residuals are zero.[5] The second result is derived from Equation (4.14); the residual is uncorrelated with the explanatory variable x. To see this, let us refer to the formula

---

[3] This statement is not true only when a perfect positive or negative correlation exists between these variables.

[4] An excellent reference for this topic is D. Freedman, R. Pisani, and R. Purves, *Statistics* (New York: Norton), 1978.

[5] This presupposes that an intercept is included in the sample regression function.

for the covariance between x and $\hat{\varepsilon}$:

$$\text{Cov}(x_i, \hat{\varepsilon}_i) = \frac{1}{n-1} \sum (x_i - \hat{\mu}_x)(\hat{\varepsilon}_i - \hat{\mu}_{\hat{\varepsilon}})$$

$$= \frac{1}{n-1} \sum (x_i - \hat{\mu}_x)\hat{\varepsilon}_i$$

since the average residual is 0 with least squares. Multiplying the bracketed expression by $\hat{\varepsilon}$ this becomes:

$$= \frac{1}{n-1}\left(\sum x_i\hat{\varepsilon}_i - \hat{\mu}_x\sum\hat{\varepsilon}_i\right)$$

Using Equations (4.13′) and (4.14′) (and therefore the normal equations), both of the terms in the bracket equal zero. Since x_i and $\hat{\varepsilon}_i$ have a zero covariance, they are uncorrelated. Note, however, that covariance measures the *linear* association between these variables. It is possible for x and $\hat{\varepsilon}$ to be nonlinearly related even though $\text{Cov}(x_i, \hat{\varepsilon}_i) = 0$.

The discussion up to this point has outlined the sample regression function, the formulas for the least squares estimators, and the correct interpretation of the coefficients of this function. We have not yet established the properties of the least squares estimators $\hat{\alpha}_0$ and $\hat{\alpha}_1$. We saw in Chapter 2 that before the properties of an estimators can be ascertained, it is necessary to make a set of assumptions about the population of interest. This is also true for the estimators considered here.

Several of the assumptions about the population regression function deal with the stochastic nature of this function. Figure 4.6 shows the proper way to view the population regression function. For each x, a probability density function of y values exists, such as those for x_1 and x_2. These are conditional probability density functions.

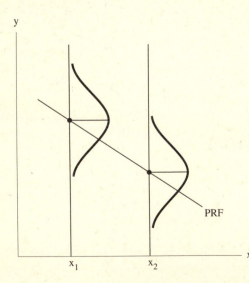

Figure 4.6 Population regression function

Each possesses a mean and a variance. The population regression function passes through the means of these functions, as indicated in the graph.

For any x, the vertical distance between an actual y value and the population regression function is the stochastic error for that observation. The error terms are thus deviations from means (of y). Because we assume that the coefficients in the population regression function pertain to all N elements of the population:

$$y_1 = \alpha_0 + \alpha_1 x_1 + \varepsilon_1$$
$$y_2 = \alpha_0 + \alpha_1 x_2 + \varepsilon_2$$
$$\cdots$$
$$y_N = \alpha_0 + \alpha_1 x_N + \varepsilon_N,$$

a probability density function of error terms exists for every x value. Accompanying each conditional distribution of y values is therefore a conditional distribution of disturbance terms.[6] The first two of the assumptions concerning the population regression function detail the parameters of these conditional distributions, while the third stipulates the independence of these errors. *Implicit in the following discussion is the presumption of a correctly specified population regression function.*

ASSUMPTIONS ABOUT THE POPULATION REGRESSION FUNCTION

1. For every x value, $E(\varepsilon_i) = 0$, or $E(\varepsilon_i|x_i) = 0$

This assumption maintains that the average error associated with each x value is zero. Since the disturbance terms are deviations from means (of y values), this assumption specifies that average deviation for a given x, which is the mean of the conditional error distribution for that x, equals 0.

The disturbance terms reflect the randomness of human behavior, omitted variables, and measurement error. A zero expected error thus indicates that the effects of all omitted factors on the mean of y exactly offset each other. Taken collectively, these exert a zero net effect on the population mean of y.

Omitting an influential variable from the estimated equation violates this assumption. If, for example, the correctly specified population regression function is:

$$y_i = \alpha_0 + \alpha_1 x_i + \alpha_2 z_i + \varepsilon_i,$$

and we omit the variable z, the population regression function based on this omission is:

$$y_i = \alpha_0 + \alpha_1 x_i + v_i,$$

---

[6] Actually, the conditional distributions for ε are origin changes of the corresponding y distributions.

where $v_i = \varepsilon_i + \alpha_1 z_i$. The mean error is then:

$$E(v_i) = E(\varepsilon_i) + E(\alpha_1 z_i)$$
$$= \alpha_1 E(z_i) \neq 0,$$

even if the assumption of a zero mean for ε_i is satisfied.[7] This is called **specification error.** When this occurs, the least squares estimators will usually lack the desirable estimator properties.[8]

2. $\text{Var}(\varepsilon_i) = \sigma_\varepsilon^2$

This assumption indicates that all of the conditional error distributions possess the same (constant) variance, σ_ε^2. This property is called **homoskedasticity**, which means "equal spread." When this premise is violated, the disturbance terms are **heteroskedastic**. Heteroskedasticity, which is primarily a cross-sectional data problem, arises when the range of y (and hence ε) values rise or fall with some variable.

An example of this can be seen by referring to the demand equation discussed earlier in this chapter. When the price of x is low, the range for quantity demanded (and thus the disturbances) may well be substantial, for real income is greater the lower the price of this good. When price rises, mean quantity demanded falls. The dispersion in q may also fall, as willingness to pay is more likely to exceed ability to pay at this price level. The error variance for the low price will then exceed that for the higher price, violating the assumption of homoskedasticity.

3. $\text{Cov}(\varepsilon_i, \varepsilon_j) = 0.$

A zero covariance between the errors in an equation is called the absence of **serial correlation**. When this assumption is satisfied, the disturbance terms are pairwise uncorrelated, and deviations of y around its mean consist entirely of random fluctuations.

Serial correlation is a time series problem, in which the disturbance term from one time period is correlated with those from other periods. Serially correlated errors thus display a nonrandom pattern, where the deviation of y from its mean in one time period is determined by previous deviations. Economic data most frequently contain positive serial correlation, where positive (i.e., above average) errors tend to follow positive errors, and vice versa. A large string of positive or negative errors is viewed as evidence of the existence of serial correlation.

---

[7] If the variable z expressed as a deviation from its mean, the expected error will then equal 0. It is assumed here that z is not in deviation form, however.

[8] The basis for this statement derives from the fact that the small sample estimator properties are repeated sampling properties. These pertain only to outcomes we can expect to observe on average; they say nothing about results for a single estimation.

4. *x* is nonstochastic, or, if stochastic, uncorrelated with ε.

When x is nonstochastic, the set of values taken by x remain fixed in repeated samples, and the values of x are totally under the control of the researcher. Unfortunately, this is more likely to be the exception rather than the rule in econometric research. However, the least squares estimators can retain their desirable properties even when this condition is violated. This assumption is utilized mainly for convenience, since it simplifies the expressions for expected values used in deriving estimator properties.

When x is nonstochastic, we may treat it as a constant when taking expected values, so that $E(x) = x$ and $E[x - E(x)] = x - E(x)$. Also, $\text{Cov}(x_i, \varepsilon_i) = 0$. We can see this using the expectation definition of covariance:

$$\text{Cov}(x_i, \varepsilon_i) = E[x_i - E(x_i)][\varepsilon_i - E(\varepsilon_i)]$$
$$= [x_i - E(x_i)]E(\varepsilon_i)$$
$$= 0 \qquad \text{(using Assumption (1))}$$

This covariance is also 0 when x is stochastic, provided that x and ε are statistically independent. In this case:

$$\text{Cov}(x_i, \varepsilon_i) = E(x_i\varepsilon_i) - E(x_i)E(\varepsilon_i)$$
$$= 0$$

since if x and ε are independent, $E(x_i\varepsilon_i) = E(x_i)E(\varepsilon_i)$.

The zero covariance between ε_i and x_i implies that the equation error is uncorrelated with the explanatory variable, and that the population regression function:

$$y_i = \alpha_0 + \alpha_1 x_i + \varepsilon_i$$

contains x and ε as distinct influences. This allows us to ascertain the individual contribution of each of these terms on y with least squares.

PROPERTIES OF THE LEAST SQUARES ESTIMATORS

Estimation of the bivariate population regression function with least squares produces the best linear unbiased estimators of α_1 and α_2 when the assumptions outlined earlier are met. This section will establish the linearity and unbiasedness of the slope estimator, $\hat{\alpha}_1$. The "best" property for both least squares estimators is based on a theorem that is cited in the next section but not proven.

We will first show that $\hat{\alpha}_1$ is a linear estimator. The linearity property is satisfied when it is possible to express $\hat{\alpha}_1$ as a linear function of the sample values of y. The slope estimator formula is:

$$\hat{\alpha}_1 = \sum x_i' y_i' / \sum x_i'^2.$$

The denominator of this expression, the sum of the squared x-deviations, is a constant. Its numerator can be expressed in terms of y_i. To see this:

$$\sum x_i' y_i' = \sum (x_i - \hat{\mu}_x)(y_i - \hat{\mu}_y)$$
$$= \sum (x_i - \hat{\mu}_x) y_i - \hat{\mu}_y \sum (x_i - \hat{\mu}_x)$$
$$\sum x_i' y_i' = \sum (x_i - \hat{\mu}_x) y_i, \tag{4.20}$$

since the sum of the x-deviations, $\sum (x_i - \hat{\mu}_x)$, equals 0. If we replace the numerator of the formula for $\hat{\alpha}_1$ with Equation (4.20):

$$\hat{\alpha}_1 = \sum x_i' y_i' / \sum x_i'^2$$

and denote $\omega_i \equiv x_i' / \sum x_i'^2$, this formula becomes:

$$\hat{\alpha}_1 = \sum \omega_i y_i = \omega_1 y_1 + \cdots + \omega_n y_n \tag{4.21}$$

Equation (4.21) shows that $\hat{\alpha}_1$ is a linear estimator. More specifically, $\hat{\alpha}_1$ is a weighted average of individual y values, with the ω_i's as weights.

Establishing the unbiasedness of $\hat{\alpha}_1$ requires that we express this formula in terms of the population parameter α_1. This is accomplished by deriving an expression for the population regression function in terms of both y_i' and α_1. The steps involved are as follows. Starting with the stochastic form of the population regression function:

$$y_i = \alpha_0 + \alpha_1 x_i + \varepsilon_i,$$

we sum both sides of this equation, then divide by n:

$$\sum y_i = \sum \alpha_0 + \sum \alpha_1 x_i + \sum \varepsilon_i$$
$$= n\alpha_0 + \alpha_1 \sum x_i + \sum \varepsilon_i$$
$$\hat{\mu}_y = \alpha_0 + \alpha_1 \hat{\mu}_x + \hat{\mu}_\varepsilon. \tag{4.22}$$

Subtracting Equation (4.22) from the population regression function:

$$(y_i - \hat{\mu}_y) = (\alpha_0 - \alpha_0) + \alpha_1 (x_i - \hat{\mu}_x) + (\varepsilon_i - \hat{\mu}_\varepsilon)$$
$$= \alpha_1 (x_i - \hat{\mu}_x) + (\varepsilon_i - \hat{\mu}_\varepsilon).$$

Stating this in deviation form:

$$y_i' = \alpha_1 x_i' + \varepsilon_i' \tag{4.23}$$

where $\varepsilon_i' \equiv (\varepsilon_i - \hat{\mu}_\varepsilon)$. Equation (4.23) is the **deviation form of the population regression function** (PRF). It is given this name since both of its variables are expressed as deviations from means. Note that the intercept is excluded since the use of x_i' and y_i' involves changing the origin of this function from $(0, 0)$ to $(\hat{\mu}_x, \hat{\mu}_y)$.

This form of the population regression function is illustrated in Figure 4.7. The vertical intercept of the original population regression function is α_0 and this function passes through the point $(\hat{\mu}_x, \hat{\mu}_y)$. The deviation form has the point of means as its origin. While α_0 no longer pertains, the slope remains equal to α_1.

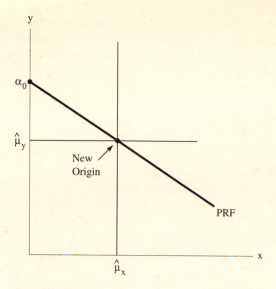

Figure 4.7 Deviation form of the population regression function

The deviation form of the population regression function expresses y_i', which is in the numerator of the formula for $\hat{\alpha}_1$, in terms of the population parameter α_1. This is an important equation that will be used many times throughout the remainder of this text. Ascertaining the properties of the least squares slope estimator can now proceed.

To show that $\hat{\alpha}_1$ is unbiased, we substitute the deviation form of the population regression function (Equation (4.23)) into the formula for $\hat{\alpha}_1$:

$$\hat{\alpha}_1 = \sum x_i' y_i' / \sum x_i'^2$$
$$= \sum x_i'(\alpha_1 x_i' + \varepsilon_i') / \sum x_i'^2$$
$$= (\alpha_1 \sum x_i'^2 + \sum x_i'\varepsilon_i') / \sum x_i'^2,$$

or

$$\hat{\alpha}_1 = \alpha_1 + (\sum x_i'\varepsilon_i' / \sum x_i'^2) \tag{4.24}$$

By manipulating Equation (4.24), we can express $\hat{\alpha}_1$ in terms of the individual errors, ε_i, and not the error deviations. Expanding the numerator of the bracketed expression on the right of Equation (4.24):

$$\sum x_i'\varepsilon_i' = \sum x_i'(\varepsilon_i - \hat{\mu}_\varepsilon)$$
$$= \sum x_i'\varepsilon_i - \hat{\mu}_\varepsilon \sum x_i'$$
$$= \sum x_i'\varepsilon_i$$

since $\sum x_i' = 0$. If we substitute this result into Equation (4.24), we can express $\hat{\alpha}_1$ as:

$$\hat{\alpha}_1 = \alpha_1 + (\sum x_i'\varepsilon_i / \sum x_i'^2) \tag{4.24'}$$

The least squares slope estimator equals its population parameter plus a term related to the equation errors. If the expected value of $\hat{\alpha}_1$ equals α_1, this estimator is unbiased. Assumptions concerning the population are required to make this determination. Specifically, it is necessary for us to invoke the set of assumptions stated earlier for the population regression function.

The expected value of Equation (4.24) is:

$$E(\hat{\alpha}_1) = \alpha_1 + E(\sum x_i' \varepsilon_i / \sum x_i'^2). \tag{4.25}$$

This estimator is unbiased if the last term on the right equals zero. This does not require that the *actual* value of this term is zero—only its expected value. The term in the bracket can be expressed as a weighted average of the ε_i values. The weights are those used to establish the linearity of $\hat{\alpha}_1$. If we again let $\omega_i \equiv x_i' / \sum x_i'^2$, the bracketed term then becomes:

$$\sum x_i' \varepsilon_i / \sum x_i'^2 = \sum \omega_i \varepsilon_i = \omega_1 \varepsilon_1 + \cdots + \omega_n \varepsilon_n,$$

which has an expected value of:

$$E(\sum \omega_i \varepsilon_i) = \omega_1 E(\varepsilon_1) + \cdots + \omega_n E(\varepsilon_n),$$
$$= \omega_1(0) + \cdots + \omega_n(0)$$
$$= 0$$

using model assumption (4), that x is a nonstochastic explanatory variable (and therefore equal to its expected value), and (1), that $E(\varepsilon_i) = 0$. When we substitute this result into Equation (4.25), we see that $\hat{\alpha}_1$ is an unbiased estimator of α_1:

$$E(\hat{\alpha}_1) = \alpha_1 + 0$$
$$= \alpha_1.$$

As long as x is either nonstochastic or uncorrelated with ε, and no major variable influencing y has been omitted from the sample regression function (so that $E(\varepsilon_i) = 0$), the least squares slope estimator is unbiased.

The unbiasedness of $\hat{\alpha}_1$ does not guarantee that individual estimates will equal α_1 every time we employ the least squares technique. Unbiasedness is a repeated sampling property. The unbiasedness of this estimator establishes only that the mean of its sampling distribution coincides with α_1. Least squares estimation of this parameter thus produces estimates equal to α_1 *on average*, when both the sampling and estimation processes are repeated a large number of times. Remember also that unbiasedness says nothing about the precision with which this parameter is estimated. The latter is determined by the variance of the sampling distribution. Figure 4.8 shows two possible sampling distributions for an unbiased estimator $\hat{\alpha}_1$. Distribution I is preferable, since the likelihood of obtaining a "very bad" estimate with a single use of least squares is smaller for that distribution. On average, both sampling distributions are associated with the value α_1, but the probability of obtaining an estimate below a or above b is greater for distribution II.

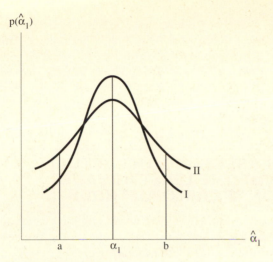

Figure 4.8 Two sampling distributions for an unbiased slope estimator

BEST LINEAR UNBIASED ESTIMATORS

The preceding discussion established that $\hat{\alpha}_1$ is a linear unbiased estimator of its population parameter, α_1. The corresponding results for $\hat{\alpha}_0$ are derived in an appendix. We have not yet shown these estimators to be best, however. Recall that an estimator is "best" if it possesses the property of efficiency; that is, it has the smallest variance of all the unbiased estimators of a parameter. The **Gauss-Markov Theorem** establishes that the least squares estimators are indeed the minimum variance linear estimators of α_0 and α_1:

GAUSS MARKOV THEOREM.   If all the assumptions regarding the population regression function are met, then the least squares estimators $\hat{\alpha}_0$ and $\hat{\alpha}_1$ are the best linear unbiased estimators of population parameters α_0 and α_1, respectively.

This statement can be viewed as evidence attesting to the fact that under *ideal* conditions, the least squares technique provides the minimum variance linear unbiased estimators of the parameters in the population regression function. This theorem does not, however, provide any guarantee for the results of a single estimation. As Chapter 2 showed, $\hat{\mu}_x$, which is a best linear unbiased estimator, can produce unsatisfactory estimates if used once or a small number of times.

These small sample estimator properties refer to the *sampling distribution* of an estimator. If one or more of the underlying assumptions are violated, the least squares estimators can lose their desirable estimator properties. A great deal of the material in the remainder of this text deals with specific violations of the assumptions.[9]

In addition to these small sample properties, the least squares estimators of α_0 and α_1 also possess the large sample property of consistency. As sample size increases, the variances of the sampling distributions of the least squares estimators fall, tending toward 0 as sample size approaches infinity. Thus, estimation precision rises as sample size is increased.

A METHOD FOR ASSESSING THE ACTUAL PERFORMANCE OF THE LEAST SQUARES TECHNIQUE: MONTE CARLO METHODS

The least squares criterion produces the best linear unbiased estimators of the parameters in the population regression function so long as the previously discussed conditions are met. The formulas for these estimators are:

$$\hat{\alpha}_0 = \hat{\mu}_y - \hat{\alpha}_1\hat{\mu}_x$$

$$\hat{\alpha}_1 = \sum x_i' y_i' / \sum x_i'^2.$$

The parameters of their sampling distributions (the variances are derived in the Appendix) are:

	MEAN	VARIANCE
$\hat{\alpha}_0$	α_0	$\sigma_\varepsilon^2 \sum x_i^2 / n \sum x_i'^2$
$\hat{\alpha}_1$	α_1	$\sigma_\varepsilon^2 / \sum x_i'^2$

We never observe the sampling distribution of an estimator in actual practice, as we utilize least squares to estimate a single set of estimates for the coefficients in the population regression function. The small sample properties of the least squares estimators reflect the outcomes that would exist on average, were we to perform many such regressions. The large sample property of consistency pertains to the added estimation precision that results from increasing sample size.

A methodology exists that can provide us with information about what the sampling distribution of an estimator actually looks like. It entails calculating many least squares estimates, and it imitates the repeated sampling context used to establish the properties of the least squares estimators. This is called the **Monte Carlo Method**. In the actual practice of econometrics, we acquire a sample of data, then use

---

[9] An analogy may be helpful. The situation here is like that of a perfectly competitive economy. If a set of assumptions are met, this economy will be run by the most efficient system possible. If assumptions are violated, problems such as market failure will result. In econometrics the similar conditions are the population regression function assumptions. Violating these might lead to "estimator failure."

least squares to estimate unknown parameters. In a **Monte Carlo Experiment** this process is reversed. We begin by selecting values for the coefficients in our population regression function. This allows us to work within a framework of *known* coefficients. We then construct data using these coefficients and the model assumptions under which the least squares estimators attain their desirable properties. When the process of data creation is complete, we next perform a number of least squares regressions. This simulates the repeated sampling context under which the small sample properties of these estimators pertain. We then judge the extent to which the actual performance of least squares estimation matches our prior expectations.

Let us illustrate the steps involved in this procedure. We will assume that the population regression function is:

$$y_i = 15 + 1.5x_i + \varepsilon_i.$$

Our known population coefficients are $\alpha_0 = 15$ and $\alpha_1 = 1.5$. The population (conditional) mean of y is therefore $E(y|x_i) = 15 + 1.5x_i$. We will use a sample size of 100 for each of 50 regressions in the initial part of this Monte Carlo Experiment. Model assumption (4) states that the observations on x are fixed in repeated samples. To satisfy this assumption, a *single* set of 100 x values was generated from the uniform random number generator in SAS. Using our population coefficients, we then calculate the conditional mean of y for this set of x values from the formula:

$$E(y|x_i) = 15 + 1.5x_i \qquad (i = 1, 2, \ldots, 100)$$

To generate the 50 sets of y observations that we will use in our regressions, we must first create 50 sets of error observations. After these have been generated, each set of 100 errors is combined with the single set of 100 values for $E(y|x_i)$ to create these dependent variable sets.

The error sets were produced using the normal distribution random number generator in SAS. Each of these has (approximately) a 0 mean and unit variance. If we denote the first set of (100) observations on the stochastic error by $\varepsilon^{(1)}$, then, the first y variable, $y^{(1)}$, is constructed in the following way:

$$y_i^{(1)} = 15 + 1.5x_i + \varepsilon_i^{(1)} \qquad (i = 1, 2, \ldots, 100)$$

These same coefficients and observations on x are used along with the remaining set of errors to derive the other 49 y variables:

$$y_i^{(2)} = 15 + 1.5x_i + \varepsilon_i^{(2)}$$
$$\cdots$$
$$y_i^{(50)} = 15 + 1.5x_i + \varepsilon_i^{(50)}$$

We now have enough data to perform 50 regressions. Of course, a great many more than 50 regressions are required to approximate these sampling distributions more closely. But, as you will soon see, very clear and distinct sampling distribution patterns appear even with this relatively small number of regressions. More important, the results of these experiments will help clarify the statements made earlier about how the error variance and the dispersion in x values affect the sampling distributions of our estimators.

Table 4.1 Monte Carlo Regression Coefficients from 50 Regressions Where the Population Regression Function Is:

$$y_i = 15 + 1.5x_i + \varepsilon_i$$

	$\hat{\alpha}_0$	$\hat{\alpha}_1$		$\hat{\alpha}_0$	$\hat{\alpha}_1$
(1)	15.0136	1.50869	(26)	15.1821	1.47520
(2)	15.2760	1.43891	(27)	14.9790	1.52966
(3)	14.8368	1.57052	(28)	14.9941	1.50673
(4)	14.7106	1.57106	(29)	15.7439	1.38393
(5)	14.8016	1.52837	(30)	15.4473	1.40231
(6)	14.9239	1.50612	(31)	14.7545	1.55850
(7)	14.9972	1.49489	(32)	14.2339	1.65311
(8)	14.6310	1.60056	(33)	14.7732	1.56149
(9)	15.1411	1.48360	(34)	15.0047	1.50319
(10)	15.2150	1.43204	(35)	14.7150	1.53634
(11)	14.3380	1.62075	(36)	14.9010	1.49593
(12)	14.7171	1.54672	(37)	15.4362	1.46455
(13)	15.2671	1.41111	(38)	14.5980	1.58558
(14)	15.3824	1.40563	(39)	14.8368	1.50907
(15)	14.6032	1.56452	(40)	15.0798	1.45679
(16)	14.8807	1.54018	(41)	14.4312	1.56911
(17)	14.6254	1.54642	(42)	14.4924	1.60725
(18)	15.2435	1.46436	(43)	15.4308	1.42700
(19)	14.8301	1.56908	(44)	15.1744	1.46603
(20)	14.8603	1.51246	(45)	15.0780	1.48625
(21)	15.3190	1.42877	(46)	14.8987	1.49987
(22)	14.9459	1.50386	(47)	15.3552	1.43206
(23)	15.3131	1.45126	(48)	15.0169	1.47518
(24)	14.7409	1.52148	(49)	14.9810	1.49968
(25)	15.1253	1.47251	(50)	14.3801	1.63890

	MEAN	VARIANCE
INTERCEPTS	14.95314281	0.10309907
SLOPES	1.50835146	0.00402339

In these equations, $n = 100$, $\hat{\sigma}_x^2 = 2.8$, $\hat{\sigma}_\varepsilon^2 = 1.1$.

Table 4.1 shows the set of 50 coefficients that are obtained from this Monte Carlo Experiment. None of these regressions replicates the population parameters exactly, although several come extremely close. Estimates of α_0 range from 14.2339 to 15.7439, with a variance of 0.103. The values of $\hat{\alpha}_1$ run from 1.3839 to 1.6531, with a variance of 0.004.

Because the least squares estimators are unbiased (we have satisfied all of the required assumptions), the average estimate from a large number of regressions should closely approximate the population parameter for each of our coefficients. The bottom of this table shows that with only 50 regressions, we have approximated this expectation very closely. The average for $\hat{\alpha}_0$, 14.953, differs from its population parameter by one-third of one percent. The mean of the slope estimates, 1.508, also diverges from its population parameter by less than one percent. Figure 4.9(**b**) illustrates the sampling distribution for the slope estimator. After performing only 50 regressions, it is apparent that this distribution is fairly symmetrical around the population parameter value of 1.5.

Another aspect of least squares estimation, which was not presented earlier, pertains to the covariance between the least squares coefficients. This is an important consideration, as it is informative to know whether the sign of the sampling error from any one of these coefficients bears any systematic relationship to that from the other coefficient. For example, if one coefficient is overestimated will the other tend to be overestimated or underestimated? The expression for this covariance is[10]:

$$\text{Cov}(\hat{\alpha}_0, \hat{\alpha}_1) = -\hat{\mu}_x(\sigma_\varepsilon^2/\sum x_i^2)$$

The term in brackets, which is the variance of $\hat{\alpha}_1$, is positive. The sign of this covariance is therefore the opposite of that for $\hat{\mu}_x$. If, for example, $\hat{\mu}_x$ is positive, which is the case for this Monte Carlo experiment, this covariance is negative. We should then expect the sampling errors of $\hat{\alpha}_0$ and $\hat{\alpha}_1$ to differ in sign. Sample regression functions that understate the slope coefficient will thus tend to overestimate the intercept, while those with underestimated intercepts will tend to overestimate the slope coefficient. This pattern is apparent in the Monte Carlo regressions of Table 4.1. Among the first ten regressions, (2), (9), and (10) overstate the intercept (overlooking rounding error). Each of these, in turn, understates the slope coefficient. Regressions (3), (4), (5), and (8) understate the intercept and overstate the intercept. Examine the remaining regressions to verify the presence of this pattern.

The Monte Carlo Method allows us to ascertain the effect of sample size on the precision of least squares estimation. The least squares estimators are consistent: as sample size rises, the variance of the sampling distribution for each estimator falls, approaching 0 as sample size continues to rise. Thus, our coefficients should be more precisely estimated the greater is sample size. Figure 4.9(**a**) shows the sampling distribution when sample size (for each of 50 regressions) is 20. Note that the estimates of $\hat{\alpha}_1$ vary over a wider range than is true for either of the other sample sizes and that this sampling distribution is not well defined. The variance of the estimated slope coefficients falls from 0.382 with this sample size, to 0.004 when sample size is 100 (Figure 4.9(**b**)), then to 0.001 for $n = 500$ (Figure 4.9(**c**)). The sampling distributions for $\hat{\alpha}_1$ thus become better defined and noticeably more compact around 1.5 as sample size increases, which is exactly what the consistency property leads us to expect.

---

[10] This is derived in J. Kmenta, *Elements of Econometrics* (2d ed.) (New York: Macmillan), 1986, pp. 226–228.

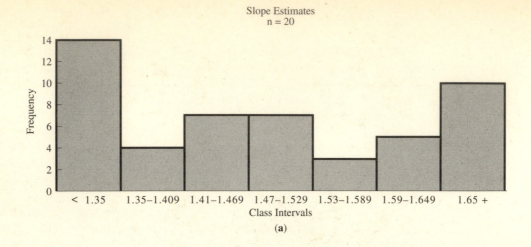

(a)

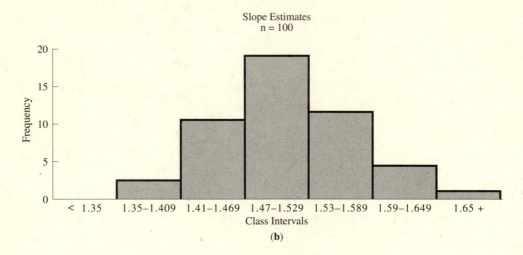

(b)

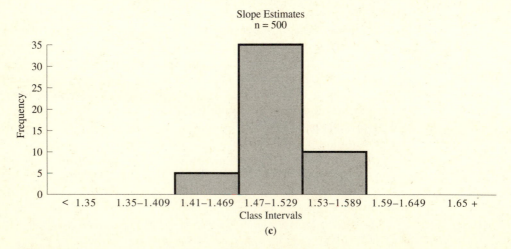

(c)

Figure 4.9

Table 4.2   Comparison of Fifteen Slope Coefficients with Sample Size of 100, Differing in Error Variance and x Variance

	ORIGINAL $(\hat{\sigma}_x^2 = 2.8, \hat{\sigma}_\varepsilon^2 = 1.1)$	$\sigma_x^2 = 2.8, \hat{\sigma}_\varepsilon^2 = 9$	$\hat{\sigma}_x^2 = 0.6, \hat{\sigma}_\varepsilon^2 = 1.1$
(1)	1.50869	1.31968	1.63428
(2)	1.43891	1.23433	1.59200
(3)	1.57052	1.48733	1.67584
(4)	1.57106	1.54078	1.63455
(5)	1.52837	1.52045	1.88366
(6)	1.50612	1.15798	1.56652
(7)	1.49489	1.16814	1.48586
(8)	1.60056	1.57779	1.57130
(9)	1.48360	1.97841	1.17820
(10)	1.43204	1.39422	1.68131
(11)	1.62075	1.01008	1.37074
(12)	1.54672	1.50449	1.23924
(13)	1.41111	1.36986	1.71136
(14)	1.40563	1.16275	1.12649
(15)	1.56452	1.73110	1.75300
	FOR ALL 50 REGRESSIONS		
Mean	1.5084	1.4763	1.507
Variance	0.004	0.044	0.049

Table 4.2 illustrates how the error variance and the dispersion in x values individually affect least squares estimation of the slope coefficient. The second column of this table reports the results of the first 15 regressions when the error variance is increased from its original value of 1 to 9. In contrast to the original fifteen regressions, where $\hat{\alpha}_1$ varies from 1.406 to 1.621, coefficient estimates now range from 1.01 to 1.978. For the entire set of regressions, the average estimate of this parameter is 1.476 when the error variance is increased, versus 1.508 with the original error dispersion. Our earlier sampling distribution discussion showed that the variance of the stochastic error is directly related to the dispersion in the sampling distribution of each coefficient. From this, we predict that the larger is σ_ε^2, the greater will be the dispersion in the sampling distribution of either least squares estimator. The results in the second column of Table 4.2 bear out this expectation: the variance of the slope estimates rises more than tenfold, from 0.004 to 0.044. The greater range of estimates reflects this. The reasoning that underlies this can be explained very simply. A large error variance reflects the existence of a great deal of random variation in y. As a result, the systematic part of y, which is represented by the equation specification, leaves a substantial portion of the actual variation in y unexplained.

The third column of Table 4.2 illustrates that a smaller dispersion in x values affects estimation precision in much the same way as did the increase in σ_ε^2. The variance of the entire 50 regressions rises from 0.004 (with the original x and error variances) to 0.049 when x displays a smaller variance. When the variation in x is small, the least squares estimators must be derived using a fairly limited amount of information about x. Relatively minor changes in x are thus given substantial importance when estimating the conditional mean of y, and the precision with which least squares can estimate the sample regression function coefficients falls. As a result, sampling distribution variances are higher than would be the case if more information about x were used in the estimation process.

Finally, Table 4.3 combines all the previously considered influences, and contrasts the results of the original regressions with those resulting from a "small" sample size, "large" error variance, and a "small" x variance. The differences between these coefficients are striking. These "Worst Case" regressions display dramatic divergences from both the original estimates and the actual coefficients. The intercept estimates range from 4.316 to 33.15, with a mean of 13.474 and a variance of 61.85.

Table 4.3 Comparison of Fifteen Monte Carlo Regressions with PRF:
$$y_i = 15 + 1.5x_i + \varepsilon_i$$

	INTERCEPT		SLOPE	
	ORIGINAL	"WORST CASE"	ORIGINAL	"WORST CASE"
(1)	15.0136	6.4060	1.50869	5.2687
(2)	15.2760	7.6889	1.43891	4.4746
(3)	14.8368	16.9250	1.57052	0.8860
(4)	14.7106	26.3459	1.57106	−3.6778
(5)	14.8016	17.3799	1.52837	0.3501
(6)	14.9239	11.4734	1.50612	3.0764
(7)	14.9972	4.3164	1.49489	5.3758
(8)	14.6310	7.1112	1.60056	5.4925
(9)	15.1411	19.6498	1.48360	−0.5927
(10)	15.2150	33.2494	1.43204	−6.8145
(11)	14.3380	19.0551	1.62075	0.0969
(12)	14.7171	27.6771	1.54672	−4.5936
(13)	15.2671	18.1649	1.41111	0.0757
(14)	15.3824	10.7272	1.40563	3.0900
(15)	14.6032	13.3413	1.56452	2.4509
	FOR ALL 50 REGRESSIONS			
Mean	14.95	13.47	1.508	2.23
Variance	0.103	61.85	0.004	12.13

In the "Worst Case" Regressions, sample size is 20 ("small"), the errors have a 0 mean and a variance of 9 ("large"); and x has a mean of 2.24 and a variance of 0.024 ("small"). In the Original regressions, $n = 100$, the error variance is smaller than that in the "Worst Case" regressions, and the variance of x is larger than in the "Worst Case" Regressions.

Sign reversal now appears with the slope coefficients. Estimates extend from -6.815 to $+5.493$. Their mean is 2.227, while the variance of these coefficients rises from 0.004 with the original model to 12.125. As this last exercise shows, least squares estimation, which produces the best linear unbiased estimators of α_0 and α_1, does not guarantee successful results whenever this technique is used.

CRITERIA FOR EVALUATING A SAMPLE REGRESSION FUNCTION

Several factors should be considered when evaluating whether the performance of a sample regression function is acceptable. One must assess the signs and magnitudes of individual coefficients, the size of the errors associated with the sample regression function, and how well the estimated equation fits the data. Each of these will now be discussed.

Coefficients

Economic theory should be employed as the basis for specifying the population regression function. Theory indicates the appropriate explanatory variable to include in this function, and often specifies the expected signs for the coefficients. In light of such prior expectations, the presence of sign reversal for either or both of the coefficients in the sample regression function is an important indicator that problems exist.

For example, an estimated demand equation with a positive slope for price signals the presence of a problem. When this occurs, it is advisable to examine the estimated equation further, attempting to detect additional problems, such as a negative intercept. The intercept estimator is the vehicle by which least squares produces a zero average residual. One author refers to this estimator as a "garbage term," since it absorbs the mean influence of omitted variables, and a nonzero mean of the estimated errors.[11] Sometimes the estimated slope coefficient does not suggest any problems, while the sign of the intercept estimator is incorrect. In this case, potential problems exist for *both* coefficients. An incorrect sign for the estimated intercept often indicates the likelihood of either measurement error problems with one or both of the variables included in the sample regression function, or the omission of important variables. Either of these complications can affect the signs or the magnitudes of the estimated coefficients.

The magnitudes of estimated coefficients are also important indicators of equation performance. Determining whether the magnitude of an estimated slope is acceptable is sometimes more difficult than checking for its expected sign. The magnitude of the intercept, which measures the estimated mean of y when x is zero,

---

[11] See H. Cassidy, *Using Econometrics: A Beginner's Guide* (Reston VA: Reston), 1981 for a discussion of this and other factors relevant to this estimator.

is less obvious yet, since this value for x is typically well outside the sample range of values for this variable.

Problems with coefficient magnitudes are related to whether these are "too small" or "too large." These terms must be given operational significance if they are to be useful when judging equations. A variable that does not belong in an equation has a zero slope coefficient in the *population* regression function. If x does not explain the behavior of y, then y will not vary as the direct result of changes in x. The slope of an equation expressing y as a function of x will therefore be zero, which, when graphed, produces a horizontal line.

If we include this "irrelevant" explanatory variable in a sample regression function, then, because $\hat{\alpha}_1$ is unbiased, we can expect to obtain the true value of 0 *on average*, but not every time we estimate the population regression function. If our estimate of α_1 is 0.003, does this indicate an acceptable or unacceptable magnitude?

Technically it is unacceptable, for this estimate implies that x belongs in the equation. The difference between $\hat{\alpha}_1$ and α_1 in this example is attributable to sampling error. On the other hand, $\hat{\alpha}_1$ does not differ that much from α_1. How do we determine when this difference is too large? This determination is made statistically, based on hypothesis testing. This topic is outlined in Chapter 5. For now, we can state two guidelines that are useful in determining the acceptability of an estimated slope coefficient. One method that assists in this determination is referencing papers or journal articles that estimate this same relationship. Compare your estimates with these and determine if and why any disparities exist. A second solution involves converting the slope coefficient into an estimated elasticity.

Sometimes we know an expected elasticity *range* for a slope coefficient, even though the reasonableness of the magnitude itself is not obvious. Consider the following demand equation for automobiles:

$$q_t = \alpha_0 + \alpha_1 p_t + \varepsilon_t,$$

where q is retail sales of automobiles (in thousands of units per year) and p is the CPI for new cars. The expected sign of α_1 is negative. If p rises by one unit how much should q decrease? The answer to this question is not obvious unless we consult existing literature on this topic. However, the demand for automobiles is price elastic. We can use this information to evaluate the magnitude of our estimator of α_1.

The sample regression function for automobile demand is:

$$q_t = \hat{\alpha}_0 + \hat{\alpha}_1 p_t + \hat{\varepsilon}_t.$$

The expected sign of $\hat{\alpha}_0$ is positive, and that of $\hat{\alpha}_1$ is negative. How do we transform $\hat{\alpha}_1$ into an estimated demand elasticity? The general formula for the elasticity of y with respect to x (η) is:

$$\eta = (\%\Delta y / \%\Delta x).$$

If we replace the numerator and denominator in this expression with the percent change formula given in Chapter 3, we can express this elasticity as:

$$\eta = (x/y)(\Delta y / \Delta x)$$

or, using p and q:

$$\eta = (p/q)(\Delta q/\Delta p).$$

The ratio $(\Delta q/\Delta p)$ is the slope of the demand equation, α_1. If we substitute this coefficient into the above formula, the elasticity is:

$$\eta = (p/q)\alpha_1$$

The least squares estimate of this elasticity uses $\hat{\alpha}_1$ in place of α_1:

$$\hat{\eta} = (p/q)\hat{\alpha}_1$$

If the (absolute) value of $\hat{\eta}_d$ exceeds 1, the demand for automobiles is price elastic, as expected. If this magnitude is less than or equal to 1, demand is inelastic or unit elastic, respectively, indicating a problem with the magnitude of $\hat{\alpha}_1$.

Values for p and q must be selected before we can calculate this elasticity. One possible choice is the mean of each variable, which produces an estimate of the elasticity at the means (η_M):

$$\hat{\eta}_M = (\hat{\mu}_p/\hat{\mu}_q)\hat{\alpha}_1$$

Other choices exist, such as values from the most recent time period, or policy-relevant values for p and q. If the absolute value of the estimated elasticity exceeds one, the slope coefficient passes this test for determining acceptable coefficient magnitudes.

The Size of Errors

The least squares technique produces a zero average residual. This technique was chosen because it minimizes the sum of the squared residuals. The sampling distributions of these estimators depend on the variance of the error term. Specifically, the numerators for the variances of both $\hat{\alpha}_0$ and $\hat{\alpha}_1$ are functions of σ_ε^2. Before we can compute the parameters of the sampling distributions of the least squares estimators, we must therefore estimate this variance.

An unbiased estimator of the population error variance is given by the following formula:

$$\hat{\sigma}_\varepsilon^2 = \sum \hat{\varepsilon}_i^2/(n - 2). \tag{4.26}$$

Some computer programs (such as SAS) refer to this estimator as the **mean square error** of the equation. This should not be confused with the mean square error property of estimators discussed in Chapter 2. The denominator in this expression is called the number of degrees of freedom. By using this in place of n, an unbiased estimator of σ_ε^2 is obtained. Note that the numerator in this expression is stated entirely in terms of estimated errors, which are known values.

The dependent variable and the error possess the same unit of measurement. The estimator given by Equation (4.26) is expressed in the same units as any variance: the square of the units for the variable it refers to. To alleviate the incompatibility between the units of measurement for y and $\hat{\sigma}_\varepsilon^2$, we utilize the standard deviation of Equation (4.26):

$$\hat{\sigma}_\varepsilon = \sqrt{\frac{\sum \hat{\varepsilon}_i^2}{(n-2)}}, \tag{4.27}$$

which is referred to as either the **standard error** of the equation, or the **root mean squared error** of the sample regression function. The unit of measurement for $\hat{\sigma}_\varepsilon$ is identical to that for y. The value of this estimator measures the average error associated with the sample regression function. The following analogy provides a more intuitive definition of the standard error:

> The sample regression function and its standard error are to a scatter diagram of data what the mean and standard deviation are to a sample of observations on a single variable.[12]

If we utilize the value of the standard error as the basis for choosing among sample regression functions, then the function with the smallest $\hat{\sigma}_\varepsilon$ should be the preferred equation. For example, if we estimate the following population regression functions:

$$y_i = \alpha_0 + \alpha_1 x_1 + \varepsilon_i$$

$$y_i = \beta_0 + \beta_1 x_1^2 + v_i,$$

then, using this criterion, we consider the sample regression function with the lower standard error to be the better equation. The important point to remember is that *the standard error has the same unit of measurement as the dependent variable. Since both of these equations have the same dependent variable, the comparison of standard errors is meaningful.* Of course, other criteria, such as signs and magnitudes of the coefficients, should be employed as well.

If we estimate the following two population regression functions:

$$y_i = \alpha_0 + \alpha_1 x_i + \varepsilon_i$$

$$\ln(y_i) = \beta_0 + \beta_1 \ln(x_i) + v_i$$

the standard errors of these equations are *not* comparable. In the first equation, $\hat{\sigma}_\varepsilon$ is measured in units of y. The standard error in the second equation, which is the log-linear form for the first equation, is expressed in units of the natural logarithm of y. If we mechanically select the equation with the smallest standard error, the log-linear equation would virtually always be chosen. Comparing $\hat{\sigma}_\varepsilon$ with $\hat{\sigma}_v$ is analogous to adding apples and oranges.

A method exists, however, that allows us to compare sample regression functions with different dependent variables. The problem in the previous example, the lack of a basis of comparison, is alleviated when we associate the standard error of

---

[12] Freedman, Pisani, and Purvis, *op. cit.*

an estimated equation with the mean of its dependent variable. This ratio is the **coefficient of variation** (C.V.):

$$C.V. = \hat{\sigma}_\varepsilon / \hat{\mu}_y,$$

or   **(4.28)**

$$C.V. = (\hat{\sigma}_\varepsilon / \hat{\mu}_y) \cdot 100$$

in percent form. The coefficient of variation measures the average error of the sample regression function relative to the mean of y. The lower the coefficient of variation, the better the performance of the sample regression function, since the average error will be low in comparison to the mean of y. Furthermore, linear and log-linear equations can be meaningfully compared using this measure. In the previous example, $\hat{\sigma}_v$, the standard error of the log-linear function, was smaller than $\hat{\sigma}_\varepsilon$ from the linear form. The coefficient of variation in the log-linear equation relates its lower standard error to the smaller mean of its dependent variable, the natural logarithm of y. The equation whose standard error is smaller relative to the mean of its dependent variable will thus have the smaller C.V. and should be the preferred equation using this criterion. One rule of thumb sometimes used to judge the overall level of the coefficient of variation is the following: *If the coefficient of variation is no greater than 0.2 (or 20 percent), the standard error in that equation is viewed as satisfactory.* Values of C.V. in excess of 0.2 (or 20 percent) indicate unacceptably high residuals.

This is not, by any means, a foolproof method for judging equation performance. The coefficient of variation in a cross-sectional equation can easily exceed this "rule of thumb" value, even when the equation is well specified. Since cross-sectional data bases often contain a great deal of random variation, relatively large values of σ_ε^2 result. At the opposite extreme, the coefficient of variation in a poorly specified time series equation can fall within this range. The coefficient of variation is thus not a flawless measure. It is advisable to evaluate an equation using the coefficient of variation as but one of *several* criteria.

Two additional points about this measure should be stated. First, sample regression functions with very low C.V.s might not perform well when used to predict future values of y. Second, some dependent variables, such as inflation rates (which are percent changes), are inherently difficult to model. A well-specified equation with this type of dependent variable might produce a high coefficient of variation, even though the equation itself is well specified. The problem arises because there is a great deal of variation in y to model. In the absence of a large econometric model, a single equation might not be able to explain a great deal of the variation in this type of dependent variable, given the current "state of the art" in econometrics.

How Well Does the Equation Account for the Behavior of the Dependent Variable?

The sample regression function can be expressed in a form that decomposes the actual value of y into a prediction from this equation plus the equation residual:

$$y_i = \hat{y}_i + \hat{\varepsilon}_i \qquad \qquad \textbf{(4.29)}$$

Looking at this in a slightly different way, Equation (4.29) divides actual y_i into an "explained" part, $\hat{y}_i = \hat{\alpha}_0 + \hat{\alpha}_1 x_i$, and an "unexplained" portion, $\hat{\varepsilon}_i$. The observed variation in y is thus accounted for by the behavior of the included explanatory variable, x, and a residual, $\hat{\varepsilon}_i$, which represents factors such as omitted variables and the randomness in human behavior. In order to gauge the performance of a sample regression function, we must develop a measure of how successfully the equation specification, and hence x, explains the observed behavior in the dependent variable. This amounts to calculating an indicator of the explained variation in y_i associated with the sample regression function.

If x does not belong in the sample regression function, then, in the absence of sampling error, the sample regression function is:

$$y_i = \hat{\alpha}_0 + \hat{\varepsilon}_i,$$

and the estimated intercept is simply $\hat{\mu}_y$. A graph of these data produces a scatter of points along a horizontal line at $\hat{\mu}_y$. The measure of explained variation in y developed here contrasts the performance of the sample regression function when x is omitted to that when this variable is included.

The total variation in y, the quantity with which we will compare the explained variation, is expressed in terms of $(y_i - \hat{\mu}_y)$. Since the sum of these terms always equals zero, we will take the sum of the squared y deviations. The resulting measure of the variation in y is called the **total sum of squares** (TSS):

$$\text{TSS} \equiv \sum(y_i - \hat{\mu}_y)^2$$
$$= \sum y_i'^2.$$

Note that TSS is $(n-1)$ times the sample variance of y. Defining the variation in y in terms of $(y_i - \hat{\mu}_y)$, requires only a slight modification to the decomposition of actual y into a predicted and residual component. Expressed in this way, Equation (4.29) becomes:

$$(y_i - \hat{\mu}_y) = (\hat{y}_i - \hat{\mu}_y) + \hat{\varepsilon}_i \qquad \textbf{(4.29')}$$

For any observation, the deviation of actual y from $\hat{\mu}_y$ consists of the difference between the predicted and mean values of y, plus the residual for that observation. In Figure 4.10, the total variation in y, $(y_i - \hat{\mu}_y)$, corresponds to the height at x_i from $\hat{\mu}_y$ to y_i. The "explained" portion of this variation in y is given by the distance from $\hat{\mu}_y$ to the sample regression function, $(\hat{y}_i - \hat{\mu}_y)$. The remaining, "unexplained" distance is accounted for by the equation residual, $\hat{\varepsilon}_i$. When x does not belong in this equation, the sample regression function coincides with the horizontal line at $\hat{\mu}_y$. All of the variation in y is then unexplained, since $\hat{y}_i$ equals $\hat{\mu}_y$, and the right side of Equation (4.29) consists of only $\hat{\varepsilon}_i$.

If we sum then square the terms in Equation (4.29'), we obtain an expression for the total sum of squares in terms of both $\hat{y}_i$ and $\hat{\varepsilon}_i$:

$$\text{TSS} = \sum(y_i - \hat{\mu}_y)^2$$
$$= \sum[(\hat{y}_i - \hat{\mu}_y) + \hat{\varepsilon}_i]^2.$$

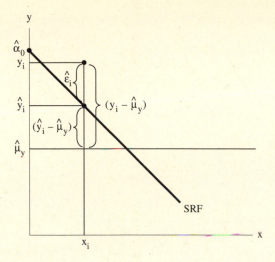

Figure 4.10 Actual, predicted, and residual values relative to $(y_i - \hat{\mu}_y)$

Squaring the bracket on the right, this becomes:

$$\text{TSS} = \sum(\hat{y}_i - \hat{\mu}_y)^2 + \sum\hat{\varepsilon}_i^2 + 2\sum(\hat{y}_i - \hat{\mu}_y)\hat{\varepsilon}_i. \tag{4.30}$$

The first term on the right is the "explained" or **regression sum of squares** (RSS):

$$\text{RSS} \equiv \sum(\hat{y}_i - \hat{\mu}_y)^2.$$

This reflects the portion of the total variation in y accounted for by the specification of the sample regression function. The second term is the **error sum of squares** (ESS):

$$\text{ESS} \equiv \sum\hat{\varepsilon}_i^2,$$

which is the "unexplained" component of TSS. The cross-product term drops out of this equation as a result of the least squares normal equations. To see this, substitute for $\hat{y}_i$ from the sample regression function:

$$\begin{aligned}
\sum(\hat{y}_i - \hat{\mu}_y)\hat{\varepsilon}_i &= \sum(\hat{\alpha}_0 + \hat{\alpha}_1 x_i - \hat{\mu}_y)\hat{\varepsilon}_i \\
&= \hat{\alpha}_0\sum\hat{\varepsilon}_i + \hat{\alpha}_1\sum x_i\hat{\varepsilon}_i - \hat{\mu}_y\sum\hat{\varepsilon}_i \\
&= 0,
\end{aligned}$$

since with least squares both $\sum\hat{\varepsilon}_i$ and $\sum x_i\hat{\varepsilon}_i$ equal 0.

By including the above results into Equation (4.30), we derive the basis for the performance measure of the sample regression function:

$$\text{TSS} = \text{RSS} + \text{ESS}. \tag{4.31}$$

The regression sum of squares indicates that part of the total variation in y that is explained by the sample regression function. However, both RSS and TSS are expressed in units of y squared. By relating RSS to TSS, we arrive at a pure number (with no units of measurement) called the **coefficient of determination** (R^2):

$$R^2 \equiv \text{RSS/TSS}.$$

R^2 measures the *proportion* of the total variation in y explained by the sample regression function. By dividing each of the terms in Equation (4.31) by TSS, we arrive at the following equation, which allows us to establish the range of values taken by R^2:

$$
\begin{aligned}
1 &= (\text{RSS/TSS}) + (\text{ESS/TSS}) \\
&= R^2 + (\text{ESS/TSS})
\end{aligned}
\tag{4.32}
$$

When the sample regression function fails to account for any of the variation in y, RSS equals 0, and all the variation in y is left unexplained: ESS = TSS. R^2 takes the value of 0, which is its lower bound, and the second term on the right of Equation (4.32) equals 1. At the opposite extreme, when the sample regression function predicts every value of y correctly, no equation errors occur. Then, all variation in y is explained, RSS equals TSS, and R^2 takes its upper bound of 1. Note that ESS is 0 in this situation.

These limits for R^2 can be employed as a gauge of how well an equation "fits" the data. R^2 is sometimes called a measure of goodness of fit. An R^2 of 0.4 is considered to be better than a value of 0.2, *but not by twice as much*. The value of 0.4 indicates that the sample regression function explains 40 percent of the variation in y. However, there are a number of potential pitfalls associated with using R^2 to judge the performance of a single equation, or as a basis for comparing several equations:

1. Spurious correlation can produce large R^2 values. While it might appear that both the explanatory variable and the equation specification are appropriate, the existence of a common time trend between x and y can produce an R^2 value greater than 0.9. Also, some variable z, which is highly correlated with x, may be the true causal factor determining the behavior of y. Even though it seems that the large R^2 reflects the importance of x in determining y, the omitted variable z may instead be responsible for this outcome. Correlation (such as R^2) is not necessarily causation. To whatever extent possible, refer to economic theory, previous empirical work, and intuition to determine a causally related variable to include in a sample regression function.

2. Time series equations almost always generate higher R^2 values than cross-section equations. In fact, the coefficients of determination in numerous published articles with well-specified cross-sectional equations are below 0.3. This arises because cross-sectional data contain a great deal of random variation, or "noise," which makes the explained variation small relative to TSS. Ironically, badly specified time series equations can have R^2s of 0.999 for the reasons indicated in (1) above. Comparisons of time series and cross-sectional equations using R^2 are therefore tenuous at best.

3. Low R^2 values are not necessarily the result of including an incorrect explanatory variable in the sample regression function. The functional form utilized to depict the relationship between x and y, when inappropriate, lowers R^2. For example, a linear specification might perform badly according to the R^2 criterion, while using x^2 instead of x produces a high R^2. A time series equation might include the correct explanatory variable, but with the wrong time period. When lags exist in the effect of x on y, an equation specification based on current x can generate a small R^2. Finally, an inappropriate choice for x can also affect R^2. In the auto demand equation discussed earlier, if the overall CPI is used to represent the purchase price of autos instead of a more appropriate choice such as the CPI for new cars, the R^2 from the resulting equation will likely be lower than that for the equation with the preferable price variable.

4. The R^2s from equations with different forms of a dependent variable are *not* comparable. This parallels the limitation concerning the standard error made previously. For example, if we estimate the following population regression functions:

$$y_i = \alpha_0 + \alpha_1 x_1 + \varepsilon_i$$
$$\ln(y_i) = \beta_0 + \beta_1 \ln(x_i) + v_i,$$

comparing their R^2s is not valid. The reason for this lies in the way we define the coefficient of determination. The R^2 for the first equation gives the proportion of the variation in y explained by x, while in the log-linear equation, R^2 states the proportion of the total variation in the *natural logarithm* of y accounted for by the explanatory variable in that equation.

By now it should be apparent that no single criterion is adequate to judge the performance of a sample regression function. When critiquing a sample regression function it is advisable to "hedge your bets"; diversify and employ several criteria simultaneously. Proficiency in the practice of applied econometrics requires expertise in critically examining estimated equations. Experience in this endeavor is predicated on practice. The examples in the remainder of this chapter are intended to illustrate the basis for specifying, estimating, and critiquing econometric equations.

Manual Calculation of Sample Regression Functions and Related Measures

This section illustrates the steps involved in manually calculating the least squares coefficients and the measures of overall equation performance that were outlined in this chapter. The two equations that are presented were originally discussed in Chapter 2. The first of these is a capacity utilization rate-unemployment rate equation, which uses time series data. The second is a cross-sectional equation, where employment by SIC is a function of real wages.

The basis for our first equation is the population regression function:

$$y_t = \alpha_0 + \alpha_1 x_t + \varepsilon_t,$$

where, in year t, y is the civilian unemployment rate; x is the capacity utilization rate in manufacturing; and ε is the stochastic error. The data are those from Chapter 2. The reader is encouraged to compare and contrast the sample regression function here with the statistical discussion given in that chapter.

Table 4.4   Calculation of Sample Regression Function for the Unemployment Rate (y) — Capacity Utilization Rate (x) Equation

YEAR	y	$(y_i - \hat{\mu}_y)$	x	$(x_i - \hat{\mu}_x)$
1979	5.8	$5.8 - 7.32 = -1.52$	84.6	$84.6 - 79.12 = 5.48$
1980	7.1	$7.1 - 7.32 = -0.22$	79.3	$79.3 - 79.12 = 0.18$
1981	7.6	$7.6 - 7.32 = 0.28$	78.2	$78.2 - 79.12 = -0.92$
1982	9.7	$9.7 - 7.32 = 2.38$	70.3	$70.3 - 79.12 = -8.82$
1983	9.6	$9.6 - 7.32 = 2.28$	73.9	$73.9 - 79.12 = -5.22$
1984	7.5	$7.5 - 7.32 = 0.18$	80.5	$80.5 - 79.12 = 1.38$
1985	7.2	$7.2 - 7.32 = -0.12$	80.1	$80.1 - 79.12 = 0.98$
1986	7.0	$7.0 - 7.32 = -0.32$	79.7	$79.7 - 79.12 = 0.58$
1987	6.2	$6.2 - 7.32 = -1.12$	81.1	$81.1 - 79.12 = 1.98$
1988	5.5	$5.5 - 7.32 = -1.82$	83.5	$83.5 - 79.12 = 4.38$

YEAR	$(x_i - \hat{\mu}_x)(y_i - \hat{\mu}_y)$	$(x_i - \hat{\mu}_x)^2$
1979	$(5.48)(-1.52) = -8.33$	30.03
1980	$(0.18)(-0.22) = -0.04$	0.03
1981	$(-0.92)(0.28) = -0.26$	0.85
1982	$(-8.82)(2.38) = -20.99$	77.79
1983	$(-5.22)(2.28) = -11.90$	27.25
1984	$(1.38)(0.18) = 0.25$	1.90
1985	$(0.98)(-0.12) = -0.12$	0.96
1986	$(0.58)(-0.32) = -0.19$	0.34
1987	$(1.98)(-1.12) = -2.22$	3.92
1988	$(4.38)(-1.82) = -7.97$	19.18
Total	-51.76	162.26

$$\hat{\alpha}_1 = \sum(x_i - \hat{\mu}_x)(y_i - \hat{\mu}_y)/\sum(x_i - \hat{\mu}_x)^2$$
$$= -51.76/162.26$$
$$= -0.319$$

$$\hat{\alpha}_0 = \hat{\mu}_y - \hat{\alpha}_1\hat{\mu}_x$$
$$= 7.32 - (-0.319)(79.1)$$
$$= 32.56$$

The sample regression function is:

$$\hat{y}_t = 32.56 - 0.319x_t.$$

Table 4.4 illustrates the set of calculations necessary to obtain $\hat{\alpha}_0$ and $\hat{\alpha}_1$. The sample regression function that results is:

$$\hat{y}_t = 32.56 - 0.319x_t.$$

The negative sign of slope estimate is consistent with prior expectations. The magnitude of this coefficient indicates that a 1 percent rise in the capacity utilization rate

Table 4.5 Actual, Predicted Values, and Residuals from the
Unemployment Rate Equation

| YEAR | UNEMPLOYMENT RATE | | RESIDUAL |
	ACTUAL	PREDICTED	
1979	5.8	$32.56 - 0.32(84.60) =$ 5.57	$5.80 -$ 5.57 $=$ 0.23
1980	7.1	$32.56 - 0.32(79.30) =$ 7.26	$7.10 -$ 7.26 $= -0.16$
1981	7.6	$32.56 - 0.32(78.20) =$ 7.61	$7.60 -$ 7.61 $= -0.01$
1982	9.7	$32.56 - 0.32(70.30) =$ 10.13	$9.70 -$ 10.13 $= -0.43$
1983	9.6	$32.56 - 0.32(73.90) =$ 8.99	$9.60 -$ 8.99 $=$ 0.61
1984	7.5	$32.56 - 0.32(80.50) =$ 6.88	$7.50 -$ 6.88 $=$ 0.62
1985	7.2	$32.56 - 0.32(80.10) =$ 7.01	$7.20 -$ 7.01 $=$ 0.19
1986	7.0	$32.56 - 0.32(79.70) =$ 7.13	$7.00 -$ 7.13 $= -0.13$
1987	6.2	$32.56 - 0.32(81.10) =$ 6.69	$6.20 -$ 6.69 $= -0.49$
1988	5.5	$32.56 - 0.32(83.50) =$ 5.92	$5.50 -$ 5.92 $= -0.42$

Other Calculations:

Error Sum of Squares (ESS):

$$ESS = (0.23)^2 + (-0.16)^2 + (-0.01)^2 + (-0.43)^2 + (0.61)^2 + (0.62)^2$$
$$+ (0.19)^2 + (-0.13)^2 + (-0.49)^2 + (-0.42)^2$$
$$= 1.5$$

Total Sum of Squares (TSS):

$$TSS = (-1.52)^2 + (-0.22)^2 + (0.28)^2 + (2.38)^2 + (2.28)^2 + (0.18)^2$$
$$+ (-0.12)^2 + (-0.32)^2 + (-1.12)^2 + (-1.82)^2$$
$$= 18.02$$

Estimated Error Variance $(\hat{\sigma}_\varepsilon^2)$: $\hat{\sigma}_\varepsilon^2 = \sum \hat{\varepsilon}_t^2/(n-2)$
$$= 1.5/8$$
$$= 0.188$$

Equation Standard Error $(\hat{\sigma}_\varepsilon)$:   0.434

Coefficient of Variation $(\hat{\sigma}_\varepsilon/\hat{\mu}_y)$: $100 = (0.433/7.32) \cdot 100$
$$= 5.923$$

Coefficient of Determination (R^2): $R^2 = 1 - (ESS/TSS)$
$$= 1 - (1.5/18.02)$$
$$= 0.917$$

in manufacturing lowers the mean civilian unemployment rate by 0.319 percent, or that a 3.13 percent increase in the capacity utilization rate is necessary to lower the mean unemployment rate by 1 percent.

Table 4.5 provides the predicted values and residuals for this equation. The equation tracks the actual unemployment rate well. This is indicated by the graph

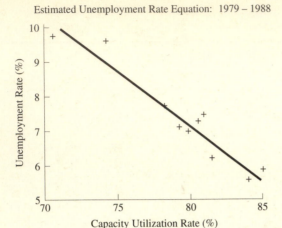

Estimated Unemployment Rate Equation: 1979 – 1988

Figure 4.11

of the scatter diagram and sample regression function given in Figure 4.11. The standard error of the equation, 0.434, is 5.92 percent of the sample mean unemployment rate. The coefficient of variation is thus below the value of 20 used as a benchmark for the acceptability of $\hat{\sigma}_\varepsilon$. Finally, the coefficient of determination, R^2, is 0.917. The sample regression function accounts for approximately 92 percent of the variation in the civilian unemployment rate over this time period.

The final equation whose calculation is illustrated here is based on a labor demand relationship that links employment (N) with real wages (w)[13]:

$$N_i = \alpha_0 + \alpha_1 w_i + \varepsilon_i$$

Cross-sectional data are utilized to estimate this equation. Calculations are presented in Tables 4.6 and 4.7. The subscript i refers to a major (two-digit) SIC category. N_i is production or nonsupervisory employment for the ith SIC category in 1983 (thousands of persons), and w_i is the real (1977 = 100) average hourly wage in 1983 for that category.

The sample regression function that is obtained is:

$$\hat{N}_i = 25,108.7 - 3,218.6 w_i.$$

The negative sign for the real wage rate is consistent with the expected sign for this coefficient. Other things being equal, a $1 increase in real hourly wages lowers mean SIC employment by 3,218,600 persons. This magnitude is large since a $1 change in

---

[13] As stated in Chapter 2, these data are usable for labor demand since it is reasonable to assume that in 1983, the first year of an economic recovery, employment was primarily demand determined. Also, by restricting the data to two-digit SIC classifications in 1983, supply bottlenecks that could make employment in some SIC classifications primarily supply determined were nonexistent.

Table 4.6 Calculation of Sample Regression Function for the Employment (N) — Real
Hourly Wage (w) Equation

	N	$(N_i - \hat{\mu}_N)$	w	$(w_i - \hat{\mu}_w)$
Manufacturing	12,581	$12{,}581 - 7{,}503 =\ \ \ 5{,}078.1$	5.39	$5.39 - 5.47 = -0.08$
Mining	678	$678 - 7{,}503 = -6{,}824.9$	6.88	$6.88 - 5.47 =\ \ \ 1.41$
Construction	3,026	$3{,}026 - 7{,}503 = -4{,}476.9$	7.28	$7.28 - 5.47 =\ \ \ 1.81$
Transportation and Public				
Utilities	4,073	$4{,}073 - 7{,}503 = -3{,}429.9$	6.59	$6.59 - 5.47 =\ \ \ 1.12$
Wholesale Trade	4,220	$4{,}220 - 7{,}503 = -3{,}282.9$	5.21	$5.21 - 5.47 = -0.26$
Retail Trade	13,951	$13{,}951 - 7{,}503 =\ \ \ 6{,}448.1$	3.50	$3.50 - 5.47 = -1.97$
Finance, Insurance, and Real				
Estate	4,066	$4{,}066 - 7{,}503 = -3{,}436.9$	4.45	$4.45 - 5.47 = -1.02$
Services	17,428	$17{,}428 - 7{,}503 =\ \ \ 9{,}925.1$	4.46	$4.46 - 5.47 = -1.01$

	$(w_i - \hat{\mu}_w)(N_i - \hat{\mu}_N)$	$(w_i - \hat{\mu}_w)^2$
Manufacturing	$(-0.08)(\ \ \ 5{,}078) =\ \ \ \ -406.3$	0.01
Mining	$(\ \ \ 1.41)(-6{,}825) =\ \ \ -9{,}623.1$	1.99
Construction	$(\ \ \ 1.81)(-4{,}477) =\ \ \ -8{,}103.1$	3.28
Transportation and Public		
Utilities	$(\ \ \ 1.12)(-3{,}430) =\ \ \ -3{,}841.5$	1.25
Wholesale Trade	$(-0.26)(-3{,}283) =\ \ \ \ \ \ \ \ 853.5$	0.07
Retail Trade	$(-1.97)(\ \ \ 6{,}448) = -12{,}702.8$	3.88
Finance, Insurance, and Real		
Estate	$(-1.02)(-3{,}437) =\ \ \ \ \ 3{,}505.6$	1.04
Services	$(-1.01)(\ \ \ 9{,}925) = -10{,}024.4$	1.02
Total	$-40{,}341.95$	12.53

$$\hat{\alpha}_1 = \sum (N_i - \hat{\mu}_N)(w_i - \hat{\mu}_w)/(w_i - \hat{\mu}_w)^2$$
$$= -40{,}341.95/12.53$$
$$= -3{,}218.6$$

$$\hat{\alpha}_0 = \hat{\mu}_N - \hat{\alpha}_1\hat{\mu}_w$$
$$= 7{,}503 - (-3{,}218.6)(5.47)$$
$$= 25{,}108.7$$

The sample regression function is:

$$\hat{N}_i = 25{,}108.7 - 3{,}218.6w_i$$

real wages is a substantial percentage of average real wages in 1983 ($5.47). It is
therefore preferable to express this slope estimate in terms of a more realistic real
wage change, say, ten cents. This real wage increase lowers mean SIC employment
by 321,860 persons.

Table 4.7 Actual, Predicted Values, and Residuals from the Employment-Real Wage Equation

	ACTUAL	PREDICTED	RESIDUAL
Manufacturing	12,581	25,109 − 3,219 (5.39) = 7,759	12,581 − 7,759 = 4,822
Mining	678	25,109 − 3,219 (6.88) = 2,962	678 − 2,962 = −2,284
Construction	3,026	25,109 − 3,219 (7.28) = 1,675	3,026 − 1,675 = 1,351
Transportation and Public Utilities	4,073	25,109 − 3,219 (6.59) = 3,896	4,073 − 3,896 = 177
Wholesale Trade	4,220	25,109 − 3,219 (5.21) = 8,338	4,220 − 8,338 = −4,118
Retail Trade	13,951	25,109 − 3,219 (3.50) = 13,843	13,951 − 13,843 = 109
Finance, Insurance, and Real Estate	4,066	25,109 − 3,219 (4.45) = 10,784	4,066 − 10,784 = −6,718
Services	17,428	25,109 − 3,219 (4.46) = 10,752	17,428 − 10,752 = 6,676

Other Calculations:

Error Sum of Squares (ESS):

$$ESS = (4,822)^2 + (-2,284)^2 + (1,351)^2 + (177)^2 + (-4,118)^2$$
$$+ (109)^2 + (-6,718)^2 + (6,676)^2$$
$$= 137,003,896$$

$$TSS = (5,078)^2 + (-6,825)^2 + (-4,477)^2 + (-3,430)^2 + (-3,283)^2$$
$$+ (6,448)^2 + (-3,437)^2 + (9,925)^2$$
$$= 266,848,525$$

Estimated Error Variance $(\hat{\sigma}_\varepsilon^2)$: $\hat{\sigma}_\varepsilon^2 = \sum \hat{\varepsilon}_t^2/(n-2)$
$$= 137,003,896/6$$
$$= 22,833,983$$

Equation Standard Error $(\hat{\sigma}_\varepsilon)$: 4,778.5

Coefficient of Variation: $(\hat{\sigma}_\varepsilon/\hat{\mu}_y) \cdot 100 = (4,778.5/7,503) \cdot 100$
$$= 63.7$$

Coefficient of Determination (R^2): $R^2 = 1 - (ESS/TSS)$
$$= 1 - (137,003,896/266,848,525)$$
$$= 0.487$$

Compared to the time series equation presented earlier, the overall performance of this equation appears at first glance to be unsatisfactory. Its standard error, for example, is almost 5,000. The coefficient of variation is 63.7. This equation accounts for less than half of the observed differences in SIC employment (the R^2 is 0.487). Because a great deal of random variation often exists with cross-sectional data, the

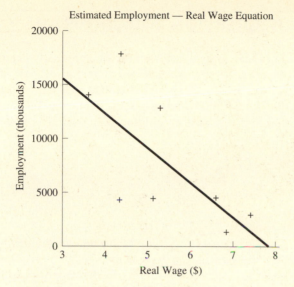

Figure 4.12

performance of this equation is not atypical for equations estimated with this type of data. Figure 4.12 gives the scatter diagram and sample regression function for this example. Judge for yourself how well this equation fits the data. Also, see if you can explain why SIC categories such as Services and Manufacturing have large residuals. Finally, Figure 4.13 graphs this sample regression function in the typical way that labor demand curves are depicted, with real wages on the vertical axis.

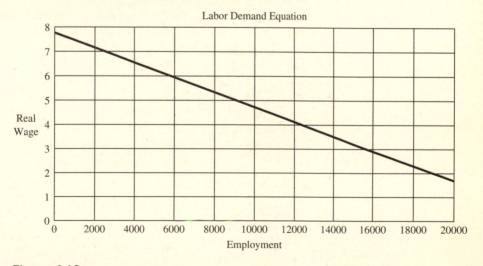

Figure 4.13

EXAMPLES OF REGRESSION EQUATIONS

■ **BETA COEFFICIENTS**   A beta coefficient is an empirically determined measure of the riskiness of an asset. These coefficients are an important part of the Capital Asset Pricing Model used in Finance. Asset risk is related to the behavior of the rate of return on an asset. The rate of return to an asset is defined as the percent change in wealth per time period that results from holding that asset. The rate of return to a stock, for example, is:

$$R_t = \frac{\Delta P_t + D_t}{P_{t-1}}$$

$$= \frac{\Delta P_t}{P_{t-1}} + \frac{D_t}{P_{t-1}}$$

where P is the price of this stock and D is the dollar value of dividends paid to its owners. The first term on the right is the percent change in the stock price, which measures its capital gain or loss. The second term, dividends as a proportion of last period's stock price, can be viewed as the dividend rate of return.

The beta coefficient of an asset such as a stock measures the sensitivity of its rate of return to changes in the rate of return to all assets (market return). The population regression function used to estimate beta coefficients expresses the rate of return on an asset at time t, R_t, as a linear function of the market return, RM_t:

$$R_t = \alpha + \beta RM_t + \varepsilon_t.$$

The coefficient of the market rate of return in this equation is the *beta coefficient* for this stock. It gives the rate of change in the mean return to this stock for a 1 percent change in market returns. The stochastic error reflects the inherent uncertainty in the return to this stock, such as the influence of unexpected events on R_t.

When β equals 1.0, the risk associated with an asset is identical to market risk, since on average, the change in R_t equals that of RM_t. When β exceeds 1, an asset is viewed as risky, since its return fluctuates more than the market rate of return. If, for example, the market return rises 5 percent, the mean return to an asset with a β of 1.6 rises by 8 percent. Finally, when β is less than 1, the return to an asset fluctuates less, on average, than the overall market return.

An example of this type of equation is given by Folger and Ganapathy, who estimated the β for IBM from monthly data for the years 1956 to 1976.[14] Their market return variable (designated x) is the University of Chicago Index of stock returns. The estimated equation is:

$$\hat{y}_t = 0.726 + 1.06x_t$$

$$R^2 = 0.471, \quad n = 240, \quad \hat{\sigma}_\varepsilon = 4.58$$

---

[14] H. Folger and S. Ganapathy, *Financial Econometrics* (Englewood Cliffs NJ: Prentice-Hall), 1982.

where $\hat{y}$ denotes the predicted rate of return to IBM stock. The estimated beta for IBM is slightly above the value used to delineate assets with average risk.[15] An explanation for this emerges when we consider the role played by IBM's stock performance as an indicator of the future course of the stock market. Since many investors base their expectations of future stock prices on the performance of IBM, the return to IBM stock should reflect the market return to stocks in general.

A 10 percent increase in the market return index is predicted to increase the mean return on IBM's stock by 10.6 percent. Several values of RM and the corresponding predicted IBM stock returns are given in the table below:

MARKET RETURN	PREDICTED RETURN TO IBM STOCK
−20	−20.47
−10	−9.87
0	0.726
10	11.33
20	21.93

Investors and portfolio managers cannot alter the market rate of return. They can influence the return to a portfolio through their selection of the types and riskiness of the included assets, and therefore to individual and portfolio betas. ■

■ **THE DEMAND FOR DOMESTIC AUTOS**   The previous discussion of demand functions can be employed as the basis for specifying and estimating a demand equation for domestic auto sales. The population regression function is assumed to take the following form[16]:

$$q_t = \alpha_0 + \alpha_1 p_t + \varepsilon_t.$$

Time series data for the years 1965 to 1984 are used to estimate this equation. Domestic retail auto sales (RSADOM), in thousands of units per year, is used as the measure of quantity demanded in this equation. The price of domestic autos is represented by the CPI for new autos. Two versions of this equation will be estimated with MicroTSP: one using this price measure with a 1967 base year (CPINC), the other using a 1982 base year (PNC82). The coefficients of these equations will be compared to see how this change of scale affects the least squares coefficients.

---

[15] The hypothesis testing procedure outlined in Chapter 5 allows us to determine whether we can view the difference between this estimate and 1.0 as being the result of chance variation.

[16] This is an admittedly oversimplified equation in that it includes a single explanatory variable and it employs a linear specification. This equation is utilized merely for the purposes of providing an example.

MicroTSP performs linear regression with the LS command. The "LS" stands for *Least Squares*. The command used to estimate the demand equation in this example is:

```
>LS RSADOM C CPINC
```

The form of this command places the name given to the dependent variable first, followed by "C," the designation for including an equation intercept, then the list of included explanatory variables. In this equation, the only included explanatory variable is CPINC. The output that results from this command is:

```
SMPL 1965 - 1984
20 Observations
LS // Dependent Variable is RSADOM
```

VARIABLE	COEFFICIENT	STD. ERROR	T-STAT.	2-TAIL SIG.
C	$10166.071 (=\hat{\alpha}_0)$	$817.84178 (=\hat{\sigma}_0)$	12.430364	0.000
CPINC	$-15.716964 (=\hat{\alpha}_1)$	$5.6962561 (=\hat{\sigma}_1)$	-2.759174	0.013

R-squared	$0.29723 (=R^2)$	Mean of dependent var	$7988.800 (=\hat{\mu}_y)$
Adjusted R-squared	0.25819	S.D. of dependent var	$1115.856 (=\hat{\sigma}_y)$
S.E. of regression	$961.069 (=\hat{\sigma}_\varepsilon)$	Sum of squared resid	$166258 (=\sum \hat{\varepsilon}^2)$
Durbin-Watson stat	1.24943	F-statistic	7.613043

The sample regression function from this output is:

$$\hat{q}_t = 10{,}166.1 - 15.72 p_t$$

$$R^2 = 0.297, \qquad \hat{\sigma}_\varepsilon = 961.1, \qquad n = 20.$$

The coefficients in this equation display the expected signs. If the CPI for new cars rises by 1 (CPINC is expressed as a percentage, such as 197.6 for 1982), mean domestic retail auto sales fall by 15,720 units per year. A 5 percent inflation rate in this price index, from its 1982 value 197.6 to 207.5, is predicted to lower mean domestic retail auto sales by 155,284 units per year.

The price coefficient appears to be somewhat low. To further investigate this coefficient, we will convert it into an estimated price elasticity. For 1982, the value of CPINC equals 197.6. Substituting this value into the sample regression function, predicted quantity is:

$$\hat{q}_{82} = 10{,}166.1 - 15.72(197.6)$$
$$= 7{,}059.8$$

The estimated price elasticity for 1982 is:

$$(p_{82}/\hat{q}_{82})(\Delta q/\Delta p) = (197.6/7059.8)(-15.72),$$

which equals -0.44. This result, that the demand for automobiles is price inelastic, lends support to our suspicion that the price sensitivity of auto demand is underestimated.

The overall performance measures for this equation display mixed signs. The coefficient of determination indicates that this equation accounts for just under 30 percent of the variation in domestic retail auto sales. This value appears to be somewhat small for a time series equation. Part of the reason for this lies with the bivariate specification used to depict the demand equation. The coefficient of variation for this equation, 12.0 ($= \{961.1/7988.8\} \cdot 100$) is within the acceptable range of 20 for this statistic.

To see how a change of scale alters the regression results, the auto demand equation is reestimated after converting the CPI for new autos to a 1982 base year. Recall (from Chapter 3) that changing the base year of annual data entails dividing the original values by that for the desired new base year, then multiplying the result by 100. Since the CPI (with a 1967 base year) takes the value of 197.6 for 1982, each of the original CPI values must be multiplied by $(1/197.6) \cdot 100$. The scale factor that links these price indexes is therefore 0.506. If we denote the original CPI as CPI_{67}, then the new CPI, CPI_{82} is:

$$CPI_{82} = 0.506 CPI_{67}.$$

Because this is a change of scale, both the mean and variance of CPI_{82} differ from those of CPI_{67}, Specifically, the mean of CPI_{82} is 0.506 times the mean of CPI_{67}, while the variance of CPI_{82} is $(0.506)^2$, or 0.256 times that of the 1967 price index.

The least squares slope coefficient in the new sample regression function, $\hat{\alpha}'_1$, is calculated from the ratio (using RSADOM for q):

$$\hat{\alpha}'_1 = Cov(CPI_{82}, RSADOM)/Var(CPI_{82})$$

which involves the covariance between the newly created price index and the dependent variable, in addition to the variance of CPI_{82}. As the methodology in Chapter 2 showed, the covariance in this equation is:

$$Cov(CPI_{82}, RSADOM) = 0.506 \cdot Cov(CPI_{67}, RSADOM).$$

Entering this information into the expression for $\hat{\alpha}'_1$ gives:

$$\hat{\alpha}'_1 = \frac{0.506 \cdot Cov(CPI_{67}, RSADOM)}{(0.506)^2 \cdot Var(CPI_{67})}$$

$$= \frac{Cov(CPI_{67}, RSADOM)}{(0.506) Var(CPI_{67})}$$

$$= 1.98 \hat{\alpha}_1,$$

where $\hat{\alpha}_1$ denotes the slope coefficient from the original equation. The new price index coefficient will therefore be approximately twice (in absolute value) as large as that in the original equation.

Should the intercept differ as the result of this scale change? To answer this question, note that the new intercept estimator, $\hat{\alpha}_0'$ is:

$$\hat{\alpha}_0' = \hat{\mu}_y - \hat{\alpha}_1' \hat{\mu}_x',$$

where y and x replace the earlier abbreviations, and x' refers to CPI_{82}. The mean of y is unaffected by this change of scale, since it pertains only to the explanatory variable. Evaluating the term on the right:

$$\hat{\alpha}_1' \hat{\mu}_x' = \frac{\hat{\alpha}_1}{(0.506)} \cdot (0.506)\hat{\mu}_x$$
$$= \hat{\alpha}_1 \hat{\mu}_x$$

which is also unchanged from its value in the original equation. Change of scale exclusively in the explanatory variable thus alters the least squares slope coefficient but not the intercept. The printout for the new equation (with the 1982 base year) is given below.

```
SMPL 1965 - 1984
20 Observations
LS // Dependent Variable is RSADOM
```

VARIABLE	COEFFICIENT	STD. ERROR	T-STAT.	2-TAIL SIG.
C	10166.071	817.84164	12.430366	0.000
PNC82	-31.056715	11.255800	-2.7591744	0.013

R-squared	0.29723	Mean of dependent var	7988.800
Adjusted R-squared	0.25819	S.D. of dependent var	1115.856
S.E. of regression	961.069	Sum of squared resid	16625754
Durbin-Watson stat	1.24943	F-statistic	7.613044

The estimated equation from this printout is:

$$\hat{q}_t = 10{,}166.1 - 31.06\text{PNC82}_t$$

$$R^2 = 0.297, \quad \hat{\sigma}_\varepsilon = 961.1, \quad n = 20$$

The price index coefficient has approximately doubled, as expected. Does this imply that the price sensitivity of domestic auto sales has also doubled? The answer is no. The scale change for the price measure lowered its values. If we increase price by 5 percent from its 1982 value (as we did with the initial equation), this raises PNC82 by only 5 units, since its value for 1982 is 100. The estimated equation predicts that this price increase lowers mean domestic auto sales by 155,284 units per year, which is identical to that in the original form of this equation. Finally, the estimated price elasticity of domestic auto sales for 1982, -0.44, is the same as that derived from the initial equation as well (verify this).

Compare the other important values in this printout and try to explain why they remain unchanged. The equation for the demand curve associated with this function, expressed in terms of price as the dependent variable is:

$$p_t = 327.3 - 0.032q_t$$

where p represents PNC82 and q is $\hat{q}$. ■

■ **A PRODUCTION FUNCTION**   The production function is one of the most basic relationships in microeconomics. This function relates maximum output attainable (q) to the inputs utilized in production. If we assume, as is often done, that there are two inputs, labor (L) and capital (k), the general form of this relationship can be expressed as:

$$q = f(k, L).$$

This equation is the *long-run production function* since both capital and labor are variable inputs. A frequently utilized function that characterizes this relationship is the *Cobb-Douglass production function*:

$$q = Ak^{\alpha}L^{\beta},$$

where the exponents α and β are constants which express the responsiveness of output to capital and labor, respectively. The term A can be viewed as an *efficiency parameter*, since the larger is A, the greater is the maximum output corresponding to any labor-capital combination.

In the short-run, the stock of capital is fixed. Firms expand output by increasing labor input while utilizing their existing plant capacity more intensively. Thus, in the short-run, output depends only on labor input, and the production function becomes:

$$q = g(L)$$

Using the Cobb-Douglass production function, and letting $k = k_0$, the short-run version of this function takes the form:

$$q = (Ak_0^{\alpha})L^{\beta}$$
$$= A_*L^{\beta},$$

where $A_* = (Ak_0^{\alpha})$.

This short-run production function is thus a bivariate relationship.[17] In its present form, this relationship cannot be estimated with least squares. Fortunately, the

---

[17] The Cobb-Douglass production function can also be converted into a bivariate relationship when its coefficients sum to one. This case, called constant returns to scale, allows us to state this equation as

$$(q/k) = f(L/k).$$

definition of linearity that pertains to least squares requires only that the equation of interest be linear in its coefficients. A multiplicative relationship such as this can be converted into the appropriate form through a logarithmic transformation. Taking the natural logarithm of both sides of this equation:

$$\ln(q) = \ln(A_*) + \beta \ln(L)$$
$$= \alpha_* + \beta \ln(L),$$

where $\alpha_* = \ln(A_*)$. If we add a stochastic error to this equation along with subscripts to denote time, it becomes:

$$\ln(q)_t = \alpha_* + \beta \ln(L)_t + \varepsilon_t$$

Had the specification of this equation been linear labor input, the slope coefficient β would equal:

$$\Delta q_t / \Delta L_t$$

which is the *marginal product of labor*. This tells the rate of change in total output as labor input varies (given k). Since the slope of a linear equation is constant, a linear production function specification restricts the marginal product of labor to a single value. The existence of *diminishing returns*, which is a positive but decreasing marginal product of labor, is therefore inconsistent with a linear production function. In the log-linear specification above, the slope coefficient indicates:

$$\Delta\ln(q)_t / \Delta\ln(L)_t$$

which, we now show, allows the marginal product of labor to vary. Consider the numerator in this expression:

$$\Delta\ln(q)_t = \ln(q)_t - \ln(q)_{t-1}.$$

According to the laws of logarithms, the right side of this equation equals $\ln(q_t/q_{t-1})$. We showed in Chapter 3 that the proportionate change in a variable is related to this quantity, specifically:

$$g_q = \frac{\Delta q_t}{q_{t-1}} = \frac{q_t}{q_{t-1}} - 1,$$

where g_q is the proportionate change (growth) in output. Solving this equation for the terms involving q, this becomes:

$$\frac{q_t}{q_{t-1}} = (1 + g_q).$$

Thus, $\Delta\ln(q)_t = \ln(1 + g_q)$. When g_q is small (less than 0.2), the right side of this expression simplifies to g_q. Thus:

$$\Delta\ln(q)_t = \ln(1 + g_q) \approx g_q.$$

Similar calculations establish that the denominator of the expression for β is the proportionate change in labor input. The slope coefficient is therefore:

$$\beta = \frac{\Delta q_t / q_{t-1}}{\Delta L_t / L_{t-1}}$$

which is the *elasticity of output with respect to labor input*. This elasticity denotes the percent change in output that results from a one percent change in labor input (given k). *The slope coefficient in a log-linear equation is therefore an elasticity.* One of the major benefits associated with this functional form is the ease with which elasticities can be calculated.

We can utilize this elasticity equation to illustrate that the principle of diminishing returns is consistent with the log-linear specification of the production function. If we drop the time subscripts and state this equation in terms of the marginal product of labor, $\Delta q/\Delta L$, we obtain:

$$\Delta q/\Delta L = \beta(q/L)$$

The ratio on the right, (q/L), which measures output per worker, is the *average product of labor*. For a Cobb-Douglass production function, the marginal product of labor is proportional to the average product of labor. The factor of proportionality is β, the elasticity of output with respect to labor input. In the short-run, as labor input expands, output also increases, but not always by the same amount. When L rises faster than q, the average product of labor declines, which, given β, causes the marginal product of labor to fall. Thus, diminishing returns can occur with this type of production function.

To illustrate the estimation and interpretation of a short-run production function, we employ monthly data for the years 1986 and 1987 on production and employment in nondurable goods manufacturing. A two-year time period is used since variations in both the stock of capital and its utilization rate are small enough that we can consider these to be constant for purposes of this illustration. The dependent variable in this equation, which represents output, is the Industrial Production Index for Nondurable Goods (1977 = 100). The labor measure is payroll employment in nondurable good manufacturing (thousands of persons). Data were obtained from the 1988 *Economic Report of the President*. The least squares equation estimated from these data is:

$$\widehat{\ln(q)}_t = -3.49 + 0.93 \ln(L)_t$$

$$R^2 = 0.967$$

$$\hat{\sigma}_\varepsilon = 0.005$$

The slope coefficient in this equation, 0.93, indicates that a one percent increase in labor input raises mean output by 0.93 percent. Because this elasticity coefficient is less than one, the response of output to labor input is inelastic.

The negative intercept in this equation does *not* express mean output when labor input is 0. Instead, this is the mean of the *logarithm* of output when $\ln(L)_t$ equals 0. Recall from above that this coefficient is the logarithm of the constant in the production function. The negative sign for this coefficient therefore does not signal the existence of a problem with the sample regression function. Our estimate of A_*, which we calculate from the intercept, is:

$$\hat{\alpha}_* = \ln(A_*)$$
$$= -3.49$$

so that

$$\hat{A}_* = e^{-3.49}$$
$$= 0.031.$$

If we enter this value along with the output elasticity into the original form of the production function, we obtain:

$$\hat{q}_t = 0.031 \cdot L_t^{0.931}.$$

Possible values for labor input along with predicted output are given in the following table:

$\hat{q}_t$	L_t	$\Delta\hat{q}_t/\Delta L_t$
108.37	6400	—
119.37	7100	0.0157
130.29	7800	0.0156
135.72	8150	0.0155

The log-linear specification thus produces a constant output elasticity, while allowing the marginal product of labor to vary. ■

■ **OKUN'S LAW**   The results of the first manually calculated equation probably raised a question in your mind concerning the estimated slope coefficient: why does a one percent increase in capacity utilization lower the mean unemployment rate by less than one percent? The answer to this question lies in the methods used to calculate the unemployment rate, along with the way in which its components change from month to month, or year to year.

The empirical relationship between changes in the state of the economy and the unemployment rate was investigated in the 1960s by Arthur Okun. His results, which are summarized by what has become known as Okun's Law, provide important insights into the sensitivity of the unemployment rate to economic growth.

One of the equations Okun estimated was a regression of changes in the quarterly unemployment rate (Δu) on the one-quarter percent change in real GNP (PCRGNP).[18] The data he used were quarterly observations from 1947:2 to 1960:4. The sample regression function he obtained is:

$$\widehat{\Delta u_t} = 0.3 - 0.3\text{PCRGNP}_t, \qquad (R^2 = 0.63).$$

The intercept in this equation indicates the mean *change* in the unemployment rate when the growth rate in the economy is 0 (PCRGNP = 0). The estimated inter-

---

[18] Arthur Okun, "Potential GNP: Its Measurement and Significance," *Proceedings* of the Business and Economic Statistics Section of the American Statistical Association, 1962, pp. 98–104.

cept reveals that the quarterly unemployment rate rises by 0.3 percent when the economy fails to grow in real terms. The negative coefficient of PCRGNP indicates that when the state of the economy improves, as represented by a positive percent change in real GNP, the mean unemployment rate falls. The magnitude of the predicted decline is, however, less than one. A one percent rise in PCRGNP is therefore associated with a fall of only 0.3 percent in the mean unemployment rate. This result is called *Okun's Law*.

The unemployment rate is the ratio of the number of unemployed persons to the civilian labor force. To understand Okun's results, it must be understood that the temporal behavior of the unemployment rate is determined by two sets of factors: **secular trends**, which are related to the long-run trend in the unemployment rate; and **cyclical trends** caused by the current state of the economy. Both the number of unemployed and the civilian labor force are influenced by secular and cyclical factors, which are summarized briefly below.

Secular trends:

(i) Productivity growth occurs as the result of new capital investment and improved production techniques. Because these tend to be labor saving, a given level of real GNP can be produced with a smaller labor input. This causes labor displacement and a rise in the number of unemployed.[19]

(ii) The size of the labor force is directly related to population growth. The result of a larger population is thus a long-term upward trend in the size of the labor force. New entrants into the labor force often enter as unemployed persons. This tends to increase the overall rate of unemployment.

(iii) The composition of the labor force is changing toward persons such as minorities, teenagers, and married women who tend to display above average unemployment rates, and away from white males with the lowest unemployment rate. This also tends to increase the unemployment rate.

The estimated intercept in the Okun equation thus indicates the necessity of real economic growth to offset increases in the unemployment rate that occur on the basis of these secular factors. The estimated slope, which is related to the rate of economic growth, depends on several cyclical factors:

Cyclical Factors:

(i) When real growth occurs, the probability of finding an acceptable job offer rises. This provides an incentive for formerly "discouraged workers" to re-enter the labor force. While unemployed, these persons were not among the officially unemployed, since, by not actively seeking employment, they were classified as being out of the labor force. Upon reentering, they are often

---

[19] The productivity measure can be viewed as the average productivity of labor: the ratio of real output to the amount of labor input. The latter is the product of hours per worker and the number of workers.

unemployed. However, if real growth persists, then after a transition period, such persons become employed, lowering the measured unemployment rate.

(ii) Because of the existence of fixed employment costs associated with employment, such as hiring, payroll, screening, and training costs, firms initially respond to increases in product demand by raising hours per worker. If real growth persists, firms eventually opt to service their manpower needs by increasing the number of workers. As this occurs, previously unemployed persons become employed, and the measured unemployment rate drops.

Both cyclical factors explain the inverse relationship between the unemployment rate and the rate of economic growth. Within the context of a growing economy, the 0.3 slope coefficient in Okun's equation pertains as the result of cyclical factor (i), that employers draw workers from an enlarged labor force; factor (ii), not all firms make the shift from overtime to additional workers simultaneously and one additional cyclical factor:

(iii) Firms undertake certain types of training investments in workers called specific human capital. These investments are repaid only if the trained employees remain on the job. If persons with specific human capital are laid off, the capital investments by firms in these persons are lost, unless firms can be assured of recalling these same persons when conditions improve. For this reason, firms tend to "hoard labor." In a recession, as output falls, labor input is reduced by a smaller proportion to preserve such human capital investments. In a recovery, as real growth occurs, firms can raise output with a *smaller* than proportionate increase in labor input, as this "hoarded labor" is more fully utilized.[20]   ■

■ THE NONINFLATIONARY RATE OF UNEMPLOYMENT (NIRU)

The empirical relationship between the rates of inflation and unemployment was investigated by A. W. Phillips. His work led to the famous Phillips Curve whose downward slope indicates the possibility of a tradeoff between the rate of inflation (π) and the rate of unemployment (U). Along the Phillips Curve given in Figure 4.14, the rate of unemployment decreases as the rate of inflation accelerates. One notable feature of this curve is its increased steepness at lower levels of unemployment. A zero unemployment rate is theoretically consistent with an infinite rate of inflation.[21] The Phillips Curve crosses the horizontal axis when π is zero. Thus, unemployment exists even when inflation is zero.

Each Phillips Curve is valid for a given rate of expected inflation (π^e). In Figure 4.14, the curve PC_1 assumes zero expected inflation. The unemployment rate that

---

[20] References on this topic are provided by a number of Labor Economics texts, such as R. Ehrenberg and R. Smith, *Modern Labor Economics* (4th ed) (New York, NY: Harper Collins Publishers Inc.), 1991.

[21] The curve asymptotically approaches the π axis as the unemployment rate decreases.

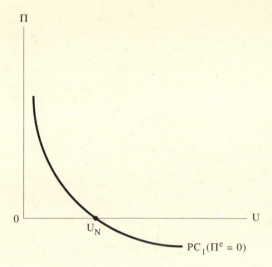

Figure 4.14 Phillips curve

prevails when actual and expected inflation are equal is called the *natural rate of unemployment*, which is labeled U_N in this diagram. The tradeoff indicated by PC_1 exists only when actual inflation differs from the expected rate (of zero).

The natural rate of unemployment can also be thought of as the rate of unemployment below which the economy's rate of inflation accelerates. As Figure 4.14 shows, this does *not* occur at a zero unemployment rate. This rate has risen from approximately 4 percent in the 1950s to about 5 percent today. The reasons for this change can be found in the secular factors discussed for Okun's Law, as well as characteristics of labor markets and government income maintenance programs. The important point for our purposes is that this rate of unemployment is empirically determined.

We can determine this level of unemployment by calculating the *Noninflationary Rate of Unemployment*, defined as the rate of unemployment at which the inflation rate neither increases nor decreases. Underlying this concept is the notion that changes in the unemployment rate cause inflation to rise or fall. This indicates that the unemployment rate is the explanatory variable in the empirical equation. The dependent variable in this equation is the *change* in the annual inflation rate:

$$(\pi_t - \pi_{t-1}).$$

Combining this information, the population regression function is:

$$(\pi_t - \pi_{t-1}) = \alpha_0 + \alpha_1 u_{t-1} + \varepsilon_t.$$

Note that this equation includes the *lagged* unemployment rate. The specification of this equation relates last year's unemployment rate to the amount by which inflation changes from its value in the previous year. If we denote $(\pi_t - \pi_{t-1})$ as π_t^*, the population regression function can be written:

$$\pi_t^* = \alpha_0 + \alpha_1 u_{t-1} + \varepsilon_t, \tag{4.33}$$

which can be estimated with least squares. Carlson estimated Equation (4.33) using annual data for the years 1952 to 1976.[22] His sample regression function is:

$$\hat{\pi}_t^* = 2.463 - 0.453u_{t-1} \qquad (R^2 = 0.15) \qquad\qquad \textbf{(4.34)}$$

The negative sign for the coefficient of lagged unemployment conforms to prior expectations (explain this). Although the coefficient of determination, 0.15, appears low, remember that the dependent variable consists of percent changes which are themselves difficult to model. Furthermore, π_t^* is the *change* in two percent changes. Both these factors produce a great deal of variation in the dependent variable, making a "low" R^2 acceptable.

The NIRU is calculated using Equation (4.34). The definition of this term implies nonincreasing (or decreasing) inflation. If we set $\hat{\pi}_t^*$ equal to zero, then:

$$\hat{\pi}_t^* = (\pi_t - \pi_{t-1}) = 0,$$

and inflation remains constant from year $t-1$ to year t. Substituting this information into Equation (4.34) gives:

$$0 = 2.463 - 0.453u_{t-1},$$

or

$$u_{t-1} = 2.463/0.453$$
$$= 5.44.$$

This is the estimated Noninflationary Rate of Unemployment for the years covered by these data.

In its present form, this equation can also be used to predict future inflation rates based on past values of inflation and unemployment. To see this, write out the original equation in full:

$$\pi_t - \pi_{t-1} = \alpha_0 + \alpha_1 u_{t-1} + \varepsilon_t.$$

If we move the term π_{t-1} to the right side of this equation, and increase the time period by one, the sample regression function becomes:

$$\pi_{t+1} = \pi_t + \alpha_0 + \alpha_1 u_t$$

The error in this equation is omitted because, based on the model assumptions, $E(\varepsilon_t) = E(\varepsilon_{t+1}) = 0$. The right side of this equation consists entirely of values known in year t. Plugging the actual rates of inflation and unemployment for a given year into this equation thus produces an estimate of the following year's inflation rate. ■

■ **A SPURIOUS EQUATION RESULT**   The causal link between the supply of money and GNP was originally established in Chapter 1. Various other aspects of this relationship have been discussed since then. A population regression function

[22] K. Carlson, "Inflation, Unemployment, and Money: Comparing the Evidence from Two Simple Models," *Review* of the Federal Reserve Bank of St. Louis, September 1978, pp. 2–7.

which expresses the contemporaneous, or same period relationship between these variables, is:

$$GNP_t = \alpha_0 + \alpha_1 M1_t + \varepsilon_t.$$

Using quarterly data from 1970:1 to 1984:1, this relationship was estimated using SAS. The SAS lines that create a data set GNPDATA containing GNP and M1, along with the commands to produce the regression above are:

```
DATA GNPDATA;
INPUT GNP M1;
CARDS;
(data here)
```

This INPUT statement presupposes free-format data entry, where the first column contains observations on GNP and the second contains values for M1. Any desired data manipulation should be placed between the INPUT and CARDS statements.

```
PROC REG;
  MODEL GNP=M1;
```

REG is the SAS procedure for linear *reg*ression. Since no data set name is indicated following REG, the most recently created data set (GNPDATA) is used. The syntax for this statement places the dependent variable on the left side and the explanatory variable(s) on the right side. *Unless otherwise specified, SAS includes an intercept in the estimated equation.* If options are requested, a slash follows the last explanatory variable and the desired options (given in the SAS manual) are then listed.

The resulting SAS printout for this sample regression function is:

```
DEP VARIABLE: GNP      NOMINAL GROSS NATIONAL PRODUCT
ANALYSIS OF VARIANCE

                   SUM OF              MEAN
SOURCE     DF     SQUARES             SQUARE       F VALUE    PROB>F
MODEL       1   30089049.98(=Σŷᵢ-μ̂ᵧ)²   30089049.98   6008.480   0.0001
ERROR      53    265411.47(=Σε̂ᵢ²)       5007.77(=σ̂ₑ²)
C TOTAL    54   30354461.45(=Σ(yᵢ-μ̂ᵧ))²

     ROOT MSE        70.76555(=σ̂ₑ)       R-SQUARE  0.9913(=R²)
     DEP MEAN      1942.589(=μ̂ᵧ)         ADJ R-SQ  0.9911
     C.V.             3.642847(=100·σ̂ₑ/μ̂ᵧ)

PARAMETER ESTIMATES
                   PARAMETER        STANDARD        T FOR H0:
VARIABLE   DF      ESTIMATE          ERROR         PARAMETER=0
INTERCEPT   1    -891.04181(=α̂₀)   37.78101952(=σ̂₀)    -23.584
M1          1       8.61729(=α̂₁)    0.11117018(=σ̂₁)     77.514
```

The sample regression function from this output (with GNP as y and M1 as x) is:

$$\hat{y}_t = -891.042 + 8.617x_t \qquad R^2 = 0.991 \quad \hat{\sigma}_\varepsilon = 70.8 \quad n = 55$$

This printout indicates satisfactory results based on several of the criteria discussed in this chapter: the expected sign of the coefficient of M1 is correct; R^2 is very high; and the coefficient of variation is well within the acceptable range. The R^2, for example, indicates this equation accounts for more than 99 percent of the variation in nominal GNP over the sample period. As you already know, this is not a good equation, for with quarterly data, the contemporaneous relationship between M1 and GNP is the result of spurious correlation and the common time trend present in these variables. How might the printout provide a clue that a problem exists?

Both the sign and magnitude of the intercept indicate a problem with this equation. According to this coefficient, mean GNP is slightly less than *minus* $900 billion when M1 is 0. The magnitude of the slope coefficient is also extremely high. This indicates that a $1 billion increase in M1 raises mean GNP *in the same quarter* by 8.6 times that amount. If you are totally unaware of the existence of lags in the effect of monetary policy, this might not seem excessive. The same is likely to be the case, if you have no idea how large the money multiplier is. This illustrates the importance of consulting critical sources of information when evaluating estimated equations: theory references, such as texts or journals; and previous empirical findings on the same, or a similar topic. The sources for the latter are also texts and journals. This combination of an underestimated intercept and overestimated slope coefficient is the result of the negative covariance between these coefficients that was discussed in the section on Monte Carlo Methods.

At any rate, let us explore the magnitude of the slope coefficient further, by considering the estimated impact of a $10 billion increase in $M1_t$ on GNP_t when both are expressed as a percentage of their respective sample means. This rise of $10 billion in $M1_t$ is 3.04 percent of its average, $328.8 billion. Based on this change, the sample regression function predicts an increase in the mean of GNP_t by $86.2 billion, which is 4.44 percent of its mean. If we refer back to the quantity theory of money:

$$M \cdot V = P \cdot Q = \text{GNP},$$

this can be expressed in percent change form as:

$$m + v = g,$$

where m, v, and g are the percent changes in M1, the velocity of circulation, and GNP, respectively. Our empirical result, that g exceeds m, can occur only if v, the growth in velocity, is positive, so that a smaller portion of income is held in the form of money balances (i.e., the ratio of M1 to GNP is falling). We can investigate this by examining the behavior of M1/GNP for the sample time period. If velocity is relatively stable, so that v is approximately 0, m should be almost identical to g—which is not the case here. One or both of these methods can be used to signal a problem with the sample regression function in question.   ■

A LOOK AHEAD.   The basic elements of regression analysis have now been set out in detail. The next two chapters incorporate statistical inference, hypothesis testing, and forecasting into this framework then extend least squares estimation to models with several explanatory variables.

The material in Chapter 5 allows us to move beyond exclusive reliance on point estimates of the coefficients in the population regression function, and provides us with two additional criteria we can use to judge estimated equations—the statistical significance of individual regression coefficients, and the forecasting performance of our sample regression function. Chapter 6 details the basics of multiple regression. As you will see there are a number of similarities between the concepts involved in multiple regression and those set out in the context of bivariate regression in this chapter.

The material on multiple regression provides the final building block for the basic infrastructure of econometric theory. All of the material that follows Chapter 6 deals either with regression model problems, or violations of the model assumptions upon which this foundation has been built.

KEY TERMS

Coefficient of determination	Ordinary least squares
Coefficient of variation	Population regression function
Deviation form of PRF	Random disturbance
Double-log	Regression sum of squares
Error sum of squares	Residual
Gauss-Markov theorem	Root mean squared error
Heteroskedastic	Sample regression function
Homoskedasticity	Serial correlation
Least squares	Specification
Log-linear specification	Specification error
Mean square error	Standard error
Monte Carlo Experiment	Stochastic error
Monte Carlo Method	Total sum of squares
Normal equations	

EXERCISES

1. (a) Show that the least squares estimator $\hat{\alpha}_0$ is a linear function of y.

    (b) Show that $\hat{\alpha}_0$ is unbiased when the model assumptions are met.

2. The coefficient of determination defines the variation of y in terms of $(y_i - \hat{\mu}_y)$, or y'_i. Suppose the following population regression function is estimated:

$$y'_i = \beta_0 + \beta_1 x_i + \varepsilon_i.$$

Will its coefficients be the same as those in the following regression function?

$$y_i = \alpha_0 + \alpha_1 x_i + v_i$$

Why (or why not)?

3. **(a)** Perform the manual calculations for the unemployment rate-capacity utilization rate equation that were done in this chapter using the short-cut formulas for $\Sigma x_i' y_i'$ and $\Sigma x_i'^2$ given in Chapter 2;

   (b) Perform the manual calculations for the employment-real wage equation using the same-short formulas as in **(a)**.

4. An outlier is an observation that is very far from the sample regression function. Suppose the equation is initially estimated using all observations, then re-estimated omitting outliers. How will the estimated slope coefficient change? How will R^2 change?

5. Obtain annual data for the Implicit Price Deflator and the Unemployment Rate.

   (a) Estimate (4.33) for the 1950s only.

   (b) Estimate (4.33) for the 1960s only.

   (c) Estimate (4.33) for the 1970s to the present.

   Calculate NIRU for each equation. What factors account for the differences in the results? Which period has the "best fitting" equation? State your criteria.

6. The standardized variable Z_x:

$$Z_x = (x - \mu_x)/\sigma_x.$$

   was introduced in Chapter 2. Z_x involves both a change of origin and scale for x. Consider the following population regression function:

$$Z_y = \alpha_0 + \alpha_1 Z_x + \varepsilon$$

   (a) What should the value of α_0 be?

   (b) Show that $\hat{\alpha}_1 = \text{Cov}(Z_x, Z_y)/\text{Var}(Z_x)$

$$= E(Z_x Z_y)$$

   (c) What is the relationship between $\hat{\alpha}_1$ and $\hat{\rho}_{xy}$?

7. Consider the relationship between the estimated error from the sample regression function, $\hat{\varepsilon}_i$, and either y_i or $\hat{y}_i$. If a least squares equation with $\hat{\varepsilon}_i$ as the dependent variable is estimated, show that:

   (a) The slope of the sample regression function with y_i as independent variable is $(1 - R^2)$.

   (b) The slope of the sample regression function with $\hat{y}_i$ as independent variable is 0. (*Hint:* Use Equation (4.16').)

8. Question 7**(b)** indicates that a plot of the least squares residuals and predicted values, with $\hat{\varepsilon}_i$ on the vertical axis and $\hat{y}_i$ on the horizontal axis should have a 0 slope. Suppose the actual plot reveals a systematic pattern, such as a U-shaped line. What might this indicate about the sample regression function?

9.   Regression equations are sometimes estimated using an explanatory variable that is a deviation from some value of interest. An example is a capacity utilization rate-unemployment rate equation, such as:

$$u_t = \alpha_0 + \alpha_1(CAP_t - CAP_t^f) + \varepsilon_t,$$

where CAP_t^f is a single value representing the capacity utilization rate corresponding to full employment (the value of 87.5 percent is sometimes used for this value).

(a) Will the estimated slope from this equation be the same or different from the equation with only CAP_t as an explanatory variable? Explain the basis for your answer. (*Hint:* Use Equations 7.16 and 7.17 for this answer.)

(b) Will the estimated intercept from this equation differ from that in the equation with CAP_t as an explanatory variable? (*Hint:* Refer to the formula for the least squares intercept.)

10.   In Appendix 4B, the term $g_i = (1/n - \hat{\mu}_x w_i)$ is used to obtain an expression for $Var(\hat{\alpha}_0)$, where $\omega_i = x_i'/\Sigma x_i'^2$. Show that:

(a) $\Sigma g_i = 1$

(b) $\Sigma g_i x_i = 0$.

APPENDIX 4A   DERIVATION OF THE LEAST SQUARES ESTIMATORS

This appendix uses calculus and matrix algebra to derive several of the formulas stated in this chapter. The reader is referred to the matrix algebra appendix in Chapter 2 and a calculus or mathematical economics text such as A. Chiang, *Fundamental Methods of Mathematical Economics* (McGraw-Hill) for necessary background.

Calculus Derivation of the Normal Equations

The two-variable sample regression equation is:

$$y_i = \hat{\alpha}_0 + \hat{\alpha}_1 x_i + \hat{\varepsilon}_i, \tag{4A.1}$$

which shows that the dependent variable (y) consists of a linear function of the explanatory variable and the equation residual. The least squares (LS) method obtains estimators of the coefficients in this function by minimizing the sum of the squared residuals in Equation (4A.1). Minimization of a function is a mathematical procedure which requires taking the first derivatives of the equation, setting these derivatives equal to zero, then solving for the coefficients of interest. Since we must obtain values for two parameters, it is necessary to take the *partial* derivatives of the function that is minimized.

The expression used to derive the least squares estimators is obtained by solving Equation (4A.1) for the error term, which allows us to depict the residual as a function of both $\hat{\alpha}_0$ and $\hat{\alpha}_1$:

$$\hat{\varepsilon}_i = y_i - \hat{\alpha}_0 - \hat{\alpha}_1 x_i. \tag{4A.2}$$

Squaring both sides of this equation, then summing, we arrive at the expression for the sum of the squared residuals (S):

$$S = \sum \hat{\varepsilon}_i^2$$
$$= \sum (y_i - \hat{\alpha}_0 - \hat{\alpha}_1 x_i)^2. \tag{4A.3}$$

This equation must be minimized with respect to both $\hat{\alpha}_0$ and $\hat{\alpha}_1$. By taking the partial derivative of Equation (4A.3) with respect to each coefficient, we obtain a set of simultaneous equations called the normal equations that provide us with the formulas for these coefficients. The chain rule is used to take the derivative of the squared term in brackets. The results are:

$$S_0 = \partial S / \partial \hat{\alpha}_0 = 2\sum (y_i - \hat{\alpha}_0 - \hat{\alpha}_1 x_i)(-1) = 0$$
$$S_1 = \partial S / \partial \hat{\alpha}_1 = 2\sum (y_i - \hat{\alpha}_0 - \hat{\alpha}_1 x_i)(-x_i) = 0 \tag{4A.4}$$

where the subscript for S denotes which partial derivative is taken. If we replace the bracket in each equation of Equation (4A.4) by $\hat{\varepsilon}_i$, these become:

$$-2\sum \hat{\varepsilon}_i = 0, \qquad \text{or } (1/n)\sum \hat{\varepsilon}_i = 0;$$
$$-2\sum \hat{\varepsilon}_i x_i = 0, \qquad \text{or } \sum \hat{\varepsilon}_i x_i = 0. \tag{4A.5}$$

The first of these shows that least squares produces a zero average residual. The second equation indicates that the residual is uncorrelated with the explanatory variable, since the expression on the right is $\text{Cov}(\hat{\varepsilon}_i, x_i)$ when $E(\hat{\varepsilon}_i) = 0$.

The following algebraic steps are used to solve the equations in Equation (4A.4) for the least squares coefficients:

For S_0:
$$\sum (y_i - \hat{\alpha}_0 - \hat{\alpha}_1 x_i) = 0$$
$$\sum y_i - n\hat{\alpha}_0 - \hat{\alpha}_1 \sum x_i = 0$$
$$(1/n)\sum y_i - (1/n)n\hat{\alpha}_0 - (1/n)\hat{\alpha}_1 \sum x_i = 0. \tag{4A.6}$$
$$\hat{\mu}_y - \hat{\alpha}_0 - \hat{\alpha}_1 \hat{\mu}_x = 0.$$

Solving for $\hat{\alpha}_0$ this becomes:

$$\hat{\alpha}_0 = \hat{\mu}_y - \hat{\alpha}_1 \hat{\mu}_x.$$

For S_1 (after dividing both sides by -2):

$$\sum (y_i - \hat{\alpha}_0 - \hat{\alpha}_1 x_i)(x_i) = 0$$
$$\sum x_i y_i - \hat{\alpha}_0 \sum x_i - \hat{\alpha}_1 \sum x_i^2 = 0. \tag{4A.7}$$

The final expression for $\hat{\alpha}_1$ involves substituting for $\hat{\alpha}_0$ into the above equation, factoring out $\hat{\alpha}_1$, then solving. Since this involves several tedious calculations, we will utilize matrix algebra to obtain the slope coefficient. This has the added benefit of illuminating several of the important matrices and topics outlined in the appendix to Chapter 2.

Matrix Algebra Solution of the Normal Equations

The normal equations of the sample regression function constitute a set of two simultaneous equations in two unknowns: $\hat{\alpha}_0$ and $\hat{\alpha}_1$. Dividing both of the equations in Equation (4A.4) by -2 gives the equation forms we work directly with:

$$\sum y_i - n\hat{\alpha}_0 - \hat{\alpha}_1 \sum x_i = 0 \tag{4A.6}$$
$$\sum x_i y_i - \hat{\alpha}_0 \sum x_i - \hat{\alpha}_1 \sum x_i^2 = 0. \tag{4A.7}$$

To put these equations into matrix form, we rewrite Equations (4A.6) and (4A.7) with the terms involving the α's on the left side. This gives:

$$n\hat{\alpha}_0 + \hat{\alpha}_1\sum x_i = \sum y_i$$
$$\hat{\alpha}_0\sum x_i + \hat{\alpha}_1\sum x_i^2 = \sum x_i y_i. \tag{4A.8}$$

This is put into the matrix form: $Z\hat{\alpha} = c$, by arranging the terms in the following way:

$$\begin{bmatrix} n & \sum x_i \\ \sum x_i & \sum x_i^2 \end{bmatrix}\begin{bmatrix} \hat{\alpha}_0 \\ \hat{\alpha}_1 \end{bmatrix} = \begin{bmatrix} \sum y_i \\ \sum x_i y_i \end{bmatrix} \tag{4A.8$'$}$$

Perform the multiplication to verify this is correct. In the matrix representation of this set of equations, $\hat{\alpha}$ is a column vector of estimated coefficients that we obtain by solving these equations. The 2×2 matrix Z on the left is the sum of the squares and cross product (SSCP) data matrix. To see this, consider the sample regression function:

$$y_i = \hat{\alpha}_0 + \hat{\alpha}_1 x_i + \hat{\varepsilon}_i. \tag{4A.1}$$

Assuming there are n observations used to estimate Equation (4A.1), we can write this in matrix form as:

$$\begin{bmatrix} y_1 \\ \vdots \\ y_n \end{bmatrix} = \begin{bmatrix} 1 & x_1 \\ \vdots & \vdots \\ 1 & x_n \end{bmatrix}\begin{bmatrix} \hat{\alpha}_0 \\ \hat{\alpha}_1 \end{bmatrix} + \begin{bmatrix} \hat{\varepsilon}_1 \\ \vdots \\ \hat{\varepsilon}_n \end{bmatrix}, \tag{4A.9}$$

or $Y = X\hat{\alpha} + \hat{\varepsilon}$. The SSCP matrix for X is obtained by performing the multiplication:

$$SSCP_x = X'X,$$

which, using the data matrix in Equation (4A.9), is:

$$SSCP_x = \begin{bmatrix} 1 & \cdots & 1 \\ x_1 & \cdots & x_n \end{bmatrix}\begin{bmatrix} 1 & x_1 \\ \vdots & \vdots \\ 1 & x_n \end{bmatrix} = \begin{bmatrix} \sum 1 = n & \sum x_i \\ \sum x_i & \sum x_i^2 \end{bmatrix} = Z.$$

The column vector on the right of Equation (4A.8) is actually $X'Y$, as the following multiplication shows:

$$X'Y = \begin{bmatrix} 1 & \cdots & 1 \\ x_1 & \cdots & x_n \end{bmatrix}\begin{bmatrix} y_1 \\ \vdots \\ y_n \end{bmatrix} = \begin{bmatrix} 1(y_1) + \cdots + 1(y_n) \\ x_1(y_1) + \cdots + x_n(y_n) \end{bmatrix} = \begin{bmatrix} \sum y_i \\ \sum x_i y_i \end{bmatrix}$$

The normal equations given by Equation (4A.8$'$) are therefore:

$$(X'X)\hat{\alpha} = X'Y, \tag{4A.10}$$

which is derived more formally in the appendix to Chapter 6.

Returning to the task at hand, the normal equations in (4A.8$'$) can be solved using the tools of the determinant and Cramer's Rule which are now outlined.

The determinant of a square matrix is a unique number associated with that matrix. If the matrix A is given by:

$$A = \begin{bmatrix} a_{11} & a_{12} \\ a_{21} & a_{22} \end{bmatrix},$$

then, the determinant of A, denoted $\det(A)$, is:

$$\det(A) = (a_{11}a_{22} - a_{12}a_{21}).$$ (4A.11)

Cramer's Rule provides a method for solving simultaneous equations such as Equation (4A.8'), which involves taking the ratio of two determinants. The denominator is the determinant of the matrix Z in Equation (4A.8'). The numerator of the expression for the first term is obtained by replacing the first column of Z by the column vector on the right side of Equation (4A.8'), which will be denoted Z_1. This becomes:

$$\hat{\alpha}_0 = \det(Z_1)/\det(Z)$$

$$= \det\begin{bmatrix} \sum y_i & \sum x_i \\ \sum x_i y_i & \sum x_i^2 \end{bmatrix} \Big/ \det\begin{bmatrix} n & \sum x_i \\ \sum x_i & \sum x_i^2 \end{bmatrix}$$ (4A.12)

$$\hat{\alpha}_0 = (\sum y_i \sum x_i^2 - \sum x_i \sum x_i y_i)/(n\sum x_i^2 - (\sum x_i)^2)$$

using the rule for determinants in Equation (4A.11).

The solution for the second coefficient, $\hat{\alpha}_1$, is obtained by creating a matrix Z_2, equal to the matrix Z with the second column replaced by the right side vector of Equation (4A.8'):

$$\hat{\alpha}_1 = \det(Z_2)/\det(Z)$$

$$= \det\begin{bmatrix} n & \sum y_i \\ \sum x_i & \sum x_i y_i \end{bmatrix} \Big/ \det\begin{bmatrix} n & \sum x_i \\ \sum x_i & \sum x_i^2 \end{bmatrix}$$ (4A.13)

$$\hat{\alpha}_1 = (n\sum x_i y_i - \sum x_i \sum y_i)/(n\sum x_i^2 - (\sum x_i)^2)$$

Substituting $n\hat{\mu}_x$ for Σx_i, $n\hat{\mu}_y$ for Σy_i, then dividing both the numerator and denominator of Equation (4A.13) by n produces:

$$\hat{\alpha}_1 = (\sum x_i y_i - n\hat{\mu}_x\hat{\mu}_y)/(\sum x_i^2 - n\hat{\mu}_x^2)$$

which can also be expressed as:

$$\hat{\alpha}_1 = \sum(x_i - \hat{\mu}_x)(y_i - \hat{\mu}_y)/\sum(x_i - \hat{\mu}_x)^2$$ (4A.14)

which is the expression given without deviation in this chapter.

APPENDIX 4B   OTHER IMPORTANT RESULTS CONCERNING THE BIVARIATE REGRESSION MODEL

Linearity and Unbiasedness of the Intercept Estimator

The equation for the least squares intercept estimator is:

$$\hat{\alpha}_0 = \hat{\mu}_y - \hat{\alpha}_1\hat{\mu}_x.$$

We can establish the linearity of this estimator by substituting the following terms into the above formula:

$$\hat{\mu}_y = \sum y_i/n$$

$$\hat{\alpha}_1 = \sum \omega_i y_i, \qquad \text{where } \omega_i \equiv x_i'/\sum x_i'^2.$$

Making these substitutions, the intercept estimator can be rewritten:

$$\hat{\alpha}_0 = \sum y_i/n - (\sum \omega_i y_i)\hat{\mu}_x.$$

Factoring out Σy_i:

$$\hat{\alpha}_0 = \sum (1/n - \hat{\mu}_x \omega_i) y_i.$$

If we denote the bracketed term g_i, this equation can be stated as:

$$\hat{\alpha}_0 = \sum g_i y_i.$$

Since we can represent $\hat{\alpha}_0$ as a linear function of the sample observations on y, it is a linear estimator.

Establishing the unbiasedness of this estimator requires that we express $\hat{\alpha}_0$ in terms of α_0. Starting with the least squares formula:

$$\hat{\alpha}_0 = \hat{\mu}_y - \hat{\alpha}_1 \hat{\mu}_x$$

we replace $\hat{\mu}_y$ with the following equation, which states $\hat{\mu}_y$ in terms of both population parameters:

$$\hat{\mu}_y = \alpha_0 + \alpha_1 \hat{\mu}_x + \hat{\mu}_\varepsilon.$$

The formula for $\hat{\alpha}_0$ then becomes:

$$\hat{\alpha}_0 = (\alpha_0 + \alpha_1 \hat{\mu}_x + \hat{\mu}_\varepsilon) - \hat{\alpha}_1 \hat{\mu}_x,$$

which, with rearrangement is:

$$\hat{\alpha}_0 = \alpha_0 + \hat{\mu}_x(\alpha_1 - \hat{\alpha}_1) + \hat{\mu}_\varepsilon. \qquad \textbf{(4B.1)}$$

This estimator is unbiased if the expected value of (4B.1) equals α_0. The expected value of this equation is:

$$E(\hat{\alpha}_0) = \alpha_0 + \hat{\mu}_x E(\alpha_1 - \hat{\alpha}_1) + E(\hat{\mu}_\varepsilon).$$

Based on assumption (4), that the values of x are fixed in repeated samples, $\hat{\mu}_x$ is a constant, which allows us to move this value outside of the expectation operator. Since $\hat{\mu}_\varepsilon$ is an unbiased estimator of the population error mean, then when model assumption (1) is met, so that $E(\varepsilon_i) = 0$, $E(\hat{\mu}_\varepsilon) = 0$, and the last term drops out. As long as the assumptions necessary to establish the unbiasedness of α_1 are satisfied, $E(\alpha_1 - \hat{\alpha}_1) = 0$. Thus, when $E(\varepsilon_i) = 0$, and x is either nonstochastic or uncorrelated with ε, all terms other than α_0 drop out of the above expression and $\hat{\alpha}_0$ is an unbiased estimator of α_0.

All the caveats discussed with reference to the unbiasedness of $\hat{\alpha}_1$ apply here. This result establishes that the mean of the sampling distribution of $\hat{\alpha}_0$ is α_0, so that on average, the least squares estimator of α_0 coincides with the latter value. Again, the unbiasedness of this estimator says nothing about the precision with which it is estimated.

Variances of the Least Squares Estimators

SLOPE ESTIMATOR.   The variance of the sampling distribution of $\hat{\alpha}_1$ is derived from the weighted average form of the expression for this estimator:

$$\hat{\alpha}_1 = \alpha_1 + \sum x_i' \varepsilon_i / \sum x_i'^2,$$

or
$\qquad\qquad\qquad\qquad\qquad\qquad\qquad\qquad\qquad\qquad\qquad\qquad\qquad$ **(4B.2)**

$$\hat{\alpha}_1 = \alpha_1 + \sum \omega_i \varepsilon_i$$

The variance of $\hat{\alpha}_1$ is given by the formula:

$$\text{Var}(\hat{\alpha}_1) = E[\hat{\alpha}_1 - E(\hat{\alpha}_1)]^2$$
$$= E[\hat{\alpha}_1 - \alpha_1]^2,$$

since $\hat{\alpha}_1$ is unbiased. If we restate Equation (4B.2) in terms of $(\hat{\alpha}_1 - \alpha_1)$, the resulting expression can be substituted into the bracketed term above:

$$(\hat{\alpha}_1 - \alpha_1) = \sum \omega_i \varepsilon_i = (\omega_1 \varepsilon_1 + \cdots + \omega_n \varepsilon_n). \tag{4B.3}$$

The variance of $\hat{\alpha}_1$ is the expected value of Equation (4B.3) squared:

$$\text{Var}(\hat{\alpha}_1) = E(\omega_1 \varepsilon_1 + \cdots + \omega_n \varepsilon_n)^2.$$

The assumption that x is nonrandom allows us to treat the weights in this expression as constants. If we assume for simplicity that $n = 2$, the final form of the expression on the right can be obtained more easily.

$$\text{Var}(\hat{\alpha}_1) = E[\omega_1 \varepsilon_1 + \omega_2 \varepsilon_2]^2$$
$$= E[\omega_1^2 \varepsilon_1^2 + \omega_2^2 \varepsilon_2^2 + 2\omega_1 \omega_2 \varepsilon_1 \varepsilon_2]$$
$$= \omega_1^2 E(\varepsilon_1^2) + \omega_2^2 E(\varepsilon_2^2) + 2\omega_1 \omega_2 E(\varepsilon_1 \varepsilon_2).$$

Based on assumptions (1) and (2) for the population regression function:

$$\text{Var}(\varepsilon_i) = E[\varepsilon_i - E(\varepsilon_i)]^2 = E(\varepsilon_i)^2 \qquad \text{since } E(\varepsilon_i) = 0$$
$$= \sigma_\varepsilon^2. \qquad \text{(from assumption (2)).}$$

The terms involving squares can thus be expressed as:

$$\omega_1^2 \sigma_\varepsilon^2 + \omega_2^2 \sigma_\varepsilon^2 = \sigma_\varepsilon^2 (\omega_1^2 + \omega_2^2).$$

The remaining term involves $E(\varepsilon_i \varepsilon_j)$, which denotes the error covariance:

$$\text{Cov}(\varepsilon_i, \varepsilon_j) = E[\varepsilon_i - E(\varepsilon_i)][\varepsilon_j - E(\varepsilon_j)] = E(\varepsilon_i \varepsilon_j) \qquad \text{from assumption (1)}$$

In the absence of serially correlated errors (assumption (2)), the covariance of ε_i and ε_j equals 0. This cross-product term in the expression for $\text{Var}(\hat{\alpha}_1)$ is therefore 0. Using this information, the variance expression can be written:

$$\text{Var}(\hat{\alpha}_1) = \sigma_\varepsilon^2 (\omega_1^2 + \omega_2^2). \tag{4B.4}$$

Finally, with $n = 2$,

$$\omega_1^2 + \omega_2^2 = \sum \omega_i^2$$

Substituting for ω in terms of x values, this is:

$$\sum \omega_i^2 = \sum (x_i' / \sum x_i'^2)^2 = \sum x_i'^2 / \sum_i x_i'^4$$

since $\Sigma x_i'^2$ is a constant. This simplifies to:

$$\sum \omega_i^2 = 1 / \sum x_i'^2 \tag{4B.5}$$

Substituting Equation (4B.5) into Equation (4B.4) gives the final expression for the slope variance:

$$\text{Var}(\hat{\alpha}_1) = \sigma_\varepsilon^2 / \sum x_i'^2 \tag{4B.6}$$

Equation (4B.6) is the formula for the variance of the sampling distribution of $\hat{\alpha}_1$. When this variance is small, the probability of obtaining an estimate "very far" from α_1 will tend to be low. In general, the smaller this variance, the more precise our estimation of α_1.[1] The variance of the sampling distribution of $\hat{\alpha}_1$ is smaller, the lower the variance of the stochastic error, σ_ε^2, and the greater the variance of x, which is related to the sum of the squared deviations of the x's in the denominator of Equation (4B.5).

INTERCEPT ESTIMATOR.
Deriving the expression for the variance of $\hat{\alpha}_0$ is more tedious than was the case for the intercept estimator. Because of this fact, only an abbreviated derivation is presented here. The starting point for this calculation is the formula for $\hat{\alpha}_0$:

$$\hat{\alpha}_0 = \hat{\mu}_y - \hat{\alpha}_1 \hat{\mu}_x,$$

which was manipulated earlier to give the following equation:

$$\hat{\alpha}_0 = \sum(1/n - \hat{\mu}_x \omega_i)y_i = g_i y_i,$$

where $g_i \equiv (1/n - \hat{\mu}_x \omega_i)$ and $\omega_i \equiv x_i'/\Sigma x_i'^2$. Substituting the right side of the population regression function for y_i into this expression allows us to state $\hat{\alpha}_0$ in terms of α_0:

$$\hat{\alpha}_0 = \sum g_i(\alpha_0 + \alpha_1 x_i + \varepsilon_i)$$
$$= \alpha_0 \sum g_i + \alpha_1 \sum g_i x_i + \sum g_i \varepsilon_i.$$

The end-of-chapter problems establish that $\Sigma g_i = 1$ and $\Sigma g_i x_i = 0$. The formula for $\hat{\alpha}_0$ thus simplifies to:

$$\hat{\alpha}_0 = \alpha_0 + \sum g_i \varepsilon_i. \tag{4B.7}$$

The formula for $\text{Var}(\hat{\alpha}_0)$ is:

$$\text{Var}(\hat{\alpha}_0) = E[\hat{\alpha}_0 - \alpha_0]^2$$

Rearranging Equation (4B.7) provides an expression for the right side of this formula:

$$E[\hat{\alpha}_0 - \alpha_0]^2 = E[\sum g_i \varepsilon_i]^2 \tag{4B.8}$$

Assuming again that $n = 2$, the bracketed term on the right is:

$$(\sum g_i \varepsilon_i)^2 = (g_1 \varepsilon_1 + g_2 \varepsilon_2)^2$$
$$= g_1^2 \varepsilon_1^2 + g_2^2 \varepsilon_2^2 + 2g_1 g_2 \varepsilon_1 \varepsilon_2.$$

Each of the g_i terms involves only n, x, and $\hat{\mu}_x$. These can be treated as constants when taking expected values. The expectation of the above expression is then:

$$E(\sum g_i \varepsilon_i)^2 = g_1^2 E(\varepsilon_1^2) + g_2^2 E(\varepsilon_2^2) + 2g_1 g_2 E(\varepsilon_1 \varepsilon_2).$$

According to the assumptions made for the population regression function:

$$E(\varepsilon_i^2) = \sigma_\varepsilon^2$$

and

$$E(\varepsilon_1 \varepsilon_2) = 0.$$

Substituting these into the expression for the variance for $\hat{\alpha}_0$:

$$E(\sum g_i \varepsilon_i)^2 = g_1^2 \sigma_\varepsilon^2 + g_2^2 \sigma_\varepsilon^2$$
$$= \sigma_\varepsilon^2 (g_1^2 + g_2^2)$$
$$= \sigma_\varepsilon^2 \sum g_i^2$$

---

[1] "Very far" will be defined precisely when hypothesis testing is discussed.

An individual g_i^2 equals:

$$g_i^2 = (1/n^2) + \hat{\mu}_x^2 \omega_i^2 - 2(1/n)\hat{\mu}_x \omega_i.$$

The sum of these terms is:

$$\sum g_i^2 = [1/n + \hat{\mu}_x^2 (1/\sum x_i'^2)],$$

which uses the fact that $\Sigma \omega_i$ is zero, and $\Sigma \omega_i^2 = 1/\Sigma x_i'^2$. Substituting this into Equation (4B.8) gives:

$$\text{Var}(\hat{\alpha}_0) = \sigma_\varepsilon^2 \left[\frac{1}{n} + \frac{\hat{\mu}_x^2}{\sum x_i'^2} \right] = \sigma_\varepsilon^2 \frac{\sum x_i^2}{n \sum x_i'^2} \tag{4B.9}$$

The expression on the right of Equation (4B.9) is derived by using the formula:

$$\sum x_i'^2 = \sum x_i^2 - n\hat{\mu}_x^2$$

Equation (4B.9) is the formula for the dispersion of the sampling distribution of $\hat{\alpha}_0$. The variance of $\hat{\alpha}_0$ is smaller, the lower is σ_ε^2, the less $\hat{\mu}_x$, the greater is sample size, n, and the larger the variance of x.

5

Extensions of the Bivariate Regression Model: Statistical Inference and Forecasting

The practice of applied econometrics does not end with calculation of the sample regression function. Our primary interest lies in ascertaining the unknown parameters of the population regression function. The least squares estimators are the source of our inferences about these values. The least squares technique produces point estimators; we approximate a population parameter with a single value (point). Because these estimators are unbiased, they coincide with their population values *on average*.[1] Any particular estimate need not equal its population value, however; the difference is the sampling error of that estimate.

Because of sampling error, any inferences we make concerning population parameters must deal explicitly with the question of whether the magnitude of sampling error is "acceptable" or "unacceptable." There is one operational problem involved in any such determination: since the population parameter is unknown, so, too, is the magnitude of the sampling error involved. Yet if sampling error is unknown, how can we make a decision regarding its acceptability?

The solution to this problem requires that we make judgments relative to *hypothesized* values of population parameters. This procedure is called **hypothesis testing**. This, together with estimation, is the core of **statistical inference**, where statements concerning actual values of population parameters are made. A key element in hypothesis testing is the **interval estimate**, where we transform a point estimate into a range of "likely" values we expect to observe as the result of sampling error. These intervals are based on the sampling distributions of the least squares estimators. "Likely" values are defined as those with a substantial probability of occurrence. Statistical inference therefore involves hypothesizing values that a population parameter might take; estimating this parameter; then using this estimate, along with knowledge

---

[1] As long as the assumptions stated in Chapter 4 are met.

of its sampling distribution, to judge the likelihood of observing the actual divergence between estimated and hypothesized parameter values.

This chapter provides the background needed to perform statistical inference on a sample regression function. The first part of this chapter associates a probability distribution with the equation errors, then outlines the method used to convert a point estimate into an interval estimate. Following this, the basic elements of hypothesis testing are set forth. Examples of different types of hypotheses are formulated then tested on estimated equations. This chapter concludes with a discussion of forecasting using a sample regression function.

THE PROBABILITY DISTRIBUTION OF THE EQUATION ERRORS

The least squares technique discussed in Chapter 4 provides a methodology for estimating a population regression function such as:

$$y_i = \alpha_0 + \alpha_1 x_i + \varepsilon_i, \tag{5.1}$$

which links an explanatory variable, x, to the dependent variable and a stochastic error, which is a random variable. To ascertain the properties of the least squares estimators, we made the following set of assumptions about the population regression function:

1. $E(\varepsilon_i) = 0$
2. $\text{Var}(\varepsilon_i) = \sigma_\varepsilon^2$
3. $\text{Cov}(\varepsilon_i, \varepsilon_j) = 0$
4. x is nonrandom, or if stochastic, uncorrelated with ε.

Assumptions (1)–(3) pertain to the conditional distributions of the disturbance terms. Each of these has a 0 mean, a constant variance, σ_ε^2, and individual errors are uncorrelated. None of these assumptions specifies the probability distribution associated with the stochastic errors. Because the stochastic error reflects the sum of a large number of factors omitted from the population regression function, we assume that:

5. each ε_i is normally distributed.

The selection of this distribution is based on the Central Limit Theorem presented in Chapter 2. Note that estimator properties such as unbiasedness are not predicated on the normal distribution of the stochastic error.

The assumption of normally distributed errors enables us to make inferences about the coefficients in the population regression function based on those in the sample regression function. As we now show, including assumption (5) among the set of population regression function assumptions makes each least squares coefficient a normally distributed random variable. To see this, recall that Equation (5.1) expresses y as a linear function of ε. By assumption (5), the disturbances are normally distributed. The dependent variable, y, is then also normally distributed since it is a linear function of a normally distributed random variable. The mean of y is:

$$E(y_i) = \alpha_0 + \alpha_1 x_i. \tag{5.2}$$

The variance of y_i is found using the formula:

$$\text{Var}(y_i) = E[y_i - E(y_i)]^2.$$

Substituting Equation (5.2) for $E(y_i)$:

$$\text{Var}(y_i) = E[(\alpha_0 + \alpha_1 x_i + \varepsilon_i) - (\alpha_0 + \alpha_1 x_i)]^2$$
$$\text{Var}(y_i) = E[(\alpha_0 - \alpha_0) + (\alpha_1 x_i - \alpha_1 x_i) + \varepsilon_i]^2$$
$$= E[\varepsilon_i]^2$$
$$= \sigma_\varepsilon^2. \tag{5.3}$$

Combining the normality of y with Equations (5.2) and (5.3) allows us to summarize the distributional information for y:

$$y_i \sim N(\alpha_0 + \alpha_1 x_i, \sigma_\varepsilon^2). \tag{5.4}$$

As Equation (5.4) shows, estimating α_0 and α_1 with least squares is equivalent to estimating the mean of the dependent variable in the population regression function.

Returning to the task of establishing that the least squares estimators are normally distributed, we will use the following notation (this was used in Chapter 4 and Appendix 4B): let $\omega_i \equiv x_i'/\Sigma x_i'^2$, where $x_i' \equiv (x_i - \hat{\mu}_x)$, and $g_i \equiv (1/n - \hat{\mu}_x \omega_i)$. Then:

$$\hat{\alpha}_0 = \sum(1/n - \hat{\mu}_x \omega_i) y_i$$
$$= \sum g_i y_i$$
$$\hat{\alpha}_1 = \sum x_i' y_i / \sum x_i'^2$$
$$= \sum \omega_i y_i.$$

Each least squares estimator is thus a linear function of y. Since y is itself a normally distributed random variable, both $\hat{\alpha}_0$ and $\hat{\alpha}_1$ are also normally distributed. The mean and variance of each of these estimators were also stated in Chapter 4. Combining this information, the normality assumption for the stochastic errors implies that:

$$\hat{\alpha}_0 \sim N(\alpha_0, \sigma_\varepsilon^2 \sum x_i^2 / n \sum x_i'^2)$$
$$\hat{\alpha}_1 \sim N(\alpha_1, \sigma_\varepsilon^2 / \sum x_i'^2). \tag{5.5}$$

The information contained in Equation (5.5) associates the normal distribution with the sampling distributions of these estimators. Each sampling distribution is centered at its population parameter, with a variance given by the second term in the above expression.[2]

---

[2] This presupposes all the caveats stated with reference to this result in Chapter 4.

Our ability to use the normal distribution when making inferences about the population coefficients from the least squares coefficients is limited, since this particular distribution presupposes knowledge of the actual variances of $\hat{\alpha}_0$ and $\hat{\alpha}_1$. For the estimators in Equation (5.5), this requires knowledge of σ_ε^2. Because this value is usually not known, it is necessary to find an alternative distribution that can be associated with the least squares coefficients. Using the distributional information contained in Equation (5.5), these coefficients can be related to the t-distribution. This will be illustrated for the slope coefficient, $\hat{\alpha}_1$.

We saw in Chapter 2 that a t-distributed random variable can be expressed as the ratio of a unit normal random variable to the square root of a chi-square variable divided by its degrees of freedom. Since $\hat{\alpha}_1$ is normally distributed, we can transform it into a unit normal random variable by standardizing it (recall from Chapter 2 that this consists of subtracting its mean then dividing the resulting expression by the standard deviation). The unit normal random variable that corresponds to $\hat{\alpha}_1$ is:

$$(\hat{\alpha}_1 - \alpha_1)/\sigma_1 \sim N(0, 1), \tag{5.6}$$

where σ_1, the population standard deviation of this estimator, equals the square root of $\sigma_\varepsilon^2/\Sigma x_i'^2$. Equation (5.6) is the numerator of the t-distributed random variable. The denominator is the square root of a chi-square random variable divided by its degrees of freedom. Using the actual and estimated variances of the equation error, the expression for this chi-square variable is:

$$(n - 2)\hat{\sigma}_\varepsilon^2/\sigma_\varepsilon^2$$

This variable has $(n - 2)$ degrees of freedom since estimating $\hat{\alpha}_1$ requires that we calculate both $\hat{\mu}_x$ and $\hat{\mu}_y$, which "uses up" 2 degrees of freedom. When we divide this expression by its degrees of freedom, the degrees of freedom terms cancel, leaving us with the ratio $\hat{\sigma}_\varepsilon^2/\sigma_\varepsilon^2$. Taking the square root of this expression:

$$\sqrt{\hat{\sigma}_\varepsilon^2/\sigma_\varepsilon^2} = \hat{\sigma}_\varepsilon/\sigma_\varepsilon \tag{5.7}$$

Equation (5.7) is the denominator of the t-distributed random variable. The ratio of Equation (5.6) to Equation (5.7) gives the t-distributed random variable that pertains for the least squares slope coefficient:

$$\frac{(\hat{\alpha}_1 - \alpha_1)}{\sigma_\varepsilon/\sqrt{\sum x_i'^2}} \left/ \frac{\hat{\sigma}_\varepsilon}{\sigma_\varepsilon} \right.$$

or

$$(\hat{\alpha}_1 - \alpha_1)/(\hat{\sigma}_\varepsilon/\sqrt{\sum x_i'^2}) = (\hat{\alpha}_1 - \alpha_1)/\hat{\sigma}_1 \sim t_{n-2}. \tag{5.8}$$

where $\hat{\sigma}_1$ is the estimated standard deviation of $\hat{\alpha}_1$. The value of this random variable denotes the number of standard deviations $\hat{\alpha}_1$ is from α_1. If, for example, the value of this statistic is 2, then $(\hat{\alpha}_1 - \alpha_1) = 2\hat{\sigma}_1$, and the estimated slope, $\hat{\alpha}_1$, is 2 standard deviations above its population parameter α_1. *The statistic given by Equation (5.8) thus designates the sampling error of an estimate, $\hat{\alpha}_1 - \alpha_1$, in units of standard deviations. We will see shortly that this value is the basis for deciding whether sampling error is "large" or of an acceptable magnitude.*

STATISTICAL INFERENCE AND HYPOTHESIS TESTING IN ECONOMETRICS

Interval Estimation: The Confidence Interval

All of the estimators discussed up to this point are **point estimators**: they approximate population parameters with single values. Examples of point estimators are the sample mean, $\hat{\mu}_x$, and the least squares coefficients, $\hat{\alpha}_0$ and $\hat{\alpha}_1$. According to the Gauss-Markov theorem, each of these is the best linear, unbiased estimator of its population parameter.[3] Except for linearity, there is no guarantee that the desirable outcomes associated with these properties will prevail for a single estimate obtained from any of these estimators. The value of an unbiased estimator, for example, coincides with its population parameter *on average*. This property offers no guidance for a single estimate, however. Sampling error, the divergence of an estimate from its population parameter, is therefore likely to occur.

On average, the sampling error of an unbiased estimator is zero. However, it is the *variance* of an estimator, which characterizes the dispersion in values we can expect to observe, that is a key determinant of the magnitude of sampling error. Estimators with large variances produce individual estimates which deviate from their population parameters more often and over a wider range than do estimators with small variances. To allow for the likelihood of sampling error, a second type of estimate, called a **confidence interval**, is constructed that defines a *range* of values that can be associated with a point estimate. These values are derived from a point estimate, its variance, and the probability distribution associated with its sampling distribution, which delineates the range of likely values we can expect point estimates to take. The other determinant of the width of this interval is the **level of confidence** that is selected. This designates the likelihood that the population parameter will fall within this interval.

The steps involved in constructing a confidence interval can be illustrated using an estimator $\hat{\alpha}$ of a random variable α, where $\hat{\alpha} \sim N(\alpha, \sigma^2)$. The standardized form of this variable is: $z = (\hat{\alpha} - \alpha)/\sigma$. Since the normal distribution applies to this estimator, we obtain the values that correspond to the desired level of confidence from the unit normal table. If, for example, we select a 95 percent level of confidence, the z value that bounds 2.5 percent (0.025) in each tail for this distribution is 1.96. Thus, 95 percent of all values for a unit normal random variable occur within the range from -1.96 (z_1) to 1.96 (z_2), or $P(z_1 < z < z_2) = 0.95$. Substituting for z in the middle of the bracketed term:

$$P(-1.96 < (\hat{\alpha} - \alpha)/\sigma < 1.96) = 0.95. \qquad (5.9)$$

On average, the inequality inside the brackets is satisfied 95 percent of the time. We obtain the formula for the 95 percent confidence interval by solving this expression

---

[3] Note that the Gauss-Markov theorem applies to the sample mean as well as to the least squares estimators.

for α (the unknown) in terms of the point estimate ($\hat{\alpha}$), the standard deviation of this estimate (σ), and the z values. The solution to the inequality

$$-1.96 < (\hat{\alpha} - \alpha)/\sigma < 1.96$$

is:

$$\hat{\alpha} - 1.96 \cdot \sigma < \alpha < \hat{\alpha} + 1.96 \cdot \sigma \qquad (5.10)$$

Equation (5.10) gives the expression for a 95 percent confidence interval for the point estimate $\hat{\alpha}$, which is often written in the form:

$$\hat{\alpha} \pm 1.96 \cdot \sigma \qquad (5.11)$$

The product of the probability (z) value and the standard deviation is sometimes referred to as the **margin for sampling error**.[4] Equation (5.11) shows how we convert the point estimate $\hat{\alpha}$ into an interval: we subtract the margin for sampling error from the point estimate to form the **lower confidence bound**, then add this quantity to our point estimate to arrive at the **upper confidence bound**.

To illustrate the steps involved in constructing a 95 percent confidence interval, let us choose the sample mean as our estimator. According to the central limit theorem, this estimator is normally distributed with mean μ and variance σ^2/n. If we utilize a sample (n) of 36 observations and assume that the population has a variance (σ^2) of 144, then the standard deviation of our estimator, $\sigma/\sqrt{n}$, equals 2. If our sample mean is 5, the 95 percent confidence interval for this estimate is:

$$5 \pm 1.96(2) = (1.08, 8.92). \qquad (5.12)$$

In this example, the margin for sampling error is 3.92 ($= 1.96 \times 2$). This value is added and subtracted from the point estimate of 5 to give an interval such as that in Equation (5.13):

$$\qquad (5.13)$$

| 1.08 | 5 | 8.92 |

The confidence interval given by Equation (5.12) does *not* indicate a 95 percent probability that μ lies between 1.08 and 8.92. The general confidence interval formula (5.10), when stated in terms of $\hat{\mu}_x$, gives a random interval, since $\hat{\mu}_x$ is a random variable. Once we substitute a specific value for $\hat{\mu}_x$, as in Equation (5.12), the interval is then fixed, and probabilistic statements are no longer valid. *The correct interpretation of a 95 percent confidence interval states that if we construct a large number of such intervals, then, on average, μ_x will be contained in 95 percent of these intervals.* Note the repeated sampling context that underlies this statement. Much of what we can correctly state about both point and interval estimators presupposes this setting.

The width of a confidence interval depends critically on the margin for sampling error involved. This, in turn, depends on the selected level of confidence and the variance of our point estimate. If we retain the values from the previous example but in-

---

[4] See G. Smith, *Statistical Reasoning* (Boston: Allyn and Bacon), 1985, for this terminology.

crease the level of confidence to 99 percent, the margin for sampling error rises. From the normal table, the probability values for this level of confidence are the z values that correspond to 0.005 in each tail: ± 2.575. The 99 percent confidence interval is:

$$5 \pm 2.575(2) = (-0.15, 10.15).$$

This is wider than the 95 percent confidence interval (1.08, 8.92), since increasing the level of confidence raises the margin for sampling error from 3.92 to 5.15. Increasing the variance of a point estimate has a similar effect on confidence interval width. If we continue to assume that sample size is 36 but the variance of x increases from 144 to 196, the standard deviation of $\hat{\mu}_x$ rises, making the 95 percent confidence interval:

$$5 \pm 1.96(14/6) = (0.43, 9.57).$$

By raising the variance of $\hat{\mu}_x$, the larger variance of x increases the margin for sampling error from 3.92 to 4.57.[5]

CONFIDENCE INTERVALS FOR REGRESSION COEFFICIENTS.   When the stochastic error in the population regression function is normally distributed, both of the least squares estimators are normally distributed with means and variances given by the expressions in (5.5). Because σ_ε^2 is unknown, the actual variances of these estimators are also unknown. We must therefore use the t-distribution to construct confidence intervals for these estimators. The distributional information for these coefficients is then:

$$(\hat{\alpha}_0 - \alpha_0)/\hat{\sigma}_0 \sim t_{n-2}$$
$$(\hat{\alpha}_1 - \alpha_1)/\hat{\sigma}_1 \sim t_{n-2},$$

where $\hat{\sigma}_0$ and $\hat{\sigma}_1$ are the estimated standard deviations of the intercept and slope estimator, respectively. Confidence intervals for $\hat{\alpha}_1$ are obtained from the following expression:

$$P(t_1 < (\hat{\alpha}_1 - \alpha_1)/\hat{\sigma}_1 < t_2) = c, \tag{5.14}$$

where c designates the level of confidence expressed as a decimal (such as 0.95). Since values from the t-distribution depend on the number of degrees of freedom, the above notation must be modified to reflect this fact. A confidence interval contains $(1 - c)/2$ percent of all probability in each tail. For example, a 95 percent confidence interval has $(1 - .95)/2$, or 0.025 in each tail. Denoting this value as p, the appropriate t-value for Equation (5.14) is $t_{p,n-2}$, which designates a t-value with $n - 2$ degrees of freedom, and probability $p = (1 - c)/2$ in each tail. Substituting this into Equation (5.14) gives:

$$P(-t_{p,n-2} < (\hat{\alpha}_1 - \alpha_1)/\hat{\sigma}_1 < t_{p,n-2}) = c, \tag{5.15}$$

---

[5] The variance of the sample mean is also affected by n. The width of a confidence interval for $\hat{\mu}_x$ is therefore affected by this value in addition to the variance of x. The implications of this factor are not pursued here, although it is not difficult to show that the margin for sampling error is inversely related to sample size.

where $t_{p,n-2}$ is $t_{0.025,n-2}$ for a 95 percent level of confidence. Solving the inequality in Equation (5.15) for α_1 gives the final expression for the confidence interval:

$$\hat{\alpha}_1 - t_{p,n-2} \cdot \hat{\sigma}_1 < \alpha_1 < \hat{\alpha}_1 + t_{p,n-2} \cdot \hat{\sigma}_1,$$

which can be rewritten as:

$$\hat{\alpha}_1 \pm t_{p,n-2} \cdot \hat{\sigma}_1. \tag{5.16}$$

The far right term in Equation (5.16), which gives the margin for sampling error associated with this estimator, is the basis for transforming the point estimator $\hat{\alpha}_1$ into an interval estimator. The margin for sampling error is the product of a probability value ($t_{p,n-2}$) and the estimated standard deviation of $\hat{\alpha}_1$. The greater either the level of confidence or the dispersion in the sampling distribution of this estimator, the larger is the margin for sampling error, and hence the width of the confidence interval. Following a similar set of steps, the confidence interval for the least squares intercept estimator is:

$$\hat{\alpha}_0 \pm t_{p,n-2} \cdot \hat{\sigma}_0. \tag{5.16'}$$

Calculating confidence intervals for the least squares estimators is straightforward. Assume the following sample regression function results are derived from an equation that uses 16 observations:

	COEFFICIENT	STANDARD DEVIATION
$\hat{\alpha}_0$	5.40	2.0
$\hat{\alpha}_1$	2.65	1.2

The correct number of degrees of freedom used in constructing confidence intervals for these estimates is $n - 2$, which, with a sample size of 16, equals 14. The 95 percent confidence intervals for these estimates thus use the value of $t_{0.025,14}$ from the t-table. This t-value, $t_{0.025,14}$, is 2.145. The 95 percent confidence intervals are:

$$\hat{\alpha}_0: \quad 5.40 \pm 2.145(2) = (1.11, 9.69)$$

$$\hat{\alpha}_1: 2.65 \pm 2.145(1.2) \ \ = (0.08, 5.22)$$

As an exercise, calculate the 99 percent confidence intervals for this example.

Our earlier discussion of confidence intervals pointed out that these vary depending on values of the point estimate, its variance, and the selected level of confidence. If we were to take repeated samples and estimate the least squares coefficients, we would obtain a number of different confidence intervals for each of these coefficients. The percentage of the resulting confidence intervals that contain the population parameter of interest would coincide with the selected level of confidence.

We now attempt to replicate this repeated sampling context with the aid of the Monte Carlo method that was originally employed in Chapter 4. We again utilize the population regression function: $y_i = 15 + 1.5x_i + \varepsilon_i$, and construct data consistent with this model. The sample size for each regression is 100, and 50 regressions are estimated in all. The errors for each regression were generated from the normal distribution random number generator of SAS. Each set of 100 errors is (approximately) normally distributed with mean 0 and unit variance. The single set of x values that is used in each of these regressions was drawn from the uniform distribution random number generator in SAS. Observations for the dependent variables in these equations are constructed according to the formula:

$$y_i^{(j)} = 15 + 1.5x_i + \varepsilon_i^{(j)} \qquad (i = 1, \ldots, 100) \qquad (j = 1, \ldots, 50),$$

where the subscript i denotes the observation, and the superscript j refers to the equation number. Table 5.1 shows the slope estimates and the 95 percent confidence

Table 5.1 95 Percent Confidence Intervals for the Slope Estimator from a Monte Carlo Experiment with a Population Regression Function

$$y_i = 15 + 1.5x_i + \varepsilon_i$$

	LOWER BOUND	POINT ESTIMATE	UPPER BOUND
(1)	1.28993	1.43603	1.58213
(2)	1.34271	1.50795	1.67319
(3)	1.30301	1.46648	1.62994
(4)	1.37053	1.52304	1.67556
(5)	1.26695	1.41932	1.57169
(6)	**1.51484**	**1.67598**	**1.83713**
(7)	1.41578	1.55909	1.70241
(8)	1.30660	1.46732	1.62804
(9)	1.21042	1.38012	1.54982
(10)	1.37721	1.52345	1.66969
(11)	1.48402	1.64157	1.79912
(12)	1.42491	1.56680	1.70870
(13)	**1.15168**	**1.31976**	**1.48783**
(14)	1.29608	1.44598	1.59587
(15)	1.21619	1.36935	1.52251
(16)	1.19147	1.34576	1.50005
(17)	1.31761	1.46347	1.60933
(18)	**1.53098**	**1.68625**	**1.84153**
(19)	1.29659	1.43136	1.56613
(20)	1.33807	1.48574	1.63341
(21)	1.35116	1.50007	1.64897
(22)	1.38333	1.54853	1.71373
(23)	1.42796	1.57515	1.72234
(24)	1.29609	1.46788	1.63968
(25)	1.29015	1.46434	1.63852

bounds for the first 25 of these regressions, which are derived from the following expression:

$$\hat{\alpha}_1^{(j)} \pm 1.96 \times (\hat{\sigma}_\varepsilon^{(j)}/\sqrt{\sum x_i'^2}) \qquad (j = 1, \ldots, 50)$$

The disparities in these intervals result exclusively from variations in both the estimated coefficients and in the margins for sampling error. Differences in the margins for sampling error occur solely as the result of divergences in equation standard errors, since with a single confidence level and a fixed set of x observations, both the value of $t_{p,n-2}$ and $\Sigma x_i'^2$ are constants.

Only three of these confidence intervals, (6), (13), and (18), exclude the population value of 1.5 for this coefficient. Two overstate this value, while one understates it. All told, only five out of the total of 50 intervals fail to contain this value. Thus, even with so small a number of regressions, which falls far short of the number assumed by the repeated sampling context of our previous statements about confidence intervals, 90 percent of the intervals contain the population parameter. We have therefore approximated the expectation of 95 percent very closely. This is far superior to the performance of the point estimates: only four of the 50 coincide (to two decimal places) with the population parameter.

Hypothesis Testing

Econometric analysis utilizes a methodology, called **hypothesis testing**, that allows us to make inferences about magnitudes of population parameters based on estimates of these values. The set of steps involved in hypothesis testing consist of:

1. setting forth a testable hypothesis relating to a possible value of a population parameter, along with an alternative for the case where the original hypothesis is rejected
2. estimating the relevant population parameter
3. developing a statistic with which to test the hypothesis and
4. defining an objective criterion that can be used to decide whether the difference between the estimate and the hypothesized parameter value is acceptable.

We will now discuss the methodology of hypothesis testing applied to econometric equations.

FORMULATING TESTABLE HYPOTHESES.   Econometric analysis involves two types of hypotheses. **Maintained hypotheses** are not subjected to empirical testing. We assume that these are met in practice. An example of a maintained hypothesis is the normal distribution of the errors in the population regression function. The other type of hypothesis, which we are concerned with here, is a **testable hypothesis**. Decisions on the accuracy of these hypotheses are made empirically.

The main hypothesis we test is the **null hypothesis**, which is denoted H_0. This hypothesis states that a population parameter takes a value that is consistent with a relationship we are interested in testing.[6] Since H_0 involves the strict equality of a population parameter and a numerical value, this is called a **simple hypothesis**. The classical method of hypothesis testing involves stating the null hypothesis as the relationship we wish to *disprove*. For example, if we are interested in establishing that an explanatory variable x belongs in the following population regression function:

$$y_i = \alpha_0 + \alpha_1 x_i + \varepsilon_i,$$

our null hypothesis states that x does *not* influence y. If H_0 is true, the coefficient of x, α_1, is 0. The null hypothesis used to test whether x belongs in this equation is, therefore:

$$H_0: \alpha_1 = 0.$$

The empirical test conducted to ascertain the validity of H_0 requires an additional hypothesis, called the **alternative hypothesis** (H_a), that we accept when available empirical evidence reveals an unacceptably low probability that H_0 is true. The alternative hypothesis can be either a simple hypothesis, involving strict equality of a population parameter with some value, or a **composite hypothesis**, which entails either non-equality or an inequality. An alternative hypothesis that can be used to test whether x belongs in the previous population regression function is:

$$H_a: \alpha_1 \neq 0.$$

If we reject H_0, we then accept the alternative hypothesis of a nonzero α_1. Alternative hypotheses stated in terms of non-equality fail to provide any guidance as to the actual magnitude of α_1, other than its being different from the value stipulated in the null hypothesis. *When theory indicates the expected sign of a variable, this information should be utilized when specifying the alternative hypothesis.* This allows more specific guidance concerning inferences about α_1 in the event we reject H_0. If x and y are inversely related, for example, then to establish whether x belongs in the equation for y, we should stipulate the following set of hypotheses:

$$H_0: \alpha_1 = 0$$

$$H_a: \alpha_1 < 0.$$

If we reject H_0, we conclude that x does in fact belong in this equation, and that it displays the expected direction of influence. When the expected sign of x is positive, the alternative hypothesis becomes:

$$H_a: \alpha_1 > 0.$$

If available empirical evidence suggests that the null hypothesis is true, do we accept this hypothesis? While the answer to this question may appear to be obvious, some elaboration is required. Uncertainty always exists in statistical inference. Sampling error almost always appears when we estimate population parameters, and new evidence that has a significant bearing on our conclusions can arise. Because of

---

[6] The null hypothesis can be a composite hypothesis. That case is not considered in this text.

this, a margin for error *always* exists in empirical work. The following quote, which makes an analogy between hypothesis testing and court trials, states this point very effectively:

> . . . a statistical test is like a trial in a court of law. A man on trial is considered innocent unless the evidence suggests *beyond a reasonable doubt* that he is guilty. Similarly a null hypothesis is regarded as valid unless the evidence suggests—also beyond a reasonable doubt—that it is not true. . . . when a statistical test is conducted, all evidence and prior information are used in accordance with predetermined rules, and a conclusion of 'reject' or 'do not reject' the null hypothesis is obtained. . . . just as a court pronounces a verdict as 'not guilty' rather than 'innocent,' so the conclusion of a statistical test is 'do not reject' rather than 'accept.'[7]

With this caveat in mind, we now present additional examples of deriving testable hypotheses from theoretical relationships, then illustrate the methodology used to evaluate these.

A number of different hypotheses can be formulated by referring to the Keynesian *consumption function*. This function expresses real personal consumption expenditure (c) as a linear function of real disposable income (y), which we can summarize with the following population regression function:

$$c_t = \alpha_0 + \alpha_1 y_t + \varepsilon_t \qquad (5.17)$$

The intercept in this equation, α_0, represents autonomous consumption, the value of consumption when disposable income equals 0. The expected sign of α_0 is positive, since we presume that individuals will draw on savings and other assets, or dissave, in order to meet subsistence requirements when y_t is 0. The slope of the Keynesian consumption function, α_1, is the rate of change in consumption as disposable income rises. This is called the marginal propensity to consume (MPC). According to Keynesian theory, the MPC is a positive fraction, so that only a portion of any increase in disposable income is consumed. Disposable income is used for consumption and savings (s) so that:

$$y_t = c_t + s_t.$$

If we substitute the right side of Equation (5.17) for c_t in this equation and omit the stochastic error, the following implied savings function results:

$$s_t = -\alpha_0 + (1 - \alpha_1)y_t$$
$$= \beta_0 + \beta_1 y_t$$

This function is "implied" since it is constructed directly from the coefficients in the consumption function. The slope of this function, β_1, is the marginal propensity to save (MPS), which is defined in an analogous fashion to the MPC. It can be shown that MPC + MPS = 1.[8]

---

[7] J. Kmenta, *Elements of Econometrics*, 2d. ed. (New York: Macmillan), 1986, pp. 112–113.

[8] The steps involved are the following: start with $y_t = c_t + s_t$, take the change (first difference) in each of the terms in this equation, then divide by Δy_t. The result is the equation given in the text.

Several hypothesis tests concerning the MPC are possible. If our interest lies in testing whether disposable income affects consumption, our null hypothesis is: $H_0: \alpha_1 = 0$. An alternative hypothesis that incorporates the expected positive sign for y_t in Equation (5.17) is: $H_a: \alpha_1 > 0$. If we wish to test whether the MPC is greater than the MPS, we must utilize the fact that MPC + MPS = 1. The null hypothesis stipulates equality between the MPC and MPS, or: $H_0: \alpha_1 = 1/2$. We can also express this as: $H_0: \alpha_1 = \beta_1$. The alternative hypothesis states what we are interested in testing, that the MPC > MPS, or that MPC > 1/2. Therefore:

$$H_0: \alpha_1 = 1/2,$$

or

$$H_a: \alpha_1 > 1/2.$$

We can utilize the unemployment rate (u)-capacity utilization rate (CAP) equation from Chapter 4 to formulate other testable hypotheses. Recall that the population regression function for this relationship is:

$$u_t = \alpha_0 + \alpha_1 CAP_t + \varepsilon_t.$$

We can test whether the capacity utilization rate in manufacturing affects the civilian unemployment rate with the null hypothesis $H_0: \alpha_1 = 0$. Our alternative hypothesis can postulate either non-equality—$H_a: \alpha_1 \neq 0$—or inequality, which reflects the expected sign of CAP—$H_a: \alpha_1 < 0$.

These hypotheses can be made more specific by referring to the theoretical discussion of Okun's Law in Chapter 4. To test whether increases in the capacity utilization rate cause less than proportionate decreases in the unemployment rate, our null hypothesis postulates a proportional negative response: $H_0: \alpha_1 = -1$. The alternative hypothesis can state either that H_0 is not true—$H_a: \alpha_1 \neq -1$—or, more appropriately, that the magnitude of this response is less than proportionate—$H_a: \alpha_1 > -1$ (less negative).

Finally, we can formulate testable hypotheses about elasticities using the log-linear production function from Chapter 4. Recall that the Cobb-Douglass production function takes the form:

$$q = Ak^{\alpha}L^{\beta},$$

where α and β are the elasticity of output with respect to capital and labor, respectively. The short-run form of this function, with constant capital ($k = k_0$), is:

$$q = (Ak_0^{\alpha})L^{\beta} = A_* L^{\beta},$$

where $A_* = (Ak_0^{\alpha})$. Using a logarithmic transformation, we can linearize this equation, then add a stochastic error, so that it is amenable to least squares estimation. The resulting equation is:

$$\ln(q_t) = \alpha_* + \beta \ln(L_t) + \varepsilon_t$$

where $\alpha_* = \ln(A_*)$. The coefficient β, the elasticity of output with respect to labor input, is the proportionate response of output to changes in labor input. If output is unit elastic, then $\beta = 1$, and any rise in labor input produces an equal percent increase in output. When output is labor inelastic, then $\beta < 1$, and variations in labor input result in less than proportionate changes in total output. Finally, output is labor elastic if $\beta > 1$, and output responds more than proportionately to changes in labor input.

Since the point of demarcation for these elasticities is the number 1, we can formulate testable hypotheses about the output elasticity using this value in the null hypothesis. Our null hypothesis is, therefore:

$$H_0: \beta = 1.$$

Note that this same value appears in the null hypothesis whether we are testing for an inelastic or elastic response. Our information about the specific elasticity range is reflected in the alternative hypothesis.

Which inequality should we select for the alternative hypothesis? We showed in Chapter 4 that:

$$\beta = \frac{\Delta q/q}{\Delta L/L}$$

$$= \frac{\Delta q/\Delta L}{q/L}$$

which indicates that this elasticity is the ratio of the marginal product of labor (MPL), $\Delta q/\Delta L$, to the average product of labor (APL), q/L:

$$\beta = \text{MPL}/\text{APL}.$$

In the short-run, profit-maximizing firms operate in the second stage of production, where both the average and marginal products of labor are decreasing. When the average product of labor is falling, the marginal product of labor is below the average product, so that $\text{MPL} < \text{APL}$, and the ratio MPL/APL, which is the elasticity of interest, is less than 1. We thus expect output to be labor inelastic, and our alternative hypothesis is:

$$H_a: \beta < 1.$$

We now present the methodology for testing these different hypotheses.

STATISTICAL TESTING OF HYPOTHESES INVOLVING LEAST SQUARES COEFFICIENTS. After the null and alternative hypotheses have been specified, we must judge the validity of the null hypothesis. The starting point for this process is our estimate of the population parameter included in the null hypothesis. This estimate seldom coincides exactly with the value stipulated by the null hypothesis. For example, the previously specified null hypothesis for the unemployment rate equation postulates a proportional negative response to changes in the capacity utilization rate, $H_0: \alpha_1 = -1$. Our estimate of this parameter (from Chapter 4) is -0.319. Testing for an inelastic response of output to labor input, we utilized the null hypothesis of unit elasticity, $H_0: \beta = 1$. Our estimate of this elasticity, from Chapter 4, is 0.93. Before any decision concerning a null hypothesis can be made, we must determine whether the deviation of a particular estimate from the population value specified in the null hypothesis is "acceptable," allowing us to attribute this difference to chance variation.

The difference between a particular estimate and its population parameter results from sampling error. Since the population parameter of interest is unknown, so too is the actual magnitude of sampling error. To circumvent this problem, hypothesis testing replaces the population parameter with its value in the null hypothesis. *Statistical testing of the null hypothesis therefore proceeds under the assumption that H_0 is correct.* Actual sampling error is thus replaced by **hypothesized sampling error**, which measures the deviation of a point estimate from the parameter value stated in the null hypothesis. If we denote the value for α_1 stipulated in the null hypothesis as α_1^0, then hypothesized sampling error equals $(\hat{\alpha}_1 - \alpha_1^0)$. *This is a known quantity.* Hypothesis testing involves determining whether the magnitude of hypothesized sampling error is "large" or not. To define "large" it is necessary that we specify a range of acceptable values for the hypothesized sampling error of an estimate. If $(\hat{\alpha}_1 - \alpha_1^0)$ falls within this range, we then consider the difference between $\hat{\alpha}_1$ and α_1^0 to be the result of chance variation. Based on this evidence, we are then unable to reject the null hypothesis. When the deviation of $\hat{\alpha}_1$ from α_1^0 falls outside the range of acceptable values, this difference is judged to be systematic. In this case, the likelihood of H_0's being true is considered unacceptably low, causing us to reject H_0 and to accept H_a.

The sampling distribution of an estimator provides us the information needed to determine whether the magnitude of hypothetical sampling error is acceptable. If the null hypothesis is $H_0: \alpha_1 = \alpha_1^0$, then, assuming this hypothesis is true, the sampling distribution of $\hat{\alpha}_1$ is centered at α_1^0, as Figure 5.1(a) shows. The hypothesized sampling error then corresponds to the horizontal distance between α_1^0 and the parameter estimate $\hat{\alpha}_1$ in Figure 5.1(b). The probability of observing a hypothesized sampling error of this size is given by the area between α_1^0 and $\hat{\alpha}_1$. The sampling distribution of an estimator thus provides us with an objective benchmark against which we can judge deviations of estimates from hypothesized values.

The **acceptance region** for a null hypothesis consists of the range of estimates that are "likely" to occur when H_0 is true. If our estimate falls within this range, we are unable to reject the null hypothesis. The acceptance region might, for example, consist of the values we expect to observe 95 percent of the time when H_0 is true. In this case, the acceptance region corresponds to the sampling distribution values for $\hat{\alpha}_1$ that bound 95 percent of all probability. The acceptance region for a hypothesis test is analogous to the confidence interval for a parameter estimate: a confidence interval defines the boundaries for an actual population parameter, while the acceptance region indicates the bounds for an estimated parameter, assuming the null hypothesis is true.

The set of values lying outside this range form the **rejection region**. In this example, 5 percent of all values occur in this region. Values that fall within the rejection region are considered "unlikely" since the probability of observing this large of a deviation of $\hat{\alpha}_1$ from α_1^0 is small when the null hypothesis is true. The value or values that separate the acceptance region from the rejection region are called **critical values**.

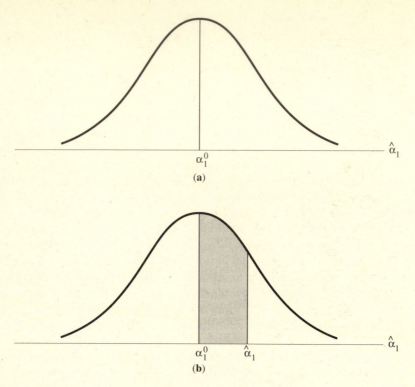

Figure 5.1

When our estimate exceeds a critical value, the magnitude of hypothesized sampling error is considered unacceptably large, forcing us to reject H_0.

The number of critical values that pertain to a hypothesis test is determined by our alternative hypothesis. The rejection region may therefore include either or both tails of the sampling distribution of our estimator. If we test the following hypotheses:

$$H_0: \alpha_1 = \alpha_1^0$$
$$H_a: \alpha_1 \neq \alpha_1^0,$$

the alternative hypothesis of non-equality implies that values very different from α_1^0, *either large or small*, constitute evidence supporting our rejection of H_0. In this case, two critical values exist, and a **two-tail test** is valid. Figure 5.2 illustrates the division of the sampling distribution for $\hat{\alpha}_1$ into an acceptance region—which consists of the values for $\hat{\alpha}_1$ that occur 95 percent of the time—and the rejection region for these hypotheses, which includes *both* tails of this distribution. Each tail contains 2.5 percent of the total probability. Acceptance and rejection regions without reference to specific probabilities are presented in Figure 5.3, along with upper critical (C_U) and lower critical (C_L) values. Using this, we can state the basis for our decision concerning

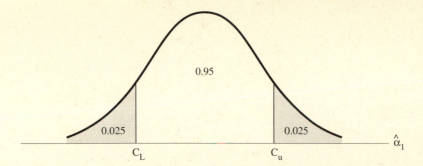

0.95

0.025

0.025

C_L

C_u

$\hat{\alpha}_1$

Figure 5.2

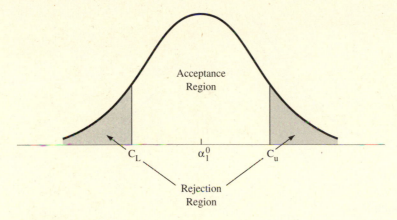

Acceptance
Region

C_L

α_1^0

C_u

Rejection
Region

Figure 5.3

the above hypotheses:

> When $\hat{\alpha}_0$ lies within the acceptance region, we do not reject the null hypothesis, since available evidence is consistent with its validity. We reject H_0 if $\hat{\alpha}_1$ falls in the rejection region. Thus when $\hat{\alpha}_1 > C_U$ or $\hat{\alpha}_1 < C_L$, the probability of observing this large a deviation of $\hat{\alpha}_1$ from α_1^0 is unacceptably low (such as 2.5 percent or less for a given tail). We then accept H_a.

When the alternative hypothesis incorporates knowledge of the expected sign of a coefficient, the rejection region for its null hypothesis differs from that in the previous discussion. If, for example, the expected sign of α_1 is positive, and we stipulate the following set of hypotheses:

$$H_0: \alpha_1 = \alpha_1^0$$

$$H_a: \alpha_1 > \alpha_1^0,$$

the statistical test of H_0 only considers unacceptably large values of $\hat{\alpha}_1$ as justification for rejecting H_0. In this case, the rejection region consists entirely of values in the

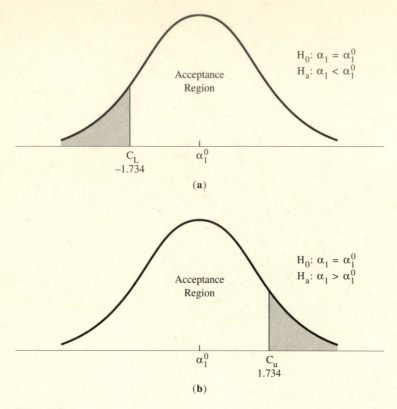

Figure 5.4

upper tail of the sampling distribution of $\hat{\alpha}_1$.[9] This results in a **one-tail test** with an upper critical value only. The basis for rejecting H_0 then becomes:

> Reject H_0 if $\hat{\alpha}_1 > C_U$, since when H_0 is true, the likelihood of observing a hypothesized sampling error of this magnitude is unacceptably small.

Had we based our alternative hypothesis on a negative expected sign for α_1, a one-tail test would still result, with a lower critical value only. Examples of the acceptance and rejection regions for each of these one-tail tests are given in Figure 5.4.

It is possible for us to reject H_0 when this hypothesis is true. The probability of this occurring is given by the **level of significance**. When the level of significance is 5 percent, the acceptance region is defined as the range within which 95 percent of all estimates fall. In this case, the probability of rejecting H_0 when this hypothesis is true is 5 percent.

---

[9] Note that the direction of the inequality in H_a points to the correct tail(s) used to define the rejection region. Think of non-equality as indicating two tails, since it divides the equal sign into two parts.

We do not use a least squares coefficient in its original form when deciding whether or not to reject the null hypothesis. Instead, we combine the distributional information associated with this coefficient and the parameter value stated in the null hypothesis to form a **test statistic**. Let us now see how the test statistics for the least squares coefficients are constructed.

Both of the least squares coefficients are normally distributed. We showed previously that $\hat{\alpha}_0 \sim N(\alpha_0, \sigma_0^2)$ and $\hat{\alpha}_1 \sim N(\alpha_1, \sigma_1^2)$. Nevertheless, the actual variances of these coefficients are unknown. If we replace these with their estimated variances, we can base our test statistics on the t-distribution. We saw earlier that:

$$(\hat{\alpha}_0 - \alpha_0)/\hat{\sigma}_0 \sim t_{n-2},$$

$$(\hat{\alpha}_1 - \alpha_1)/\hat{\sigma}_1 \sim t_{n-2}.$$

Both of these are standardized random variables. If we are to use the t-distribution, we must standardize our coefficient estimates. This is the first manipulation involved in transforming least squares estimates into test statistics.

The numerator for each of these expressions is the actual sampling error for that coefficient. A second manipulation is necessary since both α_0 and α_1 are unknown population parameters: we must replace these by the values stipulated in the null hypotheses. The null hypotheses and the resulting test statistics for the least squares coefficients are:

$$H_0: \alpha_0 = \alpha_0^0 \text{ uses } (\hat{\alpha}_0 - \alpha_0^0)/\hat{\sigma}_0 \sim t_{n-2},$$
$$H_0: \alpha_1 = \alpha_1^0 \text{ uses } (\hat{\alpha}_1 - \alpha_1^0)/\hat{\sigma}_1 \sim t_{n-2}. \tag{5.18}$$

The numerator in each of these expressions is now the *hypothesized* sampling error for that coefficient. Because such test statistics are standardized random variables, or decision about a particular null hypothesis is based on an assessment of the *relative* magnitude of the hypothesized sampling error; that is, the size of this error relative to the dispersion in the sampling distribution for this coefficient.

If the null hypotheses given in Equation (5.18) are true, then, each test statistic in Equation (5.18) follows a t-distribution with $(n-2)$ degrees of freedom. We can obtain the appropriate critical value(s) from the table for this distribution. If, for example, n equals 20, the selected level of significance is 5 percent, and we wish to test the following hypotheses:

$$H_0: \alpha_1 = \alpha_1^0$$
$$H_a: \alpha_1 \neq \alpha_1^0,$$

a two-tail test is appropriate. The critical t-values for this test delineate 2.5 percent (0.025) in each tail of this distribution for 18 $(n-2)$ degrees of freedom. These values are: $C_L = -2.101$ and $C_U = 2.101$. If the absolute value of our test statistic exceeds 2.101, we then reject H_0, since the probability of observing this large a disparity between our estimate and its hypothesized population value is 2.5 percent or less when the null hypothesis is true.

If we continue to assume this same sample size and significance level but change our alternative hypothesis to an inequality, a one-tail test is applicable. The single critical value bounds 5 percent (0.05) of the probability in the applicable tail of the t-distribution. When our alternative hypothesis is H_a: $\alpha_1 < \alpha_1^0$, the critical value, C_L, bounds 5 percent of the probability in the lower tail of this distribution. When $n = 20$, this critical t-value with 18 degrees of freedom is -1.734, as Figure 5.4(a) shows. We reject the null hypothesis if the value of our test statistic, $(\hat{\alpha}_1 - \alpha_1^0)/\hat{\sigma}_1$, falls below -1.734. If the expected sign of α_1 is positive, the alternative hypothesis changes to H_a: $\alpha_1 > \alpha_1^0$, and values substantially above α_1^0 are deemed unacceptable. This also involves a one-tail test, where the critical region lies in the right tail of the t-distribution. For $n = 20$, the single critical value with 18 degrees of freedom is $C_U = 1.734$. Test statistics that exceed this value are used as evidence favoring the rejection of H_0. The acceptance and rejection regions for this hypothesis test are given in Figure 5.4(b). Note that *the same test statistic is used in all three of these hypothesis tests. All that changes are the acceptance and rejection regions.*

Our decision concerning H_0 is predicated on a determination of whether the magnitude of hypothetical sampling error is "large." Because our test statistics are standardized random variables, their units of measurement are standard deviations. If, for example, our test statistic equals 2.8, the disparity between $\hat{\alpha}_1$ and α_1^0, or our hypothesized sampling error, is 2.8 standard deviations, since

$$(\hat{\alpha}_1 - \alpha_1^0)/\hat{\sigma}_1 = 2.8$$

implies that

$$(\hat{\alpha}_1 - \alpha_1^0) = 2.8 \cdot \hat{\sigma}_1.$$

The critical value(s) establish the limit on "acceptable" hypothesized sampling error. Using the previous one-tail critical value of 1.734, we reject H_0 if

$$(\hat{\alpha}_1 - \alpha_1^0)/\hat{\sigma}_1 > 1.734,$$

which indicates that

$$(\hat{\alpha}_1 - \alpha_1^0) > 1.734 \cdot \hat{\sigma}_1.$$

Hypothesized sampling error that exceeds 1.734 standard deviations is therefore deemed to be unlikely when the null hypothesis is true, making it unacceptably large.

This test statistic evaluates hypothesized sampling error *relative* to the dispersion of the estimate. This is important because a large value of $(\hat{\alpha}_1 - \alpha_1^0)$, which is likely to arise when $\hat{\alpha}_1$ has a substantial variance, should not by itself constitute evidence in favor of rejecting H_0. Only when $(\hat{\alpha}_1 - \alpha_1^0)$ is large relative to the variance of $\hat{\alpha}_1$ should we reject H_0, since this sizable a deviation is unlikely *given* the dispersion in the sampling distribution of this point estimate. An apparently small deviation of $\hat{\alpha}_1$ from α_1^0 can potentially provide justification for rejecting H_0. This occurs when $\hat{\sigma}_1$ is also small, which has the effect of making the "small" deviation of $\hat{\alpha}_1$ from α_1^0 large relative to $\hat{\sigma}_1$. "Large" hypothesized sampling error is therefore defined to be the number of standard deviations given by the critical value(s) for this test. In the previous example, this is $C_U \cdot \hat{\sigma}_1$, or C_U deviations of $\hat{\alpha}_1$ from α_1^0, which equals 1.734 standard deviations.

The rejection of H_0 based on a test statistic and its probability distribution provides a mechanism for establishing that the value of our estimate differs significantly from the population parameter stipulated in the null hypothesis. This methodology is not foolproof; but it is preferable to our judging deviations of $\hat{\alpha}_1$ from α_1^0 based on subjective opinion. Rejection of the null hypothesis, H_0: $\alpha_1 = \alpha_1^0$, allows us to establish that:

(i) the difference between $\hat{\alpha}_1$ and α_1^0 is **statistically significant**, meaning the probability of observing this large a deviation of $\hat{\alpha}_1$ from α_1^0 purely by chance will occur no more than the percentage given by the level of significance, or half that value for a two-tail test. This determination is based upon observing a "large" deviation of $\hat{\alpha}_1$ from α_1^0, defined in terms of standard deviations, from the probability distribution of the test statistic.

(ii) the difference between $\hat{\alpha}_1$ and α_1^0 is significantly different from 0;

(iii) $\hat{\alpha}_1$ is significantly different than α_1^0.

A special case of this procedure is utilized to determine whether an estimated coefficient is statistically significant. We saw in (ii) above that when we reject the null hypothesis, H_0: $\alpha_1 = \alpha_1^0$, we have established that the difference between α_1 and α_1^0 is significantly different from 0. In this case we say that the divergence between these values is statistically significant (using (i)). *An estimated coefficient is statistically significant if its value is significantly different from 0.*

If we continue to focus on the slope coefficient, the hypothesis test used to establish the statistical significance of this term seeks to evaluate whether α_1, the coefficient of x in the population regression function, is 0. This is nothing more than a hypothesis test to ascertain whether x influences y. The null hypothesis therefore maintains that x does not influence y—H_0: $\alpha_1 = 0$, where $\alpha_1^0 = 0$. The alternative hypothesis stipulates nonequality between these values—H_a: $\alpha_1 \neq 0$. The statistical test of these hypotheses involves a two-tail test. Its test statistic is:

$$(\hat{\alpha}_1 - 0)/\hat{\sigma}_1 = \hat{\alpha}_1/\hat{\sigma}_1 \sim t_{n-2},$$

which is simply the ratio of the coefficient estimate to its standard error. The hypothesized sampling error in this test is given by our estimate of α_1. If our null hypothesis is true, the sampling distribution of this test statistic is centered at 0. We can expect our estimate of α_1 to differ from 0 as the result of sampling error. If we assume (as before) that $n = 20$ and the level of significance is 5 percent, the critical t-values for this test are ± 2.101. If $\hat{\alpha}_1/\hat{\sigma}_1$ is either greater than 2.101 or less than -2.101, we reject this null hypothesis, for then our hypothesized sampling error exceeds 2.1 standard deviations. When this occurs, we say that $\hat{\alpha}_1$ is statistically significant. It is customary to include the significance level in this statement. Since we use the 5 percent significance level in this illustration, $\hat{\alpha}_1$ is **statistically significant at the 5 percent level**. This indicates that the deviation of our point estimate from 0 is unacceptably large, and that $\hat{\alpha}_1$ is significantly different from 0. We then conclude that the explanatory variable x does, in fact, influence y.

Before applying this material to actual equations, we must address one final topic. Hypothesis testing provides an objective basis for making inferences concerning the values of population parameters. This methodology is not without potential pitfalls, however. The first of these arises when we reject a true null hypothesis. This is called a **Type I error**. One context in which this type of error occurs is with spurious correlation, where available evidence leads us to conclude that a variable belongs in an equation (causing us to reject H_0: $\alpha_1 = 0$) when, in fact, the opposite is true. The probability of committing this type of error coincides with the size of the rejection region for our test statistic, or the selected level of significance. If the level of significance is 5 percent, we can expect to observe so large a deviation of $\hat{\alpha}_1$ from α_1^0 purely by chance no more than 5 percent of the time. Nevertheless, it is still possible for us to observe a deviation of this magnitude when H_0 is true, and to commit a Type I error. For all practical purposes this possibility always exists. We can diminish this risk by lowering the level of significance to, say, 1 percent.[10] The acceptance region then includes 99 percent of all values for our test statistic, and the probability of a Type I error falls to 1 percent. Total certainty that we will not reject a true null hypothesis still does not exist, however. Type I errors occur only when we accept the alternative hypothesis.

The other possibility concerning an incorrect decision for H_0 arises when we fail to reject a false null hypothesis, which is a **Type II error**. This type of error can occur with specification error—where the specification of an equation omits a relevant variable—and collinearity, where explanatory variables are highly correlated. Both of these complications tend to raise the estimated standard errors of the least squares coefficients, which lowers hypothesized sampling error relative to the standard deviation in our test statistic.[11] Our test statistic is then more likely to fall within the acceptance region, making the likelihood of not rejecting a false H_0—or the probability of a Type II error—larger. Type II errors arise only when we do not reject the null hypothesis.

"Rules of Thumb" and Observed Significance Levels

The procedure for hypothesis testing outlined above presupposes that the researcher selects the level of significance. Once this choice has been made, the value of the test statistic is compared to the critical value(s) that apply, and a decision regarding H_0 is made. Several "rules of thumb" based on this procedure have emerged through the years. These obviate the need to consult statistical tables when "large" samples (degrees of freedom > 30) are used to estimate the sample regression function. The

---

[10] Unless the number of observations in the data sample is increased, this decrease in the probability of a Type I error will be accompanied by a rise in the probability of a Type II error.

[11] These also affect the signs and magnitudes of estimated coefficients.

first of these states that:

> A regression coefficient is statistically significant at the 5 percent level when the absolute value of the test statistic derived from this coefficient exceeds 2.

The critical value in this rule is derived from the unit normal distribution with 2.5 percent probability in each tail, 1.96. While this rule is correct for a two-tail test, its critical value is often used in one-tail tests as well. For a one-tail test, the correct value of the unit normal distribution with a 5 percent level of significance is 1.65. A second rule pertains to statistical significance at the 1 percent level:

> A regression coefficient is statistically significant at the 1 percent level if the absolute value of the test statistic derived from this coefficient exceeds 2.8.

The value of 2.8 is derived from the t-distribution with 30 degrees of freedom (a "large" sample) and 0.005 in each tail. The correct t-value for a one-tail test (with this same number of degrees of freedom) is 2.5.

Critical values from the t-distribution are always the correct ones to use when testing hypotheses about the least squares coefficients. The rules stated above are nothing more than convenient approximations to these values. For "small" samples (degrees of freedom < 30), we must use the specific values given in the t-table, and the above rules do not apply.

A second method exists for determining the statistical significance of individual regression coefficients. This method, which is gaining increasing acceptance, reverses the process discussed above: assuming that the null hypothesis, $H_0: \alpha_j = 0$, is true (where j denotes one of our coefficients), we utilize the value of our test statistic, $\hat{\alpha}_j/\hat{\sigma}_j$, to determine the observed significance level, or **p-value**, for this hypothesis, which is the smallest level of significance at which we are able to reject H_0. The definition of a p-value for a two-tail test:

$$p(|t| \geq \text{test statistic}) = p\text{-value},$$

denotes the probability that the absolute value of a t-random variable with the appropriate degrees of freedom exceeds the value of our test statistic. Two-tail p-values equal *twice* the probability that a t-variable exceeds the test statistic, since this type of test involves both upper and lower critical regions. If, for example, our test statistic with 28 degrees of freedom equals 1.701, the probability that a t-distributed random variable exceeds this value is 0.05. The p-value for a two-tail test is the sum of the probabilities that a t-random variable exceeds 1.701 and that the variable falls below this value, which equals 2(0.05), or 0.10. p-values of less than 0.05 are used as evidence supporting the statistical significance of a coefficient in a regression equation. If a one-tail test is desired, simply divide the p-value by 2 to obtain the implied significance level for this type of test.

Several computer programs routinely provide this information (assuming a two-tail test) as part of their regression output. The p-value in the MicroTSP printout for the consumption function previously is the column labeled: "2-tail Sig." In SAS, p-values are labeled: "PROB > $|T|$." Note that p-values can be used with either "small" or "large" samples, unlike the rules of thumb discussed previously.

EXAMPLES OF HYPOTHESIS TESTS AND CONFIDENCE INTERVALS

■ THE UNEMPLOYMENT RATE-CAPACITY UTILIZATION RATE EQUATION

Our first illustration of constructing confidence intervals and testing hypotheses uses the unemployment rate (u)—capacity utilization rate (CAP) equation presented in Chapter 4. This equation is estimated using annual data for the period from 1979 to 1988. The SAS printout, along with symbols linking its entries with the notation in this text, are given below.

```
DEP VARIABLE: UR
ANALYSIS OF VARIANCE

                    SUM OF
SOURCE     DF      SQUARES          MEAN         F VALUE      PROB>F
MODEL      1      16.51409930       SQUARE        87.964      0.0001
ERROR      8(=df)  1.50190070     16.51409930
C TOTAL    9      18.01600000      0.18773759
           ROOT MSE    0.433287    R-SQUARE      0.9166
           DEP MEAN    7.32        ADJ R-SQ      0.9062
           C.V.        5.919221

PARAMETER ESTIMATES
                  PARAMETER      STANDARD      T FOR HO:
VARIABLE  DF      ESTIMATE        ERROR        PARAMETER=0    PROB>|T|
INTERCEP  1    32.561394(=α̂₀)   2.694782(=σ̂₀)  12.083(=α̂₀/σ̂₀)  0.0001
CAPUR     1    -0.319027(=α̂₁)   0.034015(=σ̂₁)  -9.379(=α̂₁/σ̂₁)  0.0001
```

The coefficient of CAP displays its expected negative sign. Its magnitude is less (in absolute value) than 1, which is also consistent with our prior expectations, based on the discussion of Okun's Law from Chapter 4. We can use the standard deviation of this coefficient, 0.034015, to construct confidence intervals for the population coefficient of the capacity utilization rate.

We obtain the degrees of freedom from the entry for DF next to ERROR in the top left of this printout. There are 8 degrees of freedom. We must therefore use the t-distribution to construct these intervals. The 95 percent confidence interval for the coefficient of the capacity utilization rate uses the t-distribution values of ± 2.306 which delineate 2.5 percent of the values for this distribution in each tail. If we denote this value $t_{0.025,8}$, which represents the value of the t-distribution with 8 degrees of freedom and 0.025 percent probability in each tail, the formulas for these intervals along with values from the printout are:

$$\hat{\alpha}_0 \pm t_{0.025,8} \cdot \hat{\sigma}_0 = 32.561 \pm 2.306(2.695)$$
$$= (26.35, 38.78)$$

$$\hat{\alpha}_1 \pm t_{0.025,8} \cdot \hat{\sigma}_1 = -0.319 \pm 2.306(0.034)$$
$$= (-0.397, -0.241)$$

The 99 percent confidence intervals differ from the above only in that the t-value now equals ± 3.355 (the value with 0.005 in each tail). These intervals are:

$$\hat{\alpha}_0 \pm t_{0.005,8} \cdot \hat{\sigma}_0 = 32.561 \pm 3.355(2.695)$$
$$= (23.52, 41.60)$$
$$\hat{\alpha}_1 \pm t_{0.005,8} \cdot \hat{\sigma}_1 = -0.319 \pm 3.355(0.034)$$
$$= (-0.433, -0.205)$$

Both sets of confidence intervals exclude 0, which, as we will see later, has a bearing on our decisions concerning hypothesis tests for these coefficients.

The first hypothesis test we conduct on this equation seeks to establish whether the coefficient of CAP is statistically significant. The hypotheses that pertain to this test are:

$$H_0: \alpha_1 = 0$$

$$H_a: \alpha_1 \neq 0.$$

This involves a two-tail test with test statistic:

$$(\hat{\alpha} - 0)/\hat{\sigma}_1 = \hat{\alpha}_1/\hat{\sigma}_1,$$

which is the ratio of the estimated coefficient to its estimated standard error. Most computer printouts routinely provide the value of this test statistic. In the printout above, this is given in the column: "T for HO: Parameter = 0." The value of this statistic for $\hat{\alpha}_1$ is -9.379 ($= -0.319/0.034$). If we select the 1 percent significance level, the critical values for this test are ± 3.355. We then reject the null hypothesis when the absolute value of hypothesized sampling error is more than 3.355 standard deviations. Since the value of our test statistic falls into the rejection region (it is below -3.355), we reject the null hypothesis and accept the alternative hypothesis that the capacity utilization rate affects the unemployment rate. The coefficient of CAP is therefore statistically significant at the 1 percent level.

The elements involved in this hypothesis test are depicted in Figure 5.5. If the null hypothesis is true, the sampling distribution of our test statistic is centered at 0. When the absolute value of this statistic exceeds 3.355, the deviation of $\hat{\alpha}_1$ from 0, or the magnitude of hypothesized sampling error, is judged to be excessive. The test statistic in this illustration indicates that the value of -0.319 for $\hat{\alpha}_1$ is 9.4 standard deviations below 0. When the sampling distribution is centered at 0, the probability of obtaining an estimate this far from 0 is so low that we reject the null hypothesis that the population coefficient of the capacity utilization rate is 0.

The next hypothesis test seeks to ascertain whether a proportional (inverse) response exists for changes in the capacity utilization rate. The set of hypotheses we test are:

$$H_0: \alpha_1 = -1$$

$$H_a: \alpha_1 > -1 \quad \text{(less negative).}$$

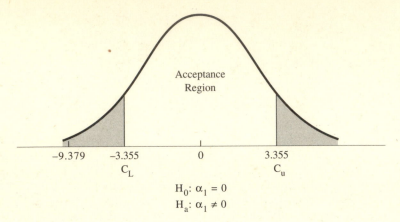

$$H_0: \alpha_1 = 0$$
$$H_a: \alpha_1 \neq 0$$

Figure 5.5

If the null hypothesis is true, the sampling distribution of $\hat{\alpha}_1$ is centered at -1 (while that for our test statistic is centered at 0). Theory leads us to expect a less than proportional response of the unemployment rate to changes in the capacity utilization rate. The alternative hypothesis is consistent with this expectation.[12] The test of these hypotheses therefore involves a one-tail test, with a single critical value in the upper tail of the sampling distribution of the test statistic. We obtain this critical value from the t-distribution with 5 percent of the probability in the upper tail: 1.86. The value of our test statistic is:

$$(\hat{\alpha}_1 - \alpha_1^0)/\hat{\sigma}_1 = [-0.319 - (-1)]/0.034$$
$$= 20.0,$$

which is well outside of the acceptance region, as shown in Figure 5.6. We therefore reject the null hypothesis that the response of u_t is of the opposite sign but equal in value to changes in the capacity utilization rate. This test also establishes that the coefficient of $\hat{\alpha}_1$ is significantly different than -1, since the probability of obtaining an estimate of α_1 equal to -0.319 when α_1 equals -1 is less than 5 percent.

Before performing hypothesis tests on the estimated intercept in this equation, we must explore the theoretical behavior of its population coefficient. The population intercept measures the mean *civilian* unemployment rate when the capacity utilization rate in *manufacturing* equals 0. This is not a very meaningful term, since we will likely never observe a situation where manufacturing capacity remains totally unutilized. Also, this possibility is far beyond the range of the sample data upon which the sample regression function is based. *In situations such as this, it is best to view the intercept as the mean of all the omitted factors that influence the dependent variable.*

---

[12] Actually, this alternative hypothesis does not rule out any value greater than -1 so that positive values are consistent with this hypothesis as well.

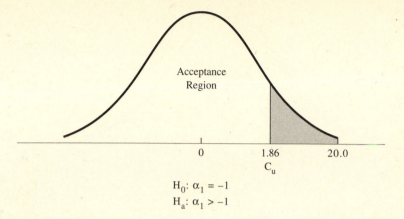

$$H_0: \alpha_1 = -1$$
$$H_a: \alpha_1 > -1$$

Figure 5.6

The expected sign of the population intercept is positive, since if our manufacturing sector were idle, positive unemployment would certainly result. The magnitude of this coefficient is expected to be less than 100, however, since the dependent variable reflects all civilian unemployment, while the explanatory variable pertains only to the manufacturing sector.[13] Our first hypothesis test thus seeks to establish that the population intercept is nonzero, which is a test of the statistical significance of the intercept in this equation. The hypotheses for this test are:

$$H_0: \alpha_0 = 0$$

$$H_a: \alpha_0 \neq 0.$$

If the null hypothesis is true, an intercept is not included in the population equation, and this function passes through the origin. The alternative hypothesis postulates our prior expectation of a nonzero intercept. A two-tail test is indicated. Using the 1 percent level of significance, the critical values of the t-distribution (with 0.005 in each tail) are ± 3.355. Our test statistic is:

$$(\hat{\alpha}_0 - 0)/\hat{\sigma}_0 = \hat{\alpha}_0/\hat{\sigma}_0 = 32.561/2.695$$
$$= 12.08,$$

which is contained in the second from the right column of the printout corresponding to INTERCEP. The value of this test statistic falls outside the acceptance region, causing us to reject H_0. The equation intercept is therefore statistically significant at the 1 percent level. Figure 5.7 shows the basis of this hypothesis test.

---

[13] This pertains to all unemployed persons included in the labor force.

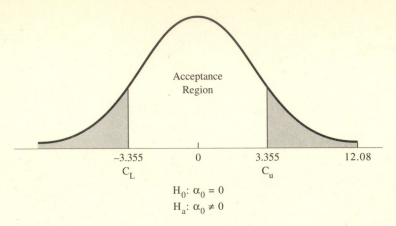

Figure 5.7

The earlier theoretical discussion leads us to expect that the population intercept is positive, but less than 100. We can therefore test this with the null hypothesis: $H_0: \alpha_0 = 100$. Our alternate hypothesis states our expectation that α_0 is less than 100—$H_a: \alpha_0 < 100$. This is a one-tail test with a lower critical value of -1.86 if the significance level is 5 percent and -2.896 for a 1 percent level of significance. Our test statistic equals:

$$(32.561 - 100.0)/2.695 = -25.0,$$

which allows us to reject the null hypothesis that if manufacturing capacity were unused, the civilian unemployment rate would rise to its maximum value. Our estimated intercept, 32.561, is 25 standard deviations below 0.

Finally, the estimated intercept in this equation appears to be underestimated. We saw in the Monte Carlo presentation of Chapter 4 that the covariance between the coefficients in a sample regression function is negative when the mean of the explanatory variable is positive, which is the case here. From this we can infer that our slope estimate is overstated, leading us to conclude that its magnitude is closer to the Okun's Law coefficient of -0.25. ■

■ **CONSUMPTION FUNCTION**   The consumption function whose Micro-TSP printout appears below is slightly different from the one discussed earlier. The data used to estimate this equation consist of annual observations for the years 1947 to 1988. Since these data span such a long time period, it is necessary to control for the effect of population growth on personal consumption expenditure. This is accomplished by expressing the variables in this equation in per capita terms. The dependent variable is therefore real per capita personal consumption expenditure (RCONSN), and the explanatory variable is real disposable personal income per capita (RDPIN). Both variables have a 1982 base year.

```
                LS // Dependent Variable is RCONSN
SMPL    1947  -  1988
42 Observations

   VARIABLE      COEFFICIENT    STD. ERROR      T-STAT(H₀:α=0)     2-TAIL SIG.
      C          25.9182(=α̂₀)   78.5447(=σ̂₀)    0.32998(=α̂₀/σ̂₀)       0.746
    RDPIN        0.90725(=α̂₁)   0.00988(=σ̂₁)    91.8552(=α̂₁/σ̂₁)       0.000

R-squared              0.995282    Mean of dependent var    7013.333
Adjusted R-squared     0.995164    S.D. of dependent var    1822.891
S.E. of regression     126.7715    Sum of squared resid     642840.3
Durbin-Watson stat     0.496588    F-statistic              8437.386
```

The intercept in this equation is our estimate of real autonomous per capita consumption expenditure. The coefficient of RDPIN is the estimated marginal propensity to consume. Its value, 0.907, is consistent with our theoretical expectation that the MPC is a positive fraction.

We will first calculate confidence intervals for the coefficients in the consumption function. The printout shows that 42 observations were used to estimate this equation, which results in 40 degrees of freedom. This places us in the range of a "large" sample, but not by very much. We will therefore utilize probability values from the t-distribution. These are:

$$t_{0.025,40} = 2.021 \text{ for 95 percent confidence intervals}$$

$$t_{0.005,40} = 2.705 \text{ for 99 percent confidence intervals.}$$

Using these values, the confidence intervals for the coefficients in the consumption function are:

95 percent:

$$\hat{\alpha}_0: 25.918 \pm 2.021(78.545) = (-132.8, 184.7)$$

$$\hat{\alpha}_1: \ \ 0.907 \pm 2.021(0.0099) = (0.887, 0.927)$$

99 percent:

$$\hat{\alpha}_0: 25.918 \pm 2.705(78.545) = (-186.5, 238.3)$$

$$\hat{\alpha}_1: \ \ 0.907 \pm 2.705(0.0099) = (0.880, 0.934)$$

The differences in these intervals for each significance level illustrate the effect of sampling distribution dispersion on confidence interval width. The standard error of the estimated MPC is so low that the 95 percent and 99 percent confidence intervals for this coefficient are almost identical. In contrast, the large dispersion in the sampling distribution of the intercept, which makes its margin for sampling error large, stretches confidence intervals for this coefficient over a wider range for both significance levels. Using the 5 percent level of significance, the margin for sampling error is only 0.02 for $\hat{\alpha}_1$, while for the estimated intercept, this value is 158.7.

The intercept in this equation, 25.92, is small relative to the mean of RCONSN, 7013.3. The estimated MPC is close to 1.0. Our sample regression function therefore resembles a 45 degree line through the origin. We can perform hypothesis tests on the coefficients in this equation to investigate this possibility.

We first determine whether our estimate of real per capita autonomous consumption is statistically significant. Our hypotheses for this test are:

$$H_0: \alpha_0 = 0$$

$$H_a: \alpha_0 \neq 0.$$

This involves a two-tail test, with the critical t-values given previously: ± 2.021 for the 5 percent significance level, and ± 2.705 for the 1 percent level. This test statistic for these hypotheses is given in the column "T-STAT" in the printout: 0.33. The value of this statistic is well below the critical values for both the 5 percent and 1 percent significance levels. This is illustrated in Figure 5.8. Thus, while the estimated intercept of 25.9 by itself appears to be very different from 0, the dispersion of the sampling

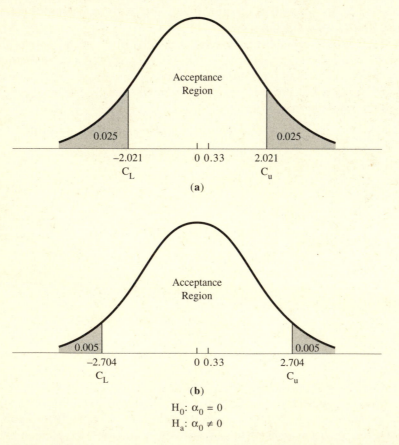

Figure 5.8

distribution of $\hat{\alpha}_0$ is also large, making the divergence of 25.9 from 0 only 0.33 standard deviations. We therefore conclude that $\hat{\alpha}_0$ is not statistically significant. The p-value from the far right column in the printout indicates a significance level of 37.3 percent for this coefficient (assuming a two-tail test). The cause of this finding can be traced back to the confidence intervals for this coefficient. Each of these intervals includes 0, which is the value for α_0 stated in the null hypothesis. The value of 0 is therefore among the "likely values" we can expect estimates of this coefficient to take when the significance level is either 5 percent or 1 percent.

The statistical significance of the slope coefficient in this equation establishes that the MPC is significantly different from 0. If we formulate an alternative hypothesis that reflects the expected positive sign for α_1, our hypotheses are:

$$H_0: \alpha_1 = 0$$

$$H_a: \alpha_1 > 0.$$

This is a one-tail test, which, using 40 degrees of freedom, has an upper critical value of 1.684 for a 5 percent significance level, and 2.423 for the 1 percent level. The value of our test statistic from this printout equals 91.9. Since the test statistic falls well outside the acceptance region, the estimated MPC is statistically significant at both the 5 percent and 1 percent levels. *In a situation such as this, the significance level we associate with the hypothesis test for a coefficient is the higher of the two tested. Here, we say that $\hat{\alpha}_1$ is statistically significant at the 1 percent level and above.*

Unlike the intercept estimate, neither of the confidence intervals for $\hat{\alpha}_1$ includes 0, the value of α_1 in H_0. We conclude that 0 is not a "likely" value to observe for either significance level. Also, while the estimated MPC appears to be small, the dispersion in its sampling distribution is also small, so that 0.907 is 91.9 standard deviations from 0.

The test of whether the consumption function is a 45 degree line uses the null hypothesis that its slope equals 1: $H_0: \alpha_1 = 1$. Our alternative hypothesis is: $H_a: \alpha_1 < 1$. The one-tail test of these hypotheses has a lower critical value of -1.684 for a 5 percent significance level, and -2.423 for the 1 percent level. The test statistic is:

$$(\hat{\alpha}_1 - \alpha_1^0)/\hat{\sigma}_1 = (0.907 - 1)/0.0099$$
$$= -9.39,$$

which falls in the rejection region for both significance levels. We conclude from this test that the MPC is significantly different from 1.

Taken together, these hypotheses provide mixed evidence supporting the proposition that the long-run consumption function differs from a 45 degree line through the origin.[14] ∎

---

[14] Establishing this actually requires testing the null hypothesis:

$$H_0: \alpha_0 = 0 \text{ and } \alpha_1 = 1$$

which involves both of the coefficients in the population regression function. Separate t-tests are not appropriate for this. The methodology for testing hypotheses such as this is presented in Chapter 6.

■ **PRODUCTION FUNCTION** Our discussion of confidence intervals and hypothesis testing concludes with a reexamination of the production function that illustrates how these tools can be applied to elasticities. Chapter 4 presented a short-run Cobb-Douglas production function for nondurable goods manufacturing that was estimated using monthly data for the years 1986 and 1987. The estimated coefficients from that equation and their standard errors are:

COEFFICIENT	ESTIMATE	STANDARD ERROR
Intercept	−3.487	3.105
$\ln(L)_t$	0.931	0.347

There are 22 degrees of freedom for this equation, since it was estimated using 24 observations. The critical t-values with 22 degrees of freedom are:

$$t_{0.025,22} = 2.074$$

and

$$t_{0.005,22} = 2.819$$

Using these, the confidence intervals for the labor elasticity are:

95 percent: $0.931 \pm 2.074(0.347) = (0.211, 1.650)$

99 percent: $0.931 \pm 2.819(0.347) = (-0.047, 1.909)$.

These intervals are fairly wide. The 95 percent confidence interval extends from the inelastic range well into the elastic region. The lower bound for the 99 percent interval is negative. If the point estimate were equal to this value, both the labor elasticity and the marginal product of labor would be negative. Our point estimate is positive, however, so the negative lower bound does not indicate this type of problem. Instead, it reveals that the estimated output elasticity is not statistically significant at the 1 percent level (for a two-tail test), since this 99 percent confidence interval includes 0.

Earlier in this chapter we outlined the set of hypotheses used to test whether output is labor inelastic. The null hypothesis states that output is unit elastic: $H_0: \beta = 1$. The alternative hypothesis reflects our prior expectation of an inelastic response: $H_a: \beta < 1$. This is a one-tail test, with critical values of -1.717 for the 5 percent level of significance and -2.508 for the 1 percent level. Our test statistic for these hypotheses is:

$$(0.931 - 1)/0.347 = -0.199.$$

Since this test statistic is above (to the right of) the critical value for each significance level, it falls within the acceptance region. We are therefore unable to reject the null hypothesis that in the short-run, the response of nondurable goods output to changes in labor input is unit elastic.

It is possible for us to formulate a number of distinct hypotheses of the form

$$H_0: \beta = \beta^0$$

and

$$H_a: \beta < \beta^0$$

that fall within the acceptance region utilized in the above test. If, for example, the hypothesized value for β is 1.1, the value of our test statistic is -0.487. When β^0 is 1.2, this statistic falls to -0.775. In fact, we can use the test statistic formula to solve for the smallest value of β^0 that would allow us to reject our null hypothesis. We reject H_0 at the 5 percent significance level if:

$$(0.931 - \beta^0)/0.347 < -1.717.$$

The solution to this inequality indicates that values of β^0 that exceed 1.527 allow us to reject our null hypothesis at the 5 percent level of significance. Thus, if β^0 equals 1.6, our test statistic, -1.93, falls outside the acceptance region for the 5 percent significance level, causing us to reject the null hypothesis, $H_0: \beta = 1.6$, and to accept the alternative hypothesis, $H_a: \beta < 1.6$. This is not a very useful set of hypotheses, since the range of β values below 1.6 encompasses all three elasticity ranges. This discussion is intended to shed additional light on the reason why we are never able to prove the validity of the hypotheses in our tests. *A single data set is often consistent with many sets of hypotheses about the parameters of a population regression function. Perfect certainty therefore never exists when testing hypotheses. When we are unable to reject a null hypothesis, we have not proven its validity; instead, we have failed to disprove it. A similar situation occurs when we accept an alternative hypothesis.* ■

PRESENTING REGRESSION EQUATION RESULTS

When a sample regression function is estimated with a canned statistical program, a great deal of information is supplied as "routine" output. A number of the sample regression functions used as examples in this chapter were obtained from either SAS or MicroTSP. The types of information each of these programs supplies is fairly typical of the output generated by canned regression packages. Values are provided that relate to both individual coefficients and measures of overall equation performance. The coefficient information generated by canned statistical programs almost always consists of values for individual regression coefficients, the standard deviation of each coefficient, and the t-statistic used to determine statistical significance. Many also include the p-value for each coefficient. While there is less standardization in the overall equation measures, almost without exception, canned statistical programs give the number of observations used to estimate the regression, the value of R^2, the standard error of the regression ($\hat{\sigma}_\varepsilon$), the mean of the dependent variable ($\hat{\mu}_y$), and the sum of the squared residuals (ESS).

Because such a substantial amount of information is produced when a sample regression function is estimated, some standardization is needed when the results of this function are presented. No universally accepted format that has been deemed "correct" exists. The specific format utilized throughout the remainder of this text will be illustrated using the MicroTSP results for the consumption function presented earlier:

$$\widehat{RCONSN}_t = 25.9 + 0.907RDPIN_t \qquad R^2 = 0.995 \quad n = 42 \quad \hat{\sigma}_\varepsilon = 126.8$$
$$\phantom{\widehat{RCONSN}_t = 2} (0.3) \quad (91.9)$$

The information provided for the coefficients in this equation consists of their estimated values and absolute values of the t-statistic used to determine their statistical significance (these are usually provided in the third column of coefficient values). The equation performance measures are the coefficient of determination (R^2), the number of observations, and the equation standard error. The statistical significance of each coefficient is fairly easy to determine using this format, since the t-statistic for each coefficient is provided.

Some formats use individual coefficients and standard errors only, while others use coefficients, standard errors, and t-statistics. It is not necessary to present all three coefficient values, since this information is redundant: when a coefficient and its t-statistic are known, the standard error can always be determined. If the standard error of coefficient $\hat{\alpha}_j$ is needed to calculate its confidence interval (j is either 0 or 1 in the example above), it can be calculated in the following way. Since a coefficient's t-statistic is the ratio of its value to its standard error:

$$t = \hat{\alpha}_j/\hat{\sigma}_j$$

its standard error is the ratio of the coefficient to the t-statistic:

$$\hat{\sigma}_j = \alpha_j/t.$$

REGRESSION WITH A TIME TREND: ESTIMATION AND PREDICTION WITH LINEAR TRENDS

We have examined several aspects of the behavior of the unemployment rate: the cyclical and secular effects that exist in the temporal behavior of this variable; and the method by which the noninflationary rate of unemployment is calculated. In this section we illustrate the technique used to determine the secular trend in a variable and then apply this to the unemployment rate.

The first step in estimating a variable's secular trend is the creation of a new variable called a **time trend**. The value of the time trend for any observation is simply the number of that observation in the data set.

Time trends have many uses in econometric equations. Besides their use in ascertaining secular trends, they are included in regression equations to account for factors that cannot be quantified, or for variables for which data do not currently exist, but whose behavior is correlated with time. Estimation of a production function, for example, requires information on technological progress. While data on this variable are unavailable, we assume that technological progress is positively correlated with time. Estimating a time series production function thus proceeds by including a time trend as an explanatory variable in a regression of output on the factors of production. In a similar manner, the secular trend in the unemployment rate is assumed to be correlated with time. Estimation of this trend is thus accomplished by regressing the unemployment rate on a time trend.

We now illustrate the estimation of the secular trend in the civilian unemployment rate using annual data for the years 1950 to 1989. The first step in this process is the creation of a time trend variable. In SAS and MicroTSP, it is always possible to create a time trend through direct data entry. The data used for this secular trend are of the form:

YEAR	u	t
1950	5.3	1
1951	3.3	2
1952	3.0	3
	. . .	
1989	5.3	40

Source: Economic Report of the President, 1990.

For either program, a shortcut exists for creating the time trend. In SAS, this data set can be created with the commands:

```
DATA UNEMP;
INPUT U;
TIME=_N_;
CARDS;
(data here)
```

The time trend is created by giving this variable its observation number, _N_. Note that this is merely another data manipulation in SAS, which must follow the **INPUT** statement, but precede the **CARDS;** entry. The remainder of this example will use MicroTSP. The next section illustrates the regression commands for SAS.

Time trends can be created in MicroTSP by using either its built-in lag function or, for more recent versions, the @TREND function. Use of the latter function will be illustrated here. To create a time trend using this function, we keep the original sample time period, 1950 to 1989, then enter the following command:

```
>GENR TIME=@TREND(50)+1
```

The expression @TREND(50) creates a trend variable with an initial value of 0 for the year or observation in the brackets (in this case 1950). Since we desire a time trend that begins with a value of 1, we must add 1 to the number created by the @TREND function.

The desired regression uses the unemployment rate, *U, which must already be in the data set*, as the dependent variable, and TIME as the single explanatory variable.

The MicroTSP regression command is:

```
>LS U C TIME
```

The resulting output is:

```
LS // Dependent Variable is U
SMPL range: 1950  -  1989
Number of observations: 40


       VARIABLE   COEFFICIENT   STD. ERROR    T-STAT.    2-TAIL SIG.

          C        3.9165385    0.4295091    9.1186397     0.000
        TIME       0.0866323    0.0182563    4.7453271     0.000


R-squared                0.372089    Mean of dependent var    5.692500
Adjusted R-squared       0.355565    S.D. of dependent var    1.660304
S.E. of regression       1.332837    Sum of squared resid    67.50530
Durbin-Watson stat       0.758943    F-statistic             22.51813
```

The estimated equation using these data is:

$$\hat{u}_t = 3.92 + 0.087t \qquad R^2 = 0.372 \quad \hat{\sigma}_\varepsilon = 1.33 \quad n = 40$$
$$\phantom{\hat{u}_t =} (9.1) \quad\;\; (4.7)$$

The coefficient of the time trend gives the estimated one-period change in the mean of the dependent variable, which is our projection of the secular trend in the unemployment rate. Our estimate of this value is 0.087 percent per year. The statistical significance of this coefficient allows us to conclude that this trend is significantly different from 0. In the present context, this indicates a non-horizontal secular trend. Predicted values of the dependent variable from this equation give the *trend rates of unemployment* for the years covered by these data, as shown in the following table:

YEAR	t	$\hat{u}_t$
1950	1	$3.92 + 0.087(1) = 4.01$
1951	2	$3.92 + 0.087(2) = 4.09$
1952	3	$3.92 + 0.087(3) = 4.18$
	. . .	
1989	40	$3.92 + 0.087(40) = 7.40$

The relationship between actual and estimated unemployment rates can be pictured more easily by referring to a time series plot of these variables. The commands

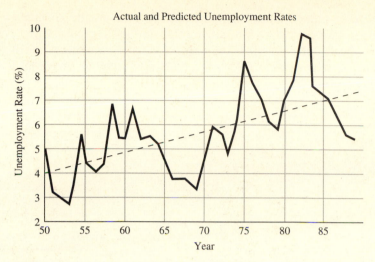

Figure 5.9

in MicroTSP that accomplish this (along with the resulting messages) are:

```
>FORCST UHAT
 Root Mean Square Error (38 obs.) = 1.299
 UHAT and RESID computed

>PLOT(A) U UHAT
```

The first command, FORCST UHAT, calculates predicted (forecasted) values of the dependent variable from the most recently run regression, using actual values of the explanatory variable. The information below this indicates the closeness of actual to predicted values (with Root Mean Square Error), and denotes the fact that two new variables, UHAT and RESID, the equation residuals are now available for use. The PLOT command includes the automatic scaling option, A. The graph of the actual and trend civilian unemployment rates is given in Figure 5.9. The dotted line represents the estimated secular trend.

The residuals from this regression, which measure deviations of actual unemployment rates from the secular trend in unemployment, can be attributed to changes in the level of economic activity.[15] In 1974, for example, the trend unemployment rate of 6.1 percent is fairly close to the actual unemployment rate of 5.6 percent. The recession that began the following year increased the unemployment rate to 8.5 percent, which is appreciably higher than the estimated trend rate of 6.18 percent.

---

[15] This statement is considered to be true in general, but not always. The assumption that a single trend line is valid for the entire set of years covered by the data is not always valid. The structure of the underlying relationship can change, resulting in the need for several trend lines. This line of thought is only briefly pursued here. Methods for allowing structural shift are presented in Chapter 9.

There is some evidence that the secular trend in the civilian unemployment changed from a positive to a negative value during the recovery that began in 1983. To investigate this possibility, the original equation was reestimated for the years 1983 to 1989. The variable TIM83 is a time trend equal to 1 in 1983. The MicroTSP printout is given below:

```
LS // Dependent Variable is U
SMPL range: 1983  -  1989
Number of observations: 7
```

VARIABLE	COEFFICIENT	STD. ERROR	T-STAT.	2-TAIL SIG.
C	9.4571430	0.4337192	21.804758	0.000
TIM83	-0.6392857	0.0969826	-6.5917592	0.001

R-squared	0.896804	Mean of dependent var	6.900000
Adjusted R-squared	0.876164	S.D. of dependent var	1.458310
S.E. of regression	0.513184	Sum of squared resid	1.316787
Durbin-Watson stat	2.023306	F-statistic	43.45129

The estimated secular trend for these years is indeed negative, equal to just above six-tenths of one percent per year. The overall performance of this equation, in terms of R^2 and coefficient of variation, are superior to those in the original equation. This should not be surprising, since the entire estimation period of the new equation consists of declines in the unemployment rate. The validity of this downward secular trend will be determined by the future behavior of the unemployment rate. The fact that the majority of the "baby boom" generation has already been absorbed into the labor force leads to the likelihood that the secular trend may indeed be decreasing.

This time trend in this last equation was recalculated so that it takes the value 1 in 1983 (t_{83}). Would the same coefficients have resulted if we had accidentally utilized the original time trend with 1950 = 1 (t_{50})? Consider the values of these time trends for the years of this regression:

	t_{83}	t_{50}
1983	1	34
1984	2	35
1985	3	36
1986	4	37
1987	5	38
1988	6	39
1989	7	40

Because the difference between these is 33 for each year, the new time trend consists of a change of origin from the original time trend, with:

$$t_{83} = t_{50} - 33.$$

Recall from Chapter 2 that change of origin leaves variances and covariances unchanged. Because of this, the slope coefficient:

$$\hat{\alpha}_1 = \text{Cov}(u_t, t_{83})/\text{Var}(t_{83})$$

remains the same when the original time trend is utilized. The intercept, which is based on the means of u and t, does change. The intercept when the new time trend is utilized, $\hat{\alpha}_0'$, is:

$$\hat{\alpha}_0' = \hat{\mu}_u - \hat{\alpha}_1 \hat{\mu}_{t83}$$
$$= \hat{\mu}_u - \hat{\alpha}_1 (\hat{\mu}_{t50} - 33)$$
$$= (\hat{\mu}_u - \hat{\alpha}_1 \hat{\mu}_{t50}) + \hat{\alpha}_1 (33)$$
$$\hat{\alpha}_0' = \hat{\alpha}_0 + 33 \cdot \hat{\alpha}_1$$
$$= \hat{\alpha}_0 - 21.1$$

using the estimated slope coefficient of -0.639 from above. As this exercise shows, when a single time trend is utilized for different sample periods, the estimated secular trend remains the same. Only the equation intercept changes. The printout using the time trend with $1950 = 1$ (TIM50) confirms this:

```
LS // Dependent Variable is U
SMPL range: 1983 - 1989
Number of observations: 7

     VARIABLE    COEFFICIENT   STD. ERROR      T-STAT.    2-TAIL SIG.

        C         30.553572     3.5935935     8.5022339     0.000
      TIM50       -0.6392857    0.0969826    -6.5917592     0.001

R-squared                0.896804    Mean of dependent var    6.900000
Adjusted R-squared       0.876164    S.D. of dependent var    1.458310
S.E. of regression       0.513184    Sum of squared resid     1.316787
Durbin-Watson stat       2.023306    F-statistic             43.45129
```

The intercept using a time trend with $1950 = 1$, 30.55, exceeds the intercept with the correct time trend, 9.46, by 21.1.

The original equation can also be used to forecast future values of the secular trend in the rate of unemployment. The predicted mean unemployment in period

$t + 1$, $\hat{u}_{t+1}$, is given by the following expression:

$$\hat{u}_{t+1} = \hat{\alpha}_0 + \hat{\alpha}_1(t + 1)$$
$$= 3.92 + 0.087(t + 1)$$

(using the coefficients from the equation with the correct time trend). To predict the mean unemployment for 1990, we substitute the value of the time trend for this year, 41, into the right side of this expression:

$$\hat{u}_{90} = 3.92 + 0.087(41)$$
$$= 7.49$$

Similarly, the predictions for the years 1991 to 1995 are:

$$\hat{u}_{91} = 3.92 + 0.087(41) = 7.49$$

$$\hat{u}_{92} = 3.92 + 0.087(42) = 7.57$$

$$\hat{u}_{93} = 3.92 + 0.087(43) = 7.66$$

$$\hat{u}_{94} = 3.92 + 0.087(44) = 7.75$$

$$\hat{u}_{95} = 3.92 + 0.087(45) = 7.84$$

A word of caution should be expressed about the use of this technique. The procedure outlined above is useful when a variable displays both cyclical and secular behavior, or secular behavior alone. The use of this technique on a purely cyclical variable does not provide a meaningful reference point for analyzing the behavior of this type of variable. Also, when the actual direction of the secular trend under consideration changes, forecasts created with this method will continue to move in the original direction, resulting in ever-increasing prediction errors. This is likely to be true for the unemployment rate equation used here, since the secular trend may have reversed its direction in 1983.

FORECASTING WITH THE TWO-VARIABLE REGRESSION MODEL

An important use of an estimated regression equation is the prediction or forecasting of possible values for the population mean of the dependent variable. The term forecast has the connotation of referring to a time-series equation, but this need not be the case. For this reason, the terms forecast and prediction are used interchangeably throughout the remainder of this text.

The type of forecast discussed here, which is called an **unconditional forecast**, entails generating predictions from an estimated equation using *actual* (known) data for the explanatory variable. The errors associated with this type of forecast are thus independent of the accuracy of the sample observations for x. Since this type of forecast deals exclusively with known values for x and y, this is an after-the-fact, or **ex-post forecast**.

We have already shown how to generate predictions by manipulating a sample regression function. If our sample regression function is:

$$\hat{y}_i = \hat{\alpha}_0 + \hat{\alpha}_1 x_i,$$

we arrive at a **forecast** or **prediction** for the population mean of y by substituting either actual, hypothetical, or predicted future values of x into the right side of this equation. This procedure implicitly assumes that the underlying structure of the relationship, which is captured by the equation specification, is equally valid for the values of x used to generate the forecast.

In a time-series context, we estimate the coefficients in the sample regression function for n periods, then utilize these, along with known values of x for periods $(n + 1)$ to the end of our forecast period to generate predicted values for y. Our forecast for period $n + \tau$ is:

$$\hat{y}_{n+\tau} = \hat{\alpha}_0 + \hat{\alpha}_1 x_{n+\tau}, \tag{5.19}$$

where τ designates the number of periods into the future our forecast extends. The ex-post forecast ends before the last time period for which actual data are available. For example, we might estimate the sample regression function for the first 10 of the last 12 years. Substituting actual values of x for years 11 $(= n + 1)$ and 12 $(= n + 2)$ into this equation, we obtain $\hat{y}_{11}$ and $\hat{y}_{12}$. A cross-section equation could use recently released data to judge how well the sample regression function predicts actual (just released) y values, or employ observed x values to compare the predicted mean of y to the values actually observed. In either case, $n + \tau$ refers to an observation with a cross-sectional equation.

The ex-post forecasting performance of an equation often provides additional information that we can use to judge its accuracy. We typically do not use a sample regression function for prediction unless its ex-post forecasting performance is deemed satisfactory. Equations that generate unsatisfactory ex-post forecasts can, however, predict out-of-sample values very accurately. This occurs when the structure of the underlying relationship between x and y is more appropriate for the beyond-sample values of x and y. It is also possible for the predictive accuracy of an equation to differ substantially among several subperiods. For example, demand for money equations that generated accurate predictions for the pre-1974 period, performed poorly starting in 1974. This led to the conclusion that a structural shift occurred in the demand for money.

Our forecast for a given observation or time period, $\hat{y}_{n+\tau}$, is a random variable. We can use this point estimate to construct confidence intervals for the actual values of y. The starting point in constructing these intervals is the forecast error $(\hat{\varepsilon}^f)$ associated with $\hat{y}_{n+\tau}$ in Equation (5.19)[16]:

$$\hat{\varepsilon}^f_{n+\tau} = \hat{y}_{n+\tau} - y_{n+\tau}$$

---

[16] Note that forecast error is defined differently than the usual equation residual, which is $(y_i - \hat{y}_i)$.

Substituting the right side of the expression for each y term gives:

$$= [\hat{\alpha}_0 + \hat{\alpha}_1 x_{n+\tau} - (\alpha_0 + \alpha_1 x_{n+\tau} + \varepsilon_{n+\tau})].$$

Upon rearranging terms, this becomes:

$$\hat{\varepsilon}^f_{n+\tau} = (\hat{\alpha}_0 - \alpha_0) + (\hat{\alpha}_1 - \alpha_1)x_{n+\tau} - \varepsilon_{n+\tau}. \tag{5.20}$$

Equation (5.20) allows us to decompose the forecast error for a given time period into:

$(\hat{\alpha}_0 - \alpha_0)$, the sampling error of $\hat{\alpha}_0$;

$(\hat{\alpha}_1 - \alpha_1)$, the sampling error of the slope coefficient, which is weighted by the value of $x_{n+\tau}$; and

$\varepsilon_{n+\tau}$, the stochastic error for this time period.

The first two of these arise as the byproduct of estimating a population regression function with sample data. Because the least squares coefficients are unbiased, the expected value of sampling error for each coefficient is 0. Actual sampling error is likely to be nonzero. The remaining source of forecast error, $\varepsilon_{n+\tau}$, represents the inherent randomness in the relationship between x and y. Improvement can be made in the first two sources of forecast error. The third is beyond our control, even when the sample regression function is properly specified.

We can determine the probability distribution of the forecast error $\hat{\varepsilon}^f_{n+\tau}$ along with the parameters of this distribution. Equation (5.20) shows that $\hat{\varepsilon}^f_{n+\tau}$ is a linear function of several normally distributed random variables ($\hat{\alpha}_0$, $\hat{\alpha}_1$, and $\varepsilon_{n+\tau}$). The forecast error is therefore normally distributed. Two parameters, a mean and variance, are associated with this distribution. The mean, or expected forecast error, is:

$$E(\hat{\varepsilon}^f_{n+\tau}) = E(\hat{\alpha}_0 - \alpha_0) + x_{n+\tau}E(\hat{\alpha}_1 - \alpha_1) - E(\varepsilon_{n+\tau})$$
$$= 0$$

since $\hat{\alpha}_0$ and $\hat{\alpha}_1$ are unbiased, and the mean stochastic error is assumed to be 0.[17] The use of least squares as the basis for forecasting thus produces a 0 error *on average*. The steps involved in deriving the formula for the forecast error variance ($\sigma^2_{f(n+\tau)}$) are complicated, and will not be presented here. The expression for this error variance is:

$$\sigma^2_{f(n+\tau)} = \sigma^2_\varepsilon \left[1 + \frac{1}{n} + \frac{(x_{n+\tau} - \hat{\mu}_x)^2}{\sum x_i'^2} \right] \tag{5.21}$$

where n is the number of observations used to estimate the sample regression function

$\hat{\mu}_x$ is the *estimation period* average of x

$\sum x_i'^2$ is the sum of squared deviations of x from $\hat{\mu}_x$ during the estimation period

σ^2_ε is the error variance for the estimated sample regression function

---

[17] Recall that these assumptions correspond to a correctly specified sample regression function, which is assumed throughout this discussion.

The variance of the forecast error is higher: the greater is the inherent randomness in the equation, as represented by σ_ε^2, the smaller is sample size n, which affects the sampling error of the least squares estimators; the farther is $x_{n+\tau}$ from $\hat{\mu}_x$, since this causes us to base our forecasts less typical x values than those used to estimate the sample regression function; and the smaller is the variance of x (and hence $\Sigma x_i'^2$). The minimum of $\sigma_{f(n+\tau)}^2$ occurs when $x_{n+\tau}$ equals $\hat{\mu}_x$, since the far-right term in the bracket then equals 0.

We can now summarize the distributional information for the forecast error:

$$\hat{\varepsilon}_{n+\tau}^f \sim N(0, \sigma_{f(n+\tau)}^2).$$

The expression for $\sigma_{f(n+\tau)}^2$ involves the unknown error variance σ_ε^2. By substituting the estimated error variance:

$$\hat{\sigma}_\varepsilon^2 = \Sigma \hat{\varepsilon}_i^2 / (n-2)$$

into Equation (5.21), we obtain an estimated forecasting error variance, $\hat{\sigma}_{f(n+\tau)}^2$, and the forecast errors now follow the t-distribution. The formula for the confidence interval corresponding to our point forecast $\hat{y}_{n+\tau}$ is, then:

$$\hat{y}_{n+\tau} \pm t_{p,n-2} \cdot \hat{\sigma}_{f(n+\tau)}, \tag{5.22}$$

where p, which denotes the probability in each tail of the t-distribution, is one-half the chosen level of significance. While the notation used in Equation (5.22) is similar to that for confidence intervals in general, it should be understood that *a separate value of* $\hat{\sigma}_{f(n+\tau)}$ *exists for each* $\hat{y}_{n+\tau}$. Furthermore, the values of $\hat{\sigma}_\varepsilon^2$, n, $\hat{\mu}_x$, and $\Sigma x_i'^2$ used to calculate each $\hat{\sigma}_{f(n+\tau)}$ pertain to the estimation period and not the forecast period.

To illustrate the ex-post forecasting technique, we utilize the consumption function from the previous section. The estimation period extends from 1947 to 1983. We then use the estimated coefficients from this equation, along with the actual values of real per capita disposable personal income (y) to forecast real per capita personal consumption expenditures (c) for the years 1984 to 1988. The estimated equation for 1947 to 1983 is:

$$\hat{c}_t = 238.4 + 0.875y_t \qquad \hat{\sigma}_\varepsilon = 87.8$$

The values of y for the years of the forecast are: 1984 = 10,419; 1985 = 10,625; 1986 = 10,929; 1987 = 11,012; 1988 = 11,286. The manually calculated predictions of real consumption expenditure are[18]:

$$1984: 238.4 + 0.875(10,419) = \quad 9,355.0$$

$$1985: 238.4 + 0.875(10,625) = \quad 9,535.3$$

$$\cdots$$

$$1988: 238.4 + 0.875(11,286) = 10,113.7$$

---

[18] The values here differ from the figures in the computer printout that is shown shortly due to rounding.

The following table gives actual and predicted real consumption expenditure, along with the forecast error for each year:

τ	YEAR	$c_{n+\tau}$	$\hat{c}_{n+\tau}$	$\hat{\varepsilon}^f_{n+\tau}$
1	1984	9,489	9,355.0	-133.98
2	1985	9,840	9,535.3	-304.73
3	1986	10,160	9,801.3	-358.73
4	1987	10,334	9,873.9	-460.10
5	1988	10,497	10,113.7	-383.35

Before we can compute the confidence interval for each prediction, we must first calculate its forecast error variance. Values for the terms in $\hat{\sigma}_{f(n+\tau)}$ are (denoting RDPIN as x): $n = 37$; $\hat{\sigma}^2_\varepsilon = 7,706.4$; $\hat{\mu}_x = 7,275.7$; and $\Sigma x_i'^2 = 107,874,795$. For 1984 ($= n + 1$) the set of calculations involved gives:

$$\hat{\sigma}_{f(n+1)}^2 = 7,706.4[1 + (1/37) + (10,419 - 7,275.7)^2/107,874,795]$$
$$= 8,620.5$$

The critical t-values for 35 degrees of freedom are 2.032 for the 95 percent level of confidence and 2.727 for the 99 percent level. The formulas for the confidence intervals in year $n + \tau$ are:

$$95 \text{ percent level: } \hat{y}_{n+\tau} \pm 2.032 \cdot \hat{\sigma}_{f(n+\tau)};$$

and

$$99 \text{ percent level: } \hat{y}_{n+\tau} \pm 2.727 \cdot \hat{\sigma}_{f(n+\tau)}.$$

Actual and predicted real per capita consumption expenditure, along with the upper and lower confidence bounds for each year are shown in the following table:

YEAR	ACTUAL	UPPER 99%	UPPER 95%	PREDICTED	LOWER 95%	LOWER 99%
1984	9,489	9,608.2	9,543.7	9,355.0	9,166.4	9,101.8
1985	9,840	9,789.9	9,725.0	9,535.3	9,345.6	9,280.7
1986	10,160	10,058.1	9,992.6	9,801.3	9,609.9	9,544.5
1987	10,334	10,131.3	10,065.7	9,873.9	9,682.1	9,616.5
1988	10,497	10,373.3	10,307.1	10,113.7	9,920.2	9,854.0

Our forecasts underestimate real per capita consumption for every year of the forecast. Actual real consumption expenditure exceeds the upper 95 percent confidence bound for all but 1984. The same is true for the 99 percent confidence intervals. Actual consumption is, with the exception of 1984, always above both the upper 95 or 99 percent confidence bounds. Should we then view these forecasts as totally unacceptable?

Several measures exist that are useful in evaluating the forecasting performance of an equation. We can obtain important insights into the relationship between actual and predicted values by considering how well the forecasts replicate the mean and variance of the actual series. Values of these statistics in the present example are shown in the following table:

VARIABLE	MEAN	STD. DEV.	MAXIMUM	MINIMUM
RCONSN	10,064	563.5	10,497	9,489
PREDICTED	9,735.8	414.1	10,113.7	9,355

While the mean of the forecasts is below the average for actual real per capita consumption, the average forecast is approximately 97 percent of the mean of actual real per capita consumption values. The dispersion in forecasted values, as measured by their standard deviation, is below that for actual real per capita consumption. The standard deviation of the forecasts is, however, less than 75 percent of the actual values. Our forecasts thus approximate the mean of real per capita consumption better than they are able to replicate the dispersion in these values.

How large of a difference in the means of these series is acceptable? One way we can evaluate the magnitude of forecast error is by calculating the percent error for each year of our forecast. For a given year, the percent error is:

$$PCTER_{n+\tau} = 100 \cdot (\hat{y}_{n+\tau} - y_{n+\tau})/y_{n+\tau}$$
$$= 100 \cdot (\hat{\varepsilon}^f_{n+\tau}/y_{n+\tau})$$

The following table gives actual and predicted values of RCONS, along with the residual (RESID) and percent error (PCTER) for each year:

YEAR	RCONS	PREDICTED	RESID	PCTER
1984	9,489	9,355.0	−133.98	−1.41
1985	9,840	9,535.3	−304.73	−3.10
1986	10,160	9,801.3	−358.73	−3.53
1987	10,334	9,873.9	−460.10	−4.45
1988	10,497	10,113.7	−383.35	−3.65

The percent errors provide a very different picture of the forecasting performance of our equation than do the actual magnitudes of the forecast errors. While the forecast errors range from −134 to −460, percent errors vary from −1.4 to −4.45 percent.

A frequently used measure of forecast accuracy is the **mean absolute percent error** (MAPE). Its use of absolute values prevents positive and negative errors from canceling, which would indicate a far better forecast performance than actually exists.

Since this measure is a percentage, it is a pure number, which is independent of the units of measurement for the dependent variable. The formula for the mean absolute percent error is:

$$\text{MAPE} = 100 \cdot (1/n_f) \sum |\hat{y}_{n+\tau} - y_{n+\tau}| / y_{n+\tau},$$

or

$$\text{MAPE} = 100 \cdot (1/n_f) \sum |\hat{\varepsilon}_{n+\tau}^f| / y_{n+\tau} \tag{5.23}$$

where n_f is the number of periods in our forecast. The value of MAPE for the consumption function is 3.23 percent. While there is no objective benchmark against which to judge MAPE, values no greater than 5 or 10 percent are often considered indicative of an acceptable forecast. This should be just one of several criteria used to judge the forecasting ability of an equation, however.

A widely used measure of forecast performance, which is provided routinely with a number of canned computer programs, is the **root mean square error** (RMSE):

$$\text{RMSE} = \sqrt{(1/n_f) \sum (\hat{y}_{n+\tau} - y_{n+\tau})^2} = \sqrt{(1/n_f) \sum (\hat{\varepsilon}_{n+\tau}^f)^2}. \tag{5.24}$$

The formula for RMSE is identical to that for the equation standard error, with the exceptions that it uses n_f in place of $(n - 2)$ in the first term of the expression, and the forecast error is calculated differently than the usual equation error. The units of measurement for RMSE are the same as those for the dependent variable. Because of this similarity between the standard error of an equation and the root mean square error of a forecast, these measures are often compared when evaluating forecasting performance. If the RMSE is substantially greater than $\hat{\sigma}_\varepsilon$, the forecasting performance of the equation is considered to be suspect, while values of RMSE close to $\hat{\sigma}_\varepsilon$ indicate acceptable forecast performance. The RMSE in this example, 345.9, is 2.73 times the estimation period equation standard error. This falls outside what is usually considered to be an acceptable range for this measure, indicating problems with our forecasts.

The root mean square error of a forecast can also be expressed in percent terms, so that its unit of measurement is a relative magnitude, and no longer that of the dependent variable. The resulting measure is the **root mean square percent error** (RMSPE):

$$\text{RMSPE} = \sqrt{(1/n_f) \sum ((\hat{y}_{n+\tau} - y_{n+\tau}) / y_{n+\tau})^2} \tag{5.25}$$

The root mean square percent error for the real per capita consumption forecast is 3.38. Note that the values of RMSPE and MAPE are fairly close in this example. Both provide measures of the average forecast error that are unaffected by the problem of positive and negative error cancellation.

This discussion of forecasting will conclude with a few remarks about the forecasting performance of the consumption function used in this section. The overall forecasting performance of this equation is unsatisfactory. Respecification is necessary before we can expect its forecasting performance to improve. The measures of forecast performance outlined in this section provide mixed evidence concerning whether or not a problem exists with this equation. While the forecast errors appear to be large, this is not the case when the values of both MAPE and RMSPE, which are expressed in percent terms, are considered. Both these values indicate an "average" forecast error of less than 3.5 percent, which is within an acceptable range for most forecasters. Problems with the performance of this equation are evident from:

1. its consistent underprediction of actual real consumption expenditures;
2. the fact that actual real per capita consumption exceeds the upper confidence bound of the forecasts (at both the 95 and 99 percent levels of confidence) for all but one year of the forecast; and
3. the root mean square error of the forecast is almost three times the standard error of the equation.

Most of the problems associated with these forecasts result from using a single explanatory variable to model the behavior of real per capita consumption expenditure. Another likely cause of these problems is the implicit assumption built into this equation that the structure of the underlying relationship is the same over the entire period covered by the data. This relationship was most likely affected by key events in both the 1970s and the 1980s: the debut of the OPEC oil cartel; the new direction of monetary policy under Paul Volker; and the recovery that began in 1983. Methods for incorporating these factors into an equation specification are presented in Chapter 9.

KEY TERMS

Acceptance region	One-tail test
Alternative hypothesis	p-Value
Composite hypothesis	Point estimator
Confidence bound (upper and lower)	Prediction
Confidence interval	Rejection region
Critical values	Root mean square error
Ex-post forecast	Root mean square percent error
Forecast	Simple hypothesis
Hypothesis testing	Statistical inference
Hypothesized sampling error	Statistically significant
Interval estimate	Test statistic
Level of confidence	Testable hypothesis
Level of significance	Time trend
Maintained hypotheses	Two-tail test
Margin for sampling error	Type I error
Mean absolute percent error	Type II error
Null hypothesis	Unconditional forecast

EXERCISES

1.   Some researchers assert that nothing has ever been proven empirically. How do the notions of Type I error and Type II error relate to this statement? Is this assertion true or false? Why?

2.   What is the relationship (if any) between spurious correlation and Type I errors?

3.   Using a graph, illustrate the appearance of the population regression function that pertains when we are unable to reject the null hypotheses for the statistical significance of $\hat{\alpha}_0$ and $\hat{\alpha}_1$.

4.   Why are the hypotheses used to test the least squares coefficients not stated in terms of estimated coefficients?

5.   Using the unemployment rate-capacity utilization rate equation in this chapter:

   (a) perform the one-tail hypotheses tests on $\hat{\alpha}_1$ at the 1 percent level of significance.

   (b) make the tests for $\hat{\alpha}_1$ two-tail tests and perform the hypotheses tests at both the 5 percent and 1 percent levels of significance.

   (c) test the following hypotheses:

   $$H_0: \alpha_0 = 0$$

   $$H_a: \alpha_0 > 0$$

   at both the 5 percent and 1 percent levels of significance.

6.   The following beta coefficient equation was presented in Chapter 4:

   $$R_t = \alpha + \beta R_{mt} + \varepsilon_t$$

   where R is the rate of return to IBM stock, and R_m is an index of the market rate of return to stocks. We now add information about the standard errors of the coefficients in this equation (note: $n = 240$):

	COEFFICIENT	STANDARD DEVIATION
Intercept	0.726	0.30
β-coefficient	1.06	0.073

   (a) Derive a 95 percent confidence interval for each coefficient.

   (b) Are these coefficients statistically significant?

   (c) Test the hypotheses $H_0: \beta = 1$ and $H_a: \beta < 1$ at the 1 percent level of significance. If we reject H_0, what does this indicate about IBM stock?

7.   Chapter 4 presented the least squares coefficients for a cross-sectional labor demand function, where employment of nonsupervisory personnel (thousands)

by two-digit SIC category in 1983 was regressed on real average hourly earnings ($1977 = 100$) in these categories for that year ($n = 8$). The information below gives those coefficients and their standard deviations:

	COEFFICIENT	STANDARD DEVIATION
Intercept	25,108.6	7,573.8
Real Wages	−3,218.6	1,349.7

(a) Derive a 99 percent confidence interval for each coefficient.

(b) Are these coefficients statistically significant?

(c) Test the hypotheses $H_0: \alpha_1 = -1,000$ and $H_a: \alpha_1 < -1,000$ at both the 5 percent and 1 percent levels of significance.

(d) What is the largest point estimate of $\hat{\alpha}_1$ for which we would be unable to reject the null hypothesis in (c)?

8. Using the estimated consumption function in this chapter, test:

$$H_0: \alpha_0 = 0$$

$$H_a: \alpha_0 > 0$$

at the 1 percent, 5 percent, and 10 percent levels of significance (use critical t-values with 40 degrees of freedom).

9. Obtain time series data on real business fixed investment (I) and an appropriate rate of interest (r).

(a) Which interest rate did you select? Why is this a valid interest rate to use?

(b) Consider the following population regression function:

$$I_t = \alpha_0 + \alpha_1 r_t + \varepsilon_t$$

(i) What are the expected signs of the coefficients in this equation? Explain the rationale for each of these signs.

(ii) How can you use this equation to estimate the interest elasticity of investment?

(c) Estimate the population regression function given in (b).

(d) Which coefficients are statistically significant? Are the signs those expected?

(e) Construct a 99 percent confidence interval for the coefficient of r_t.

(f) Use your sample data to generate ex-post forecasts of real fixed investment.

(i) Calculate a confidence interval for each of the forecast values.

(ii) Calculate the following measures for these forecasts: MAPE, RMSE, and RMSPE. How well does this equation forecast real business fixed investment?

10.   Use the data from **(9)** to estimate the log-linear version of that population regression function:

$$\ln(I)_t = \alpha_0 + \alpha_1 \ln(r)_t + \varepsilon_t.$$

The slope coefficient is the interest elasticity of investment (this follows the production function example in Chapter 4).

(a) Is the estimated interest elasticity statistically significant?

(b) Do you expect this elasticity to be elastic or inelastic? Why?

(c) Perform a hypothesis test of whether investment is interest elastic.

11.   The SAS printout for the unemployment rate equation indicates that the degrees of freedom for the entry TOTAL under the column SUM OF SQUARES equals 9. Why does this differ from the number of observations?

12.   Both of the variables in the per capita consumption function presented in this chapter have a 1982 base year. Assume that their values with a 1972 base year are a fixed multiple (k) of these original values:

$$RCONS_{72} = k \cdot RCONS_{82}$$

and

$$RDPI_{72} = k \cdot RDPI_{82}.$$

(a) Does the estimated MPC change as the result of this shift in base year? Using the formula for this coefficient, show the calculations involved in this determination.

(b) Is the estimate of mean autonomous real per capita consumption affected by this base year modification? Illustrate your answer using calculations similar to those in **(a)** above.

13.   Use the information for the production function presented in this chapter to test the following hypotheses at the 5 percent significance level:

(a) Is the intercept term in this equation statistically significant?

(b) Test whether this production function goes through the origin of the usual graph of a short-run production function, where the level of output is graphed against labor input.

6

Econometric Theory: The Multiple Regression Model

The presentation of econometric theory provided in the last two chapters focused exclusively on the bivariate regression model. Yet relatively few of the most important economic functions are bivariate. Because of this fact, we must now shift our emphasis to the more realistic setting where our population regression function includes several explanatory variables: multiple regression. This chapter provides the framework necessary to formulate, estimate, and make statistical inferences with a multiple regression equation. Many of the results from bivariate regression apply either directly, or with minor modification, to the multiple regression model. The differences outlined in this chapter are presupposed throughout the remainder of this text. After reading this material, you should have an understanding of many of the specifics that pertain to the general outline of econometrics presented in the first chapter.

THE MULTIPLE REGRESSION MODEL

Chapters 4 and 5 outlined the specifics of estimating and interpreting bivariate relationships, such as the demand curve:

$$q_x = f(p_x),$$

where q_x is the quantity of good X demanded, and p_x is the price of X. While this theoretical relationship is a deterministic function, the empirical relationship between this pair of variables is stochastic, since a range (probability density function) of p_x values exist for each q_x. As a result, we cannot state unequivocally that every person who pays a higher price for good X will consume a smaller quantity than do persons paying a lower price. Our statements about the association between these variables must therefore be restricted to the relationship that exists between q_x and p_x *on average.*

Econometric estimation of this equation consists of approximating the conditional mean of q_x, $E(q_x|p_x)$. The function expressing this relationship is the population regression model. If we postulate a linear specification for this model, and express it in stochastic form, it becomes:

$$q_x = \alpha_0 + \alpha_1 p_x + \varepsilon \tag{6.1}$$

A bivariate relationship such as Equation (6.1) is valid only if the single included explanatory variable is the primary factor influencing its dependent variable. All other factors, deemed to be of secondary importance, are then included in the error term. From model assumption (1), the net influence of these omitted variables is negligible.

Nevertheless, most of the relationships studied by economists are not bivariate but multivariate. For example, the theoretical basis for the demand curve equation given by Equation (6.1) is the demand function:

$$q_x = f(p_x, p_y, I, p^e) \tag{6.2}$$

Equation (6.2) is a multivariate relationship since it includes four explanatory variables—p_x as well as the price of a related good, p_y, income I, and the expected future price of X, p^e.

If we wish to obtain an accurate estimate of α_1 in Equation (6.1), the crucial econometric question is the following: does the least squares estimator of this coefficient obtained from the bivariate regression of q_x on p_x possess desirable properties such as unbiasedness, efficiency, and consistency? In general, the answer to this question is no.[1] The estimator of α_1 from Equation (6.1) can be expected not to attain all the desirable estimator properties. The least squares methodology must therefore be extended to allow estimation of multivariate functions.

How can we estimate the coefficient of the explanatory variable in question when "other things" (i.e., p_y, I, and p^e) are not equal? In other words, how do we control for the effects of these other variables when the data do not?

The answer to this question is based on the fact that the conditional mean of q_x is not a function of p_x alone, but of the *set* of variables p_x, p_y, I, and p^e. We can express this relationship as:

$$E(q_x|p_x, p_y, I, p^e) = f(p_x, p_y, I, p^e) \tag{6.3}$$

The population regression model therefore includes all of these variables. We can control for their influence on q_x by including *each* of these variables in our sample

---

[1] Note that when the excluded variables are totally uncorrelated with the included variable, the slope coefficient will still be unbiased; but its variance will be larger than that for his coefficient in the correctly specified equation.

regression function. If we utilize a linear relationship to depict the specification of the relationship given by Equation (6.3), the result is a multiple regression equation:

$$E(q_x|p_x, p_y, I, p^e) = \alpha_0 + \alpha_1 p_x + \alpha_2 p_y + \alpha_3 I + \alpha_4 p^e. \qquad \textbf{(6.4)}$$

The stochastic form of the population regression model (including a subscript) is:

$$q_{xi} = \alpha_0 + \alpha_1 p_{xi} + \alpha_2 p_{yi} + \alpha_3 I_i + \alpha_4 p_i^e + \varepsilon_i \qquad \textbf{(6.5)}$$

By substituting a specific value for each explanatory variable into Equation (6.4), we obtain an approximation to the mean of q_x when these values pertain. When the values of one or more of the explanatory variables in this equation change, the conditional mean of q_x also changes. The amount of change is determined by the magnitudes and signs of the coefficients involved.

The coefficients in a multiple regression equation are interpreted differently than those in a bivariate equation. The coefficient of each explanatory variable gives the slope of a graph with the dependent variable on the vertical axis and the explanatory variable on the horizontal axis, *for fixed values of the other explanatory variables*. The coefficient α_1 in Equation (6.4), for example, is the slope of the demand curve, or the rate of change in $E(q_x|p_x, p_y, I, p^e)$ when p_x changes, given the values of p_y, I, and p^e. Similarly, the coefficient α_2 is the slope of a graph with $E(q_x|p_x, p_y, I, p^e)$ on the vertical axis and p_y on the horizontal axis. This can be seen by collapsing Equation (6.4) into a bivariate equation involving only the conditional mean of q_x and p_y:

$$E(q_x|p_{xi}, p_{yi}, I_i, p_i^e) = \alpha_0^* + \alpha_2 p_{yi}$$

where $\alpha_0^* = (\alpha_0 + \alpha_1 p_{xi} + \alpha_3 I_i + \alpha_4 p_i^e)$. The correct interpretation of α_2 is the rate of change in the conditional mean of q_x as p_y changes, given p_x, I, and p^e. For example, if α_3 equals 2, and q_x is expressed in thousands of units per month, a \$1 rise in p_y increases the conditional mean of q_x by 2,000 units per month, given p_x, I, and p^e.

As this example shows, each of these coefficients indicates a rate of change. Unlike bivariate regression, however, we are now dealing with *partial* rates of change: the rate of change in the conditional mean of the dependent variable when a single variable changes, *other things being equal*. Since these coefficients designate partial rates of change, the coefficients of the explanatory variables in multiple regression are called **partial slopes**.

The specification of Equation (6.4) assumes that the major subset of variables influencing q_x are p_x, p_y, I, and p^e. If the actual data used to estimate this relationship contain any major factor in addition to these, a variable representing its influence must also be included. Variable inclusion is thus the correct way of controlling for factors that determine the behavior of the dependent variable. Because of this fact, *a single population regression function such as Equation (6.5), which is sufficient to characterize many demand relationships, is not valid for all possible equations, even if a linear specification is correct. Equation (6.5) should be viewed as a starting point based on economic theory that must be modified according to the actual data used for estimation.*

Our estimate of the population regression function is given by the sample regression function. The relationship between the population and sample regression functions with multiple regression closely parallels that for bivariate regression. If we return to the general case where our dependent variable is y and there are k explanatory (x) variables, we can express the population regression function as either:

$$E(y|x_{1i}, x_{2i}, \ldots, x_{ki}) = \alpha_0 + \alpha_1 x_{1i} + \cdots + \alpha_k x_{ki},$$

or   (6.6)

$$y_i = \alpha_0 + \alpha_1 x_{1i} + \cdots + \alpha_k x_{ki} + \varepsilon_i$$

The second of these equations, which is the stochastic form of the population regression function, contains $(k + 2)$ unknowns: the intercept α_0; the k partial slopes, $\alpha_1, \ldots, \alpha_k$; and the stochastic error term, ε. Our estimate of this equation, the sample regression function, uses estimates of the population coefficients along with values for the x's to generate predicted values for y, $\hat{y}$. These predicted values are our estimates of the conditional mean of y, $E(y|x_1, \ldots, x_k)$:

$$\hat{y}_i = \hat{\alpha}_0 + \hat{\alpha}_1 x_{1i} + \cdots + \hat{\alpha}_k x_{ki}$$ (6.7)

Actual and predicted values of y exist for each sample observation. The residual for the ith observation, $\hat{\varepsilon}_i$, is the difference between the actual and predicted value of y for that observation:

$$\hat{\varepsilon}_i = (y_i - \hat{y}_i)$$ (6.8)

Solving this equation for y allows us to express the actual value of y for this observation as the sum of our estimate of the conditional mean plus the residual:

$$y_i = \hat{y}_i + \hat{\varepsilon}_i$$ (6.9)

We arrive at the stochastic form of the sample regression function by substituting the right side of Equation (6.7) into this equation:

$$y_i = \hat{\alpha}_0 + \hat{\alpha}_1 x_{1i} + \cdots + \hat{\alpha}_k x_{ki} + \hat{\varepsilon}_i$$ (6.10)

Estimation of the coefficients in Equation (6.10) is accomplished using the least squares technique.

Before outlining the essential steps involved in obtaining the formulas for these coefficients, two points should be made. First, recall that least squares is linear regression analysis. Linearity, however, refers to the *coefficients* and not necessarily the explanatory variables in the sample regression function. Explanatory variables such as the natural logarithm of x, its absolute change, the percent change in x, or x raised to a power do not violate the linearity assumption. Only the product of individual α's, or coefficients raised to powers other than 1 violate this requirement. Second, estimation of a multiple regression equation requires positive degrees of freedom. Least squares estimation of a multiple regression equation can proceed only when the number of observations used to estimate the relationship exceeds the total number of coefficients in the equation.

LEAST SQUARES ESTIMATION OF THE MULTIPLE REGRESSION MODEL

The multiple regression model considered here includes only two explanatory variables: x and z. The population regression function using these variables, assuming a linear specification, is:

$$y_i = \alpha_0 + \alpha_1 x_i + \alpha_2 z_i + \varepsilon_i. \tag{6.11}$$

The corresponding sample regression function is:

$$y_i = \hat{\alpha}_0 + \hat{\alpha}_1 x_i + \hat{\alpha}_2 z_i + \hat{\varepsilon}_i. \tag{6.12}$$

The least squares technique involves minimizing the sum of the squared residuals, $\Sigma \hat{\varepsilon}_i^2$, then solving for the coefficients in the sample regression function. To perform this minimization, we first rearrange Equation (6.12) expressing the residual as a function of the coefficients in the sample regression function:

$$\hat{\varepsilon}_i = (y_i - \hat{\alpha}_0 - \hat{\alpha}_1 x_i - \hat{\alpha}_2 z_i).$$

We obtain the expression for the sum of the squared residuals in terms of the $\hat{\alpha}$'s by summing then squaring both sides of this equation. The least squares estimators are obtained by minimizing the resulting expression:

$$\sum \hat{\varepsilon}_i^2 = \sum (y_i - \hat{\alpha}_0 - \hat{\alpha}_1 x_i - \hat{\alpha}_2 z_i)^2 \tag{6.13}$$

with respect to $\hat{\alpha}_0$, $\hat{\alpha}_1$, and $\hat{\alpha}_2$. This minimization procedure utilizes calculus, where the partial derivative of Equation (6.13) is calculated for each $\hat{\alpha}$. Each of these, which is called a multiple regression normal equation is then set equal to 0. This set of simultaneous equations is then solved for $\hat{\alpha}_0$, $\hat{\alpha}_1$, and $\hat{\alpha}_2$, giving the formulas for the least squares coefficients. The normal equations that result are:

for $\hat{\alpha}_0$:

$$2\sum (y_i - \hat{\alpha}_0 - \hat{\alpha}_1 x_i - \hat{\alpha}_2 z_i)(-1) = 0,$$

or
$$\sum y_i - n\hat{\alpha}_0 - \hat{\alpha}_1 \sum x_i - \hat{\alpha}_2 \sum z_i = 0 \tag{6.14}$$

for $\hat{\alpha}_1$:

$$2\sum (y_i - \hat{\alpha}_0 - \hat{\alpha}_1 x_i - \hat{\alpha}_2 z_i)(-x_i) = 0,$$

or
$$\sum x_i y_i - \hat{\alpha}_0 \sum x_i - \hat{\alpha}_1 \sum x_i^2 - \hat{\alpha}_2 \sum x_i z_i = 0 \tag{6.15}$$

for $\hat{\alpha}_2$:

$$2\sum (y_i - \hat{\alpha}_0 - \hat{\alpha}_1 x_i - \hat{\alpha}_2 z_i)(-z_i) = 0,$$

or
$$\sum z_i y_i - \hat{\alpha}_0 \sum z_i - \hat{\alpha}_1 \sum z_i x_i - \hat{\alpha}_2 \sum z_i^2 = 0 \tag{6.16}$$

Solving these equations for the least squares estimators gives:

$$\hat{\alpha}_0 = \hat{\mu}_y - \hat{\alpha}_1 \hat{\mu}_x - \hat{\alpha}_2 \hat{\mu}_z \tag{6.17}$$

$$\hat{\alpha}_1 = \frac{(\sum y_i' x_i')(\sum z_i'^2) - (\sum y_i' z_i')(\sum x_i' z_i')}{(\sum x_i'^2)(\sum z_i'^2) - (\sum x_i' z_i')^2} \tag{6.18}$$

$$\hat{\alpha}_2 = \frac{(\sum y_i' z_i')(\sum x_i'^2) - (\sum y_i' x_i')(\sum x_i' z_i')}{(\sum x_i'^2)(\sum z_i'^2) - (\sum x_i' z_i')^2} \tag{6.19}$$

; and where $x_i' \equiv (x_i - \hat{\mu}_x)$, $y_i' \equiv (y_i - \hat{\mu}_y)$; and

$z_i' \equiv (z_i - \hat{\mu}_z)$.

The formula for $\hat{\alpha}_0$ indicates that the least squares sample regression function passes through the point of means, $(\hat{\mu}_x, \hat{\mu}_y, \hat{\mu}_z)$, which parallels the bivariate regression model exactly. Both partial slope formulas are more complicated than the slope expression in the bivariate regression model. Nevertheless, a common ground still exists: by dividing the numerators and denominators of Equations (6.18) and (6.19) by $(n - 1)$, we see that these formulas, like the slope expression in Chapter 4, consist of variances and covariances of the variables in the model.

The normal equations reveal several properties of least squares estimation similar to those in the bivariate model. Since the bracketed expression in each normal equation equals $\Sigma \hat{\varepsilon}_i$, simple manipulation of Equation (6.14) shows that $\Sigma \hat{\varepsilon}_i = 0$, so that the average residual is 0. The normal equation for $\hat{\alpha}_1$ can be rewritten as $\Sigma \hat{\varepsilon}_i x_i = 0$, which is $\text{Cov}(x_i, \hat{\varepsilon}_i)$ when the average residual is 0. Equation (6.16) reveals a similar result for $\hat{\alpha}_2$: $\Sigma \hat{\varepsilon}_i z_i = 0$, so that $\text{Cov}(z_i, \hat{\varepsilon}_i) = 0$. Summarizing these results:

$$\sum \hat{\varepsilon}_i = 0$$

$$\sum x_i \hat{\varepsilon}_i = 0 \tag{6.20}$$

$$\sum z_i \hat{\varepsilon}_i = 0.$$

Two additional properties of the least squares technique will be derived. The first of these establishes the equality of the average predicted value of y, $\hat{\mu}_{\hat{y}}$, and the mean of y. The predicted y for a given observation is:

$$\hat{y}_i = \hat{\alpha}_0 + \hat{\alpha}_1 x_i + \hat{\alpha}_2 z_i.$$

Substituting for $\hat{\alpha}_0$ from Equation (6.17), this becomes:

$$\hat{y}_i = (\hat{\mu}_y - \hat{\alpha}_1 \hat{\mu}_x - \hat{\alpha}_2 \hat{\mu}_z) + \hat{\alpha}_1 x_i + \hat{\alpha}_2 z_i.$$

Collecting the terms involving partial slopes:

$$\hat{y}_i = \hat{\mu}_y + \hat{\alpha}_1 (x_i - \hat{\mu}_x) + \hat{\alpha}_2 (z_i - \hat{\mu}_z). \tag{6.21}$$

Summing both sides of Equation (6.21) gives:

$$\sum \hat{y}_i = \sum \hat{\mu}_y + \hat{\alpha}_1 \sum (x_i - \hat{\mu}_x) + \sum (z_i - \hat{\mu}_z)$$

After dividing both sides of this equation by n, this simplifies to:

$$\hat{\mu}_{\hat{y}} = \hat{\mu}_y, \tag{6.22}$$

since $\Sigma(x_i - \hat{\mu}_x) = \Sigma(z_i - \hat{\mu}_z) = 0$. The average prediction of y with least squares is therefore identical to the mean of the dependent variable.

The next property is useful when critiquing the performance of a sample regression function: the residual for a given observation, $\hat{\varepsilon}_i$, is uncorrelated with the predicted y for that observation, $\hat{y}_i$. To establish this result, it is necessary to show that $\text{Cov}(\hat{\varepsilon}_i, \hat{y}_i) = 0$. The summation formula for this covariance, neglecting the term involving degrees of freedom, but using the fact that the mean residual is 0, is:

$$\text{Cov}(\hat{\varepsilon}_i, \hat{y}_i) = \sum \hat{\varepsilon}_i (\hat{y}_i - \hat{\mu}_y)$$
$$= \sum \hat{\varepsilon}_i \hat{y}_i - \hat{\mu}_y \sum \hat{\varepsilon}_i$$
$$= \sum \hat{\varepsilon}_i \hat{y}_i.$$

Substituting for $\hat{y}_i$ in this expression:

$$= \sum \hat{\varepsilon}_i (\hat{\alpha}_0 + \hat{\alpha}_1 x_i + \hat{\alpha}_2 z_i)$$
$$= \hat{\alpha}_0 \sum \hat{\varepsilon}_i + \hat{\alpha}_1 \sum \hat{\varepsilon}_i x_i + \hat{\alpha}_2 \sum \hat{\varepsilon}_i z_i$$
$$= 0$$

using the results from the least squares normal equations stated in Equation (6.20). While the residuals in a properly specified equation are uncorrelated with the predicted values of y, a scatter diagram of the values of $\hat{\varepsilon}$ and $\hat{y}$ can sometimes reveal problems with a sample regression function. Recall that the covariance measures the *linear* association between two variables. It is thus possible for $\text{Cov}(\hat{\varepsilon}_i, \hat{y}_i) = 0$ when a nonlinear association exists between $\hat{\varepsilon}_i$ and $\hat{y}_i$. This occurs either when the residual variance is not constant, which indicates heteroskedastic errors, or when a nonlinear specification is appropriate. In either case, remedial actions are called for.

The properties of the least squares estimators in the multiple regression model are ascertained relative to a set of assumptions concerning the stochastic error term and other elements of the population regression function. Much of this parallels the presentation given for the bivariate regression model. The reader is referred to the discussion in Chapter 4 if more detail is desired. The population regression function is assumed to take the form of Equation (6.11) with the two explanatory variables x and z.

MODEL ASSUMPTIONS

1. For every pair of values, (x_i, z_i), $E(\varepsilon_i) = 0$, or $E(\varepsilon_i | x_i, z_i) = 0$.

This first assumption states that the mean stochastic error equals 0, or that all of the conditional error distributions have means of 0. This is met when: (i) the variables which have been omitted from the population regression function are of secondary importance in determining the behavior of the dependent variable; and (ii) in terms of their influence on y, these variables exactly cancel each other out so that their net impact on y is 0. This assumption implies the absence of specification error in the population regression function.

2. $\text{Var}(\varepsilon_i) = \sigma_\varepsilon^2$

This is the assumption of homoskedastic errors, which requires that the error variance does not change for different values of any observations or explanatory variables.

3. $\text{Cov}(\varepsilon_i, \varepsilon_j) = 0$ for $i \neq j$

If this assumption is met, the stochastic errors are pairwise uncorrelated. In the context of time series data, this indicates the absence of serial correlation.

4. Each explanatory variable is either nonstochastic, or if it is stochastic, it is uncorrelated with the equation error.

When the variables are nonstochastic, we may consider their values as being fixed in repeated samples. Then:

$$\text{Cov}(x_i, \varepsilon_i) = [x_i - E(x_i)]E(\varepsilon_i) = 0$$

and

$$\text{Cov}(z_i, \varepsilon_i) = [z_i - E(z_i)]E(\varepsilon_i) = 0$$

and the stochastic error is uncorrelated with each of the explanatory variables in the population regression function. As a result, x, z, and ε exert separate influences on the dependent variable. This same result occurs when either x or z is stochastic but uncorrelated with ε. If this pertains to x, then:

$$\text{Cov}(x_i, \varepsilon_i) = E(x_i\varepsilon_i) - E(x_i)E(\varepsilon_i) = 0$$

since with x and ε uncorrelated, $E(x_i\varepsilon_i) = E(x_i)E(\varepsilon_i)$.

5. x and z are not perfectly collinear.

This assumption states that x and z are two separate and independent variables, so that one cannot be expressed as an exact *linear* function of the other. For example, if each z_i is one-half of the corresponding x_i, then, while it appears these are two separate variables, in reality only one set of independent observations exists. In other words, once the value of x is known, z can always be calculated. Under these circumstances, x and z are perfectly correlated and the least squares estimator is not unique.[2] We are then unable to determine the separate impacts of x and z on y. Nonlinear relationships between explanatory variables are acceptable, however. Thus, including x and x^2 in the same equation is valid. Including both $\ln(x)$ and $\ln(x^2)$ does not satisfy this assumption (think about why this is true).

---

[2] For persons familiar with matrix algebra, the least squares estimators require that the data matrix be invertible, which is violated with perfect collinearity.

6. ε_i is a normally distributed random variable.

This assumption provides the basis for performing statistical inference with the population regression function. Along with (1)–(3), this assumption implies that:

$$\varepsilon_i \sim N(0, \sigma_\varepsilon^2),$$

and the errors are independently distributed. In addition to this, y_i is also a normally distributed random variable, since the population regression function expresses y_i as a linear function of the normally distributed random variable ε_i. The distributional information for y is:

$$y_i \sim N(\alpha_0 + \alpha_1 x_i + \alpha_2 z_i, \sigma_\varepsilon^2).$$

Estimating the coefficients in the sample regression function is therefore equivalent to estimating the mean of y.

PROPERTIES OF THE LEAST SQUARES ESTIMATORS

The discussion up to this point has presented the formulas for the least squares estimators along with the general properties that accompany estimation using this technique: the average residual is 0; the least squares residuals are uncorrelated with each explanatory variable; and the average predicted value of y coincides with the mean of y. The Gauss-Markov theorem provides us with the properties of the least squares estimators:

GAUSS MARKOV THEOREM.   If assumptions (1)–(5) are met, the least squares estimators $\hat{\alpha}_0$, $\hat{\alpha}_1$, and $\hat{\alpha}_2$ are the best linear unbiased estimators of their respective population coefficients.

In this case,

$$\begin{aligned} E(\hat{y}_i) &= E(\hat{\alpha}_0 + \hat{\alpha}_1 x_i + \hat{\alpha}_2 z_i) \\ &= \alpha_0 + \alpha_1 x_i + \alpha_2 z_i \\ &= E(y_i), \end{aligned}$$

so that the predicted value of y obtained from the least squares coefficients provides an unbiased estimator of the mean of y.

AN ESTIMATOR OF THE EQUATION ERROR VARIANCE

The population regression function:

$$y_i = \alpha_0 + \alpha_1 x_i + \alpha_2 z_i + \varepsilon_i$$

contains three unknown coefficients, whose estimators have already been discussed, and an unknown error term. According to Assumption (6) of the model assumptions above, the equation error is a normally distributed random variable. Since a normally distributed random variable is fully characterized by its mean and variance, once these values are obtained, all the required information concerning this variable is known.

From model assumptions (1)–(3) and (6), individual errors are independent and normally distributed random variables with a 0 mean and a constant variance, σ_ε^2. As a result, an estimator of the error variance is all that is required for us to possess the necessary distributional information concerning the equation error. An unbiased and consistent estimator of σ_ε^2 is given by:

$$\hat{\sigma}_\varepsilon^2 = \sum \hat{\varepsilon}_i^2/(n-3), \tag{6.23}$$

The denominator of Equation (6.23) is the number of degrees of freedom for this estimator. When the sample regression function contains k estimated coefficients (*including* the intercept), there are $(n-k)$ degrees of freedom, which becomes the denominator of Equation (6.23).

The unit of measurement for this estimator is the square of the unit for the dependent variable. For this reason, the standard error of the regression, $\hat{\sigma}_\varepsilon$, is usually reported in preference to the estimated error variance, since the standard error possesses the same unit of measurement as the dependent variable. The lower the standard error of an equation, the better is the fit of the sample regression function to the data. However, the standard errors of equations with different dependent variables, such as y_i and $\ln(y)_i$, cannot be compared directly.[3] Such a comparison can be made based on the coefficient of variation (CV):

$$\text{C.V.} = \hat{\sigma}_\varepsilon/\hat{\mu}_y. \tag{6.24}$$

The square root of Equation (6.23) appears in the numerator of this statistic. When this measure is utilized as a criterion with which to judge two equations, the equation with the smaller C.V. is preferable. The "rule of thumb" (stated in Chapter 4) for this measure is: the performance of an equation is acceptable based on the use of the coefficient of variation when C.V. ≤ 0.2. However, several criteria should be employed as the basis of a more complete and reasoned analysis of a set of estimated equations.

THE COEFFICIENT OF MULTIPLE DETERMINATION

The coefficient of determination, R^2, was introduced as part of the bivariate regression model given in Chapter 4. This statistic measures the proportion of the total variation in y that is explained by the regression equation. Derivation of the related measure for multiple regression begins with the decomposition of actual y into:

$$y_i = \hat{y}_i + \hat{\varepsilon}_i,$$

where $\hat{y}_i$ is the "explained" part of y_i, and $\hat{\varepsilon}_i$ is the "unexplained" portion. In multiple regression, both $\hat{y}_i$ and $\hat{\varepsilon}_i$ are functions of the *set* of explanatory variables included

---

[3] See Chapter 4 for a more complete discussion of this point.

in the equation. Because of this fact, R^2 is called the **coefficient of multiple determination** in the multiple regression model. The total variation in y, or the total sum of squares (TSS) used in the calculation of this measure, is defined as:

$$\text{TSS} \equiv \sum (y_i - \hat{\mu}_y)^2.$$

Using the decomposition for y given in Chapter 4, TSS can be expressed as[4]:

$$\text{TSS} = \sum (y_i - \hat{\mu}_y)^2$$
$$= \sum (\hat{y}_i - \hat{\mu}_y)^2 + \sum \hat{\varepsilon}_i^2.$$

The first term on the right is the regression (explained) sum of squares (RSS), while the last term gives the error (unexplained) sum of squares (ESS). Thus:

$$\text{TSS} = \text{RSS} + \text{ESS}.$$

The coefficient of multiple determination, which gives the proportion of TSS explained by the regression equation, is therefore defined as:

$$R^2 = \text{RSS}/\text{TSS}$$
$$= 1 - \text{ESS}/\text{TSS}.$$

The value of this statistic ranges from 0 to 1. If R^2 equals 0, none of the variation in y is explained by the multiple regression equation, so that ESS = TSS. At the opposite extreme, an R^2 of 1 indicates that the regression equation accounts for all of the variation in y, and ESS = 0. The potential weaknesses of R^2 as a measure of equation performance outlined in Chapter 4 exist within the multiple regression framework as well:

1. Spurious correlation between the explanatory variables in an equation and the correct causal factors can produce high R^2 values;
2. In general, time series equations will tend to display higher R^2s than do cross-sectional equations;
3. Low R^2 values are not necessarily the result of including an incorrect explanatory variable in the sample regression function. The functional form utilized to depict the relationship between x and y, when inappropriate, lowers R^2; and
4. The R^2 values of two equations with different forms of a dependent variable, such as y_i and $\ln(y)_i$ are *not* directly comparable.

Several additional points pertain for multiple regression equations:

5. R^2 never decreases as additional explanatory variables are added to a sample regression function. When one or more new variables are added to an equation, then, even if they are not causally related to y, R^2 will at worst remain unchanged. More realistically, R^2 rises. "Padding" an equation by including additional variables thus never diminishes R^2;

---

[4] The cross-product term drops out of this equation.

6. In a multiple regression model, it is possible for R^2 to be close to 1 even though none of the included explanatory variables are statistically significant.[5]

The first four of these point to the limited usefulness of R^2 as the sole measure used in evaluating an estimated equation. However, an improvement can be made that deals with the fifth point. The reason why adding a variable never lowers R^2 can be seen if we expand the expression this measure in terms of $\hat{\varepsilon}$ and y:

$$R^2 = 1 - \sum \hat{\varepsilon}_i^2 / \sum (y_i - \hat{\mu}_y)^2$$

When we add a variable to our sample regression function, the denominator of the expression on the right remains unchanged, since it characterizes only the dispersion in y values. If, however, including this variable lowers one or more of the equation residuals, which is a very likely outcome, the numerator falls, causing R^2 to increase. An alternative measure exists that circumvents this potential for improving equation performance (as judged by R^2) through "padding." The adjusted for degrees of freedom R^2, or simply the **adjusted R^2** (denoted $\bar{R}^2$) is defined as:

$$\bar{R}^2 = 1 - \hat{\sigma}_\varepsilon^2 / \hat{\sigma}_y^2$$

$$= 1 - \frac{\sum \hat{\varepsilon}_i^2 / (n - k)}{\sum (y_i - \hat{\mu}_y)^2 / (n - 1)} \qquad (6.25)$$

If we include an additional explanatory variable in our sample regression function, then, for a given sample size (n), the denominator in the expression on the right remains unchanged (the same as with R^2). However, the numerator in Equation (6.25) can either rise, fall, or remain the same. Adding another variable raises $\bar{R}^2$ only when $\hat{\sigma}_\varepsilon^2$ falls. If, as above, several equation residuals fall as the result of including this variable, we must now weigh the decrease in $\Sigma \hat{\varepsilon}_i^2$ against the drop in the number of degrees of freedom, $(n - k)$. Adding another variable thus raises $\bar{R}^2$ only when the fall in the sum of the squared residuals more than offsets the impact of the decrease in the degrees of freedom on $\hat{\sigma}_\varepsilon^2$. Note that the formula for adjusted R^2 can also be written:

$$\bar{R}^2 = 1 - [(n - 1)/(n - k)](1 - R^2)$$

The following properties pertain to $\bar{R}^2$:

1. Increasing the number of explanatory variables in a sample regression function can either increase, decrease, or leave $\bar{R}^2$ unchanged;
2. When the sample regression function includes more than one explanatory variable, adjusted R^2 never exceeds R^2. For a single explanatory variable, $\bar{R}^2 = R^2$;
3. Adjusted R^2 can be *negative*; and
4. Adjusted R^2 is preferable to R^2 in comparing equations with the *same* dependent variable, but differing in the number of explanatory variables.

---

[5] This typically results from multicollinearity among the explanatory variables.

ASSESSING LEAST SQUARES WITH MULTIPLE REGRESSION: MONTE CARLO METHODS

We have seen that when the model assumptions are met, least squares estimation technique produces the best linear unbiased estimators of the coefficients in the population regression function. We can evaluate the accuracy of this theoretical expectation by using the Monte Carlo Method, which was detailed in Chapter 4. Recall that this methodology involves generating data that satisfy the model assumptions utilized to establish the desirable properties of the least squares estimators. The advantage of this approach is, of course, that we construct this data using *known* coefficients. It also allows us to replicate the repeated sampling context that pertains to the small sample estimator properties.

The following hypothetical population regression function is utilized as the basis for this Monte Carlo Experiment: $y_i = 15 + 1.5x_i - 3.5z_i + \varepsilon_i$. A sample size of 100 is used for each regression. In all, we perform 50 regressions. The first step consists of obtaining data for the explanatory variables in this equation. This is accomplished by deriving a *single* set of observations for x and z from the uniform random number generator of SAS. This same set of observations is used for all 50 regressions (this replicates the fixed in repeated samples assumption). In the second step, 50 sets of stochastic errors are obtained from the normal distribution random number generator in SAS. Each set has 100 observations (the value of n we are using), with a mean 0 and a variance of 2. Equipped with known coefficients, the single set of observations for x and z, and these sets of errors, we then construct observations for 50 sets of dependent variables using the formula:

$$y_i^{(j)} = 15 + 1.5x_i - 3.5z_i + \varepsilon_i^{(j)} \qquad (i = 1, \ldots, 100) \quad (j = 1, \ldots, 50),$$

where the subscript i denotes the observation, and the superscript (j) refers to the equation number. Thus, if the 100 error observations for equation (1) are denoted $\varepsilon_i^{(1)}$, we derive our first set of y observations from the following equation:

$$y_i^{(1)} = 15 + 1.5x_i - 3.5z_i + \varepsilon_i^{(1)} \qquad (i = 1, 2, \ldots, 100)$$

These same coefficients and observations for both x and z are used along with the remaining sets of errors to derive the remaining y variables:

$$y_i^{(2)} = 15 + 1.5x_i - 3.5z_i + \varepsilon_i^{(2)} \qquad (i = 1, 2, \ldots, 100)$$
$$\cdots$$
$$y_i^{(50)} = 15 + 1.5x_i - 3.5z_i + \varepsilon_i^{(50)} \qquad (i = 1, 2, \ldots, 100)$$

Our known population regression coefficients are thus: $\alpha_0 = 15$; $\alpha_1 = 1.5$, and $\alpha_2 = -3.5$.

Table 6.1 shows the results of these 50 regressions. Overall, least squares does an excellent job of estimating the coefficients in our hypothetical population regression function. Since the least squares estimators are unbiased, we expect that for a large number of regressions, the average estimate for each coefficient will coincide with its

Table 6.1   Monte Carlo Coefficients from 50 Regressions
Where the Population Regression Function Is

$$y_i = 15 + 1.5x_i - 3.5z_i + \varepsilon_i$$

	$\hat{\alpha}_0$	$\hat{\alpha}_1$	$\hat{\alpha}_2$		$\hat{\alpha}_0$	$\hat{\alpha}_1$	$\hat{\alpha}_2$
(1)	15.6365	1.67203	−3.5993	(26)	14.8987	1.49990	−3.4902
(2)	16.3572	1.48509	−3.6302	(27)	13.8052	1.59175	−3.4497
(3)	15.3016	1.54983	−3.5410	(28)	14.7569	1.52236	−3.4920
(4)	15.2232	1.41594	−3.4582	(29)	17.9076	1.49416	−3.8059
(5)	15.7898	1.60322	−3.6447	(30)	15.5388	1.37637	−3.4989
(6)	13.0948	1.62791	−3.3541	(31)	15.3829	1.40371	−3.5091
(7)	13.0508	1.44200	−3.3126	(32)	14.8008	1.46302	−3.4891
(8)	15.5027	1.47050	−3.5441	(33)	14.3740	1.48335	−3.4352
(9)	16.7251	1.58931	−3.7470	(34)	15.3664	1.56167	−3.5887
(10)	15.1458	1.51992	−3.5019	(35)	17.1614	1.49013	−3.7372
(11)	13.9820	1.54488	−3.4312	(36)	15.2810	1.45374	−3.5194
(12)	14.5306	1.69031	−3.5529	(37)	14.3516	1.52066	−3.4130
(13)	15.0610	1.41669	−3.4712	(38)	16.6589	1.39104	−3.6658
(14)	14.8599	1.80737	−3.6505	(39)	15.2408	1.28832	−3.4275
(15)	15.3656	1.42894	−3.5349	(40)	14.3513	1.60827	−3.4850
(16)	15.5631	1.46197	−3.5549	(41)	15.9893	1.55331	−3.6036
(17)	15.0282	1.48618	−3.5046	(42)	14.9613	1.65564	−3.5939
(18)	13.3477	1.42852	−3.2634	(43)	13.3456	1.77542	−3.4400
(19)	17.5570	1.34062	−3.6674	(44)	14.8802	1.53617	−3.4747
(20)	13.7435	1.62535	−3.4412	(45)	12.5919	1.64737	−3.3233
(21)	16.4807	1.33059	−3.5503	(46)	14.7584	1.67862	−3.5305
(22)	15.2215	1.41803	−3.4813	(47)	15.3401	1.44052	−3.5237
(23)	14.2062	1.53052	−3.4033	(48)	14.5923	1.44947	−3.4980
(24)	16.0761	1.58492	−3.6752	(49)	15.7577	1.40141	−3.5072
(25)	15.9162	1.29125	−3.5197	(50)	16.9880	1.53377	−3.7131

COEFFICIENT	MEAN	VARIANCE
$\hat{\alpha}_0$	15.16	1.299
$\hat{\alpha}_1$	1.512	0.131
$\hat{\alpha}_2$	−3.525	0.125

In these equations, $n = 100$, $\hat{\mu}_x = 4.5$, $\hat{\sigma}_x^2 = 2.5$, $\hat{\mu}_z = 9.4$, $\hat{\sigma}_z^2 = 3.9$.

population parameter. For only 50 observations, the mean estimate for each coefficient is already close to its population value. The mean of the intercept estimates is 15.16, which differs from the population value of α_0 by just over 1 percent. The average of the partial slope estimates are: 1.512 for α_1, and −3.525 for α_2. Both of these averages entail less than 1 percent error. Thus, when the model assumptions are met, least squares provides a very effective estimation technique *in a repeated sampling context.*

While these averages are quite good, even for just 50 regressions, individual coefficients sometimes vary substantially from population coefficients. For example, estimated intercepts range from 12.6 to 17.9. The estimated partial slopes for x vary from 1.29 to 1.78, while those for z exist within the range from -3.26 to -3.81. Thus, the behavior of an estimator on average provides no guarantee of its accuracy for a single estimate.

The least squares estimators are also consistent. Thus, as sample size rises, we expect the variance of the sampling distributions of these estimators to fall, approaching 0 as sample size approaches infinity. Tables 6.2(a) and (b) give the results of the first 10 regressions (out of a total of 50) for two different sample sizes. Part (a) gives the results for "large" regressions, where sample size is increased to 500 (everything else is kept the same), while (b) shows the results for a "small" sample size of 20 observations. Note that for both sample sizes, the 10 regression average for each of the three coefficients is relatively close to its population parameter. This occurs since unbiasedness does not depend on sample size.[6] As sample size increases from 20 to 500, the coefficient averages tend to better approximate their population parameters, and the variances of the coefficients fall, sometimes dramatically. Thus the dispersion in the sampling distributions of these estimators fall as sample size rises, which is exactly what the property of consistency leads us to expect. The intercept variance, for example, falls from 6.61 with a "small" sample to 0.34 with a "large" sample. Similar dramatic decreases in variances (in percent terms) occur with the partial slope coefficients for these different sample sizes. While there is no guarantee of an acceptable estimate with either of these sample sizes, the range of likely estimates is clearly preferable with the "large" sample.

Finally, Table 6.2(c) illustrates what results when the explanatory variables in our equation are highly correlated with each other. This is illustrated for a sample size of 100. Starting with the original x values, we construct z from the formula: $z = 2 \cdot x + v$, where v is a normally distributed random variable. Were it not for this error, perfect collinearity would exist, which would prevent us from obtaining unique estimates of the population coefficients. As we will now see, this type of correlation between our explanatory variables tends to raise the dispersion of the sampling distributions of our partial slope estimators. The variances of $\hat{\alpha}_1$ and $\hat{\alpha}_2$ can be expressed as:

$$\sigma_1^2 = \frac{\sigma_\varepsilon^2}{\sum x_i'^2 (1 - \hat{\rho}_{xz}^2)} \quad \text{and} \quad \sigma_2^2 = \frac{\sigma_\varepsilon^2}{\sum z_i'^2 (1 - \hat{\rho}_{xz}^2)} \tag{6.26}$$

Both variances are directly related to the correlation between x and z, $\hat{\rho}_{xz}$. Thus, when x and z are highly correlated, these variables tend to move together, which makes it difficult for least squares to ascertain the separate impacts of these variables on y. This intercorrelation between x and z raises the variance of the sampling distributions of $\hat{\alpha}_1$ and $\hat{\alpha}_2$. The regression coefficients from Table 6.2(c) bear this out.

---

[6] Recall that it is asymptotic unbiasedness that is a function of sample size.

Table 6.2 Monte Carlo Coefficients from the First 10 Regressions of "Small," "Large," and Collinear Observations with Population Regression Function $y_i = 15 + 1.5x_i - 3.5z_i + \varepsilon_i$

	$\hat{\alpha}_0$	$\hat{\alpha}_1$	$\hat{\alpha}_2$	
(1)	14.4675	1.52194	−3.4558	
(2)	15.6551	1.51158	−3.5653	
(3)	14.8793	1.52691	−3.4949	
(4)	14.8712	1.51108	−3.5070	
(5)	15.0032	1.53671	−3.5118	**(a)**
(6)	14.8366	1.55341	−3.5047	"LARGE"
(7)	14.1409	1.59809	−3.4674	SAMPLE
(8)	14.6631	1.55134	−3.5114	
(9)	16.2306	1.53733	−3.6362	
(10)	15.4980	1.54674	−3.5608	
Mean	15.02	1.54	−3.52	
Variance	0.338	0.0006	0.003	

In these equations, $n = 500$, $\hat{\mu}_x = 4.5$, $\hat{\sigma}_x^2 = 1.9$, $\hat{\mu}_z = 9.5$, $\hat{\sigma}_z^2 = 4.2$.

	$\hat{\alpha}_0$	$\hat{\alpha}_1$	$\hat{\alpha}_2$	
(1)	11.5805	1.40414	−3.0675	
(2)	14.2665	1.85199	−3.5861	
(3)	18.3923	1.25528	−3.7825	
(4)	14.3430	1.73576	−3.6258	
(5)	12.6549	1.89973	−3.4584	**(b)**
(6)	19.3980	1.08096	−3.7628	"SMALL"
(7)	17.8617	1.30830	−3.5968	SAMPLE
(8)	15.1072	1.40265	−3.4467	
(9)	16.2158	1.22491	−3.4687	
(10)	12.2034	1.68364	−3.2201	
Mean	15.2	1.48	−3.51	
Variance	6.61	0.074	0.045	

In these equations, $n = 20$, $\hat{\mu}_x = 4.2$, $\hat{\sigma}_x^2 = 2.3$, $\hat{\mu}_z = 9.1$, $\hat{\sigma}_z^2 = 4.3$.

	$\hat{\alpha}_0$	$\hat{\alpha}_1$	$\hat{\alpha}_2$	
(1)	11.4027	2.17740	−3.4538	
(2)	13.6007	2.74114	−3.8593	
(3)	14.9851	2.29013	−3.8945	
(4)	13.5320	2.58678	−3.9160	**(c)**
(5)	18.8279	0.71075	−3.5530	COLLINEAR
(6)	15.9621	1.37221	−3.4981	x AND z
(7)	15.8308	1.79635	−3.7244	
(8)	14.1092	2.09231	−3.6212	$z = 2 \cdot x + v$
(9)	12.9958	2.00064	−3.5483	WHERE $v \sim N(0.5, 3.5)$
(10)	17.5134	1.05937	−3.5868	
Mean	14.9	1.88	−3.67	
Variance	4.43	0.386	0.067	

In these equations, $n = 100$, $\hat{\mu}_x = 4.3$, $\hat{\sigma}_x^2 = 1.5$, $\hat{\mu}_z = 8.9$, $\hat{\sigma}_z^2 = 9.7$.

The effect of collinearity is similar to that for small sample size.[7] The variances of our estimated coefficients are greater than those for the original sample, and, the range of values for each is greater as well.

HYPOTHESIS TESTING WITH THE MULTIPLE REGRESSION MODEL

Individual Coefficients

The Gauss-Markov theorem establishes the fact that each of the least squares coefficient estimators is the best linear unbiased estimator of its population parameter, given the assumptions about the population regression function stated previously. The normality of the error in the population regression function allows us to associate this distribution with each of these coefficients, since these estimators are linear functions of y, which is itself normally distributed.[8] The partial slope coefficients in the least squares equation:

$$y_i = \hat{\alpha}_0 + \hat{\alpha}_1 x_i + \hat{\alpha}_2 z_i + \hat{\varepsilon}_i$$

are thus normally distributed random variables. Summarizing the distributional information that pertains to these coefficients:

$$\hat{\alpha}_0 \sim N(\alpha_0, \sigma_0^2),$$
$$\hat{\alpha}_1 \sim N(\alpha_1, \sigma_1^2), \qquad (6.27)$$
$$\hat{\alpha}_2 \sim N(\alpha_2, \sigma_2^2),$$

where:

$$\sigma_1^2 = \frac{\sigma_\varepsilon^2 \sum z_i'^2}{(\sum x_i'^2)(\sum z_i'^2) - (\sum x_i z_i)^2}$$
$$\qquad (6.28)$$
$$\sigma_2^2 = \frac{\sigma_\varepsilon^2 \sum x_i'^2}{(\sum x_i'^2)(\sum z_i'^2) - (\sum x_i z_i)^2}$$

Since σ_ε^2 is unknown, we must use its estimator, $\hat{\sigma}_\varepsilon^2$, to approximate both of the above variances. We then employ these estimated coefficient variances to construct confidence intervals and to test hypotheses about the coefficients in the population regression function. Recall (from Chapter 5) that when the actual variance of a random variable is unknown, and we use an estimate of this quantity, the t-distribution is the appropriate probability density function for both confidence intervals and hypothesis tests. We must therefore use this distribution with multiple regression

---

[7] Notable differences exist, however, such as the likelihood of sign reversal. This is discussed in the section on multicollinearity in Chapter 10.

[8] This result is not derived but follows easily with the matrix formulation of the least squares multiple regression model.

coefficients. However, when the number of degrees of freedom exceeds 30, we can use the normal distribution table to provide us with approximations to the relevant t-values.

Confidence intervals for individual coefficients are constructed in the same way as those presented in Chapter 5. The formulas for 95 percent confidence intervals are:

$$\hat{\alpha}_0 \pm t_{0.025,\,n-3} \cdot \hat{\sigma}_0 \text{ for the equation intercept}$$

$$\hat{\alpha}_1 \pm t_{0.025,\,n-3} \cdot \hat{\sigma}_1 \text{ for the coefficient of } x \qquad \textbf{(6.29)}$$

$$\hat{\alpha}_2 \pm t_{0.025,\,n-3} \cdot \hat{\sigma}_2 \text{ for the coefficient of } z$$

where $t_{0.025,\,n-3}$ is the value of the t-distribution for $n-3$ degrees of freedom with 0.025 in each tail. The 99 percent confidence intervals for these coefficients are identical to those in Equation (6.29), with the exception that $t_{0.005,\,n-3}$ is substituted for the t-values in these equations.

The hypothesis tests used to make inferences about the coefficients in the population regression function mirror those for bivariate regression. The null hypothesis that allows us to test whether the population intercept equals some constant, α_0^0, is $H_0: \alpha_0 = \alpha_0^0$. We can generalize this by using the subscript j to denote the population coefficient in question, where $j = 0$ is the intercept, α_0, $j = 1$ is the partial slope of x, α_1, and $j = 2$ is the coefficient of z, α_2. We therefore test whether the population coefficient α_j equals α_j^0 with the null hypothesis: $H_0: \alpha_j = \alpha_j^0$. Our alternative hypothesis can entail either the non-equality of α_j and α_j^0, or an inequality, which pertains when we have information about the expected sign of the coefficient in question. An alternative hypothesis which is stated as a non-equality requires a two-tail test, while strict inequality calls for a one-tail test. Recall that the inequality points in the direction of the appropriate tail of the distribution of the test statistic.

The test statistic utilized to make a decision concerning the null hypothesis is:

$$(\hat{\alpha}_j - \alpha_j^0)/\hat{\sigma}_j \sim t_{n-3} \qquad (j = 0, 1, 2) \qquad \textbf{(6.30)}$$

where α_j^0 is the value of α_j stipulated in the null hypothesis. The numerator of this expression therefore measures the hypothesized sampling error associated with the null hypothesis. This test statistic has a t-distribution with $n-3$ degrees of freedom.

The acceptance region for this hypothesis test is defined by the t-distribution and the desired level of significance, assuming p-values are not employed. If we select the 5 percent significance level and our alternative hypothesis requires a two-tail test, the acceptance region consists of the area under the t-distribution that encompasses 95 percent of all possible values. The critical values required to perform this test are obtained from the t-table at the end of this text. If, for example, sample size is 20, then with 17 ($= 20 - 3$) degrees of freedom, the critical values of the t-distribution (with 2.5 percent probability in each tail) are ± 2.11. In this case we are unable to reject H_0 if $(\hat{\alpha}_j - \alpha_j^0)/\hat{\sigma}_j$ is between -2.11 and 2.11, since our test statistic falls within the range of "likely" values we expect to observe when the null hypothesis is true. If the test statistic either falls above 2.11 or below -2.11, we reject H_0, since the probability of observing this large of a divergence between $\hat{\alpha}_j$ and α_j^0 (hypothesized sampling error) is deemed to be unacceptably low (less than 2.5 percent).

A variant of the above is used to ascertain the statistical significance of estimated coefficients. The test of the statistical significance of an estimated coefficient $\hat{\alpha}_j$ uses the null hypothesis: H_0: $\alpha_j = 0$. The alternative hypothesis used by canned computer programs states that the associated variable (or intercept) belongs in this equation, in which case H_a: $\alpha_j \neq 0$. If we have information about the expected sign of this coefficient, our alternative hypothesis can be either: H_a: $\alpha_j < 0$; or H_a: $\alpha_j > 0$. Since the value of α_j^0 equals 0 in these hypotheses, our test statistic simplifies to:

$$\hat{\alpha}_j / \hat{\sigma}_j \qquad (6.31)$$

which has a t-distribution with $n - 3$ degrees of freedom. The form of this test statistic is identical to that in the bivariate model. Assuming a sample size of 20, the 5 percent level of significance (the values in the above discussion), and the alternative hypothesis, H_a: $\alpha_j \neq 0$, we reject the null hypothesis when the absolute value of our test statistic exceeds 2.11. If the value of our test statistic exceeds 2.11, then:

$$(\hat{\alpha}_j - 0)/\hat{\sigma}_j > 2.11, \quad \text{or} \quad (\hat{\alpha}_j - 0) > 2.11 \cdot \hat{\sigma}_j,$$

so that a "large" deviation of $\hat{\alpha}_j$ from 0, which constitutes our basis for rejecting H_0, is defined as an estimate of α_j that is 2.11 or more standard deviations from 0. The coefficient $\hat{\alpha}_j$ is therefore statistically significant when the deviation of this estimate from 0 exceeds 2.11 standard deviations. In this case we reject H_0 and accept the alternative hypothesis. $\hat{\alpha}_j$ is then judged to be significantly different from 0.

If our hypothesis test entails a one-tail test, the acceptance region then consists of a range of possible t-values bounded by a single critical point. When our alternative hypothesis is H_a: $\alpha_j > 0$, for example, only an upper critical point exists. Assuming 17 degrees of freedom and the 5 percent level of significance, this value is 1.74. We reject H_0 if the deviation of $\hat{\alpha}_j$ from 0 exceeds 1.74 standard deviations.

The Coefficients of All Explanatory Variables Jointly

All of the hypothesis tests outlined above pertain only to *individual* coefficients. These tests are used to ascertain whether the difference between the population coefficient α_j and some constant α_j^0 (which can be 0) is statistically significant. Hypothesis tests can also be performed on more than one of the coefficients in our sample regression function. One such test ascertains the joint statistical significance of all of the partial slope coefficients in our regression equation. As illustrated below, this is a test of the statistical significance of R^2.

Other important uses exist for hypothesis tests concerning several coefficients as well. Sometimes when we estimate a sample regression function, two or more of its coefficients can fail to attain statistical significance, as determined by individual t-tests. If these variables properly belong in our equation, then deleting them will result in specification error. If we cannot establish the individual significance of these coefficients, it is still possible to show their joint significance with a hypothesis test of these coefficients *taken as a group*. Finally, we occasionally need to test whether certain linear restrictions which are implied by economic theory are valid. Since these typically involve two or more of the coefficients in our sample regression function, a multiple coefficient hypothesis test is indicated. We now discuss each of these in turn.

The null hypothesis that we use to test whether the set of explanatory variables jointly influence the dependent variable in the regression equation:

$$y_i = \alpha_0 + \alpha_1 x_{1i} + \alpha_2 x_{2i} + \cdots + \alpha_k x_{ki} + \varepsilon_i,$$

states that these variables exert no influence on y, or that:

$$H_0: \alpha_1 = \alpha_2 = \cdots = \alpha_k = 0.$$

If H_0 is true, the population regression function includes only an intercept and an error term. The alternative hypothesis postulates that at least one of the coefficients of the explanatory variables is nonzero. The test statistic for these hypotheses, which uses F-distribution, is based on the quantity:

$$RSS/ESS,$$

or the ratio of the "explained" to the "unexplained" sum of squares. If the null hypothesis is true, none of the x's influences the dependent variable in the population regression function. As a result, the "explained" portion of the total variation in y (RSS) will differ from the "unexplained" variation (ESS) only through the existence of sampling error. When the model assumptions concerning the equation errors are met, the ratio of these terms, each divided by its degrees of freedom, follows the F-distribution. Using this fact, our test statistic is:

$$\frac{RSS/(k-1)}{ESS/(n-k)} \sim F_{k-1, n-k}, \tag{6.32}$$

and the critical region is defined with respect to only the upper tail of the F-distribution based on the selected level of significance. For a 5 percent significance level, the critical point occurs where 95 percent of all probability is bounded below this value. Assuming 20 observations (n) and 3 coefficients in the equation (k), the critical F-value from the F-table with 2 degrees of freedom in the numerator, 17 degrees of freedom in the denominator is 3.59. If the value of the test statistic given by Equation (6.32) exceeds 3.59, we reject H_0 and accept the alternative hypothesis that this pair of explanatory variables jointly influences the dependent variable. If the value of Equation (6.32) is below 3.59, we are unable to reject H_0. Most computer programs routinely include the value of the test statistic for this hypothesis test as part of their default regression output.

The test statistic given by Equation (6.32) is related to R^2. The equation F-test can therefore be viewed as a **test of the statistical significance of R^2**. The relationship between the test statistic given in Equation (6.32) and R^2 can be seen if we divide both the numerator and denominator of this expression (forgetting the degrees of freedom) by the total sum of squares, TSS:

$$\frac{RSS/TSS}{ESS/TSS} = \frac{R^2}{(1-R^2)}$$

The test statistic can thus be rewritten:

$$\frac{R^2/(k-1)}{(1-R^2)/(n-k)} \tag{6.33}$$

Since it is possible for R^2 to attain large values as the result of factors such as spurious correlation, use of the equation F-statistic can sometimes result in our rejecting a true null hypothesis, causing us to commit a Type I error. At the opposite extreme, it is possible for all of the coefficients in an estimated equation to fail individual t-tests at the same time the equation F-statistic establishes the joint significance of this same set of variables. This extreme case, which results from severe multicollinearity, illustrates the need to exert caution when using both R^2 and the equation F-test as the sole criteria for evaluating the performance of an estimated equation.

A SUBSET OF EXPLANATORY VARIABLES.   The equation F-statistic is used to judge whether the entire set of explanatory variables included in an equation jointly influence the dependent variable. At the opposite extreme is the t-statistic, which is used in individual tests of the equation coefficients. For multiple regression, this pair of statistical tests is not sufficient to encompass all conceivable situations that are likely to arise. As stated above, it is possible for several of the coefficients in an estimated equation to be statistically insignificant when tested individually while the entire set of explanatory variables passes the equation F-test, establishing their joint significance. More important, variables that economic theory establishes as among those of primary importance can fail individual t-tests for statistical significance. *Their deletion, which results in specification error, can cause coefficients that were statistically significant in the initial specification to become non-significant when the equation is re-estimated!* Before dropping a set of non-significant variables from an estimated equation, it is therefore necessary to determine whether these variables are statistically significant as a group.

To outline the statistical test for a subset of coefficients, assume the population regression function is:

$$y_i = \alpha_0 + \alpha_1 x_{1i} + \alpha_2 x_{2i} + \alpha_3 x_{3i} + \alpha_4 x_{4i} + \varepsilon_i. \tag{6.34}$$

If the sample regression function passes the equation F-test but both $\hat{\alpha}_3$ and $\hat{\alpha}_4$ are not statistically significant, we can test their *joint* statistical significance using a null hypothesis which states that x_3 and x_4 do not jointly influence Y:

$$H_0\colon \alpha_3 = 0 \text{ and } \alpha_4 = 0, \quad \text{or} \quad H_0\colon \alpha_3 = \alpha_4 = 0$$

Our alternative hypothesis states that either or both of α_3 and α_4 are not 0:

$$H_0\colon \alpha_3 \neq 0 \text{ or } \alpha_4 \neq 0$$

If the null hypothesis is correct, then omitting x_3 and x_4 from our sample regression function will not increase the sum of the squared residuals appreciably. If these variables belong in the population regression function, their omission will affect both ε_i

and the sum of the squared errors, since the equation error then becomes:

$$v_i = \varepsilon_i + \alpha_3 x_{3i} + \alpha_4 x_{4i} \tag{6.35}$$

which has a nonzero expectation even if $E(\varepsilon_i) = 0.$[9]

The statistical test of these hypotheses, which is called the **Wald Test**, is based on a comparison of the sum of the squared residuals from an estimated equation that includes x_3 and x_4 with those from an equation that excludes these variables.[10] The **unrestricted equation** is the population regression function that excludes the restrictions stated in H_0. In this example, the unrestricted equation is given by Equation (6.34). The **restricted equation** is the population regression function that pertains when we impose the restrictions stated in H_0. The restricted equation here is:

$$y_i = \alpha_0 + \alpha_1 x_{1i} + \alpha_2 x_{2i} + v_i, \tag{6.36}$$

where v_i is given by Equation (6.35). If the null hypothesis is true, the sum of the squared errors from the restricted equation (ESS_{re}) will not differ substantially from that in the unrestricted equation (ESS_{ue}). The basis of the Wald test is therefore a determination of whether imposing the restrictions in the null hypothesis increases the sum of the squared residuals by a "large" amount. We therefore consider the difference in these sums:

$$(ESS_{re} - ESS_{ue}) \tag{6.37}$$

Assuming that the model assumptions for the error are met, Equation (6.37) follows the chi-square distribution with degrees of freedom equal to the number of restrictions (r).[11] This value for the degrees of freedom is derived from the additivity property of the chi-square distribution discussed in Chapter 2: the degrees of freedom for the difference between two independent chi-square random variables is the difference in their individual degrees of freedom (assuming this is a positive magnitude). Our restricted equation has $(n - k + r)$ degrees of freedom, since it contains $(k - r)$ coefficients (the original k less those whose coefficients are 0). The unrestricted equation has $n - k$ degrees of freedom. The difference in these quantities is: $(n - k + r) - (n - k) = r$. In this example, there are 2 restrictions and 5 coefficients in the unrestricted equation, so that $r = 2$ and $k = 5$.

A problem exists when Equation (6.37) is used as our test statistic. The magnitude of the sum of the squared errors in an equation is sensitive to the unit of measurement for its dependent variable. The use of Equation (6.37) as our test statistic therefore does not provide us with an unambiguous measure of when the difference between ESS_{re} and ESS_{ue} is "large." This is similar to the problem we encountered with using

---

[9] This assumes that x_3 and x_4 are not defined as deviations from means.

[10] A. Wald, "Tests of Statistical Hypotheses Concerning Several Parameters when the Number of Observations Is Large," *Transactions of the American Mathematical Society*, Vol. 54 (1943).

[11] This is a slight simplification. Actually it is $(ESS_{re} - ESS_{ue})/\sigma_\varepsilon^2$ that has a chi-square distribution. The same is true for the distribution of ESS_{ue} separately.

only the hypothesized sampling error of a coefficient, $\hat{\alpha}_j - \alpha_j^0$, to determine its statistical significance. As with t-tests, we circumvent this problem by making the value in question a *relative* magnitude. For the Wald Test, this entails evaluating the increase in the sum of squared errors that results from deleting the variables whose coefficients are included in H_0, $(ESS_{re} - ESS_{ue})$, relative to the value of ESS that occurs without any restrictions, ESS_{ue}. The sum of the squared errors from the unrestricted equation also has a chi-square distribution, with $(n - k)$ degrees of freedom.[12]

The test statistic for the Wald Test is therefore:

$$\frac{(ESS_{re} - ESS_{ue})/r}{ESS_{ue}/(n - k)} \sim F_{r,n-k} \tag{6.38}$$

which has an F distribution with r and $(n - k)$ degrees of freedom in the numerator and denominator, respectively.[13] This test statistic is constructed by the following procedure:

1. Estimate the sample regression function for the unrestricted equation, and obtain its error sum of squares, ESS_{ue}.
2. Estimate the sample regression function corresponding to the restricted equation, and obtain the sum of the squared errors, ESS_{re}.
3. Substitute these values into the test statistic formula given by Equation (6.38) and solve for the value of the test statistic.

The hypothesis test is conducted by adding the following steps:

4. Find the critical F-value for a desired level of significance with r and $(n - k)$ degrees of freedom in the numerator and denominator, respectively, from the F-distribution table.
5. Compare the value of the test statistic with this critical F-value. If the test statistic exceeds the critical F-value, omitting the variables in question results in a substantial increase in the sum of the squared residuals (relative to those in the unrestricted equation). When H_0 is true, the probability of observing this large of an increase the sum of the squared residuals is no greater than the selected level of significance. Therefore, since the test statistic exceeds the critical value for this test, we reject H_0 and accept H_a.

The test statistic given by Equation (6.38) can be restated in terms of the values of R^2 from the restricted and unrestricted equations. If we divide both the numerator and denominator of Equation (6.38) by the total sum of squares, TSS, then, since $ESS/TSS = 1 - R^2$, our test statistic becomes:

$$\frac{(R_{ue}^2 - R_{re}^2)/r}{(1 - R_{ue}^2)/(n - k)} \sim F_{r,n-k} \tag{6.39}$$

---

[12] See the previous footnote.

[13] Dividing each term in this test statistic by its degrees of freedom provides a kind of standardization, where both the numerator and denominator are expressed in quantities per degree of freedom.

When using this form of the test statistic, the only element of this hypothesis test that changes is the use of R^2 values in place of ESS in steps (1)–(3).

This statistical test is used frequently in econometrics. Estimated equations containing one or more nonsignificant coefficients are often selected as the "best" depiction of a relationship. This F-test provides us with an *objective* basis for including these non-significant variables. Also, when a multiple regression equation contains several policy variables, we can apply this F-test to establish the joint statistical significance of the set of included policy variables.

The final application of the Wald Test that is discussed here pertains to two different situations. The first of these occurs when, based on previous empirical work or economic theory, we possess information about one or more of the coefficients in our population regression function. The second arises when we are interested in testing hypotheses involving nonzero values of several coefficients. In both of these instances, the Wald Test can be utilized to ascertain the statistical validity of this information as long as it is possible for us to translate it into a linear equation (restriction) involving the coefficients in our regression equation. As an example of the second of these situations, assume that we are interested in estimating a money demand equation, with real GNP (x_1), and both a short-term and long-term interest rate (x_2 and x_3) included as explanatory variables. We may wish to test whether the interest sensitivity of money demand is the same with respect to both short-term and long-term interest rates. If the population regression function is:

$$y_i = \alpha_0 + \alpha_1 x_{1i} + \alpha_2 x_{2i} + \alpha_3 x_{3i} + \varepsilon_i, \tag{6.40}$$

where y is the real demand for money, we seek to determine whether $\alpha_2 = \alpha_3$. We can rewrite this equation as: $\alpha_2 - \alpha_3 = 0$, which is called a **linear restriction**.

We can test whether these coefficients are equal with the following hypotheses: $H_0: \alpha_2 = \alpha_3$ and $H_a: \alpha_2 \neq \alpha_3$. The first step in this test consists of incorporating this restriction into our population regression function, Equation (6.40), which becomes:

$$y_i = \alpha_0 + \alpha_1 x_{1i} + \alpha_3 x_{2i} + \alpha_3 x_{3i} + \varepsilon_i,$$

or

$$y_i = \alpha_0 + \alpha_1 x_{1i} + \alpha_3 (x_{2i} + x_{3i}) + \varepsilon_i. \tag{6.41}$$

The statistical validity of the equality of α_2 and α_3 is then determined by performing a Wald Test.[14] Equation (6.40) is the unrestricted equation for this test, and Equation (6.41) is the restricted equation. The number of restrictions in this example is 1, since we are dealing with a single relationship (equation) involving the coefficients in

---

[14] It is also possible to test this hypothesis with a t-test. The test statistic is:

$$(\hat{\alpha}_2 - \hat{\alpha}_3)/\hat{\sigma},$$

where $\hat{\sigma}$ is the standard deviation of the quantity $(\hat{\alpha}_2 - \hat{\alpha}_3)$, which equals the positive square root of $(\hat{\sigma}_2^2 + \hat{\sigma}_3^2 - 2\hat{\sigma}_{23})$.

the population regression function. The Wald test of these hypotheses is performed by estimating both of these equations with least squares, then following steps (1)–(5) above.

Least squares estimation of an equation such as Equation (6.41) that includes a linear restriction is referred to as **restricted least squares**. In this example, we perform the restricted least squares estimation of Equation (6.41) by creating the new variable $x^* = (x_2 + x_3)$, then regress y on x_1 and x^*. The coefficient of this new variable provides us with an estimate of both α_2 and α_3 in the event that we are unable to reject H_0. If the value of our test statistic (either Equation (6.38) or (6.39)) exceeds the critical F-value for this test, we reject the null hypothesis that the interest sensitivity of the demand for money is identical with respect to both short-term and long-term interest rates. The unrestricted equation, (6.40), is then selected as the sample regression function that best depicts this relationship.

A different type of information that we can use the Wald Test to evaluate occurs when our information about the population coefficients takes a form such as: $\alpha_1 + \alpha_2 + \alpha_3 = c$, where c is some nonzero constant. In contrast to the previously discussed restrictions where $c = 0$, which are formally called **homogeneous linear restrictions**, this is a **nonhomogeneous linear restriction**. The most famous example of this occurs when we wish to test for the existence of constant returns to scale with a Cobb-Douglas production function. This function can be expressed in the form:

$$q = f(k, L, m) = Ak^{\alpha}L^{\beta}m^{\gamma}$$

where q is output, k is capital input, L is labor input, and m is raw materials input. We showed in Chapter 4 that the exponents in this equation are elasticities: α, β, and γ are the elasticities of output with respect to capital and labor, and raw materials, respectively. For our present purposes, we must illustrate how to determine whether this function exhibits constant returns to scale.

A production function exhibits constant returns to scale when a proportionate change in *all* inputs alters output by the same proportion. Doubling k, L, and m therefore doubles output when constant returns to scale exist. We can express this in the following way:

$$f(2k, 2L, 2m) = 2 \cdot q,$$

or, if our proportional change in these variables is c: $f(ck, cL, cm) = cq$. If we now change all of the inputs in the Cobb-Douglas production function by c:

$$
\begin{aligned}
f(ck, cL, cm) &= A(ck)^{\alpha}(cL)^{\beta}(cm)^{\gamma} \\
&= Ac^{\alpha}k^{\alpha}c^{\beta}L^{\beta}c^{\gamma}m^{\gamma} \\
&= c^{(\alpha + \beta + \gamma)}Ak^{\alpha}L^{\beta}m^{\gamma} \\
&= c^{(\alpha + \beta + \gamma)} \cdot q.
\end{aligned}
$$

Output changes by the proportion c only when $\alpha + \beta + \gamma = 1$. In contrast to this, when output changes by a greater multiple than do all the inputs, increasing returns to scale exist. For the above production function, this occurs when $\alpha + \beta + \gamma > 1$. When output responds by proportionately less than the change in inputs, to that $\alpha + \beta + \gamma < 1$, decreasing returns to scale pertain. This last concept should not be confused with diminishing returns. Returns to scale pertain when all inputs, including capital, change. This occurs only in the long-run. Diminishing returns is defined only for fixed capital, which exists in the short-run.

Recall that we can transform the Cobb-Douglass production function into a form that is estimable with least squares if we take the natural logarithm of both sides. Adding subscripts and an error term, this function becomes:

$$\ln(q_i) = \alpha_0^* + \alpha \ln(k_i) + \beta \ln(L_i) + \gamma \ln(m_i) + \varepsilon_i \qquad (6.42)$$

where $\alpha_0^* = \ln(A)$. When the coefficients in this equation satisfy the linear restriction: $\alpha + \beta + \gamma = 1$, constant returns to scale exist in production. The hypotheses for the Wald Test of this restriction are therefore $H_0: \alpha + \beta + \gamma = 1$ and $H_a: \alpha + \beta + \gamma \neq 1$. Equation (6.42) is the unrestricted equation for this test. There are $(n - 4)$ degrees of freedom in this unrestricted equation. The restricted equation, using $\alpha = (1 - \beta - \gamma)$, is:

$$\ln(q_i) = \alpha_0^* + (1 - \beta - \gamma) \ln(k_i) + \beta \ln(L_i) + \gamma \ln(m_i) + \varepsilon_i,$$

or

$$\ln(q_i) - \ln(k_i) = \alpha_0^* + \beta\{\ln(L_i) - \ln(k_i)\} + \gamma\{\ln(m_i) - \ln(k_i)\} + \varepsilon_i$$

which can be rewritten as:

$$\ln(q/k)_i = \alpha_0^* + \beta \ln(L/k)_i + \gamma \ln(m/k)_i + \varepsilon_i \qquad (6.43)$$

Restricted least squares estimation of Equation (6.43) therefore requires that we create the variables $q^* = \ln(q/k)$, $L^* = \ln(L/k)$, and $m^* = \ln(m/k)$, then regress q^* on L^* and m^*. If adding this restriction produces a large enough increase in ESS that our test statistic exceeds the critical F value with 1 and $(n - 4)$ degrees of freedom for the selected level of significance, we then reject the null hypothesis of constant returns to scale.

Finally, this same framework can be utilized to test more than one linear restriction. We will illustrate the basis of this with the above production function. If we wish to test the following two restrictions: (i) the output elasticity of raw materials equals 0; and (ii) constant returns exist with respect to capital and labor, but not raw materials, we can translate each of these into linear restrictions that pertain to the estimable form of our production function, Equation (6.42). For the first restriction, if the elasticity of output with respect to raw material input is zero, then $\gamma = 0$. If we were interested in testing only this restriction, the t-statistic of the coefficient of $\ln(m_i)$ would serve our purposes. However, we are interested in determining the validity of this *along with* the other restriction. For the second restriction, if $q = f(k, L)$ and m does not influence q, then constant returns to scale exists when $\alpha + \beta = 1$. This is the second of our linear restrictions. Therefore, our null hypothesis is:

$$H_0: \alpha + \beta = 1 \text{ and } \gamma = 0$$

and our alternative hypothesis states that H_0 is false. We first incorporate both of these restrictions into Equation (6.42):

$$\ln(q_i) = \alpha_0^* + \alpha \ln(k_i) + (1 - \alpha) \ln(L_i) + \varepsilon_i$$

then multiply the bracketed term with $\ln(L_i)$ and rearrange, which gives us the restricted model for this hypothesis test:

$$\ln(q/L)_i = \alpha_0^* + \alpha \ln(k/L)_i + \varepsilon_i$$

Because this equation embodies two independent restrictions, $r = 2$. Our unrestricted equation is again Equation (6.42). Following the procedure for the Wald test outlined earlier, our test statistic follows the F-distribution with 2 and $(n - 4)$ degrees of freedom in the numerator and denominator, respectively.

EXAMPLES OF MULTIPLE REGRESSION EQUATIONS

■ **THE DEMAND FOR IMPORTS FROM JAPAN** The first equation that is presented is a time series model of the U.S. demand for imports from Japan. Economic theory states that import demand (m^d) is determined by the exchange rate (r) and real domestic income (y):

$$m^d = f(r, y, \varepsilon)$$

where ε is a stochastic error term.

If we express the U.S.–Japanese exchange rate in terms of yen per dollar, the expected sign of r is positive. We can illustrate the basis for this expected sign by considering what happens to import prices when the exchange rate rises by, say, 20 yen per \$1 from an initial value of 200 yen/\$1. Given the yen price of a good that Japan exports to the U.S., the exchange rate determines the number of dollars this good will sell for when purchased as an import in the United States. If a Japanese good that is exported to the United States costs 10,000 yen, then, at the original exchange rate of 200 yen per \$1, this good costs \$50 dollars in the U.S. When the exchange rate changes so that the number of yen per \$1 rises, the dollar *appreciates* relative to the yen. The Japanese good that was \$50 at the original exchange rate now costs only \$45.45 when the exchange rate is 220 yen per \$1. Thus, when the dollar appreciates relative to the yen, the dollar price of Japanese produced goods imported into the United States falls, other things being equal.

The expected sign of real income is also positive. The rationale for this sign follows from the assumption that goods imported from Japan are normal goods. When real income in the U.S. rises, our ability to pay increases, and consumption of normal goods, which includes imports from Japan, rises.

Our estimate of the import demand equation is based on annual data for the years 1979 to 1988 from the 1989 *Economic Report of the President*. The U.S. exchange rate with Japan is measured in yen per dollar. The variable y is Real GNP

(1982 = 100), which is denominated in billions of dollars. The dependent variable in this equation, real imports from Japan (billions of 1982 dollars), is the value of U.S. merchandise imports from Japan deflated by the IPD for imports (1982 = 100).

This equation was estimated using PROC REG in SAS. The output obtained for this equation is:

```
DEP VARIABLE: M
ANALYSIS OF VARIANCE
                        SUM OF          MEAN
SOURCE       DF        SQUARES         SQUARE        F VALUE   PROB>F

MODEL   (=k-1) 2      4118.35912      2059.17956     172.547   0.0001
ERROR   (=n-k) 7       83.53830880     11.93404411
C TOTAL (=n-1) 9      4201.89743

        ROOT MSE(=σ̂ₑ)    3.454569      R-SQUARE         0.9801
        DEP MEAN(=μ̂ₘ)   56.28319      ADJ R-SQ(=R̄²)    0.9744
        C.V.             6.137834


PARAMETER ESTIMATES
                     PARAMETER        STANDARD      T FOR H0:
VARIABLE      DF     ESTIMATE          ERROR        PARAMETER=0    PROB > |T|

INTERCEP      1    -243.90245(=α̂₀)   32.65043667   -7.470(=α̂₀/σ̂₀)  0.0001
EXJAPAN(=r)   1       0.09385109(=α̂₁) 0.04826212    1.945(=α̂₁/σ̂₁)  0.0929
RGNP(=y)      1       0.08077493(=α̂₂) 0.006853938  11.785(=α̂₂/σ̂₂)  0.0001
```

The resulting sample regression function, whose values are obtained from the high-lighted items in this printout, is:

$$\hat{m}_t = -243.9 + 0.094r_t + 0.081y_t$$
$$\quad\quad\quad (7.5) \quad\quad (2.0) \quad\quad (11.8)$$

$$\bar{R}^2 = 0.974 \qquad \hat{\sigma}_\varepsilon = 3.5 \qquad F = 172.5 \qquad \hat{\mu}_m = 56.3 \qquad n = 10$$

The one-tail critical t-values with 7 degrees of freedom are 1.895 for the 5 percent level of significance, and 2.998 for the 1 percent level. The estimated intercept in this equation is negative and statistically significant at the 1 percent level and above. A purely mechanical interpretation of this coefficient is that the estimated mean of real imports is negative when both the exchange rate and real GNP are 0. Since this combination of values has no economic meaning, this coefficient can be more appropriately interpreted as reflecting the mean impact of all variables omitted from this equation.

The coefficients of both explanatory variables display the correct expected sign. The coefficient of y is statistically significant at the 1 percent level and above, while that of r is significant at the 5 percent level and above. Our equation F-statistic provides further support for the results of the individual t-tests. The equation F-statistic, 172.5, exceeds the critical F-value with 2 and 7 degrees of freedom at the

1 percent significance level, 9.55. We are therefore able to reject the null hypothesis that the exchange rate and y do not jointly influence the demand for imports from Japan.

The coefficient of the exchange rate indicates that if the dollar appreciates relative to the yen, so that the exchange rate rises by 20 yen per dollar, mean real merchandise imports from Japan increase by $1.88 billion, given the level of real GNP. Another way of interpreting this coefficient is to state that it takes an appreciation of 10.64 yen per dollar to increase mean real imports by $1 billion, other things being equal. Using the sample averages for r and y of 207 and 3475.8, respectively, gives $\hat{m} = 57.1$. The estimated partial elasticity of import demand with respect to the exchange rate is then: $(207/57.1)(0.094) = 0.34$, which is inelastic.

The sensitivity of real imports to the level of economic activity is much greater. A $1 billion increase in domestic real GNP raises mean real imports from Japan by $81 million ($= 0.081$ billion), given the value of the exchange rate. Thus a $12.35 billion increase in real GNP increases mean real imports from Japan by $1 billion, other things being equal. It follows that a recession or a slowdown in the rate of economic growth can be expected to reduce our balance of trade deficit with Japan. Using the sample means of r and y, along with the resulting value for $\hat{m}$, 57.1, the partial elasticity of $\hat{m}$ with respect to y is 4.9, which indicates a highly elastic response.

The coefficients in this sample regression function reveal an important finding about the U.S. balance of trade deficit with Japan in the early 1980's: in the period following the 1982 recession until the height of dollar's strength in 1985, the deterioration in our balance of trade with Japan may have been more the result of economic growth than of dollar appreciation.   ■

■ THE DEMAND FOR IMPORTED TEXTILES AND APPAREL

The importation of both textiles and apparel into the United States has increased so dramatically since 1975 that the share of the U.S. market held by each of these has more than doubled. While a number of different explanations for this phenomenon exist, many economists attribute it to the dollar's appreciation from 1981 to 1985 that made imports of these goods relatively less expensive than american-made goods. Chmura[15] estimated separate equations for textile and apparel imports to test the empirical validity of this belief, and to determine whether exchange rate variations affect imported textiles differently than they do apparel imports. Using quarterly data from 1977:1 to 1986:1, Chmura estimated equations of the form:

$$\ln(m_t) = \alpha_0 + \alpha_1 \ln(r_{t-1}) + \alpha_2 \ln(y_{t-1}) + \varepsilon_t$$

for both textiles and apparel. The dependent variable in each of these equations is real imports (1982 = 100) for the particular good being modeled, r is the exchange

---

[15] C. Chmura, "The Effect Of Exchange Rate Variation On U.S. Textile And Apparel Imports," *Economic Review* of the Federal Reserve Bank of Richmond, May/June 1987, pp. 17–23.

rate, and y is real GNP (1982 = 100). For the reasons stated in the previous application, the expected sign of both explanatory variables is positive.

Since the U.S. imports textiles and apparel from a number of different countries, a single country's exchange rate is not sufficient to capture the effect of this variable on real imports. The Federal Reserve publishes time series data for a trade-weighted exchange rate that is, in effect, a weighted average of the exchange rates of our largest trading partners. As Chmura notes, this and similar measures deal with all imported and exported goods, which renders them inappropriate for the study of exchange rate effects for well-defined categories of goods such as textiles and apparel. Chmura remedies this by constructing a trade-weighted index based on countries that account for 84 percent of the imports of textiles and apparel during the time period for her study. This is the measure of r used in these equations.

Since quarterly data are used to estimate these equations, lags in the effect of both the trade-weighted exchange rate and real GNP are appropriate, since the separate impacts of each of these variables on real imports can be expected to extend beyond a single quarter. One-quarter lags are used for each of these explanatory variables. Chmura utilizes the log-linear functional form for these equations, which makes the coefficient of each explanatory variable a partial elasticity.

The estimated equations for textiles and apparel are:

$$\text{textiles: } \widehat{\ln(m)}_t = -29.4 + 1.33 \ln(r_{t-1}) + 2.91 \ln(y_{t-1}) \qquad R^2 = 0.87$$
$$\phantom{\text{textiles: } \widehat{\ln(m)}_t = } (11.2) \quad (3.54) \phantom{ + 1.33 \ln(r_{t-1})} (5.94)$$

$$\text{apparel: } \widehat{\ln(m)}_t = -35.1 + 1.40 \ln(r_{t-1}) + 3.69 \ln(y_{t-1}) \qquad R^2 = 0.84$$
$$\phantom{\text{apparel: } \widehat{\ln(m)}_t = } (11.4) \quad (3.39) \phantom{ + 1.40 \ln(r_{t-1})} (7.23)$$

All of the coefficients in these equations are statistically significant at the 1 percent level and above. Both equations are able to account for a substantial amount of the variation in their dependent variables, as judged by the values of R^2.

The exchange rate coefficients for both textiles and apparel display an elastic response by real imports to exchange rate variations. The statistical significance of these coefficients therefore indicates a substantial role for exchange rate variations on the importation of textiles and apparel over the 1977 to 1986 period. These estimated partial exchange rate elasticities are almost identical. Given the level of real GNP last quarter, a 1 percent increase in Chmura's trade-weighted exchange rate raises the mean real imports from 1.33 to 1.4 percent. The "income" elasticity in each equation is fairly large. Given last quarter's exchange rate, a 1 percent rise in real GNP increases mean real imports of textiles by 2.9 percent, versus 3.7 percent for apparel. The income elasticities of real import demand exceed the exchange rate elasticities for both textiles and apparel. This parallels the result for real imports from Japan discussed above. Finally, the intercepts in both equations are negative and statistically significant at the 1 percent level and above. Recall that in log-linear equations such as these, the intercept is the natural logarithm of the constant in the original (multiplicative form) equation. Thus, a negative intercept does *not* indicate a negative mean for real imports when r and y are both 0, which is true with a linear equation specification.

We will conclude this application by providing a quote from Chmura summarizing her findings:

> "The results reported here are good news for the U.S. textile and apparel industries. If . . . the exchange value of the dollar does affect imports, then the recent exchange rate depreciation should cause a decline in the quantity of imports. In addition . . . textile and apparel imports are related to income, and thus demand increases, part of the reason why imports are rising may be that the U.S. demand is expanding. If so, then the potential exists for domestic production to expand with a rise in demand . . . ."[16]

■ **A PRODUCTION FUNCTION**   We next examine an estimated Cobb-Douglas production function for the United Kingdom. Thomas used annual data for the years 1961–1981 to estimate this equation for the UK Standard Industrial Classification of "Bricks, Pottery, Glass, and Cement."[17] The particular form of the Cobb-Douglas function he utilized is:

$$q = Ae^{\gamma t}k^{\alpha}h^{\beta}$$

where q is the industrial production index for this classification; k is the value of the gross capital stock in this classification at its 1975 replacement cost; h is average weekly hours worked, and t is a time trend.

Two notable differences exist between this and the production functions discussed previously. First, the measure of labor input in this function is stated in terms of hours per worker, which is a flow variable, instead of the number of workers, which is a stock variable. Reasons for preferring h were stated in the discussion of Okun's Law in Chapter 4. Second, the time trend in this equation represents a method for capturing the effect of technological progress on production. While no variable "technological progress" exists, we assume that it is positively correlated with time. This assumption allows us to use a time trend as a proxy variable for technological progress.

Linearizing this equation with a logarithmic transformation allows us to express it in a form that is estimable with least squares. After applying this transformation, adding subscripts and an error term, it becomes:

$$\ln(q_t) = \alpha_0^* + \gamma t + \alpha \ln(k_t) + \beta \ln(h_t) + \varepsilon_t \qquad \textbf{(6.44)}$$

Since the time trend in this equation represents technological change, we will first determine the correct interpretation of the time trend coefficient. Taking the change in Equation (6.44), keeping k and h constant and overlooking the error term, we have:

$$\Delta \ln(q_t) = \gamma \, \Delta t$$

---

[16] C. Chmura, *Ibid.*, p. 22.

[17] R. L. Thomas, *Introductory Econometrics: Theory and Applications* (New York: Longman), 1985, pp. 244–249.

Recall that the left side of this equation can be expressed as: $\Delta q/q$, which is the proportionate growth rate in q. If we consider a change of one year, so that $\Delta t = 1$, then the coefficient of the time trend, which is a partial slope, indicates the proportionate growth in q per year, given the existing levels of both k and h. Thus growth in q that is unrelated to k and h is assumed to be the result of technological progress. Note that the constancy of γ assumes that technological progress occurs in a steady (linear) fashion, which is not necessarily the most realistic way of depicting this process.

The sample regression function Thomas obtained is:

$$\widehat{\ln(q)}_t = -8.57 + 0.027t + 0.46 \ln(k_t) + 1.285 \ln(h_t)$$
$$(3.3)(1.3)(1.4)(4.0)$$

$$\text{ESS} = 0.03735 \quad \bar{R}^2 = 0.889$$

The coefficient for technological progress is positive, but not statistically significant. Its value indicates that the annual increase in mean output for this industrial classification due to technological progress is 2.7 percent per year. The estimated output elasticities are 0.46 for capital and 1.285 for labor input. Other things being equal, a 1 percent increase in capital input raises mean production in this industrial classification by 0.46 percent, while a 1 percent rise in average weekly hours increases production by 1.285 percent. Of these two elasticities, only that for hours per week is statistically significant.

The sum of the estimated output elasticities in this equation is 1.745, which indicates the existence of increasing returns to scale. Thomas tests this statistically with a null hypothesis that postulates constant returns to scale: H_0: $\alpha + \beta = 1$. Incorporating this restriction into population regression Equation (6.44), it becomes:

$$\ln(q/h)_t = \alpha_0^* + \gamma t + \alpha \ln(k/h)_t + \varepsilon_t$$

which is similar to Equation (6.43) above. Restricted least squares estimation of this equation gives the following results:

$$\widehat{\ln(q/h)}_t = -5.04 + 0.0358t + 0.0439 \ln(k/h)_t$$
$$(1.41)(1.39)(1.11)$$

$$\bar{R}^2 = 0.947 \qquad \text{ESS} = 0.06385$$

An indication of the results for this F-test is provided by the non-significance of all of the coefficients in this equation. There is one restriction, so $r = 1$. A total of 21 observations were used to estimate these equations, so the degrees of freedom for the unrestricted model is 17. Using this information, the value of our test statistic is:

$$\frac{(0.06385 - 0.03735)/1}{(0.03735/17)} = 12.1.$$

The critical F-value for the 1 percent significance level with 1 and 17 degrees of freedom is 8.4. Since our test statistic exceeds this value, we reject the null hypothesis of constant returns to scale at the 1 percent level of significance. The unrestricted equation is then the basis for our production function estimates. ■

■ INTEREST RATE EQUATIONS

Short Term: The first interest rate equation that is presented is a simple multi-variate relationship whose specification explicitly considers the effect of monetary policy on short-term interest rates.[18] The short-term interest rate utilized as dependent variable is the rate on prime 4 to 6 month commercial paper (r). This is a short-term rate that reflects the rate of interest businesses pay for commercial bills, which are financial instruments used to fund production and trade. The basis of the estimated equation is the contemporaneous relationship:

$$r_t = f(d_t, (F/R)_t, \varepsilon_t),$$

where ε_t is the stochastic error. Two monetary policy variables are included as explanatory variables in this equation: the discount rate (d) and the ratio of free to required reserves (F/R). Free reserves are defined as: total reserves minus required reserves ($=$ excess reserves) less borrowed reserves.

The expected sign of d is positive. When the Federal Reserve lowers the discount rate, the cost of member-bank borrowing from the FED decreases. This serves to lower the cost of loanable funds to banks, causing interest rates to fall as banks pass on at least part of this cost decrease to borrowers. Given (F/R), this change is expected to lower r. The variable (F/R) reflects the impact of bank liquidity on r. Since this variable is a ratio, a rise in free reserves does not necessarily increase this measure of bank liquidity. Use of this variable implicitly assumes that monetary policy affects r by altering free reserves as a proportion of required reserves. For this to occur, it is necessary that free reserves change *relative* to required reserves, or that F and R vary by different proportions. The expected sign of (F/R) is negative. An increase in free relative to required reserves raises the availability of credit, other things being equal, causing short-term interest rates, and r to fall.

The estimated equation (with absolute t-statistics in parentheses) is:

$$\hat{r}_t = 0.42 + 0.994 d_t - 0.0895(F/R)_t \qquad R^2 = 0.96$$
$$(29.2) \qquad (7.6)$$

Both partial slopes display expected signs and are statistically significant at the 1 percent level and above. The estimated equation accounts for 96 percent of the variation in r. The coefficient of d indicates that a 1 percent increase in the discount rate raises the mean of r by 0.994 percent, given the ratio of free to required reserves. The magnitude of this estimated coefficient is close to 1. If the population coefficient of d equals 1, changes in the discount rate will produce equal changes in the mean of r. An objective determination of this possibility can be made using statistical inference. The set of hypotheses for this test are:

$$H_0: \text{population coefficient of } d = 1.$$

$$H_a: \text{population coefficient of } d < 1,$$

---

[18] This example is taken from M. Evans, *Macroeconomic Activity* (New York: Harper & Row), 1969.

where H_a reflects our prior expectation that only part of any decrease in the discount rate is passed on to borrowers. A one-tail t-test with a lower critical value is used for this hypothesis test. The value of the test statistic is:

$$(0.994 - 1)/0.034 = -0.18,$$

which indicates that the estimated coefficient is approximately one-fifth of one standard deviation below 1. Using the rule of thumb value of -1.65 as the critical value for this test, we are unable to reject the null hypothesis that the population-coefficient of d equals 1.

The estimated coefficient of the liquidity variable indicates that a 1 percent decrease in the ratio of free to required reserves, which could result from a mandated increase in the reserve requirement, raises the mean of r by 0.0895 percent, given the discount rate. This value implies that an 11.2 percent fall in this ratio is necessary to increase the mean of r by 1 percent. While the t-statistic for this coefficient is substantial, the t-value for the discount rate, 29.2, reflects the fact that d is the dominant explanatory variable in this equation.

Two implications emerge from this equation. First, short-term interest rates are substantially influenced by monetary policy. Second, the fact that we are unable to reject the null hypothesis that the population coefficient of the discount rate is 1 lends empirical support to the existence of an "equilibrium spread" between short-term market rates and the discount rate. When this balance is altered, actions occur that restore this differential to its equilibrium value. ∎

Long Term: The specification of the previous equation implicitly assumes that the primary determinants of short-term interest rates are under the control of the FED. Long-term bond interest rate equations entail a greater degree of complexity, since a substantial time period elapses between the issuance and maturity of long-term bonds.

The equation for long-term interest rates illustrated here was estimated by Kathleen Cooper.[19] The dependent variable is the interest rate on Moody's Aaa corporate bonds (r). The designation Aaa applies to bonds that are considered to be the least risky under the Moody rating system. The relationship she estimates is of the form:

$$r_t = f(\pi_t^e, fr_t, r_t^c, \tau_t, p_t, \varepsilon_t),$$

where π^e is a measure of expected inflation; fr is the level of nominal free reserves in the banking system; r^c is the interest cost to banks of time and saving deposits; τ is the corporate tax rate; and p measures the impact of the FED operating procedures instituted at the end of 1979 on r.

---

[19] Kathleen Cooper, "Re-Thinking the Fundamentals of Interest Rate Determination," *Business Economics*, January 1983, pp. 25–30. The ideas underlying the expected signs in this equation are also discussed in Kathleen Cooper, "Will High Real Interest Rates Persist?" *Business Economics*, April 1985, pp. 12–18.

π^e is a proxy variable for inflationary expectations, which is intended to capture the inflationary premium in long term interest rates. Other things being equal, an increase in expected inflation raises nominal interest rates, as lenders demand compensation for the anticipated loss in the purchasing power of their funds. The expected sign of π^e is thus positive.

The expectations proxy used by Cooper is a ten quarter moving average of actual rates of inflation (π), which is given by the formula:

$$\pi_t^e = (\pi_t + \pi_{t-1} + \cdots + \pi_{t-9})/10.$$

For quarter t, the current and nine previous values of π are used to calculate this average. The value of π^e for the next quarter "moves" ahead one quarter, discarding the earliest observation in the previous quarter's moving average, while adding a more recent value. The use of a moving average to represent inflationary expectations assumes that expected future inflation is based solely on the average level of current and past values of actual inflation. This is an example of **adaptive expectations**, where expectations "adapt" to changes in observed past values of a variable. In the estimated equation considered here, an increase in the average rate of inflation over the most recent 10 quarters causes the measure of expected future inflation to rise.

The variable *fr* measures the effect of bank liquidity on long-term interest rates. Other things being equal, an increase in nominal free reserves is assumed to raise the availability of bank credit, which, by increasing the supply of loanable funds, causes a decline in long-term interest rates. A potential criticism can be raised concerning the use of a nominal value of this variable as a proxy for bank liquidity. Situations can arise where *fr* rises and yet banks are *less* able to provide credit. This occurs when *real* free reserves fall. To control for the effect of price changes on bank liquidity, either real *fr* should be utilized, or an explanatory variable representing the rate of inflation should be included. Since π^e includes the current inflation rate (this is discussed below), the estimated equation indirectly controls for this influence, so this omission is not as serious as it might appear.

r^c, the interest cost to banks for time and saving deposits, is intended to represent a "deregulation effect" in long-term interest rates. In the time period prior to current interest rate regulations, the government mandated ceilings for certain interest rates. During periods of rising interest rates, such restrictions often resulted in shortages of loanable funds, since the basis for rationing shifted from cost to the availability of such funds. This had the additional effect of keeping interest rates below the free market levels they would have attained in the absence of measures such as Regulation Q. Today, interest cost is the important factor in the allocation of funds. Other things being equal, an increase in the interest cost of funds to banks raises long-term interest rates. The expected sign of r^c is therefore positive.

The remaining variable that will be discussed is τ, the corporate tax rate. The expected sign for this coefficient is positive, based on the assertion by Cooper that the tax deductibility of interest for firms issuing bonds will tend to increase their willingness to pay higher nominal rates of interest, resulting in higher observed rates of interest.

This equation was estimated using quarterly data for the period 1970:1 to 1982:2. The sample regression function is:

$$\hat{r}_t = -0.719 + 0.12\pi_t^e - 0.265fr_t + 0.428r_t^c + 3.29\tau_t + 0.494p_t + 0.538r_{t-1}$$
$$\quad\quad\quad (3.5) \quad\quad (4.0) \quad\quad (2.7) \quad\quad (1.7) \quad\quad (2.0) \quad\quad (5.0)$$

$$\bar{R}^2 = 0.98 \quad\quad \hat{\sigma}_\varepsilon = 0.3$$

Included among the explanatory variables in this equation is the value of r last quarter, r_{t-1}, which is called a **lagged dependent variable**. An estimated equation that includes a lagged dependent variable is a **short-run estimated function**. *Individual coefficients in this equation presuppose a fixed value of r last quarter.* The corresponding long-run version is obtained through algebraic manipulation, as shown below. The basis for including this type of variable in an estimated equation typically involves assumptions concerning either expectation formation, or a process of adjustment for the dependent variable that occurs over several time periods.[20] In this equation, the assumption of "partial adjustment" is utilized, so that actual r adjusts only partially toward its optimal value in a given quarter.

The long-run version of this equation is derived using the fact that when the dependent variable is in a long-run equilibrium, it remains unchanged, so that $r_t = r_{t-1}$. Using the sample regression function:

$$r_t = -0.719 + 0.12\pi^e + 0.538r_{t-1} + \cdots,$$

when this condition is met, the lagged dependent variable term can be moved to the left side, giving:

$$r_t - 0.538r_t = -0.719 + 0.12\pi^e + \cdots$$
$$r_t = [1/(1 - 0.538)](-0.719 + 0.12\pi^e + \cdots),$$

which is the **long-run equation**. Note that *the right side of the long-run equation no longer includes the lagged dependent variable.* Each of the other coefficients is multiplied by the inverse of 1 minus the coefficient of the lagged dependent variable. In the current example, the value of this "multiplier" is 2.165.

The statistically significant coefficient of π^e indicates that a 1 percent rise in expected inflation increases the mean of r in the same quarter by 0.12 percent, given the rate of interest last quarter and the values of the other explanatory variables in this equation. Economic theory leads us to believe that if inflation is correctly anticipated, then in the long run, a given rise in expected inflation will produce an equal increase in nominal interest rates. Using the multiplier of 2.165 we obtain the estimated quarterly long-run inflationary premium from this equation, 0.26. Since interest rates are expressed as annual rates, we can convert this long-run estimate to an equivalent annual value if we multiply it by 4. The result is an estimated annual

---

[20] This is covered in detail in Chapter 13.

long-run inflationary premium of 1.04, which approximates our theoretical expectation very closely.[21]

The coefficient of fr is negative and statistically significant at the 1 percent level and above. Other things being equal, a one billion dollar increase in free reserves lowers the mean of r by 0.265 percent in the short run. In the long run this estimate rises to 0.574 percent. The estimated coefficient of r^c implies that other things being equal, a 1 percent rise in the interest cost of funds to banks increases the mean of r by 0.428 percent in the short run, and by 0.93 percent in the long run. The coefficient of the corporate tax rate predicts that other things being equal, a 1 percent increase in τ raises the mean of r by 3.29 percent in the short run. While this coefficient is statistically significant at the 5 percent level, its magnitude appears too large. For example, a 3 percent increase in the corporate tax rate would raise r by just under 10 percent in the short run, using this estimate. While it is true that the real after-tax rate of interest will rise by less than the 10 percent figure, nominal interest rates did not fall in any manner consistent with this estimate during the early Reagan years when accelerated depreciation lowered effective corporate tax rates.[22]   ■

■ A MONETARY VIEW OF THE INFLATION-UNEMPLOYMENT

LINK   One of the equations presented at the end of Chapter 4 expressed a relationship between the civilian unemployment rate and changes in the rate of inflation that was used as the basis for determining the Noninflationary Rate of Unemployment (NIRU). In that equation, the unemployment rate served as a proxy variable for the amount of slack in the economy. A fall in this rate, which implies that an economy is operating closer to full employment, was shown to increase the rate of inflation. According to that model, the level of unemployment is problematic when it is at or above the NIRU.

Proponents of the monetary view of the link between inflation and unemployment believe that this empirical relationship exists only in this short run; it is merely a *transitory* relationship. According to this view, the apparent link between these variables is actually the result of changes in the supply of money, since the most important determinant of the rate of inflation is the rate of monetary expansion. The monetary view can be summarized with the following quote:

> To the extent to that there appears to be a relationship between movements in prices and unemployment, it is in fact a reflection of differential time responses to changes in the third variable. This is the monetary view, which stresses the long-run relation between money and prices, but also takes into account transitory effects of money on real product growth and unemployment.[23]

---

[21] The author would like to thank George Briden for suggesting this approach for evaluating the magnitude of the inflationary premium in this equation.

[22] The other variable in this equation, PROC, is included to measure the difference in RMB during the years with Paul Volker as head of the Federal Reserve.

[23] K. Carlson, "Inflation, Unemployment, and Money: Comparing the Evidence from Two Simple Models," *Review* of the Federal Reserve Bank of St. Louis, September 1978, pp. 2–6.

Thus, in the long run the rates of inflation and monetary growth will tend to converge, and the unemployment rate will move to its long-run equilibrium value. This unemployment rate is *not* the NIRU, however. While this value is empirically determined, the equation from which it is estimated must include a variable reflecting both monetary growth and the rate of inflation.

The underlying empirical basis for these propositions can be illustrated by referring to equations estimated by Carlson.[24] Using annual data for 1952 to 1976, Carlson derived the estimated NIRU presented in Chapter 4, 5.44 percent. He then used this value in the following equation to assess the relative importance of unemployment and monetary growth rates in the determination of inflation:

$$\widehat{\Delta INF_t} = 0.001 - 0.177(u_{t-1} - 5.44) + 0.406(m_{t-1} - \pi_{t-1})$$
$$(0.004) \quad (0.826) \qquad\qquad (3.30)$$

$$R^2 = 0.45 \qquad \hat{\sigma}_\varepsilon = 1.16$$

In this equation, ΔINF is the change in the year-to-year IPD inflation rate, u is the civilian unemployment rate, m is the year-to-year percent change in M1, and π is the year-to-year IPD inflation rate. The variable $(u_{t-1} - 5.44)$ thus represents the amount by which actual unemployment last year differed from the NIRU, while $(m_{t-1} - \pi_{t-1})$ denotes the divergence last year between the rates of monetary growth and inflation.

Both the intercept and the coefficient of the unemployment rate term fail *t*-tests of statistical significance. The nonsignificance of the unemployment term therefore provides empirical support for the view that changes in inflation cannot be systematically linked to changes in the rate of unemployment when past changes in monetary growth rates and inflation are taken into account. The coefficient of the term involving monetary growth, is, however, statistically significant. Monetary growth above the rate of inflation thus contributes to an acceleration in inflation. For every 1 percent by which monetary growth exceeds the inflation rate, mean inflation in the following year rises by 0.41 percent, given the divergence between the unemployment rate and the NIRU.

What, then, does the monetary view have to say about the unemployment rate? Both the level of unemployment and changes in its value are influenced by the supply of money in the short run. When monetary growth exceeds the inflation rate, the transitory effect of this imbalance is a decrease in the rate of unemployment. In the long run, however, as monetary growth converges to the rate of inflation, money supply growth exerts no influence on the unemployment rate, which tends to its long-run equilibrium value. How is this value determined? The following equation provides the basis for this estimate:

$$\widehat{(u_t - u_{t-1})} = 3.96 - 0.721u_{t-1} - 0.380(m_{t-1} - \pi_{t-1})$$
$$(5.08) \quad (4.86) \qquad (4.47)$$

$$R^2 = 0.61 \qquad \hat{\sigma}_\varepsilon = 0.8$$

---

[24] K. Carlson, *op. cit.*

In the long run, as monetary growth converges to the rate of inflation, m_{t-1} equals π_{t-1}, causing the term on the right to drop out of this equation. Also, since the equilibrium unemployment rate is sustainable, in long-run equilibrium, $u_t = u_{t-1}$, which makes the left side of this equation 0. The equation then becomes:

$$3.96 - 0.721u_t = 0$$

The value of u_t that satisfies this equation for its estimation period, 1952 through 1976, is 5.49. This is the estimated long-run equilibrium value of the unemployment rate for this time period.

Policy recommendations concerning the onset of inflation differ among proponents of the monetary view and those adhering to the validity of the NIRU. If the NIRU is valid, then inflation is more likely to accelerate the closer an economy comes to its noninflationary rate of unemployment. This occurs since decreases in the rate of unemployment signal greater utilization of an economy's resources, and the increased likelihood of supply bottlenecks. As a result, when demand increases, prices are more likely to rise, causing inflation to accelerate. In contrast, proponents of the monetary view look to recent rates of monetary growth as the best indicator of future inflation. This same approach applies irrespective of whether the unemployment rate is close to the NIRU. Thus advocates of the monetary view point out that it is possible to observe accelerating inflation even when the unemployment is rising above its noninflationary rate. This occurs when the supply of money continues to increase faster than existing rates of inflation. ■

KEY TERMS

Adaptive expectations	Partial slope
Coefficient of multiple determination	Restricted equation
Homogeneous linear restriction	Restricted least squares
Lagged dependent variable	Short-run estimated function
Linear restriction	Test of the statistical significance of R^2
Long-run equation	Unrestricted equation
Non-homogeneous linear restriction	Wald test

EXERCISES

1. Compare and contrast R^2 and $\bar{R}^2$ as measures of equation performance. What are the shared strengths of these measures? Their shared weaknesses?

2. In deriving the expression for R^2, we began with the equation $y_i = \hat{y}_i + \hat{\varepsilon}_i$, then subtracted the mean of y from both sides, giving the definition of the total sum of squares: TSS $= (y_i - \hat{\mu}_y) = (\hat{y}_i - \hat{\mu}_y) + \hat{\varepsilon}_i$. After summing then squaring both sides of this equation, its right side becomes the sum of the

squares of the two individual terms. Show that:

$$\sum[(\hat{y}_i - \hat{\mu}_y) + \hat{\varepsilon}_i]^2 = \sum(\hat{y}_i - \hat{\mu}_y)^2 + \sum\hat{\varepsilon}_i^2$$

3. The assumptions used to ascertain the properties of the least squares estimators include $Cov(x_i, \varepsilon_i) = Cov(z_i, \varepsilon_i) = 0$, which postulates that each explanatory variable is uncorrelated with the equation error. Does this condition also imply that $Cov(x_i, z_i) = 0$? Explain the basis for your answer.

4. The values of R^2 from equations with different forms of the same explanatory variable cannot be directly compared. If equation (I) uses y as the dependent variable, while equation (II) uses $\ln(y)$, how can the predicted and/or residual values from (II) be manipulated so that a measure comparable to the R^2 from (I) is derived?

5. This chapter briefly outlines specification error and its impact on the expected value of the error. If the population regression function is:

$$y_i = \alpha_0 + \alpha_1 x_i + \alpha_2 z_i + \varepsilon_i,$$

and the variable z is omitted, the error from the estimated population regression function is:

$$v_i = \varepsilon_i + \alpha_2 z_i.$$

Assuming $E(\varepsilon_i) = 0$, $Var(\varepsilon_i) = \hat{\sigma}_\varepsilon^2$, and that z is uncorrelated with ε, find an expression for $Var(v_i)$. Is this error homoskedastic?

6. If our population regression function is:

$$y_i = \alpha_0 + \alpha_1 x_{1i} + \alpha_2 x_{2i} + \alpha_3 x_{3i} + \alpha_4 x_{4i} + \varepsilon_i$$

derive the equation for the restricted model, and indicate the number of degrees of freedom for the Wald test of each of the following restrictions:

(a) $\alpha_1 = -\alpha_2$

(b) $\alpha_2 + \alpha_3 = 1 - \alpha_4$

(c) $\alpha_2 = 1 - \alpha_3$

(d) $\alpha_2 + \alpha_3 = 1$ and $\alpha_4 = -\alpha_3$

7. Using the following population regression function:

$$y_i = \alpha_0 + \alpha_1 x_i + \alpha_2 z_i + \varepsilon_i$$

show that the restricted equation corresponding to the nonhomogeneous linear restriction: $c_1\alpha_1 + c_2\alpha_2 = c$ is:

$$[y_i - (c/c_2)z_i] = \alpha_0 + \alpha_1[x_i - (c_1/c_2)z_i] + \varepsilon_i$$

8. If we are interested in estimating the following demand function:

$$y_i = \alpha_0 + \alpha_1 x_{1i} + \alpha_2 x_{2i} + \alpha_3 x_{3i} + \varepsilon_i,$$

where y is quantity demanded of a good, x_1 is the price of this good, x_2 is the price of a substitute good, and x_3 is income, and we wish to test whether the sensitivity of demand to own price is the same as that for the price of the substitute good:

(a) State the hypotheses that are used for this test.

(b) What is the test statistic that is used to test these hypotheses?

(c) Outline the steps involved in performing this hypothesis test.

9. Using economic theory for the demand for money (m_d):

(a) State the general functional relationship for m_d by identifying a set of explanatory variables, and explain the basis for the expected sign of each of these;

(b) Transform (a) into a linear population regression function. What is the correct interpretation for each of the coefficients in this equation?

(c) When this population regression function is graphed with m_d on the vertical axis and the interest rate on the horizontal axis, what variables constitute autonomous (of the interest rate) money demand?

(d) Derive an expression for the interest elasticity of the demand for money using the interest rate coefficient in this population regression function.

10. Answer (9) for the supply of money (m_s) instead of the demand for money.

11. For the following multivariate Keynesian saving function (absolute t-values in parentheses):

$$\hat{s}_t = -42.75 + 0.015y_t + 0.007w_t + 7.67r_t$$
$$\qquad\quad (3.30)\quad (2.09)\quad (1.75)\quad (3.81)$$

$\bar{R}^2 = 0.962 \qquad \hat{\sigma}_\varepsilon = 9.57 \qquad \hat{\mu}_y = 71.3 \qquad F = 251.5 \qquad \text{ESS} = 2470.8 \qquad n = 31$

where: s is real gross personal saving (bil \$);
y is real disposable personal income (bil \$);
w is a measure of wealth, estimated from a four-quarter moving sum of lagged real disposable personal income; and
r is a three-year Government interest rate:

(a) Derive the 95 percent and 99 percent confidence intervals for the coefficient of y, the MPS.

(b) Test the following set of hypotheses—H_0: $\alpha_1 = 0.1$ and H_a: $\alpha_1 < 0.1$—at the 5 percent level of significance (α_1 is the coefficient of y).

(c) Derive the 95 percent and 99 percent confidence intervals for the coefficient of r.

(d) Test the set of hypotheses given in **(b)** on the bivariate saving function given below:

$$\hat{s}_t = 9.4 + 0.06y_t$$
$$\quad\; (2.1)\;\; (17.2)$$

$\bar{R}^2 = 0.908 \qquad \hat{\sigma}_\varepsilon = 14.82 \qquad \hat{\mu}_y = 71.3 \qquad F = 296.4 \qquad \text{ESS} = 6372.8 \qquad n = 31$

(e) Calculate the 95 percent and 99 percent confidence intervals for the MPS given in the above equation. Compare these with the corresponding intervals from the multivariate saving equation.

12. The long-term interest rate equation illustrated at the end of this chapter uses a ten-quarter moving average as a proxy variable for inflationary expectations. Suggest a proxy variable for expected price that can be used in a demand function, and justify the basis for this choice.

APPENDIX MULTIPLE REGRESSION WITH MATRIX ALGEBRA

This appendix illustrates how the multiple regression model can be stated in matrix form and derives several of the formulas given in this chapter. It is *not* intended to provide a complete treatment of the topics covered in Chapter 6. Throughout, it is assumed that readers are familiar with the previous appendixes that deal with matrix algebra (Chapters 2 and 4). References that utilize a matrix algebra approach with the multiple regression model are:

J. Johnston, *Econometric Methods*, 3rd ed. (New York: McGraw-Hill, 1984);

G. Judge et. al., *An Introduction to the Theory and Practice of Econometrics*, 2nd ed. (New York: Wiley, 1987).

Expressing the Population Regression Function in Matrix Form

The multiple regression population regression function (PRF) can be written:

$$y_i = \alpha_1 + \alpha_2 x_{2i} + \alpha_3 x_{3i} + \cdots + \alpha_k x_{ki} + \varepsilon_i, \tag{6A.1}$$

where the intercept can be thought of as variable x_1. The PRF given by (A.6.1) is assumed to be valid for the entire set of n observations. The PRF for the set of observations is therefore:

$$
\begin{aligned}
y_1 &= \alpha_1 + \alpha_2 x_{21} + \alpha_3 x_{31} + \cdots + \alpha_k x_{k1} + \varepsilon_1 \\
&\vdots \\
y_n &= \alpha_1 + \alpha_2 x_{2n} + \alpha_3 x_{3n} + \cdots + \alpha_k x_{kn} + \varepsilon_n.
\end{aligned}
\tag{6A.2}
$$

The values taken by the dependent variable form a $(n \times 1)$ column vector, as do the stochastic errors:

$$
y = \begin{bmatrix} y_1 \\ \vdots \\ y_n \end{bmatrix} \qquad \varepsilon = \begin{bmatrix} \varepsilon_1 \\ \vdots \\ \varepsilon_n \end{bmatrix}
$$

The data matrix is the $(n \times k)$ matrix:

$$
X = \begin{bmatrix} 1 & x_{21} & \cdots & x_{k1} \\ \vdots & \vdots & & \vdots \\ 1 & x_{2n} & \cdots & x_{kn} \end{bmatrix}.
$$

The first column above denotes the fact that when the first variable is an intercept, $x_1 = 1$ for all n observations, producing a column of 1's in the data matrix. The product of the x and α terms in (6A.2) is expressed as $X\alpha$, where:

$$
\alpha = \begin{bmatrix} \alpha_1 \\ \vdots \\ \alpha_k \end{bmatrix}
$$

is a $(k \times 1)$ column vector of population coefficients to be estimated. The matrix form of (6A.2) is therefore:

$$y = X\alpha + \varepsilon. \tag{6A.3}$$

The following set of model assumptions, which stated in the text, are applied to this model:

$E(\varepsilon_i) = 0$ (for all i)

$\mathrm{Var}(\varepsilon_i) = \sigma_\varepsilon^2$ (for all i)

$\mathrm{Cov}(\varepsilon_i, \varepsilon_j) = 0$

Each x is nonstochastic, or if stochastic, uncorrelated with ε.

The x's are not perfectly collinear.

Each ε_i is normally distributed.

Within the matrix algebra framework, it is necessary to work with the mean and variance of the *vector* of errors. The mean of ε, $E(\varepsilon)$, is the expectation of a vector, which is a vector of expected values:

$$E(\varepsilon) = E\begin{bmatrix} \varepsilon_1 \\ \vdots \\ \varepsilon_n \end{bmatrix} = \begin{bmatrix} E(\varepsilon_1) \\ \vdots \\ E(\varepsilon_n) \end{bmatrix} = \begin{bmatrix} 0 \\ \vdots \\ 0 \end{bmatrix}$$

using the first model assumption. A vector of zeros is a **null vector**. The mean of the error vector is therefore a null vector if $E(\varepsilon_i) = 0$ for all observations.

The variance of a single error, ε_i, is given by the formula:

$$\mathrm{Var}(\varepsilon_i) = E[\varepsilon_i - E(\varepsilon_i)]^2 = E(\varepsilon_i^2) = \sigma_\varepsilon^2,$$

and the covariance of any pair of errors:

$$\mathrm{Cov}(\varepsilon_i, \varepsilon_j) = E[\varepsilon_i - E(\varepsilon_i)][\varepsilon_j - E(\varepsilon_j)] = E(\varepsilon_i\varepsilon_j) = 0$$

using the above assumptions. The variance of a vector such as ε is not a scalar, since it consists of n error terms, each of which has its own variance and a covariance with every other element in this vector. *The variance of a vector is thus represented by a variance-covariance matrix.* The matrix formula for the variance-covariance can be related to the variance formula for a scalar. The scalar $[\varepsilon_i - E(\varepsilon_i)]$ for a single error is replaced by the column vector $[\varepsilon - E(\varepsilon)]$. Squaring this term is accomplished using vector multiplication. Since both ε and $[\varepsilon - E(\varepsilon)]$ are column vectors, the vector multiplication that produces a matrix is that of a column vector with a row vector. Using this information, the variance-covariance matrix of ε, Σ_ε, is:

$$\sum_\varepsilon = E[\varepsilon - E(\varepsilon)][\varepsilon - E(\varepsilon)]' = E(\varepsilon\varepsilon'). \tag{6A.4}$$

Performing the multiplication and expectation in (6A.4) gives:

$$\sum_\varepsilon = E(\varepsilon\varepsilon') = E\begin{bmatrix} \varepsilon_1 \\ \vdots \\ \varepsilon_n \end{bmatrix}\begin{bmatrix} \varepsilon_1 & \cdots & \varepsilon_n \end{bmatrix}$$

$$= \begin{bmatrix} E(\varepsilon_1^2) & \cdots & E(\varepsilon_1\varepsilon_n) \\ \vdots & & \vdots \\ E(\varepsilon_n\varepsilon_1) & \cdots & E(\varepsilon_n^2) \end{bmatrix} = \begin{bmatrix} \sigma_\varepsilon^2 & \cdots & 0 \\ \vdots & & \vdots \\ 0 & \cdots & \sigma_\varepsilon^2 \end{bmatrix}$$

since the diagonal elements, $E(\varepsilon_i^2)$, are variances and off-diagonal elements, $E(\varepsilon_i \cdot \varepsilon_j)$, are co-variances. *If a null error vector is assumed along with homoskedasticity and the absence of serial correlation,* Σ_ε is the diagonal matrix above. Factoring out the scalar σ_ε^2 gives:

$$\sum{}_\varepsilon = \sigma_\varepsilon^2 \begin{bmatrix} 1 & \cdots & 0 \\ \vdots & & \vdots \\ 0 & \cdots & 1 \end{bmatrix} = \sigma_\varepsilon^2 \cdot I_n, \tag{6A.5}$$

the product of the (constant) variance and an $(n \times n)$ identity matrix, I_n. This is referred to as a **scalar-identity covariance matrix**.

The normality assumption for each ε_i allows the error vector to have a **multivariate normal distribution**:

$$\varepsilon \sim N(0, \sigma_\varepsilon^2 \cdot I_n),$$

where the null vector 0 is the mean vector, and the variance is given by the variance-covariance matrix $\sigma_\varepsilon^2 \cdot I_n$. This result is used for hypothesis testing.

The data matrix is assumed to have k independent variables. Using matrix algebra terminology, this implies that the set of explanatory variables are **linearly independent**, and that no explanatory variable can be expressed as a **linear combination** (function) of the remaining variables. For example, with the two variables x_2 and x_3, the only way to satisfy the expression:

$$\lambda_1 x_2 + \lambda_2 x_3 = 0$$

with linearly independent variables is the trivial solution $\lambda_1 = \lambda_2 = 0$. If, for example, $x_2 = (1/2)x_3$, there are two variables but only one *independent* set of observations, since if x_{2i} is known, so too is x_{3i}. In this case:

$$(1)x_2 - (1/2)x_3 = 0,$$

and $\lambda_1 = 1$ and $\lambda_2 = -1/2$. Since both of these constants are nonzero, one variable is a linear combination of the other, and x_2 and x_3 are **linearly dependent**. This is called perfect collinearity. An example of a data matrix that contains two linearly dependent variables is:

$$\begin{bmatrix} 2 & 4 \\ 4 & 8 \end{bmatrix}, \qquad \text{determinant} = 2(8) - 4(4) = 0.$$

The determinant of this matrix is 0. Thus *the determinant of a matrix with linearly dependent columns (or rows) is 0.* The **rank** of a matrix is the number of linearly independent rows and columns. If X is an $(n \times k)$ matrix then:

$$\text{rank}(X) \leq \min(n, k).$$

When there are positive degrees of freedom, $n > k$. The maximum possible rank of X is then k, or **full column rank**, which pertains when the variables in X constitute a linearly independent set of vectors. In this case, each variable provides additional information that is not derivable from linearly combining the other x's. This does *not* rule out either a set of imperfectly correlated explanatory variables or nonlinear relationships among the variables, such as $x_2 = (x_3)^2$.

Derivation of the Least Squares Estimator

The PRF given previously is:

$$y = X\alpha + \varepsilon.$$

Our estimator of this function, the sample regression function, uses an estimated coefficient vector, $\hat{\alpha}$, and a vector of estimated errors, $\hat{\varepsilon}$. This function can be expressed as either:

$$\hat{y} = X\hat{\alpha}, \quad \text{or}$$

$$y = X\hat{\alpha} + \hat{\varepsilon},$$

where $\hat{y}$ is the vector of predicted values of the dependent variable. The residual vector is:

$$\hat{\varepsilon} = (y - X\hat{\alpha}). \tag{6A.6}$$

The sum of the squared residuals (S), which is a *scalar*, is obtained from the vector multiplication: $\hat{\varepsilon}'\hat{\varepsilon}$. Substituting the right side of (6A.6) into this expression gives the function that is minimized with respect to $\hat{\alpha}$ to obtain the least squares estimators:

$$S = \hat{\varepsilon}'\hat{\varepsilon} = (y - X\hat{\alpha})'(y - X\hat{\alpha}) \tag{6A.7}$$

Before differentiating (6A.7), we will perform the matrix multiplication of the bracketed expressions in (6A.7). To do this, we make use of the following rules for transposed matrix (or vector) products:

$$(A + B)' = A' + B', \quad \text{and}$$

$$(AB)' = B' \cdot A'.$$

The transpose of a product of vectors or matrices is therefore the product of transposes *in reverse order*. This generalizes to more than two terms in the product as well. Using this rule, we can rewrite the expression for S:

$$S = (y' - \hat{\alpha}'X')(y - X\hat{\alpha}), \quad \text{or}$$

$$S = y'y - y'X\hat{\alpha} - \hat{\alpha}'X'y + \hat{\alpha}'X'X\hat{\alpha}. \tag{6A.8}$$

Note that each of the product terms on the right of (6A.8) is a scalar. Because of this fact, the two middle terms in this expression, $y'X\hat{\alpha}$ and $\hat{\alpha}'X'y$, are equal. We can therefore simplify (6A.8) to:

$$S = y'y - 2\hat{\alpha}'X'y + \hat{\alpha}'X'X\hat{\alpha}. \tag{6A.9}$$

The least squares estimator vector $\hat{\alpha}$ is obtained by partially differentiating (6A.9) with respect to $\hat{\alpha}$, setting the resulting expression equal to 0, then solving for the least squares vector, $\hat{\alpha}$. Performing these steps:

$$\partial S / \partial \hat{\alpha} = 0 - 2X'y + 2X'X\hat{\alpha} = 0,$$

so that:

$$2(X'X)\hat{\alpha} = 2(X'y), \quad \text{or}$$

$$(X'X)\hat{\alpha} = X'y. \tag{6A.10}$$

Equation (6A.10) is the basis for the multiple regression normal equations that were presented in the text. In the partial differentiation above, the 0 results from the fact that $y'y$ does not contain $\hat{\alpha}$. The last term in (6A.9), $\hat{\alpha}'X'X\hat{\alpha}$, is a **quadratic form** (Q), which involves squared terms and cross-products (SSCP) of the $\hat{\alpha}$'s. If the data matrix consists of two variables x and z, the SSCP matrix is:

$$X'X = \begin{bmatrix} \sum x_i^2 & \sum x_i z_i \\ \sum z_i x_i & \sum z_i^2 \end{bmatrix},$$

and the quadratic form that pertains is:

$$Q = [\hat{\alpha}_1 \hat{\alpha}_2] \begin{bmatrix} \sum x_i^2 & \sum x_i z_i \\ \sum z_i x_i & \sum z_i^2 \end{bmatrix} \begin{bmatrix} \hat{\alpha}_1 \\ \hat{\alpha}_2 \end{bmatrix}, \qquad \text{so}$$

$$Q = \hat{\alpha}_1^2 \sum x_i^2 + 2\hat{\alpha}_1 \hat{\alpha}_2 \sum x_i z_i + \hat{\alpha}_2^2 \sum z_i^2.$$

The partial derivative of Q with respect to the vector $\hat{\alpha}$ is the following column vector:

$$\begin{bmatrix} \partial Q / \partial \hat{\alpha}_1 \\ \partial Q / \partial \hat{\alpha}_2 \end{bmatrix} = \begin{bmatrix} 2\hat{\alpha}_1 \sum x_i^2 + 2\hat{\alpha}_2 \sum x_i z_i \\ 2\hat{\alpha}_1 \sum z_i x_i + 2\hat{\alpha}_2 \sum z_i^2 \end{bmatrix}$$

$$= 2\begin{bmatrix} \sum x_i^2 & \sum x_i z_i \\ \sum z_i x_i & \sum z_i^2 \end{bmatrix} \begin{bmatrix} \hat{\alpha}_1 \\ \hat{\alpha}_2 \end{bmatrix} = 2(X'X)\hat{\alpha},$$

which confirms the result stated in the partial derivative for S.

Solving the normal equations:

$$(X'X)\hat{\alpha} = X'y$$

for $\hat{\alpha}$ would involve dividing both sides by the first term on the left if only scalers were involved. Unfortunately, division by a matrix is not a valid operation. Since division is identical to multiplication by the inverse, we can solve (6A.10) for $\hat{\alpha}$ by premultiplying both sides of this equation by the inverse of the sum of the squares and cross-product matrix, $X'X$. The **inverse of a matrix** X, denoted X^{-1}, is a square matrix which, when multiplied by X gives the identity matrix. Thus X^{-1} must satisfy:

$$X^{-1}X = I = XX^{-1}.$$

This expression is the matrix equivalent of stating that $(1/X) \cdot X = 1$, where the matrix corresponding to 1 is the identity matrix, I.

The inverse of a matrix does not always exist. If X^{-1} exists, X is said to be **nonsingular**, or **invertible**. For X^{-1} to exist:

(i) X must be a square matrix;
(ii) the rows and columns of X must be linearly independent.

The first of these guarantees conformability in multiplication, so that X and X^{-1} can be multiplied to obtain I. The second condition requires that the rank of X equal the number of columns (and rows) in this matrix. When this condition is met, the determinant of X is nonzero.

The normal equations require that $X'X$ be invertible. Since the sample data matrix X is $(n \times k)$, $X'X$ is a $(k \times k)$ square matrix. If the columns of X are not perfectly collinear, then rank$(X) = k$, and $X'X$ exists. Returning to the normal equations:

$$(X'X)\hat{\alpha} = X'y,$$

the solution for $\hat{\alpha}$ is:

$$(X'X)^{-1}(X'X)\hat{\alpha} = (X'X)^{-1}X'y, \qquad \text{or}$$

$$\hat{\alpha} = (X'X)^{-1}X'y. \tag{6A.11}$$

When the actual calculations implied by (6A.11) are carried out, the formulas for individual $\hat{\alpha}$ terms are obtained.

Properties of the Least Squares Coefficient Vector

Establishing the unbiasedness of the least squares estimators is relatively simple using matrix algebra. Use of the algebraic formulas in the text involves considerably more detail and computational burden. One of the nicest features of the matrix approach to least squares is that the *formula (6A.11) pertains, no matter how many explanatory variables are in the sample regression function*. The algebraic formulas become rather large in merely going from one to two explanatory variables.

The procedure used to show the unbiasedness of $\hat{\alpha}$ parallels that for the algebraic determination: we first state the formula for this vector, then substitute the right side of the *population* regression function for y, which enables us to express $\hat{\alpha}$ in terms of α. Making this substitution:

$$\hat{\alpha} = (X'X)^{-1}X'y$$
$$= (X'X)^{-1}X'(X\alpha + \varepsilon)$$
$$= (X'X)^{-1}(X'X)\alpha + (X'X)^{-1}X'\varepsilon$$
$$\hat{\alpha} = \alpha + (X'X)^{-1}X'\varepsilon \tag{6A.12}$$

The least squares estimator vector therefore equals the vector of population parameters (α) plus a term related to the stochastic error. Equation (6A.12) provides the basis for establishing the normal distribution of $\hat{\alpha}$: since $\hat{\alpha}$ is a linear function of a (multivariate) normally distributed random variable (ε), $\hat{\alpha}$ is itself normally distributed. Ascertaining whether $\hat{\alpha}$ is unbiased gives the mean vector corresponding to the normal distribution of $\hat{\alpha}$.

The vector $\hat{\alpha}$ is unbiased if its mean vector equals α. Taking the expected value of both sides of (6A.12) gives:

$$E(\hat{\alpha}) = E(\alpha) + E[(X'X)^{-1}X'\varepsilon]$$

Since α is a vector of constants, $E(\alpha) = \alpha$. Assuming that the matrix X is nonstochastic, we can move the expectation operator directly to the error vector ε. Using these results:

$$E(\hat{\alpha}) = \alpha + (X'X)^{-1}X'E(\varepsilon)$$
$$= \alpha,$$

using the model assumption that $E(\varepsilon) = 0$. Least squares therefore provides an unbiased estimator vector under the set of model assumptions outlined above. Equality of these vectors requires each of their corresponding elements be the same. If we use the subscript j to denote a row of $\hat{\alpha}$, then for this to occur, $E(\hat{\alpha}_j) = \alpha_j$ for all of the elements in $\hat{\alpha}$.

Since $\hat{\alpha}$ is a vector, a variance-covariance matrix provides information needed for statistical inference on individual coefficients. The formula for the variance of an individual coefficient is:

$$\text{Var}(\hat{\alpha}_j) = E[\hat{\alpha}_j - E(\hat{\alpha}_j)]^2$$
$$= E[\hat{\alpha}_j - \alpha_j]^2$$

if $\hat{\alpha}_j$ is unbiased. In the matrix algebra framework $\hat{\alpha}$ is an unbiased column vector, so $E[\hat{\alpha} - E(\hat{\alpha})] = E[\hat{\alpha} - \alpha]$, which is also a column vector. Using this column vector to produce a matrix that corresponds to the squared term in the expression above, we multiply it (a column vector) by its transpose (a row vector). The variance-covariance matrix for $\hat{\alpha}$ thus uses the following formula:

$$\text{Var}(\hat{\alpha}) = E[\hat{\alpha} - \alpha][\hat{\alpha} - \alpha]'$$

We can obtain an expression for $(\hat{\alpha} - \alpha)$ from (6A.12):

$$(\hat{\alpha} - \alpha) = (X'X)^{-1}X'\varepsilon \tag{6A.13}$$

Substituting (6A.13) into the variance formula gives:

$$\begin{aligned}
\text{Var}(\hat{\alpha}) &= E[(X'X)^{-1}X'\varepsilon][(X'X)^{-1}X'\varepsilon]' \\
&= E[(X'X)^{-1}X'\varepsilon\varepsilon'X(X'X)^{-1}],
\end{aligned}$$

using the rule for the transpose of a product, and the fact that $(X'X)^{-1}$ is a symmetric matrix (equal to its transpose). Assuming that X is nonstochastic, we can move the expectation operator to the term $\varepsilon\varepsilon'$:

$$= (X'X)^{-1}X'E(\varepsilon\varepsilon')X(X'X)^{-1}.$$

Using the results given by (6A.4) and (6A.5), $E(\varepsilon\varepsilon') = \sigma_\varepsilon^2 \cdot I_n$. Substituting this:

$$\begin{aligned}
&= (X'X)^{-1}X'(\sigma_\varepsilon^2 \cdot I_n)X(X'X)^{-1} \\
&= \sigma_\varepsilon^2(X'X)^{-1}X'X(X'X)^{-1}, \qquad \text{so} \\
\text{Var}(\hat{\alpha}) &= \sigma_\varepsilon^2(X'X)^{-1}. \tag{6A.14}
\end{aligned}$$

The diagonal elements of this matrix contain the variances of the least squares coefficients, while its off-diagonals consist of the covariances between these coefficients. When the estimator for σ_ε^2 is substituted into (6A.14), estimated variances and covariances are obtained. This is the basis for the variance formulas given in the text.

Finally, the parameters of the (multivariate) normal distribution for $\hat{\alpha}$ are given by the results for $E(\hat{\alpha})$ and $\text{Var}(\hat{\alpha})$. Summarizing this information:

$$\hat{\alpha} \sim N(\alpha, \sigma_\varepsilon^2(X'X)^{-1})$$

Use of These Results to Obtain the Partial Slope Formulas in the Text

The population regression function used in the text includes two explanatory variables, x and z. The formulas stated in this chapter are derivable using matrices no larger than (2×2), if the starting point for the analysis is the deviation form of the population regression function:

$$y_i' = \alpha_1 x_i' + \alpha_2 z_i' + \varepsilon_i', \tag{6A.15}$$

where the variables in (6A.15) are deviations from means. The least squares intercept estimator, $\hat{\alpha}_0$, is derived once values for $\hat{\alpha}_1$ and $\hat{\alpha}_2$ are calculated using the formula:

$$\hat{\alpha}_0 = \hat{\mu}_y - \hat{\alpha}_1\hat{\mu}_x - \hat{\alpha}_2\hat{\mu}_z.$$

The data matrix (X) used to estimate (6A.15) is the $(n \times 2)$ matrix:

$$X = \begin{bmatrix} x_1' & z_1' \\ \vdots & \vdots \\ x_n' & z_n' \end{bmatrix}$$

The coefficient vector, α, consists of only two elements: α_1 and α_2. The least squares estimator vector is given by the formula:

$$\hat{\alpha} = (X'X)^{-1}X'y$$

The SSCP matrix corresponding to X is:

$$\text{SSCP} = X'X = \begin{bmatrix} \sum x_i'^2 & \sum x_i' z_i' \\ \sum z_i' x_i' & \sum z_i'^2 \end{bmatrix}$$

and the term $X'y$ equals the column vector:

$$X'y = \begin{bmatrix} \sum x_i' y_i' \\ \sum z_i' y_i' \end{bmatrix}$$

The steps involved in calculating the inverse of a (2×2) matrix are not very difficult. Readers unfamiliar with the steps involved should consult the previously cited references. The inverse of $(X'X)$ in the (2×2) case is the product of a scalar, $[1/\det(X'X)]$, and an adjoint matrix that differs from $X'X$ only in: (1) reversing the elements in the principal diagonal of $X'X$; and (2) attaching negative signs to each off-diagonal element in $X'X$. The inverse of $X'X$ is thus:

$$(X'X)^{-1} = [1/\det(X'X)] \begin{bmatrix} \sum z_i'^2 & -\sum x_i' z_i' \\ -\sum z_i' x_i' & \sum x_i'^2 \end{bmatrix}, \tag{6A.16}$$

where $\det(X'X) = \Sigma x_i'^2 \Sigma z_i'^2 - (\Sigma x_i' z_i')^2$. If we denote this determinant D, the least squares estimator vector is obtained from the following multiplication:

$$\hat{\alpha} = [1/D] \begin{bmatrix} \sum z_i'^2 & -\sum x_i' z_i' \\ -\sum z_i' x_i' & \sum x_i'^2 \end{bmatrix} \begin{bmatrix} \sum x_i' y_i' \\ \sum z_i' y_i' \end{bmatrix}$$

The reader is encouraged to perform this multiplication to verify the formulas stated in the text.

The final result given in this appendix is the variance-covariance matrix of the least squares coefficient vector. The general formula for this matrix was given by Equation (6A.14), which is modified to reflect the data matrix labelled X:

$$\text{Var}(\hat{\alpha}) = \sigma_\varepsilon^2 (X'X)^{-1}$$

The estimator $\hat{\sigma}_\varepsilon^2$ is used along with the matrix for $(X'X)^{-1}$ given by (6A.16) to obtain the estimated variance covariance matrix of $\hat{\alpha}$, Σ. The result is:

$$\Sigma = [\hat{\sigma}_\varepsilon^2 / D] \begin{bmatrix} \sum z_i' & -\sum x_i' z_i' \\ -\sum z_i' x_i' & \sum x_i' \end{bmatrix} = \begin{bmatrix} \hat{\sigma}_1^2 & \hat{\sigma}_{12} \\ \hat{\sigma}_{21} & \hat{\sigma}_2^2 \end{bmatrix}$$

where the first diagonal element gives the estimated variance of $\hat{\alpha}_1$, $\hat{\sigma}_1^2$, the second diagonal element is $\hat{\sigma}_2^2$, the variance of $\hat{\alpha}_2$, and either off-diagonal element gives the estimate of the covariance of the least squares coefficients.

7

A Guided Illustration of Variable Selection, Estimation, and the Critiquing of Multiple Regression Equations

Econometric theory, as you have likely noticed by now, is rather extensive. The practice of applied econometrics presupposes more than just this theoretical knowledge. The process of arriving at an acceptable sample regression function entails a great deal in its own right. The basis for the empirical relationship must be set out, based on economic theory or previous research; data must be gathered; and the equation must be estimated. Often the initial sample regression function is refined, based on additional information about the behavior of the dependent variable or problems with the performance of the sample regression function.

Chapters 4 through 6 provided a number of examples that were intended to illustrate the econometric theory that was presented. All these applications, however, were the final versions of relationships under consideration. As a result, the reader was only permitted to "enter" these after their completion. All of the effort and thinking that precedes this was omitted.

This chapter attempts to remedy this deficiency by illustrating the process of specifying, estimating, and critiquing an econometric relationship from beginning to end. The topic selected for this is the demand for consumer durable goods. One noteworthy addition this exercise provides to the applications in previous chapters is a detailed discussion of detecting problems with equations. After reading this chapter, you should be more thoroughly versed in the entire process of generating and judging a sample regression function.

A SUGGESTED PROCEDURE FOR SPECIFYING AND ESTIMATING AN ECONOMETRIC EQUATION

Obtaining an acceptable sample regression function requires more than merely gathering data on a few variables that appear to determine the behavior of the dependent variable of interest then running a least squares regression. Thought and planning is essential to this task. Devoting a substantial amount of time and effort *initially* to develop a properly specified equation usually saves time later, as the likelihood of omitting critical variables is reduced. An outline of the steps involved in this process will now be provided.

Specify the "Ideal" Model

Errors committed in specifying economic relationships often occur as researchers attempt to accomplish too many things at once. Frequently, persons begin this process by attempting simultaneously to specify a set of explanatory variables, identify the specific variables they will need to use, and anticipate potential problems that will be encountered with the estimated equation.

The initial step in this process should focus exclusively on identifying the explanatory variables that should appear in an "ideal" model of the dependent variable under study (where no problems gathering data exist). It is advisable to consult texts from your previous economics courses, references on applied economic topics, or articles dealing with the same or a similar topic. A useful abstract that can be used to find economic articles dealing with your topic is the *Journal of Economic Literature*. This source provides information on a wide range of articles in economic journals. The material in a number of these journals is, however, inaccessible to all but the professional economist. A suggested "short list" of the more readable journals is:

> *Applied Economics*
> *Brookings Papers on Economic Activity*
> *Business Economics*
> *Eastern Economic Journal*
> *Economic Inquiry*
> *Industrial Relations*
> *Journal of Economics and Business*
> *Land Economics*
> *National Tax Journal*
> *Quarterly Journal of Business and Economics*
> *Southern Economic Journal*

In addition to these, various Federal Reserve Banks provide monthly or quarterly publications that include empirical articles on timely topics. Among these are:

> *Economic Review* of the Federal Reserve Bank of Dallas
> *Economic Review* of the Federal Reserve Bank of Kansas City
> *Economic Review* of the Federal Reserve Bank of Richmond
> *New England Economic Review* of the Federal Reserve Bank of Boston
> *Review* of the Federal Reserve Bank of St. Louis

It is critical that you understand the underlying theoretical relationship between your dependent variable and each of the explanatory variables included in the model. If you are unable to ascertain this after consulting your initial set of references, do not hesitate to seek additional material on this topic.

The set of explanatory variables should be stated in *general terms* only. At this point, consider explanatory variables such as "the rate of interest," or "a measure of the ability to pay for this good," without referring to the specific measures that will ultimately be chosen. Also, be sure to distinguish between nominal and real values, as well as levels and growth rates (this is discussed in Chapter 3). For example, the Keynesian consumption function models the behavior of *real* consumption expenditure as a function of *real* income. The Quantity Theory of Money provides a relationship between *nominal* GNP and the *nominal* supply of money. Also, be sure to determine if your dependent variable exhibits cyclical behavior, whether it is affected by a secular trend, if both of these apply, or if neither pertains.

This initial model may differ from the final model since economic theory generally provides us with only a basic blueprint for an economic relationship. It may be necessary to add some variables to this list, based on the specific data used or the underlying nature of the dependent variable. For example, "ability to pay" in a demand function for a consumer durable good should be represented by both income and indebtedness. The acquisition cost of a durable good is best characterized by its price and an appropriate interest rate.

Finally, data gathering should *not* be undertaken at this stage. If this procedure is followed, a well conceived "ground-level" model should result.

Approximate the "Ideal" Model as Closely as Possible with Actual Data

Equipped with a basic theoretical model, we must now obtain actual data for each of the variables in this model. There are a myriad of data sources for time series data. A list of government publications for this type of data was provided in Chapter 3. A number of sources also exist for cross-sectional data. If your model can utilize the 50 states as its cross-sectional units, the *Statistical Abstract of the United States* may be an excellent data source.

If you choose to utilize time series data, it will be necessary to decide a data frequency. Data for many variables are available with frequencies ranging from weekly to annual. The choice of which to use is largely subjective. If your model includes components of GDP or the GDP price deflators, the lowest available frequency published by the government is quarterly. Should you decide to use weekly or monthly data, be aware that economic relationships tend to fluctuate more substantially for weekly or monthly data than with quarterly or annual data.

No matter which type of data you use, it is advisable to have at least three observations for each of the explanatory variables in your model. However, with data, "the more the merrier." Since the least squares estimators are unbiased and consistent (assuming a proper equation specification), estimation precision improves with a larger sample.

The suggested procedure of stating of variables in their general form in the initial step of this process guarantees that one or more of the variables in your "ideal" model will be unavailable in either the exact form you desire it, or by the same name you have assigned it. For example, the variable "ability to pay" does not exist in published data sources. Finding data on "the rate of interest" is complicated by the fact that published data exist for a number of different interest rates. It is thus necessary to make appropriate choices for these variables, or, when needed, to construct proxy variables. A few general guidelines, if followed, will make this task easier. These are:

1. When calculating a real value, select a price index that is as closely tied to the nominal value you wish to convert as possible. For time series data, use GDP deflators to convert any nominal GDP component into a real value, while the CPI can be used to convert wages or other values tied to this index (through cost of living increases). For cross-sectional data, it is preferable to use regional or local price indexes (CPIs) instead of merely dividing all observations by a single index value that pertains for the specific time period of the data.

2. Make sure that the base year for any real value (or price index) is the same for all observations. If this is not the case, use the base year change or "splicing" methods outlined in Chapter 3.

3. When gathering time series data and the data are contained in a number of different issues of a data source, always start from the *most recent* publication and work back to earlier issues. If data for a particular time period are contained in several of these issues, use the most recent publication as the basis for your information, since data revisions may well have occurred. Such revisions can sometimes result in data incompatibilities (e.g., different base years).

4. If any of your variables are derived by manipulating other variables, gather data on each variable separately and perform the calculations using the computer. For example, if real X does not exist, obtain data on nominal X and an appropriate price index; enter this data into a computer; and use the computer to calculate real X.

5. When your choice for a dependent variable is expressed as a quantity, be careful to ascertain whether it reflects demand or supply (if this is the type of function you are estimating). For example, the variable "New Construction," which is affected by demand, is a measure of supply.

6. If an interest rate belongs in your population regression function, its duration should approximate that for the interest cost being modeled. In a consumer durables equation, for example, your choice of interest rate duration should be based on that for actual loans used to finance durable good purchases, approximately three to five years.

Enter the Data on a Computer

Once data representing the variables in your ideal model have been gathered, this information must next be entered into a canned statistical program so that the empirical analysis can proceed. Chapter 3 discussed the general set of steps involved in this process, and illustrated specific commands in SAS and MicroTSP that can be used to accomplish this. No matter which program you use, *make a preliminary effort to determine the accuracy of your data entry before proceeding.* This does not necessarily require that you inspect every observation in your data set. If your data set is large, this will obviously demand a substantial amount of time. Instead, have your program generate summary statistics for each of the variables in your data set, including:

  —the number of valid observations for each variable;

  —the mean of each variable;

  —the (sample) standard deviation for each variable;

  —the minimum value for each variable; and

  —the maximum value for each variable.

When calculating a variable that entails lags, missing observations are generated. The number of missing values should correspond to the highest lag in the variable creation statement (see Chapter 3). Obtaining information on the number of observations for the entire data set allows you to determine whether each variable has the correct number of observations. If any errors occurred when entering these data, it is often possible to determine the affected variables by observing the mean, minimum, and maximum for each variable.

One data manipulation error that sometimes occurs is the result of attempting to create a new variable, the natural logarithm of an existing variable, whose values can be negative (or 0). Since the natural logarithm of a negative value or 0 does not exist, your canned computer program will respond with an error message. As an example of this, consider an explanatory variable that is the change in x: $\Delta x = x_t - x_{t-1}$. When values of x both rise and fall, some of the values for this variable will be negative. As a result, the variable $\ln(\Delta x)$ cannot be created. A solution to this exists. Instead of creating $\ln(\Delta x)$, we can define this new variable as $\ln(x_t/x_{t-1})$, which is the proportionate change (growth rate) in x. As long as x is never 0 or negative, the logarithm of the ratio x_t/x_{t-1} will always exist.

When working with time series data, it is advisable to plot your dependent variable against time. This can often assist in determining whether any seasonality exists, or if cyclical or secular trends are present. At any rate, such a plot provides a more intuitive summary of the behavior of your dependent variable than does a review of its summary statistics.

Other data plots are possible. Frequently persons create a scatter diagram with the dependent variable on the vertical axis and a particular explanatory variable on the horizontal axis as the basis for determining the expected sign of a coefficient. This is not advisable for two reasons. First, the expected sign of a coefficient should be obtained from economic theory or previous empirical research (possibly in a journal, for example). Second, the patterns provided by scatter diagrams such as this are often misleading. Consider, for example, the demand for consumer durables, which depends on, among other things, interest rates and real income. A scatter diagram of real consumer durables expenditure (vertical axis) and the selected interest rate

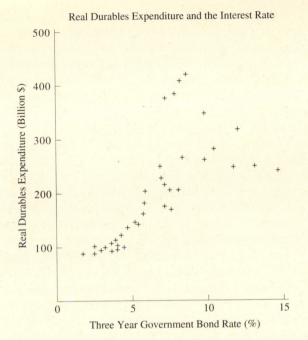

Real Durables Expenditure and the Interest Rate

Figure 7.1

(horizontal axis) will reveal a positive relationship between these variables, as Figure 7.1 shows. Using the information in this diagram as the basis for the expected sign of the interest rate results in an incorrect conclusion about the relationship between this pair of variables. This scatter diagram fails to control for factors *other than* interest rates that influence durable good demand. The upward slope occurs since rising interest rates typically accompany economic expansions, causing interest rates and real income to rise simultaneously. Because this scatter diagram does not control for rising income, its positive slope reflects the relationship between durable good demand and real income.

Estimate the Regression Relationship

The sample regression function can now be estimated. Depending on the particular canned program you use, obtain or review a number of indicators of equation performance, such as actual and predicted *y* values, a plot of residuals, and so forth.

It is critical to assess the overall performance of the sample regression function. The suggested procedure, which was outlined in Chapters 4 through 6, consists of the following sequence:

1. Assess the sign of each coefficient. If an expectation exists for a coefficient, verify that this sign is obtained. Pay special attention to the equation intercept. When its expected sign is known, an incorrect sign often reveals a likely problem with the specification of the sample regression function (see Chapters 4 and 6).

2. Evaluate the magnitude of each coefficient. Attempt to determine whether each is "reasonable." Sometimes a coefficient magnitude will appear to be large when a one-unit change is considered (the mechanical interpretation), but a typical change may be only one-tenth or one-half. If you have no idea about the reasonableness of a magnitude, consider converting the coefficient into an elasticity if you have information about the elasticity range the coefficient should fall into.

3. Determine the statistical significance of each coefficient. If an expected sign pertains, use a one-tail test. When theoretical or empirical information exists about the magnitude of a coefficient, such as a value less than 1, test a hypothesis for this value along with the usual test of statistical significance. *If a theoretical basis exists for including a particular variable in your equation, do not omit it if it fails a significance test.* Instead, reconsider whether the actual variable used provides an adequate representation of the theoretical factor it is supposed to represent. For example, use of the overall CPI when the price of a specific good is called for can result in a nonsignificant CPI coefficient (it may also display an incorrect sign). The same considerations pertain for a set of non-significant variables (see the next point).

4. If several of the coefficients in the sample regression function fail individual tests of statistical significance, test their joint significance with a Wald test (see Chapter 6). If theory establishes the importance of this set of variables, do not drop them from the estimated equation even if you are unable to establish their statistical significance with either t-tests or a Wald test.

5. Judge the overall equation performance measures: the equation standard error; the coefficient of variation (you may have to manually calculate this); the equation F-statistic; and $\bar{R}^2$. Is the equation F-value statistically significant? Is the coefficient of variation less than 0.2 (or 20)? Remember that cross-sectional equations will tend to have smaller R^2 values than time series equations. It is therefore unwise to place undue weight on the value of this measure. Additional information can be provided by an ex-post forecast of the relationship under study (see Chapter 5). Is the root mean square error of this forecast substantially larger than the in-sample equation standard error? Is the mean absolute percent error large? Do the predictions consistently underpredict or overpredict?

6. If you are comparing this equation to a previously estimated one, remember that the values of R^2 and $\hat{\sigma}_\varepsilon$ for equations with different dependent variables (such as y and $\ln(y)$) cannot be compared. Other criteria must therefore be used before this determination can be made.

7. Check the plot of residuals for outliers (large equation errors). For time series data, it is informative to observe when these occur. Outliers may result from data entry errors, so it may be worthwhile to check your data to make sure the data are correctly entered. Obtain a scatter diagram of the equation residuals (vertical axis) and predicted y (horizontal axis). Does any curvature exist within this diagram? If so, nonlinearities (in the explanatory variables) may exist. Examples of this, along with information on different equation specifications, are provided in Chapter 8.

If the initial sample regression function is deemed unsatisfactory, it might not be necessary to reconsider changing the entire sample regression function. *Because data are imperfect, a well-specified equation can possibly contain one or more coefficients with incorrect signs or nonsignificant coefficients.* If you continually estimate different variations of your original equation until obtaining a set of coefficients that display expected signs and are statistical significant, the final product may be far afield of what you started out with. The specification/estimation sequence suggested here should eliminate the need for such "data torture." An illustration of this suggested sequence that focuses on the demand for consumer durable goods is presented next.

THE DEMAND FOR CONSUMER DURABLE GOODS

The demand function for a single good can be utilized as a starting point for the specification of a time-series demand equation for consumer durable goods. The basic form of this function for a good X in time period t is:

$$q_{xt} = f(p_{xt}, p_{yt}, I_t, p_t^e, \varepsilon_t),$$

where q_x = quantity of X demanded; p_x and p_y are the prices of goods X and Y, respectively; I is income; p^e is the expected future price of X, and ε is the stochastic error. The own price variable, p_x, measures the direct cost of acquiring this good, while income represents the ability to pay for X. The expected sign of p_x is negative for the reasons stated in Chapter 4: a change in p_x alters both the relative price of X and real income (assuming p_y, I, and p^e are constant). The sign of p_y depends on whether Y is a substitute or complement for X. When Y is a substitute, the sign of p_y is positive, while a negative sign pertains when Y is a complement. The expected sign of I is positive when X is a normal good. This is certainly true for durable goods. Finally, expected future price is directly related to q_x this period.

In order for us to extend the general framework provided by demand theory to durable goods, we must add two other variables to this equation. The first of these is related to the cost of acquiring this good. The expense involved in purchasing a durable good involves a cost in addition to its purchase price. Typically it is necessary to borrow the needed funds to purchase a durable good. In this case the interest cost is an explicit cost that must be counted in addition to purchase price. If personal funds are used to purchase a durable good, the rate of interest becomes an implicit cost. In either case, a measure of the interest cost of acquiring durable goods must be added to this equation. The expected sign of this variable is negative.

The other variable that must be accounted for reflects the ability to pay for durable goods. Because of the expense involved in purchasing durable goods, ability to pay is determined by both income and the extent of indebtedness. Failure to control for the impact of debt implicitly assumes that higher income raises the ability to pay. However, when personal indebtedness is high, increases in income must be directed either exclusively or substantially toward the repayment of debt and not toward the purchase of durable goods. We must therefore include a measure of indebtedness among the explanatory variables in our equation. The level of debt should not be used for this purpose, however, as it is possible for indebtedness to rise at the same time ability to purchase durable goods increases. This occurs when debt falls relative to income. The measure of indebtedness that is utilized, which avoids this problem, is the ratio of debt to income. The expected sign of this variable is negative.

We can now add this information to the original demand function. Omitting the time subscript, our demand function becomes:

$$q_x = f(p_x, p_y, r, I, (D/I), p^e, \varepsilon)$$

where p_x and p_y are the prices of X and Y, respectively;
r is the rate of interest;
I is the level of income;
(D/I) is the debt-income ratio;
p^e is the expected future price of X; and
ε is a stochastic error.

This equation must now be adapted to aggregate time series data. The dependent variable in the estimated equation, which is our measure of consumer durable good demand, is *real* consumer durable goods expenditure, q_d. This measure is preferable to nominal durable goods expenditure because nominal expenditures, like nominal values in general, are susceptible to distortions caused by inflation. Recall that nominal expenditure is the product of price and quantity: $p \cdot q$. Real expenditure, which is obtained by dividing nominal expenditure by a price index, thus approximates q (think of the p's as canceling). Our initial specification for q_d is therefore:

$$q_d = f(p_d, p_r, r, I, (D/I), p^e, \varepsilon),$$

where p_d is a price *index* for durable goods; p_r is a price index for related goods; and the remaining terms are the same as above. Since the dependent variable is part of the National Income and Product accounts, prices most closely related to this variable are obtained using the Implicit Price Deflator. The choice for p_d is the IPD for consumer durable goods expenditure. We must next determine a specific IPD component to represent the prices of related goods. Two obvious choices for this are the overall Implicit Price Deflator, and the IPD for Personal Consumption Expenditures (p_c). Since durable good demand competes with other elements of consumption and not all goods produced in the economy, the preferable measure is p_c.

The next variable that must be specified more precisely is the measure of the interest cost of acquiring durable goods. Many interest rates exist. These differ in terms of risk and maturity. In modeling the consumer durable good purchase decision, we must approximate the actual basis of this decision as accurately as possible. Such purchases, when they involve borrowed funds, have loan durations that extend anywhere from six months to five years. We use the rate on three-year government bonds to approximate the interest cost for persons deciding whether to buy a durable good, since three years is an accurate depiction of the average durations of such loans.

However, because such a wide range of potential choices exists for our interest rate variable, the equation will be estimated with two different interest rates so that the effects of variable selection can be illustrated. The other interest rate considered is a short term interest rate, the rate on three-month treasury bills (r_s).

An appropriate measure of income is some variant of disposable personal income (DPI). The expected sign of this variable is positive, since consumer durable goods are normal goods. Additional information about this coefficient exists as well: its coefficient (the marginal propensity to consume durable goods) is expected to be less than one, and consumer durable demand is income elastic. All of this information will prove useful when judging the estimated equation. The value of DPI is not the measure of ability to pay selected for inclusion into the estimated equation, since it is a nominal value and it includes transfer payments. As the result of both of these considerations, DPI will tend to overstate the ability to purchase consumer durables. To correct this problem, real disposable personal income net of transfer paymets (y_d) is utilized as our measure of ability to pay. This variable is calculated as follows. Nominal transfer payments are converted into real values using the IPD for Personal Consumption Expenditures. The value of real transfer payments for each year is then subtracted from real disposable personal income, giving real disposable personal income net of (real) transfer payments. The expected sign of this variable is positive.

Indebtedness is represented by the ratio of real total consumer debt (calculated with the IPD for personal consumption expenditure) to real GNP (c/y).[1] Because the equation is estimated with annual data (see below), the one-period lag of this ratio is employed as the measure of indebtedness, since it is *total* debt (which takes time to accumulate) that hinders durable purchases. Note that by evaluating indebtedness relative to real GNP, the ratio (c/y) rises only when real consumer credit grows faster than the growth rate in y, the rate of economic growth. Other things being equal, an increase in real credit relative to real GNP decreases the ability to afford additional debt, resulting in lower real consumer durable expenditure. The expected sign of this indebtedness proxy is therefore negative.

A variable representing the impact of expected future price on real consumer durable expenditure is not included directly in the estimated equation. The influence of expected price is reflected in the inflationary premium included in the nominal interest rate variable. This premium measures anticipated future inflation, which is correlated with the expected future prices of durable goods.

One additional variable that is included in the estimated equation is a proxy variable that represents the influence of the expected future state of the economy, or future income uncertainty, on consumer durable purchases. A number of possible choices exist.[2] The measure utilized here is the change in the civilian unemployment

---

[1] Data for GDP became available *after* this chapter went to press. As a result, GNP is used for this equation and all of its supporting applications.

[2] Examples are the Consumer Sentiment Index from *Business Conditions Digest*, last year's unemployment rate, or a moving average of past unemployment rates.

rate (u) at time t: $\Delta u_t = (u_t - u_{t-1})$. An increase in Δu_t indicates that the unemployment rate this year has risen relative to its level for last year, which is assumed to signal a deteriorating future state of the economy, and greater uncertainty about future income. Other things being equal, this change will decrease real consumer durable expenditure. The expected sign of Δu is thus negative.

The data used to estimate the real consumer durable expenditure equation consists of annual observations for the years 1953 to 1989 from the 1990 *Economic Report of the President*. The specification of our initial equation is:

$$q_{dt} = f(p_{dt}, p_{ct}, r_{Lt}, y_{dt}, (c/y)_{t-1}, \Delta u_t, \varepsilon_t)$$

where for year t:

q_d = real consumer durable good expenditure (billions of 1982 dollars);
p_d = IPD for Consumer Durable Goods Expenditure (1982 = 100);
p_c = IPD for Personal Consumption Expenditure (1982 = 100);
r_L = interest rate on three-year Government bonds (percent);
y_d = real disposable personal income net of transfer payments (billions of 1982 dollars);
c = real total consumer credit (millions of 1982 dollars);
y = real GNP (billions of 1982 dollars);
u = civilian unemployment rate (percent); and
ε = stochastic error term.

The resulting sample regression function is given below. The value in parenthesis below each coefficient is the absolute value of its t-statistic. For 30 degrees of freedom, the critical t-value for a one-tail test is 1.697 for the 5 percent level of significance, and 2.457 for the 1 percent significance level.

$$\hat{q}_{dt} = -52.5 - 0.858p_{dt} + 1.53p_{ct} - 6.47r_{Lt} + 0.210y_{dt} - 4.67(c/y)_{t-1} - 2.91\,\Delta u_t$$
$$\quad\quad (3.0)\quad (1.1)\quad\quad (2.6)\quad\quad (6.5)\quad\quad (11.9)\quad\quad (2.5)\quad\quad\quad\quad (2.9)$$

$$\bar{R}^2 = 0.996 \quad \hat{\sigma}_\varepsilon = 6.55 \quad F = 1465.0 \quad \hat{\mu}_q = 200.7$$

All coefficients in this equation display the correct sign. Only p_d fails to attain statistical significance at either the 5 percent or 1 percent level for a one-tail test. Further investigation of the coefficient of p_{dt} indicates an additional problem: the estimated elasticity of demand is inelastic, indicating a magnitude below our prior expectation. To estimate the elasticity of durable good demand for the 1983–1989 period, we use the average of p_d for this period, 106.54, along with the resulting $\hat{q}$ (with all other variables equal to their means), 367.79:

$$\hat{\eta}_d = (p_d/\hat{q}_d)(\Delta\hat{q}_d/\Delta p_d)$$
$$= (106.54/367.79)(-0.858)$$
$$= -0.249$$

Our estimate of the elasticity of durables demand is thus in the inelastic range. No obvious problems exist with the other coefficients, or the measures of overall equation performance. How, then, should we proceed in light of this problem with the sample regression function?

If our interest lies in estimating the demand curve for durable goods or their price elasticity, we must either review the underlying basis for this relationship, find a way to work around this problem, or use the sample regression function above with some reservations. *Dropping the variable p_d from our estimated equation should not be considered as a viable option.*

The underlying theoretical basis for this equation is sound. In an attempt to work around the problem with the price coefficient, let us first see why it arises. Our sample regression function includes the prices of consumer durable goods and consumption prices as separate variables. However, when estimating a relationship such as this a potential problem can arise: a well-chosen measure of substitute good price will tend to be correlated with the price for this good. To see this, let us return to the goods X and Y. When Y is a substitute for X, the demand curve for X shifts in response to variations in p_y. This, in turn, causes p_x to change. In econometric analysis this is called multicollinearity. Multicollinearity does not always cause estimation problems, although in this particular example it does. The least squares technique attempts to estimate the *independent* effect of each price on q_d. The nature of our data limits the ability of our estimation technique to do this, since p_d and p_c tend to move together. For the estimation period, the correlation coefficient between p_d and p_c is 0.996. Because of this large correlation, the precision with which least squares is able to estimate these separate effects is adversely affected. Our estimates thus have greater variances than would be the case were there no such correlation. These greater variances, in turn, increase the range of possible estimates we can expect to obtain. The likelihood of obtaining an inelastic estimate for p_d such as the one here rises.

Excluding this variable, even though it is correlated with p_c, results in specification error. This should not be viewed as a viable solution to this problem. *You should never specify an equation "defensively."* The relevant question therefore shifts to *how* we can include p_y.

Two options exist for dealing with this potential problem: retain our original sample regression function, which includes these variables separately; or combine these into a new variable that possesses a valid economic meaning. The solution adopted here is to combine these prices into the ratio (p_d/p_c), which is called the relative price of consumer durables. Changes in this relative price are inversely related to q_d, so the expected sign of (p_d/p_c) is the same as that for p_d. The relative price of consumer durables changes if only p_d changes; if only p_c changes; if both p_d and p_c change by different proportions. Note that the demand curve for consumer durables assumes a constant value for p_c, so that any change in p_c alters the relative price of consumer durables.[3]

---

[3] Readers familiar with intermediate or advanced microeconomics should recognize that (p_d/p_c) corresponds to the absolute value of the slope of a budget constraint in commodity space, (p_x/p_y).

We now modify the specification of our equation to include the relative price of consumer durable goods. In addition to this, we estimate a second equation that differs from the first only in its inclusion of the three-month treasury bill rate, r_s, in place of the three-year rate, r_L. As indicated above, this is presented to illustrate how the "goodness of fit" of our estimated relationship is affected by the choice of the less suitable interest rate. The equations that are now estimated are:

$$q_{dt} = f\{(p_d/p_c)_t, r_{Lt}, y_{dt}, (c/y)_{t-1}, \Delta u_t, \varepsilon_{1t}\} \qquad \text{(7.1)}$$

$$q_{dt} = f\{(p_d/p_c)_t, r_{st}, y_{dt}, (c/y)_{t-1}, \Delta u_t, \varepsilon_{2t}\} \qquad \text{(7.2)}$$

The least squares estimates of these equations are presented in Table 7.1.

Both relative price coefficients are statistically significant at the 1 percent level and above, and display the expected negative sign. The estimated impact of relative price on real durable goods expenditure is similar for both equations. The estimated coefficients range from -1.95 to -2.25, for an average of -2.1. Other things being equal, a 1 percent increase in durable good prices relative to all consumption prices lowers the mean of q_d by \$2.1 billion.

Both of these coefficients indicate (relative) price inelastic durable good demand when we use the 1983–1989 averages for (p_d/p_c) (of 92.1) and the other variables in this equation, along with the resulting $\hat{q}$ (of 367.8). The estimated partial price elasticity using Equation (7.1) is:

$$\hat{\eta}_d = [(p_d/p_c)/\hat{q}_d](-2.25)$$
$$= (92.1/367.8)(-2.25)$$
$$= -0.563.$$

Note that the t-statistic of the relative price coefficient is higher in the equation that includes the three-year government interest rate as the measure of the interest cost of acquiring durable goods. Since this estimated elasticity falls outside of the expected range for relative price (we expect elastic demand), some problems with the equation in its current form are indicated. This is pursued further in Chapter 8.

Estimates of the effect of changes in the interest cost of acquiring durable goods on real durable goods expenditure differ noticeably between these equations. The interest rate coefficients vary from -6.86 when r_s is included, to -8.01 when the three-year government interest rate is used. A 1 percent increase in the interest cost of acquiring durable goods is predicted to lower mean real durable goods expenditure by \$8 billion in the equation with r_L, and by \$6.9 billion when r_s is used, other things being equal. Both coefficients are statistically significant at the 1 percent level and above. Using Equation (7.1), the estimated partial interest elasticity of durable good demand ($\hat{\eta}_r$) for the period 1983–1989 (the average of r_L is 9.08) is:

$$\hat{\eta}_r = (r_L/\hat{q}_d)(-8.01)$$
$$= (9.08/367.8)(-8.01)$$
$$= -0.198$$

which indicates that real consumer durables expenditure is interest inelastic.

Table 7.1 Dependent Variable: Real Consumer Durables Expenditure (1982 = 100)

Sample Period: 1953–1989 (Absolute values of t-statistics in parentheses)

VARIABLE	(1)	(2)
Intercept	309.2	247.6
	(3.1)	(2.1)
$(p_d/p_c)_t$	−2.25	−1.95
	(3.6)	(2.6)
r_{Lt}	−8.01	—
	(10.5)	
r_{st}	—	−6.86
		(8.3)
y_{dt}	0.207	0.203
	(7.2)	(5.9)
$(c/y)_{t-1}$	−8.43	−6.92
	(4.2)	(2.9)
Δu_t	−4.27	−4.59
	(3.2)	(2.9)

EQUATION STATISTICS		
$\bar{R}^2$	0.994	0.992
$\hat{\sigma}_\varepsilon$	7.95	9.45
ESS	1959.5	2769.5
F	1192.3	841.7
$\hat{\mu}_q$	200.7	200.7
n	37	37

EX-POST FORECAST STATISTICS (1983–1989)		
RMSE	29.18	33.23
MAPE	6.77	7.49
Mean	343.7	340.9
Std. Dev.	36.1	32.1

Estimates of the marginal propensity to consume durable goods, which correspond to the coefficients of y_d, range from 0.203 to 0.207. Both coefficients are statistically significant at the 1 percent and above. A \$1 rise in y_d increases mean real consumer durable expenditure by one-fifth of \$1, other things being equal. We can convert this into an income elasticity so that it can be judged within the framework of our prior expectations. The estimated income elasticity ($\hat{\eta}_y$) of real durable goods expenditure (1983–1989) is:

$$\hat{\eta}_y = (y_d/\hat{q}_d)(0.2)$$
$$= (2171.4/367.8)(0.2)$$
$$= 1.18,$$

where 2171.4 is the mean of y_d over this period. The demand for consumer durable goods is thus income elastic.

The indebtedness variable displays the expected negative sign. Its estimated coefficient is statistically significant at the 1 percent level and above in both equations. Parameter estimates vary from -6.92 to -8.43, with an average of -7.68. Given the relative price of consumer durables, income, interest rates, and expectations of the future state of the economy, a 1 percent increase in real consumer credit as a percent of real GNP lowers the mean of q_d in the *following* year by $8.4 billion (using Equation (7.1)).

The estimated impact of the expected future state of the economy on real durable good expenditure is negative and statistically significant at the 1 percent level and above in both equations. Values of the estimated coefficients for Δu range from -4.27 to -4.59, with an average of -4.43. Other things being equal, a 1 percent increase in the difference between the civilian unemployment rate last year and this year lowers the mean of current real durable goods expenditure by $4.3 billion (for Equation (7.1)).

Before discussing which equation is preferable, it is worthwhile to point out that while the magnitudes of many of the partial rates of change in these equations may at times appear to be small, these pertain to changes in *real* consumer durable goods expenditure. The corresponding response of nominal consumer durables expenditure to these changes is therefore larger. Their divergence is determined by the rate of inflation. If, for example, the rate of inflation remains constant at, say, 5 percent annually, then, even when real consumer durables expenditure is unchanged, its nominal value rises by 5 percent each year. To illustrate the importance of this difference, we will assume that q_d equals its predicted value of $367.8 billion, in what is defined to be the base year for this exercise. Let us assume that r_L rises from its sample mean of 9.08 percent in this base period to 10.08 percent in the next period, and that none of the other variables in Equation (7.1) change. This movement in interest rates lowers the mean of *real* consumer durables expenditure by $8 billion to $359.8 billion. Were it not for this change, then, with a 5 percent annual inflation rate, the mean of *nominal* consumer durables expenditure would have risen from $367.8 billion to $386.2 billion ($= 367.8 \cdot 1.05$), an increase of $18.4 billion. When this interest rate change occurs, the mean of nominal durable good expenditure increases from $367.8 billion to $377.8 ($= 359.8 \cdot 1.05$), a $10 billion rise. The ultimate increase in mean (nominal) expenditure is thus slightly more than half the value it would have attained were it not for the rise in interest rates.

Based on the signs, magnitudes, and statistical significance of the coefficients in each of these equations, their performance is satisfactory. Upon what basis, then, can we decide which is the preferable equation? Clearly, we must consider the measures of overall equation performance in addition to individual coefficients. An important difference in the performance of these equations emerges using this information: the values of ESS and $\hat{\sigma}_\varepsilon$ are smaller, while equation F-statistic is higher, in Equation (7.1). The values of $\bar{R}^2$, however, differ only slightly between these equations.

If we choose not to test the forecasting ability of these equations, we must base our selection of which equation is preferable on coefficient evaluation and equation statistics. Using this set of criteria, Equation (7.1) is chosen as the preferable equation, since its performance, in terms of the overall equation and individual coefficient is superior to Equation (7.2). The final decision, however, will be based on the additional information provided by the ex-post forecasting performance of these equations. Forecasts were obtained by estimating each equation for the period from 1953 to 1982, then using these in-sample coefficients along with actual values of the explanatory variables to produce forecasted values of q_d for the years 1983 to 1989. The forecast statistics are given by the bottom set of values in the equation table. The reader is referred to Chapter 5 for a discussion of these statistics.

The root mean square error (RMSE) corresponds to the standard error of the equation during the forecast period. Its unit of measurement is the same as that for q_d. Values of RMSE are 29.2 for Equation (7.1) and 33.2 for Equation (7.2). While Equation (7.1) has the smaller RMSE, it is a slightly larger multiple of $\hat{\sigma}_\varepsilon$ than is true for Equation (7.2). The RMSE for Equation (7.1) is 3.67 times its standard error, while for Equation (7.2), the RMSE is 3.52 times $\hat{\sigma}_\varepsilon$. The mean absolute percent error (MAPE) allows us to consider the relative magnitude of these forecast errors. The smaller MAPE occurs with Equation (7.1), whose average absolute forecast error is 6.77 percent of the forecast period values of the dependent variable, while the MAPE for the other equation is 7.49 percent. The final forecast criterion considered here evaluates the ability of these forecasts to replicate the mean and standard deviation of the actual values of q_d during the forecast period. While the mean and standard deviation of the predicted values from Equation (7.1) come closer to replicating the corresponding measures for actual RCDUR, they are still substantially below actual values. For example, the standard deviation in Equation (7.1), which comes closer to replicating the dispersion in q_d, is only 71 percent of that for q_d, versus a value of 63 percent for Equation (7.2) (the actual standard deviation in q_d over this period is 50.86).

Based on all of these results, Equation (7.1) is judged to be the better sample regression function. Its in-sample and ex-post performance surpass that of the other equation. Equation (7.1) is not without fault, however. The mean and standard deviation of its forecasts are unacceptably low. Its RMSE is 3.7 times the estimation period standard error. All of this points to the need for some modification of this equation to improve its overall performance. This is especially important if this equation is to be used for forecasting, since its predictions understate the actual values of RCDUR for all but one of the years in the forecast period. One possible basis for this modification can be seen by referring to Figure 7.2. The scatter diagram in (a) plots the residuals and predicted values from our preferred equation, while (b) plots the residuals and the relative price variable. Figure 7.2(b) contains some curvature, pointing to the likelihood of nonlinearity in the specification of the consumer durables demand relationship. This is pursued further in Chapter 8.

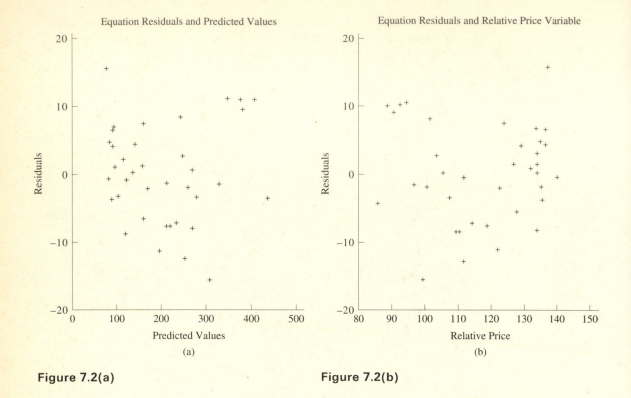

Figure 7.2(a)   Figure 7.2(b)

Finally, note how the use of ex-post forecast performance provided us with information about potential problems that the usual criteria failed to indicate. As this example illustrates, it is possible for an equation to fit the data well according to the usual (estimation period) standards, yet to perform poorly when used to forecast.

SOME ADDITIONAL DIAGNOSTIC INFORMATION: INFLUENCE STATISTICS

The consumer durables equations discussed above appeared to perform well, based on the usual criteria for judging sample regression functions. When the ex-post forecasting ability of these equations was tested, potential problems appeared. One possible explanation is that the coefficients in our sample regression functions may be influenced disproportionately by the data from 1983 to 1989 rather than that for the entire estimation period. It is also possible for particular years to influence coefficients substantially. How can we ascertain whether or when such years of significant influence occurred? Information detailing how substantially our coefficients rely on particular observations, called **influence statistics**, exist that can assist us in making this determination.[4] We will focus on four of these. The first determines whether or not an observation can be considered a "leverage point." The remaining measures evaluate the magnitude of the differences in residuals, individual coefficients, and predicted values that occur when a particular observation is omitted. We now discuss these measures.

Leverage Values

Detecting whether the explanatory variable values for a particular observation constitute an outlier with a multiple regression equation can be a difficult task. When an equation includes one or two explanatory variables, a simple plot will reveal where outliers occur. For three or more variables, this information can be obtained from a measure called the **leverage value**, or **leverage** of each data point. Essentially, these measure the distance of the x values for a particular observation from means of the x's for all observations. A large leverage value thus indicates that the x values for an observation differ substantially from the point of means for those variables. We can gain some insight into leverage values by considering the following bivariate regression[5]:

$$y_i = \alpha_0 + \alpha_1 x_i + \varepsilon_i$$

The predicted value of y for the first observation from this equation is:

$$\hat{y}_1 = \hat{\alpha}_0 + \hat{\alpha}_1 x_1$$

which, substituting for the $\hat{\alpha}$'s, can be written:

$$\hat{y}_1 = \hat{\mu}_y + \hat{\alpha}_1 (x_1 - \hat{\mu}_x)$$
$$= \sum y_i/n + x'_1(\sum x'_i y_i / \sum x_i'^2)$$

where $x'_i \equiv (x_i - \hat{\mu}_x)$.[6] Expressing this in terms of $\sum y_i$:

$$\hat{y}_1 = \sum y_i [1/n + x'_1 x'_i / \sum x_i'^2]$$

Writing this for individual y values:

$$\hat{y}_1 = [1/n + x_1'^2 / \sum x_i'^2] y_1 + [1/n + x'_1 x'_2 / \sum x_i'^2] y_2 + \cdots + [1/n + x'_1 x'_n / \sum x_i'^2] y_n,$$

---

[4] This section is based on D. Belsley, E. Kuh, and R. Welsch, *Regression Diagnostics: Identifying Influential Data And Sources of Collinearity* (New York: John Wiley), 1980, and J. Neter, W. Wasserman, and M. Kutner, *Applied Linear Statistical Models*, 3d. ed. (Homewood, IL: Richard D. Irwin), 1990.

[5] Obviously, the detection of outliers with a single explanatory variable is easily accomplished using visual inspection. This type of equation is used here because of the ease with which the values of H can be determined. Reference to a bivariate regression equation is thus for illustration purposes only.

[6] Note that in the bracketed expression for $\hat{\alpha}_1$ on the right, y_i is used in place of y'_i.

or

$$\hat{y}_1 = H_{11}y_1 + H_{12}y_2 + \cdots + H_{1n}y_n$$

where $H_{1i} \equiv [1/n + x_1'x_i'/\Sigma x_i'^2]$. As this equation shows, the predicted value of y for the first observation is a weighted average of all the values of y. The weights are the values H_{1i}. The term H_{11} in this equation, which designates the weight of y_1 in the determination of $\hat{y}_1$, is the leverage value of observation 1. The greater this value, the more influential is y_1 in the determination of $\hat{y}_1$. Given the value of n in this equation, H_{11} is large when the deviation of x_1 from $\hat{\mu}_x$ is large relative to overall dispersion in x as measured by the sum of the squared x deviations for the entire sample of x values. As indicated above, this makes x_1 an outlier.

The leverage value for an observation is also related to the variance of the residual (not the equation error) for that observation:

$$\text{Var}(\hat{\varepsilon}_i) \equiv \hat{\sigma}_{\hat{\varepsilon}_i}^2 = \sigma_\varepsilon^2(1 - H_{ii}),$$

where H_{ii} is the leverage for observation i. Leverage values are thus inversely related to residual variances. The larger H_{ii} is, the smaller $\text{Var}(\hat{\varepsilon}_i)$, which tends to make $\hat{y}_i$ close to y_i. Leverage values also possess the following properties:

    (i) $0 \le H_{ii} \le 1$; and
    (ii) $\Sigma H_{ii} = k$

where k is the number of coefficients including the intercept. Thus, if $H_{ii} = 1$, $\text{Var}(\hat{\varepsilon}_i) = 0$, and $\hat{y}_i = y_i$. Also, a leverage value is "large," meaning it is likely to indicate an influential observation, if it is two or more times the mean of the entire set of leverage values.[7] Using (ii) above, the mean leverage value is k/n. A leverage value is therefore "large" when it exceeds $2(k/n)$. A point where $H_{ii} > 2(k/n)$ is called a **leverage point**.

Studentized Residuals

The residuals for a sample regression function indicate the amount by which values of y and $\hat{y}$ diverge. Intuitively, large residuals should be indicative of "problem" or influential values for $\hat{y}$. This is not necessarily the case. An influential observation can have either a small or large residual. The previous section indicated the reason for this: since $\hat{\sigma}_{\hat{\varepsilon}_i}^2 = \hat{\sigma}_\varepsilon^2(1 - H_{ii})$, a leverage point residual will tend to be small, because it emanates from a probability density function whose variance is low. Our ability to detect influential observations using equation residuals is thus limited.

Two improvements are generally made with the equation residuals that enhance their ability to detect influential observations. While the equation errors possess a constant variance and are pairwise uncorrelated according to the multiple regression model assumptions, this is not true for the equation residuals. The set of residuals

---

[7] D. Belsley, et al., *Regression Diagnostics*, 1980, p. 17.

have unequal variances and are correlated.[8] The first improvement eliminates the unequal residual variances: the residual is standardized. The **standardized residual**, $\hat{\varepsilon}_{(s)i}$, is defined as:

$$\hat{\varepsilon}_{(s)i} = \hat{\varepsilon}_i / \hat{\sigma}_{\hat{\varepsilon}_i}$$

where $\hat{\sigma}_{\hat{\varepsilon}_i}$ is the square root of the expression: $\hat{\sigma}_{\varepsilon}^2(1 - H_{ii})$. Since the mean residual is 0 (from the multiple regression normal equations), the numerator in this expression is simply $\hat{\varepsilon}_i$. When the equation errors are normally distributed, we expect approximately 95 of them to fall within two standard deviations of 0 (their mean). Since standardized residuals follow the t-distribution, we also expect to observe 95 percent of these falling within two standard deviations of 0 for large samples. When 5 percent or more of our residuals have standardized values greater than 2 (or the relevant t-value), the normal distribution of the equation errors should be questioned. Thus, standardized residuals greater in value than 2 (or the relevant t-value with 2.5 percent in each tail) potentially indicate influential observations.

This last conclusion is not very definitive since standardized residuals are calculated using all observations, including the ones that are influential. The ability of these residuals to detect influential observations can be improved if they are instead based on a set of coefficients that is produced when influential observations are deleted. The basis for this is not difficult to establish. Least squares uses all observations, including outliers, to derive a set of coefficients. These coefficients and predicted values are thus affected by such outliers. The residual for an influential observation will tend to be small (based on its large value for H_{ii}) since the value of $\hat{y}$ for this observation will be closer to the actual y than were this observation omitted. Consider, then, a modification of this residual based on this last consideration. It is called the **deletion residual** ($\hat{\varepsilon}_{(d)i}$). Such a residual is generated as follows. We first delete observation i from our data set, then estimate our sample regression function using the remaining $n - 1$ observations. Assuming the bivariate regression equation above, we will denote the resulting coefficients as $\hat{\alpha}_0(i)$ and $\hat{\alpha}_1(i)$. The first of these, $\hat{\alpha}_0(i)$, is the estimated intercept when observation i is deleted, while $\hat{\alpha}_1(i)$ is the accompanying slope estimate. An alternative prediction for y_i can also be generated using these coefficients along with the value for the explanatory variable for this observation:

$$\hat{y}_i(i) = \hat{\alpha}_0(i) + \hat{\alpha}_1(i)x_i$$

where $\hat{y}_i(i)$ is the prediction for observation i based on the coefficients derived when this observation is deleted. The deletion residual is the difference between the actual y value for this observation and this predicted value:

$$\hat{\varepsilon}_{(d)i} = y_i - \hat{y}_i(i)$$

---

[8] See, for example, H. Theil, *Principles of Econometrics* (New York: John Wiley & Sons), 1970. In general, the residual variances are obtained from the following expression for the variance-covariance matrix of the vector of residuals, $\hat{\varepsilon}$: $\text{Var}(\hat{\varepsilon}) = \hat{\sigma}_{\varepsilon}^2 M$, where $M = (I - X(X'X)^{-1}X')$, and X is the $(n \times k)$ data matrix used to estimate the sample regression function.

This residual is related to the usual residual (based on the entire sample) in the following way:

$$\hat{\varepsilon}_{(d)i} = \hat{\varepsilon}_i/(1 - H_{ii})$$

While the residual for an influential observation will tend to be small, its leverage value, H_{ii}, will tend to be large, potentially leading to a large value for $\hat{\varepsilon}_{(d)i}$. Thus, an inspection of deleted residuals will often identify influential observations that would have been missed in an examination of ordinary residuals.

The final adjustment used to attain the desired residual measure consists of standardizing the deletion residual. The standard deviation used for this is:

$$\hat{\sigma}_{\hat{\varepsilon}_i}(i) = \hat{\sigma}_\varepsilon(i)\sqrt{(1 - H_{ii})}$$

which uses the estimated equation standard error from the regression with observation i deleted, $\hat{\sigma}_\varepsilon(i)$. We thus obtain the **studentized residual**, $\hat{\varepsilon}_{(sr)i}$:

$$\hat{\varepsilon}_{(sr)i} = (y_i - \hat{y}_i(i))/\hat{\sigma}_{\hat{\varepsilon}_i}(i)$$
$$= \hat{\varepsilon}_{(d)i}/\hat{\sigma}_{\hat{\varepsilon}_i}(i)$$

The studentized residual is more sensitive to the presence of influential observations than is the standardized residual, since the residual and equation standard error it uses are based on observation deletion. The studentized residual follows the t-distribution with $n - k - 1$ degrees of freedom. Note, however, that a studentized residual might not be large when an observation is a leverage point. This is not a perfect measure for identifying influential observations.

DFBETAS and DFFITS

The remaining influence statistics discussed here are based on differences in coefficients and predicted values that result from deleting a single observation. The first of these measures the magnitude of coefficient changes. The **DFBETA** for a coefficient is the difference between its values when the entire sample is used and when observation i is deleted. In the bivariate regression considered above we have:

$$DFBETA_0 = \hat{\alpha}_0 - \hat{\alpha}_0(i)$$

$$DFBETA_1 = \hat{\alpha}_1 - \hat{\alpha}_1(i)$$

The scale of each DFBETA is altered by dividing it by its estimated standard deviation. However, these standard deviations are derived using the estimated equation error when observation i is deleted, $\hat{\sigma}_\varepsilon^2(i)$ (it is based on $n - k - 1$ degrees of freedom). Each coefficient variance estimate uses this in place of the equation standard error from the entire set of observations. The standard deviation of $\hat{\alpha}_1 - \hat{\alpha}_1(i)$ is then the square root of:

$$\hat{\sigma}_1^2(i) = \hat{\sigma}_\varepsilon^2(i)/\sum x_i'^2$$

These scaled coefficients are called **DFBETAS**:

$$DFBETAS_0 = (\hat{\alpha}_0 - \hat{\alpha}_0(i))/\hat{\sigma}_0(i)$$

$$DFBETAS_1 = (\hat{\alpha}_1 - \hat{\alpha}_1(i))/\hat{\sigma}_1(i)$$

The DFBETAS for a coefficient indicates the change *in standard deviations* that results from omitting observation *i*. When the value of DFBETAS is "large," the coefficient in question is substantially affected by the deletion of this observation. The term "large" can be defined by what Belsley and others call a "size-adjusted cutoff," which they define as a cutoff that, ". . . would lead to exposing approximately the same proportion of potentially influential observations regardless of sample size."[9] The size-adjusted cutoff for DFBETAS is $2/\sqrt{n}$. The DFBETAS for leverage points should be examined to detect which, if any, of the coefficients in the sample regression function are substantially affected by observation deletion. The combination of a large leverage value or studentized residual and one or more large DFBETAS should be viewed as evidence of the existence of an influential observation. The combination of a high leverage value and no large DFBETAS indicates non-harmful leverage.

Predicted values of *y* also change as the result of deleting observations. This was the basis for the deletion residual defined above. The difference between actual *y* for observation *i* and its prediction based on coefficients derived when this observation is deleted is called its **DFFIT**:

$$DFFIT_i = y_i - \hat{y}_i(i)$$

Note that DFFIT is another name for the deletion residual for observation *i*. The unit of measurement for DFFIT is the same as that for *y*. To remove its reliance on a specific unit of measurement, the scale of DFFIT is changed so that it has unit variance. This scaled value, DFFITS, is:

$$DFFITS_i = (y_i - \hat{y}_i(i))/\hat{\sigma}_{\hat{y}}(i)$$

where $\hat{\sigma}_{\hat{y}}(i)$ uses the estimated equation standard error with observation *i* deleted. The DFFITS for an observation indicates the number of standard deviations predicted *y* changes when this observation is deleted. The value of DFFITS is large when it exceeds $2\sqrt{(k/n)}$. The combination of a large leverage value and a DFFITS greater than $2\sqrt{(k/n)}$ indicates an influential observation.

An Application of Influence Statistics: Durable Goods Demand

The influence statistics outlined above will now be applied to the consumer durables expenditure equation presented earlier in this chapter. Table 7.2 gives the influence statistics for the years 1978 to 1989. Part (a) of this table supplies the leverage values (*H*); studentized residuals (RSTUDENT); and DFFITS. The cutoff values for these are:

—leverage values: $2(k/n) = 2(6/37) = 0.324$

—studentized residuals: ± 2.042 (for 30 degrees of freedom)

—DFFITS: $2\sqrt{(k/n)} = 2\sqrt{(6/37)} = 0.805$

---

[9] Belsley et al., *Regression Diagnostics*, p. 17.

Table 7.2 Influence Statistics for the Consumer Durables Equation

	(a)		
	H	RSTUDENT	DFFITS
1978	0.0627	−0.4853	−0.1255
1979	0.0679	0.0464	0.0125
1980	0.1862	0.3775	0.1806
1981	*0.3358*	1.3022	*0.9259*
1982	*0.3125*	−0.3077	−0.2075
1983	0.1420	*−2.2904*	*−0.9319*
1984	0.2757	−0.2688	−0.1658
1985	0.0947	1.4870	0.4810
1986	0.1859	1.5345	0.7333
1987	0.2274	1.3938	0.7561
1988	0.1835	1.5064	0.7141
1989	*0.3487*	−0.5879	−0.4302

	(b) DFBETAS					
	INTERCEPT	(p_d/p_c)	r_L	y_d	$(c/y)_{t-1}$	Δu
1978	0.0235	−0.0222	−0.0203	−0.0222	0.0097	0.0541
1979	0.0006	−0.0011	0.0062	−0.0021	0.0039	−0.0031
1980	0.0491	−0.0560	0.1029	−0.0753	0.0847	0.0276
1981	0.0105	0.0002	*0.8122*	−0.0886	−0.0382	−0.0473
1982	0.0299	−0.0366	−0.1147	−0.0385	0.0776	−0.0985
1983	−0.2533	0.2006	−0.2267	0.0879	*0.3025*	0.1415
1984	0.0005	−0.0069	−0.0760	−0.0119	0.0528	0.0923
1985	0.0280	−0.0185	−0.0645	0.0636	−0.1457	−0.0181
1986	0.1630	−0.1794	*−0.5266*	−0.0456	0.0782	0.0305
1987	*0.3882*	*−0.4153*	*−0.4216*	*−0.3200*	*0.3353*	*−0.2228*
1988	−0.0514	0.0410	*−0.4064*	0.1711	−0.1196	0.0138
1989	0.1925	−0.1983	0.1986	*−0.2807*	*0.2635*	−0.1463

Leverage points, where H exceeds 0.324, occur in 1981 and 1989. The value of H for 1982 is fairly close to our cutoff value, so we will consider this as a potential candidate. Only one studentized residual exceeds the value of 2.042, that for 1983. Finally, two DFFITS exceed their size-adjusted cutoff, 1981 and 1983. At this point, we consider the years 1981, 1982, 1983, and 1989 as potentially influential observations.

We now turn to the DFBETAS, which are given in part (b) of Table 7.2. The cutoff for these values is $2/\sqrt{n} = 0.329$. The largest DFBETAS occurs for the interest rate coefficient (RGOV3) in 1981, which is a leverage point. The value indicates that omitting the observation for 1981 changes the interest rate coefficient by about eight-tenths of a standard deviation. None of the DFBETAS for 1982 exceed the cutoff, indicating that the leverage for this year is not harmful to the estimated coefficients.

Data Used to Estimate Consumer Durables Equation

YEAR	RCDUR	(p_c/p_d)	r_L	r_s	y_d	$(c/y)_{t-1}$	Δu
1953	80.200	140.690	2.470	1.931	830.690	7.601	−0.100
1954	81.500	135.395	1.630	0.953	837.986	8.116	2.600
1955	96.900	135.932	2.470	1.753	884.500	8.498	−1.100
1956	92.800	136.877	3.190	2.658	926.609	9.515	−0.300
1957	92.400	138.387	3.980	3.267	941.777	9.920	0.200
1958	86.900	135.443	2.840	1.839	945.572	10.018	2.500
1959	96.900	136.842	4.460	3.405	982.370	9.949	−1.300
1960	98.000	134.954	3.980	2.928	1001.434	10.607	0.000
1961	93.600	134.535	3.540	2.378	1022.599	10.942	1.200
1962	103.000	134.808	3.470	2.778	1067.840	10.942	−1.200
1963	111.800	134.593	3.670	3.157	1100.033	11.174	0.200
1964	120.800	134.286	4.030	3.549	1180.429	11.889	−0.500
1965	134.600	132.303	4.220	3.954	1248.003	12.439	−0.700
1966	144.400	129.428	5.230	4.881	1304.325	12.920	−0.700
1967	146.200	128.457	5.030	4.321	1345.594	12.581	0.000
1968	161.600	127.481	5.680	5.339	1388.450	12.481	−0.200
1969	167.800	125.366	7.020	6.677	1425.654	12.598	−0.100
1970	162.500	122.844	7.290	6.458	1467.867	12.783	1.400
1971	178.300	121.826	5.650	4.348	1502.342	12.687	1.000
1972	200.400	118.844	5.720	4.071	1554.788	13.188	−0.300
1973	220.300	114.113	6.950	7.041	1655.010	13.629	−0.700
1974	204.900	110.219	7.820	7.886	1617.038	13.994	0.700
1975	205.600	111.318	7.490	5.838	1605.518	13.339	2.900
1976	232.300	111.022	6.770	4.989	1664.418	12.845	−0.800
1977	253.900	108.996	6.690	5.265	1727.620	12.900	−0.600
1978	267.400	107.402	8.290	7.221	1826.618	13.373	−1.000
1979	266.500	104.987	9.710	10.041	1863.367	13.818	−0.300
1980	245.900	103.002	11.550	11.506	1839.358	13.926	1.300
1981	250.800	101.163	14.440	14.029	1859.488	12.656	0.500
1982	252.700	100.000	12.920	10.686	1850.900	11.928	2.100
1983	283.100	98.079	10.450	8.630	1906.732	12.038	−0.100
1984	323.100	96.022	11.890	9.580	2047.413	12.608	−2.100
1985	355.100	93.907	9.640	7.480	2103.911	13.521	−0.300
1986	384.400	92.388	7.060	5.980	2179.045	14.669	−0.200
1987	389.600	90.234	7.680	5.820	2219.004	15.187	−0.800
1988	413.600	88.434	8.260	6.690	2323.562	14.912	−0.700
1989	425.600	85.615	8.550	8.120	2420.469	14.387	−0.200

The indebtedness variable (DEBTL) has a DFBETAS close to the cutoff for 1983. Deleting the observation for this year raises this coefficient by about one-third of one standard deviation. For the last leverage point, 1989, two coefficients are close to the cutoff, those for income and indebtedness. The leverage for this year may thus be harmful to these coefficients.

Relatively large DFBETAS exist for nonleverage points as well. All of the co-efficients for 1987 except that for the income uncertainty variable (Δu) are above the 0.329 cutoff. Neither the leverage value nor the studentized residual is large for this year, however. The value of DFFITS is also below its cutoff. Deleting the observation for 1987 changes the estimated coefficients (except that for Δu) from about one-third to four-tenths of a standard deviation. The DFBETAS for the interest rate coefficient are also large for 1986 and 1988. In fact, four DFBETAS for r_L exceed the cutoff value, indicating a potentially large reliance of that coefficient on the observations from 1981 to 1989. No other variable has this many large DFBETAS. The number of large DFBETAS for the interest rate coefficient is likely to be related at least in part to the Federal Reserve operating procedures instituted by Paul Volker that resulted in greater interest rate volatility throughout this period.

The ex-post forecasting performance of this equation, which was discussed earlier, is unsatisfactory. Some insight into this can be seen from the values of DFFITS for 1983 and 1985–1989. Of the years forecasted, only 1983 is a leverage point. Omitting the observation for this year produces a nine-tenth of one standard deviation change in $\hat{y}$ for 1983. While the remaining DFFITS are below the cutoff, each is larger than the values from the earlier years (except 1981). Predicted values of y are thus affected by this set of observations. The set of large DFBETAS for 1986–1989 is also indic-ative of the relative importance of these out-of-sample observations (for forecasting purposes) on the estimated coefficients derived from the entire 1953–1989 period.

A SUGGESTED FORMAT FOR AN ECONOMETRIC PAPER

The remainder of this chapter consists of an outline for a paper format that conforms to the proposed sequence of actions discussed in this chapter.

I. INTRODUCTION. This part of the paper should be brief and to the point. It is best to write this section *last* (after results are completed). Discuss what you will attempt to do, and raise any questions you address. *Never state that you will prove anything!* End this section with: "The purpose of this paper is to . . .

II. THE MODEL. Your equation should be related to economic theory (or thinking). At this point, list only *general* variables, such as "a measure of ability to pay" instead of a specific income measure such as "real disposable personal income," or "the rate of interest" and not the specific interest rate included in the estimated equation. An example of the proper type of presentation for a demand function is:

The demand function utilized in this paper, which is based on economic theory, is given by the following equation:

$$q_{xi} = f(p_{xi}, p_{yi}, I_i, \varepsilon_i)$$

where for observation i: q_x is the quantity of good X demanded; p_x is the price of good X; p_y is the price of a related good Y; I is nominal income of consumers of good X; and ε is a stochastic error term.

Be sure that you state the expected sign of each variable (when known) and *explain* the basis for these signs. For example:

> The expected sign of p_x is negative, as postulated by the law of demand. An increase in p_x, given p_y and income, implies that the relative price of this good rises, causing consumers to increase their purchases of substitute goods for X which are now relatively less expensive. This causes q_x to fall (substitution effect). Assuming that X is a normal good, this rise in p_x also lowers the real incomes of consumers of this good, decreasing q_x as well (income effect). Thus, other things being equal, an increase in the price of this good can be expected to decrease q_x.

III. THE ESTIMATED MODEL.   Data are *always* imperfect. You, as a researcher, must therefore fit the model from Section II to the data as best you can while remaining faithful to economic theory. Include a line in this section such as the following:

> The estimated equation is:

$$y_t = \alpha_0 + \alpha_1 x_t + \alpha_2 z_t + \varepsilon_t,$$

> where: y_t is . . . , x_t is . . . , z_t is . . . , and ε_t is the stochastic error term.

This is the point in your paper where you must furnish the *specific* variable that corresponds to each of the general variables in Section II, along with the functional form chosen. Discuss the basis for your selection of this particular equation specification and provide a separate table that includes the results for the other functional forms (such as log-linear) you estimated at the end of the paper. If any of your variables are proxy variables, outline the method used to calculate them (if relevant) and how they are representative of the intended variable (e.g., for real values, give the price index used along with its base year). State the expected sign for each variable along with an explanation of the basis for this sign.

IV. THE DATA.   Discuss your data, its source(s), and any biases or measurement error that might be present. If you are using time series data, be sure to include the data frequency (e.g., annual) along with both the starting and ending time periods. For cross-sectional data, state the time period during which the data were obtained, any relevant information pertaining to the method of data collection. Be sure to provide summary statistics for the major variables in this data base. *You must describe your data clearly enough that readers will readily understand the underlying basis for the empirical results that follow.*

V. RESULTS.   In this section you present your estimated equation along with a *thorough* discussion of the empirical results. *Write this as continuous prose, and not as a separate paragraph for each coefficient.* Be sure to cover the following points: (1) discuss the sign, magnitude, and statistical significance of *each* coefficient; (2) discuss any technical problems encountered (such as multicollinearity, serial correlation, etc.) and what (if any) remedial actions were taken; and (3) discuss the performance of the *entire* equation (using $\bar{R}^2$, the F-statistic, etc.) along with a description of the basis for this assessment. A single equation can be represented in one of several ways (include a heading above it). Examples (using the preferred consumer durables equation) are:

Consumer Durables Equation: 1953–1989

$$\hat{q}_t = 309.2 - 2.25(p_d/p_c)_t - 8.01r_{Lt} + 0.21y_{dt} - 8.42(c/y)_{t-1} - 4.27\,\Delta u_t$$
$$\quad\;\;(3.1)\qquad(3.6)\qquad\quad(10.5)\quad\;(7.2)\qquad(4.2)\qquad\qquad(3.2)$$

$$N = 37 \qquad \bar{R}^2 = 0.994 \qquad F = 1192.3 \qquad \hat{\sigma}_\varepsilon = 7.95 \qquad \hat{\mu}_q = 200.7 \qquad CV = 3.96$$

Consumer Durables Equation: 1953–1989

VARIABLE	COEFFICIENT	STANDARD ERROR	t-STATISTIC
Intercept	309.2	100.50	3.1
$(p_d/p_c)_t$	−2.25	0.63	3.6
r_{Lt}	−8.01	0.76	10.5
y_{dt}	0.207	0.03	7.2
$(c/y)_{t-1}$	−8.42	1.99	4.2
Δu_t	−4.27	1.35	3.2

$$N = 37 \qquad \bar{R}^2 = 0.994 \qquad F = 1192.3 \qquad \hat{\sigma}_\varepsilon = 7.95 \qquad \hat{\mu}_q = 200.7 \qquad CV = 3.96$$

VI. CONCLUSIONS.   Be brief, summarize the major findings of this paper and any policy implications. This part of the paper should fit well with Section I.

KEY TERMS

Deletion residual

DFBETA

DFBETAS

DFFIT

Influence statistics

Leverage point

Leverage value (leverage)

Standardized residual

Studentized residual

8 Equation Specification

The least squares estimation technique is also referred to as linear regression analysis. Linearity with this method of estimation refers to coefficients and not explanatory variables. Thus, coefficients cannot be raised to powers other than one, and terms involving the product of two or more coefficients are not allowed. Independent or dependent variables such as logarithms or absolute changes are permitted. The least squares methodology is therefore not as restrictive as one might initially believe, since a large number of possible equation specifications are consistent with this framework.

Care must be exercised when selecting the specification for an estimated equation. This choice is important, since economic theory does not always provide us with guidance in selecting the appropriate specification, yet every functional form implicitly assumes a specific relationship between the dependent and explanatory variables in that equation. For example, a specification that is linear in all of its explanatory variables embodies the assumption that the partial slope of each independent variable is constant; independent of the levels of this and every other variable in the equation. However, partial elasticities differ with this specification; these depend on the values taken by the dependent and explanatory variables used to estimate the elasticity.

While this specification is adequate to model a number of different relationships, it is sometimes inappropriate. If, for example, we model a time series demand function for good X with a linear specification, and the data used to estimate this function span a substantial time period, a number of problems can be expected to arise. To see this, consider the partial slope coefficient for the price of X when the equation specification is linear. This coefficient indicates the rate of change in mean quantity demanded as the price of X changes, other things being equal. However, this specification implicitly assumes that the magnitude of this response is the same whether the price of X is $1 or $10. This is sometimes referred to as **dimensional misspecification**. In this situation, a linear specification is inappropriate. An alternative specification is therefore needed, one that allows this partial slope to depend on the specific price of X.

This chapter provides a detailed outline of the major equation specifications utilized in econometric analysis.[1] Non-calculus techniques for calculating partial slopes and elasticities are presented, along with the methodology for determining the statistical significance of partial slopes. Economic examples are integrated throughout this presentation.

FUNCTIONAL FORMS FOR EQUATION SPECIFICATION

Linear in the Explanatory Variables

The majority of equations used to illustrate the material in previous chapters employ specifications that are linear in their explanatory variables. An example of this specification with two explanatory variables, omitting the error term, is[2]:

$$y_i = \alpha_0 + \alpha_1 x_i + \alpha_2 z_i \tag{8.1}$$

In this equation, α_1 is the partial slope of x, which measures the rate of change in y for a one unit change in x, given the level of z. This is also the slope of the graph with y on the vertical axis and x on the horizontal axis:

$$y_i = (\alpha_0 + \alpha_2 z_i) + \alpha_1 x_i$$

or

$$y_i = \alpha_0^* + \alpha_1 x_i \tag{8.2}$$

This is illustrated in Figure 8.1. This specification embodies the assumptions that: (i) the partial slope of x is the same for all values taken by x; and (ii) this partial slope is independent of the levels of all other independent variables in the equation. This last point can be seen by referring to Equation (8.2) and considering the effect of a change in the value of z. An increase in z alters the term $\alpha_2 z$, causing the vertical intercept to change. While the *level* of y now differs for any x, the *rate of change* in y for a given x, or α_1, remains the same. Thus, the partial slope of x is independent of z.

An economic example of this result occurs in short-run cost theory. The total cost of production (TC) consists of total fixed cost (TFC) and total variable cost (TVC). TFC, which is independent of the level of output (q), is constant in the short-run. The value of TFC can be expressed as $r \cdot k$, where r is the user cost of capital, and k is the stock of capital, which is defined to be fixed in the short-run. Total fixed cost can thus be represented as:

$$\text{TFC} = r \cdot k_1 = \alpha_0 = \text{constant},$$

---

[1] For a more complete accounting of the various forms in a fairly readable article, the reader is referred to I. McGowan, "Choice of Functional Form in Economics," *British Review of Economic Issues*, Spring 1983, pp. 32–45.

[2] The stochastic error is omitted to simplify the presentation of the basics of functional form.

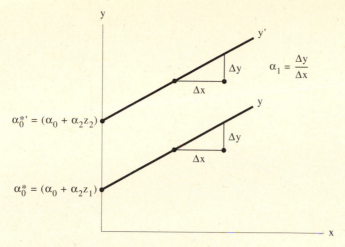

Figure 8.1 Two-dimensional representation of Equation (8.1)

where k_1 is the short-run capital stock. Total variable cost is a function of output. If we represent this by a linear relationship, then:

$$TVC = \alpha_1 q$$

Total cost is therefore:

$$TC = TFC + TVC$$
$$= \alpha_0 + \alpha_1 q \tag{8.3}$$

The slope of this curve, α_1, is the marginal cost (MC) of production:

$$\alpha_1 = \Delta TC / \Delta q$$
$$= MC$$

which is the rate of change in TC as q changes. TC only changes as the result of variable input usage, which corresponds to an increase in q. Any ΔTC thus consists entirely of variable costs, and is therefore independent of TFC (and the fixed level of k). When r (the cost of capital) rises, TFC increases, making TC higher for all values of q. The slope, or marginal cost is unaffected, as Figure 8.2 shows. Such a change affects total profits but not the profit-maximizing output of the firm.[3]

While a linear equation specification embodies the assumption of a constant partial slope, the elasticity of y with respect to x in such an equation varies depending

---

[3] Recall that the profit-maximizing condition is that marginal revenue equals MC. Since a change in TFC leaves MC unaltered, the original q is still consistent with profit-maximization, other things being equal.

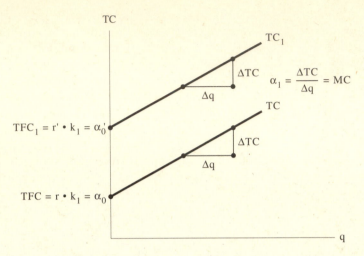

Figure 8.2 Effect of an increase in TFC on marginal cost

on the values of y and x used to estimate this magnitude. Recall that the definition of the elasticity of y with respect to x is:

$$\eta = \%\Delta y / \%\Delta x$$
$$= (x/y)(\Delta y/\Delta x)$$

For a multiple regression equation, this is a **partial elasticity**, since the second bracketed term is evaluated for *given* values of the other explanatory variables in the equation. Using the estimated coefficient for α_1 in Equation (8.1), the estimated partial elasticity is:

$$(x/y)(\hat{\alpha}_1).$$

While $\hat{\alpha}_1$ is a constant, the ratio (x/y) is not, so the partial elasticity will tend to differ depending on the particular set of x-y values chosen.

The total cost function discussed above can be used to illustrate this point. The value of $\hat{\alpha}_1$ is estimated marginal cost, which, with a linear specification, is constant. The estimated (partial) elasticity of TC with respect to q is:

$$(q/\text{TC})(\Delta\text{TC}/\Delta q) = (q/\text{TC})(\hat{\alpha}_1).$$

Even though $\hat{\alpha}_1$ is a constant, this elasticity is not constant. To see this, we can rewrite this elasticity as:

$$(\Delta\text{TC}/\Delta q)/(\text{TC}/q) = \text{MC}/(\text{TC}/q)$$

The denominator in this expression is average total cost (AC). We can therefore rewrite the elasticity expression as the ratio: MC/AC. If we let TC $= 10 + 2q$, then AC $= (10/q) + 2$, which is inversely related to q, and therefore not constant.

The value of an estimated elasticity can potentially provide us with important information about whether or not the magnitude of a coefficient is acceptable. Sometimes it is not obvious whether the magnitude of an estimated partial slope is reasonable. However, prior expectations might exist concerning the elasticity associated with the coefficient whose magnitude we are uncertain about. For example, previous empirical studies may have established that the demand for a particular good is price elastic. We can convert our estimated price coefficient into an elasticity by using the sample average for price or some other values of interest, calculate predicted quantity demanded, then see if the resulting value falls into the expected elasticity range.

One use of the linear specification that appears to be rising in popularity occurs with trended time series data. When the variables in an equation share a common time trend, spurious correlation can produce the appearance of a valid relationship between these variables when none really exists. One method of controlling for this common factor is to include a time trend as an explanatory variable. Another method analyzes the relationship between *changes* in the levels of these variables, or the first difference form of this equation. If the time trend represents long-term or secular trends present in the data, analysis of the first difference form allows short-term or cyclical factors to be examined explicitly. The estimated equation is therefore linear in the first differences of the variables. If the equation of interest is:

$$y_t = \alpha_0 + \alpha_1 x_t + \alpha_2 z_t + \varepsilon_t,$$

this equation can be lagged one period, which gives:

$$y_{t-1} = \alpha_0 + \alpha_1 x_{t-1} + \alpha_2 z_{t-1} + \varepsilon_{t-1}.$$

By subtracting this from the first equation we obtain the first difference form of the original equation:

$$(y_t - y_{t-1}) = (\alpha_0 - \alpha_0) + \alpha_1(x_t - x_{t-1}) + \alpha_2(z_t - z_{t-1}) + (\varepsilon_t - \varepsilon_{t-1}),$$

or

$$\Delta y_t = \alpha_1 \Delta x_t + \alpha_2 \Delta z_t + \Delta \varepsilon_t \qquad \textbf{(8.4)}$$

Note that the first difference form given by Equation (8.4) excludes an intercept. If, instead, the original equation includes a time trend:

$$y_t = \alpha_0 + \alpha_1 x_t + \alpha_2 z_t + \alpha_3 t + \varepsilon_t,$$

the first difference form includes α_3 as its intercept, since the α_0 terms still cancel, and:

$$\alpha_3[t - (t - 1)] = \alpha_3$$

since $\Delta t = 1$.

Technically, the coefficient α_1 in Equation (8.4) indicates the rate of change in the *change* of the mean of y for a one unit change in the *change* in x, given z. Because the first difference method is utilized to control for secular data trends, coefficients are interpreted in the usual way in light of this modification. The value of $\hat{\alpha}_1$ is therefore an estimate of the rate of change in the mean of y for a one unit change in x, given the value of z.

An example of this technique is given by Sherman and Evans, who examine the relationship between nonresidential real investment (I); real GNP (y); real corporate profits (π); and the profit rate (π/k), where k is the stock of capital.[4] Quarterly data for the period 1949–1980 gives the estimated equation:

$$\Delta \hat{I}_t = -0.78 + 0.15 \, \Delta y_t + 0.09 \, \Delta \pi_{t-2} + 0.67 \, \Delta(\pi/k)_{t-3} \qquad R^2 = 0.55$$
$$\phantom{\Delta \hat{I}_t = -0.78 + } (9.5) \qquad (3.47) \qquad\qquad (2.86)$$

Lagged values of profit and the rate of profit represent expected future values of these variables. The coefficient of Δy indicates that a \$1 billion increase in real GNP raises the mean of I by \$150 million (= 0.15 billion), given expected future profits and the expected profit rate. The other coefficients are interpreted in the same way. The intercept coefficient in this equation, -0.78, is an estimate of the time trend for a linearly specified equation.[5]

SPECIFICATIONS THAT ARE NONLINEAR IN THE EXPLANATORY VARIABLES

The Quadratic Functional Form

The constancy of partial slopes, which is presupposed by a linear specification, is not always satisfactory. The problem of dimensional misspecification alluded to earlier, which can occur when the data span a substantial time period, is one instance where this specification is likely to be invalid. However, partial slopes can vary with both time series and cross-sectional data. In a number of situations, the rate of change in y with respect to an explanatory variable x is itself a *function* of x. The impact of changes in x on the dependent variable then depends on the specific value taken by x.

One way to incorporate this assumption into the equation specification is through a quadratic functional form. An example of this is:

$$y_i = \alpha_0 + \alpha_1 x_i + \alpha_2 x_i^2 + \alpha_3 z_i + \varepsilon_i \tag{8.5}$$

Note that Equation (8.5) is quadratic in x but linear in z. *There is no rule mandating that the same specification must apply to all of the explanatory variables in an equation.* In this equation, α_1 is the **linear effect coefficient** for x, and α_2 is its **quadratic effect coefficient**. We now show how to derive the expression for the partial slope of x.

If we drop the subscript in Equation (8.5), denote the original value of y as y_0, and omit the error term, we can rewrite this equation as:

$$y_0 = \alpha_0 + \alpha_1 x_0 + \alpha_2 x_0^2 + \alpha_3 z_0 \tag{8.6}$$

If x changes by Δx, the new value of y, denoted y_1, is obtained by letting x equal $(x_0 + \Delta x)$ in Equation (8.6). Making this substitution:

$$y_1 = \alpha_0 + \alpha_1 (x_0 + \Delta x) + \alpha_2 (x_0 + \Delta x)^2 + \alpha_3 z_0,$$

---

[4] F. Sherman and G. Evans, *Macroeconomics: Keynesian, Monetarist, and Marxist Views* (New York: Harper & Row), 1984, p. 173.

[5] No *t*-statistic is provided by the authors for this coefficient.

which, after performing the indicated operations on the bracketed terms, becomes:

$$y_1 = \alpha_0 + \alpha_1 x_0 + \alpha_1 \Delta x + \alpha_2 x_0^2 + 2\alpha_2 x_0 \Delta x + \alpha_2 (\Delta x)^2 + \alpha_3 z_0.$$

This new value, y_1, consists of the terms for y_0 given by Equation (8.6) plus additional terms involving Δx:

$$y_1 = y_0 + \alpha_1 \Delta x + 2\alpha_2 x_0 \Delta x + \alpha_2 (\Delta x)^2.$$

Since the change in y equals $(y_1 - y_0)$, then, assuming that change in x is small enough to make the last term on the right negligible, we can rewrite this expression as:

$$\Delta y = \alpha_1 \Delta x + 2\alpha_2 x_0 \Delta x \qquad (8.7)$$

The partial slope of x with the quadratic specification is therefore:

$$\Delta y / \Delta x = \alpha_1 + 2\alpha_2 x, \qquad (8.8)$$

which is a linear function of x.[6] Note that Equation (8.8) is a partial slope since we have restricted z to its initial value of z_0.

The partial slope of x in the quadratic specification given by Equation (8.5) thus depends on the level of x. This allows the magnitude of this partial slope to differ for "high" and "low" values of x. Since the partial slope involves *two* equation coefficients, several major differences exist between this and a linear specification:

(a) To evaluate the partial slope of x, we must select a value for x and use this along with the estimated coefficients for α_1 and α_2. Likely choices include the sample mean of x, its most recent value, or a hypothetical value that might exist under a policy whose effect is being contemplated.

(b) The expected sign of x pertains to the sign of the *entire expression* for the partial slope of x. If, for example, x is positively related to y, this implies a positive partial slope so that $\alpha_1 + 2\alpha_2 x$ should be positive. If $\alpha_1 > 0$ this does *not* necessarily imply a positive partial slope.

(c) The values of $\hat{\alpha}_1$ and $\hat{\alpha}_2$ can differ in sign. When this occurs, the partial slope of x changes sign over possible values of x, and we must determine the range of x values over which the expected sign occurs. If, for example, the expected sign of x is positive, $\hat{\alpha}_1 = 5$ and $\hat{\alpha}_2 = -3$, then:

$$\hat{\alpha}_1 + 2\hat{\alpha}_2 x > 0 \text{ when } 5 + 2(-3)x > 0$$

which requires that $x < 5/6$ $(= \hat{\alpha}_1 / 2\hat{\alpha}_2)$. If the solution to this inequality occurs within the range of sample values for x, the expected sign of x is then obtained. If the values of x that satisfy this inequality lie entirely outside the range of sample values, the actual sign can be considered to be the opposite of that expected.

---

[6] For persons familiar with partial differentiation, this derivation provides the formula for the partial derivative $\partial y_i / \partial x_i$.

(d) The statistical significance of x in a quadratic equation is ascertained using a null hypothesis which states that x does *not* influence y. If this hypothesis is true, then *both* α_1 and α_2 are jointly 0. The hypotheses for this test are: H_0: $\alpha_1 = \alpha_2 = 0$, and H_a: at least one of these coefficients is nonzero. The test statistic for these hypotheses is the F-statistic for the subset of equation coefficients given in Chapter 6:

$$\frac{(\text{ESS}_{re} - \text{ESS}_{ue})/r}{\text{ESS}_{ue}/(n - k)}$$

where ESS is the sum of squared errors, the subscript "re" refers to the restricted equation that omits all x terms, "ue" is the full or unrestricted equation, and r is the number of restrictions ($= 2$). If the value of this test statistic exceeds the critical F value with r and $(n - k)$ degrees of freedom for the chosen level of significance, we reject H_0 in favor of H_a that x influences y. Of course, individual t-statistics should also be considered. The t-value for the coefficient of x^2 is the test statistic for the nonlinearity of the relationship between x and y.

Finally, the elasticity of y with respect to x is not constant with a quadratic specification. The formula for this value is:

$$(x/y)(\Delta y/\Delta x) = (x/y) \cdot (\text{partial slope of } x),$$

which is given by the equation:

$$(x/y)(\alpha_1 + 2\alpha_2 x) \tag{8.9}$$

We can apply this specification to the total cost function discussed earlier to see if it provides a more realistic depiction of marginal cost. If we again represent total fixed cost, which equals $r \cdot k_1$, as α_0, but now allow total variable cost to be quadratically related to output:

$$\text{TVC} = \alpha_1 q + \alpha_2 q^2$$

then the total cost function is: $\text{TC} = \alpha_0 + \alpha_1 q + \alpha_2 q^2$. Recall that the slope of this function, $\Delta \text{TC}/\Delta q$, is marginal cost. For this specification marginal cost is no longer a constant, but is instead a linear function of output:

$$\text{MC} = \alpha_1 + 2\alpha_2 q$$

The use of a quadratic specification to represent total cost therefore allows marginal cost to depend on the level of output. Is this depiction adequate? Since the slope of MC above is constant, it differs from the U-shaped marginal cost depicted in most microeconomic textbooks. A quadratic specification for total cost thus allows MC to either rise with output (if $\alpha_2 > 0$) or fall with output (if $\alpha_2 < 0$), but not to fall over the initial range of production and then rise with the onset of diminishing returns. Clearly, a continually falling short-run marginal cost curve is *not* consistent with economic theory. Which equation specification allows the expected behavior of marginal cost to occur? The answer is the **cubic specification**. If our total cost function is cubic in output, then:

$$TC = \alpha_0 + \alpha_1 q + \alpha_2 q^2 + \alpha_3 q^3$$

and the associated marginal cost function is:

$$MC = \alpha_1 + 2\alpha_2 q + 3\alpha_3 q^2 \tag{8.10}$$

which is a *quadratic* function of output. The derivation of this result is included in the exercises at the end of this chapter. Since the graph of a quadratic function results in a parabola, a U-shaped curve within the relevant range of production is clearly possible with this equation specification.

An empirical example of the quadratic specification is given by the following MicroTSP output which modifies the real consumer durable expenditure equation from Chapter 7 by making it quadratic in the variables RPCDC and RGOV3:

```
LS // Dependent Variable is RCDUR
SMPL range: 1953  -  1989
Number of observations: 37
```

VARIABLE	COEFFICIENT	STD. ERROR	T-STAT.	2-TAIL SIG.
C	731.94783	116.84990	6.2640002	0.000
RPCDC	-10.092214	1.6718948	-6.0363933	0.000
RPCDC2	0.0335814	0.0067875	4.9475409	0.000
RDPILT	0.1751225	0.0227534	7.6965431	0.000
RGOV3	-5.0614201	3.1593732	-1.6020330	0.120
RGOV32	-0.0558293	0.1676614	-0.3329882	0.742
RCRGNP(-1)	-3.7419136	1.8107634	-2.0664840	0.048
CHGUR	-3.7946002	1.0127260	-3.7469169	0.001

R-squared	0.997346	Mean of dependent var	200.6865
Adjusted R-squared	0.996706	S.D. of dependent var	102.5735
S.E. of regression	5.887232	Sum of squared resid	1005.126
Durbin-Watson stat	1.487526	F-statistic	1557.035

where: RCDUR = real consumer durable expenditure (1982 = 100); RPCDC = ratio of GNP deflator for consumer durable goods to the personal consumption deflator, or the relative price of consumer durable goods; RPCDC2 = squared value of RPCDC; RDPILT = real disposable personal income net of transfer payments (1982 = 100); RGOV3 = interest rate on 3 year government bonds; RGOV32 = squared value of RGOV3; RCRGNP = ratio of real total consumer installment credit to real GNP (both 1982 = 100); and CHGUR = annual change in the civilian unemployment rate.

Both relative price coefficients are statistically significant at the 1 percent level. Since these differ in sign, the expected negative sign does not always occur. The partial slope of RPCDC is negative when:

$$\text{partial slope of RPCDC} = -10.1 + 2(0.034)\text{RPCDC} < 0$$

or

$$\text{RPCDC} < 10.1/(2 \cdot 0.034) = 148.5.$$

Since all of the sample values for RPCDC fall below this value, the expected sign of RPCDC is attained. For the last year of data (1989), the value of RPCDC is 85.6, which gives a partial slope of -4.28: an increase of 1 in the relative price of consumer durable goods lowers the mean of RCDUR by \$4.28 billion. Finally, the estimated elasticity of RCDUR with respect to RPCDC for 1989 is:

$$(85.6/437.5)(-4.28) = -0.84,$$

where the predicted value of RCDUR for 1989, 437.5, is the denominator in the first term. The value of this estimate indicates inelastic demand.

The interest rate coefficients are both negative, but neither attains statistical significance at the 5 percent level or above. The partial slope for RGOV3 is: $-5.06 + 2(-0.056)\text{RGOV3}$. For 1989, the value of RGOV3 is 8.6, which gives an estimated partial slope of:

$$-5.06 + 2(-0.056)(8.6) = -6.0$$

The corresponding estimated interest elasticity is:

$$(8.6/437.5)(-6.0) = -0.12$$

which indicates that the demand for consumer durables is interest inelastic.

The fact that neither of the interest rate coefficients is statistically significant (based on t-statistics) does *not* constitute evidence that the demand for consumer durables is unaffected by RGOV3. To determine whether RGOV3 is statistically significant, we must use the F-statistic alluded to previously. The null hypothesis for this test states that the coefficients of RGOV3 and RGOV32 are jointly 0. The equation above is the unrestricted equation, since neither of the interest rate coefficients are restricted to being 0 (and thus omitted). The value of ESS_{ue} is thus 1005.1. The RCDUR equation was re-estimated omitting both RGOV3 and RGOV32 to obtain ESS_{re}, which equals 3849.0. The value of the test statistic is:

$$\frac{(3849.0 - 1005.1)/2}{1005.1/29} = 41.0.$$

The critical F value, $F_{2,29}$, at the 1 percent level of significance is 5.52. We can therefore reject the null hypothesis that RGOV3 does not influence RCDUR at the 1 percent level of significance. *As this example shows, it is possible for a quadratically specified variable to be statistically significant even though neither of its coefficients is individually significant.*

We conclude this section by illustrating an *F*-test for determining whether the linear specification would have been more appropriate in modeling the demand for consumer durables. The **test for the linearity of the equation specification** with a quadratic equation can be performed using a Wald Test. The null hypothesis for this test states that the quadratic effect coefficients (for RPCDC2 and RGOV32) are jointly 0. The printout above provides us with information for the unrestricted equation, with $r = 2$ and $ESS_{ue} = 1005.1$. The restricted equation is the linear version of the quadratic equation (see Chapter 7). The value of ESS_{re} obtained from the linear specification is 1959.5. The test statistic for the linearity of this equation's specification is:

$$\frac{(1959.5 - 1005.1)/2}{1005.1/29} = 13.8$$

This exceeds the critical value ($F_{2,29}$ for the 1 percent level of significance), 5.52. We are thus able to reject the null hypothesis that a linear specification is appropriate for this equation. Because we are unable to reject the nonlinear specification, the demand curve implied by this equation is not a straight line. Figure 8.3 illustrates this curve when actual 1989 values are substituted into this equation for all explanatory variables other than RPCDC (and RPCDC2). Since we are unable to reject the hypotheses that (i) RPCDC is quadratically related to RCDUR; and (ii) RGOV3 is a statistically significant determinant of RCDUR, although this relationship is not

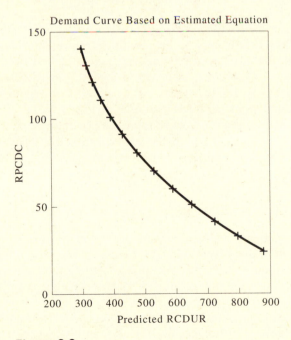

Figure 8.3

quadratic, this equation was re-estimated keeping the squared term for relative price but omitting that for RGOV3. The MicroTSP output that results is:

```
              LS // Dependent Variable is RCDUR

SMPL range: 1953  -  1989
Number of observations: 37

    VARIABLE    COEFFICIENT   STD. ERROR    T-STAT.     2-TAIL SIG.

       C          716.83562   106.06888    6.7582085     0.000
     RPCDC        -9.8651482   1.5037209   -6.5604917     0.000
     RPCDC2        0.0326946   0.0061500    5.3161903     0.000
     RDPILT        0.1769427   0.0217573    8.1325753     0.000
     RGOV3        -6.0893307   0.6626492   -9.1893734     0.000
   RCRGNP(-1)     -3.5780110   1.7165634   -2.0844036     0.046
     CHGUR        -3.8450715   0.9863695   -3.8982060     0.001

R-squared              0.997336   Mean of dependent var 200.6865
Adjusted R-squared     0.996803   S.D. of dependent var 102.5735
S.E. of regression     5.799335   Sum of squared resid  1008.969
Durbin-Watson stat     1.465008   F-statistic           1872.004
```

Note the large t-statistic for RGOV3. This is consistent with the F-test for the statistical significance of RGOV3. Compare the overall equation performance measures for this equation with that for the earlier quadratic equation and the linear version at the end of Chapter 7. Additional evidence of a nonlinear association for only RPCDC is provided by the residual plot in Figure 8.4. The first of these, Figure 8.4(a), plots the residuals from the linear equation against RPCDC. The curvature displayed by the residuals indicates the likelihood of a nonlinear association between RPCDC and RCDUR. Figure 8.4(b) plots the residuals from the linear equation with RGOV3. No such curvature is indicated, which confirms the above statistical finding of a linear association between RGOV3 and RCDUR.

Linear Specification with an Interaction Term

Situations arise in econometrics where the impact of a change in x on the dependent variable depends on the value taken by another explanatory variable. For example, the impact of unionization on earnings may differ depending on the degree of concentration in an industry. A more general possibility arises when the partial slope of x is itself a function of time.

We can allow the partial slope of x to depend on the level of another variable z (and vice versa) by using a linear specification with an interaction term:

$$y_i = \alpha_0 + \alpha_1 x_i + \alpha_2 z_i + \alpha_3 (x_i \cdot z_i) + \varepsilon_i \tag{8.11}$$

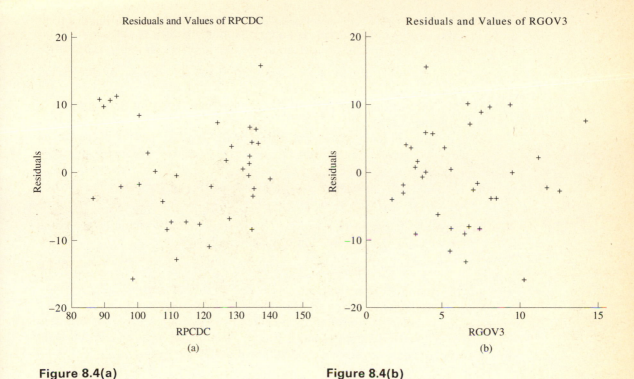

Figure 8.4(a)   Figure 8.4(b)

In this equation, α_3 is the **interaction effect coefficient**. We can derive an expression for the partial slope of x using the procedure from the previous section. If we denote the initial value of y as y_0 and replace the subscript i with 0, then omitting the error term, Equation (8.11) becomes:

$$y_0 = \alpha_0 + \alpha_1 x_0 + \alpha_2 z_0 + \alpha_3(x_0 \cdot z_0)$$

If x changes by Δx but z remains unchanged, the new value of y, y_1, is:

$$y_1 = \alpha_0 + \alpha_1(x_0 + \Delta x) + \alpha_2 z_0 + \alpha_3[(x_0 + \Delta x) \cdot z_0].$$

When we multiply the bracketed expressions and collect the terms from the original equation, this becomes:

$$y_1 = \alpha_0 + \alpha_1 x_0 + \alpha_2 z_0 + \alpha_3(x_0 \cdot z_0) + \alpha_1 \Delta x + \alpha_3 z_0 \cdot \Delta x$$

$$y_1 = y_0 + \alpha_1 \Delta x + \alpha_3 z_0 \cdot \Delta x, \text{ or}$$

$$\Delta y = (\alpha_1 + \alpha_3 z_0)\Delta x.$$

The partial slope of x is therefore:

$$\Delta y/\Delta x = \alpha_1 + \alpha_3 z \qquad\qquad\qquad \textbf{(8.12)}$$

The impact of a change in x on y thus depends on the value of z. Because this partial slope involves the level of a variable and more than one coefficient, the points of difference with the linear specification given in the previous section apply, especially:

(a) A specific value of z must be selected to obtain an estimate of this partial slope;

(b) The expected sign of x pertains to the *entire* expression on the right side of Equation (8.12);

(c) If the signs of the coefficients in Equation (8.12) differ, the sign of the partial slope will depend on the value of z selected. A positive expected sign implies $\hat{\alpha}_1 + \hat{\alpha}_3 z > 0$, or that $z > -\hat{\alpha}_1/\hat{\alpha}_3$; and

(d) The statistical significance of x is ascertained using the F-test for the null hypothesis: $H_0: \alpha_1 = \alpha_3 = 0$.

The elasticity of y with respect to x follows the general formula (x/y) (partial slope of x), which, with an interaction specification, becomes:

$$(x/y)(\alpha_1 + \alpha_3 z) = (1/y)[\alpha_1 x + \alpha_3 (x \cdot z)] \qquad \textbf{(8.13)}$$

which is the sum of all terms involving x divided by the value of y.

A paper by Weiss provides an example of this equation specification.[7] Using cross-sectional data, Weiss examined the effect of unionization on labor earnings. The degree of industry concentration is a major factor that must be controlled for in the estimated equation, since, as the author notes:

> In unconcentrated industries, strong union power might yield high wages, but in concentrated industries, where wages may already be high, unions might not add much . . . if high wages in unorganized but concentrated industries result from the threat of unionism, then concentration and unionization would represent the same force. If this is true, the combined effects of concentration and unionism would be less than the sum of the two effects taken separately.[8]

To ascertain the general relationship between unionization and earnings, Weiss uses an equation with a measure of income (I) as the dependent variable, and variables representing the extent of unionism (U) and the degree of industry concentration (CR) as explanatory variables. The income variable he utilized is private wage and salary income for 1959. This quote contains the testable hypothesis that the effect of unionism on earnings is a function of the level of industry concentration: other things being equal, the greater is the degree of concentration, the smaller is the contribution of unionization to income. The specification of Weiss' equation is linear in both CR and U with the interaction term $(U \cdot CR)$. If this hypothesis is true, the coefficient of the interaction term should be negative and statistically significant. His estimated

---

[7] L. Weiss, "Concentration and Labor Earnings," *American Economic Review*, March 1966, pp. 96–117.

[8] *Ibid.*, p. 98.

equation (with $n = 5187$) is:

$$\hat{I}_t = 1936 + 53.5CR + 23.7U - 0.44(CR \cdot U) \qquad \bar{R}^2 = 0.04 \qquad \textbf{(8.14)}$$
$$\quad (6.9) \quad (6.8) \qquad (5.7) \qquad (4.3)$$

The interaction term is statistically significant and displays the expected negative sign. The partial slope of U is $23.7 - 0.44CR$, which is positive only for concentration ratios below 53.9 percent. An industry with a relatively low concentration ratio of 20 has an estimated partial slope of 14.9 ($= 23.7 - 0.44 \cdot 20$), while a highly concentrated industry with CR equal to 60 has an estimated partial slope of -2.7 ($= 23.7 - 0.44 \cdot 60$).

The elasticity of I with respect to U is $(U/I)(23.7 - 0.44R)$. If $U = 50$ and CR $= 60$, the estimate of the mean actual income is \$5003 (substituting these values into Equation (8.14)), and the estimated elasticity is:

$$(50/5003)(-2.7) = -0.03.$$

When $U = 50$ but the industry is less concentrated with CR $= 20$, the estimate of mean income is \$3750, which gives an elasticity of:

$$(50/3750)(14.9) = 0.2.$$

A 10 percent increase in the level of unionization is therefore predicted to raise mean income by 2 percent for workers in low concentration industries, while lowering mean income by three-tenths of 1 percent for workers in more highly concentrated industries.

Quadratic Specification with an Interaction Term

Another important specification is obtained by combining the last two functional forms considered: the quadratic specification with an interaction term. This combines elements of each specification separately, so that the partial slope of x is a function of the level of x as well as the value of another explanatory variable. In the concentration and earnings equation presented above, for example, the partial slope of unionization on earnings depends only on the level of concentration. If, instead, this equation specification were quadratic in the unionization variable, the impact of unionization on earnings would then be a function of the level of industry concentration and the extent of unionization. The partial slope of unionization would thus depend on the combination of unionization and concentration that exists for different firms.

The quadratic specification with an interaction has other uses as well. If we are interested in evaluating the effect of a government program that entails several policy instruments, the partial slope of each instrument might well depend on its own level as well as that of one or more of the other instruments. This equation specification can be illustrated as:

$$y_i = \alpha_0 + \alpha_1 x_i + \alpha_2 z_i + \alpha_3 x_i^2 + \alpha_4 z_i^2 + \alpha_5 (x_i \cdot z_i) + \varepsilon_i \qquad \textbf{(8.15)}$$

if both x and z are quadratically related to y, or:

$$y_i = \alpha_0 + \alpha_1 x_i + \alpha_2 z_i + \alpha_3 x_i^2 + \alpha_4 (x_i \cdot z_i) + \varepsilon_i \qquad \textbf{(8.16)}$$

if only x is quadratically related.

The derivation of the partial slopes for these equations, which follows directly from the discussion in the previous sections, is left as an exercise. The expressions for these partial slopes are:

$$\text{Partial slope for } x \text{ in Equation (8.15):}\quad \alpha_1 + 2\alpha_3 x + \alpha_5 z = f_1(x, z)$$

$$\text{Partial slope for } z \text{ in Equation (8.15):}\quad \alpha_2 + 2\alpha_4 z + \alpha_5 x = f_2(x, z)$$

$$\text{Partial slope for } x \text{ in Equation (8.16):}\quad \alpha_1 + 2\alpha_3 x + \alpha_4 z = g(x, z)$$

$$\text{Partial slope for } z \text{ in Equation (8.16):}\quad \alpha_2 + \alpha_4 x = h(x).$$

Each of these partial slopes involves two or more coefficients and the level of one or more explanatory variables. The points of difference with the linear specification discussed for the quadratic and the interaction specifications are therefore relevant here. In addition, the first three of these partial slopes are more difficult to evaluate than those discussed previously, since each involves the levels of *two* variables. For example, if the expected sign of x in Equation (8.15) is positive, this requires that:

$$\alpha_1 + 2\alpha_3 x + \alpha_5 z > 0, \quad \text{or that} \quad x > -(\alpha_1 + \alpha_5 z)/2\alpha_3.$$

When the signs of α_1, α_3, and α_5 differ, determining the range over which the expected sign is attained can involve tedious calculations.

Finally, the elasticity of y with respect to x conforms to the basic formula: (x/y) (partial slope of x), which, using Equation (8.15) is:

$$(x/y)(\alpha_1 + 2\alpha_3 x + \alpha_5 z)$$

The Reciprocal of an Explanatory Variable

Another specification that allows the partial slope of a variable to depend on its own level involves the use of the reciprocal of that variable. For this functional form, the partial slope of a variable displays a specific behavior: the slope continually increases or decreases, approaching 0 as the level of that variable approaches infinity. An equation with the reciprocal of x as an explanatory variable is given by Equation (8.17):

$$y_i = \alpha_0 + \alpha_1 (1/x)_i + \alpha_2 z_i + \varepsilon_i \qquad \textbf{(8.17)}$$

where $(1/x)$ is the reciprocal variable for x. As the value of x increases, the reciprocal of x decreases, and y approaches $(\alpha_0 + \alpha_2 z_i + \varepsilon_i)$. This term is called the **asymptotic** or **limiting value of y**. Note that this last expression is the vertical intercept for the two-dimensional graph of y and $(1/x)$, rather than that for the usual graph of x and y. The intercept for the x-y graph is obtained by setting y equal to zero in Equation (8.17) then solving for x, which (omitting the error term) is $-[\alpha_1/(\alpha_0 + \alpha_2 z_i)]$.

An example of two reciprocal functions is given in Figure 8.5. The first of these functions is: $y = 5 + 2(1/x)$. As x increases, the value of $2(1/x)$ approaches 0, causing

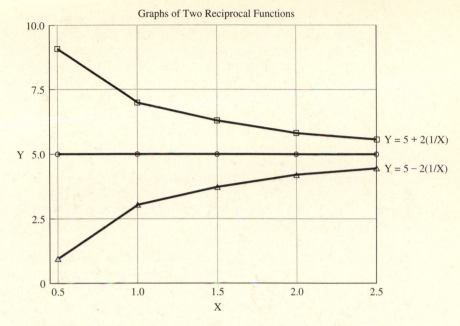

Figure 8.5

the curve to become flatter, indicating that its slope is approaching 0. The asymptotic value of y for this equation is therefore 5. Since the slope changes with the values of x, this slope is itself a function of x. *Note that when the coefficient of the reciprocal variable is positive, the function is downward sloping.*

The derivation of the partial slope of Equation (8.17) is somewhat complicated without the use of calculus. Because of this, the general expression for the partial slope with a reciprocal specification is stated without derivation[9]:

$$\text{partial slope of } x \text{ in (8.17): } -\alpha_1/x^2 \tag{8.18}$$

Since x^2 is always positive, the sign of this partial slope is the *opposite* of that for α_1. Furthermore, given the value of α_1, as x (and x^2) increase, the partial slope decreases, approaching 0, as Figure 8.5 shows. Finally, for the reciprocal specification given by Equation (8.17), the elasticity of y with respect to x takes the form:

$$(x/y)(\text{partial slope of } x) = (x/y)(-\alpha_1/x^2)$$
$$= -\alpha_1/(x \cdot y)$$

The most famous use of this functional form is the Phillips Curve, which expresses the relationship between the rate of growth in wages and the level of unemployment.

---

[9] This expression can be obtained easily with partial differentiation. Using the quotient rule for differentiation $\partial y/\partial x = \alpha_1 \cdot \partial(1/x)/\partial x = \alpha_1[-1/x^2]$, which is the expression given in the text.

As the unemployment rate decreases, approaching its full employment level, wage growth tends to accelerate as tighter labor markets cause firms to compete for labor, which is increasingly scarce at lower levels of unemployment. As unemployment rises, wage growth tends to fall, but at a decreasing rate. A point is eventually reached where further increases in unemployment have no effect on wage growth. Based on these characteristics of the relationship between wage growth and the rate of unemployment, a reciprocal specification for the rate of unemployment is appropriate, where the expected sign of the unemployment term is positive.

The original formulation of the Phillips Curve included this single explanatory variable. Economists soon came to find that this bivariate relationship was unstable, as the Phillips Curve was shifting through time. During the late 1960s and through the 1970s, we observed the joint occurrence of inflation and unemployment (this is the basis for the term "stagflation"). Theoretical developments then focused on the underlying basis of the Phillips Curve. Most notably, economists came to recognize that each curve was valid only for a specific level of expected inflation. Changes in expectations of future inflation thus alter the attainable combinations of wage growth and unemployment. The growth in compensation sought by employees for a given rate of unemployment therefore depends on worker perceptions of future inflation, since these expectations are the basis for their estimates of real wages. This modification led to the concept of the Expectations Augmented Phillips Curve.

Browne estimated the following Expectations Augmented Phillips Curve with annual data for the years 1958–1987.[10]

$$\widehat{\Delta w / w_t} = -1.8 + 0.9 p_t^e + 22.6(1/U)_t \qquad \bar{R}^2 = 0.81, \ n = 30$$
$$(1.8) \quad (11.3) \quad (5.1)$$

In this equation: $\Delta w / w$ is the annual percent change in compensation per hour, which includes wages, salaries, and benefits; p^e is a measure of expected inflation, the lagged inflation rate of the GNP deflator for personal consumption expenditures; and U is the civilian unemployment rate. Note that this measure of expected inflation presupposes the adaptive expectations framework discussed in Chapter 6.

The coefficient of the reciprocal unemployment rate is positive, as expected, and statistically significant. Using Equation (8.18), the estimated slope of the Phillips Curve is $-22.6/U^2$. A one percent increase in the civilian unemployment rate therefore lowers mean wage growth for a given level of expected inflation by 1.4 percent when U is 4 percent ($= -22.6/4^2$), by 0.6 percent when U equals 6 percent, and 0.4 percent when the unemployment rate is 8 percent.

The expected inflation variable is positive and statistically significant. Changes in p^e serve to shift the Phillips Curve and are part of the asymptotic value of wage growth (which equals $-1.8 + 0.9p^e$). Since the *level* of unemployment is inversely related to wage growth, while expected inflation is positively related, the effect of decreases in unemployment on wage growth can be offset by accompanying declines

---

[10] L. Browne, "The Labor Force, Unemployment Rates, and Wage Pressures," *New England Economic Review*, January/February 1989, pp. 21–29.

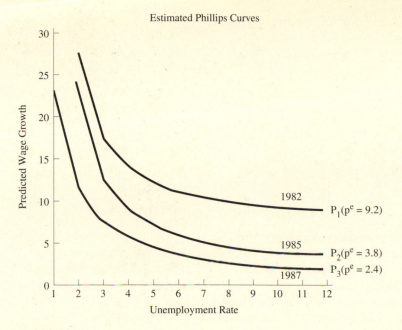

Figure 8.6

in inflationary expectations. This is the basis for one of the explanations Browne offers for the moderate wage growth that accompanied declining unemployment from 1982 to 1987 (the final year for her equation). The unemployment rate decreased from 9.7 percent in 1983 to 6.2 percent in 1987. Taken by itself, this would produce a substantial acceleration in wage demands. However, during this same period, actual and expected inflation decreased (her measure of expected inflation dropped from 9.2 percent in 1982 to 2.4 percent in 1987), which serves to moderate wage demands. A graph of the Phillips Curves implied by this equation is given in Figure 8.6. Using the value of p^e for 1982 gives the curve P_1. As the subsequent recovery proceeded, the Phillips Curve shifted down to P_2 in 1985 then to P_3 in 1987. The decreases in the unemployment rate that occurred over this period were thus consistent with moderate levels of mean wage growth.

Besides the Phillips Curve, the reciprocal specification can be used to relate the level of an explanatory variable to a dependent variable that is either a proportion or percentage. Strand and Dernburg estimated an equation where the dependent variable is the labor force participation rate, r, which is the ratio of labor force to the civilian noninstitutional population (P).[11] The explanatory variables included in

[11] K. Strand and T. Dernburg, "Cyclical Variation in Labor Force Participation," *Review of Economics and Statistics*, November 1964, pp. 378–391.

this equation are the employment rate (E/P), which is the proportion of the population that is currently employed, the ratio of unemployment insurance exhaustions (X) to P two months into the future, $(X/P)_{t+2}$, and the reciprocal of the civilian non-institutional population $(1/P)$. Their estimated monthly equation for 1947 to 1962 is[12]:

$$\hat{r}_t = \text{other terms} + 0.872(E/P)_t + 12.35(X/P)_{t+2} - 3492.2(1/P)_t$$
$$\phantom{\hat{r}_t = \text{other terms} + } (28.3) \qquad\quad (19.3) \qquad\qquad (8.3)$$

The negative sign of $(1/P)$ indicates that as population increases, the labor force participation rate increases at a decreasing rate, approaching the asymptotic value for r which equals 1.0.

Specifications Involving Logarithms

The previous sections examined various specifications where the original model is additive in the terms involving coefficients and explanatory variables. When the function of interest is multiplicative in the explanatory variables, we can utilize a logarithmic transformation to express this function in a form that is suitable for estimation with least squares. We have already seen examples of such functions in earlier chapters. For example, the stochastic Cobb-Douglas production function, $q = Ak^{\alpha}L^{\beta}e^{\varepsilon}$, can be "linearized" by taking the natural logarithm of both sides, which gives the estimable function:

$$\ln(q) = \alpha^* + \alpha \cdot \ln(k) + \beta \cdot \ln(L) + \varepsilon$$

where $\alpha^* = \ln(A)$. In this form, the least squares linearity requirement is met, so estimation can proceed with the methodology presented up to this point. A second use of logarithms arises in the context of estimating growth rates. The current value of y can be expressed as the product of its initial value, y_0, the growth rate (g) of y, and t, the number of time periods that have elapsed since the original time period. The equation based on these terms is:

$$y_t = y_0(1 + g)^t$$

which can be transformed into a form suitable for least squares estimation by applying logarithms. The resulting equation (after adding an error) is:

$$\ln(y)_t = \alpha_0 + \alpha_1 t + \varepsilon_t,$$

where $\alpha_0 = \ln(y_0)$ and $\alpha_1 = \ln(1 + g)$. To estimate this equation, we regress the natural logarithm of y on a time trend, *which is not a logarithm*. The coefficient of the time trend in this equation provides an estimate of $\ln(1 + g)$, from which we derive our estimate of the growth rate of y.

---

[12] The estimation technique is not least squares, but the results are presented to give an illustration of the use of this particular equation specification.

As these examples show, several variants of equations that utilize logarithms can be estimated with least squares: those with all variables as logarithms, the log-linear specification; and those with only some variables stated as logarithms, the **semi-log specification**. Each of the different logarithmic specifications will now be discussed.

All Variables as Logarithms: Log-Linear Specification

The general form of a **log-linear specification** with two explanatory variables is:

$$\ln(y)_i = \alpha_0 + \alpha_1 \ln(x)_i + \alpha_2 \ln(z)_i + \varepsilon_i \qquad \textbf{(8.19)}$$

The intercept in this equation is the natural logarithm of y when x and z equal 1 (the terms involving x and z then drop out, since ln(1) equals 0). This specification embodies an important feature: *the coefficient of each explanatory variable is a partial elasticity.* For example, α_1 in Equation (8.19) is the partial elasticity of y with respect to x, while α_2 is the partial elasticity of y with respect to z. The elasticities derived from this specification are therefore constant, while partial slopes are not constant. We will now establish that the coefficients α_1 and α_2 in Equation (8.19) are indeed elasticities. The discussion will proceed as follows. We first illustrate how partial slopes are determined with this specification, then enter this information into the general elasticity formula to establish that α_1 and α_2 are elasticities.

We begin this derivation by taking the first difference of Equation (8.19). Omitting the error term this is:

$$\Delta \ln(y)_t = \alpha_1 \Delta \ln(x)_t + \alpha_2 \Delta \ln(z)_t,$$

since the coefficients in this equation are constants. To derive the partial slope of x, z is assumed to be constant, which causes the last term on the right to drop out. The above equation therefore reduces to:

$$\Delta \ln(y)_t = \alpha_1 \Delta \ln(x)_t \qquad \textbf{(8.20)}$$

The change in the logarithm of y is $\ln(y)_t - \ln(y)_{t-1}$, which, according to the rules of logarithms, equals $\ln(y_t/y_{t-1})$. We can obtain an expression for the ratio in brackets by referring to the proportional growth rate formula given in Chapter 2:

$$g_y = \Delta y/y_{t-1} = (y_t/y_{t-1}) - 1$$

This can be manipulated to give the following expression for (y_t/y_{t-1}):

$$(y_t/y_{t-1}) = (1 + g_y) = 1 + \Delta y/y_{t-1} \qquad \textbf{(8.21)}$$

The change in the *natural logarithm* of y can therefore be expressed in terms of the change in the *level* of y:

$$\Delta \ln(y)_t = \ln(y_t/y_{t-1})$$
$$= \ln(1 + \Delta y/y_{t-1})$$
$$\approx \Delta y/y_{t-1} \qquad \textbf{(8.22)}$$

This approximation holds when the growth rate of y is small. Substituting the right side of Equation (8.22) and the corresponding result for $\Delta \ln(x)_t$ into Equation (8.20), that equation becomes:

$$\Delta y / y_{t-1} = \alpha_1 (\Delta x / x_{t-1})$$

The partial slope of x is (after dropping the subscripts):

$$\text{partial slope of } x: \Delta y / \Delta x = \alpha_1 (y/x)$$

Even though α_1 is constant, the ratio of y to x is generally not constant, which makes the value of this partial slope dependent on this ratio. We can obtain an expression for the partial elasticity of y with respect to x by entering this information into the general elasticity formula:

$$\text{partial elasticity of } x: (x/y)(\text{partial slope of } x) = (x/y)(\alpha_1 y / x) = \alpha_1$$

The elasticity of y with respect to x is therefore α_1, which is constant.

If we again return to log-linear form of the Cobb-Douglas production function equation given earlier:

$$\ln(q) = \alpha^* + \alpha \cdot \ln(k) + \beta \cdot \ln(L) + \varepsilon$$

where $\alpha^* = \ln(A)$. We see that α is the elasticity of output with respect to capital, which is constant, while β is the (constant) elasticity of q with respect to L. The partial slopes of capital and labor, which are marginal products, are proportional to their respective average products:

$$(\Delta q / \Delta k) = \alpha(q/k) \quad \text{and} \quad (\Delta q / \Delta L) = \beta(q/L)$$

where (q/k) and (q/L) are the average products of capital and labor, respectively. The factor of proportionality for each input is its output elasticity. For a Cobb-Douglas production function, the elasticity of ouput with respect to each input is therefore constant, and the marginal product of each input, which is proportional to the average product of that input, varies with the level of input usage.

An example of an estimated Cobb-Douglas production function for the manufacturing sector of the U.S. economy is given by Evans.[13] Evans adjusts the basic form of this function to reflect the cyclical behavior of the average product of labor. Because of the existence of fixed labor costs, such as hiring, screening, and payroll costs (see Chapter 4), employment fluctuates by a smaller proportion than does output over the course of the business cycle. This type of behavior results from "labor hoarding" (see Chapter 4). Faced with these costs, employers increase the flow of labor input by raising hours per worker (h) during the initial phase of a recovery, while not increasing the number of employees (N) until later. Because of this distinction between hours per worker and the number of workers, the total number of man-hours

---

[13] M. Evans, *Macroeconomic Activity: Theory, Forecasting, and Control* (New York: Harper & Row), 1969.

of employment, $(h \cdot N)$, is used as the labor input variable in the estimated production function. The effect of the capacity utilization rate (C_p) on capital is introduced by defining *utilized* capital, which is the product of C_p and the stock of capital (k). The basic form of the Cobb-Douglas production function that Evans estimates is:

$$q = A(h \cdot N)^{\alpha}(k \cdot C_p)^{\beta}e^{\varepsilon}$$

After applying a logarithmic transformation, this equation becomes:

$$\ln(q)_t = \alpha^* + \alpha \cdot \ln(h \cdot N)_t + \beta \cdot \ln(k \cdot C_p)_t + \varepsilon_t$$

His estimated equation is:

$$\widehat{\ln(q)_t} = 0.57 + 0.687 \ln(h \cdot N)_t + 0.283 \ln(K \cdot C_p)_t + \text{other} \qquad \bar{R}^2 = 0.98$$
$$\phantom{\widehat{\ln(q)_t} = 0.57 + } (8.8) (5.5) \text{terms}$$

where q is real gross output originating in the non-manufacturing sector (1958 = 100); N is manufacturing employment (millions); h is an index of hours per worker, with 40 hours equal to 1.0; k is the stock of capital (billions of 1958 dollars); and C_p is the capacity utilization rate in manufacturing. The coefficients of both man-hours of employment and utilized capital are positive and statistically significant. The coefficient of total man-hours, which is an estimate of the elasticity of manufacturing output with respect to labor input, indicates an inelastic value. The estimated elasticity of output with respect to utilized capital is also inelastic.

Recall from Chapter 6 that with a Cobb-Douglas production function the sum of the input coefficients measures returns to scale, which is the response of output to a proportional change in all inputs. If doubling all inputs causes output to double, constant returns to scale are said to exist, which implies constant long-run average total cost. In the estimated equation, the sum of the input coefficients equals 0.97 $(= 0.687 + 0.283)$, which provides evidence that (approximately) constant returns to scale in manufacturing existed during the time period for which the equation was estimated. A more conclusive determination of this possibility could be made by statistically testing the hypothesis of constant returns to scale.

A final example of a log-linear specification is a Keynesian demand for money function. The demand for money, or liquidity preference, as Keynes called it, consists of a transactions (and precautionary) component, which is a function of the level of income, and an asset demand component, which depends on interest rates. Estimated Keynesian money demand equations regress the real money supply (m) on the level of real GNP (y), which captures the transactions motive, one or more short-term interest rates (r), which represent the asset demand for money, and a lagged dependent variable $(m)_{t-1}$. We saw in Chapter 6 that when an equation includes a lagged dependent variable it is a short-run equation. The log-linear form is generally utilized so that each variable is a natural logarithm. The coefficient of real GNP provides an estimate of the short-run income elasticity of money demand, which is expected to be positive, while the interest rate coefficients estimate the short-run interest elasticity of the demand for money. The expected signs of the interest rate coefficients are negative, since interest rates represent the opportunity cost of holding money.

In an attempt to ascertain empirically whether the demand for money relationship has shifted since 1974, Hafer and Hein estimated three quarterly money demand equations for the period from 1960:1 to 1979:4.[14] The first of these, which is presented here, spans this entire period. The other two, which are estimated for the sub-periods 1960:1 to 1973:4 and 1974:1 to 1979:4, are discussed in Chapter 9.

$$\ln(M/P)_t = -0.28 + 0.057 \ln(y)_t - 0.019 \ln(r_c)_t - 0.039 \ln(r_s)_t + 0.962 \ln(M/P)_{t-1}$$
$$\quad\quad (2.4) \quad (2.5) \quad\quad\quad (3.5) \quad\quad\quad (1.8) \quad\quad\quad (13.6)$$

$$\bar{R}^2 = 0.874; \qquad \hat{\sigma}_\varepsilon = 0.004$$

In this equation (M/P) is the real value (1972 = 100) of the new M1 aggregate, which includes NOW, ATS, and credit union share draft accounts as part of "checkable deposits"; P is the GNP deflator (1972 = 100); y is real GNP (1972 = 100); r_c is the interest rate on commercial paper[15]; and r_s is a weighted average of interest rates on passbook savings.

The negative intercept in the estimated equation, -0.28, does not indicate the incorrect sign for this term. Since the dependent variable is a logarithm, the estimated intercept is also a logarithm. To obtain the estimated intercept for (M/P) in non-logarithmic form, it is necessary to take the antilog of this value, which entails raising e to the power of -0.28. The result is: $e^{-0.28} = 0.7558$. The estimated (short-term) income elasticity of money demand is 0.057. A one-percent increase in real GNP (such as 1500 to 1515) raises mean real money demand by just under six hundredths of one percent, given interest rates and money demand for the previous quarter. This highly inelastic estimate is substantially below the "benchmark" range of values in the demand for money literature. Because of this fact, Hafer and Hein suspect that the underlying money demand relationship has shifted during the sample period. The income elasticity of the demand for money determines the magnitude of the shift in a money demand curve, where the rate of interest (r) is on the vertical axis, such as Figure 8.7(a). This elasticity is also related to the slope of the money market equilibrium, or LM curve. This fairly low short-term elasticity implies that increases in real GNP produce relatively small rightward shifts in the money demand curve, which corresponds to a relatively flat LM curve such as that given in Figure 8.7(b). In this case, an increase in real GNP $(= y)$ requires a relatively small change in interest rates to restore money market equilibrium.

The estimated elasticities for each of the included interest rates are negative and statistically significant but small in magnitude. These values point to inelastic short-run interest elasticities. Together with the income coefficient, the implied short-run money demand curve is not very sensitive to changes in either interest rates or real

---

[14] R. W. Hafer and S. Hein, "The Shift in Money Demand: What Really Happened?," *Review*, Federal Reserve Bank of St. Louis, February 1982, pp. 11–15.

[15] Commercial paper refers to commercial bills outstanding, which are used by firms to finance production and trade. The interest rate on commercial paper is a short-term interest rate.

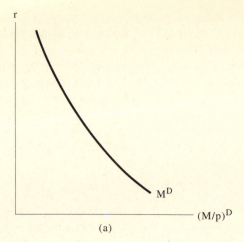

(a)

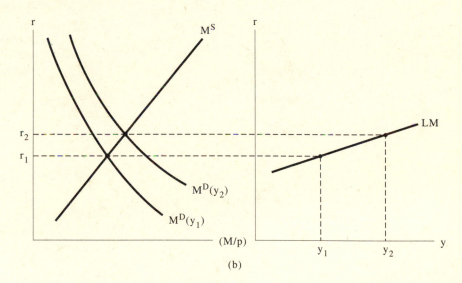

(b)

Figure 8.7 Money demand (M^D), money
supply (M^S), and LM curves

income. The interest elasticity of the demand for money is related to the effectiveness
of monetary policy. When the demand for money is interest inelastic, decreases in
the rate of interest brought about by increases in the supply of money do not induce
very substantial increases in the quantity of money demanded. As a result, the velocity
of circulation changes very little. Referring to the quantity theory of money: $M \cdot V = P \cdot Q$, increases in M are accompanied by relatively small rises in V, so that substantial

changes in total expenditure result from money supply increases. Under these circumstances, monetary policy is an effective means by which to stimulate both expenditure and nominal GNP.

Finally, the long-term money demand equation implied by the estimated equation above is obtained by assuming that money demand is in equilibrium, so that $\ln(M/P)_t = \ln(M/P)_{t-1}$. Making this substitution for $\ln(M/P)_{t-1}$ on the right side of this equation eliminates the lagged dependent variable. Each long-term coefficient is then obtained by multiplying the original coefficient by 26.3 ($= 1/(1 - 0.962)$). Substituting these long-term coefficients into the non-logarithmic form of the money demand equation we obtain:

$$\widehat{(M/P)_t} = 0.0006(y)_t^{1.5}(r_c)_t^{-0.44}(r_s)_t^{-1.03},$$

where the constant 0.0006 is e raised to the power -7.37 (the long-term equation intercept). A graph of the implied demand for money curve with $(y) = 1500$ and $r_c = 10$ percent is given by Figure 8.8. Notice that the estimated elasticities for y and r_s (1.5 and -1.03, respectively) are elastic in this long-run equation.

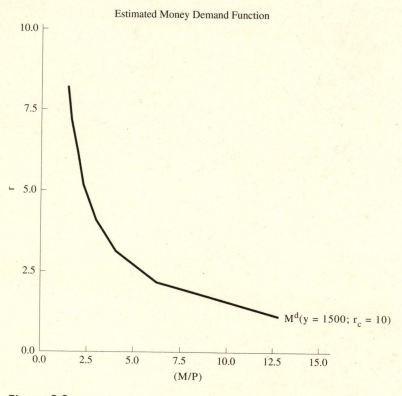

Estimated Money Demand Function

$M^d(y = 1500; r_c = 10)$

(M/P)

Figure 8.8

THE SEMI-LOG SPECIFICATION

Dependent Variable (Only) as a Logarithm

The log-linear specification is the first specification considered where the partial slope of a variable is a function of the level of the *dependent* variable. When the equation involves only y in logarithmic form, the partial slope is also a function of y. This specification is used in estimating relationships where the explanatory variables are exponentially related to y, or where interest lies in estimating the growth rate in y. When x and z are exponentially related to y, the functional form of this relationship can be expressed:

$$y = A e^{\alpha x} e^{\beta z} e^{\varepsilon}$$

where e is the constant 2.718, which is the base of the natural logarithm. When we apply a logarithmic transformation to this function, the resulting specification is logarithmic in y but linear in both x and z:

$$\ln(y) = \alpha^* + \alpha x + \beta z + \varepsilon, \tag{8.23}$$

since $\ln(e^{\alpha x}) = \alpha x$ and $\ln(e^{\beta z}) = \beta z$. We can derive the expressions for the partial slopes and elasticities of this equation using the results from the previous section. The partial slope for x is obtained by taking the first difference of Equation (8.23), assuming that z is constant (so that $\Delta z = 0$):

$$\Delta \ln(y) = \alpha \, \Delta x$$

Since $\Delta \ln(y) \approx \Delta y / y$, the above expression becomes:

$$\Delta y / y = \alpha \, \Delta x,$$

which gives the partial slope of x:

$$\Delta y / \Delta x = \alpha \cdot y.$$

For this specification, the partial slope of x is directly related to the level of y. By solving this partial slope expression for α:

$$\alpha = (\Delta y / y) / \Delta x$$

we see that the coefficient of x represents the proportional change in y for a one unit change in x, given the level of z. The partial elasticity of y with respect to x takes the form:

$$(x/y)(\text{partial slope of } x) = (x/y)(\alpha \cdot y) = \alpha \cdot x.$$

As these results show, neither the slope nor the partial elasticity of x is constant with this specification.

This particular semi-log specification is frequently used to estimate growth rates. Two possible models pertain. The first of these is stated in terms of an instantaneous growth rate for y (the rate for any point in time), while the second is based on compound growth. Each relates the current value of y, y_t, to an initial level, y_0, and a term incorporating the growth in y. The equations expressing each formulation are:

$$y_t = y_0 e^{gt} e^{\varepsilon_t} \qquad \text{instantaneous growth}$$

$$y_t = y_0 (1 + g)^t e^{\varepsilon_t} \qquad \text{compound growth}$$

Both of these equations are multiplicative, which makes them amenable to logarithmic transformations. If we take the natural logarithm of both sides of these equations we obtain:

$$\ln(y)_t = \alpha_0^* + gt + \varepsilon_t \qquad \text{instantaneous growth rate model}$$

$$\ln(y)_t = \alpha_0^* + \ln(1 + g)t + \varepsilon_t$$

$$= \alpha_0^* + \beta t + \varepsilon_t \qquad \text{compound growth rate model}$$

where $\alpha^* = \ln(y_0)$ and $\beta = \ln(1 + g)$. Note that both formulations entail regressing the natural logarithm of the dependent variable on a time trend. The difference arises in the meaning of the time trend coefficient. For the first equation, the coefficient of the time trend is itself a growth rate. It is called the **instantaneous growth rate** for y. Perhaps this can be more easily understood by referring to the meaning of the slope coefficient with this equation specification: it measures the proportionate change in y for a one unit change in x. Since x is a time trend, a one unit change in t equals 1. The slope coefficient thus measures the proportional change in y, which is equal to g.

Calculating the growth rate from the compound growth equation is slightly more complicated. The coefficient of the time trend in that equation is $\ln(1 + g)$, not the growth rate itself. We can obtain an expression for the growth rate by performing a simple manipulation. Since $\beta = \ln(1 + g)$, we can solve for g by taking the antilogarithm of both sides of the equation, then solve for β. Performing this operation:

$$e^{\beta} = e^{\ln(1 + g)}$$

$$= (1 + g)$$

The solution of this equation for g:

$$g = e^{\beta} - 1$$

is the **compound growth rate** of y.

Since regressing the natural logarithm of y on a time trend enables us either directly or indirectly to estimate a constant growth rate for y, both of these formulations are called **constant growth rate models**. Note that our estimate of y_0 in both models is obtained by raising e to the power of the estimated intercept, α^*, since the intercepts in these equations are the natural logarithm of y_0.

To illustrate the use of this specification, we will estimate the annual growth rate in real disposable personal income (y) from 1970 to 1988. Estimates of the instantaneous and compound growth rates are obtained by regressing the natural logarithm of real disposable personal income on a time trend (t). The resulting equation is:

$$\widehat{\ln(y)}_t = 7.414 + 0.0266t \qquad \bar{R}^2 = 0.984 \qquad \hat{\sigma}_\varepsilon = 0.0193$$
$$\quad\;\; (805.7) \quad (33.0) \qquad\qquad n = 19 \qquad\quad F = 1088.1$$

The coefficient of the time trend gives the estimated instantaneous growth rate in y, 2.66 percent per year. This coefficient is statistically significant at the 1 percent level. The estimated compound growth rate is:

$$e^{0.0266} - 1 = 0.0270$$

or 2.7 percent per year. Our estimate of y_0 is $e^{7.414}$, which equals 1659.0. The estimated original form of the compound growth equation is therefore:

$$\hat{y}_t = 1659(1.027)^t.$$

When $t = 1$ (in 1970), $\hat{y}$ equals 1703.8. For $t = 5$ (1974), estimated y is 1891.7, while $\hat{y}$ equals 2157.1 when $t = 10$ (in 1979).

The estimated growth rate of y need not be constant. If we regress the natural logarithm of y on a quadratic function of time, the estimated growth rate is then a function of time. If, for example, the estimated equation is:

$$\ln(y)_t = \alpha_0 + \alpha_1 t + \alpha_2 t^2 + \varepsilon_t,$$

then the partial slope is:

$$\Delta y/y = (\text{expression for quadratic partial slope}) \cdot \Delta t$$
$$= (\alpha_1 + 2\alpha_2 t)\,\Delta t$$

so that the one period growth rate in y is:

$$(\Delta y/y)/\Delta t = \alpha_1 + 2\alpha_2 t$$

This value differs depending on the time period selected. Using this specification, we again estimate the growth of real disposable personal income for the period from 1970 to 1988. The resulting equation is:

$$\widehat{\ln(y)}_t = 7.41 \quad + 0.0267t - 0.000004t^2 \qquad \bar{R}^2 = 0.983 \qquad \hat{\sigma}_\varepsilon = 0.0199$$
$$\quad\; (486.3) \quad (7.61) \qquad (0.24) \qquad\qquad n = 19 \qquad\quad F = 512.1$$

The estimated annual growth rate in RDPI is obtained from the expression: $0.0267 - 2(0.000004)t$, which gives a growth rate estimate of 2.67 percent for $t = 5$, 2.662 percent when $t = 10$, and 2.658 percent for the last time period ($t = 15$) for which the equation was estimated. The coefficient of the quadratic term in this equation is small and not statistically significant. It appears that the constant growth rate version of this equation is preferable, since the addition of t^2 improves neither the equation standard error nor the adjusted R^2.

To test the statistical significance of the time trend in this quadratic specification, it is necessary to employ an F-test based on the null hypothesis that all the coefficients of time are jointly 0. If time and its square are the only explanatory variables included in the specification, as is the case here, the equation F-statistic is the appropriate test statistic for this null hypothesis. In this example, the F value of 512.1 allows the null hypothesis to be rejected at the one-percent level and above.

This same specification has also been used with cross-sectional data. One of the equations used by Mincer to estimate the return to labor market experience for white males is[16]:

$$\widehat{\ln(y)} = 6.2 + 0.107S + 0.081t - 0.0012t^2 \qquad R^2 = 0.285$$
$$\phantom{\widehat{\ln(y)} = 6.2 + }(72.3) \quad (75.5) \quad (55.8)$$

where y is annual earnings of white males in the nonfarm sector for 1959; S is years of completed schooling; and t is the number of years of employment experience, which serves the same function as does a time trend. In this equation, the return to experience is measured by the growth in earnings for one more year of experience, given the level of completed schooling. The negative sign for t^2 indicates that additional experience increases mean earnings at a decreasing rate, given the level of schooling. The estimated return to experience in this equation is: $0.081 - 2(0.0012) \cdot t$. Because the coefficients in this expression differ in sign, the return to experience is not always positive. The expected positive sign occurs for $t < 33.75$ years, which likely encompasses virtually the entire sample used to estimate this equation.

Independent Variable (Only) as a Logarithm

For the sake of completeness, the specification where the level of y is regressed on the natural logarithm of x will be considered. The form of this equation is:

$$y_i = \alpha_0 + \alpha_1 \ln(x)_i + \alpha_2 z_i + \varepsilon_i$$

The partial slope of x is found by taking the first difference of this equation, assuming z is constant:

$$\Delta y = \alpha_1(\Delta x/x),$$

which gives the expression:

$$\text{partial slope of } x: \Delta y/\Delta x = \alpha_1/x$$

With this specification, the partial slope of x is inversely related to x. If we solve this

---

[16] J. Mincer, *Schooling, Experience, and Earnings* (New York: National Bureau of Economic Research), 1974.

expression for the coefficient of x:

$$\alpha_1 = \Delta y/(\Delta x/x),$$

we see that α_1 is the (absolute) change in y for a one percent change in x, given the level of z. Finally, the partial elasticity of y with respect to x is:

$$(x/y)(\text{partial slope of } x) = (x/y)(\alpha_1/x) = \alpha_1/y.$$

The partial slope of x is therefore inversely related to x, while the elasticity of y with respect to x is inversely related to y.

A LOOK AHEAD. This chapter has outlined the major specifications used in econometrics. However, the material presented here presupposes that the equation intercept and each partial slope pertains to every observation in the data set. Unfortunately, this is not always the case. When important demographic, regional, or temporal differences exist among the values in a database, these must often be taken into account when estimating a relationship. The effect of price on the quantity demanded of a good might differ, for example, depending on which geographic region is considered. The spending habits of males and females for a particular product may be different. Or, the return to schooling for a given level of education may differ among males and females. Chapter 9 illustrates how factors such as these (region, sex, and specific time period) can be incorporated into least squares analysis.

KEY TERMS

Asymptotic	Linear effect coefficient
Compound growth rate	Log-linear specification
Constant growth rate model	Partial elasticity
Cubic specification	Semi-log specification
Dimensional misspecification	Test for the linearity of the equation specification
First difference form	
Instantaneous growth rate	Test of structural difference
Interaction effect coefficient	Quadratic effect coefficient
Limiting value of y	

EXERCISES

1. If we were to model the production function for a particular industry with the following linear specification:

$$q_i = \alpha_1 L_i + \alpha_2 k_i + \varepsilon_i$$

(a) Indicate the theoretical problems associated with this specification.

(b) How can we test for the existence of economies of scale with this production function?

(c) If we assume that the marginal product of each input depends on the level of the other input, so that $MP_L = f(k)$ and that $MP_k = g(L)$, provide an alternative equation specification that is consistent with this behavior.

2. Provide a model of the consumption function that does not restrict the MPC to a single value, but instead, allows real consumption expenditure to rise with real income at a decreasing rate.

3. Assume that the total cost (c) function for a firm is:

$$c = Aq^\alpha w^\beta r^\gamma e^\varepsilon$$

where q is output, w is the wage rate, r is the cost of capital, and ε is a stochastic error term.

(a) From microeconomics we expect that if both w and r are doubled for a given level of output, the total cost of production should also double. This condition is not necessarily met with the function as it now stands. How must this cost function be modified to satisfy this requirement?

(b) How can this function be made estimable with least squares?

(c) Without incorporating the changes indicated in **(a)**, how can we test *statistically* whether doubling both w and r doubles q?

4. If, instead of a linear relationship between the civilian unemployment rate and the capacity utilization rate in manufacturing, we specify this relationship as:

$$u_t = \alpha_0 + \alpha_1(1/CAP)_t + \varepsilon_t$$

(a) What is the expected sign of α_1?

(b) Critique the validity of this functional form (irrespective of lags) to characterize this relationship.

5. If we are interested in estimating the impact of Unemployment Insurance on labor supply (as represented by the number of weeks unemployed, W), and there are two policy variables: the weekly replacement rate (R), which measures the proportion of pre-unemployment income that weekly benefits replace; and potential duration (PD), the maximum number of weeks to which a person is entitled to benefits, our basic relationship is:

$$W_i = f(R_i, PD_i, \varepsilon_i).$$

Prior expectations lead us to believe that the impact of each policy variable on W depends on both its own level as well as that of the other policy variable. Illustrate an equation specification that incorporates this prior expectation. Give the expected sign for each coefficient that is associated with a policy variable.

6.   Using the following data:

YEAR	(q/h)	w
1970	88.4	90.0
1971	91.0	91.8
1972	93.8	94.6
1973	95.8	96.4
1974	93.9	95.5
1975	95.7	96.1
1976	98.3	98.7
1977	100.0	100.0
1978	100.9	101.0
1979	99.4	99.3
1980	99.0	96.7
1981	100.0	96.0
1982	99.1	97.1
1983	102.0	97.8
1984	104.2	97.5
1985	105.6	98.0
1986	107.7	101.1
1987	108.9	101.2
1988	111.1	101.8
1989	112.0	102.3

where (q/h) = output per hour of the nonfarm business sector (1977 = 100), and w = real compensation per hour of the nonfarm business sector (1977 = 100),

(a) Regress w on (q/h). What is the expected sign of (q/h)? Why?

(b) Test the null hypothesis that the population coefficient of (q/h) equals 1 against the alternative hypothesis that this coefficient is less than 1 at the 5 percent significance level. What is the economic basis of this hypothesis test?

(c) Estimate the compound annual and instantaneous growth rates in real compensation per hour for the entire period 1970–1989.

(d) Test for a nonconstant growth rate in real compensation per hour.

(e) Estimate the compound annual and instantaneous growth rates for (q/h) over the entire 1970–1989 period.

(f) What are the implications of the empirical findings above for the presence of inflationary pressures in the economy? Why?

7.   If we use a cubic functional form to relate x to y (as we did for the total cost function in this chapter):

$$y_i = \alpha_0 + \alpha_1 x_i + \alpha_2 x_i^2 + \alpha_3 x_i^3 + \varepsilon_i$$

Show that: $\Delta y_i / \Delta x_i = \alpha_1 + 2\alpha_2 x_i + 3\alpha_3 x_i^2$ (hint: use the method applied to quadratic functions in the beginning of this chapter).

8. Provide some economic examples of equations for which a linear specification is inappropriate.

9. Contrast the methods used to determine the statistical significance of a variable in linear and quadratic specifications.

10. How is the estimated marginal product of labor obtained from a log-linear production function?

11. In the following equation:

$$\ln(y)_t = \alpha_0 + \alpha_1 \ln(t) + \varepsilon_t \qquad (t \text{ is a time trend})$$

(a) What is the interpretation of α_1?

(b) Obtain an expression for $\Delta y / \Delta t$.

(c) Repeat (b) when the dependent variable is y_t (and not $\ln(y_t)$).

APPENDIX   TABLE OF PARTIAL SLOPE OF *x* FOR DIFFERENT SPECIFICATIONS

SPECIFICATION	PARTIAL SLOPE	PARTIAL ELASTICITY
LINEAR: $y_i = \alpha_0 + \alpha_1 x_i + \alpha_2 z_i + \varepsilon_i$	α_1	$(x_i/y_i)\alpha_1$
QUADRATIC: $y_i = \alpha_0 + \alpha_1 x_i + \alpha_2 x_i^2 + \alpha_3 z_i + \varepsilon_i$	$\alpha_1 + 2\alpha_2 x_i$	$(x_i/y_i)(\alpha_1 + 2\alpha_2 x_i)$
QUADRATIC WITH INTERACTION TERM: $y_i = \alpha_0 + \alpha_1 x_i + \alpha_2 x_i^2 + \alpha_3 z_i + \alpha_4(x_i \cdot z_i) + \varepsilon_i$	$\alpha_1 + 2\alpha_2 x_i + \alpha_4 z_i$	$(x_i/y_i)(\alpha_1 + 2\alpha_2 x_i + \alpha_4 z_i)$
RECIPROCAL: $y_i = \alpha_0 + \alpha_1(1/x)_i + \alpha_2 z_i + \varepsilon_i$	$-\alpha_1/x_i^2$	$-\alpha_1/(x_i \cdot y_i)$
LOG-LINEAR: $\ln(y)_i = \alpha_0 + \alpha_1 \ln(x)_i + \alpha_2 \ln(z)_i + \varepsilon_i$	$\alpha_1(y_i/x_i)$	α_1
SEMI-LOG: $\ln(y)_i = \alpha_0 + \alpha_1 x_i + \alpha_2 z_i + \varepsilon_i$ $y_i = \alpha_0 + \alpha_1 \ln(x_i) + \alpha_2 z_i + \varepsilon_i$	$\alpha_1 \cdot y_i$ α_1/x_i	$\alpha_1 \cdot x_i$ α_1/y_i

9 Dichotomous Variables

The previous chapter introduced the major equation specifications that are utilized in econometrics. The use of any one of these specifications is valid only if it adequately characterizes the underlying structure of the process being modeled for all observations in the data base. Problems arise in this context when either the intercept or partial slopes vary among data divisions or subperiods within a data base. For example, the partial slope of x may differ among different demographic groups or regions. Or, the underlying structure of an equation may change as the result of price and wage controls, wars, new laws, or altered operating procedures used by the government. We must therefore consider both functional forms and the constancy of the coefficients within a selected specification before estimating a multiple regression equation. Introducing such *qualitative* considerations into an estimated equation often improves its estimation and forecasting performance.

This chapter outlines the method used to incorporate qualitative considerations into econometric equations: the use of dummy variables. The first part of this chapter describes the construction, interpretation, and use of these as explanatory variables. The final part illustrates their use as dependent variables, which results in estimating the probability that an event or qualitative consideration occurs.

DUMMY VARIABLES

Intercept Dummy Variables

The process of econometric modeling does not end with the equation specification decision. The functional form that is ultimately selected must adequately depict the underlying structure of the relationship being studied. Economic theory presents the *general outline* of an equation's specification by identifying the most important explanatory variables, and, with specific assumptions, an appropriate functional form.

We must sometimes extend this information to control for the influence of additional factors that affect our dependent variable within a specific set of data.

For an estimated equation to be valid, it is necessary that the underlying structure implied by its specification apply to all of the observations in the data base used to estimate this relationship. This can be seen with reference to the following equation:

$$y_i = \alpha_0 + \alpha_1 x_i + \alpha_2 z_i + \varepsilon_i \tag{9.1}$$

The intercept in this equation, α_0, measures the mean of y when x and z are both 0. Equation (9.1) implicitly assumes this value is valid for all of the observations in the data base. This coefficient might differ based on a specific aspect of the data used to estimate Equation (9.1). For instance, regional, demographic, or temporal differences might exist in the values of y. Examples of such differences are: the level of economic growth (y) might differ between the eastern and western regions of the United States; economic growth in the 1980s may differ from levels in earlier periods; earnings (y) are different for males and females; earnings differ for white and nonwhite employees.

All of these considerations represent *qualitative* factors, which, by themselves, are not readily quantifiable. How can we quantify such factors so that they may be entered into our regression equation? The answer to this question lies with a special type of variable, called a **dummy variable**, which captures qualitative effects by coding the different possible outcomes with numerical values. This involves little more than dichotomizing outcomes and arbitrarily assigning the values of 0 and 1 to the different possibilities. To capture such qualitative influences, we thus create a new variable D, where $D = 1$ for one of the possibilities and $D = 0$ otherwise. The choice of which category is assigned the value 1 does not alter the results. It serves merely to change the interpretation of the dummy variable coefficient, as is shown later.

The point of demarcation occurs where a meaningful difference in the behavior of y is expected to exist. Sometimes this is fairly obvious (as with demographic characteristics), while at other times the categories for D must be established by empirical testing. Using the previous examples, possible choices are: $D = 1$ for the eastern United States and $D = 0$ for the western United States; $D = 1$ from 1980 to the end of a data base while $D = 0$ for the earlier years; $D = 1$ for white employees and $D = 0$ for nonwhite employees; and $D = 1$ for males with $D = 0$ for females.

If we enter the dummy variable, D, into this equation, then:

$$y_i = \alpha_0 + \alpha_1 x_i + \alpha_2 z_i + \alpha_3 D_i + \varepsilon_i, \tag{9.2}$$

where D_i is the value of D for observation i. The correct interpretation of the coefficient of D_i can be established by taking the expected value of this equation for each value of D:

$$E(y_i | D_i = 0) = \alpha_0 + \alpha_1 x_i + \alpha_2 z_i,$$

and

$$E(y_i | D_i = 1) = \alpha_0 + \alpha_1 x_i + \alpha_2 z_i + \alpha_3(1)$$
$$= (\alpha_0 + \alpha_3) + \alpha_1 x_i + \alpha_2 z_i,$$

assuming $E(\varepsilon_i) = 0$. The coefficient of the dummy variable represents the *difference* in the equation intercept for the condition with $D = 1$, while α_0 is the intercept for observations with $D = 0$. For this reason, the observations with $D = 0$ are referred to as the **control or comparison group** with cross-sectional data and the **comparison period** with time series data. The dummy variable coefficient represents the difference in $E(y)$ when $D = 1$, given the levels of x and z, while the partial slopes of x and z equal α_1 and α_2 for all data points. In the first of the growth examples above, α_3 represents the difference between mean economic growth in the eastern and western United States, given the levels of x and z, while in the second example this coefficient indicates the difference in mean economic growth since 1980, for given values of x and z.

The two-dimensional graph of Equation (9.2) consists of a pair of parallel lines, where the height difference for any value of x equals α_3. The sign of the dummy variable coefficient determines which of these curves has the larger intercept. If α_3 is positive, the regression line for $D = 1$ will lie above that for the control group, since $E(y_i | D_i = 1)$ exceeds $E(y_i | D_i = 0)$, as shown in Figure 9.1. If y is annual earnings, x is experience, and $D = 1$ for males, 0 for females, this graph indicates that:

  (i) mean earnings of males are higher than those of females for any level of experience;
 (ii) mean earnings for any level of experience differ by the constant amount α_3; and
(iii) the return to experience, $\Delta y / \Delta x$, is identical for both males and females ($= \alpha_1$).

A dummy variable can be created in most regression programs by making use of IF statements or logical operators. Examples of the creation of this type of variable

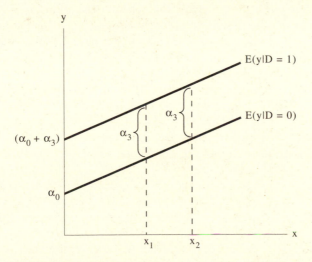

Figure 9.1 Regression lines for a dummy variable with a positive coefficient

for SAS and Micro TSP are given here:

SAS	MicroTSP

(a) Create a dummy variable equal to 1 for time periods greater than 35, 0 otherwise.

IF TIME > 35 THEN D = 1;   GENR D = (TIME > 35)
ELSE D = 0;

(b) Create a dummy variable equal to 1 for persons with income less than or equal to $50,000.

IF INCOME < = 50000 THEN D = 1;   GENR D = (INCOME < = 50000)
ELSE D = 0;

(c) Create a dummy variable equal to 1 for time periods 12 through 20, 0 otherwise.

IF 12 LE TIME LE 20 THEN D = 1;   GENR D = (12 < = TIME < = 20)
ELSE D = 0;

Note that in SAS, you are permitted to use either the inequality symbols or abbreviations. Above, LE stands for "less than or equal to."

Once the dummy variable has been created, it is ready for use in a regression equation. *The mean of this variable indicates the proportion of the sample for which D = 1.*

The sample regression function corresponding to Equation (9.2) is:

$$\hat{y}_i = \hat{\alpha}_0 + \hat{\alpha}_1 x_i + \hat{\alpha}_2 z_i + \hat{\alpha}_3 D_i$$

The coefficient $\hat{\alpha}_3$ is our estimate of the difference in the mean of y for D = 1. To test whether the actual difference in $E(y)$ is 0, or that $E(y_i|D_i = 1)$ equals $E(y_i|D_i = 0)$, we use a null hypothesis which states that the population intercept is the same for the two conditions specified in D. If the intercept is the same for both of these conditions, then $\alpha_3 = 0$. Our null hypothesis is thus: $H_0: \alpha_3 = 0$. The test of this hypothesis involves a t-test on the estimated coefficient of the dummy variable in this equation, where we ascertain whether $\hat{\alpha}_3$ is significantly different from 0. The test statistic is: $\hat{\alpha}_3/\hat{\sigma}_3$, where the denominator in this expression is the estimated standard deviation of $\hat{\alpha}_3$. If the value of this statistic exceeds the critical value for the selected level of significance, we reject the null hypothesis of identical intercepts in favor of the alternative hypothesis of different intercepts.

Beyond its simplicity, a desirable feature of the dummy variable technique is that only one degree of freedom is lost (from including the variable D) in estimating the curves for the different groups or time periods under consideration. The alternative to this technique is to divide the sample and estimate separate regressions for each group or time period. It is possible that one of these subsamples might not have enough observations to allow positive degrees of freedom, so that separate regressions are not possible.

   The unemployment rate (U) capacity utilization rate (CAP) relationship discussed since Chapter 2 can be extended to include a temporal dummy variable. Figure 9.2(a) graphs the civilian unemployment rate for the period from 1960 to 1989. Since 1974 the unemployment rate has been considerably higher than it was for the earlier years in this graph. This is, of course, the time period since OPEC came into existence. We will test the hypothesis that the mean unemployment rate has been higher since 1974 by using the dummy variable technique. The value of D is 1 for the period from 1974 to 1989 and 0 for 1960 to 1973. The expected sign of D is positive. The sample

(a)

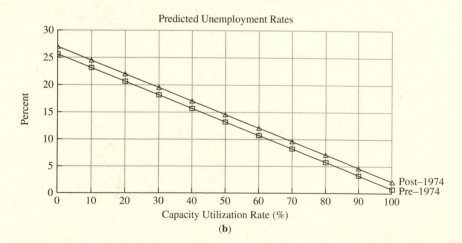

(b)

Figure 9.2

regression functions (for 1960 to 1989) with and without the dummy variable are:

Without Dummy Variable (Entire Period)

$$\hat{u}_t = 30.0 - 0.293\text{CAP}_t \qquad \bar{R}^2 = 0.761 \quad \hat{\sigma}_\varepsilon = 0.783$$
$$\phantom{\hat{u}_t = }(12.1) \quad (9.7) \qquad\qquad F = 93.6 \quad n = 30 \quad \text{ESS} = 17.2 \tag{9.3a}$$

With Dummy Variable

$$\hat{u}_t = 25.6 - 0.247\text{CAP}_t + 1.1D_t \qquad \bar{R}^2 = 0.863 \quad \hat{\sigma}_\varepsilon = 0.593$$
$$\phantom{\hat{u}_t = }(12.3) \quad (9.9) \qquad\quad (4.7) \qquad F = 92.4 \quad n = 30 \quad \text{ESS} = 9.5 \tag{9.3b}$$

The estimated coefficient of D is positive and statistically significant. The magnitude of this coefficient indicates that the mean unemployment rate corresponding to any capacity utilization rate is 1.1 percent higher after 1974. This estimate, which is approximately twice the overall equation standard error (of 0.593), indicates that a substantial shift in this relationship has occurred. Including this dummy variable affects the slope estimate as well. A 1 percent increase in the capacity utilization rate is predicted to lower the mean unemployment rate by 0.293 percent for the entire sample period, so that a 3.4 percent increase in CAP is required to reduce the mean unemployment rate by 1 percent. Contrast this with the estimate from the second equation: the sensitivity of U to changes in CAP is smaller, such that a 4 percent rise in the capacity utilization rate lowers the mean of U by 1 percent. Including the dummy variable has also improved the performance of the estimated equation: the t-statistics for both the intercept and the capacity utilization rate are higher when the dummy variable is included, and the equation standard error is lower.

The estimated equations for the two periods covered by the dummy variable (from Equation (9.3b)) are:

$$\hat{u}_t = 25.6 - 0.247\text{CAP}_t \qquad \text{for 1960 to 1973;} \tag{9.4a}$$

$$\hat{u}_t = (25.6 + 1.1) - 0.247\text{CAP}_t, \quad \text{or}$$

$$\hat{u}_t = 26.7 - 0.247\text{CAP}_t \qquad \text{for 1974 to 1989} \tag{9.4b}$$

Figure 9.2(b) plots each of these equations for the different possible values of the capacity utilization rate.

As a second example of regression with a dummy variable, we will consider an equation whose dependent variable is a natural logarithm. Tatom estimated the following potential hours per worker (HPW) equation which he then used to determine potential GNP[1]:

$$\widehat{\ln(\text{HPW})}_t = 0.797 - 0.496(U - U_f)_t + 0.177(U - U_f)_{t-1} - 0.001t + 0.014D$$
$$\phantom{\widehat{\ln(\text{HPW})}_t = }(546.1) \quad (6.1) \qquad\qquad (2.16) \qquad\qquad (57.1) \quad (7.3)$$

$$\bar{R}^2 = 0.99 \quad \hat{\sigma}_\varepsilon = 0.0032$$

---

[1] John Tatom, "Potential Output and the Recent Productivity Decline," *Review*, Federal Reserve Bank of St. Louis, January 1982, pp. 3–16.

In this equation, U is the civilian unemployment rate, U_f is the full employment rate of unemployment; t is a time trend; and D is a dummy variable equal to 1 from 1961:3 to 1967:2 and 0 for the remainder of the estimation period, which extends from 1948:2 to 1981:3. The variable $(U - U_f)$, which represents labor market slack, equals 0 when the actual unemployment rate coincides with its full employment level, or $U = U_f$. When this occurs, hours per worker attain their potential level. The time trend coefficient measures the secular growth rate in hours per worker, which is assumed to be constant. Note that with a dependent variable that is a natural logarithm, the time trend coefficient is an estimated growth rate and not the secular trend.

The coefficient of the dummy variable in this equation measures the *percent* difference in the mean of HPW for the period during which $D = 1$, given labor slack in this and the preceding period, and the secular trend in hours. This can be seen by evaluating the "partial slope" of the dummy variable:

$$\Delta \ln(\text{HPW}) = 0.014 \Delta D$$

We have seen that the change in the natural logarithm of a variable is approximately equal to the proportional change in that variable. Applying this information to the left side of the above expression, we have:

$$\Delta \text{HPW}/\text{HPW} = 0.014 \Delta D$$

and

$$\Delta \text{HPW}/\text{HPW} = 0.014$$

since $\Delta D = 1$. The positive and statistically significant dummy variable coefficient thus indicates that mean hours per worker were 1.4 percent higher for the period from 1961:3 to 1967:2. The estimated intercepts for these time periods are 0.797 for the comparison period, and 0.811 ($= 0.797 + 0.014$) when $D = 1$.

In a full employment equilibrium, $U = U_f$, so that $(U - U_f)_t = (U - U_f)_{t-1} = 0$. The terms involving labor market slack thus drop out, leaving only an intercept and a time trend. Estimates of the *logarithm* of potential hours per worker are then:

Other than 1961:3 to 1967:2: $0.797 - 0.001t$

1961:3 to 1967:2: $(0.797 + 0.014) - 0.001t = 0.811 - 0.001t$.

A final example is an equation by Jenkins and Montmarquette, who investigated the opportunity cost of displaced workers in the Canadian aircraft industry.[2] Their estimated equation is:

$$\widehat{\ln(w)_i} = 1.429 - 0.18\text{Sex}_i + 0.00011S_i + 0.0116\text{Sch}_i - 0.0004\text{Dur}_i + \text{other terms}$$
$$\quad (8.8) \quad (2.2) \quad\quad (0.2) \quad\quad (2.2) \quad\quad\quad (1.9)$$

$$\bar{R}^2 = 0.09 \quad n = 248 \quad F = 4.54$$

---

[2] Glenn Jenkins and Claude Montmarquette, "Estimating the Private and Social Opportunity Cost of Displaced Workers," *Review of Economics and Statistics*, 1978, pp. 342–353.

where, for the ith person, w is the estimated value of hourly wages in alternative employment, or the alternative wage rate (in Canadian $); Sex is a dummy variable equal to 1 for females, 0 for males; S is the number of weeks of seniority; Sch is years of completed schooling; and Dur is the duration of unemployment (in days). The coefficient of Sex is negative and statistically significant. The estimated intercept for females is 1.249 ($= 1.429 - 0.18$), which gives a nonlogarithmic value of $3.49 ($= e^{1.249}$). The corresponding value for males is $4.17 ($= e^{1.429}$). Given the level of seniority, completed schooling, and the duration of unemployment, the mean hourly alternative wage of females is 83.7 percent of that for males.

Each of these examples deals with equations that contain a single dummy variable. There is no reason why an equation cannot contain more than one dummy variable. For cross-sectional data, often-included dummy variables are sex; race; whether an observation occurred in an urban or regional setting; whether a person is a high school graduate; if the person is a college graduate; if the person is married; participation in a government program; and numerous other demographic characteristics. In addition to this, dummy variables can be created from categorical classifications. If each person in a sample is employed in one of several possible industrial classifications, a separate dummy variable can be created for each of these classifications. The single dummy variable that indicates the person's industrial classification is then set equal to 1, with all others equal to 0. For time series data, dummy variables are created for specific time periods based on factors such as the occurrence of recessions, whether price and wage controls existed, if credit conditions were imposed, if major strikes occurred, to distinguish separate countries, and so forth.

To see how multiple dummy variables are interpreted in a regression equation, we will assume that two sets of conditions exist. We create the variables $D1$ and $D2$, then enter them into the following regression equation:

$$y_i = \alpha_0 + \alpha_1 D1_i + \alpha_2 D2_i + \alpha_3 x_i + \varepsilon_i$$

Assume that $D1$ is a dummy variable that denotes the sex of an individual, with $D1 = 1$ for females, and 0 for males, and that $D2$ denotes participation in a government program, where $D2 = 1$ for participants and 0 for nonparticipants. The meaning of α_1 and α_2 in this equation can be seen by taking the expected value of y_i for each *pair* of $D1$–$D2$ values. The results, beginning with the comparison group (pair), and assuming that $E(\varepsilon_i) = 0$, is:

$E(y_i | D1 = 0 \text{ and } D2 = 0) = \alpha_0 + \alpha_3 x_i$ (the control group: male nonparticipants)

$E(y_i | D1 = 1 \text{ and } D2 = 0) = (\alpha_0 + \alpha_1) + \alpha_3 x_i$ (female nonparticipants)

$E(y_i | D1 = 0 \text{ and } D2 = 1) = (\alpha_0 + \alpha_2) + \alpha_3 x_i$ (male participants)

$E(y_i | D1 = 1 \text{ and } D2 = 1) = (\alpha_0 + \alpha_1 + \alpha_2) + \alpha_3 x_i$ (female participants)

The intercepts differ depending on sex and program participation. A purely mechanical interpretation for α_1 is the following: given the level of x, α_1 is the difference in $E(y)$ for both female and male nonparticipants, and female and male participants. *A more convenient way of viewing this coefficient is to consider it as a partial slope: the change in E(y) as D1 (sex) goes from 0 to 1 (i.e., the difference in E(y) for females), given the levels of x and D2 (participation).* Using similar reasoning, the coefficient of $D2$ (participation) is the rate change in $E(y)$ as $D2$ goes from 0 to 1 (i.e., the difference in $E(y)$ for participants), given the levels of x and $D1$ (sex).

To determine whether the equation intercept is the same for all observations, it is necessary to consider two types of statistical tests. The first of these ascertains whether the difference in the intercept is significantly different from 0 for each condition stipulated by a single dummy variable. In the above example, the first test considers whether the intercept is the same for males and females. The null hypothesis states that both sexes have the same intercept, which implies that the coefficient of $D1$ equals 0. As shown previously, this involves a t-test on the estimated coefficient of $D1$. If $\hat{\alpha}_1$ is statistically significant, the null hypothesis is rejected. The other individual test considers whether the intercept differs according to program participation. The statistical test involves a t-test for the coefficient of $D2$. The second type of test is intended to establish whether the intercept is the same for all observations. The null hypothesis for this test states that the intercept is the same for all data points, in which case α_1 and α_2 are both 0. This involves the Wald test outlined in Chapter 6, where the entire equation is the unrestricted equation, and the restricted equation omits all dummy variables.

For time series data, it is possible to include separate dummy variables for each of two nonoverlapping periods. In this case, the combination $D1 = 1$ and $D2 = 1$ never occurs, which simplifies the interpretation of the dummy variable coefficients. An example of this type of equation is given by Bordo and Choudhri, who examine the link between monetary growth and inflation in Canada for the years 1971 to 1980.[3] Their estimated equation is:

$$\hat{\pi}_t = -0.008 - 0.005\text{DUMC}_t + 0.009\text{DUMA}_t + 1.119\text{MG}_t + 0.19\text{ENINF}_t$$
$$\quad (1.7) \quad (2.1) \quad\quad\quad (2.7) \quad\quad\quad (5.8) \quad\quad\quad (2.5)$$

$$R^2 = 0.597 \quad \hat{\sigma}_\varepsilon = 0.0064$$

where π is the annual inflation rate in Canada; DUMC = 1 for the existence of price and wage controls, 1975:4 to 1978:3, 0 otherwise; DUMA = 1 for the year after the removal of price and wage controls, 1978:4 to 1979:3, 0 otherwise; MG is a 12 quarter moving average of lagged growth rates in M1, which is included to represent the direct (demand-side) effect of monetary policy on π; and ENINF is a four-quarter moving average of the ratio of a price index for energy prices to the GNP deflator, which is intended to measure the indirect (supply-side) effect of energy price effects on π. The negative and statistically significant coefficient of DUMC is consistent with a lower annual inflation rate for the period when the price and wage program was in effect. The estimated mean inflation rate is one-half of one percent (0.005) lower

---

[3] Michael Bordo and Ehsan Choudhri, "The Link Between Money and Prices in an Open Economy: The Canadian Evidence from 1971 to 1980," *Review*, Federal Reserve Bank of St. Louis, August/September 1982, pp. 13–23.

during the period of controls, given monetary policy and energy price inflation. In the year following the removal of controls, the estimated mean inflation rate increased by 0.009, which is given by the significant coefficient of DUMA. Note that this increase exceeds the estimated fall in the mean inflation rate brought about by the wage and price program.

A major pitfall exists that must be avoided when specifying equations that include dummy variables. In the examples considered up to this point, each dummy variable represents *two* possible outcomes. If, instead, a separate dummy variable is defined for each outcome, least squares estimation of a regression equation that includes an intercept will fail. To see why this occurs, let us define $D1 = 1$ for males, and 0 for females, and $D2 = 1$ for females and 0 for males. A regression equation with an intercept can be thought of as having an intercept variable, x_0, which equals 1 for every observation. The product of the intercept and this variable, or $\alpha_0(1)$, simply gives the intercept coefficient. Since every person in the sample is either male or female, when $D1 = 1$, $D2 = 0$ and vice versa. The sum $D1_i + D2_i$ thus equals 1 for every observation. Since $x_{0i} = (D1_i + D2_i)$, the intercept variable can be expressed as an exact linear function of the dummy variables. As a result, x_0, $D1$, and $D2$ constitute a perfectly collinear set of variables, which violates one of the multiple regression assumptions stated in Chapter 6. This problem is referred to as the **dummy variable trap**.

Two solutions exist for this problem. The first of these involves suppressing the intercept when the regression equation is estimated. Most regression programs include such an option.[4] *The alternative is to include an intercept and one less dummy variable than the number of possible conditions for each different qualitative variable.* This was the convention utilized in the above examples, and it is the course of action followed most frequently in econometric research.

A Note on Categorical Variables

Sometimes a data base contains information on a continuous variable that has been coded into several discrete categories. For example, information on income in a cross-sectional data set might consist only of which of several mutually exclusive categories an observation falls into. The actual (continuous) value of income might be unavailable. Variables such as this, which consist of a set of values or categories, are called **categorical variables**. In this example, the variable representing income might be defined as: 0 if income is between 0 and $19,999; 1 if income is between $20,000 and $49,999; and 2 for income greater than or equal to $50,000.[5] The correct interpretation

---

[4] In SAS, this is accomplished by including NOINT as an option after a model statement, such as: MODEL Y = X D1 D2 / NOINT;. In MicroTSP, the C is omitted from the LS statement, which gives the statement: LS Y X D1 D2.

[5] This particular coding is adopted to allow the coefficients in the expected value expressions to conform most closely to those in the dummy variable specifications. If the actual coding of a categorical variable uses the values 1 to 3, this variable can be redefined so that the values of 0 to 2 result by using a statement such as $V = V - 1$ with a computer program.

of the coefficient of a categorical variable can be understood by referring to the previous discussion of intercept-shifting dummy variables. We begin with the following regression equation:

$$y_i = \alpha_0 + \alpha_1 V_i + \alpha_2 x_i + \varepsilon_i,$$

where V is the categorical variable with the classifications given above. The intercept for each of these categories is found by taking the expected value of y for the different values of V:

$$E(y_i | V_i = 0) = \alpha_0 + \alpha_1(0) + \alpha_2 x_i = \alpha_0 + \alpha_2 x_i$$

$$E(y_i | V_i = 1) = \alpha_0 + \alpha_1(1) + \alpha_2 x_i = (\alpha_0 + \alpha_1) + \alpha_2 x_i$$

$$E(y_i | V_i = 2) = \alpha_0 + \alpha_1(2) + \alpha_2 x_i = (\alpha_0 + 2\alpha_1) + \alpha_2 x_i$$

The meaning of the coefficient of a categorical variable is thus different than that for a dummy variable. Given the level of x, the difference in the mean of y for $V = 0$ and $V = 1$ is assumed to be *identical* to the difference between $V = 1$ and $V = 2$. This can be seen by subtracting expected values:

$$E(y_i | V_i = 1) - E(y_i | V_i = 0) = \alpha_1$$

$$E(y_i | V_i = 2) - E(y_i | V_i = 1) = (\alpha_0 + 2\alpha_1 + \alpha_2 x_i) - (\alpha_0 + \alpha_1 + \alpha_2 x_i)$$

$$= \alpha_1.$$

Note also that the corresponding difference in the mean of y when going from $V = 0$ to $V = 2$ equals $2\alpha_1$. If y denotes weeks of unemployment and V is a categorical variable related to pre-unemployment earnings, this specification embodies the assumption that the difference in mean weeks unemployed is identical for persons with pre-unemployment earnings of \$10,000 and \$45,000, given the level of x. This is not likely to be a realistic assumption, even if the specification includes many explanatory variables.

As an alternative to utilizing this categorical variable, two dummy variables (the total number of categories minus one) could be included in the estimated equation. These dummy variables might be defined as: $D1 = 1$ if $V = 1$, 0 otherwise; and $D2 = 1$ when $V = 2$, 0 otherwise. In this case, the control group becomes $V = 0$, and the difference in $E(y)$ for a given level of x need not be identical for persons in the different income categories.

Multiplicative Dummy Variables

It is possible to use the dummy variable technique with only minor modification to test whether the partial slopes of explanatory variables differ among sample observations. The discussion of equation specification in Chapter 8 shows that when an interaction variable is included in an equation, the partial slope of one variable depends on the value taken by the other variable in the interaction. This result also pertains when an interaction variable is defined as the product of a dummy variable and a continuous variable. Since a dummy variable equals either 0 or 1, an interaction variable that includes a dummy variable will equal either 0 for the control group or the value of the other variable when $D = 1$.

This last point can be seen more clearly if we return to an equation with a continuous variable, x, and a dummy variable (D):

$$y_i = \alpha_0 + \alpha_1 D_i + \alpha_2 x_i + \varepsilon_i.$$

The partial slope of x in this equation equals α_2 for both the control group and the condition for which $D = 1$. If there is reason to believe that this partial slope differs for the two sets of observations that make up the dummy variable categories, we can create an interaction term, called a **multiplicative dummy variable**, where:

$$\text{multiplicative dummy variable} = (D_i \cdot x_i).$$

The value of this variable is 0 for the control group ($= 0 \cdot x_i$) and x_i ($= 1 \cdot x_i$) for the other dummy variable classification. By including this variable in our regression equation, we allow the partial slope of x to vary for the different values taken by D. The regression equation now becomes:

$$y_i = \alpha_0 + \alpha_1 D_i + \alpha_2 x_i + \alpha_3 (D_i \cdot x_i) + \varepsilon_i, \tag{9.5}$$

and, taking expected values:

$$E(y_i|D_i = 0) = \alpha_0 + \alpha_2 x_i$$
$$E(y_i|D_i = 1) = (\alpha_0 + \alpha_1) + \alpha_2 x_i + \alpha_3 x_i$$
$$= (\alpha_0 + \alpha_1) + (\alpha_2 + \alpha_3) x_i,$$

assuming $E(\varepsilon_i) = 0$. *The dummy variable coefficient in this model is interpreted differently than in the model considered earlier.* Recall that in the earlier model, the coefficient of the dummy variable denotes the difference in $E(y)$ for the two conditions considered, or $E(y_i|D_i = 1) - E(y_i|D_i = 0)$. In the model with both intercept and slope dummy variables, $E(y_i|D_i = 1) - E(y_i|D_i = 0) = \alpha_1 + \alpha_3 x_i$, which is a function of x. As a result, α_1 in Equation (9.5) no longer measures the difference in $E(y)$ for the conditions upon which D is defined. Instead, it can be viewed as either the difference in $E(y)$ when $D = 1$ *and* $x = 0$, or the difference in the equation intercept when $D = 1$.

The partial slope of x now takes two different values: α_2 for the control group, and $(\alpha_2 + \alpha_3)$ for the condition when $D = 1$. *The coefficient of the multiplicative dummy variable thus indicates the difference in the partial slope of x when $D = 1$.* To test whether the partial slope of x is the same for all observations in a data set, we utilize a null hypothesis which states that the partial slope of x is identical for all data points, or $H_0: \alpha_3 = 0$. This involves a t-test on the estimated coefficient of the multiplicative dummy variable. If this coefficient is statistically significant, the partial slope of x is judged to be significantly different for the two classifications under consideration.

In an equation such as (9.5), where there is both a dummy variable and a multiplicative dummy, the statistical significance of the dummy variable for the entire equation can no longer be ascertained using a single t-statistic. Since there are two terms involving the dummy variable, D, and $(D \cdot x)$, we must test the joint significance of α_1 and α_3. The null hypothesis for this test is: $H_0: \alpha_1 = \alpha_3 = 0$, which involves an F-test. The unrestricted equation for this test is the equation that includes both the intercept and slope dummy variables. The restricted equation excludes all terms involving the dummy variable.

The unemployment rate-capacity utilization rate relationship given in Equation (9.3**b**) was re-estimated with a multiplicative dummy variable. The dummy variable in this equation equals 1 from 1974 to 1989, and 0 prior to 1974. The estimated equation is:

$$\hat{u}_t = 19.6 + 11.0D_t - 0.175\text{CAP}_t - 0.121(D_t \cdot \text{CAP}_t) \qquad \textbf{(9.6)}$$
$$\quad\;\; (6.7) \quad (2.7) \qquad (5.0) \qquad\qquad (2.5)$$

$$\bar{R}^2 = 0.88 \quad \hat{\sigma}_\varepsilon = 0.554 \quad F = 72.2 \quad n = 30 \quad \text{SSE} = 7.98$$

The coefficients of both dummy variable terms are statistically significant at the 5 percent level and above using a t-statistic with 26 degrees of freedom. Recall that the coefficient of D in this equation must be interpreted differently than the corresponding coefficient in Equation (9.3**b**), since that equation excludes a multiplicative dummy variable. The valid interpretation of this coefficient is the difference in the mean unemployment rate from 1974 to 1989 when the capacity utilization rate is 0. It is *not* correct to state that for the period from 1974 to 1989, the mean unemployment rate corresponding to any rate of capacity utilization is 11 percent higher than it was in the earlier period.

The difference in the partial slope of CAP equals -0.121. In the period since 1974 a 1 percent increase in the capacity utilization rate lowers the mean unemployment rate by about one-eighth of 1 percent more than in the previous period. Because both of the dummy variable coefficients are statistically significant, the information in this equation can be used to separate these results into two equations. These equations are:

$$\hat{u}_t = 19.6 - 0.175\text{CAP}_t \qquad \text{from 1960 to 1973}$$
$$\hat{u}_t = (19.6 + 11.0) - (0.175 + 0.121)\text{CAP}_t$$
$$\quad = 30.6 - 0.296\text{CAP}_t \qquad \text{from 1974 to 1989}$$

Figure 9.3 graphs the predicted equations for these two periods. While the vertical intercepts differ by 11, the difference in the predicted unemployment rates decreases continually until a 90 percent capacity utilization rate. Thereafter, the pre-1974 estimated equation indicates a higher predicted value of U.

Further evidence of the validity of breaking Equation (9.6) into separate versions is obtained from a Wald Test of the hypothesis: $H_0: \alpha_2 = \alpha_4 = 0$, where α_2 is the coefficient of D, and α_4 is the coefficient of $(D \cdot \text{CAP})$. The unrestricted error sum of squares for this test is 7.98 (see Equation (9.6)). The restricted error sum of squares is 17.2. The test statistic, with 2 degrees of freedom in the numerator (the number of coefficient restrictions) and 26 degrees of freedom in the denominator, is 15.0, which exceeds the critical F-value for the 1 percent significance level of 5.53.

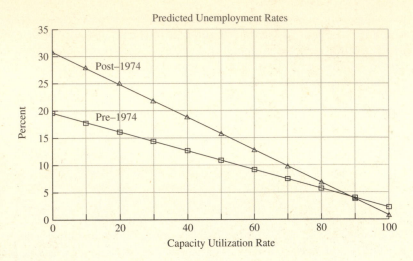

Figure 9.3

The number of dummy variables, explanatory variables, and multiplicative dummy variables included in an equation depends on the intended use of an equation. Some equations include explanatory variables along with a multiplicative dummy variable but exclude the dummy variable itself. An example of this is given by an unemployment rate equation similar to that above. To investigate the unemployment rate-capacity utilization rate relationship in Canada, Davenport estimated the following equation[6]:

$$\hat{u}_t = 0.393 - 0.307\text{CAP}_t - 0.057\text{CAP}_{t-1} + 0.00328(D \cdot t)$$
$$\quad\quad\quad\quad (4.9) \quad\quad\quad (0.9) \quad\quad\quad\quad (10.4)$$

$$\bar{R}^2 = 0.82 \quad\quad \text{(annual data: 1953 to 1981)}$$

where $D = 1$ from 1967 to 1977, 0 otherwise. By including the lagged capacity utilization rate in this equation, Davenport allows the unemployment rate to adjust to changes in production over a period of more than one year. Nevertheless, the lagged capacity utilization coefficient is not statistically significant. A notable feature of this equation is its exclusion of a dummy variable and a time trend. Only a multiplicative term involving these variables is included. This allows the equation to include a time trend only for the time period during which $D = 1$. The coefficient of this term indicates the difference in the mean unemployment rate per year from 1967 to 1977, given the current and lagged capacity utilization rate. Davenport's estimate of this value is approximately one-third of 1 percent.

[6] Paul Davenport, "Capital-Using Technical Change and Long-Run Unemployment in Canada: 1953–1981," *Journal of Post-Keynesian Economics*, Vol. 5, No. 1, Fall 1982, pp. 34–48.

A TEST FOR STRUCTURAL DIFFERENCE: THE CHOW TEST

The use of dummy variables to ascertain whether the same coefficients pertain to all of the observations in a data set is an example of a **test of structural difference**.[7] When an equation includes both a dummy variable and a separate multiplicative dummy variable for each of its explanatory variables, the intercept and each partial slope is allowed to vary, implying different underlying structures for the two conditions associated with D. In essence two equations are being estimated from the coefficients of a single equation. This technique can be extended to the case of more than one dummy variable as well. Individual t-statistics are used to test the significance of each term involving a dummy variable. The statistical significance of the dummy variable for the entire equation can be established using a Wald Test. If the value of this test statistic exceeds the critical F value, the null hypothesis that the intercept and partial slopes are identical for all data points is rejected. In this case we accept the alternative hypothesis of several different structures, which allows us to divide the equation into separate coefficients for the conditions indicated by each dummy variable (such as D_1 and D_2).

A major advantage of the dummy variable approach when testing for structural differences is that a single equation provides the set of coefficient estimates for two or more postulated structures. Furthermore, only one degree of freedom is lost for each dummy variable or multiplicative dummy variable that is added to the equation. Unless several structures are postulated to exist, this approach allows us to utilize a greater number of degrees of freedom when estimating the coefficients in these equations than the alternative of estimating separate equations for each structure. In general, this should improve the precision of the estimated coefficients.[8]

An alternative to using dummy variables as a means for determining whether separate structures exist is provided by the **Chow Test**.[9] This test consists of breaking the sample into the two or more postulated structures, then comparing the sums of squared errors from the separate equations with that from the equation estimated using all data points. We will illustrate the steps involved in this test by assuming

---

[7] The basis of using dummy variables to test for structural difference is attributed to Damodar Gujarati who outlined this process in his two papers: "Use of Dummy Variables in Testing for Equality Between Sets of Coefficients in Two Linear Regressions: A Note," *The American Statistician*, Vol. 24, No. 1, 1970, pp. 50–52; and "Use of Dummy Variables in Testing for Equality Between Sets of Coefficients in Linear Regressions: A Generalization," *The American Statistician*, Vol. 24, No. 5, 1970, pp. 18–21.

[8] With several postulated structures, the relatively large number of included variables can result in multicollinearity, so that estimation precision falls, and the statistical significance of individual terms is more difficult to ascertain. The topic of multicollinearity is covered in the next chapter. Also, the correct use of this approach requires that error variances be identical for each structure. In other words, homoskedastic errors are *necessary for the entire sample*.

[9] Gregory Chow, "Tests of Equality Between Sets of Coefficients in Two Linear Regressions," *Econometrica*, Vol. 28, No. 3, July 1960, pp. 591–605.

that we wish to test for the existence of two structures. In the application of this test that follows, we test whether the unemployment rate—capacity utilization rate relationship has remained the same since the inception of OPEC. For our present purposes, let us assume that the equations to be estimated are:

$$y_{1i} = \beta_0 + \beta_1 x_{1i} + \beta_2 z_{1i} + v_{1i}$$

$$y_{2i} = \gamma_0 + \gamma_1 x_{2i} + \gamma_2 z_{2i} + v_{2i}$$

where y_1, x_1, and z_1 refer to the observations on the equation variables for the first structure (pre-OPEC), while y_2, x_2, and z_2 are the values in the second structure (since OPEC). If there are n_1 observations in the first postulated structure and n_2 in the second structure, then, with n total observations (where $n = n_1 + n_2$), we require that both n_1 and n_2 exceed 3 ($= k$), so that positive degrees of freedom exist for each equation.[10] The degrees of freedom for each subsample need not be equal, however. The set of testable hypotheses are:

$$H_0: \beta_0 = \gamma_0, \beta_1 = \gamma_1, \text{ and } \beta_2 = \gamma_2$$

$$H_a: \beta_0 \neq \gamma_0, \beta_1 \neq \gamma_1, \text{ and } \beta_2 \neq \gamma_2$$

If the null hypothesis is correct, the corresponding coefficients in each equation are identical, in which case pooling the data and estimating the single regression equation:

$$y_i = \alpha_0 + \alpha_1 x_i + \alpha_2 z_i + \varepsilon_i$$

will produce the same results as estimating either subequation.

The test statistic for these hypotheses is the same as that for the Wald Test. A slight variation now exists, however. *The restricted equation in the Chow Test is the single equation estimated by pooling the entire set of observations, since this specification restricts the coefficients in the two subequations to be equal.* The unrestricted model consists of the *two* separate equations with (potentially) differing coefficients. The steps involved in the Chow Test are:

1. Estimate the equation:

$$y_i = \alpha_0 + \alpha_1 x_i + \alpha_2 z_i + \varepsilon_i$$

using all n observations. This is the restricted model. Obtain the sum of the squared errors from this equation, ESS_{re}, which has $(n - k)$ degrees of freedom. In the present example this equals $(n - 3)$.

2. Estimate the separate regression equations:

$$y_{1i} = \beta_0 + \beta_1 x_{1i} + \beta_2 z_{1i} + v_{1i}$$

$$y_{2i} = \gamma_0 + \gamma_1 x_{2i} + \gamma_2 z_{2i} + v_{2i}$$

---

[10] When positive degrees of freedom do not exist, this test can still be performed under certain conditions. The methodology involved is outlined in both Chow, pp. 591–605, and Franklin Fisher, "Tests of Equality Between Sets of Coefficients in Two Linear Regressions: An Expository Note," *Econometrica*, March 1970, pp. 361–366.

based on the postulated structures and obtain the sum of the squared errors from each equation. Together this pair of equations forms the unrestricted model. If we denote the sum of the squared errors from these equations as ESS_1 and ESS_2, respectively, then the unrestricted sum of squares is $ESS_{ue} = (ESS_1 + ESS_2)$. The degrees of freedom associated with ESS_{ue} equals the sum of the separate degrees of freedom: $(n_1 - k) + (n_2 - k) = (n - 2k)$, since n_1 and n_2 sum to n. In the present example, this results in $(n - 6)$ degrees of freedom.

3. The test statistic for the null hypothesis is:

$$\frac{(ESS_{re} - ESS_{ue})/k}{ESS_{ue}/(n - 2k)}$$

The number of degrees of freedom in the numerator is obtained by subtracting the unrestricted from the restricted degrees of freedom, which gives: $(n - k) - (n - 2k) = k$. In this example the test statistic is:

$$\frac{(ESS_{re} - (ESS_1 + ESS_2))/3}{(ESS_1 + ESS_2)/(n - 6)}$$

4. Compare the value of this test statistic with the critical F-value for the selected level of significance. If the null hypothesis is true, the sum of the squared errors obtained by separating the data into distinct structures (ESS_{ue}) will not differ substantially from that for the equation estimated with the entire sample (ESS_{re}). In this case the numerator of the test statistic will tend to be small, and the difference in the coefficients for the separate equations will not be statistically significant. A single equation can then be used to represent the relationship under study. If a single structure does not pertain to all observations, then the value of ESS_{ue} obtained by estimating separate equations should be significantly smaller than ESS_{re} from the pooled equation. In this case, the value of the test statistic will tend to be large, allowing us to reject the null hypothesis. Our estimate of the relationship under study is then derived from the separate equations.

This test can be easily extended to deal with more than two structures. For three postulated structures, the unrestricted model consists of the overall relationship estimated separately for each of the three structures:

$$y_{1i} = \beta_0 + \beta_1 x_{1i} + \beta_2 z_{1i} + v_{1i}$$

$$y_{2i} = \gamma_0 + \gamma_1 x_{2i} + \gamma_2 z_{2i} + v_{2i}$$

$$y_{3i} = \Theta_0 + \Theta_1 x_{3i} + \Theta_2 z_{3i} + v_{3i},$$

where these equations have n_1, n_2, and n_3 observations, respectively, that sum to the total of n sample observations. The value of ESS_{ue} is then $(ESS_1 + ESS_2 + ESS_3)$, which has $(n - 3k)$ degrees of freedom, and the test statistic is:

$$\frac{(ESS_{re} - (ESS_1 + ESS_2 + ESS_3))/2k}{(ESS_1 + ESS_2 + ESS_3)/(n - 3k)}$$

Note the number of degrees of freedom in the numerator. This value is obtained by subtracting the unrestricted from the restricted degrees of freedom, which is $(n - k) - (n - 3k) = 2k$.

We will illustrate the use of the Chow Test on the unemployment rate-capacity utilization rate equation to see if its conclusions about the existence of a structural shift in this relationship agree with those from the dummy variable test (Equation 9.6). Our null hypothesis states that the intercept and the coefficient of CAP for 1960 to 1973 are the same as those for the 1974 to 1989 period. To test this hypothesis, we first estimate the restricted equation, which is the regression of the unemployment rate on the capacity utilization rate for the entire period from 1960 to 1989. This equation, which was presented earlier (Equation (9.3a)), is:

$$\hat{u}_t = 30.0 - 0.293\text{CAP}_t \qquad \bar{R}^2 = 0.761 \quad F = 93.6 \quad \text{ESS}_{re} = 17.15 \quad n = 30$$
$$\phantom{\hat{u}_t = }(12.1) \quad (9.7)$$

We next estimate the separate equations for 1960–1973 and 1974–1989 which constitute the unrestricted model. The resulting equations are:

From 1960–1973:

$$\hat{u}_t = 19.64 - 0.175\text{CAP}_t \qquad \bar{R}^2 = 0.590 \quad F = 19.7 \quad \text{ESS}_1 = 4.69 \quad n = 14$$
$$\phantom{\hat{u}_t = }(5.9) \quad\;\; (4.4)$$

From 1974–1989:

$$\hat{u}_t = 30.63 - 0.296\text{CAP}_t \qquad \bar{R}^2 = 0.871 \quad F = 102.1 \quad \text{ESS}_2 = 3.29 \quad n = 16$$
$$\phantom{\hat{u}_t = }(13.1) \quad\;\; (10.1)$$

For the unrestricted model:

$$\text{ESS}_{ue} = 4.69 + 3.29 = 7.98$$

The value of our test statistic is:

$$\frac{(17.15 - 7.98)/2}{7.98/(30 - 4)} = 14.9$$

The critical F-value with 2 and 26 degrees of freedom for the 1 percent level of significance is 5.53. Since the value of our test statistic exceeds this critical F-value, we reject the null hypothesis of no structural shift in the unemployment rate—capacity utilization rate relationship. Our estimates of this relationship over the period from 1960 to 1989 are provided by the separate equations from the unrestricted model.

The value of this test statistic is fairly large since pooling the entire set of observations and estimating a single equation raises the sum of the squared errors substantially above the total sum of squared errors (ESS_{ue}) from the equations for the separate subperiods. Compare the unrestricted equations above with the results given by the dummy variable test in Equation (9.6). The subperiod equations for both methods are identical (except for rounding). This occurs largely as the result of the fact that there is a single period of structural shift being considered, and the number of observations in each subperiod are virtually identical. This will not always be the case, however. When several periods are being considered for the possibility of structural shift, or when the number of observations differs substantially among periods, divergent results can occur.

A NOTE ON TESTING FOR STRUCTURAL DIFFERENCE

Each of the approaches for determining structural difference presented up to this point has its advantages and disadvantages. The Chow Test ascertains whether the structures are significantly different but does not pinpoint which coefficients differ. The dummy variable technique offers the advantage of pinpointing exactly which coefficients diverge. As long as the number of postulated structures is small, the dummy variable technique allows us to use a greater number of degrees of freedom to estimate the relationship of interest. However, when the number of postulated structures is large, there are likely to be problems with either approach. One of these is multicollinearity. When there is either a large number of included explanatory variables (the dummy variable method) or subsamples with small numbers of observations (Chow Test), the likelihood of intercorrelations (multicollinearity) among the explanatory variables rises. This can potentially affect estimation performance and the quality of the estimates for each substructure. Both the dummy variable technique and the Chow Test require homoskedastic errors as well, so that pooling the entire set of observations does not violate the basic least squares assumptions. Toyoda has shown that heteroskedastic errors cause a number of serious problems with the Chow test.[11] Because homoskedastic errors are important for both approaches, it is advisable to compare estimated error variances before conducting either test. Statistical tests that determine whether the errors are homoskedastic, along with remedial measures, are outlined in Chapter 12. For now, it is sufficient to compare estimated variances and to make observational judgments as to whether these values differ.

A TIME SERIES PROCEDURE FOR DETERMINING THE LOCATION OF STRUCTURAL SHIFT

Neither the dummy variable method nor Chow Test indicates the exact location at which structural difference occurs. The researcher thus postulates one or more likely conditions, such as demographic factors or time periods, then uses one of the methods outlined above to determine whether this difference is statistically significant.

Several methods exist that can potentially determine where structural difference occurs. Visual inspection of the equation residuals can sometimes help determine the location of structural difference.[12] However, this is often much easier with time series

---

[11] Toshihisa Toyoda, "Use of the Chow Test Under Heteroskedasticity," *Econometrica*, May 1974, pp. 601–608.

[12] See Chapter 7 for a discussion of studentized residuals, which are preferable to ordinary residuals for determining the potential location of structural shift.

than cross-sectional data. Hafer and Hein have outlined a useful procedure for determining when intercept shifts occur with time series data.[13] If the basic model is:

$$y_t = \alpha_0 + \alpha_1 x_t + \alpha_2 z_t + \varepsilon_t \tag{9.7}$$

their method consists of the following steps:

1. Using the entire sample, estimate Equation (9.7) in first difference form, *omitting an intercept*:

$$\Delta y_t = \alpha_1 \, \Delta x_t + \alpha_2 \, \Delta z_t + \Delta \varepsilon_t \tag{9.8}$$

   If the intercept in our original equation has shifted at one or more points, the pattern of residuals from this first-difference form of Equation (9.7) should reflect these changes by registering increases in the magnitude of residuals as the result of each shift. Residuals that are "large" relative to the equation standard error indicate time periods that are candidates for structural shift. In other words, residuals that are a large number of standard deviations from 0, or outliers, are likely possibilities for intercept shift locations. Record the time periods during which all such large residuals occur. Also, if the slope coefficients in Equation (9.8) differ substantially from those in the original equation, these partial slopes are candidates for shifts.

2. Divide the sample into two or more *nonoverlapping* periods based on the location of outliers, and create a dummy variable for each of these periods. If, for example, a single outlier occurs for observation j, create two dummy variables with: $D1 = 1$ for periods 1 to $j - 1$, 0 otherwise; and $D2 = 1$ for periods j to n, 0 otherwise. When outliers occur in periods j and $(j + m)$, create three dummy variables with: $D1 = 1$ for observations 1 to $(j - 1)$, 0 otherwise; $D2 = 1$ from j to $(j + m - 1)$, 0 otherwise; and $D3 = 1$ from $(j + m)$ to n, 0 otherwise.

3. To determine which time period(s) significantly affect the mean of y (given x and z), include *all but one* of the dummy variables from (3) in Equation (9.7). Then, perform individual t-tests on the dummy variable coefficients. For two outliers, the equation that is estimated (using D1 as the basis for our comparison period) is:

$$y_t = \alpha_0 + \alpha_1 x_t + \alpha_2 z_t + \alpha_3 D2_t + \alpha_4 D3_t + \varepsilon_t \tag{9.9}$$

   The number of significant dummy variables determines the number of potential structures. If, for example, only one of these dummy variables is statistically significant (based on t-tests) we then proceed on the assumption that two separate structures exist. The location of structural shift then occurs at the point indicated by the outlier used to create this dummy variable.

4. Include the significant dummy variable(s) along with multiplicative dummy variables for any explanatory variable whose first-difference coefficient differs

---

[13] R. W. Hafer and S. Hein, "The Shift in Money Demand: What Really Happened?," *Review*, Federal Reserve Bank of St. Louis, February 1982, pp. 11–15.

substantially from its value in the original equation. Estimate this relationship with least squares and determine which terms are significantly different for each structure. If we make D1 the basis for our comparison period, and we suspect that both partial slopes may differ, then, the equation estimated as the final step of this procedure is:

$$y_t = \alpha_0 + \alpha_1 x_t + \alpha_2 z_t + \alpha_3 D2_t + \alpha_4(D2_t \cdot x_t) + \alpha_5(D2_t \cdot z_t)$$
$$+ \alpha_6 D3_t + \alpha_7(D3_t \cdot x_t) + \alpha_7(D3_t \cdot z_t) + \varepsilon_t \qquad \textbf{(9.10)}$$

Note that this last regression can take a different form if we choose to omit the intercept. We then include all three dummy variables and an interaction variable for each dummy variable with both x and z, but we omit the levels of x_t and z_t as explanatory variables.

Hafer and Hein use this technique to determine whether and when a structural shift in money demand occurred. Their basic equation is the money demand equation presented in the discussion of the log-linear specification in Chapter 8. The estimated equations for the periods 1960:1 to 1973:4 and the entire sample, 1960:1 to 1979:4 are[14]:

$$\widehat{\ln(M/P)_t} = -0.61 + 0.125 \ln(y)_t - 0.0161 \ln(r_c)_t - 0.0321 \ln(r_s)_t + 0.778 \ln(M/P)_{t-1}$$
$$\phantom{\widehat{\ln(M/P)_t} =} (2.8) \quad (2.7) \qquad\qquad (3.0) \qquad\qquad (2.1) \qquad\qquad (6.0)$$

$$\bar{R}^2 = 0.967; \quad \hat{\sigma}_\varepsilon = 0.004 \qquad (1960\!:\!1 \text{ to } 1973\!:\!4)$$

$$\widehat{\ln(M/P)_t} = -0.28 + 0.057 \ln(y)_t - 0.0191 \ln(r_c)_t - 0.0391 \ln(r_s)_t + 0.962 \ln(M/P)_{t-1}$$
$$\phantom{\widehat{\ln(M/P)_t} =} (2.4) \quad (2.5) \qquad\qquad (3.5) \qquad\qquad (1.8) \qquad\qquad (13.6)$$

$$\bar{R}^2 = 0.874; \quad \hat{\sigma}_\varepsilon = 0.005 \qquad (1960\!:\!1 \text{ to } 1979\!:\!4)$$

Examination of these equations reveals substantial differences in the coefficients of real GNP ($= y$) and the lagged dependent variable. The authors performed a Chow Test on the estimated equations in the pre- and post-1974 period, which allowed them to reject the null hypothesis of identical structure at the 5 percent level. Further evidence indicating structural shift was provided by the ex-post forecasting performance of the first estimated equation above. Its forecasts for 1974:1 to 1979:4 consistently overestimated the demand for money. Using the procedure outlined above, Hafer and Hein estimated the following equation:

$$\Delta \ln(M/P)_t = \alpha_1 \Delta \ln(y)_t + \alpha_2 \Delta \ln(r_c)_t + \alpha_3 \Delta \ln(r_s)_t + \alpha_4 \Delta \ln(M/P)_{t-1} + \Delta \varepsilon_t$$

Outliers were detected at 1974:2; 1975:4; and 1979:2. The following dummy variables were then created: $D1 = 1$ from 1960:1 to 1974:1, 0 otherwise; $D2 = 1$ for 1974:2 to 1975:3, 0 otherwise; and $D3 = 1$ from 1975:4 to 1979:4, 0 otherwise. When they estimated the original equation with these dummy variables (omitting D3), only the

---

[14] These equations include a correction for serial correlation. The results here are discussed as if they were estimated using least squares without such a correction.

coefficient of $D1$ was statistically significant. Their estimated equation using this dummy variable is:

$$\widehat{\ln(M/P)_t}$$

$$= -0.41 + 0.013D1_t + 0.0761 \ln(y)_t - 0.021 \ln(r_c)_t - 0.02 \ln(r_s)_t + 0.917 \ln(M/P)_{t-1}$$
$$\quad (4.0) \quad (2.9) \qquad (3.8) \qquad\qquad (4.8) \qquad\qquad (1.3) \qquad\qquad (16.1)$$

$$\bar{R}^2 = 0.96; \quad \hat{\sigma}_\varepsilon = 0.0048 \qquad (1960{:}1 \text{ to } 1979{:}4)$$

The coefficient of the dummy variable is positive and statistically significant, indicating a downward shift in the demand for money after 1974 (since $D1 = 1$ from 1960:1 to 1973:4). The coefficients of the explanatory variables look as though these might have changed as well, but the authors conclude this is not the case based on further testing.

To further illustrate this technique, we will apply it to the unemployment rate—capacity utilization rate relationship to see whether or where it indicates a structural shift in this relationship. We again use data from 1960 to 1989. The initial step involves estimating the first-difference form of this relationship with no intercept. After regressing ΔU_t on ΔCAP_t we observe outliers for 1967 and 1972. Also, the coefficient of ΔCAP, -0.221, is somewhat different from its value for the entire period. This raises the possibility that a slope shift has also occurred.

We next construct dummy variables for the different subperiods used in this technique, using 1960 to 1966 as our comparison period (so we only need to create two dummy variables). The following dummy variables are created: $D1 = 1$ from 1967 to 1971, 0 otherwise; and $D2 = 1$ from 1972 to 1989, 0 otherwise. Using these dummy variables in the original regression equation, we obtain:

$$\hat{u}_t = \;\; 26.6 \;\; - \;\; 1.1D1_t + 0.625D2_t - 0.253CAP_t \qquad \bar{R}^2 = 0.907 \quad F = 95.7$$
$$\quad\;\; (15.4) \quad (3.9) \quad\;\; (2.7) \qquad (12.4) \qquad\qquad n = 30 \quad \hat{\sigma}_\varepsilon = 0.49$$

Both dummy variables are statistically significant. We will include both of these variables in our final estimated equation along with a multiplicative dummy variable for each of these time periods. The resulting equation is:

$$\hat{u}_t = 19.9 - 0.173CAP_t + 2.35D1_t - 0.04(D1_t \cdot CAP_t) + 11.1D2_t - 0.126(D2_t \cdot CAP_t)$$
$$\quad (6.8) \quad (5.0) \qquad\quad (0.49) \quad\;\; (0.72) \qquad\qquad (3.2) \qquad\;\; (3.0)$$

$$\bar{R}^2 = 0.929 \quad F = 77.1 \quad n = 30 \quad \hat{\sigma}_\varepsilon = 0.43$$

Note that neither of the terms involving the dummy variable for 1967–1971 is statistically significant, while both terms for the period from 1972–1989 are significant. As the result of this technique, and an F-test on the joint significance of the terms involving $D2$, we conclude that:

(i) a structural shift occurred for both the slope and intercept of this relationship in 1972;

(ii) the magnitude of the intercept shift was substantial, since the estimated coefficient for $D2$ is almost 26 times the standard error of the equation;

(iii) the slope shift was also considerable, as a 1 percent rise in the capacity utilization rate lowers the unemployment rate by about one-eighth of a percent more since 1972 than it did from 1960 to 1971; and

(iv) while this technique arrived at a different point of structural shift than did our earlier conjecture (1974), the estimated equations for the two subperiods from this technique are almost identical to our earlier estimates with:

$$\hat{u}_t = 19.9 - 0.173 \text{CAP}_t \qquad \text{from 1960 to 1971}$$

$$\hat{u}_t = 31.0 - 0.299 \text{CAP}_t \qquad \text{from 1972 to 1989}$$

DICHOTOMOUS DEPENDENT VARIABLES

Up to this point we have utilized dummy variables only as explanatory variables. Used this way, they indicate differences in intercepts or slopes when specific conditions are met. Dummy variables can also be used as dependent variables. The remainder of this chapter discusses the interpretation and estimation of equations with dummy dependent variables. It concludes with several detailed examples of such equations.

The Linear Probability Model

The initial part of this chapter illustrated how the inclusion of dummy variables allows us to account for qualitative considerations in regression equations. It is also possible to use a dummy variable as a dependent variable. If a dummy variable, D, is regressed on a single explanatory variable, x, the regression equation is:

$$D_i = \alpha_0 + \alpha_1 x_i + \varepsilon_i \qquad \textbf{(9.11)}$$

In this form, the condition for which $D = 1$ is evaluated as a function of the explanatory variable, x. For example, if $D = 1$ when a person purchases a durable good, and 0 if no purchase is made, and x is income, Equation (9.11) ascertains the role of income on the decision of whether to purchase a durable good. If additional variables such as prices and demographic dummy variables are included in Equation (9.11), their influence on the durable good purchase decision can also be determined. A number of other possibilities exist for the variables in Equation (9.11). For example:

If $D = 1$ when a person votes for a measure to increase government expenditure, and $D = 0$ otherwise; and x is income, Equation (9.11) measures how income affects the decision of voting for the increased expenditure measure.

If $D = 1$ when a union wins a certification election, and $D = 0$ if the union loses the election; and x is a measure of the delay (in weeks) before an election occurs, Equation (9.11) considers how the waiting period before a certification election affects whether the union wins the election.

The expected value of Equation (9.11) has an important meaning when the dependent variable is a dummy variable. To see this, we first take the expectation of

Equation (9.11)[15]:

$$E(D_i) = \alpha_0 + \alpha_1 x_i \tag{9.12}$$

assuming that $E(\varepsilon_i) = 0$. The dependent variable we are considering can take only two values, 0 or 1. If we denote the probability that $D_i = 1$ as $p(D_i = 1)$, then we can also represent the right side of Equation (9.12) as:

$$E(D_i) = p(D_i = 1) \cdot 1 + p(D_i = 0) \cdot 0,$$

or

$$E(D_i) = p(D_i = 1) \tag{9.13}$$

The expected value of the (dummy) dependent variable thus denotes the probability that the condition for which $D = 1$ occurs. Combining the information from Equations (9.12) and (9.13) we have:

$$E(D_i) = p(D_i = 1) = \alpha_0 + \alpha_1 x_i, \tag{9.14}$$

or

$$p(D_i = 1) = \alpha_0 + \alpha_1 x_i \tag{9.15}$$

Since a regression equation with a dummy dependent variable allows a probability to be estimated, Equation (9.15) is callled the **linear probability model**.

Least squares estimation of an equation such as (9.11) encounters several problems. First, the errors from this equation are not normally distributed, although the central limit theorem pertains for large samples. Even though the errors are not normally distributed (for small samples), the least squares estimators retain their property of unbiasedness. The absence of normally distributed errors affects statistical inference with this equation. Second, the errors in Equation (9.11) are heteroskedastic. Recall that heteroskedastic errors exist when the error variance changes for different observations or values of an explanatory variable. This too, does not affect the unbiasedness of the least squares estimators. All that is affected is the minimum variance, or "best" property of the coefficient estimators. Finally, predicted values from this equation, which are estimated probabilities, can lie outside of the bounds for probabilities, 0 and 1.

The basis for the first two of these problems can be seen by expressing the errors from Equation (9.11) in terms of the possible values of its dependent variable.

For $D = 1$, $\alpha_0 + \alpha_1 x_i + \varepsilon_i = 1$ which implies that $\varepsilon_i = 1 - (\alpha_0 + \alpha_1 x_i)$

For $D = 0$, $\alpha_0 + \alpha_1 x_i + \varepsilon_i = 0$ which implies that $\varepsilon_i = -(\alpha_0 + \alpha_1 x_i)$
$$\tag{9.16}$$

As (9.16) shows, ε_i takes only two values. Since the normal distribution is continuous over the interval from minus infinity to plus infinity, the equation errors are not normally distributed.[16] This is the basis for the first point made above. For the second

---

[15] Actually, all expectations that follow are conditional expectations. Because the notation involved is sometimes complicated and potentially confusing, expected values will be portrayed without noting the condition involved.

[16] Instead, these errors follow the binomial distribution.

problem, heteroskedastic errors, we must show that the error variance is not constant. Assuming, as usual, that $E(\varepsilon_i) = 0$,

$$\text{Var}(\varepsilon_i) = E(\varepsilon_i^2)$$
$$= p(D_i = 1)(\text{value of } \varepsilon_i \text{ when } D_i = 1)^2$$
$$+ p(D_i = 0)(\text{value of } \varepsilon_i \text{ when } D_i = 0)^2$$

Substituting the information from Equation (9.16) into the expression for $\text{Var}(\varepsilon_i)$ we have:

$$\text{Var}(\varepsilon_i) = p(D_i = 1)\{1 - (\alpha_0 + \alpha_1 x_i)\}^2 + p(D_i = 0)\{-(\alpha_0 + \alpha_1 x_i)\}^2$$

Since $p(D_i = 1) = \alpha_0 + \alpha_1 x_i$, the squared expressions above can be simplified:

$$\text{Var}(\varepsilon_i) = p(D_i = 1)\{1 - p(D_i = 1)\}^2 + p(D_i = 0)\{-p(D_i = 1)\}^2$$
$$= p(D_i = 1)\{1 - p(D_i = 1)\}[\{1 - p(D_i = 1) + p(D_i = 1)\}]$$

using the fact that $p(D_i = 0) = 1 - p(D_i = 1)$. Since the bracketed term on the far right equals 1, the variance expression reduces to:

$$\text{Var}(\varepsilon_i) = p(D_i = 1)\{1 - p(D_i = 1)\} \tag{9.17}$$

Since this error variance differs among observations, heteroskedasticity exists. This proves the second point above.[17]

The possibility of unreasonable probability estimates from an equation such as (9.11), where predicted probabilities can be either negative or greater than 1, will now be illustrated using the following hypothetical data for 20 persons:

obs	D	x	obs	D	x
1	1	532.60	11	0	488.78
2	0	415.78	12	0	394.53
3	0	91.88	13	0	238.74
4	0	524.21	14	1	959.22
5	1	532.83	15	0	225.95
6	0	527.64	16	1	578.78
7	1	668.64	17	1	748.75
8	0	306.86	18	0	490.97
9	1	896.04	19	1	695.39
10	1	554.47	20	0	226.36

If we let D represent the decision of whether or not to purchase a durable good ($D = 1$ if a purchase is made, 0 otherwise), and x be weekly income, the data in the table can be viewed as sample information on a group of persons who either did or did not purchase a particular durable good from a single store. We will also assume that these

---

[17] Weighted least squares, which is discussed in Chapter 12, can be utilized to eliminate this problem.

persons faced the same prices for this durable good and its alternatives, so that the primary factor determining the purchase is income. The expected sign for x is positive, since the willingness and ability to purchase a durable good rises with income, increasing the probability of purchasing such a good.

The estimated equation (using least squares) is:

$$\widehat{p(D_i = 1)} = -0.413 + 0.0017x_i \tag{9.18}$$
$$(2.1) \qquad (4.8)$$

The intercept in this equation is negative, indicating that if weekly income is 0, the estimated probability of purchasing this durable good is *negative*! Since probabilities cannot be negative, we immediately see one of the major problems with the linear probability model. Note, however, that 0 income is an out-of-sample value for x, so the intercept here faces problems similar to those when the dependent variable in a multiple regression equation is continuous. Our alternatives are thus to simply overlook the intercept, or view it as equal to 0. The slope coefficient is positive, as expected, and statistically significant. A \$1 rise in weekly income increases the probability of purchasing a durable good by approximately one-fifth of 1 percent. Viewed slightly differently, a \$100 rise in weekly income raises the probability of purchasing this durable good by 17 percent.

The linear specification of this equation implies that a \$100 increase in weekly income raises the probability of purchasing a durable good by 17 percent, irrespective of the level of income. If we consider progressively higher levels of weekly income, the estimated probability continues to increase, eventually exceeding 1.0. The following table lists several estimated probabilities from this equation for different levels of weekly income (x):

x	$p(D_i = 1)$
100	−0.243
300	0.097
500	0.437
700	0.777
900	1.117

Based on the coefficients in our estimated equation, the probability of a durable goods purchase exceeds 1.0 when income is above \$831.18. Note that *this possibility occurs even though the coefficients in our equation are unbiased.*

These problems with the linear probability model must obviously be dealt with. Thus, while least squares estimation of an equation with a dummy dependent variable gives unbiased and consistent coefficients:

- the errors are not normally distributed
- the errors are heteroskedastic
- estimated probabilities can be negative or greater than 1.0

In addition to these complications, R^2 is not an adequate measure of equation performance, since dependent variable heights in a scatter diagram of D versus x are either 0 or 1, with nothing in between. The linear probability model will therefore tend not to fit a scatter of data points well, making relatively low values for R^2 common. The most serious of these problems, though, is the range of possible probability predictions.

IMPROVING THE LINEAR PROBABILITY MODEL.   To remedy the deficiencies of the linear probability model, an alternative is needed that constrains probabilities to values between 0 and 1. It is therefore necessary to have a nonlinear relationship between estimated probabilities and x, so that continual increases in x do not change the estimated probability by the same amount. At the same time, the alternative estimation method should not encounter the same problems with equation errors that arise with the linear probability model.

The approach that has been adopted to correct these deficiencies is to assume that the right side of the linear probability model is related to an unobserved variable, y^*, which is called a **latent variable**:

$$y_i^* = \alpha_0 + \alpha_1 x_i + \varepsilon_i \qquad (9.19)$$

Unlike the linear probability model, $\alpha_0 + \alpha_1 x_i$ corresponds to $E(y_i^*)$ and not to $E(D_i)$.[18] If we again refer to the consumer durable purchase example given earlier, y_i^* represents the willingness and ability to purchase the durable good (effective demand). Viewed differently, y_i^* might be thought of as the net benefits associated with the purchase of this good. A relationship between Equation (9.19) and the linear probability model is established by associating an observed dummy variable with the unobserved latent variable. For this purpose, it is assumed that a threshold value exists for y^*, such that the closer y^* is to this threshold, the more likely is it for $D = 1$. If we denote the threshold value of y^* for an observation as T_i, then the observed values for the dummy variable are defined as follows:

$$D_i = \begin{cases} 1 & \text{if } y_i^* > T_i \\ 0 & \text{otherwise} \end{cases} \qquad (9.20)$$

Returning again to the consumer durable example, T_i is the "critical" value of effective demand beyond which the likelihood of purchasing this good is very high.

The models discussed here utilize different probability distributions to characterize the stochastic errors in Equation (9.19). The error assumption for each involves a specific *cumulative* density function. The cumulative probability of ε, $P(\varepsilon)$, denotes the probability that ε falls in the range from minus infinity to some value ε_i. This can be denoted as:

$$P(\varepsilon_i) = p(\varepsilon \le \varepsilon_i)$$

---

[18] As noted earlier, the expectations involved are actually conditional expectations.

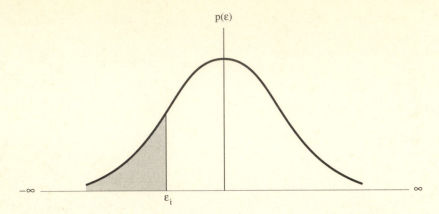

Figure 9.4 Cumulative probability

Figure 9.4 shows the cumulative probability that the random variable ε falls below ε_i. The cumulative probability density function for ε is obtained by evaluating cumulative probabilities (as in Figure 9.4) as ε takes continually larger values. This is illustrated in Figure 9.5. It should be apparent from the method by which the cumulative density function is derived that cumulative probabilities are bounded between 0 and 1. As Figure 9.5 shows, when the value of ε is small (ε_1), the value of the cumulative probability function is close to 0, while for larger values of ε (such as ε_2), the cumulative probability of ε approaches its upper bound of 1.0.[19] The reason why cumulative densities are utilized can be seen if we let T_i, the threshold value, equal 0. Then:

$$D_i = \begin{cases} 1 & \text{if } y_i^* > 0 \\ 0 & \text{otherwise} \end{cases}$$

Using this information, the probability that $D = 1$ is:

$$p(D_i = 1) = p(\alpha_0 + \alpha_1 x_i + \varepsilon_i > 0),$$

or

$$p(D_i = 1) = p(\varepsilon_i > -(\alpha_0 + \alpha_1 x_i))$$

The probability that $\varepsilon_i > -(\alpha_0 + \alpha_1 x_i)$ equals 1 minus the probability that ε_i falls below this value. This last value can also be expressed as 1 minus the probability that ε_i lies between minus infinity and $-(\alpha_0 + \alpha_1 x_i)$. Expressed this way, we see that:

$$p(D_i = 1) = 1 - P[-(\alpha_0 + \alpha_1 x_i)] \tag{9.21}$$

where $P[-(\alpha_0 + \alpha_1 x_i)]$, which denotes the probability that ε_i is between minus infinity and $-(\alpha_0 + \alpha_1 x_i)$, is the cumulative probability density function of ε. When the

---

[19] As x approaches minus infinity, cumulative probability tends to 0, while as x approaches infinity, cumulative probability approaches its upper limit of 1.0.

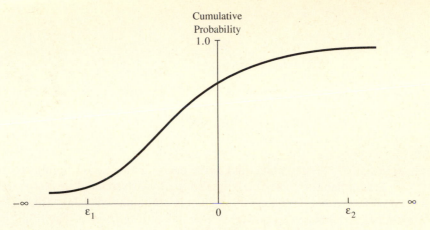

Figure 9.5 Cumulative probability density function

probability density function for ε is symmetrical, as is the case for the distributions considered below, the cumulative probability of some value $-\varepsilon_1$ equals the probability that $\varepsilon > +\varepsilon_1$. For example, the cumulative probability for the value -5 is the probability that ε ranges from minus infinity to -5. When the probability density function being considered is symmetrical, this value is the same as the probability that ε extends from $+5$ to infinity. This last probability may also be expressed as 1 minus the cumulative probability of the value $+5$. Applying this information to Equation (9.21):

$$P[-(\alpha_0 + \alpha_1 x_i)] = 1 - P(\alpha_0 + \alpha_1 x_i)$$

Substituting this result into Equation (9.21) gives:

$$p(D_i = 1) = P(\alpha_0 + \alpha_1 x_i) \tag{9.22}$$

Thus, by utilizing the latent variable framework, we can model the probability that $D = 1$ by a cumulative probability density function. When the cumulative probability density function in Equation (9.22) is represented by the logistic density function, the logit model results. If, instead, the normal distribution is utilized, the probit model emerges.

The Logit Model

The **logit model** corrects the problems with the linear probability model by representing $p(D_i = 1)$ in Equation (9.22) with the cumulative logistic density function:

$$p(D_i = 1) = \frac{1}{1 + e^{-(\alpha_0 + \alpha_1 x_i + \varepsilon_i)}} \tag{9.23}$$

where e is the base of natural logarithms ($e = 2.718$). This model for $p(D_i = 1)$ bounds probabilities between 0 and 1. Assuming that x is directly related to y^*, as x rises, approaching infinity:

$$p(D_i = 1) = \frac{1}{1 + e^{-\infty}}$$

$$= 1$$

since $e^{-\infty} = 1/e^{\infty} = 0$.[20] Similarly, when x decreases, approaching minus infinity:

$$p(D_i = 1) = \frac{1}{1 + e^{-(-\infty)}}$$

$$= 0$$

because $e^{-(-\infty)} = e^{\infty}$, which makes the denominator above infinitely large.[21]

The explanatory variable x is also nonlinearly related to $p(D_i = 1)$ in the logit model. To see this, it is necessary to manipulate Equation (9.23) so that $(\alpha_0 + \alpha_1 x_i + \varepsilon_i)$ (and not e raised to this power) can be linked to $p(D_i = 1)$. The result is:

$$\ln\left[\frac{p(D_i = 1)}{1 - p(D_i = 1)}\right] = \alpha_0 + \alpha_1 x_i + \varepsilon_i \qquad (9.24)$$

The term in brackets is the **odds ratio**, and the left side of Equation (9.24) is the **log of the odds ratio** or the logit of the event for which $D = 1$. If, for example, D represents the decision to purchase a consumer durable good, and $p(D_i = 1) = 2/3$, the odds ratio, or the odds that a consumer durable good will be purchased, is 2 to 1 ($= 2/1$). According to Equation (9.24), changes in x exert a constant (linear) impact on the *logit* of the event being considered, *not* on the probability of the event itself. The impact of a change in x on $p(D_i = 1)$ is given by the following expression:

$$\Delta p(D_i = 1)/\Delta x_i = \alpha_1 p(D_i = 1)[1 - p(D_i = 1)] \qquad (9.25)$$

As this equation shows, the effect of x on the probability that $D = 1$ depends not only on the coefficient of x, but on the probability itself. Since this probability is itself a function of x, the rate of change above is not constant.

A logit equation can include more than one explanatory variable. Examples are:

$$\ln\left[\frac{p(D_i = 1)}{1 - p(D_i = 1)}\right] = \alpha_0 + \alpha_1 x_{1i} + \alpha_2 x_{2i} + \varepsilon_i$$

$$\ln\left[\frac{p(D_i = 1)}{1 - p(D_i = 1)}\right] = \alpha_0 + \alpha_1 x_{1i} + \alpha_2 x_{2i} + \alpha_3(x_{1i} \cdot x_{2i}) + \varepsilon_i \qquad (9.26)$$

If we denote the right sides of these equations as Z_i, the expression for the partial rate of change in $p(D_i = 1)$ for a variable x_j (in Equation (9.26) x_j can be either x_1 or x_2) is given by the following formula:

$$(\Delta Z_i/\Delta x_{ji})p(D_i = 1)[1 - p(D_i = 1)] \qquad (9.27)$$

---

[20] Since knowledge of limits is not presupposed here, the presentation in the text states an equality between $1/e^{\infty}$ and 0. More correctly, as x increases, approaching infinity, the term involving e falls, approaching 0 in the limit.

[21] See the previous footnote for a more correct interpretation of the result here.

Using this formula, the partial rate of change in $p(D_i = 1)$ as x_1 changes in the second equation of (9.26) is:

$$(\alpha_1 + \alpha_3 x_{2i})p(D_i = 1)[1 - p(D_i = 1)]$$

which uses the fact that $\Delta Z_i/\Delta x_{1i} = (\alpha_1 + \alpha_3 x_{2i})$ (see Chapter 8). This partial rate of change thus depends directly on *both* x_1 and x_2.

Estimating the probability of interest with logit analysis is accomplished in two steps. Returning again to the single explanatory variable model, in the initial step, Equation (9.24) is estimated and the coefficients of interest are obtained, giving $\hat{\alpha}_0$ and $\hat{\alpha}_1$. These values are then plugged into Equation (9.23) giving the estimated probability that $D = 1$. However, the estimation technique applied to Equation (9.24), from which our estimates of $p(D_i = 1)$ are derived, is *not* least squares. That method is inappropriate since when sample values for D are used, the log of the odds ratio is either $\ln(1/0)$ (when $D = 1$) or $\ln(0/1)$ (when $D = 0$). Since both of these are meaningless, an alternative estimation method is required. The method that is actually utilized by major canned statistical programs is called **maximum likelihood estimation**. This entails selecting as our estimates values that maximize the likelihood of obtaining the sample of observations being utilized for estimation. The basic ingredient for this technique is the likelihood function (L), which is the joint probability density function of the observations being used. Mathematically, the maximum likelihood method consists of finding values of the coefficients (the $\hat{\alpha}$'s) that maximize the likelihood function for the sample of observations being analyzed. For ease of computation, it is the natural logarithm of the likelihood function (LLF) that is maximized to obtain these coefficient estimates:

The maximum likelihood estimates of the $\hat{\alpha}$'s are those that maximize LLF.

The value of the log of the likelihood function is often provided as routine output for regular least squares estimates and by most programs that perform logit analysis. This value is important since the usual R^2 and F values from regressions with continuous dependent variables should be replaced for logit equations estimated using maximum likelihood methods. Two examples of maximum likelihood logit equations will now be presented.

THE PROBABILITY OF UNION VICTORY IN CERTIFICATION ELECTIONS.

Chiaravalli and Lardaro[22] examined the determinants of the probability of a union being victorious in a contested certification election. The type of election they analyzed is a Regional Director Directed Electron (RDDE), where a regional director of the National Labor Relations Board (NLRB) holds a hearing to determine whether a certification election will be held and, if held, the appropriate bargaining unit. Because this type of election necessarily entails delays (for hearings, etc.), it is possible that whatever interest initially existed for union representation may dwindle. An important question is therefore the influence of delay on the probability of union

---

[22] R. Chiaravalli and L. Lardaro, "The Impact of Representation Case Hearings on Certification Election Outcomes," *Industrial Relations Law Journal*, Vol. 7, No. 2, April 1985, pp. 232–244.

victory in a RDDE. To ascertain this link, Chiaravalli and Lardaro utilized data from the NLRB through a Freedom of Information Act request on 45 such elections, covering approximately 5,000 eligible voters in elections between August 1979 and March 1981. The model they utilized is:

$$\ln\left[\frac{p(D_i = 1)}{1 - p(D_i = 1)}\right] = \alpha_0 + \alpha_1 \text{DELAY}_i + \alpha_2 \text{NLOCAT}_i + \alpha_3 \text{INT}_i + \alpha_4 \text{DBU}_i$$
$$+ \alpha_5 \text{NELIG}_i + \alpha_6 \text{UR}_i + \alpha_7 \text{CHALL}_i + \alpha_8 \text{PARTIC}_i + \varepsilon_i$$

where $D = 1$ if the union won the election, 0 otherwise (think of this as being related to the latent variable y^*, the net benefits of union membership); DELAY is the number of weeks between filing the petition for election and when the election is actually held; NLOCAT is the number of bargaining unit locations; INT is the percent showing of interest, which indicates the initial interest by workers for collective bargaining coverage; DBU = 1, if the bargaining unit was changed, 0 otherwise; NELIG is the number of workers eligible to vote; UR is the local unemployment rate at the time the election was held; CHALL is the number of votes challenged; PARTIC is the percentage of eligible voters who participated in the election; and ε is the stochastic error.

The expected sign for DELAY is negative. The greater is the elapsed time between filing the petition and the time of the election, the less enthusiastic will voters tend to be, as they either develop second thoughts about the potential benefits of union membership, or as a number of the people who actually vote are different from those who originally signed the petition for union representation. This last possibility can arise as the result of labor turnover. The size of a bargaining unit is represented by both NLOCAT and NELIG. The variables CHALL and PARTIC are included to control for differences in the characteristics of elections. For example, the greater is the number of votes challenged, the more highly contested is a certification election (in terms of who should make up the bargaining unit). The voter participation rate is included to control for potential differences among elections in the strength of voter beliefs about either the benefits or costs of union representation.

The logit equation that was estimated (with absolute t-statistics in parentheses) is[23]:

$$\ln\left[\frac{\widehat{p(D_i = 1)}}{1 - p(D_i = 1)}\right] = \underset{(0.3)}{-0.07} - \underset{(1.7)}{0.145\text{DELAY}_i} - \underset{(0.5)}{0.336\text{NLOCAT}_i} + \underset{(1.9)}{2.8\text{INT}_i}$$
$$- \underset{(0.7)}{0.61\text{DBU}_i} - \underset{(1.5)}{0.002\text{NELIG}_i} - \underset{(1.7)}{0.055\text{UR}_i}$$
$$+ \underset{(0.9)}{0.116\text{CHALL}_i} + \underset{(0.7)}{0.646\text{PARTIC}_i}$$

---

[23] Technically, these coefficients are asymptotically normally distributed so the statistic here is an asymptotic unit normal random variable.

The coefficients of DELAY, INT, NELIG, and UR are statistically significant at the 10 percent level and above (for one-tail tests). The coefficient of DELAY is negative, as expected. To determine the effect of a one week increase in DELAY on the probability of union victory, we must utilize a set of values for the explanatory variables in the estimated equation to obtain an estimated log-odds. Using the sample means, but with DBU = 0, we obtain:

$$\ln\left[\overbrace{\frac{p(D_i = 1)}{1 - p(D_i = 1)}}\right] = -0.07(1) - 0.145(10.6) - 0.336(1.2) + 2.8(0.688)$$
$$-0.61(0) - 0.002(107.8) - 0.055(13.1)$$
$$+ 0.116(3.7) + 0.646(0.875)$$
$$= -0.02545$$

We then substitute this value into the probability formula, Equation (9.23):

$$\widehat{p(D_i = 1)} = \frac{1}{1 + e^{-(-0.02545)}}$$
$$= 0.494$$

The estimated probability of a union victory at the sample means (with the same bargaining unit) is thus 49.4 percent. Using this value, the rate of change in $p(D_i = 1)$ with respect to DELAY is found from Equation (9.27):

$$-0.145(0.494)(1 - 0.494) = -0.036$$

A one-week increase in delay thus lowers the predicted probability of union victory by 3.6 percent. This rate of change is not always the same with a logit equation, since DELAY is nonlinearly related to $p(D_i = 1)$. To illustrate this, we let DELAY take the set of values given in the table below and show both the estimated probabilities and the partial rates of change involved (using the same procedure as outlined above):

DELAY (weeks)	PROBABILITY OF UNION VICTORY	IMPACT OF 1 WEEK INCREASE IN DELAY
8	0.587	-0.035
12	0.443	-0.036
16	0.308	-0.031
20	0.200	-0.023
26	0.095	-0.012

(values of all variables except DELAY same as earlier)

Increases in DELAY are thus associated with both a lower probability of union victory and a smaller decrease in the likelihood of union victory (the partial slope). For an 8-week delay, the estimated probability of a union winning an election is almost 60 percent, while for 16 weeks, this probability falls to only 31 percent. One additional week of delay lowers the estimated victory probability by 3.5 percent for the 8-week delay, and by 3.1 percent when delay rises to 16 weeks. Notice that for the extremely long delay of 26 weeks, the estimated likelihood of a union victory falls below 10 percent. Then, a 1-week increase in delay lowers the estimated probability of union victory by only 1.2 percent. The authors conclude from this:

> These figures reveal the substantial extent to which actions by the NLRB in terms of both definition of bargaining unit and delay are capable of altering election outcomes. For example, if NLRB actions delayed elections for 8 weeks, rather than the 10.7 week sample average observed here, the results of this study indicate that the probability of union victory would rise by about five percent, about one-tenth the value of the probability of union victory for this sample.[24]

UNEMPLOYMENT INSURANCE AND WORK DISINCENTIVES.   A number of studies have examined the labor supply effects of Unemployment Insurance (UI). The focus of much of this work has been to estimate the magnitude of the work disincentive effect of Unemployment Insurance, where the workings of this program create the incentive for unemployed persons to prolong jobless spells. Unemployment Insurance is an income maintenance program, for which longer unemployment durations are an intended outcome. As job search is subsidized, persons are able to search longer, enabling an improved matching of the skills possessed by unemployed persons and those required throughout the economy. However, the liberality of both the amount of weekly benefits offered and the allowable period over which these benefits extend can possibly contribute to inefficient job search and artificially long spells of unemployment. It is this possibility that was the concern of research in the 1970s and early 1980s.

Unemployment Insurance contributes to the duration of a given jobless spell through two policy variables: the net replacement rate, which is the proportion of after-tax weekly earnings that weekly benefits replace; and potential duration, the maximum number of weeks a person may receive benefits. While the level of weekly benefits is intended to replace 50 percent of pre-unemployment earnings, this is true only for gross earnings. Weekly benefits as a percent of *after-tax* earnings are often 67 percent or more. Thus, a great deal of income replacement often occurs with this program.

Both the net replacement rate and potential duration are related to the duration of a given unemployment spell. The provision of weekly benefits lowers the cost of leisure (non-work time) *relative* to hours worked. It also reduces the marginal rate of return to accepting employment, since the net marginal benefit of accepting a job offer is the *difference* between weekly benefits and the wages that can be received. For these reasons, increases in either weekly benefits or potential duration are expected to prolong the duration of a given unemployment spell. This was essentially how many persons viewed the labor supply disincentives of Unemployment Insurance through the 1970s.

---

[24] R. Chiaravalli and L. Lardaro, p. 240.

The potential for another labor supply effect of Unemployment Insurance also exists. Differences arise among benefit recipients not only in terms of benefit liberality or potential duration, but in the number of compensated unemployment spells as well. If the net replacement rate and potential duration provide incentives for persons to increase the number of compensated unemployment spells, then the total increase in the number of weeks unemployed will extend beyond that for a single jobless spell. The relevant empirical question, then, is whether the net replacement rate or potential duration are directly associated with increases in the number of compensated spells of unemployment.

Lardaro investigated this possibility by estimating a maximum likelihood logit equation of the probability that a benefit recipient experiences more than one compensated spell.[25] As the author notes:

> . . . individuals are able to control the number of unemployment spells they experience through choice of job (and industry), while persons with remaining benefit entitlement can opt for additional compensated spells by dropping out of the labor force, reentering later, and collecting benefits. Thus, if one examines the role played by the number of compensated spells, the possibility arises that a work disincentive effect of UI can arise from the desire of persons with a previous compensated spell (or spells) to take advantage of unused weeks of benefits before the benefit year expires by choosing . . . one or more additional compensated spells of unemployment.[26]

The model used to test this hypothesis is:

$$\ln\left[\frac{p(D_i = 1)}{1 - p(D_i = 1)}\right] = {}_2 + \alpha_1 \text{SEX}_i + \alpha_2 \text{AGE}_i + \alpha_3 \text{RACE}_i + \alpha_4 \text{STBLTY}_i$$
$$+ \alpha_5 \text{UR}_i + \alpha_6 \text{REARN}_i + \alpha_7 \text{GOTEB}_i + \alpha_8 \text{REPLACE}_i$$
$$+ \alpha_9 \text{PTNDUR}_i + \alpha_2 (\text{GOTEB} \cdot \text{REPLACE})_i$$
$$+ \alpha_{11} (\text{GOTEB} \cdot \text{PTNDUR})_i + \varepsilon_i$$

where $D = 1$ if a person experienced two or more compensated jobless spells, 0 otherwise; SEX = 1 for males, 0 otherwise; AGE = 1 for persons 20 to 24, 0 for persons 16–19; RACE = 1 for white persons, 0 otherwise; STBLTY is the ratio of base year to high quarter earnings, a measure of the regularity of pre-unemployment income; UR is the local unemployment rate; REARN is real annual earnings during the base year; GOTEB = 1 if the person received either Extended or Federal Supplemental Benefits during the 1973–1974 period, 0 otherwise; REPLACE is the net replacement rate (defined above); PTNDUR is potential duration,[27] and ε is a stochastic error.

---

[25] L. Lardaro, "Unused Benefits as a Work Disincentive: Does the Entitlement Effect of Unemployment Insurance Always Lower Unemployment?", *Proceedings* of the Thirty-Eighth Annual Meeting of the Industrial Relations Research Association (Madison WI: IRRA, 1985), pp. 409–417.

[26] Lardaro, p. 410.

[27] The actual value of PTNDUR is known for each person in this database. In a number of other studies this value had to be approximated.

The data used to estimate the above equation consist of two cross-sections of young adults (persons 16–24) from the Continuous Wage and Benefit History of Indiana. In all, a total of 2,881 persons who experienced at least one compensated jobless spell during 1973 or 1974 (the average is 1.7 spells) are included. Some of these persons received Extended and Federal Supplemental Benefits during 1974 as well. The multiplicative dummy variables in this equation are included to test whether the UI policy variables affect $p(D_i = 1)$ differently for persons receiving additional weeks of benefit entitlement.

The maximum likelihood logit equation for the probability of more than one compensated jobless spell is:

$$\ln\left[\frac{\widehat{p(D_i = 1)}}{1 - p(D_i = 1)}\right] = -1.25 + 0.153\text{SEX}_i - 0.006\text{AGE}_i$$
$$(2.4)(1.8)(0.1)$$
$$-0.236\text{RACE}_i - 0.107\text{STBLTY}_i + 0.207\text{UR}_i$$
$$(2.0)(1.9)(3.0)$$
$$+0.00007\text{REARN}_i + 1.06\text{GOTEB}_i - 0.597\text{REPLACE}_i$$
$$(1.5)(1.8)(1.1)$$
$$+0.035\text{PTNDUR}_i - 0.718(\text{GOTEB} \cdot \text{REPLACE})_i$$
$$(3.5)(0.7)$$
$$-0.032(\text{GOTEB} \cdot \text{PTNDUR})_i$$
$$(2.7)$$

For persons not receiving additional benefit entitlement (GOTEB = 0), potential duration is the only statistically significant policy variable. Neither the net replacement rate nor the multiplicative dummy variable for REPLACE are individually statistically significant.[28] The work disincentive effect of the net replacement rate thus appears to affect the duration of a given jobless spell (based on earlier research) while not inducing persons to engage in additional compensated spells. The positive and statistically significant coefficient of PTNDUR, however, indicates that additional weeks of benefit entitlement raise the likelihood of more than one jobless spell. Note that the partial effect of PTNDUR for persons not receiving Extended and Federal Supplemental Benefits is very different than that of persons for whom GOTEB = 1: for them, the partial rate of change is close to 0.

In order to calculate the magnitudes of the partial rates of change for both REPLACE and PTNDUR, the estimated probability of a person experiencing more than one compensated spell will be calculated first for persons not receiving Extended or Federal Supplemental Benefits (GOTEB = 0) then for persons receiving these benefits. Using sample averages for all continuous variables, the estimated probability

---

[28] These are also nonsignificant as a pair, based on a likelihood ratio test. The basis for this test is outlined later in this chapter.

of experiencing more than one compensated jobless spell for white (RACE = 1) males (SEX = 1) ages 20 to 24 (AGE = 1) not having additional weeks of entitlement (GOTEB = 0) is obtained by first substituting these values into the log of the odds equation above:

$$\ln\left[\overbrace{\frac{p(D_i = 1)}{1 - p(D_i = 1)}}\right] = -1.25(1) + 0.153(1) - 0.006(1) - 0.236(1)$$

$$-0.107(2.63) + 0.207(4.4) + 0.00007(2895) + 1.06(0)$$

$$-0.597(0.64) + 0.035(19.8) - 0.718(0 \cdot 0.64) - 0.032(0 \cdot 19.8)$$

$$= -0.196$$

Using this value for the log-odds, the estimated probability is then:

$$\overbrace{p(D_i = 1)} = \frac{1}{1 + e^{-(-0.196)}}$$

$$= 0.451$$

The estimated probability of a white male aged 20–24 without additional weeks of benefits experiencing more than one compensated jobless spell is thus 45.1 percent. Using the estimated probability to calculate this partial rate of change for both the net replacement rate (even though nonsignificant) and potential duration, we have:

$$\text{REPLACE: } -0.597(0.451)(1 - 0.451) = -0.1478$$

$$\text{PTNDUR: } \quad 0.035(0.451)(1 - 0.451) = \quad 0.0087$$

The estimated partial effect for REPLACE is large since this pertains for a change of 1 in the net replacement rate. This is an excessively large change. A more typical change is an increase of 0.1, or a 10 percent rise. When the net replacement rate increases by 10 percent, the estimated probability of additional jobless spells falls by 1.5 percent (one-tenth of −0.1478). An extra week of potential duration raises the estimated probability of additional jobless spells by 0.9 percent.

These partial rates of change are different for persons receiving Extended and Federal Supplemental Benefits. To evaluate the estimated probabilities involved, it is necessary to substitute a value of 1 for GOTEB and to utilize a more realistic value of PTNDUR for persons receiving such additional weeks of entitlement. For simplicity, it will be assumed that persons with Extended Benefits utilize the same percentage of the available maximum number of weeks as do persons without these benefits. Since average potential duration for persons without Extended and Federal Supplemental Benefits was 19.8 weeks out of a possible maximum of 26 weeks, the ratio of utilized to maximum weeks is 0.762. Applying this to the 39 week maximum for Extended Benefits, the value utilized for PTNDUR is 29.7. After substituting this information into the above equation, the estimated probability of more than one jobless spell falls slightly to 0.450. The estimated partial rates of change for REPLACE and PTNDUR are obtained using the formula given in Equation (9.27), where $\Delta Z_i / \Delta x_{ji}$ is the sum of the ordinary and multiplicative dummy variable coefficients for the policy variable in question:

$$\Delta Z_i/\Delta REPLACE_i = (-0.597 - 0.718)(0.45)(1 - 0.45)$$
$$= -0.3255$$

$$\Delta Z_i/\Delta PTNDUR_i = (0.035 - 0.032)(0.45)(1 - 0.45)$$
$$= 0.0007$$

Since the coefficient of $(GOTEB \cdot PTNDUR)$ is approximately equal to but opposite in sign to the coefficient for PTNDUR, the partial effect of potential duration on the probability of additional jobless spells is close to 0 for persons with Extended and Federal Supplemental Benefits. A 10-week increase in potential duration for these persons raises the predicted probability of additional jobless spells by less than 1 percent!

The Probit Model

The **probit model** differs from the logit model in its assumption about the cumulative density function that characterizes $p(D_i = 1)$. The probit model uses the cumulative normal density function to represent this value. The formula for this density function involves integral calculus, so it will not be presented here. We can depict the probability that $D = 1$ in the following way. If we again represent the relationship under study in terms of the latent variable y^*:

$$y_i^* = \alpha_0 + \alpha_1 x_i + \varepsilon_i$$

then, when y^* rises above its threshold value, the observed dummy variable is likely to take the value of 1. For probit analysis:

$$p(D_i = 1) = P(\alpha_0 + \alpha_1 x_i + \varepsilon_i),$$

where $P(\alpha_0 + \alpha_1 x_i + \varepsilon_i)$ denotes the cumulative unit normal density function evaluated at the value $\alpha_0 + \alpha_1 x_i + \varepsilon_i$. As was true for logit analysis, the value of $\alpha_0 + \alpha_1 x_i + \varepsilon_i$ is not related to $p(D_i = 1)$ itself. In probit equations, this value is linked to the inverse of the cumulative unit normal density function, which provides an estimate of the latent variable y^*.

Partial slopes with probit analysis are calculated differently than those with logit analysis. For the equation being considered here, the partial rate of change in $p(D_i = 1)$ with respect to x is:

$$\Delta p(D_i = 1)/\Delta x_i = \alpha_1 p(\alpha_0 + \alpha_1 x_i),$$

where $p(\alpha_0 + \alpha_1 x_i)$ is the value of the unit normal density function evaluated at $\alpha_0 + \alpha_1 x_i$. To calculate estimated probabilities and partial rates of change with a probit equation, it is necessary to:

1. estimate the probit equation and obtain the set of $\hat{\alpha}$'s involved;
2. using specific values for the explanatory variables in the probit equation, calculate the prediction of y^*, $\hat{\alpha}_0 + \hat{\alpha}_1 x_i$;

3. obtain the value of the cumulative unit normal density function for this value (this can be done with many canned statistical programs) this is the estimated probability of the event for which $D = 1$; and

4. the partial rate of change of $p(D_i = 1)$ with respect to x is the product of the estimated coefficient of x, $\hat{\alpha}_1$, and the value of the unit normal distribution for $\hat{\alpha}_0 + \hat{\alpha}_1 x_i$.

Alternatives to the Coefficient of Multiple Determination and the Equation *F*-Statistic for Logit and Probit Equations

When a maximum likelihood logit or probit equation has been estimated, canned computer programs generally do not provide the values of either R^2 or the equation F-statistic. We saw earlier that the nature of the date used for this type of equation tends to make R^2 small relative to its value in an equation with a continuous dependent variable. Also, because the errors do not necessarily satisfy the distributional assumptions that pertain with least squares, the F-statistic is generally omitted.

The measure used in place of the equation F-statistic also acts as a replacement for the Wald Test, since both of these are F-tests that ascertain the statistical significance of a set of equation coefficients. We will utilize the following logit equation as the basis for outlining these tests (although they apply for probit equations as well):

$$\ln\left[\frac{p(D_i = 1)}{1 - p(D_i = 1)}\right] = \alpha_0 + \alpha_1 x_{1i} + \alpha_2 x_{2i} + \cdots + \alpha_k x_{ki} + \varepsilon_i \tag{9.28}$$

The test of the statistical significance of the entire set of partial slope coefficients in Equation (9.28), which replaces the usual equation F-statistic, uses as its null hypothesis:

$$H_0: \alpha_1 = \alpha_2 = \cdots \alpha_k = 0$$

The alternative hypothesis states that H_0 is false. Equation (9.28) is the unrestricted model for this test. When the restrictions embodied in the null hypothesis are incorporated into Equation (9.28), the following restricted model results:

$$\ln\left[\frac{p(D_i = 1)}{1 - p(D_i = 1)}\right] = \alpha_0 + \varepsilon_i \tag{9.29}$$

Testing the above null hypothesis entails comparing equation performance for the restricted model with that for the unrestricted model. The measure of performance utilized for each of these equations is the log of the likelihood function (LLF). The procedure used to perform this test is:

1. Estimate the unrestricted model, Equation (9.28), with a maximum likelihood program and obtain the log of its **likelihood function**, LLF(UR), where UR denotes the fact that this is the unrestricted model.

2. Estimate the model that embodies the restrictions of the null hypothesis, Equation (9.29), and obtain the log of its likelihood function, LLF(R), where R denotes that this is the restricted model.

3. The test statistic for the null hypothesis above is:

$$-2[\text{LLF}(R) - \text{LLF}(UR)]$$

which follows the chi-square distribution with k degrees of freedom, where k is the number of coefficients whose values are restricted to 0 in the null hypothesis. If the value of this test statistic exceeds the critical chi-square value with k degrees of freedom at the selected level of significance, we reject H_0, that the set of partial slope coefficients does not influence the dependent variable. Like the situation with a "large" equation F-statistic, we then conclude that the logit or probit equation is statistically significant.

This method for ascertaining the statistical significance of the entire set of slope coefficients in either a logit or probit equation is called the **likelihood ratio test**. The value of its test statistic, which is generally used as a replacement for the equation F-statistic, is often provided as routine output in logit and probit programs.

This same procedure can be applied with only one minor modification to test a subset of coefficients in a logit or probit equation, replacing the Wald Test. If we again use Equation (9.28) as our basic, or unrestricted equation, but wish to test for the joint statistical significance of a set of coefficients, say α_1, α_2, and α_3, the null hypothesis now becomes:

$$H_0: \alpha_1 = \alpha_2 = \alpha_3 = 0$$

The alternative hypothesis again states that H_0 is false. Steps (1) and (2) above remain the same as before, the only difference being that the restricted model is now given by Equation (9.30):

$$\ln\left[\frac{p(D_i = 1)}{1 - p(D_i = 1)}\right] = \alpha_0 + \alpha_4 x_{4i} + \alpha_5 x_{5i} + \cdots + \alpha_k x_{ki} + \varepsilon_i \tag{9.30}$$

The test statistic and procedure given in step (3) is also the same, with k, the number of coefficients restricted to 0 in the null hypothesis, equal to 3 in this example. If the value of the test statistic exceeds the critical chi-square value with 3 degrees of freedom for the selected level of significance, we reject H_0 and accept H_a, that *as a set* these coefficients influence the dependent variable in our equation.

The same log likelihood function values used in the likelihood ratio test of the statistical significance of the entire set of partial slopes can be used to construct a replacement for the equation R^2. Since predicted probabilities derived from logit and probit equations often differ from 0 or 1, the conventionally calculated R^2 will only approach 1.0 when the predictions derived from these equations consist almost entirely of 0's or 1's. Since this is extremely unlikely, alternative measures of R^2 have been devised. McFadden[29] has derived a "pseudo-R^2" defined as:

$$\text{McFadden's pseudo-}R^2 = 1 - \text{LLF}(UR)/\text{LLF}(R)$$

[29] D. McFadden, "The Measurement of Urban Travel Demand," *Journal of Public Economics*, 1974, pp. 303–328.

where LLF(UR) and LLF(R) are log-likelihood functions for the unrestricted model (with all coefficients) and the restricted model (with an intercept only), respectively. Like the usual R^2, McFadden's pseudo-R^2 lies between 0 and 1.

A LOOK AHEAD.   Now that we have examined the ingredients of equation specification in detail, we next turn to a discussion of several related topics: the consequences of incorrectly specifying an equation; how measurement error in the dependent and explanatory variables affects our estimated equations; and multicollinearity. All three of these can potentially affect the signs, magnitudes and t-statistics of the coefficients in a sample regression function. Chapter 10 explains each of these topics in detail, outlines the effect of these on the properties of our estimators, and provides some useful diagnostic information. Sometimes these problems can be corrected. Unfortunately, situations arise where our best efforts to deal with these complications are unsuccessful. At any rate, we will now begin to see that the "art" of econometrics is important in its own right, and that effective practice of the "science" of econometrics often relies on various aspects of the "art" of this discipline.

KEY TERMS

Categorical variable	Linear probability model
Chow Test	Log of the odds ratio
Comparison period	Logit model
Control or comparison group	Maximum likelihood estimation
Dummy variable	Multiplicative dummy variable
Dummy variable trap	Odds ratio
Latent variable	Probit model
Likelihood function	Test of structural difference
Likelihood ratio test	

EXERCISES

1. A firm is interested in determining whether the elasticity of demand for its product varies during the summer months (June-August). Specify an equation that can be used for this purpose.

2. What does the mean of a dummy variable indicate? Its sum?

3. One method for avoiding the dummy variable trap is to omit the equation intercept. Assume that there are two qualitative conditions to be modeled. If a separate dummy variable is created for each condition and both of these are included in a regression equation that excludes an intercept, what is the correct interpretation of each dummy variable coefficient?

4. Explain how the omission of an influential (ie. significant) dummy variable can affect the estimated slope of a bivariate regression equation (hint: use a graph to explore this, and remember that OLS passes through the point of means).

5. Which of the following multiplicative dummy variables is appropriate to test for the existence of an elasticity that varies according to the conditions specified by a dummy variable: $\ln(D \cdot x)_i$ or $D_i \cdot \ln(x)_i$? Explain the basis for your choice.

6. Using the data from question 6 in Chapter 8:

(a) Test whether the compensation-productivity relationship from part 6(a) has changed over the period from 1970–1989 using: (i) the dummy variable test; and (ii) the Chow Test.

(b) Estimate the constant compound and instantaneous growth rates in w for the 1970s, then the 1980s, using the dummy variable technique. Test the null hypothesis that the growth rate in real compensation per hour was the same for both decades.

7. Explain why the graphs of the unemployment rate equations for the two periods considered in Equation (9.6) are not parallel.

8. If a categorical variable (V) contains data on the region of residence for persons in a sample, with $V = 1$ if from the northeast; $V = 2$ for the southeast; $V = 3$ for the midwest; $V = 4$ for the southwest; and $V = 5$ for the northwest; and the boundaries drawn so all areas of the contiguous 48 states are included:

(a) Define a set of dummy variables from V that deal with region of residence. How many of these dummy variables should be created?

(b) If this categorical variable itself were included in the following regression equation:

$$y_i = \alpha_0 + \alpha_1 V_i + \alpha_2 x_i + \varepsilon_i$$

what is implicitly assumed about the difference in the mean of y (for a given x) between persons in the northwest and the northeast?

9. Compare and contrast the slope assumptions in the following equations (where D is a dummy variable):

$$y_i = \alpha_0 + \alpha_1 x_i + \varepsilon_i$$

$$y_i = \alpha_0 + \alpha_1 x_i + \alpha_2 D_i + \alpha_3 (D_i \cdot x_i) + \varepsilon_i$$

$$y_i = \alpha_0 + \alpha_1 x_i + \alpha_2 D_i + \alpha_3 (D_i \cdot x_i) + \alpha_4 x_i^2 + \alpha_5 (D_i \cdot x_i^2) + \varepsilon_i$$

How is the statistical significance of the dummy variable for the entire equation tested in each of these equations?

10.   What are the major problems associated with the linear probability model? In general terms, how do logit and probit analysis deal with predicted values differently than the linear probability model?

11.   Outline two equations with dummy dependent variables that can be estimated with logit analysis. What are the expected signs of the coefficients in these equations?

12.   What is the log-odds ratio? How is the linearity of logit estimation related to this ratio?

13.   Outline the steps involved in testing the statistical significance of a subset of coefficients with a logit or probit equation.

10 Problems with the Multiple Regression Model I: Specification Error, Measurement Error, and Multicollinearity

This chapter is the first of three that detail the consequences of violating multiple regression model assumptions. The first topic discussed, specification error, occurs when the estimated equation omits one or more influential explanatory variables, when it contains explanatory variables that do not belong in the equation specification, or when included variables are measured incorrectly (measurement error). The second topic, multicollinearity, arises when the explanatory variables in an equation are highly or perfectly correlated. Although this only violates a model assumption in the extreme case of perfect multicollinearity, the existence of even moderate multicollinearity can cause problems with a sample regression function.

Both of these are potentially serious problems. This chapter outlines each of these complications, ascertains how the least squares estimators are affected, and provides useful information for detecting the presence of these problems. Detection is complicated by the fact that the warning signs for specification error (of omitting variables) are very similar to those for multicollinearity. Also, cures do not always exist. Since the evaluation and testing of multiple regression equations presupposes a correctly specified equation, the topic of specification error is discussed first. After reading this chapter you should be able to analyze an estimated equation for the presence of one or more of these problems, postulate either the direction or magnitude of bias if this is present, and possess knowledge of remedial measures where applicable.

SPECIFICATION ERROR

Omitting a Single Influential Explanatory Variable

Omitting variables of primary importance from an estimated relationship causes these variables to become part of the error in the population regression function. This, in turn, can cause one or more of the model assumptions to be violated. To examine this more completely, let us begin with the population regression function:

$$y_i = \alpha_0 + \alpha_1 x_i + \alpha_2 z_i + \varepsilon_i \qquad (10.1)$$

which, according to our maintained hypotheses, is the "correct" form of this relationship.[1] The error in Equation (10.1) is assumed to be normally distributed with 0 mean, constant variance σ_ε^2, and no serial correlation. Both of the explanatory variables are nonstochastic according to the model assumptions. If the estimated version of Equation (10.1) omits z, the estimated equation is:

$$y_i = \alpha_0 + \alpha_1 x_i + v_i \qquad (10.2)$$

In this equation, $v_i = \varepsilon_i + \alpha_2 z_i$. Based on the set of assumptions concerning Equation (10.1), the mean error from Equation (10.2) is nonzero[2]:

$$E(v_i) = E(\varepsilon_i + \alpha_2 z_i)$$
$$= \alpha_2 z_i \neq 0$$

Furthermore, when the excluded variable, z, is correlated with x, the error term in Equation (10.2) is no longer independent of the included explanatory variable.[3] As the result of both these complications, the least squares estimators of Equation (10.2) will fail to possess several desirable properties. Specifically, the least squares estimators of α_0 and α_1 are biased and inconsistent.

---

[1] In reality the "true" or "correct" population regression function is not known. Due to the process of knowledge accumulation, our perceptions of relationships such as these are incomplete and changing. The term "correct" should therefore be interpreted as referring to the most valid equation specification, based on our best information at the present time. This becomes one of our maintained hypotheses.

[2] It might be more realistic to define $E(z_i) = \mu_z$. However, since Z is assumed to be nonstochastic, we will assume that $E(z_i) = z_i$.

[3] If this equation is expressed in deviation form, the expected value of the error will be 0, but the error will still not be independent of the included explanatory variable. The deviation form of the estimated equation is:

$$y_i' = \alpha_1 x_i' + v_i'$$

where $v_i' = \varepsilon_i' + \alpha_2 z_i'$, and $z_i' \equiv (z_i - \hat{\mu}_z)$. The expected value of the error is: $E(v_i') = E(\varepsilon_i') + \alpha_2 E(z_i') = 0$, since z_i denotes a deviation from its mean, which has a zero expected value. The relationship between the residual and x is obtained from:

$$\text{Cov}(x_i', v_i') = E(x_i' v_i') - E(x_i') E(v_i') = E(x_i' v_i')$$
$$= E[x_i'(\varepsilon_i' + \alpha_2 z_i')] = \alpha_2 E(x_i' z_i')$$

since x is assumed to be independent of ε. The resulting expression is:

$$\text{Cov}(x_i', v_i') = \alpha_2 \cdot \sigma_{zx},$$

where σ_{zx} is the population covariance between x and z.

Because the estimated equation is bivariate, the formulas given in Chapter 4, which are repeated here, apply.

$$\hat{\alpha}_1 = \frac{\sum x_i' y_i'}{\sum x_i'^2}; \qquad \hat{\alpha}_0 = \hat{\mu}_y - \hat{\alpha}_1 \hat{\mu}_x$$

where $x_i' \equiv (x_i - \hat{\mu}_x)$ and $y_i' \equiv (y_i - \hat{\mu}_y)$. By substituting the deviation form of the population regression function Equation (10.1):

$$y_i' = \alpha_1 x_i' + \alpha_2 z_i' + \varepsilon_i'$$

into the formula for $\hat{\alpha}_1$, we obtain an expression for $\hat{\alpha}_1$ in terms of α_1. This allows us to ascertain whether the slope coefficient in the estimated equation is unbiased. Making this substitution:

$$\hat{\alpha}_1 = \frac{\sum x_i'(\alpha_1 x_i' + \alpha_2 z_i' + \varepsilon_i')}{\sum x_i'^2} = \alpha_1 + \frac{\alpha_2 \sum x_i' z_i'}{\sum x_i'^2} + \frac{\sum x_i' \varepsilon_i'}{\sum x_i'^2}$$

The least squares slope estimator equals its population parameter plus two additional terms. The first of these involves the omitted variable, z. The other is related to the equation error.

The second term on the right of the above equation is the least squares regression coefficient when the omitted explanatory variable, z, is regressed on the included explanatory variable x:

$$z_i = \pi_0 + \pi_{zx} x_i + \eta_i \tag{10.3}$$

A regression equation such as (10.3), where one of the explanatory variables from an equation is regressed on the remaining explanatory variables, is called an **auxiliary regression**. Since x and z are nonstochastic (by assumption), Equation (10.3) is technically a descriptive relationship. In reality, the explanatory variables in an equation are often stochastic, so that it is possible to perform the regression indicated by Equation (10.3). π_{zx} denotes the coefficient in the auxiliary regression when z is the dependent variable, and x is the explanatory variable. The least squares estimator of π_{zx} is:

$$\hat{\pi}_{zx} = \sum x_i' z_i' / \sum x_i'^2$$

which measures the rate of change in z when x changes: $\Delta z / \Delta x$.

We can express the last term on the right of the expression for $\hat{\alpha}_1$ more compactly. We saw in Chapter 4 that $\sum x_i' \varepsilon_i' = \sum x_i' \varepsilon_i$. Using the notation from that chapter, if we let $\omega_i \equiv x_i' / \sum x_i'^2$, the term involving the errors becomes $\sum \omega_i \varepsilon_i$. The expression for $\hat{\alpha}_1$ is therefore:

$$\hat{\alpha}_1 = \alpha_1 + \alpha_2 \hat{\pi}_{zx} + \sum \omega_i \varepsilon_i \tag{10.4}$$

This estimator is unbiased if its expected value equals α_1. The expected value of $\hat{\alpha}_1$ is:

$$E(\hat{\alpha}_1) = \alpha_1 + E(\alpha_2 \hat{\pi}_{zx}) + E(\sum \omega_i \varepsilon_i)$$
$$= \alpha_1 + \alpha_2 \hat{\pi}_{zx} + E(\sum \omega_i \varepsilon_i)$$

since α_1, α_2, and $\hat{\pi}_{zx}$ are constants (recall that x and z are nonstochastic, which makes $\hat{\pi}_{zx}$ nonstochastic as well). Since x is nonstochastic and $\Sigma x_i'^2$ is a constant, the expected value of the term on the right is:

$$E(\sum \omega_i \varepsilon_i) = E(\omega_1 \varepsilon_1 + \cdots + \omega_n \varepsilon_n)$$
$$= \omega_1 E(\varepsilon_1) + \cdots + \omega_n E(\varepsilon_n)$$
$$= 0$$

using model assumption (1) that $E(\varepsilon_i) = 0$. The expected value of the expression for $\hat{\alpha}_1$, which gives the mean of its sampling distribution, is then:

$$E(\hat{\alpha}_1) = \alpha_1 + \alpha_2 \hat{\pi}_{zx} \tag{10.5}$$

Since $E(\hat{\alpha}_1) \neq \alpha_1$, $\hat{\alpha}_1$ is a biased estimator of α_1. This is often referred to as **omitted variable (specification) bias**. The sampling distribution of the least squares slope estimator $\hat{\alpha}_1$ is *not* centered at α_1; on average this estimator differs from its population coefficient. The average amount by which $\hat{\alpha}_1$ diverges from α_1 is given by the bias of the least squares estimator:

$$\text{Bias}(\hat{\alpha}_1) = E(\hat{\alpha}_1) - \alpha_1 = \alpha_2 \cdot \hat{\pi}_{zx} \tag{10.6}$$

This bias corresponds to the distance between $E(\hat{\alpha}_1)$ and α_1 for the sampling distribution of the least squares estimator. When $E(\hat{\alpha}_1)$ exceeds α_1, Bias $(\hat{\alpha}_1)$ is positive, and the least squares estimator is upwardly biased. On average, $\hat{\alpha}_1$ will tend to overestimate α_1 in this case. If $E(\hat{\alpha}_1)$ is less than α_1, Bias $(\hat{\alpha}_1)$ is negative, which results in underestimation of α_1 on average. The least squares estimator is then downwardly biased. Illustrations of large and small downward bias are provided in Figure 10.1.

The coefficient of x in the correctly specified equation measures the partial slope $\Delta y / \Delta x$. Because z is omitted from the estimated equation, least squares makes no attempt to correct for the influence of this variable on y. As Equation (10.5) shows, our estimate of this coefficient, $\hat{\alpha}_1$, reflects the total effect of x on y, which consists of a *direct effect*, α_1, and an *indirect effect*, $\alpha_2 \cdot \hat{\pi}_{zx}$. Least squares thus assigns the total effect of changes in both x and z to the single included variable, x.

Recall (from Chapter 4) that the least squares slope coefficient from a bivariate equation is related to the simple correlation coefficient between the dependent and explanatory variable. If we divide both the numerator and denominator of the expression for $\hat{\pi}_{zx}$ by $(n - 1)$, it becomes:

$$\hat{\pi}_{zx} = [\text{Cov}(x, z)/\text{Var}(x)] = \hat{\sigma}_{xz}/\hat{\sigma}_x^2 \tag{10.7}$$

The formula for the sample correlation coefficient between x and z is:

$$\hat{\rho}_{zx} = \hat{\sigma}_{xz}/(\hat{\sigma}_x \cdot \hat{\sigma}_z)$$

Solving for the covariance in terms of the correlation coefficient:

$$\hat{\sigma}_{xz} = \hat{\rho}_{xz} \cdot \hat{\sigma}_x \cdot \hat{\sigma}_z$$

We next substitute this expression into the numerator of Equation (10.7):

$$\hat{\pi}_{zx} = \hat{\sigma}_{zx}/\hat{\sigma}_x^2 = \hat{\rho}_{zx}(\hat{\sigma}_z/\hat{\sigma}_x). \tag{10.8}$$

Adding this information to Equation (10.5):

$$E(\hat{\alpha}_1) = \alpha_1 + \alpha_2 \cdot \hat{\rho}_{zx}(\hat{\sigma}_z/\hat{\sigma}_x) \tag{10.9}$$

The least squares estimator $\hat{\alpha}_1$ is unbiased only when it consists exclusively of the direct effect of x on y. This condition is met when: (i) $\alpha_2 = 0$; (ii) $\hat{\rho}_{zx} = 0$; or (iii) both (i) and (ii). The first of these occurs only when z does not belong in the estimated equation, which we assume to be false. The second condition pertains when x and z are totally uncorrelated ($\hat{\rho}_{xz} = 0$). This is virtually never met since with sampling error, the sample correlation coefficient almost never equals 0 exactly. Note that when $\hat{\sigma}_x$ is large relative to $\hat{\sigma}_z$, the magnitude of $\hat{\pi}_{zx}$ approaches, but never equals, 0, making $E(\hat{\alpha}_1)$ closer to α_1. In this case, a large $\hat{\rho}_{xz}$ does not necessarily produce substantial bias.

Omitting an influential explanatory variable also biases the equation intercept. The least squares intercept for the incorrectly specified Equation (10.2) is given by the formula:

$$\hat{\alpha}_0 = \hat{\mu}_y - \hat{\alpha}_1\hat{\mu}_x$$

After substituting from the population regression function for $\hat{\mu}_y$ and manipulating the resulting terms (this is included among the exercises at the end of the chapter), the expected value of $\hat{\alpha}_0$ is:

$$E(\hat{\alpha}_0) = \alpha_0 + \alpha_2[\hat{\mu}_z - \hat{\pi}_{zx}\hat{\mu}_x] \tag{10.10}$$

The bracketed term on the right side of Equation (10.10) is the least squares estimator of the intercept in the auxiliary Equation (10.3) (which is repeated here):

$$z_i = \pi_0 + \pi_{zx}x_i + \eta_i$$

and

$$\hat{\pi}_0 = \hat{\mu}_z - \hat{\pi}_{zx}\hat{\mu}_x. \tag{10.11}$$

Adding this to the expected value of the original equation intercept, the mean of the sampling distribution of the least squares intercept estimator is:

$$E(\hat{\alpha}_0) = \alpha_0 + \alpha_2\hat{\pi}_0 \tag{10.12}$$

The expected value of this estimator equals the population parameter plus the product of the coefficient of the omitted variable (α_2) and the least squares estimator of the intercept of the auxiliary regression equation ($\hat{\pi}_0$). The least squares intercept estimator is unbiased when this second term equals 0, which occurs when: (i) $\alpha_2 = 0$, which is assumed to be false; (ii) $\hat{\pi}_0 = 0$; or (iii) both (i) and (ii). Possibility (ii) requires that: $\hat{\mu}_z - \hat{\pi}_{zx}\hat{\mu}_x = 0$, or that $\hat{\mu}_z = \hat{\pi}_{zx}\hat{\mu}_x$. *Even if x and z are totally uncorrelated (so that $\hat{\pi}_{zx} = 0$), the least squares intercept estimator is biased unless $\hat{\mu}_z$ also equals 0.* In this case, the slope estimator will have 0 bias (but not be unbiased), while the estimated intercept will be biased. In the more realistic setting where x and z are correlated, both the slope and intercept estimators will be biased (assuming that $\hat{\mu}_z \neq \hat{\pi}_{zx}\hat{\mu}_x$). The expression for the bias in this coefficient is:

$$\text{Bias}(\hat{\alpha}_0) = \alpha_2\hat{\pi}_0 \tag{10.13}$$

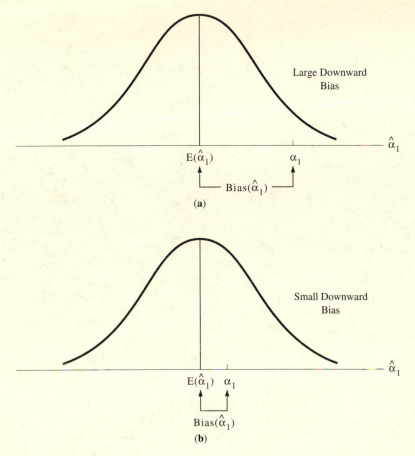

Figure 10.1

The likelihood of a biased intercept should come as no surprise, since the zero mean of the least squares residuals is achieved at the cost of producing an intercept estimator that embodies the mean effect of all omitted variables.

Omitting an influential variable therefore causes both of the least squares estimators to be biased. Since the bias in these coefficients generally does not diminish with increases in sample size, these estimators are inconsistent as well. As a result, the least squares estimators of α_0 and α_1 are both biased and inconsistent. This does not necessarily imply that least squares is totally invalid as an estimation technique, however.[4] The sign and magnitude of the bias in each coefficient should be determined. If, for example, the magnitude of bias in $\hat{\alpha}_1$ is relatively small (such as in Figure 10.1(b)), then the likelihood of obtaining an estimate equal to α_1 is relatively

---

[4] In fact, the estimators utilized at the end of this text are biased but consistent. The mean square error criterion is therefore the basis for deciding estimator preference in many instances.

high, even though the least squares estimator differs from its population parameter *on average*.

Equations (10.6) and (10.13) provide a frame of reference that allows us to evaluate the sign and possibly the magnitude of bias associated with the least squares estimators. For a single excluded variable, the bias term consists of the product of the two terms: α_2 and either $\hat{\pi}_0$ or $\hat{\pi}_{zx}$. If these possess the same sign, positive bias exists, and the least squares estimator overestimates α_0 or α_1 on average. Bias is negative when these terms are of opposite sign. In this case, the least squares estimators underestimate the population parameters on average. Empirical estimates of these terms, if available, would allow us to approximate the magnitude of bias. However, it is more likely that the direction but not magnitudes involved will be known, since estimating $\hat{\pi}_{zx}$ and $\hat{\mu}_z$ requires data on z. If this data were available, the researcher could then include this variable, avoiding the need to make this bias calculation.

As an example of a misspecified equation, consider a bivariate equation where the unemployment rate is the dependent variable and the capacity utilization rate is the explanatory variable. This relationship was explored in Chapter 4. Recall that the unemployment rate displays both cyclical and secular behavior. While this bivariate equation controls for the cyclical behavior of the unemployment rate, it omits one or more variables that represent the secular trend in this rate. If we assume that the correctly specified unemployment rate equation is the following multiple regression[5]:

$$u_t = \alpha_0 + \alpha_1 \text{CAP}_t + \alpha_2 (L/P)_t + \varepsilon_t,$$

where (L/P), the labor force participation rate of females, is utilized as a measure of the secular trend in u, omitting this variable from the estimated equation results in specification error. The expected sign of α_2 is positive. An increase in (L/P) raises the representation of "secondary workers" in the labor force, such as women, minorities, and teenagers who tend to display above-average unemployment rates. In the short term, a rise in LFP also raises u, as many women who enter the labor force do so as unemployed new entrants or unemployed re-entrants. When we omit (L/P), the expected value of α_1 is:

$$E(\hat{\alpha}_1) = \alpha_1 + \alpha_2 \hat{\pi}_{zx}, \qquad \text{(where } (L/P) \text{ is } z \text{ and CAP is } x)$$

and the bias that results from omitting (L/P) is:

$$\text{Bias}(\hat{\alpha}_1) = \alpha_2 \hat{\pi}_{zx},$$

where $\hat{\pi}_{zx}$ is the least squares estimate of the coefficient of CAP in:

$$(L/P)_t = \pi_0 + \pi_{zx}\text{CAP}_t + \eta_t.$$

Based on existing empirical evidence, the expected sign of π_{zx}, which reflects the *added worker effect*, is negative. When the capacity utilization rate falls (such as in a reces-

---

[5] The equation assumed to embody the "correct" specification here is oversimplified. Its use is intended only to illustrate the consequences of omitted variable bias when a single variable is omitted.

sion), incomes tend to fall as a number of persons who were "fully employed" either lose their jobs or are forced to work reduced hours (underemployment). This induces women, especially married females, to enter the labor force as a means of sustaining family income. As a result, (L/P) rises.[6] We can determine the sign of the bias using this information on expected signs:

$$\text{Bias}(\hat{\alpha}_1) = \alpha_2 \hat{\pi}_{zx} = (+) \cdot (-) < 0.$$

Exclusion of (L/P) therefore downwardly biases the estimated coefficient of CAP. Since the expected sign of α_1 is negative, downward bias implies a smaller value, which in this case indicates a coefficient with a greater absolute value. Determining the direction of bias for the intercept is left as an exercise.

The equations with and without (L/P) were estimated with annual data for the years 1953 to 1985. The results are:

$$\hat{u}_t = 29.9 - 0.293\text{CAP}_t \qquad \bar{R}^2 = 0.751 \quad \hat{\sigma}_\varepsilon = 0.844$$
$$\quad (2.4) \qquad (9.9) \qquad\qquad \text{SSE} = 22.1 \quad F = 97.6 \quad \hat{\mu}_u = 5.82$$

$$\hat{u}_t = 20.8 - 0.238\text{CAP}_t + 0.105(L/P)_t \qquad \bar{R}^2 = 0.877 \quad \hat{\sigma}_\varepsilon = 0.593$$
$$\quad (8.9) \qquad (10.4) \qquad\quad (5.7) \qquad\qquad \text{ESS} = 10.5 \quad F = 115.5 \quad \hat{\mu}_u = 5.82$$

The coefficient of CAP is smaller, as expected, in the first equation. The change in the magnitude of this coefficient is only 0.055. This illustrates the point made earlier that the actual size of bias is not necessarily large. Several important differences exist between the overall performance measures in these equations. The more correctly specified equation has a higher $\bar{R}^2$, since the omitted variable is statistically significant, and this equation accounts for a greater proportion of the variation in u. The sum of squared residuals (ESS) and equation standard error are substantially smaller as well. A more subtle difference, which is related to several of the above measures, lies in the values of the t-statistics for the intercept and coefficient of CAP: the t-statistic for each coefficient in the improperly specified equation is smaller than its corresponding value in the more correctly specified equation. This occurs since *the estimated standard deviation of each coefficient in the improperly specified equation is larger than its value in the equation that includes z.*[7]

The basis of this result can be seen by examining the formula for the estimated variance of $\hat{\alpha}_1$, $\hat{\sigma}_1^2$, assuming that x and z are independent.[8] Since the estimated model is a bivariate equation, the formula for $\hat{\sigma}_1^2$ given in Chapter 4 pertains:

$$\hat{\sigma}_1^2 = \hat{\sigma}_\varepsilon^2 / \sum x_i'^2 \qquad (\text{where } x_i' \equiv x_i - \hat{\mu}_x)$$

---

[6] Empirical evidence on the added worker effect dates back to the classic study by W. Bowen and T. Finegan, *The Economics of Labor Force Participation* (Princeton: Princeton University Press), 1969.

[7] Interestingly, Rao and Miller demonstrate that the actual standard deviation is smaller in the improperly specified model. See P. Rao and R. Miller, *Applied Econometrics* (New York: Macmillan), 1971.

[8] This discussion follows from J. Kmenta, *Elements of Econometrics*, 2d. ed. (New York: Macmillan), 1986, pp. 442–446.

After substitution and algebraic manipulation, the expected value of the estimated variance of $\hat{\alpha}_1$ is:

$$E(\hat{\sigma}_1^2) = \sigma_1^2 + \alpha_2^2[\textstyle\sum z_i'^2/(n-2)\sum x_i'^2] \tag{10.14}$$

The far right term in Equation (10.14) is positive. As a result the estimated variance of $\hat{\alpha}_1$ is upwardly biased. It can be shown that the estimated variance of the intercept is also upwardly biased.[9] The bias in $\hat{\sigma}_1^2$ is a byproduct of the positive bias in the estimated error variance. This explains part of the difference in the values of ESS, $\hat{\sigma}_\varepsilon$, $\bar{R}^2$, and equation F-values in the unemployment rate equations discussed above.

In addition to this, the t-ratios of variables that belong in the equation will tend to be smaller than would be the case if an unbiased estimator of $\hat{\sigma}_\varepsilon$ were used. When the magnitude of the bias in $\hat{\sigma}_1^2$ is large enough, it is possible to obtain a nonsignificant t-value for the coefficient of x. In this case we are unable to reject the false null hypothesis: H_0: $\alpha_1 = 0$. The result is a Type II error. Since both $\hat{\sigma}_0^2$ and $\hat{\sigma}_1^2$ are biased, standard t-tests are also biased, and the probability of committing a Type I error no longer coincides with the selected level of significance. Note, however, that if omitting a variable imparts substantial bias to the coefficient of an included variable, then, even though its standard deviation will be upwardly biased, its t-ratio might actually be *higher* than it would be in the correctly specified equation.

In the empirical example given previously, omitting (L/P) does not result in any obvious indication that a problem exists with the estimated equation. Both of the estimated coefficients are statistically significant, each displays the correct sign, and the equation performance measures all indicate satisfactory performance (note: CV equals 0.145, which is within generally acceptable bounds). Although it did not occur in that equation, specification bias can result in **sign reversal**. If the expected sign of α_1 is positive and the estimated coefficient contains substantial negative bias, $\hat{\alpha}_1$ can be negative. Similarly, the combination of large positive bias and a negative expected sign can result in a positive coefficient. The likelihood of sign reversal is directly related to the magnitude of Bias$(\hat{\alpha}_1)$ and the variance of the sampling distribution of this estimator.

As an example of how specification bias can produce sign reversal, let us assume we are interested in estimating the growth rate of a variable y and assume incorrectly that a constant growth rate pertains. We saw in Chapter 8 that this entails using the following specification (where t is time):

$$\ln(y)_t = \alpha_0 + \alpha_1 t + \varepsilon_t$$

instead of one that is quadratic in our explanatory variable (the time trend):

$$\ln(y)_t = \alpha_0 + \alpha_1 t + \alpha_2 t^2 + \varepsilon_t$$

The specification bias here consists of omitting the variable t^2 from our estimated equation. If the signs of α_1 and α_2 differ, the sign of $\hat{\alpha}_1$ from the linear specification

---

[9] This result is easier to establish using matrix algebra methods. For an illustration of how this result is obtained, see J. Johnston, *Econometric Methods*, 3d ed. (New York: McGraw-Hill), 1984.

can be the opposite of that expected. Consider the following equations that estimate the growth rate of inflation for the years 1970 to 1989. The dependent variable in each equation is the natural logarithm of the percent change in the IPD for Personal Consumption Expenditures (π):

$$\widehat{\ln(\pi)}_t = 1.98 - 0.026t \qquad \bar{R}^2 = 0.098 \quad \hat{\sigma}_\varepsilon = 0.39 \quad F = 3.07$$
$$\qquad\quad (11.0) \quad (1.8) \qquad\qquad\qquad n = 20$$

$$\widehat{\ln(\pi)}_t = 1.44 + 0.122t - 0.007t^2 \qquad \bar{R}^2 = 0.352 \quad \hat{\sigma}_\varepsilon = 0.33 \quad F = 6.15$$
$$\qquad\quad (5.9) \quad (2.3) \qquad (2.8) \qquad\qquad n = 20$$

Since inflation rose through the 1970s then declined during the 1980s, the assumption of a constant growth rate for inflation throughout this entire period is untenable. The estimated annual (constant) growth rate of inflation in the first equation is *minus* 2.57 percent ($= e^{-0.026} - 1$), which is not statistically significant. The $\bar{R}^2$ and F-values indicate an unsatisfactory fit of this equation to the data. The quadratic specification, which allows the growth rate to vary, reflects the upward then downward trend in the actual rates of inflation. The linear effect coefficient of the time trend in that equation is statistically significant and of the opposite sign of that in the original equation. Assuming that a quadratic specification is correct, consider the term in the bias expression given by Equation (10.6), where α_2 is the coefficient of t^2 while $\hat{\pi}_{zx}$ is the auxiliary coefficient when t^2 is regressed on t. Since $\alpha_2 < 0$ and $\hat{\pi}_{zx} > 0$, the bias here is negative. The specification bias in the first equation therefore resulted in sign reversal. The measures of overall equation performance substantially improve with the quadratic specification as well. Note that the statistical significance of the time trend in the quadratic equation, which is based on the null hypothesis that the coefficients of all terms involving the time trend are jointly zero, is given by the equation F-statistic. Further evidence supporting the validity of the quadratic specification is provided by curvature in the scatter diagram of the residuals and predicted values in the linear equation (Figure 10.2).

Omitting More Than One Influential Explanatory Variable

The consequences of specification bias with more than one influential explanatory variable parallel those from omitting a single variable fairly closely. Two major differences exist between this and the previously considered case: the direction of bias cannot always be determined a priori; and, it is possible for zero bias to result even if both of the omitted variables are correlated with the included variables.

To illustrate these points, let us begin with the following correctly specified equation:

$$y_i = \alpha_0 + \alpha_1 x_i + \alpha_2 z_{1i} + \alpha_3 z_{2i} + \varepsilon_i \qquad (10.15)$$

where the equation error follows the model assumptions outlined previously. If the estimated version of this equation omits both z_1 and z_2, the resulting equation is:

$$y_i = \alpha_0 + \alpha_1 x_i + v_i \qquad (10.16)$$

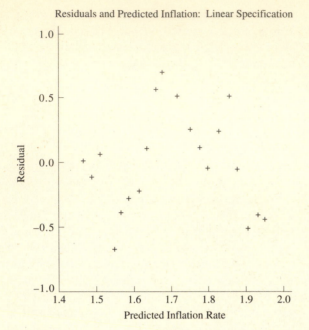

Figure 10.2

where $v_i = \varepsilon_i + \alpha_2 z_{1i} + \alpha_3 z_{2i}$. As before, all omitted variables are present in the population error. Because of this, the mean error is nonzero[10]:

$$E(v_i) = E(\varepsilon_i + \alpha_2 z_{1i} + \alpha_3 z_{2i})$$
$$= \alpha_2 z_{1i} + \alpha_3 z_{2i} \neq 0$$

Furthermore, the residual in Equation (10.16) will be correlated with x as long as *one or both* of the excluded variables are correlated with x. As a result, the least squares estimators of the coefficients in Equation (10.16) will generally not be the best linear unbiased estimators of their population parameters.

The relationship between the least squares slope estimator and its population parameter can be seen if we substitute the deviation form of Equation (10.15) into the formula for this estimator:

$$\hat{\alpha}_1 = \sum x_i' y_i' / \sum x_i'^2$$
$$= \sum x_i'(\alpha_1 x_i' + \alpha_2 z_{1i}' + \alpha_3 z_{2i}' + \varepsilon_i') / \sum x_i'^2$$
$$\hat{\alpha}_1 = \alpha_1 + \alpha_2 (\sum x_i' z_{1i}' / \sum x_i'^2) + \alpha_3 (\sum x_i' z_{2i}' / \sum x_i'^2) + \sum x_i' \varepsilon_i' / \sum x_i'^2 \quad \textbf{(10.17)}$$

---

[10] As long as the excluded variables do not have 0 means.

As before, the least squares slope estimator equals its population parameter plus terms related to the omitted variables, their coefficients, and the error in Equation (10.15). We obtain an expression for the mean of the sampling distribution of $\hat{\alpha}_1$ by taking the expected value of Equation (10.17). Assuming that all of the explanatory variables in the correctly specified equation are nonstochastic, the expected value of the least squares slope estimator is:

$$E(\hat{\alpha}_1) = \alpha_1 + \alpha_2(\sum x_i' z_{1i}'/\sum x_i'^2) + \alpha_3(\sum x_i' z_{2i}'/\sum x_i'^2) \qquad (10.18)$$

since the expected value of the term involving the error is 0. As before, the bracketed terms in Equation (10.18) are least squares coefficients from auxiliary regressions. The first of these is obtained from the auxiliary regression:

$$z_{1i} = \pi_{01} + \pi_{1x} \cdot x_i + \eta_{1i} \qquad (10.19)$$

where π_{1x} denotes the coefficient from the auxiliary regression with z_1 as the dependent variable and x the explanatory variable. The least squares estimator of π_{1x} is:

$$\hat{\pi}_{1x} = \sum x_i' z_{1i}'/\sum x_i'^2$$

The second bracketed term in Equation (10.17) is obtained from the auxiliary regression:

$$z_{2i} = \pi_{02} + \pi_{2x} \cdot x_i + \eta_{2i} \qquad (10.20)$$

where $\hat{\pi}_{2x} = \sum x_i' z_{2i}'/\sum x_i'^2$. Substituting these terms into Equation (10.17):

$$E(\hat{\alpha}_1) = \alpha_1 + \alpha_2 \hat{\pi}_{1x} + \alpha_3 \hat{\pi}_{2x} \qquad (10.21)$$

The least squares slope estimator is unbiased when $E(\hat{\alpha}_1) = \alpha_1$, which occurs when: (i) both α_2 and α_3 are 0, which is true only when neither of the omitted variables belong in the original equation; (ii) both $\hat{\pi}_{1x}$ and $\hat{\pi}_{2x}$ are 0, so that both excluded variables are totally uncorrelated with x; (iii) both (i) and (ii); and (iv) $\alpha_2 \hat{\pi}_{1x} = -\alpha_3 \hat{\pi}_{2x}$. The first of these is assumed to be false. The second is extremely unlikely, since a nonzero correlation of at least one of the excluded explanatory with x is likely to exist due to sample variation. Thus when our estimated equation excludes both z_1 and z_2, $\hat{\alpha}_1$ will have zero bias only when the separate bias components in Equation (10.21) exactly offset, so that case (iv) pertains. Fulfillment of this condition is also unrealistic. In general, the least squares estimator of α_1 will be biased. However, the existence of this possibility allows zero bias to occur even when both of the excluded variables are correlated with the included variable.

The bias in the least squares estimator of α_1 is:

$$\text{Bias}(\hat{\alpha}_1) = \alpha_2 \hat{\pi}_{1x} + \alpha_3 \hat{\pi}_{2x}, \qquad (10.22)$$

which is a weighted sum of the coefficients of the omitted variables. The weights in this expression are the auxiliary regression coefficients. If all four of the terms on the right in Equation (10.22) possess the same sign, the direction of bias is positive. If, for example, all of these terms are positive:

$$\text{Bias}(\hat{\alpha}_1) = (+)(+) + (+)(+) > 0$$

The same result occurs when all four terms are negative. Positive bias also occurs when both parts of each component possess the same sign, but the components themselves differ in sign, such as:

$$\text{Bias}(\hat{\alpha}_1) = (-)(-) + (+)(+) > 0$$

Negative bias arises when the parts of each component differs in sign:

$$\text{Bias}(\hat{\alpha}_1) = (-)(+) + (+)(-) < 0$$

In this case, the least squares estimator of α_1 underestimates this parameter on average. The sampling distribution of $\hat{\alpha}_1$ is then centered below α_1.

The least squares intercept estimator is also affected by the exclusion of these influential variables. It can be shown (this is included in the Exercises at the end of the chapter) that:

$$E(\hat{\alpha}_0) = \alpha_0 + \alpha_2 \hat{\pi}_{01} + \alpha_3 \hat{\pi}_{02} \qquad \text{(10.23)}$$

This estimator is unbiased if: (i) α_2 and α_3 are both 0; (ii) $\hat{\pi}_{01}$ and $\hat{\pi}_{02}$ are both 0; (iii) both (i) and (ii); and (iv) $\alpha_2 \hat{\pi}_{01} = -\alpha_3 \hat{\pi}_{02}$. The second of these is violated even if both of the auxiliary regression slope coefficients are zero. For example, $\hat{\pi}_{01}$ is 0 when:

$$\hat{\mu}_1 - \hat{\pi}_{1x} \cdot \hat{\mu}_x = 0$$

If $\hat{\pi}_{1x} = 0$, the above expression will differ from zero as long as $\hat{\mu}_1$ is nonzero. The same is true for $\hat{\pi}_{2x}$. Therefore, exclusion of more than one influential variable will tend to bias the least squares intercept estimator. Furthermore, the intercept estimator will be biased even when the slope estimator is not, namely when both auxiliary slope coefficients are zero. The bias of the least squares intercept estimator is:

$$\text{Bias}(\hat{\alpha}_0) = \alpha_2 \hat{\pi}_{01} + \alpha_3 \hat{\pi}_{02}.$$

All of the points discussed concerning the magnitude of the bias in $\hat{\alpha}_1$ pertain to $\hat{\alpha}_0$. The magnitude of bias can be either negative or positive, and sign reversal can occur when $\text{Bias}(\hat{\alpha}_0)$ is large and of the opposite sign of α_0.

Finally, omitting two influential variables upwardly biases the estimated error variance of the sample regression function. As a result, estimates of coefficient standard deviations and associated t-statistics will also be biased. The probability of committing a Type I error thus differs from the selected level of significance used in hypothesis tests.

When a sample regression function omits two influential variables, the direction of bias cannot always be determined a priori. This can be seen by referring to condition (iv) for the unbiasedness of each estimator: separate bias components can potentially be offsetting. In this case, the direction of bias is determinate only if the magnitude of each bias component is known, which is not often the case. An example of this situation for the least squares slope estimator is:

$$\text{Bias}(\hat{\alpha}_1) = (+)(+) + (+)(-).$$

Positive bias occurs when the magnitude of the first bias component exceeds that of the second component. In this case:

$$\alpha_2 \hat{\pi}_{1x} > \alpha_3 \hat{\pi}_{2x}$$

Negative bias results when the absolute value of the second term exceeds the first.

The difficulties associated with determining the direction of bias are compounded when our estimated equation excludes more than two influential variables. If our sample regression function includes a single variable x, but excludes the three influential variables z_1, z_2, and z_3, the bias in the least squares slope coefficient is:

$$\text{Bias}(\hat{\alpha}_1) = \alpha_2 \hat{\pi}_{1x} + \alpha_3 \hat{\pi}_{2x} + \alpha_4 \hat{\pi}_{3x}$$

where α_4 is the coefficient of z_3 in the population regression function, and $\hat{\pi}_{3x}$ is the auxiliary regression coefficient of x when z_3 is the dependent variable. Unless all the terms in the above expression possess the same sign, we cannot determine the direction of bias without knowledge of the individual magnitudes involved. When there are more than three omitted variables, the situation becomes even more complicated.

When an estimated equation includes two or more explanatory variables, the bias expressions conform to the pattern for the single explanatory variable case. Assuming the correct specification is:

$$y_i = \alpha_0 + \alpha_1 x_{1i} + \alpha_2 x_{2i} + \alpha_3 z_{1i} + \alpha_4 z_{2i} + \varepsilon_i$$

and we omit both z_1 and z_2, the estimated equation is:

$$y_i = \alpha_0 + \alpha_1 x_{1i} + \alpha_2 x_{2i} + v_i$$

where $v_i = \varepsilon_i + \alpha_3 z_{1i} + \alpha_4 z_{2i}$. In general, the estimators of α_0, α_1, and α_2 will be biased. The expected value of the least squares estimator $\hat{\alpha}_1$ is:

$$E(\hat{\alpha}_1) = \alpha_1 + \alpha_3 \hat{\pi}_{z1,x1} + \alpha_4 \hat{\pi}_{z2,x1}$$

The coefficient $\hat{\pi}_{z1,x1}$ is obtained from the regression:

$$z_{1i} = \pi_{01} + \pi_{z1,x1} \cdot x_{1i} + \pi_{z1,x2} \cdot x_{2i} + v_{1i}.$$

The coefficient $\hat{\pi}_{z2,x1}$ is derived from the auxiliary regression equation:

$$z_{2i} = \pi_{02} + \pi_{z2,x1} \cdot x_{1i} + \pi_{z2,x2} \cdot x_{2i} + v_{2i}.$$

Note that *these auxiliary regressions contain all of the included explanatory variables.* In other words, the auxiliary coefficients are now *partial* regression coefficients. The bias in the least squares estimator of α_1 is therefore:

$$\text{Bias}(\hat{\alpha}_1) = \alpha_3 \hat{\pi}_{z1,x1} + \alpha_4 \hat{\pi}_{z2,x1}$$

The expressions for the bias in the other least squares estimators are:

$$\text{Bias}(\hat{\alpha}_0) = \alpha_3 \hat{\pi}_{01} + \alpha_4 \hat{\pi}_{02}$$

$$\text{Bias}(\hat{\alpha}_2) = \alpha_3 \hat{\pi}_{z1,x2} + \alpha_4 \hat{\pi}_{z2,x2}$$

Since the bias in these coefficients will not diminish with increases in sample size, these estimators are inconsistent as well. In addition to these problems, the estimated variance of the equation error is upwardly biased. The hypothesis testing problems discussed earlier are therefore present in this case as well.

Including a Noninfluential Variable

Omitting one or more influential explanatory variables causes serious complications for the least squares estimators. If an estimated equation includes variables that are not influential, will similar complications arise? Let us assume, based on our maintained hypotheses, that the correct specification of the population regression function is:

$$y_i = \alpha_0 + \alpha_1 x_i + \varepsilon_i \tag{10.24}$$

where the stochastic error meets the assumptions in the multiple regression model. If the estimated version of this equation is:

$$y_i = \alpha_0 + \alpha_1 x_i + \alpha_2 z_i + v_i \tag{10.25}$$

a variable of secondary importance, z, is included as an explanatory variable. Note that this is the exact opposite of the case in the previous section. Normally, variables such as z are relegated to the error term.

Since z does not belong in the correctly specified equation, its population coefficient, α_2, equals 0. However, our estimate of this coefficient will most likely be non-zero as the result of sampling error. What, then, can be said about the least squares estimators in Equation (10.25)? *When an estimated equation includes noninfluential variables, the least squares estimators of the coefficients in that equation are unbiased and consistent.* In the present example:

$$E(\hat{\alpha}_0) = \alpha_0; \, E(\hat{\alpha}_1) = \alpha_1; \quad \text{and} \quad E(\hat{\alpha}_2) = 0.$$

The unbiasedness of the intercept estimator can be seen by substituting the expression for $\hat{\mu}_y$ from Equation (10.24) into the formula for $\hat{\alpha}_0$:

$$\begin{aligned}
\hat{\alpha}_0 &= \hat{\mu}_y - \hat{\alpha}_1 \hat{\mu}_x - \hat{\alpha}_2 \hat{\mu}_z \\
&= (\alpha_0 + \alpha_1 \hat{\mu}_x + \hat{\mu}_\varepsilon) - \hat{\alpha}_1 \hat{\mu}_x - \hat{\alpha}_2 \hat{\mu}_z \\
&= \alpha_0 + (\alpha_1 - \hat{\alpha}_1)\hat{\mu}_x - \hat{\alpha}_2 \hat{\mu}_z + \hat{\mu}_\varepsilon
\end{aligned}$$

Since both $\hat{\alpha}_1$ and $\hat{\alpha}_2$ are unbiased estimators, the expected value of the sampling error of $\hat{\alpha}_1$, $E(\hat{\alpha}_1 - \alpha_1) = 0$, and $E(\hat{\alpha}_2) = 0$. Also, $E(\hat{\mu}_\varepsilon) = 0$. The expected value of $\hat{\alpha}_0$ therefore coincides with its population parameter, and the least squares intercept estimator for Equation (10.25) is unbiased. Ascertaining whether the remaining coefficients are unbiased is left as an exercise.

While the coefficients in the estimated equation are unbiased and consistent, including noninfluential variables affects the variances of these coefficients. The variance of $\hat{\alpha}_1$ differs depending on whether the correctly or incorrectly specified equation is utilized. Based on the correct equation, the variance of this coefficient is:

$$\sigma_{1c}^2 = \sigma_\varepsilon^2 / \sum x_i'^2 \tag{10.26}$$

where the subscript c denotes the correct equation. Since the incorrectly specified equation is estimated, the variance of the coefficient of x is:

$$\sigma_1^2 = \frac{\sigma_\varepsilon^2 \cdot \sum z_i'^2}{(\sum x_i'^2)(\sum z_i'^2) - (\sum x_i' z_i')^2}$$

By manipulating this equation, we can express the variance of this coefficient as a function of the correlation between x and z. Dividing the numerator and denominator by $\Sigma z_i'^2$ eliminates this term from the numerator, while the denominator becomes:

$$\sum x_i'^2 - [(\sum x_i' z_i')^2 / \sum z_i'^2]$$

Multiplying the bracketed expression by $(\Sigma x_i'^2 / \Sigma x_i'^2)$, which does not alter the value of this term (since this equals 1), gives:

$$\sum x_i'^2 - \frac{[(\sum x_i' z_i')^2 (\sum x_i'^2)]}{(\sum z_i'^2)(\sum x_i'^2)}$$

The ratio on the right of this expression can be expressed as:

$$\hat{\rho}_{xz}^2 \cdot \sum x_i'^2$$

where $\hat{\rho}_{xz}^2$ is the coefficient of determination between x and z, or the square of the simple correlation coefficient between these variables. The denominator of the variance of $\hat{\alpha}_1$ in the estimated model is therefore:

$$\sum x_i'^2 (1 - \hat{\rho}_{xz}^2),$$

and the expression for this variance is:

$$\sigma_1^2 = \sigma_\varepsilon^2 / [\sum x_i'^2 (1 - \hat{\rho}_{xz}^2)] \tag{10.27}$$

which is a function of the correlation between x and z. As long as x and z are correlated, the variance of $\hat{\alpha}_1$ will differ from that in the correctly specified equation.

Because it is possible to estimate either the correctly or incorrectly specified model, two unbiased estimators of the parameter α_1 exist. As the above shows, the variances of these estimators differ. Estimator preference can therefore be decided in terms of the criterion of relative efficiency discussed in Chapter 2. Recall that an estimator is relatively more efficient than another estimator of the same parameter if both estimators are unbiased and the variance of the first estimator is smaller than that of the other. Since both estimators of α_1 considered here are unbiased, the variance of $\hat{\alpha}_1$ from the estimated model is relatively more efficient than $\hat{\alpha}_1$ in the correctly specified model if:

$$\sigma_1^2 / \sigma_{1c}^2 < 1$$

Substituting the expressions given by Equations (10.26) and (10.27) for these variances,

$$\sigma_1^2 / \sigma_{1c}^2 = 1/(1 - \hat{\rho}_{xz}^2) \geq 1$$

since $\hat{\rho}_{xz}^2$ is between 0 and 1. Equality of these variances exists only if x and z are totally uncorrelated. When x and z are correlated, the variance of $\hat{\alpha}_1$ from the estimated model exceeds σ_{1c}^2. In this case, the estimated coefficient of x is relatively less efficient than $\hat{\alpha}_1$ obtained from the correctly specified equation.

The estimator $\hat{\sigma}_\varepsilon^2$ obtained from the residuals of the estimated equation is an unbiased estimator of σ_ε^2.[11] Thus while the variance of $\hat{\alpha}_1$ from the estimated equation exceeds that from the correctly specified equation, the estimated variance of this coefficient is unbiased. In fact, the estimated variances of all three of the coefficients in the estimated equation are unbiased. As a result, t-tests on individual coefficients are valid, and the probability of committing a Type I error coincides with the selected level of significance. Because of this fact, *t-tests on the coefficients of noninfluential variables such as z can be expected to result in rejection of the null hypothesis: H_0: $\alpha_2 = 0$ only 5 percent of the time, if the chosen level of significance is 5 percent.* However, it does not necessarily follow that a coefficient with an insignificant t-value is not influential. Since coefficient variances in a multiple regression equation are affected by intercorrelations among the explanatory variables (as illustrated by Equation (10.27)), the coefficient of an influential variable can be insignificant as the result of such correlation. The problem is then one of committing a Type II error. Extreme caution must therefore be exercised before variables with nonsignificant t-values are dropped from an equation. If a noninfluential variable is dropped from an equation, then, under ideal conditions, we should expect that:

(i) the value of adjusted R^2 will rise, since degrees of freedom increase, while the sum of the squared residuals should remain virtually unchanged;

(ii) sign reversal will not occur for the coefficients of the remaining variables, nor should their magnitudes change appreciably. Were this to occur, specification bias would be indicated; and

(iii) t-statistics of the remaining variables will not change appreciably.

However, deletion of a noninfluential variable that is highly correlated with one or more of the remaining variables can alter the t-statistics of these variables. These guidelines are therefore valid only under ideal circumstances. Economic theory and previous empirical research should therefore be the most critical determinant of whether or not to delete variables from an equation.

MEASUREMENT ERROR

The discussion up to this point deals exclusively with situations where explanatory variables are either omitted or included contrary to the correct equation specification. Another possibility exists: influential variables are included in an equation, but one or more of these are measured incorrectly. When this occurs, variables used in estimating a relationship differ from correct values as the result of errors that occur

---

[11] See J. Kmenta, p. 448, for a proof of this statement.

in the measurement of these values. The general form of **measurement error** used in evaluating the consequences of this problem assumes that an included variable equals the value of the correctly measured variable plus a measurement error term, which is a random variable. Using this assumed form, measurement error is reflected in the error of the estimated equation, which can potentially cause serious estimation problems. Two cases are considered: measurement error in the dependent variable only; and measurement error only in the explanatory variable. While the second of these is considered to be the more serious problem, neither should be taken lightly.

Measurement Error in the Dependent Variable Only

We begin by assuming that the correctly specified population regression function takes the form:

$$y_i = \alpha_0 + \alpha_1 x_i + \varepsilon_i$$

but that we do not observe the actual values of y. Instead of possessing information on correct y values, available data on y contain measurement error. Observed y values, y_{io}, differ from actual y values according to the relationship:

$$y_{io} = y_i + \eta_i \tag{10.28}$$

where the measurement error in y, η_i, is a normally distributed random variable with 0 mean and constant variance σ_η^2. In order to determine the effect of measurement error on the least squares coefficients, we first solve this equation for actual y (in terms of observed y), then substitute the resulting expression into the population regression function. Solving for actual y:

$$y_i = (y_{io} - \eta_i),$$

which makes the equation based on observed y:

$$(y_{io} - \eta_i) = \alpha_0 + \alpha_1 x_i + \varepsilon_i,$$

or

$$y_{io} = \alpha_0 + \alpha_1 x_i + (\varepsilon_i + \eta_i)$$
$$= \alpha_0 + \alpha_1 x_i + v_i.$$

The stochastic error in the estimated equation also has a 0 expected value, but its variance exceeds that of the error for the equation with actual y:

$$\text{Var}(v_i) = E(\varepsilon_i + \eta_i)^2$$
$$= \sigma_\varepsilon^2 + \sigma_\eta^2,$$

assuming the measurement error in y is independent of the equation error. If measurement precision is constantly improving, both the magnitude of η and its variance will be decreasing through time.[12]

---

[12] The ironic result of such improvement, as noted by Kmenta, p. 348 is the tendency for heteroskedastic errors to occur in time series equations.

The least squares slope estimator is given by the formula:

$$\hat{\alpha}_1 = \sum x_i' y_{io}' / \sum x_i'^2$$
$$= \sum x_i'(\alpha_1 x_i' + \varepsilon_i' + \eta_i') / \sum x_i'^2$$
$$= \alpha_1 + \sum x_i' \varepsilon_i' / \sum x_i'^2 + \sum x_i' \eta_i' / \sum x_i'^2$$

and the expected value of this estimator is:

$$E(\hat{\alpha}_1) = \alpha_1 + E(\sum x_i' \eta_i' / \sum x_i'^2) \qquad \textbf{(10.29)}$$

since x is uncorrelated with ε. The second term in this expression is related to the covariance between the explanatory variable and the error in measuring y. *As long as the measurement error in y is uncorrelated with the included explanatory variable, the least squares slope estimator is unbiased.* When this condition is met, both the intercept and slope estimators are unbiased and consistent (assuming that x is correctly measured). In this case, the least squares coefficients possess all the desirable estimator properties.

A word of caution is necessary concerning the situation described here: never blindly assume that the dependent variable in an equation is measured without error, or that any error, if present, is uncorrelated with the explanatory variable(s) in that equation. While situations no doubt exist where these are viable assumptions, failure to consider such issues can result in estimation problems.

Measurement Error in the Explanatory Variable Only

Measurement error in explanatory variables can cause the least squares estimators to lose their desirable properties. We will begin with the same correct model as above:

$$y_i = \alpha_0 + \alpha_1 x_i + \varepsilon_i$$

but assume that our explanatory variable is measured incorrectly, where observed x (x_{io}) consists of actual x plus a random measurement component (η):

$$x_{io} = x_i + \eta_i$$

Using this relationship, actual x can be expressed as:

$$x_i = x_{io} - \eta_i \qquad \textbf{(10.30)}$$

which makes our estimated equation:

$$y_i = \alpha_0 + \alpha_1(x_{io} - \eta_i) + \varepsilon_i.$$

Two important facts about this equation should be noted. First, *its explanatory variable is stochastic.* Second, the measurement error in x is again reflected in the equation error. The estimated equation can be rewritten:

$$y_i = \alpha_0 + \alpha_1 x_{io} + (\varepsilon_i - \alpha_1 \eta_i)$$
$$= \alpha_0 + \alpha_1 x_{io} + v_i.$$

The least squares slope estimator is given by the formula:

$$\hat{\alpha}_1 = \sum x'_{io} y'_i / \sum x'^2_{io}$$
$$= \sum x'_{io} (\alpha_1 x'_{io} + \varepsilon'_i - \alpha_1 \eta'_i) / \sum x'^2_{io}$$
$$E(\hat{\alpha}_1) = \alpha_1 + E\left(\sum x'_{io} \varepsilon'_i / \sum x'^2_{io} - \alpha_1 \sum x'_{io} \eta'_i / \sum x'^2_{io}\right) \qquad \textbf{(10.31)}$$

Because x_{io} is stochastic, all of the terms in Equation (10.31) except α_1 are ratios of random variables. This complicates the evaluation of expected values, since the expected value of a ratio does not equal the ratio of the individual expectations. However, we can determine whether $\hat{\alpha}_1$ is unbiased in a descriptive manner, noting that the numerators in the bracketed term in Equation (10.31) are related to covariances, and determining whether population covariances for these terms are zero.

The first term in the expected value in Equation (10.31) is related to the covariance between observed x and the equation error. The expression for this covariance is:

$$\text{Cov}(x_{io}, \varepsilon_i) = E(x_{io} \cdot \varepsilon_i) \qquad (\text{since } E(\varepsilon_i) = 0)$$
$$= E[(x_i + \eta_i)\varepsilon_i] = E(x_i\varepsilon_i) + E(\eta_i\varepsilon_i).$$

Since actual x is uncorrelated with the equation error, the first expectation on the right equals 0. The remaining term is the covariance between the equation error and the measurement error in x. Assuming these errors are independent, the second expectation is zero, so that the covariance between observed x and the equation error is 0.

The second term in the expected value of Equation (10.31) is related to the covariance between observed x and the measurement error in x. This covariance equals:

$$\text{Cov}(x_{io}, \eta_i) = E(x_{io} \cdot \eta_i) \qquad (\text{since } E(\eta_i) = 0)$$
$$= E[(x_i + \eta_i)\eta_i] = E(x_i\eta_i) + E(\eta_i^2)$$
$$= \sigma_\eta^2 \neq 0$$

assuming that actual x, which is nonstochastic, is independent of the measurement error. Because this covariance is nonzero, observed x is correlated with its measurement error. The expected value of the second bracketed expression in Equation (10.31) is therefore nonzero, and the least squares slope estimator is biased. Since the magnitude of bias does not decrease with increases in sample size, the least squares slope estimator is inconsistent as well.

MULTICOLLINEARITY

Perfect Multicollinearity

In order to obtain least squares estimators of multiple regression parameters, it is necessary that the observations on each explanatory variable provide separate and independent information that can be used in estimating the equation. This requirement, which was stated as one of the multiple regression model assumptions in Chapter 6, is the absence of **perfect multicollinearity**. When this assumption is satisfied, no explanatory variable can be expressed as an *exact linear function* of one or more of the other explanatory variables in the equation.

The problems caused by perfect multicollinearity can be seen with reference to the following multiple regression equation:

$$y_i = \alpha_0 + \alpha_1 x_i + \alpha_2 z_i + \varepsilon_i \tag{10.32}$$

where hypothetical sample values of the explanatory variables are:

$$x: 2, 4, 6, 8;$$
$$z: 1, 2, 3, 4.$$

While Equation (10.32) contains two separate explanatory variables, the information provided by z is not distinct from that of x. If the value of x is known, the corresponding value z can be readily determined, since $x_i = 2z_i$. Because of this fact, z is an exact linear function of x. When this situation occurs, x and z are **linearly dependent**, which implies that the pair of variables x and z are perfectly collinear. A more formal definition of linear dependence is the following:

> Two variables x and z are linearly dependent if it is possible to express one as an exact linear function of the other. When this occurs, the expression: $\omega_1 x + \omega_2 z = 0$ can be satisfied for nonzero values of both ω_1 and ω_2.

In the present example, $x_i = 2z_i$, which can be written as:

$$(1)x + (-2)z = 0, \qquad \text{so that } \omega_1 = 1 \text{ and } \omega_2 = -2.$$

If the only solution to the above equation is $\omega_1 = \omega_2 = 0$ (the trivial solution), then x and z are **linearly independent**. The absence of perfect collinearity requires that x and z be linearly independent.[13]

When there are three explanatory variables, x_1, x_2, and x_3, linear dependence implies that one variable can be expressed as an exact linear function of *one or both* of the other variables. In this case, the expression $\omega_1 x_1 + \omega_2 x_2 + \omega_3 x_3 = 0$ can be satisfied with at least two nonzero coefficients (assuming none of the x's equal zero). An application of this equation is given by the dummy variable trap. If x_1 is the equation intercept, this variable always takes the value of 1. When x_2 and x_3 are two dummy variables used to represent a single condition (such as $x_2 = 1$ if female, 0 otherwise; $x_3 = 1$ if male, 0 otherwise), then $x_{2i} + x_{3i} = 1$, since when x_2 is 1, x_3 equals 0, and vice versa. In this case, $x_1 = x_2 + x_3$, so that $\omega_1 = 1$, $\omega_2 = -1$, and $\omega_3 = -1$, and this set of variables is linearly dependent. When intercorrelations among three or more variables are considered, this is referred to as **multicollinearity**. The dummy variable trap is thus an instance where perfect multicollinearity appears.

---

[13] The terms linear dependence and independence are used extensively in matrix algebra. Individual variables are represented by vectors, and the set of explanatory variables gives a data matrix (see the appendixes to Chapters 4 and 6). If the explanatory variables are linearly dependent, the sum of the squares and cross-products matrix, $X'X$, is singular, since the determinant of this matrix is 0. The least squares estimator vector is then indeterminate.

For more than two variables, the detection of the linear relationship is complicated by the fact that not all of the variables must be part of the linear function. However, it is *linear* dependence that causes perfect multicollinearity. Nonlinear relationships among the explanatory variables, such as the inclusion of x and x^2, will therefore not result in perfect multicollinearity.

What problems does perfect multicollinearity pose for least squares estimation of multiple regression coefficients? When this condition exists, it is impossible to obtain estimates of the separate influence of each variable involved in the linear dependency on the dependent variable. While *conceptually* the coefficients involved represent partial rates of change, the data do not allow us to determine the separate contribution of each variable holding the influence of the other variables constant, since the variables involved change in a specific manner. Thus, when perfect multi-collinearity exists, the least squares coefficient estimators do not exist.[14] This result can be seen more clearly by evaluating the expression for the least squares estimator of α_1 from Equation (10.32):

$$\hat{\alpha}_1 = \frac{(\sum y_i' x_i')(\sum z_i'^2) - (\sum y_i' z_i')(\sum x_i' z_i')}{(\sum x_i'^2)(\sum z_i'^2) - (\sum x_i' z_i')^2} \qquad \textbf{(10.33)}$$

where we assume that x and z are linearly dependent, with $z_i = \omega x_i$. Applying this to the terms involving z in Equation (10.33), these become:

$$\sum z_i'^2 = \sum(\omega x_i')^2 = \omega^2 \sum x_i'^2$$

$$\sum y_i' z_i' = \sum y_i'(\omega x_i') = \omega \sum x_i' y_i'$$

$$\sum x_i' z_i' = \sum x_i'(\omega x_i') = \omega \sum x_i'^2.$$

Substituting these expressions into Equation (10.33), the least squares estimator is:

$$\begin{aligned}
\hat{\alpha}_1 &= \frac{(\sum y_i' x_i')(\omega^2 \sum x_i'^2) - (\omega \sum x_i' y_i')(\omega \sum x_i'^2)}{(\sum x_i'^2)(\omega^2 \sum x_i'^2) - (\omega \sum x_i'^2)^2} \\[2mm]
&= \frac{[\omega^2(\sum y_i' x_i')(\sum x_i'^2)] - [\omega^2(\sum x_i' y_i')(\sum x_i'^2)]}{[\omega^2(\sum x_i'^2)^2 - \omega^2(\sum x_i'^2)^2]} \\[2mm]
&= \frac{0}{0}
\end{aligned}$$

Because the least squares estimator is the ratio of two zeros, the value of this estimator is indeterminate.

Another way of focusing on the problems associated with perfect multicollinearity is to recall (from Equation (10.27)) that the variance of each partial slope in Equation (10.32) is directly related to the simple correlation coefficient between the explanatory

---

[14] Technically, the least squares estimators are indeterminate, since the formulas for the partial slopes reduce to the ratio of two zeros, as shown below.

variables. The variance of $\hat{\alpha}_1$ is:

$$\sigma_1^2 = \sigma_\varepsilon^2 / [\sum x_i'^2 (1 - \hat{\rho}_{zx}^2)].$$

When $\hat{\rho}_{zx}$ equals 1, which is true when x and z are perfectly collinear, the variance of this partial slope is infinite. The same is true for the variance of the partial slope of z. *The inability to separate the influences of x and z on y therefore results in the total lack of precision in estimating the coefficients of these variables.*

The consequences of perfect multicollinearity are extremely serious. However, a few facts concerning this problem should be noted. The existence of intercorrelations among explanatory variables is a simple problem, assuming these variables are non-stochastic. More importantly, perfect multicollinearity seldom arises with actual data. The occurrence of perfect multicollinearity often results from correctable mistakes, such as the dummy variable trap, or including variables such as $\ln(x)$ and $\ln(x^2)$ in the same equation. The more relevant question is therefore not how to deal with perfect multicollinearity, but when *imperfect* multicollinearity is a problem, and how to deal with data that manifests this type of multicollinearity.

Imperfect Multicollinearity

Imperfect multicollinearity exists when the explanatory variables in an equation are correlated, but this correlation is less than perfect. As a practical matter, virtually every multiple regression equation contains some degree of correlation among its explanatory variables. The set of explanatory variables are therefore linearly independent, but at times these variables can be expressed as *almost* linear functions. For example, time series of nominal values frequently contain a common upward time trend, causing sample values of these variables to be highly correlated. A well chosen variable representing the price of a related good will often be highly correlated with the price of the good under investigation in a cross-sectional demand function.

Imperfect multicollinearity exists when the relationship between the two explanatory variables in Equation (10.32) is given by the expression: $z_i = \omega x_i + \eta_i$, where η is a random variable that can be viewed as the "error" in the exact linear relationship between x and z. Nonzero values of η prevent a perfect correlation between x and z, allowing us to obtain estimators of the coefficients in this equation. When imperfect multicollinearity exists:

1. the least squares estimators of the coefficients in Equation (10.32) are still the best linear unbiased estimators of their population parameters; and
2. the least squares estimators of the coefficients in Equation (10.32) are consistent estimators.

The BLUE property pertains as long as the equation is properly specified and the expected value of the error is 0. The consistency property is met when the explanatory variables are uncorrelated with the equation error. Multicollinearity does not produce such correlations where none existed previously.

The existence of imperfect multicollinearity therefore does not cause the least squares estimators to lose their desirable properties. However, a few caveats about the attainment of these properties must be stated. The unbiasedness of the least squares coefficients establishes a systematic association between these estimators and their population parameters, where the sampling distribution of each estimator is centered at its population parameter. As always, a single estimate obtained from an unbiased estimator can produce an unsatisfactory estimate. The likelihood of such an outcome is directly related to the dispersion in the sampling distribution of an estimator. Implicit in the BLUE property is the efficiency of the least squares coefficients, since this property identifies the minimum variance unbiased estimators of coefficients in the population regression function. While the least squares estimators are those with the smallest variance of all linear unbiased estimators, imperfect multicollinearity affects the attainable values of these variances, and therefore estimation precision. Since the variances of the least squares coefficients in a multiple regression equation are affected by sample correlations among the explanatory variables (as shown by Equation (10.27)), the greater is the extent of multicollinearity among a set of explanatory variables, the larger is the dispersion in the sampling distributions of these estimators. In other words, *while least squares produces linear unbiased estimators with the minimum variance property, these variances are often substantially larger than those attainable in the absence of multicollinearity.*

For three or more explanatory variables, the variance of the partial slope of a variable x_j is given by the expression:

$$\sigma_j^2 = [\sigma_\varepsilon^2 / \sum x_{ji}'^2 (1 - R_j^2)] \tag{10.34}$$

where R_j^2 is the coefficient of multiple determination from the auxiliary regression of x_j on all the other explanatory variables in the original equation. This expression can be rewritten:

$$\sigma_j^2 = (\sigma_\varepsilon^2 / \sum x_{ji}'^2)[1/(1 - R_j^2)] \tag{10.35}$$

The first term on the right side of Equation (10.35) is the variance of $\hat{\alpha}_j$ in the bivariate regression of y on x_j. The second term in this expression is the **variance inflation factor** (VIF) for x_j:

$$\text{VIF}_j = 1/(1 - R_j^2) \tag{10.36}$$

The name variance inflation factor is derived from the fact that strong intercorrelations among the explanatory variables in an equation result in a high value of R_j^2, which inflates the variance of $\hat{\alpha}_1$ relative to its value when all of the explanatory variables are totally uncorrelated. The expression for the variance of $\hat{\alpha}_j$ can therefore be written as:

$$\sigma_j^2 = (\sigma_\varepsilon^2 / \sum x_{ji}'^2)[\text{VIF}_j] \tag{10.37}$$

When no intercorrelations exist, R_j^2 equals 0, and the lower bound of 1.0 for VIF_j is attained. As R_j^2 rises, VIF_j increases at an increasing rate, approaching infinity with perfect multicollinearity ($R_j^2 = 1$). The following set of values for R_j^2 and the corresponding variance inflation factors illustrate the relationship between these magnitudes:

R_j^2	VIF_j
0	1.0
0.5	2.0
0.8	5.0
0.9	10.0
0.95	20.0
0.975	40.0
0.99	100.0
0.995	200.0
0.999	1000.0

Variance inflation factors that exceed 10 are generally viewed as evidence of the existence of problematic multicollinearity. This occurs when the coefficient of multiple determination from the auxiliary regression equations exceeds 0.9.

Multicollinearity is therefore capable of substantially diminishing the precision with which the least squares coefficients are estimated. Figure 10.3 shows two possible sampling distributions for $\hat{\alpha}_j$: one with a small variance, based on the assumption of no multicollinearity (Figure 10.3(a)); the other, with a higher variance that results from problematic multicollinearity (Figure 10.3(b)). Since multicollinearity does not bias $\hat{\alpha}_j$, both sampling distributions are centered at α_j. The probability of obtaining a "bad" estimate is larger for the estimator that is adversely affected by multicollinearity.

Because of this effect on estimation precision, multicollinearity affects the width of confidence intervals for any level of confidence. The confidence interval for a least squares coefficient is the sum of a point estimate and the margin for sampling error. Recall that the margin for sampling error is the product of a t-value and the standard deviation of the point estimate. For three explanatory variables, the 95 percent confidence interval for the coefficient of x_j is:

$$\hat{\alpha}_j \pm t_{0.025,n-4} \cdot \hat{\sigma}_j.$$

The margin for sampling error of this coefficient is directly related to the multicollinearity between the set of explanatory variables as measured by the variance inflation factor of $\hat{\alpha}_j$:

$$t_{0.025,n-4} \cdot \hat{\sigma}_j = t_{0.025,n-4} \cdot \sqrt{(\hat{\sigma}_\varepsilon^2 / \sum x_{ji}'^2)(VIF_j)}.$$

By inflating the standard deviation of $\hat{\alpha}_j$, multicollinearity therefore increases the margin for sampling error, which, in turn, widens the confidence interval for this coefficient.

Because imperfect multicollinearity alters the variances as well as the confidence intervals associated with the least squares estimators, statistical inference concerning

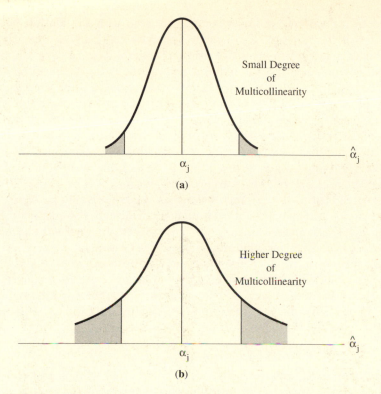

Figure 10.3

these coefficients is also affected. Both the test statistic and the acceptance region are sensitive to multicollinearity. *In general*, the *t*-statistics of the coefficients in equations with imperfect multicollinearity will tend to be smaller than those from equations where multicollinearity is absent. The statistic used to test hypotheses on the coefficient of x_j is:

$$(\hat{\alpha}_j - \alpha_j^0)/\hat{\sigma}_j,$$

where α_j^0 is the value of α_j in the null hypothesis, and the numerator denotes hypothesized sampling error. The inflated variance associated with multicollinearity raises the denominator of this statistic, causing its value to fall. Since multicollinearity widens the confidence interval associated with this point estimate, the acceptance region becomes larger as well. The probability that the hypothesized sampling error exceeds two standard deviations (using the rule of thumb value) is therefore smaller when multicollinearity is present. As a result, false null hypotheses will tend to be accepted more frequently than should be the case, causing an increased probability of Type II errors.

While the above conclusions are valid for multicollinearity in general, it does not follow that *t*-statistics for the coefficients in collinear equations will necessarily be nonsignificant. The variance of a coefficient can be small enough for statistical significance to be attained even if multicollinearity is present. While σ_j^2 is directly related to the variance inflation factor associated with x_j, this variance is smaller: (i) the larger the variance of x_j (as represented by $\Sigma x_{ji}'^2$); and (ii) the smaller σ_ε^2. If x_j is highly correlated with several of the other variables in the equation, its coefficient can still be significant if, for example, the equation fits the data well, so that the error variance is small. The same result follows when x_j has a large variance.

Another possibility exists concerning statistical inference with the coefficients of multicollinear variables. While the variance of $\hat{\alpha}_j$ tends to increase as the result of multicollinearity, so too can the value of the particular estimate used in the hypothesis test, since multicollinearity increases the likelihood of obtaining values of $\hat{\alpha}_j$ that differ substantially from α_j. If this estimate differs from zero by more than (say) two (inflated) standard deviations, the coefficient estimate will be statistically significant. In fact, if carried to the extreme, t-statistics can conceivably be *higher* with multicollinearity, as the magnitudes of estimated coefficients rise relative to the inflated variances of these values. This, however, has not been observed with as much frequency as the occurrence of insignificant t-statistics. The general expectation is thus for multicollinearity to produce nonsignificant t-statistics.

Multicollinearity affects not only the variances of the least squares estimators, but their covariances as well. By altering covariances, the possibility of sign reversal arises. For two explanatory variables (Equation (10.32)), the covariance between $\hat{\alpha}_1$ and $\hat{\alpha}_2$ is given by the expression:

$$\text{Cov}(\hat{\alpha}_1, \hat{\alpha}_2) = -[\sigma_\varepsilon^2/(\sqrt{\sum x_i'^2} \cdot \sqrt{\sum z_i'^2})][\hat{\rho}_{zx}/(1 - \hat{\rho}_{zx}^2)] \qquad \textbf{(10.38)}$$

The covariance between these coefficients equals zero when x and z are totally uncorrelated, and it is of the opposite sign of the correlation between x and z, since all the bracketed terms in Equation (10.38) except $\hat{\rho}_{zx}$ are positive. If, for example, x and z are positively related, the covariance between $\hat{\alpha}_1$ and $\hat{\alpha}_2$ is negative, indicating that overestimates of α_1 will tend to be associated with underestimates of α_2, and vice versa. One possible manifestation of a negative covariance is sign reversal, where a negative coefficient estimate is obtained when the expected sign is positive. Johnston provides an example of this.[15] Starting with a small degree of multicollinearity and estimated coefficients of: $\hat{\alpha}_1 = 1$ and $\hat{\alpha}_2 = 2$, the degree of multicollinearity was increased. The estimated coefficients with this more substantial amount of multicollinearity change to: $\hat{\alpha}_1 = -13.44$ and $\hat{\alpha}_2 = 16.4$, with sign reversal occurring for $\hat{\alpha}_1$. While the *sum* of the coefficients is virtually identical in each case, individual coefficients change dramatically. This occurs since multicollinearity affects both the variances of individual coefficients and the covariance for this pair of coefficients. The addition or deletion of just a few observations, which changes the extent of multicollinearity in the sample data, can therefore produce substantial changes in the least squares coefficients.

When the covariance between these coefficients is negative, greater multicollinearity can leave the sum of the coefficient variances unchanged. Since:

$$\text{Var}(\hat{\alpha}_1 + \hat{\alpha}_2) = \hat{\sigma}_1^2 + \hat{\sigma}_2^2 + 2\,\text{Cov}(\hat{\alpha}_1, \hat{\alpha}_2),$$

---

[15] J. Johnston, pp. 240–241.

the increase in the sum of the variances associated with multicollinearity can be offset by a more negative covariance between the set of collinear coefficients. Thus the variance for the sum of these coefficients might be the same with problematic multicollinearity.

Multicollinearity also raises the likelihood of sign reversal when there are three or more explanatory variables, as the covariances between different pairs of coefficients are affected. Nevertheless, any variables that are either totally or substantially uncorrelated with the other variables in a sample regression function will generally not be adversely affected by multicollinearity.

How are the overall measures of equation performance affected by the presence of multicollinearity? The coefficient of multiple determination, R^2, its adjusted value, $\bar{R}^2$, and the equation F-statistic are, for the most part, unaffected by the presence of imperfect multicollinearity. This result should not be surprising, since these indicators relate to the overall equation and therefore to the set of explanatory variables taken *jointly*. Nor does multicollinearity necessarily cause problems with the forecasting performance of an equation. If the pattern of explanatory variable intercorrelations is identical during both the estimation and forecast periods, forecasts generated by the equation will not be affected. Problematic multicollinearity is therefore manifested in the signs, magnitudes, and t-statistics of individual coefficients. Nonsignificant t-statistics result from the fact that the estimation technique is unable to separate the individual influence of each variable. Taken as a group, however, these same variables can fit the data extremely well, which explains the possible coexistence of large $\bar{R}^2$ and F-values. Because of this fact, it is possible for an equation to have a relatively high $\bar{R}^2$, a statistically significant F-value, but *no* statistically significant coefficients. Also, when severe multicollinearity is present, the addition or deletion of just a few sample observations can substantially change the estimated coefficients in a sample regression function. The "stability" of the least squares coefficients is therefore adversely affected by multicollinearity.

An example of problematic multicollinearity is given by the following auto demand equation:

$$s_t = f(p_{nt}, p_{ut}, y_t, r_t, D_{t-1}, A_{t-1}, \varepsilon_t),$$

where s is the demand for automobiles, measured by the total retail sales of new cars in the United States (thousands of units); p_n, the measure of own price, is the CPI for new cars (1967 = 100); p_u, substitute good price, is the CPI for used cars (1967 = 100); y, the direct measure of ability to pay, is real disposable personal income (billions of 1982 dollars); r, which represents the interest cost of acquiring the funds to purchase an auto, is the interest rate on three-year Treasury bonds; D, the indirect measure of ability to pay, is real total consumer debt as a percentage of real GNP (1982 = 100); A, which represents the condition of the existing stock of autos, is the average age of automobiles (in years); and ε is the stochastic error.

This is a demand equation for a specific durable good, so the discussion of the expected signs presented for the durable goods equation in Chapter 7 pertains. Note that several of the variables are identical to those used in that equation and that lagged values of D and A are included in this specification. The equation was estimated using annual observations for the years 1959 to 1984. The functional form utilized is log-linear. The SAS lines used to create this output are:

```
PROC REG;
MODEL LS=LPN LPU LY LR LDLAG LALAG / VIF COLLIN;
```

The letter L before each name denotes a natural logarithm. The options at the end of the MODEL statement indicate that SAS is to produce variance inflation factors (VIF) along with additional multicollinearity diagnostic measures (COLLIN) which are discussed later. The resulting output is:

```
DEP VARIABLE: LS
ANALYSIS OF VARIANCE

                    SUM OF        MEAN
SOURCE      DF     SQUARES      SQUARE      F VALUE     PROB>F
MODEL        6    0.57283974   0.09547329   13.263      0.0001
ERROR       18    0.12956783   0.007198213
C TOTAL     24    0.70240757
     ROOT MSE    0.08484228    R-SQUARE     0.8155
     DEP MEAN    9.10426       ADJ R-SQ     0.7541
     C.V.        0.9318965


PARAMETER ESTIMATES
                PARAMETER     STANDARD     T FOR HO:                 VARIANCE
VARIABLE   DF   ESTIMATE      ERROR      PARAMETER=0   PROB>|T|     INFLATION
INTERCEP    1   -4.23028281   4.67713258    -0.904      0.3777         0
LPN         1   -0.64813997   0.40874335    -1.586      0.1302      37.334889
LPU         1   -0.58959746   0.57967123    -1.017      0.3226     225.4139
LY          1    2.09842528   0.80163096     2.618      0.0174     107.3695
LR          1   -0.19291242   0.09164493    -2.105      0.0496       6.36481554
LDLAG       1    0.02744410   0.73328505     0.037      0.9706       9.78172589
LALAG       1    2.20859047   1.29362817     1.507      0.1050      35.03059
```

The adjusted R^2 for this equation is relatively high, the equation F-value, 13.2, exceeds the critical F-value of 4.01 for the 1 percent level of significance (for 6 and 18 degrees of freedom), and the equation error is less than one percent of the mean of the dependent variable. By these standards the estimated equation fits the data well. Note, however, that only two of its coefficients are statistically significant at the 5 percent level or above, and that the signs of the used car price index (LPU) and lagged indebtedness (LDLAG) are the opposite of those expected. Clearly, this equation displays the typical symptoms of problematic multicollinearity. Additional evidence supporting this contention is provided by the variance inflation factors for the explanatory variables in this equation. Four of the six variance inflation factors exceed the value of 10 considered indicative of problem multicollinearity. Thus the R^2's from their auxiliary regressions exceed 0.9. The largest VIF, 225.4, results from an R_j^2 of 0.9956 (this is obtained by solving for R_j^2 from $225.4 = 1/(1 - R_j^2)$), indicating nearly perfect multicollinearity between the CPI for used cars and several of the other explanatory variables.

At this point, it is worthwhile to contrast the consequences of specification error and multicollinearity on an estimated equation. Both the omission of influential variables and problematic multicollinearity are capable of affecting the signs, magnitudes, and variances of individual coefficients. Sign reversal, unreasonable coefficient magnitudes, and nonsignificant *t*-statistics can emerge with either of these problems. One major difference between these is the greater likelihood of observing a large $\bar{R}^2$ and statistically significant equation *F*-statistic with multicollinearity. When severe multicollinearity is present, however, the existence of these problems pertains to best linear unbiased estimators, while the opposite is true for omission of influential variables. Because of these similarities, it is possible for a researcher to conclude, based on individual coefficients, that multicollinearity is the cause of the unsatisfactory coefficients, while in fact, the problem results from an incorrectly specified equation. *Since hypothesis testing and equation evaluation proceed on the assumption that the model is correctly specified, it is necessary to critically evaluate the specification of an equation before proceeding with either formal methods for the detection of, or cures for, multicollinearity.*

This last point can be seen more vividly when the auto demand equation is re-estimated using a linear specification:

```
DEP VARIABLE: S
ANALYSIS OF VARIANCE

                  SUM OF        MEAN
SOURCE     DF    SQUARES       SQUARE      F VALUE     PROB>F
MODEL       6  43404059.76   7234009.96    13.891      0.0001
ERROR      18   9373582.88    520754.60
C TOTAL    24  52777642.64
    ROOT MSE      721.6333    R-SQUARE      0.8224
    DEP MEAN      9116.12     ADJ R-SQ      0.7632
    C.V.          7.916013

PARAMETER ESTIMATES
              PARAMETER    STANDARD     T FOR H0:                 VARIANCE
VARIABLE  DF  ESTIMATE      ERROR     PARAMETER=0   PROB>|T|     INFLATION
INTERCEP   1  -19123.99576  8998.89237   -2.125      0.0477          0
PN         1  -76.51611313  28.13533361  -2.720      0.0141      50.54008
PU         1  -31.03223064  17.91953837  -1.732      0.1004      98.95705
Y          1   12.56852896   3.46872754   3.623      0.0019      82.12462
R          1  -195.16736    114.56501    -1.704      0.1057       5.57216
DLAG       1  -466.24528    521.33470    -0.894      0.3829      11.79298
ALAG       1  4626.86739   1979.95449     2.337      0.0312      45.67195
```

The equation *F*-statistic is virtually identical with the log-linear version of this equation, while the coefficient of variation, 7.9, is higher than the initial specification but still within acceptable bounds for this measure. The major difference between the two estimated equations is the performance of the individual coefficients. All but one coefficient (DLAG) is statistically significant at the 5 percent level of significance and above for one-tail hypothesis tests. The only explanatory variable with an incorrect sign is the CPI for used cars. The negative intercept in this multivariate equation translates into a positive coefficient in the demand curve equation. Using 1984 values for all of the explanatory variables, the demand curve implied by the above equation is:

$$\hat{s}_t = 26{,}178.5 - 76.5p_{nt}.$$

Substituting the 1984 value of p_n, 208.5, gives a 10,224,100 predicted value for auto sales, which is close to the actual value of 10,391,000 for that year. Several estimated elasticities for 1984 also conform to a priori expectations. The own price elasticity estimate equals -1.56, while the estimated income elasticity is $+3.0$. Both these indicate elastic responses, which are consistent with expectations for these variables. The estimated interest elasticity for 1984, -0.2, appears to be lower than the value expected. Note that almost all of the variance inflation factors in the linear specification exceed 10, so that a potential problem with multicollinearity still exists with this functional form. However, the substantial difference in the performance of these two equations points to the necessity of treating multicollinearity only *after* the determination of appropriate functional form has been made.

Detecting Problematic Multicollinearity

OVERALL EQUATION PERFORMANCE. It is important to reiterate that multicollinearity is virtually always present in nonexperimental economic data, and that the existence of multicollinearity by itself does *not* guarantee that serious problems exist with an estimated equation. When multicollinearity is consequential, the estimated coefficients in an equation will be adversely affected, even though these are the best linear unbiased estimators of their population parameters. Keep in mind that the BLUE property pertains to a repeated sampling context. For a single estimate, the actual value of an estimator can be unsatisfactory. As the previous discussion stated, the most typical symptoms of problematic multicollinearity are one or more of the following:

—the signs of individual coefficients are the opposite of those expected;

—coefficient magnitudes are unacceptably small or large;

—affected coefficients fail to attain statistical significance;

—the addition or deletion of a few observations results in substantial changes in the estimated coefficients;

—deleting an influential variable that is highly correlated with another variable in the equation might not decrease $\bar{R}^2$.

In general, however, multicollinearity affects neither the value of $\bar{R}^2$ nor the equation F-statistic. Because of this fact, *the possibility exists that an equation with no statistically significant coefficients can itself be statistically significant (based on its F-value) and possess a large adjusted R^2*. This combination indicates that the explanatory variables taken as a *set* are statistically significant, but that data limitations prevent individual coefficients from attaining significance. Because multicollinearity increases coefficient variances, the likelihood of failing to reject the false null hypothesis that an influential variable does not belong in an equation rises, which increases the probability of Type II errors.

Keep in mind, however, that a multicollinear equation can possess none of these problems. The coefficients of highly correlated variables can be statistically significant, display correct signs, and possess reasonable magnitudes. This occurs, for example, when the equation error variance (σ_ε^2) is small enough to offset the inflating effect of intercorrelations among the explanatory variables on coefficient variances.

CORRELATION MEASURES.   Multicollinearity is caused by intercorrelations among the explanatory variables in an equation. The most logical place to seek information concerning the extent of multicollinearity would therefore appear to be the correlation coefficients for these variables. When an equation contains only two explanatory variables, the simple correlation coefficient is an adequate measure for detecting collinearity. If this value is "large," collinearity is judged to be potentially serious. The obvious problem that must be resolved before this determination can be made is the definition of "large." Most researchers appear to consider the value 0.9 as the threshold beyond which problems are likely to occur. Others have defined "large" based on the relationship between the square of $\hat{\rho}_{zx}$ and the coefficient of multiple determination for the estimated equation.

The use of such correlation measures is, however, substantially more fallible when an equation contains three or more explanatory variables. In this setting, *the use of bivariate correlations to detect problematic multicollinearity can be extremely unreliable, since an exact linear dependency can exist among three or more variables simultaneously, while no pair displays a large correlation coefficient.* Kmenta illustrates this possibility for the case of three explanatory variables that are perfectly multicollinear when taken as a set.[16] In this example, an exact linear dependency exists between these three variables, yet no bivariate correlation coefficient exceeds 0.5. Use of bivariate correlation coefficients to detect multicollinearity in this case would therefore fail. Because of this possibility, *the existence of large bivariate correlation coefficients is not a necessary condition for problematic multicollinearity when an equation contains three or more explanatory variables.* Of course, if one or more of these equal 1.0, perfect collinearity would be indicated.

To remedy this, measures of partial correlation are considered. The major defect of bivariate correlations is their inability to control for the influence of variables other than the two being considered. The most effective of the correlation methods for evaluating whether three or more variables potentially enter a linear dependency is through the use of auxiliary regressions. Candidates for dependent variables in auxiliary regressions are those displaying the symptoms of problematic multicollinearity discussed previously. If a near-linear dependency exists, the auxiliary regression will display a small equation standard error, a large R^2, and a statistically

---

[16] J. Kmenta. pp. 434–435.

significant equation F-value. The statistical significance of the auxiliary regression equation, as determined by its F-value, constitutes objective evidence of the existence of a linear relationship between the set of variables in that equation. Furthermore, the specific variables involved in the near-linear dependency can be determined on the basis of which coefficients are statistically significant. Finally, the coefficients of multiple determination in the auxiliary regressions, R_j^2, can be utilized to calculate the variance inflation factors (Equation (10.36)) associated with the dependent variables in each such regression. Once these are calculated, the rule of thumb value that problematic multicollinearity is indicated when one or more variance inflation factors equal or exceed 10 can be utilized as further evidence supporting the existence of multicollinearity in the original equation.

The use of auxiliary regressions is not a foolproof means of detecting problematic multicollinearity. If two or more of the explanatory variables in an auxiliary regression are highly correlated, problematic multicollinearity will likely manifest itself in the coefficients in that equation. As a result, one or more of the variables involved in a near-linear dependency might not be detected, since such multicollinearity can cause the t-statistics associated with these coefficients to be nonsignificant. Furthermore, *a single auxiliary regression is incapable of determining whether more than one near-linear dependency exists.* If auxiliary regression is the chosen method for determining problematic multicollinearity, then for thoroughness sake, several such regressions should be run. A more precise method for determining which auxiliary regressions should be run is outlined in the next section.

Matrix Decomposition Methods[17] (Optional)

The data used to estimate an equation can be thought of as constituting a **matrix**, which is simply a rectangular array of numbers. The **data matrix** used for least squares is a matrix, where each column represents one of the variables in the regression and each row is a single observation for these variables. For example, if the equation under consideration is given by Equation (10.32), the variables consist of: (i) an "intercept variable," which always takes the value of 1; (ii) x, which takes values: $x_1, x_2, \ldots, x_n$; and (iii) z, whose values are: $z_1, z_2, \ldots, z_n$. The data matrix for this equation, D, is therefore:

$$D = \begin{bmatrix} 1 & x_1 & z_1 \\ 1 & x_2 & z_2 \\ & \cdots & \\ & \cdots & \\ & \cdots & \\ 1 & x_n & z_n \end{bmatrix}$$

---

[17] A more complete presentation of the topics discussed here can be found in the appendixes to Chapters 3, 7, and 9. This section draws heavily on D. Belsley, E. Kuh, and R. Welsch, *Regression Diagnostics: Identifying Influential Data and Sources of Collinearity* (New York: John Wiley & Sons), 1980.

The dimension of a matrix is stated as:

(number of rows) × (number of columns)

The matrix D in this example is an ($n \times 3$) matrix. When the number of rows and columns are equal, the matrix is a **square matrix**. It is this type of matrix that is utilized to analyze multicollinearity.

The most simple square matrix to work with, a (2×2) matrix, will be employed as the basis for illustrating how matrix methods are used to detect multicollinearity. Let us consider two variables, x and z, and a sample size of two observations. If the sample values taken by these variables are: $x = 2, 4$; and $z = 1, 2$, then an exact linear dependency exists between x and z, with $x_i = 2z_i$. Using the expression from the definition of linear dependence, this implies that:

$$\omega_1 x + \omega_2 z = 0$$

is satisfied by these data for nonzero values of both ω's with:

$$(1)x + (-2)z = 0, \quad \text{or} \quad \omega_1 = 1 \quad \text{and} \quad \omega_2 = -2.$$

How can the use of matrices detect this exact linear dependency? Associated with every square matrix is a number called the **determinant** of that matrix. For the following (2×2) matrix:

$$\begin{bmatrix} a & b \\ c & d \end{bmatrix}$$

the determinant is given by the expression:

$$\text{determinant} = (a \cdot d - b \cdot c)$$

Using this information for the matrix that corresponds to the hypothetical data in this example:

$$\begin{bmatrix} x_1 & z_1 \\ x_2 & z_2 \end{bmatrix} = \begin{bmatrix} 2 & 1 \\ 4 & 2 \end{bmatrix}$$

and the determinant of this matrix is:

$$\begin{aligned} \text{determinant} &= (x_1 \cdot z_2 - z_1 \cdot x_2) \\ &= (2 \cdot 2 - 1 \cdot 4) \\ &= 4 - 4 = 0. \end{aligned}$$

The value of this determinant is no coincidence. *When the variables that make up a square matrix are linearly dependent, so that an exact linear dependence exists, the determinant of that matrix equals zero.* While the values of x and z in this example were selected to make the linear dependence obvious, when there are many variables and very large matrices involved in the estimation of the least squares coefficients, the existence of perfect multicollinearity is not at all obvious. The determinant thus provides a useful device in such situations. However, data matrices cannot be square, since if the number of observations equals the number of explanatory variables, there are 0 degrees of freedom. Furthermore, determinants are defined only for square matrices.

The square matrix that pertains to the least squares estimators involves the sum of squared observations for each variable and the products of different observations, which is called the **sum of the squares and cross-products matrix**. This particular matrix is obtained by matrix multiplication, and corresponds to D^2, if the original data matrix is D. The dimension of this matrix is: (number of explanatory variables) × (number of explanatory variables). Assuming the sample regression function does not contain an intercept, and that the data matrix contains n observations on the variables x and z, the sum of squares and cross-products matrix is:

$$\begin{bmatrix} \sum x_i^2 & \sum x_i z_i \\ \sum z_i x_i & \sum z_i^2 \end{bmatrix}$$

It is from this matrix that many of the different terms in the formulas for the $\hat{\alpha}$'s are obtained. If we assume that x and z are perfectly collinear, with $z_i = \omega x_i$, the determinant of this matrix can be shown to equal 0. Since $\sum x_i z_i = \omega \sum x_i^2$ and $\sum z_i^2 = \omega^2 \sum x_i^2$, the determinant of the sum of squares and cross-products matrix above is:

$$\text{determinant} = [(\sum x_i^2 \cdot \sum z_i^2) - (\sum x_i z_i \cdot \sum z_i x_i)]$$
$$= [(\sum x_i^2 \cdot \omega^2 \sum x_i^2) - (\omega \sum x_i^2)^2] = 0.$$

Thus, *if the variables in a data matrix are linearly dependent, the determinant of the corresponding sum of the squares and cross-products matrix will equal zero.* Many canned statistical programs provide the value of this determinant as one of their options.

This result suggests a method for determining whether perfect collinearity exists. Unfortunately, computers can commit rounding errors in the calculation of this type of matrix, so that what should be a 0 determinant is not exactly 0, but say 0.000005. For imperfect collinearity, determinants "close to 0" have been used as the basis for ascertaining whether problematic multicollinearity exists. However, the definition of "close to 0" is not precise, and various refinements, such as transforming the original variables into standardized form, have been advocated.

More recent developments in this area use another set of values that are associated with the determinant of the sum of the squares and cross-products matrix, called **eigenvalues**. For a (2 × 2) matrix such as that under consideration, two eigenvalues exist. If we denote these λ_1 and λ_2, then the relationship between these eigenvalues and the determinant of a matrix is:

$$\text{determinant} = \lambda_1 \cdot \lambda_2.$$

The determinant of a sum of the squares and cross-products matrix therefore equals the product of the eigenvalues associated with that matrix. Since a zero determinant for this matrix indicates perfect collinearity among the pair of variables in the data matrix, perfect collinearity occurs when one eigenvalue is 0. Generalizing this result: "small" or zero values for the eigenvalues of a sum of the squares and cross-products matrix are indicative of either problematic or perfect collinearity. As with so much of the discussion of the measurement or detection of multicollinearity, ambiguity in the definition of "small" again arises. Also, eigenvalues are sensitive to the units of measurement of the variables, which potentially causes further problems with such a definition.

Belsley, Kuh, and Welsch have proposed a procedure, which, while not without its critics, appears to be the most accurate diagnostic tool at the present time.[18] To determine whether a particular eigenvalue is small enough to indicate problems with the data matrix, these authors suggest as a first step that:

> the explanatory variables in the data matrix be scaled to unit length (recall this entails dividing each variable by its standard deviation) and not centered at 0 (do not subtract the mean of each variable from its values). If the equation that is to be estimated contains an intercept, be sure to include a column of 1's. Obtain the eigenvalues from the sum of the squares and cross-products matrix that incorporates all of the above features.[19]

The **condition number** of the data matrix equals the ratio:

$$\sqrt{\lambda_{max}/\lambda_{min}}$$

where "max" and "min" denote the maximum and minimum values of the *set* of all eigenvalues.[20] Extensive experimentation leads to the recommendation that if the condition number equals or exceeds 30, problematic multicollinearity is likely to be present.

For three or more explanatory variables, it is possible for a data matrix to possess more than one near-linear dependency. The use of eigenvalues can aid in the determination of exactly how many near dependencies exist. If an equation contains k explanatory variables (including the intercept), the sum of the squares and cross-products matrix will have k eigenvalues. One possible definition of the number of near-linear dependencies that exist within a data matrix is the number of small individual eigenvalues. Belsley, Kuh, and Welsch provide another criterion, based on values similar to the condition number, for this determination. If all of the eigenvalues are arranged in ascending order, a set of values called **condition indexes** is obtained. For eigenvalue j, λ_j:

$$\text{condition index } j = \sqrt{\lambda_{max}/\lambda_j} \geq 1.$$

A condition index greater than or equal to 30 indicates the potential existence of a near-linear dependency. Using this as our sole criterion, the number of near-linear dependencies is determined by the number of condition indexes equal to or greater than 30.

Relatively large condition indexes are not necessarily associated with near dependencies, however. This fact requires a modification to the above rule. The basis

---

[18] *Ibid.*

[19] The data matrix may contain a lagged dependent variable.

[20] Technically, the condition number of a matrix A measures the sensitivity of a solution vector, z, in the set of equations: $Az = c$ to changes in the matrix A and elements of the vector of constants c. Since the sum of the squares and cross-products matrix is like a matrix D^2, obtaining eigenvalues for the original data matrix D requires that square roots of the eigenvalues for the sum of the squares and cross-products matrix be taken.

for this refinement is a relationship between the eigenvalues of a data matrix and the variance of each least squares coefficient. The variance of a single least squares coefficient is the product of σ_ε^2 and the sum of k **variance proportions**, each of which is associated with a single eigenvalue of the data matrix. For each variable, the sum of the variance proportions equals 1.0. Tables providing summary information on eigenvalues, condition indexes, and variance proportions (such as those from SAS) are typically arranged with eigenvalues in *descending* order. Accompanying this is information on condition indexes, and the variance proportions for the coefficients of an equation. Since eigenvalues are arranged in descending order, the last condition index gives the condition number of the data matrix. When the explanatory variables are totally uncorrelated, the variance proportions table will look like the following:

EIGENVALUE	CONDITION INDEX	PROPORTIONS OF VARIANCE OF			
		$\hat{\alpha}_0$	$\hat{\alpha}_1$	$\cdots$	$\hat{\alpha}_k$
λ_0	$\sqrt{\lambda_0/\lambda_0}$	1.0	0	$\cdots$	0
λ_1	$\sqrt{\lambda_0/\lambda_1}$	0	1.0		0
				$\cdots$	
				$\cdots$	
				$\cdots$	
λ_k	$\sqrt{\lambda_0/\lambda_k}$	0	0	$\cdots$	1.0

In this table, the diagonal elements (from top left to bottom right) all equal 1.0, indicating that the variance of each coefficient is associated with a single eigenvalue, and therefore one variance proportion. When the explanatory variables are correlated, off-diagonal elements will not all be 0. As a result, diagonal elements will not equal 1.0, and the variance of each coefficient will be associated with two or more eigenvalues. Therefore, a single eigenvalue can play a substantial role in more than one variance. The previous rule for identifying problematic multicollinearity (in terms of large condition indexes) can now be modified with reference to variance proportions:

> When *two or more* of the variance proportions associated with a particular condition index that is in the questionable range (30 or more) are large, the implied near-linear dependency is causing problems with the coefficients in a regression equation. Large variance proportions are defined as those greater than or equal to 0.5.

This diagnostic procedure thus: (i) determines the number of near-linear dependencies in an equation by the number of condition indexes greater than or equal to 30; and (ii) identifies the variables involved in each of these near dependencies by the two or more large variance proportions for each of the large condition indexes in (i). Using this information, each linear dependency can be further investigated with an auxiliary regression.

One instance where the variance proportions fail to indicate the variables involved in a near-linear dependency is the case of a "dominating dependency." Belsley, Kuh, and Welsch indicate that:

> A dominating dependency, one with a condition index of higher order of magnitude, can become the prime determinant of the variance of a given coefficient and thus obscure information about its simultaneous involvement in a weaker dependency.[21]

A dominating dependency thus exists when the condition number associated with one eigenvalue is substantially larger than that of the others, such as 30 and 300. When such a dependency is present, it is likely that only one high variance proportion will be associated with the smaller condition indexes. This requires a final qualification to the **matrix decomposition method** outlined in this section:

> When a dominating dependency exists, a single large variance proportion associated with one of the smaller but problematic condition indexes indicates the likelihood of another near-linear dependency. Assume the variables involved are those identified with the dominating dependency along with the variable whose single variance proportion is large.

Note, however, that the existence of a single large variance proportion associated with a dominating dependency does not *by itself* constitute evidence that a particular coefficient has been adversely affected by multicollinearity. The involvement of this variable in a near dependency must be established with an auxiliary regression. The suggested procedure is to regress the variable in the dominated dependency with the single large variance proportion on the *set* of variables with large proportions in the dominating dependency. The statistical significance of this equation constitutes proof of the existence of harmful multicollinearity on the coefficient of the variable used in this auxiliary regression.

Belsley, Kuh, and Welsch suggest a procedure for forming the auxiliary regressions once the condition indexes and variance proportions have been examined. Identify the largest variance proportion for each near dependency with a condition index of 30 or above.[22] The variables that correspond to these become the "pivots," or dependent variables in the auxiliary regressions. Once these have been identified, each pivot is regressed on the *set* of nonpivot variables in the original equation.

This entire procedure can be illustrated using the output of SAS that corresponds to the COLLIN option from the linear version of the automobile demand equation.[23] Recall that this equation displays satisfactory overall performance, and that only the coefficients of p_u and D_{t-1} indicate problems: an incorrect sign for the coefficient of p_u (which is statistically significant), and a nonsignificant coefficient for D_{t-1} (but of

---

[21] Belsley et al., p. 155.

[22] This is not as easy as it appears here. For example, identical variance proportions can exist within the same near dependency. In this case, the authors suggest selecting the co-largest proportion with the remainder of its variance determined in the smallest of the problematic condition indexes. See Belsley, p. 159, for example.

[23] The actual output has been slightly modified for ease in presenting the entire set of numbers.

the correct sign). Before we can conclude that these problems are the result of problematic multicollinearity, we must first establish that these variables are involved in one or more serious near-linear dependencies.

Based on the multicollinearity diagnostics below, there is clear evidence of problematic multicollinearity with this equation. Examination of the condition indexes reveals three near dependencies, with indexes of 62.6, 125.5, and 299.7.[24] The largest of these, 299.7, is the condition number of the data matrix. This last condition index identifies a near-linear dependency involving INTERCEP, PU, Y, DLAG, and ALAG. Eigenvalues 5 and 6 each contain only one variance proportion of 0.5 or above. Thus, eigenvalue 7 is a dominating dependency. Examination of variance proportions for eigenvalue 5 point to the possibility that a second proportion, that of the coefficient of R, might also be large, but that this is hidden because of the dominating dependency. This possibility, which is investigated below, might indicate a near dependency involving both PN and R. Since this is a dominated dependency, the recommended procedure is to assume that a near dependency exists between PN, INTERCEP, and the other four variables indicated by the dominant dependency. Eigenvalue 6 identifies only DLAG as having a large variance proportion. Since DLAG is already implicated in the dominating dependency of eigenvalue 7, a near dependency between DLAG and the variables indicated in the dominating dependency has already been established. Like the situation with eigenvalue 5, however, there may be a near dependency between DLAG and the equation intercept that is masked by the dominant dependency. Finally, about 99 percent of the variance of the equation intercept is associated with the two near dependencies associated with eigenvalues 6 and 7. Any harmful effects of multicollinearity on the estimated intercept might therefore be "shared" between these dependencies.

		CONDITION			VARIANCE PROPORTIONS				
	EIGVALUE	INDEX	INTERCEP	PN	PU	Y	R	DLAG	ALAG
1	6.7416	1.0000	0.0000	0.0000	0.0000	0.0000	0.0007	0.0000	0.0000
2	0.1953	5.8750	0.0003	0.0002	0.0037	0.0000	0.0343	0.0003	0.0001
3	0.0526	11.3221	0.0000	0.0009	0.0132	0.0001	0.3649	0.0001	0.0001
4	0.0083	28.5687	0.0020	0.0081	0.0012	0.0353	0.2035	0.0043	0.0031
5	0.0017	62.5852	0.0028	*0.5812*	0.2077	0.0077	0.3463	0.0072	0.0026
6	0.0004	125.5180	0.2080	0.0726	0.0032	0.1644	0.0261	*0.4741*	0.0040
7	0.0001	299.6920	0.7870	0.3370	0.7711	0.7925	0.0242	0.5139	*0.9902*

The pivots that should serve as the dependent variables in the auxiliary regressions are indicated by an underscore: ALAG, DLAG, and PN. The nonpivot variables are the intercept, PU, Y, and R. The results of these auxiliary regressions are given

---

[24] Note that the fourth eigenvalue corresponds to a condition index of 28.6, which is close enough to the problem range of 30 to merit possible consideration as an additional near dependency. However, none of the variance proportions associated with this eigenvalue are large enough to warrant further evaluation.

in the following table:

	DEPENDENT VARIABLE		
	ALAG	DLAG	PN
INTERCEPT	6.04	7.54	62.5
	(37.1)	(13.2)	(6.99)
PU	0.009	−0.015	0.377
	(15.3)	(7.16)	(11.3)
Y	−0.001	0.005	−0.004
	(5.23)	(8.84)	(0.51)
R	0.01	−0.016	2.91
	(0.65)	(0.27)	(3.28)
$\bar{R}^2$	0.947	0.834	0.963
F	144.4	43.0	219.5
CV	1.91	3.36	5.40

These auxiliary regressions provide substantial evidence supporting the results of the matrix decomposition diagnostics. Each equation has a high adjusted R^2, a statistically significant F-value, and a small coefficient of variation. The coefficients in these equations indicate that the problems detected in the original equation are at least partially the result of multicollinearity, since both DLAG and PU are involved in one or more of the near-linear dependencies present in the data. While the coefficient of PN in the original equation does not display any obvious deficiencies, the third auxiliary regression indicates the existence of a problem with this coefficient. Furthermore, this equation establishes that eigenvalue 5, which involves only one large variance proportion, is a problematic near dependency. Note that R is only statistically significant in the auxiliary regression with PN as dependent variable, confirming the link between these variables alluded to previously.

One final word concerning the use of variance inflation factors and matrix decomposition methods is appropriate. Five of the variance inflation factors for the auto demand equation exceed the rule of thumb value of 10, indicating problems with multicollinearity in that equation. This should not be taken as evidence that five near-linear dependencies exist. The matrix decomposition methods discussed here are far more accurate at determining the number of problematic near-linear dependencies. One of the advantages of this methodology is thus its ability to determine specific auxiliary regressions that should be run as the basis for providing supporting evidence for the existence of problematic multicollinearity.

Remedial Measures

It is important to reiterate that multicollinearity does not always pose a problem. Remedial measures are only warranted *if and when* definitive proof of the existence of harmful multicollinearity has been established. The proper context for such an assessment is within the confines of a properly specified equation. It is possible for an equation to contain specification bias and multicollinearity. For example, different structures might be present within the data so that the omission of one or more dummy variables is causing problems, while at the same time, the included explanatory variables are highly interrelated. If this is the case, both the coefficients and the equation performance measures will likely be unsatisfactory. The researcher might then conclude that the major problem is multicollinearity, and undertake remedial measures consistent with this assessment. Before dealing with multicollinearity, any problems with the equation specification should first be resolved.

If the attempted remedy for multicollinearity consists of dropping nonsignificant but influential variables from the equation, the cure may be worse than the problem, since the only instance in which the omission of influential variables does not produce bias in the remaining slope coefficients (the bias is 0 then) occurs when these variables are totally uncorrelated. Dropping an influential variable involved in a nonlinear dependency thus guarantees biased coefficients (although the magnitude is not necessarily large). Viewed another way, the importance of equation specification dictates that *you should never specify an equation defensively, and fail to include a variable because you believe it will be correlated with the existing variables in that equation*. The determination of whether multicollinearity is problematic should be based on an examination of the final equation. If the variable in question is influential, based on economic theory or previous empirical research, its influence must be accounted for in the estimated equation. The more important question in this type of situation is therefore not whether but how to include an influential variable.[25]

There are several potential remedies for problematic multicollinearity. The addition of new data that are less collinear than the original sample is capable of substantially altering the performance of the coefficients in an equation. Unfortunately, such data are typically not available. It is likely that all available data have already been used to estimate the equation and that no additional data are available. For time series data, new data materializes only after a period that coincides with the frequency of the data, such as next month, next quarter, or even next year has elapsed. Deletion of the observations that are believed to be responsible for the problems might appear to be a viable solution. However, data are often so collinear that deleting all problem observations leaves too few degrees of freedom with which to estimate the relationship. Perhaps the only viable cure using additional data is the pooling of cross-sectional and time series data, which is possible when panel data are available.[26] Estimation of the parameters with such data is beyond the scope of this text.

Sometimes one of the variables responsible for the problem multicollinearity is redundant, or possibly noninfluential. The nonsignificance of the coefficient of a noninfluential variable is more the result of its irrelevance than multicollinearity. The opposite is true for the coefficient of a redundant variable, since the factor with which

---

[25] If this variable is totally uncorrelated with the existing variables in the equation, an unbiased estimate of its coefficient can be obtained from a bivariate regression of Y on that variable. However, the estimated variance of the resulting coefficient will be biased, resulting in erroneous statistical inference concerning the population coefficient.

[26] See Chapter 3 for a discussion of the different types of data that are available for econometric research.

it is redundant accounts for the same influence on the dependent variable. Both types of variables can be eliminated from the equation which may reduce multicollinearity problems. However, identifying such variables is often neither obvious nor simple. Economics journals and texts, along with previous empirical studies, can be of assistance when attempting to make this type of determination.

When none of the variables in the estimated equation are redundant, dropping variables is not a viable option, but the possibility of combining problematic variables into a form that makes economic sense exists. For example, both of the price variables in the auto demand equation discussed above are involved in near dependencies. Omitting one or both of these results in an equation specification that embodies the assumption of perfectly inelastic auto demand with respect to the omitted price variable(s). These variables can be combined to form a new variable, the relative price of new autos, p_n/p_u, which has the same negative expected sign as p_n. In general, combining variables into a ratio is acceptable as long as the partial slopes are of similar magnitude and opposite in expected sign. Another combination consists of the sum or difference of two problematic variables. For example, if an estimated equation contains both short-term and long-term interest rates, r_s and r_L, and these are highly correlated, the difference: $(r_L - r_s)$, might be effectively utilized.[27] Since each of these interest rates is the difference between the real rate of interest and the appropriate inflationary expectations, the new variable $(r_L - r_s)$ measures the gap between long-term and short-term inflationary expectations. Note that the partial slope of r_L is equal to, but of the opposite sign of the partial slope for r_s, since the regression:

$$y_i = \alpha_0 + \alpha_1(r_L - r_s) + \varepsilon_i$$

is identical to:

$$y_i = \alpha_0 + \alpha_1 r_L - \alpha_1 r_s + \varepsilon_i.$$

Variable transformations utilized to deal with problematic multicollinearity sometimes involve the dependent variable as well as the explanatory variables. One such transformation is that of first differences. If the explanatory variables x and z are highly collinear in their original form, and no combination of these makes economic sense, then estimating the original equation in first difference form (see Chapter 8) can sometimes eliminate the multicollinearity problem. Thus, when x and z are highly correlated, the absolute changes in these variables, Δx and Δz might not entail problematic multicollinearity. While this transformation might eliminate multicollinearity, it may also introduce the problem of serial correlation. This topic is discussed in the next chapter. Finally, when an explanatory variable is involved in a near-linear dependency, it is sometimes possible to convert the *dependent variable* into a ratio. For example, if the dependent variable of an equation is the level of savings (SAV), and GDP is a problematic explanatory variable, the equation can be estimated with (SAV/GDP), or the savings rate as the dependent variable. If, instead, the level of population (POP) is the problematic variable in the savings equation,

---

[27] Of course, r_s can exceed r_L, causing this difference to be negative, which precludes the use of the natural logarithm of this expression. In this case, the natural logarithm of the ratio r_L/r_s can be used.

the dependent variable can be changed to (SAV/POP), or savings per capita. While this particular remedy is potentially capable of curing heteroskedasticity problems, the partial slope of the variable used in the denominator of the dependent variable cannot be obtained, unless the reciprocal of that variable is included as an explanatory variable (such as the labor force participation equation in Chapter 8).

There will be cases where the data used to estimate a relationship are simply not adequate to allow the underlying relationship to be ascertained with much precision. Even with a properly specified equation, when remedial actions for multicollinearity have been attempted, the equation might still contain one or more unsatisfactory coefficient estimates no matter what the researcher attempts. *There is nothing wrong with including problematic coefficients in the final version of an estimated equation. If these are influential variables, the data might not allow their individual significance to be established. However, an objective basis exists for including these variables: a Wald test on the subset of nonsignificant coefficients. If the test statistic allows us to reject the null hypothesis that the joint influence of these variables is not statistically significant, then as a set, these coefficients exert a significant influence on the dependent variable, and their inclusion in the estimated equation is justified.*

KEY TERMS

Auxiliary regression	Multicollinearity
Collinearity	Omitted variable (specification) bias
Condition indexes	Perfect (imperfect) multicollinearity
Condition number	Sign reversal
Data matrix	Specification bias
Determinant	Specification error
Eigenvalue	Square matrix
Linearly dependent	Sum of the squares and cross-products matrix
Linearly independent	Variance inflation factor
Matrix	Variance proportions
Matrix decomposition methods	
Measurement error	

EXERCISES

1. If the deviation form of the correct equation is:

$$y'_i = \alpha_1 x'_i + \alpha_2 z'_i + \varepsilon'_i$$

and the influential variable z is omitted, the estimated equation is:

$$y_i = \alpha_1 x_i + v_i, \qquad \text{where } v_i = \varepsilon_i + \alpha_2 z_i,$$

When is v_i correlated with x_i (so that $\text{Cov}(x_i, v_i) \neq 0$)?

2.   Assuming the correctly specified consumption function is:

$$c_t = \alpha_0 + \alpha_1 y_t + \alpha_2 (w/p)_t + \alpha_3 r_t + \varepsilon_t,$$

where c is real personal consumption expenditures, y is real disposable personal income, (w/p) is real wealth, and r is the rate of interest:

(a) Determine the direction of bias in both the intercept and slope of the incorrectly specified consumption function: $c_t = \alpha_0 + \alpha_1 y_t + v_t$.

(b) If the two omitted variables in (a) had opposite expected signs in the consumption function, would the answer to (a) change? If so, how?

3.   Is it possible for the equation F-statistic to fall as additional variables are added to the estimated equation to eliminate specification error? Illustrate this using the formula:

$$F = [R^2/(1 - R^2)][(n - k)/(n - 1)].$$

4.   (a) Assume that the correctly specified equation is:

$$y_i = \alpha_0 + \alpha_1 x_i + \alpha_2 z_i + \varepsilon_i$$

and that the variable z is omitted when this equation is estimated. Show that the expected value of least squares intercept estimator is given by the expression in Equation (10.10):

$$E(\hat{\alpha}_0) = \alpha_0 + \alpha_2 [\hat{\mu}_z - \hat{\pi}_{zx} \hat{\mu}_x]$$

and that this is a biased estimator of α_0 when z is omitted from the regression;

(b) Now let the correctly specified equation be given by Equation (10.15), and two influential variables are omitted, making the estimated Equation (10.16). Show that Equation (10.23) is now the correct expression for $E(\alpha_0)$.

(c) Show that the least squares estimator $\hat{\alpha}_0$ is unbiased when only the dependent variable y is measured with error.

5.   If $x_i = 2z_i$, so that x and z are linearly dependent, show that $\hat{\rho}_{xz} = 1$.

6.   State the formula for $\hat{\alpha}_2$ from Equation (10.32) in the text (this is given in Chapter 6). Show that when x and z follow the linear dependency $z_i = \omega x_i$, this estimator is also indeterminate.

7.   Using Equation (10.33) in the text, show that when x and z are totally uncorrelated, the least squares formula for $\hat{\alpha}_1$ is identical to that in the bivariate model.

8.   In ascertaining the relationship between the level of schooling and earnings, Mincer[28] estimated the semi-log equation:

$$\widehat{\ln(y)}_i = 6.30 + 0.165 S_i \qquad R^2 = 0.328 \quad \hat{\sigma}_\varepsilon^2 = 0.353$$
$$(26.5)$$

---

[28] J. Mincer, *Schooling, Experience, and Earnings* (New York: National Bureau of Economic Research), 1974, p. 53.

where y is the level of earnings in 1959 for white males in the nonfarm sector, and S is the number of years of completed schooling.

(a) What is the interpretation of the coefficient of S?

(b) Mincer also estimates the above equation with an additional explanatory variable, the natural logarithm of weeks worked in 1959, $\ln(W)_i$.

    (i) What is the interpretation of the coefficient of this variable? What is its expected sign?

    (ii) When this variable is included in the estimated equation, what is the expected change in the magnitude of the coefficient of schooling?

9. The following is the SAS printout for the auto demand equation where the solution to the multicollinearity problem with the coefficient of the CPI for used cars, p_u, is to combine this variable with p_n to form a relative price variable, RPNEW:

DEP VARIABLE: S

ANALYSIS OF VARIANCE

SOURCE	DF	SUM OF SQUARES	MEAN SQUARE	F VALUE	PROB>F
MODEL	5	38841614.30	7768322.86	10.591	0.0001
ERROR	19	13936028.34	733475.18		
C TOTAL	24	52777642.64			

ROOT MSE	856.4317	R-SQUARE	0.7359	
DEP MEAN	9116.12	ADJ R-SQ	0.6665	
C.V.	9.394695			

PARAMETER ESTIMATES

VARIABLE	DF	PARAMETER ESTIMATE	STANDARD ERROR	T FOR HO: PARAMETER=0	PROB>|T|	VARIANCE INFLATION
INTERCEP	1	1582.84678	11130.63403	0.142	0.8884	0
RPNEW	1	-17.29820370	42.11906537	-0.411	0.6859	17.17128
Y	1	3.11700904	2.23475683	1.395	0.1792	24.20144
R	1	-324.03506	124.24222	-2.608	0.0173	4.65271
DLAG	1	713.31395	358.67983	1.989	0.0613	3.96325
ALAG	1	-663.16009	817.68545	-0.811	0.4274	5.53044

COLLINEARITY DIAGNOSTICS

NUM	EIGVALUE	CONDITION NUMBER	VARIANCE PROPORTIONS INTERCEP	RPNEW	Y	R	DLAG	ALAG
1	5.781019	1.000000	0.0000	0.0001	0.0001	0.0010	0.0000	0.0000
2	0.192930	5.473971	0.0001	0.0029	0.0005	0.1178	0.0001	0.0000
3	0.018838	17.518162	0.0001	0.0326	0.0289	0.5428	0.0015	0.0042
4	0.00623	30.456949	0.0007	0.0040	0.0268	0.0130	0.0555	0.1130
5	0.000801	84.949662	0.0000	0.2894	0.7651	0.1227	0.7631	0.0485
6	0.000181	178.888	0.9992	0.6710	0.1786	0.2028	0.1797	0.8342

(a) How satisfactory is the solution of combining p_n and p_u into the relative price variable? Provide the criteria you use to make this judgment.

(b) Compare and contrast this with the original equation. What are the major differences resulting from the change to the relative price variable?

(c) Has the creation of the relative price variable reduced the number of near-linear dependencies present in the data?

(d) Using the matrix decomposition methods outlined in the chapter:

    (i) Are there any dominating dependencies present in these data?

    (ii) What is the condition number of the data matrix?

    (iii) Determine the auxiliary regressions that should be run to provide further evidence of problem multicollinearity (i.e., identify the pivots).

11 Problems with the Multiple Regression Model II: Autocorrelation

The use of ordinary least squares to estimate a multiple regression model leads to best linear unbiased estimators of the parameters in such an equation when the set of assumptions outlined previously are met. Several of these assumptions relate directly to the error term in the multiple regression equation: the error for a given observation, ε_t, is assumed to be normally distributed with a mean of 0, and a constant variance, σ_ε^2. In addition, the set of errors must be pairwise independent, so that the error for one observation is independent of the error for every other observation. The material in the last chapter showed how specification error can violate the assumption of a zero mean error. In this chapter, we discuss the implications of errors that are not pairwise independent, which is autocorrelation (or serial correlation).

Autocorrelation is most likely to occur in time-series data. When the data are temporally ordered, the error from one time period can affect the error in other time periods. For example, an unexpected surge in consumer confidence can cause a consumer durable goods equation to underestimate durables consumption for two or more periods. While the errors from different observations can be correlated with cross-sectional data, no problem is likely to exist, since the particular arrangement of the data which results in such error correlation can often be changed without meaningfully altering the results.[1] This chapter discusses autocorrelation entirely in a time series context.

The method for dealing with this problem requires that we modify, but not abandon, the framework of ordinary least squares estimation. The least squares estimators remain unbiased and consistent, but these are no longer efficient (the minimum variance unbiased estimators). More important, when the errors in an equation are serially

---

[1] There are situations where this is not true. An example, called spatial autocorrelation, arises when observations on various states for a given time period, where the error from one state in a particular region may be correlated with the error from another state from the same region.

correlated, the formulas used by canned computer programs to calculate the sum of the squared residuals and the coefficient variances are incorrect. Frequently, the reported values of these statistics give a more optimistic picture of estimation results than would actually be the case if the correct formulas were used. An alternative estimation method, Generalized Least Squares (GLS), provides the best linear unbiased estimators (BLUE) of the coefficients in the multiple regression equation. Estimation with GLS utilizes least squares after transforming the model so that it conforms to the set of error assumptions under which least squares provides best linear unbiased estimators. Unbiased estimators of the residual sum of squares and coefficient variances are obtained directly from GLS results.

This chapter outlines the problems associated with least squares estimation of equations with autocorrelated errors and the basis of GLS estimation as a remedy for this problem. Methods for detecting and correcting serial correlation are also provided.

AUTOCORRELATION

The equation error for a particular time period, ε_t, is the difference between the actual and mean value of y for that observation:

$$\varepsilon_t = y_t - E(y_t).$$

When this error follows the set of assumptions in the multiple regression model: (i) the average deviation of y from its mean is zero; (ii) the difference between y_t and $E(y_t)$ in any time period is independent of all previous deviations; and (iii) the dispersion in these errors remains the same throughout the entire set of data. The second of these is the absence of autocorrelation. When this condition is violated, the deviation of y values around the population regression function ($E(y)$) is not random, but determined by other such deviations. The presence of autocorrelation thus alters the effect of errors: an error that occurs in one time period does not exert its entire influence in that period; instead, its impact carries forward to other time periods. As a result, the errors associated with the population regression function will be correlated.

The absence of autocorrelation requires that $\text{Cov}(\varepsilon_t, \varepsilon_{t-j}) = 0$, so that errors j periods apart are totally uncorrelated, or, in general, that the set of errors are pairwise independent. Autocorrelation is therefore defined as a nonzero error covariance (and correlation). Autocorrelation can be either negative or positive, although positive autocorrelation occurs more frequently with economic data. When positive autocorrelation exists, so that the covariance between errors is positive, an above average error at time t will tend to be associated with an above average error in time period $t - j$. Since the average error is 0, this implies that positive errors will tend to follow positive errors, while negative errors will tend to follow negative errors. For positive autocorrelation, the nonrandom pattern of errors thus manifests itself through strings of positive and negative errors. In general, the number of sign changes will be smaller than the number that would occur if autocorrelation were absent. Negative autocorrelation implies that above average errors will tend to follow below average errors, so that negative errors will often follow positive errors, and the number of sign changes in the equation error will exceed the number that would exist without autocorrelation.

Besides these differences in the sign of autocorrelation, a distinction also exists in the potential types of autocorrelation. **Quasi-autocorrelation** (also called impure autocorrelation) is the error correlation that occurs in a misspecified equation. The discussion of specification error in Chapter 10 demonstrated how the omission of an influential variable can result in the temporal correlation of errors, or quasi-autocorrelation. If the correctly specified equation is:

$$y_t = \alpha_0 + \alpha_1 x_t + \alpha_2 z_t + \varepsilon_t,$$

and the variable z is omitted, the estimated equation is:

$$y_t = \alpha_0 + \alpha_1 x_t + v_t,$$

where $v_t = (\varepsilon_t + \alpha_2 z_t)$. If z exhibits an upward or downward trend throughout the sample, then the error term v_t in the incorrectly specified equation will be auto-correlated.

The specification error that causes quasi-autocorrelation can result from either omitting an influential variable, as above, or the use of an incorrect functional form. If, in the above example, the correct functional form is quadratic in x, then the omitted influential variable z is x^2. In this situation the residuals will tend to exhibit positive quasi-autocorrelation. This last point can be seen with reference to Figure 11.1. The correctly specified equation, based on our maintained hypotheses, is the

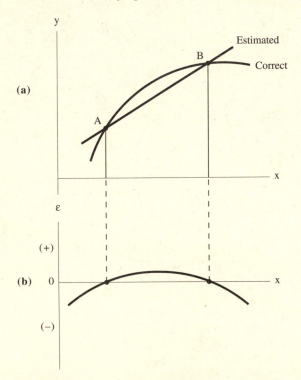

Figure 11.1

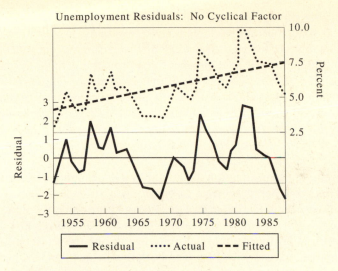

Figure 11.2

curved line, while the estimated line is linear. At points *A* and *B* where the two curves intersect, the residuals are 0. To the left of *A* is a string of negative residuals, which is followed by a string of positive residuals between points *A* and *B*, then another negative string beyond point *B*. The residuals are shown in Figure 11.1(b). This pattern of consecutive residuals with the same sign is indicative of positive autocorrelation.

Omitting an influential variable, which relegates its influence to the residual, can also produce patterns of positive quasi-autocorrelation. Figures 11.2 and 11.3 (which were produced using microTSP) illustrate two such possibilities. Figure 11.2 plots the

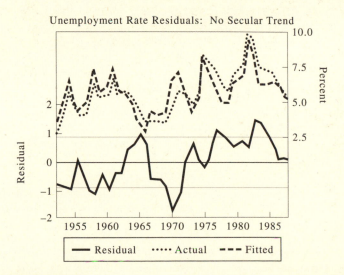

Figure 11.3

residuals of an unemployment rate equation which excludes variables that control for the cyclical nature of this variable.[2] These residuals display a cyclical pattern when plotted against the quarters over which the equation was estimated. Figure 11.3 plots the residuals from an unemployment equation that omits any factors representing the secular behavior of the rate of unemployment.[3] These residuals display an upward trend over the sample time period. *Since specification bias can cause auto-correlated errors, when serial correlation is detected it is advisable to reconsider whether the specification of the sample regression function is appropriate. This is especially important since the desirable properties of estimators and the validity of statistical inference presuppose a correctly specified equation.*

In a correctly specified equation, such temporal dependence of the errors is called **pure autocorrelation**. When the correct specification is utilized, all the variables whose influence on the dependent variable is of secondary importance are omitted, and their joint influence is felt in the equation error. Pure positive autocorrelation can therefore arise as the result of positive temporal correlation among the set of omitted but non-influential variables. Measurement error in both the included and excluded variables can also cause pure autocorrelation. The frequency of data are often reduced so that quarterly instead of monthly equations can be estimated. The method of converting monthly into quarterly data typically involves simple averaging, which results in estimated quarterly values with substantially less fluctuation than the monthly values upon which these are based. The use of this "dampened" set of observations can itself cause pure autocorrelation in the equation errors.

The discussion of autocorrelation that follows deals exclusively with positive pure autocorrelation. Restricting the focus of the discussion to positive autocorrelation is based on the greater likelihood of observing this type of error correlation in actual practice. Note that in evaluating pure autocorrelation exclusively, it is necessary to deal with only one violation of the error assumptions, that the covariance between errors in different time periods is nonzero. Two other error assumptions are often violated with quasi-autocorrelation: the expected value of the error is likely to be nonzero; and the dispersion of the errors will tend to vary for observations in the data set.[4]

MODELING AUTOCORRELATED ERRORS

The above discussion defined autocorrelation as a nonzero covariance between pairs of different errors, but added little else to the specifics of this phenomenon, other than offering a distinction between pure and quasi-autocorrelation. At this point,

---

[2] The specification of this equation is linear in a time trend, with no other explanatory variables. It was chosen only to illustrate the point under discussion, and not as an adequate depiction of a correctly specified population regression function.

[3] The estimated equation regresses the annual unemployment rate on the current capacity utilization rate in manufacturing. The same caveats stated in the previous footnote apply here.

[4] A reference that provides greater detail on this last set of points is G. Maddala, *Econometrics* (New York: McGraw-Hill), 1972, Chapter 12.

autocorrelation can be represented by the general functional relationship:

$$\varepsilon_t = f(\varepsilon_{t-1}, \varepsilon_{t-2}, \ldots, \varepsilon_{t-j}) \tag{11.1}$$

which denotes the fact that the error in one time period is related to the errors in one or more previous periods. In actual practice, the correct functional form of this relationship is unknown and must be estimated. The procedure used to deal with autocorrelation involves making simplifying assumptions about the population relationship given by Equation (11.1), then using estimated errors as the basis for inferences about the actual errors in the function under study.

The analysis of autocorrelated errors is part of a larger field called **time series analysis**. The sequence of errors, $\varepsilon_1, \varepsilon_2, \ldots, \varepsilon_t$ is called a **stochastic process**. The term "stochastic" denotes the existence of chance in the determination of these values, so that the likelihood of observing different sets of values can be ascertained from an underlying probability distribution (such as the normal distribution) that characterizes the behavior of these values.[5] The word "process" in time series analysis is analogous to the concept of the population in statistics. A process is therefore the set of all observations of a time series variable. The actual set of values we deal with, which corresponds to a sample from the population, is a **realization** from this process.

The stochastic process that generates a particular realization is unknown. We must therefore create a model of this process using a set of assumptions that enable us to obtain a reasonable approximation of it. The most critical assumption, which must be met before even attempting to model such a process is that it is a **stationary stochastic process**. The **stationarity** property of a stochastic process ensures that the underlying structure of this process does not shift through time, so that a single process creates the observed data realizations. When this condition is met, values of the stochastic process fluctuate randomly around the mean of this process. For a stochastic process to be stationary, it is necessary that:

(i) the mean of this process is constant, and does not vary with time;
(ii) the variance of this process is a finite constant that does not change with time; and
(iii) the covariance between any two values of the process depends only on the distance between them, and not on time.

The application of these requirements and the multiple regression model assumptions to the general functional relationship given by Equation (11.1) implies that:

(i) $E(\varepsilon_t) = E(\varepsilon_{t-1}) = \ldots = E(\varepsilon_{t-j}) = 0$;
(ii) $\sigma_\varepsilon^2 = E(\varepsilon_t)^2 = E(\varepsilon_{t-1})^2 = \ldots = E(\varepsilon_{t-j})^2$; and
(iii) $\text{Cov}(\varepsilon_t, \varepsilon_{t-j}) = E(\varepsilon_t \cdot \varepsilon_{t-j}) = f(j)$

The first of these follows from the multiple regression model assumption that the average error is 0. The last two require that the variance and covariance of this process are identical for values in the beginning, middle, and end of the process.

---

[5] More specifically, this refers to the joint probability density function $p(\varepsilon_1, \varepsilon_2, \ldots, \varepsilon_t)$ that generates a set of error terms.

The most widely used model of a stationary stochastic error process in econometrics assumes that the errors in the population regression function are generated by a **first-order autoregressive process**, denoted AR(1). The term "first-order" reflects the fact that the systematic relationship between errors involves a single time period, so that $\varepsilon_t = f(\varepsilon_{t-1})$. The specific form of this relationship, which is also called a (first order) **Markov process**, is given by the expression:

$$\varepsilon_t = \Theta\varepsilon_{t-1} + v_t \tag{11.2}$$

where Θ is the (first-order) **autocorrelation coefficient**, and v is an error term. For this error process to be stationary, it is necessary for us to make several assumptions about the terms in Equation (11.2). The first set of assumptions concerns the error term. This error process is assumed to consist of n independent (not autocorrelated) terms with a zero mean, and a constant variance, σ_v^2. Furthermore, the error v_t is assumed to be independent of ε (for all time periods). In other words, the error process v_t satisfies all the usual error assumptions in the multiple regression model. A "well-behaved" error process such as this is referred to as a **white noise process**. If, in addition, we assume that the data-generating process is the normal (Gaussian) distribution, the error process is called **Gaussian white noise**.

These assumptions concerning the error process v assist in establishing a zero mean error for the original error process ε_t. To see this, let us assume the relationship given by Equation (11.2) holds for all time periods. In this case:

$$\varepsilon_{t-1} = \Theta\varepsilon_{t-2} + v_{t-1}$$

$$\varepsilon_{t-2} = \Theta\varepsilon_{t-3} + v_{t-2}$$

$$\cdots$$

$$\varepsilon_{t-j} = \Theta\varepsilon_{t-j-1} + v_{t-j}$$

Substituting the expression for ε_{t-1} into Equation (11.2), this becomes:

$$\varepsilon_t = \Theta(\Theta\varepsilon_{t-2} + v_{t-1}) + v_t$$

so that

$$\varepsilon_t = \Theta^2\varepsilon_{t-2} + \Theta v_{t-1} + v_t \tag{11.3}$$

Similarly, the expression for ε_{t-2} can be substituted into Equation (11.3):

$$\varepsilon_t = \Theta^2(\Theta\varepsilon_{t-3} + v_{t-2}) + \Theta v_{t-1} + v_t$$

$$\varepsilon_t = \Theta^3\varepsilon_{t-3} + \Theta^2 v_{t-2} + \Theta v_{t-1} + v_t.$$

Continuing this process indefinitely, the error can be expressed as:

$$\varepsilon_t = \Theta^j\varepsilon_{t-j} + \Theta^{j-1}v_{t-j+1} + \cdots + \Theta v_{t-1} + v_t \tag{11.4}$$

The error process ε_t is stationary when the absolute value of Θ is less than one. Using this assumption, the term $\Theta^j\varepsilon_{t-j}$ on the right of Equation (11.4) approaches 0 as the number of previous errors increases. Since the expression Equation (11.4) can theoretically be expanded to include an infinite number of lags, the term involving ε on the right side of this expression drops out, allowing the error process ε_t to be expressed solely in terms of the white noise error v_t. Using this information, and reversing the order of the terms, the expression for ε_t becomes:

$$\varepsilon_t = v_t + \Theta v_{t-1} + \Theta^2 v_{t-2} + \cdots \tag{11.5}$$

This equation expresses the autocorrelated error process, ε_t, as the sum of an infinite number of terms involving v, where the influence of previous periods continually decreases. Equation (11.5) is referred to as the **moving average form** of the first-order autoregressive process given by Equation (11.2).

When the autoregressive nature of the error process is modeled using the assumption of a first-order autoregressive process, then using Equation (11.5), the zero mean of this error process is easily established. To see this, we take the expected value of Equation (11.5), using the fact that Θ is a constant:

$$E(\varepsilon_t) = E(v_t) + \Theta E(v_{t-1}) + \Theta^2 E(v_{t-2}) + \cdots$$

Since the white noise error process v has a zero expectation, all the terms on the right are 0, so that $E(\varepsilon_t) = 0$, satisfying the first requirement for the successful modeling of an autocorrelated error process for ε_t.

Since the mean of ε_t is zero, the expression for the variance of this error process is obtained from the expression for $E(\varepsilon_t)^2$:

$$\begin{aligned}
\sigma_\varepsilon^2 = E(\varepsilon_t)^2 &= E(\Theta\varepsilon_{t-1} + v_t)^2 \quad \text{(using 11.2)} \\
&= E(\Theta^2\varepsilon_{t-1}{}^2 + v_t^2 + 2\Theta v_t\varepsilon_{t-1}) \\
&= \Theta^2 E(\varepsilon_{t-1})^2 + E(v_t)^2 + 2\Theta E(v_t\varepsilon_{t-1}).
\end{aligned}$$

If ε_t is stationary, then its variance is constant and independent of time, so that $E(\varepsilon_{t-1})^2 = \sigma_\varepsilon^2$. The assumptions of the first-order autoregressive model include the independence of v_t and ε_{t-1}, or $E(v_t\varepsilon_{t-1}) = 0$. Including this information into the above equation, the final expression for the error variance is obtained:

$$\sigma_\varepsilon^2 = \Theta^2\sigma_\varepsilon^2 + \sigma_v^2,$$
$$\sigma_\varepsilon^2(1 - \Theta^2) = \sigma_v^2$$

so that:

$$\sigma_\varepsilon^2 = \sigma_v^2/(1 - \Theta^2) \tag{11.6}$$

Since both σ_v^2 and Θ are constants, ε_t is homoskedastic. If $\Theta = 1$, the variance of ε_t is infinite, which violates the stationary requirements. Since the variance of ε is positive, the denominator of Equation (11.6) must also be positive, or $(1 - \Theta^2) > 0$. Solving this inequality, $\Theta^2 < 1$, or $-1 < \Theta < 1$. For stationarity, it is therefore necessary that $|\Theta| < 1$, which was stated earlier.

The final requirement for the stationarity of the AR(1) error process is that the covariance between errors of different time periods be a function only of the number of time periods separating these terms. For errors one period apart:

$$\begin{aligned}
\text{Cov}(\varepsilon_t, \varepsilon_{t-1}) &= E(\varepsilon_t \cdot \varepsilon_{t-1}) \quad \text{(since } E(\varepsilon_t) = 0) \\
&= E[(\Theta\varepsilon_{t-1} + v_t)\varepsilon_{t-1}] \\
&= \Theta E(\varepsilon_{t-1})^2 + E(v_t\varepsilon_{t-1}) = \Theta E(\varepsilon_{t-1})^2
\end{aligned}$$

since, by assumption, v_t is independent of ε_{t-1}. Because $E(\varepsilon_{t-1})^2 = \sigma_\varepsilon^2$, the covariance between these errors is:

$$\text{Cov}(\varepsilon_t, \varepsilon_{t-1}) = \Theta\sigma_\varepsilon^2 \tag{11.7}$$

For errors two time periods apart:

$$\text{Cov}(\varepsilon_t, \varepsilon_{t-2}) = E(\varepsilon_t \cdot \varepsilon_{t-2}) = E[(\Theta\varepsilon_{t-1} + v_t)\varepsilon_{t-2}]$$
$$= E(\Theta\varepsilon_{t-1}\varepsilon_{t-2} + v_t\varepsilon_{t-2}) = \Theta E(\varepsilon_{t-1}\varepsilon_{t-2})$$

since v_t is independent of ε_{t-2}. Substituting for ε_{t-1} in the bracketed term, and using information on the independence between v and ε, this becomes:

$$= \Theta E[(\Theta\varepsilon_{t-2} + v_{t-1})\varepsilon_{t-2}] = \Theta^2 E(\varepsilon_{t-2})^2 = \Theta^2\sigma_\varepsilon^2.$$

If we denote by j the number of time periods separating different values of ε, then summarizing this information:

$$\text{Cov}(\varepsilon_t, \varepsilon_{t-1}) = \Theta^1\sigma_\varepsilon^2$$
$$\text{Cov}(\varepsilon_t, \varepsilon_{t-2}) = \Theta^2\sigma_\varepsilon^2,$$

and in general:

$$\text{Cov}(\varepsilon_t, \varepsilon_{t-j}) = \Theta^j\sigma_\varepsilon^2 = f(j).$$

Modeling autoregressive errors with the first-order autoregressive error process (Equation (11.1)), the assumptions about v, and the restrictions on Θ, therefore satisfies all the requirements for a stationary error process. In this model, the effect of an error in one period is carried forward in ever smaller amounts into future time periods.

The autoregression coefficient Θ is related to the correlation between errors in a first-order autoregressive model. The population correlation between errors one period apart, ρ_1, is given by the formula[6]:

$$\rho_1 = \frac{\text{Cov}(\varepsilon_t, \varepsilon_{t-1})}{\sqrt{\text{Var}(\varepsilon_t)} \cdot \sqrt{\text{Var}(\varepsilon_{t-1})}}.$$

Since ε is a stationary stochastic process, $\text{Var}(\varepsilon_t) = \text{Var}(\varepsilon_{t-1})$, so the denominator of the correlation coefficient is simply $\text{Var}(\varepsilon_t)$. From Equation (11.7), the numerator is: $\text{Cov}(\varepsilon_t, \varepsilon_{t-1}) = \Theta\sigma_\varepsilon^2$. Substituting this information, the correlation coefficient is:

$$\rho_1 = \frac{\text{Cov}(\varepsilon_t, \varepsilon_{t-1})}{\text{Var}(\varepsilon_t)} = \frac{\Theta\sigma_\varepsilon^2}{\sigma_\varepsilon^2} = \Theta \tag{11.8}$$

Thus the autocorrelation coefficient, Θ, is the population correlation coefficient between errors one period apart. Since positive autocorrelation implies a pattern of positively correlated errors, this implies that $\Theta > 0$. As can be seen from the middle term in

---

[6] The general formula for the population correlation coefficient and a discussion of this measure are given in Chapter 2.

Equation (11.8), ρ_1 is also the least squares coefficient from the bivariate regression of ε_t on ε_{t-1}.

In time-series analysis, the correlation coefficient for errors j periods apart, ρ_j is called the **autocorrelation for lag j**. The formula for this coefficient is:

$$\rho_j = \frac{\text{Cov}(\varepsilon_t, \varepsilon_{t-j})}{\sqrt{\text{Var}(\varepsilon_t)} \cdot \sqrt{\text{Var}(\varepsilon_{t-j})}}.$$

Since ε is a stationary error process, the denominator in this expression equals σ_ε^2. The numerator, as stated above, equals $\Theta^j \sigma_\varepsilon^2$. Substituting this information into the above equation, the expression for ρ_j is:

$$\rho_j = \Theta^j \sigma_\varepsilon^2 / \sigma_\varepsilon^2 = \Theta^j \qquad \textbf{(11.8′)}$$

Note that the value of ρ_j is the least squares slope coefficient from the regression of ε_t on ε_{t-j}.

Extensive use of the first-order autoregressive process dates back many years. Some authors speculate that the popularity of the AR(1) model results largely from the fact that when autocorrelated errors became a topic of concern, computers were either non-existent or not very powerful, and available data consisted mostly of annual observations.[7] Since that time, both of these considerations have become largely irrelevant. As a result, alternative models of autoregressive error processes have been developed. The two most popular of these appear to be the second order and fourth order autoregressive error processes. The expression for a **second-order autoregressive process** (AR(2)) is given by the following equation:

$$\varepsilon_t = \Theta_1 \varepsilon_{t-1} + \Theta_2 \varepsilon_{t-2} + v_t,$$

where Θ_1 and Θ_2 are the autoregression coefficients and v_t is a white noise error. The independence of v and ε is assumed for all time periods. For stationarity, restrictions are placed on the magnitudes of both Θ_1 and Θ_2.[8] The theoretical autocorrelation function for an AR(2) error process is more involved than that for the corresponding first-order process, but, as shown later, estimation when errors follow the AR(2) process is mechanically similar to that for the AR(1) process. The other type of error process gaining popularity is a special form of a fourth order autoregressive process:

$$\varepsilon_t = \Theta_4 \varepsilon_{t-4} + v_t.$$

This error process is often well suited to quarterly data without seasonal adjustment. In this case, the error from one quarter is correlated with the error one year prior to this error, since seasonal influences are captured in the error terms.

---

[7] For further discussion on this point see G. Judge, W. Griffiths, R. Hill, H. Lutkephohl, and Tsoung-Chao Lee, *The Theory and Practice of Econometrics*, 2d. ed. (New York: John Wiley), 1985, Chapter 8.

[8] The specific restrictions placed on these autocorrelation coefficients are that: $|\Theta_2| < 1$; $\Theta_1 + \Theta_2 < 1$; and $\Theta_2 - \Theta_1 < 1$. See Judge and associates.

EFFECT OF AUTOCORRELATION ON LEAST SQUARES ESTIMATION

The presence of pure autocorrelation has several consequences for least squares estimation. The OLS coefficients remain unbiased and consistent, but these are no longer best linear unbiased estimators, since they are not efficient. Furthermore, estimates of the residual sum of squares and coefficient variances obtained from canned computer programs based on the assumption of white noise errors are biased. As a result statistical inferences based on these values are invalid. Two of these propositions, the unbiasedness of the least squares estimators, and the inappropriate variance formulas, will now be illustrated.

The unbiasedness of the least squares slope estimator can be established most easily with reference to the bivariate regression model:

$$y_t = \alpha_0 + \alpha_1 x_t + \varepsilon_t \qquad (11.9)$$

where we assume the error process is first-order autoregressive: $\varepsilon_t = \Theta\varepsilon_{t-1} + v_t$. The least squares estimator of α_1 is:

$$\hat{\alpha}_1 = \sum x_t' y_t' / \sum x_t'^2,$$

where x_t' and y_t' denote deviations from means.[9] Substituting the deviation form of Equation (11.9) for y_t, the least squares slope estimator becomes:

$$\hat{\alpha}_1 = \sum x_t'(\alpha_1 x_t' + \varepsilon_t') / \sum x_t'^2$$
$$= \alpha_1 + \sum x_t' \varepsilon_t' / \sum x_t'^2$$

where $\varepsilon_t' \equiv (\varepsilon_t - \hat{\mu}_\varepsilon)$. If we let $\omega_t \equiv x_t' / \sum x_t'^2$ (which is a constant assuming x is non-stochastic) the expression for $\hat{\alpha}_1$ becomes:

$$\hat{\alpha}_1 = \alpha_1 + \sum \omega_t \varepsilon_t' \qquad (11.10)$$

The mean of the sampling distribution for this estimator is:

$$E(\hat{\alpha}_1) = \alpha_1 + E(\sum \omega_t \varepsilon_t') = \alpha_1 + \sum \omega_t E(\varepsilon_t') = \alpha_1$$

since $E(\varepsilon_t') = 0$ even with pure autocorrelation. The least squares slope estimator is therefore unbiased. Note that *the unbiasedness of this estimator is based on the zero expected value of the error, and the assumption that x and ε are independent.* Neither the presence of pure autocorrelation nor the particular order of the implied error process affect the unbiasedness property of the least squares estimators. For quasi-autocorrelation, however, both of these assumptions will most likely be violated, resulting in a biased slope estimator.

The variance of the least squares slope estimator, σ_1^2, is obtained from the expression for $E(\hat{\alpha}_1 - \alpha_1)^2$ since this is an unbiased estimator. Using Equation (11.10):

$$\sigma_1^2 = E(\hat{\alpha}_1 - \alpha_1)^2 = E(\sum \omega_t \varepsilon_t')^2.$$

---

[9] See Chapter 4 for a more complete exposition of the steps used here.

For simplicity, assume that $n = 2$. The expression on the right is then:

$$E(\sum \omega_t \varepsilon_t')^2 = E(\omega_1 \varepsilon_1' + \omega_2 \varepsilon_2')^2$$
$$= E(\omega_1^2 \varepsilon_1'^2 + \omega_2^2 \varepsilon_2'^2 + 2\omega_1 \omega_2 \varepsilon_1' \varepsilon_2')$$
$$= \omega_1^2 E(\varepsilon_1'^2) + \omega_2^2 E(\varepsilon_2'^2) + 2\omega_1 \omega_2 E(\varepsilon_1' \varepsilon_2').$$

Since ε_t is a stationary stochastic process, $E(\varepsilon_t')^2 = \sigma_\varepsilon^2$ for all time periods. Also, $E(\varepsilon_1' \varepsilon_2') = \Theta \sigma_\varepsilon^2$ from Equation (11.7). Substituting this information into the above equation:

$$E(\sum \omega_t \varepsilon_t')^2 = \omega_1^2 \sigma_\varepsilon^2 + \omega_2^2 \sigma_\varepsilon^2 + 2\omega_1 \omega_2 (\Theta \sigma_\varepsilon^2)$$

Factoring out the error variance in the first two terms on the right these become: $\sigma_\varepsilon^2 (\omega_1^2 + \omega_2^2) = \sigma_\varepsilon^2 (\Sigma \omega_t^2)$. Since $\Sigma \omega_t^2 = 1/\Sigma x_t'^2$ (see Chapter 4), the sum of the first two sum terms is $\sigma_\varepsilon^2 / \Sigma x_t'^2$, which is the variance of $\hat{\alpha}_1$ when no autocorrelation is present. This is the formula used by canned programs unless an autocorrelation option is specified.[10] Replacing ω_1 and ω_2 by their original expressions, the third term equals $2\Theta \sigma_\varepsilon^2 [x_1' x_2' / (\Sigma x_t'^2)^2]$. Putting this information together:

$$\sigma_1^2 = \sigma_\varepsilon^2 / \sum x_t'^2 + 2\Theta \sigma_\varepsilon^2 [x_1' x_2' / (\sum x_t'^2)^2] \qquad \textbf{(11.11)}$$

Thus the actual variance of the least squares slope estimator equals the no autocorrelation variance plus an additional term related to the error variance, Θ, the product of the x's, and the sum of the squared x values. The least squares coefficient variance omits the last term and is therefore biased.

The direction of bias is determined by the sign of the additional term, which depends on Θ and the product of the x's. If positive autocorrelation exists ($\Theta > 0$), and individual x terms follow an upward or downward trend, so that the product of the x terms is positive, then this entire expression is positive. In this situation, the actual variance of $\hat{\alpha}_1$ will exceed the variance that pertains in the absence of autocorrelation. The extent to which the actual variance is underestimated is a function of Θ. Canned programs that fail to allow for autocorrelation will therefore **underestimate** coefficient variances, resulting in upwardly biased t-statistics, and confidence intervals that are too narrow, *given the combination of a single explanatory variable, $\Theta > 0$, and a positive product of the x's.* In addition to this, the estimator of σ_ε^2 obtained from the least squares residuals will tend to be downwardly biased as well. The value of R^2 will thus provide an overly optimistic picture of the fit of the estimated equation to the data. Since the equation F-statistic is related to R^2, this statistic will also be unreliable.

The combination of circumstances utilized in establishing these properties are of course not the only ones possible. If, for example, $\Theta > 0$ but the x's are negatively correlated, the bias is also negative, causing deflated t-statistics and wider confidence intervals than necessary. When the x's are trendless, the direction of the bias in the coefficient variances is indeterminate a priori. Finally, with two or more explanatory variables, the determination of the direction of bias is considerably more complicated.

---

[10] Exceptions to this are PROC AUTOREG in SAS, and the inclusion of the AR(1) option in MicroTSP.

BEST LINEAR UNBIASED ESTIMATION WITH AUTOCORRELATED ERRORS

The least squares estimators of the coefficients in the population regression function:

$$y_t = \alpha_0 + \alpha_1 x_t + \varepsilon_t$$

are both unbiased and consistent when the error process is first-order autoregressive and the autocorrelation coefficient, Θ, is a known constant. However, least squares no longer provides efficient, or minimum-variance unbiased estimators. In addition to this, estimated coefficient variances, R^2, and the equation F-statistic are inaccurate. If the original equation is transformed so that its error is a white noise process, then, according to the Gauss-Markov theorem, the application of least squares to this transformed equation will yield the best linear unbiased estimators of the coefficients in this equation. This process is known as **generalized least squares (GLS) estimation**.

The steps involved in GLS estimation consist of: (i) finding a transformation, T, which, when applied to the actual errors changes them to a white noise process; (ii) applying this transformation to the original equation:

$$T \cdot y_t = T \cdot (\alpha_0 + \alpha_1 x_t) + T \cdot \varepsilon_t,$$

or

$$y_t^* = \alpha_0^* = \alpha_1 x_t^* + v_t, \qquad \textbf{(11.12)}$$

where the asterisk denotes a transformed value; and (iii) estimating the transformed equation with least squares. The transformation term is constructed so that $T \cdot \varepsilon_t$ equals the white noise error, v_t.

The appropriate transformation for an AR(1) error process is obtained by stating the white noise error process, v_t, in terms of the actual error:

$$v_t = \varepsilon_t - \Theta \varepsilon_{t-1} \qquad \textbf{(11.13)}$$

The right side of Equation (11.13), or any order autocorrelation equation can be expressed as a function of Θ using the **backshift (backward shift) operator**, B, which is defined as:

$$B \cdot \varepsilon_t \equiv \varepsilon_{t-1}; \qquad B^2 \cdot \varepsilon_t \equiv \varepsilon_{t-2}; \quad \text{and} \quad B^j \cdot \varepsilon_t \equiv \varepsilon_{t-j}.$$

Application of the backshift operator to a variable thus defines the number of periods for which this variable is lagged. Applying this operator to a parameter such as the equation intercept that does not depend on time gives the original term itself: $B \cdot \alpha_0 = \alpha_0$. Equation (11.13) can be rewritten using this operator:

$$v_t = \varepsilon_t - \Theta(B \cdot \varepsilon_t) = (1 - \Theta B)\varepsilon_t = \Theta(B)\varepsilon_t, \qquad \textbf{(11.14)}$$

where $\Theta(B)$ denotes the expression involving Θ that expresses the white noise error process, v_t, as a function of the original error process, ε_t. The transformation term, T, that is applied to the original equation for GLS estimation is $\Theta(B)$. When the error process is first-order autoregressive, $T = \Theta(B) = (1 - \Theta B)$. Using this information, the transformed equation is:

$$\Theta(B) \cdot y_t = \Theta(B) \cdot \alpha_0 + \alpha_1 \Theta(B) \cdot x_t + \Theta(B) \cdot \varepsilon_t,$$

or

$$(1 - \Theta B)y_t = (1 - \Theta B)\alpha_0 + \alpha_1(1 - \Theta B)x_t + (1 - \Theta B)\varepsilon_t \qquad \textbf{(11.15)}$$

which can be expressed as:

$$(y_t - \Theta y_{t-1}) = \alpha_0(1 - \Theta) + \alpha_1(x_t - \Theta x_{t-1}) + v_t,$$

or

$$y_t^* = \alpha_0^* + \alpha_1 x_t^* + v_t. \qquad \textbf{(11.16)}$$

Equation (11.16) is referred to as the **generalized difference form** of the original equation. Generalized least squares estimation in this context consists of the application of least squares to the generalized difference form of the original equation.

A few points should be noted about Equation (11.16). First, in converting an equation to its generalized difference form, the first observation is lost (becomes a missing value). The **Prais-Winsten correction** prevents this loss by transforming the first observation in the following manner:

$$y_1\sqrt{1 - \Theta^2} = \alpha_0\sqrt{1 - \Theta^2} + \alpha_1 x_1\sqrt{1 - \Theta^2} + v_1,$$

The remaining observations are then transformed using Equation (11.16). Second, if $\Theta = 1$, the generalized difference version of the equation coincides with the first-difference form. Often researchers utilize the first-difference form whenever autocorrelation is suspected. This procedure implicitly assumes a specific value for Θ which might not be accurate. Third, the estimated intercept in Equation (11.16), α_0^*, is an estimator for the entire expression $\alpha_0(1 - \Theta)$. The intercept from the original equation is obtained by dividing α_0^* by $(1 - \Theta)$. The variances of α_0 and α_0^* also differ. The variance of α_0^* is:

$$\text{Var}(\alpha_0^*) = \text{Var}[\alpha_0(1 - \Theta)] = (1 - \Theta)^2 \cdot \text{Var}(\alpha_0).$$

The variance of the original intercept, α_0, is obtained from the expression:

$$\text{Var}(\alpha_0) = \text{Var}(\alpha_0^*)/(1 - \Theta)^2.$$

The variance for the slope coefficient, α_1, is given by the formula:

$$\hat{\sigma}_1^2 = \sigma_\varepsilon^2 / \sum(x_t^*)^2.$$

The only difference between this and the corresponding no autocorrelation formula is the use of x^* in place of x. Finally, unless Θ is known, GLS requires the estimation of this parameter. In this case, the procedure is known as **estimated generalized least squares (EGLS) estimation**.

Least squares estimation of Equation (11.16), which provides the BLUE's of α_0 and α_1, differs from the use of least squares without any consideration of autocorrelation. The GLS slope estimator is:

$$\hat{\alpha}_1 = \sum x_t^{*\prime} y_t^{*\prime} / \sum (x_t^*)^2,$$

where $x_t^{*\prime}$ and $y_t^{*\prime}$ are deviations from means.[11] Performing the multiplication and collecting terms, the generalized least squares slope estimator equals:

$$\hat{\alpha}_1 = \frac{\sum x_t' y_t' + \sum(\text{other terms involving } \Theta)}{\sum x_t'^2 + \sum(\text{other terms involving } \Theta)}$$

The least squares estimator of α_1 therefore differs from the GLS estimator whenever autocorrelation is present, since then $\Theta \neq 0$, and the terms with Θ do not drop out. The same is true for the intercept estimator. Because of this fact, the variances of the least squares estimators exceed those of the corresponding GLS estimators, and OLS fails to provide the best linear unbiased estimators of α_0 and α_1. The efficiency of the GLS estimator results from its incorporating information on the temporal correlation of the error process directly into the parameter estimation.

The transformed equations for the other two autoregressive error processes alluded to previously can also be determined using the procedure discussed here. Consider the second-order autoregressive process:

$$\varepsilon_t = \Theta_1 \varepsilon_{t-1} + \Theta_2 \varepsilon_{t-2} + v_t.$$

Solving for the white noise error in terms of ε, this becomes:

$$v_t = \varepsilon_t - \Theta_1 \varepsilon_{t-1} - \Theta_2 \varepsilon_{t-2}.$$

Expressing this equation in terms of the backshift operator:

$$v_t = \varepsilon_t - \Theta_1 B \varepsilon_t - \Theta_2 B^2 \varepsilon_t,$$

or

$$v_t = (1 - \Theta_1 B - \Theta_2 B^2)\varepsilon_t$$

The polynomial upon which the transformation of the original equation is based, $\Theta(B) = (1 - \Theta_1 B - \Theta_2 B^2)$, is called the **characteristic polynomial** of the AR(2) error process. The transformed equation is:

$$y_t^* = \alpha_0^* + \alpha_1 x_t^* + v_t,$$

where $y_t^* = (y_t - \Theta_1 y_{t-1} - \Theta_2 y_{t-2})$; $x_t^* = (x_t - \Theta_1 x_{t-1} - \Theta_2 x_{t-2})$, and $\alpha_0^* = \alpha_0(1 - \Theta_1 - \Theta_2)$. Unless a Prais-Winsten correction is undertaken, two observations are lost in the process of creating this generalized difference form. Finally, with the AR(4) error process:

$$\varepsilon_t = \Theta_4 \varepsilon_{t-4} + v_t,$$

the characteristic polynomial is obtained from the expression:

$$v_t = \varepsilon_t - \Theta_4 \varepsilon_{t-4} \qquad \text{so that}$$

---

[11] Actually, $x_t^{*\prime} = (x_t - \hat{\mu}_x) - \Theta(x_{t-1} - \Sigma x_{t-1}/n)$, with a similar expression for $y_t^{*\prime}$. Technically, the last term on the right, $\Sigma x_{t-1}/n$ is not equal to the mean of the series for x_{t-1}, since it contains only $(n-1)$ terms. This can be remedied by beginning the summation at 0 instead of 1. However, use of this expression to illustrate that the least squares and GLS estimators differ does not require the exact expression.

$$v_t = (1 - \Theta_4 B^4)\varepsilon_t \quad \text{and}$$

$\Theta(B) = (1 - \Theta_4 B^4)$. Four observations are lost unless a Prais-Winsten correction is undertaken in this case.[12]

Estimated Generalized Least Squares Estimation: An Example of Least Squares with Stochastic Explanatory Variables

The existence of a first-order autocorrelated error process violates one of the multiple regression model assumptions. The least squares estimators of the coefficients in a multiple regression equation remain linear, unbiased, and consistent, but they are no longer efficient. If the coefficient of autocorrelation is a known constant, generalized least squares provides the BLUE's of the coefficients in an equation. Unfortunately, the coefficient of autocorrelation for a first-order autoregressive error process is almost always unknown. Because of this fact, GLS estimation is impossible, and estimated generalized least squares is the alternative for estimating the coefficients of equations with autocorrelated errors.

In form, the only substantial difference between GLS and EGLS estimation of an equation with an AR(1) error process is the use of an estimated value of Θ in the generalized difference form of the original equation. The original transformation term, T, must be replaced by an estimated transformation term, $\hat{T}$, which, of necessity, utilizes the residuals from the original equation as the basis for the estimate of Θ. The formula for an AR(1) error process with the actual errors replaced by the equation residuals provides a model from which the value of $\hat{\Theta}$ can be obtained:

$$\hat{\varepsilon}_t = \Theta\hat{\varepsilon}_{t-1} + v_t \tag{11.17}$$

Various methods for estimating Θ from this equation are discussed below. For now, we need only consider the generalized difference form of our equation using $\hat{\Theta}$ in place of Θ. The estimated transformation term is now:

$$\hat{T} = \hat{\Theta}(B) = (1 - \hat{\Theta}B) \tag{11.18}$$

Applying this transformation to Equation (11.9) gives the generalized difference form that is relevant for estimation:

$$\hat{T} \cdot y_t = \hat{T} \cdot \alpha_0 + \alpha_1(\hat{T} \cdot x_t) + \hat{T} \cdot \varepsilon_t$$

or

$$(y_t - \hat{\Theta}y_{t-1}) = \alpha_0^* + \alpha_1(x_t - \hat{\Theta}x_{t-1}) + v_t \tag{11.19}$$

where $\alpha_0^* = \alpha_0(1 - \hat{\Theta})$.

An important distinction exists between Equation (11.19), which includes an estimated value of Θ, and Equation (11.16), which utilizes a known Θ. Since $\hat{\Theta}$ is an

---

[12] For the first four observations, the Prais-Winsten correction uses: $T = \sqrt{1 - \Theta_4^2}$.

estimated value and not a known constant, it is a random variable. If we rewrite Equation (11.19) as:

$$y_t^* = \alpha_0^* + \alpha_1 x_t^* + v_t,$$ **(11.19')**

then this equation, which is the basis for estimated generalized least squares, contains a **stochastic explanatory variable**, x_t^*. Even if x_t (and x_{t-1}) are themselves nonstochastic, or fixed in repeated samples, the term $(x_t - \hat{\Theta} x_{t-1})$ is stochastic, since its value depends on $\hat{\Theta}$. Three important consequences result from this fact.

First, the EGLS estimators are no longer linear functions of the dependent variable. The least squares slope estimator for Equation (11.19') is:

$$\hat{\alpha}_1 = \sum x_t^{*\prime} y_t^{*\prime} / \sum (x_t^*)^{\prime 2}$$

If $\hat{\alpha}_1$ were a linear function of y_t^*, then it would be possible to write the above expression as:

$$\hat{\alpha}_1 = \sum \omega_t^* y_t^{*\prime},$$

where the weight for time t, $\omega_t^* = x_t^{*\prime} / \sum (x_t^*)^{\prime 2}$, is a constant. Since ω_t^* depends on $\hat{\Theta}$, this term is instead a random variable, which violates the requirement placed on the $\omega_t^{*\prime}$'s for $\hat{\alpha}_1$ to be a linear estimator. A similar result pertains for $\hat{\alpha}_0$.

Second, both of the EGLS estimators are biased. The mean of the sampling distribution of $\hat{\alpha}_1$ is given by the expression:

$$E(\hat{\alpha}_1) = \alpha_1 + E\left[\sum x_t^{*\prime} v_t / \sum (x_t^*)^{\prime 2}\right]$$ **(11.20)**

This estimator is unbiased only if the bracketed term involving x_t^* and v_t, both of which are random variables, equals 0. The expression for ω_t^* stated above provides us with a function of x_t^* that can be used to evaluate whether the expectation of the bracketed term above is 0. Using this notation, the term in brackets equals $\sum \omega_t^* v_t$. Each term in this summation is of the form $A \cdot B$, where $A = \omega_t^*$ and $B = v_t$. Recall that when A and B are independent random variables, the expectation of their product is given by the product of their individual expectations:

$$E(A \cdot B) = E(A) \cdot E(B)$$

If this result is applicable to the current example, the last term in Equation (11.20) will drop out, since $E(v_t) = 0$, making $\hat{\alpha}_1$ an unbiased estimator. However, x_t^* is a function of $\hat{\Theta}$, which itself depends on v_t. As a result, ω_t^* is not independent of v_t, and the expectation of the bracketed term is nonzero. The estimated slope coefficient $\hat{\alpha}_1$ is therefore a biased estimator of α_1. However, as sample size increases, this bias disappears, so that $\hat{\alpha}_1$ is a consistent estimator of α_1.[13] As sample size rises, this estimator also attains the property of efficiency. Estimation of the least squares slope estimator results in a biased estimator that is consistent and asymptotically efficient. The same properties also pertain to the EGLS intercept estimator.

Finally, the t-distribution no longer pertains for hypotheses tests and confidence intervals. Recall (from Chapter 5) that with least squares both $\hat{\alpha}_0$ and $\hat{\alpha}_1$ are linear

---

[13] The consistency of $\hat{\alpha}_1$ is determined from the probability limit of $\hat{\alpha}_1$.

functions of the equation error, which is a normally distributed random variable. Both of these coefficients are therefore normally distributed. When the variances of these estimators are known, the unit-normal random variable, $z_j = [\hat{\alpha}_j - E(\hat{\alpha}_j)]/\sigma_j$ ($j = 0, 1$) is applicable for hypothesis tests and confidence intervals. When the variance is unknown, z_j is replaced by the t-distributed random variable: $[\hat{\alpha}_j - E(\hat{\alpha}_j)]/\hat{\sigma}_j$ ($j = 0, 1$). However, use of the t-distribution requires as a starting point that each least squares estimator be a linear function of the equation error. The estimated generalized least squares estimators of α_0 and α_1 are not linear functions of $\hat{\Theta}$, which is itself nonlinearly related to the actual equation errors. Thus neither $\hat{\alpha}_0$ nor $\hat{\alpha}_1$ is a linear function of the normally distributed equation error, and use of the t-distribution is inappropriate for inferences concerning these values.

Fortunately, statistical inference concerning these coefficients can still be undertaken, based on the large sample, or asymptotic properties of the original t-distributed random variables. As sample size approaches infinity, the ratio $[\hat{\alpha}_j - E(\hat{\alpha}_j)]/\hat{\sigma}_j$ ($j = 0$, 1) tends toward the unit normal distribution. As a result, the latter ratio is an (asymptotically) normally distributed random variable, and the "rules of thumb" for critical values from the normal distribution can be utilized.

DETECTION OF AUTOCORRELATION

The actual error terms in a regression equation are unobserved. Residuals from the estimated equation must therefore serve as the basis for both the detection and correction of autocorrelation. The most simple, and least foolproof, method for detecting autocorrelation among the residuals of an equation consists of visually inspecting these residuals.[14] Autocorrelation manifests itself through a nonrandom residual pattern, so any obvious pattern in a time plot of residuals is a signal that a potential problem exists. For positive autocorrelation, this plot will tend to show fairly infrequent sign changes, where a series of residuals with one sign will follow a series with the opposite sign. In contrast, negatively autocorrelated residuals will tend to display an inordinately large number of sign changes. Examples of time plots for positive autocorrelation are given by Figures 11.2 and 11.3.

The most frequently utilized statistical test for the presence of autocorrelation is the **Durbin-Watson test**.[15] This test is valid when the following conditions are met:

  (i) the equation includes an intercept term;
 (ii) the error process is first-order autoregressive;
(iii) the equation excludes a lagged dependent variable; and
 (iv) none of the explanatory variables are stochastic.

---

[14] Many canned programs routinely provide these plots. In SAS, the "R" option at the end of a MODEL statement in PROC REG provides this information, such as: **MODEL Y = X Z/R;**. With MicroTSP, you may select S to see the values of predicted and actually y, along with the residuals after a regression is run. Using either the **G** selection after the regression equation is displayed, or the PLOT statement generates a time plot.

[15] J. Durbin and G. Watson, "Testing for Serial Correlation in Least Squares Regression," *Biometrika*, 1959, pp. 159–177.

Assuming the first-order error process: $\varepsilon_t = \Theta\varepsilon_{t-1} + v_t$, this test utilizes the residuals from an estimated equation to test the null hypothesis H_0: $\Theta = 0$ against either a one-tailed or two-tailed alternative hypothesis. The test statistic for this test is the **Durbin-Watson (DW) statistic**:

$$DW = \sum_{t=2}^{n} (\hat{\varepsilon}_t - \hat{\varepsilon}_{t-1})^2 \bigg/ \sum_{t=1}^{n} (\hat{\varepsilon}_t)^2 \qquad (11.21)$$

Note that the summation in the numerator starts with the second observation, since the use of the lagged residual results in the loss of one observation.

The validity of the DW statistic for testing first-order autocorrelation can be seen from an approximation derived from the manipulation of Equation (11.21). Squaring the numerator, and moving the summation sign (which begins with $n = 2$) inside to each term, the numerator equals:

$$\sum\hat{\varepsilon}_t^2 + \sum\hat{\varepsilon}_{t-1}^2 - 2\sum\hat{\varepsilon}_t\hat{\varepsilon}_{t-1}.$$

Since the sums with squared residuals differ by only one term ($\hat{\varepsilon}_t$ versus $\hat{\varepsilon}_{t-1}$), then $\sum\hat{\varepsilon}_t^2 \approx \sum\hat{\varepsilon}_{t-1}^2$. The numerator of the DW statistic can therefore be written:

$$2\sum\hat{\varepsilon}_t^2 - 2\sum\hat{\varepsilon}_t\hat{\varepsilon}_{t-1} = 2(\sum\hat{\varepsilon}_t^2 - \sum\hat{\varepsilon}_t\hat{\varepsilon}_{t-1})$$

Adding the denominator this becomes:

$$DW \approx 2\left(\sum_{t=2}^{n} \hat{\varepsilon}_t^2 - \sum_{t=2}^{n} \hat{\varepsilon}_t\hat{\varepsilon}_{t-1} \right) \bigg/ \sum_{t=1}^{n} (\hat{\varepsilon}_t)^2 \qquad (11.22)$$

Since the summations with $\hat{\varepsilon}_t^2$ in the numerator and denominator differ by only one term, these sums are approximately equal. Dividing each term in the numerator of Equation (11.22) by the denominator, the approximation for the DW becomes:

$$DW \approx 2[1 - \sum\hat{\varepsilon}_t\hat{\varepsilon}_{t-1}/\sum\hat{\varepsilon}_t^2] \qquad (11.23)$$

The summation term in Equation (11.23) is the estimated autocorrelation coefficient that is obtained by regressing the current period residuals, $\hat{\varepsilon}_t$, on the lagged residuals, $\hat{\varepsilon}_{t-1}$. From Equation (11.8), the autocorrelation for lag 1 is identical to Θ with an AR(1) error process. Utilizing this information, the approximation for the Durbin-Watson statistic is:

$$DW \approx 2(1 - \hat{\Theta}) \qquad (11.24)$$

where $\hat{\Theta}$ is the least squares estimate of Θ. Equation (11.24) links the Durbin-Watson statistic to the estimated coefficient of first-order autocorrelation.

We can obtain values of the DW statistic for the different autocorrelation possibilities using Equation (11.24). Since Θ is a correlation coefficient, its values range between -1 and $+1$. In the absence of autocorrelation, our estimate of Θ, $\hat{\Theta}$, is close to 0 and the Durbin-Watson statistic is close to 2. For perfect positive autocorrelation, $\hat{\Theta} \approx 1$, and the value of DW tends toward 0. When perfect negative autocorrelation exists, $\hat{\Theta} \approx -1$, so that the Durbin-Watson statistic is close to its upper bound of 4. Based on this approximation, the DW statistic ranges from a low of 0 (perfect positive autocorrelation), to a high value of 4 (perfect negative autocorrelation), with a value of 2 in the absence of autocorrelation. Values of the Durbin-Watson statistic close to 2.0 constitute evidence supporting the absence of autocorrelation. In fact, this value is a "rule of thumb" for many researchers.[16]

The value of the Durbin-Watson statistic is standard output in almost every major canned computer program. Manual calculation of this value is thus generally unnecessary. Once obtained, its use in a decision concerning the null hypothesis of no autocorrelation is slightly different from the usual t-tests and F-tests. Unlike the latter tests, a single critical value is not utilized, since the values of ε, and therefore DW, depend on the values taken by the explanatory variables in an equation. To allow for this fact, the determination of whether to reject the null hypothesis is based on observing whether the DW statistic falls outside of the range of values delineated by a lower value, d_L, and an upper value, d_U, which depend on the number of observations and the number of explanatory variables (k') in the estimated equation. Unfortunately, when the value of DW falls between d_L and d_U, the Durbin-Watson test is inconclusive. Values of d_L and d_U for different levels of significance are contained in the tables at the end of the text.

The procedure for carrying out the Durbin-Watson test of the null hypothesis $H_0: \Theta = 0$ against the alternative hypothesis of positive autocorrelation: $H_a: \Theta > 0$ consists of the following steps:

(i) Estimate the original equation with least squares;
(ii) obtain the value of the Durbin-Watson statistic from the residuals of this regression. If this information is not available from your canned computer program, use Equation (11.21);
(iii) consult the table at the end of the text for the critical values of the Durbin-Watson statistic, based on the number of observations, the number of explanatory variables, and the desired level of significance;
(iv) relate the value of DW to these values in the following way: if positive autocorrelation exists, then DW should be close to 0, and lie below the value of d_L obtained from the table. If, in fact, $DW < d_L$, reject the null hypothesis of no autocorrelation and accept the alternative hypothesis of positive autocorrelation. If, instead, $DW > d_U$, do not reject the null hypothesis of no autocorrelation, since the likelihood of obtaining this large a value of DW with positive autocorrelation is no greater than the selected level of significance. Finally, if the value of DW falls between the upper and lower critical values, the test is inconclusive.

As an example of the use of the Durbin-Watson test to detect positive autocorrelation, let us examine the following unemployment rate equation that is estimated with

---

[16] If, however, the equation contains a lagged dependent variable, which violates the assumptions of the Durbin-Watson test, the value of the DW statistic will tend toward 2, which gives the appearance of no autocorrelation, when in fact, this assumption may be false. A modification of the DW test statistic for the presence of lagged dependent variables is given later in this chapter.

quarterly data from 1970:2 to 1987:1:

$$\hat{u}_t = 23.1 \ - 0.078\text{CAP}_t - 0.146\text{CAP}_{t-1} + 0.043t \qquad \textbf{(11.25)}$$
$$\quad\ (15.6) \quad (2.0) \qquad\quad (3.7) \qquad\qquad (10.3)$$

$$\bar{R}^2 = 0.78 \qquad F = 78.9 \qquad \hat{\sigma}_\varepsilon = 0.677 \qquad \text{SSE} = 29.3 \qquad \text{DW} = 0.23 \qquad n = 68$$

where u is the civilian unemployment rate, CAP is the capacity utilization rate in manufacturing, and t is a time trend, with 1970:2 = 1. The specification of this equation includes variables that reflect both the cyclical and secular behavior of the unemployment rate. The variable CAP captures cyclical influences, which are assumed to occur over two quarters, while the time trend controls for the secular trend in u during the estimation period. The Durbin-Watson statistic from this equation, 0.23, is close to 0, indicating the likelihood of positive autocorrelation. The critical values of the DW statistic for the 1 percent level of significance and 70 observations (which is closest to the n of 68) with three explanatory variables ($k' = 3$) are $d_L = 1.37$ and $d_U = 1.55$. Since the actual value of the test statistic falls below d_L, we reject the null hypothesis, $H_0: \Theta = 0$ in favor of the alternative hypothesis that the error process is positively autocorrelated.

The Durbin-Watson Test requires only a slight modification for negative autocorrelation. The critical values of the Durbin-Watson Test are adjusted, based on the upper value of 4 for the test statistic. The lower critical value becomes $d'_L = (4 - d_L)$, while the upper value changes to $d'_U = (4 - d_U)$. The set of hypotheses that are tested are: $H_0: \Theta = 0$ and $H_a: \Theta < 0$. Steps (i), (ii), and (iii) remain the same. The final step is:

(iv)' obtain the appropriate values of d_L and d_U from the table at the end of the text, and calculate $d'_L = (4 - d_L)$ and $d'_U = (4 - d_U)$. Note that d'_U is less than d'_L. If the equation DW exceeds d'_L (the larger of the two critical values), reject the null hypothesis of no autocorrelation, and accept the alternative that $\Theta < 0$. Do not reject H_0 when DW is below d'_U. Finally, if DW falls between d'_U and d'_L, the test is inconclusive.

The unemployment rate Equation (11.25) can be used to illustrate the Durbin-Watson Test for negative autocorrelation. The test statistic from that equation is 0.23, and from the DW table, $d_L = 1.37$ and $d_U = 1.55$. The new critical values of the test are therefore: $d'_L = (4 - 1.37) = 2.63$; and $d'_U = (4 - 1.55) = 2.45$. Since the DW statistic is below d'_U, we reject the alternative hypothesis of negative autocorrelation.

Figure 11.4 shows the acceptance, rejection, and inconclusive regions for the Durbin-Watson Test. The DW statistic is symmetrically distributed around its no autocorrelation value of 2. For test statistic values between d_U and d'_U, we are unable to reject the null hypothesis of zero autocorrelation. When DW either falls below d_L or above d'_L, the null hypothesis is rejected. Finally, there are two inconclusive regions, one for each one-sided alternative hypothesis. Using the information contained in Figure 11.4, the two-tail Durbin-Watson Test can be detailed. The null hypothesis remains $H_0: \Theta = 0$, while the alternative is: $H_a: \Theta \neq 0$. Do not reject the null hypothesis if $d_U < \text{DW} < d'_U$, which places the test statistic above the upper range for positive autocorrelation and below the lower value for negative autocorrelation. The null

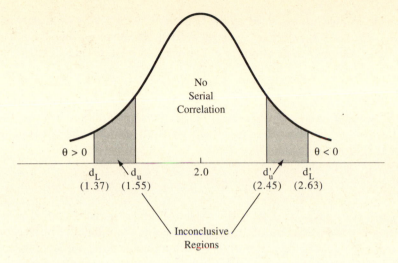

Figure 11.4

hypothesis is rejected if $d'_L < \mathrm{DW} < d_L$, so that the test statistic is either below the lower bound for positive autocorrelation, or above the upper bound for negative autocorrelation. When a two-tail test is performed on the unemployment rate Equation (11.25), the null hypothesis of a nonzero Θ is rejected in favor of the alternative hypothesis of an autocorrelated error process, since the value of the test statistic, 0.23, falls below d_L.

   A variant of this methodology allows the testing of fourth-order autocorrelation (generally with quarterly data). Assuming that the error can be characterized by the following AR(4) process:

$$\varepsilon_t = \Theta_4 \varepsilon_{t-4} + v_t.$$

Wallis[17] has extended the framework of the Durbin-Watson Test to allow the testing of this specific type of autocorrelation. Starting with the null hypothesis: $H_0 \colon \Theta_4 = 0$, the **Wallis test of Fourth-Order Autocorrelation** uses the following test statistic:

$$\mathrm{W4} = \sum_{t=5}^{n} (\varepsilon_t - \varepsilon_{t-4})^2 / \sum_{t=1}^{n} \varepsilon_t^2$$

The summation in the numerator runs from $t = 5$ to n, since four observations are lost with this type of autocorrelation. Wallis derived the upper and lower significance points for this test. The reader is referred to Kmenta for a more in-depth discussion of Wallis' text and the tables that are utilized.[18]

---

[17] K. F. Wallis, "Testing for Fourth-Order Autocorrelation in Quarterly Regression Equations," *Econometrica* 40 (1972): 617–36.

[18] J. Kmenta, *Elements of Econometrics* (2nd ed), (New York: Macmillan Publishing Co, 1986), pp. 325–6.

The framework provided by the Durbin-Watson Test is valid only when the estimated equation excludes a lagged dependent variable. Durbin[19] has devised a test for first-order autocorrelation for equations that include lagged dependent variables, such as:

$$y_t = \alpha_0 + \alpha_1 x_t + \alpha_2 y_{t-1} + \varepsilon_t$$

The **Durbin h test**, as this is called, utilizes the same null and alternative hypotheses as the original Durbin-Watson Test. Its test statistic, the **Durbin h-statistic**, is defined by the following formula:

$$h = \left(1 - \frac{DW}{2}\right)\sqrt{\frac{n}{1 - n(\hat{\sigma}_2^2)}} \qquad \textbf{(11.26)}$$

where n is sample size, DW is the Durbin-Watson statistic, and $\hat{\sigma}_2^2$ is the estimated variance of the coefficient of the lagged dependent variable.[20] For large samples, this test statistic follows the unit normal distribution when the null hypothesis of no autocorrelation is true. Because of this, a single critical value is utilized to make a decision concerning the null hypothesis. A one-tail Durbin h test for positive autocorrelation uses the set of hypotheses: H_0: $\Theta = 0$; and H_a: $\Theta > 0$. If the h-statistic exceeds the critical value for a unit normal random variable with the desired level of significance, the null hypothesis of no autocorrelation is rejected in favor of H_a.

The Durbin-Watson statistic tests only for the presence of first order serial correlation. Breusch and Godfrey have proposed a more general test for autocorrelation that can be employed when the order of the error's autoregressive processes extends beyond the first order. Furthermore, no modification (such as the Durbin-h test) is required when a lagged dependent variable appears in an equation, and there is no inconclusive region for their test statistic. The **Breusch-Godfrey test** is a statistical test of the joint significance of a set of autocorrelation coefficients.[21] If the error process is jth order autoregressive:

$$\varepsilon_t = \Theta_1 \varepsilon_{t-1} + \Theta_2 \varepsilon_{t-2} + \cdots + \Theta_j \varepsilon_{t-j} + v_t$$

where v is a white noise error process, the Breusch-Godfrey test ascertains whether the set of coefficients Θ_1 to Θ_j is significantly different from 0. The null hypothesis for their test is thus:

$$H_0: \Theta_1 = \Theta_2 = \cdots = \Theta_j = 0$$

---

[19] J. Durbin, "Testing for Serial Correlation in Least Squares Regressions When Some of the Regressors Are Lagged Dependent Variables," *Econometrica* 38 (1970): 410–21.

[20] Note that the denominator in this test statistic is negative when $\hat{\sigma}_2^2$ exceeds $1/n$. In this case, the test cannot be performed.

[21] T. S. Breusch, "Testing Autocorrelation in Dynamic Linear Models," *Australian Economic Papers* 17 (1978): 334–55; and L. G. Godfrey, "Testing Against Autoregressive and Moving Average Error Models when the Regressors Include Lagged Dependent Variables," *Econometrica* 46 (1978): 1293–1302.

The basis for conducting this test is the likely correlation of $\hat{\varepsilon}_t$ with its own lags when the error process is serially correlated. The steps involved are:

1. Estimate the original equation with least squares and obtain the residuals from that equation, $\hat{\varepsilon}_t$.
2. Using the residuals from this regression, calculate the set of lagged residuals that correspond to the order of the autoregressive process postulated in the null hypothesis. Here, we calculate $\hat{\varepsilon}_{t-1}$ through $\hat{\varepsilon}_{t-j}$. Note that only $(n-j)$ observations then exist, since j missing values occur when creating these lagged residuals.
3. Regress $\hat{\varepsilon}_t$ on the set of explanatory variables included in the original equation *plus* the lagged residuals created in step (2). If, for example, the original equation includes x and z as explanatory variables, we regress $\hat{\varepsilon}_t$ on an intercept, $x_t, z_t, \hat{\varepsilon}_{t-1}, \hat{\varepsilon}_{t-2}, \ldots, \hat{\varepsilon}_{t-j}$.
4. The test statistic for this test, $(n-j)R^2$, follows the chi-square distribution with j degrees of freedom, where j is the postulated order of the autoregressive process and $(n-j)$ is the number of observations used to estimate this equation. If the value of this statistic exceeds the critical chi-square value for the selected level of significance, we reject the null hypothesis of no serial correlation. In that case, we accept the alternative hypothesis of autocorrelated errors, where at least one Θ is different from 0.

Two potential difficulties exist when using this test. First, the order of the autoregressive process is generally not known. The researcher must therefore decide on an appropriate value for j. Second, when the original equation contains a large number of explanatory variables, the degrees of freedom used to estimate the equation in step (3), $n-k-j$ (where k is the number of coefficients in the original equation), might not be positive. As the frequency of data decreases (from monthly to annual), this becomes less of a problem since j likely falls. In spite of these difficulties, a major strength of the Breusch-Godfrey test is that it has no inconclusive region. When the Durbin-Watson test is inconclusive, it can be employed to ascertain the existence of autocorrelated errors.

A methodology exists for detecting autocorrelation that combines visual inspection of information obtainable from the estimated errors with a statistical test of the null hypothesis of no autocorrelation. This procedure is the identification portion of the Box-Jenkins[22] time series analysis. In the present context, the starting point for this methodology is the use of the least squares residuals to estimate two functions that provide important clues about the specific type of error generating process in our equation. The first of these is called the **theoretical autocorrelation function (TACF)**. This function summarizes the relationship between different lags, j, and the corresponding autocorrelations, Θ_j. The graph of this function is known as a **correlogram**.

---

[22] G. Box and G. Jenkins, *Time Series Analysis: Forecasting and Control*, 2d. ed. (San Francisco: Holden-Day), 1976.

The theoretical autocorrelation function is symmetrical, so that $\Theta_{-j} = \Theta_j$. Because of this fact, it is necessary only to evaluate the pattern of autocorrelations for positive lags. For an AR(1) error process, the theoretical autocorrelation function declines exponentially to 0, since (from Equation (11.8′)) the autocorrelation at lag j equals Θ^j, which approaches 0 as j increases. The TACF and correlogram for this type process with $\Theta = 0.8$ are given in Figure 11.5. The theoretical autocorrelation functions for smaller values of Θ approach 0 more rapidly, as the autocorrelations die off more quickly. When Θ is negative, the theoretical autocorrelation function oscillates between negative and positive autocorrelations, which decline to 0 exponentially.

The theoretical autocorrelation function for an AR(2) error process can display one of several possible patterns. The distinction between a first-order and second-order autoregressive error processes is therefore not always apparent from the TACF. The additional information needed to distinguish between these error processes is

Theoretical Autocorrelation Function
And Correlogram

j	θ_j
1	0.800
2	0.640
3	0.512
4	0.410
5	0.328
6	0.262
7	0.210
8	0.168
9	0.134
10	0.107

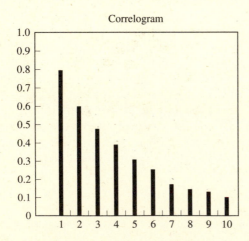

Figure 11.5

obtained through the use of partial autocorrelation coefficients. The **partial autocor-relation for lag j** shows the autocorrelation between ε_t and ε_{t-j} after controlling for the influence of all intermediate lagged errors. The partial autocorrelation for lag 1, φ_1, which is identical to the autocorrelation for lag 1, is obtained from the equation:

$$\varepsilon_t = \varphi_1 \varepsilon_{t-1} + v_t.$$

Higher-order partial autocorrelations are obtained from multivariate error regressions. For example, the partial autocorrelation for lag 2 is the coefficient of ε_{t-2} in the following regression equation:

$$\varepsilon_t = \varphi_1 \varepsilon_{t-1} + \varphi_2 \varepsilon_{t-2} + v_t.$$

The term φ_2 is a partial slope, which indicates the relationship between ε_t and ε_{t-2} after controlling for the influence of ε_{t-1} on ε_t. Similarly, the partial autocorrelation for lag 3 is the coefficient of ε_{t-3} in the equation:

$$\varepsilon_t = \varphi_1 \varepsilon_{t-1} + \varphi_2 \varepsilon_{t-2} + \varphi_3 \varepsilon_{t-3} + v_t.$$

The **theoretical partial autocorrelation function (TPACF),** summarizes the pattern of partial autocorrelations for different lags. This function plays a critical role in the identification of the order of an autoregressive process. To see why this is so, consider an AR(1) error process. The partial autocorrelation for lag 1 with this type error process is nonzero. However, the partial autocorrelations for lags 2 and above all equal 0, since with a first-order autoregressive process ε_t is correlated only with its value from the previous period.[23] Similarly, with an AR(2) error process, both φ_1 and φ_2 are nonzero, while all partial autocorrelation coefficients above φ_2 are zero. The usefulness of the TPACF in identifying the order of an autoregressive error process thus results from the fact that:

> The order of an autoregressive error process is given by the number of non-zero partial autocorrelation coefficients in the theoretical partial autocorrelation function.

Identification of whether or not an error process is autoregressive, and the order of the process is therefore accomplished using both the theoretical autocorrelation function, and the theoretical partial autocorrelation function.

The population autocorrelations and partial autocorrelations are, however, unknown, and must be estimated using the least squares residuals, $\hat{\varepsilon}_t$, from a sample regression function. Inferences about the underlying error generating process therefore utilize both the **sample autocorrelation function (SACF)** and the **sample partial autocorrelation function (SPACF)**. Identification of the order of the error-generating process entails comparing each of the above sample functions to their corresponding

---

[23] Recall that ε_t is related to an infinite number of lagged terms and to the white noise error process, v_t.

SMPL 1970.2 – 1987.1
68 Observations
IDENT RESID

Autocorrelations	Partial Autocorrelations		ac	pac
I **********	I **|********	1	0.848	0.848
I *********	I * I	2	0.705	−0.050
I ********	I * I	3	0.606	0.075
I *******	I I	4	0.520	−0.011
I *****	I ** I	5	0.393	−0.185
I ****	I * I	6	0.307	0.071
I ***	I ** I	7	0.209	−0.142
I * I	I ** I	8	0.082	−0.166
I I	I * I	9	0.009	0.111
I I	I * I	10	−0.014	0.045
I * I	I * I	11	−0.065	−0.090
I ** I	I * I	12	−0.144	−0.108
I ** I	I * I	13	−0.169	0.055
I ** I	I I	14	−0.172	0.020
I ** I	I * I	15	−0.190	−0.048
I ** I	I * I	16	−0.180	0.060
I ** I	I * I	17	−0.178	−0.113

Q–Statistic	(17 lags)	158.837	S.E. of Correlations 0.121

Figure 11.6

theoretical functions. Figure 11.6 shows the correlogram along with sample autocorrelations (ac) and sample partial autocorrelations (pac) for residuals from the unemployment rate equation used in the illustration of the Durbin-Watson Test. The dotted lines in both correlograms indicate values that are two standard deviations from 0.[24] Statistics constructed from these estimated standard deviations enable us to test whether individual sample autocorrelations and partial autocorrelations are significantly different from 0. Sample values of either type autocorrelation that exceed two standard deviations allow us to reject the null hypothesis of a zero autocorrelation (or partial autocorrelation) for that lag. Only one of the partial autocorrelations in Figure 11.6 is significantly different from 0. The nonzero values for the remaining partial autocorrelations result from sampling error that produces a divergence between the theoretical and sample partial autocorrelation functions. The sample autocorrelations conform to the typical pattern for an AR(1) error process with a positive Θ. The correlogram for the SACF in this example indicates that the sample autocorrelations continually decrease, and die off (become nonsignificant) after 7 lags.

---

[24] The formulas for these standard deviations are given in A. Pankratz, *Forecasting With Univariate Box-Jenkins Models: Concepts and Cases* (New York: John Wiley & Sons), 1983, Chapter 3. This diagram was produced using microTSP.

The visual evidence provided by the patterns of autocorrelations and partial autocorrelations can be augmented by a statistical test of whether the error process is autoregressive. The null hypothesis for this test, which focuses on the *set* of autocorrelations, is:

$$H_0: \Theta_1 = \Theta_2 = \cdots = \Theta_j = 0$$

where j is the number of autocorrelations considered. Box and Jenkins suggest using $n/4$ values.[25] The test statistic for this null hypothesis is the **Box-Pierce Q-Statistic**,[26] given by the equation:

$$Q = n\sum \hat{\Theta}_i^2$$

where the summation goes from $i = 1$ to j. For large n, Q is approximately chi-square distributed with j degrees of freedom when the null hypothesis is true. The null hypothesis of no autocorrelation is therefore rejected if Q exceeds the critical chi-square value with j degrees of freedom, since then the autocorrelations *taken as a set* are significantly different from 0. The value of the Q-statistic from the data for Figure 11.6 is 158.84. For the 1 percent level of significance, the critical chi-square value with 17 degrees of freedom is 33.4. Since the test statistic exceeds this critical value, we can reject the null hypothesis of no autocorrelation in favor of the alternative hypothesis.

One limitation of the Box-Pierce Q-Statistic is its reliance on a large sample size. For moderate samples, an improvement over this test statistic has been proposed by Ljung and Box.[27] The modified Box-Pierce Statistic, or **Ljung-Box Q-statistic (LQ)** is given by the formula:

$$LQ = n(n + 2)\sum \frac{\hat{\Theta}_i^2}{(n - i)}$$

where the summation again runs from 1 to j. This test statistic also follows the chi-square distribution with j degrees of freedom.[28] Since $(n + 2)/(n - i)$ is greater than 1, the value of the Ljung-Box statistic exceeds that of the Box-Pierce statistic, or $LQ > Q$. As a result, use of the Box-Pierce statistic will lead to less frequent rejection of the null hypothesis of no autocorrelation than does the Ljung-Box statistic.

---

[25] G. Box and G. Jenkins, p. 33.

[26] G. Box and D. Pierce, "The Distribution of Residual Autocorrelations in Autoregressive Integrated Moving Average Time Series Models," *Journal of the American Statistical Association* 65 (1970).

[27] G. M. Ljung and G. E. P. Box, "On a Measure of Lack of Fit in Time Series Models," *Biometrika* 65 (1978): 67–72.

[28] See the earlier footnote for a comment on the number of degrees of freedom for this test statistic.

METHODS FOR ESTIMATING THE COEFFICIENT OF AUTOCORRELATION

Several widely utilized methods exist for estimating the autocorrelation coefficient when the error process is first-order autoregressive. The major difference between these is whether the estimate of Θ is obtained from a single calculation, or as the result of several such calculations, called either iteration or grid-search. For some persons, the technique used is ultimately determined by the canned computer program utilized. MicroTSP, for example, uses an iterative method (the Cochrane-Orcutt procedure). When the researcher can select the method to apply, it is generally preferable to utilize the specific grid-search method presented below, the Hildreth-Lu technique. Both types of estimates will now be outlined.

Non-Iterative Methods

The most widely utilized non-iterative method for estimating Θ uses the Durbin-Watson statistic. Equation (11.24) shows that the Durbin-Watson statistic can be related to Θ: $DW \approx 2(1 - \hat{\Theta})$. Solving this expression for our estimate of Θ provides the needed information:

$$\hat{\Theta} \approx (1 - DW/2) \qquad (11.27)$$

When the value of DW is close to its non-autocorrelation value of 2.0, the estimate of Θ obtained from Equation (11.27) is close to 0. As the value of DW approaches its lower limit of 0, which is indicative of positive autocorrelation, $\hat{\Theta}$ approaches 1.

As an example of estimating Θ by this method, let us refer to the unemployment rate equation presented earlier. The Durbin-Watson statistic from that equation is 0.23. The estimate of Θ from this DW is:

$$\hat{\Theta} = (1 - 0.23/2) = 0.885.$$

Using this information, along with the correlogram that identified the error process as first-order autoregressive, our estimate of the true autoregressive error process in the unemployment rate equation is: $\varepsilon_t = 0.885\hat{\varepsilon}_{t-1} + \hat{v}_t$. Based on this value of $\hat{\Theta}$, the estimated transformation that converts the original equation to generalized difference form (for all but the first observation) is:

$$\hat{T} = \hat{\Theta}(B) = (1 - 0.885B).$$

Multiplying the original equation by $\hat{T}$ we obtain:

$$u_t^* = \alpha_0^* + \alpha_1 CAP_t^* + \alpha_2 CAP_{t-1}^* + \alpha_3 t^* + v_t,$$

where $u_t^* = (u_t - 0.885u_{t-1})$, $CAP_t^* = (CAP_t - 0.885CAP_{t-1})$, $CAP_{t-1}^* = (CAP_{t-1} - 0.885CAP_{t-2})$, $t^* = (t - 0.885(t - 1))$, $\alpha_0^* = \alpha_0(1 - 0.885) = 0.115\alpha_0$, and v_t is an estimated white noise error. A Prais-Winsten correction was utilized with this equation, so the first observations for u, CAP, CAP_{t-1}, and t were multiplied by $\sqrt{1 - 0.885^2} =$

0.466. The resulting estimated generalized least squares unemployment equation is:

$$\hat{u}_t^* = 2.4 \quad - 0.132\text{CAP}_t^* - 0.052\text{CAP}_{t-1}^* + 0.021t^* \tag{11.28}$$
$$\quad\quad (13.5) \quad (7.4) \quad\quad\quad (2.9) \quad\quad\quad\quad (1.5)$$

$\bar{R}^2 = 0.628 \quad\quad \text{SSE} = 4.46 \quad\quad \hat{\sigma}_\varepsilon = 0.27 \quad\quad F = 38.1 \quad\quad \text{DW} = 1.64 \quad\quad \text{LQ} = 24.4$

The intercept Equation (11.28), which is an estimate of $\alpha_0(1 - \Theta)$, must be manipulated to arrive at an estimate of α_0. This estimate is:

$$\hat{\alpha}_0 = \hat{\alpha}_0^*/(1 - \hat{\Theta}) = 2.4/0.115 = 20.9$$

The t-statistic for the estimated intercept should also be considered. The estimated variance of $\hat{\alpha}_0^*$ from the above equation is 0.0314. The estimated variance of α_0 is then:

$$\text{Var}(\alpha_0) = \text{Var}(\alpha_0^*)/(1 - \hat{\Theta})^2 = 0.0314/(0.115)^2 = 2.38$$

Using this information, the t-statistic for the estimated intercept, $\hat{\alpha}_0$ is:

$$t = 20.9/\sqrt{2.38} = 13.5,$$

which is identical to the test statistic for $\hat{\alpha}_0^*$

The coefficients of the explanatory variables in Equation (11.28) are different from those in the original equation. The temporal pattern in the adjustment of the unemployment rate to changes in the capacity utilization rate has been reversed. In the original equation, a 1 percent increase in CAP decreased the mean unemployment rate by a greater amount in the second rather than the first quarter following such a change. Equation (11.28) indicates the greater impact on the mean unemployment rate during the quarter in which the change in CAP occurs. Also, the coefficient of time, which indicates the secular trend in U, is now half its size in the original equation, and no longer statistically significant. Finally, the Durbin-Watson statistic from this equation is in the inconclusive range. The Ljung-Box Q-statistic for 17 lags, 24.4, is less than the critical chi-square value for 17 degrees of freedom and a 5 percent significance level of 27.6. We are thus unable to reject the null hypothesis of no autocorrelation based on the LQ-statistic.

Theil and Nagar recommend a small sample modification to the estimate of Θ based on the Durbin-Watson statistic.[29] This modification is appropriate as long as the explanatory variables tend to move in a smooth manner, which implies that both first and second differences should be small relative to the original values of these variables. This precludes equations with dummy variables and explanatory variables that are first differences. The Theil-Nagar estimate of Θ, $\hat{\Theta}_{\text{TN}}$, is:

$$\hat{\Theta}_{\text{TN}} = [n^2(\hat{\Theta}_{\text{DW}}) + k^2]/(n^2 - k^2), \tag{11.29}$$

[29] H. Theil and A. Nagar, "Testing the Independence of Regression Disturbances," *Journal of the American Statistical Association* 56 (1961): 793–806.

where n is the number of observations used to estimate the original equation, $\hat{\Theta}_{DW}$ is the estimate of Θ from the Durbin-Watson statistic, and k is the number of estimated coefficients *including the intercept*. For large samples, the estimates of Θ based on the Theil-Nagar modification and the Durbin-Watson statistic are close in value. This fact can be demonstrated by calculating $\hat{\Theta}_{TN}$ for the unemployment rate equation. For that equation, $n = 68$, $k = 4$, and $\hat{\Theta}_{DW} = 0.885$. Substituting this information into Equation (11.29), the Theil-Nagar estimate of Θ is:

$$\hat{\Theta}_{TN} = [68^2 \cdot 0.885 + 4^2]/(68^2 - 4^2) = 0.892,$$

which differs only slightly from the value of $\hat{\Theta}_{DW}$. If, however, the unemployment equation had utilized only 20 observations, then assuming the original value of $\hat{\Theta}_{DW}$, the Theil-Nagar estimate of Θ would be 0.964, which differs substantially from the value of $\hat{\Theta}_{TN}$ when $n = 68$.

The remaining non-iterative methods discussed here are based on the direct use of least squares. The first of these is the **two-step Cochrane-Orcutt procedure**.[30] The initial step in this procedure consists of estimating Θ from the least squares regression (without an intercept) of current period residuals on their lagged values:

$$\hat{\varepsilon}_t = \Theta \hat{\varepsilon}_{t-1} + v_t$$

The least squares estimate of Θ from this equation is:

$$\hat{\Theta} = \sum \hat{\varepsilon}_t \hat{\varepsilon}_{t-1} / \sum \hat{\varepsilon}_{t-1}^2 \qquad \text{(for } t = 2, 3, \ldots)$$

The value of $\hat{\Theta}$ obtained from this regression is then utilized to transform the original equation into its generalized difference form, which is estimated with least squares. Application of this methodology to the unemployment rate equation produces a statistically significant estimate of Θ:

$$\hat{\hat{\varepsilon}}_t = 0.908 \hat{\varepsilon}_{t-1}$$
$$(15.1)$$

where $\hat{\hat{\varepsilon}}$ is our estimate of $\hat{\varepsilon}$. This estimate of Θ, 0.908, is used to transform the original equation to generalized difference form. The resulting estimated generalized least squares equation (using a Prais-Winsten correction) is:

$$\hat{u}_t^* = 1.93 \; - 0.132 CAP_t^* - 0.051 CAP_{t-1}^* + 0.015t^* \qquad \textbf{(11.30)}$$
$$\quad\;\; (12.9) \quad (7.5) \qquad\quad (2.9) \qquad\qquad (0.8)$$

$$\bar{R}^2 = 0.628 \qquad SSE = 4.37 \qquad \hat{\sigma}_\varepsilon = 0.26 \qquad F = 38.1 \qquad DW = 1.60$$

Because the estimate of Θ from the first step in this process is close to that derived from the Durbin-Watson statistic, this equation differs very little from Equation (11.28). The value of DW again falls into the inconclusive range.

---

[30] D. Cochrane and G. Orcutt, "Application of Least Squares Regressions to Relationships Containing Autocorrelated Error Terms," *Journal of the American Statistical Association* 44 (1949): 32–61.

The last noniterative method for estimating Θ is known as the **Durbin Procedure**, which entails a rearrangement of the generalized difference form of the original equation as the basis for obtaining an estimate of Θ.[31] Assuming the original equation contains the two explanatory variables x and z, the generalized difference form of this equation is:

$$(y_t - \Theta y_{t-1}) = \alpha_0^* + \alpha_1(x_t - \Theta x_{t-1}) + \alpha_2(z_t - \Theta z_{t-1}) + v_t.$$

If the terms in brackets are separated out and this equation is expressed with y_t as the dependent variable, then y_{t-1} becomes an explanatory variable whose coefficient is Θ, the coefficient of autocorrelation:

$$
\begin{aligned}
y_t &= \Theta y_{t-1} + \alpha_0^* + \alpha_1 x_t - \alpha_1 \Theta x_{t-1} + \alpha_2 z_t - \alpha_2 \Theta z_{t-1} + v_t \\
&= \Theta y_{t-1} + \alpha_0^* + \alpha_1 x_t + \beta_1 x_{t-1} + \alpha_2 z_t + \beta_2 z_{t-1} + v_t,
\end{aligned}
$$

where $\beta_1 = -\alpha_1 \Theta$ and $\beta_2 = -\alpha_2 \Theta$. The coefficient of y_{t-1} from the least squares regression of y_t on y_{t-1}, x_t, x_{t-1}, z_t, and z_{t-1} is the estimate of $\hat{\Theta}$ from the Durbin procedure. This value is then utilized in the generalized difference form of the original equation for estimated GLS estimation of the parameters of that equation. The value of $\hat{\Theta}$ for the unemployment rate equation with this procedure is 0.919. The coefficients in the generalized difference form of the original equation using this estimate are very similar to those presented earlier. However, the variables in the unemployment rate equation require that the problem of perfect collinearity be dealt with before the estimated of Θ is obtained. The basis for this problem is included along with the exercises at the end of this chapter.

Iterative and Grid-Search Methods

All the above methods for estimating Θ share a common characteristic: a single estimate of Θ is produced without attempting to improve on this value by considering the residuals in the generalized difference equation. Other methods for estimating Θ exist that evaluate several intermediate values of $\hat{\Theta}$ before arriving at a final estimate. **Iterative methods** calculate new estimates of Θ based on the residuals from the generalized difference equation. This process continues (iterates) until the new estimate of Θ differs only slightly from the previous estimate. The particular iterative method considered here is the **iterative Cochrane-Orcutt method**.[32] This essentially extends the two-step Cochrane-Orcutt procedure by estimating subsequent regressions of current on lagged residuals. Assuming the original equation contains the two explanatory

[31] J. Durbin, "Estimation of Parameters in Time-Series Regression Models," *Journal of the Royal Statistical Society* 22 (1960, Series B): 139–53.

[32] D. Cochrane and G. Orcutt, pp. 32–61.

variables x and z, the set of steps involved in this method are:

1. Perform the two-step Cochrane-Orcutt procedure: estimate the original equation with least squares, then regress the current period residuals from that equation, $\hat{\varepsilon}_t$, on their lagged values, $\hat{\varepsilon}_{t-1}$ (without an intercept). The coefficient of the lagged residual is the first-round estimate of Θ, $\hat{\Theta}_{(1)}$. Substitute this estimate of Θ into the generalized difference form of the original equation, and estimate the generalized difference equation with least squares.
2. Use the least squares estimates of the coefficients in the generalized difference equation (which includes correcting the intercept) with the *original* variables to produce a new set of residuals, $\hat{\varepsilon}_{(2)t} = y_t - \hat{\alpha}_0 - \hat{\alpha}_1 x_t - \hat{\alpha}_2 z_t$. Note that the values of $\hat{\varepsilon}_{(2)t}$ are not the residuals from the generalized difference equation estimated in step (1). The second-round estimate of Θ, $\hat{\Theta}_{(2)}$, is the least squares slope coefficient from the regression of $\hat{\varepsilon}_{(2)t}$ on $\hat{\varepsilon}_{(2)t-1}$ (without an intercept).
3. Use $\hat{\Theta}_{(2)}$ to estimate the generalized difference form of the original equation. If the second-round estimate of Θ differs from $\hat{\Theta}_{(1)}$ by less than some prespecified tolerance level, such as 0.01, then $\hat{\Theta}_{(2)}$ is the final estimate of Θ used for estimated generalized least squares, and the process stops. Otherwise, step (2) is repeated until either the difference between successive estimates of Θ differ by some acceptable amount, or if the maximum number of desired iterations has occurred.

Let us apply the iterative Cochrane-Orcutt method to the unemployment rate Equation (11.25). The residuals from this equation were regressed on their lagged values to produce the estimate $\hat{\Theta}_{(1)} = 0.908$ that was given for the two-step Cochrane-Orcutt procedure. This value is then used to estimate the original equation in generalized difference form, given by Equation (11.30). The estimate of α_0 from this equation is: $1.93/(1 - 0.908) = 21.1$. Using this and the other estimated coefficients in the generalized difference equation, the second-round residuals are obtained from the expression:

$$y_t - 21.1 - (-0.132\text{CAP}_t) - (-0.051\text{CAP}_{t-1}) - 0.015t.$$

Regressing these residuals on their lagged values produces the second-round estimate of Θ:

$$\hat{\varepsilon}_{(2)t} = 0.939\hat{\varepsilon}_{(2)t-1} + \hat{v}_t$$
$$(26.3)$$

This new estimate of Θ, $\hat{\Theta}_{(2)} = 0.939$, is then used to re-estimate the generalized difference form of the original equation. The result is:

$$\hat{u}_t^* = 1.33 - 0.132\text{CAP}_t^* - 0.050\text{CAP}_{t-1}^* + 0.0002t^*$$
$$(11.0) \quad (7.6) \qquad\qquad (2.9) \qquad\qquad\qquad (0.01)$$

$$\bar{R}^2 = 0.631 \qquad \text{SSE} = 4.30 \qquad \hat{\sigma}_\varepsilon = 0.26 \qquad F = 38.6 \qquad \text{DW} = 1.67$$

The third-round residuals are then calculated from this equation: $y_t - 21.8 - (-0.132\text{CAP}_t) - (-0.050\text{CAP}_{t-1}) - 0.0002t$. Regressing these residuals on their lagged values produces the third-round estimate of Θ:

$$\hat{\varepsilon}_{(3)t} = 0.947\hat{\varepsilon}_{(3)t-1} + \hat{v}'_t$$
$$(35.2)$$

This estimate, $\hat{\Theta}_{(3)} = 0.947$, differs from $\hat{\Theta}_{(2)}$ by only 0.009, which is within the usual range for ending an iterative process. The final version of the equation based on this estimate of Θ is then:

$$\hat{u}^*_t = 1.18 \quad - 0.132CAP^*_t - 0.050CAP^*_{t-1} - 0.006t^*$$
$$(10.0) \quad (7.6) \qquad (2.9) \qquad\qquad (0.20)$$

$$\bar{R}^2 = 0.632 \qquad SSE = 4.29 \qquad \hat{\sigma}_\varepsilon = 0.26 \qquad F = 38.8 \qquad DW = 1.69$$

The corrected intercept is 22.3 ($= 1.18/(1 - 0.947)$). The **Ljung-Box Q-statistic** for 17 lags obtained from this equation is 23.4. This is below the critical chi-square value for 17 degrees of freedom at the 5 percent significance level of 27.6. Based on the Box-Pierce test we are unable to reject the null hypothesis of no autocorrelation.

In contrast to the iterative method presented above, the grid-search method does not estimate the set of $\hat{\Theta}$ values used in generalized difference equations. Instead, a range (grid) of possible values for Θ are selected and each of these is used to estimate a separate generalized difference equation. The generalized difference form with the smallest sum of squared residuals is then selected as the preferable equation, and its $\hat{\Theta}$ is the estimate of the first-order autocorrelation coefficient. This is called the **Hildreth-Lu procedure**.[33] The grid of values within which $\hat{\Theta}$ is allowed to vary depends on limitations in terms of time and resources, and the type of software utilized. The most desirable grid is the set of values between -1 and $+1$, since Θ is a correlation coefficient. The increment between successive values of $\hat{\Theta}$ used to determine the final equation is also at the discretion of the researcher. Frequently, an increment of 0.1 is utilized.

The Hildreth-Lu procedure was used to determine an estimate of $\hat{\Theta}$ for the unemployment rate equation. The initial set of values used for $\hat{\Theta}$ along with the corresponding sum of the squared errors (ESS) are given below:

$\hat{\Theta}$	ESS	$\hat{\Theta}$	ESS
0.2	20.13	0.8	5.06
0.3	16.38	0.9	4.40
0.4	13.12	**0.95**	**4.2895**
0.5	10.34	**0.96**	**4.2868**
0.6	8.06	**0.965**	**4.2879**
0.7	6.29	0.97	4.290

[33] G. Hildreth and J. Lu, "Demand Relations with Autocorrelated Disturbances," *Michigan State University Agricultural Experiment Station, Technical Bulletin 276*, November 1960.

This table suggests that a new grid of $\hat{\Theta}$ values between 0.95 and 0.965 be evaluated to establish more precisely where the minimum of ESS actually occurs. Upon further investigation, this value was determined to be 0.9593. The final version of the generalized difference equation using this value for $\hat{\Theta}$ is:

$$\hat{u}_t^* = 0.95 - 0.132\text{CAP}_t^* - 0.049\text{CAP}_{t-1}^* - 0.022t^*$$
$$\quad (8.3) \quad (7.7) \qquad\qquad (2.9) \qquad\qquad\quad (0.55)$$

$$\bar{R}^2 = 0.634 \qquad \text{ESS} = 4.28 \qquad \hat{\sigma}_\varepsilon = 0.26 \qquad F = 39.2 \qquad \text{DW} = 1.71$$

The major differences between this and the final equation for the iterative Cochrane-Orcutt procedure are the negative sign for the coefficient of time and a different estimated intercept ($\hat{\alpha}_0 = 23.2$). Based on the Hildreth-Lu procedure, we are again unable to reject the null hypothesis of no autocorrelation. The Ljung-Box Q-statistic for 17 lags, 23.1, provides further evidence of the absence of autocorrelation in the residuals of this equation.

Before moving on to a discussion of forecasting with serially correlated errors, it is appropriate to illustrate that equation misspecification can result in serially correlated errors. The importance of this illustration lies in the fact that all of the serial correlation corrections that have been presented are appropriate only when the equation is correctly specified. Serial correlation correction is therefore not a substitute for a correctly specified sample regression function. Consider the consumer durables expenditure equation presented with a linear specification in Chapter 7. The sample regression function is:

$$\hat{y}_t = 309.2 - 2.25(p_{cd}/p_c)_t - 8.01r_t + 0.21yd_t - 8.43(c/y)_{t-1} - 4.27\,\Delta u_t$$
$$\quad (3.1) \quad\;\; (3.6) \qquad\qquad (10.5) \quad\; (7.2) \qquad (4.2) \qquad\qquad (3.2)$$

$$\bar{R}^2 = 0.994 \qquad \text{ESS} = 1959.5 \qquad n = 37 \qquad \hat{\sigma}_\varepsilon = 7.95 \qquad F = 1192.3 \qquad \text{DW} = 1.04$$

where y is real consumer durable good expenditure, (p_{cd}/p_c) is the relative price of consumer durables, r is the interest rate on 3 year government bonds, yd is real disposable personal income less transfer payments, (c/y) is the ratio of indebtedness to GNP, and u is the civilian unemployment rate. The Durbin-Watson statistic for this equation, 1.04, is fairly low, indicating the likelihood of positive serial correlation. The appropriate lower significance point for the Durbin-Watson statistic (at the 5 percent level) with $k' = 5$ and $n = 37$ is 1.190. Since the value of DW falls below this value, we are able to reject the null hypothesis of no autocorrelation.

We next perform the Breusch-Godfrey test, assuming a second-order autoregressive process, where $\varepsilon_t = \Theta_1 \varepsilon_{t-1} + \Theta_2 \varepsilon_{t-2} + v_t$ and $j = 2$. The null hypothesis for this test postulates no serial correlation:

$$H_0: \Theta_1 = \Theta_2 = 0$$

After calculating the residuals from the least squares regression above, we obtain $\hat{\varepsilon}_{t-1}$ and $\hat{\varepsilon}_{t-2}$, then regress $\hat{\varepsilon}_t$ on an intercept, (p_{cd}/p_c), r, yd, $(c/y)_{t-1}$, Δu, $\hat{\varepsilon}_{t-1}$ and $\hat{\varepsilon}_{t-2}$.

The resulting equation is:

$$\hat{\varepsilon}_t = 18.9 - 0.108(p_{cd}/p_c)_t + 0.45r_t - 0.009yd_t + 0.349(c/y)_{t-1}$$
$$\quad (0.2) \quad (0.2) \qquad\quad (0.6) \qquad (0.3) \qquad\quad (0.2)$$

$$\quad - 1.54\,\Delta u_t + 0.657\hat{\varepsilon}_{t-1} - 0.258\hat{\varepsilon}_{t-2}$$
$$\qquad (1.1) \qquad\quad (3.2) \qquad\quad (1.3)$$

$$(n - j) = 35 \qquad R^2 = 0.2749$$

The test statistic for the Breusch-Godfrey test is $(n - j)R^2 = 35(0.2749) = 9.62$. The critical chi-square value with 2 $(= j)$ degrees of freedom for the 5 percent significance level is 5.99. Since the value of our test statistic exceeds this critical value, we can reject the null hypothesis of no serial correlation. This general conclusion agrees with that for the Durbin-Watson test. However, the order of serial correlation (second order) may be greater than that which is detectable with the Durbin-Watson test.

Instead transforming this equation, we replace the above specification with one that is quadratic in relative price, which was presented in Chapter 8:

$$\hat{y}_t = 716.8 - 9.9(p_{cd}/p_c)_t + 0.033(p_{cd}/p_c)_t^2 - 6.09r_t$$
$$\quad (6.8) \quad (6.6) \qquad\quad (5.3) \qquad\qquad (9.2)$$

$$\quad + 0.177y_t - 3.6(c/y)_{t-1} - 3.8\,\Delta u_t$$
$$\qquad (8.1) \qquad\quad (2.1) \qquad\quad (3.9)$$

$$\bar{R}^2 = 0.997 \qquad \text{ESS} = 1009.0 \qquad n = 37 \qquad \hat{\sigma}_\varepsilon = 5.80 \qquad F = 1872.0 \qquad \text{DW} = 1.48$$

Not only do the various measures of equation performance improve with this specification (t-statistics, ESS, $\hat{\sigma}_\varepsilon$, and F), but the DW rises substantially. Its current value, 1.48, places it in the inconclusive range (with $d_L = 1.131$ and $d_U = 1.870$ for $k' = 6$ and $n = 37$). In order to resolve this inconclusive result, we regress the current period residuals on their lags:

$$\hat{\varepsilon}_t = 0.230\hat{\varepsilon}_{t-1} + \hat{v}_t \qquad \bar{R}^2 = 0.045$$
$$\quad (1.3)$$

The estimate of Θ from this equation is not statistically significant. Furthermore, the Ljung-Box Q-statistic using 9 lags, 8.6, lies within the acceptance region for the null hypothesis of no serial correlation (the critical chi-square value at the 5 percent significance level is 16.9). It thus appears that the improved specification does not possess serially correlated errors.

FORECASTING WITH SERIALLY CORRELATED ERRORS

We have seen that our usual estimation method, least squares, can be improved upon when the error process in an equation is serially correlated. By utilizing the information contained in the error correlations, the generalized least squares technique produces estimators with smaller variances than does least squares. In a similar manner, it is possible for us to improve the accuracy of forecasting when serially correlated errors are present.

We will begin with the following bivariate equation:

$$y_t = \alpha_0 + \alpha_1 x_t + \varepsilon_t \tag{11.31}$$

and the assumption that ε is a first-order autoregressive error process:

$$\varepsilon_t = \Theta \varepsilon_{t-1} + v_t$$

When serial correlation is absent, $\Theta = 0$, and least squares produces best linear unbiased forecasts of y:

$$\hat{y}_{t+1} = \hat{\alpha}_0 + \hat{\alpha}_1 x_{t+1}$$

Since $E(\varepsilon_t)$ is assumed to equal 0 for all past, present, and future time periods, we assign the residual this value for period $t + 1$. The error term (and residual) thus fail to contain any information that we can use to improve the forecasting performance of this equation. For first-order autocorrelation, this is no longer the case. Our "forecast" of ε_{t+1} need no longer be 0, but should instead be based on past errors. Since:

$$\varepsilon_t = \Theta \varepsilon_{t-1} + v_t$$

then next period's error, ε_{t+1}, is:

$$\varepsilon_{t+1} = \Theta \varepsilon_t + v_{t+1}$$

Since v is a white noise error process with a 0 mean, we use only $\Theta \varepsilon_t$ to depict ε_{t+1}. Incorporating this information into our forecasting equation, it becomes:

$$\hat{y}_{t+1} = \hat{\alpha}_0 + \hat{\alpha}_1 x_{t+1} + \hat{\Theta} \hat{\varepsilon}_t \tag{11.32}$$

This equation can be linked to the generalized difference form of the sample regression function that corresponds to Equation (11.31). To see this, we first express the error in Equation (11.32) in terms of that sample regression function:

$$\hat{\Theta} \hat{\varepsilon}_t = \hat{\Theta}(y_t - \hat{\alpha}_0 - \hat{\alpha}_1 x_t)$$
$$= \hat{\Theta} y_t - \hat{\Theta} \hat{\alpha}_0 - \hat{\alpha}_1 \hat{\Theta} x_t$$

Rewriting Equation (11.32) using this information:

$$\hat{y}_{t+1} = \hat{\alpha}_0 + \hat{\alpha}_1 x_{t+1} + (\hat{\Theta} y_t - \hat{\Theta} \hat{\alpha}_0 - \hat{\alpha}_1 \hat{\Theta} x_t)$$

our forecast for period $t + 1$ is:

$$\hat{y}_{t+1} = \hat{\Theta} y_t + \hat{\alpha}_0(1 - \hat{\Theta}) + \hat{\alpha}_1(x_{t+1} - \hat{\Theta} x_t),$$

or

$$\hat{y}_{t+1} = \hat{\Theta} y_t + \hat{\alpha}_0^* + \hat{\alpha}_1 x_{t+1}^* \tag{11.33}$$

When α_0, α_1, and Θ are known, the use of Equation (11.33) produces best linear unbiased forecasts of future y values.[34] Since all of these are parameters unknown, the properties of Equation (11.33) as an estimator of $\hat{y}_{t+1}$ pertain strictly to large samples.

---

[34] A. Goldberger, "Best Linear Unbiased Prediction in the Linear Regression Model," *Journal of the American Statistical Association* 57 (1962): 369–75.

To illustrate the use of Equation (11.33) for forecasting, we will utilize the consumption function presented in Chapter 5. The estimated version of that equation for the period 1947–1988 is:

$$\hat{c}_t = 25.9 + 0.907 \text{RDPI}_t$$
$$(0.3) \quad (91.9)$$

$$\bar{R}^2 = 0.995 \quad \hat{\sigma}_\varepsilon = 126.8 \quad n = 42 \quad F = 8437.4 \quad \text{DW} = 0.49$$

where c is real consumption and RDPI is real disposable personal income both in per-capita terms. The Durbin-Watson statistic from this equation, 0.49, is very low, and well below the lower critical point (at the 5 percent level) of 1.44. We thus conclude that positive serial correlation is present. This is confirmed by visual inspection of the autocorrelation functions for this equation (this is from MicroTSP):

```
IDENT RESID
SMPL range: 1947  -  1988
Number of observations: 42

      Autocorrelations        Partial Autocorrelations      ac      pac

          *********                    *********        1   0.665   0.665
          *******                    * .                2   0.503   0.108
          ****                     .   *                3   0.340  -0.056
          ** .                     . **                 4   0.166  -0.130
          ** .                     .   **               5   0.151   0.136
          ** .                     .                    6   0.116   0.026
          * .                      .   *                7   0.065  -0.066
          * .                      .     *              8   0.090   0.067
        .                          . **                 9  -0.032  -0.184
      . **|                        . **|               10  -0.154  -0.178

Box-Pierce Q-Stat   38.28   Prob   0.0000   SE of Correlations  0.154
Ljung-Box  Q-Stat   42.34   Prob   0.0000
```

The single large partial autocorrelation and the gradual fading of the autocorrelations points to first-order serial correlation. The Ljung-Box Q-statistic of 42.3 exceeds the critical chi-square value at the 5 percent level of 18.3. To assess the forecasting performance of this equation both with and without serial correlation correction, we estimate it with both least squares and estimated GLS for the period from 1947–1983. The coefficients from those equations are then used to generate ex-post forecasts for the period 1984–1988. OLS forecasts are created using the following equation:

$$\hat{c}_{t+\tau} = 238.4 + 0.875 \text{RDPI}_{t+\tau}$$

which is based on the least squares coefficients from the estimation period (1947–1983). The forecast for 1984 is:

$$\hat{c}_{84} = 238.4 + 0.875(10{,}419) = 9{,}355$$

Forecasts for 1985–1988 are derived by changing only the value of RDPI. The serial correlation corrected forecasts are derived from Equation (11.33):

$$\hat{c}_{t+\tau} = \hat{\Theta}c_t + \hat{\alpha}_0^* + \hat{\alpha}_1 \text{RDPI}_{t+\tau}^*$$

The coefficients in this equation are obtained using the iterative Cochrane-Orcutt technique on the consumption function. The estimated serial correlation coefficient is $\hat{\Theta} = 0.4677$ and the sample regression function (in generalized difference form) is:

$$\hat{c}_t^* = 81.9 + 0.885\text{RDPI}_t^*$$
$$(1.4) \quad (60.1)$$

$$\bar{R}^2 = 0.997 \quad \hat{\sigma}_\varepsilon = 75.5 \quad n = 36 \quad F = 6888.6 \quad \text{DW} = 1.89$$

The forecast for 1984 is calculated as follows:

$$\hat{c}_{84} = 0.4677(c_{83}) + 81.9 + 0.885\text{RDPI}_{84}^*$$

Using actual values for the variables on the right side:

$$\hat{c}_{84} = 0.4677(9,139) + 81.9 + 0.885(10,419 - 0.4677(9,930))$$
$$= 9,466.8$$

The remaining forecasts were calculated in a similar manner. Figure 11.7 contrasts actual real personal consumption per capita for the period 1984–1988 with the forecasts generated with least squares (denoted OLS) and those from estimated GLS (EGLS). Note that while the EGLS forecasts are an improvement over those generated with OLS, they are still problematic, since they consistently underestimate the values of real per-capita consumption.

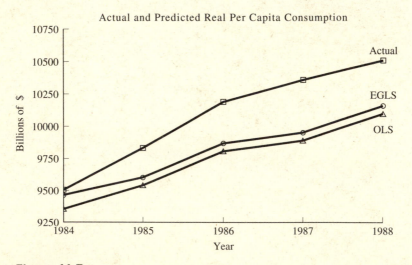

Figure 11.7

KEY TERMS

Autocorrelation

Autocorrelation coefficient

Autocorrelation for lag j

Backshift (backward shift) operator

Box-Pierce Q-Statistic

Breusch-Godfrey test

Characteristic polynomial

Correlogram

Durbin h-statistic

Durbin h-test

Durbin Procedure

Durbin-Watson (DW) statistic

Durbin-Watson test

Estimated generalized least squares (GLS) estimation

First-order autoregressive process

Gaussian white noise

Generalized difference form

Generalized least squares

Generalized least squares (GLS) estimation

Hildreth-Lu procedure

Iterative Cochrane-Orcutt method

Iterative methods

Ljung-Box Q-statistic (LQ)

Markov process

Moving average form

Partial autocorrelation for lag j

Prais-Winsten correction

Pure autocorrelation

Quasi-autocorrelation

Realization

Sample autocorrelation function (SACF)

Sample partial autocorrelation function (SPACF)

Second-order autoregressive process

Stationarity

Stationary stochastic process

Stochastic explanatory variable

Stochastic process

Theoretical autocorrelation function (TACF)

Theoretical partial autocorrelation function (TPACF)

Time series analysis

Two-step Cochrane-Orcutt procedure

Wallis Test of Fourth-Order Autocorrelation

White noise process

EXERCISES

1. This chapter noted that omitting an influential variable can sometimes cause autocorrelated errors. To pursue this point further, assume that an equation incorrectly excludes a dummy variable that has a positive expected sign (there is an upward shift for (say) the second half of the data). Using a graph, illustrate how the omission of this dummy variable can produce serially correlated errors. Do you expect there to be positive or negative autocorrelation? Why?

2. What is the importance of the distinction between pure and quasi-autocorrelation for econometric estimation?

3. What relationship (if any) exists between heteroskedastic errors and the stationarity of the error process for an equation?

4. State the appropriate data transformation, $T = \Theta(B)$, that is needed to perform estimated generalized least squares estimation for each of the error processes below, where v is a white noise error process:

    (a) $\varepsilon_t = \Theta_1 \varepsilon_{t-1} + \Theta_2 \varepsilon_{t-2} + \Theta_3 \varepsilon_{t-3} + \Theta_4 \varepsilon_{t-4} + v_t$.

    (b) $\varepsilon_t = \Theta_1 \varepsilon_{t-1} + \Theta_4 \varepsilon_{t-4} + v_t$.

    (c) $\varepsilon_t = \Theta \varepsilon_{t-1} + v_t$.

    (d) $\varepsilon_t = \Theta \varepsilon_{t-12} + v_t$.

5. Assume that the errors in an equation are second-order autoregressive.

    (a) Contrast the different methods discussed in this chapter for detecting serial correlation for such an equation.

    (b) If the Durbin-Watson test is used to detect serial correlation in this case, what problems are likely to occur?

    (c) If the partial autocorrelation function is used to detect serial correlation here, what specific pattern should exist?

    (d) What is the appropriate transformation that must be applied to the original equation to correct for this second-order serial correlation?

    (e) If estimated generalized least squares estimation of this equation is undertaken based on the transformation given in (d), will the coefficient estimates be unbiased? Explain why or why not.

    (f) What adjustment must be made to $\hat{\alpha}_0$ to obtain an estimate of α_0? Must we also manipulate the standard deviation of $\hat{\alpha}_0$? Its t-statistic?

6. What is an iterative method for estimating serial correlation coefficient(s)? A grid-search method? Compare and contrast the Hildreth-Lu and Cochrane-Orcutt procedures for estimating equations with serially correlated errors.

7. Explain how forecasts can be improved over the usual method (as in Chapter 5) when the errors in an equation are serially correlated. Contrast the method for producing such forecasts for a first-order and second-order autoregressive error process.

8. If the Durbin-Watson test proves to be inconclusive when testing for autocorrelation, what alternatives exist to determine whether serial correlation exists?

12 Problems with the Multiple Regression Model III: Heteroskedasticity

Since detailing multiple regression, we have shown how a number of the multiple regression assumptions can be violated, along with detection and remedial measures should violations exist. Much of this material deals with the set of assumptions made about the errors in the population regression function. In the last chapter we formalized this information, characterizing such "well behaved" errors as a white noise error process, where the mean of this process is constant, the errors are pairwise independent, the error variance is a finite constant, and all of these do not change with time. In that chapter we illustrated how to detect and correct violations of the requirements pertaining to error covariances, assuming that the error terms had a mean of zero and constant variance. In this chapter, we detail the consequences of violating the constant error variance requirement and present a number of possible remedies.

HETEROSKEDASTICITY

In the context of multiple regression analysis, the requirement of a constant error variance implies that all of the conditional error distributions possess the same variance. This property, which is called **homoskedasticity**, is illustrated in Figure 12.1. When the errors in an equation are homoskedastic, the dispersion of individual errors around the population regression function is the same for every observation. If, instead, this dispersion changes for different values of an explanatory variable in an equation, the error dispersion is not constant, and the error terms are **heteroskedastic**. In this case, **heteroskedasticity** is said to exist.

Examples of equations with heteroskedastic errors are not difficult to find. This problem tends to arise more with cross-sectional than time series data. The reason for this can be traced to the nature of cross-sectional data. Since this type of data consists of observations for a single time period, the likelihood of having widely differing values for one or more explanatory variables is greater than with time series

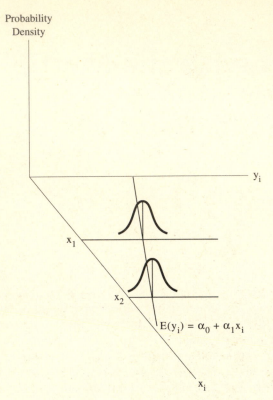

Figure 12.1

data, where observations through time are often of similar magnitudes. Time series heteroskedasticity can arise, however. If, for example, the data span a very long time period, the magnitudes of explanatory variables can differ appreciably. Also, over very long time periods, improvements in the accuracy with which many macroeconomic variables are measured can, ironically, result in heteroskedastic errors. In the discussion that follows, we present· heteroskedasticity entirely within the context of cross-sectional data.

We can illustrate the nature of heteroskedasticity by referring to a bivariate demand function, where the quantity demanded of good x is stochastically related to the price of good x for a cross-section of individuals: $q_{xi} = f(p_{xi}, \varepsilon_i)$. If we assume that nominal income is constant, it is quite possible for this equation to have heteroskedastic errors, where the error variance falls with p_x. When the price of x is low, the range of values for q_x (and thus the dispersion in the errors) will tend to be substantial, since real income is greater the lower the price of a good. As p_x rises, both the willingness and ability to purchase good x will tend to decrease, causing mean quantity demanded to fall. The variance of q_x (and the errors) may well fall, since the willingness to pay for good x is more likely to exceed the ability to pay for this good at high prices (given nominal income). In this situation, the errors in the demand equation are heteroskedastic. As Figure 12.2(a) illustrates, the error variance is a decreasing function of p_x: $\sigma_{\varepsilon i}^2 = g(p_{xi})$.

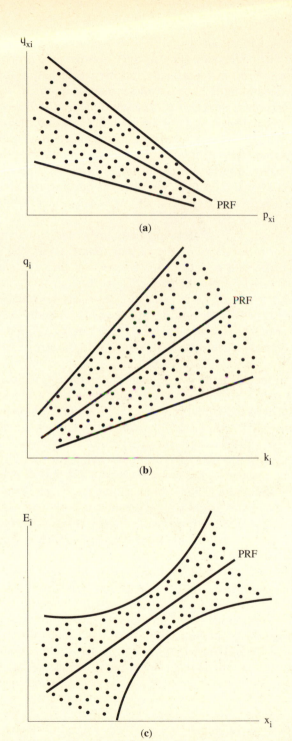

Figure 12.2

Heteroskedastic disturbances can also arise with production functions. If we attempt to estimate a production function (such as the Cobb-Douglas production function) for a cross-section of firms in a particular industry, then output (q) for the ith firm is stochastically related to both labor (L) and capital (k) inputs: $q_i = f(L_i, k_i, \varepsilon_i)$. Included in the error term of this function is the entrepreneurial ability of managers, the different skill levels of employees, and disparities in the ages and efficiencies of the tools, equipment, and factories that are lumped into the single input capital. While factors such as these can be expected to vary among firms of all sizes, the extent to which variation exists will tend to be greater for larger firms. As a result, the errors in this production function will tend to be heteroskedastic, and the error variance will increase with the size of the capital stock: $\sigma_{\varepsilon i}^2 = f(k_i)$. This is illustrated in Figure 12.2(b).

Examples of cross-sectional heteroskedasticity exist for nonmicroeconomic topics as well. Consider an equation for the rate of return (R) on the stocks of a cross-section of firms.[1] The rate of return on the stock of firm i is stochastically related to the profits of that firm (π), the dividends it pays out (DV), and the debt of that firm (D): $R_i = f(\pi_i, \mathrm{DV}_i, D_i, \varepsilon_i)$. If lower dividends are an indication of less stable returns, then the dispersion in returns, and thus their conditional error distributions, will tend to be larger the smaller is DV. The rate of return equation can therefore be expected to display heteroskedastic errors, with the error variance falling for larger values of DV: $\sigma_{\varepsilon i}^2 = f(\mathrm{DV}_i)$.

The final example given here pertains to human capital theory. Mincer has shown that heteroskedasticity can arise with earnings functions.[2] For a cross section of individuals, the earnings of an individual (E_i) are a function of the number of years of completed schooling for this person, S_i, and the amount of labor market experience possessed, X_i: $E_i = f(S_i, X_i, \varepsilon_i)$. The stochastic error in this relationship includes factors such as preferences for particular types of jobs, the willingness to forego current earnings during a training period before being rewarded with higher earnings later, location preferences for jobs, and attitudes about retirement. Given the level of completed schooling, the variances of errors will be greater for both low and high levels of experience, while for intermediate experience levels, the error variance will be smaller. For persons with relatively little job market experience (given S_i), substantial choices exist about the types of jobs one should take and amounts of training to acquire. The dispersion in errors will tend to be large in this experience range, since many different job choices are made, resulting in a substantial variation in earnings at this stage of labor market involvement. Over the middle of the experience spectrum, the earnings of persons who earlier opted for training (at lower initial wages) will more closely approximate the earnings of those who did not, so the observed dispersion in earnings will be smaller than that for the smaller experience level. Finally, when job market experience is substantial, error dispersion becomes larger, as some

---

[1] This example was obtained from H. Folger and S. Ganapathy, *Financial Econometrics* (Englewood Cliffs: Prentice-Hall), 1982, pp. 76–77.

[2] J. Mincer, *Schooling, Experience and Earnings* (New York: National Bureau of Economic Research), 1974.

persons opt to remain at their current location and to forego more lucrative jobs elsewhere, differences in health become more pronounced, and differences in early retirement incentives appear. This example is different from those earlier in that the error variances do not exhibit **monotonic heteroskedasticity**, where they either rise or fall. In this example the variance falls, reaches a minimum, then rises thereafter, as Figure 12.2(c) shows.

When the errors in an equation are heteroskedastic, it is necessary to identify the different error *variances* by including a subscript (i) that denotes the particular cross-sectional observation under consideration. The error variance for observation i is therefore denoted $\sigma_{\varepsilon i}^2$. The set of error assumptions used to evaluate least squares estimators are now:

$$E(\varepsilon_i) = 0; \qquad \text{Cov}(\varepsilon_i, \varepsilon_j) = E(\varepsilon_i \cdot \varepsilon_j) = 0; \qquad \text{Var}(\varepsilon_i) = E(\varepsilon_i^2) = \sigma_{\varepsilon i}^2$$

and ε_i is normally distributed.

The implications of heteroskedasticity for least squares estimation, which we discuss next, parallel those for serial correlation very closely.

EFFECT OF HETEROSKEDASTICITY ON LEAST SQUARES ESTIMATION

Heteroskedasticity affects neither the linearity, unbiasedness nor the consistency of the least squares estimators. Its impact is felt entirely in the efficiency of these estimators. In the presence of heteroskedasticity, the least squares estimators are no longer the minimum variance estimators of the coefficients in the population regression function. Furthermore, both the residual sum of squares and the estimated coefficient variances obtained from canned computer programs are totally inappropriate when the errors in an equation are heteroskedastic.

To show that heteroskedasticity does not affect the unbiasedness of the least squares slope estimator, we use the following bivariate regression equation:

$$y_i = \alpha_0 + \alpha_1 x_i + \varepsilon_i$$

The least squares slope estimator is given by the formula:

$$\hat{\alpha}_1 = \sum x_i' y_i' / \sum x_i'^2$$

where x' and y' denote deviations from means. Substituting for y_i' from the deviation form of the population regression function, we can express the above equation as:

$$\hat{\alpha}_1 = \alpha_1 + \sum x_i' \varepsilon_i' / \sum x_i'^2$$
$$= \alpha_1 + \sum \omega_i \varepsilon_i'$$

again denoting the weight for the ith observation, ω_i, as $\omega_i \equiv x_i' / \sum x_i'^2$ and $\varepsilon_i' \equiv (\varepsilon_i - \hat{\mu}_\varepsilon)$. The mean of the sampling distribution of $\hat{\alpha}_1$ is:

$$E(\hat{\alpha}_1) = \alpha_1 + E(\sum \omega_i \varepsilon_i')$$
$$= \alpha_1 + \sum \omega_i E(\varepsilon_i') \qquad \text{since the } x\text{'s are nonstochastic}$$
$$= \alpha_1$$

since $E(\varepsilon_i') = 0$ even with heteroskedastic errors. Thus *the least squares slope estimator is unbiased when the assumption of homoskedasticity is violated. Just as we saw with serial correlation, the unbiasedness of this estimator depends on the zero expected value of the equation error and the assumption that x is either nonstochastic or uncorrelated with the equation error.* The same conclusions pertain for the intercept estimator.

The variance of the least squares slope estimator, σ_1^2, is obtained from the expression for $\hat{\alpha}_1$ above:

$$\sigma_1^2 = E(\hat{\alpha}_1 - \alpha_1)^2 = E(\textstyle\sum \omega_i \varepsilon_i')^2$$

If we assume that $n = 2$, this expression becomes:

$$\sigma_1^2 = E(\omega_1 \varepsilon_1' + \omega_2 \varepsilon_2')^2$$
$$= E(\omega_1^2 \varepsilon_1'^2 + \omega_2^2 \varepsilon_2'^2 + 2\omega_1 \omega_2 \varepsilon_1' \varepsilon_2')$$
$$= \omega_1^2 E(\varepsilon_1'^2) + \omega_2^2 E(\varepsilon_2'^2) + 2\omega_1 \omega_2 E(\varepsilon_1' \varepsilon_2').$$

Since the errors are not serially correlated, the last term on the right is 0. When heteroskedasticity exists, the expected value of each squared error term differs. Since $E(\varepsilon_i'^2) = \sigma_{\varepsilon i}^2$, the right side of the variance expression is:

$$= \omega_1^2 \sigma_{\varepsilon 1}^2 + \omega_2^2 \sigma_{\varepsilon 2}^2$$
$$\sigma_1^2 = \textstyle\sum \omega_i^2 \sigma_{\varepsilon i}^2$$

Unlike the similar derivation for serially correlated errors, we can no longer factor out the variance terms, since they differ with heteroskedastic errors. No further simplifications are therefore possible. Substituting back into the original expressions for the ω's the variance of $\hat{\alpha}_1$ is:

$$\sigma_1^2 = \textstyle\sum \{x_i' / \textstyle\sum x_i'^2\}^2 \cdot \sigma_{\varepsilon i}^2$$
$$= \textstyle\sum x_i'^2 \sigma_{\varepsilon i}^2 / (\textstyle\sum x_i'^2)^2 \tag{12.1}$$

which is different from the appropriate formula for homoskedastic errors:

$$\sigma_1^2 = \sigma_\varepsilon^2 / \textstyle\sum x_i'^2$$

We can depict the slope variance in a form that allows us to compare it more readily to that with homoskedastic errors. If we denote the variance of an individual error as consisting of two parts—the mean of all error variances ($\hat{\mu}_\sigma$) and a deviation from that mean (Φ_i')—we then have: $\sigma_{\varepsilon i}^2 = \hat{\mu}_\sigma + \Phi_i'$. Substituting this into Equation (12.1) it becomes:

$$\sigma_1^2 = \textstyle\sum x_i'^2 (\hat{\mu}_\sigma + \Phi_i') / (\textstyle\sum x_i'^2)^2$$
$$= \hat{\mu}_\sigma / \textstyle\sum x_i'^2 + \textstyle\sum x_i'^2 \Phi_i' / (\textstyle\sum x_i'^2)^2 \tag{12.2}$$

If we think of $\hat{\mu}_\sigma$ as corresponding to σ_ε^2, then the above expression allows us to decompose the actual variance of $\hat{\alpha}_1$ into the variance that pertains when the errors are homoskedastic plus a term related to the different error variances that arise with heteroskedastic errors. When an equation has heteroskedastic errors, the usual formulas for standard errors and t-statistics are therefore meaningless since they omit the second term on the right of Equation (12.2). This problem is exacerbated when we consider the fact that each estimated coefficient variance uses an estimate of σ_ε^2 in place of its actual value. Kmenta has shown that the usual estimate of the error variance is itself biased.[3] Canned computer programs that fail to account for heteroskedasticity therefore produce biased error sums of squares and coefficient variances. Confidence intervals and hypothesis tests based on such values are therefore also biased. Since the numerator in the second term of Equation (12.2) is related to the covariance between the error variances and x, the direction of bias (for $n > 2$) is opposite in sign to this covariance. Thus when $\sigma_{\varepsilon i}^2$ rises with x, which is often the case with economic data, estimated standard errors will tend to be downwardly biased. As a result, the probability of rejecting true null hypotheses will exceed the selected level of significance.

The loss of efficiency for the least squares estimators results from the weighting scheme implicit in that estimation technique. Recall that least squares estimators are obtained by minimizing the sum of the squared residuals (S): $S = \Sigma \hat{\varepsilon}_i^2 = \Sigma(y_i - \hat{\alpha}_0 - \hat{\alpha}_1 x_i)^2$ with respect to both $\hat{\alpha}_0$ and $\hat{\alpha}_1$ then solving the resulting normal equations to obtain expressions for each estimator. Least squares thus accords each squared residual an equal weight ($= 1$), and each $\hat{\varepsilon}_i$ is assumed to provide equally valid information as to where the population regression function lies. This is valid when the errors are homoskedastic, since then each conditional error distribution has an identical variance. For heteroskedastic errors, however, the conditional error variances rise or fall with different values of the explanatory variable x. In the demand curve example, the error variance falls with p_{xi} (given income). For the production function, $\sigma_{\varepsilon i}^2$ rises with the stock of capital, k_i. This rising error dispersion means that the residuals for "large" values of the explanatory variable will tend to be located increasingly far from the population regression function, causing them to provide less reliable information about its location. Furthermore, the squared values of these "large" residuals will tend to dominate the sum of the squared residuals.

Ideally, we would like our estimation technique to accord such increasingly distant residuals less weight when deriving our estimators than those from smaller variance conditional error distributions that lie closer to the population regression function. Unfortunately, least squares fails to do this, so the inefficiency of this estimation technique, along with the inappropriateness of its residual sum of squares and coefficient variances, remains.

BEST LINEAR UNBIASED ESTIMATION WITH HETEROSKEDASTIC ERRORS

Least squares estimation with heteroskedastic errors still produces linear unbiased estimators, but these are no longer the best linear unbiased estimators of the parameters of the population regression function. The problem arises, as we saw above,

---

[3] J. Kmenta, *Elements of Econometrics* (2nd ed.), (New York: Macmillan Publishing Co., 1986), pp. 254–255.

from the weighting scheme used to derive these estimators. Estimation efficiency can be gained if our technique weights the residuals from lower variance conditional error distributions more heavily than those from distributions with higher variances. This implies a weighting scheme that is inversely related to the variance of the conditional error distribution from which a residual comes.

Best linear unbiased estimators can therefore be obtained by transforming the original equation so that it incorporates this weighting scheme, and at the same time, satisfies all of the model assumptions required for the Gauss-Markov Theorem to apply. The gain in efficiency over least squares results from incorporating the information about the different error variances directly into our estimation technique. This estimation technique is generalized least squares.

Generalized least squares estimation of an equation with heteroskedastic errors entails defining a transformation, T, which, when applied to our original equation: (i) causes each observation to be weighted by a value that is inversely related to the variance of its conditional error distribution; and (ii) results in a homoskedastic error term (as well as a 0 mean error and no serial correlation). For the ith observation, let us assume that the known variance of the error term is:

$$\text{Var}(\varepsilon_i) = E(\varepsilon_i^2) = \sigma_{\varepsilon i}^2$$

Our transformation term must convert the original error into one that is homoskedastic. We thus require that the transformed error, $\varepsilon_i^* = T \cdot \varepsilon_i$, be homoskedastic:

$$\text{Var}(\varepsilon_i^*) = \text{Var}(T \cdot \varepsilon_i) = k^2 \text{ (a constant)}$$

If T is itself nonrandom, then: $\text{Var}(\varepsilon_i^*) = T^2 \cdot \text{Var}(\varepsilon_i)$, which, using the variance assumption above, becomes: $\text{Var}(\varepsilon_i^*) = T^2 \cdot \sigma_{\varepsilon i}^2 = k^2$. Solving for T, the transformation expression is:

$$T = k/\sigma_{\varepsilon i}$$

If, for simplicity, we select $k = 1$, our transformation term is:

$$T = 1/\sigma_{\varepsilon i} \tag{12.3}$$

Using the bivariate regression equation above:

$$y_i = \alpha_0 + \alpha_1 x_i + \varepsilon_i$$

the transformed equation is:

$$T \cdot y_i = T \cdot \alpha_0 + \alpha_1(T \cdot x_i) + T \cdot \varepsilon_i,$$

or

$$y_i^* = \alpha_0 x_{0i}^* + \alpha_1 x_i^* + \varepsilon_i^* \tag{12.4}$$

where $y_i^* = (y_i/\sigma_{\varepsilon i})$; $x_{0i}^* = (1/\sigma_{\varepsilon i})$; $x_i^* = (x_i/\sigma_{\varepsilon i})$; and $\varepsilon_i^* = (\varepsilon_i/\sigma_{\varepsilon i})$. As required, the error in (12.4) weights the original error term by a value that is inversely related to its variance. Note that Equation (12.4) no longer contains an intercept, since the transformation creates a new variable x_0. Consider now the transformed error term:

$$E(\varepsilon_i^*) = E(\varepsilon_i/\sigma_{\varepsilon i})$$
$$= (1/\sigma_{\varepsilon i})E(\varepsilon_i)$$
$$= 0.$$

The transformed error thus retains a 0 mean. It is also not autocorrelated:

$$E(\varepsilon_i^* \cdot \varepsilon_j^*) = E\{(\varepsilon_i/\sigma_{\varepsilon i}) \cdot (\varepsilon_j/\sigma_{\varepsilon j})\}$$
$$= \{1/(\sigma_{\varepsilon i} \cdot \sigma_{\varepsilon j})\} \cdot E(\varepsilon_i \cdot \varepsilon_j)$$
$$= 0$$

since with no serial correlation, $E(\varepsilon_i \cdot \varepsilon_j) = 0$. Finally this error is homoskedastic:

$$\text{Var}(\varepsilon_i^*) = \text{Var}(\varepsilon_i/\sigma_{\varepsilon i})$$
$$= (1/\sigma_{\varepsilon i}^2) \cdot \text{Var}(\varepsilon_i)$$
$$= \sigma_{\varepsilon i}^2/\sigma_{\varepsilon i}^2$$
$$= 1$$

The transformed equation therefore satisfies all of the conditions required for the Gauss-Markov Theorem to apply. Generalized least squares (GLS) estimation of the original equation, which consists of estimating the transformed equation with least squares, therefore provides the best linear unbiased estimators of α_0 and α_1.

Generalized least squares estimation of equations with heteroskedastic errors entails weighting the variables in the original equation. Because of this, it is called **weighted least squares**. As with ordinary least squares, the GLS estimators are obtained by minimizing the sum of squared residuals. The difference is that these residuals are now weighted, based on the appropriate transformation term. For the example above, the weight, ω_i, is $1/\sigma_{\varepsilon i}$, and the weighted residual sum of squares (S_w) is $S_w = \Sigma \hat{\varepsilon}_i^{*2} = \Sigma(\omega_i \hat{\varepsilon}_i)^2$, where the term in brackets is $(\hat{\varepsilon}_i/\sigma_{\varepsilon i})$. Residuals from high variance conditional distributions therefore receive smaller weights than do residuals with smaller variances. The residual sum of squares and coefficient variances produced by generalized least squares are unbiased. Statistical inference and hypothesis testing are not afflicted with the same problems that OLS is.

We will analyze heteroskedasticity by assuming that **multiplicative heteroskedasticity** exists, where the error variance for the ith observation can be expressed in terms of the following multiplicative form:

$$\text{Var}(\varepsilon_i) = \sigma_\varepsilon^2 \cdot \Theta_i \qquad \text{(12.5)}$$

which is the product of a constant (σ_ε^2) and a term Θ_i, that is a function of one or more variables that are not necessarily in our equation. Equation (12.5) postulates heteroskedastic variances that are proportional to Θ, where the constant σ_ε^2 is the factor of proportionality. For our present purposes, we assume that Θ is related to our single included explanatory variable x, so $\Theta = \Theta(x)$. Our transformation term, T, is thus a function of Θ. We desire that the variance of the transformed error,

$\varepsilon_i^* = T \cdot \varepsilon_i$, equals σ_ε^2. But the variance of ε_i^* is:

$$\text{Var}(\varepsilon_i^*) = \text{Var}(T \cdot \varepsilon_i)$$
$$= T^2 \cdot \text{Var}(\varepsilon_i)$$

For this variance to be homoskedastic and equal to σ_ε^2, we seek:

$$T^2 \cdot \text{Var}(\varepsilon_i) = \sigma_\varepsilon^2$$

so that

$$T^2 = \sigma_\varepsilon^2 / \text{Var}(\varepsilon_i)$$

Substituting for the denominator from Equation (12.5), we obtain the expression for T:

$$T^2 = \sigma_\varepsilon^2 / (\sigma_\varepsilon^2 \cdot \Theta_i)$$

and

$$T = 1/\sqrt{\Theta_i} \tag{12.6}$$

The appropriate transformation term is thus the reciprocal of the square root of Θ_i. Note that *the factor of proportionality, σ_ε^2, cancels out in this derivation, so that our transformation term is independent of that value. To model multiplicative heteroskedasticity, it is only necessary to model Θ.*

The most common form utilized for Θ is:

$$\Theta(x) = x_i^2$$

which makes the variance expression:

$$\text{Var}(\varepsilon_i) = \sigma_\varepsilon^2 \cdot x_i^2 \tag{12.7}$$

The appropriate transformation term is then: $T = 1/x_i$. Generalized least squares then consists of estimating the following equation with least squares:

$$(y_i/x_i) = \alpha_0(1/x_i) + \alpha_1 + (\varepsilon_i/x_i), \tag{12.8}$$

or

$$y_i^* = \alpha_1 + \alpha_0 x_i^* + \varepsilon_i^*$$

To estimate this equation it is necessary to create the two new variables, $y_i^* = (y_i/x_i)$ and $x_i^* = (1/x_i)$, then to regress y_i^* on x_i^*. *Note that the intercept in this transformed equation is the coefficient of x, while the intercept in the original equation is the coefficient of x_i^*.*

The transformed variables used with this particular transformation often have economic meaning. Assume, for example, that we are interested in estimating a cross-sectional savings function, where individual observations are countries, the dependent variable is the level of savings (S) for the ith country, and the explanatory variable is GDP for that country. If the error variances are believed to be related to population (POP) (so that $\Theta = \text{POP}_i^2$), the transformed equation is then:

$$(S_i/\text{POP}_i) = \alpha_0(1/\text{POP}_i) + \alpha_1(\text{GDP}_i/\text{POP}_i) + (\varepsilon_i/\text{POP}_i)$$

The dependent variable in this equation is per-capita savings, while the transformed GDP variable measures per-capita GDP. In this example, a variable that was excluded from the original equation was used as the basis for the transformation term.

One must consider whether this is valid, or if POP should have been included in the original equation specification. Situations do arise where y and x are not strongly related, but when using some other variable z (as we did above) to define ratios, y/z is highly correlated with x/z as the result of spurious correlation.[4] It is, however, common practice for many researchers to routinely specify equations such as the one above in per-capita terms. For the current example, this would consist of regressing per-capita savings on per-capita GDP *with an intercept term*.

Several other forms for Θ have been utilized. Two of these will be presented here. The first is: $\Theta_i = x_i$, which is based on the assumption that:

$$\text{Var}(\varepsilon_i) = \sigma_\varepsilon^2 \cdot x_i \qquad (12.9)$$

In this case, $T = 1/\sqrt{x_i}$ and the transformed equation is:

$$(y_i/\sqrt{x_i}) = \alpha_0(1/\sqrt{x_i}) + \alpha_1(\sqrt{x_i}) + (\varepsilon_i/\sqrt{x_i}) \qquad (12.10)$$

In order to estimate this equation, we must regress $(y_i/\sqrt{x_i})$ on $(1/\sqrt{x_i})$ and $\sqrt{x_i}$ *without an intercept*. The coefficient of $(1/\sqrt{x_i})$ provides us with an estimate of the intercept in the original equation, while the coefficient of $\sqrt{x_i}$ gives the estimated slope.

The last form for Θ considered here is: $\Theta_i = E(y_i)^2$. Since $E(y) = \beta_0 + \beta_1 x_i$, this particular assumption for Θ is consistent with:

$$\text{Var}(\varepsilon_i) = \sigma_\varepsilon^2 \cdot (\beta_0 + \beta_1 x_i)^2 \qquad (12.11)$$

The transformation term that pertains is then: $T = 1/(\beta_0 + \beta_1 x_i)$, and the transformed equation estimated to obtain GLS estimates is:

$$(y_i/(\beta_0 + \beta_1 x_i))$$
$$= \alpha_0(1/(\beta_0 + \beta_1 x_i)) + \alpha_1(x_i/(\beta_0 + \beta_1 x_i)) + (\varepsilon_i/(\beta_0 + \beta_1 x_i)) \qquad (12.12)$$

This estimated equation also excludes an intercept. Our estimated intercept is the coefficient of the newly constructed variable $(1/(\beta_0 + \beta_1 x_i))$.

In actual practice, the exact form of heteroskedasticity is not known. Researchers generally relate this unknown variance to the size of one or more variables. Note that *the variables considered need not be restricted to the explanatory variables in the equation being estimated*. For example, the amount of some good exported by a particular country is related to the inputs used to produce that good as well as factor endowment of that country. If we regress exports on a series of inputs, heteroskedasticity may result from differences in the sizes of endowments among countries. One way to allow for this is to postulate that the overall resource endowment of a country, and thus the error variances in the export equation, is related to its GDP, which is not included among the explanatory variables in the export equation.[5]

---

[4] See E. Kuh and J. Meyer, "Correlation and Regression Estimates When the Data Are Ratios," *Econometrica*, October 1955, pp. 400–416.

[5] This example is based on the work of E. Leamer, *Sources of International Comparative Advantage: Theory and Evidence* (Cambridge MA: MIT Press), 1984.

ESTIMATED GENERALIZED LEAST SQUARES ESTIMATION WITH HETEROSKEDASTIC ERRORS

Generalized least squares estimation provides the framework within which best linear unbiased estimators of the coefficients in the population regression function are obtained. However, GLS estimation is only possible when the exact form of heteroskedasticity is known. Since it is usually necessary for us to make assumptions about the specific form of heteroskedasticity, and to estimate one or more parameters of the transformation term utilized to eliminate this problem, our estimation alternative is estimated generalized least squares (EGLS).

The substantial differences between GLS and EGLS estimation with heteroskedastic errors concern the form of the equation we must estimate, the properties of the resulting estimators, and the probability distribution that pertains for statistical inference. Looking at the first of these, EGLS involves applying an estimated transformation term, $\hat{T}$, in place of T. Using the result from the previous section, the general expression involved is: $\hat{T} = 1/\sqrt{\hat{\Theta}}$. We can generalize the appropriate transformation term when Θ consists of x raised to some power γ: $\Theta_i = x_i^\gamma$. Then:

$$\text{Var}(\varepsilon_i) = \sigma_\varepsilon^2 \cdot x_i^\gamma \tag{12.13}$$

so that $T = 1/x_i^{\gamma/2}$, and the transformed equation is:

$$(y_i/x_i^{\gamma/2}) = \alpha_0(1/x_i^{\gamma/2}) + \alpha_1(x_i^{1-\gamma/2}) + (\varepsilon_i/x_i^{\gamma/2}) \tag{12.14}$$

If, for example, $\gamma = 2$, the assumed form of heteroskedasticity is: $\sigma_{\varepsilon i}^2 = \sigma_\varepsilon^2 \cdot x_i^2$; when $\gamma = 1$, $\sigma_{\varepsilon i}^2 = \sigma_\varepsilon^2 \cdot x_i$. Since the value of γ is unknown, we must obtain an estimate, $\hat{\gamma}$, and use this value in place of γ. The form of the above equation we actually estimate is then:

$$(y_i/x_i^{\hat{\gamma}/2}) = \alpha_0(1/x_i^{\hat{\gamma}/2}) + \alpha_1(x_i^{1-\hat{\gamma}/2}) + (\varepsilon_i/x_i^{\hat{\gamma}/2})$$

$$y_i^* = \alpha_0 x_{0i}^* + \alpha_1 x_i^* + \varepsilon_i^* \tag{12.15}$$

Note that if the actual value of γ is 1.0 or 2.0, our estimate is likely to differ from this value as the result of sampling error, although on average, we would obtain the correct values if our method of estimation is unbiased. If the assumed form of heteroskedasticity is $\sigma_{\varepsilon i}^2 = \sigma_\varepsilon^2 \cdot E(y_i)$, our estimate of $E(y_i)$ is $\hat{\alpha}_0 + \hat{\alpha}_1 x_i$, which equals $\hat{y}_i$.

In either of the above cases, the estimated value for Θ is a random variable. This affects the properties of the EGLS estimators. When we use an estimated value for either γ or $E(y_i)$ to derive the weighted variables used in the estimation process, we now have a regression equation with stochastic regressors. The exception to this occurs when we use either $1/x_i$ or $1/\sqrt{x_i}$ as our weighting term without estimating these values, and the variable x is fixed in repeated samples. Then, x_i^* is nonstochastic.

When we utilize one or more stochastic explanatory variables, the estimated generalized least squares estimators are no longer linear. This occurs because it is not possible to express each estimator as a linear function of the y values *with fixed weights*. If we consider a transformed equation with an intercept (not a variable x_{0i}) and a single explanatory variable, x_i^*, the EGLS slope estimator is:

$$\hat{\alpha}_1 = \sum x_i^{*'} y_i^{*} / (\sum x_i^{*'})^2 \tag{12.16}$$

By defining the "weight" for an observation i as $\omega_i^* \equiv x_i^{*'} / (\Sigma x_i^{*'})^2$ (this is not the same as the weight involving $\hat{y}$), this estimator can be expressed as:

$$\hat{\alpha}_1 = \sum \omega_i^* y_i^*$$

If these weights were constants, then the EGLS estimator of α_1 would indeed be a linear estimator. However, since ω_i^* is a function of $\hat{y}$ which is stochastic, these weights are themselves stochastic, violating the requirement of constant weights for linearity to pertain.

The EGLS estimators are also biased. Using Equation (12.16) above, by substituting for y_i^* from the population regression function, we have:

$$\hat{\alpha}_1 = \alpha_1 + \sum x_i^{*'} \varepsilon_i^* / (\sum x_i^{*'})^2$$

This estimator is unbiased only if the expected value of the term on the right is 0. However, both x_i^* and ε_i^* are random variables. Because of this, we can no longer move the term $x_i^{*'} / (\Sigma x_i^{*'})^2$ outside of the expectation operator, making its expected value: $\Sigma \omega_i^* E(\varepsilon_i^*)$, which has an expectation of zero. The expected value of this term is therefore in the nature of $E(A \cdot B)$, with $A = \omega_i^*$, and $B = \varepsilon_i^*$. Recall from Chapter 2 that if A and B are independent random variables, then $E(A \cdot B) = E(A) \cdot E(B)$. In the present context, if ω_i^* is independent of ε_i^*, the EGLS estimator will be unbiased, because this expression reduces to $E(\omega_i^*) \cdot E(\varepsilon_i^*)$, which equals 0 since $E(\varepsilon_i^*) = 0$. Unfortunately, this is not the case. Since $x_i^{*'}$ (and thus ω_i^*) is a function of $\hat{y}$, which itself depends on ε_i^*, the estimated generalized least squares estimator $\hat{\alpha}_1$ is biased. However, the EGLS estimator of α_1 is consistent. For large samples, the estimated generalized least squares estimator is also efficient. *The desirable properties attained by the EGLS estimators for heteroskedastic equations therefore pertain only for large samples: consistency and asymptotic efficiency.*

Because the EGLS estimators possess only large sample properties, the t-distribution is no longer valid for calculating confidence intervals and performing hypothesis tests. The equation errors are still normally distributed, but the EGLS estimators of $\hat{\alpha}_0$ and $\hat{\alpha}_1$ are no longer linear functions of these errors, which is required for the t-distribution to pertain. Statistical inference and hypothesis testing can still be performed. Now it is necessary to utilize the asymptotic, or large sample probability distribution that applies to the original t-distributed random variables. As sample size rises, the t-distribution random variable $[\hat{\alpha}_i - E(\hat{\alpha}_i)]/\hat{\sigma}_i (i = 1, 2)$ tends toward the unit normal distribution. The t-statistics calculated by canned statistical programs are therefore asymptotically normally distributed, so the rule of thumb values for the normal distribution can be used to determine statistical significance.

DETECTION OF HETEROSKEDASTICITY

A number of methods exist for detecting heteroskedasticity. Since the actual errors from an equation are not observed, the detection of heteroskedastic errors must be based on the residuals obtained from least squares estimation of the relationship under study.

We will use the data in Table 12.1 to illustrate the detection and correction of heteroskedasticity. The data in this table are the values of shipments (s), employment (N), and new capital expenditures (E) for 39 four-digit SICs (Standard Industrial Classifications) in 1977. The SICs included encompass the classifications "Machinery Except Electrical" (the 35's) and "Electric and Electronic Equipment" (the 36's). The basis for the population regression function that uses these data is: $s_i = f(N_i, E_i, \varepsilon_i)$, where i pertains to a four-digit SIC. The variable E, new capital expenditure, is a proxy for the stock of capital. The expected signs of both N and E are positive (explain the basis for these signs). Utilizing a linear specification for this relationship, the sample regression function is:

$$\hat{s}_i = 294.6 + 34.4N_i + 9.6E_i \qquad \bar{R}^2 = 0.915 \quad \hat{\sigma}_\varepsilon = 1025.2 \quad n = 39 \quad F = 205.2$$
$$\quad (1.2) \quad\;\; (6.7) \qquad (4.5)$$

Both partial slopes display positive expected signs and are statistically significant at the 1 percent level and above. The intercept is not significant. Finally, both the adjusted R^2 and F-statistic indicate that the sample regression function fits the data well. Using this information, we now discuss how to determine: (i) whether the errors in this function are heteroskedastic; and (ii) if so, whether they are related to N, E, or both of these variables.

The most obvious method for detecting heteroskedastic errors, which is considered first, consists of visually inspecting graphs of different pairs of variables associated with the equation of interest. For a single explanatory variable, a scatter diagram of y versus x can potentially reveal heteroskedastic errors, if the dispersion in y changes for the different values of x. A scatter diagram or plot of the residuals from the regression of y on x is also useful. Changes in the dispersion of the residuals provides an indication of the possibility of heteroskedastic errors. When there are several explanatory variables, this procedure becomes more complicated. First of all, it is not always obvious which variable, if any, is causing heteroskedasticity. A separate scatter diagram of y with each explanatory variable will often be needed. Also, heteroskedasticity might be associated with more than one explanatory variable (related to $E(y)$, for example). If this is the case, a scatter diagram of $\hat{\varepsilon}$ and $\hat{y}$ may well be useful. In either case, the method of visually inspecting data can be deceptive, leading one to a false conclusion as the result of sample data variation that either gives or fails to provide the appearance of heteroskedastic errors.

Figures 12.3(a) and (b) illustrate scatter diagrams of the value of shipments and each of the explanatory variables in the shipments equation presented above. The scatter diagram in Figure 12.3(a), which contrasts shipments with employment, contains some evidence of heteroskedasticity, although the dispersion in shipments values does not appear to change that appreciably. The same is not true for the scatter diagram of shipments and new capital expenditures (Figure 12.3(b)). As capital

Table 12.1 The Value of Shipments, Employment, and New Capital Expenditures for Selected SICs in 1977

SIC	VALUE OF SHIPMENTS (MIL $)	NUMBER OF EMPLOYEES (THOUSANDS)	NEW CAPITAL EXPENDITURES (MIL $)
3633	1,793	19	27
3524	1,575	20	29
3644	1,422	26	33
3535	1,898	33	35
3631	1,707	25	36
3641	1,651	29	37
3564	1,431	28	38
3678	1,105	26	40
3511	2,730	41	44
3551	1,787	36	47
3632	2,577	36	47
3555	1,351	26	47
3634	2,531	47	48
3671	1,582	37	53
3643	1,795	44	56
3563	2,076	32	56
3622	2,511	55	58
3693	1,885	31	63
3612	2,209	43	67
3532	1,997	31	67
3613	3,563	72	74
3545	2,385	54	77
3541	2,819	60	82
3651	5,732	75	106
3579	2,720	42	112
3691	1,983	26	122
3561	3,774	63	124
3562	2,567	51	133
3694	3,647	64	146
3621	4,463	97	163
3544	3,901	106	176
3661	7,858	124	217
3585	9,638	139	233
3533	3,912	59	258
3523	10,282	131	342
3674	5,327	114	409
3662	14,886	334	471
3531	12,629	155	498
3573	12,924	193	652

(Source: *Statistical Abstract of the United States, 1985.*)

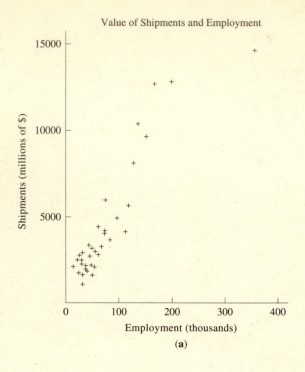

(a)

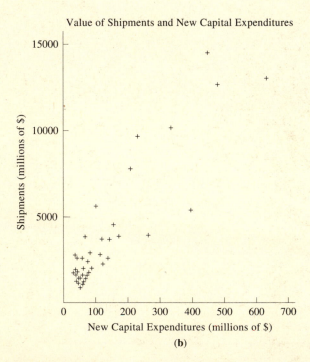

(b)

Figure 12.3

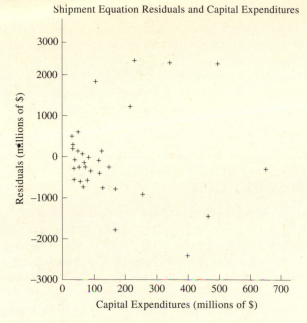

Shipment Equation Residuals and Capital Expenditures

Figure 12.4

expenditures rise above $200 million, the dispersion in shipments clearly increases. Figure 12.4 is a scatter diagram of the residuals from the shipments regression equation and new capital expenditures. Again, the likelihood of heteroskedastic errors is evident. This is even more apparent in Figure 12.5, where the bottom graph plots the

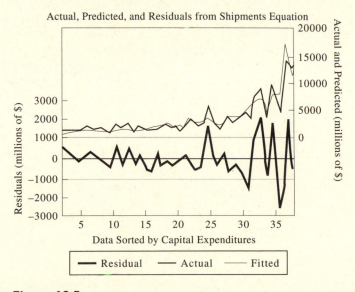

Actual, Predicted, and Residuals from Shipments Equation

Figure 12.5

residuals (their scale is on the left axis) against sorted capital expenditures (in terms of increasing magnitudes). Notice how the residual variance increases starting with the twenty-third observation. Visual evidence clearly supports the existence of heteroskedastic errors in this equation.

Visual inspection methods can provide false signals as to whether heteroskedasticity exists. Statistical tests are therefore the preferred method of detecting heteroskedasticity since they provide us with an objective (but not foolproof) framework within which we can proceed.

STATISTICAL TESTS FOR THE PRESENCE OF HETEROSKEDASTICITY

Four statistical tests for detecting heteroskedasticity will be outlined here. The first of these, the Goldfeld-Quandt Test, is valid for either "small" or "large" samples, meaning it is not merely a large-sample, or asymptotic test. The next test that is outlined, the Park and Glejser tests, actually consists of two separate methodologies for using the least squares residuals as the basis for estimating possible forms of heteroskedasticity. The remaining tests, the Breusch-Pagan Test and the White Test, are asymptotic, so that they are, strictly speaking, valid only as sample size approaches infinity.

The Goldfeld-Quandt Test

The **Goldfeld-Quandt Test** is probably the most well known test for heteroskedasticity.[6] Assuming that we can identify the "problem" variable which is causing heteroskedastic errors, and that the pattern of heteroskedasticity consists of either continuously rising or falling error variances, this test determines whether the difference in the error variances estimated from two different parts of the sample is statistically significant. The null hypothesis for this test is homoskedastic errors: $H_0: \sigma_{\varepsilon i}^2 = \sigma_\varepsilon^2$ ($i = 1, 2, \ldots, n$), while the alternative hypothesis postulates heteroskedasticity *with continually rising error variances*. If the null hypothesis is true, the error variances are identical for all data points. If we break the sample into two parts and estimate separate error variances, the differences in these values should result entirely from sampling error. The steps involved in this test are:

1. Identify the "problem" explanatory variable thought to be causing heteroskedasticity. *Sort the data set so that the error variance increases with this variable.* If, for example, x is the key variable, and $\sigma_{\varepsilon i}^2$ is thought to increase with x, sort the data set so that the first observation corresponds to the smallest x, and the last observation pertains to the largest x. If, instead, the error variance is inversely related to x, sort the data set so that the first observation is the largest x value, and so on.

---

[6] S. Goldfeld and R. Quandt, "Some Tests for Homoskedasticity," *Journal of the American Statistical Association* 60 (1965), pp. 539–547.

2. Divide the overall sample into two subsamples, omitting anywhere from one-sixth to one-third of the observations *from the middle of the data set*. The resulting subsamples will have n_1 and n_2 observations, respectively, where n_1 corresponds to the initial set of observations (with a smaller error variance), and n_2 to the larger error variances. It is necessary that the number of coefficients in our regression equation (k) be less than either n_1 or n_2.

3. Estimate separate regressions for each subsample, and obtain the residual sum of squares (ESS) from these equations. We will denote these ESS$_1$ (for the smaller error variance observations) and ESS$_2$ (for the larger variances). If the errors from the original equation are normally distributed, the quantity:

$$\text{ESS}_i/\sigma_{\varepsilon i}^2 \qquad (i = 1, 2)$$

follows the chi-square distribution with $(n_i - k)$ degrees of freedom. By performing two separate regressions, we have obtained two such independent random variables. Omitting the central observations accentuates their differences.

4. The test statistic for the Goldfeld-Quandt Test is obtained by taking the ratio of the two independent chi-square random variables above, dividing each by its degrees of freedom. The ratio:

$$\frac{(\text{ESS}_2/\sigma_{\varepsilon 2}^2)/(n_2 - k)}{(\text{ESS}_1/\sigma_{\varepsilon 1}^2)/(n_1 - k)}$$

follows the F-distribution with $(n_2 - k)$ degrees of freedom in the numerator and $(n_1 - k)$ in the denominator. If the null hypothesis of homoskedasticity is true, $\sigma_{\varepsilon 1}^2 = \sigma_{\varepsilon 2}^2$, which reduces the test statistic above to:

$$\frac{\text{ESS}_2/(n_2 - k)}{\text{ESS}_1/(n_1 - k)} = \frac{\hat{\sigma}_2^2}{\hat{\sigma}_1^2} \sim F_{(n_2 - k, n_1 - k)}$$

We then expect the value of this test statistic to be approximately equal to 1. If this test statistic exceeds the critical F-value for $(n_2 - k)$ and $(n_1 - k)$ degrees of freedom in the numerator and denominator, respectively, for the selected level of significance, we reject the null hypothesis of homoskedasticity.

The shipments equation was tested for heteroskedasticity using the Goldfeld-Quandt Test. The data were sorted according to the values of new capital expenditures (this was judged to be the problematic variable based on Figures 12.3 and 12.4). In the first step of this test, the sample was broken into three subsamples: observations 1–15, the middle 9 observations, and observations 25–39. Separate regressions were run for observations 1–15, which produced ESS$_1$ = 31,583,709, and observations 25–39, from which we obtained ESS$_2$ = 1,266,588. Our test statistic is:

$$\frac{31,583,709/(15 - 3)}{1,266,588/(15 - 3)} = 24.9$$

The critical F-value with 12 degrees of freedom in both the numerator and denominator is 4.16 for the 1 percent significance level, and 2.69 for the 5 percent level. Since the value of our test statistic exceeds both of these critical values, we are able to reject the null hypothesis of homoskedastic errors. The likelihood of observing this large a difference in estimated error variances if the null hypothesis is true is therefore less than 1 percent. *Since we have concluded that heteroskedastic errors exist, we can no longer be confident that the explanatory variables in this equation, which least squares indicated were statistically significant, are in fact significant. Caution must also be exercised regarding the validity of* $\hat{\sigma}_{\varepsilon}^2$.

The Park and Glejser Tests

The Goldfeld-Quandt Test is useful in detecting heteroskedasticity, but it fails to provide us with information about the specific form of the error variances. The tests proposed by Park and Glejser can be used to both detect the presence of heteroskedasticity and approximate its form. The **Park test** assumes multiplicative heteroskedasticity similar to Equation (12.13)[7]:

$$\sigma_{\varepsilon i}^2 = \sigma_{\varepsilon}^2 x_i^{\gamma} e^{v_i} \quad \bullet \tag{12.17}$$

The coefficient γ provides critical information about the form of heteroskedasticity that can be used to define estimated weights. Since Equation (12.17) is multiplicative, it can be linearized by a logarithmic transformation:

$$\ln(\sigma_{\varepsilon i}^2) = \ln(\sigma_{\varepsilon}^2) + \gamma \ln(x_i) + v_i$$

which becomes:

$$\ln(\sigma_{\varepsilon i}^2) = \beta_0 + \gamma \ln(x_i) + v_i \tag{12.18}$$

where $\beta_0 = \ln(\sigma_{\varepsilon}^2)$. Equation (12.18) is amenable to least squares estimation, except for the fact that $\sigma_{\varepsilon i}^2$, which is part of the dependent variable, is unknown. We can overcome this obstacle using the fact that in the present context, $E(\varepsilon_i^2) = \sigma_{\varepsilon i}^2$. We do not know ε_i^2, but we can use the least squares residuals of the original equation to approximate this value: $\hat{\varepsilon}_i^2$. Making this substitution, the estimable form of Equation (12.18) used for the Park test is:

$$\ln(\hat{\varepsilon}_i^2) = \beta_0 + \gamma \ln(x_i) + v_i \tag{12.19}$$

When $\gamma = 0$, homoskedastic errors exist. If γ in this equation is nonzero, heteroskedasticity is present. This information is the statistical basis of Park's test for heteroskedasticity. The null hypothesis for this test states that the errors in our original equation are homoskedastic: $H_0: \gamma = 0$. The alternative hypothesis postulates heteroskedastic errors: $H_a: \gamma \neq 0$. The test of these hypotheses is a t-test on the estimated coefficient of γ. The steps involved in the Park test are:

1. Estimate the original equation $y_i = \alpha_0 + \alpha_1 x_i + \alpha_2 z_i + \varepsilon_i$, with least squares, and obtain the residuals, $\hat{\varepsilon}_i$.

---

[7] R. Park, "Estimation with Heteroskedastic Error Terms," *Econometrica* 34 (October 1966), p. 888.

2. Calculate the squared residuals, $\hat{\varepsilon}_i^2$, and two other variables: the natural logarithm of $\hat{\varepsilon}_i^2$, $\ln(\hat{\varepsilon}_i^2)$, and the logarithm of the explanatory variable suspected of being involved in Equation (12.17), $\ln(x_i)$.
3. Use these newly created variables to estimate Equation (12.19), and perform a t-test of the coefficient $\hat{\gamma}$. If $\hat{\gamma}$ is statistically significant, reject the null hypothesis of homoskedastic errors, and conclude that heteroskedasticity exists.

If we conclude that our original equation has heteroskedastic errors, we can use $\hat{\gamma}$ to construct an expression for the error variances: $\sigma_{\varepsilon i}^2 = \sigma_{\varepsilon}^2 x_i^{\hat{\gamma}}$. Our estimated transformation term is then: $\hat{T} = 1/x_i^{\hat{\gamma}/2}$.

We will illustrate this test using the new shipments equation above. The residuals from that equation were used to estimate Equation (12.19) with new capital expenditures as the problematic explanatory variable. The results are:

$$\widehat{\ln(\varepsilon_i^2)} = 3.99 + 1.69 \ln(E_i) \qquad \bar{R}^2 = 0.251 \quad n = 39 \quad F = 13.8$$
$$\phantom{\widehat{\ln(\varepsilon_i^2)} = } (1.9) \quad (3.7)$$

The estimate of γ from this equation, 1.69, is statistically significant at the 1 percent level and above. We are therefore able to reject the null hypothesis of homoskedastic errors in the new shipments equation with the Park test. The estimated error variance that results from this test is: $\sigma_{\varepsilon i}^2 = \sigma_{\varepsilon}^2 E_i^{1.69}$, which gives $\hat{T} = 1/E_i^{0.845}$ as our estimate of the transformation term.

A similar test exists that does not require multiplicative heteroskedasticity, but instead assumes **additive heteroskedasticity**. The **Glejser Test** tests for heteroskedasticity by regressing least squares residuals on different possible specifications involving the explanatory variable thought to be related to $\sigma_{\varepsilon i}^2$.[8] The residuals themselves are not used in this regression, however, since the one of the least squares normal equations is: $\Sigma x_i \hat{\varepsilon}_i = 0$. It is therefore not possible to fit a regression of $\hat{\varepsilon}_i$ on x_i. To overcome this, the Glejser test uses the absolute values of the residuals, $|\hat{\varepsilon}_i|$, as the dependent variable. The recommended regressions for this test are:

$$|\hat{\varepsilon}_i| = \gamma_0 + \gamma_1 x_i + v_i \tag{12.20a}$$

$$|\hat{\varepsilon}_i| = \gamma_0 + \gamma_1 (1/x_i) + v_i \tag{12.20b}$$

$$|\hat{\varepsilon}_i| = \gamma_0 + \gamma_1 \sqrt{x_i} + v_i \tag{12.20c}$$

Heteroskedasticity is present when $\gamma_1 \neq 0$. If heteroskedasticity exists, it can also involve γ_0. The Glejser test therefore involves t-tests of *both* of the coefficients in Equations (12.20a,b,c). This test is performed in the following way:

1. Estimate the original equation: $y_i = \alpha_0 + \alpha_1 x_i + \alpha_2 z_i + \varepsilon_i$ with least squares, and obtain the residuals, $\hat{\varepsilon}_i$.
2. Create the three new variables: $|\hat{\varepsilon}_i|$, $(1/x_i)$, and $\sqrt{x_i}$. Estimate Equations (12.20a)–(12.20c) with least squares. Select the equation with the highest $\bar{R}^2$ and lowest standard error as the best representation of heteroskedasticity.

[8] H. Glejser, "A New Test for Heteroskedasticity," *Journal of the American Statistical Association* 64 (1969), 316–323.

3. Using the preferred equation from step (2), perform t-tests on $\hat{\gamma}_0$ and $\hat{\gamma}_1$. If only $\hat{\gamma}_1$ is statistically significant, we reject the null hypothesis of homoskedasticity, and conclude that heteroskedastic errors are present. Our estimated error variance is then: $\text{Var}(\varepsilon_i) = \hat{\gamma}_1^2 \{f(x_i)\}^2$, where $f(x_i)$ is either x_i, $(1/x_i)$, or $\sqrt{x_i}$, and the estimated transformation term is: $\hat{T} = 1/f(x_i)$. If, for example, the preferred equation is (12.20a), our estimate of the error variance is: $\text{Var}(\varepsilon_i) = \hat{\gamma}_1^2 x_i^2$, and our estimated transformation term is: $\hat{T} = 1/x_i$. If both $\hat{\gamma}_0$ and $\hat{\gamma}_1$ are statistically significant when Equation (12.20a) is estimated, we reject the null hypothesis of homoskedasticity and obtain as our estimate of the error variance: $\text{Var}(\varepsilon_i) = (\gamma_0 + \gamma_1 x_i)^2$, which makes our estimated transformation: $\hat{T} = 1/(\hat{\gamma}_0 + \hat{\gamma}_1 x_i)$.

The Glejser test was performed on the new shipments equation, with new capital expenditure as the problematic variable. Each of the specifications in Equation (12.20) were estimated. The results are:

$$|\hat{\varepsilon}_i| = 247.2 + 3.0 E_i \qquad\qquad \bar{R}^2 = 0.344 \quad \hat{\sigma}_v = 601.7 \quad F = 20.9$$
$$\phantom{|\hat{\varepsilon}_i| = 2}(1.9) \quad\;\; (4.6)$$

$$|\hat{\varepsilon}_i| = 1296.3 - 42579.0(1/E_i) \qquad \bar{R}^2 = 0.302 \quad \hat{\sigma}_v = 620.6 \quad F = 17.4$$
$$\phantom{|\hat{\varepsilon}_i| = 1}(7.1) \qquad\;\; (4.2)$$

$$|\hat{\varepsilon}_i| = -318.6 + 93.2\sqrt{E_i} \qquad\quad \bar{R}^2 = 0.417 \quad \hat{\sigma}_v = 567.1 \quad F = 28.2$$
$$\phantom{|\hat{\varepsilon}_i| = }(1.6) \qquad (5.3)$$

Based on the measures of overall equation performance, the third equation provides the best fit. In that equation, the intercept is not statistically significant, while the slope term is significant. We are therefore able to reject the null hypothesis of homoskedasticity in the new shipments equation. The estimated error variance expression from the Glejser test is $\sigma_{\varepsilon i}^2 = (93.2)^2 \cdot E_i$, and the appropriate transformation term is: $\hat{T} = 1/\sqrt{E_i}$.

The Park and Glejser tests are fairly straightforward to perform. If heteroskedastic errors are detected, each provides information about the specific form of the error variance. In spite of their simplicity, several problems exist with these tests. Goldfeld and Quandt have shown that the errors in both the Park and Glejser tests are themselves heteroskedastic.[9] This is a potentially serious complication since the means by which they detect heteroskedasticity, t-tests on specific coefficients, is unreliable due to the biased coefficient variances caused by heteroskedasticity. In addition to this, the residuals from the Glejser test have a nonzero mean and are serially correlated.[10] Glejser has found that when the functions given by the equations in (12.20) are used as the basis for modeling heteroskedasticity, his methodology provides satisfactory estimates when the sample size utilized is large. Both the Park and

---

[9] S. Goldfeld and R. Quandt, *Nonlinear Methods in Econometrics* (Amsterdam: North Holland, 1972), Ch. 3.

[10] Goldfeld and Quandt.

Glejser tests should therefore be used cautiously with their results serving to provide insights into the likely pattern of heteroskedasticity.

The Breusch-Pagan Test

The final two tests outlined here are large sample, or asymptotic tests for heteroskedasticity. The first of these is the **Breusch-Pagan test**.[11] This test assumes that the errors in the original equation are normally distributed with 0 mean, there is no serial correlation, and the error variance can be expressed as:

$$\sigma_{\varepsilon i}^2 = f(\gamma_0 + \gamma_1 v_1 + \cdots + \gamma_k v_k), \tag{12.21}$$

where the v's are a set of variables believed to be related to the heteroskedastic errors. The specific form of $f(\cdot)$ need not be expressed explicitly to perform this test. It is only necessary to specify the variable(s) that we believe are related to the heteroskedasticity problem. Possible choices include variables from our original equation as well as other variables which were omitted. The null hypothesis for the Breusch-Pagan test states that the errors in our original equation are homoskedastic, which can be stated: $H_0: \gamma_1 = \gamma_2 = \cdots \gamma_k = 0$. If the null hypothesis is true, $\sigma_{\varepsilon i}^2 = f(\gamma_0)$, which indicates homoskedastic errors, since γ_0 is a constant. The steps involved in this test are:

1. Estimate the equation of interest: $y_i = \alpha_0 + \alpha_1 x_i + \alpha_2 z_i + \varepsilon_i$ by least squares and obtain the residuals, $\hat{\varepsilon}_i$.
2. Using these residuals, calculate the quantity $\hat{\sigma}^2 = \Sigma \hat{\varepsilon}_i^2 / n$ (note that this is *not* the same as $\hat{\sigma}_\varepsilon^2$, which uses the number of degrees of freedom as its denominator) and the variable that serves as the dependent variable in the second regression, $(\hat{\varepsilon}_i^2 / \hat{\sigma}^2)$.
3. Specify the variable(s) thought to be associated with the heteroskedastic errors. If $v_1 = x_i$ and $v_2 = z_i$, we perform the following regression:

$$(\hat{\varepsilon}_i^2 / \hat{\sigma}^2) = \gamma_0 + \gamma_1 x_i + \gamma_2 z_i + v_i \tag{12.22}$$

and obtain the regression (explained) sum of squares, RSS, which can be calculated from the equation: RSS = TSS − ESS, where TSS is the total sum of squares, $\Sigma(y_i - \hat{\mu}_y)^2$, and ESS is the sum of squared residuals. If the errors from the original equation are normally distributed, then, when the null hypothesis is true, the quantity RSS/2 follows the chi-square distribution as n approaches infinity with degrees of freedom equal to the number of slope coefficients in Equation (12.22). If the value of our test statistic, RSS/2, exceeds the critical chi-square value for the appropriate degrees of freedom and selected level of significance, we reject the null hypothesis of homoskedastic errors.

---

[11] T. Breusch and A. Pagan, "A Simple Test for Heteroskedasticity and Random Coefficient Variation," *Econometrica* 47 (1979), 1287–1294.

The Breusch-Pagan test was performed on the shipments equation using new capital expenditure as the single variable included in step (3): $v_i = E_i$. The regression equation: $(\hat{\varepsilon}_i^2 / \hat{\sigma}^2) = \gamma_0 + \gamma_1 E_i + v_i$ has as its regression sum of squares 48.5. The test statistic is therefore: $48.5/2 = 24.25$. The critical chi-square value for the 1 percent level of significance with 1 degree of freedom is 6.63. Since the value of our test statistic exceeds this critical value, we are able to reject the null hypothesis of homoskedasticity with the Breusch-Pagan test.

White's Test for Heteroskedasticity

One caveat is associated with the Breusch-Pagan test: it is highly dependent on the normal distribution of the error terms in the original regression equation. When these errors depart from normality, the effectiveness of the Breusch-Pagan test falls. **White's test for heteroskedasticity** is also an asymptotic test, but, unlike the Breusch-Pagan test, it utilizes a specific form for $\sigma_{\varepsilon i}^2$, and it is not closely tied to the normal distribution of the errors in the original equation.[12] To perform White's test:

1. Estimate the original equation, $y_i = \alpha_0 + \alpha_1 x_i + \alpha_2 z_i + \varepsilon_i$ with least squares, obtain the residuals, $\hat{\varepsilon}_i$, and create a new variable equal to the squared residuals, $\hat{\varepsilon}_i^2$.
2. Using $\hat{\varepsilon}_i^2$ as a proxy variable for $\sigma_{\varepsilon i}^2$, estimate the regression:

$$\hat{\varepsilon}_i^2 = \gamma_0 + \gamma_1 x_i + \gamma_2 z_i + \gamma_3 x_i^2 + \gamma_4 z_i^2 + \gamma_5 (x_i \cdot z_i) + v_i \qquad \textbf{(12.23)}$$

and use the sample size, n, and the *unadjusted* coefficient of multiple determination, R^2, to construct the test statistic for this test: $n \cdot R^2$. If the null hypothesis is true, then as n approaches infinity, $n \cdot R^2$ follows the chi-square distribution with 5 degrees of freedom. If the value of this test statistic exceeds the critical chi-square value with 5 degrees of freedom for the selected level of significance, we reject the null hypothesis of homoskedasticity.

Note that if the original equation contains a dummy variable (D), the regression in step (2) cannot be run with both D and D^2 included, since this will result in perfect multicollinearity. In this situation only the dummy variable itself should enter step (2).

The degrees of freedom for this test coincide with the number of partial slope coefficients in Equation (12.23). If the original equation contains only one explanatory variable, the estimation of Equation (12.23) entails regressing $\hat{\varepsilon}_i^2$ on x_i and x_i^2, and there are 2 degrees of freedom. For three explanatory variables, $\hat{\varepsilon}_i^2$ is regressed on (say) $x_1, x_2, x_3, x_1^2, x_2^2, x_3^2, x_1 \cdot x_2, x_1 \cdot x_3$, and $x_2 \cdot x_3$. It should be apparent that with a large number of explanatory variables, there may not be enough degrees of freedom to estimate Equation (12.23). When this occurs, the linear terms may be omitted, but the squared and interaction variables should be retained.

---

[12] H. White, "A Heteroskedasticity-Consistent Covariance Matrix and a Direct Test for Heteroskedasticity," *Econometrica* 48 (1980), 817–838.

The shipments equation was examined for heteroskedasticity using White's test. In the version of Equation (12.23) that was estimated, x_i is the SIC employment level, and z_i corresponds to new capital expenditure. Using 39 observations (n), the coefficient of determination was 0.579. The value of the test statistic for the White test is therefore: $39(0.579) = 22.6$. The critical chi-square value with 5 degrees of freedom for the 1 percent level of significance is 15.1. We are therefore able to reject the null hypothesis of homoskedasticity with the White test.

ESTIMATION WITH HETEROSKEDASTIC ERRORS

When the errors in an equation are heteroskedastic, the least squares estimators are not best linear unbiased estimators. They are, however, unbiased. The two most troublesome aspects of least squares estimation, coefficients that are not the minimum variance estimators, and estimated coefficient variances that are biased, severely limit our ability to perform hypothesis tests and to construct confidence intervals. White has provided the basis for alleviating the second of these problems with statistical inference by developing consistent estimators of the variances of the least squares coefficients.[13] This feature is now incorporated into a number of canned statistical programs. When estimating an equation with least squares, such programs will, unless otherwise instructed, use formulas that presuppose a constant error variance to calculate coefficient variances. For the bivariate regression $y_i = \alpha_0 + \alpha_1 x_i + \varepsilon_i$, the estimated slope variance they use is:

$$\mathrm{Var}(\hat{\alpha}_1) = \hat{\sigma}_\varepsilon^2 / \sum x_i'^2$$

We saw earlier that this is a biased estimator of σ_1^2. The correct formula for this variance is given by Equation (12.1):

$$\sigma_1^2 = \sum x_i'^2 \sigma_{\varepsilon i}^2 / (\sum x_i'^2)^2$$

White's heteroskedasticity consistent variance estimator has this formula as its basis. It replaces the unknown error variances, $\sigma_{\varepsilon i}^2$, with the squared residuals, $\hat{\varepsilon}_i^2$. The formula for White's variance estimator is thus:

$$\hat{\sigma}_1^2 = \sum x_i'^2 \hat{\varepsilon}_i^2 / (\sum x_i'^2)^2 \tag{12.24}$$

If the standard deviation of Equation (12.24) is utilized to perform hypothesis tests and to construct confidence intervals for $\hat{\alpha}_1$, the resulting expressions will be correct asymptotically.

The use of this variance estimator does not alleviate the first concern expressed above, that the least squares estimators are not efficient when the errors in an equation are heteroskedastic. Efficient estimation requires generalized least squares. Implementing this technique consists of transforming the heteroskedastic equation in

---

[13] White, pp. 817–838. Although we only discuss White's variance estimator here, he has developed consistent estimators for the covariances of coefficients as well.

such a way that its errors satisfy the requirements of the Gauss-Markov theorem, then estimating this transformed equation with least squares. If the error variances are known, and $\text{Var}(\varepsilon_i) = \sigma_{\varepsilon i}^2$, we saw with Equation (12.3) that the appropriate transformation term is $T = 1/\sigma_{\varepsilon i}$. Assuming a single explanatory variable, the equation that is estimated with least squares is:

$$(y_i/\sigma_{\varepsilon i}) = \alpha_0(1/\sigma_{\varepsilon i}) + \alpha_1(x_i/\sigma_{\varepsilon i}) + (\varepsilon_i/\sigma_{\varepsilon i}) \tag{12.25}$$

The transformation term defines the weight that must be applied to each of the variables in the heteroskedastic equation. The estimated coefficients from this equation are best linear unbiased estimators. This estimation method also generates unbiased estimates of individual coefficient variances, something that least squares estimation of the untransformed equation is unable to do.

As a practical matter, the actual form of heteroskedasticity is not known. We must therefore use the residuals from an estimated equation to determine whether heteroskedasticity exists, and to make assumptions about the specific form it takes should our test lead us to conclude that heteroskedasticity is present. If we estimate any parameters that enable us to approximate the function that pertains to the error variances, we then move into the realm of estimated generalized least squares estimation.

Since we are assuming that heteroskedasticity exists, one possible assumption is for multiplicative heteroskedasticity, with a general form given by Equation (12.5): $\text{Var}(\varepsilon_i) = \sigma_\varepsilon^2 \cdot \Theta_i$, where Θ_i is a function of either the variables in our estimated equation or some other variables we are aware of. If we assume that $\Theta_i = x_i^\gamma$, then our variance expression is: $\sigma_{\varepsilon i}^2 = \sigma_\varepsilon^2 \cdot x_i^\gamma$, and we can use the Park test to obtain an estimate of the exponent γ. Our estimated transformation term is then: $\hat{T} = 1/x_i^{\hat{\gamma}/2}$, which defines the weights applied to each of the variables in our heteroskedastic equation. The equation that was used to perform the Park test on the shipments equation, restated here, is:

$$\widehat{\ln(\hat{\varepsilon}_i^2)} = 3.99 + 1.69 \ln(E_i) \qquad \bar{R}^2 = 0.251 \quad n = 39 \quad F = 13.8$$
$$\phantom{\widehat{\ln(\hat{\varepsilon}_i^2)} = } (1.9) \quad (3.7)$$

Our estimate of γ from this equation is 1.69, which makes $\hat{T} = 1/E_i^{0.845}$. The transformed shipments equation thus becomes:

$$(s_i/E_i^{0.845}) = \alpha_0(1/E_i^{0.845}) + \alpha_1(N_i/E_i^{0.845}) + \alpha_2(E_i^{0.155}) + (\varepsilon_i/E_i^{0.845})$$

where the exponent of E_i, 0.155, is $1 - 0.845$. Estimation of this equation requires that we create four new variables: $s_i^* = (s_i/E_i^{0.845})$; $x_{0i}^* = (1/E_i^{0.845})$; $N_i^* = (N_i/E_i^{0.845})$; and $E_i^* = E_i^{0.155}$; then regress s_i^* on x_{0i}^*, N_i^*, and E_i^* *without an intercept*. The resulting sample regression function is:

$$\hat{s}_i^* = 387.5x_{0i}^* + 37.0N_i^* + 7.1E_i^* \qquad n = 39 \quad F = 21.1 \quad \bar{R}^2 = 0.514$$
$$\phantom{\hat{s}_i^* = } (2.4) \qquad (5.2) \qquad (2.0)$$

All three of the coefficients in this equation are statistically significant at the 5 percent level and above. The F-statistic is significant as well. Using the coefficients from this equation, our EGLS estimate of the *untransformed* equation using the information from the Park test, is:

$$\hat{s}_i = 387.5 + 37.0N_i + 7.1E_i \qquad (12.26)$$
$$\phantom{\hat{s}_i = } (2.4) \quad\ (5.2) \quad\ (2.0)$$

Note that *the relevant value of R^2 is not derived from the transformed equation, since that indicates the proportion of the total variation in the transformed value of shipments explained by the variables x_{0i}^*, N_i^*, and E_i^*.* Also, the actual residuals and predicted values should be obtained from Equation (12.26). The residuals are thus calculated using the formula: $\hat{s}_i - (387.5 + 37.0N_i + 7.1E_i)$, where the term in brackets is the predicted value of new shipments.

If we assume additive heteroskedasticity, we can use the results of the Glejser test to estimate the form of heteroskedasticity, then perform weighted least squares on the shipments equation. Of the three equations estimated to perform the Glejser test, the third performed the best. That equation, which is repeated here, is:

$$|\hat{\varepsilon}_i| = -318.6 + 93.2\sqrt{x_i} \qquad \bar{R}^2 = 0.417 \quad \hat{\sigma}_v = 567.1 \quad F = 28.2$$
$$\phantom{|\hat{\varepsilon}_i| = } (1.6) \quad\ \ (5.3)$$

The intercept in this equation is not statistically significant. The form of heteroskedasticity suggested by this equation is therefore:

$$\sigma_{\varepsilon i}^2 = (93.2)^2 \cdot E_i$$

which has as its transformation term: $1/\sqrt{E_i}$. The form of the transformed equation is an example of that in Equation (12.10):

$$(s_i/\sqrt{E_i}) = \alpha_0(1/\sqrt{E_i}) + \alpha_1(N_i/\sqrt{E_i}) + \alpha_2\sqrt{E_i} + (\varepsilon_i/\sqrt{E_i})$$

The estimated equation that results is:

$$\hat{s}_i^* = 293.9x_0^* + 37.4N_i^* + 8.1E_i^* \qquad n = 39 \quad \bar{R}^2 = 0.672 \quad F = 39.9$$
$$\phantom{\hat{s}_i^* = } (1.7) \qquad\ (6.0) \qquad (3.0)$$

which, when untransformed, is:

$$\hat{s}_i = 293.9 + 37.4N_i + 8.1E_i$$
$$\phantom{\hat{s}_i = } (1.7) \quad\ (6.0) \qquad (3.0)$$

Both employment and new capital expenditures are statistically significant at the 1 percent level, while the intercept term is significant at the 5 percent level only for a one-tail test. Both partial slopes are higher than the corresponding coefficient for the equation derived using the Park test results. The same caveats discussed for the earlier equation pertain here as well.

If heteroskedasticity is assumed to be related to the expected value of shipments, $E(s)$: $\sigma_{\varepsilon i}^2 = \sigma_\varepsilon^2 \cdot [E(s)]^2$, we can use predicted shipments from our original equation, $\hat{s}_i$, as an estimate of $E(s)$. The appropriate transformation term is then: $\hat{T}_i = 1/\hat{s}_i$, and the equation we estimate is:

$$(s_i/\hat{s}_i) = \alpha_0(1/\hat{s}_i) + \alpha_1(N_i/\hat{s}_i) + \alpha_2(E_i/\hat{s}_i) + (\varepsilon_i/\hat{s}_i)$$

The least squares estimate of this equation is:

$$\hat{s}_i^* = 327.8 + 39.5N_i^* + 6.2E_i^* \qquad \bar{R}^2 = -0.007 \quad \hat{\sigma}_v = 0.21 \quad F = 0.9$$
$$\phantom{\hat{s}_i^* = }(2.0) \quad\;\; (5.8) \qquad (2.3)$$

The performance of this equation is unsatisfactory overall, as its F-statistic, 0.9, is not statistically significant, and its adjusted R^2 is negative (note: this does not indicate a negative $\bar{R}^2$ for the original equation).

It is possible to perform estimated generalized least squares estimation using the information from White's test. The basis of this method consists of defining weights, $w_i = 1/\hat{\sigma}_i$, where $\hat{\sigma}_i$ is an estimate of the $\sigma_{\varepsilon i}$ that allows us to obtain consistent estimates of the coefficients in the original equation and their standard deviations. The steps involved are as follows[14]:

1. Perform White's test for heteroskedasticity as outlined earlier: estimate the original equation with least squares; calculate the residuals, $\hat{\varepsilon}_i$; square these to obtain $\hat{\varepsilon}_i^2$; then regress $\hat{\varepsilon}_i^2$ on the variables in the original equation, their squares and cross-products (including an intercept).

2. Since $\hat{\varepsilon}_i^2$ is an estimator of σ_ε^2, calculate the predicted values of $\hat{\varepsilon}_i^2$ from this equation, $\hat{\sigma}_{1i}^2$. Use these as the basis for an initial transformation term, $\hat{T} = 1/\hat{\sigma}_{1i}^2$, with which to re-estimate the regression of $\hat{\varepsilon}_i^2$ on the variables, their squares and cross-products from step (1). Using the shipments equation whose variables are s_i, N_i, and E_i, we regress $(\hat{\varepsilon}_i^2/\hat{\sigma}_{1i}^2)$ on a constant, $(N_i/\hat{\sigma}_{1i}^2)$, $(E_i/\hat{\sigma}_{1i}^2)$, $(N_i^2/\hat{\sigma}_{1i}^2)$, $(E_i^2/\hat{\sigma}_{1i}^2)$, and $((N_i \cdot E_i)/\hat{\sigma}_{1i}^2)$. This provides us with another estimate of $\hat{\sigma}_{\varepsilon i}^2$; call it $\hat{\sigma}_{2i}^2$.

3. The final estimated transformation term for this method is: $\hat{T} = 1/\hat{\sigma}_{2i}$. Apply this to the variables in the original equation and estimate the transformed equation with least squares. For the shipments equation, our transformed equation is:

$$(s_i/\hat{\sigma}_{2i}) = \alpha_0(1/\hat{\sigma}_{2i}) + \alpha_1(N_i/\hat{\sigma}_{2i}) + \alpha_2(E_i/\hat{\sigma}_{2i}) + (\varepsilon_i/\hat{\sigma}_{2i})$$

The estimated coefficients in this equation are consistent, as are the estimated coefficient standard deviations.

Since the weights used in this transformation are estimated standard deviations, it is necessary that all of the values for both $\hat{\sigma}_{1i}^2$ and $\hat{\sigma}_{2i}^2$ be positive. If negative values arise for either (or both) of these estimated variances, the following modification is added:

(2a) If values of $\hat{\sigma}_{1i}^2$ are negative, keep the original explanatory variables but use the natural logarithm of the squared residuals, $\ln(\hat{\varepsilon}_i^2)$, as the dependent variable. The predicted variances with this method, $\hat{\sigma}_{1i}^2$, are obtained from the

---

[14] The description of the steps involved here follows the presentation in R. Ramanathan, *Introductory Econometrics With Applications*, (San Diego: Harcourt Brace, Jovanovich), 1989, pp. 460–461.

expression: $\hat{\sigma}_{1i}^2 = \exp(\widehat{\ln(\varepsilon_i^2)})$, where exp is the exponential function. Then, the transformation term used in step (3) is: $\hat{T} = 1/\hat{\sigma}_{1i}$.

(2b) If all of the values of $\hat{\sigma}_{1i}^2$ are positive but $\hat{\sigma}_{2i}^2$ includes negative values, use the natural logarithm of $(\hat{\varepsilon}_i^2/\hat{\sigma}_{1i}^2)$ as the dependent variable in the final part of step (2). Then, $\hat{\sigma}_{2i}^2 = \exp(\ln(\hat{\varepsilon}_i^2/\hat{\sigma}_{1i}^2))$, and the transformation term used in step (3) is: $\hat{T} = 1/\hat{\sigma}_{2i}$.

When this method was used to estimate the shipments equation, negative values occurred for $\hat{\sigma}_{1i}^2$, necessitating the use of step (2a). This consisted of regressing $\ln(\hat{\varepsilon}_i^2)$ on an intercept, N_i, E_i, N_i^2, E_i^2, and $(N_i \cdot E_i)$. Applying the exponential function to the predicted values of this equation the values of $\hat{\sigma}_{1i}^2$ were obtained, along with the weights, $\hat{T} = 1/\hat{\sigma}_{1i}$, that are used to create the transformed equation. The estimated generalized least squares shipments equation is then:

$$\hat{s}_i^* = 417.1 + 33.3N_i^* + 8.6E_i^* \qquad \bar{R}^2 = 0.821 \quad \hat{\sigma}_v = 1.94 \quad F = 88.4$$
$$\quad (2.8) \quad\;\; (4.9) \qquad (3.7)$$

This equation has the highest F-statistic of any presented thus far. The t-statistics for the intercept and new capital expenditures were the largest as well. The intercept in this equation differs substantially from the unweighted least squares equation (of 294.6), but is fairly close to the estimated intercept obtained using the results of Park's test to transform the original equation.

The final method presented for estimating an equation with heteroskedastic errors does not involve generalized least squares. Instead, the transformation it utilizes is natural logarithms. Use of the log-linear specification can reduce or eliminate heteroskedasticity. Since heteroskedasticity is often related to the size of one or more variables, applying a logarithmic transformation to the variables in an equation reduces such disparities in size. For the shipments data, we concluded that heteroskedasticity was associated with the values of new capital expenditures. The values of this variable range from 27 to 652, with a standard deviation of 148.3. If we transform this variable into a natural logarithm, its values extend from 3.3 to 6.5, with a standard deviation of only 0.9. As this shows, applying a logarithmic transformation can substantially reduce the dispersion in problematic variables.

The log-linear version of the shipments equation was estimated. The resulting equation is:

$$\widehat{\ln(s)}_i = 4.23 \; + 0.72 \ln(N)_i + 0.21 \ln(E)_i$$
$$\quad (20.9) \quad (6.2) \qquad\quad (2.3)$$

$$n = 39 \quad \bar{R}^2 = 0.906 \quad \hat{\sigma}_\varepsilon = 0.211 \quad F = 183.2$$

The performance of this specification is very good. All three coefficients are statistically significant at the 1 percent level, the adjusted R^2 is high, as is the equation F-statistic. The coefficients of $\ln(N)_i$ and $\ln(E)_i$, which are elasticities, indicate that shipments are inelastic with respect to both employment and new capital expenditures. Actual and predicted values, along with the residuals for this equation are

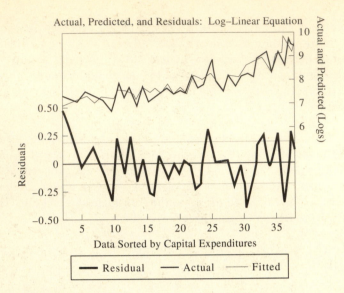

Figure 12.6

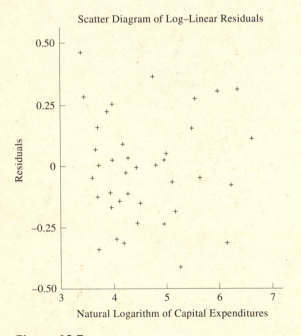

Figure 12.7

given in Figure 12.6, while a scatter diagram of the log-linear residuals and new capital expenditures is shown in Figure 12.7. Based on visual inspection, there does not appear to be heteroskedastic errors when the logarithmic transformation is applied to these data. Statistical testing of this preliminary conclusion is included in the exercises.

It should be noted in closing that use of the logarithmic transformation is not always possible. If one or more of the variables in an equation have negative values or values of 0, this transformation cannot be applied. Before using this equation specification, it is important to make sure that it provides an appropriate depiction of the relationship under study.

KEY TERMS

Additive heteroskedasticity

Breusch-Pagan Test

Glejser Test

Goldfeld-Quandt Test

Heteroskedastic

Homoskedasticity

Monotonic heteroskedasticity

Multiplicative heteroskedasticity

Park Test

Weighted least squares

White's heteroskedasticity consistent variance estimator

White's test for heteroskedasticity

EXERCISES

1. Explain why the visual inspection of residuals can cause one to arrive at an incorrect solution about the presence of heteroskedasticity.

2. Using the real wage-employment data from the manual calculation problem at the end of Chapter 4, test for the existence of heteroskedasticity using: (i) the Goldfeld-Quandt test; (ii) Park's test; (iii) Glejser's test; (iv) the Breusch-Pagan test; and (v) White's test.

3. What problems arise using the Breusch-Pagan and White tests for heteroskedasticity in question (2) above?

4. Test the log-linear form of the shipments equation for heteroskedasticity using the tests listed in question (2).

5. One of the forms Glejser suggested as a possibility for the error variances is $|\varepsilon_i| = \sqrt{\alpha_0 + \alpha_1 x_i} + v_i$. What problems exist in estimating the parameters in this equation with least squares?

6. Explain why it is only necessary to consider the error variance up to a factor of proportionality when modelling heteroskedastic errors.

7. Describe the weighted least squares estimation technique. How does this attain a more accurate depiction of a population regression function?

8. Besides using a log-linear specification, it may be possible to reduce or eliminate heteroskedasticity by changing the origin of a "problem" variable. Consider, for example, a variable x with values such as: 1,245,677. If we change the scale of this variable to millions, how might heteroskedasticity be reduced?

9. Is it possible to obtain the same estimated coefficients with least squares and weighted least squares when the errors in an equation are heteroskedastic? Explain your answer.

10. Outline the essential differences between generalized least squares and estimated generalized least squares estimation for equations with heteroskedastic errors.

11. How does the existence of heteroskedasticity affect forecasts generated by an equation? Confidence intervals for these forecasts?

13 Equations with Lagged Variables: The Distributed Lag and Autoregressive Models

The interactions that characterize many economic relationships often occur over a number of time periods. It is not uncommon to find situations where a considerable amount of time elapses before changes in one variable exert an appreciable impact on a related variable. Often stressed examples of this are the lags in the effects of monetary and fiscal policy on the level of economic activity. The full impact of changes in a variable might, instead, occur over several time periods. In either of these situations, lags exist in the relationship between the variables under study.

In this chapter we detail two different, but not unrelated, situations where lagged variables are included in the specification of an equation. The first of these deals with equations that include one or more lagged explanatory variables, such as:

$$y_t = \beta + \alpha_0 x_t + \alpha_1 x_{t-1} + \alpha_2 x_{t-2} + \cdots + \alpha_k x_{t-k} + \varepsilon_t$$

The second type of equation we examine includes a lagged dependent variable:

$$y_t = \alpha_0 + \alpha_1 x_t + \alpha_2 y_{t-1} + \varepsilon_t$$

This last specification pertains when considerations such as momentum or habit formation are relevant. Methods for estimating these different types of equations are presented, along with economic examples. Complications are noted, and modifications to concepts presented earlier (especially for serial correlation) are discussed.

LAGGED EXPLANATORY VARIABLES: THE DISTRIBUTED LAG MODEL

Whenever we model the behavior of a dependent variable with a multiple regression equation, we must determine both proper functional form and the relevant set of explanatory variables to include. For time series data, the process of selecting explanatory variables is complicated by the fact that we must identify not only the variables themselves, but the correct temporal linkage between these and the dependent variable. If all of the explanatory variables in an equation are contemporaneously related to the dependent variable, then an equation such as:

$$y_t = \alpha_0 + \alpha_1 x_t + \alpha_2 z_t + \varepsilon_t \tag{13.1}$$

is relevant. Equation (13.1) implicitly assumes that whenever x or z change, the entire impact on y is felt in the same period during which this change occurs.

The appropriateness of Equation (13.1) is partly related to the frequency of the data used to estimate this relationship. A contemporaneous equation may be correct for annual data if the adjustment of y occurs within one year. For either monthly or quarterly data, however, it may be necessary to include lags of one or both of the explanatory variables. If, for example, we are using quarterly data, and the impact of x on y is felt over a six-month period while z works within the same quarter, the appropriate form of Equation (13.1) is:

$$y_t = \alpha_0 + \alpha_1 x_t + \alpha_2 x_{t-1} + \alpha_3 z_t + \varepsilon_t \tag{13.2}$$

As a variant of this example, if x is a monetary policy instrument, such as the monetary base, and y is a measure of overall economic activity, then with quarterly data, current period x should be excluded. Milton Friedman has shown that the initial impact of monetary policy is not felt for at least two quarters. Assuming that this impact occurs from periods $t - 2$ to $t - k$, Equation (13.2) becomes (after rearrangement):

$$y_t = \alpha_0 + \alpha_1 z_t + \alpha_2 x_{t-2} + \alpha_3 x_{t-3} + \cdots + \alpha_k x_{t-k} + \varepsilon_t \tag{13.2'}$$

Of course, lags can be appropriate for equations with any data frequency. We used a specification with the form of Equation (13.2) to model the unemployment rate (u) earlier in the text. Using annual data, the cyclical behavior of u was represented by the capacity utilization rate (CAP). It was assumed that the unemployment rate responds to changes in the capacity utilization rate over a two-year period, while z, the labor force participation rate of females (LFPF), which represents the secular trend in unemployment, was contemporaneously related to y:

$$u_t = \alpha_0 + \alpha_1 CAP_t + \alpha_2 CAP_{t-1} + \alpha_3 LFPF_t + \varepsilon_t \tag{13.3}$$

There are a number of reasons why lags appear in econometric equations. The more important among these are:

1. **Imperfect Information.** Economic agents do not possess perfect information about all aspects of their activities. Because of this, it is necessary for them to expend time and effort gathering information about key economic variables such as prices, quantities, the availabilities of resources, etc. Expectations about future values of key variables also tend to be related to past experience with these same variables. In addition, it is often necessary to distinguish whether a change in some variable of interest is temporary or permanent. Because acquiring such information takes time, adjustments to changes in economic circumstances often occur over several time periods. For policy

makers, it takes time to decipher whether or not the economy is in need of economic stimulus. They might be unaware that a recession is taking place for up to six months after its beginning. Policy makers must also determine whether a slowdown is temporary or of a long-term nature. This is called the recognition lag.

2. **Adjustment Costs.** When the optimal amount of an input for a firm changes, the adjustment from the existing to this new quantity frequently takes several periods. Consider a desired increase in manhours, for example. Firms can attain this desired higher level of manhours by increasing hours per worker, the number of workers, or both. However, different costs are associated with each of these alternatives. The existence of fixed employment costs (see Chapter 4) gives firms a basis for preferring increases in hours per worker over greater numbers of workers in the short-run. If there is an increase in the demand for a firm's product, that firm might not be able to find enough qualified persons in a single period. Or, if they hire a number of people but the increase in demand turns out to be temporary, the resulting layoffs involve costs (such as unemployment insurance). In either case, the adjustment from current to desired manhours will likely occur over several time periods. A similar situation pertains for capital and the long-run adjustment to an increase in demand. If the desired capital stock of a firm rises in response to higher demand, say, a new factory is desired, the firm might well be able to build this factory in a single period. However, adhering to this single period schedule likely entails massive amounts of overtime pay, requires the use of sub-optimal capital and equipment, and necessitates rushing the planning involved. The added marginal costs of completing this project in a single period will generally more than offset the added marginal benefits involved, leading to its completion after several time periods. A number of periods will thus lapse before supply adjusts completely to an increase in demand.

3. **The Existence of Contracts.** Firms are often tied to contracts for labor, raw materials, or intermediate goods supplies that extend over several years. Collective bargaining agreements with unions or natural gas contracts, which are examples of this, typically span periods of from one to three years. The existence of such contracts can slow the ability of firms to enter new markets, as they are forced to enter on a smaller scale than would be the case in the absence of such contractually obligated commitments. Once allowed to enter into new contracts, firms can then become more completely committed to the new markets. This will occur over several years, however.

4. **Habit Formation.** People develop preferences for different goods, and firms have preferred ways of producing goods. Such preferences tend to slow the adjustments of persons and firms to changes in their economic environments. In time, persons or firms will eventually make the needed adjustments.

5. **Inertia.** A number of economic processes have a built-in inertia, where past values determine present values. The inflation rate is an example. A momentum exists with inflation, so that the rate of inflation in one period is related to past rates of inflation.

Of course, the above headings are not mutually exclusive. Inertia for economic relationships involving individuals entails habit formation. Adjustment costs are clearly related to the existence of imperfect information.

Other lags exist as well. For fiscal policy, once the need for a course of action has been agreed upon, a period of time lapses as both the legislative and executive branches arrive at a package of acceptable fiscal measures. This is often called the administrative lag. For both monetary and fiscal policy, once the desired measures have been undertaken, there is a lag of at least two quarters before these have an appreciable impact on the target variables upon which they act. This is the operational lag. For example, a tax cut will impact disposable incomes immediately, while its effects on spending, output and employment occur over a number of periods. Similarly, for monetary policy, if the supply of money is increased, its impact on output and employment are felt only after interest rates and investment are affected.

To outline the methodology for dealing with lagged relationships, we will portray the multiple regression equation for y in the following way:

$$y_t = \beta + \alpha_0 x_t + \alpha_1 x_{t-1} + \cdots + \alpha_k x_{t-k} + \varepsilon_t \qquad (13.4)$$

where the single explanatory variable x is included. The impact of x on y in this equation occurs (is distributed) over a finite number of different time periods. For this reason, the above equation is called a **finite distributed lag model**. A more compact way of writing Equation (13.4) is:

$$y_t = \beta + \sum_{i=0}^{k} \alpha_i x_{t-i} + \varepsilon_t \qquad (13.5)$$

Note that the symbol β is used to denote the intercept in this equation. This allows the α's to pertain exclusively to the different periods for x. The coefficient α_0 denotes the impact of a one unit change in x on the mean of y *in the same period*, given the values of x_{t-1}, x_{t-2}, and so forth. It is called the **impact (short-run) multiplier**.[1] The coefficients α_1 to α_k, which relate changes in x from previous periods to the mean of y this period, are called **interim multipliers**. The coefficient α_1, for example, denotes the effect of a one unit change in x last period on the mean of y in the current period, given x_t, x_{t-2}, and all of the other lagged values of x. It is called the **interim multiplier of order 1**.[2] If this one unit increase in x is maintained indefinitely, the mean of y changes by α_0 in the initial period, and by $(\alpha_0 + \alpha_1)$ after two periods. The latter sum denotes the **two-period interim multiplier**. Similarly, the j-period interim multiplier is: $(\alpha_0 + \alpha_1 + \cdots + \alpha_{j-1})$. The total (cumulative) impact of an indefinitely maintained one-unit increase in x on the mean of y is the sum of the impact and the interim

---

[1] Technically, the impact multiplier is the partial derivative of y_t with respect to x_t: $\partial y_t / \partial x_t$.

[2] The interim multiplier of order j is the partial derivative of y_t with respect to x_{t-j}: $\partial y_t / \partial x_{t-j}$.

multipliers:

$$\alpha = \sum_{i=0}^{k} \alpha_i$$

This sum, α, is the **equilibrium or long-run multiplier**.[3] The underlying basis of this multiplier can be seen by considering the long-run equilibrium for either Equation (13.4) or (13.5). In this setting, x maintains its equilibrium value indefinitely, so that: $x_t = x_{t-1} = \cdots = x_{t-k}$. If we denote this equilibrium value x_e, then the long-run equilibrium value of y, y_e, is (with $\varepsilon_t = 0$):

$$y_e = \beta + (\alpha_0 + \alpha_1 + \cdots + \alpha_k)x_e$$

or

$$y_e = \beta + \alpha x_e$$

When x changes by one unit, the mean of y thus changes by α units in the long-run. A time path exists for this adjustment. In the initial period, the mean of y changes by α_0. In the second period, this change is $(\alpha_0 + \alpha_1)$, etc.

We can illustrate these concepts by utilizing an equation that depicts the cyclical behavior of the unemployment rate (u), relating it to the current and three lags of the capacity utilization rate in manufacturing (CAP). The estimated equation, using annual data for 1955–1989 and a Cochrane-Orcutt serial correlation correction (with $\hat{\Theta} = 0.807$), is:

$$\hat{u}_t = 34.6 - 0.239\text{CAP}_t - 0.059\text{CAP}_{t-1} - 0.028\text{CAP}_{t-2} - 0.025\text{CAP}_{t-3}$$
$$\quad (10.6) \quad (14.6) \qquad (3.8) \qquad\qquad (1.8) \qquad\qquad (1.7)$$

$$\bar{R}^2 = 0.944 \quad n = 35 \quad \hat{\sigma}_\varepsilon = 0.37 \quad F = 116.6$$

All of the coefficients of CAP are negative, as expected, and statistically significant (for one-tail tests). The impact multiplier is -0.239, which indicates that if the capacity utilization rate in manufacturing rises by 1 percent, the mean unemployment rate this period falls by approximately one-fourth of 1 percent. The following table summarizes the various multipliers:

MULTIPLIER		VALUE
Impact:		-0.239
Interim for:		
two periods	$(-0.239 - 0.059)$	$= -0.298$
three periods	$(-0.239 - 0.059 - 0.028)$	$= -0.326$
Long-run:	$(-0.239 - 0.059 - 0.028 - 0.025)$	$= -0.351$

---

[3] This assumes that the sum is finite.

The long-run multiplier for this equation is -0.351, so that a 1 percent rise in CAP sustained indefinitely lowers the mean unemployment rate by about one-third of 1 percent. Note that the lag coefficients in this equation decrease (in absolute value). This pattern does not always occur for lag distributions.

Another piece of information often derived from the lag distribution of a variable is the average, or **mean lag**, which is defined as:

$$\text{Mean lag} = \sum_{i=0}^{k} i \cdot \alpha_i \bigg/ \sum_{i=0}^{k} \alpha_i \qquad \textbf{(13.6)}$$

The mean lag is simply a weighted average of the α_i's, where these values do not necessarily sum to 1. Note that the denominator in Equation (13.6) is the long-run multiplier. The mean lag denotes the average number of periods during which a sustained change in x influences y. In the above example $k = 3$, so the mean lag is:

$$\text{Mean lag} = \{(1)(-0.059) + (2)(-0.028) + (3)(-0.025)\}/(-0.351)$$
$$= 0.54$$

This implies that on average, the lag for the effect of CAP on u is six months. This appears to be somewhat low. It results from the relatively large value of α_0 and the fact that the other α_i's continually decrease (in absolute value). This can be seen by deriving the proportion of the long-run multiplier accounted for by each α_i. For the impact multiplier, this proportion is:

$$-0.239/-0.351 = 0.681$$

so that 68 percent of the impact of a sustained change in CAP on the mean of u is felt in the same year. For the one year lag, the proportionate share is 16.8 percent ($-0.059/-0.351$). The remaining proportions are 8 and 7.1 percent, respectively. Note that when the α_i's differ in sign, the mean lag can give an unsatisfactory value.

METHODS FOR ESTIMATING FINITE DISTRIBUTED LAG MODELS

Technically, least squares estimation of distributed lag equations does not entail any estimation difficulty. As long as the explanatory variable x is nonstochastic (or independent of the equation error), the least squares coefficients β and α_0 to α_k are the best linear unbiased estimators of the coefficients in the population regression function. Several practical difficulties exist, however. First, if too few lagged x's are included in the estimated equation, specification error occurs, leading to biased and inconsistent parameter estimates. If too many lags are included, the "irrelevant" x's will not produce bias or inconsistency, but they will potentially contribute to a multicollinearity problem since current and lagged x's will likely be correlated. This can adversely affect the magnitudes of lagged x coefficients as well as their t-statistics. Second, the larger is the time period over which the lags extend, k, the fewer will be the number of degrees of freedom available to estimate the relationship. For each lagged x included in our equation, one degree of freedom is lost. If k is larger than

n, there will not be enough degrees of freedom to estimate the equation. Finally, when k is large, including the correct number of lagged x's will likely produce problematic multicollinearity. The t-statistics of the coefficients will tend to be too low as the result of the variance inflation caused by multicollinearity (see Chapter 10). This raises the likelihood of committing Type II errors, where the probability of rejecting a false hypothesis (that $\alpha_j = 0$) does not correspond to the selected level of significance. It is likely that the number of lags involved will be underestimated if we base this determination on t-statistics.

The common factor underlying each of these considerations is the potential loss of estimation precision from the simple application of least squares to a distributed lag equation. *This occurs even if we know the correct value of k.* However, we generally do not know this value, which further complicates matters, since we run the dual risks of both multicollinearity and specification error. In general, research has attempted to find ways of estimating distributed lag relationships with a relatively small number of parameters. Four methods for estimating distributed lags will be presented. The first of these pertains when the maximum value for k is known. The second is a method for ascertaining k using cross-correlations between the variables of interest. The remaining two impose assumptions about the shape of the lag distribution.

Estimation When Maximum Lag Length Is Known[4]

If an upper bound for lag length (M) is known, and this does not entail estimating a large number lagged x coefficients, two procedures are generally utilized. Both consist of estimating the relationship sequentially, starting with y_t and x_t, then regressing y_t on x_t and x_{t-1}, and proceeding until y_t is regressed on $x_t, x_{t-1}, \ldots, x_{t-M}$. The first procedure consists of the following steps:

1. Omit the initial M values. Estimation will proceed using only observations $M + 1, M + 2, \ldots, n$.
2. Estimate the set of regression equations:

$$y_t = \beta + \alpha_0 x_t + \varepsilon_t$$

$$y_t = \beta + \alpha_0 x_t + \alpha_1 x_{t-1} + \varepsilon_t$$

$$y_t = \beta + \alpha_0 x_t + \alpha_1 x_{t-1} + \alpha_2 x_{t-2} + \varepsilon_t$$

$$\cdots$$

$$y_t = \beta + \alpha_0 x_t + \alpha_1 x_{t-1} + \cdots + \alpha_M x_{t-M} + \varepsilon_t$$

and obtain the adjusted R^2 from each equation.

---

[4] Both of the methods outlined below are presented in greater detail in G. Judge, R. Hill, W. Griffiths, H. Lutkerpohl, and T. Lee, *Introduction to the Theory and Practice of Econometrics*, 2d. ed. (New York: John Wiley & Sons), 1988, Ch. 17. This section draws heavily on the material in that reference.

3. Since:

$$\bar{R}^2 = 1 - \frac{\hat{\sigma}_\varepsilon^2}{\sum(y_t - \hat{\mu}_y)^2/(n - M - 1)}$$

where the denominator is the sample variance of y based on the $n - M$ observations used, this denominator is the same for each of the above regression equations. Maximizing $\bar{R}^2$ is therefore equivalent to minimizing the estimated error variance, $\hat{\sigma}_\varepsilon^2$. The equation with the largest $\bar{R}^2$ is thus selected as the one with the best lag representation.

Note that this approach to lag length estimation still potentially suffers from the multicollinearity problems mentioned above. While the value of $\bar{R}^2$ is unaffected by multicollinearity, individual coefficients may well be. It is therefore possible to arrive at an appropriate lag length using this procedure, but to have a number of non-significant coefficients, or values with incorrect signs.

The second procedure treats the selection of lag length as one of proper variable inclusion since it is assumed that maximum lag length is known. Since there is a logical ordering for the lagged variables, a set of sequential hypotheses can be set up and tested. If we denote the actual lag length L, and the maximum lag length M, we can set up the following set of hypotheses:

$$H_{0(1)}: L = M - 1; \quad \text{and} \quad H_{a(1)}: L = M$$
$$H_{0(2)}: L = M - 2; \quad \text{and} \quad H_{a(2)}: L = M - 1$$
$$\cdots$$
$$H_{0(j)}: L = M - j; \quad \text{and} \quad H_{a(j)}: L = M - j + 1$$

The first null hypothesis, $H_{0(1)}$, pertains to the equation:

$$y_t = \beta + \alpha_0 x_t + \alpha_1 x_{t-1} + \cdots + \alpha_M x_{t-M} + \varepsilon_t \tag{13.7}$$

If this null hypothesis is true, the coefficient of x_{t-M} is zero: $\alpha_M = 0$. The second null hypothesis, $H_{0(2)}$, pertains to the model:

$$y_t = \beta + \alpha_0 x_t + \alpha_1 x_{t-1} + \cdots + \alpha_{M-1} x_{t-M+1} + \varepsilon_t \tag{13.8}$$

where the variable x_{t-M} has been omitted. Since these are sequential hypotheses, if we are unable to reject $H_{0(1)}$, we assume in this second hypothesis test that $\alpha_M = 0$. If $H_{0(2)}$ is true, then $\alpha_{M-1} = 0$. Proceeding through the remaining null hypotheses is accomplished in a similar fashion. These hypotheses are evaluated using an F-distributed test statistic that is based on the differences in the sum of squared residuals from omitting successive lag terms. The steps involved are:

1. Omit the initial M values. Estimation will proceed using only observations $M + 1, M + 2, \ldots, n$. We will denote this total of $(n - M)$ observations as T.

2. Estimate the set of regression equations:

$$y_t = \beta + \alpha_0 x_t + \varepsilon_t$$

$$y_t = \beta + \alpha_0 x_t + \alpha_1 x_{t-1} + \varepsilon_t$$

$$y_t = \beta + \alpha_0 x_t + \alpha_1 x_{t-1} + \alpha_2 x_{t-2} + \varepsilon_t$$

$$\cdots$$

$$y_t = \beta + \alpha_0 x_t + \alpha_1 x_{t-1} + \cdots + \alpha_M x_{t-M} + \varepsilon_t$$

and obtain the residual sum of squares (ESS) from each equation.

3. For the first null hypothesis, we use Equations (13.7) and (13.8). These can be thought of as the unrestricted and restricted equations, respectively. If $H_{0(1)}$ is true, then omitting x_{t-M} should not cause a substantial increase in the residual sum of squares. Since the sum of squared residuals is sensitive to the unit of measurement for y, the change in its value is viewed relative to the residual sum of squares when the restriction $\alpha_M = 0$ is ignored. The test statistic is then:

$$\frac{(\text{ESS}_{M-1} - \text{ESS}_M)/1}{\text{ESS}_M/(T - M - 2)} \sim F_{1,(T-M-2)}$$

where the subscript on ESS denotes the lag length utilized. Note that there are $T - M - 2$ degrees of freedom in the equation with lag length M, since there are M lag coefficients along with β and α_0. In general, the degrees of freedom in the denominator of the test statistic is (T − number of lags in denominator − 2).

4. Obtain the critical F-value with 1 and $(T - M - 2)$ degrees of freedom in the numerator and denominator, respectively. If the test statistic exceeds this critical value, we reject H_0 and accept the alternative hypothesis that lag length is M. If the test statistic falls below the critical F-value, we proceed to test the next hypothesis (step (5)).

5. We next contrast the equations with lags up to periods $M - 1$ and $M - 2$. The test statistic is:

$$\frac{(\text{ESS}_{M-2} - \text{ESS}_{M-1})/1}{\text{ESS}_{M-1}/(T - M - 1)} \sim F_{1,(T-M-1)}$$

Continue with this process, calculate the test statistic for each lag and obtain the critical F-value. Locate the first test statistic that exceeds its critical value. If we assume this value occurs for lag j, we are able to reject the null hypothesis: $H_{0(j)}: \alpha_{M-j} = 0$. The estimated lag length is then $M - (j + 1)$.

Both of these tests were applied to an unemployment rate equation expressed in terms of a distributed lag of the capacity utilization rate in manufacturing. Annual data for the years 1955 to 1989 were used (all regressions began with 1955). For purposes of illustration, we assume the maximum lag length that characterizes this relationship is 7 years. The relevant data are expressed below:

k	ESS	df	$\bar{R}^2$	TEST STATISTIC
7	7.138	26	0.88954	
6	7.414	27	0.88951	1.01 (for $H_{0(1)}$: $M = 6$)
5	7.754	28	0.8886	1.24 (for $H_{0(2)}$: $M = 5$)
4	8.864	29	0.8770	4.01 (for $H_{0(3)}$: $M = 4$)
3	10.033	30	0.8654	3.82 (for $H_{0(4)}$: $M = 3$)
2	12.121	31	0.8427	6.24 (for $H_{0(5)}$: $M = 2$)
1	15.033	32	0.8110	7.45 (for $H_{0(6)}$: $M = 1$)

A lag length of 7 was selected using the maximum adjusted-R^2 criterion. For the F-test outlined above, each of the critical F-values for the 5 percent significance level is approximately equal to 4.2. We will use this as the critical value for the F-test. The first null hypothesis we are able to reject is $H_{0(5)}$. Our estimated lag length is therefore 3.

Both of these tests arrive at different lag lengths. Unfortunately, this is not an uncommon occurrence. Also, when selecting the preferred equation based on the results of either test, problematic multicollinearity may arise, so that the coefficients of several lagged x's can have incorrect signs or not be statistically significant.

A Method for Approximating the Number of Lags

The discussion of serial correlation detection in Chapter 11 introduced the method of visually inspecting the sample autocorrelation function of the residuals from a least squares equation. This has become a widely used tool for persons working with time series data. The field of time series analysis utilizes another tool, the **cross-correlation function**, to determine whether lags of x are related to y. Essentially, this function consists of the different correlation coefficients between y_t and successive lags of x, where *it is necessary that both y and x be stationary*. Assuming this condition is met, the cross-correlation between x and y, ρ_{xy}, is defined as:

$$\rho_{xy}(i) = E[(x_t - \mu_x)(y_{t+i} - \mu_y)]/(\sigma_x \cdot \sigma_y) \qquad \text{for } i = 0, \pm 1, \pm 2, \ldots$$

where σ_x and σ_y are the standard deviations of x and y, respectively. Like any correlation function, this is a scaled covariance. The value of i, which indicates the number of periods examined, can be either negative or positive. If i is positive, future values of y are correlated with current x values, indicating the presence of a distributed lag between y and x. When i is negative, past y is correlated with current x, which designates x as a predictor of y. Many canned computer programs include a feature that computes and graphs the cross-correlation function. For MicroTSP, the CROSS command is used to obtain this function. Using 1950 to 1989 as our sample period, we obtain the cross-correlation function for the unemployment rate (UR) and the capacity utilization rate (CAPUR) for 10 periods (years) with the command:

```
>CROSS(10) D(UR) CAPUR[↵]
```

The first difference operator, D( ), was applied to the unemployment rate to make it stationary.[5] The resulting output is:

```
 COR{D(UR),CAPUR(-i)}    COR{D(UR),CAPUR(+i)}      i    lag   lead

 ********|    .          ********|    .             0  -0.577 -0.577
     .   |****            .  *****|   .             1   0.295 -0.347
     .   |*****           .     * |   .             2   0.362 -0.113
     .   |***.            .       |   .             3   0.198 -0.017
     .   |** .            .       |*  .             4   0.192  0.074
     .   |*  .            .     **|   .             5   0.040 -0.176
     .   |** .            .      *|   .             6   0.125 -0.098
     .   |** .            .       |   .             7   0.120 -0.028
     .   |*  .            .       |   .             8   0.064 -0.023
     .   |*  .            .       |*  .             9   0.114  0.109
     .   |   .            .       |*  .            10  -0.029  0.068

                           SE of Correlations   0.158
```

The graph on the left, along with the entries in the column labeled "lag" are used to determine whether lagged CAPUR is correlated with UR, and the number of periods involved. Relatively strong correlations are indicated starting from current CAPUR up to a 5-year lag. The entry "SE of Correlations" gives the large-sample standard deviation for each of these correlations, which equals $1/\sqrt{n}$, where n is sample size (here $n = 40$).

It is possible to test for the joint significance of L cross-correlations. The null hypothesis states that each of the first L cross-correlations equals 0. The test statistic for this test is[6]:

$$LQ = n(n + 2) \sum_{i=1}^{L} \frac{\rho_{xy}^2(i)}{n - i}$$

which follows the chi-square distribution with L degrees of freedom. The numerator in this expression is the squared cross-correlation coefficient for the ith lag. As before, n is sample size.

---

[5] The property of stationarity was given in Chapter 11. For a time series to be stationary its mean must be constant and independent of time, its variance must be a finite constant that is the same for the entire time series and the covariance between any two values must be a function of only the number of periods between these observations. What is referred to as stationarity here is actually weak stationarity.

[6] G. Ljung and G. Box, "On a Measure of Lack of Fit in Time Series Models," *Biometrika* 65 (August 1978), 297–303.

This test statistic was calculated so that the joint significance of the first 7 lags for UR and CAPUR could be ascertained. The value of this statistic, 14.6, exceeds the critical chi-square value with 7 degrees of freedom at the five percent significance level, 14.1. We can therefore reject the null hypothesis that the first 7 lags are jointly 0. Note that several of these cross-correlations are not individually statistically significant (using a one-tail test). This chi-square test can, however, serve as a basis for defining the maximum lag length to consider, as in the previous section.

The Polynomial Distributed Lag

The most serious problems that can befall the methods outlined above are the likelihood of encountering serious multicollinearity and the need to estimate an equation with relatively few degrees of freedom. Both of these complications arise because of the potentially large number of coefficients we must estimate with least squares. If we can characterize the lag structure for the coefficients of interest, such as strictly increasing or decreasing, or rising at first then falling, we can circumvent these problems and estimate the lag distribution with a relatively small number of parameters. This entails approximating the shape of the lag distribution with a polynomial, then incorporating this information into the general distributed lag equation we wish to estimate.

Let us assume that we are dealing with the same distributed lag equation as before:

$$y_t = \beta + \alpha_0 x_t + \alpha_1 x_{t-1} + \cdots + \alpha_k x_{t-k} + \varepsilon_t$$

If, for successive lags, the α's in this equation initially increase, reach a maximum value, then decrease thereafter (until period k), we have a set of coefficients such as those in Figure 13.1. An important theorem in mathematics states that it is possible to approximate curves with shapes such as that in Figure 13.1 by a polynomial of suitable degree. *The degree of the polynomial should be one more than the number of turning points in the shape of interest.* For a straight line, there are no turning points,

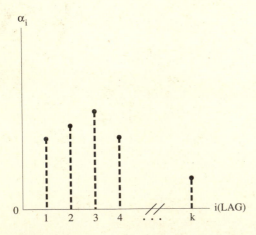

Figure 13.1

so the appropriate polynomial is first degree. Since we are depicting the relationship between α_i and different lags, i, we have: $\alpha_i = f(i)$. A first degree polynomial based on this relationship is:

$$\alpha_i = f(i) = \gamma_0 + \gamma_1 \cdot i$$

which is simply a linear equation. For Figure 13.1, one turning point exists, so a second degree polynomial is relevant:

$$\alpha_i = f(i) = \gamma_0 + \gamma_1 \cdot i + \gamma_2 \cdot i^2 \tag{13.9}$$

This is a quadratic equation. To generalize, when $(j - 1)$ turning points exist, a jth degree polynomial pertains, and the equation for α_i is:

$$\alpha_i = f(i) = \gamma_0 + \gamma_1 \cdot i + \gamma_2 \cdot i^2 + \cdots + \gamma_j \cdot i^j \tag{13.10}$$

Since this technique entails depicting lag structures with polynomials, representations such as Equations (13.9) and (13.10) are called **polynomial distributed lags**. Returning to the second degree polynomial that characterizes the lag structure in Figure 13.1, we can express each α in terms of different γ values. These are derived by setting i equal to the desired value in Equation (13.9):

$$
\begin{aligned}
\alpha_0 &= \gamma_0 & (\alpha_0 = f(0)) \\
\alpha_1 &= \gamma_0 + \gamma_1 \cdot (1) + \gamma_2 \cdot (1)^2 & (\alpha_1 = f(1)) \\
&= \gamma_0 + \gamma_1 + \gamma_2 \\
\alpha_2 &= \gamma_0 + \gamma_1 \cdot (2) + \gamma_2 \cdot (2)^2 & (\alpha_2 = f(2)) \\
&= \gamma_0 + 2\gamma_1 + 4\gamma_2 \\
&\quad \cdots \\
\alpha_k &= \gamma_0 + \gamma_1 \cdot (k) + \gamma_2 \cdot (k)^2 & (\alpha_k = f(k)) \\
&= \gamma_0 + k\gamma_1 + k^2\gamma_2
\end{aligned}
\tag{13.11}
$$

Using the expressions for each α from Equation (13.11) we substitute into our original distributed lag equation:

$$y_t = \beta + \gamma_0 x_t + (\gamma_0 + \gamma_1 + \gamma_2)x_{t-1} + \cdots + (\gamma_0 + k\gamma_1 + k^2\gamma_2)x_{t-k} + \varepsilon_t$$

Next, we factor out the different γ values:

$$
\begin{aligned}
y_t = \beta &+ \gamma_0(x_t + x_{t-1} + \cdots + x_{t-k}) + \gamma_1(1 \cdot x_{t-1} + \cdots + k \cdot x_{t-k}) \\
&+ \gamma_2[1^2 \cdot x_{t-1} + \cdots + k^2 \cdot x_{t-k}] + \varepsilon_t
\end{aligned}
\tag{13.12}
$$

We can simplify this equation by using summations for the bracketed expressions involving the different lags of x. The results are:

$$\text{for } \gamma_0 \colon x_t + x_{t-1} + \cdots + x_{t-k} = \sum_{i=0}^{k} x_{t-i} \equiv x_{1t}$$

$$\text{for } \gamma_1 \colon 1 \cdot x_{t-1} + \cdots + k \cdot x_{t-k} = \sum_{i=1}^{k} i \cdot x_{t-i} \equiv x_{2t}$$

$$\text{for } \gamma_2 \colon 1^2 \cdot x_{t-1} + \cdots + k^2 \cdot x_{t-i} = \sum_{i=1}^{k} i^2 \cdot x_{t-i} \equiv x_{3t}$$

Using these newly created variables, we substitute back into Equation (13.12):

$$y_t = \beta + \gamma_0 x_{1t} + \gamma_1 x_{2t} + \gamma_2 x_{3t} + \varepsilon_t \tag{13.13}$$

Equation (13.13) can be estimated with least squares. To do this, it is necessary to create the new variables x_1, x_2, and x_3, then to regress y on these variables with an intercept. This procedure is known as the **Almon lag technique**.[7]

By representing the lag structure in Figure 13.1 with a second degree polynomial, we have reduced the number of coefficients that must be estimated from $k + 1$ (α_0 through α_k) to 4 (β, γ_0, γ_1, and γ_2). Potential problems with degrees of freedom and multicollinearity are substantially reduced by following this procedure. However, the explanatory variables in Equation (13.13) are likely to be correlated based on the way in which they are constructed. Since they are linear functions of the different lags of an explanatory variable, some multicollinearity problems might still occur.

We will illustrate the mechanics of estimating a polynomial distributed lag using the unemployment rate-capacity utilization rate data. For simplicity, a second degree polynomial with three lags will be used:

$$u_t = \beta + \alpha_0 CAP_t + \alpha_1 CAP_{t-1} + \alpha_2 CAP_{t-2} + \alpha_3 CAP_{t-3} + \varepsilon_t$$

The first step in estimating the α's in this equation is to create the variables x_1, x_2, and x_3 from Equation (13.13). These are constructed in the following way:

$$x_{1t} = CAP_t + CAP_{t-1} + CAP_{t-2} + CAP_{t-3}$$

$$x_{2t} = CAP_{t-1} + 2CAP_{t-2} + 3CAP_{t-3}$$

$$x_{3t} = CAP_{t-1} + 4CAP_{t-2} + 9CAP_{t-3}$$

Next, the unemployment rate is regressed on these variables with an intercept. The equation that results is:

$$\hat{u}_t = 39.1 - 0.237x_{1t} + 0.207x_{2t} - 0.050x_{3t}$$
$$\qquad (16.1) \quad (11.1) \qquad (5.0) \qquad (3.7)$$

$$\bar{R}^2 = 0.869 \quad n = 35 \quad \hat{\sigma}_\varepsilon = 0.571 \quad F = 76.2$$

The distributed lag coefficients are constructed using the values: $\hat{\gamma}_0 = -0.237$; $\hat{\gamma}_1 = 0.207$; and $\hat{\gamma}_2 = -0.050$. The estimated coefficients (using Equation (13.11)) are:

$$\hat{\alpha}_0 = \hat{\gamma}_0 = -0.237$$

$$\hat{\alpha}_1 = \hat{\gamma}_0 + \hat{\gamma}_1 + \hat{\gamma}_2 = (-0.237 + 0.207 - 0.050) = -0.080$$

$$\hat{\alpha}_2 = \hat{\gamma}_0 + 2\hat{\gamma}_1 + 4\hat{\gamma}_2 = \{-0.237 + 2(0.207) + 4(-0.050)\} = -0.023$$

$$\hat{\alpha}_3 = \hat{\gamma}_0 + 3\hat{\gamma}_1 + 9\hat{\gamma}_2 = \{-0.237 + 3(0.207) + 9(-0.050)\} = -0.066$$

---

[7] S. Almon, "The Distributed Lag Between Capital Appropriations and Expenditures," *Econometrica* 33 (January 1965), 178–196.

Substituting these into the original equation we have:

$$\hat{u}_t = 39.1 - 0.237\text{CAP}_t - 0.080\text{CAP}_{t-1} - 0.023\text{CAP}_{t-2} - 0.066\text{CAP}_{t-3}$$

The Almon lag technique requires that both lag length and the appropriate degree of the polynomial that defines lag weights be known. Knowledge of both (or either of) these values is seldom had in actual practice. Because of this, a number of practical approaches to estimating polynomial distributed lags have emerged over the years. Kelejian and Oates suggest the following procedure[8]:

1. Select a polynomial degree that is large enough to characterize the likely pattern of the α_i's. They recommend a third or fourth-order polynomial.
2. Determine what is likely to be the maximum lag length (M) for the relationship being modeled. For quarterly or monthly data, they recommend the equivalent of 3 to 4 years of data.
3. If we denote the polynomial degree by p, consecutively estimate the equation, each time with a different number of lag periods, but with a polynomial of degree p using only observations $M + 1$ to n. In the first regression, the maximum included lag equals p. For subsequent regressions, the maximum lag runs from $p + 1$ and concludes with M.
4. Since the same set of observations are used for each of these regressions, we can use the adjusted R^2 values to select the equation that fits the data best.[9] Recall from the discussion earlier, this is equivalent to selecting the equation with the smallest σ_ε^2. The value of k is obtained from the equation which maximizes $\bar{R}^2$.

The use of this procedure can be illustrated using the unemployment rate-capacity utilization rate data. The labor force participation rate of females (LFPF) is included to represent the secular trend in U. A polynomial of degree 3 was selected along with a maximum lag length of 7. This value was obtained from the cross-correlation analysis presented earlier. MicroTSP was used to calculate the regression equations along with the implied lag weights. The least squares command includes a polynomial distributed lag by adding PDL( ), where the name of the variable to which the Almon lag is to be applied appears in parentheses. For the data used here, the command is:

```
>LS  U  C  LFPF  PDL(CAP)[↵]
```

When this is entered, MicroTSP prompts the user for the lag length, the polynomial degree, and whether any endpoint restrictions are desired. Since no endpoint information is known, no restrictions are placed on the lag distribution. The entries for the

---

[8] H. Kelejian and W. Oates, *Introduction to Econometrics: Principles and Applications*, 3d. ed. (New York: Harper & Row), 1989, pp. 175–176.

[9] Actually, Kelejian and Oates recommend the use of R^2. Adjusted R^2 is used here to be consistent with the discussion earlier in this chapter.

first regression performed are:

```
PDL parameters for CAPUR:
Number of lags // 3[  ]
Order of polynomial // 3[  ]
╞═══════╡ Zero Constraints ╞═══════
(0) None
(1) Near
(2) Far
(3) Both
 F1 Break - cancel procedure
```

The adjusted R^2 values, along with the lag lengths estimated were as follows:

k	$\bar{R}^2$
3	0.888
4	0.895
5	**0.898**
6	0.896
7	0.889

Adjusted R^2 is maximized for a lag length of 5. The MicroTSP output for this equation is:

```
LS // Dependent Variable is U
SMPL range: 1955 - 1989
Number of observations: 35
```

VARIABLE	COEFFICIENT	STD. ERROR	T-STAT.	2-TAIL SIG.
C	37.268249	3.7368974	9.9730456	0.000
LFPF	0.0295820	0.0163896	1.8049290	0.079
PDL1	-0.0247297	0.0112317	-2.2017824	0.034
PDL2	0.0229033	0.0116677	1.9629689	0.057
PDL3	-0.0256873	0.0051658	-4.9725549	0.000
PDL4	0.0062329	0.0027162	2.2947095	0.027

R-squared	0.912844	Mean of dependent var	5.934286
Adjusted R-squared	0.897817	S.D. of dependent var	1.576471
S.E. of regression	0.503935	Sum of squared resid	7.364557
Durbin-Watson stat	1.665217	F-statistic	60.74757

The variables PDL1 to PDL4 are similar, but not identical, to the x variables in Equation (13.13). Each of these is statistically significant for a two-tail test (their expected signs are unknown) at approximately the 5 percent level. MicroTSP calculates the implied lag coefficients from these variables along with their t-statistics. The output that corresponds to this equation is:

Lag Distribution of CAPUR	Lag	Coef	S.E.	T-Stat
*	0	-0.22315	0.01905	-11.7138
*	1	-0.07955	0.01297	-6.13296
*	2	-0.02473	0.01123	-2.20178
*	3	-0.02128	0.01107	-1.92316
*	4	-0.03181	0.01313	-2.42214
*	5	-0.01892	0.01885	-1.00353
O Sum		-0.39944	0.03922	-10.1838

All of the coefficients are negative and statistically significant up to the fifth period lag. The sum of the coefficients, -0.399, which is the long-run multiplier, is also statistically significant. The final version of the estimated equation is:

$$\hat{u}_t = 37.3 + 0.030\text{LFPF}_t - 0.223\text{CAP}_t - 0.080\text{CAP}_{t-1} - 0.025\text{CAP}_{t-2}$$
$$\quad (10.0) \quad (1.8) \qquad (11.7) \qquad (6.1) \qquad\qquad (2.2)$$

$$\quad - 0.021\text{CAP}_{t-3} - 0.032\text{CAP}_{t-4} - 0.019\text{CAP}_{t-5}$$
$$\qquad (1.9) \qquad\qquad (2.4) \qquad\qquad (1.0)$$

$$\bar{R}^2 = 0.898 \quad n = 35 \quad \hat{\sigma}_\varepsilon = 0.504 \quad F = 60.7$$

If lag length (L) is known, we can use a sequential testing procedure similar to the one presented earlier to arrive at the polynomial degree. This entails estimating the equation first with a polynomial of degree L, then with consecutively smaller degrees, and testing these restrictions with an F-test. If we continue to denote polynomial degree by p, the sequence of hypotheses that are tested are:

$$H_{0(1)}: p = L - 1; \quad \text{and} \quad H_{a(1)}: p = L$$
$$H_{0(2)}: p = L - 2; \quad \text{and} \quad H_{a(2)}: p = L - 1$$
$$\cdots$$
$$H_{0(j)}: p = L - j; \quad \text{and} \quad H_{a(j)}: p = L - j + 1$$

Each null hypotheses is conditional; that is, it assumes the previous null hypothesis is true.

The test statistic for these hypotheses is based on the change in the sum of the squared residuals that results from incorporating the implied restrictions on the polynomial degree. The value of p is obtained from the last null hypothesis we are unable to reject. The procedure is as follows:

1. Discard the first L observations. Estimate the equation first with lag length L and a polynomial degree L, then with lag length L and polynomial degree $L - 1$. Obtain the sum of the squared residuals from each of these regressions.

2. If we denote the sums of the squared residuals from (1) as ESS_L and ESS_{L-1}, respectively, the first null hypothesis is tested using the test statistic:

$$\frac{(ESS_{L-1} - ESS_L)/1}{ESS_L/(df_L)}$$

where df_L denotes the number of degrees of freedom from the estimated equation with lag length and polynomial degree L. This test statistic follows the F-distribution with 1 and df_L degrees of freedom in the numerator and denominator, respectively. If the value of the test statistic exceeds the critical F-value for 1 and df_L degrees of freedom, reject $H_{0(1)}$ that $p = L - 1$ and accept the alternative hypothesis that the polynomial is of degree L. If we are unable to reject $H_{0(1)}$, proceed to the next step.

3. If $H_{0(1)}$ is not rejected, we next test $H_{0(2)}$, assuming $H_{0(1)}$ is correct. We thus estimate the equation with L lags using polynomial degrees $L - 1$ and $L - 2$. Obtain the sum of the squared residuals from these regressions, calculate the test statistic:

$$\frac{ESS_{L-2} - ESS_{L-1}}{ESS_{L-1}/(df_{L-1})}$$

and compare this with the critical F-value for the selected level of significance. If we are unable to reject $H_{0(2)}$, repeat this step by decreasing polynomial degrees by 1, and so forth.

4. When we are able to reject a null hypothesis, the polynomial degree that is selected is given by the null hypothesis *in the previous test* (the last value for L we were unable to reject).

Since the value of L is generally unknown, a common practice is to use the estimated lag length in place of this value when performing this test. Estimated maximum lag length has also been used. When this type of joint testing is utilized to determine both lag length and polynomial degree, the Type I error for this procedure is unknown.[10]

Estimating polynomial degree with this test might seem like an overly difficult way to proceed. Since increasing polynomial degree by 1 for a given lag length requires the addition of one more variable (such as x_{3t} for going from a second to third degree polynomial), it is tempting to estimate polynomial degree by continually adding one more degree to the polynomial, then performing a t-test on the coefficient of the newly added variable. The likely problem with this approach is multicollinearity among the x variables. As noted above, each x is a linear function of current or lagged values of the variable of interest, which tends to build intercorrelations into

---

[10] See G. Judge, et al., Ch. 17.

these variables. This can be seen by again referring to the unemployment rate-capacity utilization rate data. Using a lag length of 5 years, the equation was estimated for polynomial degrees 2, 3, then 4. All of the x variables were statistically significant with degrees 2 and 3. For the fourth degree polynomial, x_{4t} was statistically significant, while x_{5t} was not. The fact that x_{5t} was not significant seems to indicate that it does not belong in the equation, allowing us to conclude that the correct polynomial is of degree 3. To test for the presence of multicollinearity that may be responsible for the low t-statistic of this variable, an auxiliary regression of x_{5t} on the other x's was performed. The results of this regression were:

$$\widehat{x_{5t}} = 108.4 \; - 2.5x_{1t} - 6.0x_{2t} + 4.8x_{3t} + 2.0x_{4t}$$
$$(127.4) \quad (4.4) \quad\;\; (9.9) \quad\;\; (18.1) \quad\;\; (14.4)$$

$$R^2 = 0.9971 \quad \bar{R}^2 = 0.997 \quad \hat{\sigma}_\varepsilon = 26.1 \quad F = 2572.8 \quad CV = 0.0028$$

All four of the variables in this regression are statistically significant, the value of R^2 is close to 1, the equation F is highly significant, and the coefficient of variation is close to 0, indicating a "small" equation standard error. The variance inflation factor for x_{5t} (see Chapter 8) is:

$$\text{VIF}_5 = 1/(1 - 0.9971) = 344.0.$$

This far exceeds the usual benchmark of 10 considered to indicate the possibility of problematic multicollinearity. It thus appears that the standard error of the coefficient of x_{5t} in the original equation was inflated, causing its t-statistic to be understated. As this example shows, this particular method for determining polynomial degree is prone to problems with multicollinearity. As a basis for determining polynomial degree, it will likely *underestimate* the correct degree, since the likelihood of our failing to reject a false null hypothesis for the last included x variable (a Type II error) will tend to be large as the result of the variance inflating effects of multicollinearity.

We have seen that the Almon lag technique can be applied to equations where one or more of the explanatory variables are not subjected to polynomial lags. The Almon lag technique can also be applied to more than one of the variables in a regression equation. Batten and Thornton[11] illustrate this for the St. Louis Equation, which was developed by Andersen and Jordan in 1968 to assess the relative importance of monetary and fiscal policy on the level of economic activity. The original Andersen-Jordan equation was:

$$\Delta Y_t = \beta + \sum_{i=0}^{3} \alpha_i \Delta M_{t-i} + \sum_{i=0}^{3} \gamma_i \Delta G_{t-i} + \sum_{i=0}^{3} \tau_i \Delta R_{t-i} + \varepsilon_t$$

where Y is nominal GNP; M is a monetary aggregate such as M1; G is a measure of high employment federal government expenditures; and R is a measure of high employment federal tax revenues. First differences of the variables in this equation are

---

[11] D. Batten and D. Thornton, "Polynomial Distributed Lags and the Estimation of the St. Louis Equation," *Review* of the Federal Reserve Bank of St. Louis 65 (April 1983), 13–25.

utilized since this specification potentially avoids spurious correlations among Y and the explanatory variables that arise as the result of common trends. Andersen and Jordan utilized a fourth degree polynomial to characterize the lag distributions of each of the explanatory variables (with both endpoints restricted to 0). Subsequent research pointed out that the use of first differences can result in heteroskedastic errors. This can be avoided by using annual rates of change in place of first differences, which has become the accepted method for specifying the variables in this equation.

After experimenting with polynomial degree and lag length, Batten and Thornton arrived at a ninth degree polynomial for M with 10 lags, and a seventh degree polynomial for G with 9 lags. Their estimated equation omits R. Using quarterly data for the period 1962:2 to 1982:3, and compound annual growth rates for Y, M, and G (these are represented by lowercase letters), their estimated equation is:

VARIABLE	COEFFICIENT	(t-STAT)	VARIABLE	COEFFICIENT	(t-STAT)
Intercept	2.342	1.56			
$m(t)$	0.767	4.61	$g(t)$	0.110	2.34
$m(t-1)$	0.635	3.66	$g(t-1)$	0.056	1.24
$m(t-2)$	0.295	1.80	$g(t-2)$	-0.095	2.11
$m(t-3)$	-0.377	2.36	$g(t-3)$	0.028	0.61
$m(t-4)$	0.233	1.38	$g(t-4)$	-0.001	0.03
$m(t-5)$	-0.127	0.68	$g(t-5)$	-0.042	0.90
$m(t-6)$	-0.134	0.79	$g(t-6)$	0.095	1.93
$m(t-7)$	-0.126	0.74	$g(t-7)$	0.047	0.92
$m(t-8)$	0.297	1.69	$g(t-8)$	-0.116	2.32
$m(t-9)$	0.230	1.15	$g(t-9)$	-0.116	2.33
$m(t-10)$	-0.530	2.77			
$\Sigma m(t)$	1.163	4.50	$\Sigma g(t)$	-0.034	0.26

$\bar{R}^2 = 0.47$ $\hat{\sigma}_\varepsilon = 3.21$

The lag distributions for the money growth and government expenditure growth coefficients are given in Figure 13.2. Six of the eleven monetary coefficients are statistically significant, while five of the nine fiscal policy coefficients are significant. Both lag distributions range from positive to negative values. Other things being equal, a one percent rise in the growth rate of money increases the mean growth rate of GNP by 0.77 percent, given past rates of monetary growth, and current and past growth rates of high employment government expenditure. This impact multiplier for monetary policy is substantially larger than that for fiscal policy, 0.11. The long-run multiplier for monetary policy, 1.163, is statistically significant at the 1 percent level and above. This multiplier is close to 1, indicating that other things being equal, a sustained one percent rise in monetary growth will, in the long-run, raise the growth rate of GNP by approximately the same amount. The long-run fiscal policy multiplier

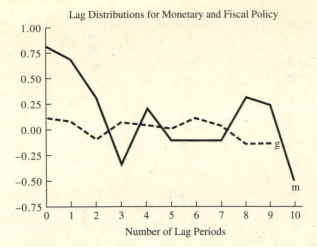

Figure 13.2

is both small and statistically insignificant. Thus, other things being equal, the effect of a sustained one percent rise in high employment government spending on GNP growth is not significantly different from 0. Based on these results, Batten and Thornton conclude:

> ... the long-run effectiveness of money growth and the long-run ineffectiveness of growth in high-employment government expenditures are substantiated by ordinary least squares estimates of model parameters ... Thus, there is no evidence that the conclusion of the St. Louis equation can be traced to ... econometric misspecification.

Before moving on to the discussion of infinite distributed lag estimation, it is worthwhile to note the consequences of incorrectly specifying either the lag length or degree of polynomial when estimating an Almon lag[12]:

If the lag length that is utilized is correct, but the polynomial degree is incorrect: the distributed lag coefficients are unbiased but inefficient when the polynomial degree is greater than the correct degree; the distributed lag coefficients are biased when the polynomial degree is understated.

If the polynomial degree is correct, but the lag length is incorrect: the distributed lag coefficients will generally be biased when the lag length is too short; the distributed lag coefficients will be biased when the lag length that is utilized overstates the correct lag length by an amount greater than or equal to the degree of the polynomial.

---

[12] See G. Judge et al., Chapter 17.

THE ESTIMATION OF INFINITE DISTRIBUTED LAG MODELS

We have only considered finite distributed lags such as Equation (13.2′) up to this point. However, it is theoretically possible for an infinite number of lags to occur as y adjusts to a sustained change in x. If this is true, the distributed lag model is:

$$y_t = \beta + \alpha_0 x_t + \alpha_1 x_{t-1} + \alpha_2 x_{t-2} + \cdots + \varepsilon_t \qquad \textbf{(13.14)}$$

In its present form, Equation (13.14) is not estimable, since it entails an infinite number of parameters. A positive number of degrees of freedom would therefore never exist. Before we can estimate the parameters in an infinite distributed lag equation, we must therefore find a way to reduce the number of parameters that must be estimated to a manageable number. Koyck illustrated one such method.[13] If we assume that the coefficients in the infinite distributed lag model continually diminish, so that the influence of successively distant values of x become smaller, and, that these weights decrease geometrically, the coefficient for the ith period lag of x, α_i, can be expressed as:

$$\alpha_i = \alpha_0 \lambda^i \qquad (i = 0, 1, \ldots) \qquad \textbf{(13.15)}$$

where α_0 is the coefficient x in the current period and λ is a constant. If $\lambda = 1$, $\alpha_i = \alpha_0$ for all time periods, which violates the assumption of declining lag coefficients. When $\lambda = 0$, $\alpha_i = 0$ for all time periods, and y is not a function of x. For geometrically declining weights to exist, it is therefore necessary for λ to be a positive fraction, or $0 < \lambda < 1$. The constant λ indicates the **rate of decay** for the distributed lag. The closer λ is to 1, the slower is the decrease in successive lag coefficients, while for small values of λ, the coefficients fall more rapidly. The following table shows values of α_i for different λ's, assuming $\alpha_0 = 3$.

LAG	$\lambda = 0.9$	$\lambda = 0.4$
0	$3(0.9)^0 = 3.00$	$3(0.4)^0 = 3.00$
1	$3(0.9)^1 = 2.70$	$3(0.4)^1 = 1.20$
2	$3(0.9)^2 = 2.43$	$3(0.4)^2 = 0.48$
3	$3(0.9)^3 = 2.19$	$3(0.4)^3 = 0.19$
	$\cdots$	
9	$3(0.9)^9 = 1.16$	$3(0.4)^9 = 0.0008$

Figure 13.3 graphs these two lag distributions. The quantity $(1 - \lambda)$ is called the **speed of adjustment**, which indicates the rate at which successive lag coefficients decrease. For the first column above, which has the slower rate of decay, the speed

---

[13] L. Koyck, *Distributed Lags and Investment Analysis* (Amsterdam: North Holland) 1954.

of adjustment is 0.1, while for $\lambda = 0.4$, the speed of adjustment is 0.6. When the speed of adjustment is large, lag coefficients decrease rapidly, and the influence of x on y dies out quickly. This is apparent in Figure 13.3 for the curve depicting $\lambda = 0.4$. While the influence of past values of x on y decreases for both of the values of λ in this figure, the impact of lags farther in the past is more substantial with the lag distribution whose speed of adjustment is more gradual. Eventually, past values of x exert an insignificant impact on y, no matter what the value of λ.

We can now analyze how this set of assumptions about the lag distribution of x allows us to estimate the infinite lag model, Equation (13.14). First, we substitute the values of α from Equation (13.15) into Equation (13.14):

$$y_t = \beta + (\alpha_0\lambda^0)x_t + (\alpha_0\lambda^1)x_{t-1} + (\alpha_0\lambda^2)x_{t-2} + \cdots + \varepsilon_t$$

As it now stands, this equation is still not estimable, since it contains an infinite number of regressors and its specification is non-linear in the parameters (λ is raised to powers and α_0 is multiplied by λ). Further simplification is therefore necessary. We next factor out the common term α_0:

$$y_t = \beta + \alpha_0\{x_t + \lambda x_{t-1} + \lambda^2 x_{t-2} + \cdots\} + \varepsilon_t \qquad \textbf{(13.16)}$$

Now, apply the backshift operator defined in Chapter 11 to the bracketed expression. Recall that the backshift operator, B, is defined as

$$Bx_t \equiv x_{t-1};$$

$$B^2x_t \equiv x_{t-2};$$

and in general:

$$B^i x_t \equiv x_{t-i}$$

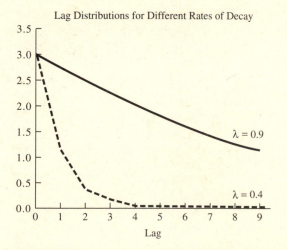

Lag Distributions for Different Rates of Decay

Figure 13.3

This operator allows us to express lagged values of x in terms of current period x and an exponent of its value. Applying this operator to Equation (13.16):

$$y_t = \beta + \alpha_0 x_t \{1 + (\lambda B) + (\lambda B)^2 + \cdots\} + \varepsilon_t$$

Since the value of λ is less than one, the bracketed expression involves an infinite sequence whose sum is:

$$\{1 + (\lambda B) + (\lambda B)^2 + \cdots\} = \frac{1}{(1 - \lambda B)}$$

Equation (13.16) may therefore be written:

$$y_t = \beta + \frac{\alpha_0 x_t}{(1 - \lambda B)} + \varepsilon_t$$

Multiplying both sides of this equation by the term $(1 - \lambda B)$, it becomes:

$$y_t(1 - \lambda B) = \beta(1 - \lambda B) + \alpha_0 x_t + \varepsilon_t(1 - \lambda B)$$

or

where $\beta(1 - \lambda B) = \beta(1 - \lambda)$ since β does not have a time subscript. Finally, rearranging the terms in this equation, we may express it as:

$$y_t = \beta(1 - \lambda) + \alpha_0 x_t + \lambda y_{t-1} + (\varepsilon_t - \lambda \varepsilon_{t-1}) \qquad \textbf{(13.17)}$$

There are several noteworthy features of Equation (13.17). First, the error in this equation is a moving average error (see Chapter 11). If we denote this error as ε_t^*, and let $\beta(1 - \lambda) \equiv \beta^*$, we can rewrite Equation (13.17) as:

$$y_t = \beta^* + \alpha_0 x_t + \lambda y_{t-1} + \varepsilon_t^* \qquad \textbf{(13.18)}$$

This method of transforming an infinite distributed lag equation into one with the form of Equation (13.18) is called a **Koyck transformation**. Equation (13.18) is estimable with least squares. However, even if the original errors satisfy all the usual assumptions (i.e., $E(\varepsilon_t) = 0$; $\text{Var}(\varepsilon_t) = \sigma_\varepsilon^2$; and $\text{Cov}(\varepsilon_t, \varepsilon_{t-j}) = 0$), the moving average errors in a Koyck transformation will fail to satisfy all of these properties. Specifically, *the moving average errors in Equation (13.18) will be serially correlated even when the original errors, ε_t, are not*. To see this, recall that serial correlation exists when the covariance between errors in different periods is nonzero. For errors one period apart, we have:

$$\begin{aligned}
E(\varepsilon_t^* \cdot \varepsilon_{t-1}^*) &= E[(\varepsilon_t - \lambda \varepsilon_{t-1})(\varepsilon_{t-1} - \lambda \varepsilon_{t-2})] \\
&= E[\varepsilon_t \varepsilon_{t-1} - \lambda \varepsilon_t \varepsilon_{t-2} - \lambda \varepsilon_{t-1}^2 + \lambda^2 \varepsilon_{t-1} \varepsilon_{t-2}] \\
&= E[-\lambda \varepsilon_{t-1}^2] \\
&= -\lambda \sigma_\varepsilon^2 \\
&\neq 0
\end{aligned}$$

since we are assuming that ε is not serially correlated, which makes the expected value of each $\varepsilon_t \varepsilon_{t-j}$ equal to 0. Since this covariance is non-zero, the errors in Equation (13.18) are serially correlated. Second, Equation (13.18), which contains a lagged dependent variable, is an **autoregressive equation**. The Koyck transformation entails modifying an infinite distributed lag equation such as Equation (13.14) into an autoregressive equation. The long-run multiplier for x in Equation (13.14) is easily estimable with a Koyck lag. This value is:

$$\sum_{i=0}^{\infty} \alpha_i = \sum_{i=0}^{\infty} (\alpha_0 \lambda^i)$$

$$= \alpha_0 \sum_{i=0}^{\infty} \lambda^i$$

$$= \frac{\alpha_0}{1 - \lambda} \tag{13.19}$$

Our estimate of this multiplier is obtained by dividing the coefficient of x, $\hat{\alpha}_0$, by the estimated speed of adjustment, which is one minus the coefficient of the lagged dependent variable. The mean lag with a Koyck lag is:

$$\text{Mean Lag} = \frac{\lambda}{1 - \lambda}$$

If $\lambda = 3/4$, the speed of adjustment is 1/4, and the mean lag is 3 periods. This indicates that for a sustained change in x, three-fourths of the change in y occurs after 3 periods. Finally, the Koyck transformation reduces the number of parameters that must be estimated from an infinite number to only three: β^*, α_0, and λ.

While the Koyck Lag has a number of important features, most notably its dramatic reduction in the number of parameters that must be estimated, it is essentially a mathematical solution to the problem of estimating an infinite lag. As such, it lacks an economic basis. However, two different economic models exist whose mathematical representation produces equations that are either identical to or very similar to that for the Koyck Lag.

Adaptive Expectations

The correct specification of an equation often includes the expected level of an explanatory variable, and not its actual value. If, for example, y is a function of z and the *expected* level of x (x_t^*), we may express this relationship as:

$$y_t = \alpha_0 + \alpha_1 z_t + \alpha_2 x_t^* + \varepsilon_t \tag{13.20}$$

As an example of this type of relationship, consider real business fixed investment (I). This type of expenditure, which consists of spending by firms on factories and equipment, is related to interest rates (r) and profits. However, since the revenues and costs associated with such investments occur over a number of future time periods, it is *expected* future profit (π_t^*) that determines such expenditure. Thus, we can express the equation for real fixed investment as:

$$I_t = \alpha_0 + \alpha_1 r_t + \alpha_2 \pi_t^* + \varepsilon_t$$

Another example of this type of equation is given by the Keynesian liquidity preference (money demand) function. The real demand for money (m^d) depends on both interest rates and real income. Interest rates can and often do change rapidly, causing a great deal of uncertainty concerning their future values. The real demand for money therefore depends on expected interest rates (r^*) and real income (y):

$$m_t^d = \alpha_0 + \alpha_1 r_t^* + \alpha_2 y_t + \varepsilon_t$$

The underlying basis for these relationships results from factors such as imperfect information and the existence of transactions costs. How can we estimate such an equation, since data on the expected value of x (such as expected future profits) often do not exist? One method for accomplishing this is to assume a specific basis for expectations formation. If we assume that the expected level of x is determined by its past and present levels, and that such expectations are modified when errors are committed estimating this variable, we may utilize the **adaptive expectations** model:

$$x_t^* - x_{t-1}^* = \lambda(x_t - x_{t-1}^*) \tag{13.21}$$

In Equation (13.21), the unobserved variable, x_t^*, is stated in terms of its actual value, x_t. λ is the **expectation coefficient**, where it is assumed that $0 < \lambda \le 1$. The left side of this equation denotes the change in expected x. The term in brackets on the right is the difference between last period's expectation of x and its value this period. According to the adaptive expectations model in Equation (13.21), expected x each period changes (adapts) by a proportion, λ, of the gap between the current value of x and its expectation last period.

We can rewrite Equation (13.21) expressing x_t^* as a weighted average of actual x and last periods expectation of this variable:

$$x_t^* = \lambda x_t + (1 - \lambda)x_{t-1}^* \tag{13.22}$$

The weights in this equation are stated in terms of the expectations coefficient, λ. The basis for the restrictions placed on the values of λ can be seen by substituting the values of 0 and 1 into this equation. When the expectations coefficient is 0, Equation (13.22) reduces to $x_t^* = x_{t-1}^*$, so that the expected value of x this period remains unchanged from its value last period. This is referred to as **static expectations**. If $\lambda = 1$, $x_t^* = x_t$, and the expected value of x this period adjusts completely to its current value. It should be evident that the larger is λ, the more rapid is the adjustment of expected x to the actual values of this variable.

Since Equation (13.22) involves the expectations for x in periods t and $t - 1$, we can eliminate the lag of x_t^* in this equation by utilizing the backshift operator. We first move all the terms involving expected x to the left side:

$$x_t^* - (1 - \lambda)x_{t-1}^* = \lambda x_t$$

Applying the backshift operator to the left side of this equation:

$$x_t^*\{1 - (1 - \lambda)B\} = \lambda x_t$$

we can express x_t^* as:

$$x_t^* = \frac{\lambda x_t}{\{1 - (1 - \lambda)B\}} \tag{13.23}$$

The right side of Equation (13.23) provides us with an expression for x_t^* that can be substituted into our original equation for y. If we utilize the following bivariate relationship for simplicity, with y as a function of x^*:

$$y_t = \beta + \alpha x_t^* + \varepsilon_t$$

We can express y as a function of *actual* x:

$$y_t = \beta + \alpha \left[\frac{\lambda x_t}{\{1 - (1 - \lambda)B\}} \right] + \varepsilon_t$$

Multiplying both sides of this equation by $\{1 - (1 - \lambda)B\}$ and multiplying through the bracketed terms we arrive at an equation that can be estimated using least squares:

$$y_t\{1 - (1 - \lambda)B\} = \beta\{1 - (1 - \lambda)B\} + (\alpha\lambda)x_t + \{1 - (1 - \lambda)B\}\varepsilon_t$$

$$y_t - (1 - \lambda)y_{t-1} = \lambda\beta + (\alpha\lambda)x_t + \varepsilon_t - (1 - \lambda)\varepsilon_{t-1}$$

$$y_t = \beta^* + \alpha^* x_t + (1 - \lambda)y_{t-1} + \varepsilon_t^* \qquad \textbf{(13.24)}$$

where $\beta^* = \lambda\beta$; $\alpha^* = \alpha\lambda$; and $\varepsilon_t^* = \varepsilon_t - (1 - \lambda)\varepsilon_{t-1}$. Applying the adaptive expectations model to a bivariate equation, where y is a function of expected x, therefore results in an autoregressive equation with a moving average error. Equation (13.24) is identical (for estimation purposes) to the Koyck Lag model discussed above, where y is regressed on x and lagged y. Also, the errors in Equation (13.24), like those in the Koyck model, will be serially correlated.

There is another similarity between these models as well. If we continually substitute for x_{t-1}^* in Equation (13.22), we obtain the following expression for expected x:

$$x_t^* = \lambda \sum_{i=0}^{\infty} (1 - \lambda)^i x_{t-i}$$

The expected value of x according to the adaptive expectations model is therefore an infinite distributed lag of actual x values, with geometrically decreasing weights.

The correct interpretation of the coefficient of x in Equation (13.24) is different from that in the original model which was stated in terms of the expected value of x. In that equation, α measures the impact on the mean of y of a one unit change in *expected* x. For Equation (13.24), α^* measures the effect of a one-unit change in *actual* x on the mean of y, given the value of y last period. To make this comparable to the coefficient for expected x, we must divide $\hat{\alpha}^*$ by $\hat{\lambda}$, our estimate of the expectation coefficient.

When the original equation is multivariate, such as in Equation (13.20), the form of the equation that is estimated includes not only x, z, and lagged y, but the lag of z as well. This result is derived by substituting Equation (13.23) into Equation (13.20).

The adaptive expectations model has also been stated in forms other than that of Equation (13.21). An alternative formulation of this model is:

$$x_t^* - x_{t-1}^* = \lambda(x_{t-1} - x_{t-1}^*) \qquad \textbf{(13.25)}$$

According to this equation, the change in expected x is a proportion of the expectation error committed last period $(x_{t-1} - x_{t-1}^*)$. Note that when $\lambda = 1$, $x_t^* = x_{t-1}$, and a model similar to the Koyck equation does not result. The bivariate equation of y on x^* then becomes:

$$y_t = \alpha_0 + \alpha_1 x_{t-1} + \varepsilon_t$$

If y is quantity supplied and x is price, the above equation is the Cobweb Model that has been studied extensively in agricultural economics. In that model, current supply decisions are based on past prices (which are the basis for expected future price). Systematic errors can occur, as price expectations fail to change in response to expectation errors from previous periods.

This last possibility, of committing systematic errors, is perhaps the most serious objection to the adaptive expectations framework. As Begg points out:

> ... the hypothesis is entirely backward looking ... Suppose that OPEC is meeting next week but that the outcome of the deliberations is a formality; everyone knows that they will announce a doubling of oil prices. Surely economists will be predicting higher inflation from the moment at which news of the prospective oil price increase becomes available. Yet the hypothesis of Adaptive Expectations asserts that individuals raise inflation expectations only after higher inflation has gradually fed into the past data from which they extrapolate ... Using such a rule, individuals would make systematic mistakes, underpredicting the actual inflation rate for many periods after the oil price rise.[14]

As an example of this, assume that the inflation rate, which was originally constant and correctly anticipated at 0 percent, changes to 10 percent then remains at that level. If we use Equation (13.25), and assume that $\lambda = 3/4$, expected inflation is 0 in the first period after the increase, 7.5 percent in the second period, 9.4 percent in the next period, then 9.85 percent. Thus, even when the inflation rate is constant, persons will continue to underanticipate the actual rate of inflation for a number of time periods.

The attempt to model expectations without the problem of systematic errors has led economists to develop a number of alternative models. Perhaps the most famous of these is the *rational expectations hypothesis*, which was introduced by Muth in 1961.[15] According to this hypothesis, individuals act in their own self-interest when setting expectations, using all available information. Unlike adaptive expectations, rational expectations is not predicated on a purely mechanical formula. When relevant information appears, it is incorporated directly and immediately into future expectations.

Before moving on to the next economic justification for the Koyck model, two more points will be made about adaptive expectations. First, there is no theoretical

---

[14] D. Begg, *The Rational Expectations Revolution in Macroeconomics: Theories and Evidence* (Baltimore: The Johns Hopkins University Press), 1982, p. 26.

[15] J. Muth, "Rational Expectations and the Theory of Price Movements," *Econometrica* 29 (July 1961), 315–335.

basis for the value of λ in the adaptive expectations model. Instead, it is viewed as a value to be determined empirically. The only *a priori* restrictions placed on this value are those presented above, that λ is a positive fraction. Second, the expectation coefficient is not necessarily constant. It may instead be a function of one or more variables that influence past and future values of expected x. Examples are:

$$x_t^* - x_{t-1}^* = \lambda(z_t - z_{t-1}^*)$$
$$x_t^* - x_{t-1}^* = \lambda_1(x_t - x_{t-1}^*) + \lambda_2(z_t - x_t)$$

In the first of these, expected x changes by a proportion of the difference between actual and lagged values of a related variable z. In the other, expected x is modified based on its own values and those of a related variable, z. A macroeconomic example of this last adjustment equation can be seen by referring to expected inflation. Expected inflation may change based on the gap between current and past inflation (x) *as well as* the difference between the current rate of monetary growth (z_t) and the current inflation rate.

The Partial (Stock) Adjustment Model

A number of instances arise when the dependent variable in an equation represents an equilibrium or optimal value. Such equations are often derived using calculus to maximize or minimize some function of interest. For example, minimizing the cost of producing a given level of output (assuming a specific production function) allows us to derive an expression for the optimal (i.e., cost-minimizing) employment of labor and capital.

If we let y^* denote the optimal or equilibrium value of y, and the equation for optimal y is:

$$y_t^* = \alpha_0 + \alpha_1 x_t + \alpha_2 z_t + \varepsilon_t \tag{13.26}$$

we must make an assumption about the relationship between actual y and y^*, since y_t^* is unobserved. It is generally assumed that actual y adjusts to its optimal or equilibrium over a number of time periods. This period of adjustment is the result of factors such as the existence of transactions costs that place limits on the amount of information possessed, and technical constraints.

Technically, Equation (13.26) provides an expression for the long-run level of y, since it is stated in terms of the optimal or equilibrium level of that variable. The **partial adjustment model**, which allows us to estimate an equation such as the one we are considering, may be stated as:

$$y_t - y_{t-1} = \lambda(y_t^* - y_{t-1}) \tag{13.27}$$

Unlike the adaptive expectations model, this model states the change in *actual y* in terms of its optimal value: the change in actual y each period is a proportion (λ) of the desired change in y ($= y_t^* - y_{t-1}$). The coefficient λ, which is called the **adjustment coefficient**, denotes the rate at which the desired change in y occurs each period. This value is restricted so that: $0 < \lambda < 1$. These restrictions are applied since if $\lambda = 0$,

$y_t = y_{t-1}$, indicating that no adjustment in y occurs. When $\lambda = 1$, $y_t = y_t^*$, and the entire adjustment of actual y to its optimal level occurs in a single period. The larger is λ, the more rapid is the adjustment of y to y^*. If, for example, $\lambda = 0.7$, then the change in actual y each period is 70 percent of the desired change.

The partial adjustment model in Equation (13.27) can be expressed in a slightly different way:

$$y_t = \lambda y_t^* + (1 - \lambda)y_{t-1} \tag{13.28}$$

This shows that actual y is a weighted average of its optimal and previous values, where the adjustment coefficient is the basis for the weights. By substituting Equation (13.26) into Equation (13.28), we obtain an expression for y in terms of observable variables:

$$
\begin{aligned}
y_t &= \lambda(\alpha_0 + \alpha_1 x_t + \alpha_2 z_t + \varepsilon_t) + (1 - \lambda)y_{t-1} \\
&= \lambda\alpha_0 + (\lambda\alpha_1)x_t + (\lambda\alpha_2)z_t + (1 - \lambda)y_{t-1} + \lambda\varepsilon_t
\end{aligned}
$$

so that:

$$y_t = \alpha_0^* + \alpha_1^* x_t + \alpha_2^* z_t + \alpha_3 y_{t-1} + \varepsilon_t^* \tag{13.29}$$

where $\alpha_0^* = \lambda\alpha_0$; $\alpha_1^* = \lambda\alpha_1$; $\alpha_2^* = \lambda\alpha_2$; $\alpha_3 = (1 - \lambda)$; and $\varepsilon_t^* = \lambda\varepsilon_t$. Equation (13.29) is the short-run equation for y, since it is stated in terms of actual y and the entire adjustment of actual to optimal y does not occur in a single period (based on the restrictions for λ). Note that the error in this equation is *not* a moving average error, but a multiple of the original error.

The short-run equation for the partial adjustment model has a number of similarities and differences with the corresponding equation for adaptive expectations. Both are autoregressive equations. However, the errors in these equations are very different. In the adaptive expectations model, the moving average error is serially correlated (this was shown earlier). In the partial adjustment model, the error will be serially correlated only when ε_t itself suffers from this problem. To see this, we determine the covariance between the values of ε_t^* for two different periods assuming that ε_t is a white noise error process:

$$
\begin{aligned}
\text{Cov}(\varepsilon_t^*, \varepsilon_{t-j}^*) &= E[(\lambda\varepsilon_t)(\lambda\varepsilon_{t-j})] \qquad \text{since } E(\varepsilon_t^*) = 0 \\
&= \lambda^2 E(\varepsilon_t \cdot \varepsilon_{t-j}) \\
&= 0
\end{aligned}
$$

The errors in the partial adjustment model are therefore less likely to be problematic than those in the adaptive expectations model. Also, when the long-run equation contains two or more explanatory variables, the short-run equation does not require that lags be added for these variables. Recall, this is not the case with adaptive expectations. For that model, when $y = f(x^*, z, \varepsilon)$, the resulting short-run equation is stated in terms of x, z, lagged y, and lagged z.

Once we have estimated the short-run Equation (13.29), our estimate of the adjustment coefficient is obtained by calculating 1 minus the estimated coefficient of the lagged dependent variable, since $\alpha_3 = 1 - \lambda$. If this estimate is either negative or greater than 1, the restrictions placed on this value are violated, indicating the likelihood of problems with the estimated equation.

To transform the short-run equation into its long-run form, we drop the lagged dependent variable and divide each of the estimated coefficients by $\hat{\lambda}$. Alternatively, this process can be viewed as the result of using the fact that in equilibrium, $y_t = y_{t-1}$. Substituting y_t for y_{t-1} in our estimated function eliminates the lagged dependent variable and causes a "multiplier" equal to $1/\hat{\lambda}$ to be applied to each of the remaining coefficients.

When the specification of Equation (13.26) is log-linear, a slight modification of the partial adjustment model pertains. Instead of stating the absolute difference in y as a function of the desired change, the proportional difference in y, $\ln(y_t/y_{t-1})$, is used:

$$\ln(y_t/y_{t-1}) = \ln(y_t^*/y_{t-1})^\lambda$$

or

$$\ln(y)_t - \ln(y)_{t-1} = \lambda[\ln(y^*)_t - \ln(y)_{t-1}] \tag{13.30}$$

This can also be expressed as a weighted average of the log of actual y and the log of its equilibrium value:

$$\ln(y)_t = \lambda \ln(y^*)_t + (1 - \lambda) \ln(y)_{t-1} \tag{13.31}$$

With this formulation of the partial adjustment model, λ denotes the *percentage* by which actual y adjusts to its optimal value per period.

As an example of this, consider again the Keynesian liquidity preference function, where the real demand for money (m^d) is stochastically related to interest rates (r) and real income (y):

$$m_t^d = f(r_t, y_t, \varepsilon_t)$$

When interest rates or real income change, actual cash balances adjust to their new desired levels. This adjustment occurs over a number of periods. We can therefore use the partial adjustment framework to model the demand for money. The correct dependent variable is desired money demand, m^*. Demand for money functions are typically estimated using a log-linear specification:

$$\ln(m^*)_t = \alpha_0 + \alpha_1 \ln(r)_t + \alpha_2 \ln(y)_t + \varepsilon_t$$

To transform this equation into an estimable short-run money demand function, we utilize Equation (13.31), which, following Goldfeld, is known as the real adjustment mechanism[16]:

$$\ln(m)_t = \lambda \ln(m^*)_t + (1 - \lambda) \ln(m)_{t-1}$$

---

[16] S. Goldfeld, "The Case of Missing Money," *Brookings Papers on Economic Activity* 3 (1976), 683–730.

Substituting for $\ln(m^*)_t$ we have:

$$\ln(m)_t = \lambda\{\alpha_0 + \alpha_1 \ln(r)_t + \alpha_2 \ln(y)_t + \varepsilon_t\} + (1 - \lambda) \ln(m)_{t-1}$$

which becomes:

$$\ln(m)_t = \alpha_0^* + \alpha_1^* \ln(r)_t + \alpha_2^* \ln(y)_t + \alpha_3 \ln(m)_{t-1} + \varepsilon_t^*$$

In this equation, α_1^* is the short-run interest elasticity of money demand, α_2^* is the short-run income elasticity, and $1 - \alpha_3$ gives the adjustment coefficient. The corresponding long-run elasticities are derived by dividing each short-run elasticity by $1 - \alpha_3 \; (= \lambda)$.

Thornton estimated this function using quarterly data from 1974:1 to 1984:2.[17] His sample regression function is:

$$\widehat{\ln(m)}_t = -0.069 - 0.023 \ln(r)_t + 0.096 \ln(y)_t + 0.894 \ln(m)_{t-1}$$
$$ (0.2) (4.2) (4.1) (16.1)$$

$$h = -0.14 \quad \bar{R}^2 = 0.880 \quad \hat{\sigma}_\varepsilon = 0.001$$

The interest rate utilized is the commercial paper rate while y is real income. Both short-run elasticities display the correct signs and are statistically significant. The estimated adjustment coefficient is 0.106 ($= 1 - 0.894$), which indicates that about 11 percent of the adjustment of actual to desired money balances occurs each quarter. The estimated short-run interest elasticity of money demand is -0.023, while the short-run income elasticity is 0.096. Both indicate inelastic responses. The value for h above is the Durbin-h statistic, which is used to test for autocorrelation when an equation contains a lagged dependent variable (see Chapter 11). Based on its value, we are unable to reject the null hypothesis of no serial correlation.

To derive the long-run money demand function, we can either set $\ln(m)_t = \ln(m)_{t-1}$ and manipulate the equation, or drop the lagged dependent variable and divide each of the remaining coefficients by the estimated adjustment coefficient, 0.106. This makes each long-run elasticity 9.4 ($= 1/0.106$) times the corresponding short-run elasticity. The resulting equation is:

$$\widehat{\ln(m)}_t = -0.651 - 0.217 \ln(r)_t + 0.906 \ln(y)_t$$

Both long-run elasticities are inelastic, although the income elasticity is close to 1.0. Other things being equal, a one percent rise in the commercial paper rate lowers mean money demand by 0.023 percent in the short-run, and by 0.217 percent in the long-run. Similarly, a one percent rise in real income raises mean money demand by 0.096 percent in the short-run and by 0.906 percent in the long-run.

Two other examples of partial adjustment equations will now be presented. The first of these provides the basis for modeling expenditures on consumer durables. The starting point for this model is the existence of an optimal stock of consumer

---

[17] D. Thornton, "Money Demand Dynamics: Some New Evidence," *Review* of the FED St. Louis 67 (March 1985), 14–23.

durables, s^* (this is a dollar value). This stock is related to income, prices, and other key variables:

$$s_t^* = \alpha_0 + \alpha_1(p_{cd}/p_c)_t + \alpha_2 y_t + \alpha_3 r_t + \alpha_4 D_t + \varepsilon_t \qquad (13.32)$$

where p_{cd} denotes the prices of consumer durables, p_c represents other consumption prices, y is real income, r is the interest rate, D is a measure of indebtedness, and ε is a stochastic error. The stock adjustment mechanism is used here. Each period the stock of durables is assumed to change by a proportion of the gap between the desired and actual stock:

$$s_t - s_{t-1} = \lambda(s_t^* - s_{t-1})$$

Part of the expenditure each period on consumer durables is used for additions to the existing stock. A second type of consumer durables expenditures exists—replacement purchases. This expenditure is necessitated by the depreciation of the existing stock of durables. If we assume that replacement purchases (R) are a constant fraction of the existing stock of durables, then:

$$R_t = \gamma s_{t-1}$$

Total expenditures on consumer durables (P) therefore consist of regular purchases (additions to the existing stock) and replacement purchases:

$$P_t = s_t - s_{t-1} + R_t$$
$$= \lambda(s_t^* - s_{t-1}) + \gamma s_{t-1}$$

so that:

$$P_t = \lambda s_t^* + (\gamma - \lambda)s_{t-1}$$

Substituting for s_t^* from Equation (13.32) we have:

$$P_t = \alpha_0^* + \alpha_1^*(p_{cd}/p_c)_t + \alpha_2^* y_t + \alpha_3^* r_t + \alpha_4^* D_t + \alpha_5 s_{t-1} + \varepsilon_t^*$$

where $\alpha_5 = (\gamma - \lambda)$

Hymans estimated an equation similar to this for automobile expenditure.[18] His equation for the desired stock of autos (A^*) is:

$$A_t^* = \alpha_0 + \alpha_1 y_{t-1} + \alpha_2 \text{UM}_{t-1} + \alpha_3(p_a/p_c)_t + \varepsilon_t$$

where y is real disposable personal income net of transfers (1958 = 100); UM is the unemployment rate for males 20 and older; p_a is the implicit auto price deflator (1958 = 100); and p_c is the GNP deflator for personal consumption expenditure (1958 = 100). Total real automobile expenditure (E) consists of additions to the existing stock, $A_t - A_{t-1}$, and replacement expenditure, γA_{t-1}, where γ is the rate of depreciation:

$$E_t = \lambda(A_t^* - A_{t-1}) + \gamma A_{t-1}$$

---

[18] S. Hymans, "Consumer Durables Spending: Explanation and Prediction," *Brookings Papers on Economic Activity* 2 (1970), 173–199.

Rearranging the terms in this equation:

$$E_t = \lambda A_t^* + (\gamma - \lambda)A_{t-1}$$

By substituting for A_t^*, we arrive at the estimable form of the automobile expenditures equation:

$$E_t = \alpha_0^* + \alpha_1^* y_{t-1} + \alpha_2^* \mathrm{UM}_{t-1} + \alpha_3^*(p_a/p_c)_t + \alpha_4 A_{t-1} + \varepsilon_t^*$$

Although it does not appear that a lagged dependent variable appears in this equation, Hymans' method for calculating the existing stock of automobiles uses lagged values of E. To obtain an estimate of A_{t-1}, Hymans makes the following assumptions: (i) the rate of auto depreciation per quarter, γ, is constant; and (ii) after a fixed number of quarters (q) an automobile is considered scrap, and is no longer a part of A. Using these assumptions:

E_{t-i} represents gross purchases of autos i quarters ago;

and

$(1 - \gamma)^i E_{t-i}$ is the surviving portion of purchases i quarters ago

Also:

$$A_t = \sum_{i=0}^{q} (1 - \gamma)^i E_{t-i}$$

To obtain a depreciation rate, Hymans assumes a scrap value of 0.04, or 4.0 percent of the original price of an auto, and that the life expectancy of an auto is 10 years ($q = 40$). Using this information, a value for γ is obtained:

$$(1 - \gamma)^{40} = 0.04, \qquad \text{which implies that } \gamma = 0.078$$

Hymans therefore approximates the existing stock of autos by the following equation:

$$A_t = \sum_{i=0}^{40} (1.0 - 0.078)^i E_{t-i}$$

This is a 40-period weighted moving average of past auto expenditure levels with geometrically declining weights. Since the values of A_t use E_{t-1}, last period's auto expenditure does in fact enter into this equation.

Using quarterly data from 1954:1 to 1968:4, Hymans' equation (which was corrected for serial correlation with $\hat{\Theta} = 0.643$) is:

$$\hat{E}_t = 19.0 + 0.32 y_{t-1} - 0.75 \mathrm{UM}_{t-1} - 25.9(p_a/p_c)_t - 0.157 A_{t-1} + 1.65 S_t$$
$$\quad (2.9) \quad (9.1) \qquad (3.7) \qquad\qquad (4.4) \qquad\quad (6.3) \qquad\quad (3.9)$$

$$\bar{R}^2 = 0.961 \quad \hat{\sigma}_\varepsilon = 1.13$$

where E is real expenditure on autos and parts exclusive of mobile homes (1958 = 100) and S is a dummy variable that indicates the occurrence of auto strikes in 1964 and 1967. Recall that the coefficient of A_{t-1} in this equation is *not* $1 - \lambda$ as was the case with the earlier models, but $\gamma - \lambda$. Our estimate of the adjustment coefficient therefore uses the estimate of γ above, 0.078, and the coefficient in the estimated equation, -0.157:

$$0.078 - \lambda = -0.157$$

so that

$$\hat{\lambda} = 0.235$$

Based on this estimate, the actual auto stock adjusts by 23.5 percent of the discrepancy between it and the desired stock each quarter. This indicates approximately a one-year period for the actual stock of autos to adjust to its desired level.

The final example of the use of the partial adjustment model pertains to the derivation of a labor demand function. A demand for labor function defines the "optimal" amount of labor demanded as a function of a number of related variables. The term "optimal" is defined based on the behavioral assumptions used to derive this function. If we assume that firms attempt to minimize the cost of producing a given level of output, and utilize a specific functional form to represent production, we can show how such a function is derived.

We will base this model on two inputs, labor (L) and capital (k), and denote the cost per unit of labor (the wage rate) as w, and the cost per unit capital (the rental price of capital) as r. Total costs (C) are then:

$$C = wL + rk$$

which consists of labor costs (wL) and capital costs (rk). If we utilize the Cobb-Douglas production function:

$$q = Ak^{\alpha}L^{\beta}$$

we now have the basis for constructing the optimization procedure used to derive the labor demand function. Although this process involves multivariate calculus, the essential elements will be traced out.

Technically, this is an example of **constrained minimization**, where we minimize costs subject to the constraint that output equals a given level (q_1). For the functions above, the expression that is minimized, which is called the **objective function**, is set up. This consists of the following expression:

$$\mathscr{L} = wL + rK - \mu(Ak^{\alpha}L^{\beta} - q_1)$$

where μ is a **Lagrangean multiplier**. After partially differentiating this expression with respect to L, k and μ, then manipulating the resulting equations, an expression for optimal L (L^*) is obtained:

$$L^* = v(w/r)^{-\Theta}q^{\Omega}$$

where the terms v, Θ, and Ω are functions of α and β. Since this is a multiplicative function, we can linearize it by applying logarithms. Adding subscripts for time and an equation error, the result is:

$$\ln(L^*)_t = \ln(v) - \Theta \ln(w/r)_t + \Omega \ln(q)_t + \varepsilon_t$$

Optimal labor input is therefore a positive function of output and negatively related to the ratio of input prices, w/r. This last term is called the wage-rental ratio. It measures the price of labor *relative* to the price per unit of capital. That the cost of labor in this function is stated in relative terms is important, since it implies that a rise in w (given q) does not necessarily cause L^* to fall. L^* falls (given q) only when w rises relative to r. Thus if both w and r change by the same proportion (such as doubling), the optimal labor input for a given level of output remains unchanged.

As it now stands, we have an expression for optimal labor input, which is unobserved. To state this function in terms of actual labor input we use the partial adjustment model given by Equation (13.31):

$$\ln(L)_t = \lambda \ln(L^*)_t + (1 - \lambda) \ln(L)_{t-1}$$

Substituting for $\ln(L^*)_t$ this becomes:

$$\ln(L)_t = \lambda\{\ln(v) - \Theta \ln(w/r)_t + \Omega \ln(q)_t + \varepsilon_t\} + (1 - \lambda) \ln(L)_{t-1}$$

$$\ln(L)_t = \alpha_0 + \alpha_1 \ln(w/r)_t + \alpha_2 \ln(q)_t + \alpha_3 \ln(L)_{t-1} + \varepsilon_t^* \qquad \textbf{(13.33)}$$

where $\alpha_0 = \lambda \ln(v)$; $\alpha_1 = -\lambda\Theta$; $\alpha_2 = \lambda\Omega$; $\alpha_3 = 1 - \lambda$; and $\varepsilon_t^* = \lambda\varepsilon_t$. Equation (13.33) is the short-run demand for labor function. The coefficient α_1 measures the short-run elasticity of output with respect to the wage-rental ratio. It indicates the sensitivity of labor demand to a 1 percent change in the relative price of labor, given output and employment last period. α_2 is the short-run output elasticity of labor demand.

LEAST SQUARES ESTIMATION OF AUTOREGRESSIVE EQUATIONS

We have shown how equations with distributed lags of explanatory variables can result in autoregressive equations. The discussion earlier in the chapter also showed that this type of equation can result from the existence of momentum, habit formation, and so forth. We now discuss how to estimate autoregressive equations.

We begin by assuming that the function we are interested in estimating is of the form:

$$y(t) = \alpha_0 + \alpha_1 y(t - 1) + \varepsilon(t) \qquad \textbf{(13.34)}$$

In this equation, we have replaced the time period subscript, either t or $t - 1$, with a bracket around this value. This notation allows us to avoid confusing the number of an observation with the variable name, since both y_t and y_{t-1} are variables in the above equation and different observations of the variable y_t. We will assume for now that $\varepsilon(t)$ is a white noise error process. We thus have the following data for the variables $y(t)$, $y(t - 1)$, and $\varepsilon(t)$ (starting from $t = 2$):

$y(t)$	$y(t-1)$	$\varepsilon(t)$
y_2	y_1	ε_2
y_3	y_2	ε_3
y_4	y_3	ε_4
$\cdots$		
y_n	y_{n-1}	ε_n

The first thing to note about Equation (13.34) is that the lagged dependent variable, $y(t-1)$, cannot be viewed as being fixed in repeated samples. It is a stochastic explanatory variable. We encountered this type of variable earlier (in Chapters 11 and 12), when estimated generalized least squares estimation was discussed. The least squared estimator of α_1 in Equation (13.34) is:

$$\hat{\alpha}_1 = \sum y(t-1)'y(t)'/\sum y(t-1)'^2$$
$$= \alpha_1 + \sum y(t-1)'\varepsilon(t)/\sum y(t-1)'^2$$

where $y(t-1)'$ and $y(t)'$ are deviations from means. Our estimator consists of the population parameter plus a term related to the covariance between $y(t-1)$ and $\varepsilon(t)$ and the variance of $y(t-1)$. If we let $\omega(t) \equiv y(t-1)'/\sum y(t-1)'^2$, we can rewrite the least squares estimator of α_1 as:

$$\hat{\alpha}_1 = \alpha_1 + \sum \omega(t)\varepsilon(t)$$

Note that the weights in this equation, $\omega(t)$, are themselves stochastic. Both of the variables in the summation are thus random variables. $\hat{\alpha}_1$ is an unbiased estimator only if the expected value of the summation term equals 0. Since both $\omega(t)$ and $\varepsilon(t)$ are random variables:

$$E\left[\sum \omega(t)\varepsilon(t)\right] \neq \sum \omega(t)E[\varepsilon(t)]$$

The expectation of this sum is 0 only if $\omega(t)$ is distributed independently of $\varepsilon(t)$. If this is true, then $E[\sum \omega(t)\varepsilon(t)] = E[\sum \omega(t)]E[\varepsilon(t)] = 0$. This is unfortunately not the case. From (13.34), $y(t) = f(\varepsilon(t))$. Lagging this equation by one period, $y(t-1) = f(\varepsilon(t-1))$. In the table of observations above, each row of $y(t-1)$ is independent of the *corresponding row* of $\varepsilon(t)$. But, $y_2 = f(\varepsilon_2)$; $y_3 = f(\varepsilon_3), \ldots, y_{n-1} = f(\varepsilon_{n-1})$, so the jth row for $y(t-1)$ is correlated with the $(j-1)$st row for $\varepsilon(t)$. The variable $\varepsilon(t)$ is therefore correlated with terms in the numerator and denominator of the estimator expression. In addition to this, since the least squares formula for $\hat{\alpha}_1$ is stated in terms of deviations from means, a number of individual errors are correlated with the mean of either $y(t)$ or $y(t-1)$. For these reasons, $\omega(t)$ and $\varepsilon(t)$ are not independent, and *least squares estimation of an equation with a lagged dependent variable leads to biased estimators.* The least squares estimators of the parameters in Equation (13.34) are consistent, however.[19] Statistical inference can therefore proceed using asymptotic results as their basis: in the limit, the least squares estimators are normally distributed.

If the errors in the original equation are serially correlated, which pertains for both the Koyck transformation and the adaptive expectations model, least squares estimation loses the property of consistency. To see this, assume the errors in (13.34) are first-order autocorrelated, or AR(1):

$$\varepsilon(t) = \Theta\varepsilon(t-1) + v(t),$$

---

[19] In the limit, as sample size approaches infinity, the variable $y(t)$ is a function of y_0, an initial value taken as fixed, and $\varepsilon_1, \varepsilon_2, \ldots, \varepsilon_t$. Thus, the lagged dependent variable, $y(t-1)$ is a function of $y_0, \varepsilon_1, \varepsilon_2, \ldots, \varepsilon_{t-1}$ and is independent of $\varepsilon(t)$. In the limit, $y(t-1)$ and $\varepsilon(t)$ are said to be contemporaneously uncorrelated.

where $v(t)$ is a white noise error process, with $E(v(t)) = 0$, $\text{Var}(v(t)) = \sigma_v^2$, and $\text{Cov}(v(t), v(t-1)) = 0$. Since $\varepsilon(t) = f(\varepsilon(t-1))$, the explanatory variable $y(t-1)$ is also a function of $\varepsilon(t-1)$. Thus the explanatory variable in Equation (13.34) is correlated with the error term, and least squares estimation of this equation produces biased estimators. Since this correlation exists for all sample sizes, the least squares estimators are also inconsistent. To summarize this information:

The least squares estimators of the coefficients in an autoregressive equation such as Equation (13.34) are biased whether or not the error term is serially correlated.

If the errors in this equation are *not* serially correlated, the least squares estimators are biased but consistent. The normal distribution is then asymptotically valid for statistical inference.

If the equation has serially correlated errors, the least squares estimators are both biased and inconsistent.

In this last case, it is necessary to *discard* the estimated coefficients because they are invalid, even asymptotically. The normal distribution is then not a proper basis for statistical inference.

DETECTING SERIAL CORRELATION IN EQUATIONS WITH LAGGED DEPENDENT VARIABLES

The potential validity of least squares as an estimation technique for autoregressive equations depends critically on whether the errors are themselves autoregressive. The detection of serial correlation is therefore a major concern in the present context. In Chapter 11 these detection methods were outlined in detail and illustrated. Recall that the Durbin-Watson test, which is the most well known of these tests, is not valid when an equation contains one or more stochastic explanatory variables, as is the case here. When an equation contains a lagged dependent variable, the Durbin-Watson statistic tends toward 2, giving the impression that serial correlation is absent when this might not be the case. For such equations, the correct statistic is the Durbin h-statistic:

$$h = \hat{\Theta}\sqrt{n/v}$$

where $\hat{\Theta}$ is the estimated autocorrelation coefficient, $v = 1 - n\hat{\sigma}_1^2$, and $\hat{\sigma}_1^2$ is the estimated variance of the coefficient of the lagged dependent variable. Typically, $\hat{\Theta}$ is obtained from the Durbin-Watson statistic (DW):

$$\hat{\Theta} \approx 1 - \text{DW}/2$$

In the limit (generally for $n > 30$), the h-statistic follows the unit normal distribution. If the null hypothesis states no first-order serial correlation: $H_0: \Theta = 0$; and the alternative is (say) positive serial correlation: $H_a: \Theta > 0$, we reject the null hypothesis at the 5 percent significance level if h exceeds 1.645. If, instead, the alternative hypothesis is nonequality: $H_a: \Theta \neq 0$, H_0 is rejected at the 5 percent level if $|h| > 1.96$.

Durbin's h-statistic can be used in equations with large numbers of explanatory variables, including a series of lags of the dependent variable. To calculate this statistic, we need only use the estimated variance for the one-period lag of the dependent variable. The potential problem with the h-statistic is that v can be negative, which results in a negative square root. Specifically, $v < 0$ when $n\hat{\sigma}_1^2 > 1$. If this occurs, Durbin has suggested an alternative method for determining whether first-order serial correlation exists. If our equation (dropping the previous notation) is:

$$y_t = \alpha_0 + \alpha_1 x_t + \alpha_2 y_{t-1} + \varepsilon_t \tag{13.35}$$

we first estimate this with least squares and calculate the residuals, $\hat{\varepsilon}_t$. We then regress $\hat{\varepsilon}_t$ (the dependent variable) on x_t, y_{t-1}, and $\hat{\varepsilon}_{t-1}$:

$$\hat{\varepsilon}_t = \gamma_0 + \gamma_1 x_t + \gamma_2 y_{t-1} + \gamma_3 \hat{\varepsilon}_{t-1} + v_t$$

The test for first-order serial correlation consists of a t-test on the coefficient of $\hat{\varepsilon}_{t-1}$. If this is statistically significant, we conclude that the errors in our equation are first-order autoregressive, and we must view these estimators as invalid.

Serially correlated errors are not always first-order autoregressive. Breusch has proposed a test for higher order serial correlation that can be used in equations such as those we are considering.[20] If the error process is:

$$\varepsilon_t = \Theta_1 \varepsilon_{t-1} + \Theta_2 \varepsilon_{t-2} + \cdots + \Theta_m \varepsilon_{t-m} + v_t$$

where v is a white noise error process, Breusch's test considers the joint statistical significance of Θ_1 to Θ_m. The null hypothesis for this test is $H_0: \Theta_1 = \cdots = \Theta_m = 0$. If the null hypothesis is correct, $\varepsilon_t = v_t$, and the errors are white noise. The alternative hypothesis states that at least one Θ is non-zero. The steps involved (referring to Equation (13.35)) are:

1. Estimate Equation (13.35) with least squares and obtain the residuals, $\hat{\varepsilon}_t$.
2. Regress $\hat{\varepsilon}_t$ on x_t, y_{t-1}, $\hat{\varepsilon}_{t-1}, \ldots, \hat{\varepsilon}_{t-m}$, and obtain the *unadjusted* R^2. This is accomplished using only $(n - m)$ values, since with lags up to period m, m missing values occur.
3. The test statistic for this test is $(n - m)R^2$, which follows the chi-square distribution with m degrees of freedom. If the value of the test statistic exceeds the critical chi-square value with m degrees of freedom for the selected level of significance, we reject H_0 and accept the alternative hypothesis of serially correlated errors.

The degrees of freedom for this test correspond to the number of restrictions implied by the null hypothesis. One particular variant of this test can be used with quarterly data. If we suspect that the error process is:

$$\varepsilon_t = \Theta_4 \varepsilon_{t-4} + v_t$$

---

[20] T. Breusch, "Testing for Autocorrelation in Dynamic Linear Models," *Australian Economic Papers* 17 (1978), 334–355.

then the Durbin h-test will likely fail to detect serial correlation. To test for this form of serial correlation, the null hypothesis is: H_0: $\Theta_4 = 0$, step (2) above is modified so that $\hat{\varepsilon}_t$ is regressed on only x_t, y_{t-1}, and $\hat{\varepsilon}_{t-4}$, and the critical chi-square value has one degree of freedom. Also, the equation will be estimated with $(n - 4)$ observations, so our test statistic is $(n - 4)R^2$.

A NOTE ON SERIAL CORRELATION AND THE EXISTENCE OF DISTRIBUTED LAGS

It is possible for an equation to give the appearance of being a distributed lag relationship when in fact it is not. This results from the existence of serially correlated errors. Assume that the correct specification of the equation for y is:

$$y_t = \alpha_0 + \alpha_1 x_t + \varepsilon_t$$

but the error term in this equation is serially correlated, with:

$$\varepsilon_t = \Theta \varepsilon_{t-1} + v_t$$

where v_t is a white noise error process. To transform the equation for y so that its errors are no longer serially correlated, we apply the transformation: $T = \Theta(B) = (1 - \Theta B)$, which gives the relationship:

$$y_t - \Theta y_{t-1} = \alpha_0(1 - \Theta) + \alpha_1 x_t - (\alpha_1 \Theta)x_{t-1} + v_t,$$

or

$$y_t = \alpha_0^* + \alpha_1 x_t + \alpha_2 x_{t-1} + \alpha_3 y_{t-1} + v_t \qquad \textbf{(13.36)}$$

The form of Equation (13.36) is identical to the partial adjustment model, where $y_t^* = f(x_t, x_{t-1}, \varepsilon_t)$, and similar to the Koyck transformation. It differs from the Koyck model by its inclusion of the variable x_{t-1}. It is this difference that allows us to test whether a distributed lag exists, or if it is serial correlation that is causing the appearance of such a lag structure.

The coefficient of x_{t-1} in Equation (13.36), α_2, is the negative of the product of α_1, the coefficient of current period x and Θ, the lagged dependent variable coefficient:

$$\alpha_2 = -\alpha_1 \cdot \Theta \qquad \textbf{(13.37)}$$

To test whether the relationship between y and x entails a distributed lag, Griliches suggests estimating Equation (13.36) with least squares and determining whether the coefficient of *lagged* x approximately satisfies Equation (13.37).[21] If:

$$\hat{\alpha}_2 \approx -\hat{\alpha}_1 \cdot \hat{\Theta}$$

and the residuals are not serially correlated we can conclude that the relationship between y and x does *not* involve a distributed lag. Our estimate of Equation (13.36) is then an estimated generalized least squares equation, where the estimated coefficient

---

[21] Z. Griliches, "Distributed Lags: A Survey," *Econometrica* 35 (January 1967), 16–49.

for x is $\hat{\alpha}_1$, the coefficient of y_{t-1} serves as our estimate of the first-order serial correlation coefficient, and the estimated intercept for the original equation is $\hat{\alpha}_0^*/(1 - \hat{\Theta})$.

THE ESTIMATION OF AUTOREGRESSIVE EQUATIONS WITH SERIALLY CORRELATED ERRORS

A number of procedures have been developed to deal with the problem outlined above, allowing consistent estimation of parameters in autoregressive equations with serially correlated errors. All of these eliminate the correlation between explanatory variables and the equation error as sample size approaches infinity. Several of these are non-iterative methods, while others involve iteration.

Noniterative Estimation Methods

The first noniterative method considered, the **instrumental variable technique**, uses a proxy variable to eliminate the difficulties that arise with least squares estimation. The basis for this technique will be presented by referring to the deviation form of a bivariate autoregressive equation:

$$y_t' = \alpha_1 y_{t-1}' + \varepsilon_t' \tag{13.38}$$

Recall that the least squares estimators are derived by solving a set of simultaneous equations, called normal equations, which arise as part of the mathematical procedure of minimizing the sum of the squared residuals. One normal equation exists for each estimator. The normal equation for $\hat{\alpha}_1$ in Equation (13.38) is derived by multiplying the terms in this equation by y_{t-1}' then summing:

$$\sum y_t' y_{t-1}' = \alpha_1 \sum y_{t-1}'^2 + \sum y_{t-1}' \varepsilon_t'$$

If y_{t-1} were independent of ε_t, the expectation of the last term on the right would be 0, and we could use the remaining terms to define our estimator of α_1. This would give the usual normal equation for $\hat{\alpha}_1$. Solving for $\hat{\alpha}_1$:

$$\hat{\alpha}_1 = \sum y_t' y_{t-1}' / \sum y_{t-1}'^2$$

Least squares encounters problems here because y_{t-1}, which is a stochastic explanatory variable, is correlated with the equation error. This affects the normal equation for this estimator. In the present context, the least squares estimator $\hat{\alpha}_1$ is both biased and inconsistent since the expectation of $\sum y_{t-1}' \varepsilon_t'$ is not 0. If, however, we were to use a variable in place of y_{t-1} that is uncorrelated asymptotically with ε_t, we could at least salvage the property of consistency. This is the basis for the instrumental variable technique.

The first step in this procedure consists of finding a proxy variable for y_{t-1}, called an **instrumental variable**, that satisfies two conditions:

1. It is highly correlated with the "problem" variable, y_{t-1}.
2. It is asymptotically uncorrelated with the equation error.

If we denote such a variable z_t, then we can modify the normal equation presented above by replacing it with the product of z_t and Equation (13.38):

$$\sum z_t' y_t' = \alpha_1 \sum z_t' y_{t-1}' + \sum z_t' \varepsilon_t' \qquad (13.39)$$

The way in which the instrumental variable z_t is defined makes it asymptotically uncorrelated with the equation error. Thus, for large samples, the expected value of $\sum z_t' \varepsilon_t'$ is 0. Overlooking this term in Equation (13.39), we can then solve for the estimator of α_1:

$$\hat{\alpha}_1 = \sum z_t' y_t' / \sum z_t' y_{t-1}' \qquad (13.40)$$

Equation (13.40), which is the instrumental variable estimator of α_1, is a consistent estimator of α_1. *This estimator is not the same as that derived by replacing y_{t-1} in the original equation with z_t.* If y were regressed on z, the denominator of $\hat{\alpha}_1$ would instead be $\sum z_t'^2$, and the resulting estimator would not be consistent. Note that the equation intercept in the nondeviation form of Equation (13.38) is obtained in the usual way.

This framework can be extended to equations with more than one explanatory variable. If our equation expresses y as a function of x, which is nonstochastic and y_{t-1}, then in deviation form:

$$y_t' = \alpha_1 x_t' + \alpha_2 y_{t-1}' + \varepsilon_t' \qquad (13.41)$$

The two "adjusted" normal equations that serve as the basis for the instrumental variable estimators of α_1 and α_2 are derived by multiplying Equation (13.41) by x_t' and z_t' then summing:

$$\sum x_t' y_t' = \alpha_1 \sum x_t'^2 + \alpha_2 \sum x_t' y_{t-1}' + \sum x_t' \varepsilon_t' \qquad \text{(same as usual OLS)}$$

$$\sum z_t' y_t' = \alpha_1 \sum z_t' x_t' + \alpha_2 \sum z_t' y_{t-1}' + \sum z_t' \varepsilon_t'$$

For large samples, the expected value of the term involving ε in each of these equations is 0. The instrumental variable estimators are obtained by solving this set of simultaneous equations (omitting the terms involving ε) for α_1 and α_2. Note that since x is not a "problem" variable in this procedure, it serves as its own instrument.

The choice of which variable to use as an instrument is not always obvious. If we consider the regression of y on x and y_{t-1}, a suitable choice for an instrument, which was suggested by Liviatin, is x_{t-1}.[22] Since $y_t = f(x_t, y_{t-1})$, y_{t-1} is correlated with x_{t-1}. Also, since x is nonstochastic, it is uncorrelated asymptotically with ε. The lag of x thus meets both requirements for an instrumental variable. A potential problem with this choice is collinearity that may exist between x_t and x_{t-1}.

A final choice for an instrument is a stochastic variable created from y_t. If we regress y_t on a series of lags of x, we can generate a new variable, the predicted value of y, $\hat{y}$. The instrumental variable is then the lag of this variable: $\hat{y}_{t-1}$.

---

[22] N. Liviatin, "Consistent Estimation of Distributed Lags," *International Economic Review* 4 (January 1963), 44–52.

The final noniterative method that will be presented was set forth by Hatanaka.[23] This two-step method, which produces consistent and asymptotically efficient estimators, is related to the instrumental variable technique. We will assume that the equation to be estimated is:

$$y_t = \alpha_0 + \alpha_1 x_t + \alpha_2 y_{t-1} + \varepsilon_t \tag{13.42}$$

although there can be a number of x's and different lags of y. The error term is assumed to be first-order autoregressive. The steps in this procedure are:

1. Create an instrumental variable for y_{t-1} by regressing y_t on x_t and lags of x:

$$y_t = \gamma_0 + \gamma_1 x_t + \gamma_2 x_{t-1} + \cdots + \eta_t$$

The number of lags can be determined by maximizing $\bar{R}^2$. Obtain the predicted y series, $\hat{y}_t = \hat{\gamma}_0 + \hat{\gamma}_1 x_t + \hat{\gamma}_2 x_{t-1} + \cdots$, then lag $\hat{y}$ one period to obtain $\hat{y}_{t-1}$.

2. Estimate Equation (13.42) *with the instrumental variable technique,* using $\hat{y}_{t-1}$ created in (1) in place of y_{t-1}. In other words, estimate:

$$y_t = \alpha'_0 + \alpha'_1 x_t + \alpha'_2 \hat{y}_{t-1} + \varepsilon'_t$$

and obtain the residuals from this equation, $\hat{\varepsilon}'_t$.

3. A consistent estimator of the coefficient of serial correlation, $\hat{\Theta}$, is obtained by regressing $\hat{\varepsilon}_t$ on $\hat{\varepsilon}_{t-1}$ without an intercept:

$$\hat{\varepsilon}_t = \Theta \hat{\varepsilon}_{t-1} + v_t$$

4. Use the estimate of Θ from step (3) to transform Equation (13.42) in the usual way for serial correlation:

$$(y_t - \hat{\Theta} y_{t-1}) = \alpha_0(1 - \hat{\Theta}) + \alpha_1(x_t - \hat{\Theta} x_{t-1}) + \alpha_2(y_{t-1} - \hat{\Theta} y_{t-2}) + v_t$$

$$y_t^* = \alpha_0^* + \alpha_1 x_t^* + \alpha_2 y_{t-1}^* + v_t$$

The final equation that is estimated is a variant of this:

$$y_t^* = \alpha_0^* + \alpha_1 x_t^* + \alpha_2 y_{t-1}^* + \alpha_3 \hat{\varepsilon}_{t-1} + v_t \tag{13.43}$$

where $\hat{\varepsilon}_{t-1}$ is the set of residuals used in step (3).

5. The consistent and asymptotically efficient estimators are:

$\hat{\alpha}_1$ for the partial slope of x;

$\hat{\alpha}_2$ for the coefficient of the lagged dependent variable;

$\hat{\Theta}^* = \hat{\Theta} + \hat{\alpha}_3$ for the serial correlation coefficient; and

$\hat{\alpha}_0 = \hat{\alpha}_0^*/(1 - \hat{\Theta}^*)$ for the equation intercept.

The standard errors and t-statistics from Equation (13.43) are asymptotically valid (the standard error for $\hat{\alpha}_0^*$ must be adjusted in the way indicated in Chapter 11).

---

[23] M. Hatanaka, "An Efficient Two-Step Estimator For the Dynamic Adjustment Model with Autoregressive Errors," *Journal of Econometrics* 2 (1974), 199–220.

The estimators in step (5) are known as **Hatanaka's Residual Adjusted Estimator**. Unlike the instrumental variable technique outlined earlier, Hatanaka's two-step procedure deals simultaneously with the serially correlated errors and the estimation problems associated with the lagged dependent variable.

An Iterative Estimation Method

It might appear that the problems with serial correlation in autoregressive equations can be eliminated by using a more simple procedure such as the Cochrane-Orcutt technique. However, Betancourt and Kelejian have shown that the use of this technique when a lagged dependent variable is present can result in inconsistent estimates.[24] This occurs when the estimated serial correlation coefficient is not associated with an overall (global) minimum of the sum of the squared residuals. To avoid this potential difficulty, consistent estimates are obtained using a grid search method such as the Hildreth-Lu procedure.

To illustrate this technique, we will assume that first-order serial correlation exists and use Equation (13.42) as our equation of interest. Based on the serial correlation assumption, the appropriate transformation term is: $T = \Theta(B) = (1 - \Theta B)$. The transformed equation that is estimated is:

$$y_t^* = \alpha_0^* + \alpha_1 x_t^* + \alpha_2 y_{t-1}^* + v_t \tag{13.44}$$

where $y_t^* = (y_t - \Theta y_{t-1})$; $x_t^* = (x_t - \Theta x_{t-1})$; $y_{t-1}^* = (y_{t-1} - \Theta y_{t-2})$; and $\alpha_0^* = \alpha_0(1 - \Theta)$. The values utilized for Θ range from -1 to $+1$, differing by 0.1 for each regression. We first use $\Theta = -1$, create y_t^*, x_t^*, and y_{t-1}^* using this value, estimate Equation (13.44), then record the sum of squared residuals for that equation. Next, we use $\Theta = -0.9$, and repeat this procedure for $\Theta = -0.8, -0.7, \ldots, 1.0$. We then determine the smallest sum of squared residuals for all these regressions and fine-tune further. The estimated equation with the smallest residual sum of squares is selected as the sample regression function corresponding to Equation (13.42). The estimated coefficients from this equation are consistent. The estimated intercept, though, must be modified, such that $\hat{\alpha}_0 = \hat{\alpha}_0^*/(1 - \hat{\Theta})$, where $\hat{\Theta}$ is the estimated serial correlation coefficient corresponding to the minimized residual sum of squares.

EXAMPLES OF AUTOREGRESSIVE EQUATIONS WITH SERIALLY CORRELATED ERRORS

■ **UNEMPLOYMENT RATE EQUATION**   Earlier in this chapter we utilized the unemployment rate-capacity utilization rate relationship as the basis for exploring distributed lags. We will again make use of this equation, but in a different context.

---

[24] R. Betancourt and H. Kelejian, "Lagged Endogenous Variables and the Cochrane-Orcutt Procedure," *Econometrica* 49 (1981), 1073–1078.

The civilian unemployment rate (u) is determined by both cyclical and secular factors. The cyclical component of u is related to the state of the economy. We will model this influence in our equation by including the capacity utilization rate in manufacturing (CAP). The secular trend in the unemployment rate can be modeled by including a variable representing the labor force participation of "secondary workers." We will capture this effect by including the labor force participation rate of females (LFPF). The response of the unemployment rate to changes in either the cyclical or secular factors is not instantaneous. Based on adjustment costs, such as the fixed employment costs discussed in Chapter 4, and the existence of transaction costs, which is related to imperfect information by both employers and job seekers, we can apply the partial adjustment model to this relationship. The equilibrium, or optimal unemployment rate (u^*), can be specified as:

$$u_t^* = \alpha_0 + \alpha_1 CAP_t + \alpha_2 LFPF_t + \varepsilon_t$$

Using the partial adjustment model, we have an expression for u_t^*:

$$u_t = \lambda u_t^* + (1 - \lambda)u_{t-1}$$

Combining these equations we arrive at the following empirically estimable unemployment rate function:

$$u_t = (\lambda\alpha_0) + (\lambda\alpha_1)CAP_t + (\lambda\alpha_2)LFPF_t + (1 - \lambda)u_{t-1} + \lambda\varepsilon_t$$

or

$$u_t = \alpha_0^* + \alpha_1^* CAP_t + \alpha_2^* LFPF_t + \alpha_3 u_{t-1} + \varepsilon_t^*$$

Least squares estimation of this equation was accomplished using annual data for the years 1955–1989 from the 1990 *Economic Report of the President*. The resulting sample regression function is:

$$\hat{u} = 20.3 \underset{(12.7)}{} - \underset{(13.0)}{0.22 CAP_t} + \underset{(1.8)}{0.02 LFPF_t} + \underset{(7.0)}{0.41 u_{t-1}}$$

$$\bar{R}^2 = 0.932 \quad n = 35 \quad \hat{\sigma}_\varepsilon = 0.41 \quad F = 155.5 \quad h = 2.2$$

The Durbin h-statistic, 2.2, indicates the presence of serial correlation. The coefficients in this equation are therefore biased and inconsistent and must be discarded.

Consistent estimators of the coefficients in this equation were obtained using the Hildreth-Lu grid search technique. Examination of the sample autocorrelation function indicated the presence of first-order serial correlation, so this pattern was utilized to transform the original equation. The grid of values for this search ranged from -1 to $+1$ in increments of 0.1. The minimum residual sum of squares occurred for $\hat{\Theta} = 0.6$. The transformed sample regression function using this value is:

$$\hat{u}_t^* = 8.92 \underset{(12.7)}{} - \underset{(15.0)}{0.239 CAP_t^*} + \underset{(1.5)}{0.034 LFPF_t^*} + \underset{(4.5)}{0.268 u_{t-1}^*}$$

$$n = 34 \quad F = 85.3 \quad \hat{\sigma}_\varepsilon = 0.36$$

The estimated adjustment coefficient from this equation is 0.732 ($= 1 - 0.268$), which indicates that approximately three-fourths of the adjustment of the actual to the equilibrium unemployment rate occurs in one year. This estimate is about one-third less than that in the first equation above. In the short-run, a 1 percent rise in the capacity utilization lowers the mean unemployment rate by approximately one-fourth of 1 percent (0.239 percent), given the secular trend in the unemployment rate and the value of u last year. In the long-run, the corresponding fall in the mean unemployment rate is about one-third of one percent ($= -0.239/0.732 = -0.326$). Note that this estimate of $\hat{a}_1$ indicates the sensitivity of the *equilibrium* (*or long-run*) *unemployment rate* to changes in the capacity utilization rate, given the secular trend in unemployment. It is related to the long-run equation above (before the partial adjustment model is applied).

The coefficients in this regression equation are asymptotically normally distributed. Using the one-tail critical normal value of 1.65 for the 5 percent significance level, all of these coefficients are statistically significant with the exception of LFPF. The short-run estimate of the secular trend in u is 0.034 percent, while the corresponding long-run estimate is 0.046 ($= 0.034/0.732$). Finally, the estimated intercept for the short-run equation is 22.3 ($= 8.92/(1 - \hat{\Theta})$). ■

■ **CONSUMPTION FUNCTION**   The Keynesian consumption function is one of the foundations of the Keynesian model. According to this relationship, real consumption expenditure (c) is determined primarily by the level of real income (y). A number of other factors affect c in addition to y. These are captured in the stochastic error. If we model this relationship with a linear equation we have:

$$c_t = \alpha_0 + \alpha_1 y_t + v_t$$

In this equation, α_0 is autonomous consumption expenditure while α_1 is the marginal propensity to consume. According to Keynesian theory, α_1 is a positive fraction, and α_0 is positive.

Through the years this simple depiction of personal consumption expenditure was expanded and the income variable was refined. A distinction was made between current, or transitory income, as in the equation above, and permanent, or long-run income. This distinction is important because people tend to respond very differently to one-time changes in income and changes that are expected to persist. This difference is particularly important for fiscal policy, since tax changes affect personal consumption expenditure. If a $100 fall in taxes is temporary, spending might not be stimulated, thus frustrating the actions of policy makers.

In light of this discussion, it is more accurate to link real consumption expenditure to long-term or real permanent income (y^p):

$$c_t = \beta_0 + \beta_1 y_t^p + \varepsilon_t \tag{13.45}$$

The variable permanent income does not exist. It is therefore necessary to either find an existing variable that can serve as a proxy for this variable, or to model permanent income. The method utilized here employs the adaptive expectations framework.[25] We postulate that c is a function of y^p, where permanent real income per capita now corresponds to long-run expected income. The behavior of y^p is thus assumed to follow the adaptive expectations model using Equation (13.21):

$$y_t^p - y_{t-1}^p = \lambda(y_t - y_{t-1}^p)$$

where y is actual (observable) real income per capita. Solving for y_t^p in terms of y_t (similar to Equation (13.23)):

$$y_t^p = \frac{\lambda y_t}{\{1 - (1 - \lambda)B\}}$$

We now substitute the right side of this equation for y_t^p into Equation (13.45) and obtain an estimable form of the consumption function which is stated in terms of actual y:

$$c_t = \alpha_0^* + \alpha_1^* y_t + \alpha_2 c_{t-1} + \varepsilon_t^* \tag{13.46}$$

where $\alpha_0^* = \lambda\beta_0$; $\alpha_1^* = \lambda\beta_1$; $\alpha_2 = (1 - \lambda)$; and $\varepsilon_t^* = \varepsilon_t - (1 - \lambda)\varepsilon_{t-1}$. In the present context, Equation (13.45) is the long-run consumption function, while Equation (13.46) is the short-run consumption function. α_1^* is the short-run MPC, while $\alpha_1 = \alpha_1^*/\lambda$ is the long-run MPC. Note that *the form of Equation (13.46) is exactly the same as what we would have arrived at by applying the partial adjustment model to the original consumption function* (the one with actual y). The correct interpretation of each coefficient is, however, significantly different.

Least squares estimation of Equation (13.46) using annual data for 1955–1989 from the 1990 *Economic Report of the President* produced the following sample regression function:

$$\hat{c}_t = -95.9 + 0.514 y_t + 0.456 c_{t-1} \qquad \bar{R}^2 = 0.996 \quad n = 35 \quad \hat{\sigma}_\varepsilon = 104.9 \tag{13.47}$$
$$\phantom{\hat{c}_t = }(1.1) \quad (4.4) \qquad (3.6) \qquad\qquad\qquad h = 4.6 \quad F = 4472.2$$

The Durbin h-statistic from this equation is 4.6. This clearly exceeds the critical normal distribution value of 1.65 for a one-tail test at the 5 percent significance level. We thus reject the null hypothesis on no first-order serial correlation in favor of the alternative hypothesis of positive autocorrelation. The coefficients in Equation (13.47) are therefore biased and inconsistent. We must discard these and attempt to obtain consistent estimators.

Two methods for obtaining consistent estimates of Equation (13.46) will now be illustrated. The first of these is Hatanaka's Residual Adjusted Estimator. The initial step of this procedure consists of generating an instrumental variable for the lagged dependent variable. This was accomplished by regressing c_t on five lags of y (the number of y's was determined using the maximum-$\bar{R}^2$ criterion). The predicted dependent

---

[25] Other methods also exist, such as regressing current real per-capita consumption on its own lags and using predicted consumption as a proxy for permanent income. This technique will not be discussed here.

variable from this regression was then lagged, giving $\hat{c}_{t-1}$, which serves as the instrumental variable for c_{t-1}. The resulting estimates of the coefficients in Equation (13.46) are: $\alpha_0^* = -176.8$; $\alpha_1^* = 0.9702$; and $\alpha_2 = -0.0456$. Using these coefficients, the residuals were obtained, and the regression of $\hat{\varepsilon}_t$ on $\hat{\varepsilon}_{t-1}$ yielded:

$$\hat{\varepsilon}_t = 0.6765\hat{\varepsilon}_{t-1} \qquad \bar{R}^2 = 0.476$$
$$(5.5)$$

The value of 0.6765 is now used to transform c, y, and $\hat{c}$ so that serial correlation is eliminated. The final step of Hatanaka's procedure is the creation of:

$$c_t^* = (c_t - 0.6765c_{t-1}); \qquad y_t^* = (y_t - 0.6765y_{t-1}) \qquad \hat{c}_{t-1}^* = (\hat{c}_t - 0.6765\hat{c}_{t-1})$$

The dependent variable, c_t^*, is regressed on y_t^*, $\hat{c}_{t-1}^*$, and $\hat{\varepsilon}_{t-1}$. The resulting regression equation is:

$$\hat{c}_t^* = -63.7 + 0.741y_t^* + 0.213\hat{c}_{t-1}^* - 0.035\hat{\varepsilon}_{t-1} \qquad \textbf{(13.48)}$$
$$(0.9) \quad (6.6) \qquad (1.75) \qquad (0.3)$$

$$\bar{R}^2 = 0.977 \quad \hat{\sigma}_\varepsilon = 87.2 \quad n = 34 \quad F = 476.4$$

The estimated expectation coefficient in this equation is 0.787 ($= 1 - 0.213$). The short-run MPC estimate is 0.741, which indicates that a \$1 increase in *actual* real income per capita raises the mean of c by approximately 75 cents, given the value of c last period. The estimated long-run MPC, which relates a change in real *permanent* income per capita to c, is 0.941 ($= 0.741/0.787$): a \$1 increase in y sustained indefinitely raises mean real consumption per capita by about 95 cents. This last estimate reveals an important benefit associated with the use of the adaptive expectations framework: even though we do not observe permanent income, use of the adaptive expectations model along with available data allows us to infer the sensitivity of c to changes in this unobserved variable.

The estimated serial correlation coefficient from Hatanaka's procedure is the sum of the $\hat{\varepsilon}_{t-1}$ coefficients from the regression of $\hat{\varepsilon}_t$ on $\hat{\varepsilon}_{t-1}$ and the above equation. Thus, $\hat{\Theta} = 0.6765 - 0.035 = 0.6415$. This value is utilized to derive the estimated intercept $\hat{z}$, which is $-63.7/(1 - 0.6415) = -177.8$. This estimate of real autonomous consumption per capita displays the opposite sign of that expected, but is not statistically significant.

The coefficients in Equation (13.48) are substantially different from those in Equation (13.47). In the earlier equation, the estimated short-run MPC was 0.514, which is about 45 percent smaller than the corresponding value when Hatanaka's procedure was employed. The coefficient of c_{t-1} is about 50 percent smaller in Equation (13.48). Surprisingly, this combination makes the estimated long-run MPC almost identical for both equations: 0.945 for the original least squares equation and 0.941 for the equation adjusted with Hatanaka's method.

The final procedure used to obtain consistent estimates of Equation (13.46) is a Hildreth-Lu grid search. Based on the presumption of first-order serial correlation, the transformation term applied to (13.46) is $T(\Theta) = (1 - \Theta B)$. The generalized dif-

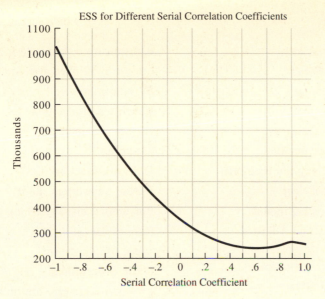

ESS for Different Serial Correlation Coefficients

Figure 13.4

ference form of the equation is then:

$$(c_t - \Theta c_{t-1}) = \alpha_0(1 - \Theta) + \alpha_1(y_t - \Theta y_{t-1}) + \alpha_2(c_{t-1} - \Theta c_{t-2}) + v_t$$

This equation was estimated with different values of the first-order serial correlation coefficient, Θ, ranging from -1 to $+1$ in increments of 0.1. The lowest residual sums of squares occurred for values of Θ between 0.5 and 0.7. A finer grid was then applied, which resulted in a minimum sum of squared residuals for $\Theta = 0.63$ (ESS $= 236,035$). A graph of ESS versus the different values of Θ is given in Figure 13.4. The sample regression function for this value of Θ is:

$$\hat{c}_t^* = -51.4 + 0.743y_t^* + 0.204c_{t-1}^*$$
$$(0.8) \quad (6.7) \quad \ (1.7)$$

$$\hat{\sigma}_\varepsilon = 85.9 \quad F = 990.0 \quad n = 35$$

The estimated short-run MPC in this model is almost identical with that from the equation using Hatanaka's procedure (0.743 versus 0.741), as is the estimated expectation coefficient (0.796 here versus 0.787 with Hatanaka's residual adjusted estimator). Because these estimates are similar, the estimated long-run MPC's are also close (0.934 for the grid-search and 0.941 for Hatanaka's method). Thus, both methods for obtaining consistent estimates produce similar estimates of the consumption function, and each differs substantially from the equation estimated with least squares and no serial correlation correction. ■

KEY TERMS

Adaptive expectations	Instrumental variable technique
Adjustment coefficient	Interim multiplier of order 1
Almon lag technique	Interim multiplier
Autoregressive equation	Koyck transformation
Constrained minimization	Lagrangean multiplier
Cross-correlation function	Mean lag
Equilibrium or long-run multiplier	Objective function
Expectation coefficient	Partial adjustment model
Finite distributed lag model	Polynomial distributed lag
Hatanaka's Residual Adjusted Estimator	Rate of decay
	Speed of adjustment
Impact (short-run) multiplier	Static expectations
Instrumental variable	Two-period interim multiplier

EXERCISES

1. Provide two examples of relationships involving distributed lags, one microeconomic the other macroeconomic.

2. Compare and contrast the adaptive expectations model and the partial adjustment model. What are the major differences between these?

3. Given the following model:

    $$y_i = \alpha_0 + \alpha_1 x_i + \alpha_2 z_i + \varepsilon_i$$

    where ε is a white noise error process:

    (a) Assume that x is the expected level of some variable v: $x_i = v_i^*$. Derive the short-run equation for this model (stated in terms of actual v). What estimation problems arise with this equation?

    (b) Now assume that x is no longer the expected level of v, but that y is the optimal level of q: $y_i = q_i^*$. Derive the short-run equation that corresponds to this partial adjustment model. Are there any estimation difficulties that arise with this model? Compare the estimation of this model to that in part **(a)**.

4. Use the following data to answer this question, where c is real personal consumption expenditure per capita (thousands $) and y is real disposable personal income per capita (thousands $) (source: *Economic Report of the President*, 1990):

YEAR	c	y	YEAR	c	y
1955	5287	5714	1973	7972	9042
1956	5349	5881	1974	7826	8867
1957	5370	5909	1975	7926	8944
1958	5357	5908	1976	8272	9175
1959	5331	6027	1977	8551	9381
1960	5561	6036	1978	8808	9735
1961	5579	6113	1979	8904	9829
1962	5729	6271	1980	8783	9722
1963	5855	6378	1981	8794	9769
1964	6099	6727	1982	8818	9725
1965	6362	7027	1983	9139	9930
1966	6607	7280	1984	9489	10419
1967	6730	7513	1985	9840	10625
1968	7003	7728	1986	10123	10905
1969	7185	7891	1987	10303	10970
1970	7275	8134	1988	10546	11337
1971	7409	8322	1989	10724	11681
1972	7726	8562			

(a) Estimate the following consumption functions:

$$c_t = \alpha_0 + \alpha_1 y_t + \varepsilon_t$$

$$c_t = \alpha_0 + \alpha_1 y_t + \alpha_2 c_{t-1} + \varepsilon_t$$

Compare and contrast the MPC's and estimates of autonomous consumption from these equations. Is there any basis to prefer one over the other?

(b) Assuming that the second of these equations has first-order serially correlated errors, which test(s) can be used to detect this? If the order of the autoregressive process is (say) 3, how can this be tested?

(c) If the first equation is valid, explain how serially correlated errors can make it appear that a distributed lag is involved in this relationship.

(d) Using the preferred estimate of the second equation above (with any serial correlation corrected), calculate the coefficients of lagged y based on the Koyck lag method.

(e) Now regress c_t on a polynomial distributed lag of y (with no y_{t-1}). Start with a third degree polynomial and use the method suggested by Kelejian and Oates earlier in the chapter. What is the value of the long-term multiplier?

5. The previous question considered the existence of a distributed lag of income in the consumption function. Provide several theoretical reasons why such a relationship may exist.

6. What is the sample cross-correlation function? How can this be used to detect the number of lags for a distributed lag relationship?

7. What is the instrumental variable technique? Why is this needed for the estimation of an autoregressive equation with serially correlated errors?

8. What is implied when the coefficient of a lagged dependent variable is greater than 1?

9. Sometimes the relationship between y and x is such that an infinite lag of x values pertains. How is such an infinite lag estimated?

10. What is the major *theoretical* flaw of the adaptive expectations hypothesis? Give an exmple of why this flaw is a problem.

14 An Introduction to Simultaneous Equation Models

We now arrive at the final topic that will be covered in this text, simultaneous equations. Throughout all of the previous chapters, it has been assumed that the causation involved in any relationship runs in only one direction, from the explanatory variable(s) to the dependent variable. Thus, when any explanatory variable changed, we viewed this as altering the dependent variable in a predictable way when the expected sign of a variable was known.

This approach is valid when all explanatory variables are nonstochastic, or if stochastic, uncorrelated with the equation errors. This distinction between stochastic and nonstochastic variables is an important one, since not all stochastic variables are uncorrelated with the error term in an equation.

An example of this can be seen by referring to the demand curve relationship that has been utilized for exposition throughout this text:

$$q_x = \alpha_0 + \alpha_1 p_x + \varepsilon$$

where q is the quantity demanded of some good X, p is the price of X, and ε is a stochastic error term. When p increases, q decreases, based on the Law of Demand. We have assumed up to now that this is the only causation involved. To see whether this is true, let us assume that preferences or some variable *other than* price changes, resulting in a larger stochastic error. This causes the demand curve to shift right (a higher quantity demanded for any price), which, given supply, raises the price of good X. The change in q (an increase in demand) has therefore *caused* the explanatory variable, p_x, to change. The causation involved in this demand relationship is therefore *bidirectional*. The price of good X and q_x are thus *jointly* (simultaneously) determined. As a result, the explanatory variable in this equation is stochastic and correlated with the error term. As this illustrates, this "simple" demand relationship is more complicated than it appears.

What are the implications of this dual-directional causation? There are three primary considerations. First, since q_x and p_x are jointly determined, it is no longer valid to model this relationship with a single equation. In the example here, a second equation is needed. Since price and quantity are jointly determined through the interaction of demand and supply, a supply equation must be added. Together, the demand and supply equations constitute a simultaneous equation model. Second, because more than one behavioral relationship is involved here, proper estimation of the demand function requires certainty about the relationship that is being modeled. This is called equation identification. Finally, the jointly determined variable, price, can be expected to be correlated with the error in the demand equation. This violates an important model assumption, causing least squares estimation to lose its desirable properties.

These last two chapters outline the nature, identification, and estimation of simultaneous equation relationships. A number of examples are included that should provide a more thorough understanding of the different elements involved.

AN INTRODUCTION TO SIMULTANEOUS EQUATION MODELS

The single equation models studied up to this point generally view explanatory variables as both fixed in repeated samples (nonstochastic) and independent of the equation error. This implicitly assumes that the direction of causation involved runs exclusively from explanatory variables to the dependent variable in an equation. In this context, it is meaningful to characterize variables as either dependent or independent. The validity of this distinction breaks down when simultaneous equations are considered. The basis for this will be presented by discussing the demand curve relationship, then revising it in light of several added complications.

The demand curve relationship that has been discussed throughout this text is:

$$q_x = \alpha_0 + \alpha_1 p_x \tag{14.1}$$

Equation (14.1) is a theoretical relationship between quantity demanded (q_x) and price (p_x), where for each price a single quantity demanded exists. This deterministic relationship is depicted by the curve D in Figure 14.1. When the price of X is p_1, quantity demanded is q_1. If price rises to p_2, quantity demanded falls to q_2. In this model of the demand for a single product, quantity demanded and price are related through a one-to-one relationship, where q responds to changes in price. The direction of causation involved in this relationship runs from p_x to q_x. Quantity demanded is the dependent variable, since its values are determined by the particular price that pertains. Values of price are not assumed to be related to quantity; these are viewed as being given in the demand model, and thus independent of q. Because of this, the explanatory variable, price, is an independent variable.

There are a number of factors in addition to price that determine the quantity of a good that is demanded. It is thus more accurate to depict the demand relationship above as a stochastic function, where the stochastic error term reflects the set of factors other than price that influence q. The stochastic demand curve relationship

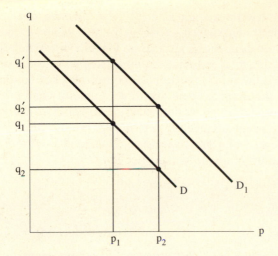

Figure 14.1

can be expressed as:

$$q_x = \alpha_0 + \alpha_1 p_x + \varepsilon \qquad\qquad (14.1')$$

Factors such as preferences enter this function through the equation error (ε). If we assume that preferences for X improve, the error term in Equation (14.1') rises, resulting in a higher quantity demanded for each price. This produces the new demand curve, D_1, in Figure 14.1. While we can continue to discuss a relationship between q_x and price, this changes slightly with a stochastic function; we must now consider the conditional means of q that correspond to different prices. Also, the demand curve in this stochastic case is the population regression function. If price is p_1, the conditional mean of q is now q_1', while for the higher price, the mean quantity demanded falls to q_2'.

However, in the context of a shifting demand curve, it is unrealistic to continue viewing these different prices as determined in isolation from quantity demanded. From microeconomic theory we know that when the demand curve for a good shifts, the price of that good rises, given supply. In this more realistic setting, the increase in quantity (rightward shift in demand) *causes* price to rise. The causation involved in the demand curve relationship thus extends in both directions, as the diagram below indicates:

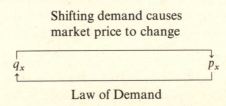

Shifting demand causes
market price to change

Law of Demand

The price of X is not determined independently of q_x. Instead, quantity and price constitute a pair of **jointly determined variables**. In this context, the distinction between dependent and independent variables is no longer valid. When there are two jointly determined variables, a second relationship exists that must be modeled. The second relationship here is the supply function. By considering both of these relationships, we can model the simultaneous determination of quantity and price. Thus, the single demand equation used throughout this text is in reality part of a *set* of equations, where price and quantity are simultaneously determined. In this example, the demand and supply functions are part of a **simultaneous equation model**. A more appropriate model for the determination of quantity and price is:

$$q_x^d = \alpha_0 + \alpha_1 p_x + \varepsilon_1 \qquad \text{(demand)}$$

$$q_x^s = \beta_0 + \beta_1 p_x + \varepsilon_2 \qquad \text{(supply)} \qquad \textbf{(14.2)}$$

$$q_x^d = q_x^s = q_x \qquad \text{(equilibrium condition)}$$

The first two equations above are called **structural equations**, since they detail the underlying structure of the model under study. The third, which is not a behavioral relationship, is an **equilibrium condition**. Equilibrium in this market is determined by market clearing. By including this equilibrium condition, we can denote quantity demanded or quantity supplied as the quantity of X (it is actually the equilibrium quantity of X). Substituting q_x for the dependent variables above gives the following two equation simultaneous equation model (assuming, for now, that the structural coefficients remain the same):

$$q_x = \alpha_0 + \alpha_1 p_x + \varepsilon_1 \qquad \textbf{(14.3)}$$

$$q_x = \beta_0 + \beta_1 p_x + \varepsilon_2$$

There are two important factors to consider when dealing with simultaneous equation models. First, since the distinction between dependent and independent variables used in previous models is not meaningful in this context, it is necessary to rename the types of variables we will be dealing with. **Endogenous variables** are those whose values are determined within the model under study. Included in this category are dependent variables and all jointly determined explanatory variables. In equation set (2) above, q and p are both endogenous variables. **Exogenous variables** are variables whose values are taken as given, or determined outside of the model. Unidirectional causation exists for this type of variable. Earlier in the text, all explanatory variables were assumed to be exogenous. Second, if a behavioral equation has one or more endogenous explanatory variables, it is actually part of a *set* of equations. Furthermore, a separate equation exists linking each endogenous explanatory variable with the dependent variable in this equation. A simultaneous equation system is **complete** if the total number of equations equals the number of endogenous variables. We will study only complete sets of simultaneous equations in these last two chapters.

How do we ascertain whether an explanatory variable is endogenous? This is accomplished by determining whether a **feedback loop**, or systematic association between that explanatory variable and the dependent variable exists. The basis for such a systematic association is usually provided by economic theory. The designation of explanatory variables as endogenous or exogenous also depends on the intended uses for the model being studied.

To illustrate these points, we will refer to the simple Keynesian model. In principles-level courses, monetary considerations are integrated into this model with the introduction of the monetary transmission mechanism. This is illustrated in Figure 14.2. Given the real supply and demand for money (M^d and M^s, respectively), the equilibrium interest rate (r) is r_1. When the interest rate is r_1, planned investment

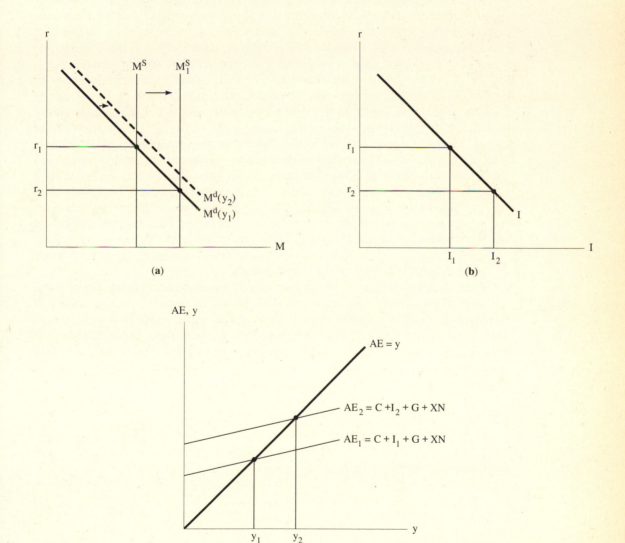

Figure 14.2

is I_1, which makes aggregate expenditure $AE_1 = C + I_1 + G + XN$, where C, G, and XN are real consumption, real government purchases, and real net exports, respectively. If the real money supply rises to M_i^S, the rate of interest falls to r_2. Given this lower interest rate, planned investment rises from I_1 to I_2, which increases both aggregate expenditure and equilibrium real GNP (y). According to the Keynesian monetary transmission mechanism, a rise in the real money supply lowers interest rates, which, in turn, increases planned investment and equilibrium real GNP.

The causation in this model extends from the interest rate, which is taken as given, or exogenous, to real GNP. In reality, as Figure 14.2 shows, we are dealing with *two* markets: a money market, in which the real supply and demand for money determine the equilibrium interest rate; and a product market, where equilibrium real GNP is determined based on aggregate expenditure. Thus, r and Y constitute a pair of jointly determined variables; their determination is not sequential.

The basis for this joint determination of r and Y (and thus the endogeneity of r) arises from the linkage between the product and money markets. In the money market, the real demand for money depends on both *r and Y*. The demand for money is therefore linked to the state of the economy (through Y). The position of the money demand curve is determined simultaneously with equilibrium in the product market. The previous illustration of the monetary transmission mechanism shows that as the real supply of money increases, Y also rises. However, this increase in Y causes the money demand curve to shift. The location of the new money demand curve is based on $y = y_2$ (see Figure 14.2). As the real demand for money increases, the interest rate then rises above r_2, which, in turn, lowers both planned investment and equilibrium Y. Eventually, a final equilibrium emerges for this *pair* of endogenous variables. *As long as either real money demand or the real money supply is a function of Y in this model, the interest rate is endogenous.*

Explicit consideration of the endogeneity of interest rates in this model forms the basis of the *general equilibrium model* of the macro economy usually studied in intermediate macroeconomics courses. A macroeconomic equilibrium exists only when both the product and money markets are in equilibrium. Separate equations exist for the product market (which determines Y) and the money market (which determines r). This is called the *IS-LM model*. The endogeneity of both y and r is illustrated in Figure 14.3.

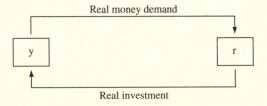

Figure 14.3

EXAMPLES OF SIMULTANEOUS EQUATION MODELS

We will now present several additional examples of simultaneous equation models. The analysis that follows is more algebraic than has been the case up to this point. Also, different variations of several of these models are analyzed. This presentation of "variations of a theme" illustrates how the designation of variables as being exogenous or endogenous often depends on the intended use for a model.

■ **THE SIMPLE KEYNESIAN MODEL WITHOUT MONEY I** The basic Keynesian model of income determination can be depicted in a number of ways, depending on how detailed one wishes to be. Perhaps the simplest representation of this model is:

$$C_t = \alpha_0 + \alpha_1 Y_t + \varepsilon_t \tag{14.4}$$

$$Y_t = C_t + I_t + G_t + XN_t \tag{14.5}$$

Equation (14.4) is the Keynesian Consumption Function that was presented in Chapter 5. According to this relationship, real personal consumption expenditure (C) is a function of real income (Y). The intercept of this function, α_0, is autonomous consumption, while its slope, α_1, is the marginal propensity to consume (MPC). According to the Keynesian model, $0 < \alpha_1 \leq 1$. The second equation above is an **identity**. In this model, C and Y are endogenous, while real investment (I), real government purchases (G) and real net exports (XN) are exogenous.

The endogeneity of Y in the consumption function can be seen by referring to the income identity (Equation (14.5)). We saw earlier that an explanatory variable is endogenous if a feedback loop exists so that if the dependent variable changes, that explanatory variable changes in a systematic way. Here, Y is endogenous if changes in real consumption produce changes in real income. In Equation (14.5), if C rises, then Y also rises given I, G, and XN. In this model real consumption and real income are therefore jointly determined.

The equilibrium values of C and Y in this model are obtained by substituting the structural equation for consumption (Equation (14.4)) into the income identity:

$$Y_t = (\alpha_0 + \alpha_1 Y_t + \varepsilon_t) + I_t + G_t + XN_t$$

$$Y_t = (\alpha_0 + I_t + G_t + XN_t) + \alpha_1 Y_t + \varepsilon_t$$

Solving for Y_t we have:

$$Y_t - \alpha_1 Y_t = (\alpha_0 + I_t + G_t + XN_t) + \varepsilon_t$$

$$Y_t(1 - \alpha_1) = (\alpha_0 + I_t + G_t + XN_t) + \varepsilon_t$$

$$Y_t^* = \frac{1}{1 - \alpha_1}(\alpha_0 + I_t + G_t + XN_t) + \frac{\varepsilon_t}{1 - \alpha_1} \tag{14.6}$$

where Y_t^* denotes equilibrium real income. The value of Y_t^* is the product of a term related to the MPC, the different types of spending in this model, and the stochastic error term. Since α_0, I, G, and XN are independent of real income, these are called autonomous values (independent of Y). The expression in parentheses, $(\alpha_0 + I_t + G_t + XN_t)$, is total autonomous spending. The term $1/(1 - \alpha_1)$ is the Keynesian (income) multiplier. Note from Equation (14.6) that the endogenous variable Y can be expressed entirely in terms of exogenous variables and the stochastic error. This equation is called a **reduced form**. A reduced-form equation exists for each endogenous variable in a simultaneous equation model such as the one we are considering.[1] A reduced-form equation also exists for real consumption. It is obtained by substituting Equation (14.6) for Y_t into the consumption function.

By rewriting Equation (14.6), the nature of the Keynesian income multiplier can be seen more easily:

$$Y_t^* = \frac{1}{1 - \alpha_1} \alpha_0 + \frac{1}{1 - \alpha_1} I_t + \frac{1}{1 - \alpha_1} G_t + \frac{1}{1 - \alpha_1} XN_t + \varepsilon_t^* \qquad \textbf{(14.7)}$$

where $\varepsilon_t^* = \varepsilon_t/(1 - \alpha_1)$. The income multiplier denotes the amount by which *equilibrium* Y changes in response to a rise or fall in autonomous spending. Taking the first difference of Equation (14.7) we obtain an expression for the change in real income:

$$\Delta Y_t^* = \frac{1}{1 - \alpha_1} \Delta\alpha_0 + \frac{1}{1 - \alpha_1} \Delta I_t + \frac{1}{1 - \alpha_1} \Delta G_t + \frac{1}{1 - \alpha_1} \Delta XN_t + \Delta\varepsilon_t^* \qquad \textbf{(14.8)}$$

A separate income multiplier exists for each type of autonomous expenditure. For example, the investment multiplier indicates the change in equilibrium real income that results from a $1 rise in real investment:

$$\text{investment multiplier} \equiv \Delta Y_t^*/\Delta I_t$$

To obtain an expression for this multiplier in terms of the parameters of our model, we assume that α_0, G, and XN are constant (i.e., have changes of 0). Omitting the error term, this reduces Equation (14.8) to:

$$\Delta Y_t^* = \frac{1}{1 - \alpha_1} \Delta I_t \qquad \textbf{(14.9)}$$

Since $\alpha_1 < 1$, the term $1/(1 - \alpha_1)$ exceeds 1, so that a $1 rise in I increases Y_t^* by more than $1. Dividing both sides of Equation (14.9) by ΔI_t we obtain the expression for the investment multiplier:

$$\frac{\Delta Y_t^*}{\Delta I_t} = \frac{1}{1 - \alpha_1} \qquad \textbf{(14.10)}$$

The rise in Y_t^* corresponding to a $1 increase in I is thus directly related to the MPC (the only spending propensity in this model). If, for example, $\alpha_1 = 0.8$, the investment multiplier is 5 $(= 1/(1 - 0.8))$, and a $1 rise in real investment increases Y^* by $5.

---

[1] This is true for linear models but not necessarily for nonlinear models.

In this model, real income is contemporaneously related to C. If, instead, the consumption function is:

$$C_t = \alpha_0 + \alpha_1 Y_t + \alpha_2 Y_{t-1} + \varepsilon_t \qquad (14.4')$$

where a lagged variable is present in the model, then the equilibrium value of Y_t is a function of autonomous spending, the error term and real income last period. This is an example of a **dynamic model**. When investment rises by \$1 in a dynamic model, the adjustment of Y^* occurs over several periods and a time path exists for each endogenous variable. ■

■ **THE SIMPLE KEYNESIAN MODEL WITHOUT MONEY II**   The model given by Equations (14.4) and (14.5) is a very simple one in that the government sector, investment and foreign trade are exogenous. The amout of detail involved in a model depends on the intended uses for that model. If we are interested in real consumption and real income, the previous model may be adequate. It is also possible to develop this model even further while keeping I, G, and XN exogenous. Since real personal consumption expenditure consists of real expenditure on durable goods, non-durable goods and services, it is possible to model each of these components individually, then to obtain real consumption as the sum of these elements. As an example of this, consider the following model:

$$C_{dt} = \alpha_0 + \alpha_1 Y_t + \alpha_2 p_{dt} + \alpha_3 r_t + \alpha_4 D_t + \alpha_5 C_{d,t-1} + \varepsilon_{1t} \qquad (14.11)$$

$$C_{nt} = \beta_0 + \beta_1 Y_t + \beta_2 p_{nt} + \beta_3 p_{ct} + \varepsilon_{2t} \qquad (14.12)$$

$$C_{st} = \gamma_0 + \gamma_1 Y_t + \gamma_2 p_{st} + \gamma_3 t + \varepsilon_{3t} \qquad (14.13)$$

$$C_t = C_{dt} + C_{nt} + C_{st} \qquad (14.14)$$

$$Y_t = C_t + I_t + G_t + XN_t \qquad (14.15)$$

where C_d, C_n, and C_s are real consumption expenditure on durables, nondurables, and services, respectively; p_d, p_n, and p_s are the implicit price deflators for durable goods, nondurable goods, and services, respectively; r is the interest rate; D is indebtedness; p_c is the deflator for personal consumption expenditures; t is a time trend; and ε_1, ε_2, and ε_3 are stochastic errors. Equation (14.14) is a consumption identity, while Equation (14.15) is the income identity. In this model there are five endogenous variables: C_d, C_n, C_s, C, and Y; and eleven exogenous variables: p_d, p_n, p_s, p_c, r, D, $C_{d,t-1}$, t, I, G, and XN. The time trend in the equation for consumption spending on services is intended to capture the secular trend in service expenditure. The lagged dependent variable in the durable goods equation is consistent with the partial adjustment framework discussed in Chapter 13. In simultaneous equation models, lagged dependent variables are called **predetermined variables** and are counted among the set of exogenous factors.

Equations (14.11)–(14.15) constitute a complete dynamic simultaneous equation model of personal consumption expenditure (and its components) and real income. To see why real income is endogenous in Equation (14.11) we will assume that C_{dt}

rises. Using the consumption identity, Equation (14.14), this increases personal consumption expenditure (given C_{nt} and C_{st}), which, in turn, raises Y_t (from the income identity). In each of the structural equations of this model (Equations (14.11)–(14.13)), real income is thus endogenous.

While this model is more in-depth than the original model, it is still possible to add more equations. Interest rates, for example, are assumed to be exogenous in this model. However, large changes in durable goods purchases can exert upward pressure on interest rates as is often true during the later stages of economic recoveries. One possibility, then, is to add an interest rate equation that would make both Y and r endogenous in the durable goods equation. ■

■ THE SIMPLE KEYNESIAN MODEL WITH MONEY: THE IS-LM MODEL

Macroeconometric models based on Keynesian analysis include equations for the components of expenditure that were viewed as exogenous in the earlier models. An example of such a model with exogenous net exports is the following:

$$C_t = \alpha_0 + \alpha_1 Y_{dt} + \varepsilon_{1t} \tag{14.16}$$

$$I_t = \beta_0 + \beta_1 r_t + \beta_2 Y_t + \varepsilon_{2t} \tag{14.17}$$

$$T_t = \tau_0 + \tau_1 Y_t \tag{14.18}$$

$$Y_{dt} = Y_t - T_t \tag{14.19}$$

$$Y_t = C_t + I_t + G_t + XN_t \tag{14.20}$$

In this model investment is now endogenous, based on Equation (14.17), which links real investment to interest rates (r) and real income. Equation (14.18) is a tax function, where τ_0 is real autonomous tax revenue and τ_1 is the marginal tax rate (with $\tau_1 > 0$). As long as $\tau_1 \neq 0$, tax revenue (T) is endogenous. Equation (14.19) is an identity that defines real disposable income (Y_{dt}) as the difference between real income and real tax revenue. Finally, Equation (14.20) is the income identity. This model contains five endogenous variables ($C, I, Y, T,$ and Y_d) and three exogenous variables ($r, G,$ and XN).

The endogeneity of Y_d in the consumption and investment functions should be apparent by this point. The endogeneity of real income in the tax function may be less obvious. To establish this, we must show that a feedback effect exists from T to Y. If real tax revenue rises, real disposable income falls (from Equation (14.19)) for any Y. As a result, real consumption falls (from Equation (14.16)), which lowers real income (from the income identity). Real taxes and real income are thus jointly determined in this model.

The above model is generally used to portray the product market in a closed economy. The reduced form equation for Y can be obtained through a series of algebraic manipulations. We first substitute Equation (14.18) into Equation (14.19) and use the resulting expression for Y_d in the consumption function:

$$C_t = \alpha_0 + \alpha_1(Y_t - \tau_0 - \tau_1 Y_t) + \varepsilon_{1t},$$

or

$$C_t = (\alpha_0 - \alpha_1\tau_0) + \alpha_1(1 - \tau_1)Y_t + \varepsilon_{1t} \qquad \textbf{(14.21)}$$

Substituting Equations (14.21) and (14.17) into the income identity, we obtain:

$$Y_t = \alpha_0 - \alpha_1\tau_0 + \alpha_1(1 - \tau_1)Y_t + \varepsilon_{1t} + \beta_0$$
$$+ \beta_1 r_t + \beta_2 Y_t + \varepsilon_{2t} + G_t + \mathrm{XN}_t$$
$$Y_t\{1 - \alpha_1(1 - \tau_1) - \beta_2\} = (\alpha_0 - \alpha_1\tau_0 + \beta_0) + \beta_1 r_t$$
$$+ G_t + \mathrm{XN}_t + (\varepsilon_{1t} + \varepsilon_{2t})$$
$$Y_t^* = \alpha_0^* + \alpha_1^* r_t + \alpha_2^* G_t + \alpha_3^* \mathrm{XN}_t + \varepsilon_t^* \qquad \textbf{(14.22)}$$

where $\alpha_0^* = (\alpha_0 - \alpha_1\tau_0 + \beta_0)/(1 - \alpha_1(1 - \tau_1) - \beta_2)$; $\alpha_1^* = \beta_1/(1 - \alpha_1(1 - \tau_1) - \beta_2)$; $\alpha_2^* = \alpha_3^* = 1/(1 - \alpha_1(1 - \tau_1) - \beta_2)$; and $\varepsilon_t^* = (\varepsilon_{1t} + \varepsilon_{2t})/(1 - \alpha_1(1 - \tau_1) - \beta_2)$. Equilibrium real income in this model is thus a function of the interest rate, real government purchases, real net exports, and the errors in the structural equations of this model.[2] Equation (14.22) is called the IS model. It allows us to identify all combinations of interest rates and real income that are consistent with product market equilibrium.

A geometric depiction of the IS model, which constitutes only the deterministic part of this model, is given in the bottom diagram of Figure 14.4, where r is on the vertical axis and y on the horizontal axis. Given the interest rate r_1, planned real investment is I_1 (Figure 14.4(a)), which makes aggregate expenditure AE_1 (Figure 14.4(b)). The term $I_1(r_1)$ in the expression for AE_1 denotes its linkage with the interest rate r_1. The resulting equilibrium y is y_1. The pair, r_1 and y_1, is thus an equilibrium combination in the product market. It is labeled point A in the lower diagram. If the interest rate falls to r_2, planned investment rises to I_2, increasing aggregate expenditure to AE_2. Equilibrium real income now rises to y_2 and the point B on the lower diagram results.

The direction of causation in the IS model runs from r to Y: a decrease in r stimulates real planned investment, which, in turn, raises equilibrium Y. Since there is no money market in this model, interest rates are exogenous. For a *given* interest rate, aggregate expenditure is determined, which is then associated with an equilibrium level of real income. Technically, every point on the IS curve in Figure 14.4 indicates an equilibrium point: equilibrium in the product market. But the general equilibrium is *not* obtainable from the product market alone. For macroeconomic equilibrium, it is necessary that both the money market and the product market be in equilibrium. Further information is required before we can determine which point on the IS curve is the general equilibrium for an economy.

This additional information is a model of the money market. While the IS model embodies the assumption of a unidirectional causation from r to Y, in reality, this pair of variables is jointly determined. To make the model of r and Y complete, a

---

[2] Assuming fixed levels of the different types of autonomous expenditure, α_0 and β_0, and autonomous tax revenue, τ_0.

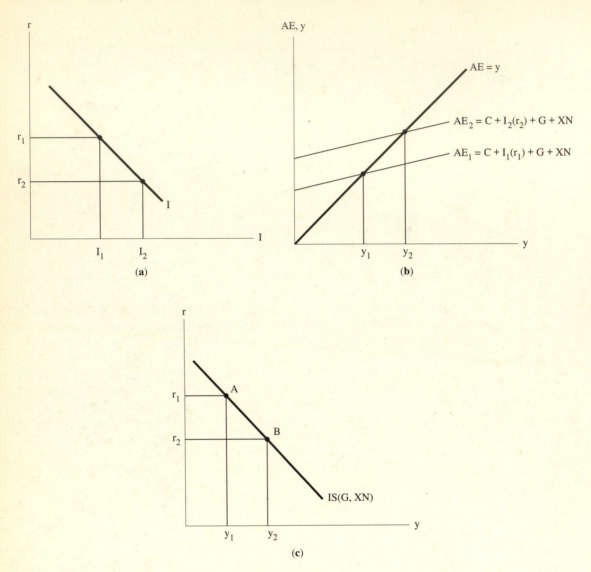

Figure 14.4

second relationship is therefore needed. We now add the following set of equations:

$$M_t^d = \gamma_0 + \gamma_1 r_t + \gamma_2 Y_t + \varepsilon_{3t} \tag{14.23}$$

$$M_t^d = M_t^s \tag{14.24}$$

Equation (14.23) is a money demand equation called the Keynesian Liquidity Preference Function. In this equation, the real demand for money (M_t^d) is negatively related to the interest rate (the speculative motive for holding money) and directly related to real income (the precautionary and transactions motives). Equation (14.24) is an equilibrium condition for the money market: the money market is in equilibrium when the real demand for money equals the real money supply. In this model, the real supply of money is exogenous. Substituting M_t^s for M_t^d in Equation (14.23), the money market can be represented as:

$$M_t^s = \gamma_0 + \gamma_1 r_t + \gamma_2 Y_t + \varepsilon_{3t},$$

which, with rearrangement, is:

$$r_t = -(\gamma_0/\gamma_1) - (\gamma_2/\gamma_1)Y_t + (1/\gamma_1)M_t^s - (\varepsilon_{3t}/\gamma_1),$$

or

$$r_t = \gamma_0^* + \gamma_1^* Y_t + \gamma_2^* M_t^s + \varepsilon_{3t}^*, \tag{14.25}$$

where $\gamma_0^* = -(\gamma_0/\gamma_1)$; $\gamma_1^* = -(\gamma_2/\gamma_1)$; $\gamma_2^* = 1/\gamma_1$; and $\varepsilon_{3t}^* = -(\varepsilon_{3t}/\gamma_1)$. Equation (14.25) gives the combinations of interest rates and real income that result in money market equilibrium. This is called the LM model. It is derived in Figure 14.5 (omitting the error term). When real income is y_1, the demand for money curve in Figure 14.5(a) is $M^d(y_1)$. Given the real supply of money, the equilibrium interest rate is r_1. This gives point C in Figure 14.5(b). When real income rises to y_2, the real demand for money increases to $M^d(y_2)$, raising the equilibrium interest rate to r_2. Point D in Figure 14.5(b) results. These combinations trace out the upward sloping LM curve on the right.

The direction of causation in the LM model, which is unidirectional, runs from Y to r. Given the level of Y, the real demand for money is determined. Assuming a constant real money supply, an equilibrium interest rate results. Every point on the LM curve is an equilibrium point. However, like the IS model, this single relationship

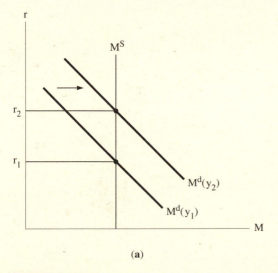

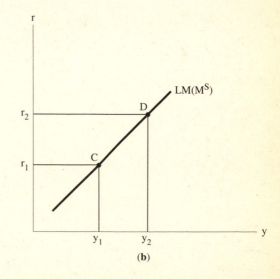

(a) (b)

Figure 14.5

does not contain enough information to determine the economy's general equilibrium. At point C in Figure 14.5(b), for example, the money market is in equilibrium. The product market is not necessary in equilibrium at this point, however.

This inability to determine the economy's overall equilibrium from each model (curve) separately is eliminated when these relationships are combined into a simultaneous equation model. Together, the IS and LM functions constitute a complete model of the joint determination of r and Y, two structural equations in two endogenous variables:

$$Y_t = \alpha_0^* + \alpha_1^* r_t + \alpha_2^* G_t + \alpha_3^* XN_t + \varepsilon_t^* \qquad \text{(14.22 repeated)}$$

$$r_t = \gamma_0^* + \gamma_1^* Y_t + \gamma_2^* M_t^s + \varepsilon_{3t}^* \qquad \text{(14.25 repeated)}$$

The IS-LM model is depicted in Figure 14.6 (omitting the errors). The point of intersection of these curves, which denotes the algebraic solution of equations (14.22) and (14.25), is the simultaneous (general) equilibrium of an economy, which is based on equilibrium in both the product *and* money markets.

A number of analytical benefits result when r and Y are viewed as a pair of jointly determined variables. One of these can be seen by considering the effect of an exogenous increase in real government purchases on equilibrium Y. In the simple Keynesian model without money, this impact is derived from the first difference form of Equation (14.22) assuming r and XN are constant:

$$\Delta Y_t^* = \alpha_2^* \, \Delta G_t,$$

or

$$\Delta Y_t^* = \frac{1}{1 - \alpha_1(1 - \tau_1) - \beta_2} \, \Delta G_t \qquad \textbf{(14.26)}$$

Assuming a constant interest rate, equilibrium real income rises by the product of the multiplier, α_2^*, and the change in real government purchases. This is illustrated in

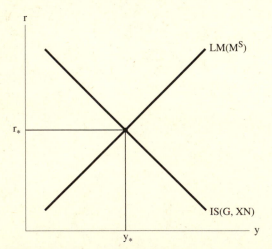

Figure 14.6

Figure 14.7, where the IS curve shifts right to IS_1 based on higher real government purchases of G'. The economy moves from point A to point B, where the magnitude of the rise in real income, $\Delta Y_t^* = (Y'_* - Y_*)$, is given by Equation (14.26).

No feedback from the increase in Y_* to the rate of interest occurs when r is exogenous. Note, however, that while point B is consistent with product market equilibrium, it is not on the LM curve. The money market is therefore out of equilibrium, and point B is not sustainable. When real income is Y'_*, the money market is in equilibrium at point C on the LM curve. If the economy is at point B, the interest rate r_* is too low for money market equilibrium.

In the more valid context where both interest rates and real income are endogenous, the rise in real income produced by this fiscal stimulus increases the demand for money. Given the real supply of money, as money demand rises, interest rates also increase. By including the money market, we now move along the new IS curve. As the increase in Y stimulates the real demand for money, interest rates rise, lowering both investment and real income. The new equilibrium occurs at point D where both the product and money markets are in equilibrium. This is the general equilibrium for the economy.

When real government purchases rise, private spending, specifically real investment, is also affected when interest rates are endogenous. The final change in aggregate expenditure is thus less than the initial change in G:

$$\Delta AE = \Delta G - \Delta I$$

In this model, a rise in G *causes* private spending (in terms of I) to fall through an endogenous increase in the interest rate. This decline in I is called crowding out.

Fiscal policy is less effective in stimulating real income when interest rates are endogenous. Perhaps less obvious, the ultimate impact of fiscal policy on equilibrium Y depends in part on money market considerations (here, the sensitivity of money

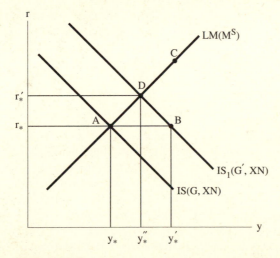

Figure 14.7

demand to Y and r). An expression for the total impact of this change in G on equilibrium real income can be obtained from the reduced form equation for Y in the IS-LM model. To obtain this reduced form, we substitute the LM equation, Equation (14.25), into the IS model, Equation (14.22), for r_t:

$$Y_t = \alpha_0^* + \alpha_1^*[\gamma_0^* + \gamma_1^* Y_t + \gamma_2^* M_t^s + \varepsilon_{3t}^*] + \alpha_2^* G_t + \alpha_3^* XN_t + \varepsilon_t^*$$

$$Y_t = [\alpha_0^* + \alpha_1^* \gamma_0^*] + \alpha_1^* \gamma_1^* Y_t + \alpha_1^* \gamma_2^* M_t^s + \alpha_2^* G_t + \alpha_3^* XN_t + (\varepsilon_t^* + \alpha_1^* \varepsilon_{3t}^*)$$

$$Y_t = \left[\frac{\alpha_0^* + \alpha_1^* \gamma_0^*}{1 - \alpha_1^* \gamma_1^*}\right] + \left[\frac{\alpha_1^* \gamma_2^*}{1 - \alpha_1^* \gamma_1^*}\right] M_t^s + \left[\frac{\alpha_2^*}{1 - \alpha_1^* \gamma_1^*}\right] G_t$$

$$+ \left[\frac{\alpha_3^*}{1 - \alpha_1^* \gamma_1^*}\right] XN_t + \left[\frac{\varepsilon_t^* + \alpha_1^* \varepsilon_{3t}^*}{1 - \alpha_1^* \gamma_1^*}\right]$$

This can be expressed more compactly as:

$$Y_t^* = \pi_0 + \pi_1 M_t^s + \pi_2 G_t + \pi_3 XN_t + \varepsilon_t^{**} \qquad \textbf{(14.27)}$$

Like all reduced forms, this gives an expression for an endogenous variable in terms of the set of exogenous variables in the entire model. The impact of G_t on the general equilibrium of Y is given by the reduced form coefficient, π_2:

$$\Delta Y_t^* = \pi_2 \Delta G_t$$

The government purchases multiplier, π_2, indicates the *total* effect of a change in real government purchases on equilibrium real income. Note that this multiplier is defined in terms of various structural equation coefficients. Substituting back to the original expressions for the starred terms, this multiplier is:

$$\frac{\Delta Y_t^*}{\Delta G_t} = \frac{1}{1 - \alpha_1(1 - \tau_1) - \beta_2 + \beta_1(\gamma_2/\gamma_1)} \qquad \textbf{(14.28)}$$

The denominator of the government purchases multiplier with exogenous interest rates excludes the term $\beta_1(\gamma_2/\gamma_1)$, which involves the interest sensitivity of investment (β_1), and the sensitivity of real money demand to the interest rate (γ_1) and real income (γ_2), respectively. Since $\beta_1 < 0$, $\gamma_1 < 0$, and $\gamma_2 < 0$, the sign of this term is positive, which makes the denominator for this multiplier larger than that in the earlier model. As a result, the government purchases multiplier is smaller in the endogenous interest rate model. ■

■ **INTERNATIONAL TRADE**   The macroeconomic models discussed above all viewed net exports as exogenous. We will now model net exports in the context of a simultaneous equations model. Net exports is the difference between exports (X) and imports (M). Consistent with the earlier analysis, we will view both of these in real terms. Each is a demand relationship, where imports reflect domestic demand, while exports indicate foreign demand for goods and services. Since foreign prices are involved with both imports and exports, the translation of these values into domestic prices is relevant. This makes the exchange rate (ER) a significant consideration.

Income is also an important factor for both exports and imports. However, a different type of income is relevant for each relationship. For imports, domestic income (Y) pertains, while with exports, foreign income (Y_f) is applicable. In general terms, then, the functions for real imports and exports can be stated as:

$$X = X(\text{ER}, Y_f, \varepsilon_1) \tag{14.29}$$

$$M = M(\text{ER}, Y, \varepsilon_2) \tag{14.30}$$

where ε_1 and ε_2 are stochastic error terms. Since real net exports is the difference between real exports and real imports, this relationship can be expressed as:

$$\text{XN} = \text{XN}(\text{ER}, Y, Y_f, v_1),$$

which, using a linear specification, is:

$$\text{XN}_t = \alpha_0 + \alpha_1 \text{ER}_t + \alpha_2 Y_t + \alpha_3 Y_{ft} + v_{1t} \tag{14.31}$$

If we model U.S. net exports with Japan, and define ER as Japanese yen per \$1, then a fall in ER, which indicates fewer yen per \$1, denotes dollar depreciation. By raising the dollar prices of Japanese imports in the United States and lowering the yen prices of United States exports to Japan, net exports for the United States rise (see Chapter 6 for a discussion of this).

The exchange rate is not determined independently of net exports. If XN changes, both the supply and demand for dollars are affected, causing the exchange rate to change as well. The exchange rate and net exports are therefore a pair of jointly determined variables and the net exports equation is part of a set of simultaneous equations. An exchange rate equation is:

$$\text{ER}_t = \beta_0 + \beta_1 \text{XN}_t + \beta_2(r - r_f)_t + \beta_3(\text{GGNP} - \text{GGNP}_f)_{t-1} + v_{2t} \tag{14.32}$$

where r and r_f are U.S. and Japanese interest rates, respectively; GGNP is the growth rate in United States real income; GGNP_f is the growth rate of Japanese real income; and v_2 is a stochastic error. In this equation, *differentials* in interest rates and lagged rates of real income growth affect the exchange rate. An increase in XN, given these differentials, is expected to raise the number of yen per \$1, increasing ER. The complete model for net exports and the exchange rate is now:

$$\text{XN}_t = \alpha_0 + \alpha_1 \text{ER}_t + \alpha_2 Y_t + \alpha_3 Y_{ft} + v_{1t}$$

$$\text{ER}_t = \beta_0 + \beta_1 \text{XN}_t + \beta_2(r - r_f)_t + \beta_3(\text{GGNP} - \text{GGNP}_f)_{t-1} + v_{2t}$$

It is not difficult to expand the equation for net exports into separate equations for exports (X) and imports (M). When this is done, the net exports equation becomes an identity:

$$X_t = \gamma_{01} + \gamma_{11} \text{ER}_t + \gamma_{21} Y_{ft} + \varepsilon_{1t} \tag{14.29'}$$

$$M_t = \gamma_{02} + \gamma_{12} \text{ER}_t + \gamma_{22} Y_t + \varepsilon_{2t} \tag{14.30'}$$

$$\text{ER}_t = \beta_0 + \beta_1 \text{XN}_t + \beta_2(r - r_f)_t + \beta_3(\text{GGNP} - \text{GGNP}_f)_{t-1} + v_{2t} \tag{14.32}$$

$$\text{XN}_t = X_t - M_t \tag{14.31'}$$

In this more elaborate model, there are four equations in four endogenous variables (X, M, ER, and XN) and four exogenous variables (Y_f, Y, $(r - r_f)$, and $(\text{GGNP} - \text{GGNP}_f)_{t-1}$). Further modifications are possible. Perhaps the most obvious changes deal with the implicit assumption in this model that interest rates and domestic real income are exogenous. This is pursued in the Exercises at the end of this chapter. ∎

PROBLEMS ESTIMATING STRUCTURAL EQUATIONS WITH LEAST SQUARES: LEAST SQUARES BIAS

We now have seen a number of structural equations that depict microeconomic and macroeconomic relationships. The most notable difference between these and the econometric equations from earlier chapters has to do with the distinction between dependent and independent variables: this distinction is not meaningful for structural equations, since the direction of causation no longer runs exclusively from the right-hand side variables to the dependent variable. When one or more explanatory variables are endogenous, their joint determination with the dependent variable violates one of the regression model assumptions, as we now show.

To see this, let us again illustrate why least squares is an appropriate estimation technique for non-structural equations. We will refer to the demand curve equation, Equation (14.1′), but assume for now that the price of X is exogenous:

$$q_x = \alpha_0 + \alpha_1 p_x + \varepsilon$$

The model assumptions made earlier (in Chapter 4 for this bivariate model) relate to the stochastic error and the included explanatory variable:

Error Assumptions

$$E(\varepsilon_i) = 0 \qquad \text{Var}(\varepsilon_i) = \sigma_\varepsilon^2 \qquad \text{Cov}(\varepsilon_i, \varepsilon_j) = 0$$

Explanatory Variable Assumption

> The explanatory variable is either nonstochastic, or, if stochastic, uncorrelated with the equation error

The least squares estimator of α_1 in this equation, dropping the subscript x, and adding the subscript i, is:

$$\hat{\alpha}_1 = \frac{\sum (p_i - \hat{\mu}_p)(q_i - \hat{\mu}_q)}{\sum (p_i - \hat{\mu}_p)^2} = \frac{\sum p_i' q_i'}{\sum p_i'^2}$$

where $\hat{\mu}_p$ and $\hat{\mu}_q$ are the sample means of price and quantity, respectively, and p_i' and q_i' denote deviations from means. Substituting for q_i' from the deviation form of the population regression function:

$$q_i' = \alpha_1 p_i' + \varepsilon_i'$$

we have:

$$\hat{\alpha}_1 = \frac{\sum p_i'(\alpha_1 p_i' + \varepsilon_i')}{\sum p_i'^2}$$

$$= \alpha_1 + \frac{\sum p_i' \varepsilon_i'}{\sum p_i'^2} \tag{14.33}$$

This slope estimator equals its population parameter plus a term related to the co-variance between p_x and ε, and the variance of p_x. It is possible to express this term as a weighted average of the equation errors. Letting $\omega_i \equiv p_i'/\Sigma p_i'^2$, Equation (14.33) can be written:

$$\hat{\alpha}_1 = \alpha_1 + \sum \omega_i \varepsilon_i' \tag{14.34}$$

Note that we have proceeded up to this point without invoking any of the model assumptions.

The unbiasedness of $\hat{\alpha}_1$ requires that $E(\hat{\alpha}_1) = \alpha_1$. The expected value of Equation (14.34) is:

$$E(\hat{\alpha}_1) = \alpha_1 + E\left[\sum \omega_i \varepsilon_i'\right] \tag{14.35}$$

Before the expected value of the bracketed term on the right can be taken, model assumptions must be used. If p_x is exogenous, it can be treated as a constant with respect to mathematical expectation. Then:

$$E(\hat{\alpha}_1) = \alpha_1 + \sum \omega_i E(\varepsilon_i')$$

$$= \alpha_1$$

since $E(\varepsilon_i') = 0$. In this case, $\hat{\alpha}_1$ is unbiased.

We next allow p_x to be stochastic but independent of the equation error. Now, both p_x and ε are random variables, and:

$$E\left[\sum \omega_i \varepsilon_i'\right] \neq \sum \omega_i E(\varepsilon_i')$$

Each of the terms in the brackets must be treated as a random variable when taking expected values. The term $\Sigma \omega_i \varepsilon_i'$ can be viewed as the product of two random variables y_1 and y_2, where y_1 represents the term with ω_i (related to p_x) and y_2 denotes ε_i'. Equation (14.35) is now:

$$E(\hat{\alpha}_1) = \alpha_1 + \sum E[y_1 \cdot y_2] \tag{14.36}$$

We saw in Chapter 2 that when two random variables are independent, the expectation of their product equals the product of their individual expectations. Equation (14.36) thus becomes:

$$E(\hat{\alpha}_1) = \alpha_1 + \sum E(y_1) \cdot E(y_2)$$

when p_x is stochastic but independent of the equation error. Substituting back from the y's to the original terms, the expected value of $\hat{\alpha}_1$ is:

$$E(\hat{\alpha}_1) = \alpha_1 + \sum E(\omega_i) E(\varepsilon_i')$$

$$= \alpha_1$$

again, since $E(\varepsilon_i') = 0$. When p_x is stochastic, $\hat{\alpha}_1$ is thus an unbiased estimator *as long as p_x is independent of the equation error.*

The consistency of the least squares estimator for α_1 will be demonstrated descriptively by analyzing the normal equation for $\hat{\alpha}_1$. This equation can be obtained by summing the deviation form of the sample regression function then multiplying each term by p_i':

$$\sum q_i' p_i' = \hat{\alpha}_1 \sum p_i'^2 + \sum \varepsilon_i' p_i' \tag{14.37}$$

As noted in Chapter 4, the summation terms above are related to variances and covariances. Using the model assumption that the explanatory variable is either nonstochastic, or, if stochastic, uncorrelated with the equation error, the term on the far right tends to 0 as sample size rises, since it is related to the covariance between p and ε. We can thus overlook this term when defining the formula for $\hat{\alpha}_1$. The normal equation (14.37) can thus be viewed as expressing the following relationship:

$$\sum q_i' p_i' = \hat{\alpha}_1 \sum p_i'^2 \tag{14.38}$$

from which the formula for $\hat{\alpha}_1$ is derived:

$$\hat{\alpha}_1 = \sum q_i' p_i' / \sum p_i'^2$$

This equation can be manipulated to express $\hat{\alpha}_1$ in terms of α_1 (similar to Equation (14.33)):

$$\hat{\alpha}_1 = \alpha_1 + \sum p_i' \varepsilon_i' / \sum p_i'^2$$

Recall that an estimator is consistent if it is unbiased (or asymptotically unbiased) and its variance falls as sample size (n) rises, so that its sampling distribution collapses to a single value given by its population parameter as n approaches infinity.[3] In this example, $\hat{\alpha}_1$ is unbiased, so it satisfies the first of these conditions. To examine the behavior of $\hat{\alpha}_1$ as sample size is increased, we divide both the numerator and denominator above by $(n-1)$:

$$\hat{\alpha}_1 = \alpha_1 + \frac{\sum p_i' \varepsilon_i' / (n-1)}{\sum p_i'^2 / (n-1)} \tag{14.39}$$

As n approaches infinity, the numerator in Equation (14.39) tends toward the population covariance between the explanatory variable and the error term, $\sigma_{p\varepsilon}$. The denominator tends toward the population variance of p_x, σ_p^2. Thus:

$$\hat{\alpha}_1 = \alpha_1 + \sigma_{p\varepsilon} / \sigma_p^2 \qquad \text{as } n \text{ approaches infinity}$$

If, as n approaches infinity, $\hat{\alpha}_1$ tends in probability toward α_1, then $\hat{\alpha}_1$ is a consistent estimator.[4] By "tends in probability toward α_1" is meant the sampling distribution

---

[3] The combination of unbiasedness (or asymptotic unbiasedness) and a falling variance constitute a sufficient condition for consistency.

[4] This is actually a statement about the probability limit of $\hat{\alpha}_1$: $\hat{\alpha}_1$ is a consistent estimator of α_1 if $\text{plim}(\hat{\alpha}_1) = \alpha_1$. Since the notion of the probability limit has not been covered in this text, a descriptive analysis of this concept is made in this chapter.

of $\hat{\alpha}_1$ collapses to the single value α_1 for larger sample sizes. In the present context, $\hat{\alpha}_1$ is a consistent estimator of α_1 when, as n approaches infinity, the second term on the right of the above expression tends to 0. Thus, as n approaches infinity, when: (i) $\sigma_{p\varepsilon} = 0$; and (ii) σ_p^2 is nonzero, $\hat{\alpha}_1$ is a consistent estimator of α_1. Based on the model assumption concerning the explanatory variable, both of these requirements are met. Thus, the least squares estimator of $\hat{\alpha}_1$ is consistent when p_x is either exogenous, or, if stochastic, uncorrelated with the equation error.

In the context of an endogenous price of X, the equation error is no longer independent of p_x. We will establish this using the equation set of which the demand curve function is part (Equation (14.2)). Omitting the subscript x, these equations are:

$$q_i^d = \alpha_0 + \alpha_1 p_i + \varepsilon_{1i}$$

$$q_i^s = \beta_0 + \beta_1 p_i + \varepsilon_{2i}$$

$$q_i^d = q_i^s$$

If price is uncorrelated with ε_1, then, in the demand function, $\text{Cov}(p_i, \varepsilon_{1i}) = 0$. We can derive an expression for this covariance using the expected value formula:

$$\text{Cov}(p_i, \varepsilon_{1i}) = E[p_i - E(p_i)][\varepsilon_{1i} - E(\varepsilon_{1i})]$$
$$= E[p_i - E(p_i)]\varepsilon_{1i}$$

since $E(\varepsilon_{1i}) = 0$ by the regression model assumptions. Since p_i is endogenous, we can derive an expression for it by calculating its reduced form equation. To obtain this, we utilize the equilibrium condition and equate the right sides of the demand and supply equations:

$$\alpha_0 + \alpha_1 p_i + \varepsilon_{1i} = \beta_0 + \beta_1 p_i + \varepsilon_{2i}$$

$$p_i(\alpha_1 - \beta_1) = (\beta_0 - \alpha_0) + (\varepsilon_{2i} - \varepsilon_{1i})$$

$$p_i = \left[\frac{\beta_0 - \alpha_0}{\alpha_1 - \beta_1}\right] + \left[\frac{\varepsilon_{2i} - \varepsilon_{1i}}{\alpha_1 - \beta_1}\right], \tag{14.40}$$

or

$$p_i = \pi_0 + \varepsilon_i^* \tag{14.40'}$$

Using Equation (14.40'): $E(p_i) = \pi_0$, since $E(\varepsilon_i^*) = 0$. We thus have an expression for the price term in the covariance formula:

$$[p_i - E(p_i)] = [\pi_0 + \varepsilon_i^* - \pi_0] = \varepsilon_i^*$$

Substituting this into the covariance expression, we have:

$$\text{Cov}(p_i, \varepsilon_{1i}) = E(\varepsilon_i^* \cdot \varepsilon_{1i})$$

$$= E\left[\frac{(\varepsilon_{2i} - \varepsilon_{1i}) \cdot \varepsilon_{1i}}{\alpha_1 - \beta_1}\right]$$

Since the population coefficients α_1 and β_1 are constants, they can be moved outside the expectation operator, making this expression:

$$\text{Cov}(p_i, \varepsilon_{1i}) = \frac{1}{\alpha_1 - \beta_1} E\{(\varepsilon_{2i} - \varepsilon_{1i}) \cdot \varepsilon_{1i}\}$$

$$= \frac{1}{\alpha_1 - \beta_1} \{E(\varepsilon_{2i} \cdot \varepsilon_{1i}) - E(\varepsilon_{1i})^2\}$$

If the errors for these equations are uncorrelated for a given observation, $E(\varepsilon_{2i}\varepsilon_{1i}) = 0$. In a time series context, this indicates that the equation errors are **contemporaneously uncorrelated**, or uncorrelated for a given time period. Denoting $E(\varepsilon_{1i}^2) = \sigma_{\varepsilon_1}^2$, the covariance above reduces to:

$$\text{Cov}(p_i, \varepsilon_{1i}) = \frac{-\sigma_{\varepsilon_1}^2}{\alpha_1 - \beta_1} \neq 0 \qquad \textbf{(14.41)}$$

The fact that price is correlated with ε_1 should come as no surprise, in light of the fact that the reduced form for p (Equation (14.40)) expresses price as a function of ε_1. Generalizing the result contained in Equation (14.41): *when an equation contains one or more endogenous explanatory variables, its error term will tend to be correlated with the endogenous variables in that equation.*

The basis for this result is illustrated in Figure 14.8. If ε_{1i} rises as the result of an exogenous improvement in preferences for X, the demand curve for X shifts right, as q_x is now higher for any p_x. Because p_x is endogenous, and jointly determined along with q_x, this increase in the demand for X, given the supply of X, causes the market price of X to rise. Thus, as ε_{1i} rises, q_x also rises, resulting in a new p_x. The systematic relationship between q_x and p_x, which constitutes the feedback loop from

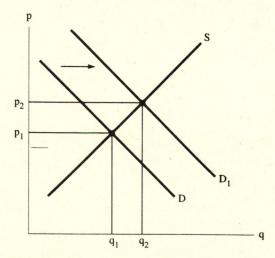

Figure 14.8

q_x to p_x, produces a correlation between ε_1 and p_x. The explanatory variable and equation error are therefore correlated. The expression for the covariance of these terms is given by Equation (14.41).

This correlation between p_x and ε_1 affects both the unbiasedness and consistency of the least squares estimators of the coefficients in this equation. Returning again to Equation (14.36):

$$E(\hat{\alpha}_1) = \alpha_1 + \sum E[y_1 \cdot y_2]$$

where y_1 corresponds to ω_i and y_2 to ε_1. Based on the existence of a correlation between the explanatory variable, p_x, and the equation error formalized in Equation (14.41), y_1 is *not* independent of y_2. Because of this, no simplification can be made with the expectation term on the right. Thus, when p_x is endogenous, our demand function is a structural equation, and:

$$E(\hat{\alpha}_1) = \alpha_1 + E\left[\sum p_i' \varepsilon_i' / \sum p_i'^2\right] \neq \alpha_1$$

The least squares estimator of α_1 is therefore biased. The bias of this estimator is given by the expression:

$$\text{Bias}(\hat{\alpha}_1) = E(\hat{\alpha}_1) - \alpha_1$$
$$= E\left[\sum p_i' \varepsilon_i' / \sum p_i'^2\right]$$

Since this correlation between p_x and ε_1 cannot be expected to disappear with larger sample sizes, this estimator is asymptotically biased as well. The existence of this problem is called **least squares bias**: the application of least squares to a structural equation produces biased coefficient estimators. This is sometimes referred to as **simultaneous equation bias**.

Not only are the least squares estimators of structural equations biased, they are inconsistent as well. If we refer again to Equation (14.39), but replace ε_i from the original demand equation with ε_{1i} from the structural demand equation:

$$\hat{\alpha}_1 = \alpha_1 + \frac{\sum p_i' \varepsilon_{1i}' / (n-1)}{\sum p_i'^2 / (n-1)}$$

then, as sample size approaches infinity, this relationship tends toward:

$$\hat{\alpha}_1 = \alpha_1 + \sigma_{p\varepsilon} / \sigma_p^2 \tag{14.42}$$

where the population covariance between p and ε_{1i} is denoted $\sigma_{p\varepsilon}$. We have seen that $\sigma_{p\varepsilon}$ is nonzero when p_x is endogenous. Thus, as n approaches infinity, even if $\sigma_p^2 \neq 0$, the second term on the right does *not* approach 0. As a result, $\hat{\alpha}_1$ based on least squares estimation does not tend in probability toward α_1 (as n approaches infinity). Instead, the sampling distribution of $\hat{\alpha}_1$ tends toward $\alpha_1 + \sigma_{p\varepsilon} / \sigma_p^2$, and the least squares estimator of α_1 is inconsistent.

The value towards which this estimator tends can be expanded using the expression for $\text{Cov}(p_i, \varepsilon_{1i})$ given by Equation (14.41):

$$\text{Cov}(p_i, \varepsilon_{1i}) = \sigma_{p\varepsilon} = \frac{-\sigma_{\varepsilon_1}^2}{\alpha_1 - \beta_1}$$

Substituting this into Equation (14.42) we have:

$$\hat{\alpha}_1 = \alpha_1 + \frac{-\sigma_{\varepsilon_1}^2}{\sigma_p^2(\alpha_1 - \beta_1)} \tag{14.43}$$

In Equation (14.43), $\sigma_{\varepsilon_1}^2$, σ_p^2, and β_1 are positive, while $\alpha_1 < 0$. The second term on the right of Equation (14.43) is therefore the ratio of two negative values, which is positive. Thus, as n approaches infinity, the least squares estimator of α_1 in the structural demand equation will tend to overstate this value.

These problems with least squares estimation can be seen from a different perspective if we consider the normal equation for $\hat{\alpha}_1$ in the structural demand equation. This is derived in a manner similar to Equation (14.37), except that ε_i is replaced by ε_{1i}:

$$\sum q_i' p_i' = \hat{\alpha}_1 \sum p_i'^2 + \sum \varepsilon_{1i}' p_i'$$

When price is uncorrelated with the equation error, the term $\Sigma \varepsilon_{1i}' p_i'$ tends to 0, allowing us to ignore it when defining the formula for $\hat{\alpha}_1$. Since this condition is not met when p_x is endogenous, simply dividing $\Sigma q_i' p_i'$ by $\Sigma p_i'^2$ and omitting the other term results in a biased and inconsistent estimator. The consistency property can still be salvaged if a variable is used in place of the endogenous explanatory variable p_x that is (at least) uncorrelated with ε_{1i} for large n. This suggests the use of an instrumental variable estimator (as discussed in Chapter 13). We will return to this in Chapter 15.

LEAST SQUARES ESTIMATION OF REDUCED FORM EQUATIONS

We saw above that the application of least squares to structural equation coefficients produces biased and inconsistent estimators. Is the same true when reduced form coefficients are estimated with least squares?

A reduced form equation expresses one of the endogenous variables in an equation system in terms of the *set* of exogenous variables in that system. Included among the exogenous variables are lagged endogenous variables. Recall that these are called predetermined variables. What happens when we estimate such a relationship with least squares? To answer this question, we will utilize the following reduced form equation, which expresses an endogenous variable y_1 in terms of the exogenous variable x:

$$y_{1i} = \pi_0 + \pi_1 x_i + v_i$$

The least squares estimator of π_1 is:

$$\hat{\pi}_1 = \sum x_i' y_{1i} / \sum x_i'^2$$

Substituting for y_1 from the population reduced form:

$$y_{1i}' = \pi_1 x_i' + v_i'$$

we have:

$$\hat{\pi}_1 = \sum x_i'(\pi_1 x_i' + v_i')/\sum x_i'^2$$
$$= \pi_1 + \sum x_i' v_i'/\sum x_i'^2 \qquad \textbf{(14.44)}$$

The expected value of this estimator is:

$$E(\hat{\pi}_1) = \pi_1 + E(\sum x_i' v_i'/\sum x_i'^2)$$

The second term on the right can be expressed as a weighted average of the reduced form error terms. If we let $\omega_i \equiv x_i'/\sum x_i'^2$, this expected value is:

$$E(\hat{\pi}_1) = \pi_1 + E(\sum \omega_i v_i') \qquad \textbf{(14.44')}$$

Recall that a reduced form error is a function of the *set* of structural equation errors in the system under consideration. Since the variable x is exogenous, it is either non-stochastic, or if stochastic, uncorrelated with the structural equation errors. Because of this fact:

$$E(\sum \omega_i v_i') = \begin{cases} \sum \omega_i E(v_i') & \text{if } x \text{ is exogenous} \\ \sum E(\omega_i) E(v_i') & \text{if } x \text{ is stochastic and uncorrelated with the} \\ & \qquad \text{structural equation errors} \end{cases}$$

Either way, x is uncorrelated with the reduced form error, and the expectation term on the right of Equation (14.44') is 0. Thus:

$$E(\hat{\pi}_1) = \pi_1$$

so that least squares estimation of a reduced form equation produces unbiased coefficients.

As sample size approaches infinity, the sampling distribution of this estimator tends toward π_1 as well, so that least squares estimation of reduced form equations produces consistent estimators. Rewriting Equation (14.44) in a form similar to Equation (14.39) we have:

$$\hat{\pi}_1 = \pi_1 + \frac{\sum x_i' v_i'/(n-1)}{\sum x_i'^2/(n-1)} \qquad \textbf{(14.45)}$$

As n approaches infinity, the numerator in Equation (14.45) approaches the population covariance between v and x. The denominator approaches the population variance of x. If, as sample size rises, the reduced form error is uncorrelated with x and the population variance of x is finite and non-zero, the sampling distribution of $\hat{\pi}_1$ tends toward the single value π_1, making it a consistent estimator. When x is exogenous, these conditions are satisfied, and $\hat{\pi}_1$ is a consistent estimator.

These conclusions about the unbiasedness and consistency of the least squares estimators of the reduced form coefficients are true *in general*, but not always. The exception occurs when the reduced form equation contains one or more lagged dependent variables and the reduced form errors are serially correlated. To illustrate this, we will assume the first structural equation is:

$$y_{1t} = \alpha_0 + \alpha_1 y_{2t} + \alpha_2 x_t + \alpha_3 y_{1,t-1} + \varepsilon_{1t} \qquad \textbf{(14.46)}$$

where y_2 is an endogenous variable, and x is exogenous. If the structural error above is first-order autocorrelated, where:

$$\varepsilon_{1t} = \Theta \varepsilon_{1,t-1} + \eta_t \qquad (14.47)$$

then the lagged dependent variable in Equation (14.46) will be correlated with the structural equation error. This can be seen by noting that since y_{1t} is a function of ε_{1t}, then, lagging these by one period, $y_{1,t-1}$ is a function of $\varepsilon_{1,t-1}$. Substituting Equation (14.47) into Equation (14.46) we have:

$$y_{1t} = \alpha_0 + \alpha_1 y_{2t} + \alpha_2 x_t + \alpha_3 y_{1,t-1} + \Theta \varepsilon_{1,t-1} + \eta_t$$

The lagged dependent variable $y_{1,t-1}$ is therefore correlated with the structural equation error, ε_{1t}, as a result of the correlation between ε_{1t} and $\varepsilon_{1,t-1}$. *When a structural equation with a lagged dependent variable has serially correlated errors, the error term and the lagged dependent variable will thus tend to be correlated. This correlation renders invalid the designation of the lagged dependent variable as being exogenous. In this situation, the lagged dependent variable must be treated as an endogenous variable.*

This problem with least squares estimation of a reduced form equation arises from the fact that in the situation above, $y_{1,t-1}$ is a stochastic variable that is correlated with both the structural and reduced form errors. If we make reference to Equation (14.44′), the reduced form error, v, is a function of ε_1 along with all of the other structural errors in the system for which Equation (14.46) is a part and:

$$E(\textstyle\sum \omega_i v_i') \neq \sum E(\omega_i) E(v_i')$$

Since there is no reason to believe that this expectation is 0, the least squares estimator of π_1 is therefore biased. Least squares estimation of a reduced form equation in this situation produces biased coefficient estimators. Some autocorrelation correction is therefore warranted to eliminate this problem.

A LOOK AHEAD. This chapter has outlined the nature of simultaneous equation models and provided a number of examples from microeconomics and macroeconomics. Within this framework, the distinction between dependent and independent variable loses its significance, since the direction of causation is no longer unidirectional. It is now more appropriate to view variables as being either endogenous or exogenous.

Structural equations, which characterize the underlying structure of the economic model under study, have at least one endogenous variable among the set of explanatory variables. A feedback loop therefore exists from the dependent variable to any endogenous explanatory variable. This feedback produces a correlation between the structural equation error and the endogenous explanatory variable(s), violating one of the regression model assumptions. Least squares estimation of a structural equation results in biased and inconsistent estimators. In contrast, as long as the reduced form errors are not serially correlated, least squares is an appropriate technique for estimating reduced form coefficients.

The last chapter of this text details the estimation of structural equation parameters. While an unbiased estimation technique does not currently exist, consistent estimation is possible using a variant of least squares. As was true for equations with autocorrelated or heteroskedastic errors, this entails transforming the equation to correct the major problem that exists (here, of the correlation between endogenous explanatory variables and the equation error), then applying least squares to the transformed equation. In this context, the estimation technique is called two-stage least squares.

One other element is involved. Before applying this estimation technique to a structural equation, we must be sure that it is identified—we must be able to distinguish it from the other equations that constitute that simultaneous equation system. The next chapter therefore deals with the identification and estimation of structural equations and simultaneous equation models.

KEY TERMS

Complete

Contemporaneously uncorrelated

Dynamic model

Endogenous variable

Equilibrium condition

Exogenous variable

Feedback loop

Identity

Jointly determined variables

Least squares bias

Predetermined variable

Reduced form

Simultaneous equation bias

Simultaneous equation model

Structural equations

EXERCISES

1. Obtain the reduced form for C_t from the simple Keynesian model given by Equations (14.4) and (14.5).

2. In the simultaneous equation model given by Equations (14.11)–(14.15), what variables other than r might be made endogenous in Equations (14.11)–(14.13)? Explain the *economic* basis for the modifications involved.

3. In the section on International Trade, a four-equation model of exports, imports, net exports, and the exchange rate is given, where interest rates are assumed to be exogenous. Add an equation for the interest rate and explain the feedback effect between this and the exchange rate.

4. A student asked: "Since we are dealing with simultaneous equation models, where a particular structural equation is part of a set of equations, why don't we include a variable 'the supply of X' in the structural demand equation?" Explain how supply enters into the demand functions considered in this chapter.

5.   In terms of economic theory, what is the difference between a structural equation coefficient and a reduced form coefficient?

6.   The reduced form equation error in Equation (14.40′) is $\varepsilon_t^* = (\varepsilon_{2i} - \varepsilon_{1i})/(\alpha_1 - \beta_1)$.

Using the general model assumptions:

(a) Show that ε_t^* has a 0 expectation.

(b) Is this error term homoskedastic?

(c) When will ε_t^* be autocorrelated?

7.   Will least squares estimation of a reduced form equation from a dynamic model result in biased estimators?

8.   Explain the nature and causes of least squares bias.

9.   Use the following set of equations to answer these questions:

$$XN_t = \alpha_0 + \alpha_1 ER_t + \alpha_2 Y_t + \alpha_3 Y_{ft} + v_{1t}$$

$$Y_t = C_t + I_t + G_t + XN_t$$

The first equation models real net exports (XN) as a function of the exchange rate (ER), domestic real income (Y) and real foreign income (Y_f), while the second equation is the (domestic) real income identity.

(a) List the endogenous variables in this set of equations.

(b) Which variables are exogenous?

(c) Derive the reduced form equations for this model.

(d) Explain the economic basis of the real foreign income multiplier from part (c).

(e) Which variables that are presently exogenous in this model could be made endogenous? Provide the economic rationale for each of these newly endogenous variables.

10. Using the results from this chapter, explain why least squares estimation of a demand function can sometimes produce a *positive* coefficient for the price of X.

11. In the simultaneous equations for the money market given by Equations (14.23) and (14.24), the money supply is assumed to be exogenous. Modify this model and provide a structural equation for the real supply of money.

(a) How many endogenous models are in this model now?

(b) Is this a complete model?

(c) Derive the reduced forms of M_t and r_t.

15 The Identification and Estimation of Simultaneous Equation Models

The econometric framework outlined in this text began with bivariate regression. A progression to multiple regression was necessary, since modeling the behavior of many variables entails more interrelationships than an equation with a single explanatory variable is capable of handling. When modeling such variables, it is necessary to explicitly consider a number of explanatory factors, not just one.

The final progression that is detailed in this text, from single equation models to simultaneous equation systems, is similar in a number of ways to the one we made in moving from bivariate to multiple regression. Modeling the behavior of a variable of interest often involves not only a number of different explanatory variables, but several interrelationships as well. Just as the realism of bivariate models was enhanced by adding explanatory variables, we must now include additional *equations* to account for the different interrelationships this variable is involved in.

An example of this is provided by the demand function for a good. This was first viewed as a bivariate relationship (in Chapter 4), with quantity demanded as a function of price. When nonexperimental data are used to estimate this relationship, it is necessary to control for the effects of a number of additional factors of primary importance, by including them as explanatory variables. The result is a multivariate function. The multiple regression techniques outlined in Chapter 6 deal with the estimation and interpretation of this type of function.

The framework of Chapter 6 overlooks one of the interrelationships that exists between quantity demanded and price. If price changes, quantity demanded also changes, given the explanatory variables in the demand equation. However, the response of quantity demanded to this price change itself produces a change in price. This is the feedback loop that exists since price is endogenous (see Chapter 14). To model this interaction, it is necessary to specify additional equations. The result is a set of simultaneous equations: a demand function; a supply function; and an equilibrium condition. Within this framework it is possible to model the joint determination of price and quantity.

This chapter outlines methods for estimating structural equations such as a demand function, where one or more explanatory variables are endogenous. Before this can be done, it is necessary to specify the *set* of relationships involved, or the equations that constitute a simultaneous equation model. Since there is necessarily more than one equation involved in a set of equations, it is imperative that a particular equation be statistically "different" from the other equations in that set. This is called equation identification. A structural equation cannot be estimated unless it satisfies criteria for identification. Since identification must be met before estimation can proceed, this chapter begins with a discussion of equation identification. Once the rules for identification have been stated, methods for estimating structural equations are then outlined. A number of estimated equations are then presented to illustrate the identification and estimation of simultaneous equation relationships.

EQUATION IDENTIFICATION

A General Overview of Equation Identification

Several examples of simultaneous equation models were described in Chapter 14. Of these, the supply and demand model will be used in the presentation that follows. Focusing on a bivariate demand relationship, if we obtain data on the price of a good (p) and the quantity bought and sold (q), the bivariate demand relationship that results is:

$$q_i = \alpha_0 + \alpha_1 p_i + \varepsilon_{1i} \tag{15.1}$$

We have been using this function in some form since Chapter 4. According to economic theory, price is inversely related to quantity demanded, other things being equal. While the "other things being equal" assumption is valid for theoretical discussions, it is not necessarily valid when conducting an empirical investigation. If Equation (15.1) does, in fact, depict a demand function, then how can we estimate the supply curve for this good, since quantity supplied is also a function of price? In other words, if we regress quantity on price, are we guaranteed that the resulting sample regression function will provide us with an estimate of a demand function? The answer to this question is that we cannot be sure whether Equation (15.1) is a demand function or a supply function. Thus if our estimate of α_1 is positive, this does not necessarily indicate sign reversal for the demand slope. It may instead reflect the positive slope of the supply curve for this good.

The basis for these statements can be better understood by referring to Figure 15.1 and considering the equation set of which Equation (15.1) is a part:

$$q_i = \alpha_0 + \alpha_1 p_i + \varepsilon_{1i} \qquad \text{(demand)} \tag{15.1}$$

$$q_i = \beta_0 + \beta_1 p_i + \varepsilon_{2i} \qquad \text{(supply)} \tag{15.2}$$

where q_i is the quantity bought and sold, which denotes equilibrium quantity. Both demand and supply are functions of price and a stochastic error. Each point in Figure 15.1 is therefore an equilibrium price-quantity combination, the intersection of a demand and supply curve. If we regress q_i on p_i we may indeed obtain a negative estimate

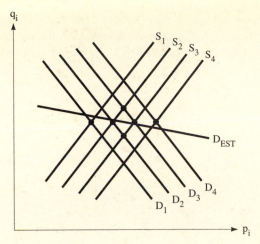

Figure 15.1

of α_1. However, with random fluctuations in the error terms of the demand and supply functions, we are *not* estimating the demand for this good. Nor are we estimating supply! We are instead estimating a combination of the demand and supply curves, a "hodgepodge function" that contains some of each but which is not exclusively either function. This "hodgepodge" function is denoted D_{EST} in Figure 15.1.

The problem involved here is that Equations (15.1) and (15.2) are **observationally equivalent**. This is the statistical version of the saying, "If you've seen one, you've seen them all." Statistically, the above equations are identical; the dependent variable in each, quantity, is expressed as a linear function of price and an error term. The fact that the coefficients in Equation (15.1) are α's while those in Equation (15.2) are β's makes no difference. Should a firm base an important pricing decision on the estimated "demand" relationship given by D_{EST}, whose slope is much flatter than the actual demand curves in Figure 15.1, its managers would likely be upset by the results of their decision. If, for example, the firm lowers price in the expectation that quantity demanded will rise substantially, they will instead see quantity rise by much less than their expectations, since the demand curves D_1 to D_4 are steeper than the hodgepodge function D_{EST}. Matters would be even worse, if this firm concluded that demand is elastic over the relevant range when it is actually inelastic. Then, total revenue would fall, not rise, in response to this price decrease.

We can establish the underlying algebraic basis of the discussion above if we express Equations (15.1) and (15.2) in deviation form[1]:

$$q_i' = \alpha_1 p_i' + \varepsilon_{1i}' \qquad \text{(demand)} \qquad \textbf{(15.3)}$$

$$q_i' = \beta_1 p_i' + \varepsilon_{2i}' \qquad \text{(supply)} \qquad \textbf{(15.4)}$$

---

[1] This illustration draws on the material in W. Merrill and K. Fox, *Introduction to Economic Statistics* (New York: John Wiley & Sons, Inc., 1970), pp. 517–521.

where q'_i, p'_i, ε'_{1i} and ε'_{2i} denote deviations from means. We must use these equations to obtain an expression for $\hat{\alpha}_1$. Assuming market equilibrium, we can obtain the reduced form equation for price by equating the right sides of Equations (15.3) and (15.4):

$$\alpha_1 p'_i + \varepsilon'_{1i} = \beta_1 p'_i + \varepsilon'_{2i}$$

$$p'_i = \frac{\varepsilon'_{2i} - \varepsilon'_{1i}}{\alpha_1 - \beta_1} \tag{15.5}$$

Substituting Equation (15.5) into the demand equation, Equation (15.3), we have:

$$q'_i = \alpha_1 \left[\frac{\varepsilon'_{2i} - \varepsilon'_{1i}}{\alpha_1 - \beta_1} \right] + \varepsilon'_{1i}$$

which, with rearrangement becomes:

$$q'_i = \frac{\alpha_1 \varepsilon'_{2i} - \beta_1 \varepsilon'_{1i}}{\alpha_1 - \beta_1} \tag{15.6}$$

When q_i is regressed on p_i, the slope estimator, $\hat{\alpha}_1$, is:

$$\hat{\alpha}_1 = \sum p'_i q'_i / \sum p'^2_i \tag{15.7}$$

Substituting the reduced form expressions given by Equations (15.5) and (15.6) for q'_i and p'_i into Equation (15.7) gives the following:

$$\hat{\alpha}_1 = \frac{\sum \left[\dfrac{\varepsilon'_{2i} - \varepsilon'_{1i}}{\alpha_1 - \beta_1} \right] \left[\dfrac{\alpha_1 \varepsilon'_{2i} - \beta_1 \varepsilon'_{1i}}{\alpha_1 - \beta_1} \right]}{\sum \left[\dfrac{\varepsilon'_{2i} - \varepsilon'_{1i}}{\alpha_1 - \beta_1} \right]^2}$$

The terms involving $\alpha_1 - \beta_1$ cancel, leaving:

$$\hat{\alpha}_1 = \frac{\sum (\varepsilon'_{2i} - \varepsilon'_{1i})(\alpha_1 \varepsilon'_{2i} - \beta_1 \varepsilon'_{1i})}{\sum (\varepsilon'_{2i} - \varepsilon'_{1i})^2}$$

Performing the multiplication and exponentiation indicated in this expression, moving the summation terms in the numerator and denominator to each term, and omitting the subscript i, we have:

$$\hat{\alpha}_1 = \frac{\alpha_1 \sum \varepsilon'^2_2 - \beta_1 \sum \varepsilon'_2 \varepsilon'_1 - \alpha_1 \sum \varepsilon'_1 \varepsilon'_2 + \beta_1 \sum \varepsilon'^2_1}{\sum \varepsilon'^2_2 + \sum \varepsilon'^2_1 - 2 \sum \varepsilon'_1 \varepsilon'_2}$$

Grouping the terms above when needed and dividing both the numerator and denominator by n it becomes:

$$\hat{\alpha}_1 = \frac{\alpha_1 \sigma^2_2 - (\beta_1 + \alpha_1)\sigma_{12} + \beta_1 \sigma^2_1}{\sigma^2_1 + \sigma^2_2 - 2\sigma_{12}} \tag{15.8}$$

where σ^2_1 and σ^2_2 are the variances of ε_1 and ε_2, respectively, and σ_{12} is the covariance between ε_1 and ε_2.

Equation (15.8) expresses the estimated demand slope in terms of the error variances for this set of equations. One final modification will be made to this equation. By expressing σ_{12} in terms of the correlation coefficient for the demand and supply errors:

$$\rho_{12} = \frac{\sigma_{12}}{\sigma_1 \cdot \sigma_2}$$

so that

$$\sigma_{12} = \rho_{12} \cdot \sigma_1 \cdot \sigma_2 \qquad \text{(see Chapter 2)}$$

Equation (15.8) is now:

$$\hat{\alpha}_1 = \frac{\alpha_1 \sigma_2^2 - (\beta_1 + \alpha_1)\rho_{12} \cdot \sigma_1 \cdot \sigma_2 + \beta_1 \sigma_1^2}{\sigma_1^2 + \sigma_2^2 - 2\rho_{12} \cdot \sigma_1 \cdot \sigma_2} \tag{15.9}$$

If the demand curve does not shift, but supply shifts, then: $\sigma_1 = \sigma_1^2 = 0$ and $\sigma_2^2 \neq 0$. Equation (15.9) then becomes:

$$\hat{\alpha}_1 = \alpha_1 \sigma_2^2 / \sigma_2^2 = \alpha_1$$

In this situation, regressing quantity on price results in a correctly estimated equation, where $\hat{\alpha}_1$ correctly estimates the demand curve slope. This is illustrated in Figure 15.2, where supply is assumed to continually increase.

Unfortunately, this last outcome is not the only one possible. Consider what happens when demand is shifting (so that $\sigma_1^2 \neq 0$) but supply is not ($\sigma_2 = \sigma_2^2 = 0$), as in Figure 15.3. Equation (15.9) then reduces to:

$$\hat{\alpha}_1 = \beta_1 \sigma_1^2 / \sigma_1^2 = \beta_1$$

In this case, the attempt to estimate the slope of the demand function results in an estimate of the supply slope, which is the opposite of what the researcher desires. It is definitely a valid possibility, however.

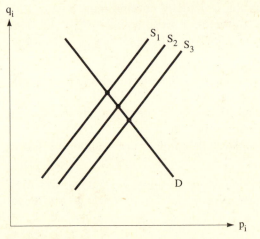

Figure 15.2

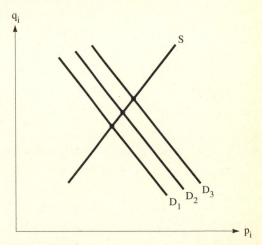

Figure 15.3

In the more realistic case, where both the demand and supply curves are shifting simultaneously, our estimated demand curve slope is given by Equation (15.9), which is a combination of both slopes. We have therefore estimated the "hodgepodge" function given by D_{EST} in Figure 15.1. The difference between $\hat{\alpha}_1$ and α_1 here is related to least squares bias (see Chapter 14).

This illustration indicates that it is possible for us to successfully approximate the slope of interest. Essentially, since the demand and supply functions are observationally equivalent, we cannot be sure of exactly which relationship we are estimating unless we possess further information about the *other* equation(s) in a set of simultaneous equations. This is the essence of the **identification problem**. Before we can estimate one or more of the structural equations in a set of simultaneous equations, we must solve this identification problem. Based on this discussion, one possible definition of equation identification is the following:

> An equation is **identified** if it is possible to distinguish it *statistically* from the other behavioral equations (not identities) in a set of simultaneous equations. In other words, the equation in question cannot be observationally equivalent to the other equation(s) in the set of equations.

In light of the correct result obtained by manipulating Equation (15.9), we may state a second definition of equation identification:

> An equation is identified if it is possible for the *other* equation(s) in the system to shift when it does not, allowing it to be traced out (identified).

The second definition pertains to Figure 15.2. A shifting supply curve traces out a stable demand curve, allowing the identification of demand. Note, however, that it is the behavior of the *other* equation in the system, supply, that allows demand to be identified. This is sometimes referred to as the **paradox of identification**.[2]

We now have two definitions of equation identification that can be used as the basis for moving to a more formal analysis of this topic. Before we proceed, it should be kept in mind that equation identification is actually nothing more than a form of equation specification, which, in the context of a set of equations, entails *model formulation*. Equation identification can therefore be attained if one or more of the following exists:

1. information exists about the error variances in different equations, for example, demand fluctuates less than supply (as above);
2. one or more variables are excluded from each of the equations in a system, allowing some functions to shift when others do not;
3. linear restrictions pertain to the coefficients in one or more equations in a set of equations.

The first of these will not be discussed here. More advanced texts cover this topic in detail. The third will be analyzed when methods for testing linear restrictions is

---

[2] A. Koutsoyiannis, *Theory of Econometrics*, 2d. ed. (Totowa NJ: Barnes & Noble, 1977), p. 349.

presented later in this chapter. The discussion that follows will therefore focus on the second point, the exclusion of variables from different equations.

We will analyze this by referring back to the situation outlined earlier where the demand slope was correctly estimated. We saw that when demand does not shift while the supply function does, demand is identified. One instance where this occurs is when supply contains a variable not present in demand, such as the costs of production (C). If we respecify the set of equations considered earlier:

$$q_i = \alpha_0 + \alpha_1 p_i + \varepsilon_{1i} \qquad \text{(demand)}$$

$$q_i = \beta_0 + \beta_1 p_i + \beta_2 C_i + \varepsilon_{2i} \qquad \text{(supply)}$$

(15.10)

the demand curve is unchanged from its original form, while supply is now a function of both price and production costs. If wages or raw material costs fall, the supply curve will shift right. Since demand is not a function of production costs, it will not shift in response to these changes. This is the case depicted in Figure 15.2, where a rightward shifting supply curve traces out the stable demand curve, allowing demand to be identified. It illustrates the paradox of identification, since the specification of the supply function permits demand to be identified. Thus, the identification of demand occurs not as the result of what the demand function includes, but on what it *excludes* (costs). Variable exclusions such as this are called **zero restrictions**, since the exclusion of a variable from an equation can be thought of as the restriction that its coefficient equals zero.

It should be pointed out that while demand is not directly affected by the costs of production, it is *indirectly* affected. When production costs fall, supply shifts right, which, given demand, lowers market price. While demand does not shift in response to this change, *quantity* demanded rises. Thus, in a sense demand is a function of supply: a change in cost affects demand by altering price. The distinction between demand and quantity demanded that is stressed so heavily in principles-level courses is necessitated by the endogeneity of price: supply affects demand through market price.

The identification of demand in Equation (15.10) can also be established by utilizing the first definition of identification above, where an equation must not be observationally equivalent to the other equations in a system. We saw earlier that it is possible for us to be dealing with a hodgepodge of the set of equations instead of the relationship of interest. We can represent this hodgepodge function as a linear combination of the equations in an equation set, with the first equation multiplied (weighted) by ω_1 and the second multiplied by ω_2. If we define these weights so that $\omega_1 + \omega_2 = 1$, then $\omega_1 q_i + \omega_2 q_i = (\omega_1 + \omega_2)q_i = q_i$, since these weights sum to 1. Thus, the original dependent variable is the dependent variable in the hodgepodge equation as well. We will thus apply these weights only to the right side of the hodgepodge equation. Using this information, the hodgepodge equation for system (15.10) can be expressed as:

$$q_i = \omega_1(\alpha_0 + \alpha_1 p_i + \varepsilon_{1i}) + \omega_2(\beta_0 + \beta_1 p_i + \beta_2 C_i + \varepsilon_{2i})$$
$$= (\omega_1\alpha_0 + \omega_2\beta_0) + (\omega_1\alpha_1 + \omega_2\beta_1)p_i + (\omega_2\beta_2)C_i + (\omega_1\varepsilon_{1i} + \omega_2\varepsilon_{2i})$$
$$q_i = \gamma_0 + \gamma_1 p_i + \gamma_2 C_i + \varepsilon_i^*$$

(15.11)

where $\gamma_0 = (\omega_1\alpha_0 + \omega_2\beta_0)$, $\gamma_1 = (\omega_1\alpha_1 + \omega_2\beta_1)$, $\gamma_2 = \omega_2\beta_2$, and $\varepsilon_t^* = (\omega_1\varepsilon_{1i} + \omega_2\varepsilon_{2i})$. The demand function in Equation (15.10) is clearly distinguishable from the hodgepodge function of Equation (15.11) since it excludes C. The same is not true for the supply function in this equation set. Since supply is a function of price, cost, and an error term, it is observationally equivalent to the hodgepodge function. As a result, supply is not identified. This is generally expressed by stating that supply is either **underidentified** or **unidentified**.

Another explanation for the unidentification of supply can be stated in terms of the second definition of identification above: in Equation (15.10), it is not possible for demand to shift when supply does not. As a result, shifting demand cannot trace out a stable supply function. This occurs since the supply function does not exclude any of the variables in Equation (15.10). Again, the role of variable exclusion in equation identification can be seen.

The concept of identification pertains to sets of equations as well as to individual equations:

A *set* of equations is identified if each of its behavioral equations is identified.

In the example above, the set of equations given in (15.10) is unidentified, since the supply function is unidentified. This definition stresses the fact that we are only interested in the identification of behavioral equations, since these are the ones we wish to estimate. It is not necessary for us to identify or estimate either identities or equilibrium conditions.

We next modify the demand function in Equation set (15.10) by adding income (y) as an explanatory variable, while leaving the supply function unchanged. The result is:

$$q_i = \alpha_0 + \alpha_1 p_i + \alpha_2 y_i + \varepsilon_{1i} \qquad \text{(demand)}$$
$$q_i = \beta_0 + \beta_1 p_i + \beta_2 C_i + \varepsilon_{2i} \qquad \text{(supply)}$$

(15.12)

Even though the supply function has not changed, it is now identified. In fact, demand, supply, and this system of equations are identified. The identification of supply can be seen by examining the demand function. Demand now includes a variable, income, which is excluded from the supply function. As a result, when income grows, the demand curve will shift right while supply does not shift, allowing a stable supply curve to be identified.[3] This corresponds to Figure 15.3. Demand remains identified since it excludes the costs of production. As production costs fall, supply shifts right when demand does not shift, identifying demand as before.

The identification of these equations can also be established by referring to the hodgepodge function that corresponds to (15.12):

$$q_i = \omega_1(\alpha_0 + \alpha_1 p_i + \alpha_2 y_i + \varepsilon_{1i}) + \omega_2(\beta_0 + \beta_1 p_i + \beta_2 C_i + \varepsilon_{2i})$$
$$q_i = \gamma_0 + \gamma_1 p_i + \gamma_2 y_i + \gamma_3 C_i + \varepsilon_i^*$$

(15.13)

---

[3] This assumes that the good in question is a normal good.

where the coefficients and error in Equation (15.13) are defined similarly to those in Equation (15.11). Since demand excludes the costs of production, the demand function is statistically distinguishable from Equation (15.13), allowing it to be identified. Supply excludes income, which differentiates it from Equation (15.13), allowing its identification.

The requirement for equation identification should now be clear. At this point, a necessary condition for equation identification, called the **order condition**, can be stated:

> **Order Condition:** In an equation set consisting of G behavioral equations, an equation is identified if it excludes at least $(G - 1)$ variables, either endogenous or exogenous, that are present in the *other* behavioral equations in that system.

In the examples above, $G = 2$, since there is a demand and supply equation. According to the order condition, each equation is identified if it excludes at least $1 (= G - 1)$ variable. When fewer than $(G - 1)$ variables are excluded, an equation is under-identified.

This requirement can be linked with the definitions of identification presented earlier. When an equation in a two equation set excludes one or more variables, the other equation can shift when this function does not, allowing it to be traced out (identified). Also, when variables are excluded from such an equation, it is statistically distinguishable from the hodgepodge function corresponding to that set of equations. The equation is therefore identified.

An important point should be mentioned at this juncture: *even though both of the equations in Equation set (15.12) are identified, their estimation by least squares is still inappropriate, since the endogenous explanatory variable in each equation is correlated with the error term in that equation. Least squares bias will therefore result. Thus, equation identification is only the first step in the estimation of structural equations.*

It is not possible to estimate an unidentified equation. This does *not* mean that a mechanical regression of quantity on price is impossible. Instead, the attempt to estimate demand by merely regressing quantity on price does not necessarily result in estimation of the demand function. This point can be demonstrated by referring to Equations (15.1) and (15.2):

$$q_i = \alpha_0 + \alpha_1 p_i + \varepsilon_{1i} \quad \text{(demand)} \tag{15.1}$$

$$q_i = \beta_0 + \beta_1 p_i + \varepsilon_{2i} \quad \text{(supply)} \tag{15.2}$$

According to the order condition, with two structural equations, each equation must exclude at least one variable for it to be identified. Since neither demand nor supply excludes any variables, both are unidentified according to the order condition. We can see this by forming the hodgepodge function for this set of equations:

$$q_i = \omega_1(\alpha_0 + \alpha_1 p_i + \varepsilon_{1i}) + \omega_2(\beta_0 + \beta_1 p_i + \varepsilon_{2i})$$
$$q_i = \gamma_0 + \gamma_1 p_i + \varepsilon_i^* \tag{15.14}$$

Both supply and demand are statistically identical to Equation (15.14). As a result, neither equation is identified, and the regression of quantity on price can be expected to result in the estimation of a hodgepodge of supply and demand.

The unidentification of an equation indicates that the *set* of equations of which it is part does not contain enough information to permit unique estimation of that relationship. An identified equation can also be **overidentified**: more than enough information may exist to identify an equation. If we modify Equation (15.13) by adding a new variable, z, such as weather, to the supply function:

$$q_i = \alpha_0 + \alpha_1 p_i + \alpha_2 y_i + \varepsilon_{1i} \qquad \text{(demand)}$$

$$q_i = \beta_0 + \beta_1 p_i + \beta_2 C_i + \beta_3 z_i + \varepsilon_{2i} \qquad \text{(supply)}$$

(15.15)

the demand function now excludes two variables: C and z. According to the order condition, demand is identified, since it excludes at least one variable. The supply function can shift as the result of fluctuations in either or both of C and z, permitting a stable demand function to be identified. The overidentification of demand indicates that more than one way exists for demand to be identified, shifts in C or z. Supply is also identified, as before. However, there is only one way the demand function in Equation (15.15) can shift when supply does not: changes in income. Supply thus excludes only one $(= G - 1)$ variable. Here, the supply function is **exactly identified**, since there is exactly enough information available in the system for it to be identified. In light of these distinctions, the following classifications can be added to the order condition:

> In an equation set consisting of G behavioral equations, an equation is under-identified if it excludes fewer than $(G - 1)$ variables, either endogenous or exogenous, that are present in the other behavioral equations in that system; exactly identified if $(G - 1)$ variables are excluded; and overidentified if it excludes more than $(G - 1)$ variables.

The order condition is only a necessary condition for equation identification. It must be met for an equation to be identified. However, the order condition is not a sufficient condition. This means that it is possible for an equation that satisfies the order condition not to be identified. This possibility generally arises when there are three or more structural equations in a equation system. For identification with such systems, a second "status check" must also be made. This is called the rank condition. The name of this condition reflects the fact that it involves matrix algebra, where the rank of a matrix is evaluated. Since this text does not presuppose a matrix algebra background, we will demonstrate how to carry out this test in a descriptive manner only.

The rank test determines whether an equation is identified by evaluating whether the other equations in the system include the variable(s) omitted by this equation and that no linear dependency exists among this set of excluded variables. This condition can be stated in the following descriptive way:

> **Preliminary Rank Condition:** An equation is identified if each variable it excludes is included in at least one other equation, and that every other equation in the system contains at least one of these excluded variables.

The idea behind this condition is ultimately the same as that for the order condition: that the other behavioral equations in a system must be able to shift when a particular equation does not, allowing it to be identified. However, with more than one other equation to consider, further refinement is called for. To perform this test, we must determine whether the variables omitted from the equation whose identification we are testing are present in the other equations of the system. To do this, we first set up a table of coefficients for the entire set of equations, then examine the entries for the other equations that correspond to the variables excluded from the equation of interest. To illustrate this we will use the following set of three equations:

(1) $$y_{1i} = \alpha_0 + \alpha_1 y_{2i} + \alpha_2 y_{3i} + \alpha_3 x_{1i} + \alpha_4 x_{2i} + \varepsilon_{1i}$$

(2) $$y_{2i} = \beta_0 + \beta_1 y_{1i} + \beta_2 y_{3i} + \beta_3 x_{2i} + \beta_4 x_{3i} + \varepsilon_{2i}$$

(3) $$y_{3i} = \gamma_0 + \gamma_1 y_{1i} + \gamma_2 y_{2i} + \gamma_3 x_{3i} + \gamma_4 x_{4i} + \varepsilon_{3i}$$

where the y variables are endogenous and the x's are exogenous and predetermined. This is a complete system, with three equations and three endogenous variables. We will examine the identification of the first of these equations. Before making up the table to examine whether the variables excluded from that equation, x_3 and x_4, are present in the other equations, it is helpful to rearrange the equations above to align terms with the different variables in the system. We will arrange terms in the following order: y_1, y_2, y_3, x_0 (the "intercept variable"), x_1, x_2, x_3, and x_4. These equations are rearranged with the x and y terms set equal to the error in each equation. The intercept for each equation is viewed as the coefficient of a variable x_0. The rearranged equations are:

(1) $$y_{1i} - \alpha_1 y_{2i} - \alpha_2 y_{3i} - \alpha_0 - \alpha_3 x_{1i} - \alpha_4 x_{2i} \qquad\qquad = \varepsilon_{1i}$$

(2) $$-\beta_1 y_{1i} + y_{2i} - \beta_2 y_{3i} - \beta_0 \qquad - \beta_3 x_{2i} - \beta_4 x_{3i} \qquad = \varepsilon_{2i}$$

(3) $$-\gamma_1 y_{1i} - \gamma_2 y_{2i} + y_{3i} - \gamma_0 \qquad\qquad - \gamma_3 x_{3i} - \gamma_4 x_{4i} = \varepsilon_{3i}$$

The resulting table of coefficients is:

	y_1	y_2	y_3	x_0	x_1	x_2	x_3	x_4
(1)	1	$-\alpha_1$	$-\alpha_2$	$-\alpha_0$	$-\alpha_3$	$-\alpha_4$	0	0
(2)	$-\beta_1$	1	$-\beta_2$	$-\beta_0$	0	$-\beta_3$	$-\beta_4$	0
(3)	$-\gamma_1$	$-\gamma_2$	1	$-\gamma_0$	0	0	$-\gamma_3$	$-\gamma_4$

The first equation omits the variables x_3 and x_4. According to the order condition, at least two variables must be excluded for this equation to be identified. Since it excludes two variables, it is exactly identified according to the order condition. We now form a second table that features the columns corresponding to 0 entries in this equation (excluded variables) for the *other* equations in the set. This is based on the columns for x_3 and x_4 for equations (2) and (3) above:

	x_3	x_4
(2)	$-\beta_4$	0
(3)	$-\gamma_3$	$-\gamma_4$

According to this table, the variable x_3 is present in both equations (2) and (3), while x_4 appears only in the third equation. Now if x_3 changes, equations (3) and (4) both shift, while a change in x_4 shifts only equation (3).

For identification purposes, there must be at least one nonzero entry in each row and each column of this table.[4] To see why this is so, let us consider a few cases where this is violated. If the above table were:

	x_3	x_4
(2)	0	0
(3)	0	0

the variables excluded from the equation (1) would not appear in any of the other equations in the model. It should be obvious that this equation would not be identified. While it excludes two variables, these same variables are absent from the rest of the equation system as well. Thus, the other equations are unable to shift when this equation does not, and identification does not occur. A second case is the following:

	x_3	x_4
(2)	0	0
(3)	0	$-\gamma_4$

One of the variables (x_4) excluded from equation (1) is present in another equation. Thus, equation (3) can shift when equation (1) does not. But as the result of such a shift, it can trace out *either* equation (1) or (2). Problems with identification also occur

---

[4] This does not necessarily result in identification, as noted below.

if the table were instead:

	x_3	x_4	
(2)	$-\beta_4$	0	or
(3)	0	0	

	x_3	x_4
(2)	0	0
(3)	$-\gamma_3$	$-\gamma_4$

since when either x_3 or x_4 change, only one equation shifts. Thus, if there is not an entry in every row and every column of this table, equation (1) is not identified, even if it passes the order test.

Returning to the original table for equation (1):

	x_3	x_4
(2)	$-\beta_4$	0
(3)	$-\gamma_3$	$-\gamma_4$

this equation is identified as long as β_4 is not zero (since this would make the first row above all zeros), or γ_4 is not zero (then the second column would be all zeros).[5]

The table above can be made into a matrix, which is simply a rectangular array of numbers. The resulting matrix is:

$$\begin{bmatrix} -\beta_4 & 0 \\ -\gamma_3 & -\gamma_4 \end{bmatrix}$$

This is referred to as a 2×2 matrix (the "$\times$" is read as "by"), since there are two rows and two columns. When the number of rows and columns of a matrix are equal, the matrix is a square matrix. The determinant of a matrix is a unique number obtained by manipulating a square matrix such as the one above. *Its value here allows us to determine whether there is enough information contained in the entire set of equations to allow this equation to be identified.* The determinant of a 2×2 matrix is given by the following formula, which denotes the locations of the matrix values used:

(top left)(bottom right) − (bottom left)(top right)

The determinant of the above matrix is thus:

$$(-\beta_4)(-\gamma_4) - (-\gamma_3)(0) = \beta_4 \cdot \gamma_4$$

---

[5] It is also required that these both not be zero.

When the determinant of this matrix is zero, the variables omitted from this equation are linearly dependent.[6] This indicates that it is possible to express one of the omitted variables from this equation as an exact linear function of the other, and that the set of equations does not obtain enough information to identify this equation. The attempt to estimate the coefficients in this function thus produces an estimate of a hodgepodge function of the entire set of equations in the system. Individual coefficients are then linear functions of all of the coefficients in this model.

We can see from the expression above that the determinant of interest is zero when either β_4 or γ_4 is zero, or if both are zero. Recall that this would make the entire set of entries for a column or row of the coefficient table zero. Using the concept of a determinant, the **rank condition** can now be stated more accurately:

> **Rank Condition:** In a system of G equations and G endogenous variables, an equation is identified if it is possible to form at least one nonzero determinant of size $(G - 1) \times (G - 1)$ from the coefficients of variables excluded from this equation but included in the other equations. The coefficients in these determinants can pertain to either endogenous or exogenous variables. If all such determinants equal 0, the equation is underidentified.

By combining the rank and order conditions, we have a necessary and sufficient condition for equation identification:

> If the rank condition is satisfied and an equation excludes $(G - 1)$ variables, that equation is exactly identified. When the rank condition is met and more than $(G - 1)$ variables are excluded from an equation, that equation is over-identified. When fewer than $(G - 1)$ variables are excluded, the equation is underidentified.

Before applying this condition to economic examples, we will consider one last possibility for the table discussed above. If this table were instead:

	x_3	x_4
(2)	$-\beta_4$	$-\beta_5$
(3)	$-\gamma_3$	$-\gamma_4$

The determinant that would pertain for the rank condition is:

$$(-\beta_4)(-\gamma_4) - (-\gamma_3)(-\beta_5)$$

Even though no row or column in the table consists entirely of zeros, it is still possible for the rank condition to be violated. This occurs if:

$$\beta_4\gamma_4 = \gamma_3\beta_5$$

---

[6] The name "rank test" is derived from the fact that the rank of the matrix of omitted variable coefficients is evaluated. If the determinant above is zero, the rank of that matrix is less than the total number of omitted variables, indicating that the omitted variables are linearly dependent.

As this illustration shows, the rank condition is capable of ascertaining patterns among the coefficients in a set of equations that might not be detectable with visual inspection. Unfortunately, the calculation of determinants for matrices larger than 2×2 can be very cumbersome, and is beyond the scope of this text. For our present purposes, we will consider the determinant of matrices larger than 2×2 to be nonzero as long as there is at least one nonzero value in each row and each column. When there are four or more equations and an equation is (potentially) overidentified, there will be several $(G - 1) \times (G - 1)$ determinants that can be evaluated. It is not necessary for all of these to be nonzero. All that is required is that at least one be nonzero.

To illustrate the use of the rank condition, we will apply it to two different economic models. The first of these is a supply and demand model with the equilibrium condition included:

$$q_i^d = \alpha_0 + \alpha_1 p_i + \alpha_2 I_i + \varepsilon_{1i} \qquad \text{(demand)}$$

$$q_i^s = \beta_0 + \beta_1 p_i + \beta_2 C_i + \varepsilon_{2i} \qquad \text{(supply)}$$

$$q_i^d = q_i^s \qquad \text{(equilibrium condition)}$$

where I is income and C is production cost. There are three equations (G) and three endogenous variables in this system. Both supply and demand exclude two variables. We next rearrange the variables in this system:

$$q_i^d \qquad - \alpha_1 p_i - \alpha_0 - \alpha_2 I_i \qquad = \varepsilon_{1i}$$

$$+ q_i^s - \beta_1 p_i - \beta_0 \qquad - \beta_2 C_i = \varepsilon_{2i}$$

$$q_i^d - q_i^s \qquad = 0$$

The table used with the rank condition is:

q_i^d	q_i^s	p_i	x_0	I_i	C_i	
1	0	$-\alpha_1$	$-\alpha_0$	$-\alpha_2$	0	(demand)
0	1	$-\beta_1$	$-\beta_0$	0	$-\beta_2$	(supply)
1	-1	0	0	0	0	(equilibrium)

The demand function excludes two variables, q^s and C. To determine whether it is identified by the rank condition, we form the 2×2 matrix using the columns for q^s and C in the supply and equilibrium equations:

$$\begin{bmatrix} 1 & -\beta_2 \\ -1 & 0 \end{bmatrix}$$

The determinant of this matrix is:

$$(1)(0) - (-1)(-\beta_2) = -\beta_2$$

The demand function satisfies the rank condition as long as $\beta_2 \neq 0$, which indicates that the costs of production appears in the supply function. Since there are three

$(=G)$ equations, and two $(=G-1)$ variables are excluded, the demand equation is exactly identified.

We next apply the rank condition to the supply function. Using the table above, we select columns 1 and 5, which correspond to the variables omitted from supply, q^d and I. The rows utilized are for the demand and equilibrium equations:

$$\begin{bmatrix} 1 & -\alpha_2 \\ 1 & 0 \end{bmatrix}$$

The determinant of this matrix is:

$$(1)(0) - (1)(-\alpha_2) = \alpha_2$$

Supply is identified according to the rank condition as long as income appears in the demand function. Since supply excludes two variables and it satisfies the rank condition, it is exactly identified.

The second application for the rank condition is the model of international trade given in Chapter 14, where exports (X) (Equation (14.29′)), imports (M) ((14.30′)), the exchange rate (ER) (equation (14.32)); and net exports (XN) (identity (14.31′)) are jointly determined. There are four equations $(=G)$ and four endogenous variables in this system. The equations themselves and the manipulations required to form the table for the rank test will not be presented here. These are left as an exercise. Since all of the behavioral equations contain intercepts, the "intercept variable," x_0, is omitted. The table used for the rank test is:

	X	M	ER	XN	Y	Y_f	$(r - r_f)$	$(\text{GGNP} - \text{GGNP}_f)_{t-1}$
(14.29′)	1	0	$-\gamma_{11}$	0	0	$-\gamma_{21}$	0	0
(14.30′)	0	1	$-\gamma_{12}$	0	$-\gamma_{22}$	0	0	0
(14.32)	0	0	1	$-\beta_1$	0	0	$-\beta_2$	$-\beta_3$
(14.31′)	-1	-1	0	1	0	0	0	0

We will perform the rank test on the export equation, Equation (14.29′). Five variables are omitted from the exports equation, so it is possible to form *several* 3×3 determinants. We will construct a matrix based on the first three omitted variables M, XN, and Y:

$$\begin{bmatrix} 1 & 0 & -\gamma_{22} \\ 0 & -\beta_1 & 0 \\ -1 & 1 & 0 \end{bmatrix}$$

Since there is at least one value in every row and column of this matrix, we conclude that its determinant is not zero and the rank condition is satisfied.[7] Since the exports equation excludes five variables $(>G-1)$, it is overidentified.

---

[7] For persons familiar with matrix algebra, the determinant of this matrix is $\gamma_{22} \cdot \beta_1$.

A More Formal Presentation of Equation Identification

The different possibilities for identification presented in the last section are particularly relevant when a more formal definition of identification is considered. The setting in which this occurs considers the relationship between the set of structural coefficients in a set of equations and the reduced form coefficients obtained from that model. We will illustrate this by referring to the IS-LM model presented in Chapter 14. Recall that the IS-LM model is a general equilibrium macroeconomic model, where real income (y) and the interest rate (r) are jointly determined. In the product market, the interest rate determines investment spending. This, in turn, defines aggregate expenditure and equilibrium real income. For the money market, the level of real income determines real money demand, which, given the real supply of money, produces an equilibrium rate of interest. A simple IS-LM model similar to Equations (14.22) and (14.25) is:

$$y_i = \alpha_0 + \alpha_1 r_i + \varepsilon_{1i} \qquad \text{(product market equilibrium)}$$
$$r_i = \beta_0 + \beta_1 y_i + \varepsilon_{2i} \qquad \text{(money market equilibrium)}$$

(15.16)

There are four structural coefficients to be estimated in this system of equations. If the reduced form equations for this system are calculated, we have:

$$y_i = \pi_{01} + v_{1i}$$
$$r_i = \pi_{02} + v_{2i}$$

(15.17)

where $\pi_{01} = (\alpha_0 + \alpha_1 \beta_0)/(1 - \alpha_1 \beta_1)$ and $\pi_{02} = (\beta_0 + \beta_1 \alpha_0)/(1 - \alpha_1 \beta_1)$. The reduced form coefficients are thus functions of the set of structural equation coefficients. The definition of identification considered here relates the number of reduced form coefficients to the number of structural equation coefficients:

> An equation is identified if there are at least as many reduced form coefficients as there are structural equation coefficients.

The two reduced form coefficients in (15.17), which are functions of the α's and β's, constitute two equations in the four unknowns, α_0, α_1, β_0, and β_1. Since there are fewer equations (reduced form coefficients) than unknown structural coefficients, Equation system (15.16) is under-identified.

The choice of which variable is designated the dependent variable when y and r are jointly determined does not really matter. This model could have been depicted by two equations where y is a function of r. Viewed this way, the product market function is observationally equivalent to the money market function, which explains the under-identification of both equations and the equation set.

We now modify the IS-LM equations in the following way:

$$y_t = \alpha_0 + \alpha_1 r_t + \alpha_2 G_t + \varepsilon_{1t} \qquad \text{(product market equilibrium)}$$
$$r_t = \beta_0 + \beta_1 y_t + \beta_2 M_t + \varepsilon_{2t} \qquad \text{(money market equilibrium)}$$

(15.18)

where G is real government purchases and M is the real money supply. There are now six structural equation coefficients. The reduced form equations for Equation set (15.18) are:

$$y_t = \frac{\alpha_0 + \alpha_1\beta_0}{1 - \alpha_1\beta_1} + \frac{\alpha_2}{1 - \alpha_1\beta_1}G_t + \frac{\alpha_1\beta_2}{1 - \alpha_1\beta_1}M_t + \frac{\varepsilon_{1t} + \alpha_1\varepsilon_{2t}}{1 - \alpha_1\beta_1}$$

$$r_t = \frac{\beta_0 + \beta_1\alpha_0}{1 - \alpha_1\beta_1} + \frac{\beta_1\alpha_2}{1 - \alpha_1\beta_1}G_t + \frac{\beta_2}{1 - \alpha_1\beta_1}M_t + \frac{\varepsilon_{2t} + \beta_1\varepsilon_{1t}}{1 - \alpha_1\beta_1}$$

which, in the usual notation, can be written:

$$y_t = \pi_{01} + \pi_{11}G_t + \pi_{21}M_t + \varepsilon_{1t}^*$$

$$r_t = \pi_{02} + \pi_{12}G_t + \pi_{22}M_t + \varepsilon_{2t}^*$$

There are now six reduced form coefficients available to estimate the six structural coefficients. Since the number of equations (reduced form coefficients) coincides with the number of unknowns (structural coefficients), the coefficients of the structural equations can be uniquely obtained. This set of equations is therefore exactly identified. The expressions for the structural coefficients in this equation set are:

$$\alpha_0 = \pi_{01} - (\pi_{21}/\pi_{22})\pi_{02}$$

$$\alpha_1 = \pi_{21}/\pi_{22}$$

$$\alpha_2 = \pi_{11} - \pi_{21}(\pi_{12}/\pi_{22})$$

$$\beta_0 = \pi_{02} - (\pi_{12}/\pi_{11})\pi_{01}$$

$$\beta_1 = \pi_{12}/\pi_{11}$$

$$\beta_2 = \pi_{22} - \pi_{12}(\pi_{21}/\pi_{11})$$

The final case considered here pertains when a set of equations has fewer structural coefficients than the number of reduced form coefficients. This can be seen by altering the money market equation in Equation (15.18):

$$y_t = \alpha_0 + \alpha_1 r_t + \alpha_2 G_t + \varepsilon_{1t} \qquad \text{(product market equilibrium)}$$

$$r_t = \beta_0 + \beta_1 y_t + \beta_2 M_t + \beta_3 r_t^e + \varepsilon_{2t} \qquad \text{(money market equilibrium)}$$

(15.19)

where r^e is the expected rate of interest (which is assumed to be independent of current r). There are seven structural equation coefficients in (15.19). The reduced form equations for this system are:

$$y_t = \frac{\alpha_0 + \alpha_1\beta_0}{1 - \alpha_1\beta_1} + \frac{\alpha_2}{1 - \alpha_1\beta_1}G_t + \frac{\alpha_1\beta_2}{1 - \alpha_1\beta_1}M_t + \frac{\alpha_1\beta_3}{1 - \alpha_1\beta_1}r_t^e + \frac{\varepsilon_{1t} + \alpha_1\varepsilon_{2t}}{1 - \alpha_1\beta_1}$$

$$r_t = \frac{\beta_0 + \beta_1\alpha_0}{1 - \alpha_1\beta_1} + \frac{\beta_1\alpha_2}{1 - \alpha_1\beta_1}G_t + \frac{\beta_2}{1 - \alpha_1\beta_1}M_t + \frac{\beta_3}{1 - \alpha_1\beta_1}r_t^e + \frac{\varepsilon_{2t} + \beta_1\varepsilon_{1t}}{1 - \alpha_1\beta_1}$$

which can be written:

$$y_t = \pi_{01} + \pi_{11}G_t + \pi_{21}M_t + \pi_{31}r_t^e + \varepsilon_{1t}^*$$

$$r_t = \pi_{02} + \pi_{12}G_t + \pi_{22}M_t + \pi_{32}r_t^e + \varepsilon_{2t}^*$$

We now have eight reduced form coefficients that can be used to estimate seven structural coefficients. Because the number of equations (reduced form coefficients) exceeds the number of unknown structural coefficients, values for the structural coefficients can be obtained, but the solutions for these coefficients will not be unique. For example, the coefficient α_1 can be expressed as either of the following:

$$\alpha_1 = \pi_{21}/\pi_{22} \qquad \text{(same as for Equation (15.18))}$$

$$\alpha_1 = \pi_{31}/\pi_{32}$$

Equation set (15.19) is therefore overidentified. We stated in the previous section that when an equation is overidentified, there is more than enough information contained in the set of equations to identify it. As the approach to identification in this section shows, overidentification results in an overabundance of estimators for structural equation coefficients. The reduced form coefficients for Equation (15.19) are therefore consistent with several different sets of structural coefficients.

The results of this section provide some insight into possible methods for estimating structural equations. Since least squares estimation of reduced form equations generally produces unbiased and consistent estimators, the estimated reduced form coefficients can be used to solve for structural coefficients.[8] This approach is called **indirect least squares**. This technique does not work when an equation is underidentified, for then there are too few reduced form coefficients to solve for the set of structural parameters. In contrast, for a set of overidentified equations, a number of different solutions exist for the structural coefficients. The only situation where indirect least squares works well is with exactly identified equations. Then, the number of reduced form coefficients coincides exactly with the number of structural parameters, leading to unique estimates of the structural coefficients. Even when the equations are exactly identified, the indirect least squares estimators are not unbiased, however. This can be seen by considering the estimator of α_1 from Equation (15.18):

$$\hat{\alpha}_1 = \hat{\pi}_{21}/\hat{\pi}_{22}$$

The expected value of $\hat{\alpha}_1$ is:

$$E(\hat{\alpha}_1) = E(\hat{\pi}_{21}/\hat{\pi}_{22})$$

Since both estimated reduced form coefficients are random variables:

$$E(\hat{\alpha}_1) \neq E(\hat{\pi}_{21})/E(\hat{\pi}_{22})$$

The indirect least squares estimators are therefore biased.[9] It can be shown, however, that these are consistent estimators.[10]

---

[8] The exception occurs when lagged endogenous variables are present and the reduced form errors are serially correlated.

[9] This result occurs since the expectation operator is a linear operator. As such, the expected value of the ratio of two random variables is not equal to the ratio of individual expected values.

[10] This is accomplished by taking the probability limit of the expression for $\hat{\alpha}_1$. Unlike the expectation operator, the probability limit of a ratio is the ratio of individual probability limits.

As we have seen, indirect least squares is not a satisfactory estimation technique for equation sets with overidentified equations. However, overidentified equations occur very frequently in applied econometric research. Because of this, a different estimation method is required. While unbiased estimators for structural equation coefficients do not currently exist, several consistent estimators are available for both exactly identified and overidentified equations. We now turn to a discussion of these.

CONSISTENT ESTIMATION OF STRUCTURAL EQUATIONS

Least squares estimation of a structural equation produces biased and inconsistent estimators, since the endogenous explanatory variable(s) are correlated with the equation error. This correlation affects not only the coefficients of the endogenous explanatory variables, but *all* of the coefficients in that equation. To eliminate this problem, it is necessary to find an alternative estimation technique where this correlation disappears, at least for large samples.

One possible technique, the method of indirect least squares, was detailed in the last section. When an equation is exactly identified, indirect least squares can be used to provide consistent estimates of structural coefficients, after the reduced form coefficients have been estimated and the required algebraic substitutions have been made to arrive at expressions for the structural coefficients. Obviously, this entails a great many calculations, especially when there are a large number of variables in a structural equation. This technique does not pertain for all identified equations, however, since such equations can be either exactly identified or overidentified. For overidentified equations, the indirect least squares estimators are not unique.

In light of these complications, indirect least squares is generally not used to estimate structural equations. The actual methods that are used vary. These generally fall under the headings of either single equation, or **limited information methods**, which are considered here, or system methods, called **full-information methods**. Limited information estimation techniques allow us to deal with one equation at a time, alleviating the need to solve the set of all equations as a method for estimating a structural equation.

The limited information methods detailed here are instrumental variable methods that pertain to either exactly or over-identified equations. To derive our estimation methods, we will utilize the structural demand equation in the following model:

$$q_i = \alpha_0 + \alpha_1 p_i + \varepsilon_{1i} \qquad \text{(demand)}$$

$$q_i = \beta_0 + \beta_1 p_i + \beta_2 C_i + \varepsilon_{2i} \qquad \text{(supply)} \qquad \textbf{(15.20)}$$

where C is the costs of production. According to the order condition, the demand function is exactly identified since it excludes one variable (C). Rewriting this equation in deviation form:

$$q_i' = \alpha_1 p_i' + \varepsilon_{1i}' \qquad \textbf{(15.21)}$$

the normal equation for $\hat{\alpha}_1$ is obtained by multiplying this equation by p_i' then summing each term:

$$\sum q_i' p_i' = \alpha_1 \sum p_i'^2 + \sum \varepsilon_{1i}' p_i'$$

If p_i were not correlated with ε_{1i}, we could exclude the last term on the right when deriving the formula for $\hat{\alpha}_1$:

$$\hat{\alpha}_1 = \sum q_i' p_i' / \sum p_i'^2$$

This is the least squares estimator of α_1, which we know is biased and inconsistent since p is correlated with ε_1. The problem with this estimator is that it omits the term above related to $\text{Cov}(\varepsilon_1, p)$ that is nonzero. This omission can be viewed as a type of specification error that occurs as the result of the endogeneity of price in the demand function.

A solution to this problem is found by utilizing a proxy variable for p that is: (i) correlated with p; and (ii) uncorrelated with ε_1 for large samples. This is called an instrumental variable (see Chapter 14). If we denote this instrumental variable z, then the normal equation for $\hat{\alpha}_1$ is obtained by multiplying Equation (15.21) by z_i' then summing:

$$\sum q_i' z_i' = \alpha_1 \sum p_i' z_i' + \sum \varepsilon_{1i}' z_i' \qquad \textbf{(15.22)}$$

Since by the nature of our instrumental variable, $\text{Cov}(\varepsilon_1, z)$ approaches zero as sample size increases, we can overlook the term on the right in Equation (15.22) and define the instrumental variable estimator of α_1 as:

$$\hat{\alpha}_1 = \sum q_i' z_i' / \sum p_i' z_i' \qquad \textbf{(15.23)}$$

The estimator given in Equation (15.23) is a consistent estimator of α_1.

Many potential choices exist for the instrumental variable, z. No endogenous variable from an equation set should be used for this purpose, since it would fail to meet the second requirement above. It is important that the choice for z be highly correlated with the variable it replaces (p). The reason for this can be seen by dividing each of the terms in Equation (15.22) by $\Sigma p_i' z_i'$:

$$\frac{\sum q_i' z_i'}{\sum p_i' z_i'} = \alpha_1 + \frac{\sum \varepsilon_{1i}' z_i'}{\sum p_i' z_i'}$$

The more highly correlated z is with p, the larger is the term in the denominator on the right, $\Sigma p_i' z_i'$, making the formula used to obtain the instrumental variable estimator of α_1 closer to that value.

Technically, z can be almost any variable, as long as it is exogenous. However, some choices are better than others. Since the instrumental variable estimator is consistent, any suitable choice for z, whether highly or weakly correlated with p, will result in a consistent estimator of α_1. For the sample sizes typically used to estimate such relationships, some choices perform noticeably better than others. This is the basis for the desirability of the high correlation between p and z stated above. The practice that has evolved through the years is to restrict this choice to an exogenous variable in the system of equations of which the equation is part. For an exactly identified equation such as the demand function in Equation (15.20), there is then only one choice for z: the variable excluded from demand but included in supply, C. Using this variable, $\hat{\alpha}_1$ is obtained from (normal) Equation (15.23), where z is replaced by C:

$$\sum q'_i C'_i = \alpha_1 \sum p'_i C'_i + \sum \varepsilon'_{1i} C'_i$$

Since the costs of production are exogenous and uncorrelated with ε_1, the term $\Sigma \varepsilon'_{1i} C'_i$ can be omitted, giving:

$$\hat{\alpha}_1 = \sum q'_i C'_i / \sum p'_i C'_i \qquad \textbf{(15.24)}$$

as the instrumental variable estimator of α_1. This estimator can be obtained in two steps:

1. Regress the endogenous variable, price, on the costs of production:

$$p_i = \gamma_0 + \gamma_1 C_i + v_i$$

and obtain the predicted values of price from this equation, $\hat{p}_i$.

2. Perform the least squares regression of q on *predicted* price:

$$q_i = \alpha_0 + \alpha_1 \hat{p}_i + \varepsilon^*_{1i}$$

The coefficients from this equation are the instrumental variable estimators of α_0 and α_1, which are consistent.

This procedure for obtaining instrumental variables with exactly identified equations is called two-step or **two-stage least squares**.

The consistency of the instrumental variable estimators in this equation can be seen in the following way. From step (1) above:

$$p_i = \hat{p}_i + \hat{v}_i$$

According to the properties of least squares, $\hat{v}$ is uncorrelated with $\hat{p}$. Substituting the right side of the above expression into the structural demand function, we obtain the equation used in the second stage:

$$q_i = \alpha_0 + \alpha_1(\hat{p}_i + \hat{v}_i) + \varepsilon_{1i},$$

or

$$q_i = \alpha_0 + \alpha_1 \hat{p}_i + (\alpha_1 \hat{v}_i + \varepsilon_{1i})$$

In the second step above, $\varepsilon^*_{1i} = \alpha_1 \hat{v}_i + \varepsilon_{1i}$. The explanatory variable in step (2), $\hat{p}$, is both stochastic and likely to be correlated with the structural equation errors ε_{1i} for small samples. As a result, the instrumental variable estimator is biased. This correlation between $\hat{p}$ and ε_1 approaches zero as sample size rises. Thus:

$\hat{v}_i$ is uncorrelated with $\hat{p}_i$ (according to least squares properties)

and

$\hat{p}_i$ is uncorrelated with ε_{1i} as sample size rises

For large samples $\hat{p}$ is therefore uncorrelated with ε^*_{1i}, and estimators obtained from the procedure outlined above are consistent.

One important point should be made about the two-step procedure above. While the estimated coefficients in the second step equation are consistent, both the estimated error variance and coefficient standard errors are not. A consistent estimator of the error variance from the equation in the second step above is:

$$\hat{\sigma}_\varepsilon^2 = \sum (q_i - \hat{\alpha}_0 - \hat{\alpha}_1 p_i)^2 / (n - 2)$$

Note that *this is calculated by replacing the explanatory variable used in instrumental variable estimation, $\hat{p}$, with the actual values of price, p.*

The supply function in Equation (15.20) cannot be estimated using the instrumental variable method. This equation is under-identified according to the order condition, since it does not exclude any of the variables in the system. As should be apparent, a link exists between the identification and estimation of a structural equation. For an under-identified equation, such as the supply function in Equations (15.20), no suitable instrument from within the system exists that can be used in place of the endogenous explanatory variable, price. Why not perform the first step above by regressing price on costs then use the predicted values of price in the second step? Let us assume this procedure is followed. The first step estimates the following equation by least squares:

$$p_i = \lambda_0 + \lambda_1 C_i + v_i$$

The predicted values for price are an exact linear function of C:

$$\hat{p}_i = \hat{\lambda}_0 + \hat{\lambda}_1 C_i$$

When these values of $\hat{p}$ are substituted into the original equation in the second step, we have:

$$q_i = \alpha_0 + \alpha_1 \hat{p}_i + \alpha_2 C_i + \varepsilon_{1i}^*,$$

or

$$q_i = \alpha_0 + \alpha_1(\hat{\lambda}_0 + \hat{\lambda}_1 C_i) + \alpha_2 C_i + \varepsilon_{1i}^* \tag{15.25}$$

The explanatory variables in Equation (15.25) are perfectly collinear, since predicted price is an exact linear function of the other explanatory variable in this equation. Thus a multiple regression assumption is violated when under-identification exists. If this were an identified equation, predicted price would be a function not only of costs but of some variable excluded from supply as well, allowing perfect collinearity to be avoided.

If we now modify the above equations so that both demand and supply are exactly identified, there are two explanatory variables in each of the equations of our system:

$$q_i = \alpha_0 + \alpha_1 p_i + \alpha_2 I_i + \varepsilon_{1i} \qquad \text{(demand)}$$
$$q_i = \beta_0 + \beta_1 p_i + \beta_2 C_i + \varepsilon_{2i} \qquad \text{(supply)} \tag{15.26}$$

where income (I) and costs (C) are exogenous. To estimate the demand function, we now need two normal equations. The exogenous variable in this equation, income, can serve as its own instrument. We again use the costs of production as the other instrument. The normal equations (using the deviation form of the demand function) are then:

$$\sum q_i' C_i' = \alpha_1 \sum p_i' C_i' + \alpha_2 \sum I_i' C_i' + \sum \varepsilon_{1i}' C_i'$$
$$\sum q_i' I_i' = \alpha_1 \sum p_i' I_i' + \alpha_2 \sum I_i'^2 + \sum \varepsilon_{1i}' I_i'$$

The second of these is identical to the least squares normal equation for $\hat{\alpha}_2$. We now have two equations and two unknowns, α_1 and α_2. Since both income and production costs are exogenous, the terms involving the error on the right of each normal equation tend to zero for large sample sizes, allowing us to omit these terms when solving for $\hat{\alpha}_1$ and $\hat{\alpha}_2$. The estimated coefficients in the demand function can either be obtained by solving these normal equations or by utilizing two-stage least squares. In the present context, that procedure is carried out in the following way:

1. Estimate:

$$p_i = \gamma_0 + \gamma_1 I_i + \gamma_2 C_i + v_i$$

   by ordinary least squares and obtain the predicted values of p from this equation, $\hat{p}_i$.
2. Use these predicted values in place of p_i when estimating the structural demand equation:

$$q_i = \alpha_0 + \alpha_1 \hat{p}_i + \alpha_2 I_i + \varepsilon_{1i}^*$$

Estimation of the structural supply function proceeds in a similar way, where predicted price, which is obtained from the regression in step (1) above, is used in place of price in the supply function.

The steps involved in instrumental variable estimation allow us to see that the identification and estimation of structural equations corresponds to specification and estimation of a single equation model. To estimate a structural equation, we need as many normal equations as there are explanatory variables in that equation. However, only exogenous variables from the *other* equations in a system can serve as instruments for the endogenous explanatory variables in this equation. If a structural equation does not exclude any of the variables present in the other equations in a system, it is under-identified. As a result, no instruments exist within the system to replace the endogenous explanatory variables in that equation, and that equation cannot be estimated. As stated earlier in this chapter, this does *not* mean that a regression using the variables in that equation is impossible. Instead, the result of such a regression is more likely to be a hodgepodge of the set of equations than the equation of interest itself.

This relationship between the number of exogenous variables excluded from a structural equation and the number of included endogenous explanatory variables allows us to state another requirement for estimation of a structural equation:

> The number of exogenous variables in the *set* of equations must be at least as great as the total number of variables included in this equation minus 1.

Note that the requirement on exogenous variables pertains to the *entire set of equations*, not just the other equations in a system. This must be the case, since the exogenous variables in an equation, which are included among the entire set of exogenous variables in the system, can serve as their own instruments. Based on this, the order condition can be restated:

> **Order Condition:** A structural equation is identified if the number of exogenous variables it excludes (which can serve as instruments) is at least as great as the number of included endogenous variables minus 1.

The reason why the "minus one" keeps appearing should be apparent. By designating one of the endogenous variables in an equation the dependent variable, we are imposing the restriction that its coefficient is 1 (or -1, depending on the notation used). This is called a **normalizing restriction**. Once such a restriction is imposed, an instrument is no longer needed for that variable. As a result, we require one fewer instrument than the total number of variables in that equation for estimation purposes.

Working with overidentified equations adds some complication to the results above. If we are working with a set of overidentified equations, which occurs quite frequently in applied econometric work, the choice of which variables to use as instruments is less obvious than when dealing with exactly identified equations. If we utilize the following demand and supply model:

$$q_i = \alpha_0 + \alpha_1 p_i + \alpha_2 I_i + \alpha_3 p_i^r + \varepsilon_{1i} \qquad \text{(demand)}$$
$$q_i = \beta_0 + \beta_1 p_i + \beta_2 C_i + \beta_3 p_{t-1} + \varepsilon_{2i} \qquad \text{(supply)} \tag{15.27}$$

where p^r, the price of a related good in consumption, is exogenous, both equations are overidentified, since each excludes two $(> G - 1)$ variables. Before demand can be estimated, we must find a suitable instrument for the endogenous explanatory variable, price. But since demand is overidentified, more than one choice exists. We can use either costs, lagged price, or some combination of these variables. If we use only one of these variables, we are, in effect, throwing out some of the information contained in the set of equations. By combining both variables to form an instrument we avoid this problem. Since many ways exist for combining these variables, what procedure should we follow? To answer this question, we will outline the appropriate two-step procedure. The application of two-stage least squares to an overidentified equation proceeds in the following way:

1. Regress each of the endogenous explanatory variables in a structural equation on the *entire set of exogenous variables in the system of equations*. Note that this consists of estimating the reduced form equation for each endogenous explanatory variable. Obtain the predicted values for each of these variables.
2. Estimate the structural equation of interest by least squares after replacing all endogenous explanatory variables with their predicted values generated in step (1). The coefficients obtained from this technique are biased but consistent.

The uniqueness of these estimates is derived from step (1), where each endogenous explanatory variable is regressed on the set of exogenous variables in the system.

The efficiency gain that accrues to two-stage least squares results from using the reduced form equations in step (1). *The caveat mentioned earlier about the equation standard error and coefficient error variances still pertains here.* However, canned statistical programs that contain a two-stage least squares procedure routinely make this correction.

The steps required to estimate the demand-supply system of Equation (15.27) by two-stage least squares are:

1. Regress price on all exogenous variables in the system: I, p^r, C, and p_{t-1}, and obtain predicted price, $\hat{p}$. Note, however, that p_{t-1} should only be considered exogenous if the errors in the reduced form equation are not autocorrelated (see Chapter 14).

2. Estimate the demand function by performing least squares on:

$$q_i = \alpha_0 + \alpha_1 \hat{p}_i + \alpha_2 I_i + \alpha_3 p_i^r + \varepsilon_{1i}^*$$

The supply function is estimated by applying least squares to:

$$q_i = \beta_0 + \beta_1 \hat{p}_i + \beta_2 C_i + \beta_3 p_{t-1} + \varepsilon_{2i}^*$$

It can be shown that, for an exactly identified equation, the instrumental variable and two-stage least squares estimators are identical. Also, if one of the structural equations is underidentified, then utilizing this technique will result in perfect multicollinearity between $\hat{p}$ and the other exogenous variables in the equation estimated.

We have shown that the two-stage least squares estimators are biased but consistent. In light of this, estimated standard errors for coefficients that are derived in the way stated earlier pertain for large samples only, and the coefficient test statistics follow the asymptotic normal distribution. Thus, when a computer program with a two-stage least squares routine is utilized to estimate a structural equation, the calculated t-statistics it lists pertain to an asymptotic unit normal random variable.

When an equation system consists of a large number of equations and exogenous variables, two-stage least squares estimation may not be possible, since the number of observations available to estimate a set of equations may be less than the total number of variables in step (1). When this occurs, methods for reducing the number of variables (which preserve degrees of freedom) are needed. One of these methods is **principal components analysis**, where the group of exogenous variables is reduced to a smaller set by calculating linear combinations of exogenous variables. Another technique, **structurally ordered instrumental variables**, fine tunes the set of exogenous variables used to create each predicted endogenous variable by restricting the possible choices to the set of exogenous variables appearing in the equation for that endogenous variable along with those most closely related to it, based on an examination of the set of structural equations.[11] Since this is not likely to be a problem for persons using this text, these techniques will not be dealt with here.

---

[11] See R. Wonnacott and T. Wonnacott, *Econometrics* (2nd ed), (New York: John Wiley & Sons), 1979, pp. 295–96.

FORECASTING WITH A SIMULTANEOUS EQUATION MODEL

The process of generating forecasts with a simultaneous equation model is similar in a number of ways to forecasting with a single equation. The major difference is the way we obtain predicted values for the variables in our sample regression function. We will assume that the following simultaneous equation model of supply and demand has been estimated:

$$q_t = \alpha_0 + \alpha_1 p_t + \alpha_2 I_t + \alpha_3 p_t^r + \varepsilon_{1t}$$
$$q_t = \beta_0 + \beta_1 p_t + \beta_2 C_{1t} + \beta_3 C_{2t} + \varepsilon_{2t} \tag{15.28}$$

where I is income, p^r is the price of a related good, and C_1 and C_2 are two different types of production costs (e.g., wages and raw materials costs). To forecast demand in future time periods, we use our sample regression function expressed with different time subscripts:

$$\hat{q}_{t+\tau} = \hat{\alpha}_0 + \hat{\alpha}_1 p_{t+\tau} + \hat{\alpha}_2 I_{t+\tau} + \hat{\alpha}_3 p_{t+\tau}^r \tag{15.29}$$

where τ is the number of time periods into the future the forecast extends (see Chapter 5). Once we have values for p, I, and p^r for the future time periods, we plug these values into our sample regression function and obtain predicted values of quantity demanded. Since income and the price of a related good are exogenous, this entails obtaining values from some source or possibly using hypothetical values. Because price is endogenous, and thus jointly determined along with q, we cannot follow this same procedure to obtain its future values. As we saw in Chapter 14, values for endogenous variables in a simultaneous equation system are obtained from the set of exogenous variables in the *system* of equations. The reduced form equation is therefore the means by which we obtain future values for price. In the present example, the relevant reduced form is:

$$\hat{p}_t = \hat{\pi}_0 + \hat{\pi}_1 I_t + \hat{\pi}_2 p_t^r + \hat{\pi}_3 C_{1t} + \hat{\pi}_4 C_{2t}$$

which, when its time subscripts are changed, becomes:

$$\hat{p}_{t+\tau} = \hat{\pi}_0 + \hat{\pi}_1 I_{t+\tau} + \hat{\pi}_2 p_{t+\tau}^r + \hat{\pi}_3 C_{1,t+\tau} + \hat{\pi}_4 C_{2,t+\tau} \tag{15.30}$$

Predicted values of price from Equation (15.30) are then substituted into Equation (15.29) along with predictions for I and p^r to produce estimates of future quantity demanded. This method for calculating forecasts is called **unrestricted estimation**, since it entails simply regressing the endogenous explanatory variables on the set of exogenous variable without utilizing any of the specific information (restrictions) from the set of structural equations.

An alternative method exists for producing forecasts of endogenous explanatory variables. Instead of merely estimating their reduced forms separately (as in Equation (15.30)), it is possible to derive reduced form coefficients by substituting estimated structural coefficients into the algebraic expressions for the various reduced form coefficients. Since this method utilizes information from the structural coefficients directly, it is called **restricted estimation**. While this is sometimes complicated, for example, when the system is very large, it is generally preferred to unrestricted estimation when the computations involved are not excessive.

Some sets of equations, those in dynamic models, contain lagged endogenous variables. If, for example, the variable p^r is instead lagged price, p_{t-1}, the reduced form for price is then:

$$\hat{p}_t = \hat{\pi}_0 + \hat{\pi}_1 I_t + \hat{\pi}_2 p_{t-1} + \hat{\pi}_3 C_{1t} + \hat{\pi}_4 C_{2t}$$

For future time periods, this equation is:

$$\hat{p}_{t+\tau} = \hat{\pi}_0 + \hat{\pi}_1 I_{t+\tau} + \hat{\pi}_2 p_{t+\tau-1} + \hat{\pi}_3 C_{1,t+\tau} + \hat{\pi}_4 C_{2,t+\tau}$$

When forecasting two or more periods into the future, values for lagged price are needed. When these are obtained by lagging forecasted values for price from the model itself, the method of obtaining forecasts is called **dynamic simulation**. A number of canned computer programs have routines that "solve" such equations and the systems of which they are part.

LINEAR RESTRICTIONS IN SIMULTANEOUS EQUATION MODELS

Testing linear restrictions within the framework of a simultaneous equation model can be carried out using the Wald Test. The steps involved are essentially those outlined in Chapter 6. The only difference lies in the way in which the Wald Test statistic is calculated. Before applying the Wald Test to structural equations, we will review how it is carried out for nonstructural equations. If the equation of interest is:

$$y_i = \alpha_0 + \alpha_1 x_{1i} + \alpha_2 x_{2i} + \alpha_3 x_{3i} + \varepsilon_i$$

and we wish to test the following null hypothesis: H_0: $\alpha_1 = \alpha_2$, against the alternative hypothesis that H_0 is false, we utilize the following procedure:

1. Incorporate the restriction from the null hypothesis into our equation. Here, we obtain:

$$y_i = \alpha_0 + \alpha_1(x_{1i} + x_{2i}) + \alpha_3 x_{3i} + \varepsilon_i$$

   To estimate this restricted equation, we calculate the new variable: $x_i^* = (x_{1i} + x_{2i})$, then regress y on x^* and x_3 using least squares. From this we obtain the error sum of squares, ESS_{re}.

2. Estimate the original (unrestricted) equation with least squares and obtain its error sum of squares, ESS_{ue}.

3. The test statistic for the Wald Test is:

$$\frac{(\text{ESS}_{re} - \text{ESS}_{ue})/r}{\text{ESS}_{ue}/(n-k)}$$

where r, the number of restrictions, is 1 in this example, and k is the total number of coefficients in the unrestricted equation (here $k = 4$). If the value of this test statistic exceeds the critical F-value with r and $(n - k)$ degrees of freedom, we reject H_0 and accept the alternative hypothesis that α_1 differs from α_2.

Some applications of the Wald test are:

the determination of whether constant returns to scale exist in a Cobb-Douglas production function; and

ascertaining the joint statistical significance of a subset of explanatory variables whose t-statistics are not significant (this may be the result of multicollinearity).

In a simultaneous equation setting, it is possible for linear restrictions to pertain either to a single equation or across equations within the system of equations. Also, structural equations are estimated with two-stage least squares, not least squares. Because of these differences, the Wald Test is carried out differently when simultaneous equations are involved.

Linear restrictions, such as those tested with the Wald Test, can permit structural equations that are otherwise under-identified to become identified.[12] If we consider the following set of simultaneous equations:

$$y_{1i} = \alpha_0 + \alpha_1 y_{2i} + \alpha_2 x_{1i} + \alpha_3 x_{2i} + \varepsilon_{1i}$$

$$y_{2i} = \beta_0 + \beta_1 y_{1i} + \beta_2 x_{1i} + \beta_3 x_{2i} + \varepsilon_{2i}$$

neither equation is identified, since both contain y_1, y_2, x_1, and x_2. The only restriction in each equation is the normalizing restriction that defines its dependent variable. If economic theory leads us to believe that $\alpha_2 = \alpha_3$, we can test this hypothesis statistically with the Wald Test. Our null hypothesis is: $H_0: \alpha_2 = \alpha_3$. The restricted equation for this hypothesis test is:

$$y_{1i} = \alpha_0 + \alpha_1 y_{2i} + \alpha_2(x_{1i} + x_{2i}) + \varepsilon_{1i},$$

or

$$y_{1i} = \alpha_0 + \alpha_1 y_{2i} + \alpha_2 x_i^* + \varepsilon_{1i}$$

where $x^* = (x_1 + x_2)$. This equation is now identified, since it is possible to distinguish it from a linear combination of the two equations in this system. Another way of viewing this is to note that two restrictions pertain to this equation: the normalizing restriction and the linear restriction contained in the null hypothesis.

The presence of the variable x^* does not indicate that a third independent explanatory variable is now present in this model, since the new variable x^* is the sum of the other two variables. As such, it is not independent of both x_1 and x_2. Two possibilities therefore exist for exogenous instrumental variables: x^* and *either* x_1 or x_2.[13] Note that the second equation in the system is still underidentified.

---

[12] This example follows from the presentation in R. Bacon, *A First Course in Econometric Theory* (Oxford: Oxford University Press), 1988, p. 257.

[13] Were we to form three normal equations from these variables, only two would be independent.

To illustrate the steps involved in carrying out the Wald Test in a simultaneous equation setting, we will utilize the following equation system:

$$y_{1i} = \alpha_0 + \alpha_1 y_{2i} + \alpha_2 x_{1i} + \alpha_3 x_{2i} + \alpha_4 x_{3i} + \varepsilon_{1i}$$

$$y_{2i} = \beta_0 + \beta_1 y_{1i} + \beta_2 x_{2i} + \beta_3 x_{3i} + \beta_4 x_{4i} + \varepsilon_{2i}$$

(15.31)

Both of these equations are exactly identified according to the order condition. If we wish to test the following null hypothesis: H_0: $\alpha_3 = \alpha_4 = 0$, against the alternative hypothesis that H_0 is false, our restricted first equation is:

$$y_{1i} = \alpha_0 + \alpha_1 y_{2i} + \alpha_2 x_{1i} + \varepsilon_{1i}$$

(15.32)

This equation is then estimated with two-stage least squares, where the predicted value of y_2 replaces its actual value. The unrestricted equation is shown in (15.31). The test statistic for the Wald Test in this example has the same form as that given earlier with one exception: its numerator, $\text{ESS}_{re} - \text{ESS}_{ue}$, is calculated using $\hat{y}_{2i}$ to produce the values of ESS.[14] The denominator of the test statistic is calculated in the usual way, utilizing *actual* y_2 when calculating ESS. To distinguish the values of ESS_{ue} in the numerator and denominator of this test statistic, we will denote these as $\text{ESS}_{ue(n)}$ and $\text{ESS}_{ue(d)}$, respectively. The steps involved in this test are then:

1. Generate $\hat{y}_2$ by regressing y_2 on all of the exogenous variables in the set of equations, x_1, x_2, x_3, and x_4.
2. Estimate the restricted equation:

$$y_{1i} = \alpha_0 + \alpha_1 \hat{y}_{2i} + \alpha_2 x_{1i} + v_{1i}^*$$

and obtain $\text{ESS}_{re} = \Sigma(y_{1i} - \hat{\alpha}_0 - \hat{\alpha}_1 \hat{y}_{2i} - \hat{\alpha}_2 x_{1i})^2$.

3. Estimate the unrestricted equation to obtain the value of $\text{ESS}_{ue(n)}$. To do this, estimate:

$$y_{1i} = \alpha_0 + \alpha_1 \hat{y}_{2i} + \alpha_2 x_{1i} + \alpha_3 x_{2i} + \alpha_4 x_{3i} + \varepsilon_{1i}^*$$

with least squares (this is two-stage least squares) and obtain:

$$\text{ESS}_{ue(n)} = \Sigma(y_{1i} - \hat{\alpha}_0 - \hat{\alpha}_1 \hat{y}_{2i} - \hat{\alpha}_2 x_{1i} - \hat{\alpha}_3 x_{2i} - \hat{\alpha}_4 x_{3i})^2$$

4. Obtain $\text{ESS}_{ue(d)}$ for the denominator of the test statistic using the coefficients estimated in step (3), but actual y_2:

$$\text{ESS}_{ue(d)} = \Sigma(y_{1i} - \hat{\alpha}_0 - \hat{\alpha}_1 y_{2i} - \hat{\alpha}_2 x_{1i} - \hat{\alpha}_3 x_{2i} - \hat{\alpha}_4 x_{3i})^2$$

5. Use the values for ESS from steps (1)–(4) to calculate the following test statistic:

$$\frac{(\text{ESS}_{re} - \text{ESS}_{ue(n)})/2}{\text{ESS}_{ue(d)}/(n - k)} \sim F_{2,(n-k)}$$

---

[14] This test is discussed in T. Wallace and J. Silver, *Econometrics: An Introduction* (Reading: MA, Addison-Wesley Publishing Co.), 1988, pp. 353–54.

Here, k equals 5. If the value of this test statistic exceeds the critical F value with 2 and $(n - k)$ degrees of freedom in the numerator and denominator, respectively, at the selected level of significance, we reject the null hypothesis.

TWO-STAGE LEAST SQUARES WITH AUTOCORRELATED ERRORS

The estimation of structural equations with time series data can encounter problems if errors are autocorrelated. The correction of autocorrelation is fairly straightforward, as the framework and methods outlined in Chapter 11 pertain. To detail two-stage least squares estimation when one of the equations has autocorrelated errors, we will use the following model:

$$y_{1t} = \alpha_0 + \alpha_1 y_{2t} + \alpha_2 x_{1t} + \varepsilon_{1t}$$
$$y_{2t} = \beta_0 + \beta_1 y_{1t} + \beta_2 x_{2t} + \varepsilon_{2t}$$

$$(15.33)$$

where we assume that ε_1 is a white noise error process, but ε_2 is first-order auto-correlated:

$$\varepsilon_{2t} = \Theta \varepsilon_{2,t-1} + v_{2t} \qquad (15.34)$$

The error term in the second equation is a function of its value in the previous period, $\varepsilon_{2,t-1}$, and the white noise error, v_{2t}. To eliminate the autocorrelated errors in the second equation above, we express Equation (15.34) in terms of the white noise error, v_{2t}:

$$v_{2t} = \varepsilon_{2t} - \Theta \varepsilon_{2,t-1}$$

Applying the backshift operator to the right side of this expression we have:

$$v_{2t} = (1 - \Theta B)\varepsilon_{2t}$$

The bracketed term in this equation defines the transformation term that must be applied to the second structural equation to remove its autocorrelated errors:

$$T = (1 - \Theta B) \qquad (15.35)$$

Multiplying structural Equation (15.33) by Equation (15.35) we have:

$$(T \cdot y_{2t}) = T \cdot \beta_0 + \beta_1(T \cdot y_{1t}) + \beta_2(T \cdot x_{2t}) + T \cdot \varepsilon_{2t} \text{ or}$$
$$(1 - \Theta B) \cdot y_{2t} = (1 - \Theta B) \cdot \beta_0 + \beta_1(1 - \Theta B) \cdot y_{1t} + \beta_2(1 - \Theta B) \cdot x_{2t} + (1 - \Theta B) \cdot \varepsilon_{2t}$$

This gives the appropriate generalized difference form of Equation (15.33) whose errors are no longer autocorrelated:

$$(y_{2t} - \Theta y_{2,t-1}) = \beta_0(1 - \Theta) + \beta_1(y_{1t} - \Theta y_{1,t-1})$$
$$+ \beta_2(x_{2t} - \Theta x_{2,t-1}) + v_t \qquad (15.36)$$

Two-stage least squares estimation of Equation (15.36) requires that we obtain predicted values for y_1 for use in the second-stage estimation. Unlike the original structural equation, (15.33), the set of exogenous variables now consists of x_{1t}, x_{2t}, and $x_{2,t-1}$. The reduced form from which predicted y_1 is generated is thus:

$$y_{1t} = \pi_0 + \pi_1 x_{1t} + \pi_2 x_{2t} + \pi_3 x_{2,t-1} + \eta_t$$

Once $\hat{y}_1$ is created, the term involving y_1 in Equation (15.36) is constructed as:

$$(\hat{y}_{1t} - \Theta y_{1,t-1})$$

Note that predicted y_1 is only used in the first term above. Using this information, the form of Equation (15.36) that is estimated is:

$$\begin{aligned}(y_{2t} - \Theta y_{2,t-1}) = \beta_0(1 - \Theta) &+ \beta_1(\hat{y}_{1t} - \Theta y_{1,t-1}) \\ &+ \beta_2(x_{2t} - \Theta x_{2,t-1}) + v_t^*\end{aligned} \qquad \textbf{(15.37)}$$

If possible, a Prais-Winsten correction should be applied to the first observation. Equation (15.37) can be estimated by either the Cochrane-Orcutt method or the Hildreth-Lu grid search method. If the Hildreth-Lu method is utilized, Equation (15.37) is estimated for different values of Θ ranging from -1 to $+1$ in increments of 0.1. The equation with the lowest sum of squared residuals is the equation that is utilized.

Autocorrelated errors in a structural equation can be other than first-order. A number of alternatives to the Durbin-Watson test were presented in Chapter 11 that can be used to determine if the order of autocorrelation in higher than AR(1). Among these is the identification procedure employed in time series analysis and the Breusch-Godfrey test. If such tests reveal second-order autocorrelation, where:

$$\varepsilon_{2t} = \Theta_1 \varepsilon_{2,t-1} + \Theta_2 \varepsilon_{2,t-2} + v_t$$

the transformation term that must be applied to Equation (15.33) is:

$$T = (1 - \Theta_1 B - \Theta_2 B^2)$$

and the generalized difference form of Equation (15.33) becomes:

$$\begin{aligned}(y_{2t} - \Theta_1 y_{2,t-1} - \Theta_2 y_{2,t-2}) = \beta_0(1 - \Theta_1 - \Theta_2) &+ \beta_1(y_{1t} - \Theta_1 y_{1,t-1} - \Theta_2 y_{1,t-2}) \\ &+ \beta_2(x_{2t} - \Theta_1 x_{2,t-1} - \Theta_2 x_{2,t-2}) + v_t\end{aligned}$$

The creation of $\hat{y}_1$ now entails the regression of y_1 on x_{1t}, x_{2t}, $x_{2,t-1}$, and $x_{2,t-2}$. The term involving y_1 in the generalized difference form of Equation (15.33) above is:

$$\hat{y}_{1t} - \Theta_1 y_{1,t-1} - \Theta_2 y_{1,t-2}$$

As before, the generalized difference form of Equation (15.33) can be estimated using the Cochrane-Orcutt or Hildreth-Lu methods.

If both structural equations have autocorrelated errors, the appropriate transformation term is applied to each equation. The set of exogenous variables that must be included in the reduced form equations for y_1 and y_2 are contained in the generalized difference form for these structural equations. If, for example, both equations have first-order autocorrelated errors, both y_1 and y_2 are then regressed on x_{1t}, x_{2t}, $x_{1,t-1}$ and $x_{2,t-1}$ to generate $\hat{y}_1$ and $\hat{y}_2$. The term with an endogenous explanatory variable on the right of each equation is:

$$\hat{y}_{2t} - \Theta_{(1)}y_{2,t-1} \qquad \text{(for the first equation)}$$

$$\hat{y}_{1t} - \Theta_{(2)}y_{1,t-1} \qquad \text{(for the second equation)}$$

where $\Theta_{(1)}$ and $\Theta_{(2)}$ are the autocorrelation coefficients in the first and second structural equations, respectively.

Correcting for autocorrelation is more complicated when a lagged dependent variable is present in a structural equation. Fair has shown that applying the autocorrelation methods outlined above to such an equation results in inconsistent estimators.[15] He proposed a method that allows consistent estimation of structural equations with lagged dependent variables and autocorrelated errors. The essential elements of his methodology will be outlined here.

We illustrate Fair's method using the following set of simultaneous equations:

$$y_{1t} = \alpha_0 + \alpha_1 y_{2t} + \alpha_2 x_{1t} + \varepsilon_{1t}$$
$$y_{2t} = \beta_0 + \beta_1 y_{1t} + \beta_2 x_{2t} + \beta_3 y_{2,t-1} + \varepsilon_{2t} \tag{15.38}$$

where the errors in the second equation are autocorrelated, with:

$$\varepsilon_{2t} = \Theta\varepsilon_{2,t-1} + v_t \tag{15.39}$$

For a particular choice of Θ, $\hat{\Theta}$, the equation for y_{2t} in (15.38) can be expressed as:

$$(y_{2t} - \hat{\Theta}y_{2,t-1}) = \beta_0(1 - \hat{\Theta}) + \beta_1(y_{1t} - \hat{\Theta}y_{1,t-1}) + \beta_2(x_{2t} - \hat{\Theta}x_{2,t-1})$$
$$+ \beta_3(y_{2,t-1} - \hat{\Theta}y_{2,t-2}) + \{(\hat{\Theta} - \Theta)\varepsilon_{2,t-1} + v_t\} \tag{15.40}$$

The first term in the expression for the error of this equation, $(\hat{\Theta} - \Theta)\varepsilon_{2,t-1}$, results from the fact that $\hat{\Theta}$ does not necessarily coincide with Θ. Problems estimating Equation (15.40) arise since $\varepsilon_{2,t-1}$ is correlated with $y_{2,t-1}$ *as well as* $y_{1,t-1}$ (and any other lagged endogenous variables in this equation). If we replace y_{1t} with $\hat{y}_{1t}$ and estimate Equation (15.40) with two-stage least squares, this correlation between the equation error and the lagged endogenous variables will still exist. As a result, two-stage least squares estimation of Equation (15.40) produces biased and inconsistent estimators of the coefficients of this equation.

Fair's method for obtaining consistent estimators of the coefficients in Equation (15.40) consists of the following steps:

1. Select as instruments those variables that are uncorrelated with v. The list of instruments must include *at least* $y_{2,t-1}$ (the lagged dependent variable in this equation), the lags of any other endogenous variables in this equation, the exogenous variables included in this equation and their lags. Regress each

---

[15] R. Fair, "The Estimation of Simultaneous Equation Models with Lagged Endogenous Variables and First-Order Serially Correlated Errors," *Econometrica* 38 (May 1970), pp. 507–516.

endogenous explanatory variable on this list of instruments. For Equation (15.40), this entails performing the following regression:

$$y_{1t} = \pi_0 + \pi_1 y_{2,t-1} + \pi_2 x_{1t} + \pi_3 x_{2t} + \pi_4 y_{1,t-1} + \pi_5 y_{2,t-2} + \pi_6 x_{2,t-1} + \eta_t$$

and obtaining the predicted values of y_1, $\hat{y}_1$.

2. Select a value for $\hat{\Theta}$, say $\hat{\Theta}_{(1)}$, and estimate Equation (15.40) using least squares, where the term $(y_{1t} - \hat{\Theta} y_{1,t-1})$ is replaced with $(\hat{y}_{1t} - \hat{\Theta}_{(1)} y_{1,t-1})$. Do *not* use the predicted value of $y_{1,t-1}$ in this expression. Calculate the sum of squared residuals from this equation.

3. Repeat step (2) for different values of $\hat{\Theta}$ between -1 and $+1$ with increments of 0.1 (this is a Hildreth-Lu grid search). Select as the final equation the one with the smallest sum of squared residuals.

The consistency of this procedure can be seen in the following way. When the sum of squared residuals is minimized, $\hat{\Theta} = \Theta$, causing the "problem" term in the error of Equation (15.40), $(\hat{\Theta} - \Theta)\varepsilon_{2,t-1}$, which is correlated with the explanatory variables, to drop out. Since the residual in the final equation, v, is uncorrelated with the explanatory variables in that equation, consistent estimation of Equation (15.40) results.

EXAMPLES OF SIMULTANEOUS EQUATION MODELS

■ A MODEL OF PERSONAL CONSUMPTION EXPENDITURES

Ray Fair has specified and estimated a large macroeconometric model of the U.S. economy.[16] We will present a part of that model here, the set of equations that determine personal consumption expenditures based on each of its three components. This model is similar to the one based on Equations (14.11)–(14.14) in Chapter 14.

In Fair's model, consumption expenditure and labor supply are jointly determined as part of constrained utility maximization by households. Because this model views labor supply and consumption spending as jointly determined, Fair distinguishes between after-tax wages, total nonlabor income, and the value of transfer payments received. Changes in nonlabor income affect labor supply differently than do wage changes, since increases or decreases in nonlabor income leave the *relative* cost of leisure (the cost of leisure relative to the prices of goods) unaffected. In contrast, when wages change, both the cost of leisure (relative to the consumption of goods) and the amount of income generated for any number of work hours change (this results in a substitution and income effect).

Fair utilized economic theory to specify his behavioral equations. The equations below contain lagged dependent variables, indicating the presumption of a partial adjustment framework. Fair's overall framework differs from that for partial adjustment

---

[16] R. Fair, *Specification, Estimation, and Analysis of Macroeconometric Models* (Cambridge, MA: Harvard University Press), 1984, pp. 103–122.

presented in Chapter 13, however. Since the portions of Fair's model considered here are based on a consumption-labor supply framework, the existence of constraints on the number of hours persons are able to work, based on labor market tightness, can sometimes restrict the amount of consumption expenditure that occurs. If we let c_j^* denote unconstrained consumption expenditure for category j (either nondurables, durables, or services), Fair postulates that:

$$c_j^* = f(y_1, x_1, x_2, \ldots) \tag{15.41}$$

where y_1 is an observed endogenous variable, and the x's are observed exogenous variables. When the labor market is not very tight, for example when the unemployment rate is high, desired hours may not coincide with the actual number of hours worked. This divergence constrains attainable consumption expenditure. Fair models this in the following way:

$$c_j = c_j^* + \gamma Z + \varepsilon \tag{15.42}$$

where c_j is actual consumption expenditure for category j, c_j^* is desired consumption, Z is a labor market tightness variable (with $\gamma > 0$), and ε is a stochastic error. When labor markets are tight, $c_j = c_j^*$. No divergence exists between actual and desired hours, allowing actual consumption to correspond to its unconstrained value. In this case, $Z = 0$. Below a critical value of labor market tightness, $Z < 0$, making $c_j < c_j^*$. Substituting Equation (15.41) into Equation (15.42) we have an expression for actual consumption in terms of a set of observed variables and the labor tightness variable, Z:

$$c_j = f(y_1, x_1, x_2, \ldots) + \gamma Z + \varepsilon \tag{15.43}$$

In the empirical estimation of his model, Fair defines Z based on the detrended ratio of hours paid to the total population 16 and over.[17]

The specification of each of Fair's equations, which corresponds to the term $f(y_1, x_1, x_2, \ldots)$ on the right of Equation (15.43), is the result of a specific procedure he utilized. Starting with an initial set of variables, different versions of each behavioral equation were estimated. The performance of several versions of an equation were then judged. These equations differed in terms of their inclusion of either: (i) lagged or current period values of variables; (ii) total nonlabor income or transfer payments; (iii) short-term or long-term interest rates (either nominal or real); and (iv) real or nominal wages.[18] When appropriate, Fair also corrected for autocorrelation, assuming a first-order process. Variables which were dropped from equations either continued to display the incorrect sign, or, if the correct sign appeared, failed to attain statistical significance. For example, the IPD for services was dropped from the consumption of services equation since it consistently displayed the wrong sign.

---

[17] Detrended hours are called JJ*. Fair's formula for Z is:

$$Z = (1 - 337/JJ^*)$$

Note that this definition of Z satisfies the restrictions for this value outlined above.

[18] These steps are outlined in R. Fair, p. 115.

The consumption equations in Fair's model, which he estimated using quarterly data for the period from 1954:1 through 1982:3, are:

$$\hat{c}_{st} = 0.0002 + 0.020w_t + 0.007y_{nt} - 0.001r_{st} + 0.0001\text{WLTH}_{t-1}$$
$$\phantom{\hat{c}_{st} =} (0.1) \qquad (2.1) \qquad (0.4) \qquad\quad (5.9) \qquad\qquad (2.4)$$
$$\phantom{\hat{c}_{st} =} + 0.023Z_t + 0.986c_{s,t-1}$$
$$\phantom{\hat{c}_{st} = +} (1.9) \qquad (61.5)$$
$$R^2 = 0.999 \qquad \hat{\sigma}_\varepsilon = 0.002$$

$$\hat{c}_{nt} = 0.109 - 0.047p_{nt} + 0.185w_t + 0.064y_{nt} - 0.001r_{st} + 0.002\text{WLTH}_{t-1}$$
$$\phantom{\hat{c}_{nt} =} (4.0) \qquad (2.2) \qquad\quad (2.5) \qquad (2.1) \qquad\quad (1.1) \qquad\qquad (5.1)$$
$$\phantom{\hat{c}_{nt} =} + 0.083Z_t + 0.666c_{n,t-1}$$
$$\phantom{\hat{c}_{nt} = +} (3.5) \qquad (10.0)$$
$$R^2 = 0.994 \qquad \hat{\sigma}_\varepsilon = 0.003$$

$$\hat{c}_{dt} = 0.074 - 0.104p_{dt} + 0.405w_t + 0.067y_{Rt} - 0.006r_{Lt} + 0.002\text{WLTH}_{t-1}$$
$$\phantom{\hat{c}_{dt} =} (3.6) \qquad (3.1) \qquad\quad (4.1) \qquad (1.2) \qquad\quad (8.0) \qquad\qquad (6.2)$$
$$\phantom{\hat{c}_{dt} =} + 0.123Z_t + 0.458c_{d,t-1}$$
$$\phantom{\hat{c}_{dt} = +} (3.3) \qquad (6.0)$$
$$R^2 = 0.989 \qquad \hat{\sigma}_\varepsilon = 0.004$$

where c_s, c_n, and c_d are real per-capita consumption expenditures on services, non-durable goods, and durable goods, respectively; p_n and p_d are the Implicit Price Deflators for nondurable and durable goods, respectively; w is the after-tax wage rate; WLTH is real per-capita wealth; r_s and r_L are after-tax short-term and long-term interest rates, respectively; y_n is real per-capita non-labor income; y_R is real per-capita transfer payment income; and Z is the labor market slack variable discussed above.

To make this set of equations consistent with the model given by Equations (14.11)–(14.14) in Chapter 14, a consumption identity could also be added to this set of equations:

$$c_t = c_{st} + c_{nt} + c_{dt}$$

where c_t is total personal consumption expenditures. Because the equations above contain real after-tax wages and not real disposable personal income, the wage co-efficient in each coefficient is not an estimated marginal propensity to consume. Remember that the test statistic indicated below each coefficient is the value for an asymptotically normally distributed random variable, since two-stage least squares estimators are biased but possess the large sample property of consistency. Values from the normal distribution table can therefore be used to determine the statistical significance of these coefficients. In the above equations, after-tax wages are statisti-cally significant in every equation. The same is not true for non-labor income and transfer payment income: one of these measures is statistically significant for only the nondurable goods equation. In contrast, lagged per-capita real wealth is statistically significant in every equation above, as is the labor market slack variable, Z. ∎

■ **A MODEL OF PROTECTIONISM**   Salvatore examined the effect of protectionist pressures on import penetration in the United States by focusing on a specific type of nontariff barrier to trade—the escape clause petition for protection.[19] An escape clause petition can be filed when imports of a good that was previously granted some form of concessions in a trade agreement rise substantially enough to threaten domestic producers of that good. When an investigation into the validity of such a petition determines that domestic producers were injured, the original trade concessions can be either changed or withdrawn.[20] Salvatore focuses on this type of measure, since, unlike other measures of nontariff protection, it is readily quantifiable.

Salvatore's model is a simultaneous equation system of the joint determination of import penetration into the United States, measured by imports as a proportion of GNP (M); the number of escape clause petitions filed in a year (N); and the proportion of successful escape clause petitions (S). As Salvatore notes, the number of petitions filed is a measure of protectionist pressure, while the proportion of successful petitions corresponds to the extent of actual protectionism. His estimated equations, which use annual data for the years 1948 to 1985, are:

$$\hat{M}_t = 0.004 - 0.0004N_t - 0.008S_t + 0.002E_{t-1} + 0.988M_{t-1}$$
$$\phantom{\hat{M}_t = 0.004 - }(2.2)(1.6)(1.0)(24.4)$$
$$R^2 = 0.96 \qquad \hat{\sigma}_\varepsilon = 0.005 \qquad h = 0.19$$

$$\hat{N}_t = 12.1 - 0.084Y_t - 91.60M_t - 2.74S_t - 6.16D6374_t + 4.04D7579_t$$
$$\phantom{\hat{N}_t = 12.1 - }(3.1)(1.0)(1.0)(3.5)(2.9)$$
$$R^2 = 0.68 \qquad \hat{\sigma}_\varepsilon = 2.49 \qquad DW = 2.07$$

$$\hat{S}_t = 0.075 + 2.24M_t - 0.019XN_t - 0.107D6374_t - 0.0002D7579_t$$
$$\phantom{\hat{S}_t = 0.075 + }(0.9)(0.1)(2.5)(0.1)$$
$$R^2 = 0.40 \qquad \hat{\sigma}_\varepsilon = 0.154 \qquad DW = 2.05$$

where: M, N, and S are defined above; E is a dummy variable equal to 1 when the dollar was deemed to be overvalued, 1958–1960, 1969–1972, 1975–1977, and 1982–1985, 0 otherwise; Y is real GNP; XN is real merchandise net exports; D6374 is a dummy variable equal to 1 from 1963–1974, 0 otherwise; and D7579 is a dummy variable equal to 1 from 1975–1979, 0 otherwise. The dummy variables are included to test whether the mean number of petitions or proportion of successful petitions differs significantly during the periods of either the Trade Expansion Act of 1962 (D6374), or for the Trade Act of 1974 (D7579).

---

[19] D. Salvatore, "Import Penetration, Exchange Rates, and Protectionism in the United States," *Journal of Policy Marketing* 9 (1987), 125—141.

[20] This discussion oversimplifies the entire process involved, since only the basic information is needed before a discussion of the empirical investigation can proceed.

In the import penetration equation, both the number of petitions filed and the proportion of successful petitions are expected to be negatively related to import penetration. Thus, as either protectionist pressure (N) or the extent of protectionism (S) rise, imports are expected to fall as a percentage of GNP. Also, mean import penetration is expected to be higher when the dollar is overvalued, giving a positive expected sign to E. This variable is lagged since exchange rate changes require a number of months before imports can make substantial inroads into the U.S. market (this is sometimes called the *J*-curve effect). For the number of petitions equation, both import penetration and the proportion of successful petitions have positive signs. The greater is import penetration, the more likely are "violations" to trade agreements to occur. Also, an increase in S signals a greater likelihood of winning concessions as the result of filing escape clause petitions, resulting in a greater number of petitions filed. The number of petitions is inversely related to real GNP, since, as the domestic economy expands, job losses to imports are offset somewhat by gains in domestic sales. Finally, the proportion of successful petitions is expected to be positively related to import penetration, based on the belief that greater import penetration raises the extent of actual protectionism, and negatively related to real merchandise net exports.

A major problem with Salvatore's results is that none of the endogenous explanatory variables in the equations for the number of petitions and proportion of successful petitions are statistically significant (their asymptotic Z values are 1.0 or less). In fact, the only statistically significant variable in the proportion of successful petitions equation is a dummy variable. Salvatore included this equation in his model to determine

> ... if the interpretation and enforcement of the trade laws in the United States are affected by the international position of the nation, as measured by the level of import penetration and trade balance after explicitly taking into consideration the changes in the trade laws themselves.[21]

His theoretical presumption about the joint determination of M, N, and S may well be correct. Quite possibly, the equation for S is inadequately specified, leading to problems with the predicted endogenous variables in the other equations. It is reasonable to believe that a "momentum" can exist for successful petitions, leading to the conclusion that the lagged value of S should appear in the proportion of successful petitions equation. Also, the receptiveness of different presidents to escape clauses is likely to vary. This is certainly true for the Reagan administration. Thus a dummy variable for the years 1981 to the end of Salvatore's data may well be appropriate. Finally, Salvatore notes these problems with individual coefficients in his model. He further tested it with a series of dynamic simulations, in which lagged import penetration was replaced by values predicted from the model (after one period). The overall performance of this model was satisfactory in this setting, thus vindicating the performance of individual equations somewhat. ■

---

[21] D. Salvatore, p. 133.

■ A MODEL OF SHORT-TERM INTEREST RATES

Clarida and Fried-man developed a small macroeconometric model to explain the relatively high short-term interest rates in the early 1980s.[22] During the early part of the 1980s, nominal interest rates set record highs several times. Then, when inflation began its decline from double-digit levels, high real interest rates resulted. The concern by Clarida and Friedman was that the recovery, which was in its early stages at the time of their article, might be cut short by such high real interest rates, as was the case for the relatively short recovery from the 1980 recession.

Clarida and Friedman formulated a six-equation model (five behavioral equations and an identity) to analyze the behavior of short-term interest rates and to seek answers to the following questions: (i) Are short-term interest rates higher than they would have been if historical trends continued to exist?; and (ii) If the answer to (i) is yes, can the different behavior of short-term interest rates be explained within the "typical" framework of macroeconomic analysis?

To some extent, the relatively high interest rates of the early 1980s resulted from the operating procedure utilized by Paul Volker at the FED. Prior to his arrival, the FED concentrated largely on stabilizing interest rates. Volker's approach, which was necessary to combat the inflation that existed when he assumed the position of FED Chairman, focused on stabilizing monetary growth rates within target ranges. The outcome of this operating procedure was, unfortunately, to cause greater volatility in interest rates. In addition to this, interest rates rose to levels exceeding those that would have been allowed under the previous operating procedure. By utilizing an econometric model, Clarida and Friedman attempt to simulate what interest rate behavior would have been had the previous operating procedure continued after 1979. The ability to perform such simulations is one of the major benefits of econometric models.

The basis for Volker's operating procedure can be seen by manipulating the equation for the Quantity Theory of Money (see Chapter 1):

$$M \cdot V = P \cdot Q$$

where M is the nominal money supply; V is the (income) velocity of circulation; P is the price level; and Q is real GNP. Manipulation of this equation allows each term to be expressed as a growth rate. To do this, we first apply a logarithmic transformation to both sides of this equation:

$$\ln(M) + \ln(V) = \ln(P) + \ln(Q)$$

then take the first difference of the resulting equation:

$$\Delta \ln(M) + \Delta \ln(V) = \Delta \ln(P) + \Delta \ln(Q)$$

---

[22] R. Clarida and B. Friedman, "Why Have Short-Term Interest Rates Been So High?," *Brookings Papers on Economic Activity* 2 (1983), 553–578.

Recall, from Chapter 3, that the change in the natural logarithm of a variable is related to its growth rate. Applying this to the term involving M above:

$$\Delta \ln(M) = \ln(M)_t - \ln(M)_{t-1}$$
$$= \ln(M_t/M_{t-1})$$
$$= \ln(1 + g_M)$$

where g_M is the proportionate growth rate in M. For small values of g_M:

$$\ln(1 + g_M) \approx g_M$$

Applying this information to the first difference equation above:

$$g_M + g_V = g_P + g_Q$$

The proportional change in the money supply plus that in velocity equals the inflation rate (g_P) plus the rate of economic growth (g_Q). If we assume that velocity is either constant or stable and predictable, we may omit the term g_V. To obtain a rule for monetary growth that does not result in inflation, we set the inflation term, g_P, equal to 0. The equation then reduces to:

$$g_M = g_Q$$

For noninflationary monetary growth when velocity is constant or predictable, the nominal supply of money should grow at the same rate as Q, or at the overall rate of economic growth. This is called the monetary rule. Monetary growth in excess of the economy's rate of growth will tend to produce demand-pull inflation, where "too much money chases too few goods." Were the FED to stabilize interest rates in times of high or rising inflation, the result would often require $g_M > g_Q$, exacerbating inflation. Thus, Volker's operating procedure in the early 1980s was based on the monetary rule.

The equations formulated by Clarida and Friedman that are reported here use quarterly data from 1961:1 to 1979:3 for estimation. Dynamic simulations were then run for the period 1979:4 (Volker's arrival) to 1983:2. The variables in all but one of these equations are stated in terms of proportionate growth rates, or changes in the natural logarithms of these variables. Each equation includes a lagged dependent variable. In light of problems encountered with autocorrelated errors, Clarida and Friedman estimated these equations with Fair's method for dealing with two-stage least squares with autocorrelated errors and lagged dependent variables. The resulting equations are:

Aggregate Demand:

$$\widehat{\Delta \ln(Q)_t} = 0.006 - 0.103\Delta \ln(r_L)_t + 0.102\Delta \ln(E)_t$$
$$\quad (4.8) \quad (2.9) \quad\quad\quad\quad (2.0)$$
$$- 0.069\Delta \ln(P_M)_{t-1} + 0.440\Delta \ln(Q)_{t-1}$$
$$\quad (2.2) \quad\quad\quad\quad (5.0)$$
$$\bar{R}^2 = 0.49 \quad\quad \hat{\sigma}_\varepsilon = 0.008 \quad\quad \hat{\Theta} = -0.4$$

Aggregate Supply:

$$\widehat{\Delta \ln(P)_t} = 0.090\Delta \ln(Q)_{t-1} + 0.054\Delta \ln(P_M)_{t-1} + 0.870\Delta \ln(P)_{t-1}$$
$$\qquad (3.4) \qquad\qquad (3.9) \qquad\qquad\qquad (25.2)$$
$$\bar{R}^2 = 0.88 \qquad \hat{\sigma}_\varepsilon = 0.003 \qquad \hat{\Theta} = -0.1$$

Money Demand:

$$\widehat{\Delta(\ln(M) - ln(P))_t} = 0.119\Delta \ln(Q)_t - 0.041\Delta \ln(r_s)_t + 0.870\Delta(\ln(M) - \ln(P))_{t-1}$$
$$\qquad\qquad (1.9) \qquad\qquad (3.9) \qquad\qquad\qquad (7.7)$$
$$\bar{R}^2 = 0.53 \qquad \hat{\sigma}_\varepsilon = 0.007 \qquad \hat{\Theta} = -0.5$$

Money Supply:

$$\widehat{\Delta \ln(M)_t} = 0.003 + 0.212\Delta \ln(R)_{t-1} + 0.010\Delta \ln(r_s)_t - 0.023\Delta \ln(r_D)_t + 0.763\Delta \ln(M)_{t-1}$$
$$\quad (2.3) \quad (2.1) \qquad\qquad (0.6) \qquad\qquad (1.3) \qquad\qquad (8.6)$$
$$\bar{R}^2 = 0.53 \qquad \hat{\sigma}_\varepsilon = 0.005 \qquad \hat{\Theta} = -0.2$$

Term Structure of Interest Rates:

$$\widehat{\Delta \ln(r_L)_t} = 0.047 + 0.144\Delta \ln(r_s)_t - 0.058\Delta \ln(r_s)_{t-1}$$
$$\qquad (1.4) \quad (1.1) \qquad\qquad (0.5)$$
$$+ 0.138\Delta(\ln(D_L) - \ln(D_s))_{t-1} + 0.910\Delta \ln(r_L)_{t-1}$$
$$\qquad (2.3) \qquad\qquad\qquad (37.0)$$
$$\bar{R}^2 = 0.98 \qquad \hat{\sigma}_\varepsilon = 0.020 \qquad \hat{\Theta} = 0.4$$

Nominal Income Identity:

$$\Delta \ln(y)_t \equiv \Delta \ln(Q)_t + \Delta \ln(P)_t$$

The aggregate demand equation, which is stated in terms of the growth of real GNP (Q) includes an endogenous long-term interest rate, r_L, which is the rate on Moody's Baa corporate bonds. The inclusion of this variable makes this equation consistent with the IS model framework. In addition to the interest rate, aggregate demand includes a fiscal policy variable, E, high employment federal government expenditures, and the IPD for imports, P_M. Since this is a first difference equation with an intercept, the estimated intercept can be viewed as the coefficient of a time trend (see Chapter 8). The aggregate supply function is a relationship between the proportionate growth rate in the Implicit Price Deflator (P) and lagged growth rates in real GNP (Q) and the IPD for imports (P_M).

The monetary segment of this model consists of a money demand function, a money supply function, and a term structure of interest rates equation that links short-term with long-term interest rates. The dependent variable in the money demand equation, the growth in the real demand for money is $\Delta(\ln(M) - \ln(P))$, which equals $\Delta \ln(M/P)$, where M is nominal money stock M1. This is a function of the rate of economic growth ($\Delta \ln(Q)$), which determines the transactions demand for money, a short-term interest rate (r_s), the three-month Treasury Bill rate, which represents the opportunity cost of holding money, and a lagged dependent variable, which is consistent with the partial adjustment framework that is fairly typical for money demand equations. The money supply function is stated in terms of growth in the nominal money supply ($\Delta \ln(M)$). This is related to nonborrowed reserves (R); short-term interest rates (r_s); the discount rate (r_D); and the lagged money supply. This formulation of the money supply function allows for different possible monetary growth rates resulting from either growth in non-borrowed reserves, changes in borrowed reserves, which occur through discount rate effects, and the impact of short-term interest rates on desired levels of excess reserves.

The term structure of interest rates equation expresses a linkage between long-term and short-term interest rates. Note that most of the variables in this equation are not expressed in first difference (logarithmic) form. This equation is an important feature of this model's applicability to the IS-LM framework, since with this equation, the interest rate that affects aggregate demand (r_L) is jointly determined along with the rate that pertains for the demand and supply of money (r_s). This equation also links long-term interest rates to the differences in growth between long-term and short-term federal government debt (D_L and D_s, respectively). Thus the accumulation of national debt as the result of expansionary fiscal policy increases long-term interest rates affecting aggregate demand.

The final equation in this model, the nominal income identity, expresses growth in nominal income as the sum of real income growth ($\Delta \ln(Q)$) and inflation ($\Delta \ln(P)$). *Since this is an identity and not a behavioral relationship, it is not necessary to estimate this equation. Its coefficients are all 1.0.*

The endogenous variables in this model (forgetting natural logarithms and changes) are Q, y, P, M, r_L, and r_s. These are determined by the set of exogenous variables: E; P_M; R; r_D; D_L; D_s; $r_{s,t-1}$; and the lagged dependent variables in these equations. To explore the basis for Clarida and Friedman's investigation of the behavior of short-term interest rates in the early 1980s, we will trace out the effects of a slowing of monetary growth that results from an exogenous decrease in non-borrowed reserves (R). To simplify this, we will view the levels of the different variables involved and not their growth rates.

An exogenous fall in R, brought about by the FED's more recent operating procedure, lowers the supply of money. As a result of this action, short-term interest rates rise, which both lowers the real demand for money and increases long-term interest rates (from the term structure equation). The existence of higher long-term interest rates depresses aggregate demand, causing reductions in both Q (through the aggregate demand equation) and y (from the income identity).

Clarida and Friedman utilized their model for a number of historical simulations which they used to answer the questions posed earlier. Their results showed consistent underprediction of short-term interest rates. Their conclusion, based on this is: "The analysis reveals that short-term interest rates since October 1979 have been 'too high' . . . the familiar story of relatively little money for the prevailing levels of economic activity . . . goes a long way toward explaining why this has been so . . . ."[23]

■

---

[23] Clarida and Friedman, p. 556.

■ A MODEL OF THE UNEMPLOYMENT RATE AND REAL COMPENSATION GROWTH

The behavior of the unemployment rate has been analyzed throughout this text. Starting with a simple bivariate relationship between the unemployment rate and the capacity utilization rate in Chapter 2, this framework was then extended to include a secular trend, after which it was stated in terms of a polynomial distributed lag of capacity utilization rates. We now extend our modeling of this variable one step further: into a simultaneous equations context.

The model discussed here focuses on the joint determination of the unemployment rate and the growth rate in real compensation. The basic information in this model is summarized by the following structural equations:

$$U_t = f_1(GW_t, CAP_t, ST_t, \Delta HPW_t, U_{t-1}, \varepsilon_{1t}) \tag{15.44}$$

$$GW_t = f_2(U_t, GP_t, t, \Delta U_{t-1}, \varepsilon_{2t}) \tag{15.45}$$

where U is the civilian unemployment rate; GW is the annual percent change in real hourly compensation in the non-farm business sector (1982 = 100); CAP is the capacity utilization rate in manufacturing; ST is a measure of the secular trend in the unemployment rate; HPW is hours per worker in the non-farm business sector; GP is the annual growth rate in output per worker of all persons in the non-farm business sector; and t is a time trend.

There are two endogenous variables in this model: the unemployment rate and the growth rate real hourly compensation are jointly determined. The basis for their joint determination will be established by referring to Equation (15.44). If GW rises, then given the state of the economy (CAP); the secular trend in U (ST); changes in hours per worker (ΔHPW); and last period's U, firms are filling their labor requirements by increasing the number of workers, causing the unemployment rate to fall. This causation is not unidirectional. When the unemployment rate falls, the amount of labor market slack decreases, which raises upward pressure on real wages, causing GW to rise. The joint determination of U and GW can therefore be summarized in the following way:

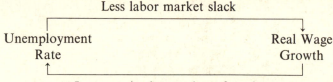

Less labor market slack

Unemployment   Real Wage
Rate   Growth

Increases in the number of workers

Equations (15.44) and (15.45) were given linear specifications, then estimated by two-stage least squares using annual data for the period from 1955 to 1990. The resulting equations are:

$$\hat{U}_t = 7.67 - 0.123GW_t - 0.080CAP_t + 0.071t - 0.001t^2$$
$$\phantom{\hat{U}_t =} (2.5) \quad (1.7) \qquad\quad (2.4) \qquad\quad (1.5) \qquad (1.6)$$

$$\phantom{\hat{U}_t =} - 0.304\,\Delta HPW_t - 0.136D6773_t + 0.775U_{t-1}$$
$$\phantom{\hat{U}_t =} (4.4) \qquad\qquad (0.5) \qquad\qquad (6.6)$$

$$\bar{R}^2 = 0.962 \qquad n = 36 \qquad \hat{\sigma}_\varepsilon = 0.304 \qquad F = 127.3 \qquad h = -1.4$$

$$\widehat{GW}_t = 4.27 - 0.182U_t + 0.357GP_t - 0.092t - 23.6D8086_t$$
$$(4.6)(1.9)(2.7)(4.4)(3.2)$$
$$+ 0.649(D8086 \cdot t)_t + 0.245\,\Delta U_{t-1}$$
$$(3.3)(1.5)$$
$$\bar{R}^2 = 0.719 \qquad n = 36 \qquad \hat{\sigma}_\varepsilon = 0.946 \qquad F = 16.0 \qquad DW = 1.96$$

The secular trend in the unemployment rate equation is represented by a quadratic function of the time trend. The statistical significance of this secular trend (and thus the time trend) is ascertained using a Wald Test performed as outlined earlier with the residual sum of squares in the numerator calculated differently than that in the denominator. The value of the resulting test statistic is 19.3, which exceeds the critical F-value for 2 and 28 degrees of freedom at the 5 percent significance level. The time trend is therefore statistically significant in the unemployment rate equation. The partial slope of the time trend in that equation (the estimated secular trend in U) is obtained from the following expression (see Chapter 8):

$$0.071 - 2(0.001)t$$

This is simply the partial slope expression for a quadratically specified variable. This secular trend is upward until the last year of data ($t = 36$), when it becomes negative.

The coefficient of the growth in real compensation in this equation is negative, as expected, and statistically significant at the 5 percent level for a one-tail test (based on the asymptotic normal value of -1.65). The same is true for the capacity utilization rate and the change in hours per worker. The coefficient of the lagged unemployment rate is positive and less than one, which is consistent with the restrictions that pertain for lagged dependent variables. The dummy variable D6773, which is included to test for differences in the mean unemployment rate over the period from 1967 to 1973 (when it equals 1) is not statistically significant. The Durbin-h statistic from the unemployment rate equation indicates the absence of autocorrelated errors in that equation.

The coefficient of U in the growth in compensation equation is negative and statistically significant for a one-tail test. The sign of ΔU_{t-1} is the opposite of that expected and statistically insignificant. The growth in productivity variable, GP, is positively related to compensation growth and statistically significant. Other things being equal, increases in productivity raise real compensation, causing GW to rise. The time trend in this equation is multiplicative with the dummy variable D8086, which allows the trend in compensation growth to differ over those years. For the period from 1980 to 1986 (when D8086 equals 1), the coefficient of the time trend is:

$$-0.092 + 0.649 = +0.557$$

The statistical significance of the variable (D8086 · t) indicates that the *difference* in the trend rate for real compensation growth from 1980 to 1986 is statistically significant. The Durbin-Watson statistic for this equation is consistent with nonautocorrelated errors.

Two different sets of ex-post forecasts of the endogenous variables in this model were generated. For each of these, the model was estimated from 1955–1986, then forecasts were produced for 1987 through 1990. Since this model contains lagged endogenous variables, this is a dynamic equation system. To obtain predicted values for the unemployment rate and the growth in real compensation, the system of equations (which includes a difference equation) must be solved. The predictions generated for this exercise are based on a dynamic simulation, where, after the first year of the forecast (1987), values of the lagged unemployment rate are based on predictions of the unemployment rate from the solved set of equations.

The first simulation uses actual values of the exogenous variables to predict the endogenous variables (after solving the model). Figure 15.4 shows the actual and ex-post forecasts of the unemployment rate. Figure 15.5 is a similar graph for real compensation growth. As these figures illustrate, the model predicts the endogenous variables well, though the unemployment equation tracks the actual data better than does the compensation growth equation. From 1988 to 1990, predicted compensation growth is consistently above actual values.

The second simulation attempts to determine the differences in these endogenous variables if, instead of the actual values for the capacity utilization rate, that rate remained at 84 percent throughout the entire forecast period. Although the capacity utilization rate appears only in the unemployment rate equation, changes in its level

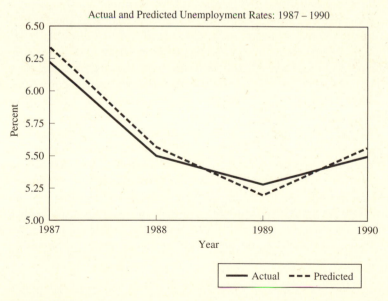

Figure 15.4

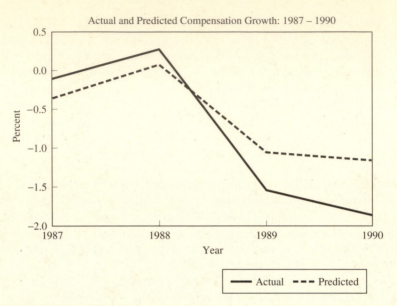

Actual and Predicted Compensation Growth: 1987 – 1990

Figure 15.5

also affect real compensation growth, since the unemployment rate and real compensation growth are jointly determined. Figure 15.6 shows the actual unemployment rate and the two sets of predictions, one with the actual capacity utilization rate, the other assuming an 84 percent rate. As expected, the predicted unemployment rate is consistently lower with this higher capacity utilization rate. The difference between these predictions grows larger toward the end of the forecast period. Figure 15.7 contrasts the actual growth in real compensation with the two sets of forecasts. Predicted compensation growth is larger with the higher capacity utilization rate, since labor markets are tighter in this scenario than the one based on actual capacity utilization rates. The differences between these two sets of predictions are not very large, however.

This last forecasting exercise illustrates one of the important uses of econometric models: simulating values of endogenous variables under different scenarios. Above, we contrasted predictions of the unemployment rate and the rate of real compensation growth under two different scenarios, one based on actual values of the exogenous variables, the other for hypothetical values. Other possibilities also exist. Often, different policy actions are simulated with an econometric model, then the range of possible outcomes is studied. From this, government policy makers can develop "best case" and "worst case" scenarios for events they are likely to encounter in the near future. While exercises such as these are imperfect, and subject to some error, their greatest advantage is that they are *systematic*. If such simulations are used for policy analysis or decision-making, and errors occur, policy makers can check their model to see where the problems lie, then attempt to correct these. For example, they might determine that their model is too aggregated. To improve future forecasts, they might

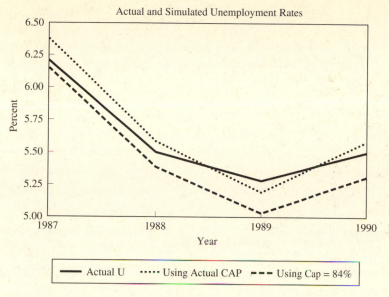

Figure 15.6

then reformulate the model with less aggregation, which entails the use of more endogenous variables and a larger model (such as breaking total consumption expenditure into its three components). They might also change the classifications of one or
more variables that were previously exogenous to endogenous in the reformulated

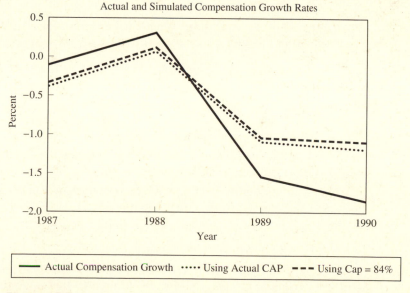

Figure 15.7

model. This also results in a larger model. While these examples point to making models larger, it is sometimes necessary to reduce the size of a model to improve its forecast performance. In both cases, experience working with and analyzing the performance of a particular model is probably the most important prerequisite for improving its performance. ■

KEY TERMS

Determinant

Dynamic simulation

Exactly identified

Full-information methods

Identification problem

Identified

Indirect least squares

Limited information methods

Normalizing restriction

Observationally equivalent

Order condition

Overidentified

Paradox of identification

Principal components analysis

Rank condition

Restricted estimation

Structurally ordered instrumental variable

Two-stage least squares

Under-identified

Unidentified

Unrestricted estimation

Zero restriction

EXERCISES

1. What is equation identification? Why is it important for estimating simultaneous equation models?

2. Using the following set of equations, where the y's are endogenous and the x's are exogenous:

$$y_{1i} = \alpha_0 + \alpha_1 y_{2i} + \alpha_2 x_{1i} + \alpha_3 x_{2i} + \alpha_4 x_{3i} + \varepsilon_{1i}$$

$$y_{2i} = \beta_0 + \beta_1 y_{1i} + \beta_2 x_{2i} + \varepsilon_{2i}$$

    (a) Which of these equations are identified based on the order condition? If one is under-identified, explain why this occurs.

    (b) If a linear restriction exists for the first equation, where $\alpha_2 + \alpha_3 = 1$, does this affect the identification of that equation?

    (c) How can the linear restriction stated in (b) be tested?

    (d) Derive the reduced form equations for y_1 and y_2.

3. If we assume that the error in the second equation above is first-order auto-correlated, where $\varepsilon_{2t} = \Theta \varepsilon_{2,t-1} + v_t$, illustrate how this equation is estimated with two-stage least squares. If this equation also contained a lagged depen-

dent variable, would that variable be exogenous when autocorrelation was present?

4. What is indirect least squares? When is this an appropriate estimation technique? When is it inappropriate (or impractical)?

5. Is least squares estimation of an exactly identified equation appropriate? Explain why (or why not).

6. How is autocorrelation detected in structural equations? If it exists, how is autocorrelation corrected?

7. Explain how equation identification is related to the existence of potential instruments for instrumental variable estimation techniques such as two-stage least squares.

8. Contrast restricted with unrestricted estimation as methods for generating forecasts from simultaneous equation models.

9. In the short-term interest rate model of Clarida and Friedman presented earlier in this chapter, there is a term structure of interest rates equation, where long-term interest rates are a function of (endogenous) short-term rates. Explain the theoretical basis for the "feedback loop" from long-term to short-term interest rates in that equation which establishes the endogeneity of short-term rates.

10. Contrast the steps involved in performing the Wald Test between structural and non-structural equations. Where do the differences arise?

APPENDIX   MicroTSP and SAS Commands to Perform Two-Stage Least Squares

This chapter detailed how to estimate structural equations using two-stage least squares and presented several examples that employ this technique. This appendix illustrates the commands needed to perform this analysis for the two canned computer programs discussed throughout this text: MicroTSP and SAS.

The simultaneous equation model used as the basis for this illustration is the following:

$$y_{1t} = \alpha_0 + \alpha_1 y_{2t} + \alpha_2 x_{1t} + \alpha_3 x_{3t} + \varepsilon_{1t}$$

$$y_{2t} = \beta_0 + \beta_1 y_{1t} + \beta_2 x_{2t} + \beta_3 x_{4t} + \varepsilon_{2t}$$

where the y's are endogenous variables and the x's are exogenous. Both of these equations are overidentified based on the order condition. Two-stage least squares estimation of this equation set proceeds in the following way:

1. Regress each endogenous explanatory variable, y_1 and y_2, on the set of exogenous variables in this entire system, x_1, x_2, x_3 and x_4 (this estimates the reduced-form equation for each of these endogenous variables), and obtain the predicted values for these variables: $\hat{y}_1$ and $\hat{y}_2$. These predicted values serve as the instrumental variables for actual y_1 and y_2 in the next step.

2. Estimate each structural equation with least squares using the newly created instrumental variables in place of the actual endogenous explanatory variables. In other words, estimate the following equations with least squares:

$$y_{1t} = \alpha_0 + \alpha_1 \hat{y}_{2t} + \alpha_2 x_{1t} + \alpha_3 x_{3t} + \varepsilon_{1t}^*$$

$$y_{2t} = \beta_0 + \beta_1 \hat{y}_{1t} + \beta_2 x_{2t} + \beta_3 x_{4t} + \varepsilon_{2t}^*$$

Consistent estimates of the sum of the squared errors and individual coefficients variances must use the two-stage least squares coefficients and *actual* y_1 and y_2, not their predicted values. Generally, canned statistical programs that include a two-stage least squares routine proceed in this way by design. We now turn to each computer program.

MicroTSP

MicroTSP uses the TSLS command to produce two-stage least squares estimates. This command begins with the same syntax that is used for least squares estimation. Additional information is needed so that MicroTSP can determine which explanatory variable is endogenous and the set of regressors to include in the first-stage regression. The general form of this command is:

TSLS *dep* C *explanatory variables* @ *list of exogenous variables*

where *dep* denotes the dependent variable, and C is used if an intercept is desired. The command for the first structural equation above is:

```
>TSLS Y1 C Y2 X1 X3 @ C X1 X2 X3 X4
```

Since the variable Y2 is not included in the list of exogenous variables after the "@" sign, MicroTSP regresses this variable on the list of exogenous variables. Keep in mind that for two-stage least squares estimation of overidentified equations, the set of *all* exogenous variables in the set of equations must be included after the "@" sign. If only the exogenous variables from the equation being estimated are included, the result will be perfect multicollinearity. MicroTSP will respond with the statement:

```
Near Singular Matrix
```

which indicates that the variables that make up the data set are linearly dependent.

A separate TSLS command is required for each structural equation that is to be estimated. The command for the second structural equation above is:

```
>TSLS Y2 C Y1 X2 X4 @ C X1 X2 X3 X4
```

Note that the variable list after each "@" sign is identical for both of these commands, as required.

SAS

SAS accomplishes two-stage least squares estimation as part of its PROC for *systems* of *linear* equations, PROC SYSLIN. The user informs SAS that two-stage least squares is desired by including the 2SLS option in the PROC SYSLIN statement:

```
PROC SYSLIN 2SLS;
```

The regression model statement for each structural equation in this PROC is identical to that for least squares estimation in PROC REG:

MODEL *dep = list of explanatory variables*;

where *dep* is the name of the dependent variable. For the first structural equation above, this statement is:

```
MODEL Y1=Y2 X1 X3;
```

There must be a separate MODEL statement for each structural equation that is to be estimated. If this were the only information provided, SAS would have no way of knowing which of the explanatory variables are endogenous and which are exogenous. MicroTSP determines this with the inclusion of "@" followed by a list of exogenous variables. SAS uses two separate statements that define the exogenous and endogenous variables. These statements are:

INSTRUMENTS *list of exogenous variables*;

ENDOGENOUS *list of endogenous variables*;

For this example, these statements are:

```
INSTRUMENTS X1 X2 X3 X4;
ENDOGENOUS Y1 Y2;
```

Equipped with this information, SAS will regress any explanatory variable in a MODEL statement that is included in the ENDOGENOUS list on the set of variables in the INSTRUMENTS statement.

The complete set of SAS statements used to obtain two-stage least squares estimates of the set of equations above is:

```
PROC SYSLIN 2SLS;
  MODEL Y1=Y2 X1 X3;
  MODEL Y2=Y1 X2 X4;
 INSTRUMENTS X1 X2 X3 X4;
 ENDOGENOUS Y1 Y2;
```

S tatistical Tables

Probabilities in the Right Tail of the Standard Normal Distribution

Z	PROB	Z	PROB	Z	PROB	Z	PROB	Z	PROB	Z	PROB
0.00	0.500	0.50	0.309	1.00	0.159	1.50	0.067	2.00	0.023	2.50	0.006
0.01	0.496	0.51	0.305	1.01	0.156	1.51	0.066	2.01	0.022	2.51	0.006
0.02	0.492	0.52	0.302	1.02	0.154	1.52	0.064	2.02	0.022	2.52	0.006
0.03	0.488	0.53	0.298	1.03	0.152	1.53	0.063	2.03	0.021	2.53	0.006
0.04	0.484	0.54	0.295	1.04	0.149	1.54	0.062	2.04	0.021	2.54	0.006
0.05	0.480	0.55	0.291	1.05	0.147	1.55	0.061	2.05	0.020	2.55	0.005
0.06	0.476	0.56	0.288	1.06	0.145	1.56	0.059	2.06	0.020	2.56	0.005
0.07	0.472	0.57	0.284	1.07	0.142	1.57	0.058	2.07	0.019	2.57	0.005
0.08	0.468	0.58	0.281	1.08	0.140	1.58	0.057	2.08	0.019	2.58	0.005
0.09	0.464	0.59	0.278	1.09	0.138	1.59	0.056	2.09	0.018	2.59	0.005
0.10	0.460	0.60	0.274	1.10	0.136	1.60	0.055	2.10	0.018	2.60	0.005
0.11	0.456	0.61	0.271	1.11	0.134	1.61	0.054	2.11	0.017	2.61	0.005
0.12	0.452	0.62	0.268	1.12	0.131	1.62	0.053	2.12	0.017	2.62	0.004
0.13	0.448	0.63	0.264	1.13	0.129	1.63	0.052	2.13	0.017	2.63	0.004
0.14	0.444	0.64	0.261	1.14	0.127	1.64	0.051	2.14	0.016	2.64	0.004
0.15	0.440	0.65	0.258	1.15	0.125	1.65	0.050	2.15	0.016	2.65	0.004
0.16	0.436	0.66	0.255	1.16	0.123	1.66	0.049	2.16	0.015	2.66	0.004
0.17	0.433	0.67	0.251	1.17	0.121	1.67	0.048	2.17	0.015	2.67	0.004
0.18	0.429	0.68	0.248	1.18	0.119	1.68	0.047	2.18	0.015	2.68	0.004
0.19	0.425	0.69	0.245	1.19	0.117	1.69	0.046	2.19	0.014	2.69	0.004
0.20	0.421	0.70	0.242	1.20	0.115	1.70	0.045	2.20	0.014	2.70	0.004
0.21	0.417	0.71	0.239	1.21	0.113	1.71	0.044	2.21	0.014	2.71	0.003
0.22	0.413	0.72	0.236	1.22	0.111	1.72	0.043	2.22	0.013	2.72	0.003
0.23	0.409	0.73	0.233	1.23	0.109	1.73	0.042	2.23	0.013	2.73	0.003
0.24	0.405	0.74	0.230	1.24	0.108	1.74	0.041	2.24	0.013	2.74	0.003
0.25	0.401	0.75	0.227	1.25	0.106	1.75	0.040	2.25	0.012	2.75	0.003
0.26	0.397	0.76	0.224	1.26	0.104	1.76	0.039	2.26	0.012	2.76	0.003
0.27	0.394	0.77	0.221	1.27	0.102	1.77	0.038	2.27	0.012	2.77	0.003
0.28	0.390	0.78	0.218	1.28	0.100	1.78	0.038	2.28	0.011	2.78	0.003
0.29	0.386	0.79	0.215	1.29	0.099	1.79	0.037	2.29	0.011	2.79	0.003
0.30	0.382	0.80	0.212	1.30	0.097	1.80	0.036	2.30	0.011	2.80	0.003
0.31	0.378	0.81	0.209	1.31	0.095	1.81	0.035	2.31	0.010	2.81	0.003
0.32	0.375	0.82	0.206	1.32	0.093	1.82	0.034	2.32	0.010	2.82	0.002
0.33	0.371	0.83	0.203	1.33	0.092	1.83	0.034	2.33	0.010	2.83	0.002
0.34	0.367	0.84	0.201	1.34	0.090	1.84	0.033	2.34	0.010	2.84	0.002
0.35	0.363	0.85	0.198	1.35	0.089	1.85	0.032	2.35	0.009	2.85	0.002
0.36	0.359	0.86	0.195	1.36	0.087	1.86	0.031	2.36	0.009	2.86	0.002
0.37	0.356	0.87	0.192	1.37	0.085	1.87	0.031	2.37	0.009	2.87	0.002
0.38	0.352	0.88	0.189	1.38	0.084	1.88	0.030	2.38	0.009	2.88	0.002
0.39	0.348	0.89	0.187	1.39	0.082	1.89	0.029	2.39	0.008	2.89	0.002
0.40	0.345	0.90	0.184	1.40	0.081	1.90	0.029	2.40	0.008	2.90	0.002
0.41	0.341	0.91	0.181	1.41	0.079	1.91	0.028	2.41	0.008	2.91	0.002
0.42	0.337	0.92	0.179	1.42	0.078	1.92	0.027	2.42	0.008	2.92	0.002
0.43	0.334	0.93	0.176	1.43	0.076	1.93	0.027	2.43	0.008	2.93	0.002
0.44	0.330	0.94	0.174	1.44	0.075	1.94	0.026	2.44	0.007	2.94	0.002
0.45	0.326	0.95	0.171	1.45	0.074	1.95	0.026	2.45	0.007	2.95	0.002
0.46	0.323	0.96	0.169	1.46	0.072	1.96	0.025	2.46	0.007	2.96	0.002
0.47	0.319	0.97	0.166	1.47	0.071	1.97	0.024	2.47	0.007	2.97	0.002
0.48	0.316	0.98	0.164	1.48	0.069	1.98	0.024	2.48	0.007	2.98	0.001
0.49	0.312	0.99	0.161	1.49	0.068	1.99	0.023	2.49	0.006	2.99	0.001
										3.00	0.001

Critical Values for the Student's t Distribution
Probabilities in Right Tail

PROBABILITY

df	0.100	0.050	0.025	0.010	0.005
1	3.178	6.314	12.706	31.821	63.637
2	1.866	2.920	4.303	6.965	9.925
3	1.638	2.353	3.182	4.541	5.841
4	1.533	2.132	2.776	3.747	4.604
5	1.476	2.015	2.571	3.365	4.032
6	1.440	1.943	2.447	3.143	3.707
7	1.415	1.895	2.365	2.998	3.499
8	1.397	1.860	2.306	2.896	3.355
9	1.383	1.833	2.262	2.821	3.250
10	1.372	1.812	2.228	2.764	3.169
11	1.363	1.796	2.201	2.718	3.106
12	1.356	1.782	2.179	2.681	3.055
13	1.350	1.771	2.160	2.650	3.012
14	1.345	1.761	2.145	2.624	2.977
15	1.341	1.753	2.131	2.602	2.947
16	1.337	1.746	2.120	2.583	2.921
17	1.333	1.740	2.110	2.567	2.898
18	1.330	1.734	2.101	2.552	2.878
19	1.328	1.729	2.093	2.539	2.861
20	1.325	1.725	2.086	2.528	2.845
21	1.323	1.721	2.080	2.518	2.831
22	1.321	1.717	2.074	2.508	2.819
23	1.319	1.714	2.069	2.500	2.807
24	1.318	1.711	2.064	2.492	2.797
25	1.316	1.708	2.060	2.485	2.787
26	1.315	1.706	2.056	2.479	2.779
27	1.314	1.703	2.052	2.473	2.771
28	1.313	1.701	2.048	2.467	2.763
29	1.311	1.699	2.045	2.462	2.756
30	1.310	1.697	2.042	2.457	2.750
40	1.303	1.684	2.021	2.423	2.704
60	1.296	1.671	2.000	2.390	2.660
120	1.289	1.658	1.980	2.358	2.617
∞	1.282	1.645	1.960	2.326	2.576

Critical Values for the Chi-Square Distribution
Probabilities in Right Tail

PROBABILITY

df	0.10	0.05	0.01
1	2.71	3.84	6.63
2	4.61	5.99	9.21
3	6.25	7.81	11.30
4	7.78	9.49	13.30
5	9.24	11.10	15.10
6	10.60	12.60	16.80
7	12.00	14.10	18.50
8	13.40	15.50	20.10
9	14.70	16.90	21.70
10	16.00	18.30	23.20
11	17.30	19.70	24.70
12	18.50	21.00	26.20
13	19.80	22.40	27.70
14	21.10	23.70	29.10
15	22.30	25.00	30.60
16	23.50	26.30	32.00
17	24.80	27.60	33.40
18	26.00	28.90	34.80
19	27.20	30.10	36.20
20	28.40	31.40	37.60
21	29.60	32.70	38.90
22	30.80	33.90	40.30
23	32.00	35.20	41.60
24	33.20	36.40	42.00
25	34.40	37.70	44.30
26	35.60	38.90	45.60
27	36.70	40.10	47.00
28	37.90	41.30	48.30
29	39.10	42.60	49.60
30	40.30	43.80	50.90
60	74.40	79.10	88.40
100	118.00	124.00	136.00

Critical Values of the F-Distribution
5 Percent Probability in Right Tail

DEGREES OF FREEDOM IN NUMERATOR

		1	2	3	4	5	6	7	8	9	10	20	100	∞
D	1	161	200	216	225	230	234	237	239	241	242	248	253	254
e	2	18.51	19.00	19.16	19.25	19.30	19.33	19.36	19.37	19.38	19.39	19.44	19.49	19.50
g	3	10.13	9.55	9.28	9.12	9.01	8.94	8.88	8.84	8.81	8.78	8.66	8.56	8.53
r	4	7.71	6.94	6.59	6.39	6.26	6.16	6.09	6.04	6.00	5.96	5.80	5.66	5.63
e	5	6.61	5.79	5.41	5.19	5.05	4.95	4.88	4.82	4.78	4.74	4.56	4.40	4.36
e	6	5.99	5.14	4.76	4.53	4.39	4.28	4.21	4.15	4.10	4.06	3.87	3.71	3.67
s	7	5.59	4.74	4.35	4.12	3.97	3.87	3.79	3.73	3.68	3.63	3.44	3.28	3.23
	8	5.32	4.46	4.07	3.84	3.69	3.58	3.50	3.44	3.39	3.34	3.15	2.98	2.93
o	9	5.12	4.26	3.86	3.63	3.48	3.37	3.29	3.23	3.18	3.13	2.93	2.76	2.71
f	10	4.96	4.10	3.71	3.48	3.33	3.22	3.14	3.07	3.02	2.97	2.77	2.59	2.54
	11	4.84	3.98	3.59	3.36	3.20	3.09	3.01	2.95	2.90	2.96	2.65	2.45	2.40
F	12	4.75	3.88	3.49	3.26	3.11	3.00	2.92	2.85	2.80	2.76	2.54	2.35	2.30
r	13	4.67	3.80	3.41	3.18	3.02	2.92	2.84	2.77	2.72	2.67	2.46	2.26	2.21
e	14	4.60	3.74	3.34	3.11	2.96	2.85	2.77	2.70	2.65	2.60	2.39	2.19	2.13
e	15	4.54	3.68	3.29	3.06	2.90	2.79	2.70	2.64	2.59	2.55	2.33	2.12	2.07
d	16	4.49	3.63	3.24	3.01	2.85	2.74	2.66	2.59	2.54	2.49	2.28	2.07	2.01
o	17	4.45	3.59	3.20	2.96	2.81	2.70	2.62	2.55	2.50	2.45	2.23	2.02	1.96
m	18	4.41	3.55	3.16	2.93	2.77	2.66	2.58	2.51	2.46	2.41	2.19	1.98	1.92
	19	4.38	3.52	3.13	2.90	2.74	2.63	2.55	2.48	2.43	2.38	2.15	1.94	1.88
i	20	4.35	3.49	3.10	2.87	2.71	2.60	2.52	2.45	2.40	2.35	2.12	1.90	1.84
n	21	4.32	3.47	3.07	2.84	2.68	2.57	2.49	2.42	2.37	2.32	2.09	1.87	1.81
	22	4.30	3.44	3.05	2.82	2.66	2.55	2.47	2.40	2.35	2.30	2.07	1.84	1.78
D	23	4.28	3.42	3.03	2.80	2.64	2.53	2.45	2.38	2.32	2.28	2.04	1.82	1.76
e	24	4.26	3.40	3.01	2.78	2.62	2.51	2.43	2.36	2.30	2.26	2.02	1.80	1.73
n	25	4.24	3.38	2.99	2.76	2.60	2.49	2.41	2.34	2.28	2.24	2.00	1.77	1.71
o	26	4.22	3.37	2.89	2.74	2.59	2.47	2.39	2.32	2.27	2.22	1.99	1.76	1.69
m	27	4.21	3.35	2.96	2.73	2.57	2.46	2.37	2.30	2.25	2.20	1.97	1.74	1.67
i	28	4.20	3.34	2.95	2.71	2.56	2.44	2.36	2.29	2.24	2.19	1.96	1.72	1.65
n	29	4.18	3.33	2.93	2.70	2.54	2.43	2.35	2.28	2.22	2.18	1.94	1.71	1.64
a	30	4.17	3.32	2.92	2.69	2.53	2.42	2.34	2.27	2.21	2.16	1.93	1.69	1.62
t	40	4.08	3.23	2.84	2.61	2.45	2.34	2.25	2.18	2.12	2.07	1.84	1.59	1.51
o	100	3.94	3.09	2.70	2.46	2.30	2.19	2.10	2.03	1.97	1.92	1.68	1.39	1.28
r	∞	3.84	2.99	2.60	2.37	2.21	2.09	2.01	1.94	1.88	1.83	1.57	1.24	1.00

Critical Values of the F-Distribution
1 Percent Probability in Right Tail

DEGREES OF FREEDOM IN NUMERATOR

		1	2	3	4	5	6	7	8	9	10	20	100	∞
D	1	4052	4999	5403	5625	5764	5859	5928	5981	6022	6056	6208	6334	6366
e	2	98.49	99.01	99.17	99.25	99.30	99.33	99.34	99.36	99.38	99.40	99.45	99.49	99.50
g	3	34.12	30.81	29.46	28.71	28.24	27.91	27.67	27.49	27.34	27.23	26.69	26.23	26.12
r	4	21.20	18.00	16.69	15.98	15.52	15.21	14.98	14.80	14.66	14.54	14.02	13.57	13.46
e	5	16.26	13.27	12.06	11.39	10.97	10.67	10.45	10.27	10.15	10.05	9.55	9.13	9.02
e	6	13.74	10.92	9.78	9.15	8.75	8.47	8.26	8.10	7.98	7.87	7.39	6.99	6.88
s	7	12.25	9.55	8.45	7.85	7.46	7.19	7.00	6.84	6.71	6.62	6.15	5.75	5.65
	8	11.26	8.65	7.59	7.01	6.63	6.37	6.19	6.03	5.91	5.82	5.36	4.96	4.86
o	9	10.56	8.02	6.99	6.42	6.06	5.80	5.62	5.47	5.35	5.26	4.80	4.41	4.31
f	10	10.04	7.56	6.55	5.99	5.64	5.39	5.21	5.06	4.95	4.85	4.41	4.01	3.91
	11	9.65	7.20	6.22	5.67	5.32	5.07	4.88	4.74	4.63	4.54	4.10	3.70	3.60
F	12	9.33	6.93	5.95	5.41	5.06	4.82	4.65	4.50	4.39	4.30	3.86	3.46	3.36
r	13	9.07	6.70	5.74	5.20	4.86	4.62	4.44	4.30	4.19	4.10	3.67	3.27	3.16
e	14	8.86	6.51	5.56	5.03	4.69	4.46	4.28	4.14	4.03	3.94	3.51	3.11	3.00
e	15	8.68	6.36	5.42	4.89	4.56	4.32	4.14	4.00	3.89	3.80	3.36	2.97	2.87
d	16	8.53	6.23	5.29	4.77	4.44	4.20	4.03	3.89	3.78	3.69	3.25	2.86	2.75
o	17	8.40	6.11	5.18	4.67	4.34	4.10	3.93	3.79	3.68	3.59	3.16	2.76	2.65
m	18	8.28	6.01	5.09	4.58	4.25	4.01	3.85	3.71	3.60	3.51	3.07	2.68	2.57
	19	8.18	5.93	5.01	4.50	4.17	3.94	3.77	3.63	3.52	3.43	3.00	2.60	2.49
i	20	8.10	5.85	4.94	4.43	4.10	3.87	3.71	3.56	3.45	3.37	2.94	2.53	2.42
n	21	8.02	5.78	4.87	4.37	4.04	3.81	3.65	3.51	3.40	3.31	2.88	2.47	2.36
	22	7.94	5.72	4.82	4.31	3.99	3.76	3.59	3.45	3.35	3.26	2.83	2.42	2.31
D	23	7.88	5.66	4.76	4.26	3.94	3.71	3.54	3.41	3.30	3.21	2.78	2.37	2.26
e	24	7.82	5.61	4.72	4.22	3.90	3.67	3.50	3.36	3.25	3.17	2.74	2.33	2.21
n	25	7.77	5.57	4.68	4.18	3.86	3.63	3.46	3.32	3.21	3.13	2.70	2.29	2.17
o	26	7.72	5.53	4.64	4.14	3.82	3.59	3.42	3.29	3.17	3.09	2.66	2.25	2.13
m	27	7.68	5.49	4.60	4.11	3.79	3.56	3.39	3.26	3.14	3.06	2.63	2.21	2.10
i	28	7.64	5.45	4.57	4.07	3.76	3.53	3.36	3.23	3.11	3.03	2.60	2.18	2.06
n	29	7.60	5.52	4.54	4.04	3.73	3.50	3.33	3.20	3.08	3.00	2.57	2.15	2.03
a	30	7.56	5.39	4.51	4.02	3.70	3.47	3.30	3.17	3.06	2.98	2.55	2.13	2.01
t	40	7.31	5.18	4.31	3.83	3.51	3.29	3.12	2.99	2.88	2.80	2.37	1.94	1.81
o	100	6.90	4.82	3.98	3.51	3.20	2.99	2.82	2.69	2.59	2.51	2.06	1.59	1.43
r	∞	6.64	4.60	3.78	3.32	3.02	2.80	2.64	2.51	2.41	2.32	1.87	1.36	1.00

Durbin–Watson Statistic
5 Percent Significance Points of d_L and d_U[a]

n	k = 1		k = 2		k = 3		k = 4		k = 5		k = 6		k = 7		k = 8		k = 9		k = 10	
	d_L	d_U	d_L	d_U	d_L	d_U	d_L	d_U	d_L	d_U	d_L	d_U	d_L	d_U	d_L	d_U	d_L	d_U	d_L	d_U
6	0.610	1.400																		
7	0.700	1.356	0.467	1.896																
8	0.763	1.332	0.559	1.777	0.368	2.287														
9	0.824	1.320	0.629	1.699	0.455	2.128	0.296	2.588												
10	0.879	1.320	0.697	1.641	0.525	2.016	0.376	2.414	0.243	2.822										
11	0.927	1.324	0.758	1.604	0.595	1.928	0.444	2.283	0.316	2.645	0.203	3.005								
12	0.971	1.331	0.812	1.579	0.658	1.864	0.512	2.177	0.379	2.506	0.268	2.832	0.171	3.149						
13	1.010	1.340	0.861	1.562	0.715	1.816	0.574	2.094	0.445	2.390	0.328	2.692	0.230	2.985	0.147	3.266				
14	1.045	1.350	0.905	1.551	0.767	1.779	0.632	2.030	0.505	2.296	0.389	2.572	0.286	2.848	0.200	3.111	0.127	3.360		
15	1.077	1.361	0.946	1.543	0.814	1.750	0.685	1.977	0.562	2.220	0.447	2.472	0.343	2.727	0.251	2.979	0.175	3.216	0.111	3.438
16	1.106	1.371	0.982	1.539	0.857	1.728	0.734	1.935	0.615	2.157	0.502	2.388	0.398	2.624	0.304	2.860	0.222	3.090	0.155	3.304
17	1.133	1.381	1.015	1.536	0.897	1.710	0.779	1.900	0.664	2.104	0.554	2.318	0.451	2.537	0.356	2.757	0.272	2.975	0.198	3.184
18	1.158	1.391	1.046	1.535	0.933	1.696	0.820	1.872	0.710	2.060	0.603	2.257	0.502	2.461	0.407	2.667	0.321	2.873	0.244	3.073
19	1.180	1.401	1.074	1.536	0.967	1.685	0.859	1.848	0.752	2.023	0.649	2.206	0.549	2.396	0.456	2.589	0.369	2.783	0.290	2.974
20	1.201	1.411	1.100	1.537	0.998	1.676	0.894	1.828	0.792	1.991	0.692	2.162	0.595	2.339	0.502	2.521	0.416	2.704	0.336	2.885
21	1.221	1.420	1.125	1.538	1.026	1.669	0.927	1.812	0.829	1.964	0.732	2.124	0.637	2.290	0.547	2.460	0.461	2.633	0.380	2.806
22	1.239	1.429	1.147	1.541	1.053	1.664	0.958	1.797	0.863	1.940	0.769	2.090	0.677	2.246	0.588	2.407	0.504	2.571	0.424	2.734
23	1.257	1.437	1.168	1.543	1.078	1.660	0.986	1.785	0.895	1.920	0.804	2.061	0.715	2.208	0.628	2.360	0.545	2.514	0.465	2.670
24	1.273	1.446	1.188	1.546	1.101	1.656	1.013	1.775	0.925	1.902	0.837	2.035	0.751	2.174	0.666	2.318	0.584	2.464	0.506	2.613
25	1.288	1.454	1.206	1.550	1.123	1.654	1.038	1.767	0.953	1.886	0.868	2.012	0.784	2.144	0.702	2.280	0.621	2.419	0.544	2.560
26	1.302	1.461	1.224	1.553	1.143	1.652	1.062	1.759	0.979	1.873	0.897	1.992	0.816	2.117	0.735	2.246	0.657	2.379	0.581	2.513
27	1.316	1.469	1.240	1.556	1.162	1.651	1.084	1.753	1.004	1.861	0.925	1.974	0.845	2.093	0.767	2.216	0.691	2.342	0.616	2.470
28	1.328	1.476	1.255	1.560	1.181	1.650	1.104	1.747	1.028	1.850	0.951	1.958	0.874	2.071	0.798	2.188	0.723	2.309	0.650	2.431
29	1.341	1.483	1.270	1.563	1.198	1.650	1.124	1.743	1.050	1.841	0.975	1.944	0.900	2.052	0.826	2.164	0.753	2.278	0.682	2.396
30	1.352	1.489	1.284	1.567	1.214	1.650	1.143	1.739	1.071	1.833	0.998	1.931	0.926	2.034	0.854	2.141	0.782	2.251	0.712	2.363
31	1.363	1.496	1.297	1.570	1.229	1.650	1.160	1.735	1.090	1.825	1.020	1.920	0.950	2.018	0.879	2.120	0.810	2.226	0.741	2.333
32	1.373	1.502	1.309	1.574	1.244	1.650	1.177	1.732	1.109	1.819	1.041	1.909	0.972	2.004	0.904	2.102	0.836	2.203	0.769	2.306
33	1.383	1.508	1.321	1.577	1.258	1.651	1.193	1.730	1.127	1.813	1.061	1.900	0.994	1.991	0.927	2.085	0.861	2.181	0.795	2.281
34	1.393	1.514	1.333	1.580	1.271	1.652	1.208	1.728	1.144	1.808	1.080	1.891	1.015	1.979	0.950	2.069	0.885	2.162	0.821	2.257
35	1.402	1.519	1.343	1.584	1.283	1.653	1.222	1.726	1.160	1.803	1.097	1.884	1.034	1.967	0.971	2.054	0.908	2.144	0.845	2.236
36	1.411	1.525	1.354	1.587	1.295	1.654	1.236	1.724	1.175	1.799	1.114	1.877	1.053	1.957	0.991	2.041	0.930	2.127	0.868	2.216
37	1.419	1.530	1.364	1.590	1.307	1.655	1.249	1.723	1.190	1.795	1.131	1.870	1.071	1.948	1.011	2.029	0.951	2.112	0.891	2.198
38	1.427	1.535	1.373	1.594	1.318	1.656	1.261	1.722	1.204	1.792	1.146	1.864	1.088	1.939	1.029	2.017	0.970	2.098	0.912	2.180
39	1.435	1.540	1.382	1.597	1.328	1.658	1.273	1.722	1.218	1.789	1.161	1.859	1.104	1.932	1.047	2.007	0.990	2.085	0.932	2.164
40	1.442	1.544	1.391	1.600	1.338	1.659	1.285	1.721	1.230	1.786	1.175	1.854	1.120	1.924	1.064	1.997	1.008	2.072	0.945	2.149
45	1.475	1.566	1.430	1.615	1.383	1.666	1.336	1.720	1.287	1.776	1.238	1.835	1.189	1.895	1.139	1.958	1.089	2.022	1.038	2.088
50	1.503	1.585	1.462	1.628	1.421	1.674	1.378	1.721	1.335	1.771	1.291	1.822	1.246	1.875	1.201	1.930	1.156	1.986	1.110	2.044
55	1.528	1.601	1.490	1.641	1.452	1.681	1.414	1.724	1.374	1.768	1.334	1.814	1.294	1.861	1.253	1.909	1.212	1.959	1.170	2.013
60	1.549	1.616	1.514	1.652	1.480	1.689	1.444	1.727	1.408	1.767	1.372	1.808	1.335	1.850	1.298	1.894	1.260	1.939	1.222	1.984
65	1.567	1.629	1.536	1.662	1.503	1.696	1.471	1.731	1.438	1.767	1.404	1.805	1.370	1.843	1.336	1.882	1.301	1.923	1.266	1.964
70	1.583	1.641	1.554	1.672	1.525	1.703	1.494	1.735	1.464	1.768	1.433	1.802	1.401	1.837	1.369	1.873	1.337	1.910	1.305	1.943
75	1.598	1.652	1.571	1.680	1.543	1.709	1.515	1.739	1.487	1.770	1.458	1.801	1.428	1.834	1.399	1.867	1.369	1.901	1.339	1.935
80	1.611	1.662	1.586	1.688	1.560	1.715	1.534	1.743	1.507	1.772	1.480	1.801	1.453	1.831	1.425	1.861	1.397	1.893	1.369	1.925
85	1.624	1.671	1.600	1.696	1.575	1.721	1.550	1.747	1.525	1.774	1.500	1.801	1.474	1.829	1.448	1.857	1.422	1.886	1.396	1.916
90	1.635	1.679	1.612	1.703	1.589	1.726	1.566	1.751	1.542	1.776	1.518	1.801	1.494	1.827	1.469	1.854	1.445	1.881	1.420	1.908
95	1.645	1.687	1.623	1.709	1.602	1.732	1.579	1.755	1.557	1.778	1.535	1.802	1.512	1.827	1.489	1.852	1.465	1.877	1.442	1.902
100	1.654	1.694	1.634	1.715	1.613	1.736	1.592	1.758	1.571	1.780	1.550	1.803	1.528	1.826	1.506	1.850	1.484	1.874	1.462	1.898
150	1.720	1.746	1.706	1.760	1.693	1.774	1.679	1.788	1.665	1.802	1.651	1.817	1.637	1.832	1.622	1.847	1.608	1.862	1.594	1.877
200	1.758	1.778	1.748	1.789	1.738	1.799	1.728	1.810	1.718	1.820	1.707	1.831	1.697	1.841	1.686	1.852	1.675	1.863	1.665	1.874

Continued

Durbin–Watson Statistic (Continued)
5 Percent Significance Points of dL and dU[a]

n	k'=11 dL	k'=11 dU	k'=12 dL	k'=12 dU	k'=13 dL	k'=13 dU	k'=14 dL	k'=14 dU	k'=15 dL	k'=15 dU	k'=16 dL	k'=16 dU	k'=17 dL	k'=17 dU	k'=18 dL	k'=18 dU	k'=19 dL	k'=19 dU	k'=20 dL	k'=20 dU
16	0.098	3.503	—	3.557	—	—	—	—	—	—	—	—	—	—	—	—	—	—	—	—
17	0.138	3.378	0.087	3.441	—	—	—	—	—	—	—	—	—	—	—	—	—	—	—	—
18	0.177	3.265	0.123	3.335	0.078	3.603	—	—	—	—	—	—	—	—	—	—	—	—	—	—
19	0.220	3.159	0.160	3.234	0.111	3.496	0.070	3.642	—	—	—	—	—	—	—	—	—	—	—	—
20	0.263	3.063	0.200	3.141	0.145	3.395	0.100	3.542	0.063	3.676	—	—	—	—	—	—	—	—	—	—
21	0.307	2.976	0.240	3.057	0.182	3.300	0.132	3.448	0.091	3.583	0.058	3.705	—	—	—	—	—	—	—	—
22	0.349	2.897	0.281	2.979	0.220	3.211	0.166	3.358	0.120	3.495	0.083	3.619	0.052	3.731	—	—	—	—	—	—
23	0.391	2.826	0.322	2.908	0.259	3.128	0.202	3.272	0.153	3.409	0.110	3.535	0.076	3.650	0.048	3.753	—	—	—	—
24	0.431	2.761	0.362	2.844	0.297	3.053	0.239	3.193	0.186	3.327	0.141	3.454	0.101	3.572	0.070	3.678	0.044	3.773	—	—
25	0.470	2.702	0.400	2.784	0.335	2.983	0.275	3.119	0.221	3.251	0.172	3.376	0.130	3.494	0.094	3.604	0.065	3.702	0.041	3.790
26	0.508	2.649	0.438	2.730	0.373	2.919	0.312	3.051	0.256	3.179	0.205	3.303	0.160	3.420	0.120	3.531	0.087	3.632	0.060	3.724
27	0.544	2.600	0.475	2.680	0.409	2.859	0.348	2.987	0.291	3.112	0.238	3.233	0.191	3.349	0.149	3.460	0.112	3.563	0.081	3.658
28	0.578	2.555	0.510	2.634	0.445	2.805	0.383	2.928	0.325	3.050	0.271	3.168	0.222	3.283	0.178	3.392	0.138	3.495	0.104	3.592
29	0.612	2.515	0.544	2.592	0.479	2.755	0.418	2.874	0.359	2.992	0.305	3.107	0.254	3.219	0.208	3.327	0.166	3.431	0.129	3.528
30	0.643	2.477	0.577	2.553	0.512	2.708	0.451	2.823	0.392	2.937	0.337	3.050	0.286	3.160	0.238	3.266	0.195	3.368	0.156	3.465
31	0.674	2.443	0.608	2.517	0.545	2.665	0.484	2.776	0.425	2.887	0.370	2.996	0.317	3.103	0.269	3.208	0.224	3.309	0.183	3.406
32	0.703	2.411	0.638	2.484	0.576	2.625	0.515	2.733	0.457	2.840	0.401	2.946	0.349	3.050	0.299	3.153	0.253	3.252	0.211	3.348
33	0.731	2.382	0.668	2.454	0.606	2.588	0.546	2.692	0.488	2.796	0.432	2.899	0.379	3.000	0.329	3.100	0.283	3.198	0.239	3.293
34	0.758	2.355	0.695	2.425	0.634	2.554	0.575	2.654	0.518	2.754	0.462	2.854	0.409	2.954	0.359	3.051	0.312	3.147	0.267	3.240
35	0.783	2.330	0.722	2.398	0.662	2.521	0.604	2.619	0.547	2.716	0.492	2.813	0.439	2.910	0.388	3.005	0.340	3.099	0.295	3.190
36	0.808	2.306	0.748	2.374	0.689	2.492	0.631	2.586	0.575	2.680	0.520	2.774	0.467	2.868	0.417	2.961	0.369	3.053	0.323	3.142
37	0.831	2.285	0.772	2.351	0.714	2.464	0.657	2.555	0.602	2.646	0.548	2.738	0.495	2.829	0.445	2.920	0.397	3.009	0.351	3.097
38	0.854	2.265	0.796	2.329	0.739	2.438	0.683	2.526	0.628	2.614	0.575	2.703	0.522	2.792	0.472	2.880	0.424	2.968	0.378	3.054
39	0.875	2.246	0.819	2.309	0.763	2.413	0.707	2.499	0.653	2.585	0.600	2.671	0.549	2.757	0.499	2.843	0.451	2.929	0.404	3.013
40	0.896	2.228	0.840	2.291	0.785	2.391	0.731	2.473	0.678	2.557	0.626	2.641	0.575	2.724	0.525	2.808	0.477	2.892	0.430	2.974
45	0.988	2.156	0.938	2.225	0.887	2.296	0.838	2.367	0.788	2.439	0.740	2.512	0.692	2.586	0.644	2.659	0.598	2.733	0.553	2.807
50	1.064	2.103	1.019	2.163	0.973	2.225	0.927	2.287	0.882	2.350	0.836	2.414	0.792	2.479	0.747	2.544	0.703	2.610	0.660	2.675
55	1.129	2.062	1.087	2.116	1.045	2.170	1.003	2.225	0.961	2.281	0.919	2.338	0.877	2.396	0.836	2.454	0.795	2.512	0.754	2.571
60	1.184	2.031	1.145	2.079	1.106	2.127	1.068	2.177	1.029	2.227	0.990	2.278	0.951	2.330	0.913	2.382	0.874	2.434	0.836	2.487
65	1.231	2.006	1.195	2.049	1.160	2.093	1.124	2.138	1.088	2.183	1.052	2.229	1.016	2.276	0.980	2.323	0.944	2.371	0.908	2.419
70	1.272	1.986	1.239	2.026	1.206	2.066	1.172	2.106	1.139	2.148	1.105	2.189	1.072	2.232	1.038	2.275	1.005	2.318	0.971	2.362
75	1.308	1.970	1.277	2.006	1.247	2.043	1.215	2.080	1.184	2.118	1.153	2.156	1.121	2.195	1.090	2.235	1.058	2.275	1.027	2.315
80	1.340	1.957	1.311	1.991	1.283	2.024	1.253	2.059	1.224	2.093	1.195	2.129	1.165	2.165	1.136	2.201	1.106	2.238	1.076	2.275
85	1.369	1.946	1.342	1.977	1.315	2.009	1.287	2.040	1.260	2.073	1.232	2.105	1.205	2.139	1.177	2.172	1.149	2.206	1.121	2.241
90	1.395	1.937	1.369	1.966	1.344	1.995	1.318	2.025	1.292	2.055	1.266	2.085	1.240	2.116	1.213	2.148	1.187	2.179	1.160	2.211
95	1.418	1.929	1.394	1.956	1.370	1.984	1.345	2.012	1.321	2.040	1.296	2.068	1.271	2.097	1.247	2.126	1.222	2.156	1.197	2.186
100	1.439	1.923	1.416	1.948	1.393	1.974	1.371	2.000	1.347	2.026	1.324	2.053	1.301	2.080	1.277	2.108	1.253	2.135	1.229	2.164
150	1.579	1.892	1.564	1.908	1.550	1.924	1.535	1.940	1.519	1.956	1.504	1.972	1.489	1.989	1.474	2.006	1.458	2.023	1.443	2.040
200	1.654	1.885	1.643	1.896	1.632	1.908	1.621	1.919	1.610	1.931	1.599	1.943	1.588	1.955	1.576	1.967	1.565	1.979	1.554	1.991

[a] k' is the number of regressors excluding the intercept.

Source: N. Savin and K. White, "The Durbin–Watson Test for Serial Correlation with Extreme Sample Sizes or Many Regressors," Econometrica, Vol. 45, November 1977, pp. 1989–1996. Reprinted with permission of the Econometric Society.

Durbin–Watson Statistic

1 Percent Significance Points of d_L and d_U[a]

n	$k'=1$ d_L	$k'=1$ d_U	$k'=2$ d_L	$k'=2$ d_U	$k'=3$ d_L	$k'=3$ d_U	$k'=4$ d_L	$k'=4$ d_U	$k'=5$ d_L	$k'=5$ d_U	$k'=6$ d_L	$k'=6$ d_U	$k'=7$ d_L	$k'=7$ d_U	$k'=8$ d_L	$k'=8$ d_U	$k'=9$ d_L	$k'=9$ d_U	$k'=10$ d_L	$k'=10$ d_U
6	0.390	1.142	—	—	—	—	—	—	—	—	—	—	—	—	—	—	—	—	—	—
7	0.435	1.036	0.294	1.676	—	—	—	—	—	—	—	—	—	—	—	—	—	—	—	—
8	0.497	1.003	0.345	1.489	0.229	2.102	—	—	—	—	—	—	—	—	—	—	—	—	—	—
9	0.554	0.998	0.408	1.389	0.279	1.875	0.183	2.433	—	—	—	—	—	—	—	—	—	—	—	—
10	0.604	1.001	0.466	1.333	0.340	1.733	0.230	2.193	0.150	2.690	—	—	—	—	—	—	—	—	—	—
11	0.653	1.010	0.519	1.297	0.396	1.640	0.286	2.030	0.193	2.453	0.124	2.892	—	—	—	—	—	—	—	—
12	0.697	1.023	0.569	1.274	0.449	1.575	0.339	1.913	0.244	2.280	0.164	2.565	0.105	3.053	—	—	—	—	—	—
13	0.738	1.038	0.616	1.261	0.499	1.526	0.391	1.826	0.294	2.150	0.211	2.490	0.140	2.838	0.090	3.182	—	—	—	—
14	0.776	1.054	0.660	1.254	0.547	1.490	0.441	1.757	0.343	2.049	0.257	2.354	0.183	2.667	0.122	2.981	0.078	3.287	—	—
15	0.811	1.070	0.700	1.252	0.591	1.464	0.488	1.704	0.391	1.967	0.303	2.244	0.226	2.530	0.161	2.817	0.107	3.101	0.068	3.374
16	0.844	1.086	0.737	1.252	0.633	1.446	0.532	1.663	0.437	1.900	0.349	2.153	0.269	2.416	0.200	2.681	0.142	2.944	0.094	3.201
17	0.874	1.102	0.772	1.255	0.672	1.432	0.574	1.630	0.480	1.847	0.393	2.078	0.313	2.319	0.241	2.566	0.179	2.811	0.127	3.053
18	0.902	1.118	0.805	1.259	0.708	1.422	0.613	1.604	0.522	1.803	0.435	2.015	0.355	2.238	0.282	2.467	0.216	2.697	0.160	2.925
19	0.928	1.132	0.835	1.265	0.742	1.415	0.650	1.584	0.561	1.767	0.476	1.963	0.396	2.169	0.322	2.381	0.255	2.597	0.196	2.813
20	0.952	1.147	0.863	1.271	0.773	1.411	0.685	1.567	0.598	1.737	0.515	1.918	0.436	2.110	0.362	2.308	0.294	2.510	0.232	2.714
21	0.975	1.161	0.890	1.277	0.803	1.408	0.718	1.554	0.633	1.712	0.552	1.881	0.474	2.059	0.400	2.244	0.331	2.434	0.268	2.625
22	0.997	1.174	0.914	1.284	0.831	1.407	0.748	1.543	0.667	1.691	0.587	1.849	0.510	2.015	0.437	2.188	0.368	2.367	0.304	2.548
23	1.018	1.187	0.938	1.291	0.858	1.407	0.777	1.534	0.698	1.673	0.620	1.821	0.545	1.977	0.473	2.140	0.404	2.308	0.340	2.479
24	1.037	1.199	0.960	1.298	0.882	1.407	0.805	1.528	0.728	1.658	0.652	1.797	0.578	1.944	0.507	2.097	0.439	2.255	0.375	2.417
25	1.055	1.211	0.981	1.305	0.906	1.409	0.831	1.523	0.756	1.645	0.682	1.776	0.610	1.915	0.540	2.059	0.473	2.209	0.409	2.362
26	1.072	1.222	1.001	1.312	0.928	1.411	0.855	1.518	0.783	1.635	0.711	1.759	0.640	1.889	0.572	2.026	0.505	2.168	0.441	2.313
27	1.089	1.233	1.019	1.319	0.949	1.413	0.878	1.515	0.808	1.626	0.738	1.743	0.669	1.867	0.602	1.997	0.536	2.131	0.473	2.269
28	1.104	1.244	1.037	1.325	0.969	1.415	0.900	1.513	0.832	1.618	0.764	1.729	0.696	1.847	0.630	1.970	0.566	2.098	0.504	2.229
29	1.119	1.254	1.054	1.332	0.988	1.418	0.921	1.512	0.855	1.611	0.788	1.718	0.723	1.830	0.658	1.947	0.595	2.068	0.533	2.193
30	1.133	1.263	1.070	1.339	1.006	1.421	0.941	1.511	0.877	1.606	0.812	1.707	0.748	1.814	0.684	1.925	0.622	2.041	0.562	2.160
31	1.147	1.273	1.085	1.345	1.023	1.425	0.960	1.510	0.897	1.601	0.834	1.698	0.772	1.800	0.710	1.906	0.649	2.017	0.589	2.131
32	1.160	1.282	1.100	1.352	1.040	1.428	0.979	1.510	0.917	1.597	0.856	1.690	0.794	1.788	0.734	1.889	0.674	1.995	0.615	2.104
33	1.172	1.291	1.114	1.358	1.055	1.432	0.996	1.510	0.936	1.594	0.876	1.683	0.816	1.776	0.757	1.874	0.698	1.975	0.641	2.080
34	1.184	1.299	1.128	1.364	1.070	1.435	1.012	1.511	0.954	1.591	0.896	1.677	0.837	1.766	0.779	1.860	0.722	1.957	0.665	2.057
35	1.195	1.307	1.140	1.370	1.085	1.439	1.028	1.512	0.971	1.589	0.914	1.671	0.857	1.757	0.800	1.847	0.744	1.940	0.689	2.037
36	1.206	1.315	1.153	1.376	1.098	1.442	1.043	1.513	0.988	1.588	0.932	1.666	0.877	1.749	0.821	1.836	0.766	1.925	0.711	2.018
37	1.217	1.323	1.165	1.382	1.112	1.446	1.058	1.514	1.004	1.586	0.950	1.662	0.895	1.742	0.841	1.825	0.787	1.911	0.733	2.001
38	1.227	1.330	1.176	1.388	1.124	1.449	1.072	1.515	1.019	1.585	0.966	1.658	0.913	1.735	0.860	1.816	0.807	1.899	0.754	1.985
39	1.237	1.337	1.187	1.393	1.137	1.453	1.085	1.517	1.034	1.584	0.982	1.655	0.930	1.729	0.878	1.807	0.826	1.887	0.774	1.970
40	1.246	1.344	1.198	1.398	1.148	1.457	1.098	1.518	1.048	1.584	0.997	1.652	0.946	1.724	0.895	1.799	0.844	1.876	0.789	1.956
45	1.288	1.376	1.245	1.423	1.201	1.474	1.156	1.528	1.111	1.584	1.065	1.643	1.019	1.704	0.974	1.768	0.927	1.834	0.881	1.900
50	1.324	1.403	1.285	1.446	1.245	1.491	1.205	1.538	1.164	1.587	1.123	1.639	1.081	1.692	1.039	1.748	0.997	1.805	0.955	1.864
55	1.356	1.427	1.320	1.466	1.284	1.506	1.247	1.548	1.209	1.592	1.172	1.638	1.134	1.685	1.095	1.734	1.057	1.785	1.018	1.841
60	1.383	1.449	1.350	1.484	1.317	1.520	1.283	1.558	1.249	1.598	1.214	1.639	1.179	1.682	1.144	1.726	1.108	1.771	1.072	1.823
65	1.407	1.468	1.377	1.500	1.346	1.534	1.315	1.568	1.283	1.604	1.251	1.642	1.218	1.680	1.186	1.720	1.153	1.761	1.120	1.802
70	1.429	1.485	1.400	1.515	1.372	1.546	1.343	1.578	1.313	1.611	1.283	1.645	1.253	1.680	1.223	1.716	1.192	1.754	1.162	1.792
75	1.448	1.501	1.422	1.529	1.395	1.557	1.368	1.587	1.340	1.617	1.313	1.646	1.284	1.682	1.256	1.714	1.227	1.746	1.199	1.785
80	1.466	1.515	1.441	1.541	1.416	1.568	1.390	1.595	1.364	1.624	1.338	1.653	1.312	1.683	1.285	1.714	1.259	1.745	1.232	1.777
85	1.482	1.528	1.458	1.553	1.435	1.578	1.411	1.603	1.386	1.630	1.362	1.657	1.337	1.685	1.312	1.714	1.287	1.743	1.262	1.773
90	1.496	1.540	1.474	1.563	1.452	1.587	1.429	1.611	1.406	1.636	1.383	1.661	1.360	1.687	1.336	1.715	1.312	1.741	1.288	1.759
95	1.510	1.552	1.489	1.573	1.468	1.596	1.446	1.618	1.425	1.642	1.403	1.666	1.381	1.690	1.358	1.717	1.336	1.741	1.313	1.757
100	1.522	1.562	1.503	1.583	1.482	1.604	1.462	1.625	1.441	1.647	1.421	1.670	1.400	1.693	1.378	1.722	1.357	1.741	1.335	1.755
150	1.611	1.637	1.598	1.651	1.584	1.665	1.571	1.679	1.557	1.693	1.543	1.708	1.530	1.722	1.515	1.737	1.501	1.752	1.486	1.757
200	1.664	1.684	1.653	1.693	1.643	1.704	1.633	1.715	1.623	1.725	1.613	1.735	1.603	1.746	1.592	1.757	1.582	1.768	1.571	1.779

Continued

Durbin–Watson Statistic (Continued)
1 Percent Significance Points of d_L and d_U[a]

n	$K'=11$ d_L	$K'=11$ d_U	$K'=12$ d_L	$K'=12$ d_U	$K'=13$ d_L	$K'=13$ d_U	$K'=14$ d_L	$K'=14$ d_U	$K'=15$ d_L	$K'=15$ d_U	$K'=16$ d_L	$K'=16$ d_U	$K'=17$ d_L	$K'=17$ d_U	$K'=18$ d_L	$K'=18$ d_U	$K'=19$ d_L	$K'=19$ d_U	$K'=20$ d_L	$K'=20$ d_U
16	0.060	3.446	—	3.506	—	—	—	—	—	—	—	—	—	—	—	—	—	—	—	—
17	0.084	3.286	0.053	3.358	—	3.557	—	—	—	—	—	—	—	—	—	—	—	—	—	—
18	0.113	3.146	0.075	3.227	0.047	3.420	—	3.601	—	—	—	—	—	—	—	—	—	—	—	—
19	0.145	3.023	0.102	3.109	0.067	3.297	0.043	3.474	—	3.639	—	—	—	—	—	—	—	—	—	—
20	0.178	2.914	0.131	3.004	0.092	3.185	0.061	3.358	0.038	3.521	—	3.671	—	—	—	—	—	—	—	—
21	0.212	2.817	0.162	2.914	0.119	3.084	0.084	3.252	0.055	3.412	0.035	3.562	—	3.700	—	—	—	—	—	—
22	0.246	2.729	0.194	2.823	0.148	2.991	0.109	3.155	0.077	3.311	0.050	3.459	0.032	3.597	—	3.725	—	—	—	—
23	0.281	2.651	0.227	2.744	0.178	2.906	0.136	3.065	0.100	3.218	0.070	3.363	0.046	3.501	0.029	3.629	—	3.747	—	—
24	0.315	2.580	0.260	2.674	0.209	2.829	0.165	2.982	0.125	3.131	0.092	3.274	0.065	3.410	0.043	3.538	0.027	3.657	—	3.766
25	0.348	2.517	0.292	2.610	0.240	2.758	0.194	2.906	0.152	3.050	0.116	3.191	0.085	3.325	0.060	3.452	0.039	3.572	0.025	3.682
26	0.381	2.460	0.324	2.552	0.272	2.694	0.224	2.836	0.180	2.976	0.141	3.113	0.107	3.245	0.079	3.371	0.055	3.490	0.036	3.602
27	0.413	2.409	0.356	2.499	0.303	2.635	0.253	2.772	0.208	2.907	0.167	3.040	0.131	3.169	0.100	3.294	0.073	3.412	0.051	3.524
28	0.444	2.363	0.387	2.451	0.333	2.582	0.283	2.713	0.237	2.843	0.194	2.972	0.156	3.098	0.122	3.220	0.093	3.338	0.068	3.450
29	0.474	2.321	0.417	2.407	0.363	2.533	0.313	2.659	0.266	2.785	0.222	2.909	0.182	3.032	0.146	3.152	0.114	3.267	0.087	3.379
30	0.503	2.283	0.447	2.367	0.393	2.487	0.342	2.609	0.294	2.730	0.249	2.851	0.208	2.970	0.171	3.087	0.137	3.201	0.107	3.311
31	0.531	2.248	0.475	2.330	0.422	2.446	0.371	2.563	0.322	2.680	0.277	2.797	0.234	2.912	0.196	3.026	0.160	3.137	0.128	3.246
32	0.558	2.216	0.503	2.296	0.450	2.408	0.399	2.520	0.350	2.633	0.304	2.746	0.261	2.858	0.221	2.969	0.184	3.078	0.151	3.184
33	0.585	2.187	0.530	2.266	0.477	2.373	0.426	2.481	0.377	2.590	0.331	2.699	0.287	2.808	0.246	2.915	0.209	3.022	0.174	3.126
34	0.610	2.160	0.556	2.237	0.503	2.340	0.452	2.444	0.404	2.550	0.357	2.655	0.313	2.761	0.272	2.865	0.233	2.969	0.197	3.071
35	0.634	2.136	0.581	2.210	0.529	2.310	0.478	2.410	0.430	2.512	0.383	2.614	0.339	2.717	0.297	2.818	0.257	2.919	0.221	3.019
36	0.658	2.113	0.605	2.186	0.554	2.282	0.504	2.379	0.455	2.477	0.409	2.576	0.364	2.675	0.322	2.774	0.282	2.872	0.244	2.969
37	0.680	2.092	0.628	2.164	0.578	2.256	0.528	2.350	0.480	2.445	0.434	2.540	0.389	2.637	0.347	2.733	0.306	2.828	0.268	2.923
38	0.702	2.073	0.651	2.143	0.601	2.232	0.552	2.323	0.504	2.414	0.458	2.507	0.414	2.600	0.371	2.694	0.330	2.787	0.291	2.879
39	0.723	2.055	0.673	2.123	0.623	2.210	0.575	2.297	0.528	2.386	0.482	2.476	0.438	2.566	0.395	2.657	0.354	2.748	0.315	2.838
40	0.744	2.039	0.694	2.104	0.645	2.189	0.597	2.272	0.551	2.357	0.505	2.444	0.461	2.531	0.418	2.619	0.377	2.708	0.338	2.797
45	0.835	1.972	0.790	2.044	0.744	2.118	0.700	2.193	0.655	2.269	0.612	2.346	0.570	2.424	0.528	2.503	0.488	2.582	0.448	2.661
50	0.913	1.925	0.871	1.987	0.829	2.051	0.787	2.116	0.746	2.182	0.705	2.250	0.665	2.318	0.625	2.387	0.586	2.456	0.548	2.526
55	0.979	1.891	0.940	1.945	0.902	2.002	0.863	2.059	0.825	2.117	0.786	2.176	0.748	2.237	0.711	2.298	0.674	2.359	0.637	2.421
60	1.037	1.865	1.001	1.914	0.965	1.964	0.929	2.015	0.893	2.067	0.857	2.120	0.822	2.173	0.786	2.227	0.751	2.283	0.716	2.338
65	1.087	1.845	1.053	1.889	1.020	1.934	0.986	1.980	0.953	2.027	0.919	2.075	0.886	2.123	0.852	2.172	0.819	2.221	0.786	2.272
70	1.131	1.831	1.099	1.870	1.068	1.911	1.037	1.953	1.005	1.995	0.974	2.038	0.943	2.082	0.911	2.127	0.880	2.172	0.849	2.217
75	1.170	1.819	1.141	1.856	1.111	1.893	1.082	1.931	1.052	1.970	1.023	2.009	0.993	2.049	0.964	2.090	0.934	2.131	0.905	2.172
80	1.205	1.810	1.177	1.844	1.150	1.878	1.122	1.913	1.094	1.949	1.066	1.984	1.039	2.022	1.011	2.057	0.983	2.097	0.955	2.135
85	1.236	1.803	1.210	1.834	1.184	1.866	1.158	1.898	1.132	1.931	1.106	1.965	1.080	1.999	1.053	2.033	1.027	2.068	1.000	2.104
90	1.264	1.798	1.240	1.827	1.215	1.856	1.191	1.886	1.166	1.917	1.141	1.948	1.116	1.979	1.091	2.012	1.066	2.044	1.041	2.077
95	1.290	1.793	1.267	1.821	1.244	1.848	1.221	1.876	1.197	1.905	1.174	1.934	1.150	1.963	1.126	1.993	1.102	2.023	1.079	2.054
100	1.314	1.790	1.292	1.816	1.270	1.841	1.248	1.868	1.225	1.895	1.203	1.922	1.181	1.949	1.158	1.977	1.136	2.006	1.113	2.034
150	1.473	1.783	1.458	1.799	1.444	1.814	1.429	1.830	1.414	1.847	1.400	1.863	1.385	1.880	1.370	1.897	1.355	1.913	1.340	1.931
200	1.561	1.791	1.550	1.801	1.539	1.813	1.528	1.824	1.518	1.836	1.507	1.847	1.495	1.860	1.484	1.871	1.474	1.883	1.462	1.896

[a] K' is the number of regressors excluding the intercept.

Source: N. Savin and K. White, "The Durbin–Watson Test for Serial Correlation with Extreme Sample Sizes or Many Regressors," Econometrica, Vol. 45, November 1977, pp. 1989–1996. Reprinted with permission of the Econometric Society.

Index